WileyPLUS

ileyPLUS is a research-based online environment for effective teaching and learning.

WileyPLUS builds students' confidence because it takes the guesswork out of studying by providing students with a clear roadmap:

- what to do
- how to do it
- if they did it right

It offers interactive resources along with a complete digital textbook that help students learn more. With *WileyPLUS*, students take more initiative so you'll have greater impact on their achievement in the classroom and beyond.

WileyPLUS

CONTEMPORARY
BUSINESS

CANADIAN EDITION

LOUIS E. BOONE
University of South Alabama

MICHAEL H. KHAN
University of Toronto

DAVID L. KURTZ
University of Arkansas

BRAHM M. CANZER
John Abbott College

...at the speed of business

WILEY

Library and Archives Canada Cataloguing in Publication

Contemporary business / Louis E. Boone ... [et al.]. — Canadian ed.
Includes bibliographical references and indexes.
ISBN 978-1-118-16173-9 (bound).—ISBN 978-1-118-49870-5 (pbk.)
    1. Management—Textbooks.   2. Business—Textbooks.   I. Boone, Louis E
HD31.C637 2012   658   C2012-904906-9

Production Credits

Vice President & Publisher:	Veronica Visentin	Editorial Assistant:	Laura Hwee
Acquisitions Editor:	Darren Lalonde	Production Coordinator:	Lynda Jess
Marketing Manager:	Anita Osborne	Permissions Coordinator:	Kristiina Paul
Editorial Manager:	Karen Staudinger	Typesetting:	MPS Limited
Production Manager:	Tegan Wallace	Cover Design:	Joanna Vieira
Developmental Editor:	Joanne Sutherland	Cover Image:	© Corepics/depositphotos
Media Editor:	Channade Fenandoe		

Printing and binding: Friesens
Printed and bound in Canada.

1 2 3 4 5 FP 17 16 15 14 13

John Wiley & Sons Canada, Ltd.
6045 Freemont Blvd.
Mississauga, Ontario L5R 4J3

Visit our website at: www.wiley.ca

WILEY

BRIEF CONTENTS

CONTENTS

PART 5

Managing Technology and Information   389

Chapter 14

Using Technology to Manage Information   390

Inside Business
Stock-Trak: Learning about the Stock
Market through Simulation

Hit & Miss
Business Intelligence Software Helps
with Information Overload

Business Etiquette
Courteous Communications via
Wireless Devices

Going Green
Can Cloud Computing Also
Be "Green" Computing?

**Solving an Ethical
Controversy**
Should Employers Monitor
Employees' Internet Use?

Hit & Miss
Cisco Systems Tackles
Cloud Security

PART 6

Managing Financial Resources   415

Chapter 15

Understanding Accounting and Financial Statements   416

Inside Business
Cooking the Books

Hit & Miss
Forensic Accountants:
Fraud Busters

PREFACE

Canadian college and university students have questions about business and the role business-people play. Some questions relate to their personal experiences, and others concern understanding issues we all face as Canadians living in an increasingly global society. Students want answers to these questions and more:

- What products are "made in Canada" and why can't we make more?
- Why do Canadian consumers pay more than Americans for many products and services?
- Why did Research In Motion lose its global leadership role in smartphone technology?
- Who caused the 2008–10 financial collapse?
- Why are some countries wealthy and others not?
- Which Canadian businesses will provide job opportunities for me when I graduate?
- Should I start my own business?

Contemporary Business, Canadian edition, is a comprehensive introductory textbook. Rooted in the basics of business, this textbook provides students with a foundation upon which to build a greater understanding of current business practices and issues that affect their lives.

At the Speed of Business

Business has always been about change; but in today's business world, change seems to be in over-drive. In many industries, products and strategies come and go faster than ever before. This rate of change in business is recognized in the theme of this textbook—*"at the speed of business."*

Chapter 1 opens with a close-up look at the role of the Internet and social media in launching Justin Bieber's career. The changes brought on by Internet and other technologies are illustrated throughout the textbook. As regular users of the Internet, students understand first-hand how the Internet has changed their behaviour—starting with communications and digital media. We use this familiarity to build an understanding of businesses that have been affected by the Internet, such as Research In Motion, discussed in Chapter 7. We also examine Canadian businesses that have succeeded in large part due to the marketing power of the Internet, such as Halo in Chapter 6 and StockTrak in Chapter 14.

Another theme throughout the textbook is globalization and the growing challenges facing Canadian businesses as they compete not only against American and Mexican firms in North America but against firms everywhere in the world. We look at changes in production of tangibles and intangibles, the use of automation, and the growing trend of outsourcing to lower-cost countries, such as China and India. Chapter 8 opens with a closer examination of the decline of the Canadian apparel industry and how some apparel companies, such as Lululemon Athletica and Halo, have managed to succeed by focusing on niche markets.

Responsible Business

A current topic of major interest is the use of business ethics and corporate social responsibility (CSR). Chapter 2 is rich in content related to CSR. It opens with a look at Canada's world-renowned Cirque du Soleil and its model of global CSR. Throughout the textbook, and particularly in each chapter's *Solving an Ethical Controversy* feature, we focus on ethical issues and CSR. Similarly, each chapter's *Going Green* feature looks at green issues, including conservation, pollution, recycling, and reusing.

Student-focused

In this first Canadian edition, we present Canadian content that speaks directly to students about the world of business. We asked a group of undergraduate business students to suggest content that would appeal to first-year students. Many examples included in this textbook were inspired by student peers. From Canadian superstar Justin Bieber to lesser known success stories across Canada, this textbook brings Canadian business and businesspeople face-to-face with students so that the roles played by businesspeople in our economy can be better understood, questioned, and debated. Students said they wanted to understand business beyond the simple concepts of profit as a goal or maximizing the provision of services for not-for profit organizations. We believe we have produced a textbook that meets these needs.

Contemporary Business, Canadian edition, is written in a conversational style that has been thoroughly edited for plain language to ensure readability for all students, including students for whom English is their second language.

ACKNOWLEDGEMENTS

Contemporary Business, Canadian edition, is the result of the efforts of many people who rightfully need acknowledgement. We would first like to thank our publishing team, beginning with our developmental editor, Joanne Sutherland, for her suggestions on style and content throughout the writing effort. We thank Mariko Obokata for an excellent job on the copy edit, Leslie Saffrey for her accurate proofreading, Kristiina Paul for her creative photo research, and Amy Kwan for her dedicated work as research coordinator on the project. Special thanks also go to Irene Wiecek.

We wish to thank the Wiley team on the business side of the project, beginning with Darren Lalonde, Veronica Visentin, and all of the marketing representatives whose field knowledge of marketplace needs helped to focus our efforts.

We especially want to thank our academic colleagues for their suggestions and constructive criticisms on the drafts of the manuscript as we progressed toward our completed product. We know we could not have produced the quality and calibre of this textbook without their contributions.

Editorial Advisory Board:

Colin Boyd, University of Saskatchewan

Dave Fleming, George Brown College

Radha Koilpillai, St. Mary's University

Hugh Laurence, University of Toronto, Scarborough

Margaret Mason, Fanshawe College

Valerie Miceli, Seneca College

Frank Saccucci, Grant MacEwan University

David Swanston, University of Toronto, Mississauga

Kent Walker, University of Windsor

Reviewers:

Scott Cawfield, York University

David Delcorde, University of Ottawa

Gordon McFarlane, Langara College

Donna McRae-Murphy, Eastern College

Peter Mombourquette, Mount Saint Vincent University

Paul Myers, St. Clair College

Hyacinth Randall, Seneca College

Andrea Rennie, Seneca College

Al Ruggero, Seneca College

Ronnalee Rylance, CDI College

Drew Smylie, Centennial College

Michael Wade, Seneca College

Claudia Zhang, Grant MacEwan University

Finally, we extend special thanks to the following group of University of Toronto students for their insightful and invaluable contributions to the text.

Back row (left to right): Faris Al-Natour, Brett Payne, Liliana Monroy del Valle, Maryam Akhtar, Umair Ammad
Front row (left to right): Amy Kwan, Bianca Adewolu, Anni Huang, Laura Sofia Garzón, Sarah Israr, Amir Sariri Khayatzadeh
Absent: Megan Kennedy

This book is lovingly dedicated to my wife Carole, son Matthew, and daughter Sarah.

Brahm Canzer

This is book is dedicated to my parents, for all they have given me; my wife Asma, who supports me in all of my endeavours; my children, Khadijah and Zakariyah, who always bring a smile to my face; and to all of my friends and family who have supported me throughout the years.

Michael Khan

ABOUT THE AUTHORS

Dave Kurtz

During Dave Kurtz's high school days, no one in Salisbury, Maryland, would have mistaken him for a scholar. In fact, he was a mediocre student, so bad that his father steered him toward higher education by finding him a succession of backbreaking summer jobs. Thankfully, most of them have been erased from his memory, but a few linger, including picking peaches, loading watermelons on trucks headed for market, and working as a pipefitter's helper. Unfortunately, these jobs had zero impact on his academic standing. Worse yet for Dave's ego, he was no better than average as a high school athlete in football and track.

But four years at Davis & Elkins College in Elkins, West Virginia, turned him around. Excellent instructors helped get Dave on a sound academic footing. His grade point average soared—enough to get him accepted by the graduate business school at the University of Arkansas, where he met Gene Boone. Gene and Dave became longtime co-authors; together they produced more than 50 books. In addition to writing, Dave and Gene were involved in several entrepreneurial ventures.

This long-term partnership ended with Gene's death in 2005. But, this book will always be Boone & Kurtz's *Contemporary Business*.

Today, Dave is back teaching at the University of Arkansas, after tours of duty in Ypsilanti, Michigan; Seattle, Washington; and Melbourne, Australia. He is the proud grandfather of six "perfect" kids and a sportsman with a golf handicap too high to mention. Dave, his wife, Diane, and four demanding canine companions (Daisy, Lucy, Molly, and Sally) live in Rogers, Arkansas. Dave holds a distinguished professorship at the Sam M. Walton College of Business in nearby Fayetteville, home of the Arkansas Razorbacks.

Michael Khan

Michael Khan is a lecturer in accounting at the Rotman School of Management at the University of Toronto. He teaches in both the MBA and Commerce programs and has won awards for excellence in teaching at both the graduate and undergraduate levels. His involvement in professional accounting training includes teaching at the Institute of Chartered Accountants of Ontario's annual School of Accountancy. Michael is a Chartered Accountant (CA) and holds an MBA from the Schulich School of Business, York University. He also has specialized professional designations in the field of Information Technology Audit and Governance (CISA – Certified Information Systems

Auditor and CGEIT – Certified in the Governance of Enterprise Information Technology). His professional experience includes internal and external audit, accounting, and consulting positions at Ernst & Young, Deloitte, Rogers Communications, and George Weston Limited. In his spare time, he enjoys travelling and scuba diving.

Brahm Canzer

Brahm Canzer currently teaches business management courses to John Abbott College students in Montreal. He is also an adjunct lecturer at McGill University and Concordia University. During his teaching career, he has also taught undergraduate courses in a corporate learning program under the auspices of the University of Toronto. Brahm received his PhD (1995) and MBA (1976) from Concordia University in Montreal. His strong interest in the use of the Internet technology in education led him to be among the first pioneers to design and teach online MBA courses for Simon Fraser University. He is a contributing author to several business textbooks and author of *eBusiness: Strategic Thinking and Practice*. He has helped create a variety of web-based supplemental learning materials in academic and corporate learning settings. Brahm also provides consulting services to businesses seeking assistance as they explore web-based opportunities and solutions for improving their operations.

FEATURES OF THIS BOOK

Numbered *Learning Objectives* at the opening of each chapter guide student learning. These are repeated in the margin at the start of each major chapter section and appear again in the *Summary of Learning Objectives* at the end of the chapter.

1 | THE CHANGING FACE OF BUSINESS

LEARNING OBJECTIVES

LO 1.1 Distinguish between business and not-for-profit organizations.

LO 1.2 Identify and describe the factors of production.

LO 1.3 Describe the private enterprise system, including basic rights and entrepreneurship.

LO 1.4 Identify the six eras of business, and explain how the relationship era—including alliances, technology, and environmental concerns—influences contemporary business.

LO 1.5 Explain how today's business workforce and the nature of work itself are changing.

LO 1.6 Identify the skills and attributes managers need to lead businesses in the 21st century.

LO 1.7 Outline the characteristics that make a company admired by the business community.

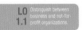

WHAT IS BUSINESS?

What do you think of when you hear the word *business*? Do you think of big corporations like Rogers Communications or TD Bank? Or do you think about the local bakery or shoe store? Maybe you recall your first summer job. *Business* is a broad, all-inclusive term that can be applied to many kinds of enterprises. Businesses provide most of our employment opportunities and most of the products that we enjoy every day.

SUMMARY OF LEARNING OBJECTIVES

LO 1.1 Distinguish between business and not-for-profit organizations.

Business consists of all profit-seeking activities that provide goods and services necessary to an economic system. Not-for-profit organizations are business-like establishments whose primary objectives involve social, political, governmental, educational, or similar functions—instead of profits.

✓ ASSESSMENT CHECK ANSWERS

1.1.1 **What activity lies at the heart of every business endeavour?** At the heart of every business endeavour is an exchange between a buyer and a seller.

1.1.2 **What are the primary objectives of a not-for-profit organization?** Not-for-profit organizations place public service above profits, although they need to raise money to operate and achieve their social goals.

LO 1.3 Describe the private enterprise system, including basic rights and entrepreneurship.

The private enterprise system is an economic system that rewards firms for being able to perceive and serve the needs and demands of consumers. Competition in the private enterprise system means success for firms that satisfy consumer demands. Citizens in a private enterprise economy enjoy rights to private property, profits, freedom of choice, and competition. Entrepreneurship drives economic growth.

✓ ASSESSMENT CHECK ANSWERS

1.3.1 **What is an alternative term for private enterprise system?** *Capitalism* is an alternative word for *private enterprise system.*

1.3.2 **What is the most basic freedom under the private enterprise system?** The most basic freedom is the right to private property.

Assessment Check questions correspond to each of the numbered *Learning Objectives* and appear at the end of each major section in the chapter. *Assessment Check Answers* can be found in the *Summary of Learning Objectives* at the end of the chapter.

---

l then sets up a plan to earn those private shopping club for women scounted sale prices to members and typically lasts only 48 hours. lembers are notified by e-mail in : Rack's customer base has grown ry leader in the emerging field of

lled the *private enterprise system*. ig competition, private property,

entrepreneurship the willingness to take risks to create and operate a business.

✓ ASSESSMENT CHECK

1.2.1 Identify the four basic inputs to an economic system.

1.2.2 List four types of capital.

INSIDE BUSINESS

Justin Bieber: Reflecting the changing face of the music business

It may be hard to believe, but Justin Bieber was a virtual unknown in 2007. That was, until his growing YouTube video fan base came to the attention of talent agent Scooter Braun.

Today, Justin Bieber is well known as a Canadian-born and -raised international singing sensation and an icon of today's younger music market. But, at only 13 years of age, Justin Bieber was pretty much an unknown until he was discovered through YouTube, the online video-sharing service. When he was discovered, Bieber was already a talented artist and had many fans. Then, he gained the attention of an agent, and he was on his way to the next step in his climb to the top in the music business. Braun viewed several of the "Mom-produced" videos Bieber's mother had uploaded to YouTube. He then persuaded Bieber's mother, Patricia Mallette, to allow him to represent Justin. So began Bieber's introduction to the industry insiders who would make his dream of a music career a reality. Bieber soon recorded several demos in Atlanta and was introduced to singer and producer Usher. The connections were made, and Bieber was signed to a record label.

The Internet plays a major role linking the various players in the music industry. Talented new artists, like Justin Bieber, can perform to the online universe of potential fans and take their first steps toward their musical career development. A close connection with fans is made easier by posting personal comments, articles, interviews, television shows, music videos, and other content. Such posts help to build the critical "buzz" that draws the attention of agents like Scooter Braun.

The Internet has become a showplace for musical entertainment. As a result, the Internet has dramatically drawn advertising dollars away from traditional media such as radio, television, and magazines. These traditional media depend on large audiences to justify their high advertising costs. The Internet's social media sites succeed by providing content to much smaller niche markets. For

A vignette that looks *Inside Business* opens each chapter and is revisited at the end of the chapter in *Return to Inside Business*. Questions for Critical Thinking help students apply concepts discussed in the chapter to this real business case.

26 PART 1 Business in a Global Environment

RETURN TO INSIDE BUSINESS

Justin Bieber: Reflecting the changing face of the music business

The Internet has changed the way artists, like Justin Bieber, are discovered and how they communicate and develop their relationships with their fan base. Justin Bieber uses a variety of tools such as blogs, tweets, and videos to develop and maintain his relationship with fans.

QUESTIONS FOR CRITICAL THINKING

1. How would you improve Justin Bieber's web presence?
2. What is another type of business that could use the Internet to improve communications between participants?

Solving an Ethical Controversy feature boxes discuss an ethical issue in debate format. Students are presented with pro and con arguments and then a summary of the controversial subject.

SOLVING AN **ETHICAL** CONTROVERSY

Would Prescription Drug Advertisements Be Helpful or Harmful to Canadians?

Currently, direct-to-consumer advertising (DTCA) by drug manufacturers is banned in Canada. Since 1985 in the United States, drug manufacturers have used DTCA to market name-brand prescription drugs. DTCA increased dramatically after 1997, when the U.S. Food and Drug Administration (FDA) no longer required detailed lists of possible side effects. In 2009, pharmaceutical companies spent $4.5 billion on advertising. New Zealand is the only other developed country where DTCA is legal.

Americans now spend more on prescription drugs than on any other area of health care. One reason is the sheer number of prescriptions. Another is that advertising costs have raised the prices of brand-name prescription drugs. Drug companies also market heavily to doctors. The medical community has voiced concern that DTCA may be harming both the public and the healthcare system.

Would direct-to-consumer advertising benefit Canadians?

PRO

1. DTCA encourages people to ask their doctors about potentially harmful conditions that may be helped by nonsurgical treatment if caught early enough.

2. Drug companies use their profits to develop new drugs. This process involves considerable research and testing to win Health Canada's approval of drugs that can improve or even save lives.

CON

1. Drug advertisements appeal to people's emotions while minimizing potential side effects. Advertisements may even persuade people to ask for unnecessary treatments.

2. Pharmaceutical companies usually advertise new drugs that have not been tested over time and are more expensive than slightly different, older drugs with well-known side effects. DTCA sometimes backfires.

Summary

The Health Council of Canada and other agencies have conducted studies on DTCA. These studies show that most doctors felt pressured to prescribe advertised drugs. After a recent U.S. ad campaign for Tegaserod, a drug for irritable bowel syndrome, sales to English-speaking Canadians increased 42 percent. So, despite DTCA being currently banned in Canada, U.S. advertising affects drug sales in Canada. Pharmaceutical companies have tried to introduce DTCA in Europe, but European Union countries voted overwhelmingly against even the "information to patients" section of a proposed regulation.

Sources: "U.S. Ad Spending Down Nine Percent . . . , Nielsen says," The Nielsen Company, February 24, 2010, http://en-us.nielsen.com; http://www.nytimes.com; "Should Prescription Drugs Be Advertised Directly to Consumers?" ProCon.org, http://prescriptiondrugs.procon.org, accessed February 12,2010; Dennis Thompson, "As TV Drug Ads Increase, So Do Concerns," U.S. News & World Report, October 4, 2009, http://www.usnews.com; World Health Organization, "Direct-to-Consumer Advertising Comes under Fire," Bulletin of the World Health Organization 87:8 (August 2009), http://www.who.int, accessed February 12, 2010; Natasha Singer, "Lawmakers Seek to Curb Drug Commercials," New York Times, July 26, 2009; Barbara Mintzes, What Are the Public Health Implications? Direct-to-Consumer Advertising of Prescription Drugs in Canada, January 2006, http://healthcouncilcanada.ca/docs/papers/2006/hcc_dtc-advertising_200601_e_v6.pdf, accessed February 22, 2011; Canadian Family Physician website, http://www.cfp.ca/, accessed February 22, 2011.

BUSINESS ETIQUETTE

Social Networking

Most young people hear a lot of career advice. One reliably good tip is to build a network of personal contacts in your chosen field. Online social networks make this task especially easy—but the Internet's informality can make it tricky to network in a professional way. Here are suggestions for presenting yourself in a positive light on sites like Facebook, LinkedIn, Twitter, and others.

1. Know the purpose of the networking site you choose. Most people consider Facebook more social, while LinkedIn purposely maintains a more professional look and feel.

2. Remember that potential employers, mentors, and other professionals will check your Facebook page to learn about you, despite the site's mostly fun-oriented profile. Look objectively at what they'll see there.

3. Review and edit your posted photos to make sure they present the image of yourself you want others to see.

4. Resist the impulse to share. Keep your posts brief and neither overly detailed nor overly personal. People you hope to tap for potential job leads don't need to know what you ate for breakfast. Limit the information about your family, too.

5. To network with someone you haven't met, first find someone you have in common and ask that person to make an online introduction.

6. Contribute to the community. "Help the people around you and you help yourself," advises one author. Posting interesting information about your area of professional expertise is one way to both help the community and build relationships.

7. Avoid posting any information or opinions about your current or past employers.

8. Always remember that everything you post is as public as the newspaper's front page. Edit yourself, and check your privacy settings.

Sources: G. Lynch "Facebook Etiquette: Five Dos and Don'ts," PCWorld, http://www.pcworld.com, accessed March 2010; Jimmy Wales and Andrea Weckerle, "Keep a Civil Cybertongue," Wall Street Journal, December 29, 2009, p. A19; Laura M. Holson, "Short Outbursts? Big Problem," New York Times October 8, 2009, p. E1C.

Business Etiquette feature boxes provide students with insight and tips on how to communicate effectively and professionally in the contemporary business world.

Two *Hit & Miss* feature boxes in each chapter profile the successes and failures of a wide variety Canadian and international businesses. Students are asked to evaluate each case by answering Critical Thinking Questions.

The growing importance and influence of environmental issues on contemporary business decisions is examined in the *Going Green* feature boxes.

HIT & MISS

Microsoft and Google Square Off on the Web

Google took a big step into Microsoft territory when it introduced home and office tools—Gmail and Google Docs, and especially its own operating system, Chrome OS. These tools challenge Microsoft's long-running Windows series. Google even has a Web browser, also called Chrome, which competes with Microsoft's Internet Explorer. Meanwhile, Microsoft challenges Google's own dominance in Internet searches by promoting its new search engine, Bing.

Google has long supported Web-based applications, as opposed to the desktop applications that have been Microsoft's specialty, but Microsoft is fighting back. Microsoft is creating browser-based versions of its desktop Office products, including Word, Excel, and PowerPoint, to compete with Google's cloud-computing tools. Microsoft's applications are often known for growing by adding more and more features in each new generation. But Microsoft will now need to also match Google's successful focus on speed and ease of use. Google highlights these characteristics to promote a great user experience with its PC products. Google hopes to import this advantage into the business applications market. "We want to spoil people like heck in their personal lives," says Google's vice president of product management. "Then when they go to work, they should be asking the question, 'Why are things so hard?'"

Google credits some of its success to its design teams' unwillingness to settle for the ordinary. "I don't think our Docs team has ever been fundamentally happy with their product," said the president of the company's enterprise group. That restlessness means that weakness in any Google product's performance may be short-lived. Google Docs, for instance, can't yet match Microsoft Word's editing and page layout features, while Google Spreadsheets offers limited performance and scaling capabilities.

Google is so determined to solve such problems that it's helping to shape the creation of the World Wide Web's new HTML5 language, the standard language for structuring and presenting content on web pages and Web-based documents. "We view the Web as a platform," says Google's enterprise product management director. "We don't view it as a companion to the desktop . . . We want the vast majority of users of Microsoft Office to be able to easily switch to Google Docs."

Critical Thinking Questions

1. What feature or features has Google identified as the basis for its competitive differentiation?

2. Some companies are considering using Google's Android operating system for their tablet PCs and netbooks. How do you expect Microsoft to react if Google succeeds in entering the market for desktop applications in this way?

Sources: M. Merrill, "Microsoft Bing, Google Compete with Health Maps," *Healthcare IT News*, www.healthcareitnews.com, June 2, 2010; Thomas Claburn, "Microsoft Web Apps Will Force Google's Hand," InformationWeek, www.informationweek.com, April 10, 2010; Nick Bilton, "A Big-Picture Look at Google, Microsoft, Apple and Yahoo," *New York Times*, www.nytimes.com, January 22, 2010.

GOING GREEN TAX CREDITS FOR AN ENERGY STAR

For the past several decades, the Government of Canada has promoted its EnerGuide labelling program. This program supports energy conservation by helping consumers to understand the heavy energy consumed by washing machines, dryers, stoves, refrigerators, computers, and air conditioners. Energy conservation helps to reduce air pollution caused by energy-producing technologies such as coal- and gas-driven power plants. Energy conservation also helps to reduce the need to build more production facilities, which are typically a government responsibility. Energy is needed to drive the economy. If our economy is to grow, then governments must find the funds needed to develop more energy. A better way to control the costs of supplying energy is to reduce the demand for energy. Governments often use both the "carrot" and "the stick." Higher prices are "the stick" that helps to reduce energy use. Energy use also drops when consumers learn about how much energy they use, often when they purchase new appliances. Tax incentives are "the carrot" that helps consumers to make better and more energy-efficient choices. Recently, the government has offered tax credits to people who buy hybrid gas–electric vehicles, vehicles that use alternative fuels, and plug-in electric vehicles.

Canada's Energy Efficiency Act was passed in 1992. This act sets the minimum energy-efficiency standards for some energy-consuming products, including appliances imported to Canada and those traded between provinces and territories. The "ENERGY STAR" program was introduced in 1992. This program

encourages Canadians to save energy and reduce pollution. The ENERGY STAR symbol goes one step further and identifies the specific models that meet or exceed the highest levels of energy efficiency.

In many communities, when you replace certain appliances with qualified appliances, you receive a rebate and lower your utility bills. Your local government may help you to choose from among boilers, central or room air conditioners, washing machines, dishwashers, freezers, oil and gas furnaces, heat pumps (air source and geothermal), refrigerators, and water heaters. Whether your community takes part depends on climate, geography, and other factors.

Certain kinds of home improvements can receive tax credits, including the replacement of furnaces, windows, hot-water tanks, and insulation. To get an idea of the scale of incentives, visit Natural Resources Canada's Office of Energy Efficiency website.

Questions for Critical Thinking

1. How does paying rebates and granting tax credits stimulate the economy?

2. Which would you prefer to receive—an income-tax credit or a rebate? Why?

Source: Natural Resources Canada's Office of Energy Efficiency website at http://oee.nrcan.gc.ca/, accessed February 8, 2011.

28   PART 1 Business in a Global Environment

BUSINESS TERMS YOU NEED TO KNOW

business 4	private enterprise system 8	brand 14	offshoring 20
profits 4	capitalism 8	transaction management 14	nearshoring 20
not-for-profit organizations 5	competition 8	relationship era 14	vision 21
factors of production 6	competitive differentiation 8	relationship management 15	critical thinking 22
natural resources 6	private property 9	technology 16	creativity 22

Key terms are bolded in the chapter and appear in the adjacent margin with their definitions. Key terms are also listed in *Business Terms You Need to Know* at the end of the chapter with page references.

Chapter 1 The Changing Face of Business   15

Managing Relationships through Technology

Increasingly, businesses focus on **relationship management**, the collection of activities that build and maintain ongoing, mutually beneficial ties with customers and others. At its core, relationship management requires two steps: first, the gathering of knowledge of customer needs and preferences and then applying that understanding to get as close to the customer as possible. Many of these activities are based on **technology**, or the business application of knowledge that is based on scientific discoveries, inventions, and innovations. In managing relationships with customers, technology most often takes the form of communication, via the Internet and cellphone.

relationship management the collection of activities that build and maintain ongoing, mutually beneficial ties with customers and others.

technology the business application of knowledge based on scientific discoveries, inventions, and innovations.

End-of-Chapter Questions and Exercises

Review Questions encourage students to review their understanding of the chapter content.

REVIEW QUESTIONS

1. What do the terms *business ethics* and *social responsibility* mean? Why are they important components of a firm's overall philosophy in conducting business?

2. How do individuals make a difference in a firm's commitment to ethics? Describe the three stages an individual goes through when developing ethical standards.

3. Identify the ethical dilemmas in each of the following situations. (A situation might involve more than one dilemma.)

   a. Due to the breakup with a client, an advertising agency finds itself working with rival companies.

   b. A newly hired employee learns that the office manager plays computer games on company time.

   c. A drug manufacturer offers a doctor an expensive gift to encourage the doctor to prescribe a new brand-name drug.

   d. An employee is told to destroy documents that show a firm's role in spreading pollution.

   e. A company spokesperson agrees to a media conference that puts a positive spin on the firm's use of underpaid labour.

4. Describe how ethical leadership helps to develop each of the other ethical standards.

5. How do firms demonstrate their social responsibility?

6. What are the four major areas where businesses have responsibilities to the general public? How can meeting these responsibilities lead to a competitive edge?

7. Describe the four basic rights that consumerism tries to protect. How has consumerism improved the contemporary business environment? What challenges has consumerism created for businesses?

PROJECTS AND TEAMWORK APPLICATIONS

1. Write your own personal code of ethics. Create standards for your behaviour at school, in personal relationships, and on the job. Assess how well you meet your own standards. Revise your code of ethics, if necessary.

2. On your own or with a classmate, visit the website of one of the following firms, or choose another that interests you. Use what you can learn about the company from the website to construct a chart or figure that shows examples of the firm's ethical awareness, ethical education, ethical actions, and ethical leadership. Present your findings to class.

   a. Tim Hortons

   b. the National Hockey League (NHL), or any major professional sports league

   c. TELUS Mobility

   d. RBC Financial Group

   e. Research In Motion

   f. RONA

   g. IKEA

3. Using the company you studied for question 2 (or another company), conduct a social audit. Do your findings match the firm's culture of ethics? If not, what are the differences, and why did they occur?

4. On your own or with a classmate, go online, flip through a magazine, or surf television channels to identify a firm that uses green marketing. If you see a commercial on television, go to the firm's website to learn more about the product or process advertised. Does the firm make claims that comply with the Competition Bureau's guidelines? Present your findings in class.

5. As a consumer, you expect the companies you do business with will have a certain level of responsibility toward you. Describe a situation when you felt that a company did not recognize your rights as a consumer. How did you handle the situation? How did the company handle it? What was the final outcome?

WEB ASSIGNMENTS

1. Ethical standards. Go to the website listed below. It summarizes the ethical standards for all TELUS employees. Read the material and then write a brief report that compares TELUS's ethical standards to the discussion on corporate ethics in this chapter. In addition, consider how TELUS's ethical standards are integrated into the firm's overall efforts at global citizenship.

   http://about.telus.com/governance/downloads/2010_Ethics_Policy_EN.pdf

2. Starting a career. Each year, *Canada's Top 100* rates the best companies to work for. Visit the *Canada's Top 100* website and review the most recent list. What criteria did *Canada's Top 100* use when building this list? What role does ethics and social responsibility play?

   http://www.canadastop100.com/

3. Social responsibility. Footwear manufacturer La Canadienne is one of the few companies in its industry that still manufactures products in the Canada. Go to the website listed below to learn more about the firm's commitment to Canadian manufacturing. Prepare a report that relates this commitment to the firm's other core values.

   http://www.lacanadienneshoes.com/

Projects and Teamwork Applications encourage active learning and give students the chance to work in groups. Projects can be used either in or out of the classroom.

Web Assignments ask students to research chapter topics using resources on the Internet.

Launching Your... Career at the end of each part of the book explores resources and opportunities available for careers in contemporary business including: Global Business and Economics, Entrepreneurial Pursuits, Marketing, Management, Technology and Information, and Finance.

1 LAUNCHING YOUR . . .

GLOBAL BUSINESS AND ECONOMICS CAREER

In Part 1, "Business in a Global Environment," you learned about the role of contemporary business in today's society. You also learned about the major forces that shape contemporary business. The part includes four chapters that discuss the changing face of business, business ethics and social responsibility, economic challenges facing contemporary business, and competing in world markets. Business has always been an exciting career field. You can choose to start your own company, work at a local business, or take a position with a multinational corporation. Today's business opportunities are very attractive. Businesses are expanding to compete in a global economy—and they need loyal and talented people to help them reach their goals. Professional and business service jobs are found in some of the fastest-growing industries in the North American economy. These jobs are projected to grow by more than 23 percent over a decade.[1] Now is the time to learn about several career options that can lead you to your dream job. Each part in this text includes a profile of some of the many opportunities available in business. Here are a few opportunities related to Chapters 1 through 4.

Appendixes

APPENDIX A
ADDITIONAL CASES

Part 1 Business in a Global Environment

SAS Is Still a Great Place to Work

SAS is a global leader in analytics and statistical software solutions. The company employs thousands of employees around the world, including many working in major cities across Canada. SAS employees enjoy the benefits that come with working for a company that values loyal employees and treats them particularly well. So much so, that in 2011 and 2012, SAS headed the list of *Fortune* magazine's Top 100 Companies to work for. To get an idea of why employees rate the company so highly, let's look at the company's 300-acre (120-hectare) main campus located in Raleigh, North Carolina. Here you will find a gym, weight room, meditation garden, sauna, and Olympic-size swimming pool. It seems unlikely any of the complex's 4,200 employees would fall ill with such health-building options to choose from, but just in case, there's a healthcare centre with a staff of 56, including four doctors, 10 nurses, physical therapists, and a psychologist. All care is free. "We charge you for one thing," says the health service director, "if you miss your appointment and don't give us notice. That's $10."

Additional Cases related to the concepts presented in each of the six parts in the book are provided in Appendix A. Each case profiles a different company and asks students to apply what they have learned in answering Critical Thinking Questions about the case.

APPENDIX B
VIDEO CASES

Part 1 Business in a Global Environment

Secret Acres: Selling Comics Is Serious Business

Just about everyone remembers a favourite comic book hero from childhood—whether it was Spiderman, Tin Tin, or even Garfield. Leon Avelino and Barry Matthews readily admit that they are kids in grown-up bodies with real day jobs (Avelino works for *Sports Illustrated* and Matthews is an accountant for an e-commerce firm). They just happen to love comic books and their latest form—graphic novels. Their love for comics in all forms—and their desire to start their own business—led them to found Secret Acres, a comic book and graphic novel publisher based in New York City. Secret Acres has published several works from up-and-coming authors (they have eight books on their list so far). The company also sells books from independent distributors. Often asked whether they think Secret Acres will succeed or fail in the next few years, Avelino quips, "People think we're too small to fail." He laughs but then adds, "That pisses me off. I think we can totally fail."

Appendix B contains Video Cases based on the Wiley Business Video Series. The video cases feature successful companies like ZipCar, Comet Skateboards, Secret Acres, and Pet Airways, and focus on management issues discussed within one of the book's six parts.

The other five appendixes at the end of the book discuss Business Law, Insurance and Risk Management, Personal Financial Planning, Developing a Business Plan, and Careers in Contemporary Business.

SUPPLEMENTS

A wide assortment of supplements and tools are available to instructors and students using *Contemporary Business*, Canadian edition. All the resources and personal support you will need are available on *WileyPLUS*.

WileyPLUS is an innovative, research-based online environment for effective teaching and learning.

WileyPLUS builds students' confidence because it takes the guesswork out of studying by providing students with a clear roadmap: what to do, how to do it, if they did it right. This interactive approach focuses on:

CONFIDENCE: Research shows that students experience a great deal of anxiety over studying. That's why we provide a structured learning environment that helps students focus on what to do, along with the support of immediate resources.

MOTIVATION: To increase and sustain motivation throughout the semester, *WileyPLUS* helps students learn how to do it at a pace that's right for them. Our integrated resources—available 24/7—function like a personal tutor, directly addressing each student's demonstrated needs with specific problem-solving techniques.

SUCCESS: *WileyPLUS* helps to assure that each study session has a positive outcome by putting students in control. Through instant feedback and study objective reports, students know if they did it right, and where to focus next, so they achieve the strongest results.

With *WileyPLUS*, our efficacy research shows that students improve their outcomes by as much as one letter grade. *WileyPLUS* helps students take more initiative, so you'll have greater impact on their achievement in the classroom and beyond.

What do students receive with *WileyPLUS*?

- The complete digital textbook, saving students up to 60% off the cost of a printed text.
- Question assistance, including links to relevant sections in the online digital textbook.
- Immediate feedback and proof of progress, 24/7.
- Integrated, multimedia resources—including audio summaries, video cases, interactive case studies, crosswords, flashcards, animated figures, and much more—that provide multiple study paths and encourage more active learning.

What do instructors receive with *WileyPLUS*?

- Reliable resources that reinforce course goals inside and outside of the classroom.
- The ability to easily identify those students who are falling behind.
- Media-rich course materials and assessment content including—Instructor's Manual, Test Bank, Computerized Test Bank, PowerPoint® Slides, PRS Questions, Video Cases, Study Guide Solutions, and much more.

www.wileyplus.com. Learn More.

© Can Stock Photo Inc./iofoto

PART 1

BUSINESS IN A GLOBAL ENVIRONMENT

1 | THE CHANGING FACE OF BUSINESS

LEARNING OBJECTIVES

LO 1.1 Distinguish between business and not-for-profit organizations.

LO 1.2 Identify and describe the factors of production.

LO 1.3 Describe the private enterprise system, including basic rights and entrepreneurship.

LO 1.4 Identify the six eras of business, and explain how the relationship era—including alliances, technology, and environmental concerns—influences contemporary business.

LO 1.5 Explain how today's business workforce and the nature of work itself are changing.

LO 1.6 Identify the skills and attributes managers need to lead businesses in the 21st century.

LO 1.7 Outline the characteristics that make a company admired by the business community.

INSIDE BUSINESS

© ZUMA Wire Service/Alamy

Justin Bieber: Reflecting the changing face of the music business

It may be hard to believe, but Justin Bieber was a virtual unknown in 2007. That was, until his growing YouTube video fan base came to the attention of talent agent Scooter Braun.

Today, Justin Bieber is well known as a Canadian-born and -raised international singing sensation and an icon of today's younger music market. But, at only 13 years of age, Justin Bieber was pretty much an unknown until he was discovered through YouTube, the online video-sharing service. When he was discovered, Bieber was already a talented artist and had many fans. Then, he gained the attention of an agent, and he was on his way to the next step in his climb to the top in the music business. Braun viewed several of the "Mom-produced" videos Bieber's mother had uploaded to YouTube. He then persuaded Bieber's mother, Patricia Mallette, to allow him to represent Justin. So began Bieber's introduction to the industry insiders who would make his dream of a music career a reality. Bieber soon recorded several demos in Atlanta and was introduced to singer and producer Usher. The connections were made, and Bieber was signed to a record label. He was on his way to becoming an international teen star.

His break-out single, "One Time," was released in 2009. His first album, "My World 2.0," soon followed in 2010. Both went platinum, and his hit, "Baby," ranks as the most viewed YouTube video ever. It is an understatement to say that YouTube and social media led to Bieber's discovery and career development. Social media have made it easier for talented young artists to seek recognition and a chance at stardom. Agents like Scooter Braun use the Internet to search for new talent. Online popularity and an online fan base can be early signs of likely success.

The Internet plays a major role linking the various players in the music industry. Talented new artists, like Justin Bieber, can perform to the online universe of potential fans and take their first steps toward their musical career development. A close connection with fans is made easier by posting personal comments, articles, interviews, television shows, music videos, and other content. Such posts help to build the critical "buzz" that draws the attention of agents like Scooter Braun.

The Internet has become a showplace for musical entertainment. As a result, the Internet has dramatically drawn advertising dollars away from traditional media such as radio, television, and magazines. These traditional media depend on large audiences to justify their high advertising costs. The Internet's social media sites succeed by providing content to much smaller niche markets. For example, when viewers want to see Justin Bieber perform, they can log onto his dedicated YouTube channel, which is also available on mobile devices like smartphones. And, unlike television or radio, YouTube allows customers to not only listen to songs but also purchase the songs through sites such as Apple's iTunes Store.

Today, the Internet delivers samples of an artist's work to fans. It also delivers related content to help develop a relationship with fans and provides a direct channel for customers to purchase products. The Internet's promotional power speaks to the new world of music and entertainment today.[1]

CHAPTER 1 OVERVIEW

Business is the nation's engine for growth. A growing economy is an economy that produces more goods and services but uses fewer resources over time. Growing economies are important because they yield income for business owners, their employees, and shareholders. A country depends on the wealth its businesses generate, from large enterprises like Research In Motion to start-ups like Justin Bieber, and from venerable firms like BCE to powerhouses like the Royal Bank of Canada. These companies and many others share a creative approach to meeting society's needs and wants.

Businesses solve our transportation problems by marketing cars, tires, gasoline, and airline tickets. They bring food to our tables by growing, harvesting, processing, packaging, and shipping everything from spring water to cake mix and frozen shrimp. Restaurants buy, prepare, and serve food, and some even deliver. Construction companies build our schools, homes, and hospitals, while real estate firms bring property buyers and sellers together. Clothing manufacturers design, create, import, and deliver our jeans, sports shoes, work uniforms, and party wear. Hundreds of firms work at entertaining us during our leisure hours. They create, produce, and distribute films, television shows, video games, books, and music downloads.

To succeed, business firms must know what their customers want, and they must supply it quickly and efficiently. The products that firms produce often reflect changes in consumer tastes, such as the growing preference for sports drinks and vitamin-fortified water. But firms can also *lead*, by promoting technology and other changes. Firms have the resources, the know-how, and the financial incentive to bring about real innovations, such as smartphones, new cancer treatments, and alternative energy sources like wind power. Thus, when businesses succeed, everybody wins.

You'll see throughout this book that businesses require physical inputs such as auto parts, chemicals, sugar, thread, and electricity. They also need the accumulated knowledge and experience of their managers and employees. Businesses also rely heavily on their own ability to change with the times and with the marketplace. Flexibility is a key to long-term success—and to growth.

Business is a leading force in our economy—and *Contemporary Business* is right there with it. This book explores the strategies that allow companies to grow and compete in today's interactive marketplace. This book also explores the skills you will need to turn ideas into action for your own success in business. This chapter sets the stage for the entire text by defining what business is and describing its role in society. The chapter's discussion illustrates how the private enterprise system encourages competition and innovation while preserving business ethics.

WHAT IS BUSINESS?

LO 1.1 Distinguish between business and not-for-profit organizations.

What do you think of when you hear the word *business*? Do you think of big corporations like Rogers Communications or TD Bank? Or do you think about the local bakery or shoe store? Maybe you recall your first summer job. *Business* is a broad, all-inclusive term that can be applied to many kinds of enterprises. Businesses provide most of our employment opportunities and most of the products that we enjoy every day.

business all profit-seeking activities and enterprises that provide goods and services necessary to an economic system.

Business consists of all profit-seeking activities and enterprises that provide goods and services necessary to an economic system. Some businesses produce tangible goods, such as automobiles, breakfast cereals, and digital music players; others provide services, such as insurance, hair styling, and entertainment, ranging from theme parks and sports events to concerts.

Business drives the economic pulse of a nation. It provides the means for improving a nation's standard of living. At the heart of every business is an exchange between a buyer and a seller. A buyer has a need for a good or service and trades money with a seller to receive that product or service. The seller hopes to gain a profit—a main ingredient in reaching the goal of continuously improving the standard of living.

profits rewards for businesspeople who take the risks involved to offer goods and services to customers.

Profits are rewards for businesspeople who take the risks involved in blending people, technology, and information to create and market want-satisfying goods and services. In contrast, accountants think of profits as the difference between a firm's revenues and the expenses it incurs in generating these revenues. More generally, however, profits serve as incentives for people to start companies, expand them, and provide consistently high-quality competitive goods and services.

The quest for profits is a central focus of business: without profits, a company could not survive. But businesspeople also recognize their social and ethical responsibilities. To succeed in the long run, companies must deal responsibly with employees, customers, suppliers, competitors, government, and the general public.

Not-for-Profit Organizations

What is a common feature of Simon Fraser University's athletic department, the Canadian Society for the Prevention of Cruelty to Animals, the Canadian Red Cross, and your local library? They are all **not-for-profit organizations**, business-like establishments that have primary goals other than returning profits to their owners. These organizations play important roles in society by placing public service above profits. It is important

A business survives because of the exchange between buyer and seller. In this hair salon, the exchange occurs between the customer and the stylist.

to understand that these organizations need to raise money to operate and to achieve their social goals. Not-for-profit organizations operate in both the private and public sectors. Private-sector not-for-profits include museums, libraries, trade associations, and charitable and religious organizations. Government agencies, political parties, and labour unions are not-for-profit organizations that are part of the public sector.

not-for-profit organizations organizations whose primary aims are public service, not returning a profit to its owners.

Not-for-profit organizations form a large part of the Canadian economy. The not-for-profit field is an industry just like any other industry: revenues are raised and employees earn incomes by providing services. Canada has more than 160,000 registered not-for-profit organizations, in categories ranging from arts and culture to science and technology. Most are local organizations that provide sports and recreational activities. Not-for-profits receive funding from both government sources and private sources, including donations. These organizations are commonly exempt from federal, provincial, and local taxes. Not-for-profits raise more than $112 billion in revenues and employ more than 2 million people. Approximately one-third of these jobs are in hospitals, universities, and colleges. About half of all revenue comes from government grants, mostly provincial. These organizations also receive more than $8 billion in donations from individuals and require more than 2 billion volunteer hours, the equivalent of more than 1 million full-time jobs.[2]

Managers of not-for-profit organizations focus on goals other than making profits, but they face many of the same challenges as executives of for-profit businesses. Without funding, organizations cannot do research, obtain raw materials, or provide services. Toronto's Hospital for Sick Children (SickKids) is one of the world's top healthcare institutions for children. It is Canada's leading centre dedicated to children's health by uniting patient care, research, and education. SickKids was founded in 1875 and is affiliated with the University of Toronto. It is one of Canada's most research-intensive hospitals: its more than 600 staff researchers operate within a $140 million budget.[3]

Other not-for-profits organize their resources to respond to emergencies. For example, the Red Cross and Doctors without Borders (also known as Médecins Sans Frontière, or MSF) acted quickly when the earthquake in Haiti left hundreds of thousands of families homeless. Relief agencies around the world worked hard to supply enough tents and tarpaulins for immediate shelter. These agencies then turned their attention to constructing more permanent living spaces.[4]

Some not-for-profits sell merchandise or set up profit-making side businesses to sell goods and services that people are willing and able to pay for. For example, college bookstores sell products with the school logo—everything from sweatshirts to coffee mugs. SickKids supports learning for families and healthcare providers by selling parenting books, many of which are Canadian

Jean-Luc Luyssen/ABACAPRESS.COM/The Canadian Press

The Red Cross organizes its efforts to respond to the earthquake disaster in Haiti.

 ASSESSMENT CHECK

1.1.1 What activity lies at the heart of every business endeavour?

1.1.2 What are the primary objectives of a not-for-profit organization?

bestsellers.[5] The Lance Armstrong Foundation has sold more than 40 million yellow LiveStrong wristbands. It also sells sports gear and accessories for men, women, and children. All funds raised through these sales are used to fight cancer and support patients and their families.[6]

Merchandising programs and fundraising campaigns need managers who have effective business skills and experience. As a result, many of the concepts discussed in this book apply both to not-for-profit organizations and to for-profit firms.

LO 1.2 Identify and describe the factors of production.

factors of production four basic inputs for effective operation: natural resources, capital, human resources, and entrepreneurship.

natural resources all production inputs that are useful in their natural states, including agricultural land, building sites, forests, and mineral deposits.

capital production inputs consisting of technology, tools, information, and physical facilities.

FACTORS OF PRODUCTION

An economic system requires certain inputs for successful operation. Economists use the term **factors of production** to refer to the four basic inputs: natural resources, capital, human resources, and entrepreneurship. Table 1.1 identifies each of these inputs and the type of payment received by firms and individuals who supply them.

Natural resources include all production inputs that are useful in their natural states. Examples of the inputs are agricultural land, building sites, forests, and mineral deposits. Calgary-based Encana Corporation is a leading Canadian developer of natural gas supply in North America. Toronto-based Barrick Gold Corporation is the global gold industry leader. Its 25 operating mines and projects are located in five continents and include African Barrick Gold. The world's largest wind farm, the Roscoe Wind Complex near Roscoe, Texas, generates enough power to support almost a quarter million homes. Natural resources are the basic inputs required in any economic system.

Capital, another key resource, includes technology, tools, information, and physical facilities. *Technology* refers to such machinery and equipment as computers and software, telecommunications, and inventions designed to improve production. Information, which is frequently improved by technological innovations, is another critical factor. Both managers and employees require accurate, timely information to effectively perform their assigned tasks. Technology plays an important role in the success of many businesses. Technology can lead to a new product, such as hybrid autos that run on a combination of gasoline and electricity. In recent years, most major car companies have introduced hybrid versions of their bestselling models.

Table 1.1 Factors of Production and Their Factor Payments

FACTOR OF PRODUCTION	CORRESPONDING FACTOR PAYMENT
Natural resources	Rent
Capital	Interest
Human resources	Wages
Entrepreneurship	Profit

Technology can help a company improve a product. Amazon's popular wireless reading device, the Kindle, uses a high-speed wireless network so its readers don't need a computer to download e-books. The latest Kindle model is small and comfortable enough to be held in your hands. It now has improved battery life and storage capacity and weighs less than 170 g. The Kindle reflects light for ease of reading and generates little heat.[7]

Technology can also help a company to operate more smoothly by tracking deliveries, providing more efficient communication, analyzing data, or training employees. Canada Post cut costs by expanding the electronic side of its business. Customers can now track their own registered mail online.

To remain competitive, a firm needs to continually acquire, maintain, and upgrade its capital. All these activities need money. A company's funds may come from the owner's investments, profits that are turned back into the business, or loans from others. Money is used to build factories; purchase raw materials and component parts; and to hire, train, and pay employees. People and firms that supply capital receive factor payments in the form of interest.

Human resources represent another important input in every economic system. Human resources include anyone who works, from the chief executive officer (CEO) of a huge corporation to a self-employed editor. Their input includes both physical labour and intellectual effort. Companies rely on their employees' ideas, innovation, and physical effort. Some companies ask for employee ideas through traditional means, such as through staff meetings and by setting up an online "suggestion box." Others encourage creative thinking during company-sponsored events, such as hiking or rafting trips, or during social gatherings. Effective, well-trained human resources can provide firms with a significant competitive edge. Competitors cannot easily match another company's talented, motivated employees in the same way they can buy the same computer system or purchase the same grade of natural resources.

Competent, effective human resources can be a company's best asset. Providing perks to those employees to keep them is in a company's best interest, as proven by software provider SAS.

Hiring and keeping the right people matters, as we'll see later, in the case at the end of this chapter. SAS continues to be a great place to work in part due to the attention the firm pays to retain their employees.[8]

Entrepreneurship is the willingness to take risks to create and operate a business. An entrepreneur is someone who sees an opportunity to make a profit and then sets up a plan to earn those profits and achieve success. Montreal-based Beyond the Rack is a private shopping club for women and men. Authentic designer merchandise is offered at deep discounted sale prices to members through limited-time events. Each event starts at a specific time and typically lasts only 48 hours. After each event ends, the merchandise is no longer available. Members are notified by e-mail in advance of each event that matches their preferences. Beyond the Rack's customer base has grown to more than 2.5 million members and is recognized as an industry leader in the emerging field of online marketing.[9]

Canadian businesses operate within an economic system called the *private enterprise system*. The next section looks at the private enterprise system, including competition, private property, and the entrepreneurship alternative.

human resources production inputs consisting of anyone who works, including both the physical labour and the intellectual inputs contributed by workers.

entrepreneurship the willingness to take risks to create and operate a business.

✔ **ASSESSMENT CHECK**

1.2.1 Identify the four basic inputs to an economic system.

1.2.2 List four types of capital.

**LO
1.3**   Describe the private enterprise system, including basic rights and entrepreneurship.

THE PRIVATE ENTERPRISE SYSTEM

No business operates on its own. All businesses operate within a larger economic system that directs how goods and services are produced, distributed, and consumed. The type of economic system used in a society also affects the patterns of resource use. Some economic systems, such as communism, enforce strict controls on business ownership, profits, and resources to accomplish government goals.

In Canada, businesses function within the **private enterprise system**, an economic system that rewards firms for their ability to identify and serve the needs and demands of customers. The private enterprise system minimizes government interference in business activity. Businesses that are skillful at satisfying customers will gain access to the necessary factors of production and earn profits.

Another name for the private enterprise system is **capitalism**. Adam Smith, often called the father of capitalism, first described the concept of capitalism in his book *The Wealth of Nations*, published in 1776. Smith believed that an economy is best regulated by the "invisible hand" of **competition**, which is the battle among businesses for consumer acceptance. Smith thought that competition among firms would lead to consumers' receiving the best possible products and prices because less efficient producers would gradually be driven from the marketplace.

The idea of the "invisible hand" is a basic principle of the private enterprise system. In Canada, competition shapes much of economic life. To compete successfully, each firm must find a basis for its **competitive differentiation**, the unique combination of organizational abilities, products, and approaches that sets one company apart from its competitors in the minds of customers. Businesses in a private enterprise system must keep up with changing marketplace conditions. Firms that fail to adjust to shifts in consumer preferences and firms that ignore their competitors risk failure. Google, for instance, continues to challenge Microsoft's leading position in the market for business word-processing and spreadsheet software. Google is expected to enable its Marketing Solutions website to sell third-party software to Google Apps customers. In the short time since Google expanded into enterprise business applications, it has added almost 2 million organizations for Gmail and Google Docs. This aggressive launch will push Microsoft to respond.[10]

In early 2010, Google launched the Nexus One in an effort to compete in the smartphone market; see the "Hit & Miss" feature.

Our discussion in this book focuses on the tools and methods that 21st-century businesses apply to compete and differentiate their goods and services. We also discuss many of the ways that market changes will affect business and the private enterprise system in the future.

Basic Rights in the Private Enterprise System

For capitalism to operate effectively, the citizens of a private enterprise economy must have certain rights. As shown in Figure 1.1, these include the rights to private property, profits, freedom of choice, and competition.

private enterprise system an economic system that rewards firms for their ability to identify and serve the needs and demands of customers.

capitalism an economic system that rewards firms for their ability to perceive and serve the needs and demands of consumers; also called the private enterprise system.

competition the battle among businesses for consumer acceptance.

competitive differentiation the unique combination of organizational abilities, products, and approaches that sets one company apart from its competitors in the minds of customers.

FIGURE 1.1 Basic Rights within a Private Enterprise System

HIT & MISS

Microsoft and Google Square Off on the Web

Google took a big step into Microsoft territory when it introduced home and office tools—Gmail and Google Docs, and especially its own operating system, Chrome OS. These tools challenge Microsoft's long-running Windows series. Google even has a Web browser, also called Chrome, which competes with Microsoft's Internet Explorer. Meanwhile, Microsoft challenges Google's own dominance in Internet searches by promoting its new search engine, Bing.

Google has long supported Web-based applications, as opposed to the desktop applications that have been Microsoft's specialty, but Microsoft is fighting back. Microsoft is creating browser-based versions of its desktop Office products, including Word, Excel, and PowerPoint, to compete with Google's cloud-computing tools. Microsoft's applications are often known for growing by adding more and more features in each new generation. But Microsoft will now need to also match Google's successful focus on speed and ease of use. Google highlights these characteristics to promote a great user experience with its PC products. Google hopes to import this advantage into the business applications market. "We want to spoil people like heck in their personal lives," says Google's vice president of product management. "Then when they go to work, they should be asking the question, 'Why are things so hard?'"

Google credits some of its success to its design teams' unwillingness to settle for the ordinary. "I don't think our Docs team has ever been fundamentally happy with their product," said the president of the company's enterprise group. That restlessness means that weakness in any Google product's performance may be short-lived. Google Docs, for instance, can't yet match Microsoft Word's editing and page layout features, while Google Spreadsheets offers limited performance and scaling capabilities.

Google is so determined to solve such problems that it's helping to shape the creation of the World Wide Web's new HTML5 language, the standard language for structuring and presenting content on web pages and Web-based documents. "We view the Web as a platform," says Google's enterprise product management director. "We don't view it as a companion to the desktop . . . We want the vast majority of users of Microsoft Office to be able to easily switch to Google Docs."

Critical Thinking Questions

1. What feature or features has Google identified as the basis for its competitive differentiation?

2. Some companies are considering using Google's Android operating system for their tablet PCs and netbooks. How do you expect Microsoft to react if Google succeeds in entering the market for desktop applications in this way?

Sources: M. Merrill, "Microsoft Bing, Google Compete with Health Maps," *Healthcare IT News*, www.healthcareitnews.com, June 2, 2010; Thomas Claburn, "Microsoft Web Apps Will Force Google's Hand," InformationWeek, www.informationweek.com, April 10, 2010; Nick Bilton, "A Big-Picture Look at Google, Microsoft, Apple and Yahoo," *New York Times*, www.nytimes.com, January 22, 2010.

The right to **private property** is the most basic freedom in the private enterprise system. Every participant has the right to own, use, buy, sell, and hand down most forms of property, including land, buildings, machinery, equipment, patents on inventions, individual possessions, and intangible properties.

The private enterprise system also guarantees business owners the right to all after-tax profits they earn through their activities. Although a business is not assured of earning a profit, its owner is legally and ethically entitled to any income it makes that is greater than its costs.

Freedom of choice means that a private enterprise system relies on citizens to choose their own employment, purchases, and investments. They can change jobs, discuss and agree on wages, join labour unions, and choose among many different brands of goods and services. People living in the capitalist nations of North America, Europe, and other parts of the world are so conditioned to having this freedom of choice that they sometimes forget how important it is. A private enterprise economy maximizes individual wealth by providing options. Other economic systems sometimes limit the freedom of choice to accomplish government goals, such as by increasing industrial production of certain items or by military strength.

The private enterprise system also allows fair competition by allowing the public to set the rules for competitive activity. For this reason, the Canadian government has passed laws to prohibit excessively aggressive competitive practices designed to remove the competition. The Canadian government has established ground rules that make the following illegal: price discrimination, fraud in financial markets, and deceptive advertising and packaging. For example, in early 2011, the Canadian Radio-television and Telecommunications Commission (CRTC) issued a decision that increased the costs charged to small Internet Service Providers (ISPs) that buy access to the larger ISP networks of Bell and Bell Aliant, mainly in Ontario and Quebec. The CRTC allowed the larger ISPs to control network traffic especially high-volume traffic from the smaller ISPs. The CRTC also

private property the most basic freedom under the private enterprise system; the right to own, use, buy, sell, and hand down land, buildings, machinery, equipment, patents, individual possessions, and various intangible kinds of property.

began charging "usage-based billing." The smaller ISPs who sold popular unlimited packages before were forced to introduce limits, charge more for bandwidth, and change their infrastructure strategy. These changes ended their competitive advantage over the bigger ISPs, which typically charge more for high-volume users. By the end of 2011, after much complaining from the smaller ISP customers, a compromise pricing model was introduced. The new pricing model limits usage but still allows the smaller ISPs to offer unlimited usage packages to those customers that demanded them.[11]

The Entrepreneurship Alternative

entrepreneur a person who seeks a profitable opportunity and takes the necessary risks to set up and operate a business.

The entrepreneurial spirit beats at the heart of private enterprise. An **entrepreneur** is a risk taker in the private enterprise system. You hear about entrepreneurs all the time—two college students starting a software business in their dorm room or a mom who invents a better baby carrier. Many times, their success is modest, but once in a while, the risk pays off in huge profits, as it did for Justin Bieber. People who can see marketplace opportunities are able to use their capital, time, and talents to pursue those opportunities for profit. The willingness of people to start new ventures leads to economic growth and keeps pressure on existing companies to continue to satisfy customers. If no one were willing to take economic risks, the private enterprise system wouldn't exist.

The entrepreneurial spirit leads to growth in the Canadian economy. Of all new businesses created in Canada, 99 percent are small businesses, defined as privately owned and operated companies with fewer than 500 employees and total annual revenue between $30,000 and $5 million. Thousands of new businesses start each year. The Canadian economy depends on small businesses for their growth and strength. Statistics Canada data suggest that 5 percent of all businesses employ fewer than five employees, and 95 percent employ fewer than 50. The small business sector creates 80 percent of all new jobs and generates 45 percent of Canada's economic output. Thus, Canada's small businesses are the majority of all Canadian businesses.[12]

So where are the jobs in Canada? Figure 1.2 shows that the most employment is in the retail trade, followed by accommodation and food services. Notice that small businesses are major employers in these and other segments.[13]

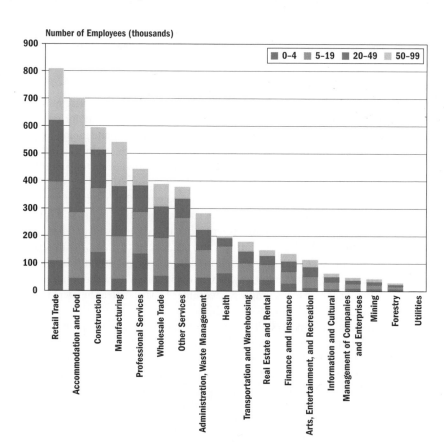

FIGURE 1.2 Number of Private-Sector Employees by Industry and Size of Business Enterprise, 2009

Source: Statistics Canada, *Survey of Employment, Payrolls and Hours* (SEPH), and calculations by Industry Canada. Industry data are classified in accordance with the North American Industry Classification System (NAICS).

Entrepreneurship creates jobs and sells products. Entrepreneurship also leads to innovation. In contrast to more established firms, start-up companies tend to innovate in fields of technology that are new and have few competitors. Because small companies are more flexible than large companies, they can change their products and processes more quickly than larger corporations. Entrepreneurs often find new ways to use natural resources, technology, and other factors of production. Often, they find these new ways because they have to—they may not have enough money to build an expensive prototype or launch a nationwide ad campaign. Sometimes, an entrepreneur may innovate by simply tweaking an existing idea or technology. For example, in 2011, Quebec-based ExoPC introduced the Ciara Vibe tablet to the North American market, after selling earlier versions in Europe and Asia. Software engineer Jean-Baptiste Martinoli adapted Microsoft's Windows 7 operating system to make it able to function with a touch screen. By making the screen larger and adding some additional features, he created another competitor for Apple's iPad. By collaborating with Microsoft, this small business created a niche for itself in a global marketplace. The company was bought in 2010 by Montreal-based Groupe Hypertec Inc. and its CiaraTech division handles manufacturing and distribution. Time will tell whether the marketplace has room for smaller tablet competitors. Sales are just beginning to take off, so we have good reason to believe the firm will be successful.[14]

Apple invites entrepreneurs of all kinds to develop applications for the iPhone. If the new apps are successful, then Apple profits from those efforts.

Entrepreneurship is also important to existing companies. More and more, large firms are realizing the value of entrepreneurial thinking among their employees. These companies hope to benefit from enhanced flexibility, improved innovation, and new market opportunities. Apple also reaches out to its customers, by inviting entrepreneurs of all kinds to develop applications for the iPhone. If the new apps are successful, then Apple profits from those efforts. Already, the iPhone has more than 140,000 different applications, including some developed by Apple. Together, all the apps have been downloaded billions of times.[15]

As the next section explains, entrepreneurs have played a vital role in the history of Canadian business. They have helped create new industries, developed successful new business methods, and improved Canadian standing in global competition.

✓ **ASSESSMENT CHECK**

1.3.1 What is an alternative term for *private enterprise system*?

1.3.2 What is the most basic freedom under the private enterprise system?

1.3.3 What is an entrepreneur?

SIX ERAS IN THE HISTORY OF BUSINESS

LO 1.4 Identify the six eras of business, and explain how the relationship era—including alliances, technology, and environmental concerns—influences contemporary business.

In the 400 or so years since the first Europeans settled on the North American continent, amazing changes have occurred in the size, focus, and goals of Canadian businesses. As Figure 1.3 indicates, North American business history is divided into six distinct time periods: (1) the Colonial period, (2) the Industrial Revolution, (3) the age of industrial entrepreneurs, (4) the production era, (5) the marketing era, and (6) the relationship era. The next sections describe how events in each of these time periods have influenced business practices.

Era	Main Characteristics	Time Period
Colonial Period	Primarily agricultural	Prior to 1776
Industrial Revolution	Mass production by semiskilled workers, aided by machines	1760-1850
Industrial entrepreneurs	Advances in technology and increased demand for manufactured goods, leading to enormous entrepreneurial opportunities	Late 1800s
Production	Emphasis on producing more goods faster, leading to production innovations such as assembly lines	Through the 1920s
Marketing	Consumer orientation, seeking to understand and satisfy needs and preferences of customer groups	Since 1950s
Relationship	Benefits derived from deep, ongoing links with individual customers, employees, suppliers, and other businesses	Began in 1990s

FIGURE 1.3 Six Eras in Business History

The Colonial Period

Colonial society featured rural and agricultural production. Colonial towns were small compared with European cities, and they functioned as marketplaces for farmers and craftspeople. The economic focus of North America centred on rural areas because success depended on the output of farms. The success or failure of crops influenced every aspect of the economy.

Colonists depended on Europe for manufactured items and for financial help for their infant industries. Surprising to some, even after the American Revolutionary War (1776–1783), the United States maintained close economic ties with England. The Canadian experience is more understandable. In Canada, British investors continued to provide much of the money needed for developing the North American business system. This financial influence continued well into the 19th century.

The Industrial Revolution

The Industrial Revolution began in England around 1750. It changed how businesses operated. Instead of a focus on independent, skilled workers who specialized in building products one by one, businesses moved to a factory system that mass-produced items by using numerous semiskilled workers. The factories made profit from the savings created by large-scale production and by increasing their use of machines. As businesses grew, they could often purchase raw materials more cheaply in larger lots. Production was also improved by specialization of labour, such as by limiting each worker to a few specific tasks in the production process.

Because of these events in England, Canadian businesses also began a time of rapid industrialization. Agriculture became mechanized, and factories set up in cities. During the mid-1800s, the pace of the revolution increased as newly built railroad systems provided fast, economical transportation. The railroads opened up the West and transported people and the agricultural products they grew, the timber they felled, and furs they trapped to markets back east and on to Europe.

The Age of Industrial Entrepreneurs

The Industrial Revolution created opportunities, and those opportunities increased entrepreneurship in Canada.

Inventors created new production methods and a virtually endless number of commercially useful products. Many of these products are famous today:

- Alexander Graham Bell; his father, Melville; and friend Reverend Thomas Henderson started basic short-distance telephone service between office buildings and warehouses in 1877. The company later became Bell Canada Inc.

- In the United States, Eli Whitney introduced the idea of interchangeable parts, which later led the way to mass production on a previously impossible scale.

The entrepreneurial spirit of this golden age in business advanced the Canadian business system and increased the overall standard of living for Canadians. That market transformation, in turn, created new demand for manufactured goods.

The Production Era

Demand for manufactured goods continued to increase in the 1920s. Businesses focused even more attention on the activities needed to produce those goods. Work became more specialized, and huge, labour-intensive factories were common in North America. Henry Ford started using assembly lines, which later became commonplace in major industries. Business owners turned over their responsibilities to a new group of managers who had been trained in operating companies. These new managers were able to produce even more goods by using quicker methods.

During the production era, business focused their attention on internal processes instead of external influences. Marketing was rare, used only to distribute a business's products. Little attention was paid to what the consumer wanted or needed. Instead, businesses decided what products were available to purchase. If you wanted to buy a Ford Model T automobile, your colour choice was black—the only colour the company made.

The Marketing Era

The Great Depression of the early 1930s changed Canadian businesses yet again. When most people's incomes dropped, businesses could no longer count on selling everything they produced. Managers

In 1877, Alexander Graham Bell assigned 75 percent of the Canadian telephone patents rights to his father, Melville Bell. He and his friend Reverend Thomas Henderson then began leasing out pairs of wooden hand telephones for use on private lines. These lines were constructed by their clients between close locations, such as between a store and warehouse.

© INTERFOTO / Alamy

began to pay more attention to the markets for their goods and services, and sales and advertising became important activities. During this period, selling often meant the same as marketing.

After World War II, demand increased for all kinds of consumer goods. After nearly five years without new automobiles, appliances, and other items, consumers were buying again. At the same time, competition was also increasing. Businesses soon began to think of marketing as more than just selling; managers thought about a process of deciding what consumers wanted and needed first, and then designing products to meet those needs. In short, they developed a **consumer orientation**.

Businesses began to analyze consumer desires before beginning any production. Consumer choices skyrocketed. Automobiles were sold in a wide variety of colours and styles, and car buyers could choose their favourite colour. Companies also learned how important it was for their goods and services to stand out from those of competitors. **Branding** is the process of creating in consumer's minds an identity for a good, service, or company. Branding is an important marketing tool in contemporary business. A **brand** can be a name, term, sign, symbol, design, or some combination that identifies the products of one firm and shows how they differ from competitors' offerings.

The Home Depot, the world's largest home improvement specialty retailer, operates more than 2,200 retail stores in the United States, Canada, Mexico, and China. It also exports products around the world. Its carefully guarded brand name stands for excellent customer service, an entrepreneurial spirit, and the desire to give back to the communities where it operates. The company sells thousands of products, some under its own sub-brands including RIDGID® tools, BEHR® paint, LG® appliances, and Toro® lawn equipment.[16]

The marketing era has had a huge effect on the way business is conducted today. Even the smallest business owners recognize the importance of understanding what customers want and the reasons they buy.

The Relationship Era

In the 21st century, a major change is taking place in the ways companies relate with their customers. Since the Industrial Revolution, most businesses have concentrated on building and promoting products in the hope that enough customers will buy the products to cover costs and earn acceptable profits. This approach is called **transaction management**.

In contrast, in the **relationship era**, businesses are taking a different, longer-term approach to how they relate with customers. Firms now look for ways to actively promote customer loyalty by carefully managing every interaction. These firms earn huge paybacks for their efforts. A company that keeps its customers over the long term reduces its advertising and sales costs. Because customer spending tends to increase over time, the firm's revenues also grow. Companies with long-term customers often find they no longer need to offer price discounts to attract new business. Instead, they find that many new customers are referred by their loyal customers.

Business owners gain several advantages when they develop ongoing relationships with customers. Serving existing customers is less costly than trying to attract new customers. Thus, businesses that develop long-term customer relationships can reduce their overall costs. Long-term relationships with customers mean that businesses can improve their understanding of what customers want and prefer from the company. As a result, these businesses increase their chances of holding on to real advantages through competitive differentiation.

The relationship era is an age of connections—between businesses and customers, employers and employees, technology and manufacturing, and even between separate companies. More and more, the world economy is interconnected, as businesses expand beyond their national boundaries. In this new environment, techniques for managing networks of people, businesses, information, and technology are critically important to contemporary business success. As you begin your own career, you will soon see the importance of relationships, including your online presence. See the "Business Etiquette" feature for suggestions on presenting yourself in a positive way through social networking.

---

consumer orientation a business philosophy that focuses first on consumers' unmet wants and needs, and then designs products to meet those needs.

branding the process of creating in consumers' minds an identity for a good, service, or company; a major marketing tool in contemporary business.

brand a name, term, sign, symbol, design, or some combination that identifies the products of one firm and shows how they differ from competitors' offerings.

transaction management building and promoting products in the hope that enough customers will buy them to cover costs and earn profits.

relationship era the business era where firms seek to actively promote customer loyalty by carefully managing every interaction.

Managing Relationships through Technology

Increasingly, businesses focus on **relationship management**, the collection of activities that build and maintain ongoing, mutually beneficial ties with customers and others. At its core, relationship management requires two steps: first, the gathering of knowledge of customer needs and preferences and then applying that understanding to get as close to the customer as possible. Many of these activities are based on **technology**, or the business application of knowledge that is based on scientific discoveries, inventions, and innovations. In managing relationships with customers, technology most often takes the form of communication, via the Internet and cellphone.

Blogs are growing more important as a link between companies and their customers, and more companies are beginning to take advantage of blogs' directness. Some companies connect with their customers in a positive way through their company blogs, including Walmart, Patagonia, and LinkedIn.[17] Google used its corporate blog both to announce its new Buzz social networking product and to calm angry users by announcing needed changes in the service; see the "Hit & Miss" feature for an example of relationship-building through technology.

relationship management the collection of activities that build and maintain ongoing, mutually beneficial ties with customers and others.

technology the business application of knowledge based on scientific discoveries, inventions, and innovations.

BUSINESS ETIQUETTE

Social Networking

Most young people hear a lot of career advice. One reliably good tip is to build a network of personal contacts in your chosen field. Online social networks make this task especially easy—but the Internet's informality can make it tricky to network in a professional way. Here are suggestions for presenting yourself in a positive light on sites like Facebook, LinkedIn, Twitter, and others.

1. Know the purpose of the networking site you choose. Most people consider Facebook more social, while LinkedIn purposely maintains a more professional look and feel.

2. Remember that potential employers, mentors, and other professionals will check your Facebook page to learn about you, despite the site's mostly fun-oriented profile. Look objectively at what they'll see there.

3. Review and edit your posted photos to make sure they present the image of yourself you want others to see.

4. Resist the impulse to share. Keep your posts brief and neither overly detailed nor overly personal. People you hope to tap for potential job leads don't need to know what you ate for breakfast. Limit the information about your family, too.

5. To network with someone you haven't met, first find someone you have in common and ask that person to make an online introduction.

6. Contribute to the community. "Help the people around you and you help yourself," advises one author. Posting interesting information about your area of professional expertise is one way to both help the community and build relationships.

7. Avoid posting any information or opinions about your current or past employers.

8. Always remember that everything you post is as public as the newspaper's front page. Edit yourself, and check your privacy settings.

Sources: G. Lynch "Facebook Etiquette: Five Dos and Don'ts," *PCWorld*, http://www.pcworld.com, accessed March 2010; Jimmy Wales and Andrea Weckerle, "Keep a Civil Cybertongue," *Wall Street Journal*, December 29, 2009, p. A19; Laura M. Holson, "Short Outbursts? Big Problem," *New York Times* October 8, 2009, p. E1C.

Strategic Alliances

Businesses are also finding that they must form partnerships with other organizations to take full advantage of opportunities. One form of partnership between organizations is a **strategic alliance**, which creates a competitive advantage for the businesses involved.

E-business has created a new type of strategic alliance. A firm whose entire business is conducted online, such as Amazon or Overstock.com, may team up with traditional retailers who have expertise in distribution and in buying the right amount of the right merchandise. Overstock.com, based in Salt Lake City, Utah, is an online-only retailer for bargain hunters looking for discount prices on brand-name consumer goods, including clothing, appliances, electronics, and sporting goods. Overstock.com partners with manufacturers and distributors that gain a new outlet for reducing their inventory; in return, Overstock.com sells more than 2 million different products on its website. Overstock.com earned revenues of more than $800 million in one recent year and received several top customer service awards.[18]

The Green Advantage

Another way to build relationships is to have your business address some of the issues that your customers care about. For example, environmental concerns now influence consumers' choices of everything from yogurt to clothing to cars and light bulbs; many observers say the question about "going green" is no longer whether, but how. The need to develop environmentally friendly products and processes is a major new force in business today. Companies

 HIT & MISS

Google Buzz a Bust?

As originally conceived, Google's Buzz must have sounded like a great idea: "a new way to start conversations about things you find interesting" that was "built right into Gmail, so you don't have to peck out an entirely new set of friends from scratch—it just works." Unfortunately, the features designed to make adopting Buzz effortless created an instant uproar over users' privacy.

Buzz was planned to compete with Facebook and Twitter. Buzz offered users a ready-made social network through an "auto-follow" function that automatically networked users with their most frequent Gmail contacts. It also automatically connected users with Picasa photo albums and links and videos shared on Google Reader. Tens of millions of people around the world reportedly sampled the new service in its first two days, posting more than 9 million messages and comments. Most users, however, were angry and dismayed to discover how much personal information was made public by the auto-follow and the network's other features.

Within 48 hours, Google announced steps to correct privacy concerns, including changing to an auto-suggest feature and making it easier for users to modify or disable the program. "We're very sorry for the concern we've caused and have been working hard ever since to improve things based on your feedback," Buzz's product manager told users. "We'll continue to do so."

Though some observers still worried that "Gmail users are being driven into a social networking service . . . they didn't sign up for," others conceded the high level of interest in Buzz suggested "Google might have a minor hit on its hands already." The debate was settled in late 2011 when Google announced the end of Buzz.

Questions for Critical Thinking

1. Can a company carry its efforts at customer relationship-building too far?

2. Why do you think Google could not recover customers' goodwill after introducing new privacy features into its Buzz network?

Sources: Chloe Albanesius, "The Year in Review: Google," *PCMag*, December 26, 2011, http://www.pcmag.com/article2/0,2817,2398051,00.asp; Miguel Helft, "Anger Leads to Apology from Google About Buzz," *New York Times*, February 15, 2010, http://www.nytimes.com; David Coursey, "Google Apologizes for Buzz Privacy Issues," *PC World*, February 15, 2010, http://www.pcworld.com; "Millions of Buzz Users, and Improvements Based on Your Feedback," company website, February 11, 2010, http://gmailblog.blogspot.com; "Introducing Google Buzz," company website, February 9, 2010, http://googleblog.blogspot.com.

in every industry are researching how to save energy, cut emissions and pollution, reduce waste, and, of course, how to save company money and increase profits. Endura Energy is an Ontario-based developer of large-scale rooftop solar energy systems. This company works with building owners to capture value from unused roof space and to promote green energy. Using the Ontario government's Feed-in-Tariff program, Endura Energy is building a 100-kilowatt (kW) rooftop solar power system in Richmond Hill. This system will generate approximately 110,000 kilowatt hours (kWh) of clean energy each year, equivalent to reducing approximately 85 tonnes of carbon emissions annually. The owners of the building do not need to contribute financially, which will make it easier to develop more rooftop systems that will contribute to the electric grid.[19]

Energy is among the biggest costs for most firms. Traditional carbon-based fuels such as coal are responsible for most of the additional carbon dioxide in the atmosphere. Ford Motor Company is upgrading lighting fixtures in its manufacturing facilities. The old inefficient equipment will be replaced with fluorescent lighting that saves energy and money. The new lighting will include motion detectors to reduce energy use during periods of low activity.[20] Clean solar energy is becoming more common and may soon be easier to set up and more widely available. Endura Energy is currently developing more than 5 megawatts (MW) of projects covering more than 93,000 square metres of roof space across 20 separate sites. The Ontario government's Feed-in-Tariff program guarantees the purchase of electricity produced at set rates. Thus, we will likely see more projects built on available rooftops.[21]

Some "green" initiatives can be costly for firms. General Electric, though, has found a hit in its Ecomagination line of environmentally friendly products. For General Electric, thinking "green" satisfies not only consumers' environmental concerns but also shareholders' concerns about saving money and earning profits. "We've sold out in eco-certified products for [a year in advance]," says Bob Corcoran, the company's vice president for corporate citizenship. The company's energy-saving wind turbines are backordered for two years. GE believes it is doing what its shareholders expect it to do. "No good business can call itself a good corporate citizen if it fritters away shareholder money," Corcoran says.[22]

In each new era in business history, managers have had to re-examine their tools and techniques. Tomorrow's managers will need creativity and vision to stay on top of rapidly changing technology and to manage complex relationships in the global business world of the fast-paced 21st century. As green operations become more cost-effective, and as consumers and shareholders demand more responsive management, few firms will want to be left behind. For a look at management issues in the energy industry, see the "Going Green" feature.

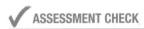

ASSESSMENT CHECK

1.4.1 What was the Industrial Revolution?

1.4.2 During which era was the idea of branding developed?

1.4.3 What is the difference between transaction management and relationship management?

GOING GREEN GREEN **ENERGY ISN'T CHEAP**

Ontario's Green Energy Act was introduced in 2009. At the time, the government promised to close aging coal-generating plants and replace them with alternative green sources of energy. New nuclear power stations, solar-panelled rooftops, and wind farms were expected to produce green energy and jobs by using a new generation of technology. However, some Ontario consumers and businesses have seen their energy bills double, and many communities have been in conflict over the location of wind farms and on issues with respect to nuclear power safety.

A different experience occurred in one U.S. region, where the shift to nuclear technology appears to have been successful.

"Time is not our friend with respect to global climate change . . . the usual approach—doing too much, too late—will not work." So says John Rowe, CEO of the utility company Exelon, a recent winner of the National Safety Council's Green Cross for Safety. Exelon is betting on the world's growing demand for renewable energy sources to create a sound financial future for the company and its stakeholders while minimizing its environmental impact.

Exelon was created in 2000 from a merger between utility companies in Chicago and Philadelphia. After the merger, Exelon sold most of its underperforming coal plants to focus on nuclear power generation. Its fleet of 17 reactors is the world's third-largest, topped only by utilities in France and Russia. Exelon earns $17 billion in sales and almost $3 billion in profits each year. As a result, it returns more than twice as much to shareholders as other utilities. Its nuclear plants produce about 130 billion kWh of electricity each year. Greenhouse gas emissions have been reduced more than 35 percent from earlier levels. That's equivalent to taking 1 million passenger cars off the road.

Legislation to cap or more heavily regulate carbon emissions will force Exelon's carbon-dependent competitors to increase their prices. "I thought climate legislation would come sooner or later and that I'd rather have my money in the nuke fleet," says Rowe. The company plans to further shrink its carbon footprint by 2020 by eliminating more than 15 million metric tons of potential greenhouse gas emissions every year.

Questions for Critical Thinking

1. Exelon has tried and failed to acquire three smaller rival companies. What role, if any, might strategic partnerships play in the company's future?

2. Exelon is the most valuable U.S. utility company in terms of market value. It derives 92 percent of its power from nuclear plants. Is being environmentally aware and being profitable compatible goals for a business? Why or why not?

3. Canadian power supply is typically owned entirely or partially by provincial governments. Does government ownership make a difference to company managers when they make major decisions?

Sources: Andy Frame, "It's Not Easy (or Cheap) Going Green," *Hamilton Spectator*, January 26, 2011, http://www.thespec.com/opinion/editorial/article/477815--it-s-not-easy-or-cheap-going-green,; Exelon Company website, www.exeloncorp.com, accessed February 12, 2010; Julie Schmit, "Exelon CEO: Deal with Emissions Now," *USA Today*, January 25, 2010, www.usatoday.com; Jonathan Fahey, "Exelon's Carbon Advantage," *Forbes*, January 18, 2010, http://www.forbes.com; "National Safety Council Names Exelon Nuclear as Recipient of 2010 Green Cross for Safety Medal," *PR Newswire*, January 5, 2010.

Scott Olson/Staff/Getty Images News/Getty Images

Companies in every industry are researching how to save energy, cut emissions, reduce waste, and save company money. Clean solar energy is one option that is becoming more common and may soon be easier to set up and more widely available.

LO 1.5 Explain how today's business workforce and the nature of work itself are changing.

TODAY'S BUSINESS WORKFORCE

A skilled and knowledgeable workforce is an essential resource for keeping pace with the rapid rate of change in today's business world. Employers need reliable workers who are dedicated to promoting strong ties with customers and partners. Employers need to build workforces that are capable of efficient, high-quality production, which is needed to compete in global markets. Smart business leaders also realize that the brainpower of employees plays a vital role in a firm staying on top of new technologies and innovations. In short, a first-class workforce can be the foundation of a firm's competitive differentiation, providing important advantages over competing businesses.

Changes in the Workforce

Companies face several trends that challenge their skills for managing and developing human resources. These challenges include the aging of the population and a shrinking labour pool, the growing diversity of the workforce, the changing nature of work, the need for flexibility and mobility, and the need to work with others to innovate.

Aging of the Population and a Shrinking Labour Pool

As people retire from the workforce, they take their experience and expertise with them. As Figure 1.4 shows, the Canadian population as a whole is aging. Today, though, many of those from the Baby Boom generation, the huge number of people born between 1946 and 1964, are still hitting the peaks of their careers. At the same time, members of so-called Generation X (born from 1965 to 1981) and Generation Y (born from 1982 to 2005) are building their careers. As a result, employers are finding more generations together in the workforce than ever before. This broad age diversity brings management challenges, such as the need to accept a variety of work–life styles, the changing expectations of work, and varying levels of technological expertise. Still, despite the wide range of ages in the workforce today, some economists predict the Canadian labour pool could soon fall short as the Baby Boomers retire.

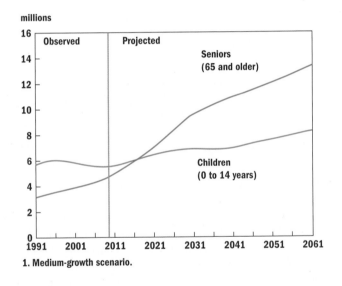

FIGURE 1.4
Population Projections, Children and Seniors

Source: Statistics Canada, CANSIM tables 051-001 and 052-005.

Technology has intensified the hiring challenge by requiring workers to have ever-more advanced skills. Although the number of college-educated workers has increased, the demand for these workers is still greater than the supply. Because of these changes, companies are increasingly seeking—and finding—talent at the extreme ends of the working-age spectrum. Teenagers are entering the workforce sooner, and some seniors are working longer—or seeking new careers after retiring from their primary careers. Many older workers work part-time or flexible hours. Meanwhile, for those older employees who do retire, employers must look after a variety of retirement planning and disability programs, retraining, and insurance benefits.

Increasingly Diverse Workforce

The Canadian workforce is growing more diverse, in age and in other ways, too. Two-thirds of Canada's population growth is due to international immigration, particularly from Asia. As illustrated in Figure 1.5, Chinese immigration is closely followed by immigration from India and other Asian countries.

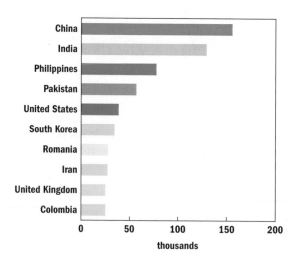

FIGURE 1.5 Top 10 Birthplaces of Immigrants Who Landed in Canada from 2001 to 2006

Source: Statistics Canada, 2006 Census of Population.

diversity the blending of individuals of different genders, ethnic backgrounds, cultures, religions, ages, and physical and mental abilities to enhance a firm's chances of success.

Diversity is the blending of individuals of different genders, ethnic backgrounds, cultures, religions, ages, and physical and mental abilities. Having a diverse workplace can enhance a firm's chances of success. Some firms that recently made the top 10 in a list of "Top 50 Companies for Diversity" were also leaders and innovators in their industries, including Johnson & Johnson (number one on the list), AT&T, the accounting firm Ernst & Young, Marriott International, The Coca-Cola Company, and IBM.[23] Several studies have shown that diverse employee teams and workforces tend to perform tasks more effectively. They also develop better solutions to business problems than homogeneous employee groups. This result is due in part to the varied perspectives and experiences that promote innovation and creativity in multicultural teams.

Practical managers also know that attention to diversity issues can help them avoid damaging legal battles. Losing a discrimination lawsuit can be very costly; yet, in a recent survey, a majority of executives from racial and cultural minorities said they had seen discrimination in work assignments.[24]

Outsourcing and the Changing Nature of Work

The Canadian workforce is changing, but so is the nature of work. Manufacturing once accounted for most of Canada's annual output, but most Canadian employment has now shifted to services such as financial management and communications. Because of this change, firms must now rely on well-trained service workers who have knowledge, technical skills, the ability to communicate and deal with people, and a talent for creative thinking. The Internet offers another business tool for increasing employment flexibility. **Outsourcing** is the use of outside vendors to produce goods or fulfill services and functions that were previously handled in-house or in-country. In the best situation, outsourcing can reduce costs and allow a firm to concentrate on what it does best, while accessing expertise it may not have. But outsourcing also creates its own challenges, such as differences in language or culture.

outsourcing using outside vendors to produce goods or fulfill services and functions that were previously handled in-house or in-country.

offshoring the relocation of business processes to lower-cost locations overseas.

Offshoring is the relocation of business processes to lower-cost locations overseas. Offshoring can involve both production and services. In recent years, China has emerged as a prime location for production offshoring, whereas India has become the key player in offshoring services. Some companies are now structured so that entire divisions or functions are developed and staffed overseas—the jobs were never in Canada to start with. Another trend in some industries is **nearshoring**, outsourcing production or services to nations near a firm's home base.

nearshoring the outsourcing of production or services to locations near a firm's home base.

Flexibility and Mobility

Younger workers are looking for an experience different from the work-comes-first lifestyle of the Baby Boom generation. Workers of all ages are exploring different work arrangements, such as telecommuting from remote locations and sharing jobs among two or more employees.

Employers are also hiring more temporary and part-time employees, some of whom are less interested in climbing the career ladder and more interested in using and developing their skills. The cubicle-filled office will likely never disappear, but technology has made certain tasks easier. For example, employees can take part in productive networking and virtual teams because technology allows people to work where they choose and to easily share knowledge, a sense of purpose or mission, and a free flow of ideas across any geographical distance or time zone.

Managers of such spread-out workforces need to work hard to build and earn the trust of their staff. Managers aim to retain valued employees and to ensure that all members are acting ethically and contributing their share without the day-to-day supervision of a conventional workplace. These managers, and their employees, need to be flexible and sensitive to change, while work, technology, and the relationships between them continue to evolve.

Innovation through Collaboration

Some observers also see a trend toward more collaborative work in the future, as opposed to individuals working alone. Businesses that use teamwork hope to build a creative setting where all members contribute their knowledge and skills to solve problems or seize opportunities.

The old relationship between employers and employees was simple: workers arrived at a certain hour, worked at their jobs, and went home every day at the same time. Companies rarely laid off workers, and employees rarely left for a job at another firm. But all that—and more—has changed. Employees are no longer likely to remain with a single company throughout their entire careers. Employees do not expect lifetime loyalty from the companies they work for, and they do not expect to give that loyalty to any company either. Instead, today's employees build their own careers however and wherever they can. These changes mean that many firms now recognize the value of a partnering with employees to encourage creative thinking and problem solving and to reward risk taking and innovation.

✔ **ASSESSMENT CHECK**

1.5.1 Define outsourcing, offshoring, and nearshoring.

1.5.2 Describe the importance of collaboration and employee partnership.

THE 21ST-CENTURY MANAGER

LO 1.6 Identify the skills and attributes managers need to lead businesses in the 21st century.

Today's companies look for managers who are intelligent, highly motivated people who can create and sustain a vision of how an organization can succeed. The 21st-century manager must apply critical-thinking skills and creativity to business challenges and lead change.

Importance of Vision

To thrive in the 21st century, businesspeople need **vision**, the ability to perceive marketplace needs and what an organization must do to satisfy them. Canadian James Cameron is the Oscar–award winning writer and director of blockbuster sci-fi films, including *The Terminator, Aliens, The Abyss,* and the all-time most successful film, *Avatar.* Cameron has an uncanny ability to know what audiences want and how to produce it. After he exceeded the budgets for *Titanic,* Cameron persuaded his financial backers to continue funding the project. To show his confidence that *Titanic* would succeed, he offered to give up his fees for writing the screenplay and directing, in exchange for receiving a percentage of box office sales. His financial backers recognized his motivation to complete the film, and their funding of the film proved to be a good decision. *Titanic* earned more than $25 million the first weekend of its release and went on to replace George Lucas's *Star Wars* as the biggest money-making film in history. Cameron's futuristic 3-D creation *Avatar* broke through that milestone and won 11 Oscars.[25]

vision the ability to perceive marketplace needs and what an organization must do to satisfy them.

Film director, writer, and inventor James Cameron knows how to entertain audiences.

Importance of Critical Thinking and Creativity

Critical thinking and creativity are essential characteristics of workers in the 21st century. Today's businesspeople need to look at a wide variety of situations, draw connections between dissimilar information, and develop future-oriented solutions. This need applies to top executives, mid-level managers, and entry-level workers.

critical thinking the ability to analyze and assess information to pinpoint problems or opportunities.

Critical thinking is the ability to analyze and assess information to pinpoint problems or opportunities. The critical-thinking process includes activities such as determining the authenticity, accuracy, and worth of information, knowledge, and arguments. It involves looking beneath the surface for deeper meaning and connections that can help identify critical issues and solutions. Without critical thinking, a firm may encounter serious problems.

creativity the capacity to develop novel solutions to perceived organizational problems.

Creativity is the capacity to develop novel solutions to perceived organizational problems. Most people think of creativity in terms of writers, artists, musicians, and inventors, but that definition is very limited. In business, creativity refers to being able to see better and different ways of doing business. A computer engineer who solves a glitch in a software program is performing a creative act, as is a shipping clerk who finds a way to speed delivery of the company's overnight packages. Sometimes, a crisis calls for creative leadership. For example, Captain Chesley Sullenberger famously guided US Airways Flight 1549 to a safe landing in New York's Hudson River. In doing so, he had already made immediate and critical decisions when both his plane's engines quit after hitting birds upon takeoff. Sullenberger's quick thinking and years of training saved the lives of his passengers and crew members and the people on the ground. "Losing thrust on both engines, at low speed, at a low altitude, over one of the most densely populated areas on the planet. Yes, I knew it was a very challenging situation," he said. As the plane lost altitude, Sullenberger ruled out returning to LaGuardia Airport or attempting to land at a nearby New Jersey airport. Instead, he opted to splash down in the river, close to a ferry terminal. "I needed to touch down with the wings exactly level . . . the nose slightly up . . . [and] just above our minimum flying speed, but not below it." He accomplished those seemingly impossible feats and saved all 155 people on board.[26]

Some practice and mental exercise can cultivate your own ability to think creatively. See Figure 1.6 for some exercises and guidelines to improve your creativity.

Creativity and critical thinking must do more than generate new ideas. They must lead to action. In addition to creating an environment in which employees can nurture ideas, managers must give employees opportunities to take risks and try new solutions.

- In a group, brainstorm by listing ideas as they come to mind. Don't criticize other people's ideas, but build on them. Wait until later to evaluate and organize the ideas.

- Think about how to make familiar concepts unfamiliar. A glue that doesn't stick very well? That's the basis for 3M's popular Post-it® notes.

- Plan ways to rearrange your thinking by asking simple questions such as, "What features can we leave out?" or by imagining what it feels like to be the customer.

- Cultivate curiosity, openness, risk, and energy as you meet people and encounter new situations. View these encounters as opportunities to learn.

- Treat failures as additional opportunities to learn.

- Get regular physical exercise. When you work out, your brain releases endorphins, and these chemicals stimulate creative thinking.

- Pay attention to your dreams and daydreams. You might find that you already know the answer to a problem.

FIGURE 1.6
Exercises and Guidelines to Promote Creative Thinking

Ability to Lead Change

Today's business leaders must guide their employees and organizations through the changes brought about by technology, marketplace demands, and global competition. Managers must be skilled at recognizing employee strengths and motivating people to move toward common goals as members of a team. Throughout this book, real-world examples show how companies have initiated major change initiatives. Most, if not all of these companies, have been led by managers who are comfortable with making the tough decisions that are needed in today's fluctuating conditions.

Factors that require organizational change can come from both external and internal sources; successful managers must be aware of both types of factors. External forces might include feedback from customers, developments in the international marketplace, economic trends, and new technologies. Internal factors might arise from new company goals, emerging employee needs, labour union demands, or production problems.

✔ **ASSESSMENT CHECK**

1.6.1 Why is vision an important managerial quality?

1.6.2 What is the difference between creativity and critical thinking?

WHAT MAKES A COMPANY ADMIRED?

LO 1.7 Outline the characteristics that make a company admired by the business community.

Who is your hero? Is it someone who has achieved great feats in sports, government, entertainment, or business? Why do you admire this person—does he or she run a company, earn a lot of money, or give back to the community and society? Every year, business magazines and organizations publish lists of companies that they consider to be "most admired." Companies, like individuals, may be admired for many reasons. Some of these reasons might include solid profits, stable growth, a safe and challenging work environment, high-quality goods and services, and business ethics and social responsibility. *Business ethics* refers to the standards of conduct and moral values involved in decisions made in the work environment. *Social responsibility* is a management philosophy that includes contributing resources to the community, preserving the natural environment, and developing or participating in not-for-profit programs designed to promote the well-being of the general public. We explore these topics more deeply in Chapter 2. You'll also find business ethics and social responsibility examples throughout this book. For businesses to behave ethically and responsibly, their employees need strong moral guidance. The "Solving an Ethical Controversy" feature debates the responsibility of watchdogs—the people and organizations that monitor companies—when they fail to perform their duties.

ASSESSMENT CHECK

1.7.1 Define *business ethics* and *social responsibility*.

1.7.2 Identify three criteria used to judge whether a company might be considered admirable.

As you read this text, you'll be able to make up your mind about why companies should—or should not—be admired. *Fortune* publishes two lists of most-admired companies each year, one for U.S.-based firms and one for the world. The list is compiled from surveys and other research conducted by the Hay Group, a global human resources and organizational consulting firm. Criteria for making the list include innovation, people management, use of corporate assets, social responsibility, quality of management, and quality of products and services.[27] *Fortune* ranked Apple as the number one most admired company in 2011. Their complete "Top Ten" list can be found online.

SOLVING AN **ETHICAL** CONTROVERSY

Securities Oversight?

In Canada and the United States, the laws on the buying and selling of securities, such as stocks and bonds, require full disclosure of information to discourage fraud. Enforcement is typically by authorities and the businesspeople who earn their living persuading investors to undertake risks with their money. This arrangement has worked well enough that extreme cases of abuse of trust are very rare.

A whopping $65-billion securities fraud came to light during the economic downturn that began in 2008. The investment company run by Bernard Madoff turned out to be the biggest Ponzi scheme of all time. Madoff used new investors' funds to pay off the older investors. The investment profits that Madoff claimed were only an illusion. Independent investigator Harry Markopolos told Congress he had been warning the U.S. securities authority, the SEC, about Madoff's activities for years. "I gift-wrapped and delivered the largest Ponzi scheme in history to them and somehow they couldn't be bothered to conduct a thorough and proper investigation because they were too busy on matters of higher priority," Markopolos testified. Thousands of individual and institutional investors faced financial ruin as Madoff's scheme evaporated.

If the SEC was not doing its job, does it bear part of the blame for investors' losses?

PRO

1. A $65-billion fraud could flourish only under a flawed regulatory system. "Our current fragmented regulatory system can allow bad actors to engage in misconduct outside the view and reach of some regulators," said an officer of the securities industry's watchdog organization. "It is undeniable that . . . the system failed to protect investors."

2. "The SEC is . . . captive to the industry it regulates, and it is afraid of bringing big cases against the largest, most powerful firms," said Markopolos. "Clearly the SEC was afraid of Mr. Madoff."

CON

1. The SEC's director of enforcement told a Senate committee, "We don't turn a blind eye to fraud. If we see it and we suspect it, we pursue it. We don't want fraudsters out there."

2. The director also said the SEC doesn't have enough resources to pursue all the tipoffs of potential fraud that come before it: "If we had more resources, we could clearly do more." Other regulators blamed lack of coordination among government agencies for the lapses in oversight that allowed Madoff to operate.

Summary

Madoff pled guilty to charges of felony securities fraud and was sentenced to 150 years in prison. The SEC is conducting an internal investigation to learn why it failed to act on information that Markopolos and others had provided over the years.

Sources: Jenny Anderson and Zachery Kouwe, "SEC Enforcers Focus on Avoiding Madoff Repeat," *New York Times*, February 8, 2010, www.nytimes.com; SEC website, U.S. Securities and Exchange Commission, "The Investor's Advocate: How the Sec Protects Investors, Maintains Market Integrity, and Facilitates Capital Formation," http://www.sec.gov/about/whatwedo.shtml, accessed February 13, 2009; Linda Sandler, "Madoff Said Only Brother Could Do Audit, Witness Tells Congress," *Bloomberg News*, February 5, 2009, http://www.bloomberg.com; Allan Chernoff, "Madoff Whistleblower Blasts SEC," *CNNMoney*, February 4, 2009, http://www.cnnmoney.com; Dana B. Henriques, "Witness on Madoff Tells of Fear for Safety," *New York Times*, February 4, 2009, http://www.nytimes.com; Julian Cummings, "Madoff: SEC Defends Its Role," *CNNMoney*, January 28, 2009, http://www.cnnmoney.com; Liz Moyer, "How Regulators Missed Madoff," *Forbes*, January 27, 2009, http://www.forbes.com.

WHAT'S AHEAD

As business speeds along in the 21st century, new technologies, population shifts, and shrinking global barriers will alter the world at a frantic pace. Businesspeople trigger many of these changes, by creating new opportunities for individuals who are prepared to take action. Studying contemporary business will help you prepare for the future.

Throughout this book, you'll be exposed to the real-life stories of many businesspeople. You'll learn about a range of business careers and the daily decisions, tasks, and challenges that businesspeople face. By the end of the course, you'll understand how marketing, production, accounting, finance, and management work together to provide competitive advantages for firms. This knowledge can help you become a more capable employee and enhance your career potential.

Now that this chapter has introduced some basic terms and issues in the business world of the 21st century, Chapter 2 takes a detailed look at the ethical and social responsibility issues facing contemporary business. Chapter 3 deals with economic challenges, and Chapter 4 focuses on the difficulties and opportunities faced by firms competing in world markets.

RETURN TO INSIDE BUSINESS

Justin Bieber: Reflecting the changing face of the music business

The Internet has changed the way artists, like Justin Bieber, are discovered and how they communicate and develop their relationships with their fan base. Justin Bieber uses a variety of tools such as blogs, tweets, and videos to develop and maintain his relationship with fans.

QUESTIONS FOR CRITICAL THINKING

1. How would you improve Justin Bieber's web presence?

2. What is another type of business that could use the Internet to improve communications between participants?

SUMMARY OF LEARNING OBJECTIVES

LO 1.1 Distinguish between business and not-for-profit organizations.

Business consists of all profit-seeking activities that provide goods and services necessary to an economic system. Not-for-profit organizations are business-like establishments whose primary objectives involve social, political, governmental, educational, or similar functions—instead of profits.

✓ ASSESSMENT CHECK ANSWERS

1.1.1 **What activity lies at the heart of every business endeavour?** At the heart of every business endeavour is an exchange between a buyer and a seller.

1.1.2 **What are the primary objectives of a not-for-profit organization?** Not-for-profit organizations place public service above profits, although they need to raise money to operate and achieve their social goals.

LO 1.2 Identify and describe the factors of production.

The factors of production have four basic inputs: natural resources, capital, human resources, and entrepreneurship. Natural resources include all productive inputs that are useful in their natural states. Capital includes technology, tools, information, and physical facilities. Human resources include anyone who works for the firm. Entrepreneurship is the willingness to take risks to create and operate a business.

✓ ASSESSMENT CHECK ANSWERS

1.2.1 **Identify the four basic inputs to an economic system.** The four basic inputs are natural resources, capital, human resources, and entrepreneurship.

1.2.2 **List four types of capital.** Four types of capital are technology, tools, information, and physical facilities.

LO 1.3 Describe the private enterprise system, including basic rights and entrepreneurship.

The private enterprise system is an economic system that rewards firms for being able to perceive and serve the needs and demands of consumers. Competition in the private enterprise system means success for firms that satisfy consumer demands. Citizens in a private enterprise economy enjoy rights to private property, profits, freedom of choice, and competition. Entrepreneurship drives economic growth.

✓ ASSESSMENT CHECK ANSWERS

1.3.1 **What is an alternative term for *private enterprise system*?** *Capitalism* is an alternative word for *private enterprise system*.

1.3.2 **What is the most basic freedom under the private enterprise system?** The most basic freedom is the right to private property.

1.3.3 **What is an entrepreneur?** An entrepreneur is a risk taker who is willing to start, own, and operate a business.

LO 1.4 Identify the six eras of business, and explain how the relationship era—including alliances, technology, and environmental concerns—influences contemporary business.

The six historical eras are the Colonial period, the Industrial Revolution, the age of industrial entrepreneurs, the production era, the marketing era, and the relationship era. In the Colonial period, businesses were small and rural, emphasizing agricultural production. The Industrial Revolution brought factories and mass production to business. The age of industrial entrepreneurs built on the Industrial Revolution through an expansion in the number and size of firms. The production era focused on the growth of factory operations through assembly lines and other efficient internal processes. During and following the Great Depression, businesses concentrated on finding markets for their products through advertising and selling, giving rise to the marketing era. In the relationship era, businesspeople focus on developing and sustaining long-term relationships with customers and other businesses. Technology promotes innovation and communication, while alliances create a competitive advantage through partnerships. Concern for the environment also helps build strong relationships with customers.

 ASSESSMENT CHECK ANSWERS

1.4.1 What was the Industrial Revolution? The Industrial Revolution began around 1750 in England. It moved business operations from an emphasis on independent, skilled workers to a factory system that mass-produced items.

1.4.2 During which era was the idea of branding developed? The idea of branding began in the marketing era.

1.4.3 What is the difference between transaction management and relationship management? Transaction management focuses on building, promoting, and selling enough products to cover costs and earn profits. Relationship management is the collection of activities that build and maintain ongoing ties with customers and other parties.

LO 1.5 Explain how today's business workforce and the nature of work itself are changing.

The workforce is changing in several significant ways: (1) it is aging and the labour pool is shrinking, and (2) it is becoming increasingly diverse. The nature of work has shifted toward services and a focus on information. More firms now rely on outsourcing, offshoring, and nearshoring to produce goods or to fulfill services and functions that were previously handled in-house or in-country. Today's workplaces are also becoming increasingly flexible, allowing employees to work from different locations and through different relationships. Companies promote innovation through teamwork and collaboration.

 ASSESSMENT CHECK ANSWERS

1.5.1 Define outsourcing, offshoring, and nearshoring. Outsourcing involves using outside vendors to produce goods or to fulfill services and functions that were once handled in-house. Offshoring is the relocation of business processes to lower-cost locations overseas. Nearshoring is the outsourcing of production or services to nations near a firm's home base.

1.5.2 Describe the importance of collaboration and employee partnership. Businesses are increasingly focusing on collaboration, rather than on individuals working alone. No longer do employees just put in their time at a job they hold

their entire career. The new employer–employee partnership encourages teamwork and creative thinking, problem solving, and innovation. Managers are trained to listen to and respect employees.

LO 1.6 Identify the skills and attributes managers need to lead businesses in the 21st century.

Today's managers need vision, which is the ability to perceive both marketplace needs and the way their firm can satisfy those needs. Critical-thinking skills and creativity allow managers to pinpoint problems and opportunities and plan novel solutions. Finally, managers are dealing with rapid change, and they need skills to help lead their organizations through shifts in external and internal conditions.

 ASSESSMENT CHECK ANSWERS

1.6.1 Why is vision an important managerial quality? Managerial vision allows a firm to innovate and adapt to meet changes in the marketplace.

1.6.2 What is the difference between creativity and critical thinking? Critical thinking is the ability to analyze and assess information to pinpoint problems or opportunities. Creativity is the capacity to develop novel solutions to perceived organizational problems.

LO 1.7 Outline the characteristics that make a company admired by the business community.

A company is usually admired for its solid profits, stable growth, a safe and challenging work environment, high-quality goods and services, and business ethics and social responsibility.

 ASSESSMENT CHECK ANSWERS

1.7.1 Define *business ethics* **and** *social responsibility*. Business ethics refers to the standards of conduct and moral values involved in decisions made in the work environment. Social responsibility is a management philosophy that includes contributing resources to the community, preserving the natural environment, and developing or participating in not-for-profit programs designed to promote the well-being of the general public.

1.7.2 Identify three criteria used to judge whether a company might be considered admirable. Criteria in judging whether companies are admirable include the following: solid profits, stable growth, a safe and challenging work environment, high-quality goods and services, and business ethics and social responsibility.

BUSINESS TERMS YOU NEED TO KNOW

business 4

profits 4

not-for-profit organizations 5

factors of production 6

natural resources 6

capital 6

human resources 7

entrepreneurship 7

private enterprise system 8

capitalism 8

competition 8

competitive differentiation 8

private property 9

entrepreneur 10

consumer orientation 14

branding 14

brand 14

transaction management 14

relationship era 14

relationship management 15

technology 16

strategic alliance 16

diversity 20

outsourcing 20

offshoring 20

nearshoring 20

vision 21

critical thinking 22

creativity 22

REVIEW QUESTIONS

1. Why is business so important to a country's economy?

2. In what ways are not-for-profit organizations a substantial part of the Canadian economy? What challenges do not-for-profits face?

3. Identify and describe the four basic inputs that make up the factors of production. Give an example of each factor of production that an auto manufacturer might use.

4. What is a private enterprise system? What four rights are critical to the operation of capitalism? Why would capitalism function poorly in a society that does not ensure these rights for its citizens?

5. In what ways is entrepreneurship vital to the private enterprise system?

6. Identify the six eras of business in North America. How were businesses changed during each era?

7. Describe the focus of the most recent era of business. How is this era different from previous eras?

8. Define *partnership* and *strategic alliance*. How might a motorcycle dealer and a local radio station benefit from an alliance?

9. Identify the major changes in the workforce that will affect the way managers build a world-class workforce in the 21st century. Why is brainpower so important?

10. Identify four qualities required by the "new" managers of the 21st century. Why are these qualities important in a competitive business environment?

PROJECTS AND TEAMWORK APPLICATIONS

1. The entrepreneurial spirit fuels growth in the Canadian economy. Choose a company that interests you—one you have worked for or dealt with as a customer—and read about the company in the library or visit its website. Learn what you can about the company's early history: Who founded it and why? Is the founder still with the organization? Do you think the founder's original vision is still embraced by the company? If not, how has the vision changed?

2. Brands distinguish one company's goods or services from its competitors. Each company you purchase from hopes that you will become loyal to its brand. Some well-known brands are Tim Hortons, Burger King, Coca-Cola, Hilton, and Old Navy. Choose a type of good or service you use regularly and identify the major brands associated with it. Are you loyal to a particular brand? Why or why not?

3. More and more businesses are forming strategic alliances to become more competitive. Sometimes, businesses pair up with not-for-profit organizations in a relationship that is beneficial to both. Choose a company whose goods or services interest you, such as Lululemon Athletica, Timberland, FedEx, General Mills, or Target. On your own or with a classmate, research the firm on the Internet to learn about its alliances with not-for-profit organizations. Describe one of the alliances, including the goals and benefits to both parties. Create a presentation for your class.

4. This chapter describes how the nature of the workforce is changing: the population is aging, the labour pool is shrinking, the workforce is becoming more diverse, the nature of work is changing, the workplace is becoming more flexible and mobile, and employers are promoting innovation and collaboration among their employees. Form teams of two to three students. Select a company and research how that company is responding to changes in the workforce. When you have completed your research, be prepared to present it to your class. Choose one of the following companies or select your own: BCE, Telus, 3M, Marriott, or Dell.

5. Many successful companies today use technology to help them improve their relationship management. Suppose a major grocery store chain's management team has asked you to assess its use of technology for this purpose. On your own or with a classmate, visit one or two local grocery stores and explore their corporate websites. Note the ways in which firms in this industry already use technology to connect with their customers. List at least three new ways these firms can use technology to connect with their customers, or list three improvements to their existing methods. Present your findings to the class as if you were presenting to the management team.

WEB ASSIGNMENTS

1. Using search engines. Gathering information is one of the most popular applications of the Internet. Using two of the major search engines, such as Google and Bing, search the Internet for information pertaining to brand and relationship management. Sort through your results—you're likely to gets thousands of "hits"—and identify the three most useful. What did you learn from this experience regarding the use of a search engine?

http://www.google.com

http://www.bing.com

2. Companies and not-for-profits. In addition to companies, virtually all not-for-profit organizations have websites. Four websites are listed below, two for companies (Alcoa and Sony) and two for not-for-profits (Humane Society of Canada and National Audubon Society). What is the purpose of each website? What type of information is available? How are the sites similar? How are they different?

http://www.alcoa.com

http://www.sony.com

http://www.humanesociety.com

http://www.audubon.org

3. Characteristics of the Canadian workforce. Visit the website listed below. It is the home page for the *Canada Year Book*. Published annually by Statistics Canada, the *Canada Year Book* is a good source of basic demographic and economic data. Use the relevant data tables to prepare a brief profile of the Canadian workforce (gender, age, educational level, etc.). How is this profile expected to change over the next 10 to 20 years?

http://www.statcan.gc.ca/pub/11-402-x/index-eng.htm

WILEY **PLUS**
www.wileyplus.com

Access your WileyPLUS course for:

- The complete digital textbook.

- Question assistance, including links to relevant sections in the online digital textbook.

- Immediate feedback and proof of progress, 24/7

- Integrated, multi-media resources – including MP3 downloads, visual exhibits, animations, and much more – that provide multiple study paths and encourage more active learning.

QUIZ YOURSELF

Note: Internet Web addresses change frequently. If you don't find the exact sites listed, you may need to access the organization's home page and search from there or use a search engine such as Bing or Google.

2 | BUSINESS ETHICS AND SOCIAL RESPONSIBILITY

LEARNING OBJECTIVES

LO 2.1 Explain the concepts of business ethics and social responsibility.

LO 2.2 Describe the factors that influence business ethics.

LO 2.3 Discuss how organizations shape ethical behaviour.

LO 2.4 Describe how businesses' social responsibility is measured, and summarize the responsibilities of business to the general public, customers, and employees.

LO 2.5 Explain why investors and the financial community are concerned with business ethics and social responsibility.

INSIDE BUSINESS

Cirque du Soleil: A Class Act in Social Responsibility

© JHP Attractions/Alamy

Have you ever attended a Cirque du Soleil (Cirque) performance? If you have, you've seen creativity, ingenuity, and perseverance throughout the show from beginning to end. Maybe you saw "O" at the Bellagio, where performers dive into and out of a 5.7-million-litre pool. Or perhaps "Michael Jackson, the Immortal World Tour." Cirque puts on a great show and is a hard act for its imitators to follow.

How creative can a company like Cirque be, in terms of social responsibility? Cirque prides itself on impressing audiences. But what can it do to impress the wider community?

Cirque's founder, Guy Laliberté, has an idea. He is convinced that the company can become a leader in promoting social responsibility. Then, a trickle-down effect will inspire other companies to follow suit. Cirque has decided to publicize its efforts. It hopes to encourage other companies to be more socially responsible. Cirque also wants to keep its stakeholders aware of its plans.

Cirque's work on Global Citizenship affects the community, the environment, the workplace, business partners, and suppliers.

Cirque du Monde (one of Cirque's social action programs) can be found in nearly 80 communities in 20 countries. The company spends, on average, 1 percent of its earnings on cultural and social action programs. Laliberté set up the One Drop Foundation, which works with Oxfam and others to provide sanitation and access to water to countries in need. Project Haïti began after the 2010 earthquake and is expected to cost more than $5 million. Cirque du Monde also helps at-risk youth to regain their self-confidence. These youth are invited to attend personal development programs presented by circus instructors and social workers.

Cirque has also been a major innovator in the area of environmental responsibility. The rate of global warming has been increasing, especially over the past two decades, which were the hottest in more than 400 years. Cirque has started many projects to reduce its carbon footprint and protect the environment. Yannick Spierkel, Cirque's tour general manager, believes Cirque can "influence the lives and buying habits of employees and even set up awareness campaigns with clients." At home, Cirque chose to build its Montreal headquarters on a recovered landfill. Recently, Cirque was able to reduce its headquarters' water consumption by 20 percent, or 8.4 million litres (equivalent to the water in 168 swimming pools). Cirque reduced water use by installing rainwater collection basins in the parking lot and on the building's seventh floor and by replacing plumbing fixtures with low-flow models. When Cirque goes on tour, Green Committees look at how the group can continue to operate in an environmentally responsible manner in the cities it visits. For example, in Las Vegas, the staff of *Mystère* has been given the task of going completely paperless by rethinking all of their work habits.

Cirque is well aware that its responsibility to the community begins with its own staff right at its international headquarters. Marie Trottier, the senior building services director says: "Working for a company that promotes and facilitates environmental initiatives and provides the means to make a difference has certainly influenced me personally." For example, Cirque takes pride in ensuring its staff is well taken care of. Cirque has no dress code, so staff can come to work wearing whatever feels comfortable. This physical comfort suits the workplace's sense of creativity. Staff can watch the performers practise and thus see the result of their efforts behind the scenes. "Wherever you go, you can feel creativity, you can smell it, you can touch it, because that is what we are about," says Murielle Cantin, senior vice-president of creative content. Staff can relax on couches or have lunch from a low-cost cafeteria that serves vegetables grown in in-house gardens.

Companies can indirectly have a large impact on their community and the environment through their suppliers. Cirque takes an extra step to ensure that its relationships with business partners also include an attitude of social responsibility. Cirque is part of Business for Social Responsibility (BSR). This global network of more than 250 companies seeks to develop and maintain sustainable business strategies and solutions. As a result, Cirque has reduced its deliveries to tour destinations by approximately 40 percent. It also groups its inbound shipments to warehouses to reduce transportation-related emissions. A tool has also been developed to help buyers select more environmentally friendly materials. Formal training sessions ensure that buyers are trained on how to purchase supplies in an environmentally responsible manner.

Cirque is trying to create a ripple effect with its business partners. Cirque has made social responsibility a requirement when selecting future business partners. It has also built a social responsibility clause into all its partnership agreements. This clause applies to employee relations, working conditions, ethical sourcing, environmental protection, and social and cultural actions in the community. Éric Choquette, Cirque's merchandising director explains: "The objective is to keep the bottom line in mind while making increasingly responsible choices."[1]

CHAPTER 2 OVERVIEW

Cirque du Soleil's efforts to create sustainable operations are not unique in the world of business. Many companies are concerned about the environment and their societies. This concern may lead to action, such as growing more slowly than they might have or reducing short-term profits for longer, sustainable benefits. Cirque du Soleil changed its own operations to help the environment while still maintaining a reasonable profit.

Most organizations strive to combine ethical behaviour with profitable operation. Some have had difficulties overcoming major ethical errors in recent years. Ethical failures in many large and well-known firms have led to lawsuits, indictments, and judgements against firms. We have all seen news reports of executives receiving millions of dollars in pay while their companies struggle to operate. This kind of news has damaged the image of the chief executive officer (CEO)—and of business in general.

Sometimes, bad news leads to good news. As a result of such bad news stories, both the government and companies have made changes. They have renewed their efforts to behave in an ethical manner to show their responsibility to society, to consumers, and to the environment. In 2010, Industry Canada began a new voluntary standard on social responsibility, known as ISO SR26000. It focuses on seven principles (accountability, transparency, ethical behaviour, stakeholder interests, rule of law, international norms of behaviour, and human rights). This new standard has led to more firms paying attention to creating clearer standards and procedures for ethical behaviour. Companies now understand the enormous impact of setting a good example instead of a bad one. Today, you are likely to hear about the goodwill produced by such companies as CIBC, TELUS, and Tim Hortons. These companies create goodwill when they give back to their communities by funding youth camping programs and recycling or energy-conservation programs, or by paying fair prices to suppliers.[2]

As we discussed in Chapter 1, the basic aim of business is to serve customers at a profit. Most companies try to do more than that. Most companies want to give back to customers, society, and the environment. Sometimes, though, they face difficult questions. When does a company's self-interest work against society's and customers' well-being? Does the goal of seeking profits always work against having high principles of what is right and wrong? Many businesses of all sizes answer no.

LO 2.1 Explain the concepts of business ethics and social responsibility.

CONCERN FOR ETHICAL AND SOCIETAL ISSUES

business ethics standards of conduct and moral values regarding right and wrong actions in the business environment.

An organization that wants to do well over the long term should consider its **business ethics**. Business ethics refers to the standards of conduct and moral values that lead to our actions and decisions in the business environment. Businesses also must consider a wide range of social issues, including how a decision will affect the environment, employees, and customers. These issues are at the heart of *corporate social responsibility (CSR)*. CSR's primary objective is to enhance society's well-being through philosophies, policies, procedures, and actions. In other words, businesses must find a balance between doing what is right and doing what is profitable. In 2011, IKEA Canada decided to stop selling traditional incandescent bulbs, one year before the federal requirement in 2012. "Eliminating incandescent bulbs is another simple step IKEA is taking to help our customers save energy and reduce emissions. It's a small step, with a big impact," says Kerri Molinaro, president of IKEA Canada. IKEA Canada sees this action as a "win-win" situation for both consumers and the environment. Replacing five incandescent bulbs with compact fluorescent light bulbs (CFLs) can save up to $30 per year and can reduce greenhouse gases by up to 150 kg (kilograms) per year. IKEA Canada now provides many efficient lighting options, including LED, halogen, and solar-powered lamps.[3]

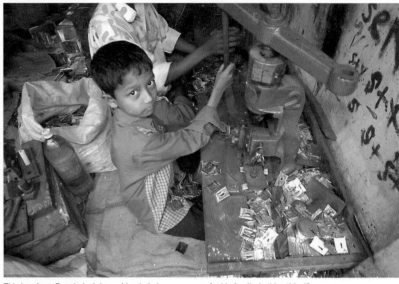

This boy from Bangladesh is working to help earn money for his family. Is this ethical?

© Dan Vincent/Alamy

In business, as in life, deciding what is right or wrong is not always an easy choice. Firms have many responsibilities—to customers, to employees, to investors, and to society as a whole. Trying to serve the different needs of these groups can lead to conflicts. The ethical values of executives and individual employees at all levels can influence a business's decisions and actions. In your own career, you will encounter many situations where you will need to weigh right and wrong before making a decision or taking action. We begin our discussion of business ethics by focusing on individual ethics.

The concept of right and wrong can be complex. It is certainly not "black and white." Business ethics are also shaped by the ethical climate within an organization or even within a country. For example, an acceptable age to start working may be 16 in a developed country but could be 10 in a developing country. Ethics also goes beyond what is legal and what is not legal. Codes of conduct and ethical standards play important roles in businesses that support and applaud doing the right thing. This chapter shows how a firm can create a framework to encourage—and even demand—high standards of ethical behaviour and social responsibility from its employees. The chapter also considers the complex questions of what business owes to society and how society's forces shape the actions of businesses. Finally, this chapter examines the influence of business ethics and social responsibility on global businesses.

✔ **ASSESSMENT CHECK**

2.1.1 To whom do businesses have responsibilities?

2.1.2 If a firm is meeting all its responsibilities to others, why do ethical conflicts arise?

THE CONTEMPORARY ETHICAL ENVIRONMENT

LO 2.2 Describe the factors that influence business ethics.

Business ethics is now in the spotlight as never before. Companies realize that they need to work harder to earn the public's trust. Many companies have taken on the challenge as if their survival depends on it. This movement toward *corporate social responsibility* should benefit everyone—consumers, the environment, and the companies themselves.

Most business owners and managers have built and maintained successful companies without breaking the rules. One example of a firm with a long-term commitment to ethical practice is Johnson & Johnson, the giant multinational manufacturer of healthcare products. It is the most admired pharmaceutical maker and the fourth-most-admired company in the world, according to *Fortune*. Johnson & Johnson has worked with the same basic code of ethics, its well-known credo, for more than 50 years (see Figure 2.1).[4]

Our Credo

We believe our first responsibility is to the doctors, nurses and patients, to mothers and fathers and all others who use our products and services. In meeting their needs everything we do must be of high quality. We must constantly strive to reduce our costs in order to maintain reasonable prices. Customers' orders must be serviced promptly and accurately. Our suppliers and distributors must have an opportunity to make a fair profit.

We are responsible to our employees, the men and women who work with us throughout the world. Everyone must be considered as an individual. We must respect their dignity and recognize their merit. They must have a sense of security in their jobs. Compensation must be fair and adequate, and working conditions clean, orderly and safe. We must be mindful of ways to help our employees fulfill their family responsibilities. Employees must feel free to make suggestions and complaints. There must be equal opportunity for employment, development and advancement for those qualified. We must provide competent management, and their actions must be just and ethical.

We are responsible to the communities in which we live and work and to the world community as well. We must be good citizens—support good works and charities and bear our fair share of taxes. We must encourage civic improvements and better health and education. We must maintain in good order the property we are privileged to use, protecting the environment and natural resources.

Our final responsibility is to our stockholders. Business must make a sound profit. We must experiment with new ideas. Research must be carried on, innovative programs developed and mistakes paid for. New equipment must be purchased, new facilities provided and new products launched. Reserves must be created to provide for adverse times. When we operate according to these principles, the stockholders should realize a fair return.

FIGURE 2.1 Johnson & Johnson Credo

Source: "Our Company: Our Credo," Johnson & Johnson website, accessed February 4, 2010, http://www.jnj.com, © Johnson & Johnson.

Many business schools include programs on ethics and social responsibility in their course curriculum. MBA students from the University of Ottawa's Telfer School of Management are now required to swear an ethics-related oath upon graduation (see Figure 2.2).

As a manager my actions will affect the well being of all stakeholders; accordingly, I will strive to create and sustain value over the long term while maintaining a commitment to social, ethical and global values.

I will be responsible to all stakeholders, and this will include employees, shareholders, customers, the community in which I operate, and all those that may be affected by my actions.

I will act with integrity and respect in all my dealings, making transparency paramount and demanding the same in return.

I will allow neither ego nor malice to play a role in my decision making process.

I will conduct my activities in an environmentally sustainable manner, and will consider the true societal costs when making investment and operating decisions.

I will maintain the same care and vigilance when dealing with public money, as I would if it were my own.

I will obey and uphold local and international laws wherever and with whomever I engage in commercial activities with, whether personally or on behalf of a corporate, government, or nonprofit entity.

I will similarly oppose corruption and any dishonest practices whether or not prohibited by local or international law.

I will accept and take responsibility for my actions, honestly and without exception I pledge to perpetuate the text and spirit of this oath to those present, to my classmates, my community, and my world.

We, the Telfer MBA Class of [year of graduation] hereby take this Oath, as professional managers.

FIGURE 2.2 Telfer School of Management MBA Oath

Source: Telfer School of Management, "Telfer School Grads Take the MBA Oath," http://www.telfer.uottawa.ca/en/latest-news/1829-telfer-school-grads-take-the-mba-oath, accessed February 14, 2011.

Many companies are aware of how ethical standards can translate into concern for the environment and society at large.

According to David Cheesewright, president and CEO of Walmart Canada, the company has grouped its social responsibility priorities into four broad categories:

1. Environment

2. People

3. Responsible Sourcing

4. The Community

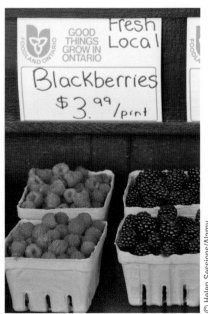

Walmart Canada has started selling fresh produce. The company has developed an efficient, cost-effective, and more sustainable process by sourcing produce locally, where possible. Local sourcing means lower transportation costs and reduced transportation-related emissions. Local sourcing also supports local suppliers, addressing many concerns that shopping at Walmart leads to lost Canadian jobs.[5]

Walmart also surveyed its suppliers about their sustainability practices. This survey was a first step in developing a "sustainability index" to help its customers measure the impact of Walmart products—on the environment and on society. Also, 40 Walmart stores make use of photovoltaic solar cells that generate electricity directly from sunlight. CSR is important for Walmart because of the ongoing controversy about some of its business practices.[6]

Walmart Canada has started sourcing produce locally to increase efficiency, lower costs, and reduce greenhouse emissions.

Not all companies set and meet high ethical standards, but the ethical climate is improving despite the recent recession. A recent study found that 49 percent of employees surveyed "witnessed misconduct on the job" in 2009, down from 56 percent in 2007. More employees said they reported misconduct when they saw it, up to 63 percent in 2009 from 58 percent in 2007. However, about 25 percent of employees said the recession had a negative impact on their company's ethics culture. In those companies, misconduct rose 16 points. About 10 percent of employees said their company had lowered its ethical standards to survive the recession.[7]

Sarbanes-Oxley and Bill 198

In the United States, the **Sarbanes-Oxley Act of 2002** established new rules and regulations for securities trading and accounting practices. Companies are now required to publish their code of ethics, if they have one, and inform the public of any changes made to it. The law may actually motivate even more firms to develop written codes and guidelines for ethical business behaviour. The provisions of this act apply to Canadian companies who trade on any American stock exchange. Similar legislation has been enacted in Canada known as Bill 198 of 2003, which has come to be referred to as "C-SOX" or the Canadian version of Sarbanes-Oxley.

Today's ethical environment for business also includes new corporate officers, who are appointed to deter wrongdoing and ensure that ethical standards are met. Ethics compliance officers are responsible for conducting employee training programs that help spot potential fraud and abuse, investigating sexual harassment and discrimination charges, and monitoring potential conflicts of interest. Practising corporate social responsibility is more than just monitoring behaviour. Many companies now adopt a three-pronged approach to ethics and social responsibility:

1. engaging in traditional corporate philanthropy, such as giving to worthy causes

2. anticipating and managing risks

3. identifying opportunities to create value by doing the right thing.[8]

Individuals Make a Difference

In today's business environment, individuals can make the difference in ethical expectations and behaviour. Executives, managers, and employees show their personal ethical principles—or lack of ethical principles. In turn, their behaviour can affect the expectations and actions of those who work for them and with them.

What is the current state of individual business ethics in Canada? Ethical behaviour can be difficult to track or define in all situations. The evidence suggests that some individuals act unethically

Sarbanes-Oxley Act of 2002
U.S. federal legislation designed to deter and punish corporate and accounting fraud and corruption. It is also designed to protect the interests of workers and shareholders by requiring enhanced financial disclosures, criminal penalties for CEOs and CFOs who defraud investors, and safeguards for whistle-blowers. The act also established a new regulatory body for public accounting firms.

or illegally on the job. Their behaviour includes putting their own interests ahead of the organization, lying to employees, misreporting hours worked, Internet abuse, and safety violations.[9]

Technology may have expanded the range and impact of unethical behaviour. For example, anyone who has computer access to data may be able to steal or manipulate the data or shut down the system, even from a remote location. Recently, Radisson Hotels alerted customers that its credit-card security system had experienced a data breach in some Canadian and U.S.-based hotels. The cost of dealing with a data breach can add up to $6.6 million per incident.[10] Although some people might not be concerned about these breaches, they can affect how investors, customers, and the general public view a firm. It can be difficult to rebuild trust. The company may also lose some long-term customers.

Nearly every employee, at every level, faces ethical questions at some time. Some people explain questionable behaviour by saying, "Everybody's doing it." Others act unethically because they feel pressured in their jobs or because they need to meet performance goals. Yet some avoid unethical acts because they don't fit with their personal values and morals. We all use different ways to make our ethical choices. The next section focuses on how we develop our personal ethics and morals.

Development of Individual Ethics

An individual's moral and ethical development is the result of many factors. Experiences shape our responses to different situations. Our family, educational, cultural, and religious backgrounds also play a role, as does the environment within the firm. We also have different styles of deciding ethical dilemmas, no matter what our stage of moral development.

This textbook can help you understand and prepare for the ethical dilemmas you may face in your career. Let's take a closer look at the factors that can help you to solve ethical questions on the job.

BUSINESS ETIQUETTE

How to Handle Ethical Dilemmas at Work

How Can Business Support an Ethical Environment?

"Doing well begins with doing right," according to Sharon Allen, Deloitte LLP's board chair. Her advice to companies in the current economy is to focus on ethics. By encouraging employees to work to high ethical standards, the organization will end up with strong performers.

Unethical behaviour in the workplace can lead to lost earnings and damaged personal lives. This effect was seen in two Canadian companies, Nortel and Livent.

Employees are eager to work for companies that demonstrate good corporate social responsibility and high standards for ethical business conduct. Customers also have more trust in those organizations. To ensure good ethical conduct for both employees and customers, companies should have ethical leaders, a code of ethics or similar policies, and ethics training for employees.

What Can You Do about an Ethical Dilemma?

The business journalist Suzy Welch claims that ethical dilemmas are difficult to resolve because we tend to make conclusions based on little information. Welch suggests taking the following steps if you suspect unethical behaviour in the office:

1. Get all the facts. Ask tactful questions of people you know are trustworthy—do not rely on rumours or gossip. In return, be careful of revealing anything told to you in confidence. Talk to your company's human resources department. Be investigative, not aggressive.

2. When you have the facts, ask yourself, Is this situation a moral dilemma? Or, is it a case of office politics? What may look like an ethical problem might be a power play in disguise.

3. If the situation really is an ethical dilemma, explain the issue to a trusted friend outside the company—and outside your family. That person may be able to take an unbiased view and advise you about what to do next.

Sources: Suzy Welch, "What to Do When Facing Ethical Problems at Work," *CNN*, www.cnn.com, August 3, 2009; Sharon Allen, "The New ROE: Return on Ethics," *Forbes.com*, www.forbes.com, July 21, 2009.

On-the-Job Ethical Dilemmas

In the fast-paced world of business, you will sometimes be asked to consider the ethics of decisions. These decisions can affect not just your own future but can also affect the futures of your co-workers, your company, and its customers. As we already mentioned, deciding what is right and wrong can be difficult in many business situations. The decision is especially tricky when the needs and concerns of two or more parties conflict. In the recent past, some CEOs (or their companies) who were accused of wrongdoing simply claimed that they had no idea crimes were being committed. Today's top executives make a greater effort to be aware of all activities taking place in their firms.

Many clothing retailers donate unworn, unsold garments to charities such as clothing banks. In January 2010, a graduate student discovered that the H&M store on New York's 34th Street was destroying unsold clothing. She tried to speak to store officials and then tried to speak to someone at the company's headquarters in Sweden. Her requests for information and her offer to put H&M in contact with aid organizations went unanswered. She then contacted the *New York Times*. The newspaper published a story about how H&M—among other retailers—was damaging unsold garments before discarding them. The damage was intended to make the clothing unsalable by street vendors or other black-market sellers. The New York City Clothing Bank, founded by the city's mayor during the 1980s, accepts unsold garments and slightly defaces them— not to destroy them, but to protect retailers by negating the garments' street value. When the story was published, H&M promised to stop destroying unsold clothing and instead donate the garments to charity. A company spokeswoman in New York declared, "It will not happen again. We are committed 100 percent to make sure this practice is not happening anywhere else, as it is not our standard practice."[11]

FIGURE 2.3 Common Business Ethical Challenges

Businesses sometimes refuse to purchase goods or services from a particular country because of civil rights abuses by that country's government. Some of the world's largest and most prestigious jewellers, including Cartier and Tiffany & Co., announced they would not purchase rubies and other gems from Myanmar (formerly Burma). Their boycott is the result of that government's civil rights violations and the severe measures it has taken against protests by students and monks. The United States and the European Union have also agreed to ban the import of gems from Myanmar.[12]

Solving ethical dilemmas is not easy. Often, each possible decision can lead to both good and bad outcomes, which must be considered. The ethical issues that face manufacturers who have unsold merchandise are one example of many different types of ethical situations in the workplace. Figure 2.3 identifies four of the most common ethical challenges that businesspeople face: conflict of interest, honesty and integrity, loyalty versus truth, and whistle-blowing.

Conflict of Interest

A **conflict of interest** occurs when a businessperson is faced with a situation where an action that benefits one person or group has the potential to harm another. Conflicts of interest may pose ethical challenges when they involve the businessperson's own interests and the interests of a person or party to whom the businessperson has a duty. For example, lawyers, business consultants, and advertising agencies face a conflict of interest if they represent two competing companies: a strategy that might benefit one client might harm the other client. Similarly, a real estate agent would face an ethical conflict by representing both the buyer and seller in a transaction. Handling the situation responsibly is possible, but is also difficult. A conflict may also exist between someone's personal interests and the interests of an organization or its customers. An offer of gifts or bribes for special treatment can lead to a situation where the buyer may benefit personally, but the company may not.

A conflict of interest may also occur when one person holds two or more similar jobs in two different workplaces. Conflicts of interest can be handled ethically by (1) avoiding them and (2) disclosing them. Some companies have policies against taking on clients who are competitors

conflict of interest a situation in which an employee must choose between a business's welfare and personal gain.

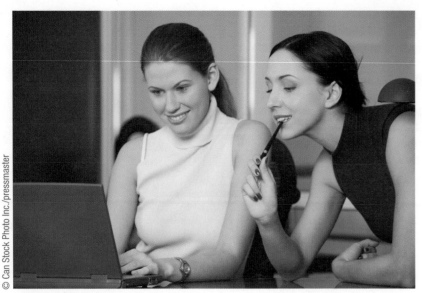

Employers and employees value honesty and integrity, but what should happen when employees misuse their Internet privileges for personal purposes?

© Can Stock Photo Inc./pressmaster

of existing clients. Most businesses and government agencies have written policies that either prevent employees from accepting gifts or specify a maximum gift value. A member of a board of directors or a committee member might abstain from voting when he or she has a personal interest in the decision. In other situations, people state their potential conflict of interest so that others can decide whether to use another source instead.

Honesty and Integrity

Employers highly value honesty and integrity. An employee who is honest can be relied on to tell the truth. An employee with **integrity** goes beyond truthfulness. Having integrity means behaving according to one's deeply felt ethical principles in business situations. It includes doing what you say you will do and accepting responsibility for your mistakes. Behaving with honesty and integrity inspires trust. As a result,

integrity behaving according to one's deeply felt ethical principles in business situations.

integrity can help to build long-term relationships with customers, employers, suppliers, and the public. Employees, in turn, want their managers and the company as a whole to treat them honestly and with integrity.

Unfortunately, violations of honesty and integrity are common. Some people misrepresent their academic standing and previous work experience on their résumés or job applications. Although it may be tempting to lie on a résumé in a competitive job market, it shows a lack of honesty and integrity—and eventually the lies will catch up with you. An ADP survey revealed that one in five Canadians lies on his or her résumé. Recently, it was learned that an Osgoode Hall law student, Quami Frederick, had purchased a fake undergraduate degree to gain admission to law school. She also submitted an Osgoode Hall transcript with inflated grades to obtain an articling position at the Bay Street law firm Wildeboer Dellelce, LLP. Frederick now faces a disciplinary hearing that will likely result in her expulsion from Osgoode Hall. The law firm has withdrawn its offer.[13]

Some employees steal from their employers by taking home supplies or products without permission or by carrying out personal business when they are being paid to work. For example, Internet misuse during the workday is increasing. Employees use the Internet during work hours for personal e-mail, shopping, gaming, and for visiting bulletin boards and blogs or social networking sites such as Facebook and YouTube. The use of laptops, cellphones, and other wireless devices makes this misconduct easier to hide.[14] The frequency of such activity varies widely. Employers may feel more strongly about taking strong measures on some activities than on others. Most people will agree that Internet misuse is a problem. Some employers have resorted to electronic monitoring and surveillance. These employers have another reason to monitor their employees: complying with the laws regarding the privacy and security of client information.

Loyalty versus Truth

Businesspeople expect their employees to be loyal and to act in the best interests of the company. But when the truth about a company is not favourable, an ethical conflict can arise. Individual employees may need to decide between loyalty to the company and truthfulness in business relationships. People resolve such dilemmas in various ways. Some place the highest value on loyalty, even at the expense of truth. Others avoid volunteering negative information but answer truthfully when asked a direct question. People may emphasize truthfulness and actively disclose negative information, especially when the cost of silence is high, such as when operating a malfunctioning aircraft or selling tainted food.

Whistle-Blowing

When an employee encounters unethical or illegal actions at work, that employee must decide what action to take. This person may conclude that the only solution is to "blow the whistle." **Whistle-blowing** is usually an employee's disclosure to company officials, government authorities, or the media of illegal, immoral, or unethical practices.

In February 2004, former Olympic athlete Myriam Bédard said she had been fired from her marketing job at Via Rail after questioning invoices for advertising work by Groupaction, the company that was the main focus in the sponsorship scandal. Bédard said she wrote to Prime Minister Paul Martin when she saw him on TV urging Canadians to come forward with whatever information they had about the sponsorship program. Via Rail Chair Jean Pelletier was later fired for having called Bédard a "pitiful, single woman," saying she was trying to draw attention to herself with the allegations.

When the sponsorship inquiry got underway in March 2004, Bédard appeared before the Parliamentary committee that was looking into the scandal. She made some shocking statements:

- That Canadian race-car driver Jacques Villeneuve had secretly been paid $12 million from the sponsorship fund to wear a Canadian logo.

- Her domestic partner, Nima Mazhari, had persuaded then–Prime Minister Jean Chrétien not to join the U.S. invasion of Iraq.

- Then–Via President Marc LeFrançois had told her Groupaction was involved in drug trafficking.[15]

Although no specific law protects whistle-blowers in Canada, many Canadian companies, such as Air Canada, have policies to protect whistle-blowers. In 2004, Bill C-25, The Public Servants Disclosure Protection Act, was introduced. This bill was intended to protect people who expose problems in the government's bureaucracy. The government said this act will help ensure "transparency, accountability, financial responsibility and ethical conduct."[16]

Despite these protections, whistle-blowing has its risks. Zues Yaghi, from Edmonton, blew the whistle on casino video slot machines. He said the machines could be made to pay on demand. Yaghi claimed that the computer program had a "back door" that would allow players to collect jackpots after making a few clicks. Yaghi was sued by the company for $10 million. A warrant was issued to search Zaghi's home. A few days later, a gag order was issued to prevent him from saying how a player could make the slots pay out. The company offered him $50,000 to remain quiet about the issue but Yaghi asked for more money.[17]

Obviously, whistle-blowing and other ethical issues are rare in firms that have strong organizational climates of ethical behaviour. The next section examines how a business can develop an environment that discourages unethical behaviour among individuals.

whistle-blowing disclosure to company officials, government authorities, or the media of illegal, immoral, or unethical practices committed by an organization.

✓ **ASSESSMENT CHECK**

2.2.1 What is the role of a firm's ethics compliance officer?

2.2.2 What factors influence the ethical environment of a business?

HOW ORGANIZATIONS SHAPE ETHICAL CONDUCT

LO 2.3 Discuss how organizations shape ethical behaviour.

No individual makes decisions in a vacuum. Most organizations have established standards of conduct. These standards strongly influence the choices that employees make. Most ethical lapses in business reflect the values in the firms' corporate cultures.

As shown in Figure 2.4, a corporate culture that supports business ethics develops on four levels:

1. ethical awareness

2. ethical reasoning

3. ethical action

4. ethical leadership

If any of these four factors is missing, the ethical climate in an organization will weaken.

code of conduct a formal statement that defines how an organization expects its employees to resolve ethical issues.

Ethical Awareness

The foundation of an ethical climate is ethical awareness. As we have already seen, ethical dilemmas occur frequently in the workplace. Employees need help in identifying ethical problems when they occur. They also need guidance about how the firm expects them to respond.

One way for a firm to provide this support is to develop a **code of conduct**. This formal statement defines how the organization expects its employees to resolve ethical questions. Johnson & Johnson's credo, presented in Figure 2.1, is such a code. At the most basic level, a code of conduct may simply be the ground rules for acceptable behaviour, such as the laws and regulations that employees must obey. Other companies use their codes of conduct to identify key corporate values and provide frameworks that guide employees as they resolve moral and ethical dilemmas.

Air Canada is headquartered in Montreal, Quebec, and has offices around the world. Its code of conduct defines the company's values and helps employees to put these values into practice. The code of conduct emphasizes "honesty and integrity" and treating employees with fairness, dignity, and respect. The code applies to "all directors, officers and employees." Portions of the policy even include retirees who have travel pass privileges. All employees at every level are expected to treat fellow employees, suppliers, and customers with dignity and respect. They are also expected to comply with environmental, health, and safety regulations. The code of conduct reminds leaders that their language and behaviour must not even seem to put pressure on their employees that might suggest they should perform a task differently from the standards in the code. The code of conduct also outlines how to report violations to a supervisor or the corporate secretary. Employees are promised confidentiality and nonretaliation for problems reported in good faith. Air Canada requires all employees to sign this code of conduct. It is also posted on the Air Canada website.[18]

Air Canada requires all of its directors, officers, employees, and even some of their retirees to sign a code of conduct to promote ethical behaviour.

The Canadian Press/Ryan Remiorz

Other firms incorporate similar codes in their policy manuals or mission statements; some issue a code of conduct or statement of values in the form of a small card that employees and managers can carry with them. For example, Harley-Davidson has developed a brief code of ethics that employees can apply both at work and in their personal lives. It reads: "Tell the truth, keep your promises, be fair, respect the individual and encourage intellectual curiosity."

Ethical Education

A code of conduct can provide an overall framework, but it does not have a solution for every ethical situation. Some ethical questions have black-and-white answers, but others do not. Businesses must provide the tools employees need to evaluate the options and arrive at suitable decisions.

Many firms have started their own ethics training programs. Other firms have hired organizations such as The Skald Group, based in Hamilton, Ontario, which provides outsourced ethics programs to businesses.[19] Other organizations, such as SAI Global, host employee-reporting services that offer an anonymous hotline and an ethics case management system. SAI Global also helps companies to develop ethics codes and customizes ethics training to each company's needs, including specialized online, interactive training systems.[20]

Many have debated whether ethics can be taught. Ethics training is helpful, though, because employees can practise applying ethical values to sample situations before they face real-world situations. Similar strategies are used in many business schools, where case studies and practical scenarios work best. Walter Pavlo is a convicted white-collar criminal and a former employee at the telecommunications firm MCI. He speaks at colleges and universities about his experiences, both in the firm and in prison. Pavlo once worked with other MCI staff to hide $6 million in offshore accounts. Today, though, he speaks about his actions to warn students of the consequences of cheating.

Ethical Action

Codes of conduct and ethics training help employees to recognize and reason through ethical problems. In addition, firms must provide structures and approaches that allow decisions to be turned into ethical actions. Texas Instruments gives its employees a reference card to help them make ethical decisions on the job. The card is the size of a standard business card and lists the following guidelines:

- Is the action legal?
- Does it comply with our values?
- If you do it, will you feel bad?
- How will it look in the newspaper?
- If you know it's wrong, don't do it!
- If you're not sure, ask.
- Keep asking until you get an answer.

Businesses often set goals for the whole business and for individual departments and employees. These goals can affect ethical behaviour. For example, a firm's managers may set unrealistic goals for employee performance. These goals may lead to an increase in cheating, lying, and other misdeeds, as employees attempt to protect themselves. In today's Internet economy, a high value is often placed on speed. But valuing speed can lead to a climate where ethical behaviour is challenged. Ethical decisions often require careful and quiet thought, which can be a challenging task in today's fast-paced business world.

Some companies encourage ethical action. These companies provide support for employees faced with dilemmas. One common tool is an employee hotline, which is a telephone number that employees can call anonymously for advice or to report unethical behaviour they have seen. As already mentioned, some firms have ethics compliance officers, who guide employees through difficult ethical issues.

Ethical Leadership

Executives must not just talk about ethical behaviour; they also need to show it in their actions. Employees need to be personally committed to the company's core values, and they must be willing to base their actions on those values. The recent recession exposed executive-level misdeeds that damaged or even destroyed entire organizations. Some people lost their life savings. After hearing of these misdeeds, two students at the Harvard Business School interviewed corporate leaders they regarded as being highly moral. The students concluded that these "ethical mavericks" follow a moral code with three simple characteristics:

1. use clear, explicit language rather than euphemisms for corrupt behaviour
2. encourage behaviour that generates and fosters ethical values
3. practise moral absolutism, insisting on doing right, even if it proves financially costly.[21]

However, ethical leadership should also go one step further. Each employee at every level should be charged with the responsibility to be an ethical leader. Everyone should be aware of problems and be willing to defend the organization's standards.

Unfortunately, not all organizations can build a solid framework of business ethics. Because the damage from ethical misconduct can powerfully affect a firm's **stakeholders**—customers, investors, employees, and the public—businesses are pressured to act in acceptable ways. But when businesses fail, the law must step in to enforce good business practices. Many of the laws that affect specific industries or individuals are described in other chapters in this book. For example, legislation affecting international business operations is discussed in Chapter 4. Laws designed to assist small businesses are examined in Chapter 5. Laws related to labour unions are described in Chapter 8. Legislation related to banking and the securities markets is discussed in Chapters 16 and 17. Finally, for an examination of the legal and governmental forces designed to safeguard society's interests when businesses fail at self-regulation, see Appendix C, "Business Law."

---

stakeholders customers, investors, employees, and public affected by or with an interest in a company.

✓ **ASSESSMENT CHECK**

2.3.1 For an employee, when does loyalty conflict with truth?

2.3.2 How does ethical leadership contribute to ethical standards throughout a company?

LO 2.4 Describe how businesses' social responsibility is measured, and summarize the responsibilities of business to the general public, customers, and employees.

social responsibility business's consideration of society's well-being and consumer satisfaction, in addition to profits.

ACTING RESPONSIBLY TO SATISFY SOCIETY

A second major issue affecting business is the question of social responsibility. In a general sense, **social responsibility** is management's acceptance of its obligation, when evaluating firm performance, to consider profit to be of equal value as qualitative indicators, such as employee satisfaction, consumer satisfaction, and societal well-being. Businesses may exercise social responsibility for many reasons: because such behaviour is required by law, because it enhances the company's image, or because management believes it is the ethical course of action. The "Going Green" feature discusses Starbucks' efforts to introduce environmentally sound practices.

STARBUCKS INTRODUCES A NEW STORE–DESIGN STRATEGY

In June 2009, the coffee-selling giant Starbucks announced that the company will design new stores and renovate existing stores worldwide with two goals in mind: to reflect the character of the neighbourhood and to reduce environmental impact.

The project is part of Starbucks' efforts to reposition itself. Arthur Rubinfeld, the president of Starbucks Global Development, said, "We recognize the importance of continuously evolving with our customers' interests, lifestyles and values in order to stay relevant over the long term."

The company will make each store unique by employing local artisans and local materials, including recycled and reclaimed items. It has also committed to conserving water and energy, recycling where possible, and using "green" construction methods. Among its goals are:

- to use renewable resources for 50 percent of the energy used in its stores
- to make its stores 25 percent more energy efficient to reduce greenhouse gas emissions

- to meet U.S. Green Building Code LEED (Leadership in Energy and Environmental Design) certification standards for all its new stores

- to implement a 100 percent reusable or recyclable cup supply by 2015

- to have recycling in stores where it controls waste collection by 2015.

The company has already met some of these goals. For instance, it reduces its prices by 10 cents for customers who bring their own travel cup. The company is also replacing incandescent light bulbs with LED bulbs to save energy and expense. Signage will be installed in new and renovated stores to explain their "green" and sustainable features and construction methods.

This new strategy is shaping Starbucks stores in more than 40 countries, including Hong Kong, Saudi Arabia, Spain, and Argentina.

Questions for Critical Thinking

1. How do Starbucks' new plans for its stores reflect its sense of social responsibility?

2. How has Starbucks involved its customers in these efforts?

Sources: Starbucks website, http://www.starbucks.com, accessed February 2010; Brian Clark Howard, "5 Major Companies Innovate by Going Green," *Daily Green*, November 18, 2009, http://www.thedailygreen.com; Sharon van Schagen, "Starbucks Brews Global Green-Building Plan, Renovates Seattle Shop," *Grist*, June 30, 2009, http://www.thedailygreen.com; "Starbucks Reinvents the Store Experience to Speak to the Heart and Soul of Local Communities," June 25, 2009, http://news.starbucks.com; Starbucks, "Make a Difference," http://www.starbucks.com/thebigpicture, accessed January 31, 2012.

A business is often judged by its interactions with the community. To demonstrate their social responsibility, many corporations highlight their charitable contributions and community service in their annual reports and on their websites. PricewaterhouseCoopers Canada has a "Team Volunteering" program that regularly sets up teams to work with charities throughout Canada in day-long projects. In 2010, this program's volunteers "helped build 18 houses, sorted 575 bags of clothing, created 5,400 hospital play-kits, distributed 8,200 snowsuits to children and sorted 73,600 pounds [more than 33,000 kg] of food."[22]

The Tim Horton Children's Foundation was established in 1974. It provides camp environments for children from disadvantaged homes. Each year, one day is set aside as Camp Day, when every Tim Hortons store in Canada and the United States donates the value of all that day's coffee sales to the Tim Horton Children's Foundation. In 2009, Camp Day raised more than $9.4 million to fund community outreach programs.[23]

Some firms measure social performance by conducting **social audits**, formal procedures that identify and evaluate all company activities that relate to social issues, such as conservation, employ-

social audits formal procedures that identify and evaluate all company activities that relate to social issues, such as conservation, employment practices, environmental protection, and philanthropy.

ment practices, environmental protection, and philanthropy. The social audit tells management how well the company is performing in these areas. After seeing this information, management may decide to revise its current programs or develop new ones.

Outside groups may do their own evaluations of businesses. Various environmental, religious, and public-interest groups have created standards of corporate performance. Reports on many of these evaluations are available to the general public. The Canadian Business for Social Responsibility (CBSR) organization offers CSR assessments that examine the internal activities of a company and compare them to industry CSR best practices. The CBSR also offers advisory services to assist firms in creating a companywide CSR strategy.

Tim Hortons Camp Day highlights the company's commitment to the community and allows the company to fulfill its social responsibility.

© Aurora Photos/Alamy

Business's

| To the General Public | To Customers |
| To Investors and the Financial Community | To Employees |

Social Responsibilities

FIGURE 2.5 Business's Social Responsibilities

As Figure 2.5 shows, business's social responsibilities can be divided by their relationships to the general public, customers, employees, investors, and other members of the financial community. Many of these relationships extend beyond national borders.

Responsibilities to the General Public

The responsibilities of business to the general public include dealing with public health issues, protecting the environment, and developing the quality of the workforce. Many argue that businesses also have responsibilities to support charitable and social causes and organizations that work toward the greater public good. In other words, businesses should give back to the communities in which they earn profits. Such efforts are called *corporate philanthropy*.

Public Health Issues

As business addresses its ethical and social responsibilities to the general public, one of its most complex issues is public health. Central to the public health debate is what businesses should do about dangerous products such as tobacco and alcohol. Many cities have banned smoking not only in public places but also in commercial businesses such as restaurants. A 10-year study in Toronto revealed that cardiovascular hospital admissions dropped by 39 percent after smoking was banned in public places.[24]

Rates of heart disease, diabetes, and obesity have been increasing. These three conditions are now major public health issues. Approximately 1.6 million Canadian children (or 26 percent) are overweight or obese.[25] Three-quarters of obese teenagers will become obese adults at risk for heart disease and diabetes. Jared Fogle became famous for losing 111 kg over a two-year period through exercise and a diet that included SUBWAY sandwiches.[26]

To do their part to aid the general public, SUBWAY and the Jared Foundation focus on encouraging children to eat healthfully in the hopes of avoiding obesity problems later in life.

Substance abuse is another serious public health problem worldwide. Many of the drugs used by athletes are similar to chemicals that are naturally present in the body. As a result knowing whether an athlete has used drugs can be extremely difficult. Professional players who fail drug tests face tough penalties. The most disappointing drug use scandal involving a Canadian athlete was likely when Ben Johnson was stripped of his gold medal for the 100 metres at the 1988 Olympics for having used the anabolic steroid stanozolol. The "Solving an Ethical Controversy" feature explores a related public health issue: Are advertisements for prescription drugs informative or harmful to consumers?[27]

SOLVING AN **ETHICAL** CONTROVERSY

Would Prescription Drug Advertisements be Helpful or Harmful to Canadians?

Currently, direct-to-consumer advertising (DTCA) by drug manufacturers is banned in Canada. Since 1985 in the United States, drug manufacturers have used DTCA to market name-brand prescription drugs. DTCA increased dramatically after 1997, when the U.S. Food and Drug Administration (FDA) no longer required detailed lists of possible side effects. In 2009, pharmaceutical companies spent $4.5 billion on advertising. New Zealand is the only other developed country where DTCA is legal.

Americans now spend more on prescription drugs than on any other area of health care. One reason is the sheer number of prescriptions. Another is that advertising costs have raised the prices of brand-name prescription drugs. Drug companies also market heavily to doctors. The medical community has voiced concern that DTCA may be harming both the public and the healthcare system.

Would direct-to-consumer advertising benefit Canadians?

PRO

1. DTCA encourages people to ask their doctors about potentially harmful conditions that may be helped by nonsurgical treatment if caught early enough.

2. Drug companies use their profits to develop new drugs. This process involves considerable research and testing to win Health Canada's approval of drugs that can improve or even save lives.

CON

1. Drug advertisements appeal to people's emotions while minimizing potential side effects. Advertisements may even persuade people to ask for unnecessary treatments.

2. Pharmaceutical companies usually advertise new drugs that have not been tested over time and are more expensive than slightly different, older drugs with well-known side effects. DTCA sometimes backfires.

Summary

The Health Council of Canada and other agencies have conducted studies on DTCA. These studies show that most doctors felt pressured to prescribe advertised drugs. After a recent U.S. ad campaign for Tegaserod, a drug for irritable bowel syndrome, sales to English-speaking Canadians increased 42 percent. So, despite DTCA being currently banned in Canada, U.S. advertising affects drug sales in Canada. Pharmaceutical companies have tried to introduce DTCA in Europe, but European Union countries voted overwhelmingly against even the "information to patients" section of a proposed regulation.

Sources: "U.S. Ad Spending Down Nine Percent . . ., Nielsen says," The Nielsen Company, February 24, 2010, http://en-us.nielsen.com; http://www.nytimes.com; "Should Prescription Drugs Be Advertised Directly to Consumers?" ProCon.org, http://prescriptiondrugs.procon.org, accessed February 12,2010; Dennis Thompson, "As TV Drug Ads Increase, So Do Concerns," *U.S. News & World Report*, October 4, 2009, http://www.usnews.com; World Health Organization, " Direct-to-Consumer Advertising Comes under Fire," *Bulletin of the World Health Organization* 87:8 (August 2009), http://www.who.int, accessed February 12, 2010; Natasha Singer, "Lawmakers Seek to Curb Drug Commercials, *New York Times*, July 26, 2009; Barbara Mintzes, *What Are the Public Health Implications? Direct-to-Consumer Advertising of Prescription Drugs in Canada*, January 2006, http://healthcouncilcanada.ca/docs/papers/2006/hcc_dtc-advertising_200601_e_v6.pdf, accessed February 22, 2011; Canadian Family Physician website, http://www.cfp.ca/, accessed February 22, 2011.

Recycling can help companies do their part to protect the environment. Best Buy stores will take your old TVs, DVD players, computers, cellphones, and other electronic devices to avoid having them end up in landfills.

Canadian Tire demonstrates its commitment to preserving the environment through its "Take Back the Light" program. Consumers can take their old CFLs and fluorescent tube light bulbs to Canadian Tire for safe disposal.[30]

Protecting the Environment

Businesses consume huge amounts of energy, which increases the use of fossil fuels, such as coal and oil, for energy production. This activity introduces carbon dioxide and sulphur into the earth's atmosphere. Meanwhile, the sulphur from fossil fuels combines with water vapour in the air to form sulphuric acid. The acid rain that results can travel across continents, killing fish and trees and polluting groundwater. Although acid rain has been tracked for many decades, companies are still being identified and punished for their violations. Suncor, a large oil sands firm in Alberta, was recently fined $200,000 for dumping harmful materials into a river in Northern Alberta. This dumping took place on the same day that Ottawa promised to improve environmental monitoring of the Canadian oil sands.[28]

Other production and manufacturing methods leave behind large quantities of waste materials. These materials can further pollute the environment and fill already bulging landfills. Some products are difficult to reuse or recycle, particularly electronics that contain toxins such as lead and mercury. Few manufacturers are equipped to deal with recycled materials; some refurbish products and sell them abroad—where they are less likely to be recycled. Hewlett-Packard, however, is making its scanners with a combination of new and recycled plastics. Lead, mercury, and cadmium will soon be banned from new equipment manufactured in Europe. As we gain stricter laws on electronic recycling, many manufacturers and retailers are offering take-back, mail-in, and trade-in programs for discarded electronic equipment. For example, many Best Buy stores now accept televisions, DVD players, computer monitors, cellphones, and other electronic devices. The stores charge a small fee for televisions 81 cm and under, CRTs (cathode ray tubes, now obsolete), monitors, and laptops, but will give customers a gift card in an equal amount.[29]

For many managers, minimizing pollution and other environmental damage caused by their products or their operating processes is an important economic, legal, and social issue. When General Motors unveiled the Chevrolet Volt, the new car instantly became more popular than conventional hybrids that use a combination of electricity and gasoline. The Volt is entirely electric. After its battery runs down, a gasoline engine powers an on-board generator that recharges the battery. General Motors decided on a 64-km range for the battery because studies have shown that more than three-quarters of commuters drive about that distance to and from work every day, and half drive even less. GM's Vehicle Line Director Tony Posawatz notes, "The beauty of the Volt is the size of the battery."[31] The introduction of the Volt has led to many other automobile manufacturers attempting to produce superior technology. In 2011, Nissan introduced the Nissan Leaf, which has a range of a range of 160 km, more than twice the Volt's range.

Despite difficulties, companies find they can be environmentally friendly and profitable, too. Another solution to the problems of pollutants is **recycling**—reprocessing used

recycling reprocessing of used materials for reuse.

materials for reuse. Recycling can sometimes provide much of the raw material that manufacturers need, thereby conserving the world's natural resources and reducing the need for landfills.

According to Statistics Canada, the diversion of discarded electronic items away from landfill sites has increased by 115 percent in two years.[32] Manufacturers and federal agencies are struggling to devise a workable system to further manage the problem of electronic waste. In some provinces, consumers pay a surcharge on certain electronics purchases, such as computers, monitors, fax machines, and televisions. In Ontario, this surcharge is part of the Waste Electrical and Electronic Equipment (WEEE) Program.[33] In the meantime, Best Buy, Staples, and other retailers accept all gadgets for recycling, no matter where they were purchased. Manufacturers Hewlett-Packard and Dell have agreed not to send waste materials overseas. The "Hit & Miss" feature describes a company that puts a creative twist on recycling. Pacific Diesel turns used restaurant oil and grease into clean, biodegradable biodiesel fuel.

Many consumers like to support environmentally conscious businesses. To target these customers, companies often use **green marketing**, a marketing strategy that promotes environmentally safe products and production methods. But a business cannot simply claim that its goods or services are environmentally friendly. The Competition Bureau of Canada (CB) has guidelines for environmental claims. For example, a firm must be able to prove that any environmental claim can

green marketing a marketing strategy that promotes environmentally safe products and production methods.

HIT & MISS

Pacific Biodiesel Recycles Oil from French Fries to Fuel

In 1980, Robert King founded King Diesel on the island of Maui in Hawaii. The company used conventional diesel fuel to run the generators at the Central Maui Landfill. In 1995, King became concerned about the large amounts of used cooking oil being dumped. He contacted Daryl Reece at the University of Idaho. Reece helped develop a process that successfully converted used restaurant oils into biodiesel fuel. Together, King and Reece founded Pacific Biodiesel. This company uses biodiesel to run the generators at the landfill in one of America's first commercially viable, community-based biodiesel plants. Today, Pacific Biodiesel and its associated companies produce and sell biodiesel fuel. They also design, build, and support biodiesel plants throughout the United States.

Biodiesel fuel is biodegradable and nontoxic and can be used in any diesel engine. This fuel is produced from renewable resources such as used cooking oil and soybean oil. If not converted to fuel, these oils would be dumped in landfills or down drains. Biodiesel significantly reduces many pollutants and reduces dependence on foreign oil.

On Maui, restaurants pay haulers to take their used cooking oil to the landfill. The haulers pay the county of Oahu for the right to dump garbage at waste facilities. Pacific Biodiesel's facility at the landfill is rent-free. The haulers' fees cover most of the county's payment to Pacific Biodiesel for processing the waste. Shipping this waste off the island would be much more expensive; recycling the oil prolongs the useful life of the landfills and guarantees a local source

of energy. On Maui alone, Pacific Biodiesel recycles about 757,000 litres of oil and grease each year.

King says, "We definitely took a leap of faith, but . . . we wanted to do more . . . something to contribute to society . . . [I]t is important to do . . . something that brings you happiness—because the feeling you get by 'doing the right thing' never disappears."

Canadian Pacific and Natural Resources Canada have recently partnered in a pilot project to test the effectiveness of biodiesel in Canada's cold weather regions. So far, these tests have indicated that biodiesel could work effectively despite Canada's colder climate.

Questions for Critical Thinking

1. How might Pacific Biodiesel spread the message that recycling is good business and good for the environment? How might it reach out to other industries?

2. How does Pacific Biodiesel fulfill its responsibilities to the general public?

3. Would Canadian Pacific likely be as successful as Pacific Biodiesel in making a public impact, given that a U.S. competitor has already established the technology?

Sources: Pacific Biodiesel website, http://biodiesel.com/, accessed February 2010; U.S. Environmental Protection Agency, "Food to Fuel: Pacific Biodiesel, Inc.," http://www.epa.gov/; Deidre Tegarden, "Pacific Biodiesel," *Maui Weekly*, November 26, 2009, http://www.mauiweekly.com; Canadian Pacific, "Cold Weather Biofuel Testing," http://www.cpr.ca/en/in-your-community/environment/Pages/cold-weather-biodiesel-testing.aspx, accessed March 2, 2012.

be supported by reliable scientific evidence. In addition, as shown in Table 2.1, the CB states how various environmental terms can be used in advertising and marketing.[34]

sustainable the capacity to endure in ecology.

Many firms focus on other environmental issues, such as finding renewable sources of clean energy and developing **sustainable** agriculture. Vinod Khosla, founder of Sun Microsystems, is working with a group of high-powered entrepreneurs and investors in the Silicon Valley. They hope to develop a new generation of energy.[35] They're not alone. Many entrepreneurs, large energy firms, and small engineering companies are developing solar energy, geothermal energy, biodiesel, and wind power. As we saw in the "Hit & Miss" feature, Pacific Biodiesel started with one plant and now has branches across the United States. Canadian Pacific is likely to match Pacific Biodiesel's growth in Canada.

The Tim Hortons Coffee Partnership works with the Hanns R. Neumann Stiftung Foundation to contribute to the sustainability of the coffee sector in Guatemala, Colombia, Brazil, Honduras, and El Salvador by working with both the private sector (primarily coffee roasters) and the public sector (donors).[36]

Table 2.1 Competition Bureau of Canada's Guidelines for Environmental Claims in Green Marketing

IF A COMPANY SAYS A PRODUCT IS . . .	THE PRODUCT OR PACKAGE MUST . . .
Degradable	be photodegradable or biodegradable within a short period of time under normal disposal conditions for that type of product of package.
Compostable	biodegrade, generating a relatively homogeneous and stable humus-like substance.
Recyclable	be able to be processed and returned to use in the form of raw materials or products.
Refillable	be reusable for their original purpose.

Source: Competition Bureau of Canada website, *Environmental Claims: A Guide for Industry and Advisors*, June 2008, http://www.competitionbureau.gc.ca/eic/site/cb-bc.nsf/eng/02701.html#s10_2, accessed February 18, 2011.

Developing the Quality of the Workforce

In the past, a nation's wealth was often based on its money, production equipment, and natural resources. But a country's true wealth is in its people. An educated, skilled workforce provides the know-how needed to develop new technology, improve productivity, and compete in the global marketplace. To remain competitive, Canadian businesses must take more responsibility for enhancing the quality of its workforce, including encouraging diversity of all kinds.

In developed economies, such as Canada, many new jobs require university or college education. Demand is high for workers with advanced skills. That means the difference between the highest-paid and lowest-paid workers is increasing. Education plays an important role in earnings, despite success stories of those who dropped out of college or high school to start businesses. Workers with professional degrees earn an average of $2,750 a week, whereas those with some high school but no diploma earn about $450. Businesses must encourage students to stay in school, continue their education, and sharpen their skills. Tim Hortons provides 220 post-secondary scholarships each year to students who "believe in giving back to the community (through volunteer work)." These scholarships are valued at $1,000 each and are awarded to students in Canada and the United States.[37]

Organizations also face responsibilities for helping women, members of various cultural groups, and those who are physically challenged to contribute fully to the economy. Failure to do so is not only a waste of more than half the nation's workforce but may be harmful to a firm's public image. Some socially responsible firms also encourage diversity in their business suppliers. COSTI Immigrant Services, based in Toronto, has set up programs to assist immigrant women move into strong roles in the workforce. COSTI helps women of diverse backgrounds overcome economic challenges and cultural barriers. COSTI has been helping new immigrants for over 50 years.[38]

The Coca-Cola Company is committed to developing employee diversity. It strives to create an inclusive atmosphere, offers diversity training for employees and managers, and encourages regular dialogue among colleagues, suppliers, customers, and stakeholders. "By building an inclusive workplace environment, The Coca-Cola Company seeks to leverage its worldwide team, which is rich in diverse people, talent, and ideas," according to the company's website.[39] For any global organization to function competitively, diversity is vital.

Corporate Philanthropy

As noted in Chapter 1, not-for-profit organizations play an important role in society by serving the public good. They provide the human resources that enhance the quality of life in communities around the world. To fulfill this mission, many not-for-profit organizations rely on financial donations from the business community. Firms donate billions of dollars each year to not-for-profit organizations. This **corporate philanthropy** includes cash contributions, donations of equipment and products, and supporting the volunteer efforts of company employees. Recipients include cultural organizations, adopt-a-school programs, community development agencies, and housing and job training programs.

corporate philanthropy an organization's contribution to the communities where it earns profits.

Corporate philanthropy can have many positive benefits beyond the "feel-good" rewards of giving. Corporate philanthropy can lead to higher employee morale, enhanced company image, and improved customer relationships. Each year, CIBC and other Canadian companies sponsor the CIBC Run for the Cure, Canada's largest single-day, volunteer-led fundraising event specifically for breast cancer research, education, and awareness. This event not only raises funds for a very important cause but also increases the corporate profiles of CIBC and the other corporate sponsors.[40]

Companies often want to tie their marketing efforts to their charitable giving. For example, many firms contribute to the Olympics; they then create advertising that features the company's sponsorship. This type of advertising is known as *cause-related marketing*. In a recent survey, nearly nine out of ten young people said they believed companies had a duty to support social causes. Nearly seven in eight said they would switch brands to reward a company that supported social causes. Consumers will often pay more for a product if they know the proceeds are going to a good cause. KitchenAid Canada started a "Cook for the Cure" campaign. It donates $75 of the $470 selling price of its pink line of stand mixers to the Canadian Breast Cancer Foundation.[41]

The Canadian Press/Halifax Chronicle Herald/Ingrid Bulmer

CIBC has taken the lead in the CIBC Run for the Cure, which encourages many other businesses to also participate.

Another form of corporate philanthropy is volunteerism. Thousands of businesses encourage their employees to contribute their time to such projects as Habitat for Humanity, the Red Cross, and the Humane Society. These programs make tangible contributions to the well-being of other citizens. These programs also create public support and goodwill for the companies and their employees. Sometimes, the volunteer work takes place when employees are off the job. Other times, firms allow their employees to volunteer during regular working hours. Volunteers with special skills are always needed. After the earthquake in Haiti, the pilots' union at UPS volunteered to transport supplies and personnel as part of the relief effort.[42]

Responsibilities to Customers

consumerism public demand that a business consider the wants and needs of its customers when making decisions.

Businesspeople share a social and ethical responsibility to treat their customers fairly and to act in a way that does not cause harm. **Consumerism** is the public demand that a business consider the wants and needs of its customers when making decisions. Consumerism has gained wide acceptance. It is based on the belief that consumers have certain rights. In 1962, U.S. President John F. Kennedy extolled four basic consumer rights, later called The Consumer Bill of Rights. Figure 2.6 summarizes these consumer rights. The Consumers' Association of Canada (CAC) was formed in 1947. It helps to educate and inform consumers on issues related to buying products and services. It also helps people to solve consumer problems by working with government and industry.[43]

The Right to Be Safe

product liability the responsibility of manufacturers for injuries and damages caused by their products.

Today's businesspeople have moral and legal obligations to ensure their products are safe to use. Consumers should know that the products they purchase will not cause injuries in normal use. **Product liability** refers to the responsibility of manufacturers for injuries and damages caused by their products. Items that lead to injuries, either directly or indirectly, can have lasting consequences for their manufacturers.

Many companies test their products thoroughly to avoid safety problems. Still, testing cannot check for every possible problem. Companies must try to think of all possible problems and warn consumers of any potential dangers. When a product poses a threat to customer safety, a responsible manufacturer responds quickly. The manufacturer can either correct the problem or recall the dangerous product. We often take for granted that our food supply is safe. But contamination can leak in, causing illness or even death. Maple Leaf Foods had a listeria outbreak at one of its Toronto plants. The company recalled 220 packaged meats in August 2008. Maple Leaf had direct costs of more than $20 million. This amount did not include the loss of future customer goodwill. At least 42 cases of listeriosis were confirmed, and at least 15 deaths were blamed on the outbreak.[44]

FIGURE 2.6
Commonly Referred-to Consumer Rights

The Right to Be Informed

Consumers should be able to get enough education and product information to make responsible buying decisions. Companies can easily forget consumers' right to be fully informed while they are busy promoting and selling their goods and services. The Competition Act contains provisions against false or misleading representations and deceptive marketing. The Competition Act has rules and regulations that lead to advertising truthfulness. These rules keep businesses from making unproven claims about how its products perform or why its products are superior. The act also requires businesses to avoid misleading consumers. Businesses that don't follow these rules may face questions from the CB and consumer protection organizations. Persons who are guilty can face criminal penalties of up to 14 years in prison and fines, or both. On a civil level, if a person is found to be liable, the fine could be up to $1 million, $15 million for corporations. For instance, Rogers Communications Inc. (RCI) aired ads that its new discount text-and-talk service, Chatr, has fewer dropped calls than its competitors. In 2010, the CB started an investigation. It is seeking a $10 million fine against RCI. The CB says that RCI's claims are misleading according to the Competition Act. "We take misleading advertising very seriously," says Melanie Aitken, commissioner of competition. "Consumers deserve accurate information when making purchasing decisions and need to have confidence they are not being misled by false advertising campaigns." RCI also aired ads that claimed it had Canada's most reliable network. Competitor TELUS took RCI to court, and RCI pulled the ads.[45]

Health Canada supports the Food and Drug Act (FDA). This act defines the standards for safety and advertising to be followed by makers of drugs, cosmetics, and therapeutic devices. The act also requires that all ingredients be listed on product labels so consumers are fully informed.[46]

The business responsibility to maintain consumers' right to be informed goes beyond avoiding advertising that misleads. All communications with customers—from salespeople's comments to warranties and invoices—must be checked so that they clearly and accurately inform customers. The labels of most packaged goods, personal computers, and other products include toll-free customer service telephone numbers so that consumers can get answers to their questions.

The Right to Choose

Consumers should have the right to choose the goods and services they need and the goods they want to purchase. Socially responsible firms try to preserve this right, even if it means they need to reduce their own sales and profits. Brand-name drug makers have taken a defensive stand in an issue being discussed by provincial governments, insurance companies, consumer groups, unions, and major employers such as General Motors. These groups want to force down the rising price of prescription drugs. They believe that the government should ensure that consumers have the right and the opportunity to buy cheaper generic brands of drugs. In 2011, however, the Province of Ontario enacted regulations stopping pharmacies, such as Shoppers Drug Mart, Rexall, and PharmaPlus, from selling their lower-priced generic alternatives to brand-name drugs. The reason? Experts claimed these savings were unlikely to be passed onto the consumers.[47]

The Right to Be Heard

Consumers should be able to express their valid complaints to the appropriate people. Many companies spend much effort to ensure that consumers' complaints receive a full hearing. The auction website eBay assists buyers and sellers who believe they were unfairly treated in transactions that occur through the site. It uses a 200-employee team to work with eBay users and law enforcement agencies to fight against fraud. The company has strict guidelines for buyers and sellers. It also has rules about leaving feedback about a buyer or seller. For example, sellers must only sell items that are included on a list of acceptable goods for sale. They cannot offer such items as alcohol, pornography, drugs, counterfeit currency, or artifacts from cave formations or graves. The protection of copyrights is also an important part of eBay's policy.[48]

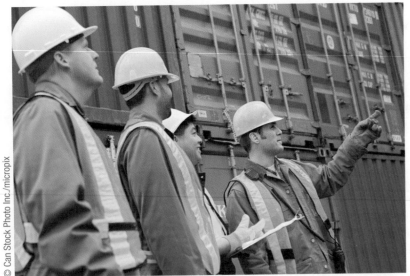

© Can Stock Photo Inc./micropix

Workplace safety is an important business responsibility. Workers are required to wear hard hats when in potentially dangerous areas.

Responsibilities to Employees

Companies that can attract skilled and know-ledgeable employees are better able to meet the challenges of competing globally. In return, businesses have wide-ranging responsibilities to their employees, both here and abroad. These responsibilities include workplace safety, quality-of-life issues, ensuring equal opportunity on the job, avoiding age discrimination, and preventing sexual harassment and sexism.

Workplace Safety

The safety and health of workers on the job is now an important business responsibility. The Canadian Centre for Occupational Health and Safety (CCOHS) promotes workplace health and safety. Workers' compensation programs are managed mostly at the provincial level by organizations such as the Workplace Safety and Insurance Board in Ontario, the Workers' Compensation Board in Nova Scotia, and the Workers' Compensation Board of Alberta. These organizations are responsible for setting workplace safety and health standards. These standards range from broad guidelines on storing hazardous materials to specific standards for worker safety in industries such as construction, manufacturing, and mining. These organizations track and investigate workplace accidents and pay claims to employees who are injured on the job.

According to a 2010 research study, each year, one in every 53 employed workers was injured and received workers' compensation.[49] Many people die every year in Canada as a result of work-related injuries. Most of these fatalities occur because of unsafe equipment, inadequate safety training, and dangerous work that is illegal or inappropriate for youth. Provincial workers' compensation boards, labour ministries, and the CCOHS are working to educate employers and young workers about safety, health, and a positive work environment.

Quality-of-Life Issues

Balancing work and family is becoming harder for many employees. They work long hours then go home to face child-care tasks, caring for their elderly parents, and solving other family crises. A *sandwich generation* of households has arisen. This term refers to people caring for two generations—their children and their aging parents. The population is growing older, and more and more Canadians provide some type of care to a relative or friend age 50 or older. At the same time, most mothers spend more time working outside the home. That means they have fewer hours to spend on their family.

The employees who juggle work with life's other demands aren't just working mothers. Childless couples, single people, and men all say they are frustrated with having to balance work with family and personal needs. Some employers are trying to help their employees find a work–life balance. They do this by offering flexible work schedules so that parents can do their jobs *and* meet the needs of their children (or aging parents). Each year, the editors of Canada's Top 100 Employers organize a competition called Canada's Top Family-Friendly Employers. Employers who make the top 100 have made a big commitment to help their employees balance work and family commitments. Some of the employers who made this list in 2012 were University of Toronto, Manitoba Hydro, and BMO Financial Group.[50]

Increasingly, women are starting their own businesses so they can set their own hours and goals. The "Hit & Miss" feature describes one woman who started her own business so she could provide her ailing son with the care he needed.

HIT & MISS

Balancing Life and Work with a Cup of Tea

In 2000, Zhena Muzyka, a 25-year-old single mother had an infant son who needed kidney surgery. Muzyka had no health insurance and only a few dollars in the bank. As a young girl, she had watched her Rom (gypsy) grandmother tend a huge garden and blend teas. Muzyka had always been interested in herbal medicine, so she borrowed money from her parents and her brother and started Zhena's Gypsy Tea. She started selling tea from a cart in a friend's antique store. At first, she worked with her son, Sage, in a baby carrier, at her side. When her teas became popular—and Sage outgrew the carrier—she knew she had reached a turning point.

Muzyka searched for new sources and started blending her own loose-leaf teas. She added essential oils for their medicinal value. She learned that none of the teas she was buying were organic or **fair trade**. She made the change to fair trade teas after learning that infant mortality rates among tea pickers on non–fair trade farms can reach 70 percent. Fair trade tea workers have guaranteed health care, clean water, education, and maternity leave and child care.

As Zhena's Gypsy Tea has grown and diversified, Muzhaka has searched for new ways to put her values into practice. Her Pink Tea for Women's Health is a partner of the Breast Cancer Research Foundation. The company now uses corn silk for its teabags. It buys wind credits, even though it lowers profits. Muzyka says, "[Zhena's Gypsy Tea] is the most 'worth it' thing I've ever done. Knowing that we're sincerely making a difference for people and helping them out of poverty—while providing a delicious cup of tea for consumers here—is pretty satisfying."

And Sage? After three operations, he had a clean bill of health in 2007.

Questions for Critical Thinking

1. How did Zhena Muzyka translate her life experiences into her company's ethics culture?

2. Do you have an idea for starting your own business? If so, brainstorm some ideas for balancing your life and values with your work.

3. What key provincial or federal legislation would you need to be aware of especially if your business was to grow and employ a significant number of staff members?

Sources: Gypsy Tea website, http://www.gypsytea.com, accessed February 2010; Eve Gumpel, "Gypsy Tea Steeped in Health and Fun," *Women Entrepreneur.com*, January 24, 2010, http://www.womenentrepreneur.com; "Oh, That's So Yesterday: A California Tea Company Gets a Brand Makeover," *Inc.*, December 2009/January 2010.

Some companies have come up with truly innovative ways to deal with work schedules, including paid time off for vacation or illness. At some of its locations, IBM has done away with vacation time altogether—instead, the focus is on results. Employees have an informal agreement with their supervisors about when they will be out of the office. This time away is based on their ability to complete their work on schedule. The number of days they take off is not tracked; instead, vacation time is considered open-ended. But the catch is, the work needs to be done. With some surprises, the firm found that employees put in just as many hours, if not more hours, under the new program. According to an IBM representative, "there is no policing, and employees are empowered to take vacation when they want."[51]

fair trade a market-based approach of paying higher prices to producers for goods exported from developing countries to developed countries in an effort to promote sustainability and to ensure the people in developing countries receive better trading conditions.

Ensuring Equal Opportunity on the Job

Businesspeople face many challenges when managing an increasingly diverse workforce in the 21st century. Technological advances are expanding the ways people with physical disabilities can contribute in the workplace. Businesses also need to find ways to responsibly recruit and manage older workers and workers with varying lifestyles. In 1982, Lotus Development (later Lotus Software) was the first major company to offer full benefits to its employees' partners, regardless of sexual orientation. This means that the company offers such benefits as health insurance to its employees' unmarried domestic partners if it also offers the same benefits to its employees' married spouses. Companies that now offer these gender-neutral benefits include Avon Products, Costco Wholesale, Disney, General Mills, and Mattel. Companies such as WestJet and Research In Motion advertise that their hiring practices do not discriminate in terms of sexual orientation, colour, race, religion, etc.[52]

Table 2.2 Protections Designed to Ensure Equal Opportunity

FOCUS	LAW	KEY PROVISIONS
Equal Rights	Canadian Charter of Rights and Freedoms, 1982	Every individual is equal before and under the law and has the right to the equal protection and equal benefit of the law without discrimination and, in particular, without discrimination based on race, national or ethnic origin, colour, religion, sex, age, or mental or physical disability.
Physical and Mental Disabilities	Canadian Human Rights Act and Provincial Human Rights Codes	Forbids age discrimination in employment—with exceptions in some cases regarding mandatory retirement and bona fide occupational requirements. Requires employers to make reasonable accommodations for employees with new or pre-existing mental or physical disabilities.
Equal Pay for Equal Work	Provincial Employment Standards Acts	Ensures equal pay for equal work when work is substantially the same, requires the same effort, and is performed under the same working conditions at the same establishment.
Physical and Mental Disabilities	Canadian Disability Vocational Rehabilitation Program and Provincial Vocational Rehabilitation Acts	Provides work and personal adjustment training and support for people with disabilities who seek gainful employment.
Pregnancy and Parental Leave	Provincial Labour Ministries	Employers cannot penalize employees for taking pregnancy or parental leave. Employees who take such leaves have the right to earn credit toward their length of service. They typically must be returned to their job after their pregnancy or parental leave is over.
Family Medical Leave	Provincial Labour Ministries	Allows an employee to take up to 8 weeks of unpaid leave in a 26-week period to care for a seriously ill family member.
Reservists	Provincial Labour Ministries	Employees who are reservists and deployed on an operation are to be granted unpaid leave without benefits. While on leave, their seniority and length of service will accumulate.

discrimination biased treatment toward a job candidate or employee.

Employment Equity Act (EEA) an act created (1) to increase job opportunities for women and members of minority groups and (2) to help end discrimination based on race, colour, religion, disability, gender, or national origin.

The Canadian Charter of Rights and Freedoms is an all-encompassing act that addresses **discrimination** in Canada. Section 15 states: "Every individual is equal before and under the law and has the right to the equal protection and equal benefit of the law without discrimination and, in particular, without discrimination based on race, national or ethnic origin, colour, religion, sex, age or mental or physical disability." Table 2.2 describes other specific types of equal opportunity employee protections.[53]

The **Employment Equity Act (EEA)** was created for two reasons: to increase job opportunities for women and members of minority groups and to help end discrimination in any personnel action that is based on race, colour, religion, disability, gender, or national origin. To enforce fair-employment laws, this act is overseen by the Canadian Human Rights Commission, which investigates charges of discrimination and harassment. The EEA can also help employers set up programs to increase job opportunities for women, members of minority groups, people with disabilities, and people in other protected categories.

Age Discrimination

The average age of Canadian workers is steadily rising. In a few years, more than half the workforce will be age 40 or older. Some employers find it less expensive to hire and retain younger workers. These younger employees generally have lower medical bills and typically receive lower salaries and benefits packages. But many older workers have training and skills that younger workers lack. The Canadian Human Rights Act (CHRA) prohibits age discrimination except in very specific cases.

In 2008, Kim Ouwroulis, age 44, was an exotic dancer at the New Locomotion club in Mississauga, Ontario. She filed a complaint with the Human Rights Commission of Ontario, claiming she was fired due to her age. These types of cases require the employer to prove that "sex appeal is the essence of the job," says Denise Reaume, a University of Toronto professor who specializes in discrimination law. "This is tricky because sexual response is as variable as human beings are."[54]

Legal issues aside, employers should consider not only the experience that older workers bring to the workplace but also their enthusiasm. "Job satisfaction is especially high among those 65 and over because most people working at that age are not forced to still work, due to financial reasons, but choose to do so because they like their jobs," says the leader of a recent study. Nearly 75 percent of people over age 65 who were interviewed said they were very happy with their jobs.[55]

Employers are responsible for avoiding age discrimination in the workplace. As the average age of workers rises, employers will benefit from the older generation's knowledge.

In all cases, employers need to plan ahead for the aging of the workforce. Such planning includes finding ways to retain accumulated business wisdom, preparing for the demand for health services, and being ready for growth in the industries that serve seniors. The number of people aged 55 to 64 has increased by almost 30 percent in the past few years. By 2017, it is predicted that more people will be at an age they can leave the labour market than those at an age to enter it.[56] These numbers show a coming shift in the workforce and in the goods and services needed.

Sexual Harassment and Sexism

Every employer has a responsibility to ensure that all workers are treated fairly and are safe from sexual harassment. **Sexual harassment** refers to unwelcome and inappropriate actions of a sexual nature. It is a form of sex discrimination that violates the CHRA, which gives both men and women the right to file lawsuits for intentional sexual harassment. Thousands of sexual harassment

sexual harassment unwelcome and inappropriate actions of a sexual nature.

complaints are filed each year, and many complaints are filed by men. Thousands of other cases are either handled internally by companies or never reported.

The workplace has two types of sexual harassment. The first type occurs when an employee is pressured to go along with unwelcomed advances and requests for sexual favours in return for job security, promotions, and raises. The second type results from a hostile work environment, where an employee feels hassled or degraded because of unwelcome flirting, lewd comments, or obscene jokes. The courts have ruled that allowing sexually oriented materials in the workplace can create a hostile atmosphere that interferes with an employee's ability to work. Employers are also legally responsible to protect employees from sexual harassment by customers and clients. The Canadian Human Rights Commission's website helps employers and employees by listing the criteria for identifying sexual harassment and how it should be handled in the workplace.

Firms should prevent sexual harassment for ethical and legal reasons. But did you know that sexual harassment can also be costly? The cost in settlements or fines can be huge. It makes good business sense for firms to prevent this kind of behaviour. Many firms have set up policies and employee education programs aimed at preventing such problems. An effective harassment prevention program should include the following:

- A specific policy statement prohibiting sexual harassment

- A complaint procedure for employees to follow

- A work atmosphere that encourages sexually harassed staffers to come forward

- A commitment to investigate and resolve complaints quickly and to take disciplinary action against harassers

These components need to be supported by top management; otherwise, sexual harassment is difficult to get rid of.

Sexual harassment is often part of the broader problem of **sexism**—discrimination against members of either sex, but usually against women. One important sexism issue is equal pay for equal work.

On average, a Canadian woman earns 70.5 percent of what a man earns.[57] The difference can't be explained by differences in education, occupation, work hours, or other factors. The only explanation seems to be being female.[58] In some extreme cases, differences in pay and advancement can lead to sex discrimination suits. These suits, like sexual harassment suits, can be costly and time-consuming to settle. As in all business practices, it is better to act legally and ethically in the first place.

sexism discrimination against members of either sex, but usually against women.

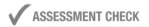

✓ ASSESSMENT CHECK

2.4.1 What is meant by social responsibility, and why do firms pay attention to it?

2.4.2 What is green marketing?

2.4.3 What are the four main consumer rights?

LO 2.5 Explain why investors and the financial community are concerned with business ethics and social responsibility.

RESPONSIBILITIES TO INVESTORS AND THE FINANCIAL COMMUNITY

A fundamental goal of any business is to make a profit for its shareholders. But investors and the financial community also demand that businesses behave ethically and legally. When firms fail in this responsibility, thousands of investors and consumers can suffer.

Provincial regulators such as the Ontario Securities Commission and the Alberta Securities Commission are primarily responsible for protecting investors from financial misdeeds. These provincial regulators investigate suspicions of unethical or illegal behaviour by publicly traded firms. They look into accusations that a business is using faulty accounting practices to inaccurately report its financial resources and profits to investors. Recall that legislation, such as Bill 198 in Canada and the Sarbanes-Oxley Act of 2002 in the United States, protect investors from unethical accounting practices. In 2009, Garth Drabinski and Myron Gottlieb were found guilty of preparing fraudulent accounting information at Toronto-based Livent Inc. They defrauded investors of approximately $500 million. Livent was well known as the producer of *The Phantom of the Opera*, Toronto's longest running musical.[59] Chapter 17 discusses securities trading practices further.

WHAT'S AHEAD

The decisions and actions of businesspeople are often influenced by outside forces, such as the legal environment and society's expectations about business responsibility. Firms are also affected by the economic environment where they operate. The next chapter discusses the broad economic issues that influence businesses around the world. Our discussion will focus on how certain factors—supply and demand, unemployment, inflation, and government monetary policies—pose both challenges and opportunities when firms seek to compete in the global marketplace.

✔ **ASSESSMENT CHECK**

2.5.1 Why do firms need to do more than just earn a profit?

2.5.2 What is the role of the provincial securities regulators?

RETURN TO INSIDE BUSINESS

Cirque du Soleil: A Class Act in Social Responsibility

Businesses in today's corporate environment try to operate in a socially responsible manner. Companies like the Cirque du Soleil have taken significant measures to both operate in a socially responsible manner and publicize their efforts.

QUESTIONS FOR CRITICAL THINKING

1. Do you feel that corporate social responsibility has significant impact on Cirque du Soleil's success, or is it just a "nice-to-have"?

2. Does a firm need to publicize its corporate social responsibility efforts? Or, does company-sponsored publicity make it appear that these efforts are solely to generate revenues through positive public relations?

SUMMARY OF LEARNING OBJECTIVES

LO 2.1 Explain the concepts of business ethics and social responsibility.

Business ethics are the standards of conduct and moral values that businesspeople rely on to guide their actions and decisions in the workplace. Businesspeople must consider a wide range of social issues when making decisions. Social responsibility is management's acceptance of the obligation to put an equal value on profit, consumer satisfaction, and societal well-being when evaluating the firm's performance.

 ASSESSMENT CHECK ANSWERS

2.1.1 To whom do businesses have responsibilities? Businesses have responsibilities to customers, employees, investors, and society.

2.1.2 If a firm is meeting all its responsibilities to others, why do ethical conflicts arise? Ethical conflicts arise because business must balance doing what is right and doing what is profitable.

LO 2.2 Describe the factors that influence business ethics.

Many factors shape individual ethics, including personal experience, peer pressure, and organizational culture. Individual ethics are also influenced by family, cultural, and religious standards. The culture of the workplace can also be a factor.

 ASSESSMENT CHECK ANSWERS

2.2.1 What is the role of a firm's ethics compliance officer? Ethics compliance officers must discourage wrongdoing and ensure that ethical standards are met.

2.2.2 What factors influence the ethical environment of a business? Individual ethics and technology influence the ethical environment of a business.

LO 2.3 Discuss how organizations shape ethical behaviour.

Conflicts of interest occur when an action that benefits one person may harm another person. For example, a businessperson's own interests may conflict with the interests of a customer. Honesty and integrity are valued qualities that lead to trust, but a person's immediate self-interest may lead to actions that go against these principles. Loyalty to an employer sometimes conflicts with being truthful. When misconduct occurs in the workplace, some employees may think about being whistle-blowers but the personal costs may be high. Employees are strongly influenced by the standards of conduct already set up and supported in their workplace. Businesses can help shape ethical behaviour by using codes of conduct that define what they expect from employees. Organizations can also use this training to develop employees' ethics awareness and reasoning. Employers can promote ethical action by providing decision-making tools, supporting goals that are consistent with ethical behaviour, and by setting up advice hotlines. Executives must also provide ethical leadership by showing ethical behaviour in all their decisions and actions.

 ASSESSMENT CHECK ANSWERS

2.3.1 For an employee, when does loyalty conflict with truth? Truth conflicts with loyalty when the truth about a company or a situation is unfavourable.

2.3.2 How does ethical leadership contribute to ethical standards throughout a company? When leaders and managers behave ethically, employees are more likely to commit to the company's core values.

LO 2.4 Describe how businesses' social responsibility is measured, and summarize the responsibilities of business to the general public, customers, and employees.

Today's businesses are expected to weigh two things: their qualitative impact on consumers and society and their quantitative economic contributions in terms of sales, employment levels, and profits. Social responsibility can be measured by charitable contributions and compliance with labour laws and consumer protection laws. Some businesses choose to conduct social audits. Public-interest groups also create standards for measuring companies' performance. A business's responsibilities to the general public include protecting public health and the environment and developing the quality of the workforce. Some also argue that businesses have a social responsibility to support charitable and social causes in the communities where they earn profits. Business must also treat customers fairly and protect consumers. Businesses do this by upholding consumers' rights to be safe, to be informed, to choose, and to be heard. Businesses have wide-ranging responsibilities to their employees. They need to ensure that the workplace is safe, address quality-of-life issues, ensure equal opportunity, and prevent sexual harassment and other forms of discrimination.

 ASSESSMENT CHECK ANSWERS

2.4.1 What is meant by social responsibility, and why do firms pay attention to it? Social responsibility is management's responsibility to consider profit, consumer satisfaction, and society's well-being as having equal value when evaluating the firm's performance. Businesses pay attention to it for many reasons: because it is required by law, because it enhances the company's image, and because it is the right thing to do.

2.4.2 What is green marketing? Green marketing is a marketing strategy that promotes environmentally safe products and production methods.

2.4.3 What are the four main consumer rights? The four main consumer rights are the rights to be safe, to be informed, to choose, and to be heard.

LO 2.5 Explain why investors and the financial community are concerned with business ethics and social responsibility.

Investors and the financial community demand that businesses behave ethically and legally in their handling of financial transactions. Businesses must be honest in reporting their profits and financial performance to avoid misleading investors. Provincial securities regulators investigate suspicions that publicly traded firms have engaged in unethical or illegal financial behaviour.

 ASSESSMENT CHECK ANSWERS

2.5.1 Why do firms need to do more than just earn a profit? Firms need to do more than just earn a profit for two reasons: because the law requires them to behave in a legal and ethical manner and because investors and shareholders demand such behaviour.

2.5.2 What is the role of the provincial securities regulators? Among other functions, provincial securities regulators investigate suspicions of unethical or illegal behaviour by publicly traded firms.

BUSINESS TERMS YOU NEED TO KNOW

business ethics 32	social responsibility 42	product liability 50
Sarbanes-Oxley Act of 2002 35	social audits 43	fair trade 53
conflict of interest 37	recycling 46	discrimination 54
integrity 38	green marketing 47	Employment Equity Act (EEA) 54
whistle-blowing 39	sustainable 48	sexual harassment 55
code of conduct 40	corporate philanthropy 49	sexism 56
stakeholders 42	consumerism 50	

REVIEW QUESTIONS

1. What do the terms *business ethics* and *social responsibility* mean? Why are they important components of a firm's overall philosophy in conducting business?

2. How do individuals make a difference in a firm's commitment to ethics? Describe the three stages an individual goes through when developing ethical standards.

3. Identify the ethical dilemmas in each of the following situations. (A situation might involve more than one dilemma.)

   a. Due to the breakup with a client, an advertising agency finds itself working with rival companies.

   b. A newly hired employee learns that the office manager plays computer games on company time.

   c. A drug manufacturer offers a doctor an expensive gift to encourage the doctor to prescribe a new brand-name drug.

   d. An employee is told to destroy documents that show a firm's role in spreading pollution.

   e. A company spokesperson agrees to a media conference that puts a positive spin on the firm's use of underpaid labour.

4. Describe how ethical leadership helps to develop each of the other ethical standards.

5. How do firms demonstrate their social responsibility?

6. What are the four major areas where businesses have responsibilities to the general public? How can meeting these responsibilities lead to a competitive edge?

7. Describe the four basic rights that consumerism tries to protect. How has consumerism improved the contemporary business environment? What challenges has consumerism created for businesses?

8. What five major responsibilities do companies have to their employees? What changes in society are affecting these responsibilities?

9. Which equal opportunity laws or acts protect the following workers:

   a. an employee who must care for an elderly parent

   b. a Canadian Armed Forces member who is returning from deployment overseas

   c. a job applicant who is HIV positive

   d. a person who is over 40 years old

   e. a woman who has been sexually harassed on the job

   f. a woman who has a family history of breast cancer

10. How does a company show its responsibility to investors and to the financial community?

PROJECTS AND TEAMWORK APPLICATIONS

1. Write your own personal code of ethics. Create standards for your behaviour at school, in personal relationships, and on the job. Assess how well you meet your own standards. Revise your code of ethics, if necessary.

2. On your own or with a classmate, visit the website of one of the following firms, or choose another that interests you. Use what you can learn about the company from the website to construct a chart or figure that shows examples of the firm's ethical awareness, ethical education, ethical actions, and ethical leadership. Present your findings to class.

   a. Tim Hortons

   b. the National Hockey League (NHL), or any major professional sports league

   c. TELUS Mobility

   d. RBC Financial Group

   e. Research In Motion

   f. RONA

   g. IKEA

3. Using the company you studied for question 2 (or another company), conduct a social audit. Do your findings match the firm's culture of ethics? If not, what are the differences, and why did they occur?

4. On your own or with a classmate, go online, flip through a magazine, or surf television channels to identify a firm that uses green marketing. If you see a commercial on television, go to the firm's website to learn more about the product or process advertised. Does the firm make claims that comply with the Competition Bureau's guidelines? Present your findings in class.

5. As a consumer, you expect the companies you do business with will have a certain level of responsibility toward you. Describe a situation when you felt that a company did not recognize your rights as a consumer. How did you handle the situation? How did the company handle it? What was the final outcome?

WEB ASSIGNMENTS

1. **Ethical standards**. Go to the website listed below. It summarizes the ethical standards for all TELUS employees. Read the material and then write a brief report that compares TELUS's ethical standards to the discussion on corporate ethics in this chapter. In addition, consider how TELUS's ethical standards are integrated into the firm's overall efforts at global citizenship.

   http://about.telus.com/governance/downloads/2010_Ethics_Policy_EN.pdf

2. **Starting a career**. Each year, *Canada's Top 100* rates the best companies to work for. Visit the *Canada's Top 100* website and review the most recent list. What criteria did *Canada's Top 100* use when building this list? What role does ethics and social responsibility play?

   http://www.canadastop100.com/

3. **Social responsibility**. Footwear manufacturer La Canadienne is one of the few companies in its industry that still manufactures products in the Canada. Go to the website listed below to learn more about the firm's commitment to Canadian manufacturing. Prepare a report that relates this commitment to the firm's other core values.

   http://www.lacanadienneshoes.com/

Note: Internet addresses change frequently. If you don't find the exact sites listed, you may need to access the organization's home page and search from there or use a search engine such as Bing or Google.

Access your WileyPLUS course for:

- The complete digital textbook.

- Question assistance, including links to relevant sections in the online digital textbook.

- Immediate feedback and proof of progress, 24/7

- Integrated, multi-media resources – including MP3 downloads, visual exhibits, animations, and much more – that provide multiple study paths and encourage more active learning.

QUIZ YOURSELF

3 | ECONOMIC CHALLENGES FACING CONTEMPORARY BUSINESS

LEARNING OBJECTIVES

LO 3.1 Distinguish between microeconomics and macro-economics. Explain the factors that drive demand and supply.

LO 3.2 Describe the four different types of market structures in a private enterprise system, and compare the three major types of economic systems.

LO 3.3 Identify and describe the four stages of the business cycle. Explain how productivity, price level changes, and employment levels affect the stability of a nation's economy.

LO 3.4 Discuss how monetary policy and fiscal policy are used to manage an economy's performance.

LO 3.5 Describe the major global economic challenges of the 21st century.

INSIDE BUSINESS

© Can Stock Photo Inc./sgoodwin4813

Vancouver's 2010 Olympic Village: Seemed like a great idea at the time

The idea was simple—build condominium apartments to house athletes during the Vancouver 2010 Olympic Games and then sell the apartments and make a profit. And it had seemed like a good idea to most people in business and government. The public–private apartment development with Millennium Development Corporation was part of an environmentally positive effort to reclaim polluted land in Vancouver's False Creek area.

But timing is everything. Sometimes real estate markets are hot and prices are high, and sometimes they're not. The expected buyers didn't step forward. Everyone accepted that the market forces of supply and demand were at work in Vancouver's real estate market. One year later, only 30 units had been sold. The Olympic Village went into receivership. The appointed receiver, Ernst and Young, looked at how to sell units in the overpriced complex. Its study suggested cutting prices on 230 of the 1,100 units and renting 127 units. This plan would increase occupancy to 70 percent of the complex. It would also help to kick-start more interest in buying. According to some analysts, the City of Vancouver might lose $50 million to $150 million as the $500 million loan repayment by project developer Millennium will be reduced by any losses.

Real estate is usually a sure route to lower-cost housing for Canadians—in the long run. Most homeowners can expect to pay more than renters for the first seven to 10 years of a mortgage. Then, the financial benefit shifts from the renter to the homeowner. This pattern is generally true because rents continue to rise but the cost of owning rises at a slower pace. This effect is mostly because of the fixing of the price of the real estate at the time of sale, whereas rents may go up or down, depending on the demand and supply for rental property.

Many people think that buying real estate is a "no brainer" and that they can't really lose when they make mortgage payments instead of paying rent. After all, what do you have after paying rent year after year? But it is different for homeowners. After homeowners pay down a mortgage loan for a few years, they are closer to full ownership of their real estate investment.

But is that always true? Many people do not understand how supply and demand work in the real estate and rentals markets. Sometimes, it's clearly better to buy than to rent. But, sometimes, during a short time of only a few years, it can make little financial difference. And sometimes renting is the best financial choice. According to some analysts, we might now be in a longer than usual period of poor performance for real estate, when buying is financially equivalent to renting.

Think about today's market forces: the demand for real estate is highly linked to changes in population. After all, the more population grows in an area, and the more incomes increase, the greater the demand for a place to live. Many factors affect the demand for home ownership, such as homeowners' ages and their number of children. We also need to think about whether people plan to stay around for a long time or if they are only moving in for a short time before moving on again. When it's time to move, it's a lot easier to hand the keys of a rental over to the landlord than to have to sell a property.

On the supply side is the amount of real estate available. If there is not enough housing for the people who need it, prices will rise; but, if people are moving away, the market will have difficulty keeping prices stable.

Maybe the greatest influence on whether to buy real estate is the expectation of profit. One way people can better decide whether to buy or rent is to compare the total cost of renting for say, a 10-year period, to the costs of owning the same property. Predicting rents over a 10-year period is difficult. Predicting changes to the value of the property, interest rates on the mortgage loans, and local taxes is even more of a challenge.

From 1992 until 2002, Vancouver real estate prices were virtually flat, showing very little upward movement. The trend broke in 2003. Prices have continued to grow higher until now.

Some people think that prices might have increased too much. Others think that prices might flatten out for a long period, as they did from 1992 to 2002. Some fear prices might take a sudden drop. The only certain thing is that prices, high or low, will affect the relative business success of the Olympic condominium properties.[1]

CHAPTER 3 OVERVIEW

When we look at the exchanges that companies and societies make as a whole, we are focusing on the *economic systems* in different nations. These systems show the combination of a nation's policies and how it divides its resources among its citizens. Countries divide up their scarce resources in different ways.

Economics studies the choices people and governments make when dividing up their scarce resources. Economics affects each of us because everyone is involved in producing, distributing, or consuming goods and services. Your life is affected by economics every day. When you decide what product to buy, what services to use, or what activities to fit into your day, you are making economic choices. An important part of economics is understanding how the activities of one industry affect the activities of other industries, and how these activities fit into the overall picture of a country.

The choices you make may have international effects. For example, if you want to buy a new car, you might visit several dealers on the same street—Ford, Chrysler, Honda, Hyundai, and General Motors. You might decide to buy a car from Toyota, a Japanese firm, but your car might have been made in Canada, using parts from all over the world. Firms sometimes advertise the Canadian origin of their products in hopes that consumers will buy their products to support the Canadian economy. But many products are made of parts imported from several nations.

Businesses and not-for-profit organizations also make economic decisions when they choose how to use human and natural resources; how to invest in equipment, machinery, and buildings; and how to form partnerships with other firms. **Microeconomics** is the study of small economic units, such as individual consumers, families, and businesses.

The study of a country's overall economic issues is called **macroeconomics** (*macro* means "large"). Macroeconomics studies how an economy uses its resources and how government policies affect standards of living. For example, using ethanol in place of gasoline or biodiesel instead of diesel fuel has macroeconomic outcomes. It affects the Canadian economy and suppliers around the world. Macroeconomics studies not just the economic policies of individual nations but how those individual policies affect the overall world economy. Much business takes place around the world, so a law in one country can easily affect a transaction in another country. Macroeconomic issues have broad effects. They also help shape the decisions made by individuals, families, and businesses every day.

This chapter introduces economic theory and the economic challenges facing individuals, businesses, and governments in the global marketplace. We begin by discussing the microeconomic concepts of supply and demand and their effect on the prices for goods and services. Next we explain the various types of economic systems and the tools for comparing and evaluating their performance. Then we look at how governments try to manage economies to create stable business environments. The final section looks at some of the driving economic forces currently affecting people's lives.

economics the social science that studies the choices people and governments make when dividing up their scarce resources.

microeconomics the study of small economic units, such as individual consumers, families, and businesses.

macroeconomics the study of a nation's overall economic issues, such as how an economy maintains and divides up resources and how a government's policies affect its citizens' standards of living.

MICROECONOMICS: THE FORCES OF DEMAND AND SUPPLY

Think about your own economic activities. You shop for groceries, subscribe to a cellphone service, pay tuition, and fill your car's tank with gas. Now think about your family's economic activities. When you were growing up, your parents might have owned a home or rented an apartment. You might have taken a family vacation. Your parents may have shopped at discount clubs or local stores. These decisions about spending money relate to the study of microeconomics. The choices about where to spend money help to set both the prices of goods and services and the amounts sold. Information about these activities is important to companies because staying in business and growing means they need to sell enough products priced high enough to cover costs and earn profits. The same information is also important to consumers who need to decide what to buy and where to buy it. Consumers' decisions are usually based on the prices and the supply of the goods and services they need.

At the heart of every business is an exchange between a buyer and a seller. The buyer needs or wants a good or service—such as a hamburger or a haircut—and is willing to pay a seller for that good or service. The seller needs the exchange to earn a profit and stay in business. The exchange process involves both demand and supply. **Demand** is the willingness and ability of buyers to purchase goods and services at different prices. The other side of the exchange is **supply**, the amount of goods and services for sale at different prices. When you understand the factors that lead to demand and supply, and how demand and supply work together, you then know more about the many actions and decisions made by individuals, businesses, and government. This section takes a closer look at these ideas.

demand the willingness and ability of buyers to purchase goods and services.

supply the willingness and ability of sellers to provide goods and services.

You shop for groceries, subscribe to a cellphone service, pay tuition, and fill your car's tank with gas. These decisions about spending money relate to the study of microeconomics. The choices about where to spend money also help to set the prices of goods and the amounts sold.

© Can Stock Photo Inc./monkeybusiness

Demand is driven by consumer tastes and preferences and by economic conditions. Consumers tend to fill up their gas tanks more frequently when the per-litre price is low.

Factors Driving Demand

For most of us, economics is a balance between what we want and what we can pay. Each person must choose how much money to save and how much to spend. We must also decide what to buy from all the goods and services available. Suppose you want to buy a smartphone. You have to choose one smartphone from many brands and models. You also have to decide where to go to buy your smartphone. After shopping around, you might decide you don't want a smartphone. You might decide to purchase something else or to save your money.

Demand is driven by many factors that affect how people decide to spend their money. Demand can be driven by price or by what consumers like best. It may also be driven by outside conditions or by larger economic events. During the 2008–10 recession, 2009 sales in the video game industry—including portable players and consoles, software, and associated items—dropped 8 percent from the previous year. Nevertheless, the past several years were the strongest years for video game sales.[2]

Demand can also increase the number of certain types of websites and services. For example, major Canadian satellite and cable distributors, such as Rogers and Bell, are increasing the number of "on demand" programs that customers can view. Also, after many popular television programs have aired, they can be viewed from their television websites, such as Citytv.com. In the American television market, the popularity of Google's YouTube has led to networks NBC and Fox teaming up to launch an advertising-supported online video site. The site, called Hulu.com, offers full-length movies and television shows. It also hosts programming from NBC and Fox and shows from Sony and Metro-Goldwyn-Mayer. (Disney joined later.)[3] Hulu is not yet available in Canada, but the service will likely someday be channelled through Canadian providers or replicated by a Canadian source.

In general, when the price of a good or service goes up, people buy smaller amounts. In other words, as price rises, the quantity demanded declines. At lower prices, consumers are generally willing to buy more of a good. A **demand curve** is a graph showing the amount of a product that buyers will purchase at different prices. Demand curves typically slope downward because lower and lower prices attract larger and larger purchases.

Gasoline prices are a classic example of how demand curves work. The left side of Figure 3.1 shows a possible demand curve for the total amount of gasoline that people will purchase at different prices. The prices shown may not be the actual prices in your location today, but they still show how the demand curve works. When gasoline is priced at $1.39 per litre, drivers may fill up their tanks once or twice a week. At $1.69 per litre, many drivers start reducing the gas they use. They may combine errands or carpool. The quantity of gasoline demanded at $1.69 per litre is lower than the amount demanded at $1.39 per litre. The opposite happens when gas prices drop to $1.09 per litre. More gasoline is sold at $1.09 per litre than at $1.39 per litre because people choose to run more errands or to take more weekend trips. However, as noted earlier, other factors may lead to consumers paying higher prices. They may have already made vacation plans and do not want to cancel them or they may need to drive to work every day.

Economists make it clear that changes in the quantity demanded at various prices are different from changes in overall demand. A change in quantity demanded, such as the change that occurs at different gasoline prices, is simply movement along the demand curve. A change in overall demand is different. This kind of change results in an entirely new demand curve. Businesses are always trying to predict both kinds of demand, and making the wrong decision can lead to problems. For example, gasoline is made from crude oil, which means many factors come into play. One major impact is the growing investment in and development of alternative fuels, such as biodiesel, wind, and solar power. If these alternative fuels are developed and readily available, then demand for oil may decrease. Another issue is the Canadian economy. When a downturn occurs, the demand decreases for oil and other goods. But changes in the energy sources can have the opposite effect. For example, political unrest in oil-rich nations, such as Nigeria, or extreme weather that closes refineries can increase the demand for the oil that is available.[4]

demand curve a graph of the amount of a product that buyers will purchase at different prices.

Figure 3.1 shows how the increased demand for gasoline worldwide has created a new demand curve. The new demand curve shifts to the right of the old demand curve. This shift means that overall demand has increased at every price. A demand curve can also shift to the left. This shift means the demand for a good or service has decreased. However, the demand curve still has the same shape.

Although a change in price leads to movement along a demand curve, many factors can combine to change the overall demand for a product. The shape and position of the demand curve show the demand for a product. Demand is affected by customer preferences and incomes, the prices of substitute and complementary items, the number of buyers in a market, and the strength of the buyers' outlook for the future. Changes in any of these factors lead to a new demand curve.

Changes in household income also change demand. When consumers have more money to spend, firms can sell more products at every price. The demand curve has shifted to the right. When income drops, nearly everyone has a tougher time, and the demand curve shifts to the left. For example, higher-end Canadian retailers, such as Holt Renfrew, experienced a decrease in demand for their luxury goods because consumers thought twice about buying designer handbags, shoes, and clothing. Meanwhile, discount retailers, such as Walmart, increased their sales, so their demand curves shifted to the right.[5] Table 3.1 describes how a demand curve is likely to respond to each of these changes.

FIGURE 3.1 Demand Curves for Gasoline

For a business to succeed, its managers must carefully watch the factors that may affect demand for the goods and services it hopes to sell. Costco sets up free sampling stations in its stores so customers can try small portions of foods prepared on site. These sampling stations encourage customers to buy something in the department where they are sampling.

Table 3.1 Expected Shifts in Demand Curves

FACTOR	DEMAND CURVE SHIFTS	
	TO THE RIGHT *IF*:	TO THE LEFT *IF*:
Customer preferences	Increase	Decrease
Number of buyers	Increase	Decrease
Buyers' incomes	Increase	Decrease
Prices of substitute goods	Increase	Decrease
Prices of complementary goods	Decrease	Increase
Future expectations become more	Optimistic	Pessimistic

Factors Driving Supply

Economic factors also affect supply, which is the willingness and ability of firms to provide goods and services at different prices. Consumers must decide how to spend their money, and businesses must decide what products to sell, and how to sell them.

supply curve a graph that shows the relationship between different prices and the amount of goods that sellers will offer for sale, regardless of demand.

Sellers would like to charge higher prices for their products. A **supply curve** shows the relationship between different prices and the amount of goods that sellers will offer for sale at those prices, regardless of demand. Movement along the supply curve is the opposite of movement along the demand curve: as price rises, the quantity that sellers are willing to supply also rises. At lower and lower prices, the quantity supplied decreases. In Figure 3.2, a supply curve for gasoline shows that increasing prices for gasoline should bring increasing supplies to market.

Businesses need certain inputs to operate effectively. As discussed in Chapter 1, these *factors of production* include natural resources, capital, human resources, and entrepreneurship. Natural resources include land, building sites, forests, and mineral deposits. Capital refers to resources such as technology, tools, information, physical facilities, and financial capabilities. Human resources include employees' physical labour and intellectual inputs. Entrepreneurship is the willingness to take risks to create and operate a business. Factors of production play a central role in the overall supply of goods and services.

A change in the cost or availability of any inputs can shift the entire supply curve, by either increasing or decreasing the amount available at every price. For example, suppose the cost of land increases. A firm might not be able to purchase land to build a more efficient manufacturing plant, which would have lowered production levels and shifted the supply curve to the left. But if the company can find a way to speed up the production process, then it can make more products with less labour. The change in production can reduce the overall cost of the finished products, which shifts the supply curve to the right.

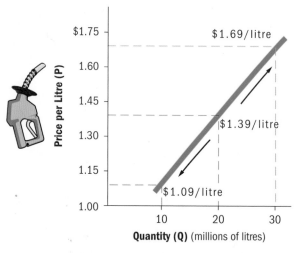

FIGURE 3.2 Supply Curve for Gasoline

Table 3.2 shows how changes in four factors can affect the supply curve. Forces of nature can also affect the supply curve. During a record-breaking freeze in 2010, much of Florida's fruit crop was severely damaged. Because the oranges and lemons could not be harvested and shipped, the supply dropped.[6]

Table 3.2 Expected Shifts in Supply Curves

FACTOR	SUPPLY CURVE SHIFTS	
	TO THE RIGHT *IF*:	TO THE LEFT *IF*:
Costs of inputs	Decrease	Increase
Costs of technologies	Decrease	Increase
Taxes	Decrease	Increase
Number of suppliers	Increase	Decrease

The agriculture industry has often had similar shifts in the supply curve. As consumers increase their demand for locally grown produce, farmers are trying to supply more produce. For example, farmers in colder regions are making the growing season longer by using heated greenhouses to grow vegetables and fruits normally available only during the summer. Winter farming—some of it organic—can help rural economies by creating new jobs that bring new income to an area. A Vancouver company, Spud.ca, is an online grocery retailer. It is trying to meet the increased demand for locally grown organic produce. More than 50 percent of Spud's products are sourced locally. In an average grocery store or natural foods store, only 15 to 20 percent of the items are locally sourced. The company's website has a "meet our local suppliers" link. It lets customers view photos of the owners, read about them, and click through to their websites. Spud.ca is also a founding member of Eat Local, a not-for-profit organization that promotes buying locally by organizing public markets.[7]

How Demand and Supply Interact

Separate shifts in demand and supply can affect prices and the availability of products. In the real world, changes do not take turns affecting first demand and then supply. Several factors often change at the same time—and they keep changing. Sometimes changes in more than one factor can lead to conflicting pressures on prices and quantities. Other times, the final upward or downward direction of prices and quantities depends on the factor that has changed the most. Most of our examples show how demand and supply affect products but demand and supply can also affect employment.

Figure 3.3 shows the interaction of both supply and demand curves for gasoline on a single graph. Notice that the two curves intersect at *P*. The law of supply and demand states that prices (*P*) are set by the intersection of the supply and demand curves. The point where the two curves meet identifies the **equilibrium price**, the current market price for an item.

equilibrium price the current market price for an item.

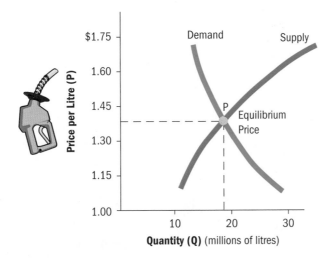

FIGURE 3.3 Law of Supply and Demand

If the actual market price differs from the equilibrium price, buyers and sellers tend to make purchase choices that restore the equilibrium level. The price of gold hit a record high in December 2009, but gold prices dropped when the U.S. Federal Reserve Bank raised interest rates and the U.S. dollar gained strength against the euro. Economists say that investors always seem to return to gold as a safe standard. Consumers who want to buy jewellery will usually continue to do so, but they may buy more or fewer pieces depending on the price of gold.[8] Gold buyers and sellers seemed to have found an equilibrium at about $500 per ounce from 2002 to 2006 but since then the price has continued an upward trend to increasingly higher record breaking levels (see Figure 3.4).[9]

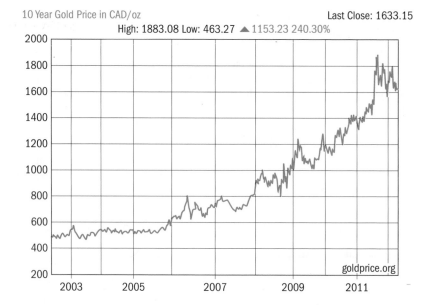

10 Year Gold Price in CAD/oz

High: 1883.08 Low: 463.27 ▲ 1153.23 240.30%

Last Close: 1633.15

goldprice.org

FIGURE 3.4 Price of Gold over the Past 10 Years

Source: "10 Year Gold Price in CAD/oz," http://goldprice.org/charts/history/gold_10_year_o_cad.png, accessed May 2, 2012.

Sometimes, suppliers react to market changes by reducing prices. For many years, fast-food chains such as McDonald's and Wendy's attracted customers by offering everyday value menus and coupons. The 2008–10 recession and the resulting economic downturn meant people were eating at home more and going out less. As a result, the fast-food chains saw a drop in their profits. Although some say the recession is over, economic recovery takes time. Competition among the

HIT & MISS

Five Guys Burgers and Fries: A Simple Recipe for Success

Jerry Murrell's two oldest sons told him they were not going to college. Murrell wanted to keep the boys close to home and at work. He and his wife, Janie, used the money they had saved for their tuition to open a hamburger take-out shop. Five Guys and a Burger (named for Murrell's five sons) soon grew to 570 franchises in the United States and Canada. All the Murrells' sons joined the company, and the family still owns and runs it.

Murrell knew it would be hard to compete with the fast-food chains. He decided Five Guys would need to focus on the food. All the restaurants have the same simple, red-and-white-tile décor. The meat for the burgers—80 percent lean—is always fresh, never frozen. Burgers are made to order, and diners can choose from 17 toppings. To make the buns tastier, they are toasted on a grill, not in a bun toaster. The Murrells buy potatoes from northern Idaho, where they grow more slowly. The fries are cut from these potatoes and then cooked in peanut oil. Five Guys insists on buying the highest-quality ingredients. That means its food prices change depending on what the company pays its suppliers.

The family tried some dishes that didn't sell, such as serving coffee and a chicken sandwich. Aside from a few hot dogs, they have stayed with the original burger-and-fries formula that first brought them success.

The food-industry research firm Technomic named Five Guys the fastest growing chain for a recent year. That same year, the company took in an estimated $570 million—up 50 percent from the previous year. "We figure our best salesman is our customer," Murrell says. "Treat that person right, he'll walk out the door and sell for you."

Questions for Critical Thinking

1. Why do you think Five Guys and a Burger prospered during the 2008–2010 recession?

2. How might supply and demand lead to the price the company pays its suppliers?

Sources: Five Guys Burgers and Fries website, http://www.fiveguys.com, accessed April 10, 2010; Jerry Murrell, "How I Did It," *Inc.com*, April 1, 2010, http://www.inc.com; "Business Opening: Five Guys Burgers and Fries," *greenbaypressgazette*, March 25, 2010, http://www.greenbaypressgazette.com; Ashley Miller, "Five Guys Named Fastest Growing Chain Restaurant," *examiner.com*, March 30, 2010, http://www.examiner.com; Roger Yu, "Fast-Growing Five Guys Burger Chain Sticks to Basic, Fresh Food," *USA Today*, June 8, 2009, http://www.usatoday.com.

chains, which was already strong, could grow even stronger, depending on how long the economic recovery takes.[10] One fast-food chain that did well during the recession is the Five Guys Burgers and Fries chain. Read about this chain in the "Hit & Miss" feature.

As noted earlier, the forces of demand and supply can be affected by many different factors. One important variable is the larger economic situation. The next section explains how macroeconomics and economic systems influence market forces and, ultimately, affect demand, supply, and prices.

ASSESSMENT CHECK

3.1.1 Define microeconomics and macroeconomics.

3.1.2 Explain demand and supply curves.

3.1.3 How do factors of production affect the overall supply of goods and services?

MACROECONOMICS: ISSUES FOR THE ENTIRE ECONOMY

LO 3.2 Describe the four different types of market structures in a private enterprise system, and compare the three major types of economic systems.

Every country needs to decide how to best use the four basic factors of production. Each nation's policies and choices help to shape its economic system. Every country has different political, social, and legal conditions, so no two countries have exactly the same economic system. In general, these economic systems can be divided into three categories: private enterprise systems; planned economies; and mixed economies, which are a bit of both. Business is becoming increasingly global, so it is important to understand the main features of the world's economic systems.

Capitalism: The Private Enterprise System and Competition

Most industrialized nations operate economies that are based on the *private enterprise system*, also known as *capitalism* or a *market economy*. A private enterprise system rewards businesses for meeting the needs and demands of consumers. Government tends to prefer a hands-off position when it comes to controlling business ownership, profits, and resource allocations. Instead, competition manages economic life, by creating opportunities and challenges that businesspeople must deal with to succeed.

The relative competitiveness of an industry is important for every firm to think about. Relative competitiveness affects the cost of doing business and how easy it is to do business in that industry. Four basic types of competition take shape in a private enterprise system: pure competition, monopolistic competition, oligopoly, and monopoly. Table 3.3 shows the main differences among these types of competition.

Table 3.3 Types of Competition

CHARACTERISTICS	TYPES OF COMPETITION			
	PURE COMPETITION	MONOPOLISTIC COMPETITION	OLIGOPOLY	MONOPOLY
Number of competitors	Many	Few to many	Few	No direct competition
Ease of entry into industry by new firms	Easy	Somewhat difficult	Difficult	Regulated by government
Similarity of goods or services offered by competing firms	Similar	Different	Similar or different	No directly competing products
Control over price by individual firms	None	Some	Some	Considerable in a pure monopoly; little in a regulated monopoly
Examples	Small-scale farmer in Ontario	Local fitness centre	Telecommunications companies like Bell and Rogers	Rawlings Sporting Goods, exclusive supplier of major-league baseballs

© Can Stock Photo Inc./javarman

Fishing is a good example of pure competition. Clams gathered by one person are similar to those gathered by others, so the price for clams rises and falls with changes in supply and demand. When a poisonous "red tide" of algae infests the clam beds, the supply of fresh clams drops and the price increases.

pure competition a market structure where large numbers of buyers and sellers exchange similar products, and no single participant has a large influence on price.

monopolistic competition a market structure where large numbers of buyers and sellers exchange similar products so each participant has some control over price.

oligopoly a market situation where relatively few sellers compete and high start-up costs act as barriers to keep out new competitors.

monopoly a market situation where a single seller controls trade in a good or service, and buyers can find no close substitutes.

Pure competition is a market structure, such as the structure of small-scale agriculture or fishing. Large numbers of buyers and sellers exchange similar products, and no single participant has a large influence on price. Instead, prices are set by the forces of supply and demand. Firms can easily enter or leave a purely competitive market because no single company controls the market. In pure competition, buyers see little difference between the goods and services offered by competitors.

Fishing and agriculture are good examples of pure competition. The wheat grown and sold by one farmer in Manitoba is about the same as the wheat sold by others. Rainfall and temperatures can affect crop growth, and the price for wheat rises or falls, depending on the law of supply and demand. The same idea applies to the shellfish industry that gathers clams and mussels off the east and west coasts. The "red tide" of algae sometimes means part of the season's supply of shellfish can't be eaten just when summer tourists want fresh shellfish. The rising demand and short supply can mean rapid price increases.

Monopolistic competition is a market structure similar to the structure for retailing: large numbers of buyers and sellers exchange distinct and differentiated (dissimilar) products, so each participant has some control over price. The sellers can show that their products are different from competing offerings because of price, quality, or other features. In an industry that features monopolistic competition, a firm can begin or stop selling a good or service relatively easily. The success of one seller often attracts new competitors. Individual firms also have some control over how their goods and services are priced.

One example of monopolistic competition is the market for pet food. Consumers can choose from private-label products (store brands such as Loblaw's President's Choice Nutrition First pet foods) and brand-name products, such as Purina in bags, boxes, and cans. Producers of pet food and the stores that sell it have wide range when setting prices. Consumers can choose the store or brand with the lowest prices, or sellers can convince consumers that a more expensive offering (for example, the Fromm brand) is worth more because it offers better nutrition, more convenience, or other benefits.

An **oligopoly** is a market situation where few sellers compete and high start-up costs act as barriers to keep out new competitors. In some oligopolistic industries, such as the paper and steel industries, competitors offer similar products. In others, such as the aircraft and automobile industries, competitors sell different models and features. The huge investment needed to enter an oligopoly market tends to discourage new competitors. The limited number of sellers also increases the control these firms exercise over price. Competing products in an oligopoly usually sell for very similar prices because any major price competition can reduce profits for all firms in the industry. That means a price decrease by one firm in an oligopoly will usually mean its competitors will lower their prices. But prices can vary from one market to another, just as they can vary from one country to another.

The final type of market structure is a **monopoly**, where a single seller controls trade in a good or service, and buyers can find no close substitutes. A pure monopoly occurs when a firm has unique features so important to competition in its industry that these features act as barriers to prevent entry by would-be competitors. Many view Microsoft and Google as two modern-day monopolies, but they are expanding into each other's territory. Google launched Google Apps, an online suite of business applications. These applications were designed to compete with Microsoft's Exchange Server. Microsoft launched its own search engine, Bing, to compete against Google. Later, Microsoft and Yahoo Inc. announced plans to team up to challenge Google's control of the Internet search market. The competition between Microsoft and Google may ultimately benefit consumers.[11]

Many firms create short-term monopolies when research breakthroughs allow them to receive exclusive patents on new products. In the pharmaceuticals industry, big drug companies such as Merck and Pfizer invest billions of dollars in research and development. When the research leads to successful new drugs, the companies can benefit from their patents: they can set prices without fear of competitors undercutting them. After the patent expires, generic substitutes enter the market, and prices decrease.

Because a monopoly market lacks the benefits of competition, many governments control monopolies. The Canadian government issues patents for new applications and limits the life of patents. The Canadian government also makes most pure monopolies illegal by passing antitrust legislation such as the Competition Act. The government applies these laws against monopoly behaviour and by not allowing some large companies to merge, such as our banks. In other cases, the government allows some monopolies to be in businesses in exchange for controlling their activities.

Microsoft and Google are expanding into each other's territory. Microsoft launched its own search engine, Bing. It also announced plans to team up with Yahoo! to challenge Google's control of the Internet search market.

A **regulated monopoly** is a firm that is granted exclusive rights in a specific market by a local, provincial, or federal government. Pricing decisions—mainly rate-increase requests—are subject to control by regulatory authorities such as the Ontario Energy Board that sets electricity and natural gas rates.

regulated monopoly a firm that is granted exclusive rights in a specific market by a local, provincial, or federal government.

During the 1980s and 1990s, the U.S. government tried to avoid regulated monopolies and instead preferred deregulation. Regulated monopolies that have been deregulated include long-distance and local telephone services, cable television services, cellphone services, and electric utilities. The idea is to improve customer service and to reduce consumer prices by increasing competition. This trend has not been followed as much in Canada, which partly explains the different prices paid for products and services in each country. To illustrate the differences, the Canadian Radio-television and Telecommunications Commission (CRTC) recently set rules for video-on-demand providers. These rules require that no less than 5 percent of English-language feature films are Canadian, no less than 8 percent of French-language films are Canadian, and no less than 20 percent of all programming (other than feature films) is Canadian. In another licence condition, video-on-demand services must contribute 5 percent of their gross annual revenues to a Canadian program production fund. These requirements and their related expenses are passed along in the form of higher rates charged to Canadian customers.[12]

Planned Economies: Socialism and Communism

A **planned economy** is an economic system where business ownership, profits, and resource allocation are shaped by a plan to meet government goals, not goals set by individual firms. Two forms of planned economies are communism and socialism.

Socialism is an economic system where the government owns and operates the major industries, such as energy or communications. Socialists believe that major industries are too important to a society to be left in private hands. They also believe that government-owned businesses can serve the public's interest better than private firms. Socialism allows private ownership in industries considered less important to social welfare, such as retail shops, restaurants, and some manufacturing facilities. Scandinavian countries, such as Denmark, Sweden, and Finland, have many socialist features in their societies, as do some African nations and India.

The writings of Karl Marx in the mid-1800s formed the basis of communist theory. Marx believed that private enterprise economies created unfair conditions. He believed these conditions led to workers being taken advantage of because business owners controlled most of society's

planned economy an economic system where business ownership, profits, and resource allocation are shaped by a plan to meet government goals, not goals set by individual firms.

socialism an economic system where the government owns and operates the major industries, such as communications.

communism an economic system where all property is shared equally by the people in a community under the direction of a strong central government.

resources *and* reaped most of the economy's rewards. Instead, Marx suggested an economic system called **communism**. In this economic system, all property would be shared equally by the people in a community under the direction of a strong central government. Marx believed that getting rid of private ownership of property and businesses would mean a classless society that would be good for everyone. Each individual would contribute to the nation's overall economic success, and resources would be divided up depending on each person's needs. Under communism, the central government owns the means of production, and the people work for state-owned enterprises. The government decides what people can buy because it controls what is produced in the nation's factories and farms.

Several nations adopted communist-like economic systems during the early 20th century. These nations wanted to correct abuses they believed existed in their previous systems. In practice, though, these new economic systems usually gave people less freedom of choice in terms of their jobs and purchases. These governments might be best described as totalitarian socialism. These nations often made mistakes in dividing up resources to compete in the growing global marketplace. Government-owned monopolies often suffer from inefficiency.

Consider the former Soviet Union, where large government bureaucracies controlled nearly every aspect of daily life. Shortages happened all the time because producers had little or no incentive to satisfy their customers. The quality of goods and services also suffered for the same reason. When Mikhail Gorbachev became the last president of the Soviet Union, he tried to improve the quality of Soviet-made products. But the Soviet Union faced severe financial problems. It was shut out of trading in the global marketplace and got caught up in a costly arms race with the United States. Eventually, these events led to the collapse of Soviet communism and the breakup of the Soviet Union.

Today, communist-like systems exist in just a few countries, such as North Korea. Even the People's Republic of China now has a more market-oriented economy. Its national government has given local government and individual plant managers more say in business decisions. Some private businesses are now allowed in China. Households now have more control over agriculture, in contrast to the collective farms where many people once worked. Today, Chinese workers make products for export to other countries. Western products such as McDonald's restaurants and Coca-Cola are now part of Chinese consumers' lives.

Mixed Market Economies

mixed market economy an economic system that draws from both private enterprise economies and planned economies, to different degrees.

Private enterprise systems and planned economies use opposite approaches to operating economies. In reality, though, many countries operate a **mixed market economy**, an economic system that draws from both types of economies, to different degrees. Some nations are generally considered to have a private enterprise economy. In these countries, government-owned firms frequently operate beside private enterprises. In Canada, health care, education, and electricity generation are run by the government.

France has blended socialist and free enterprise policies for hundreds of years. The nation's energy production, public transportation, and defence industries are run as nationalized industries and are controlled by the government. Meanwhile, a market economy operates in other industries. Over the past two decades, the French government has loosened its hold on state-owned companies, inviting both competition and private investment into industries that once operated as government monopolies.

privatization the conversion of government-owned and -operated companies to privately held businesses.

The percentages of private and public enterprise can vary widely in mixed economies, and the mix changes. Dozens of countries have converted government-owned and -operated companies into privately held businesses. This trend is known as **privatization**. Even Canada has seen discussions of privatizing everything from public transportation to roads, schools, and hospitals.

Governments may privatize state-owned enterprises so they can raise funds and improve their economies. The objective is to cut costs and run the operation more efficiently. For most of its history, Air Canada has been a federal government–owned airline. In 1989, the airline became fully privatized. In 2000, the firm acquired Canadian Airlines International and became the world's 10th-largest international air carrier. Air Canada now has an extensive global network. It flies to the United States, Europe, the Middle East, Asia, Australia, the Caribbean, Mexico, and South America.[13]

Table 3.4 compares the alternative economic systems by ownership and management of enterprises, rights to profits, employee rights, and worker incentives.

ASSESSMENT CHECK

3.2.1 What is the difference between pure competition and monopolistic competition?

3.2.2 Which economic system is the Canadian economy based on?

3.2.3 What is privatization?

Table 3.4 Comparison of Alternative Economic Systems

SYSTEM FEATURES	CAPITALISM (PRIVATE ENTERPRISE)	PLANNED ECONOMIES		
		COMMUNISM	SOCIALISM	MIXED ECONOMY
Ownership of enterprises	Businesses are owned privately, often by large numbers of people. Very little government ownership means that production is in private hands.	Government owns the means of production with few exceptions, such as small plots of land.	Government owns basic industries, but private owners operate some small enterprises.	A strong private sector works with public enterprises.
Management of enterprises	Enterprises are managed by owners or their representatives, with very little government involvement.	Centralized management controls all state enterprises in line with three- to five-year plans. Planning now is being decentralized.	Much government planning is involved in socialist nations. State enterprises are managed directly by government bureaucrats.	Management of the private sector resembles the management under capitalism. Professionals may also manage state enterprises.
Rights to profits	Entrepreneurs and investors are allowed to receive all profits (minus taxes) that their firms earn.	Profits are not allowed under communism.	Only the private sector of a socialist economy generates profits.	Entrepreneurs and investors are allowed to receive private-sector profits, although they often must pay high taxes. State enterprises are also expected to produce returns.
Rights of employees	Employees have the rights to choose their own occupation and to join a labour union. These rights have long been recognized.	Employee rights are limited in exchange for promised protection against unemployment.	Workers may choose their occupations and join labour unions, but the government influences many people's career decisions.	Workers may choose their own jobs and may join a labour union. Unions often become quite strong.
Worker incentives	Large incentives motivate people to perform at their highest levels.	Incentives are emerging in communist countries.	Incentives usually are limited in state enterprises but are used to motivate workers in the private sector.	Capitalist-style incentives operate in the private sector. More limited incentives influence public-sector activities.

EVALUATING ECONOMIC PERFORMANCE

LO 3.3 Identify and describe the four stages of the business cycle. Explain how productivity, price level changes, and employment levels affect the stability of a nation's economy.

Ideally, an economic system should provide two important benefits for its citizens: a stable business environment and sustained growth. In a stable business environment, the overall supply of needed goods and services matches the overall demand for these items. There are no wild ups or downs in price or availability to make economic decisions difficult. Consumers and businesses have access to supplies of desired products at affordable prices and also have money to buy the items they demand.

Growth is another important economic goal. An ideal economy is always changing because it is always expanding the amount of goods and services it produces from the nation's resources. Growth leads to expanded job opportunities, improved wages, and a rising standard of living.

Flattening the Business Cycle

A nation's economy usually flows through several stages of a business cycle: prosperity, recession, depression, and recovery. Canada has not had a true economic depression since the 1930s. Most economists believe that effective economic policies should prevent future depressions. Thus, economists expect recessions to lead to a time of economic recovery. The "Solving an Ethical Controversy" feature looks at whether developing alternative sources of energy will create new jobs to stimulate the economy.

— SOLVING AN **ETHICAL** CONTROVERSY —

Should Alternative Energy Development Be Relied on to Create New Jobs?

Someday, we will run out of fossil fuels such as oil and coal. We need to look at developing more alternative energy sources: solar, wind, ethanol, biodiesel, geothermal, and nuclear power. Developing alternative energy could create thousands of new jobs, help revive the economy, and slow down global warming.

Some people are critical of alternative energy development. They say the cost of government subsidies to make these businesses competitive is too high and does not make good economic sense. For example, in Ontario, the cost of the energy produced is estimated at 13.5 cents per kilowatt hour (kWh) for wind farms and 44.5 cents per kWh for solar power. But the cost of a natural gas generator is only 7.5 cents per kWh. Critics also estimate the Government of Ontario would need to pay a subsidy of more than $200,000 per job to make these business projects viable for their owners.

In the United States, a study paid for by American renewable-energy corporations urges Congress to pass a federal standard of 25 percent reliance on alternative energy by 2025. Supporters claim that a national Renewable Electricity Standard (RES) of 25 percent would create hundreds of thousands of jobs in renewable energy fields. China is now the world's leading manufacturer of wind turbines, ahead of Denmark, Germany, Spain, and the United States. Don Furman, of Iberdrola Renewables, says, "Without a strong RES, the U.S. wind industry will see no net job growth, and will likely lose jobs to overseas competitors."

Should we develop alternative energy sources to help economic recovery and create jobs?

PRO

1. Investing in clean, alternative sources of energy could create new "green" jobs for North Americans. Some energy sources—for example, wind and solar power—are renewable and sustainable.

2. Clean, renewable energy will help end North America's dependence on foreign oil. Fossil fuels cause environmental destruction, and their prices are not stable.

CON

1. Fossil fuels will last for many more years. Continual advances could make these fuels a more energy-efficient, less expensive choice.

2. Alternative energy sources are still in early development. More time and more costly research are needed before alternative energy is less expensive and practical on a national scale.

Summary

Canada and the United States are not alone in developing "green" energy sources. Several European countries along the North Sea have joined to create an environmentally clean "supergrid." These countries will receive their energy from green sources in Scotland, Germany, and Norway through energy-efficient undersea cables. Canada enjoys the financial benefits of having huge reserves of oil and natural gas. Some provinces, such as Quebec and Newfoundland and Labrador, produce surplus hydro-electricity that they export to the U.S. market.

Sources: Terrance Corcoran, "Ontario Burns up More Green Cash, *National Post*, February 25, 2011, p. FP11; "Stronger National Renewable Electricity Standard Needed for Significant Clean Energy Job Stability and Growth, Study Finds," American Wind Energy Association, February 4, 2010, http://www.awea.org; "Can Alternative Energy Effectively Replace Fossil Fuels?" ProCon, http://alternativeenergy.procon.org, accessed February 4, 2010; Keith Bradsher, "China Leading Global Race to Make Clean Energy," *New York Times*, January 30, 2010, http://www.newyorktimes.com; "Renewable Energy 'Supergrid' Coming to Europe," *Energy Economy*, December 31, 2009, http://www.alternative-energy-news.info.

Both business decisions and consumer buying patterns differ at each stage of the business cycle. In times of prosperity, unemployment is low, consumers are confident about the future and make more purchases, and businesses expand. Businesses hire more employees, invest in new technology, and purchase new technology to take advantage of new opportunities.

A **recession** is a cycle of economic contraction that lasts for six months or longer. During a recession, consumers often wait before making major purchases. They also shift what they buy, preferring basic, practical products at low prices. Businesses do something similar. They slow production, decide to wait before expanding, reduce their stock, and often reduce the number of employees. During recessions, consumers may worry about being laid off and using up their savings. Many consumers become more careful in how they spend money. Some wait before making luxury purchases and taking vacations. Others start to shop at lower-priced retailers, such as Costco, Walmart, and Target. Some people sell their cars, jewellery, and shares to help pay their bills.

During a recession, consumers may shift what they buy, preferring to buy basic, practical products at low prices. Consumers may worry about being laid off and using up their savings. Many consumers become more careful in how they spend money. Some people sell their cars, jewellery, and shares to help pay the bills.

Peter Power/The Globe and Mail/The Canadian Press

Sometimes, an economic slowdown continues in a downward spiral over a long period of time. When that happens, the economy falls into depression. Many Canadians have heard stories about their great-grandparents who lived through the Great Depression of the 1930s. During this time, food and other basic products were hard to find, and many people were out of work.

In the recovery stage of the business cycle, the economy comes out of the recession and consumers start spending again. Businesses often still need part-time and other temporary workers during the early stages of a recovery. Unemployment begins to decline as business activity starts up again and firms seek more workers to meet growing production demands. Slowly, the concerns of recession begin to disappear, and consumers start spending again: eating out at restaurants, booking vacations, and purchasing new cars.

recession a cycle of economic contraction that lasts for six months or longer.

Productivity and the Nation's Gross Domestic Product

Every economy focuses on **productivity**, the relationship between the goods and services produced and the inputs needed to produce them. In general, as productivity rises, an economy's growth increases and its citizens' wealth increases. In a recession, productivity stalls and may decline.

Productivity describes the relationship between the number of units produced and the number of human and other production inputs needed to produce them. Productivity is a ratio of output to input. When a steady amount of inputs creates an increased number of outputs, productivity has increased.

Total productivity looks at all inputs needed to produce a specific amount of outputs. It can be written as an equation:

productivity the relationship between the number of units produced and the number of human and other production inputs needed to produce them.

$$\text{Total Productivity} = \frac{\text{Output (goods or services produced)}}{\text{Input (human/natural resources, capital)}}$$

Many productivity ratios focus on only one input in the equation: labour productivity or output per labour-hour. An increase in labour productivity means that the same amount of work produces more goods and services than before. Many gains in Canadian productivity are because of technology. In recent years, Canada's economy has done well because of technology and productivity. Productivity can also be increased by outsourcing work to lower-cost employees. For example, many businesses have shifted their manufacturing to countries such as China and India, where labour is cheaper. The Internet makes it easy to provide services from anywhere in the world. Overseas workers can use the Internet to provide customer service, accounting, engineering design, and even legal processing. We will discuss this globalization of business activity more in the next chapter.

Productivity is often used to measure a company's efficiency. The total productivity of a nation's businesses measures a country's economic strength and standard of living. Economists call this measure the country's **gross domestic product (GDP)**. GDP is the total of all goods and services produced within a country. The GDP per-capita output of a country is the total national output divided by the number of citizens. GDP per capita is better than GDP for measuring the average wealth of any individual citizen of a country. As Figure 3.5 shows, the United States is the world's largest economy as measured by GDP. The differences between the countries are interesting, especially when you look at each country's GDP per capita.[14]

gross domestic product (GDP) the sum of all goods and services produced within a country during a specific time period, such as a year.

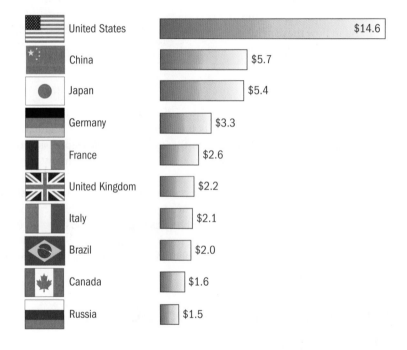

FIGURE 3.5 Nations with Highest Gross Domestic Products (GDP Measured in Trillions of U.S. Dollars)

Source: Central Intelligence Agency, "Field Listing—GDP (Official Exchange Rate)," *World Factbook*, accessed February 3, 2011, https://www.cia.gov/library/publications/the-world-factbook/fields/2195.html?countryName=&countryCode=&regionCode=%3E

United States		$14.6
China	$5.7	
Japan	$5.4	
Germany	$3.3	
France	$2.6	
United Kingdom	$2.2	
Italy	$2.1	
Brazil	$2.0	
Canada	$1.6	
Russia	$1.5	

Price-Level Changes

inflation rising prices caused by a combination of excess consumer demand and higher costs of raw materials, component parts, human resources, and other factors of production.

core inflation rate the inflation rate after energy prices and food prices are removed.

hyperinflation an economic situation marked by soaring prices.

The general level of prices is another important indicator, or measure, of an economy's stability. For the last 100 years, economic decision makers have focused on **inflation**, rising prices caused by a combination of excess consumer demand and higher costs of raw materials, component parts, human resources, and other factors of production. The **core inflation rate** is the inflation rate of an economy after energy prices and food prices are removed. This measure is often an accurate estimate of the inflation rate that consumers, businesses, and other organizations can expect in the near future.

Excess consumer demand creates *demand-pull inflation*. Increases in the costs of factors of production create *cost-push inflation*. North America's most severe inflationary period of the last half of the 20th century peaked in 1980. General price levels increased almost 14 percent in one year. An economy may experience **hyperinflation**—an economic situation marked by soaring prices. Hyperinflation has occurred in South America and in the countries that once formed the Soviet Union.

Inflation devalues money because the constant price increases mean that people can purchase fewer goods and services with a given amount of money. It is bad news for many people: those whose earnings do not keep up with inflation, those who live on fixed incomes, and those who have investments that pay a fixed rate of interest. Inflation can be good news for people whose income is rising and those with debts at a fixed rate of interest. A homeowner with a fixed-rate mortgage during inflationary times is paying off that debt with money that is worth less and less each year. Over the past decade, inflation and a strong stock market increased the number of North American millionaires to more than 7.8 million.[15] But inflation also means being a millionaire does not mean the same as it once did. To live like a 1960s millionaire, you need almost $7 million today.

When increased productivity keeps prices steady, it can have a major positive impact on an economy. In a low-inflation environment, businesses can make long-range plans without worrying about sudden inflationary shocks. Low interest rates encourage firms to invest in research and development and in capital improvements. Both are likely to produce productivity gains. Consumers can purchase growing stocks of goods and services with the same amount of money. Low interest rates encourage people to make major purchases, such as new homes and cars. But some people have concerns. The changing cost of oil—which is used to produce many goods—is a continuing issue. Businesses need to raise prices to cover their costs. Also, smaller firms have gone out of business or have been merged with larger companies. Thus, the amount of competition has been reduced and the purchasing power of the larger corporations has increased. Business owners continue to keep an eye on signs of inflation.

Increased productivity keeps prices steady. It can also have a major positive impact on the economy. Low interest rates encourage firms to invest in capital improvements—such as building a new company headquarters or expanding its existing space. These improvements are likely to lead to productivity gains.

The opposite situation—**deflation**—occurs when prices keep falling. In Japan, deflation has been a reality for several years. Shoppers pay less for many products, ranging from groceries to homes. Lower prices may sound like good news to consumers, but they can weaken the economy. The housing industry and auto makers need to keep prices strong to support all the businesses that depend on them. Think about it for a moment. Would you want to buy a house today if you thought the price would be lower in a year?

deflation the opposite of inflation, occurs when prices continue to fall.

Measuring Price Level Changes

The Canadian government tracks price changes with the **Consumer Price Index (CPI)**. The CPI measures the monthly average change in the prices of goods and services. Statistics Canada calculates the CPI each month, using the prices of a "market basket," a mix of the goods and services commonly purchased. Figure 3.6 shows the categories in the CPI market basket. Each month, price checkers visit thousands of stores, service businesses, rental units, and doctors' offices all over Canada to price the items in the CPI market basket. The prices they collect are used to create the CPI. Thus, the CPI provides a running measurement of changes in consumer prices.

Consumer Price Index (CPI) a measurement of the monthly average change in prices of goods and services.

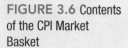

FIGURE 3.6 Contents of the CPI Market Basket

Source: Information from Statistics Canada.

HIT & MISS

Vancity Provides a "Microcredit Toolkit" to Local Not-for-Profit Organizations

Individual economic progress can often be helped by small loans to people who can use the money to purchase the equipment or training they need. Many new immigrants want to start a small business or add to their incomes by starting a micro business. But they can face difficulty when trying to borrow money because they may lack collateral (to back up the loan), personal credit history (to show they have paid back previous loans), and full-time employment.

Vancity wants to change this. It provides a Microcredit Toolkit to local not-for-profit organizations that help new immigrants through a partnership with MOSAIC, a Vancouver not-for-profit organization that works with new immigrants and refugees. The Toolkit helps new immigrant entrepreneurs to have better access to financial services. Vancity is Canada's largest credit union. It has 400,000 members and $14.5 billion of assets to manage. Vancity views the MOSAIC arrangement as a socially responsible way to serve people who would face great difficulty in getting a loan, even a small one, without this help. The average loan to a MOSAIC client is $3,200. More than 98 per cent of the loans have been repaid. Many loans are used to pay for retraining programs and for help to obtain Canadian certification.

MOSAIC was the first to use the kit. The organization received a $167,000 grant from Vancity to develop its Peer Lending Program and to translate the Toolkit into other languages. "We are excited about being the first non-profit to use the Toolkit. Every day we see people who could benefit from this program. People who are highly motivated with skills and talents, but who don't qualify for support from a traditional financial institution," says Sherman Chan of MOSAIC. "By removing those barriers we can help our clients achieve financial independence."

For example, Dharmasena (Sena) Yakadawela has 13 years of legal experience and had been a judge in Sri Lanka. After he couldn't find work in his profession, he took a job at a 24-hour convenience store. But Sena met with MOSAIC and learned about Vancity's *Back to Work* microloan program. It helps skilled immigrants such as Sena by loaning the funds to retrain in Canada. Sena's microloan helped him to go to the University of British Columbia. There, he studied for his Certificate of Immigration Consultants. After graduation, a second loan allowed him to write the exam with the Canadian Society of Immigration Consultants and pay the membership registration fees. Soon afterward, Sena started his own business. He now helps overseas healthcare professionals to obtain Canadian work permits.

Peer Lending is Vancity's unique credit arrangement. A small group of borrowers guarantee loans for each other instead of using collateral. The program looks at commitment and ability, not financial assets. Vancity is the only financial institution in Canada to offer a program like this. The Peer Lending loans range from $1,000 to $5,000.

Since the Peer Lending program was introduced seven years ago, it has helped about 700 people. More than half have generated $500 to $1,000 additional income per month, and 10 percent now have enough skills to leave the program to take new jobs or grow their small businesses.

Questions for Critical Thinking

1. How does this program benefit the borrower, lender, and society in general?

2. Why do you think that the payback rate on microloans is so high?

Sources: Vancity, "All Great Businesses Start with a Little Help: Microloans Fund Big Dreams," https://www.vancity.com/MyCommunity/NotForProfit/Microloans/, accessed February 3, 2011; Microfinance website, www.microfinance.ca, accessed February 3, 2011.

Employment Levels

People need money to buy the goods and services produced in an economy. Most consumers earn that money by working, so the number of people who are working is an important measure of how well the economy is doing. In general, employment has increased over the past few years, but there have been some decreases. The services producing sector has seen some increases, but manufacturing hasn't had much change.[16] The "Hit & Miss" feature discusses how immigrants to Canada can receive small loans to help get started in their new country.

Economists use a nation's **unemployment rate** as an indicator, or measure, of its economic health. The unemployment rate is usually shown as a percentage of the total workforce actively seeking work but currently unemployed. The total labour force includes all people who are willing and available to work at the going market wage. It includes people who currently have jobs and those who are seeking work. Statistics Canada tracks unemployment rates and measures so-called discouraged workers. These individuals want to work but have given up looking for jobs, for various reasons. Unemployment can be grouped into the four categories shown in Figure 3.7: frictional, seasonal, cyclical, and structural.

Frictional unemployment describes the joblessness of people in the workforce who are temporarily not working but are looking for jobs. These potential workers include new graduates, people who have left jobs for any reason and are looking for work, and former workers who have decided to return to work. **Seasonal unemployment** is the joblessness of people in a seasonal industry. Construction workers, farm labourers, fishing boat operators, and landscape employees may have times of seasonal unemployment when weather conditions keep them from working.

unemployment rate the percentage of the total workforce actively seeking work but currently unemployed.

frictional unemployment the joblessness of people in the workforce who are temporarily not working but are looking for jobs.

seasonal unemployment the joblessness of workers in a seasonal industry.

Frictional Unemployment
- Temporarily not working
- Looking for a job

Example: New graduates entering the workforce

Seasonal Unemployment
- Not working during some months
- Not looking for a job

Example: Farm workers needed only when a crop is in season

Structural Unemployment
- Not working due to no demand for skills
- May be retraining for a new job

Example: Assembly line employees whose jobs are now done by robots

Cyclical Unemployment
- Not working due to economic slowdown
- Looking for a job

Example: Executives laid off during corporate downsizing or recessionary periods

FIGURE 3.7 Four Types of Unemployment

Cyclical unemployment describes the joblessness of people who are out of work because of a cyclical contraction in the economy. During periods of economic expansion, overall employment is likely to rise, but when growth slows and a recession begins, more people are unemployed. Even workers who have good job skills may face temporary unemployment. Workers in high-tech industries, air travel, and manufacturing have all faced unemployment during economic contraction.

Structural unemployment describes the joblessness of people who are unemployed for long periods of time. These people often have little hope of finding a job. Some of these workers don't have the skills needed for available jobs or their skills are no longer in demand. For example, technology has increased the need for people with computer-related skills but technology has also led to structural unemployment for manual labourers and workers who are injured and cannot return to work.

cyclical unemployment the joblessness of people who are out of work because of a cyclical contraction in the economy.

structural unemployment the joblessness of people who remain unemployed for long periods of time, often with little hope of finding a job.

 ASSESSMENT CHECK

3.3.1 Describe the four stages of the business cycle.

3.3.2 What do economists use to measure the health of an economy?

LO 3.4 Discuss how monetary policy and fiscal policy are used to manage an economy's performance.

MANAGING THE ECONOMY'S PERFORMANCE

monetary policy a government plan to increase or decrease the money supply and to change banking requirements and interest rates to affect bankers' willingness to make loans.

expansionary monetary policy a plan to increase the money supply to try to decrease the cost of borrowing. Lower interest rates encourage businesses to make new investments, which leads to employment and economic growth.

restrictive monetary policy a plan to reduce the money supply to control rising prices, overexpansion, and concerns about overly rapid economic growth.

fiscal policy a plan of government spending and taxation decisions designed to control inflation, reduce unemployment, improve the general welfare of citizens, and encourage economic growth.

Government can use two policies—monetary policy and fiscal policy—to fight unemployment, increase business and consumer spending, and reduce the length and severity of economic recessions. For example, the Bank of Canada can increase or decrease interest rates; and the federal government can cut taxes, offer tax rebates, or propose other changes.

Monetary Policy

A common way for a government to affect economic activity is to use a policy. A **monetary policy** is a government plan to increase or decrease the money supply and to change banking requirements and interest rates to affect spending by changing bankers' willingness to make loans.

An **expansionary monetary policy** increases the money supply to try to decrease the cost of borrowing. Lower interest rates encourage businesses to make new investments, which leads to employment and economic growth. By contrast, a **restrictive monetary policy** reduces the money supply to control rising prices, overexpansion, and concerns about overly rapid economic growth.

The Bank of Canada Governor, Mark Carney, is responsible for the country's monetary policy. He works independently of the current government. In the United States, the Federal Reserve System ("the Fed") is responsible for American monetary policy. It is headed by a chairman and a board of governors, all of whom are nominated by the U.S. President. The current chairman is Ben Bernanke, who is also chairman of the Federal Open Market Committee, the Fed's main agency for monetary policymaking. Just as Canadian banks function alongside the Bank of Canada, all American banks must be members of the Fed.

The Bank of Canada uses various tools to control the economy. By changing the required percentage of chequing and savings accounts that banks must deposit with the Bank of Canada, the Governor can expand or shrink the funds available to lend. The Bank of Canada also lends money to Canadian banks. The banks then make loans at higher interest rates to businesses and individuals. When the Bank of Canada changes the interest rates charged to commercial banks, it affects the interest rates charged to borrowers. Changing the interest rates affects borrowers' willingness to borrow.

Fiscal Policy

Governments also affect economic activities by making decisions about taxes and spending. The government applies **fiscal policy** through revenues and expenses. Fiscal policy is the second technique that governments use to control inflation, reduce unemployment, improve the general standard of living, and encourage economic growth. Increased taxes may limit economic activities, while lower taxes and increased government spending usually increase spending and profits, cut unemployment rates, and encourage economic expansion. Sometimes, the federal government issues tax rebates to individuals and businesses to try to stimulate investment and spending. The "Going Green" feature discusses federal tax credits for energy-efficient products.

The Canadian Press/Tom Hanson

The Bank of Canada uses various tools to control the economy. The Bank of Canada lends money to Canadian banks. The banks then make loans to businesses and individuals.

GOING GREEN TAX CREDITS FOR AN ENERGY STAR

For the past several decades, the Government of Canada has promoted its EnerGuide labelling program. This program supports energy conservation by helping consumers to understand the heavy energy consumed by washing machines, dryers, stoves, refrigerators, computers, and air conditioners. Energy conservation helps to reduce air pollution caused by energy-producing technologies such as coal- and gas-driven power plants. Energy conservation also helps to reduce the need to build more production facilities, which are typically a government responsibility. Energy is needed to drive the economy. If our economy is to grow, then governments must find the funds needed to develop more energy. A better way to control the costs of supplying energy is to reduce the demand for energy. Governments often use both "the carrot" and "the stick." Higher prices are "the stick" that helps to reduce energy use. Energy use also drops when consumers learn about how much energy they use, often when they purchase new appliances. Tax incentives are "the carrot" that helps consumers to make better and more energy-efficient choices. Recently, the government has offered tax credits to people who buy hybrid gas–electric vehicles, vehicles that use alternative fuels, and plug-in electric vehicles.

Canada's Energy Efficiency Act was passed in 1992. This act sets the minimum energy-efficiency standards for some energy-consuming products, including appliances imported to Canada and those traded between provinces and territories. The "ENERGY STAR" program was introduced in 1992. This program encourages Canadians to save energy and reduce pollution. The ENERGY STAR symbol goes one step further and identifies the specific models that meet or exceed the highest levels of energy efficiency.

In many communities, when you replace certain appliances with qualified appliances, you receive a rebate and lower your utility bills. Your local government may help you to choose from among boilers, central or room air conditioners, washing machines, dishwashers, freezers, oil and gas furnaces, heat pumps (air source and geothermal), refrigerators, and water heaters. Whether your community takes part depends on climate, geography, and other factors.

Certain kinds of home improvements can receive tax credits, including the replacement of furnaces, windows, hot-water tanks, and insulation. To get an idea of the scale of incentives, visit Natural Resources Canada's Office of Energy Efficiency website.

Questions for Critical Thinking

1. How does paying rebates and granting tax credits stimulate the economy?

2. Which would you prefer to receive—an income-tax credit or a rebate? Why?

Source: Natural Resources Canada's Office of Energy Efficiency website at http://oee.nrcan.gc.ca/, accessed February 8, 2011.

International Fiscal Policy

Canada and other nations in the industrial world are trying to help developing nations to improve their economies. Many African countries have large debts. One idea is to forgive the debts of some of these countries to help their economies to grow. But not all fiscal experts agree. Some say that any debt forgiveness should also have certain conditions so that these countries can build their own fiscal policies. Countries need to lower their tax rates, avoid devaluing their currencies, plan for new business start-ups, and reduce trade barriers. They also need to allow citizens to own property and should encourage home ownership. In addition, they must improve agriculture, education, and health care so their citizens can begin to set and reach financial goals. The World Bank offers low-interest loans and interest-free credit and grants to developing countries. The World Bank has been involved in helping Haiti recover from the catastrophic earthquake of 2010.[17]

The Federal Budget

Each year, the federal government presents a **budget** to Parliament for approval. The budget is a plan for how the government will raise and spend money during a specific period of time, often the coming year. The federal budget includes numerous spending categories, ranging from defence to interest payments on the national debt. The decisions about what to include in the budget have a direct effect on the economy. During a recession, the federal government may increase spending

budget an organization's plan for how it will raise and spend money during a specific period of time.

budget deficit a situation where the government spends more than it raises through taxes.

national debt the money owed by government to individuals, businesses, and government agencies who purchase Treasury bills, Treasury notes, and Treasury bonds.

budget surplus the excess funding when government spends less than it raises through taxes and fees.

balanced budget a situation where total revenues raised by taxes and fees equal the total proposed government spending for the year.

 ASSESSMENT CHECK

3.4.1 What is the difference between an expansionary monetary policy and a restrictive monetary policy?

3.4.2 What are the three primary sources of government funds?

3.4.3 Does a balanced budget erase the federal debt?

on highway repairs to improve transportation and increase employment in the construction industry. During prosperity, the government may fund scientific research on new medical treatments or alternative fuels.

The main sources of government funds to pay for the annual budget are taxes, fees, and borrowing. The overall total of these funds and how these funds are combined can have major effects on the economic well-being of the nation. Governments can raise money by setting taxes on sales, income, and other sources. But increasing taxes means that people and businesses have less money to spend. Raising taxes might reduce inflation, but overly high taxes can slow economic growth. Governments often try to balance taxes so that people can receive the services they need without slowing economic growth.

Taxes don't always bring in enough funds to cover every government spending project. When the government spends more than it raises through taxes, it creates a **budget deficit**. To cover the deficit, the government borrows money by selling Treasury bills, Treasury notes, and Treasury bonds to investors. This borrowing makes up the **national debt**. If the government takes in more money than it spends, it has a **budget surplus**. In a **balanced budget**, total revenues raised by taxes equal the total proposed spending for the year.

Balancing the budget—or even having a budget surplus—does not erase the national debt. Canadian politicians are always discussing how quickly the nation should use revenues to reduce its debt. We can think about the national debt on a personal level. Most families want to wipe out debt—from credit cards, automobile purchases, and college. Canada has approximately 33 million people. Our national debt is about $1 trillion. That works out to about $30,303 per person. The United States has approximately 310 million citizens and a national debt of $13.9 trillion. Thus, each American's share of debt is about $44,839.[18]

The decision is more complex for the federal government. When the government raises money by selling Treasury bills, it makes safe investments available to investors worldwide. If foreign investors cannot buy Treasury notes from Canada, they might turn to other countries. Then, the money flowing into Canada is reduced. The government uses part of the funds it borrows to invest in public infrastructures, such as highways, hospitals, and hydro-electric dams.

LO 3.5 Describe the major global economic challenges of the 21st century.

GLOBAL ECONOMIC CHALLENGES OF THE 21ST CENTURY

Businesses face many important economic challenges in the 21st century. The economies of countries around the world are becoming more interconnected. Governments and businesses must now compete and will need to meet several challenges to stay competitive in the global market. Table 3.5 shows five key global economic challenges: (1) international terrorism, (2) the shift to a global information economy, (3) the aging of the world's population, (4) the growth of China and India, and (5) efforts to enhance the competitiveness of every country's workforce.

Today, we have a global economy. No country is an economic island. An ever-increasing stream of goods and services crosses national borders. More and more businesses are becoming true multinational firms, by operating manufacturing plants and other facilities around the world. Global trade and investments continue to grow, so events in one nation can set off effects around the world. The "Business Etiquette" feature offers some tips for international travel.

World trade has its risks, but Canadian firms can profit from expanding around the world. Canada is home to only a small portion of the world's 7 billion people. Canadian companies that want to grow need to look toward the world market.[19] Canadian businesses can also benefit from the lower labour costs in other parts of the world. Some businesses are successful at importing goods and services from foreign firms. But, it is very important for Canadian firms to track the foreign firms that supply their products. Canadian firms recently had to recall thousands of toys made by Chinese manufacturers. The toys contained lead paint that can be harmful to children. The Associated Press did some research and found that some Chinese manufacturers had used cadmium in place of lead in children's jewellery sold in North America. Cadmium is known to cause cancer. Like lead, cadmium impairs brain development in young children. Federal government agencies warned Asian firms not to use other toxic substances in place of lead. They also began looking into products sold in North America that might contain cadmium or other toxic heavy metals. However, many products we buy are now being made by businesses that operate far away. We need to be careful when looking for lower-priced *and* quality-made products from other places in the world.[20]

BUSINESS ETIQUETTE

Tips for International Travel

Good manners and good communication have always been important in business. Both are even more important as global business increases. If your work takes you to a foreign country—or even to an international videoconference— you need to understand the manners and etiquette of the country you are visiting, either actually or virtually. These useful tips for international business travel are based on suggestions by Dana Persia of DP Image Consulting.

Before Leaving

1. Research the business etiquette and customs of the country you will visit. Travel guides have lots of tips. Also, look on the Internet. The Foreign Affairs and International Trade Canada website is very helpful.

2. If you don't know the country's language, learn a few important phrases. Your hosts will thank you for your effort, even if you can't say the words exactly right.

3. Research what you should wear in the country you are visiting. The standards for women are stricter in many countries. In general, try to fit in as best you can.

Getting There

1. If you can, arrange your flight so you arrive early. You will need to get used to the time-zone change, especially before an important conference or meeting.

2. Get enough sleep before you travel to help reduce the effects of jet lag.

3. Drink water before, during, and after your flight to help with jet lag. Avoid alcohol and caffeine. Both are dehydrating and make the effects of jet lag worse.

When You Arrive

Remember the research you did. Remind yourself that other cultures look differently at gender roles, especially for women. Think about when and where to talk about business. Knowing the etiquette about business cards, alcohol, and gifts is also important. What is accepted in one country may be unacceptable somewhere else!

Sources: DP Image Consulting website, http://www.dpimageconsulting.com, accessed February 4, 2010; International Business Etiquette and Manners, http://www.cyborlink.com, accessed February 4, 2010; U.S. Department of State website, http://www.state.gov, accessed February 4, 2010; Phillip Khan-Panni, "20 Tips on International Business Etiquette," *Eacademy*, June 12, 2009, http:www.eacademy.com; Foreign Affairs and International Trade Canada website, http://www.international.gc.ca/international/index.aspx , accessed February 8, 2011.

Table 3.5 Global Economic Challenges

CHALLENGE	FACTS AND EXAMPLES
International terrorism	• Many nations assist in locating and holding known terrorists. • Most nations cooperate by changing their banking laws to cut off funds to terrorist organizations. • Many countries are concerned about the safety of mass-transit systems after bombings in Moscow and elsewhere.
Shift to a global information economy	• Half of all North American workers hold jobs in information technology or in industries that intensively use information technology goods and services. • The software industry in India expects to employ more than 2.3 million people. • The number of Internet users in Asia and Western Europe has more than doubled in five years.
Aging of the world's population	• The median age of Canadians is 39-plus. By 2030, the median could reach 44. More than 25% of people will be 65 or older—nearly double today's number.[a] This aging population will increase demands for health care, retirement benefits, and other support services. Governments will need to deal with extra budget pressures. • As the baby boomers begin to retire, businesses around the world will need to replace their workplace skills.
Growth of India and China straining commodity prices	• China and India make up more than one-third of the world's population. China's economic growth has been in the industrial sector, and India has focused on services. Both countries now consume more oil and other commodities. Their increasing use means higher demand, which can increase prices.
Enhancing competitiveness of every country's workforce	• Leaner organizations (those with fewer supervisors) need employees who have the skills to control, combine, and supervise work operations.

[a]Statistics Canada, "Canada's Population Estimates: Age and Sex," July 9, 2009, http://www.statcan.gc.ca/daily-quotidien/091127/dq091127b-eng.htm, accessed February 8, 2011.

 ASSESSMENT CHECK

3.5.1 Why is no country an economic island today?

3.5.2 Describe two ways in which global expansion can benefit a Canadian firm.

WHAT'S AHEAD

Global competition is a key factor in today's economy. In Chapter 4, we focus on the global dimensions of business. We cover basic concepts of doing business internationally and look at how nations can ready themselves to benefit from the global economy. Then we describe the specific ways that individual businesses expand beyond their national borders to compete successfully in the global marketplace.

RETURN TO INSIDE BUSINESS

Vancouver's 2010 Olympic Village: Seemed like a great idea at the time

Vancouver was trying to get people and businesses to move to the former Olympic Village. The early response from people and businesses seemed to be positive. As more buyers and renters moved into the empty condominium units, several businesses opened, including a bank, grocery stores, and drug stores. The people who moved there like their new community. It seems to be changing into a neighbourhood, instead of being just a collection of buildings. Vancouver's real estate market seems to be dealing with the higher supply of property contributed by the Olympic Village conversion to condominiums. Overall prices have changed very little.

QUESTIONS FOR CRITICAL THINKING

1. How do you expect condominium prices to change over the next 10 years?

2. What primary factors will affect these price changes the most?

SUMMARY OF LEARNING OBJECTIVES

LO 3.1 Distinguish between microeconomics and macroeconomics. Explain the factors that drive demand and supply.

Microeconomics is the study of economic behaviour among individual consumers, families, and businesses. Together, their overall behaviour in the marketplace leads to the quantity of goods and services that are demanded and supplied at different prices. Macroeconomics is the study of the broader economic picture. It looks at how an economic system maintains and divides up its resources. Macroeconomics focuses on how a government's monetary and fiscal policies affect the overall operation of an economic system.

Demand is the willingness and ability of buyers to purchase goods and services at different prices. Several factors drive demand for a good or service: customer preferences, the number of buyers and their incomes, the prices of substitute goods, the prices of complementary goods, and consumer expectations about the future. Supply is the willingness and ability of businesses to offer products for sale at different prices. Supply depends on the cost of inputs and technology resources, taxes, and the number of suppliers in the market.

✓ ASSESSMENT CHECK ANSWERS

3.1.1 Define microeconomics and macroeconomics. *Microeconomics* is the study of economic behaviour among individual consumers, families, and businesses. Together, their overall behaviour in the marketplace leads to the quantity of goods and services that are demanded and supplied at different prices. *Macroeconomics* is the study of the broader economic picture. It looks at how an economic system maintains and divides up its resources.

3.1.2 Explain demand and supply curves. A demand curve is a graph showing the amount of a product that buyers will purchase at different prices. A supply curve shows the relationship between different prices and the amount of goods that sellers will offer for sale at those prices, regardless of demand.

3.1.3 How do factors of production affect the overall supply of goods and services? A change in the cost or availability of any of the factors of production can shift the entire supply curve, by either increasing or decreasing the amount available at every price.

LO 3.2 Describe the four different types of market structures in a private enterprise system, and compare the three major types of economic systems.

Four basic types of competition take shape in a private enterprise system: pure competition, monopolistic competition, oligopoly, and monopoly. Pure competition is a market structure, such as the structure of small-scale agriculture. Large numbers of buyers and sellers exchange similar products, and no single participant has a large influence on price. Monopolistic competition is a market structure, similar to the structure for retailing: large numbers of buyers and sellers exchange distinct and differentiated (dissimilar) products, so each participant has some control over price. Oligopolies are market situations, such as the steel and airline industries, where just a few sellers compete. High start-up costs form barriers to keep out new competitors. In a monopoly, one seller controls trade in a good or service, and buyers can find no close substitutes.

The major economic systems are private enterprise systems, planned economies (such as communism or socialism), and mixed economies. In a private enterprise system, individuals and private businesses pursue their own interests without too much governmental restriction. In a planned economy, the government has stronger control over business ownership, profits, and the resources needed to accomplish governmental and societal goals, not goals set by individual firms. Socialism is one type of a planned economic system where the government owns and operates the major industries. Communism is a planned economic system without private property. Under communism, goods are owned in common, and factors of production and production decisions are controlled by the state. A mixed market economy blends government ownership and private enterprise, drawing from both planned and private enterprise economies.

3.2.1 What is the difference between pure competition and monopolistic competition? Pure competition is a market structure where large numbers of buyers and sellers exchange similar products. Monopolistic competition is a market structure where large numbers of buyers and sellers exchange differentiated products.

3.2.2 Which economic system is the Canadian economy based on? The Canadian economy is based on the private enterprise system.

3.2.3 What is privatization? Privatization is the conversion of government-owned and -operated agencies to privately held businesses.

LO 3.3 Identify and describe the four stages of the business cycle. Explain how productivity, price level changes, and employment levels affect the stability of a nation's economy.

The four stages of the business cycle are prosperity, recession, depression, and recovery. During prosperity, unemployment is low and there is strong consumer confidence. In a recession, consumers often wait before making major purchases, may worry about being laid off, and may use up their savings. A depression occurs when an economic slowdown continues in a downward spiral over a long period of time. During recovery, consumers start spending again. Business activity increases, and more people have jobs.

As productivity rises, an economy's growth increases and its citizens' wealth increases. In a recession, productivity stalls and may decline. Changes in general price levels— inflation or deflation—are important indicators of an economy's general stability. The Canadian government measures price-level changes by using the Consumer Price Index. A nation's unemployment rate is an indicator of both overall stability and growth. The unemployment rate shows, as a percentage of the total labour force, the number of people actively seeking employment who are unable to find jobs.

✓ ASSESSMENT CHECK ANSWERS

3.3.1 Describe the four stages of the business cycle. The four stages are prosperity, recession, depression, and recovery. During prosperity, unemployment is usually low and there is strong consumer confidence. In a recession, consumers may wait before making major purchases, may worry about being laid off, and may use up their savings. A depression occurs when an economic slowdown continues in a downward spiral over a long period of time. During recovery, consumers start spending again. Business activity increases, and more people have jobs.

3.3.2 What do economists use to measure the health of an economy? To measure the health of an economy, economists use gross domestic product (GDP), the general level of prices, the core inflation rate, the Consumer Price Index, and the unemployment rate.

LO 3.4 Discuss how monetary policy and fiscal policy are used to manage an economy's performance.

Monetary policy is a government's plan to control the size of the nation's money supply. Increasing or decreasing the overall money supply can affect interest rates, which also affects borrowing and investment decisions. By changing the size of the money supply, a government can encourage growth or control inflation. Fiscal policy involves decisions about government revenues and expenditures. Changes in government spending affect economic growth and employment levels in the private sector. A government must also raise money, through taxes or borrowing, to finance its spending. The taxes paid by individuals and businesses are funds that would have been spent on goods and services. Thus, any taxation changes also affect the overall economy.

✓ ASSESSMENT CHECK ANSWERS

3.4.1 What is the difference between an expansionary monetary policy and a restrictive monetary policy? An expansionary monetary policy increases the money supply to try to decrease the cost of borrowing. A restrictive monetary policy reduces the money supply to control rising prices, overexpansion, and concerns about overly rapid economic growth.

3.4.2 What are the three primary sources of government funds? The Canadian government acquires funds through taxes, fees, and borrowing.

3.4.3 Does a balanced budget erase the federal debt? No, a balanced budget does not erase the national debt. In a balanced budget, total revenues raised by taxes equal the total proposed spending for the year.

LO 3.5 Describe the major global economic challenges of the 21st century.

Businesses face five key global economic challenges in the 21st century: (1) international terrorism; (2) the shift to a global information economy; (3) the aging of the world's population; (4) the growth of India and China; and (5) efforts to enhance the competitiveness of every country's workforce.

 ASSESSMENT CHECK ANSWERS

3.5.1 Why is no country an economic island today? No business or country is an economic island because many goods and services travel across national borders. Many companies now are becoming multinational firms.

3.5.2 Describe two ways in which global expansion can benefit a Canadian firm. A firm can benefit from global expansion by attracting more customers and by using less expensive labour and production to produce goods and services.

BUSINESS TERMS YOU NEED TO KNOW

economics 64

microeconomics 64

macroeconomics 64

demand 65

supply 65

demand curve 66

supply curve 68

equilibrium price 69

pure competition 72

monopolistic competition 72

oligopoly 72

monopoly 72

regulated monopoly 73

planned economy 73

socialism 73

communism 74

mixed market economy 74

privatization 74

recession 77

productivity 77

gross domestic product (GDP) 78

inflation 78

core inflation rate 78

hyperinflation 78

deflation 79

Consumer Price Index (CPI) 79

unemployment rate 81

frictional unemployment 81

seasonal unemployment 81

cyclical unemployment 81

structural unemployment 81

monetary policy 82

expansionary monetary policy 82

restrictive monetary policy 82

fiscal policy 82

budget 83

budget deficit 84

national debt 84

budget surplus 84

balanced budget 84

REVIEW QUESTIONS

1. How does microeconomics affect business? How does macroeconomics affect business? Why is it important for businesspeople to understand the basics of microeconomics and macroeconomics?

2. Draw supply and demand graphs that estimate what will happen to demand, supply, and the equilibrium price of coffee if these events occur:

    a. Widely reported medical studies suggest that coffee drinkers are less likely to develop certain diseases.

    b. The cost of manufacturing paper cups increases.

    c. The government sets a new tax on takeout beverages.

    d. The biggest coffee chain leaves the area.

3. Describe the four different types of competition in the private enterprise system. Which type of competition is most likely for the following businesses?

    a. a large drugstore chain

    b. a small yoga studio

    c. a steel mill

    d. a large farm whose major crop is corn

    e. Microsoft

4. Distinguish between the two types of planned economies. What factors keep them from working in today's environment?

5. What are the four stages of the business cycle? What stage do you believe the Canadian economy is in now? Why?

6. What is the gross domestic product? What is its relationship to productivity?

7. What are the effects of inflation on an economy? What are the effects of deflation? How does the Consumer Price Index work?

8. What does a nation's unemployment rate show? Describe what type of unemployment is most likely for each of the following:

    a. a discharged armed forces veteran

    b. a bus driver who has been laid off due to cuts in the city transit budget

    c. a worker who was injured on the job and must start a new career

    d. a lifeguard

    e. a dental hygienist who has quit one job and is looking for another

9. Explain the difference between monetary policy and fiscal policy. How does the government raise funds to cover the costs of its annual budget?

10. What is the difference between the budget deficit and the national debt? What are the benefits of paying down the national debt? What are the negative effects?

PROJECTS AND TEAMWORK APPLICATIONS

1. Describe a situation when you had to make an economic choice to try to balance your wants with limited means. What factors helped you to reach your decision?

2. Choose one of the following products. Describe the factors that might affect its supply and demand.

   a. UGG boots

   b. a Kindle

   c. Miles by MasterCard credit card

   d. a newly created name-brand drug

   e. a bicycling tour in Europe

3. Go online to research one of the following government departments or agencies. Read about its responsibilities, its budget, and the like. Make the case for privatizing it:

   a. Veterans Affairs Canada

   b. Statistics Canada

   c. Library and Archives Canada

   d. Transport Canada

   e. Canadian Radio-television and Telecommunications Commission

4. Some businesses always experience seasonal unemployment. But more and more, owners of these businesses are trying to increase demand—and employment—during the off-season. Choose a classmate to be your business partner. Together, select one of the following businesses. Create a plan for increasing business and keeping employees for a season when your business does not usually operate:

   a. a children's summer camp

   b. a ski lodge

   c. an inn located near a beach resort

   d. a house-painting service

   e. a greenhouse

5. On your own or with a classmate, go online to research the economy of one of the following countries. Learn about the type of economy the country has, its major industries, and its competitive issues. (Note which industries or services are privatized and which are government-owned.) Take notes on unemployment rates, monetary policies, and fiscal policies. Present your findings to the class.

   a. China

   b. New Zealand

   c. India

   d. Sweden

   e. Mexico

   f. United States

   g. Brazil

WEB ASSIGNMENTS

1. **Credit card regulations**. Several new federal regulations recently were passed governing credit cards. Visit the website listed here. After reviewing these rules, prepare a brief report highlighting the most significant changes.

   http://www.actionplan.gc.ca/initiatives/eng/index.asp?initiativeID=47&mode=2

2. **Unemployment**. Statistics Canada compiles and publishes data on Canada's unemployment. Go to the Statistics Canada website (http://www40.statcan.gc.ca/l01/ind01/l3_2621_1803-eng.htm?hili_lfss01). Read through the most recent reports and answer the following questions:

   a. What is the current unemployment rate in Canada? How does it compare with the rates of other developed countries?

   b. Which province has the highest unemployment rate? Which province has the lowest unemployment rate?

   c. What is the so-called underemployment rate?

3. **Gross domestic product**. Visit the Statistics Canada website (http://www40.statcan.gc.ca/l01/cst01/dsbbcan-eng.htm). Access the most recent statistics on the Canadian GDP. Prepare a brief report. What is the current GDP? What is the difference between real and nominal GDP? What individual components make up GDP?

www.wileyplus.com

Access your WileyPLUS course for:

- The complete digital textbook.
- Question assistance, including links to relevant sections in the online digital textbook.
- Immediate feedback and proof of progress, 24/7
- Integrated, multi-media resources – including MP3 downloads, visual exhibits, animations, and much more – that provide multiple study paths and encourage more active learning.

QUIZ YOURSELF

Note: Internet Web addresses change frequently. If you don't find the exact sites listed, you may need to access the organization's home page and search from there or use a search engine such as Bing or Google.

London   Hong Kong   Seoul

KE

KOSPI

1,158.19

4 | COMPETING IN WORLD MARKETS

LEARNING OBJECTIVES

LO 4.1 Explain the importance of international business and the primary reasons nations trade, and discuss the concepts of absolute and comparative advantage in international trade.

LO 4.2 Describe how nations measure international trade and the significance of exchange rates.

LO 4.3 Identify the major barriers that confront global businesses.

LO 4.4 Explain how international trade organizations and economic communities reduce barriers to international trade.

LO 4.5 Compare the different levels of involvement used by businesses when entering global markets.

LO 4.6 Distinguish between a global business strategy and a multidomestic business strategy.

INSIDE BUSINESS

PotashCorp: Genesis for Economic Development

Where does wealth come from? How did Canada become the complex economic society it is today? Why do some countries have wealth while others seem to always be living in poverty? What roles do Canadian businesses play in the challenge to generate and distribute wealth in our country and around the world? We need to understand these questions, concepts, and our framework for how business and economic development work. Let's take a closer look at just one international Canadian business.

PotashCorp of Saskatoon, Saskatchewan, is one of many businesses that generate wealth by producing commodities for Canadian and international customers. Commodities are basic products like oil, natural gas, gold, silver, forest products, and many other resources that businesses need to make the products they sell.

Sometimes a commodity is used directly in production. For example, natural gas is burned in kilns to dry fresh-cut lumber when making building materials like 2×4 wall studs. But commodities can also be ingredients in a recipe for producing an important product—fertilizer.

PotashCorp is the world's largest producer of fertilizer. It has about 20 percent of the entire global capacity and annual sales of about $6 billion. Fertilizer replaces the nutrients in the soil that are absorbed by crops. In simple terms, the key recipe ingredients of fertilizer—potash, phosphate, and nitrogen—are put back in the soil so that the soil can continue to produce higher-yield crops. Potash and phosphate are mined, and nitrogen is extracted from the air. This simple, but important product has allowed PotashCorp to grow into a $50 billion giant. It has global operations and part ownership in businesses in China, Chile, Israel, and Jordan.

The demand for fertilizer is directly related to two factors: the demand for agricultural products and the ability of the growers to

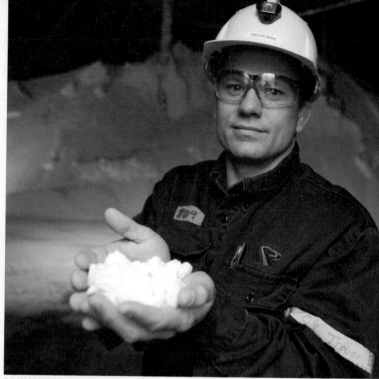

DAVID STOBBE/Reuters/Landov

pay. The growing demand for agricultural products is clearly associated with population growth. For example, the populations of India and China together make up more than one-third of the world's population. As these countries grow economically richer, they are more able to afford the cost of fertilizers to better feed their growing populations.

Let's think about what happened during the global financial crises that occurred between 2008 and 2010. Around the world, demand dropped for all commodities, particularly in India and China. As a result, sales and prices of commodities, including fertilizers, also dropped. Mining of the ingredients decreased, and some mines were closed until prices and demand became profitable again.

At the same time, PotashCorp's shares dropped from $233 per share on June 20, 2008 down to $67 per share on December 5, 2008. By January 2011, demand and prices had recovered to increase the share value to $170, which meant the business could be profitable again.

China has the world's largest population, estimated to be more than 1.3 billion people. China is also the world's largest user of fertilizer, using 28 percent of all available fertilizer. China's own potash production is limited. Historically, 75 percent of potash used in China is imported. As incomes have grown in China, the Chinese agribusinesses have increased their use of fertilizers to meet the growing demand for more food, and for meat products in particular. India, with an estimated 1.1 billion people, is the second largest consumer of fertilizer. It needs about 13 percent of the world demand for fertilizer. Brazil has an estimated population of 200 million people. It imports 90 percent of the potash it needs, and uses 7 percent of the world's fertilizer. North America has an estimated population of about 340 million people. It needs about 14 percent of the world's fertilizer. North American demand has been more stable than in these other markets. Demand for fertilizer has increased by 85 percent in China, India, Southeast Asia, and Brazil over the past 20 years. These figures closely match food production trends during that time.

Some countries are rich in highly valued commodities. These countries have an immediate source of wealth on which they can build more economic activity. The countries that are not rich in these commodities must look for other strategies or face the economic consequences. Canada has an economic advantage over other countries because of our rich natural resources. Canadians benefit from the sale of commodities to customers and in other countries wherever they may be in the world.[1]

CHAPTER 4 OVERVIEW

Take a moment and think about how many products you used today that came from outside Canada. Did you drink Brazilian coffee with your breakfast? Are your clothes manufactured in China? Did you drive to class in a German or Japanese car fuelled by gasoline refined from Venezuelan crude oil? Or did you watch a movie on a television set assembled in Mexico for a Japanese company such as Sony? A fellow student in Germany may be wearing Zara jeans, using a BlackBerry smartphone, and drinking Pepsi.

Canadian and foreign companies know the importance of international trade to their future success. Economic interdependence is increasing throughout the world as companies look for new markets for their goods and services and the most cost-effective locations to set up factories. Businesses cannot rely only on sales in their home country. Today, Canadian manufacturing, agricultural, and service firms need foreign sales. Other countries are sources of new markets and profit opportunities. Foreign companies also look to Canada when they need new markets.

Thousands of products cross national borders every day. The automobiles that Canadian manufacturers sell in the United States are **exports**, domestically produced goods and services sold in markets in other countries. **Imports** are foreign-made products purchased by domestic consumers. Together, Canadian exports and imports make up about 30 percent of Canadian gross domestic product (GDP). Canada is the world's tenth largest exporter. Canada's exports and imports are worth more than $400 billion each. Those total amounts have remained steady over the past 10 years and peaked in 2008, at just under $500 billion of exports and $450 billion of imports, just as the 2008–2010 financial crisis set in.[2]

Sometimes goods are bought and sold across national boundaries. Companies that do business with other countries need to work with new social and cultural practices, different economic and political environments, and legal restrictions. Before entering world markets, companies must take the business plans they use in their home market and change them to work with the markets in other countries.

This chapter looks at the world of international business. We will see how large and small companies deal with globalization. First, we look at why nations trade, the importance of the global marketplace, the features of the global marketplace, and how nations measure international trade. Then we look at barriers to international trade as a result of cultural and environmental differences. To reduce these barriers, countries turn to organizations that promote global business. Finally, we look at the strategies firms use for entering foreign markets and how they create international business strategies.

exports domestically produced goods and services sold in other countries.

imports foreign goods and services purchased by domestic customers.

WHY NATIONS TRADE

LO 4.1 Explain the importance of international business and the primary reasons nations trade, and discuss the concepts of absolute and comparative advantage in international trade.

When their home markets mature and sales slow, companies in every industry know the importance of expanding business to other countries. TD Ameritrade is Toronto Dominion Bank's online brokerage business in the United States. It was set up when TDBank acquired Ameritrade in 2006. Lululemon Athletica is based in Vancouver, B.C., but operates stores in United States. Bombardier sells jet aircraft to companies around the world. These are only a few of the thousands of Canadian companies selling their products in other countries. These firms take advantage of large populations, healthy resources, and rising standards of living abroad that increase foreign interests in their goods and services. Likewise, the Canadian market's high purchasing power attracts thousands of foreign companies to its shores.

International trade is vital to a nation and its businesses. Trading with other countries increases economic growth in two ways: by providing a new market for products and by providing access to needed resources. Companies can expand their markets, seek growth opportunities in other nations, and make their production and distribution systems more efficient. They can also reduce their dependence on the economies of their home nations.

International Sources of Factors of Production

Business decisions to operate abroad depend on the basic factors of production in the other country: the availability, price, and quality of labour, natural resources, capital, and entrepreneurship. Indian colleges and universities produce thousands of highly qualified computer scientists and engineers each year. To take advantage of this talent, many global computer software and hardware firms have set up operations in India. Many other companies outsource their information technology and customer service jobs to Indian companies.

Trading with other countries also allows a company to spread risk because different nations may be at different stages of the business cycle or in different phases of development. If demand falls in one country, the company may find strong demand in other nations. In India and China, sales of automobiles for personal use are just getting started. For many years, companies such as General Motors, Kellogg's, and IKEA have used international sales to balance lower sales at home.

Size of the International Marketplace

We have discussed that companies choose international trade because of the benefits to human and natural resources, entrepreneurship, and capital. Companies are also attracted to international business because of the size of the global marketplace. The world's population is approximately 7 billion now. Only one in six people live in a well-developed country. The portion of the world's population living in less developed countries will increase in the coming years because more developed nations have lower birthrates. But the global birthrate is slowing overall. Today's average woman has half as many children as the average woman had 35 years ago.[3]

When firms in developing nations increase their global business, they also increase their ability to reach new groups of customers. Firms that are looking for new revenue are usually attracted to giant markets, such as China and India. China has a population of about 1.3 billion, and India's population is 1.2 billion. But people alone do not create a market. Consumer demand also needs purchasing power. Table 4.1 shows that population size does not guarantee economic prosperity. Of the 10 countries with the highest population, only one country also has a GDP on the top-10 list—the United States. Note also that countries with smaller populations can create great wealth for their citizens, as measured by GDP per capita. Where does Canada rank? With a population of 34 million people, Canada places 36th from the top of the population rankings but 11th with $45,888 per-capita GDP.

People in the developing nations have lower per-capita incomes than people in the highly developed economies of North America and Western Europe. Despite having lower incomes, the huge populations in developing countries represent profitable markets for some companies. The higher-income group may only be a small percentage of the entire country's population, but their numbers still represent important and growing markets.

Table 4.1 The World's Top 10 Nations

	BASED ON POPULATION			BASED ON WEALTH	
Rank	COUNTRY	POPULATION (IN MILLIONS)	Rank	COUNTRY	PER-CAPITA GDP (IN U.S. DOLLARS)
1	China	1,323	1	Luxembourg	$104,390
2	India	1,156	2	Norway	$84,543
3	United States	308	3	Qatar	$74,422
4	Indonesia	240	4	Switzerland	$67,074
5	Brazil	199	5	Denmark	$55,113
6	Pakistan	175	6	Australia	$54,869
7	Bangladesh	156	7	Sweden	$47,667
8	Nigeria	150	8	UAE	$47,132
9	Russia	140	9	United States	$47,132
10	Japan	127	10	Netherlands	$46,418
36	Canada	33	11	Canada	$45,888

Sources: U.S. Census Bureau, International Data Base, "Countries and Areas Ranked by Population" www.census.gov, accessed March 8, 2010; International Monetary Fund, "World Economic Outlook Database—October 2010," www.imf.org, accessed February 27, 2011.

Many developing countries have typically posted high growth rates in their annual GDP. Until the 2008–10 economic slowdown, U.S. and Canadian GDP rates grew at an annual rate of about 4 percent. By contrast, GDP growth in less developed countries was much greater—China's GDP growth rate averaged 10.1 percent over a recent three-year period, and India's averaged 7.5 percent.[4] These countries represent opportunities for global businesses, even though their per-capita incomes are lower than in more developed countries. Many North American firms are setting up operations in these and other developing countries. They want to benefit from local sales as a result of expanding economies and rising standards of living. For example, Walmart has opened dozens of new stores in developing countries from China to Brazil. It now has nearly 4,000 stores in 15 different countries worldwide. One Walmart executive says the company is "progressing from being a domestic company with an international division to being a global company."[5]

Canada's trade is overwhelmingly tied to the United States, and U.S. trade is tied to Canada. Both countries are similar in their social and cultural values. That means that when a business finds a market in one country, it will most likely find the buyers in the other country, too. Almost all of Canada's population is spread along the American border. The closeness of the two countries makes it easier to transport goods and to communicate, and that helps develop the cross-border trade.

Figure 4.1 shows Canada's top trade partners. Notice the amount of trade Canada has with the United States. Much of our trade with United States is resource-based. Canada's energy supply of oil, natural gas, and hydro-electricity will continue to grow as the United States continues to need safe, secure, and reliable supplies of energy.

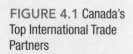

FIGURE 4.1 Canada's Top International Trade Partners

Source: Statistics Canada, CANSIM table 228-0003; Statistics Canada, Table 20.a "Canada's Top International Trade Partners, 2009," http://www.statcan.gc.ca/pub/11-402-x/2010000/pdf/international-eng.pdf, accessed February 27, 2011.

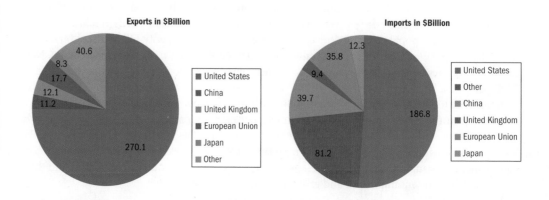

Absolute and Comparative Advantage

Few countries can produce all the goods and services they need. For centuries, trading has helped countries to meet the demand for goods and services. A country can focus on producing what it does best. It can then export the extra output and buy foreign products that it doesn't have or cannot produce efficiently. The foreign sales of a product depend on whether the country has an absolute advantage or a comparative advantage.

A country has an *absolute advantage* in making a product when it has a monopoly on making that product or when it can produce the product at a lower cost than any other country. China has had an absolute advantage in silk production for centuries. Silk is woven from fibres from silkworm cocoons. Silk is a prized raw material in high-quality clothing. European demand for silk led to the famous Silk Road, an 8,000-kilometre link between Rome and the ancient Chinese capital city of Xian.

Today, absolute advantages are rare. Some countries almost have absolute advantages in some products. For example, climate differences can give some nations or regions an advantage in growing certain plants. Saffron may be the world's most expensive spice. It costs around $4,650 per kilogram. Saffron is the stigma of a flowering plant in the crocus family. It is native to the Mediterranean, Asia Minor, and India. Today, saffron is grown mainly in Spain, where the plant thrives in the Spanish soil and climate. Attempts to grow saffron in other parts of the world have generally been unsuccessful.[6]

A nation can develop a *comparative advantage* when it can supply its products more efficiently and at a lower price than it can supply other goods, compared with the outputs of other countries. China profits from its comparative advantage in producing textiles. A nation can also develop a comparative advantage in skilled human resources by ensuring that its people are well educated. India, for example, has a comparative advantage in software development because of its highly educated workforce and low wage scale. Several companies have moved part or all of their software development to India.

IBM wanted to increase its longstanding advantage in research and innovation as global competition increased. The company took the unusual step of forming six global research collaborations with companies, universities, and governments in Saudi Arabia, China, Switzerland, Ireland, Taiwan, and India. IBM hopes to sign at least four more international partnerships. Working with these countries breaks the tradition of doing research in secret. "The world is our lab now," says IBM's director of research.[7]

© Can Stock Photo Inc./Dream79

Saffron is possibly the world's most expensive spice. This pricey spice is extracted from crocus flowers. The plants grow well in Spain but don't grow well in most other countries. Spain has a near absolute advantage in saffron production.

✓ ASSESSMENT CHECK

4.1.1 Why do nations trade?

4.1.2 What are some measures of the size of the international marketplace?

4.1.3 How does a nation acquire a comparative advantage?

MEASURING TRADE BETWEEN NATIONS

LO 4.2 Describe how nations measure international trade and the significance of exchange rates.

International trade provides competitive advantages to both the countries and the individual companies involved. But how do we measure global business activity? We need to look at two ideas—the balance of trade and the balance of payments. These two ideas can help us to understand what the trade inflows and outflows mean for a country. Another important factor is the currency exchange rates for the trading countries.

A nation's **balance of trade** is the difference between its exports and imports. When a country exports more than it imports, it has a positive balance of trade, called a *trade surplus*. When a country imports more than it exports, it produces a negative balance of trade, called a *trade deficit*. Canada tends to maintain a balance between exports and imports by running a trade surplus with the United States and a trade deficit with other trading partners, particularly China.[8] The United States has run a trade deficit every year since 1976. The United States is one of the world's top exporters, but it has an even greater demand for foreign-made goods, which creates a trade deficit.

balance of trade the difference between a nation's exports and imports.

balance of payments the overall money flows into and out of a country.

A nation's balance of trade plays a central role in shaping its **balance of payments**—the overall flow of money into or out of a country. The balance of payments is also affected by overseas loans and borrowing, international investments, profits from international investments, and foreign aid payments. To calculate a nation's balance of payments, subtract the monetary outflows from the monetary inflows. A positive balance of payments, or a *balance-of-payments surplus*, means more money has moved into a country than out of it. A negative balance of payments, or *balance-of-payments deficit*, means more money has gone out of the country than entered it.

Major Canadian Exports and Imports

The global economy has grown to more than $74 trillion of total GDP. Canada's economy represents about $1.3 trillion, and the U.S. economy represents about $14.7 trillion. Trade is an important reason why global GDP has grown and keeps growing.[9]

Canada's top exports in 2010 were industrial goods and materials ($95 billion), energy products ($93 billion), and machinery and equipment ($69 billion). Figure 4.2 shows the major changes in these categories and other categories since 2000. Energy product exports have increased 72 percent over the 10-year period. These increases result from both increased export quantities and the dramatic increase in market prices for oil. The average price of oil in 2000 was about $27 per barrel and was about $71 in 2010.[10] In contrast, Canadian manufacturing export sales have decreased. The exports of Canadian automobile products, particularly trucks, have been reduced because of growing sales by foreign companies.

FIGURE 4.2 Major Canadian Imports and Exports in 2000 and 2010

Source: Data from the website of Foreign Affairs and International Trade Canada, *Annual Statistics on Merchandise Imports and Exports, by Country and Commodity, Recorded on a Customs Basis*, Table 228-0043, "Merchandise Imports and Exports by Sector," http://www.international.gc.ca/economist-economiste/statistics-statistiques/merchandise-marchandises.aspx?lang=eng accessed March 2, 2011.

On the import side, Canada's top imports were machinery and equipment ($113 billion), industrial goods and materials ($85 billion), and automotive products ($68 billion). Imports have changed over the past decade. For example, imports of energy products have increased 122 percent. Although Canada is a net exporter of energy, we also increased our imports of energy.

The United States leads the world in the international trade of goods and services. It has combined exports and imports of about $2.5 trillion. The goods exchanged by U.S. exporters and importers range from machinery and vehicles to crude oil and chemicals. Strong U.S. demand for imported goods partly reflects the American ability to produce a wide range of products for world consumption.

Although the United States imports more goods than it exports, the opposite is true for services. U.S. exporters sell more than $507 billion in services annually. Much of that money comes from travel and tourism—money spent by foreign nationals visiting the United States.[11] The increase in exported services is significant because the U.S. dollar has declined and, in recent years, has continued to rise and fall in terms of foreign currencies. U.S. service exports also include business and technical services, such as engineering, financial services, computing, legal services, and entertainment, in addition to royalties and licensing fees.

U.S. annual imports are nearing $2 trillion, making the United States the world's leading importer. Like Canadians, Americans demand foreign-made goods, for everything from clothing to consumer electronics. These preferences show up as huge trade deficits with the two nations that export the most consumer goods to North America—China and Japan.

Exchange Rates

An **exchange rate** is the value of one country's currency in terms of the currencies of other countries. We need to learn how foreign exchange works because we live in a global community. The value of currency is an important economic measure for every country. Each currency's exchange rate is usually stated in terms of another currency. For example, about 12 Mexican pesos are needed to purchase one Canadian dollar. A Canadian dollar can also be exchanged for approximately $1 in the United States. The euro is the currency used in most European Union (EU) member countries. The euro has had ups and downs in value. European consumers and businesses use the euro to pay bills by cheque, credit card, or bank transfer. Euro coins and notes are also used in many EU member-countries.

exchange rate the value of one country's currency in terms of the currencies of other countries.

Many factors can affect foreign exchange rates: economic and political conditions, actions by the central bank, balance-of-payments position, and speculation over future currency values. Currency values fluctuate, or "float," depending on the supply and demand for each currency in the world market. In this system of *floating exchange rates*, currency traders create a market for the world's currencies based on each country's trade and the likelihood of investments. The idea is that exchange rates can go up and down freely as supply and demand change. But exchange rates do not float in total freedom. National governments often step in to change their exchange rates.

Nations can affect exchange rates in other ways. They may form currency blocs by linking their exchange rates to each other. Many governments practise protectionist policies that try to protect their economies against trade imbalances. For example, nations sometimes take actions to

Because we live in a global community, we need to understand how currency exchange rates work. Many factors affect foreign exchange rates.

© Can Stock Photo Inc./iofoto

devaluation a reduction in a currency's value in terms of other currencies or in terms of a fixed standard.

devalue their currencies. It is a way to increase exports and encourage foreign investment. **Devaluation** is a reduction in a currency's value in terms of other currencies or in terms of a fixed standard. Brazil devalued its currency. Investing in Brazil became less costly than investing in other countries. After the devaluation, foreign investment in Brazil increased. Pillsbury bought Brazil's Brisco, a company that makes *pao de queijo*, a cheese bread formed into rolls and served with morning coffee. Other foreign companies invested in Brazil's construction, tourism, banking, communications, and other industries.

For an individual business, the impact of currency devaluation depends on where the business buys its materials and where it sells its products. Usually, business transactions use the currency of the country where the transactions take place. When business takes place in Japan, the transactions will likely be in yen. In the United Kingdom, transactions are in pounds. Many EU countries now use the euro, so fewer currencies are used in Europe. Today, the EU member-countries that use the euro include Austria, Belgium, Cyprus, Estonia, Finland, France, Germany, Greece, Ireland, Italy, Luxembourg, Malta, the Netherlands, Portugal, Slovakia, Slovenia, and Spain. Other currencies include the British pound, the Australian dollar, the Indian rupee, the Brazilian real, the Mexican peso, the Taiwanese dollar, and the South African rand.

Exchange rate changes can quickly create—or destroy—a competitive advantage. They are important factors when investors decide whether to invest in other countries. In Europe, a declining dollar means that a price of 10 euros is worth more, so European companies are pressured to lower their prices in order to keep foreign customers. When the value of the dollar falls, European vacations are more costly for Canadian tourists because their dollars are worth less in terms of the euro.

Use the Internet to find currency converters. You can find some at http://beginnersinvest. about.com/od/currencycalc/Currency_Calculator.htm. They can help you to make money conversions. They also can help you to understand the spending power of a Canadian dollar in other countries.

Currencies that easily convert into other currencies are called *hard currencies*. Examples of hard currencies are the euro, the U.S. dollar, and the Japanese yen. The Russian ruble and many central European currencies are soft currencies because they cannot be converted as easily. Exporters that trade with these countries sometimes prefer to barter, or accept payment not in cash but in goods, such as oil, timber, or other commodities. They then resell these goods in exchange for payment in hard currencies.

The foreign currency market is the largest financial market in the world. Its daily volume is more than US$3 trillion.[12] This amount is about 10 times the size of all the world's stock markets combined. The foreign exchange market is the most liquid and most efficient financial market in the world.

✔ **ASSESSMENT CHECK**

4.2.1 Compare balance of trade and balance of payments.

4.2.2 Explain the function of an exchange rate.

4.2.3 What happens when a currency is devalued?

LO 4.3 Identify the major barriers that confront global businesses.

BARRIERS TO INTERNATIONAL TRADE

All businesses face barriers, whether they sell only to local customers or trade in international markets. Some countries, such as Australia and New Zealand, set rules for the hours and days that retailers can open. International companies must follow a variety of laws and exchange currencies. They may also need to change their products to suit different tastes in other countries. Kraft recently won nearly a quarter of China's $1.6 billion cookie market. Kraft had to make its Oreo cookies less sweet to suit local tastes. The company also launched new products such as Oreo Wafer Sticks, Wafer Rolls, Soft Cakes, and Strawberry Cremes.[13]

Companies that do international business face social and cultural differences, economic barriers, and legal and political barriers. Some of the barriers are shown in Figure 4.3. Some of these barriers are easy to deal with, but other barriers require a company to make major changes in its business strategy. To be successful in global markets, companies and their managers need to understand not only how these barriers affect international trade but also how to overcome these barriers.

FIGURE 4.3 Barriers to International Trade

Social and Cultural Differences

The social and cultural differences among nations range from language and customs to educational background and religious holidays. Understanding and respecting these differences are important for international business success. Businesspeople who understand the host country's cultures, languages, social values, and religious attitudes and practices are prepared for the marketplace and the negotiating table. Businesspeople can win customers and meet their business goals by being sensitive to local views, to how people like to be addressed, and to suitable ways of dressing, using body language, and being on time or late. It is not only Canadian executives who need to adapt to the global business environment. Many business deals are made on the golf course. Chinese students at Xiamen University learn golf, in addition to studying business and law. Peking University is building a practice green. The "Business Etiquette" feature offers suggestions for understanding the Japanese culture.

BUSINESS ETIQUETTE

Tips for Understanding Japanese Culture

Japan's 127 million people live in a fairly small area. The people tend to be reserved and introverted. Their culture emphasizes conformity more than the culture in Canada. The Japanese literacy rate is nearly 100 percent; 95 percent of Japanese people have completed high school. Buddhism and Shintoism are the main religions. Here are some tips for respecting Japanese culture. These tips will help you in your global business dealings.

- Dress to impress. Casual wear is not suitable in work situations.

- You will often remove your shoes when you step indoors. Choose slip-on style shoes that you can easily put on and take off.

- Avoid large hand movements and pointing. Japanese people do not talk with their hands. They may find hand movements distracting.

- Respect other people's personal space. Handshakes are becoming more common, but bowing is still the traditional greeting.

- In Japan, a smile can mean many things, including anger, sorrow, or embarrassment.

- Japanese people don't make a lot of eye contact. They are also comfortable with silence. Do not feel you need to talk during a pause in conversation.

- Business entertaining usually takes place in bars and restaurants at the end of the workday. Tipping is not required.

- If you are invited to a Japanese home, you are very honoured.

- Remember to give and receive business cards using both hands. Show respect for a business card you receive by looking at it carefully.

- Always wrap gifts. In Japan, it's best to ask the store to wrap your gifts. The stores will make sure the paper and other details are suitable. For example, white symbolizes death.

- Remember that Japanese people do not like criticism. They also don't like to say no. They may say yes when they really mean no.

Sources: "Japanese Etiquette," *Cultural Savvy.com*, www.culturalsavvy.com, accessed March 17, 2010; "Japan," *Cyborlink.com*, www.cyborlink.com, accessed March 9, 2010; Emily Maltby, "Expanding Abroad? Avoid Cultural Gaffes," *Wall Street Journal*, January 19, 2010, p. B5.

Language

English is the second most widely spoken language in the world, followed by Hindustani, Spanish, Russian, and Arabic. Only Mandarin Chinese is more common than English. In other countries, some students whose first language is not English take eight years of English language classes in elementary and high school. Understanding a business colleague's primary language can make the difference between closing an international business transaction and losing the sale. Company workers in foreign markets not only must choose the correct and suitable words but also need to translate words correctly so they say what they want to say. Some firms rename their products or rewrite slogans for foreign markets.

Some communication barriers involve more than bad translations. Companies may make mistakes by presenting messages using unsuitable media, overlooking local customs and regulations, or ignoring differences in taste. One executive recently lost a deal in China. His mistake? He gave the prospective client a set of four antique clocks wrapped in white paper. But the number four and the Chinese word for clock sound like the word "death." And white is the traditional colour for funerals.[14] Cultural sensitivity is especially important in cyberspace. Website developers need to remember that website visitors come from anywhere in the world. Some icons that seem friendly to Canadian Internet users may shock people from other countries. For example, a person making a high-five hand signal would be insulting people in Greece. Also not suitable are making a circle with the thumb and index finger in Brazil, using a thumbs-up sign in Egypt, and showing a two-fingered peace sign with the back of the hand facing out in Great Britain.

Gift-giving traditions use the language of symbolism. For example, in Latin America, knives and scissors are not suitable gifts because they represent the severing of friendship. Flowers are generally acceptable, but Mexicans use yellow flowers in their Day of the Dead activities, so yellow flowers are linked to death.

Values and Religious Attitudes

Today's world is shrinking in many ways, but people in different countries do not always share the same values or religious feelings. Major differences can exist between people - even those living in the same country.

North American society places a higher value on business efficiency and lower unemployment than European society. But in Europe, employee benefits are more valued. In Canada, vacation time is decided on by each provincial government. For example, in Ontario, the Employment Standards Act states that employees earn two weeks' vacation after working for a 12-month vacation entitlement period. In contrast, the EU gives employees a minimum paid vacation of four weeks per year, but most Europeans have five or six weeks. When a Canadian company opens a factory in an EU country, it can hire local employees only if it offers vacation time as set by that nation's business practices.

North American culture values national unity and accepts regional differences. Canada and the United States are seen as separate national markets that have independent economies. European countries that are part of the 27-member EU are trying to create a similar marketplace. But many people don't like the idea of being European citizens first and British, Danish, or Dutch citizens second. British consumers differ from Italian consumers in important ways. Canadian companies that don't understand these differences and that don't change their activities to suit the other country will face problems with being accepted.

Religion plays an important role in every society. Businesspeople must also learn to be sensitive to the major religions in countries where they operate. International businesspeople need to understand religious cycles and the timing of major holidays. Their knowledge can help prevent embarrassing moments when booking meetings, trade shows, conferences, and events such as the opening of a new factory. People who do business in Saudi Arabia need to remember Islam's month-long observance of Ramadan, when work ends at noon. Friday is the Muslim Sabbath, so the Saudi workweek runs from Saturday through Thursday. Also, Muslims don't drink alcohol and think of pork as being unclean. That means gifts of pigskin or liquor would not be welcomed.

Economic Differences

North American business opportunities usually do well in densely populated countries such as China and India. There, the local consumers eagerly buy Western products. Although selling products there is tempting for Canadian firms, managers must think about the economic factors of doing business in China and India: the country's size, its per-capita income, and its stage of economic development. These economic factors are important to think about when deciding whether a country is right for an international business venture. For example, Tata is thinking about selling its car to Western auto buyers, even as it works on selling its low-cost Nano car in its home market in India. See the "Hit & Miss" feature for details.

Infrastructure

Businesses that compete in world markets need to think about the host country's economic measures, including its **infrastructure**. Infrastructure refers to the basic systems of communication (telecommunications, television, radio, and print media), transportation (roads and highways, railroads, and airports), and energy facilities (power plants and gas and electric utilities). The Internet and technology use can also be considered part of infrastructure.

infrastructure the basic systems of a country's communication, transportation, and energy facilities.

India's industrialization is growing. A recent forecast says that India will soon have 30 million air passengers each year. India's civil aviation minister says that means India will soon need at least 400 new airports. The Indian aviation industry is growing at nearly 20 percent a year, so 3,000 new planes will also be needed. It will take about one year to complete the bidding process for contractors to work on building a new airport in the capital city of Mumbai. "Our job is not over by creating infrastructure for aviation industry to grow," said the minister. "We need safe and secure aviation. Indian aviation will not grow at the cost of safety and security." Part of India's new air travel security is a CT scanner that inspects luggage at India's biggest new airport in New Delhi, which was built in only three years.[15]

 HIT & MISS

The Tiny Nano—A Potential Hit for Tata Motors

The Tata Nano is a tiny car that sells for $2,500 in India. When the Tata Nano arrived in North America it wasn't on the road; it was on display at the Cooper-Hewitt National Design Museum in New York. "As the world's most affordable car, it is a design achievement," said a museum director.

The Nano is a safe and sturdy vehicle. But more important, it is a major step in changing transportation for millions of Indian families that can't afford the high price of most cars. Tata built "the people's car," by using existing parts and a simple design to keep costs down.

"My particular fascination about the Nano is what I refer to as the 'Nano effect' on the rest of the world's vehicle industry," said one research director. He thinks that people everywhere will ask, "If Indians can buy a four-door car for $2,500, why can't I?"

Maybe they soon can. Tata is a $63-billion Indian company. It backed the Nano during legal issues over the land needed for a factory. The legal issues delayed production for two years. The recent recession also meant Tata had its first financial losses in seven years. About the same time, it faced heavy debts after having bought the money-losing Jaguar and Land Rover brands from Ford.

Tata's strategic plan is still to achieve international standing by solving the transportation problems of low-income car markets in the developing world. Tata will sell the Nano in Nigeria next. It has already passed Europe's crash-safety test. In just a few years, you may see slightly higher-priced Nanos on the streets of Europe and even in North America.

Questions for Critical Thinking

1. Do you think Tata's goal of making transportation affordable in developing countries is realistic? Why or why not?

2. Can you think of any disadvantages for low-income markets if thousands of cars suddenly show up on the road?

Sources: Phil Patton, "A Tata Nano Takes Manhattan," *New York Times*, www.nytimes.com, February 11, 2010; April K. Gupta and Haiyan Wang, "Tata Nano: Not Just a Car But Also a Platform," *BusinessWeek*, www.businessweek.com, January 20, 2010; Madhur Singh, "India's Top Automaker, Tata Motors, Hits a Rough Patch," *Time*, www.time.com, February 24, 2009.

Financial systems provide a type of infrastructure for businesses. In Canada, buyers have widespread access to cheques, credit cards, and debit cards, and to the electronic systems needed to process these payments. In many African countries, such as Ethiopia, local businesses do not accept credit cards. Visitors to Ethiopia's capital city, Addis Ababa, are warned to bring plenty of cash and traveller's cheques.

Currency Conversion and Shifts

Countries share many similarities in their infrastructure. But businesses that cross national borders face basic economic differences: national currencies. Foreign currency fluctuations, or ups and downs, may mean more problems for global businesses. As explained earlier in the chapter, the values of the world's major currencies rise and fall in relation to each other. Rapid and unexpected currency shifts can make it difficult to price items in the local currency. Shifts in exchange rates can also affect business decisions. A devalued currency may make a nation less desirable as a country to export to because of reduced demand in that country. But devaluation can also make the nation desirable as an investment opportunity. Investments there will be a bargain in terms of the buying power of the investor's currency.

Political and Legal Differences

We have discussed how social, cultural, and economic differences can build barriers to international trade. Legal and political differences can also act as barriers. In China, the government is very strict about Internet use. Many Chinese websites are now registering overseas to try to avoid government censorship.[16] The government's use of censorship can be a threat to companies thinking about doing business there.

To compete in today's world marketplace, managers in international businesses need to be familiar with the legislation that affects their industries. Some countries have general trade restrictions. Others have detailed rules that state how foreign companies can operate.

Political Climate

In any international business investment, an important factor is the stability of the political situation. The political structures of many nations promote stability similar to the political stability in Canada. Other nations have very different political structures that change frequently. This is the situation in Indonesia, Congo, and Bosnia. Host nations often pass laws to protect their own interests, sometimes at the expense of foreign businesses. See the "Ethical Controversy" feature for a look at how fair trade laws work.

The political structures have had huge changes in Russia, Turkey, the former Yugoslavia, Hong Kong, and in several central European countries, including the Czech Republic and Poland. Such political changes almost always bring changes in the legal environment. Hong Kong is considered to be part of China. Thus, political developments have led to changes in Hong Kong's legal and cultural environments. Since the collapse of the Soviet Union, Russia has struggled to develop a new market structure and political processes.

Legal Environment

When doing business internationally, managers must be familiar with three dimensions of the legal environment: Canadian law, international regulations, and the laws of the countries in which they plan to trade. Some laws protect the rights of foreign companies to compete in Canada. Others spell out the actions allowed for Canadian companies doing business in foreign countries.

Canada's Corruption of Foreign Public Officials Act (CFPOA) and the American Foreign Corrupt Practices Act (FCPA) make it illegal for companies to bribe foreign officials, political candidates, and government representatives. These acts set out the fines and jail time for managers who are aware of illegal payoffs. Until recently, many countries, including France and Germany, accepted the practice of bribing foreign officials in countries where such practices were

SOLVING AN **ETHICAL** CONTROVERSY

How Fair Is Fair Trade?

Although demand for candy remains high, the price of cocoa is near a 30-year-high. One reason is that to win the much wanted "fair trade" description for their products, chocolate makers pay small cocoa farmers an extra $150 per ton for the raw ingredient and accept a price of at least $1,600 a ton overall. Nestlé recently announced its popular Kit Kat chocolate bars will now include only fair trade chocolate from West Africa. Still, many people find fault with the company for supposedly not dealing with other possible problems, such as child labour.

Is "fair trade" fair enough?

PRO

1. Nestlé is one of the world's largest buyers of cocoa beans. The company is taking a strong lead in social responsibility. But its high prices for fair-trade cocoa are "going to put pressure on our business," said the firm's U.K. head.

2. Nestlé's efforts will provide poor cocoa farmers with cash, trees, and training. It will also help these farmers to keep their children in school.

CON

1. If a company allows child labour in its overseas businesses, then its fair trade claims are meaningless.

2. Firms can and should ensure that all their actions are socially responsible at every level, at home and abroad.

Summary

The share of fair trade chocolate sold in the United Kingdom is expected to soon rise to about 10 percent of all chocolate sold, a ten-fold increase, in part resulting from Nestlé's efforts. Nestlé has promised to plant millions of disease-resistant cocoa trees in Africa. It will also spend at least $445 million on sustainable farming projects. Nestlé has also agreed to a global plan to improve cocoa farmers' access to health care and to fight child labour.

Sources: Roberta Cruger, "Is Fair Trade Chocolate Fair Enough?" *Independent/RelaxNews*, www.treehugger.com, February 14, 2010; Thomas Muller, "Nestle Sees Stagnant U.K. Chocolate Market as Cocoa Prices Soar," *Bloomberg.com*, www.bloomberg.com, December 12, 2009; "Organizations Question Nestlé's Commitment to Fair Trade Cocoa," Laborrights.org, www.laborrights.org, December 7, 2009; Deborah Ball, "Nestle Moves to Fair-Trade Chocolate for KitKat Candy in U.K.," *Wall Street Journal*, www.online.wsj.com, December 7, 2009.

customary—and allowed tax deductions for these expenses. Canada, the United States, the United Kingdom, France, Germany, and 35 other countries have signed the Organisation for Economic Co-operation and Development's Anti-Bribery Convention. Many police forces do not actively enforce this law, but this agreement makes offering or paying bribes a criminal offence. It also ends the tax deduction for bribes.[17]

Corruption continues to be an international problem. The commonness of bribing and the international rules against bribery create difficulties for Canadian businesspeople who want to do business in foreign countries. Chinese pay *huilu*, and Russians rely on *vzyatka*. In the Middle East, palms are greased with *baksheesh*. Figure 4.4 compares 179 countries on measures of supposed corruption. This Corruption Perceptions Index is computed by Transparency International, a Berlin-based organization that rates the degree of corruption observed by businesspeople and the general public.

The growth of online business has introduced new elements to the legal situation of international businesses. Patents, brand names, trademarks, copyrights, and other intellectual property are difficult to keep watch over, given the availability of information on the Internet. Some countries have laws to protect information obtained by electronic contacts. Malaysia has stiff fines and long jail terms for people convicted of illegally accessing computers and using the information that passes through them.

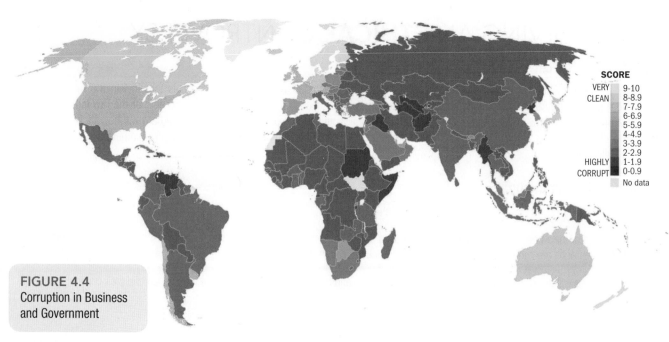

SCORE	
VERY CLEAN	9-10
	8-8.9
	7-7.9
	6-6.9
	5-5.9
	4-4.9
	3-3.9
	2-2.9
HIGHLY CORRUPT	1-1.9
	0-0.9
	No data

FIGURE 4.4
Corruption in Business and Government

Source: Data from Transparency International, "Corruption Perceptions Index 2011," http://www.transparency.org. Copyright 2012 Transparency International: the global coalition against corruption. Used with permission. For more information, visit http://www.transparency.org.

The 2011 Corruption Perceptions Index measures the perceived levels of public sector corruption in 183 countries and territories around the world. Countries are scored from 0 (perceived to be very corrupt) to 10 (perceived to be very clean).

International Regulations

To make international commerce more standard, Canada and many other countries have treaties and signed agreements that describe the expected conduct of international business and protect some of its activities. Canada has entered into many *friendship, commerce, and navigation treaties* with other nations. These treaties describe many aspects of international business relations, including the right to conduct business in the treaty partner's home market. Other international business agreements involve product standards, patents, trademarks, tax policies, export controls, international air travel, and international communications. One area has no international regulations—the use and protection of water supplies. IBM is stepping in to help provide the international community with water-management methods and tools, as we see in the "Going Green" feature.

After China was granted full trade relations with the United States, China agreed to lower its trade barriers, including subsidies that hold down the prices of food exports, restrictions on where foreign law firms can open offices, and taxes charged on imported goods. In exchange for China's promise to halve these taxes, called *tariffs*, the United States granted Chinese businesses access to U.S. markets equal to the access enjoyed by most other countries.

Many rules affect the actions of managers that do business in international markets. Worldwide producers and marketers must keep required minimum levels of quality in all countries where they operate. They must also comply with numerous local regulations. In Britain, advertisers cannot encourage children to engage in unhealthy behaviour such as overeating or skipping regular meals and having candy and snack foods instead. Malaysia's Censorship Board outlaws nudity and swearing on TV. Germany and France let publishers set the prices that retailers charge for books.

The British government is fighting violence against women. It recently commissioned a report that shows children and teens are being increasingly exposed to unhealthy pressures by "hyper-sexualised images" in the media. "They are facing pressures that children in the past simply did not have to face," the report said. One of the pressures is the idea that they need to look "hot" and "sexy." The report suggests that parental controls in new videogame consoles and mobile phones be switched on before they are sold, that men's magazines carry age warnings, and that sexually oriented music videos be broadcast only late in the evening.[18]

IBM HELPS KEEP WATER FLOWING

Did you know it takes 42 litres of water to make one slice of bread, and 133 litres to make a single cup of coffee? Water is one of our greatest resources, but it is under much stress. One in five people worldwide lack access to safe drinking water.

IBM is taking major steps to protect the world's supply of water. Water exists worldwide, but there is no global market for it. There is also very little international or national information about how to conserve water. "Water is about quantity, quality, space, and time," says IBM's Global Innovation Outlook report on the world's water management problems. "Whether you have a big problem or not depends entirely on where you live."

IBM is dealing with the future of water management in several ways. It is setting up meters and sensors that use special IBM software to monitor the capacity and quality of water systems that serve nations, communities, organizations, and individual homes. The company is working to ensure that treated drinking water doesn't come into contact with waste from thousands of kilometres of old underground pipes. IBM's acoustic technology helps to find the worst leaks so they can be repaired right away. IBM is also collecting information on pollution, marine life, and waves for commercial fishermen. It is also working to improve filters that can take arsenic and salt from drinking water for low cost in developing countries.

"We're not going to create water where there is none," says the vice president of IBM's Big Green Innovations. "But where we know water is under stress, we need to monitor what's going on and better manage it."

Questions for Critical Thinking

1. *Fast Company* magazine recently voted IBM 18th in the world in innovation because of IBM's water-management efforts. What makes IBM particularly suitable for this award?

2. IBM is an information services company. What can other socially responsible firms learn from IBM's water-management efforts?

Sources: "Advanced Water Management," www-935.ibm.com, accessed March 23, 2010; "Smarter Water Management," www.ibm.com, accessed March 23, 2010; "Chuck Salter, #18. IBM," *Fast Company*, www.fastcompany.com, February 17, 2010; Mary Tripsas, "Everybody in the Pool of Green Innovation," *New York Times*, www.nytimes.com, November 1, 2009.

Types of Trade Restrictions

Trade restrictions include taxes on imports and complicated administrative procedures. These trade restrictions create additional barriers to international business. They may limit the products and services available to consumers and can increase the costs of foreign-made products. Trade restrictions are also used to protect citizens' security, health, and jobs. A government may limit exports of strategic and defence-related goods to unfriendly countries to protect its country's own security. A government may also ban imports of farm products that have been contaminated by insecticide to protect people's health. Imports are also restricted to protect domestic jobs in the importing country.

Other restrictions are used to promote trade with certain countries. Still other restrictions protect countries from unfair competition. Trade restrictions may be used for different political reasons, but most are in the form of tariffs. Governments also impose some nontariff barriers, also called administrative barriers. These barriers include quotas, embargoes, and exchange controls.

Tariffs

Taxes, surcharges, and duties on foreign products are referred to as **tariffs**. Governments assess two types of tariffs—revenue tariffs and protective tariffs. Both tariffs make imports more expensive for domestic buyers. Revenue tariffs generate income for the government. For example, Canadian leisure travellers who have been outside Canada for 24 to 48 hours can bring back only up to $200 worth of goods free of duty and tax, and after 48 hours or more, $800 worth of goods. Any amounts greater are charged revenue tariffs.[19]

A protective tariff has one purpose: to raise the retail price of imported products to match or top the prices of similar products made in the home country. In other words, protective tariffs try to limit imports and give local competitors an equal chance to succeed.

Tariffs are a disadvantage to companies that want to export to the countries that have the tariffs. Governments do not always agree on the reasons behind protective tariffs. As a result, tariffs do not always have the desired effect. Canada, like most countries, has a tariff on foreign competitors selling products in Canada at prices lower than Canadian manufacturers charge.

tariffs taxes imposed on imported goods.

Nontariff Barriers

Nontariff trade barriers are also called administrative trade barriers. These barriers restrict imports without using the strict rules that tariffs use. Nontariff trade barriers may be in the form of quotas on imports, restrictive standards for imports, and export subsidies. Many countries have recently reduced their tariffs or removed them entirely. These countries can use nontariff barriers to control the flow of imported products.

Quotas limit the amounts of particular products that countries can import during specified time periods. Limits may be set as quantities, such as the number of cars or bushels of wheat. Limits can also be set as values, such as dollars' worth of cigarettes.

quota a limit set on the amounts of particular products that can be imported.

International trade restrictions include *quotas*, or limits, on the amount of a product that can be imported into a country.

dumping selling products in other countries at prices below production costs or below typical prices in the home market to capture market share from domestic competitors.

embargo a total ban on importing specific products or a total stop to trading with a particular country.

exchange control a restriction on importing certain products or a restriction against certain companies to reduce trade and the spending of foreign currency.

Quotas help prevent **dumping**. In one form of dumping, a company sells products in other countries at prices below the cost of production. In another form of dumping, a company exports a large quantity of a product at a lower price than the same product in the home market. This action drives down the price of the domestic product. Dumping benefits domestic consumers in the importing market, but it hurts domestic producers. Dumping is also a way for companies to gain quick entry to foreign markets.

An **embargo** is more severe than a quota. An embargo is a total ban on importing a specified product. It can also be a total stop to trading with a particular country. Many countries, including Canada, have long-standing trade embargoes with North Korea and Iran. Embargo durations can vary depending on changes in foreign policy.

Another form of administrative trade restriction is **exchange control**. A central bank or government agency applies the exchange controls, which affect both exporters and importers. Firms that gain foreign currencies by exporting must sell those currencies to the central bank or another agency. Importers must buy foreign currencies to pay for their purchases from the same agency. The exchange control authority then assigns, expands, or restricts foreign exchange, depending on the national policy.

✓ **ASSESSMENT CHECK**

4.3.1 How can values and attitudes form a barrier to trade, and how can these barriers be overcome?

4.3.2 What is a tariff? What is its purpose?

4.3.3 Why is dumping a problem for companies marketing goods internationally?

REDUCING BARRIERS TO INTERNATIONAL TRADE

Although tariffs and administrative barriers restrict trade, the world is generally moving toward free trade. Several types of organizations ease barriers to international trade, such as groups that monitor trade policies and practices and institutions that offer monetary assistance. The multinational economic community, like the European Union, is another type of federation that is designed to ease trade barriers. This section looks at the roles these organizations play.

Organizations Promoting International Trade

The **General Agreement on Tariffs and Trade (GATT)** is an international trade accord. Since GATT began more than 60 years ago, it has sponsored a series of negotiations, called rounds, which have greatly reduced worldwide tariffs and other barriers. Major industrialized nations founded the multinational organization in 1947. GATT's aim is to work toward reducing tariffs and relaxing import quotas. The last set of completed negotiations—the Uruguay Round—cut average tariffs by one-third, or by more than $700 billion; reduced farm subsidies; and improved protection for copyright and patent holders. Also, international trading rules now apply to various service industries. Finally, the new agreement established the **World Trade Organization (WTO)** to succeed GATT. This organization includes representatives from 157 countries.

General Agreement on Tariffs and Trade (GATT) an international trade accord that has greatly reduced worldwide tariffs and other trade barriers.

World Trade Organization

Since 1995, the WTO has monitored GATT agreements among the member-nations. It has also mediated disputes and continues GATT's aim to reduce trade barriers throughout the world. Unlike the provisions in GATT, the WTO's decisions are final and must be followed by all parties involved in disputes.

World Trade Organization (WTO) a 157-member international institution that monitors GATT agreements and mediates international trade disputes.

The WTO has led to much debate in recent years. Much disagreement has come from WTO decisions that affect working conditions and the environment in member-nations. Many are concerned that the WTO's focus on lowering trade barriers encourages businesses to keep costs down by using methods that may increase both pollution and human rights abuses. Some find it troubling that the organization's member-countries must agree on policies. The problem is that developing countries do not want to lose their low-cost advantage by agreeing to stricter labour and environmental policies. Other critics say that if wealthy firms such as fast-food chains, entertainment companies, and Internet retailers can freely enter foreign markets, they may mean the end of smaller foreign businesses that serve the unique tastes and practices of other countries' cultures.

Trade unions in developed nations complain about the WTO's support of free trade. They say free trade makes it easier to export manufacturing jobs to low-wage countries. Canadian textile manufacturing has just about disappeared. U.S. glassmaking is in a long decline that began in the 1990s, aided by increased imports and bigger profits to be made overseas.[20]

The most recent round of WTO talks was called the Doha Round, after the city in Qatar where it began. After several years of heated discussions and negotiations that fell apart, the eight leading industrial nations recommitted themselves to successfully conclude the talks. The discussion included ways to improve global agricultural trade and trade among developing countries. The leaders worked to reduce domestic price supports, eliminate export subsidies, and improve market access for goods. Such changes can help farmers in developing countries compete in the global marketplace.[21]

World Bank

Soon after the end of World War II, industrialized nations formed an organization to lend money to less developed and developing countries. The **World Bank** primarily funds projects that build or expand nations' infrastructure. These projects include transportation, education, and medical systems and facilities. The World Bank and other development banks provide the largest source of

World Bank an organization established by industrialized nations to lend money to less developed countries.

advice and assistance to developing nations. In exchange for granting loans, the World Bank often sets requirements that are meant to help build the economies of borrower nations.

Some say the World Bank makes loans with conditions that ultimately hurt the borrower nations. When developing nations need to balance government budgets, they are sometimes forced to cut vital social programs. Critics also say that the World Bank should consider the impact of its loans on the environment and working conditions.

International Monetary Fund

International Monetary Fund (IMF) an organization created to promote trade, eliminate barriers, and make short-term loans to member-nations that are unable to meet their budgets.

The **International Monetary Fund (IMF)** was established a year after the World Bank. It was created to promote trade through financial cooperation and, in the process, eliminate barriers. The IMF makes short-term loans to member-nations that cannot meet their expenses. It operates as a lender of last resort for troubled nations. In exchange for these emergency loans, IMF lenders frequently require the borrowing nations to address the problems that led to the crises. These steps may include limiting imports or devaluing currencies. Since it began, the IMF has worked to prevent financial crises by warning the international business community when countries face difficulty meeting their financial obligations. Often, the IMF lends to countries to keep them from defaulting on prior debts. These loans also help to prevent an economic crisis in one country from spreading to other countries.

Some countries owe more money than they can ever hope to repay. The debt payments make it impossible for their governments to deliver desperately needed services to their citizens. After a devastating earthquake in Haiti, the G7 countries (the world's most industrialized nations, including the United States, Canada, and France) promised to cancel any remaining debt owed to them by Haiti. The World Bank not only decided to financially support Haiti but also chose to drop the payments on Haiti's debt for five years. It was also looking for a way to cancel the remaining debt.[22]

International Economic Communities

International economic communities reduce trade barriers and promote working together to create regions that share economic benefits. In the simplest approach, countries may establish a *free-trade area* where they trade freely among themselves without tariffs or trade restrictions. Each country maintains its own tariffs for trade outside this area. A *customs union* sets up a free-trade area and specifies a tariff structure for members' trade with nonmember nations. In a *common market*, or economic union, members go beyond a customs union and try to bring all of their trade rules into agreement.

North American Free Trade Agreement (NAFTA) an agreement among the United States, Canada, and Mexico to break down tariffs and trade restrictions.

One example of a free-trade area is the **North American Free Trade Agreement (NAFTA)** agreed to by the United States, Canada, and Mexico. Other examples of regional trading blocs include the MERCOSUR customs union (joining Brazil, Argentina, Paraguay, and Uruguay) and the 10-country Association of Southeast Asian Nations (ASEAN).

AP Photo/Pablo Martinez Monsivais/The Canadian Press

NAFTA permits free trade for the United States, Canada, and Mexico. The amount of goods and services traded is healthy for the economy both in Canada and in the United States.

NAFTA

NAFTA became effective in 1994. It created the world's largest free-trade zone with the United States, Canada, and Mexico. North America has a combined population of more than 450 million and a total GDP of more than $15 trillion. North America is one of the world's most attractive markets. The United States is the single largest market, and it controls much of North America's business. Although fewer than 1 person in 20 lives in the United States, the nation's more than $14 trillion GDP represents about one-fifth of total world output.[23]

Canada is far less densely populated but has reached a similar level of economic standing. Canada's economy has been growing at a faster rate than the

U.S. economy in recent years. More than two-thirds of Canada's GDP is generated in the services sector. That makes sense because three of every four Canadian workers work in service occupations. Canada's per-capita GDP places it among the top nations in terms of its spending power. Canada's economy is fuelled by trade with the United States, and its home markets are strong. The United States and Canada are each other's biggest trading partners. About 78 percent of Canada's exports and about 53 percent of its imports involve the United States.[24] U.S. business is also attracted to Canada's human resources. For example, all major U.S. automakers have large production facilities in Canada.

Mexico is moving from being a developing nation to gaining industrial nation status, because of NAFTA. Mexico's trade with the United States and Canada has tripled since the signing of NAFTA. But 18 percent of the country's 111 million people live below the poverty line, and Mexico's per-capita income is about a quarter of the per-capita income in the United States. Mexico's border with the United States is busy with a stream of traffic moving goods from Mexican factories into the United States. The United States is Mexico's largest trading partner. The United States receives about 80 percent of Mexico's total exports and supplies almost 50 percent of all Mexico's imports.[25]

United States, Canada, and Mexico got rid of all trade barriers and investment restrictions over a 15-year period. NAFTA opened more doors for free trade. The agreement also eased rules about services, such as banking, and set up standard legal requirements for protecting intellectual property. The three nations can now trade with one another without tariffs or other trade barriers. It is now easier to ship goods across the partners' borders. Standardized customs and labelling regulations create economic efficiencies. They also help to make importing and exporting easier. Trade among the partners has increased. Trade is now more than double what it was before NAFTA took effect.

CAFTA-DR

The **Central America–Dominican Republic Free Trade Agreement (CAFTA-DR)** created a free-trade area among the United States, Costa Rica, the Dominican Republic (the DR of the title), El Salvador, Guatemala, Honduras, and Nicaragua. The agreement ends most tariffs on nearly $33 billion in products traded between the United States and its Latin American neighbours. Agricultural producers such as corn, soybean, and dairy farmers stand to gain under the relaxed trade rules. U.S. sugar producers fought against CAFTA-DR's passage. These sugar producers had been supported by subsidies that kept their prices higher than in the rest of the world. Labour unions complained that the agreement would lower labour standards and export millions more jobs to lower-wage countries. Overall, CAFTA-DR's effects should be positive. It is expected to increase both exports and imports, much as NAFTA did.

Central America–Dominican Republic Free Trade Agreement (CAFTA-DR) an agreement among the United States, Costa Rica, the Dominican Republic, El Salvador, Guatemala, Honduras, and Nicaragua to reduce tariffs and trade restrictions.

European Union

The best-known example of a common market is the **European Union (EU)**. The EU combines 27 countries, nearly 500 million people, and a total GDP of roughly $12.28 trillion to form a huge common market.[26] As Figure 4.5 shows, 12 countries are the latest EU members—Cyprus, Malta, Estonia,

European Union (EU) a 27-nation European economic alliance.

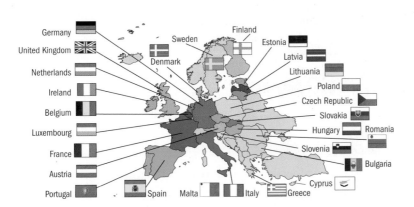

FIGURE 4.5 The 27 Nations of the European Union

Latvia, Lithuania, Hungary, Poland, the Czech Republic, Slovakia, Slovenia, Bulgaria, and Romania. The Treaty of Lisbon took effect in 2009. Its goal is to make the union governance more efficient.

The EU's goals are to promote economic and social progress, to introduce European citizenship as a complement to national citizenship, and to give the EU a major role in international affairs. To achieve its goal of a borderless Europe, the EU is first removing barriers to free trade among its members. This highly complex process involves standardizing business regulations and requirements, standardizing import duties and taxes, and getting rid of customs checks so that companies can transport goods from England to Italy or Poland as easily as goods can be moved from St. John's to Vancouver.

Bringing standards and laws together can contribute to economic growth. But NAFTA had scared people in Canada and the United States who weren't sure about free trade with Mexico. Some people in Western Europe feel the same. They are worried that opening trade with such countries as Poland, Hungary, and the Czech Republic will cause jobs to flow to those lower-wage economies.

The EU also introduced the euro to replace currencies such as the French franc and Italian lira. For the 17 member-states that have adopted the euro, potential benefits include eliminating the economic costs of currency exchange and simplifying price comparisons. Businesses and their customers now make cheque and credit-card transactions in euros and use euro notes and coins in making cash purchases.

✔ ASSESSMENT CHECK

4.4.1 What international trade organization succeeded GATT, and what is its goal?

4.4.2 Compare and contrast the goals of the World Bank and the International Monetary Fund.

4.4.3 What are the goals of the European Union, and how do these goals promote international trade?

LO 4.5 Compare the different levels of involvement used by businesses when entering global markets.

GOING GLOBAL

Expanding into overseas markets can increase profits and marketing opportunities. It can also make a firm's business operations more complex. Before deciding to go global, a company must make many key decisions. These are the first decisions to be made:

- which foreign market(s) to enter
- the costs of entering a new market
- the best way to organize the overseas operations.

These issues have more or less importance depending on the level of involvement a company chooses. Education and employee training in the host country are much more important for an electronics manufacturer building an Asian factory than for a firm that plans to export Canadian-made products.

Before deciding which markets to enter, companies usually take time to do research. This research focuses on local demand for the firm's products, availability of needed resources, and ability of the local workforce to make world-class, quality products. Other factors are existing and potential competition, tariff rates, currency stability, and investment barriers. Government and other sources can help this research process. A good starting place is the CIA's *World Factbook*. It contains country-by-country information on geography, population, government, economy, and infrastructure.

Foreign Affairs and International Trade Canada and the U.S. Department of Commerce have counsellors who work at district offices. These counsellors offer a full range of international business advice, including computerized market data and names of business and government contacts in dozens of countries. As Table 4.2 shows, the Internet provides access to many resources for international trade information.

Levels of Involvement

After a firm has completed its research and has decided to do business overseas, it can choose one or more strategies:

- exporting or importing
- entering into contract-based agreements such as franchising, licensing, and subcontracting deals
- choosing direct investment in the foreign market through acquisitions, joint ventures, or by setting up an overseas division.

Table 4.2 International Trade Research Resources on the Internet

WEBSITE AND ADDRESS	GENERAL DESCRIPTION
Foreign Affairs and International Trade Canada http://www.international.gc.ca/	Gateway to Canadian international trade and foreign activities involving businesses
BusinessWeek – Asia http://www.businessweek.com/global-economics/asia	Business news in Asia, featuring articles on Asian countries from India to Japan
Europages http://www.europages.com	Directory of and links to Europe's top 500,000 companies in 33 European countries
World Trade Organization http://www.wto.int	Details on the trade policies of various governments
CIA *World Factbook* https://www.cia.gov/ library/ publications/the-world-factbook	Basic facts about the world's nations, from geography to economic conditions
STAT- USA http://www.usa.gov/Topics/Reference-Shelf/Data.shtml	Extensive trade and economic data, information about trends, daily intelligence reports, and background data (access requires paid subscription to the service)
The Canadian Trade Commissioner Service http://www.tradecommissioner.gc.ca/eng/home.jsp	Valuable information that will help companies prepare an export plan and develop a market entry strategy. Foreign Affairs and International Trade Canada's trade commissioners, located in more than 150 cities worldwide, can help implement strategies and provide advice on how to take advantage of international business opportunities.
Canadian Trade Data Online http://www.ic.gc.ca/eic/site/ic1.nsf/eng/home	Customized reports can be generated on Canada and U.S. trade in goods with over 200 countries.
Canada's Gateways http://www.canadasgateways.gc.ca/index2.html	Information on Canada's National Policy Framework for Strategic Gateways and Trade Corridors, which supports strategies to strengthen Canada's position in international commerce. Here you will find links to Canada's three main Gateway and Corridor Initiatives and information on Foreign Trade Zones.

The company's risk increases with the level of its global involvement. But its overall control of all aspects of producing and selling its goods or services also increases.

Importers and Exporters

An importer is a firm that brings in goods produced abroad to sell at home. Exporters are companies that produce or purchase goods at home and sell them in other countries. An importing or exporting strategy provides the most basic level of international involvement and the least risk and control.

Exports are often handled by export trading companies. These firms search out competitively priced local merchandise. They then resell these items abroad at prices high enough to cover expenses and earn profits. Suppose a retail chain such as Pier 1 Imports wants to purchase West African products to sell in its stores. It may contact an export trading company that deals in a country such as Ghana. The local firm monitors the quality of goods, packs the order for overseas shipment, arranges transportation, and completes customs paperwork and other steps to move the product from Ghana to Canada.

Exporting can be one of two types: indirect or direct. A company uses *indirect exporting* when it makes a product, such as an electronic component, that becomes part of another product sold in foreign markets. The second method is *direct exporting*. This type of exporting occurs when a company tries to sell its products in markets outside its own country. Direct exporting is often the first step for companies entering foreign markets. It is also the most common form of international business. Firms that succeed at direct exporting may then move on to other strategies.

Export trading companies are one way to reach foreign markets. Two other methods are to use export management companies or offset agreements. An *export management company* can give an exporting firm advice and expertise. These international specialists help the exporter to complete paperwork, make contacts with local buyers, and comply with local laws for labelling, product safety, and performance testing. The exporting firm retains more control than it would if it used an export trading company.

An *offset agreement* matches a major international firm with a smaller business. The smaller firm basically becomes a subcontractor to the larger firm. For example, Bombardier might contract with a small American supplier of electrical cables used to manufacture aircraft made in Canada and exported to the U.S. Both firms benefit from the agreement and the smaller firm can often gain international experience.

Countertrade

countertrade a barter agreement whereby trade between two or more nations involves payment made in the form of local products instead of currency.

International trade often involves payments made in the form of local products, not currency. This system of international bartering agreements is called **countertrade**.

A common reason for using international barter is poor access to the needed foreign currency. To complete an international sales agreement, the seller may agree to accept part or all of the purchase cost in merchandise instead of in currency. The seller may try to find a buyer for the bartered goods before the transaction is completed. To make this task easier, several international buyers and sellers sometimes join together in a single agreement.

Countertrade is sometimes a firm's only way to enter a certain market. Many developing countries simply cannot get enough credit or financial help to afford the imports that their people want. Countries that have heavy debt also use countertrade. Russian buyers sometimes find their currency is less acceptable to foreign traders than the stronger currencies of the United States, Great Britain, Japan, and EU countries. Thus, Russian buyers may trade local products, ranging from crude oil to diamonds to vodka. These products become the payments when the foreign companies selling goods do not want to receive Russian rubles. Other countries, such as China, may restrict imports. For those countries, countertrade may be the only practical way to get government approval to import needed products.

Contract-based Agreements

After a company gains some experience in international sales, it may decide to enter into contract-based agreements with local parties. These agreements can include franchising, foreign licensing, and subcontracting.

franchise a contract-based agreement in which a franchisee can produce and/or sell the franchisor's products under that company's brand name if the franchisee agrees to the operating terms and requirements.

Franchising   Franchising is common among Canadian and U.S. companies. Franchising can also work well for companies that want to expand into international markets. A **franchise** is a contract-based agreement in which a wholesaler or retailer (the franchisee) can sell the franchisor's products under that company's brand name if the franchisee agrees to the operating terms and requirements. The franchisor also helps the franchisee with marketing, management, and business services. Franchises are common in the leading fast-food brands, such as Tim Hortons and McDonald's. In 1995, Tim Hortons merged with Wendy's International, Inc., which helped Tim Hortons to gain entry into the United States. Tim Hortons can be found in Michigan, Maine, Connecticut, Ohio, West Virginia, Kentucky, Pennsylvania, Rhode Island, Massachusetts, and New York. Tim Hortons' Canadian operation is 95 percent franchise-owned and -operated. The company plans to use the same strategy in the United States as it opens more locations there. Currently, Tim Hortons has more than 3,000 restaurants across Canada and more than 600 locations in the United States.[27] Franchising is described in detail in Chapter 5.

foreign licensing agreement international agreement in which one firm allows another firm to produce or sell its product, or use its trademark, patent, or manufacturing processes, in a specific geographical area, in return for royalties or other compensation.

Foreign Licensing   In a **foreign licensing agreement**, one firm allows another firm to produce or sell its product, or use its trademark, patent, or manufacturing processes, in a specific geographical area. In return, the firm receives a royalty or other compensation.

Licensing can be good for a small manufacturer that wants to launch a well-known product overseas. The small manufacturer gets a proven product from another market, and just a little or no investment is needed to start operating. Licensing can also allow a company entry into a market that would otherwise be closed to imports due to government restrictions. Sometimes a licensing agreement can ensure product freshness by allowing manufacturing to take place in the local market. Morinaga, a Japanese food manufacturer, holds licences to produce Lipton teas, Kraft cheeses, and Sunkist fruit drinks and desserts in Japan.[28]

Subcontracting   The third type of contract-based agreement is **subcontracting**. This agreement involves hiring local companies to produce, distribute, or sell goods or services. Subcontracting allows a foreign firm to use the subcontractor's expertise in local culture, contacts, and regulations. Subcontracting works equally well for mail-order companies. They can hire local businesses to fill the orders and to serve customers. Manufacturers use subcontracting to save money on import duties and labour costs. Businesses choose to subcontract to market products that are best sold by locals in a given country.

The key downside of subcontracting is that companies cannot always control their subcontractors' business practices. Several major companies have been embarrassed by reports that their subcontractors used child labour to manufacture clothing.

> **subcontracting** an agreement that involves hiring other companies to produce, distribute, or sell goods or services; in international subcontracting, local companies in a specific country or geographical region are hired to produce, distribute, or sell goods or services.

Offshoring

Offshoring is not generally considered to be a way of starting business internationally. *Offshoring* is the moving of business processes to a lower-cost location overseas. It has become a widespread practice. China is the preferred location for production offshoring. India is the preferred location for services offshoring. Many business leaders support offshoring. They believe that global firms must keep their costs as low as possible to stay competitive. The apparent link between jobs sent overseas and jobs lost at home has led to much debate about offshoring.

Offshoring shows no signs of slowing down. But it is changing, mostly for manufacturers. Mexico, India, and Vietnam are now the countries with the lowest manufacturing costs. "There was huge momentum and almost herd behaviour around going to China back in 2005 or 2006," says one consultant. "China was more competitive than other low-cost countries and had more infrastructure. Now, some of that has changed. Rising transportation costs and material costs, which hurt China in 2007 and 2008, applied to a much lesser degree in Mexico." If companies are setting up factories abroad to sell to foreign markets, offshoring may make some sense. But it doesn't make sense to make heavy or bulky products abroad and then ship them to North American markets. The time needed to move the goods is also a factor. Offshoring to a few different low-cost locations may be an international firm's lowest-risk strategy. "If the rupee strengthens," says the consultant, "you can shift some work to Vietnam. If transportation costs go crazy, you can move some more work to Mexico."[29]

International Direct Investment

The highest level of control is investing directly in another country's production and marketing. Over time, a firm may become successful at doing business in other countries through exporting and contract-based agreements. Its managers may then decide to start manufacturing in those countries, open branch offices, or buy ownership in local companies. A good example is Toyota. It makes cars in countries outside Japan, including in Canada and the United States. See the "Hit & Miss" feature for a description of Toyota's recent public relations troubles when it recalled millions of cars.

In an *acquisition*, a company purchases another firm in the host country. An acquisition means a mostly domestic business operation can quickly become an international company. The big U.S. retailer Target recently paid $1.8 billion to Hudson Bay Co. to acquire Canadian retailer Zellers. Target gained a quick entry to prime locations in the Canadian market. Some Zellers stores will be closed. But others will be updated to become part of the highly successful Target chain. Canadian shoppers no longer need to cross the border to shop at Target.[30]

In a **joint venture**, a company shares risks, costs, profits, and management responsibilities with one or more host-country companies. By setting up an *overseas division*, a company can do much of its business overseas. This strategy differs from a multinational company's strategy. A firm with overseas divisions stays primarily a domestic organization with international operations. Matsushita established Panasonic Automotive Systems Asia Pacific to develop and sell new technology products in India, Thailand, Indonesia, Malaysia, the Philippines, and Vietnam.

> **joint venture** a partnership between companies for a specific activity.

HIT & MISS

Toyota's Recall Woes

Toyota Motor Company had huge growth in the last decade. It doubled its production capacity while trying to become the world's top automaker. Rapid growth doesn't excuse the recent recall of millions of Toyotas worldwide due to possible faulty accelerator pedals. But rapid growth could help explain why the public relations part of the recall made the company stumble so badly. Extensive research by Toyota, the U.S. Congress, NASA, and the U.S. Department of Transportation's National Highway Traffic Safety Administration (NHTSA) unit found some accelerator pedal mechanisms stuck under specific temperature and humidity conditions. The mechanism remained at about 15 percent of full throttle because moisture prevented a smooth return action. But, overall, the problems were traced to human error. The problem was mostly that owners inserted unsuitable floor mats that interfered with the proper working of the pedals. Toyota seemed to have a hard time handling the concerns raised by their dealers, customers, and potential customers. "What they did this week, they should've done last … You want to rip off that Band-Aid all at once," said one public relations expert. But Toyota first denied the accelerator pedals had mechanical problems. It insisted that customers had incorrectly installed their floor mats so they interfered with the pedals. Even when the problem became clear, Toyota was slow to react. Customers were left confused and angry—as they waited for more information and repairs.

Finally CEO Akio Toyoda told the world, "I apologize from the bottom of my heart for all the concern that we have given to so many of our customers." Writing in the *Washington Post*, he also said, "We have not lived up to the high standards you have come to expect from us. I am deeply disappointed by that and apologize. As the president of Toyota, I take personal responsibility."

Time will tell whether the world's number-one automaker can recover from what one observer called "the worst-handled auto recall in history." The recall will cost Toyota more than $2 billion in repairs and lost sales.

Questions for Critical Thinking

1. Do you think Toyota could have or should have used social media like Twitter and Facebook to alert customers about the problem and solution? Why or why not?

2. Why do you think Toyota's CEO felt he had to apologize? What effect do you think his actions had on Toyota owners?

Sources: CBSNews.com, "Toyota Recall Recap: Floormats, Sticky Pedals, AND User Error," February 28, 2011, http://newyork.cbslocal.com/2011/02/28/toyota-recall-recap-floormats-sticky-pedals-and-user-error/, accessed March 04, 2011; Bill Saporito, "Behind the Troubles at Toyota," *Time*, www.time.com, February 11, 2010; "Toyota's Recall Woes," editorial, *New York Times*, www.nytimes.com, February 9, 2010; Matthew Phillips, "Toyota's Digital Disaster," *Newsweek*, www.newsweek.com, February 3, 2010.

---

multinational corporation (MNC) a firm with many operations and marketing activities outside its home country.

✓ ASSESSMENT CHECK

4.5.1 Name three possible strategies for beginning overseas operations.

4.5.2 What is countertrade?

4.5.3 Compare and contrast licensing and subcontracting.

4.5.4 Describe joint ventures.

LO 4.6 Distinguish between a global business strategy and a multidomestic business strategy.

From Multinational Corporation to Global Business

A **multinational corporation (MNC)** is an organization with many foreign operations. Table 4.3 shows China with two companies on the list, and the United Kingdom, Brazil, and the Netherlands each have one company on the list.

Many U.S. multinationals, including Nike and Walmart, have expanded their overseas operations. They believe that domestic markets are peaking, and foreign markets offer greater potential for sales and profit. Other MNCs are making large investments in developing countries, partly because these countries provide low-cost labour compared with the wages in North America and Western Europe. In addition, many MNCs are locating high-tech facilities in countries that have large numbers of technical school graduates.

DEVELOPING A STRATEGY FOR INTERNATIONAL BUSINESS

Managers need to develop a framework from which to conduct international business. But managers must first evaluate their corporate objectives, organizational strengths and weaknesses, and strategies for product development and marketing. They can choose to combine these elements in either a global strategy or a multidomestic strategy.

Table 4.3 The World's Top 10 Leading Companies (Based on a Combined Ranking for Sales, Profits, Assets, and Market Value)

RANK	COMPANY	BUSINESS	COUNTRY OF ORIGIN
1	JPMorgan Chase	Banking	United States
2	HSBC Holdings	Banking	United Kingdom
3	General Electric	Conglomerate	United States
4	ExxonMobil	Oil and gas operations	United States
5	Royal Dutch Shell	Oil and gas operations	Netherlands
6	PetroChina	Oil and gas operations	China
7	ICBC	Banking	China
8	Berkshire Hathaway	Investment Services	United States
8	Petrobras-Petroleo Brasil	Oil and gas operations	Brazil
10	Citigroup	Banking	United States

Source: "The Global 2000," *Forbes*, http://www.forbes.com/global2000, accessed March 30, 2012.

Global Business Strategies

In a **global business strategy** (or a *standardization strategy*), a firm sells the same product in basically the same way all over the world. Many companies simply change their domestic business strategies by translating promotional brochures and instructions into the languages of the host nations.

A global marketing perspective can be suitable for some goods and services and for market segments that are common to many nations. The approach works for products with nearly universal appeal, for luxury items such as jewellery and for commodities such as chemicals and metals. Alcoa, for example, is the world's biggest producer of aluminum for use in aerospace and automotive building and construction, consumer electronics, packaging, and commercial transportation. In many applications, aluminum's strength and light weight mean there are no good substitutes for it. The company forecasts a long-term increase in global demand, especially in China, India, Russia, the Middle East, and Latin America. It also sees itself as committed to a global strategy that blends sustainability. That means it will "build financial success, environmental excellence, and social responsibility through partnerships in order to deliver net long-term benefits to our shareowners, employees, customers, suppliers, and the communities in which we operate."[31]

global business strategy the offering of a standardized, worldwide product and the selling of it in basically the same way throughout a firm's domestic and foreign markets.

multidomestic business strategy a plan to develop and market products to serve different needs and tastes in separate national markets.

Multidomestic Business Strategies

In a **multidomestic business strategy** (or an *adaptation strategy*), the firm treats each national market in a different way. It develops products and marketing strategies that appeal to the customs, tastes, and buying habits of specific national markets. Some companies do not change their strategy for different markets. These companies don't pay attention to the global nature of the Internet, which can cause problems for potential customers. For example, European consumers were slow to order products online. But Internet use in Western Europe has had huge growth. All types of companies have seen increases in the number of website visitors and in their Internet revenues.

 ASSESSMENT CHECK

4.6.1 What is a global business strategy? What are its advantages?

4.6.2 What is a multidomestic business strategy? What are its advantages?

WHAT'S AHEAD

The examples in this chapter show that both large and small businesses rely on world trade, not just major corporations. Chapter 5 looks at the special advantages and challenges facing small-business owners. A critical decision facing any new business is choosing the most suitable form of business ownership. Chapter 5 also looks at the major ownership structures—sole proprietorship, partnership, and corporation—and measures the pros and cons of each. The chapter closes by discussing recent trends affecting business ownership, such as the growing impact of franchising and business consolidations through mergers and acquisitions.

Internet users in Western Europe now make online purchases for such items as railroad tickets. This businesswoman enjoys being able to work on the train. She may be using her online connection to purchase her return ticket.

RETURN TO INSIDE BUSINESS

PotashCorp: Genesis for economic development

PotashCorp is a good example of a resource business that has a comparative advantage. Canadian mines are very profitable operating at today's commodity prices. The firm can expand globally by using its expertise at other mines around the world. As mentioned earlier, potash is a commodity, which means the product is the same whether it comes from this mine or that mine. That means PotashCorp can sell potash throughout its distribution network. International mining firms sometimes merge or acquire other firms to grow the business and increase profits. PotashCorp was the object of a takeover bid by Australian mining giant BHP Billiton, which also operates in Saskatchewan.

QUESTIONS FOR CRITICAL THINKING

1. What are the upsides and downsides to a company that sells a commodity in competitive international markets?

2. Is PotashCorp an MNC or an global business?

SUMMARY OF LEARNING OBJECTIVES

LO 4.1 Explain the importance of international business and the primary reasons nations trade, and discuss the concepts of absolute and comparative advantage in international trade.

The world's economies are becoming increasingly global. That means Canadian and other foreign businesses have opportunities to expand into new markets for their goods and services. Doing business globally provides new sources of materials and labour. Trading with other countries reduces a company's dependence on economic conditions in its home market. Countries that encourage international trade usually have higher levels of economic activity, employment, and wages than countries that restrict international trade.

Nations usually benefit if they specialize in producing certain goods or services. A country has an absolute advantage if it holds a monopoly or if it produces a good or service at a lower cost than other nations. It has a comparative advantage if it can supply one product more efficiently or at a lower cost than it can produce other products.

✓ ASSESSMENT CHECK ANSWERS

4.1.1 Why do nations trade? Nations trade because trading increases economic growth. Trade provides a new market for products and access to needed resources. Trading makes production and distribution systems more efficient and reduces dependence on the economy of the domestic market.

4.1.2 What are some measures of the size of the international marketplace? Developing countries have lower per-capita incomes than developed nations in North America and Western Europe, but developing nations have populations that are large and growing. China's population is about 1.3 billion and India's is roughly 1.1 billion.

4.1.3 How does a nation acquire a comparative advantage? A nation has a comparative advantage when it can supply a product more efficiently and at a lower price than it can supply other goods, compared with the outputs of other countries.

LO 4.2 Describe how nations measure international trade and the significance of exchange rates.

Countries measure their level of international trade by comparing exports and imports. They then calculate whether they have a trade surplus or a trade deficit. The balance of trade is the difference between a country's exports and its imports. The term *balance of payments* refers to the overall flow of money into or out of a country. It includes overseas loans and borrowing, international investments, and profits from such investments. An exchange rate is the value of one country's currency in terms of the currency of another country. Currency values fluctuate, or "float," depending on the supply and demand for each currency in the world market. When the value of the dollar falls compared with other currencies, the cost paid by foreign businesses and households for Canadian products declines, and demand for exports may rise. An increase in the value of the dollar raises the prices of Canadian products sold abroad, but it reduces the prices of foreign products sold in Canada.

✓ ASSESSMENT CHECK ANSWERS

4.2.1 Compare balance of trade and balance of payments. Balance of trade is the difference between exports and imports; balance of payments is the overall flow of money into or out of a country.

4.2.2 Explain the function of an exchange rate. A nation's exchange rate is the rate at which its currency can be exchanged for the currencies of other nations. An exchange rate makes it easier for countries with different currencies to trade with each another.

4.2.3 What happens when a currency is devalued? Devaluation is a reduction in a currency's value in terms of other currencies or in terms of a fixed standard.

LO 4.3 Identify the major barriers that confront global businesses.

Businesses face several barriers in the global marketplace. Companies that operate in other countries need to be sensitive to social and cultural differences, such as languages, values, and religions. Economic differences include standard-of-living variations and levels of infrastructure development. Legal and political barriers are difficult to judge. Each country sets its own laws for business practices. Trade restrictions such as tariffs and administrative barriers are also barriers to international business.

 ASSESSMENT CHECK ANSWERS

4.3.1 How can values and attitudes form a barrier to trade, and how can these barriers be overcome? Marked differences in values and attitudes, such as religious attitudes, can form barriers between traditionally capitalist countries and countries adapting new capitalist systems. Many of these barriers can be overcome by learning about the values and attitudes in other cultures and by respecting such differences.

4.3.2 What is a tariff? What is its purpose? A tariff is a surcharge or duty charged on foreign products. Its purpose is to protect domestic producers of those items.

4.3.3 Why is dumping a problem for companies marketing goods internationally? Dumping is selling products in other countries at prices below production costs or below typical prices in the home market. Dumping decreases the cost of products in the market where they are dumped. Thus, dumping hurts the domestic producers of those products.

LO 4.4 Explain how international trade organizations and economic communities reduce barriers to international trade.

Many international organizations try to promote international trade by reducing trade barriers among nations. Some of these organizations are the World Trade Organization, the World Bank, and the International Monetary Fund. Multinational economic communities create partnerships to remove barriers to the flow of goods, capital, and people across the borders of its member-countries. Three economic agreements are the North American Free Trade Agreement, CAFTA-DR, and the European Union.

 ASSESSMENT CHECK ANSWERS

4.4.1 What international trade organization succeeded GATT, and what is its goal? The World Trade Organization (WTO) succeeded GATT. Its goals are to monitor GATT agreements, mediate disputes, and to continue GATT's aim to reduce trade barriers throughout the world.

4.4.2 Compare and contrast the goals of the World Bank and the International Monetary Fund. The World Bank funds projects that build or expand nations' infrastructure. These projects include transportation, education, and medical systems and facilities. The International Monetary Fund makes short-term loans to member-nations that cannot meet their expenses. The fund operates as a lender of last resort for troubled nations.

4.4.3 What are the goals of the European Union, and how do these goals promote international trade? The European Union's goals are to promote economic and social progress, to introduce European citizenship as a complement to national citizenship, and to give the EU a major role in international affairs. Bringing standards and laws together can contribute to international trade and economic growth.

LO 4.5 Compare the different levels of involvement used by businesses when entering global markets.

The first level of involvement in international business is exporting and importing. This strategy involves the lowest degree of both risk and control. Companies may use export trading companies or management companies to help distribute their products. Other options are contract-based agreements, such as franchising, foreign licensing, and subcontracting. Franchising and licensing are especially suitable for services. Companies may also use local subcontractors to produce goods for local sales. The highest level of control is investing directly in another country's production and marketing, known as international direct investment. This strategy also has the greatest risk. Firms make direct investments by acquiring foreign companies or facilities, forming joint ventures with local firms, or setting up their own overseas divisions.

 ASSESSMENT CHECK ANSWERS

4.5.1 Name three possible strategies for beginning overseas operations. Three strategies are exporting or importing; using contract-based agreements such as franchising, licensing, or subcontracting; and making direct investments in foreign markets through acquisition, joint venture, or setting up an overseas division.

4.5.2 What is countertrade? Countertrade is an agreement to make payments in the form of local products, not in currency.

4.5.3 Compare and contrast licensing and subcontracting. In a foreign licensing agreement, one firm allows another firm to produce or sell its product or use its trademark, patent, or manufacturing process in a specific geographical area. In return, the firm receives royalty payments or other compensation. In international subcontracting, a firm hires local companies in other countries to produce, distribute, or sell its goods and services.

4.5.4 Describe joint ventures. In a joint venture, a company shares risks, costs, profits, and management responsibilities with one or more host-country companies.

LO 4.6 Distinguish between a global business strategy and a multidomestic business strategy.

A company that adopts a global strategy (or a standardization strategy) develops a single, standardized product and marketing strategy for worldwide sales. The firm sells the same product in basically the same way in all countries where it operates. Under a multidomestic strategy (or an adaptation strategy), the firm treats each foreign market in a different way. It develops products and marketing strategies that appeal to the customs, tastes, and buying habits of specific nations.

✓ **ASSESSMENT CHECK ANSWERS**

4.6.1 What is a global business strategy? What are its advantages? A global business strategy is a standardized competitive strategy. The firm sells the same product in basically the same way all over the world. This strategy works well for goods and services that are common to many nations. The firm can market the products to many countries without making many changes.

4.6.2 What is a multidomestic business strategy? What are its advantages? In a multidomestic business strategy, the firm treats each foreign market in a different way. The firm tries to appeal to the customs, tastes, and buying habits of specific national markets. This strategy allows the firm to change its marketing appeals to suit individual cultures or areas.

BUSINESS TERMS YOU NEED TO KNOW

exports 94

imports 94

balance of trade 97

balance of payments 98

exchange rate 99

devaluation 100

infrastructure 103

tariffs 107

quota 108

dumping 108

embargo 108

exchange control 108

General Agreement on Tariffs and Trade (GATT) 109

World Trade Organization (WTO) 109

World Bank 109

International Monetary Fund (IMF) 110

North American Free Trade Agreement (NAFTA) 110

Central America–Dominican Republic Free Trade Agreement (CAFTA-DR) 111

European Union (EU) 111

countertrade 114

franchise 114

foreign licensing agreement 114

subcontracting 115

joint venture 115

multinational corporation (MNC) 116

global business strategy 117

multidomestic business strategy 117

REVIEW QUESTIONS

1. How does a business decide whether to trade with a foreign country? What are the key factors for participating in the information economy on a global basis?

2. Why are developing countries such as China and India becoming important international markets?

3. What is the difference between absolute advantage and comparative advantage? Give an example of each.

4. Can a nation have a favourable balance of trade and an unfavourable balance of payments? Why or why not?

5. Identify several potential barriers to communication when a company attempts to do business in another country. How might these be overcome?

6. Identify and describe briefly the three dimensions of the legal environment for global business.

7. What are the major nontariff restrictions affecting international business? Describe the difference between tariff and nontariff restrictions.

8. What is NAFTA? How does it work?

9. How has the EU helped trade among European businesses?

10. What are the key choices a company must make before reaching the final decision to go global?

PROJECTS AND TEAMWORK APPLICATIONS

1. In 1997, Britain transferred Hong Kong to China. China agreed to grant Hong Kong a high degree of autonomy as a capitalist economy for 50 years. Do you think this agreement is holding up? Why or why not? Consider China's economy, population, infrastructure, and other factors in your answer.

2. The huge growth of online business has introduced new legal concerns for international business. Patents, brand names, copyrights, and trademarks are difficult to monitor because of the Internet has no boundaries. What steps can businesses take to protect their trademarks and brands online? Come up with at least five suggestions. Compare your list with your classmates' lists.

3. The WTO monitors GATT agreements, mediates disputes, and continues the effort to reduce trade barriers all over world. But many are concerned that the WTO's focus on lowering trade barriers encourages businesses to keep costs down by using methods that may lead to pollution and human rights abuses. Others argue that human rights should not be linked to international business. Do you think environmental and human rights issues should be linked to trade? Why or why not?

4. Describe briefly the EU and its goals. What are the pros and cons of the EU? Do you think the European alliance will hold up over the next 20 years? Why or why not?

5. Find the most recent edition of "The *Fortune* Global 500." It is usually published in *Fortune* magazine in late July or early August. You can also go to *Fortune*'s online version at http://money.cnn.com/magazines/fortune/global500. Use the Global 500 to answer the following questions.

    a. On what is the Global 500 ranking based (e.g., profits, number of employees, revenues)?

    b. List the home countries of the world's 10 largest corporations.

    c. For the following industry classifications identify the top-ranked company, its Global 500 ranking, and country: Food and Drug Stores; Industrial and Farm Equipment; Petroleum Refining; Utilities: Gas and Electric; Telecommunications; Pharmaceuticals.

WEB ASSIGNMENTS

1. **WTO.** Visit the website of the World Trade Organization (http://www.wto.org). Research two current trade disputes. Which countries and products are involved? Do the two disputes have anything in common? What steps does the WTO follow to resolve trade disputes between member-countries?

2. **EU.** Europa.eu is the Web portal for the European Union. Go to the following website (http://europa.eu/index_en.htm) and answer the following questions:

    a. What steps must a country take to become a member of the EU?

    b. How many EU members have adopted the euro? Which countries will be adopting the euro over the next few years?

    c. What is the combined GDP of EU members? Which EU member has the largest GDP? Which has the smallest GDP?

3. **Nestlé.** Nestlé is one of the world's largest global corporations. Visit the firm's website (http://www.nestle.com). Where is the company headquartered? What are some of its best-known brands? Are these brands sold in specific countries, or are they sold worldwide? List three or four issues Nestlé faces as a global corporation.

Access your WileyPLUS course for:

- The complete digital textbook.

- Question assistance, including links to relevant sections in the online digital textbook.

- Immediate feedback and proof of progress, 24/7

- Integrated, multi-media resources – including MP3 downloads, visual exhibits, animations, and much more – that provide multiple study paths and encourage more active learning.

QUIZ YOURSELF

Note: Internet Web addresses change frequently. If you do not find the exact sites listed, you may need to access the organization's or company's home page and search from there or use a search engine such as Bing or Google.

1 LAUNCHING YOUR . . .

GLOBAL BUSINESS AND ECONOMICS CAREER

In Part 1, "Business in a Global Environment," you learned about the role of contemporary business in today's society. You also learned about the major forces that shape contemporary business. The part includes four chapters that discuss the changing face of business, business ethics and social responsibility, economic challenges facing contemporary business, and competing in world markets. Business has always been an exciting career field. You can choose to start your own company, work at a local business, or take a position with a multinational corporation. Today's business opportunities are very attractive. Businesses are expanding to compete in a global economy—and they need loyal and talented people to help them reach their goals. Professional and business service jobs are found in some of the fastest-growing industries in the North American economy. These jobs are projected to grow by more than 23 percent over a decade.[1] Now is the time to learn about several career options that can lead you to your dream job. Each part in this text includes a profile of some of the many opportunities available in business. Here are a few opportunities related to Chapters 1 through 4.

If you're good at numbers and are interested in how societies and companies work, then you may be suited to a career as an *economist*. Economists study how resources are divided up, research information by collecting and studying data, watch economic trends, and develop forecasts. Economists study the cost of energy, foreign trade and exchange between countries, the effect of taxes, and employment levels—both from a national or global viewpoint and from the viewpoint of individual businesses. Some economists work for corporations to help them run more efficiently. Others work for consulting firms to offer their special knowledge, or for government agencies to oversee economic decision-making. Usually, economists need advanced degrees to work in top-level positions. Economists usually earn more than $80,000 per year.[2]

Are you interested in global business? Many companies search the world for the best employees, supplies, and markets. You could work in Canada for a foreign-based firm such as Nokia or Toyota. Or, you could work in Australia, Asia, Europe, or Latin America for a Canadian-based firm such as Royal Bank of Canada. You could also use computer networks to work with overseas coworkers to develop new products for a firm such as General Electric. Today's technology and telecommunications mean that distance is no longer a barrier to doing business. Global business careers can be found in all the areas you will read about in this text—business ownership, management, marketing, technology, and finance.

Global business leaders are not born, they're made. So how can you start on that career path? Businesses consider three areas when hiring employees for overseas assignments:

- *competence*—technical knowledge, language skills, leadership ability, experience, and past performance

- *adaptability*—interest in overseas work, communication skills and other personal skills, empathy for other cultures, and appreciation for varied management styles and work environments

- *personal characteristics*—education, experience, and social compatibility with the host country.[3]

Solid experience in your field or company is the most needed skill. Firms want employees who are skilled in their business and are loyal to the firm. Only the best are hired to represent the firms overseas. People who obtain their master's of business administration (MBA) degree are doing well financially: in a recent year, the average salary for MBA graduates a few years out of school was $126,000.[4] Companies don't usually want to send new graduates overseas immediately. Instead, they invest in training to make sure employees are suited to the new assignment.

The second-highest skill that companies look for is two-fold: knowledge of and interest in other languages and cultures. Businesspeople need to be able to work smoothly in another society, so they are selected for their abilities with other languages and cultures. China is a business hotspot, so some people have become fluent in Mandarin Chinese to increase their career prospects. Some school systems offer Chinese language classes in addition to the standard offerings of French, German, and Spanish.

Finally, employees are assessed on their personal characteristics. After all, firm want to be certain that employees will fit well in their new country. A person's talent is still the most important factor when assigning work, but executives with cross-cultural skills are in high demand.[5]

CAREER ASSESSMENT EXERCISES IN ECONOMICS AND GLOBAL BUSINESS

1. The Canadian economy has had many ups and downs. As a result, economists are often in the news. The head of the Bank of Canada, Mark Carney, has been managing the country's general financial condition. To learn about the role economists play in a federal government agency, research Carney's background and qualifications. Assess how he is performing at the Bank of Canada. Now make a list of your own skills. Are there areas where your skills match his? What do you need to change?

2. To see the effect of the global economy in your community, visit a major retailer. List the countries that make the products on the shelves. Compare your list with your classmates' list. See who found the most countries and what goods those countries made. Go online to research the career opportunities at the retailer's website.

3. To learn more about other countries, go online and research a country you are interested in. The following sources may be useful:

- *The World Factbook*, published by the Central Intelligence Agency, https://www.cia.gov/library/publications/the-world-factbook/index.html. This publication is updated yearly. It contains much information about countries—geography and climate, population statistics, cultural and political information, transportation and communications methods, and economic data.
- *BusinessWeek* magazine, http://www.businessweek.com. Use the Global Economics tab to link to business news in other countries, where you can find breaking news and information on global companies.
- Online news sites Yahoo! News and Google News, http://news.yahoo.com and http://news.google.com. Both of these online news sites have links to global business news.

Write a one-page summary of the information you found. List the abilities and skills you would need to function well as a businessperson in that country. Focus on the areas of competence, adaptability, and personal characteristics. Now formulate a plan to gain those skills.

© Can Stock Photo Inc./mangostock

PART 2
STARTING AND GROWING YOUR BUSINESS

5 | FORMS OF BUSINESS OWNERSHIP AND ORGANIZATION

LEARNING OBJECTIVES

LO 5.1 Distinguish between small and large businesses.

LO 5.2 Discuss the contributions of small businesses to the economy.

LO 5.3 Discuss the survival rate of small businesses.

LO 5.4 Describe the features of an effective business plan.

LO 5.5 Describe funding opportunities for small businesses, including the role of the Business Development Bank of Canada (BDC).

LO 5.6 Explain how franchising provides opportunities for both franchisors and franchisees.

LO 5.7 Outline the three main legal forms of business ownership and summarize the features of not-for-profit organizations.

LO 5.8 Describe public and collective (co-operative) business ownership.

LO 5.9 Describe the ownership structure of corporations and the levels of corporate management.

LO 5.10 Describe mergers, acquisitions, and joint ventures.

INSIDE BUSINESS

Pi Athlete Management Inc.: Advising athletes about their careers and more

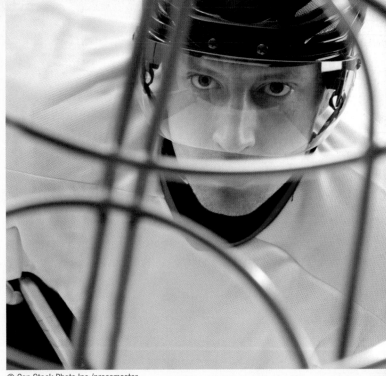

© Can Stock Photo Inc./pressmaster

Young athletes and their families face many challenges. Take a moment and imagine their complex world of information and decision-making. Most successful athletes are very young when they first realize they have talent in a sport. These athletes and their families need to figure out how to encourage further athletic development *and* plan for higher education. The smart players know the value of education and think about what they can do if a sports career doesn't work out. Coaches and trainers remind them that injuries have ended many sports careers and will continue to do so—just ask Sidney Crosby. At some point, aging brings all athletic careers to an end. Professional athletes often retire by their early thirties—if they can stay healthy and active. Hockey players Gordie Howe and Chris Chelios played into their forties but their long careers are a rarity.

Some athletes want to work at a career in sports while getting a college or university education. These athletes need to look for scholarship programs, especially programs affiliated with the National Collegiate Athletic Association (NCAA). Some amateur athletes succeed and become professional athletes. These athletes will face contract negotiations, relocation costs, and many financial, tax, and legal issues. Amateur athletes cannot be represented directly by agents. Usually, their families act as the go-between: these family members deal with the agents and consulting firms until the athlete becomes a professional.

During their careers, athletes use their public recognition to make extra money through endorsements and speaking engagements. Some athletes develop products such as games, books, and equipment. Sports personalities often earn more money through their activities off the field than on. For example, Tiger Woods has earned more than $100 million through tournament winnings but more than $1 billion when you include his earnings from product endorsements, especially his profitable relationship with Nike.

So where do athletes find a team of consultants to help manage their careers and advise them along the way? Pi Athlete Management Inc. of Montreal offers a full set of services under one roof.

The firm has a team of consultants to advise athletes and their families when making decisions related to education, athletic training, media relations, marketing and endorsements, and financial planning. This firm provides services and develops trusting relationships with athletes and their families—and hopes to share in their professional success. Receiving fees for services helps to pay the bills, but the big money is earned when a sports professional starts earning big salaries, bonuses, and revenues from endorsements. Agents who manage this part of the business activity usually earn money on a commission. The average player's salary is high: in basketball, $5.15 million; in baseball, $3.3 million; in hockey, $2.4 million; and in football, $1.9 million. It is easy to understand why athletes, their families, and their agents are all attracted to the dream of a professional sports career.

For example, 22-year-old Marc Bourgeois, from Granby, Quebec, signed as a free agent with the Arizona Diamondbacks in 2011. He played for the University of Southern Mississippi, and then was drafted by the Minnesota Twins in 2009. His friend and former teammate from Granby, Michael Carbone, suffered a back injury that ended his dream of a sports career. But today, Michael Carbone is an agent (working with Pi Athlete Management Inc.), and Marc Bourgeois receives public relations help from the firm's expert and co-founder, Daniel Smajovits.

The formal structure of the business requires a contract with the consultants and agents that provide services on behalf of Pi Athletic Management Inc. According to Marty Bindman, one of the founding partners of Pi Athlete Management Inc., "every member of our team, with the exception of the founding partners, can be considered as an independent contractor. They operate under our brand as affiliates and receive our support. In exchange, they are paid a referral fee and we cover their expenses. Daniel Smajovits and I are involved in all meetings with clients and potential clients. Client contracts are entered into with Pi. Michael Carbone is affiliated with us in just such a capacity. He is heading up our baseball initiative. He recently graduated with an MBA in sports management under an NCAA baseball scholarship. His

career was cut short by a back injury. Marc Bourgeois came to us through Michael. He was not happy with his previous representation and asked us to take over after signing with the Diamondbacks organization."

As more athletes and their families share their stories with others who need management services, word-of-mouth will help build the enterprise.[1]

CHAPTER 5 OVERVIEW

Do you want to work for a big company or a small one? Do you plan to start your own business? If you want to start your own company, you're not alone. Every day, more North Americans are starting a new business than those who are getting married or having a baby. Before you enter the business world—as an employee or an owner—you need to know a few things: the industry the company operates in and the size and framework of the firm. For example, Pi Athlete Management Inc. is a small company that has many associates. These associates and the founders bring to the firm their knowledge and past work experience with professional sports management.

Several factors affect how a business is organized, including how easily it can be set up, its access to financing, its tolerance of financial risk, its strengths and weaknesses, and the strengths and weaknesses of competing firms.

This chapter begins by focusing on small-business ownership, including the advantages and disadvantages of small-business ventures, the contributions of small business to the economy, and the reasons small businesses fail. The chapter examines the services provided by the Business Development Bank of Canada (BDC), the role of women and members of minority groups in small business, and alternatives for small businesses, such as franchising.

The chapter then discusses the forms of private business ownership—sole proprietorships, partnerships, and corporations. In addition, we discuss the features of not-for-profit organizations. Public and collective ownership are also examined. The chapter concludes with an explanation of structures and operations typical of larger companies, and a review of the major types of business alliances.

LO 5.1 Distinguish between small and large businesses.

MOST BUSINESSES ARE SMALL BUSINESSES

When we hear the term *business*, many of us think of big corporations, such as Bell Canada Enterprises (BCE), Royal Bank of Canada, and Rogers Communications. But most businesses are small businesses. In fact, more than 97 percent of all Canadian businesses employ fewer than 100 people. Small businesses employ people other than the owner but other businesses are self-employed businesses. Canada has 2.7 million self-employed individuals. Setting up a self-employed business is not the same as running a business that employs other people. Interestingly,

Statistics Canada reports that the numbers of self-employed people have been quite steady for the past decade.[2]

What Is a Small Business?

How can you tell a small business from a large one? The definition varies depending on the source, but Statistics Canada defines a **small business** as an "independent business having fewer than 100 employees and revenues not more than $2 million."[3]

Nutrisoya is a Quebec-based manufacturer of tofu and soy milk. It sells products under the brand name Natur-a. The company is making products that meet North Americans' growing demand for natural and healthy foods and beverages. Today, this industry is valued at more than $4 billion in revenue, 10 times what it was 15 years ago. When the company was acquired in 1988, its revenue was only about $400,000. That made it a small business by Statistics Canada's definition. Today, Nutrisoya's revenue is more than $30 million annually. The firm is both a small business and a mid-sized business. Its revenue places it above the cut-off revenue for small businesses but its 20 employees fall within the definition for a small company. Many businesses fall into this sort of hybrid definition: when trying to classify the business, one requirement conflicts with another requirement. Whether a company is small or medium-sized does not really matter unless the firm is applying for work, grants, or loans. Then, a means test is used to decide which firms qualify.[4]

Government agencies offer benefits to help small businesses compete with larger firms. Thus, small-business owners will want to know whether their companies meet the standards for being a small business. If a company qualifies, it may be able to receive government loans or take part in government programs that encourage purchasing goods and services from smaller suppliers. Some companies that receive such assistance might one day expand to other areas of the country, and eventually become a larger business.

small business an independent business with fewer than 100 employees and revenues less than $2 million, not dominant in its market.

Typical Small-Business Ventures

Small businesses have always competed against each other and against some of the world's largest organizations. John Stanton created a retail concept for runners and walkers like himself in 1981, when sports retailing didn't try to meet the needs of such small markets like they do today. North America has 100 Running Room retail stores that employ more than 1,200 people. The Edmonton-based firm continues to grow, profiting from the popularity of walking and running. John Stanton uses the firm's website to build on personal relationships with loyal followers who support healthier living and giving back to the communities where they live. That formula seems to have been successful for Stanton. The Running Room is one of Canada's 50 Best Managed companies.[5]

John Stanton has built The Running Room into one of Canada's 50 Best Managed Companies.

The Canadian Press/Jeff McIntosh

In the past 15 years, many small businesses have closed because larger firms have bought out the small independent businesses and replaced them with larger operations. For example, we have fewer independent bookstores and hardware stores because bigger chains, such as Chapters, Indigo Books, and The Home Depot have increased the size and number of their stores. Some businesses are not very likely to be gobbled up by bigger firms: businesses that sell personalized services, rely on certain locations, and keep their overhead costs low.

Small businesses account for more than two-thirds of employment in five Canadian industry categories: non-institutional health care, construction, accommodation and food, forestry, and other services. Approximately 25 percent of small businesses operate in Canadian goods-producing industries; the remaining 75 percent operate in service industries.[6]

Small firms have created an important space for themselves: they provide busy consumers with customized services that range from pet-sitting to personal shopping. These businesses meet the needs of individual customers in a way that big firms can't.

Small business also plays a major role in agriculture. Canada has 68 million hectares of farmland. Most of this land is owned by large corporate farms, but most of Canada's 327,000 farms are owned by individual farmers or their families. The family farm is a classic example of a small-business operation. It is independently owned and operated. It also employs a limited number of people, including family members.[7]

Figure 5.1 shows the distribution of business ownership in the goods-producing and service-producing sectors and by numbers of employees. The "indeterminate" category consists of incorporated or unincorporated businesses that do not have a Canada Revenue Agency payroll deductions account. The workforce of such businesses may consist of contract workers, family members and/or owners. About 25 percent of all business establishments produce goods; the remainder provide services. Small firms make up 98 percent of goods-producing businesses and 98 percent of all service-producing businesses.

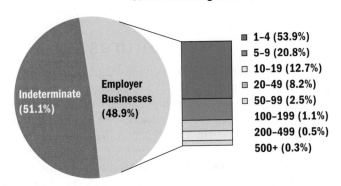

FIGURE 5.1
Distribution of Business Establishments in the Goods-Producing and Service-Producing Sectors by Firm Size (Number of Employees), December 2009

Source: Statistics Canada, Business Register, December 2009, http://www.ic.gc.ca/eic/site/sbrp-rppe.nsf/eng/rd02493.html#table2, accessed March 21, 2012.

home-based businesses firms operated from the residence of the business owner.

Many small businesses are **home-based businesses**—firms that operate from the business owner's residence. People often choose to operate home-based firms to have more control over both their business and their personal time. People who run home-based businesses can be morning people or night people, but they can usually choose to work when it suits them best. A home-based business is easier to run because of access to the Internet and communications devices such as the BlackBerry and other smartphone technology. People who run home-based businesses don't need to worry about overhead costs such as leasing office or warehouse space. The downside is isolation and less visibility to customers—except, of course, if customers visit online. Those customers don't care where your office is located.

Many small businesses become more competitive because of the Internet. The Internet doesn't guarantee success—there are so many websites that a small firm needs to find ways to make its online presence effective. Setting up a website is generally less expensive than opening a retail store. A website can also reach a wider range of customers.

North American business history has many stories of great inventors who started their companies in barns, garages, warehouses, and attics. For example, Steve Jobs and Steve Wozniak, who founded Apple Computer, Inc., used a family garage to transform their technical idea into a commercial reality. The impact of today's entrepreneurs, including home-based businesses, is discussed in more depth in Chapter 6.

✔ **ASSESSMENT CHECK**

5.1.1 How does Statistics Canada define *small business*?

5.1.2 In what industries do small businesses play a significant role?

CONTRIBUTIONS OF SMALL BUSINESS TO THE ECONOMY

LO 5.2 Discuss the contributions of small businesses to the economy.

Small businesses are important to the Canadian economy. Together, they generate more than 29 percent of the nation's gross domestic product (GDP). This rate is highest in British Columbia at 34 percent and lowest in Newfoundland at 18 percent.[8] Small businesses account for $83 billion (20 percent) of Canada's total value of exports, with an average value of $2 million per firm. Medium-sized businesses account for $60 billion (14 percent) of the total value of exports, with an average value of $13.8 million per firm. Large businesses account for $257 billion (62 percent) of the total value of exports, with an average value of $188.7 million per firm.[9]

Creating New Jobs

Small businesses make significant contributions to the Canadian economy and to society as a whole. One major contribution is the number of new jobs that small businesses create each year. The number of new jobs varies from year to year, but, in many years, more than half of all new jobs are created by companies with fewer than 100 employees. A significant share of these jobs—about 7 percent—are created by the smallest companies, those with four or fewer employees.[10]

Small businesses also help the economy by hiring people who have difficulty finding jobs at larger firms. Some of these employees are people returning to the workforce after a period of not working, people who receive social assistance, and workers with various challenges.

You might never want to start your own company, but you will probably work for a small business sometime in your career, especially in your first few jobs. Small firms often hire the youngest workers. Table 5.1 shows some of the newest jobs in both traditional and new industries. Many of these jobs are found in small businesses.

Table 5.1 New Job Opportunities for Small Businesses

INDUSTRY	JOBS
Green energy	Wind-farm engineers, solar installers and technicians, green-collar specialists and consultants
Health care	Informatics specialists (workers cross-trained in health care and information technology)
Management	Business continuity planners (consultants who help businesses plan strategies for dealing with natural disasters, cyberattacks, and other security breaches); spa managers
Education	Distance-learning coordinators (staff who prepare and help run online courses for colleges, trade schools, charter schools, and companies)
Media	User-experience designers (Web-savvy people who focus on improving user experiences with interactive media)

Sources: Larry Buhl, "Newest Professions, Growing Salaries," *Yahoo! Hot Jobs*, accessed June 23, 2010, http://hotjobs.yahoo.com/jobseeker; Mary Nemko and Liz Wolgemuth, "Choosing the Career Path Less Traveled," *U.S. News & World Report*, May 2009, pp. 22–24.

Creating New Industries

Small firms give businesspeople the opportunity and outlet for developing new ideas. Sometimes these new ideas become entirely new industries. Many of today's largest and most successful firms, such as Whole Foods, Google, and Amazon, began as small businesses. Facebook co-founders Mark Zuckerberg, Dustin Moskovitz, Chris Hughes, and Eduardo Saverin launched their new business from their college dorm room. In five years, Facebook had more than 300 million users. It had successfully positioned itself as a leader in the new industry of social networking.[11]

New industries are sometimes created when small businesses shift their focus to provide needed services to a larger corporate community. Corporate downsizing creates a demand for activities previously handled by in-house employees. These support businesses may become an industry themselves. For example, the need for wireless communication devices and services to support businesses has led to a huge number of small businesses trying to meet this demand.

New industries can be created when small businesses shift their focus to meet consumer interests and preferences. For example, many North Americans are too busy working to shop for the things they need. New businesses are created to meet this demand by offering customized services. The Trunk Club is an online shopping service that uses Web cams to meet with men who are too busy to shop for clothes. The company interviews customers to learn about their clothing needs, and then selects new clothing and sends it directly to the customer.[12]

New industries can also be created when both the business world and consumers see a need for change. For example, environmental responsibility has changed how we do things—from recycling and reusing goods to reducing the amount of energy we use. These changes have led to a new industry of green goods and services. Small companies provide many of these goods and services. The "Going Green" feature describes one small-business owner who uses her passion and talent to provide environmentally responsible services.

TRUNK CLUB
MEN'S OUTFITTERS

HOW IT WORKS   GET STARTED »

HAND-SELECTED OUTFITS SHIPPED TO YOUR DOOR.

The traditional shopping process, whether in stores or online, doesn't work for men. Trunk Club is different. We start with an assortment of the best brands in men's fashion, and then personally hand select a "trunk" of clothes for you based on your preferences.

SIGN UP

SKIP THE STORES IN 3 STEPS

TELL US ABOUT YOURSELF
Build your profile online, or talk to an expert via phone or email.

WE PACK YOUR TRUNK
Based on your tastes and needs, a Trunk Club Expert will handpick your order.

KEEP WHAT YOU LOVE
Try everything on and send back returns with the pre-paid FedEx label.

Courtesy of TrunkClub.com

New industries can be created when small businesses shift their focus to meet consumer interests and preferences. The Trunk Club is an online shopping service that uses Web cams to interview men who are too busy to shop for clothes. The Trunk Club then selects new clothing and sends it to the customer.

Innovation

Small businesses are good at innovation—developing new and improved goods and services. Innovation is often the entire reason for starting a new business. In a typical year, small firms develop twice as many product innovations per employee as larger firms. Small firms also produce 13 times more patents per employee than larger firms.[13]

GOING GREEN

GREEN MAMA: SMALL BUSINESS WITH A BIG MESSAGE

The Green Mama isn't a mythical figure. She's a consultant, writer, and environmentalist who believes the world can be made more sustainable, one mom at a time. Manda Aufochs Gillespie had been living and promoting an environmentally conscious lifestyle for several years when she was featured in a *Chicago Tribune* article. Suddenly, Gillespie became a guru for like-minded parents who also wanted to improve the health and lives of their families while reducing their impact on the planet. Since then she has launched a website, www. thegreenmama.com. She also hosts a weekly playgroup/seminar for parents, the Green Mama Café; writes a blog; consults for day-care businesses and educational institutions; gives workshops;

appears on television; and provides everyday advice to consumers. She's also a mom.

The website is the centre of Gillespie's green universe. "The site is for people who are trying to be green parents in any major city," she explains. "It's a tool for living." Visitors to the site can get shopping tips for the best cloth diapers, learn how to clean their floors with white vinegar (instead of commercial cleaners), become informed about buying local produce, and learn about everything from the effectiveness of hand sanitizers to the cost of organic produce. No question is too simple for Gillespie. She also suggests how to save money—and reduce waste—such as by re-gifting gently used children's clothing to another child, instead of buying new clothing for a birthday gift.

How does her philosophy become a business? It's not just the $5 that each mom pays for one of Gillespie's workshops at the Green Mama Café, or her consulting fees. Marketing experts say that these moms represent some 20 million consumers who are now demanding green goods and services. It's not just cloth diapers and natural floor cleaners. These consumers now look carefully at every item they put in their reusable shopping bags. If they have to pay a bit more for those products, they will—because they are usually saving money somewhere else. "It turns out that what saves money also saves resources and what is better for the environment can also make parenting easier, if you have the right mindset," says one mom who goes to Gillespie's Green Mama seminars. These green moms have nearly $210 billion in purchasing power—and manufacturers, media, and service providers are paying attention.

Questions for Critical Thinking

1. Manda Gillespie owns one of many small businesses that are creating a whole new industry: green goods and services for parents. What factors will contribute to the success of these businesses? What risks do these businesses face?

2. As a consumer, do you purchase any green goods or services? Why or why not? Have these goods and services been offered by small or large companies?

Sources: Green Mama website, http://www.thegreenmama.com, accessed April 2, 2010; Jessica Levco, "The Green Mama Speaks," *Chicago Magazine*, May 2009, http://www.chicagomag.com; Robyn Monaghan, "Green Mamas Unite," *Chicago Parent*, March 20, 2009, http://www.chicagoparent.com.

In the 20th century, small businesses developed several major innovations: the airplane, the personal computer, soft contact lenses, and the zipper. In the 21st century, small businesses are developing innovations that involve social networking, security, and green energy industries. The "Business Etiquette" feature offers tips for using online social networking successfully.

✓ **ASSESSMENT CHECK**

5.2.1 What are the three key ways that small businesses contribute to the economy?

5.2.2 How are new industries formed?

LO 5.3 Discuss the survival rate of small businesses.

WHY SMALL BUSINESSES FAIL

Small businesses play a huge role in the Canadian economy. One of the reasons they are so successful is the same reason they fail—the willingness to take a risk. The most common difficulties for a small firm are management inexperience, inadequate financing, and the challenge of meeting government regulations.

About 96 percent of small businesses (1–99 employees) that enter the marketplace are in business for one full year, 85 percent are in business for three years, and 70 percent are in business for five years.[14] Let's see why this happens.

Management Shortcomings

One of the most common causes of small-business failure is management inexperience. For example, managers may not have the right people skills, may not have much knowledge of finance, may not be able to track inventory or sales, may be poor at judging their competition, or may simply not have enough time to do everything that needs to be done. Large firms are often big enough that they can hire specialists in marketing and finance, but the owner of a small business often has to take on all the firm's roles at the same time.

Trying to do all the business functions can lead to bad decisions that can end in the firm's failure. Krispy Kreme was once a small business that expanded too fast because its management made poor decisions. The company's near failure had nothing to do with its doughnuts. Instead, as the company grew bigger, so did its debt. Some blamed management misconduct. At the same time, consumers began to turn their attention away from doughnuts and toward more healthful snacks and breakfast foods. Krispy Kreme is now recovering. It has new management and is operating on a smaller scale.[15]

Owners of small businesses can increase their chances of success by learning the principles of business; knowing the industry they operate in; developing good interpersonal skills; understanding their own limitations; hiring motivated employees; and asking for professional advice on finance, regulations, and other legal matters.[16]

BUSINESS ETIQUETTE

How to Use Social Networking in Your Job Search

Online social networking is likely part of your everyday life. But you can also use this technology to look for a job. During one recent year, networking sites, such as LinkedIn, registered 1 million new users each month. Worried you'll get lost when so many other people are also using social networking? Use a few simple tips to stand out from the millions of others who have discovered the benefits of social networking.

- *Research a network before jumping in.* Some networks, such as Facebook, are mainly for connecting with friends. Others, such as LinkedIn, are stronger networks when looking for work. Twitter attracts both types of users. To decide on what is right for you—and to make the most of a social network—learn about it before you log on to look for work.

- *Complete your online profile.* Help prospective employers by filling out your online profile. Update your bio as often as you can. Provide a link to your own blog or web page. Don't try to be perfect—if you know your weaknesses or if you made a mistake in a previous job, describe how you've improved or learned from your mistakes.

- *Share information.* Be willing to share information about companies or career opportunities with other job seekers. You can help an online employer find the right person—even if it's not you.

- *Search for people.* First, look for companies that interest you. Next, talk to your friends, family members, classmates, alumni—anyone who might know someone at those companies. A specific job might not be available now, but a personal connection can help you when that job does open up.

- *Respect privacy.* You want to provide only certain information about yourself online, so respect the privacy of potential employers and colleagues. Read about the privacy settings of a social networking site and abide by them.

Sources: DeLynn Senna, "Recruiters Reveal Pet Peeves About Job Seekers," *Yahoo! Hot Jobs*, http://hotjobs.yahoo.com, accessed April 2, 2010; Alex Williams, "Mind Your BlackBerry or Mind Your Manners," *New York Times*, June 21, 2009; David LaGesse, "Turning Social Networking into a Job Offer," *U.S. News & World Report*, May 2009, pp. 44–45.

Inadequate Financing

Money is the foundation of any business. Every business—large or small—needs some financing to operate, thrive, and grow. Another big problem of small businesses is inadequate financing. First-time business owners often assume that their firms will make enough money from their initial sales to finance continuing operations. But building a business takes time. Products need to be developed, employees need to be hired, a website needs to be constructed, distribution needs to be planned, and office or retail space may need to be rented or purchased. Most small businesses—even those with minimal start-up costs—sometimes don't turn a profit for months or even years.[17]

We have all heard about people starting firms with just a few hundred dollars borrowed from a friend or with a cash advance from a credit card. But most small businesses get their start-up money from commercial banks and other financial institutions. This type of financing includes credit lines and loans for nonresidential mortgages, vehicles, specialized equipment, and leases.[18]

Credit cards have high interest rates. Still, they are an important source of financing for small businesses. The heaviest users of credit cards for business financing are firms with fewer than 10 employees. Inadequate financing can make management shortcomings worse by making it more difficult for small businesses to attract and keep talented people. Typically, a big company can offer a better benefits package and a higher salary.

Successful small companies need to be creative to operate with less money to spend on employees, marketing, inventory, and other business costs. Asafumi Yamashita started his business with $500. He used the money to buy specialty vegetable seeds from Japan. In his own greenhouse, he planted Japanese spinach, radishes, and other special produce. Yamashita had become friends with the head chef at a Japanese restaurant in Paris. The chef told Yamashita that these vegetables were nearly impossible to buy locally. Within a year of planting those first seeds, Yamashita was supplying several top restaurants in Paris. Others heard about Yamashita's high-quality vegetables, and he now supplies his vegetables to only the most exclusive restaurants. Yamashita has limited his number of customers and has no employees. This means he needs less financing and maintains control over all the vegetables that leave his garden.[19]

Government Regulation

Small-business owners say that meeting the terms of government regulations is one of their biggest challenges. Some firms close because of how difficult it is to deal with government regulations. Small businesses spend billions of dollars in paperwork each year. A large company has an easier time dealing with all the government forms and reports. Larger firms can often hire or contract specialists to deal with specific regulations, such as employment law and workplace safety requirements. But small businesses often have difficulty paying the costs of government paperwork because they have fewer staff and smaller budgets. Statistics Canada is doing research to help reduce the problem. In a recent year, small- and medium-sized businesses in five sectors spent $1.17 billion filling out forms to meet 11 key government information requirements, such as filing income tax forms and paying federal and provincial sales taxes.[20]

Taxes are another big expense for a small business. All employers pay provincial and federal income taxes. They must also pay taxes for workers' compensation insurance, pension payments, and unemployment benefits. Although large companies have the same expenses, most have more resources to pay their taxes. The government has created tax incentives to help small businesses. These incentives include the Small Business Investor Tax Credit that returns a 30 percent tax credit to an investor to a maximum $75,000 credit.[21]

© FLPA/Alamy

Asafumi Yamashita started his business with $500. He used the money to buy specialty vegetable seeds from Japan. Within a year, Yamashita was supplying several top restaurants in Paris. Yamashita has limited his number of customers and has no employees. This means he needs less financing and maintains control over all the vegetables he grows.

✓ ASSESSMENT CHECK

5.3.1 What percentage of small businesses are still operating five years after starting?

5.3.2 What are the three main causes of small-business failure?

THE BUSINESS PLAN: A FOUNDATION FOR SUCCESS

Large or small, every business needs a plan to succeed. We sometimes hear about firms that started with an idea scribbled on a restaurant napkin or sketched out on graph paper in a dorm room. But a business idea must have a solid plan to become reality. A **business plan** is a formal document that details a company's goals, the methods it will use to achieve these goals, and the standards it will use to measure its achievements. Firms often need a business plan to obtain financing. The business plan also creates a framework for the organization.

Business plans give the organization a sense of purpose. They identify the firm's mission and goals. Business plans create measurable standards and outline a strategy for reaching company objectives. A typical business plan includes the following sections:

- an *executive summary* that briefly answers the who, what, where, when, why, and how questions for the business

- an *introduction* that includes a general statement of the concept, purpose, and objectives of the business

- separate *financial* and *marketing sections* that describe the firm's target market, marketing plan, and detailed financial forecasts of the need for funds and when the firm is expected to break even—the level of sales where revenues equal costs

- *résumés of principals*—especially important in plans written to obtain financing.

LO 5.4 Describe the features of an effective business plan.

business plan a formal document that details a company's goals, methods, and standards.

Firms often need a business plan to obtain financing. Business plans identify the firm's mission and goals. They create measurable standards and outline a strategy for reaching company objectives. The business plan also creates a framework for the organization.

An effective business plan uses the five sections above, contains the company's mission, and addresses the following issues:

- *The company's mission and the vision of its founders.* Look at the home page of any firm's website and you will find its mission. At the website for TOMS Shoes, visitors learn that "TOMS shoes was founded on a simple premise: With every pair you purchase, TOMS will give a pair of new shoes to a child in need. One for one. Using the purchasing power of individuals to benefit the greater good is what we're all about."[22] This simple statement says why the company was founded and what it intends to achieve.

- *An outline of why the company is unique.* Why start a business that's just like hundreds of others? An effective business plan describes why the firm and its products differ from the rest of the pack. TOMS Shoes illustrates a unique business model with its "one-for-one" donation program.

- *The customers.* A business plan identifies who the firm's customers will be and how the firm will serve their needs.

- *The competition.* A business plan addresses its existing and potential competitors. It then suggests a strategy for creating better or unique offerings. A firm can study the competition to learn valuable information about what works and what doesn't work.

- *Financial evaluation of the industry and market conditions.* This knowledge helps develop a reasonable financial forecast and budget.

- *Assessment of the risks.* Every business undertaking involves risks. A solid business plan acknowledges these risks and outlines a strategy for dealing with them.[23]

One firm may want to change an entire industry, while another firm wants to improve the lives of children by giving them shoes. Both firms need a business plan to be a success. For more information on how to write a business plan, see Appendix F, "Developing a Business Plan," on page 567.

✔ **ASSESSMENT CHECK**

5.4.1 What are the five main sections of a business plan?

5.4.2 Why is an effective business plan important to the success of a firm?

LO 5.5 Describe funding opportunities for small businesses, including the role of the Business Development Bank of Canada (BDC).

ASSISTANCE FOR SMALL BUSINESSES

Financing is an important part of setting up a small business. After writing a business plan, the business owner needs to look for loans and other types of financing. Government agencies and private investors often provide the needed funds. Many people want to start a business, which means the government can provide funds only to some firms. But not everyone agrees that the government makes the right choices, as discussed in the "Solving an Ethical Controversy" feature.

Business Development Bank of Canada

The **Business Development Bank of Canada (BDC)** is a government agency that assists, counsels, and protects the interests of small businesses in Canada. BDC was created by an act of Parliament in 1944. It operates across Canada through offices and resource centres that provide long-term financial assistance and management counselling. The BDC also provides training, technical assistance, and education to help small businesses prepare for doing business in foreign markets. Statistics show that most failures in small businesses happen because of poor management. For this reason, the BDC works to improve the management skills of small-business owners and managers. The BDC offers individual counselling, courses, conferences, workshops, and a wide range of publications. BDC's management courses cover all the functions, duties, and roles of managers. Instructors may be teachers from local colleges or universities. They may also be management consultants, bankers, lawyers, and accountants. Fees for these courses are low. The most popular course is a general survey of eight to 10 areas of business management. Businesspeople can then focus on one or more of these areas, depending on their strengths and weaknesses. The BDC sometimes offers one-day conferences. These conferences are aimed at keeping owner–managers up-to-date on new management developments, tax laws, and the other helpful information.[24]

The Small Business Administration (SBA) is the main American government agency that helps small U.S. firms. The SBA is the advocate, or supporter, for small businesses within the U.S. federal government. Many small business resources are available at the websites of both organizations.

Business Development Bank of Canada (BDC) a governmental agency that assists, counsels, and protects the interests of small businesses in Canada.

Fisker Automotive received government loans to build a plug-in hybrid sports car called the Karma. It sounds like a win–win situation—investment in alternative energy vehicles, creation of new jobs, rejuvenation of the auto industry—but the new car will be built in Finland and priced around $89,000, more than most people can pay.

SOLVING AN **ETHICAL** CONTROVERSY

Good Karma or Bad Karma?

During the recent economic downturn, many businesses—large and small—received funds from government to survive and ultimately grow. The bankrupt General Motors Corp. was restructured with funding from several North American sources, including the Canadian and Ontario governments. When a business is not about to close, should governments help one business more than another?

Fisker Automotive, a California start-up automaker, received $528 million in U.S. government loans to build a plug-in hybrid sports car called the Karma. It sounded like a win–win situation for everyone—investment in vehicles powered by alternative energy, the creation of new jobs, rejuvenation of the auto industry. But some people do not agree with the government funding. Their reason? The new car will be built in Finland—and will be priced at about $89,000, more than most people can pay.

Should government funds be used to support firms that manufacture luxury goods overseas?

PRO

1. According to Fisker Automotive, no government funds will be used for overseas work. Instead, much of the loan money will be used to buy parts from U.S. suppliers and to pay for engineering and design—in the United States. The U.S. Department of Energy says the loans will save or create about 5,000 jobs.

2. Although the Karma carries a big price, the car will attract buyers who might have purchased a traditional sports car that has high fuel consumption and high levels of emissions. Fisker says that because of the projected tax credits, the final cost of the Karma will be around $39,000.

CON

1. It is not a fair use of government funds to invest in a product that only the wealthiest car buyers can buy. "This is not for average Americans," argues a spokesperson for Citizens Against Government Waste. "It's a status symbol thing."

2. Other firms applied for much smaller loans to develop alternatively powered vehicles at a lower price point, but were turned down. A fairer distribution of funds could have supported more companies, created more jobs, and sold more hybrid cars to average car buyers.

Summary
Fisker says it will repay the government loans with interest and will offer a superior product to luxury car buyers. The firm says the launch of the Karma, the world's first production plug-in hybrid car, will "put the American auto industry ahead of foreign competition." But others say that government funds should be reserved for firms that produce goods and services to benefit a wider range of consumers.

Sources: Fisker Automotive website, http://karma.fiskerautomotive.com, accessed April 2, 2010; Josh Mitchell and Stephen Power, "Gore-Backed Car Firm Gets Large U.S. Loan," *Wall Street Journal*, September 25, 2009, http://online.wsj.com; Ken Thomas, "California Automaker Receives $528.7 Million Government Loan," *Associated Press*, September 23, 2009, http://autos.yahoo.com.

Financial Assistance

Most small businesses borrow money directly from Canada's financial institutions. These banks, trust companies, and credit unions actively believe in lending money to small businesses. The Canada Small Business Financing Program (CSBFP) is typical of federal and provincial government assistance. When a bank loans money to a small business and is not paid back, the government will guarantee payment for as much as 85 percent of the loan. Some small businesses cannot borrow from traditional lending institutions because they don't have a financial history. These small businesses may be funded by the BDC or other organizations that may want to help higher-risk firms.

The CSBFP tries to increase the number of loans for establishing, expanding, modernizing, and improving small businesses. It does this by encouraging financial institutions to make their financing available to small businesses. By sharing the risk with financial institutions, the program may help businesses to obtain loans of up to $500,000. The loans can cover 90 percent of the costs to purchase or improve land or property, to purchase leasehold improvements or improve leased property, or to purchase new equipment or improve used equipment. Eligible small businesses must be operating for profit in Canada and must have annual gross revenues less than $5 million.[25]

Business Incubators

business incubator a local program designed to provide low-cost, shared business facilities to small start-up companies.

Some community agencies want to encourage business development. These agencies use a concept called a **business incubator** to provide low-cost, shared business facilities to small start-up companies. A typical incubator might section off space in an abandoned plant and rent it to various small firms. Tenants often share clerical staff, computers, and other business services. The goal is that, after a few months or years, the new business will be ready to move out and operate on its own.

The Canadian Association of Business Incubation (CABI) is a national association of member organizations. CABI supports the growth of new and early stage businesses. According to CABI and Statistics Canada research, Canada has at least 83 operating business incubators that generate more than $45 million in funds. Their almost 900 client firms raised more than $93 million in revenue and created full- and part-time jobs for more than 13,000 people. Incubation firms make a positive impact. After one year, 2,958 client companies had generated revenues.[26]

Private Investors

venture capital money invested in a business by another business or a group of individuals in return for an ownership share.

A small business may start with cash from a personal savings account or a loan from a family member. But small-business owners need larger sums of money to continue operating and to grow. They may want to continue receiving funds from private investors. **Venture capital** is money invested in the small business by another business or a group of individuals in return for an ownership share. Venture capital (VC) can give the small business the funding it needs to succeed. Even when the economy is slow, venture capitalists are looking for companies to invest in. Canada's Venture Capital and Private Equity Association reports that Canadian VC investment in 2010 increased 10 percent from the year before, to $1.1 billion. The story is similar in the United States. There, the U.S. National Venture Capital Association reported that venture capitalists had invested more than $7 billion in small start-up firms despite a slow economy. These investors preferred funding small-business owners who had a previous successes and for those proposing new ways to commercialize such products as solar energy, low-emission cars, and new medications. These investors have high requirements for a solid business plan. They also expect small-businesses owners to run lean operations.[27]

Small-Business Opportunities for Women

© ZUMA Wire Service/Alamy

The number of women-owned firms in Canada has increased over the past few decades. Today, nearly half of all small- and medium-sized enterprises (SMEs) in Canada have at least one female owner. Women also hold majority ownership in 18 percent of SMEs. Women-owned firms also contribute significantly to employment. About one-third of all self-employed people in Canada are women.

Women, like men, start their own companies for many different reasons. Some have a unique business idea that they want to bring to life. Others decide to form their own company when they lose their job or become frustrated with the working conditions in large companies. Many women start their own companies in hopes of finding a better balance between family and work.

The presence of women in business ownership means more than just more jobs. Majority women-owned SMEs produce annual commercial revenues of more than $72 billion. These sales represented approximately 8 percent of all revenues from Canada's SMEs. Women are present across all sectors of the Canadian economy, although most work in service industries. Today, 80 percent of majority women-owned SMEs operate in the services sector, compared with 59 percent of SMEs owned by men.[28]

Arlene Dickinson started working at Venture Communications in 1988. She took full ownership of the marketing firm 10 years later. Her success in marketing and communications led her to the panel of *Dragons' Den*, the CBC's popular business show. On the show, entrepreneurs compete for funding and partnership with the panel members. Dickinson is also in demand as an author and speaker at events that highlight her entrepreneurial ability and success.[29]

✓ **ASSESSMENT CHECK**

5.5.1 What are the various ways the BDC helps small businesses?

5.5.2 What are business incubators?

5.5.3 Why are small businesses good opportunities for women?

(HIT) & MISS

CBC's *Dragons' Den* Highlights Entrepreneurial Thinking and Investing

The CBC's popular reality show *Dragon's Den* is the Canadian version of a show that is seen around the world. The format is the same in every country. Entrepreneurs present their ideas for a new business to a panel of venture capitalists. The entrepreneurs hope to make a deal. The idea is to partner with one or more panel members to improve the chances the business will be developed successfully.

The show succeeds partly because of the entertainment value: the viewers at home act as armchair-panellists. The show is also educational. Viewers watch the panellists review the presentations. They quickly learn about business valuation, patents, and the managerial mindset that venture capital partners like to see.

Many viewers are probably thinking about starting a business of their own. The biggest lesson that all viewers learn is the role of expertise and knowledge to move the business to the "next level."

The entrepreneurs that make deals with the dragons are usually business owners who have been successful but need help to grow the business. They now need the dragons' expertise and business connections as much as they need their investment funds. Having the dragons on their side can help take their business to a higher level.

Questions for Critical Thinking

1. Why is the show successful in Canada and around the world?

2. How would the show differ in other countries?

Sources: *Dragons Den* website, http://www.cbc.ca/dragonsden/, accessed March 18, 2012; "*Dragon's Den*," Financial Post website, http://business.financialpost.com/tag/dragons-den/, accessed March 18, 2012; "Business Titans Jim Treliving and W. Brett Wilson Jump at FROGBOX Offering," *Marketwire*, January 27, 2011, http://www.marketwire.com/press-release/business-titans-jim-treliving-and-w-brett-wilson-jump-at-frogbox-offering-1386326.htm, accessed March 18, 2012; "Dragon's Den & Venture Capital," Financial Blogger, February 13, 2012, http://www.thefinancialblogger.com/dragons-den-venture-capital/, accessed March 18, 2012.

**LO
5.6** Explain how franchising provides opportunities for both franchisors and franchisees.

FRANCHISING

Franchising combines large and small businesses into a single entity. It is also a major factor in the growth of small businesses. **Franchising** is a contract-based business arrangement between a manufacturer, or another supplier, and a dealer, such as a restaurant operator or a retailer. The contract spells out how the dealer will market the supplier's product. Franchises can involve both goods and services, such as food and wait staff.

Starting a small, independent company can be risky, time-consuming work, but franchising can reduce the amount of time and effort needed to grow. The parent company has already developed and tested the concept, and the brand is often familiar to customers. Figure 5.2 lists Canada's top 10 franchises.

franchising a contract-based business arrangement between a manufacturer or other supplier, and a dealer, such as a restaurant operator or retailer.

FIGURE 5.2 The Top 10 Canadian Franchises

1. Hampton Hotels	6. Denny's Inc.
2. McDonald's	7. Jan Pro Franchising International, Inc.
3. Days Inn	8. Kumon Math & Reading Centers
4. Vanguard Cleaning Systems	9. Liberty Tax Service
5. SUBWAY	10. Jazzercise Inc.

Source: Franchise Canada, "The Top 10 Canadian Franchises," August 17, 2011, http://franchisecanada.org/top-10-canadian-franchises/, accessed March 18, 2012.

The Franchising Sector

Canada has the second largest franchise industry in the world, after the United States. Canadians are as familiar with American franchise businesses in Canada, such as McDonald's, as they are with Canadian franchises, such as Tim Hortons.

The franchise industry has more than $100 billion in sales each year. Approximately one out of five consumer dollars is spent on goods and services at a franchise business. Canada has approximately 76,000 individual franchise businesses operating under 900 different brand names. These franchises employ more than 1 million people. One out of every 14 working Canadians is employed by a franchise.

The average franchise fee is $23,000, and the average franchisee investment is $160,000. Of all the franchises opened in Canada within the last five years, 86 percent are under the same ownership, and 97 percent are still in business. Ontario leads the rest of Canada in franchising: 56 percent of Canadian franchises are based in Ontario, mostly in the Greater Toronto Area, and 65 percent of all Canadian franchise outlets are in Ontario. The hospitality industry is the largest franchised sector, making up almost 40 percent of all Canadian franchised brand names. The franchise industry is active in more than 30 business, service, and retail sectors.[30]

Franchised businesses are also a huge part of the U.S. economy. There, franchises account for nearly 50 percent of all retail sales. The International Franchise Association reports that franchising is responsible for 760,000 businesses, 18 million jobs, and more than $500 billion in payroll. Total franchise sales continue to grow and now approach $2 trillion. A new franchise is opened every eight minutes every business day.[31]

Franchising overseas is also a growing trend for businesses who aim to expand into foreign markets. You can go almost anywhere in the world and find a McDonald's burger. Other international franchises are also becoming more common. Baskin-Robbins, now owned by Dunkin' Brands, has more than 6,000 stores in more than 35 countries, including Australia, Canada, China, Japan, Malaysia, and Russia. Japan has more than 850 Baskin-Robbins ice cream stores. Baskin-Robbins holds the 13th rank of top U.S.-based franchises.[32]

Franchising Agreements

A franchising agreement is a contract between the franchisee and the franchisor. The individual or business firm that buys the franchise is called the **franchisee**. This business owner agrees to sell the franchisor's goods or services under certain terms. The **franchisor** is the firm whose products are sold by the franchisee. For example, Tim Hortons Inc. is a franchisor. Your local Tim Hortons restaurant owner is a franchisee.

Franchise agreements can be complex. They involve an initial purchase fee plus agreed-on start-up costs. Because the franchisee represents the franchisor's brand, the franchisor can require the franchisee to purchase certain ingredients or equipment, use standard pricing, and market the business in a certain way. McDonald's is one of the more expensive franchises—total start-up costs can be more than $1 million. In contrast, the total start-up

International franchises are becoming more common. Baskin-Robbins has more than 6,000 stores in more than 35 countries, including Australia, Canada, China, Japan, Vietnam, and Russia.

cost for a SUBWAY franchise may reach $228,000.[33] Because of the costs, businesspeople often work together to purchase a more expensive franchise.

franchisee the individual or business firm purchasing a franchise.

franchisor the firm whose products are sold to customers by the franchisee.

Benefits and Problems of Franchising

Like other businesses, franchising has its upsides and downsides. The upsides for the franchisor include being able to expand a business, which might not be possible without the franchise. A franchised business can move into new locations, including overseas, at less cost than a traditional business. In other countries, franchises employ local workers and businesspeople who know what consumers like. A good franchisor can manage a much larger and more complex business—with fewer direct employees—than a traditional business. Most franchisees pay attention to how their franchises are managed because they have a stake in the company as business owners. If the business is run efficiently, the franchisor will probably make more money on the investment than if the firm were run entirely as a company-owned chain of retail shops, restaurants, or service providers.

A successful franchisor has financial strength and can usually bargain for better deals on ingredients, supplies, and even real estate. This strength is also a benefit for the franchisees if the savings are passed on to them.[34]

Franchising can be the quickest way to become a business owner. Some people say that it's also the least risky way to own a business. Franchisees benefit from having a business name that people know, such as McDonald's, Tim Hortons, SUBWAY, Pizza Hut, or Super 8 hotels. Having a familiar name usually means a loyal following of customers. The franchisor has already set up a management system, and it has already shown that it can be successful. Franchisors provide a support to franchisees, including financing, assistance in obtaining a location, business training, supplies, and marketing tools.[35]

Franchisees say they like the idea of franchising because it combines the freedom of business ownership with the support of a large company. Like other small-business owners, franchisees want to make their own business decisions and decide on their own work hours. They also want to have more control over the amount of money they make, instead of taking what they might earn in a salaried job. In an economic slowdown, franchisees might be former executives who

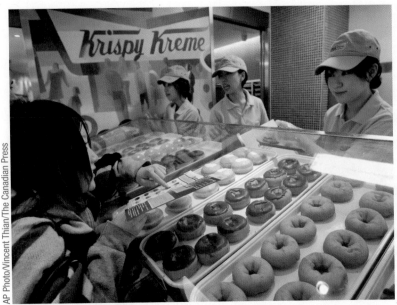

Krispy Kreme is a franchised company that stumbled after overexpanding.

AP Photo/Vincent Thian/The Canadian Press

have been laid off. These highly trained and motivated businesspeople are looking for a way to restart their careers.[36] Sometimes, the ideas or successes of individual franchisees can be good for the entire company. That's what happened with SUBWAY, as described in the "Hit & Miss" feature.

Franchising can have its downside—for both franchisors and franchisees. If franchisees fail, their failure reflects on the franchisor's brand and the bottom line. The same is true for the franchisee: a firm that is mismanaged at the top level, by the franchisor, can be bad for the smaller business owners, who are running the individual locations. When a firm decides to offer franchise opportunities, it may lose money for several years. Of course, by offering franchise opportunities, the franchisor—often the founder of what was once a small business—loses control over every aspect of the business. Not having control can make it difficult to select the right franchisees to carry out the company's mission.[37]

HIT & MISS

One Small Franchise Produces One Big Idea

SUBWAY has enjoyed top franchise rankings consistently for more than a decade. SUBWAY has 30,000 sandwich restaurants in nearly 80 countries. The firm is set to become the single largest fast-food chain in the world. But SUBWAY is made up of many small businesses—franchises. Sometimes, a small idea by one franchisee can change the entire organization.

Stuart Frankel is a SUBWAY franchisee, and his idea was simple: on weekends, he wanted to charge a special price of $5 for a footlong SUBWAY sandwich. This special price was about $1 less per sandwich than the regular price. It took some time for Frankel and two other Florida SUBWAY franchisees to convince the corporate franchisor that the idea was a good one. The economy was slow, food costs were increasing, and SUBWAY shops were almost empty because people were eating at home to save money. Frankel's employees stood around at their stations, and sandwich sales decreased. But after some time, Frankel got the OK from corporate headquarters. From there, a chain reaction began.

"I like round numbers," said Frankel about the $5 price. SUBWAY customers liked the number, too. When the special pricing was announced, customers returned for the $5 sandwiches. Sales increased by double digits. Employees made sandwiches as fast as they could. SUBWAY's corporate marketing team pushed the $5 promotion nationwide—franchises from New York to New Orleans began offering $5 footlongs. When the initial four-week promotion was up, marketing executives extended it to seven weeks. When that time was up, they extended it indefinitely but with a limited number of sandwich variations.

Something else happened. Demand for the $5 footlongs was so great that franchise owners began to run out of certain ingredients. They couldn't get enough bread, turkey, ham, or tuna. One franchisee recalls being in a panic. "The whole thing took on a life of its own," said Jeff Moody, CEO of SUBWAY's advertising.

With one motion, Stuart Frankel had a great idea for consumers who wanted to eat out and get a good deal at the same time. "There are only a few times when a chain has been able to scramble up the whole industry, and this is one of them," notes restaurant consultant Jeffrey T. Davis. "It's huge." Sometimes a small idea is really big.

Questions for Critical Thinking

1. Why was Stuart Frankel's idea successful with consumers? Would it have been as successful during a different economic time? Why or why not?

2. A franchise company is only as good as its franchisees. And a franchisee's success is based in part on the decisions and support of corporate leadership. If the $5 footlong promotion had failed, how would that failure have affected Frankel's franchise business? How might it have affected SUBWAY?

Sources: "Subway Brand Ranked Number One Provider of Healthy Options in Zagat Survey," http://www.subway.com, accessed April 2, 2010; "Subway Restaurants Again Named #1 Worldwide Franchise Opportunity for 2009," http://www.subway.com, accessed April 2, 2010; Matthew Boyle, "The Accidental Hero," *BusinessWeek*, November 10, 2009, http://www.businessweek.com.

The franchisee has many cash expenses: the initial investment, franchise fees, supplies, maintenance, leases, and so on. The most expensive franchises are usually franchises that involve hotels and resorts. These franchises can cost millions of dollars.[38] It is not unusual for groups of businesspeople to purchase a franchise (or several franchise locations).[39] The franchisees' payments to the franchisor can add to the difficulty of keeping the business going until the owner begins to earn a profit. Choosing a low-cost start up such as Guard-a-Kid may be a good alternative option. Guard-a-Kid is the largest child-identity franchise in North America. It offers franchisees a complete start-up kit. The kit includes two days of training and supplies, such as a laptop computer, digital camera, logo T-shirts, and personalized business cards. The fee to the franchisee is $10,000 to $20,000, depending on the territory size.[40] But it's important for potential franchisees to check carefully how much profit they can make after they pay their expenses.

Franchises are closely linked to their brand, so franchisors and franchisees must work together to maintain standards of quality in their goods and services. If customers are unhappy with their experience at one franchise location, they might not stop at another location several kilometres away, even if the second location is owned and operated by someone else. This is especially true where food is involved. The discovery of bad meat or produce at one franchise restaurant can cause panic to spread throughout the entire chain of restaurants. A potential franchisee is smart to thoroughly research the financial performance and reputation of the franchisor. This research can be done using resources such as other franchisees, the Better Business Bureau, Industry Canada, the U.S. Federal Trade Commission, and the Canadian Franchise Association (CFA). The CFA is a trade association representing franchisors. CFA members agree to a review before they are accepted as members. They also agree to follow the association's code of ethics.

Some franchisees have found the franchising agreement to be too confining. As the saying goes, you can't add a tuna salad sandwich to the menu at McDonald's no matter how many stores you own. The agreements are usually strict, which helps to maintain the brand's good standing. Some franchise companies control promotional activities, select the site location, or are even involved in hiring decisions. These activities may seem overly controlling to some franchisees, especially those who want more independence and freedom.

Controls can also cost franchisees more than they feel is fair. Recently, the National Franchise Association, a group of more than 80 percent of Burger King's U.S. franchisees, sued Burger King. The lawsuit was because Burger King forced its franchisees to offer consumers a $1 double cheeseburger, which supported the company's promotional efforts. While the $1 burger offering may seem like a great way to attract and serve hungry consumers, BK franchisees said the promotion has cost them a loss of at least 10 cents per burger. In other words, it costs most franchises $1.10 to make and serve a cheeseburger but the franchisor told them they must charge $1.[41]

✔ ASSESSMENT CHECK

5.6.1 What is the difference between a franchisor and a franchisee?

5.6.2 How does franchising benefit both parties?

5.6.3 What are the potential downsides of franchising for both parties?

LO 5.7 Outline the three main legal forms of business ownership and summarize the features of not-for-profit organizations.

FORMS OF PRIVATE BUSINESS OWNERSHIP

No matter how big or small, most businesses are organized as one of three legal structures: sole proprietorship, partnership, or corporation. Each legal structure offers unique advantages and disadvantages. In addition to the three main legal structures, there is the option of creating and running a not-for-profit organization.

Sole Proprietorships

The most common, oldest, and simplest form of business ownership is the **sole proprietorship**. In a sole proprietorship, the sole proprietor's status as an individual is not legally separate from his or her status as a business owner. Although sole proprietorships are common in many industries, they are found mostly among small businesses such as repair shops, small retail stores, and service providers such as plumbers, hairstylists, and photographers.

sole proprietorship a business ownership in which the sole proprietor's status as an individual is not legally separate from his or her status as a business owner.

Sole proprietorships have some unique advantages. Because sole proprietorships have a single owner, they are easy to form *and* dissolve. A sole proprietorship gives the owner the most management flexibility. The owner also has the right to all profits after paying business-related bills and taxes. A highly motivated owner of a sole proprietorship directly receives all the benefits of his or her hard work.

It is easy to enter and exit a sole proprietorship because there are very few legal requirements. The owner registers the business or trade name to make sure that another firm does not use the same name. The owner next pays for any necessary licences. Local governments require certain licences for businesses, such as restaurants, motels or hotels, and retail stores. Some occupational licences require that business owners have specific insurance, such as liability coverage.

Sole proprietorships are also easy to dissolve. This factor is particularly important to temporary or seasonal businesses that set up for a limited period of time. It's also helpful if the owner needs or wants to close the business for any reason—for example, to relocate or to accept a full-time position with a larger firm.

Management flexibility is another advantage of a sole proprietorship. The owner can make decisions without reporting to a manager, take quick action, and keep trade secrets. A sole proprietorship always bears the individuality, or style, of its owner, whether it's a certain way of cutting hair or how a store window is decorated.

The greatest disadvantage of the sole proprietorship is the owner's personal financial liability for the business's debts. Also, the business must operate with financial resources that are limited to the owner's personal funds and to money that he or she can borrow. Such financing limitations can keep the business from expanding.

Another disadvantage is that the owner must handle a wide range of management and operational tasks. He or she may not have skills in every area, which may keep the firm from growth or may even cause the firm damage. Sole proprietors may also face a higher chance of being audited by the Canada Revenue Agency (CRA). Finally, a sole proprietorship usually lacks long-term continuity because a change in personal circumstances or finances can terminate the business on short notice.

Partnerships

partnership an association of two or more persons who operate a business as co-owners by voluntary legal agreement.

Another option for organizing a business is to form a partnership. A **partnership** is an association of two or more persons who operate a business as co-owners by voluntary legal agreement. Many small businesses begin as partnerships between co-founders.

Partnerships are easy to form. The partners need to register the business name and obtain any necessary licences. Having a partner usually means greater financial capability and someone to share in the tasks and decision making. It's even better if one partner has a particular skill, such as design, while the other is good at finance.

Most partnerships have the downside of being exposed to unlimited financial liability. Each partner bears full responsibility for the debts of the firm, and each is legally liable for the actions of the other partners. If the firm fails and has debt, every partner is responsible for those debts. It doesn't matter if the debts are the fault of only one partner. If one partner defaults, the others are responsible for the firm's debts, even if they have to use their personal funds. To avoid these problems, many firms set up a limited-liability partnership. This type of partnership limits the liability of partners to the value of their interests in the company.

Breaking up a partnership is more complicated than dissolving a sole proprietorship. The partner who wants to leave cannot just withdraw his or her portion of the funds from the bank. Instead, the partner who wants out may need to find a new partner to buy his or her interest in the firm. The death of a partner also threatens the business. A new partnership must be formed, and the estate of the deceased can take a share of the firm's value. To ease the possible financial difficulties, business planners suggest life insurance coverage for each partner, combined with a buy–sell agreement. The insurance proceeds can be used to repay the deceased partner's heirs. That way, the surviving partners can retain control of the business. Businesses that are based on partnerships risk having personal conflicts. Partners need to choose each other carefully. Best friends sometimes don't make the best partners. Good partners work hard and try to plan for the future.

Corporations

A **corporation** is a legal organization that has assets and liabilities separate from the assets and liabilities of its owners. A corporation can be a large or small business. It can be Air Canada or a local auto repair shop.

Corporate ownership offers many advantages. Because a corporation is a separate legal entity, its shareholders have only limited financial risk. If the firm fails, the shareholders lose only the money they invested. The same goes for the firm's managers and executives. Because they are not the sole proprietors or partners in the business, their personal savings are not at risk if the company closes or goes bankrupt. This protection also extends to legal risk. Class-action suits against automakers, drug manufacturers, and food producers are filed against the companies, not the owners of those companies.[42]

Corporations offer other advantages. They can gain access to more funding because they can offer direct outside investments such as sales of shares. A large corporation can legally raise internal funds for projects by transferring money from one part of the corporation to another.

One major disadvantage for a corporation is the double taxation of corporate earnings. A corporation pays federal and provincial income taxes on its profits. But its owners (the shareholders) also pay personal taxes on dividends, the distributions of profits they receive from the corporation.

corporation a legal organization with assets and liabilities separate from the assets and liabilities of its owners.

Not-for-Profit Corporations

The same business concepts that apply to commercial companies also apply to **not-for-profit corporations**—organizations whose goals do not include pursuing a profit. Canada has about 160,000 not-for-profits, including charitable groups, social-welfare organizations, government agencies, and religious congregations. Not-for-profit corporations also include museums, libraries, hospitals, conservation groups, and private schools.

Governments have separate legal provisions for organizational structures and operations of not-for-profit corporations. These organizations do not issue shares because they do not pay dividends to owners, and their ownership rarely changes. They are also exempt from paying income taxes. However, they must meet very strict guidelines to keep their not-for-profit status.

Montreal's Sun Youth Organization was founded in 1954 by a small group of kids tired of the few sports and recreational activities in the St. Lawrence Blvd./boul. Saint Laurent area (now Le Plateau). The entrepreneurial kids created a handwritten newspaper called the *Clark Street Sun*. They sold the newspaper door to door to raise funds to pay for the sports activities. The children themselves organized most of the activities. Finally, they were able to purchase equipment and uniforms for the increasing number of children involved. As these early groups of children grew older, Sun Youth became the social services organization known and supported by Montrealers of every language and ethnic background. Today, the organization works with schools, police officers, firefighters, medical professionals, corporations, and volunteers to deal with referrals from more than 170 social service agencies from the Greater Montreal area.[43]

not-for-profit corporations organizations whose goals do not include pursuing a profit.

✓ **ASSESSMENT CHECK**

5.7.1 What are the key differences between sole proprietorships and partnerships?

5.7.2 What is a corporation?

5.7.3 What is the main characteristic of a not-for-profit corporation?

PUBLIC AND COLLECTIVE OWNERSHIP OF BUSINESS

LO 5.8 Describe public and collective (co-operative) business ownership.

Most businesses in Canada are owned by the private sector, but some firms are owned and operated by local, provincial, or federal governments. For example, Manitoba Hydro, New Brunswick Power, and many other electricity utility companies are owned entirely or partially by governments.[44]

In another type of ownership structure, groups of customers can collectively own a company. At the end of the year, after paying suppliers, employees, and operating costs, the co-op returns any remaining funds to members as patronage shares. In another collective ownership structure, smaller firms can group together to own a larger organization. Both types of collective ownership structures are called co-operatives.

Mountain Equipment Co-op is a collectively owned retailer that sells outdoor gear and clothing.

Deborah Baic/The Globe and Mail/The Canadian Press

Public (Government) Ownership

One alternative to private ownership is some form of *public ownership*. In public ownership, a government unit or agency owns and operates an organization. In Canada, local governments often own the city's bus companies, parking structures, and water systems. The Toronto Transit Commission operates the network of buses, subways, and streetcars that serve the city of Toronto. People who support public ownership believe that services can be provided to more people when profits are turned back to the company to provide more services. However, some people disagree. These people say the supporters' belief has no proof. There is evidence to support parts of both sides of the argument.

Sometimes, public ownership results when private investors are unwilling to invest in a high-risk project—or when operating an important service is simply unprofitable. VIA Rail Canada operates the national passenger rail service for the Government of Canada. VIA was established as an independent Crown Corporation in 1977. It provides public transportation by operating trains that serve 450 communities across the country. Each year, VIA carries more than 4 million customers on a fleet of 400 passenger cars.[45]

Collective (Co-operative) Ownership

Collective ownership sets up an organization called a *co-operative* (or *co-op*). The owners work together to operate all or part of the activities in their firm or industry. Currently, about 100 million people are employed by co-operatives around the world.[46] Co-operatives allow small businesses to pool their resources for purchases, marketing, equipment, and distribution. Discount savings can be split among members. Co-operatives often share equipment and expertise. During difficult economic times, members of a co-operative find a variety of ways to support each other.

Canada has more than 8,400 co-ops. These co-ops employ more than 152,000 people: more than 87,000 work in non-financial co-operatives and more than 32,000 work in the agricultural sector. Canada has 5.9 million co-operative members, which means that four of every 10 Canadians are members of a co-operative. At least seven co-ops are listed in the top 500 companies in Canada. Several financial co-operatives, such as Vancouver's Vancity Credit Union network, have been rated among the best places to work in Canada.[47]

✓ **ASSESSMENT CHECK**

5.8.1 What is public ownership?

5.8.2 What is collective ownership? Where are co-operatives typically found, and what benefits do they provide small businesses?

LO 5.9 Describe the ownership structure of corporations and the levels of corporate management.

ORGANIZING A CORPORATION

A corporation is a legal structure. It also requires a more complex organizational structure than a sole proprietorship or a partnership. This complexity explains why we often think of a corporation as a large entity, even though it does not have to be a big company.

Where and How Businesses Incorporate

Businesses owners who want to incorporate must decide where to locate their headquarters. They must also follow the correct procedure for filling out the legal document that sets up the corporation.

Where to Incorporate

The business decision of where to incorporate—and establish headquarters—may be based on a number of factors. Most businesses want to be near their customers. Other factors are real estate prices, public transportation, and communications networks. Access to a good source of employees is another reason for choosing a location. Online businesses such as Amazon.ca and eBay don't need to worry about being located near their customers, but they should think about the local source of employees.

Most small- and medium-sized businesses are incorporated in the provinces where they operate, but a Canadian firm can actually incorporate in any province it chooses. The founders of large corporations, or the founders of corporations that do business nationwide, often compare the benefits—such as tax incentives. Some provinces are considered to be more "business friendly" than others. For example, Alberta has one of the lowest taxes for incorporated businesses in Canada.

- Name and Address of the Corporation
- Corporate Objectives
- Type and Amount of Stock to Issue
- Expected Life of the Corporation
- Financial Capital at the Time of Incorporation
- Provisions for Transferring Shares of Stock among Owners
- Provisions for Regulating Internal Corporate Affairs
- Address of the Business Office Registered with the Province
- Names and Addresses of the Initial Board of Directors
- Names and Addresses of the Incorporators

FIGURE 5.3
Traditional Articles of Incorporation

The Corporate Charter

A corporation is like an artificial person created by law, with most of the legal rights of a real person. These rights include the rights to start and operate a business, to buy or sell property, to borrow money, to sue or be sued, and to enter into binding contracts.

Incorporation of a business can be done at the federal or provincial level. Legally, if you incorporate provincially, your corporation has the right to carry on business only in the province where your business is incorporated. This rule is not a problem for restaurants and other businesses that have a fixed location, but it might be a problem for others. Federally incorporated businesses are permitted to operate everywhere in Canada.

Each province has a specific process for incorporating a business. For example, the individual or individuals who create the corporation must select a name that is different from the names used by other businesses. Figure 5.3 lists the 10 elements that are typically required for chartering a corporation.

The information in the articles of incorporation forms the basis on which a government grants a *corporate charter*. This charter is the legal document that formally establishes a corporation. After securing the charter, the owners prepare the company's bylaws, which set out the rules for operation.

FIGURE 5.4 Levels of Management in a Corporation

Corporate Management

Every corporation, large or small, has levels of management and ownership. Figure 5.4 illustrates the typical levels—although a smaller firm might not have all five levels. These levels range from shareholders down to supervisory management.

Stock Ownership and Shareholder Rights

shareholders owners of a corporation as a result of their purchase of shares in the corporation.

At the top of Figure 5.4 are **shareholders**. They buy shares of stock in the corporation, which makes them part owners. Some companies, such as many family businesses, are owned by only a few shareholders, and the shares are generally unavailable to outsiders. In such a firm, known as a *closed* or *closely held corporation*, the shareholders also control and manage all of the company's activities.

An open corporation, also called a *publicly held corporation*, is different. It sells shares to the general public, which sets up a diversified ownership. This type of ownership often leads to a broader range of operations than in a closed corporation. Publicly held corporations usually hold annual shareholders' meetings. During these meetings, managers report on corporate activities, and shareholders vote on decisions that require their approval, including elections of officers.

Shareholders' role in the corporation depends on the class of stock they own. Shares are usually either common shares or preferred shares. Although owners of **preferred shares** have limited voting rights, they receive dividends before the holders of common shares. If the corporation is dissolved, the owners of preferred shares have first claims on assets, once all debtors are repaid. Owners of **common shares** have voting rights but only residual claims on the firm's assets. That means they are the last to receive any income distributions. Because one share is typically worth only one vote, small shareholders generally have little influence on corporate management actions.

Board of Directors

Shareholders elect a **board of directors**—the governing body of a corporation. The board sets overall policy, authorizes the corporation's major transactions, and hires the chief executive officer (CEO). Most boards include both inside directors (corporate executives) and outside directors—people who are not employed by the organization. Sometimes, the corporation's top executive also chairs the board. Generally, outside directors are also shareholders, so they have a financial stake in the company's performance.

Corporate Officers and Managers

The CEO and other members of top management, such as the chief operating officer (COO), the chief financial officer (CFO), and the chief information officer (CIO), make most major corporate decisions. Managers at the next level down, the middle management, handle the ongoing operational functions of the company. At the first tier of management, supervisory personnel coordinate day-to-day operations, assign tasks to employees, and evaluate job performance.

Today's CEOs and CFOs work under stricter regulations than in the past. They must verify in writing the accuracy of their firm's financial statements. The process for nominating candidates for the board has also become more complex. In short, more checks and balances are in place for the governance of corporations.

WHEN BUSINESSES JOIN FORCES

LO 5.10 Describe mergers, acquisitions, and joint ventures.

Today's business environment includes many complex relationships among businesses and not-for-profit organizations. Two firms may team up to develop a product or to co-market products. One company may buy another company. Large corporations may split into smaller units. The list of alliances can be as varied as the organizations themselves, but the major trends in corporate ownership are mergers and acquisitions (M&A) and joint ventures.

Mergers and Acquisitions (M&A)

The terms *merger* and *acquisition* are often used interchangeably, but their meanings are different. In a **merger**, two or more firms combine to form one company. In an **acquisition**, one firm purchases the other. This purchase means that the buyer acquires the firm's property and assets *and* takes on the firm's debt. Acquisitions also occur when one firm buys a division or a subsidiary from another firm. A recent study looked at mergers and acquisitions in the global mining sector. The study suggests Canadian firms are major players in this sector. Canadian firms were involved in 36 percent of the almost 3,000 deals that represented more than $113 billion in value.[48]

Mergers can be classified as vertical, horizontal, or conglomerate. A **vertical merger** combines firms operating at different levels in the production and marketing process. For example, the combination of a manufacturer and a large retailer is a vertical merger. A vertical merger pursues one of two main goals: (1) to ensure adequate flows of raw materials and supplies needed for a firm's products or (2) to increase distribution. Microsoft is well known for acquiring small firms that have developed products with strong market potential, such as Teleo, a provider of voice over

preferred shares shares that give owners limited voting rights and the right to receive dividends or assets before owners of common shares.

common shares shares that give owners voting rights but only residual claims to the firm's assets and income distributions.

board of directors the governing body of a corporation.

✓ **ASSESSMENT CHECK**

5.9.1 What are the two key elements of the incorporation process?

5.9.2 Identify the five main levels of corporate ownership and management.

merger an agreement in which two or more firms combine to form one company.

acquisition an agreement in which one firm purchases another.

vertical merger a merger that combines firms operating at different levels in the production and marketing process.

Internet protocol (VoIP) software and services that can be used to make phone calls via the Internet.

A **horizontal merger** joins firms in the same industry. Firms use a horizontal merger to diversify, to increase their customer base, to cut costs, or to expand product lines. This type of merger is popular in the auto industry. India-based Tata Motors bought the Jaguar and Land Rover brands from Ford Motor Corp. Volkswagen owns Audi and Porsche.

A **conglomerate merger** combines unrelated firms. The most common reasons for a conglomerate merger are to diversify, to increase sales, or to spend a cash surplus to avoid a takeover attempt. Conglomerate mergers may join firms in totally unrelated industries. General Electric is well known for its conglomerate mergers, including its ownership of healthcare services and household appliances. Experts debate whether conglomerate mergers are a good idea. Those in favour of such mergers say that a company can use its management expertise to succeed in a variety of industries. But the obvious downside is that a huge conglomerate can spread its resources too thin to be successful in any one market.

Toronto Star/Ron Bull/The Canadian Press

Joint ventures between for-profit firms and not-for-profit organizations provide great benefits for both parties. Becel has been the title sponsor for the Heart and Stroke Foundation's Ride for Heart for the past 19 years, helping to raise funds supporting research and education on heart disease and stroke.

Joint Ventures: Specialized Partnerships

A **joint venture** is a partnership between companies for a specific activity. Sometimes a company enters into a joint venture with a local firm to share the operation's costs, risks, management, and profits. This type of joint venture is common when a firm wants to start a business in a foreign market. A joint venture can also help companies to solve a common problem.

Joint ventures between for-profit firms and not-for-profit organizations are becoming common. These partnerships provide benefits for both parties. Not-for-profit organizations receive the funding, marketing exposure, and sometimes the staff they might not have on their own. The CIBC, New Balance, East Side Mario's, the Running Room, Canpar, and Revlon are some of the Canadian businesses that have partnered with the Canadian Breast Cancer Foundation's Run for the Cure. The annual event raised $33 million across the country.[49]

Joint ventures between not-for-profits and for-profit firms are often good for businesses, too. Firms that partner with environmental groups can cut costs, save energy, and reduce waste. For example, McDonald's partnered with the Environmental Defense Fund. McDonald's was then successful in phasing out harmful packaging, converting much of its cooking oil to biodiesel, getting rid of more than 136 million kg of packaging, and reducing restaurant waste by more than 30 percent.[50]

WHAT'S AHEAD

The next chapter focuses on the driving forces that lead to new businesses: entrepreneurs. It examines the differences between a small-business owner and an entrepreneur. It also identifies the personality traits common to most entrepreneurs. The chapter also describes the process of launching a new venture, including identifying opportunities, locating financing, and turning good ideas into successful businesses. Finally, the chapter explores a method for infusing the entrepreneurial spirit into established businesses—intrapreneurship.

RETURN TO INSIDE BUSINESS

Pi Athlete Management Inc.: Advising athletes about their careers and more

According Daniel Smajovits of Pi Athlete Management, the firm avoids "hustling" athletes. Instead, it relies on word-of-mouth referrals to attract new clients.

"Our short game is to represent professional athletes. The athletes come to us via word of mouth and through athletes whom we currently represent. We are not actively trying to poach other athletes from their agents for two reasons: 1) We are trying to eliminate the sleaze factor in this industry. I do not want to be the guy in the hotel lobby passing out business cards to currently represented players. 2) We do not want to take on more than we can handle. If an athlete comes to us, we will see what we can do for him: while it might sound nice to say that we represent 20 professional athletes, if I can't be there equally for each guy, then it's all smoke and mirrors. If we know that an athlete is unhappy with his current representation, we would love to speak with him as we know we can do better by him, but it's not something we actively pursue.

Additionally, for our professional athletes, one unique selling point about us is that we can take care of all their off-field needs in house. We're working with one lawyer and one CA/CPA, both with a tremendous amount of experience and a vast international network, so all their legal, financial and tax work can be handled by us. My background in marketing and PR is vital to provide media training, to seek out marketing opportunities and coordinate media appearances."

QUESTIONS FOR CRITICAL THINKING

1. What other professional consulting services would be helpful for Pi Athlete Management to offer to athletes?

2. What else can Pi Athlete Management do to increase its network of consultants and athletes?

SUMMARY OF LEARNING OBJECTIVES

LO 5.1 Distinguish between small and large businesses.

A small business is an independently owned business that has fewer than 50 employees and revenues less than $2 million. A small business is not usually the leading business in its field. It meets industry-specific size standards for income or number of employees. A business is classified as large when its number of employees or revenue exceeds these standards.

 ASSESSMENT CHECK ANSWERS

5.1.1 How does Statistics Canada define *small business*? Statistics Canada defines a small business as an independent business that has fewer than 100 employees and revenues not more than $2 million.

5.1.2 In what industries do small businesses play a significant role? Small businesses provide many jobs in construction, agriculture, wholesale trade, services, and retail trade.

LO 5.2 Discuss the contributions of small businesses to the economy.

Small businesses create new jobs and new industries. They often hire people who have difficulty finding jobs at larger firms. Small firms give businesspeople the opportunity and outlet for developing new ideas. Sometimes these new ideas become entirely new industries. Small businesses also develop new and improved goods and services.

 ASSESSMENT CHECK ANSWERS

5.2.1 What are the three key ways that small businesses contribute to the economy? Small businesses create new jobs, create new industries, and provide innovation.

5.2.2 How are new industries formed? New industries are formed when small businesses shift their focus to meet consumer interests and preferences. Innovation and new technology can play a significant role. In addition, new industries can be created when both the business world and consumers see a need for change.

LO 5.3 Discuss the survival rate of small businesses.

About 96 percent of small businesses (1–99 employees) that enter the marketplace are in business for one full year, 85 percent are in business for three years, and 70 percent are in business for five years. Failure is often attributed to management inexperience, inadequate financing, and difficulty meeting government regulations.

 ASSESSMENT CHECK ANSWERS

5.3.1 What percentage of small businesses are still operating five years after starting? About 70 percent are in business after five years.

5.3.2 What are the three main causes of small-business failure? The three main causes of small-business failure are management inexperience, inadequate financing, and difficulty meeting government regulations.

LO 5.4 Describe the features of an effective business plan.

A complete business plan contains an executive summary, an introduction, financial and marketing sections, and résumés of the business principals. An effective business plan uses these five sections and includes the company's mission, an outline of what makes the company unique, identification of customers and competitors, financial evaluation of the industry and market, and an assessment of the risks.

 ASSESSMENT CHECK ANSWERS

5.4.1 What are the five main sections of a business plan? The five sections are the executive summary, introduction, financial section, marketing section, and résumés of the principals.

5.4.2 Why is an effective business plan important to the success of a firm? The business plan puts in writing all the reasons the firm can be successful. It contains the company's mission and addresses many issues, including the vision of its founders and why the company is unique. It is the document that is needed to obtain financing. The business plan also creates a framework for the organization.

LO 5.5 Describe funding opportunities for small businesses, including the role of the Business Development Bank of Canada (BDC).

The Business Development Bank of Canada (BDC) is a government agency that assists, counsels, and protects the interests of small businesses in Canada. BDC was created by an act of Parliament in 1944. It operates across Canada through offices and resource centres that provide long-term financial assistance and management counselling. The BDC also provides training, technical assistance, and education to help small businesses prepare for doing business in foreign markets. Statistics show that most failures in small businesses happen because of poor management. For this reason, the BDC works to improve the management skills of small-business owners and managers.

 ASSESSMENT CHECK ANSWERS

5.5.1 What are the various ways the BDC helps small businesses? The BDC provides long-term financial assistance and management counselling. It also provides business information, advice, and training to owners of small businesses.

5.5.2 What are business incubators? Business incubators are programs that community agencies set up to help small businesses get started. Their services can include low-cost rental space, shared clerical staff, and shared office equipment, such as computers.

5.5.3 Why are small businesses good opportunities for women? Women feel they can achieve more as small-business owners and can balance family and work more easily if they own their own firms.

LO 5.6 Explain how franchising provides opportunities for both franchisors and franchisees.

A franchisor is a large firm that allows a small-business owner (a franchisee) to market and sell the larger firm's products under its brand name, in return for a fee. The franchisor's opportunities include the possibilities of expansion and greater profits. The franchisee's benefits include name recognition, quick start-up, support from the franchisor, and the freedom of small-business ownership.

 ASSESSMENT CHECK ANSWERS

5.6.1 What is the difference between a franchisor and a franchisee? A franchisor permits a small-business owner (the franchisee) to market and sell the franchisor's products under its brand name, in return for a fee.

5.6.2 How does franchising benefit both parties? Benefits to the franchisor include opportunities for expansion and greater profits. Benefits to the franchisee include name recognition, quick start-up, support from the franchisor, and the freedom of small-business ownership.

5.6.3 What are the potential downsides of franchising for both parties? The downsides for the franchisor include franchisees' mismanagement and failure, overexpansion, and loss of control over the business. Downsides for the franchisee include the initial expenses, failure of the franchisor or other franchisees, and overly controlling franchise agreements.

LO 5.7 Outline the three main legal forms of business ownership and summarize the features of not-for-profit organizations.

The three legal forms of business ownership are sole proprietorships, partnerships, and corporations. A sole proprietorship is owned and operated by one person. Sole proprietorships are easy to set up and offer great operating flexibility, but the owner is personally liable for all of the firm's debts and legal responsibilities. In a partnership, two or more individuals share responsibility for owning and running the business. Partnerships are relatively easy to set up, but they do not protect either partner from liability. A corporation is a separate legal entity from its owners. Investors receive shares of stock in the firm. Owners have no legal and financial liability beyond their individual investments. The legal structure of a not-for-profit corporation requires that its goals do not include earning a profit.

 ASSESSMENT CHECK ANSWERS

5.7.1 What are the key differences between sole proprietorships and partnerships? Sole proprietorships have more management flexibility and are easier to dissolve than partnerships. Partnerships require shared workload and decision making, whereas sole proprietorships are entirely the responsibility of one business owner.

5.7.2 What is a corporation? A corporation is a legal organization that has assets and liabilities separate from the assets and liabilities of its owners. A corporation can be a large or small business.

5.7.3 What is the main characteristic of a not-for-profit corporation? A not-for-profit corporation is an organization whose goals do not include pursuing a profit. Governments have separate legal provisions for organizational structures and operations of not-for-profit corporations. They are also exempt from paying income taxes.

LO 5.8 Describe public and collective (co-operative) business ownership.

In public ownership, a government unit or agency owns and operates an organization. Collective ownership sets up an organization called a co-operative. The owners join forces to operate all or part of the activities in their firm or industry.

 ASSESSMENT CHECK ANSWERS

5.8.1 What is public ownership? Public ownership occurs when a unit or agency of government owns and operates an organization.

5.8.2 What is collective ownership? Where are co-operatives typically found, and what benefits do they provide small businesses? Collective ownership sets up an organization called a *co-operative* (or *co-op*). The owners work together to operate all or part of the activities in their firm or industry. Co-operatives are frequently found among agricultural businesses. They can also occur in retail. Co-operatives allow small firms to pool their resources, share equipment and expertise, and help each other through difficult times.

LO 5.9 Describe the ownership structure of corporations and the levels of corporate management.

Shareholders are the owners of a corporation. In return for their financial investments, they receive shares of stock in the company.

Shareholders elect a board of directors, who set overall policy. The board hires the chief executive officer (CEO), who then hires the managers.

 ASSESSMENT CHECK ANSWERS

5.9.1 What are the two key elements of the incorporation process? The two key elements are where to incorporate and the corporate charter.

5.9.2 Identify the five main levels of corporate ownership and management. The five levels are the shareholders, the board of directors, top management, middle management, and supervisory management.

LO 5.10 Describe mergers, acquisitions, and joint ventures.

In a merger, two or more firms combine to form one company. A vertical merger combines firms operating at different levels in the production and marketing process. A horizontal merger joins firms in the same industry. A conglomerate merger combines unrelated firms. An acquisition occurs when one firm purchases another. A joint venture is a partnership between companies for a specific activity.

 ASSESSMENT CHECK ANSWERS

5.10.1 Distinguish between a merger and an acquisition. In a merger, two or more firms combine to form one company. In an acquisition, one firm purchases another company. The buyer acquires the firm's property and assets *and* takes on the firm's debt. Acquisitions also occur when one firm buys a division or a subsidiary from another firm.

5.10.2 What are the different kinds of mergers? Mergers can be classified as vertical, horizontal, or conglomerate. A vertical merger combines firms operating at different levels in the production and marketing process. A horizontal merger joins firms in the same industry. A conglomerate merger combines unrelated firms.

5.10.3 What is a joint venture? A joint venture is a partnership between organizations formed for a specific activity.

BUSINESS TERMS YOU NEED TO KNOW

small business 129	venture capital 138	corporation 145	merger 149
home-based businesses 130	franchising 140	not-for-profit corporation 145	acquisition 149
business plan 135	franchisee 141	shareholders 148	vertical merger 149
Business Development Bank of Canada (BDC) 137	franchisor 141	preferred shares 149	horizontal merger 150
	sole proprietorship 143	common shares 149	conglomerate merger 150
business incubator 138	partnership 144	board of directors 149	joint venture 150

REVIEW QUESTIONS

1. Describe how a small business might use innovation to create new jobs.

2. Why do so many small businesses fail before they reach their fifth year?

3. What are the benefits of developing and writing an effective business plan?

4. What is the Business Development Bank of Canada? How does it assist small companies, financially and in other ways?

5. Describe how local governments and business incubators help small firms to set up and grow.

6. Why are so many small-business owners attracted to franchising? When would it be better to start an entirely new business instead of purchasing a franchise?

7. What are the upsides and downsides of traditional corporate structure?

8. Co-operatives appear frequently in agriculture. Describe another industry where collective ownership would work well, and explain why.

9. In a sole proprietorship and in partnerships, the owners and the managers are the same people. How are ownership and management separated in corporations?

10. How can a joint venture between a commercial firm and a not-for-profit organization help both parties to achieve their goals?

PROJECTS AND TEAMWORK APPLICATIONS

1. Research a large firm to learn more about its beginnings as a small business. Who founded the company? Does the firm still produce its original product or service, or does it provide a new product or service?

2. Go to the website Entrepreneur.com to research franchises. Choose a franchise that interests you and look up its start-up requirements. Would you run a franchise in a partnership with someone you know? Why or why not? Present your findings in class.

3. Think of an idea for a small business. Research the industry and the major competition online. Draft a business plan. Will your firm be a sole proprietorship or a partnership? Include this decision in your business plan.

4. Identify an organization that is owned by a unit or agency of government, such as VIA Rail or BC Hydro. Imagine that you have been hired by as a consultant. You must decide whether the organization should remain publicly owned. Research its successes and failures. Write a memo to explain your conclusion.

5. Identify a business and a not-for-profit organization that could form a joint venture that would have good for both parties. Write a proposal or create an advertisement for the event or activity that the organizations could present.

WEB ASSIGNMENTS

1. **Small-business successes.** Visit the website at http://www.businessweek.com/smallbiz/successstories/. Scroll through the titles of success stories and choose one that interests you. Read the feature and prepare a brief report answering these questions:

   a. What does the firm do?

   b. Where did the idea come from?

   c. What expertise does the owner have?

   d. How did the business begin?

   e. Who are its competitors?

2. **Business Development Bank of Canada (BDC).** Go to the BDC's website at http://www.bdc.ca/EN/Pages/home.aspx. Click on Advice Centre and have a look at the articles. Identify one article that you believe provides the most useful information for a small business owner. Write a summary of the article's highlights.

Note: Internet Web addresses change frequently. If you do not find the exact sites listed, you may need to access the organization's or company's home page and search from there.

Access your WileyPLUS course for:

- The complete digital textbook.

- Question assistance, including links to relevant sections in the online digital textbook.

- Immediate feedback and proof of progress, 24/7

- Integrated, multi-media resources – including MP3 downloads, visual exhibits, animations, and much more – that provide multiple study paths and encourage more active learning.

QUIZ YOURSELF

© Can Stock Photo Inc./mangostock

6 | STARTING YOUR OWN BUSINESS: THE ENTREPRENEURSHIP ALTERNATIVE

LEARNING OBJECTIVES

LO 6.1 Define the term *entrepreneur*, and distinguish among entrepreneurs, small-business owners, and managers.

LO 6.2 Identify the different types of entrepreneurs.

LO 6.3 Explain why people choose to become entrepreneurs.

LO 6.4 Discuss factors that support and expand opportunities for entrepreneurs.

LO 6.5 Identify personality traits that typically characterize successful entrepreneurs.

LO 6.6 Summarize the process of starting a new venture.

LO 6.7 Explain how organizations promote intrapreneurship.

INSIDE BUSINESS

Halo by Shoshana: An Entrepreneurial Success Story in Fashion Accessories

Courtesy of Shoshana Finn

How can a woman highlight her clothing to create a fashionable look? It's simple—use accessories. The right accessories do more than just match an outfit. The right accessories can create a one-of-a-kind image.

That's just what Montreal-based Shoshana Finn thought. She designs custom-made head and hair accessories for New York theatres. But she decided to also make accessories for every woman that could transform the ordinary into the extraordinary. Halo by Shoshana shows once again that the entrepreneurial spirit is alive and well. Shoshana has succeeded in one of the most challenging industries—the fashion world. Of course, it probably helps that Shoshana's parents and grandparents were also Montreal garment makers. It probably helps even more that she learned about the business on the inside as the industry was changed by global competitive forces.

The Canadian apparel industry is the 10th largest manufacturing sector in Canada. According to Statistics Canada, this industry comprises 2,150 mostly small business manufacturers. Most are located in Quebec, Ontario, Manitoba, and British Columbia. Quebec has 55 percent of all industry activity. More than 1,000 apparel businesses are located in Montreal, the historical capital of the industry. These businesses employ more than 33,500 people in Montreal. For more than a century, local people and new immigrants have worked in this industry, mostly at semi-skilled jobs, such as sewing. Only 5 percent of Montreal-based apparel businesses employ more than 100 people; 95 percent employ fewer than 100 people; 66 percent employ fewer than 10 employees; and the average is only 29 employees per company. Why are these companies so small? Many apparel businesses outsource some steps in the production process to other local firms that specialize in an area and have invested in labour-saving machines.

The Canadian industry employs about 70,000 workers and ships over $5.5 billion worth of clothing. About 39.5 percent of the clothing made is exported, mainly to the U.S. market. Smaller Canadian producers are helped by their closeness to American customers, smaller production runs, and quick delivery times. However, the industry is facing more and more difficulties due to rising costs for labour, fabrics, marketing, and the rising exchange rate on the American dollar. The lower-valued Canadian dollar acted as a subsidy for exporters in 2003 when it was worth US$0.65. But the increase in the exchange rate means the Canadian dollar is worth closer to US$1. The higher exchange rate is a challenge to Canadian manufacturers, who now compete with lower-costing imports from China and India.

Less than 20 years ago, about 70 percent of the textile and clothing products sold in Canada were made in Canada. But Canadian manufacturing has changed. The biggest reason for the change is the removal of barriers to multilateral trade. At the Uruguay Round of negotiations, World Trade Organization member-countries agreed to remove all quotas in four stages, from 1995 to 2005. With the end of quotas, Canadian manufacturers were no longer protected from imports. According to the Canadian Apparel Federation, the clothing manufacturing industry lost more than 40,000 jobs from 2001 to 2006.

In response, Canadian manufacturers have increased their investment in more efficient machinery and equipment. They have automated more of the production process, focused on fewer lines of products, and increased marketing effort into new markets. They have also started to outsource more large-scale production runs to China and India, where labour costs are much lower.

Another response is more smaller-scale specialty businesses like Halo by Shoshana. Shoshana's business focuses on a specialized product with unique value for fashion-conscious customers.

Halo by Shoshana can compete because it offers unique quality and design. The marketing power of the Internet also helps. The firm's website shows high-quality *haute couture* photographs of models. If visitors like what they see, they can order online. The site also shows the products for retailers who might decide to carry the accessories in their stores.[1]

CHAPTER 6 OVERVIEW

You think you want to start and run your own company. Like Shoshana Finn who founded Halo by Shoshana, you've got a great idea for a new business and you dream of fame and fortune. If you are entrepreneurial, you're not alone. More than ever, people like you, your classmates, and your friends are choosing to be entrepreneurs.

How do you become an entrepreneur? Experts advise people who want to be entrepreneurs to learn as much as possible about business. Take courses and complete academic programs such as the one you are currently taking. Try to gain practical experience by working part-time or full-time. Shoshana Finn learned about the fashion business while she was growing up. Both her grandfather and father ran successful garment manufacturing businesses. You can also learn about the upsides and downsides of entrepreneurship by reading newspaper and magazine articles and biographies of successful entrepreneurs. You will learn how entrepreneurs handle the challenges of starting their businesses. Need advice on how to launch and grow a new venture? Turn to magazines such as *Entrepreneur*, *Forbes*, *Fast Company*, *Success*, and *Inc*. You can also get assistance from entrepreneurship associations, such as the Canadian Federation of Independent Business (CFIB). Anyone who wants to be an entrepreneur should visit the websites listed in Figure 6.1.

Canada Business	www.canadabusiness.ca
Business Development Bank	www.bdc.ca
Entrepreneur.com	www.entrepreneur.com
Canadian Chamber of Commerce	www.chamber.ca
U.S. Chamber of Commerce	www.uschamber.com
Kauffman Foundation	www.kauffman.org
U.S. Small Business Administration	www.sba.gov
The Wall Street Journal Small Business	http://online.wsj.com/small-business

FIGURE 6.1
Internet Resources for Entrepreneurs

In this chapter, we focus on how to enter the world of entrepreneurship. This chapter describes the activities of entrepreneurs, the different kinds of entrepreneurs, and the reason more and more people are choosing to be entrepreneurs. We will discuss the business environment where entrepreneurs work, the characteristics that help entrepreneurs succeed, and how they start new ventures. The chapter ends with a discussion of how large companies try to keep the entrepreneurial spirit alive and well.

LO 6.1 Define the term *entrepreneur*, and distinguish among entrepreneurs, small-business owners, and managers.

entrepreneur a person who seeks a profitable opportunity and takes the necessary risks to set up and operate a business.

WHAT IS AN ENTREPRENEUR?

An **entrepreneur** is a risk taker in the private enterprise system, a person who seeks a profitable opportunity and takes the necessary risks to set up and operate a business. Think about Vancouver's Jim Pattison, founder of the Jim Pattison Group. He started by purchasing a car dealership in 1961. Today, he is head of a private Canadian corporation that had 2010 revenues of about $7.2 billion. The company works in the automotive, media, packaging, food sales and distribution, magazine distribution, entertainment, export, and financial industries. Today, the Jim Pattison Group is Canada's third largest private company.[2]

Entrepreneurs differ from many small-business owners. Many small-business owners share the same drive, creative energy, and desire to succeed. But entrepreneurs are different because one of their major goals is expansion and growth. (Many small-business owners want to keep their businesses small.) Jim Pattison wasn't happy having just one successful business, so he purchased and developed others. Entrepreneurs combine their ideas and drive with money, employees, and other resources to create a business that meets a need.

Entrepreneurs also differ from managers. Managers are employees who direct others to reach an organization's goals. Owners of some small start-up firms work as owner-managers to carry out their plans for their businesses and to make up for human resource limitations at their new

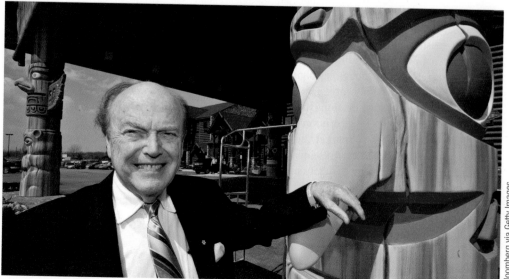

Vancouver's Jim Pattison is founder of the Jim Pattison Group. In 1961, he purchased a car dealership. Today, he is head of Canada's third largest private corporation.

Bloomberg via Getty Images

companies. Entrepreneurs may also perform a managerial role, but their main responsibility is to use the resources of their organizations—employees, money, equipment, and facilities—to accomplish their goals.

Studies have identified certain personality traits and behaviours common to entrepreneurs that differ from the traits and behaviours needed for managerial success. One of these traits is the willingness to take on the risks of starting a new venture. Some take that risk because they need to—they've left or lost their previous jobs or just need a way to make money. Others, like Jim Pattison, want a challenge or a different quality of life. Entrepreneurial characteristics are examined in detail later in this chapter.

✓ **ASSESSMENT CHECK**

6.1.1 What tools do entrepreneurs use to create a new business?

6.1.2 How do entrepreneurs differ from managers?

CATEGORIES OF ENTREPRENEURS

LO 6.2 Identify the different types of entrepreneurs.

Entrepreneurs use their talents in different situations. These differences can be classified into three categories: classic entrepreneurs, serial entrepreneurs, and social entrepreneurs.

Classic entrepreneurs see business opportunities and set aside resources to gain access to those markets. Shoshana Finn of Halo by Shoshana is a classic entrepreneur. She saw a niche in the fashion accessories market and designed unique products. Her one-of-a-kind accessories soon brought her attention—and customers who want to enhance their wardrobe and style.

A classic entrepreneur starts a new company by seeing a business opportunity and setting aside resources to gain access to a new market. **Serial entrepreneurs** are different. They start one business, run it, and then start and run more businesses, one after another. Juha Christensen is a serial entrepreneur. He never earned a college degree but gained experience working in his family's small aviation company outside Copenhagen. At age 17, he started a computer-reselling business. For more than two decades he has been a big player in the wireless sector: he helped lead the way for personal digital assistants before there was a Palm Pilot; he persuaded some of the world's top cellphone makers to use a common operating system called Symbian; he headed Microsoft's move into smartphones; a few years later, he moved on to Web start-up Macromedia and made millions when the company was sold to Adobe Systems. Then he created Sonopia, which leases part of the radio communications spectrum owned by Verizon Wireless and resells it to other companies

classic entrepreneur a person who sees a business opportunity and sets aside resources to gain access to that market.

serial entrepreneur a person who starts one business, runs it, and then starts and runs more businesses, one after another.

social entrepreneur a person who sees societal problems and uses business principles to develop new solutions.

✓ ASSESSMENT CHECK

6.2.1 What do classic entrepreneurs and social entrepreneurs have in common?

6.2.2 Is a social entrepreneur simply a philanthropist who gives to good causes to help others?

who sign up their own customers. Using customized handsets and customer support provided by Sonopia, small, diverse organizations can become phone companies with their own networks. Recently, Christensen became a venture partner at Sunstone Capital, a leading European venture capital firm that provides funding for start-ups.[3]

Some entrepreneurs focus on solving society's challenges through their businesses. **Social entrepreneurs** see a societal problem and use business principles to develop new solutions. Social entrepreneurs develop new solutions that help humanity. More than 50 years ago, a group of seven Indian women gathered one afternoon to roll out dough to make traditional crackers. They saw an opportunity to make and market these crackers for a wider audience. They set up a women's cooperative that was based on this idea. They called their business Lijjat Papad and hoped to empower Indian women entrepreneurs. Since then, the cooperative's president, Jyoti Naik, has led the cooperative to become one of India's most successful business ventures. The company now produces a wide variety of bakery products, spices, and flour. It has 62 branches across India. The cooperative brand is one of the most popular and trusted in India. It is viewed as the best-run small-village cooperative in the nation.[4]

LO 6.3 Explain why people choose to become entrepreneurs.

REASONS TO CHOOSE ENTREPRENEURSHIP AS A CAREER PATH

If you want to run your own business, you have lots of company. During one recent year, about 23,000 new businesses were created each month in Canada. The United States has more people and created more businesses—there, 530,000 new businesses were created each month. In both countries, new businesses in services and the construction industry had the highest rates of activity.[5]

In the past few decades, more people have shown interest in entrepreneurial careers. They may have been encouraged in part by publicity around the successes of entrepreneurs such as Mark Zuckerberg. He launched the global social-networking website Facebook while he was a student at Harvard University.

As shown in Figure 6.2, people become entrepreneurs for one or more of four major reasons: a desire to be their own boss, a desire to succeed financially, a desire to attain job security, and a desire to improve their quality of life. Each of these reasons is described in more detail in the following sections.

Being Your Own Boss

One of the biggest reasons for becoming an entrepreneur is the chance to be your own boss. Entrepreneurs have the freedom to make all the decisions. In Montreal's West Island area, Carmine Petrillo has made Monster Gym an inviting community-oriented gym for people who are serious and not-so-serious about exercise. When gym clients need to decide whether to renew their memberships or join another club, they often consider the condition of the exercise equipment. For gym owners, deciding when to upgrade to new equipment is an expensive decision: a single exercise machine can cost thousands of dollars. Monster Gym clients are lucky. Carmine has made such decisions on his own since opening his doors in 1994. He is good at looking ahead to keep meeting the needs of his suburban clientele. After all, they have grown used to having the latest and best exercise equipment. Carmine's decision to upgrade equipment often and regularly has helped grow the client base to 4,500 people.[6]

Being your own boss usually means having to make all the important decisions. It also means engaging in most—if not all—of the communication related to your business, including dealing with customers, suppliers, distributors, retailers, and others. The "Business Etiquette" feature offers tips for professional-style communication—even if you're on the run and using your thumbs.

Desire to Be One's Own Boss

Desire to Succeed Financially

Desire for Job Security

Desire for an Improved Quality of Life

FIGURE 6.2 Why People Become Entrepreneurs

Carmine Petrillo created Monster Gym, an inviting community-oriented gym for people who are serious and not-so-serious about exercise. For many people, the main reason for being an entrepreneur is to control when, where, and how they work.

BUSINESS ETIQUETTE

Communicating by E-mail, Text Message, or Social Networking Updates: You Don't Have to Be All Thumbs

Most entrepreneurs use e-mail, texting, social networking updates, and other electronic communications to reach their customers, suppliers, distributors, employees, and others. That communication often takes place on the run; when you are your own boss, you are busy taking care of many tasks. You may think of yourself as being fast with the cellphone or smartphone keyboard, and maybe you can send off an e-mail in no time. Still, it might be a good idea to review a few etiquette tips to make sure your messages sound professional.

- Don't write in all caps. Using all capital letters makes the message look frantic, or as if you are yelling.

- On the subject line, do *not* write "Important—Please Read." That kind of message is likely to end up in a "delete" box, unread. Also, try to avoid sending any kind of "forwarded" messages—for the same reason. Instead, use a short but descriptive subject line so the person you are emailing knows what the message is about. An example is "Review of Tuesday's Meeting."

- Avoid slang expressions and shorthand, such as "LOL," "ru," and "L8." Also don't use smiley or sad-face icons.

- Be friendly but not too familiar. Never include jokes in a business e-mail or text message.

- Be brief. A short message is more helpful than a long message. If you need to say more, then end the e-mail by saying you will follow up with a phone call.

- Remember that your computer and your phone are like a tape recorder. Messages can be saved and stored. You do *not* want to make an unprofessional comment that could cause problems later. Never add personal messages to professional messages. Avoid complaints or criticisms that could hurt your company's image or the reputation of others.

Sources: Mark Grossman, "Email Etiquette Is Important," *Grossman Law Group*, http://www.ecomputerlaw.com, accessed March 16, 2010; "Business Email Etiquette: What You Should Know BEFORE You Hit Send," http://www.evancarmichael.com/Women-Entrepreneurs, accessed March 16, 2010; Karl Stolley and Allen Brizee, "Email Etiquette," *Purdue Owl*, http://owl.english.purdue.edu, accessed March 16, 2010; Nina Kaufman, "Making it Legal," Entrepreneur.com, http://legal.entrepreneur.com, accessed March 16, 2010.

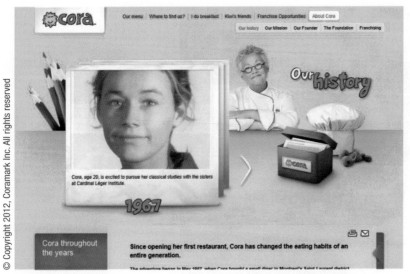

In 1987, Cora Tsouflidou opened her first restaurant in Montreal. She offered a big-breakfast menu of crepes, omelettes, fruits, and cereals. Her recipe of high-quality, healthier food was a hit with customers. Today, the family-run company has 120 Chez Cora franchise locations across Canada. Family members actively manage the firm and enjoy their financial success.[7]

Financial Success

Entrepreneurs create wealth. Many start their ventures with the specific goal of becoming rich—or at least financially successful. Entrepreneurs often believe they have an idea for a better product. They want to be the first to bring it to market—and to receive the financial rewards as a result. Entrepreneurs believe they won't achieve their greatest success by working for someone else—and they're generally right. Of course, the downside is that when they fail, they become unemployed.

Job Security

The demand for skilled employees remains high in many industries. But working for a company, even a *Fortune* 500 firm, is no guarantee of job security. In fact, over the past 10 years, large companies have looked for efficiencies by downsizing and getting rid of more jobs than they created. As a result, more and more workers—both first-time job seekers and laid-off long-term employees—are deciding to create their own job security by starting their own businesses. Having your own business doesn't guarantee job security, but research has found that most newly created jobs come from small businesses. Many of those new jobs are in new companies.[8]

Economies are changing overseas. Workers there are discovering the benefits of entrepreneurship compared with being employed by big firms. In China, entire industries are government-owned, such as banking, steel, and telecommunications. Many young Chinese businesspeople are starting their own small firms. China has nearly 500 million people under the age of 30. Their role models are Bill Gates and Michael Dell, reports an entrepreneurship professor at the Europe International Business School in Shanghai.[9]

Quality of Life

Entrepreneurship is a good career option for people who want to improve their quality of life. Starting a business means independence and some freedom to decide when, where, and how to work. A **lifestyle entrepreneur** is a person who starts a business for two reasons: to gain flexibility in work hours and to gain control over his or her life. It does *not* mean working fewer hours or easier work. Generally it is the opposite—people who start their own businesses often work longer and harder than ever before, at least in the beginning. But they enjoy being successful, both materially and in the way they live their lives.

Zhena Muzyka, a single mom, needed a job that gave her flexibility and earning power. Her young son, "needed operations [for kidney disease], and the insurance wasn't going to cover them. I had to come up with a job where I could have him with me because he had special needs," Muzyka explains. So she combined her interest in herbal medicine with fair-trade practices. That's how she started her firm, Gypsy Tea. Today, Muzyka's son is healthy, and Gypsy Tea is a multimillion-dollar firm. It produces flavoured teas grown on fair-trade farms in Peru, India, and other countries. Workers at these farms receive health care, clean water, maternity leave, child care, and other benefits. New products have been added to the Gypsy Tea line, including candles and beads. "It's the most 'worth-it' thing I've ever done," says Muzyka of Gypsy Tea.[10] Another group of entrepreneurs also found a way to make their business fit their lifestyle and their creative interest in home fragrance products. Read about Fruits & Passion co-owners Jean Hurteau; his wife, France Menard; and brother, Guy Hurteau, in the "Hit & Miss" feature.

lifestyle entrepreneur a person who starts a business to reduce work hours and create a more relaxed lifestyle.

 ASSESSMENT CHECK

6.3.1 What are the four main reasons people choose to become entrepreneurs?

6.3.2 What factors affect the entrepreneur's job security?

(HIT) & MISS

Fruits & Passion for Lifestyle Products

Fruits & Passion is a popular beauty, body, and lifestyle products retailer. This business is the result of a great success story in a very competitive global marketplace. The firm creates unique fragrances for oils, candles, other personal care products. It uses ingredients gathered from around the world to make its products and then wraps them in attractive packaging.

Fruits & Passion was started in 1991 by Jean Hurteau; his wife, France Menard; and his brother, Guy Hurteau. The threesome believed that the "lifestyle market" for personal luxuries was beginning to grow, and they wanted to be part of it. Stores like The Body Shop were leading the way in the personal care market. But the partners sensed that people's desire for personal lifestyle quality would also lead to demand for other products for the home. For example, small decorative candles could enhance a room's quality if the design and fragrance were just right. Little things could make a big difference in their kitchens, bathrooms, and bedrooms.

Before long, the firm was selling its creative products through a dozen Canadian retail stores, which they still own and operate today. But, to truly realize the potential sales, the company needed a large retail distribution network to provide products to customers in more markets.

Currently, the firm sells its products through 150 Fruits & Passion retailers—93 are in Canada—and through more than 2,000 independent retailers around the world. Fruits & Passion franchise retailers can be found in England, Taiwan, China, Morocco, Mexico, France, the United States, and Canada. The company's website helps people to learn about the variety of products it sells and is set up for online sales.

Questions for Critical Thinking

1. Why do these products sell so well around the world?

2. What entrepreneurial characteristics do you think were needed to make this business a success?

Sources: Company website, http://www.fruits-passion.ca/, accessed January 18, 2012.

THE ENVIRONMENT FOR ENTREPRENEURS

LO 6.4 Discuss factors that support and expand opportunities for entrepreneurs.

Are you ready to start your own company? Do some research about the environment where you want to do business. You'll need to think about several important overall factors. First is the economy—whether it is stalled or booming, you may find opportunities. Think about where you want to locate your business.

The general attitude toward entrepreneurs in North America is positive. In addition to favourable public attitudes and more financing options, four additional factors also support and expand opportunities for entrepreneurs: globalization, education, information technology, and demographic and economic trends (see Figure 6.3). Each of these factors is discussed in the following sections.

Globalization

The rapid globalization of business has created many opportunities for entrepreneurs. Entrepreneurs market their products abroad and hire international talent. Most of the fastest-growing small Canadian companies have international sales—usually to the United States. For example, despite being in Montreal, Halo by Shoshana sells handmade hair accessories all over the world, including to celebrities. Shoshana Finn's hair accessories have been worn by models in such fashion magazines as *Marions-Nous*, *Chatelaine*, and *Lou Lou*.[11]

Entrepreneurship is growing around the world. The role of entrepreneurs is growing in most industrialized countries, in newly industrialized countries, and in the emerging free-market countries in central and eastern Europe. However, the level of entrepreneurship varies. Worldwide,

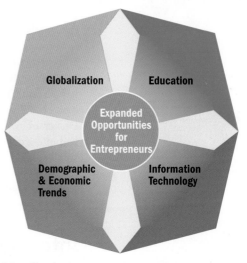

FIGURE 6.3 Factors Supporting and Expanding Opportunities for Entrepreneurs

more than 9 percent of adults are starting or managing a new business. Thailand leads in the number of adults engaged in entrepreneurial activity (27 percent), followed by Peru (26 percent), Colombia (23 percent), Venezuela (20 percent), Dominican Republic (17 percent), and China (16 percent).[12]

India has experienced a big increase in the number of female entrepreneurs. Shahnaz Husain knew the effects that chemical-based beauty care products can have on consumers—and on the environment. In 1971, she opened India's first professional herbal salon on the balcony of her house in Delhi. She now runs a respected beauty care empire called Ayurvedic. Husain's Ayurvedic products contain natural ingredients, ranging from vegetables to diamond dust. "The ancient Indian system of Ayurveda is the oldest and most organized system of herbal healing in the world. I was convinced that it could offer ideal answers to cosmetic care," explains Husain. "I entered highly competitive international markets, without commercial advertising or fancy packaging." Ayurvedic supplies its products to high-end stores in London, Paris, and Milan, and in shops located in Spain and Japan.[13]

Education

In the past 20 years, more educational opportunities have been offered for would-be entrepreneurs. Today, students at many colleges and universities can take a major in entrepreneurship. Dozens of other colleges and universities offer an emphasis in entrepreneurship, and hundreds more offer one or two courses in how to start a business.

Many schools offer opportunities to intern with a start-up or to work toward launching a company. Most large universities in Canada, such as Simon Fraser University's Beedie School of Business, host entrepreneurial centres for research and development of new business. The school recently hosted an event that included two expert judges from the CBC program *Dragons' Den*, Jim Treliving and Bruce Croxon.[14]

In addition to schools, many other organizations have opened in recent years to teach entrepreneurship to young people. The Kauffman Center for Entrepreneurial Leadership offers training programs for learners from kindergarten through community college. The center's Entreprep summer program is taught in cooperation with local colleges and universities. This summer program teaches high-school juniors how to start and manage a company. Students in Free Enterprise (SIFE) is a worldwide not-for-profit organization. College students work with faculty advisors to teach grade-school and high-school students and others the value of private enterprise and entrepreneurship.[15] The Association of Collegiate Entrepreneurs has chapters on many school campuses in Canada and the United States.

You don't have to major in business to become an entrepreneur, but students who major in entrepreneurship or take entrepreneurship courses are three times more likely to start their own business or to help someone else to start a business.[16] You don't have to wait for graduation to launch your first start-up, and your business idea doesn't have to change the world. Record numbers of college students are launching their own businesses—while still in school. When Ryan Dickerson was a junior living in a small dorm room at university, he figured out how to turn his bed into a couch during the day. It was a good idea that gave him the furniture he needed for the small space. He designed a special bolster pillow that was the same length as his bed. During the day, this pillow became the "back" of the couch. He called his invention the Rylaxer. The pillows were first made locally and sold on campus. Dickerson immediately drew up a business plan for selling them nationwide.[17]

Information Technology

The explosion in information technology (IT) has been one of the biggest advances for entrepreneurs. Computer and communications technologies have merged, and their costs have dropped. Low-cost technology has given entrepreneurs the tools they need to help them compete with large companies. Information technology helps entrepreneurs to work quickly and efficiently and to provide immediate and helpful customer service. Information technology also increases sales and gives businesses a professional image. In fact, technology has made it possible for a dorm-room innovator like Ryan Dickerson to compete with a much larger firm. Technology has also assisted in the huge increase of *homepreneurs*—entrepreneurs who run home-based businesses. These successful ventures are described in the "Hit & Miss" feature.

Social networking has also changed the business environment for entrepreneurs. According to a recent study, more than 90 percent of successful companies now use at least one social media tool. Many entrepreneurs have included the use of sites such as Twitter, LinkedIn, and Facebook in their business strategy. They believe that social media will help them reach more customers and grow faster. Social media will give these entrepreneurs a competitive edge. Eric Mattson, a researcher for *Inc.* magazine, believes that social networking is more useful to small firms run by entrepreneurs than to larger firms because "in smaller organizations, there is more room for innovation because it requires [fewer] processes to adopt."[18]

Demographic and Economic Trends

Who else is starting a business? Two groups are most likely to start their own businesses: immigrants to North America and people between the ages of 55 and 64.[19] As baby boomers continue to age and control a large share of North American wealth, the trend is expected to continue. Older entrepreneurs will also have access to their retirement funds and home equity for financing. Many boomers plan to work after retiring from their traditional jobs or careers. Some just want to keep working; others want to add to their income and savings.

As mentioned earlier, more college and university students are becoming entrepreneurs. Ted Livingston, the founder and chief executive officer (CEO) of Waterloo-based Kik Interactive

HIT & MISS

Businesses Based at Home Are Booming

The idea itself makes perfect sense: you've been laid off from your full-time job, or you've recently moved to a new area, or you just had a baby. Working from home seems like the ideal solution. But until a few years ago, home-based businesses were not really considered to be real businesses by many in the business community. Most people viewed home-based work as no more challenging—or successful—than stuffing envelopes. All that has changed. Today, more than 6.6 million home-based businesses contribute at least half of their owners' household income. *Homepreneurs* are estimated to employ about one in every 10 private-sector workers—and their businesses are competitive. Technology has made all this possible.

Some homepreneurs run businesses that are entirely based on technology, such as Web development. Stephen Labuda is president of Agency3. He is a former programmer for Deutsche Bank, a large international banking firm. Labuda built websites on the side for several years. Then he quit his job and made Agency3 his full-time, home-based career. The firm's revenues are in the millions, and Labuda has about half a dozen employees. Labuda loves working from home. "I'm not intending to go rent office space," he notes.

Other homepreneurs rely on technology to reach customers, fulfill orders, ship goods, and provide other services. When Michael and Mary Ferrari retired, they realized they needed to supplement their savings—and they didn't want to stop working. So they formed UnusualThreads.com, a company that sells fashions worn by celebrities. The couple still only works the site part-time, but they earn enough money to add to their savings and can take time off to travel. Another homepreneur is Marco Barberini, who launched OvernightPetTags.com several years ago. He now grosses more than $8,000 a month. Barberini discovered how to manufacture and ship pet-identification tags cheaper than his competition. Barberini echoes the advice of every successful homepreneur. "Most people give up too quickly," he says. "Just make sure that [your product] is going to be something that's in demand, and do it."

Questions for Critical Thinking

1. Could any of these home-based businesses succeed without the heavy use of information technology? Why or why not?

2. Outline your own idea for a home-based business that relies on technology.

Sources: Steven Berglas, "Wake-up Call for Newly Hatched Entrepreneurs," Forbes.com, February 6, 2010, http://www.forbes.com; Carol Tice, "Homepreneur Winners Keep Growing Despite Downturn," Entrepreneur.com, February 1, 2010, http://blog.entrpreneur.com; John Tozzi, "The Rise of the Homepreneur," *BusinessWeek*, accessed January 8, 2010, http://www.businessweek.com.

✓ **ASSESSMENT CHECK**

6.4.1 To what extent is entrepreneurship possible in different countries, and what opportunities does globalization create for today's entrepreneurs?

6.4.2 Identify the educational factors that help expand current opportunities for entrepreneurs.

6.4.3 Describe current demographic trends that suggest new goods and services for entrepreneurial businesses.

Inc., studied mechatronics engineering at the University of Waterloo between 2005 and 2009. He founded Kik (then called Unsynced) while in the VeloCity residence in the winter term of 2009. VeloCity is a student residence–based start-up incubator that was set up in September 2008 at the University of Waterloo. VeloCity is a community that educates and connects talented, like-minded students with each other and with the surrounding start-up community for support and mentorship. At age 23, Livingston showed his appreciation by donating $1 million to VeloCity.[20]

Demographic trends can create opportunities for entrepreneurs. For example, the aging of the population, the growth of ethnic groups, and two-income families can lead to new markets for products and services. Services designed for older consumers, foods that cater to ethnic preferences, and convenience products for busy parents all have an opportunity for success. As the economy rises and falls, entrepreneurs who are flexible and can adapt quickly have the best chance for success. When consumers are less willing to spend money, certain businesses do well. For example, a shoe-repair shop will likely see an increase in business. The Play It Again chain of North American stores sells used sports equipment. This retail chain's business will also likely increase. Skates and protective hockey gear are often used for only one or two seasons before a child has outgrown them. The slightly used equipment will be a great bargain for another family looking to outfit the next Sidney Crosby in their family.[21]

LO 6.5 Identify personality traits that typically characterize successful entrepreneurs.

CHARACTERISTICS OF ENTREPRENEURS

People who start a business of their own are true innovators. They aren't satisfied with things the way they are but want to achieve certain goals on their own terms. Successful entrepreneurs often have parents who were entrepreneurs—or who had dreams of starting their own business. Most entrepreneurs share some specific personality traits. Researchers have studied successful entrepreneurs and report that they are more likely to be curious, passionate, self-motivated, honest, courageous, and flexible. The eight traits shown in Figure 6.4 are especially important for people who want to succeed as entrepreneurs.

Entrepreneurial Personality

Vision

High Energy Level

Need to Achieve

Self-Confidence and Optimism

Tolerance for Failure

Creativity

Tolerance for Ambiguity

Internal Locus of Control

FIGURE 6.4
Characteristics of Entrepreneurs

Vision

Entrepreneurs generally begin with a *vision*—an overall idea for how to make their business idea a success. Then they follow this vision with energy and excitement. Bill Gates and Paul Allen launched Microsoft with the vision of a computer on every desk and in every home, all running Microsoft software. Their vision helped Microsoft become the world's largest marketer of computer software. It guided the company and provided clear direction for employees. This kind of direction was especially helpful as Microsoft grew, adapted, and prospered during huge technological changes.

It can be said that every invention, from the light bulb to the cellphone, started with someone having a vision—viewing the world in a slightly different way. Some inventions have been created out of need or because of a mistake. True entrepreneurs can turn these situations into opportunities. In the healthcare field, penicillin was created by accident. Products with narrower markets have also found success. Jodi Pliszka has an autoimmune disorder that causes baldness. She's an athlete who spent years searching for a product that would keep her head cool and dry under helmets and during exercise. She couldn't find anything, but instead of giving up, she invented what she needed. The result is called HeadlineIt, a thin, lightweight disposable liner worn under helmets, wigs, and hats. Within a few years, Pliszka received a design patent for her product, and sales hit the $1 million mark. Pliszka was first a clinical therapist and an author. Now she is also a successful entrepreneur.[22]

High Energy Level

Entrepreneurs work long and hard to make their visions a reality. Many entrepreneurs work full-time at their regular day jobs and spend weeknights and weekends launching their start-ups. Many entrepreneurs work alone or with a very small staff. That means that the entrepreneurs themselves do most—if not all—of the work needed to get the business going. This work includes tasks related to the start-up's design, marketing, sales, and finances. Most entrepreneurs spend at least 70 hours a week on their new business. This time can affect their other job (if they have one) and their personal life—at least in the beginning.[23] Thus, entrepreneurs need a high level of energy if they want to succeed.

Need to Achieve

Entrepreneurs work hard because they want to do well. Their strong desire to compete helps them to enjoy the challenge of reaching difficult goals. It also promotes a commitment to personal success. A poll by About.com showed Oprah Winfrey as the most admired entrepreneur among adults. She is the first African American woman to become a billionaire. Winfrey has built an empire that includes television, magazines, and radio. Her own words best illustrate her strong drive: "I don't think of myself as a poor, deprived ghetto girl who made good. I think of myself as somebody who from an early age knew I was responsible for myself, and had to make good."[24] But when teens were polled by Junior Achievement, they picked Apple founder Steven Jobs as their most admired entrepreneur. Teens said that Jobs "made a difference in/improved people's lives or made the world a better place."[25] Both of these entrepreneurs have achieved very high goals.

Self-Confidence and Optimism

Entrepreneurs believe that they can succeed, and their self-confidence and excitement leads to optimism in others. Their optimism can seem like fearlessness in the face of difficult odds. They see opportunities where others see danger. Ishita Khanna founded her not-for-profit organization, Ecosphere, in one of the harshest living areas on the planet, the Spiti valley in Tibet. But this valley is also one of the most beautiful—and searched for—locations for eco-travellers. Khanna believed that if small entrepreneurial businesses in Tibet—especially those run by women—could be linked, they would have more power. She knew it wouldn't be easy. "Spiti's geographical isolation and poor communication infrastructure has been one of the major hurdles," Khanna now admits. But Khanna didn't give up, and Ecosphere recently received the Green Livelihoods Achievement Award from The Sierra Club. "There are numerous doubts that plague one before one takes the plunge," Khanna says. "But if you are passionate about what you want to do, that is half the battle won already."[26]

© Richard Drew/AP/Wide World Photos

Tolerance for Failure

Entrepreneurs often succeed because of their strong will and because they continue to try again and again when others would give up. They also view setbacks and failures as learning experiences. They are not easily discouraged or disappointed when things don't go as planned. Bobbi Brown has built a big name in the cosmetics industry. Estée Lauder bought her company, and Brown stayed on in an active role. The brand faced some setbacks after its acquisition. Sales decreased, but Brown never gave up. She met with the CEO, who said the problem was that the cosmetics were not setting themselves apart from the competition. Brown tried to understand the criticism, learned from the setback, and decided to change the culture of the company. She made the advertising photographs more editorial, and approached the cosmetics business as if it were a magazine. The company's numbers improved and hit half a billion dollars.[27]

Entrepreneurs often succeed simply because they won't give up. When sales of Bobbi Brown's cosmetics line slowed, she moved the company to a new location and updated its advertising. In the process, she successfully made her company stand out from the competition.

When things go well, it's easy to take personal credit. But when poor business decisions result in failure, it's more difficult. Truly successful entrepreneurs are willing to take responsibility for their mistakes. That is why an important part of launching any new business is establishing a code of ethics, as discussed in the "Solving an Ethical Controversy" feature.

Creativity

Entrepreneurs think of new ideas for goods and services. They also devise new ways to overcome difficult problems and situations. When we look at the top entrepreneurs in the world, we can see that creativity is a common trait. *Inc.* magazine presents an annual list of the 500 top small businesses, most of which were started by entrepreneurs. The word *solution* is one of the most common words in the names of these companies.

Some entrepreneurs find creative solutions to problems; others find creative ways to complete a task or provide a service. Still others create entirely new products. Aaron Patzer started Mint.com because he and his friends and family were frustrated with Intuit's Quicken products. He believed that he could develop a more user-friendly personal-finance software—and he did. Two years later, Patzer sold his website to Intuit for $170 million.[28]

SOLVING AN **ETHICAL** CONTROVERSY

Entrepreneurs and Ethics: It's Good Business

When you're starting a new business, it's easy to get caught up in the excitement: a fresh start, a new idea, visions of fame and fortune. It might seem harmless to present an overly optimistic sales picture or to be a bit vague about where and how your product will be produced. After all, once your invention hits the stores, sales will skyrocket and everyone will forgive what you said before. But experts in every industry warn against unclear communication and decision-making. Your business could fall flat, and failure may come in the form of a damaged image or legal problems. You might be someone who can tolerate some failures, but a wise entrepreneur knows how to prevent other failures—such as a failure of ethics.

Should every new business have a formal code of ethics?

PRO

1. A code of ethics "embodies the ethical commitments of your organization," writes business author Chris MacDonald. "It tells the world who you are, what you stand for, and what to expect when conducting business with you." It also shows leadership.

2. A code of ethics is a necessity in today's business environment. Without it, when a difficult incident or event happens, a small firm may be exposed to "greater risk from regulatory and prosecutorial authorities," observes Michael Connor, publisher of *Business Ethics*.

CON

1. Not every entrepreneurial enterprise, particularly those run by one person, needs a formal code of ethics. A person's word or a handshake is just as effective. The important thing is to convey honesty and integrity about the way your firm will do business.

2. There are too many stories in the media about businesspeople who have failed to make ethical decisions—and not enough stories about the many entrepreneurs who conduct business every day in an ethical manner. A code of ethics will not make a bad person good; nor will lack of a code turn a good person bad.

Summary

Some people argue that writing a formal code of ethics takes too much time; others recommend outsourcing the task to a consultant or another third party. However, the overwhelming majority of business experts advise taking the time and effort to develop a code of ethics. If a company has more than one employee, then all employees should be required to become familiar with the code. As an entrepreneur, you will face many challenges and probably a few failures; but none should be a failure of ethics.

Sources: "Business Ethics," Small Business Administration, http://www.sba.gov, accessed March 16, 2010; Carter McNamara, "Complete Guide to Ethics Management," *Management Help*, http://www.managementhelp.org, accessed March 16, 2010; Chris MacDonald, "Considerations for Writing a Code of Ethics," *Streetwise Small Business Book of Lists*, accessed March 16, 2010; Josh Spiro, "How To Write a Code of Ethics for Business," Inc.com, February 24, 2010, http://www.inc.com; Don Knauss, "The Role of Business Ethics in Relationships with Customers," Forbes.com, January 19, 2010, http://www.forbes.com.

Tolerance for Ambiguity

Entrepreneurs take in stride the uncertainties of launching a business. Dealing with unexpected events is normal for most entrepreneurs. Tolerance for ambiguity is different from the love of risk-taking that many people relate to entrepreneurship. Successful entrepreneurship is not at all like gambling. Entrepreneurs look for strategies that they believe have a good chance of success. When a strategy isn't working, they quickly make changes. An important way entrepreneurs manage ambiguity is by staying close to customers so that they can change their offerings to match customer desires. One such entrepreneur is Kevin Mitnick. In the mid-1990s, Mitnick was arrested by the FBI for computer hacking, after which he served five years in prison. When he was released, Mitnick could have hidden his identity and started a new life—or gone on to further crimes. Instead, Mitnick went legitimate, opening his own computer security consulting company. He maintains a solid relationship with the businesses whose systems he once might have compromised. "The lifestyle of an entrepreneur is not so different from that of a hacker," quips Mitnick. "The only thing lacking is the sneakiness, the seduction of adventure." His firm, Mitnick Security Company, is earning more than $750,000 a year.[29]

Internal Locus of Control

Entrepreneurs have an internal locus of control. That means they believe that they control their own future. You won't find entrepreneurs blaming others or outside events for their successes or failures—they own it all.

Ralph Braun was diagnosed with a degenerative illness when he was 6 years old. By the time he was 14, he was in a wheelchair. Braun attended college but for only one year. He had to drop out because he couldn't get around the large campus in his wheelchair. So he decided to design his own transportation. Within about four months, he had built his first scooter. Then he got a job at a local automotive supply factory. There, he was able to get around easily on his scooter. People noticed and told him about friends or family members who needed a scooter like that. He started building them to order. Braun then began to focus on the van he was driving. He redesigned the interior to include a wheelchair/scooter lift that is now standard on buses and other mass transit. Again, he received requests to convert the vans of other wheelchair-bound drivers. Eventually Braun quit his factory job to focus on his business full-time. BraunAbility is now a $200 million empire. When he began building scooters, Braun recalls, "everyone told me it wasn't going to work. But when it comes to commonsense engineering, I'm very blessed. I think it is a [natural] ability." Braun is clearly in charge of his fate.[30]

✓ **ASSESSMENT CHECK**

6.5.1 What do we mean when we talk about an entrepreneur's vision?

6.5.2 Why is it important for an entrepreneur to have a high energy level and a strong need for achievement?

6.5.3 How do entrepreneurs generally feel about the possibility of failure?

STARTING A NEW VENTURE

LO 6.6 Summarize the process of starting a new venture.

Entrepreneurs can start a business in many different ways. This section discusses how to choose an idea for a new venture and how to turn a good idea into a working business.

Selecting a Business Idea

When choosing an idea for your business, remember the two most important things: (1) find something you love to do and are good at doing and (2) find an idea that meets a need in the marketplace. People willingly work hard doing something they love, and the experience will bring personal fulfillment. The old sayings "Do what makes you happy" and "Be true to yourself" are the best guidelines for deciding on a business idea.

Success also depends on customers. Would-be entrepreneurs need to be sure that the idea they choose will interest customers in the marketplace. The most successful entrepreneurs tend to work in industries where lots of change is taking place. These are usually the same industries where customers have difficulty deciding on their exact needs. In these industries, entrepreneurs can make use of their strengths, such as creativity, hard work, and tolerance of ambiguity. They can use these strengths to build customer relationships. But outstanding entrepreneurial success happens in every industry. Maybe you want to build a business based on your grandmother's cookie recipes, or maybe you have a better idea for tax-preparation software. Whatever your idea is, you are more likely to succeed if you ask yourself the right questions from the beginning.

Consider the guidelines in Figure 6.5 as you think about your business ideas.

FIGURE 6.5
Guidelines for Selecting a Business Idea

- List your interests and abilities. Include your values and beliefs, your goals and dreams, things you like and dislike doing, and your job experiences.
- Make another list of the types of businesses that match your interests and abilities.
- Read newspapers and business and consumer magazines. Learn about demographic and economic trends that discuss future needs for products that no one yet offers.
- Carefully evaluate existing goods and services. Look for ways to improve them.
- Decide on a business that matches what you want and offers profit potential.
- Do marketing research to decide whether your business idea will attract enough customers to earn a profit.
- Learn as much as you can about the industry in which your new venture will operate, your product or service, and your competitors. Read surveys that project growth in different industries.

Many entrepreneurs invent new products or new ways of doing things. The inventor–entrepreneur needs to protect the rights to his or her invention by obtaining a patent. In Canada, the Patent Office is part of the Canadian Intellectual Property Office (CIPO), an agency of Industry Canada. The U.S. Patent and Trademark Office provides information about this process from an American perspective.

Corin and Brian Mullins are the founders of Hapi Foods Group. Their company uses organic ingredients to make two artisan cereals, Holy Crap and Skinny B. The mom-and-pop start-up business is located in Sechelt, on the Sunshine Coast of British Columbia. This start-up is doing well in the very competitive breakfast cereal market. Read their story in the "Going Green" feature.

Buying an Existing Business

Some entrepreneurs prefer to buy established businesses instead of taking on the risks of starting new businesses. Buying an existing business brings many advantages: employees are already in place to serve regular customers and to deal with familiar suppliers, the good or service is already known in the marketplace, and the necessary permits and licences have already been obtained. It is easier to get financing for an existing business than for most start-ups. Some sellers may even help the buyers by providing financing and by offering to stay on as consultants. Most people want to buy a healthy business so that they can build on its success. But an experienced entrepreneur might buy a struggling business with the idea of turning it around. Entrepreneurs who are thinking about buying a business can use many resources, ranging from information provided by government agencies to websites listing actual companies for sale.

Buying a franchise is similar to buying an established business. Both are a less risky way to begin a business than starting an entirely new firm. But franchising (which was discussed in detail in Chapter 5) involves risks. It is a good idea to do thorough research before making any decision to start a new business.

GOING GREEN

HOLY CRAP: CORIN AND BRIAN MULLINS SURE KNOW HOW TO PICK A NAME FOR THEIR ORGANIC CEREALS

They named their cereals "Holy Crap" and "Skinny B." Everyone remembered these names when the couple appeared on the CBC's *Dragons' Den*. But the brand name was only one of several smart business decisions made by the Mullins. Their product is a good choice for customers who want a good-tasting organic cereal that (to be polite) helps with digestion and moving things along on the inside. Holy Crap has no genetically modified organisms (GMOs). It is made from all-natural ingredients: organic chia, hulled hemp hearts, organic buckwheat, organic cranberries, organic raisins, organic apple bits, and organic cinnamon.

The recipe is perfect for physically active young adults who want foods that fit with their lifestyle and taste good. Customers post "taste-imonials" on the company's website. Their comments show how much they believe in the products. For example, Will Kelsay is a professional XTERRA triathlete from Boulder, Colorado. His profile is titled "Holy Crap Cereal Is Rocket Fuel for Triathletes." It shows photos of Will in competition and bylines like "Will loves Holy Crap and the benefits of its super food ingredients." Will describes his belief in the product this way:

"The key ingredient of Holy Crap is chia, or Salvia Hispanica L. This oil seed crop is considered a perfect food because it's one of the few vegetarian sources of complete protein. The Aztecs valued it more highly than gold. Holy Crap cereal is a chia based wheat free, gluten free, lactose free breakfast cereal. The Tarahumara Indians in Copper Canyon, Mexico, the greatest long distance runners on the planet, have had a long history of using this slow burning rocket fuel for both athletes and warriors alike. The main cereal ingredient is Chia or Salvia Hispanica L., which typically contains 20% protein, 34% oil, and 25% dietary fiber. Salvia Hispanica L. contains the highest Omega-3 nutrient source found in nature with perfectly balanced Omega 3, 6, 9 profiles and ratios. The next most abundant ingredient is hulled hemp hearts, which are low in carbohydrates, contain more protein than milk, meat or eggs and are suitable for those unable to digest gluten, sugar, milk, nuts and meat." This kind of comment helps promote the cereals to serious athletes and to not-so-serious athletes that want to be like serious athletes—at least in what they eat.

The company has a warm relationship with its customers. It continues to do well because of brand name recognition. The company has retail distribution across North America at health food stores, specialty grocery stores, and through online shopping from their website.

Questions for Critical Thinking

1. Will the brand name help or hurt the company as it tries to grow further?

2. What are some other products that the company should consider developing and what names would you give them?

Sources: Company website, http://holycrap.ca/, accessed January 20, 2012; Julie Greco, "Is Holy Crap Cereal Milking the Hype?" *St. Catharines Standard*, November 26, 2010, http://www.stcatharinesstandard.ca/ArticleDisplay.aspx?e=2862817, accessed April 13, 2012; Allison Cross, "Sales Explode for Cereal with Cheeky Name," *Toronto Star*, November 23, 2010, http://www.thestar.com/living/article/895792--sales-explode-for-cereal-with-cheeky-name, accessed April 13, 2012; Remy Scalza, "Holy Crap: Local Cereal with Funny Name Goes Global," December 27, 2011, http://www.insidevancouver.ca/2011/12/27/holy-crap-local-cereal-goes-global/, accessed April 13, 2012.

Creating a Business Plan

In the past, many entrepreneurs launched their businesses without writing formal business plans. Planning is an important part of managing in contemporary business. But entrepreneurs often go after opportunities as they arise and then they change course when they need to. Flexibility seems to be the key to business start-ups, especially in rapidly changing markets. But starting a business has many risks. Doing at least some planning is not just advisable but necessary, especially when an entrepreneur needs to look for funds from outside sources.

Appendix F discusses business plans in more detail. The Internet also offers a variety of resources for creating business plans. Table 6.1 lists some of these online resources.

Table 6.1 Online Resources for Preparing a Business Plan

AllBusiness.com http://www.allbusiness.com	Under the Finance tab, select Business Planning for links to business plan examples, templates, and tips.
Inc. http://www.inc.com	Under the Start-Up tab, select Writing a Business Plan. There, you'll find articles on how to structure a business plan and how to write a mission statement. You'll also find a tutorial that shows how to use your business plan as a tool.
MoreBusiness.com http://www.morebusiness.com	To see sample plans, select "Write a Business Plan" under "Starting a Business."

Finding Financing

seed capital the initial funding needed to launch a new venture.

A key issue in any business plan is financing. The need for **seed capital**, the funds used to launch a company, depends on the nature of the business. Seed capital can range as high as several million—say, for the purchase of a McDonald's franchise in a lucrative area—or as low as $1,000 for a website design. Many entrepreneurs use personal savings. Some ask for loans from business associates, family members, or even friends to use as start-up funds. In fact, 82 percent of start-ups are self-financed, the greatest source by far.[31]

Debt Financing

debt financing borrowed funds that entrepreneurs must repay.

Entrepreneurs sometimes use **debt financing**, borrowed money that they must repay. Debt financing includes loans from banks, finance companies, credit-card companies, and family or friends. Some entrepreneurs charge business expenses to their personal credit cards, which are relatively easy to obtain. But high interest rates on credit cards mean that this source of funding is expensive. It is usually better to find other methods of funding.

Many banks turn down people who apply for loans to fund start-ups. The banks are fearful of the high risk of starting a new business. Over the last several years, more and more banks have turned down loan requests. Only a small percentage of start-ups raise seed capital through bank loans. Much planning and preparation is needed when applying for a bank loan. Bank loan officers want to see a business plan and will evaluate the entrepreneur's credit history. Because a start-up has not yet established a business credit history, banks often base lending decisions on the entrepreneurs' personal credit histories. Banks are more willing to make loans to three kinds of entrepreneurs: those who have been in business for a while, those whose businesses show a profit on rising revenues, and those who need funds to finance expansion. Some entrepreneurs find that local community banks or credit unions are more interested in their loan applications than are the major national banks.

Even entrepreneurs who have previously received funding from banks—and have maintained a good relationship with their lenders—have experienced credit difficulties in recent years. A line of credit is an approved loan that a business can borrow from when funds are needed. Without that money, some businesses would not be able to pay for the materials they need to make the products that customers have already ordered. The 2008–10 economic slowdown was made worse by the reduction in credit and (in many cases) the refusal to offer more credit to businesses that could no longer function without normal levels of credit.

Equity Financing

equity financing funds invested in new ventures in exchange for part ownership.

venture capitalists business firms or groups of individuals that invest in new and growing firms in exchange for an ownership share.

In **equity financing**, entrepreneurs exchange a share of ownership in their company for money supplied by one or more investors. Entrepreneurs invest their own money and the funds supplied by the other people and firms that become co-owners of the start-ups. An entrepreneur does not have to repay equity funds. Instead, the investors share in the success of the business. Sources of equity financing include family and friends, business partners, venture capital firms, and private investors.

Some entrepreneurs team up with a partner who has funds to invest. This arrangement may be good for an entrepreneur who has a great business idea and skills but little or no money. Some investors also have business experience. These investors will be eager to share their knowledge because if the company succeeds, they will succeed. But, like borrowing, equity financing has its downsides. For example, investment partners may not agree on the future direction of the business. When the disagreement happens in a partnership, and the partners cannot resolve their differences, one partner may have to buy out the other to keep operating.

Venture capitalists are business organizations or groups of private individuals that invest in early stage, high-potential, growth companies. Venture capitalists usually back companies

Some entrepreneurs find creative ways to obtain equity financing. Gavin McClurg's venture, Offshore Odysseys, is a sailing expedition aboard a catamaran named *Discovery*. Investors buy timeshare segments for between $20,000 and $30,000. During the journey, they might swim across the equator or paraglide above Tahiti.

Jody MacDonald Photography

in high-technology industries such as biotechnology. In exchange for taking a risk with their own funds, these investors expect high rates of return and a share of the company. Typical terms for accepting venture capital include agreeing on how much the company is worth, how much stock both the investors and the founders will retain, control of the company's board, payment of dividends, and the period of time during which the founders are prohibited from "shopping" for further investments.[32] Venture capitalists want to invest in companies that have a combination of extremely rare qualities: the use of innovative technology, a potential for rapid growth, a well-developed business model, and an impressive management team.

Angel investors are wealthy individuals who invest money directly in new ventures in exchange for an equity share. These investors are a larger source of investment capital for start-up firms. In contrast to venture capitalists, angels focus mostly on new ventures. Many angel investors are successful entrepreneurs who want to help would-be business owners get through the familiar difficulties of launching their businesses. Angel investors fund a wide variety of new ventures. Most entrepreneurs have trouble finding wealthy private investors. Angel networks have formed to match business angels with start-ups in need of capital.

You can learn about entrepreneurship and angel investors by watching CBC's television program *Dragons' Den*.

angel investors wealthy individuals who invest directly in a new venture in exchange for an equity stake.

Government Support for New Ventures

All levels of government support new ventures in many ways, as discussed in Chapter 5. Various local agencies and business incubators offer information, resources, and sometimes even access to financing for entrepreneurs.

Another way to encourage entrepreneurship is through *enterprise zones,* specific geographic areas set aside for economic renewal. Enterprise zones encourage investment, often in troubled areas, by offering tax advantages and incentives to businesses locating within the zone.

Long Plain First Nation's second urban reserve is located in Winnipeg at 480 Madison Street. An *urban reserve* is an economic zone within a municipality. It is an area that the federal government has set aside as First Nation reserve land. This economic zone allows for Aboriginal commercial ventures that enjoy tax exemptions offered to traditional reserves. Yellowquill College moved into a converted two-storey, 25,000-square-foot former Manitoba Hydro office building on the Long Plain urban reserve. Plans for the urban reserve include a gas station, a convenience store, and a five-storey, 80,000-square-foot office tower. Also in the plans is a depot for First Nations buyers to take delivery of tax-free goods purchased in the city.

Many First Nations are located in rural and remote areas. These areas are usually some distance from cities and towns where jobs and wealth are created. The distance creates challenges for First Nations who are trying to be economically self-sufficient. The federal government reports that Canada had 120 urban reserves as of 2008. The Winnipeg urban reserve is Long Plain's second urban reserve. Long Plain has operated an urban reserve in Portage la Prairie since the 1980s.[33]

✓ ASSESSMENT CHECK

6.6.1 What are the two most important considerations when choosing an idea for a new business?

6.6.2 What is the difference between debt financing and equity financing?

6.6.3 What is seed capital?

INTRAPRENEURSHIP

LO 6.7 Explain how organizations promote intrapreneurship.

Established companies try to keep the entrepreneurial spirit alive by encouraging **intrapreneurship**, the process of promoting innovation within their organization. In today's business world, things can change very quickly. Established firms need to innovate continually to hold onto their competitive advantages.

Many companies encourage intrapreneurship. In fact, 30 percent of large firms now set aside funds to support intrapreneurship.[34] Perhaps no business has benefited more from intrapreneurship than 3M. To foster creativity, 3M encourages engineers to "bootleg," or borrow, up to 15 percent of their time from other assignments to explore new product ideas of their choosing. Bootlegging has led to some of 3M's most successful products, including Scotch tape and Post-it notes.[35]

intrapreneurship the process of promoting innovation within the structure of an existing organization.

ASSESSMENT CHECK

6.7.1 Why do large companies support intrapreneurship?

6.7.2 What is a skunkworks?

Established companies such as 3M support intrapreneurial activity in varied ways. In addition to allowing bootlegging time for traditional product development, 3M implements two intrapreneurial approaches: skunkworks and pacing programs. A *skunkworks* project is initiated by an employee who has an idea and then recruits resources from within 3M to turn it into a commercial product. *Pacing programs* are company-initiated projects. They focus on a few products and technologies that 3M sees as having potential for success. The company provides financing, equipment, and people to support such pacing projects.[36]

WHAT'S AHEAD

In upcoming chapters, we look at other trends that are shaping the business world of the 21st century. In the next part of *Contemporary Business*, we explore the critical issues of how companies organize, lead, and manage their work processes; manage and motivate their employees; empower their employees through teamwork and enhanced communication; handle labour and workplace disputes; and create and produce world-class goods and services.

RETURN TO INSIDE BUSINESS

Halo by Shoshana: An Entrepreneurial Success Story in Fashion Accessories

Entrepreneurial success is like a recipe for success. Given the right ingredients and business conditions, the entrepreneur is more likely to succeed. Those ingredients include the character of the entrepreneur, the uniqueness of the product, and the price customers are willing to pay. Many small businesses are successful at filling a unique need, similar to the way Halo is successful in the fashion industry.

QUESTIONS FOR CRITICAL THINKING

1. Can bigger businesses in the fashion industry learn any lessons by looking at the success of Halo by Shoshana?

2. Develop a business idea that follows the Halo model of ingredients for success.

SUMMARY OF LEARNING OBJECTIVES

LO 6.1 Define the term *entrepreneur*, and distinguish among entrepreneurs, small-business owners, and managers.

Unlike many small-business owners, entrepreneurs typically own and run their businesses with the goal of building significant firms that create wealth and add jobs. Entrepreneurs are visionaries. They see opportunities and take the initiative to gather the resources they need to start their businesses quickly. Both managers and entrepreneurs use the resources of their companies to achieve the goals of their organizations.

 ASSESSMENT CHECK ANSWERS

6.1.1 What tools do entrepreneurs use to create a new business? Entrepreneurs combine their ideas and drive with money, employees, and other resources to create a business that meets a need.

6.1.2 How do entrepreneurs differ from managers? Managers direct others to reach an organization's goals. Entrepreneurs have the drive and impatience that make their companies successful. These qualities may hurt their ability to manage.

LO 6.2 Identify the different types of entrepreneurs.

A classic entrepreneur sees a business opportunity and sets aside resources to gain access to that market. A serial entrepreneur starts one business, runs it, and then starts and runs more businesses, one after another. A social entrepreneur uses business principles to solve social problems.

 ASSESSMENT CHECK ANSWERS

6.2.1 What do classic entrepreneurs and social entrepreneurs have in common? They both see opportunities and then set aside resources to develop new solutions.

6.2.2 Is a social entrepreneur simply a philanthropist who gives to good causes to help others? A philanthropist usually supports human welfare through charitable donations.

A social entrepreneur develops new ways to advance social causes and thus enhance social welfare.

LO 6.3 Explain why people choose to become entrepreneurs.

People choose to become entrepreneurs for many reasons. Four of the common reasons are a desire to be one's own boss, a desire to achieve financial success, a desire for job security, and a desire to improve one's quality of life.

 ASSESSMENT CHECK ANSWERS

6.3.1 What are the four main reasons people choose to become entrepreneurs? People usually choose to become entrepreneurs because they want to be their own boss, they believe they will achieve greater financial success, they believe they have more control over job security, and they want to enhance their quality of life.

6.3.2 What factors affect the entrepreneur's job security? An entrepreneur's job security depends on the decisions of customers and investors. It also depends on the cooperation and commitment of the entrepreneur's own employees.

LO 6.4 Discuss factors that support and expand opportunities for entrepreneurs.

Several factors contribute support opportunities for entrepreneurs: a favourable public perception, availability of financing, the falling cost and widespread availability of information technology, globalization, entrepreneurship education, and changing demographic and economic trends.

 ASSESSMENT CHECK ANSWERS

6.4.1 To what extent is entrepreneurship possible in different countries, and what opportunities does globalization create for today's entrepreneurs? More than 9 percent of adults worldwide are starting or managing a new business. Globalization makes it possible for entrepreneurs to market their products abroad and to hire international talent. Many of the fastest-growing small Canadian companies have international sales, especially to the United States.

6.4.2 Identify the educational factors that help expand current opportunities for entrepreneurs. Many universities offer majors in entrepreneurship, dozens of others offer an entrepreneurship emphasis, and hundreds more offer courses in how to start a business. Some organizations encourage and teach entrepreneurship, such as the Kauffman Center for Entrepreneurial Leadership, Entreprep, and Students in Free Enterprise.

6.4.3 Describe current demographic trends that suggest new goods and services for entrepreneurial businesses. The aging of the North American population and the growth of two-income families are creating opportunities for entrepreneurs to market new goods and services.

LO 6.5 Identify personality traits that typically characterize successful entrepreneurs.

Successful entrepreneurs share several typical traits, including vision, high energy levels, the need to achieve, self-confidence and optimism, tolerance for failure, creativity, tolerance for ambiguity, and an internal locus of control.

 ASSESSMENT CHECK ANSWERS

6.5.1 What do we mean when we talk about an entrepreneur's vision? Entrepreneurs begin with a vision, which is an overall idea for how to make their business idea a success. They then follow this vision with energy and excitement.

6.5.2 Why is it important for an entrepreneur to have a high energy level and a strong need for achievement? Start-up companies usually have a small staff and have a difficult time raising enough capital. The entrepreneur needs to make up the difference by working long hours. A strong need for achievement helps entrepreneurs to enjoy the challenge of reaching difficult goals. It also promotes dedication to personal success.

6.5.3 How do entrepreneurs generally feel about the possibility of failure? They view failure as a learning experience and are not easily discouraged or disappointed when things don't go as planned.

LO 6.6 Summarize the process of starting a new venture.

Entrepreneurs must choose an idea for their business, develop a business plan, obtain financing, and organize the resources they need to operate their start-ups.

 ASSESSMENT CHECK ANSWERS

6.6.1 What are the two most important considerations when choosing an idea for a new business? The two important considerations are finding something you love to do and are good at doing and finding an idea that meets a need in the marketplace.

6.6.2 What is the difference between debt financing and equity financing? Debt financing is money borrowed that must be repaid. Equity financing is an exchange of ownership shares in a company for money supplied by one or more investors.

6.6.3 What is seed capital? Seed capital is the money that is used to start a company.

LO 6.7 Explain how organizations promote intrapreneurship.

Organizations encourage intrapreneurial activity within the company in a variety of ways, including through hiring practices, dedicated programs such as skunkworks, providing access to resources, and giving employees freedom to innovate within established firms.

 ASSESSMENT CHECK ANSWERS

6.7.1 Why do large companies support intrapreneurship? Large firms support intrapreneurship to keep an entrepreneurial spirit alive and to promote innovation and change.

6.7.2 What is a skunkworks? A skunkworks project is initiated by an employee who has an idea and then recruits resources from within the company to turn the idea into a commercial product.

BUSINESS TERMS YOU NEED TO KNOW

entrepreneur 158

classic entrepreneur 159

serial entrepreneur 159

social entrepreneur 160

lifestyle entrepreneur 162

seed capital 172

debt financing 172

equity financing 172

venture capitalists 172

angel investors 173

intrapreneurship 173

REVIEW QUESTIONS

1. Identify the three categories of entrepreneurs. How are they different from each other? How might an entrepreneur belong to more than one category?

2. People often become entrepreneurs because they want to be their own boss, and they want to be in control of most or all of the major decisions related to their business. How might these desires relate to potential financial success? Are there any downsides? If so, what are they?

3. How have globalization and information technology created new opportunities for entrepreneurs? Describe current demographic trends that suggest new goods and services for entrepreneurial businesses.

4. Identify the eight characteristics that are attributed to successful entrepreneurs. Which trait or traits do you believe are the most important for success? Why? Are there any traits that might contribute to potential failure? If so, which traits? Why might they contribute to failure?

5. When selecting a business idea, why is it important to follow the advice to "do what makes you happy" and "be true to yourself"?

6. Suppose an entrepreneur is considering buying an existing business or franchise. Which of the eight entrepreneurial traits would most likely apply to this person, and why?

7. Imagine that you and a partner are planning to launch a business that sells backpacks, briefcases, and soft luggage made from recycled materials. You'll need seed capital for your venture. Outline how you would use that seed capital.

8. Describe the two main types of financing that entrepreneurs may seek for their businesses. What are the risks and benefits of each?

9. What is an enterprise zone? Describe what types of businesses might benefit from opening in an enterprise zone. How might their success be interconnected?

10. What is intrapreneurship? How does it differ from entrepreneurship?

PROJECTS AND TEAMWORK APPLICATIONS

1. Interview an entrepreneur. You can do the interview in person, by e-mail, or by phone. The person can be a local shop or restaurant owner, a hair salon owner, a pet groomer, a consultant—any field is fine. Find out why that person decided to become an entrepreneur. Ask whether his or her viewpoint has changed since starting the business. Decide whether the person is a classic, serial, or social entrepreneur. Present your findings to the class.

2. Certain demographic trends can represent opportunities for entrepreneurs—the aging of the North American population, the increasing diversity of the population, the growth in population of some areas, and the large number of two-income families, to name a few. On your own or with a classmate, choose a demographic trend and brainstorm for business ideas that can profit from the trend. Create a poster or a PowerPoint presentation to present your idea—and its relationship to the trend—to your class.

3. Review the eight characteristics of successful entrepreneurs. Which characteristics do you have? Do you think you would be a good entrepreneur? Why or why not? Create an outline of the traits you believe are your strengths—and the traits that might be your weaknesses.

4. Many entrepreneurs turn a hobby or an area of interest into a business idea. Others get their ideas from situations or daily problems when they believe they have a solution—or a better solution than those already tried. Think about an area of personal interest or a problem you think you can solve with a new good or service. Create the first part of a potential business plan, which is the introduction to your new company and its offerings. Outline briefly what kind of financing you think would work best for your business, and what steps you would take to obtain the funds.

5. Enterprise zones are designed to revitalize economically distressed areas. Choose an area you are familiar with. It may be as close as a local neighbourhood, or as far away as a city, where you might like to live. Do some online research about the area. Outline your own plan for an enterprise zone. Include businesses that you think would do well in the area, jobs that might be created, housing creation, and other factors.

WEB ASSIGNMENTS

1. **Tools for entrepreneurs.** American Express has established what it calls "Open Forum" to allow entrepreneurs and small-business owners to communicate with one another and share ideas. Visit the Open Forum website and review the material. Prepare a short report on how Open Forum can help an entrepreneur to start and grow a business.

   http://www.openforum.com/

2. **Venture capitalists.** Venture capital firms are an important source of financing for entrepreneurs. Most actively look for funding proposals. Go to the website shown below to learn more about venture capital. What are some of the famous businesses that were originally financed by venture capitalists?

   http://www.nvca.org/

3. **Getting started.** Visit the website of *Entrepreneur* magazine. Explore the information on how to research a business idea. What are the steps involved in getting a product to market?

   http://www.entrepreneur.com

Access your WileyPLUS course for:

- The complete digital textbook.
- Question assistance, including links to relevant sections in the online digital textbook.
- Immediate feedback and proof of progress, 24/7
- Integrated, multi-media resources – including MP3 downloads, visual exhibits, animations, and much more – that provide multiple study paths and encourage more active learning.

QUIZ YOURSELF

Note: Internet Web addresses change frequently. If you don't find the exact sites listed, you may need to access the organization's home page and search from there or use a search engine such as Bing or Google.

2 LAUNCHING YOUR . . .

ENTREPRENEURIAL CAREER

In Part 2, "Starting and Growing Your Business," you learned the many ways that business owners have achieved their dreams of owning their own company and being their own boss. The two chapters in Part 2 introduced the wide variety of entrepreneurial or small businesses; the forms these businesses can take (sole proprietorship, partnership, or corporation); and the reasons that some new ventures succeed and others fail. You learned that entrepreneurs are visionaries who build firms that create wealth. They share qualities such as vision and creativity, high energy, optimism, a strong need to achieve, and a tolerance for failure. You might wonder how you can use this information. Here are some career ideas and opportunities in the small-business and e-business areas.

First, think about the field that attracts you as a future business owner. Try to gain experience in the industry by first working for someone else. The information and skills you learn will be valuable when you start out on your own. Remember that lack of experience is often the leading reason for small-business failure.[1]

Next, look for a good fit between your own skills, abilities, and qualities and a market need, or niche. For example, the number of older people in the population is increasing, and more and more young families find themselves running short on time. As a result, the need for childcare and eldercare services will increase—and so will the opportunities for new businesses in those areas. Watch these trends to find ideas that you can use or adapt.

Do you like the idea of being your own boss but worry about risking your savings to start a new and untried business? Then you might want to think about owning a franchise, such as Quiznos or Dunkin' Donuts. Franchising can be less risky than starting a new business from scratch, but it still means hard work. You need to understand the franchise resources you can access and the franchise responsibilities you will take on. Filling a market need is important for success. To find more information about franchising, access the Business Development Bank of Canada's review of franchising at http://www.bdc.ca/EN/advice_centre/ask_professionnal/buy_business/Pages/franchises.aspx?question=3.

Are you skilled in a certain area of business, technology, or science? Consulting firms offer their expertise to clients in private, government, not-for-profit, and foreign business operations. Business consultants influence clients' decisions in marketing, finance, manufacturing, information systems, e-business, human resources, and many other areas, including corporate strategy and organization. Technology consultants support businesses in all fields. They might set up a secure website, train employees in the use of new software, manage an off-site help desk, or plan for disaster recovery. Science consulting firms find work in the field of environmental consulting. They help businesses to deal with pollution cleanup and control, habitat protection, and help them to meet government environmental regulations and standards.

But maybe you prefer to tinker with gears and machinery or with computer graphics and code. If you think you have the ideas and creativity to invent something completely new, you need to learn about patents, trademarks, and copyright laws to protect your ideas.[2] Patents, trademarks, and copyright each offer different protections for your work, but none will guarantee success. Again, hard work, persistence, and a little bit of luck will help you succeed.

CAREER ASSESSMENT EXERCISES IN ENTREPRENEURSHIP AND BUSINESS OWNERSHIP

1. Find out whether you have what it takes to be an entrepreneur. Review the material on the Business Development Bank of Canada's website: http://www.bdc.ca/EN/advice_centre/benchmarking_tools/Pages/entrepreneurial_self_assessment.aspx

Answer the questions there. After you've finished, use the scoring guides to see how ready you are to start your own business. What weak areas did your results show? What can you do to strengthen those areas?

2. Find an independent business or franchise in your area. Make an appointment to talk to the owner about his or her start-up experience. Prepare a list of questions for a 10- to 15-minute interview. Remember to ask about details, such as the number of hours worked per week, the approximate start-up costs, the goals of the business, the available resources, the lessons learned since opening, and the rewards of owning the business. How do the owner's answers differ from what you expected?

3. Search online for information about how to file for a patent, trademark, or copyright. A good starting point is BDC's website: http://www.bdc.ca/EN/advice_centre/articles/Pages/a_quick_refresher_on_patents_trademarks_for_business_services.aspx

Assume you have an invention you want to protect. Find out what forms are required; what fees are needed; how much time is usually needed to complete the legal steps; and the rights and protections you will gain from the patent, trademark, or copyright.

ColorBlind Images/Getty Images

PART 3

MANAGEMENT: EMPOWERING PEOPLE TO ACHIEVE BUSINESS GOALS

7 | MANAGEMENT, LEADERSHIP, AND THE INTERNAL ORGANIZATION

LEARNING OBJECTIVES

LO 7.1 Define *management* and the three types of skills necessary for managerial success.

LO 7.2 Explain the role of vision and ethical standards in business success.

LO 7.3 Summarize the major benefits of planning, and distinguish among strategic planning, tactical planning, and operational planning.

LO 7.4 Describe the strategic planning process.

LO 7.5 Contrast the two major types of business decisions, and list the steps in the decision-making process.

LO 7.6 Define *leadership,* and compare different leadership styles.

LO 7.7 Discuss the meaning and importance of corporate culture.

LO 7.8 Identify the five major forms of departmentalization and the four main types of organization structures.

INSIDE BUSINESS

Bloomberg via Getty Images

Research In Motion: A Question of Management?

It is hard for many people to understand how Waterloo, Ontario–based Research In Motion Ltd. (RIM) could fall from the height of success. It was even harder for shareholders and industry analysts who watched as the firm's management seemed unable to cope in a competitive environment where RIM once was the leader.

By 2012, RIM had an estimated 75 million global subscribers and was generating $20 billion in revenues. The company was profitable, posting more than $3.4 billion in profit in 2011. But analysts could see that RIM was losing customers to new product offerings from Apple, Google, and others.

RIM had early success with its 1998 introduction of the BlackBerry. The product's reliability and RIM's superior customer support made it popular and led to its success. To use a BlackBerry device, wireless service providers need to buy into the system that RIM is selling. The individual customer buys a BlackBerry device, but the wireless service provider must buy the software and other technology from RIM. Then, the software and technology together make it possible for customers to use these products and products licensed to other manufacturers by RIM.

The business model worked well. In fact, it still works well in many markets around the world where voice and data (text) communication meet the primary needs of mostly business subscribers. But then Apple introduced the iPhone. Software developers began creating hundreds and hundreds of special applications (apps) to run on the iPhone. RIM's smartphone devices lost their appeal as more and more consumers purchased iPhones instead of BlackBerry smartphones.

By the time the late Steve Jobs introduced the iPad, Apple's mobile tablet device, RIM was trying to catch up. RIM launched its PlayBook, but it was poorly received. The trend for future growth—especially in the bigger consumer market—pointed away from RIM and toward Apple and other producers. Apple and Google chose to focus on digital content sales. It seemed that RIM's management was losing touch with what customers wanted. The hardware device was less important to generating revenue. Instead, digital content was becoming the source of growth.

By January 2012, unhappy shareholders had seen their stock value fall to $15 per share from highs of more than $150 per share in 2008. The shareholders demanded major leadership changes at RIM. The board of directors removed the two top management figures, who had led to RIM's original success. Mike Lazaridis and Jim Balsillie were not out, but they were no longer setting the vision and direction for the company they had built from scratch. Thorsten Heins was named president and chief executive officer replacing Mike Lazaridis. Jim Balsillie stepped down as co-CEO. He initially remained on the board of directors, but then stepped down from that position in late March 2012.

As the company's press release put it:

Mr. Heins said he looks forward to continuing to work with Mr. Lazaridis, globally recognized as a technology pioneer. He said, "Mike created a whole new way of communicating and I look forward to continuing our close collaboration."

Lazaridis commented on Heins's transition to CEO:

There comes a time in the growth of every successful company when the founders recognize the need to pass the baton to new leadership. Jim and I went to the Board and told them that we thought that time was now. With BlackBerry 7 now out, PlayBook 2.0 shipping in February and BlackBerry 10 expected to ship later this year, the company is entering a new phase, and we felt it was time for a new leader to take it through that phase and beyond. Jim, the Board and I all agreed that leader should be Thorsten Heins.[1]

CHAPTER 7 OVERVIEW

Many students in introductory business courses dream about the challenges of a management career. When you ask business students about their career goals, many will say, "I want to be a manager." You may think that being a manager means being the boss. But in today's business world, companies want managers to be more than bosses. They want managers who understand technology, adapt quickly to change, can skillfully motivate employees, and realize the importance of satisfying customers. Managers who can master those skills will be in great demand. Managers who have strong commitments can improve their firms' performance.

This chapter begins by looking at how successful organizations use management to turn visions into reality. It describes the levels of management, the skills that managers need, and the functions that managers perform. The chapter explains how the first of these functions—planning—helps managers in two ways: to meet the challenges of a rapidly changing business environment and to develop strategies that guide a company's future. Other sections of the chapter explore the types of decisions that managers make, the role of managers as leaders, and the importance of corporate culture. The chapter concludes by examining the second function of management—organizing.

LO 7.1 Define *management* and the three types of skills necessary for managerial success.

management the process of achieving organizational goals through people and other resources.

WHAT IS MANAGEMENT?

Management is the process of achieving organizational goals through people and other resources. The manager's job is to combine human and technical resources in the best way possible to achieve the company's goals.

Management principles and concepts apply to both not-for-profit organizations and for-profit firms. The managerial functions described in this chapter are performed by a city mayor, the president of the YMCA, and a superintendent of schools. Management takes place at many levels, from the level of a manager at a family-owned restaurant to the level of a national sales manager for a major manufacturer.

The Management Hierarchy

Your local grocery store has a fairly simple organization: a store manager, several assistant managers or department managers, and employees who may be baggers, cashiers, or stock clerks. If your grocery store is part of a regional or national chain, it will also have corporate managers who are ranked above the store manager. Loblaw is Canada's largest food distribution company. It operates more than 1,000 grocery stores across Canada. It has headquarters in Brampton, Ontario. Each store has managers for everything, from the meat department to human resources. At Loblaw headquarters, you'll find top-level managers for finance, consumer affairs, real estate, information technology, sales and operations, pharmacy, and other areas.[2]

All these managers combine human and other resources to meet Loblaw goals. But their jobs differ because they work at different levels of the organization.

A firm's management usually has three levels: top, middle, and supervisory. These levels of management form a management hierarchy, as shown in Figure 7.1. The hierarchy is the traditional structure found in most organizations. Managers at each level perform different activities.

The highest level of management is *top management*. Top managers include such positions as chief executive officer (CEO), chief financial officer (CFO), and executive vice-president. Top managers spend most of their time developing long-range plans for their organizations. They decide whether to introduce new products, purchase other

Top Management
- Chief Executive Officer
- Chief Financial Officer
- Premier, Mayor

Middle Management
- Regional Manager
- Division Head
- Director, Dean

Supervisory (First-Line) Management
- Supervisor
- Department Chairperson
- Program Manager

FIGURE 7.1
The Management Hierarchy

companies, or enter new geographical markets. Top managers set a direction for their organization. They also inspire the company's executives and employees to achieve their vision for the company's future.

The job isn't easy. Many top managers must steer their firms through an economic downturn, a slump in sales, or a crisis in quality. TD Bank's Ed Clark was recently named outstanding CEO of the Year. This recognition was, in part, because of his success in steering Canada's second largest bank through one of the worst global financial crisis in history (2008–2010) and back to continued growth. The bank's stock market value returned to pre-crisis levels, likely because of two factors: uninterrupted dividend payouts to shareholders and investors' confidence in future growth.[3]

Middle management is the second level in the management hierarchy. It includes general managers, plant managers, division managers, and branch managers. Middle managers focus their attention on specific operations, products, or customer groups. They develop detailed plans and procedures to carry out the firm's strategic plans. For example, suppose top management decides to increase distribution of a product. A sales manager will decide on how many salespeople are needed. Middle managers will focus on the products to be sold and on the customers who will buy the products and lead to the profit growth the CEOs expect. The middle managers might budget money for product development, identify new uses for existing products, and improve the ways they train and motivate salespeople. Middle managers are more familiar with day-to-day operations than CEOs. That's why middle managers often come up with new ways to increase sales or solve company problems.

Supervisory management, or first-line management, includes supervisors, section chiefs, and team leaders. These managers assign specific jobs to nonmanagerial employees and assess their performance. Managers at this first level of the hierarchy work directly with the employees who produce and sell the firm's goods and services. They carry out middle managers' plans by motivating workers to accomplish daily, weekly, and monthly goals. In a study of top-ranked customer service firms, all firms had first-line managers who carried out the firms' strategies to provide superior customer service.[4]

For the past six years, TD Canada Trust has ranked highest in customer satisfaction among the big five Canadian retail banks, according to J.D. Power and Associates. The first-line managers make sure that customer service is the main concern for all employees.

Skills Needed for Managerial Success

Managers at every level in the management hierarchy use three basic types of skills: technical, human, and conceptual. All managers must acquire these skills, but the importance of each skill changes at each management level.

Technical skills are the manager's ability to understand and use the techniques, knowledge, tools, and equipment of a specific department or area of study. Technical skills are especially important for first-line managers. They are less important at higher levels of the management hierarchy. But most top executives started out as technical experts. The résumé of a vice-president for information systems probably lists jobs as a computer analyst. A vice-president for marketing usually has a background in sales. Many firms, such as The Home Depot and Dell, have increased their training programs for first-line managers to increase their technical skills and productivity. Cold Stone Creamery operates franchises for its premium ice-cream stores in Alberta and Saskatchewan. This company carefully trains managers and crew members in the art of preparing its specialty ice cream for hungry customers. "We set high standards and provide world-class training," says the company.[5]

Human skills are interpersonal skills that help managers to work effectively with people. Human skills include the ability to communicate with, motivate, and lead employees to complete their assigned activities. Managers need human skills to interact with people both inside and outside the organization. People without these skills will probably have a difficult time trying to be a successful manager. Human skills must be adapted to different forms. For example, human skills include mastering and communicating effectively with staff using e-mail, cellphones, pagers, faxes, and text messaging. All these forms of communication are widely used in today's offices. As you can imagine, managers at Cold Stone Creamery ice cream stores need to have excellent human skills, not only with customers but also with employees.

Conceptual skills help a manager to see the organization as a single unit and to understand how each part of the overall organization interacts with other parts. People with conceptual skills can see the big picture by acquiring, analyzing, and interpreting information. Conceptual skills are especially important for top-level managers, who must develop long-range plans for the future direction of their organization. Tony Hsieh sold his own company, LinkExchange, to Microsoft for $265 million. He then joined Zappos as an advisor and later became its CEO. Hsieh's conceptual skills helped Zappos to grow its sales to more than $1 billion annually while also winning praises for being an excellent place to work. Recently, Hsieh sold Zappos to Amazon in a deal worth $1.2 billion.[6]

Managerial Functions

In the course of a typical day, managers meet and talk with people, read, think, and send text or e-mail messages. As they perform these activities, managers carry out four basic functions: planning, organizing, directing, and controlling. Planning activities set out the basics for activity, and the other functions carry out the plans.

Planning

planning the process of looking forward to future events and conditions and deciding on the courses of action for achieving organizational goals.

Planning is the process of looking forward to future events and conditions and deciding on the courses of actions for achieving organizational goals. Effective planning helps a business to focus its vision, avoid costly mistakes, and seize opportunities. Planning should be flexible and responsive to changes in the business environment. It should also involve managers from all levels of the organization. Planning for the future is more important than ever because global competition is getting stronger, technology continues to expand, and firms are bringing new innovations to market faster. For example, a CEO and other top-level managers need to plan for succession—for those who will follow in their footsteps. Some CEOs don't want to do this kind of planning, fearing that it might shorten their time leading a company. Management experts advise firms to plan ahead for the next generation of management, so they can keep the company's position in the marketplace.[7]

Frank Stronach led Magna International from its start in 1969 to become the largest automotive parts manufacturer in North America with sales over $23 billion. Stronach decided to step down as CEO. He announced his decision before a shareholders' vote on his position. Although the company had returned to profitability after the financial crisis, which hit the auto industry hard, many thought that it was time for new leadership at the firm.[8]

Organizing

After plans have been developed, the next step in the management process is **organizing**— the process of blending human and material resources through a formal structure of tasks and authority: arranging work, dividing tasks among employees, and coordinating them to ensure plans are carried out and goals are met. Organizing involves classifying and dividing work into manageable units with a structure that makes sense. Managers staff the organization with the best possible employees for each job. Sometimes, the organizing function requires studying a company's existing structure and deciding whether to restructure it to operate more efficiently, cost-effectively, or sustainably.

organizing the process of blending human and material resources through a formal structure of tasks and authority: arranging work, dividing tasks among employees, and coordinating them to ensure plans are carried out and goals are met.

Directing

After an organization has been set up, managers focus on **directing**, or guiding and motivating employees to accomplish organizational goals. Directing can include training (or retraining), setting up schedules, assigning tasks, and monitoring progress. For example, an office manager might need to meet the goal of reducing the office electricity bill. This manager might do the following: assign incandescent light bulbs to be replaced by compact fluorescents, ask employees to turn off the lights when they leave a room, and direct the information technology (IT) staff to program all computer screens to turn off after 15 minutes of inactivity.[9]

Some managers take time to listen to their employees. These managers gain an understanding of their employees, and the employees feel that the manager cares about their work. Weekly meetings with employees allow for the exchange of information, and individuals can make their views known. Such meetings can help to motivate employees and provide an opportunity for comments about the direction the firm is moving.

directing guiding and motivating employees to accomplish organizational goals.

Controlling

The **controlling** function assesses an organization's performance against its goals. Controlling assesses the success of the planning function and provides feedback for future rounds of planning.

Controlling has four basic steps: setting performance standards, monitoring actual performance, comparing actual performance with the standards, and making corrections if needed. For example, according to the Sarbanes-Oxley Act, CEOs and CFOs must monitor the performance of the firm's accounting staff more closely than was done in the past. CEOs and CFOs must personally confirm the truth of financial reports filed with the U.S. Securities and Exchange Commission. Many Canadian firms, such as Magna International, are listed on American stock exchanges. These Canadian firms are also required to comply with Sarbanes-Oxley.

controlling the function of assessing an organization's performance against its goals.

 ASSESSMENT CHECK

7.1.1 What is management?

7.1.2 Describe the differences in the jobs of top managers, middle managers, and supervisory managers.

7.1.3 What is the relationship between the manager's planning and controlling functions?

SETTING A VISION AND ETHICAL STANDARDS FOR THE FIRM

LO 7.2 Explain the role of vision and ethical standards in business success.

A business begins with a **vision**, its founder's ability to perceive marketplace needs and what an organization must do to satisfy them. Vision is a focus for a firm's actions. Vision helps to direct the company toward opportunities and sets it apart from its competitors. The current vision for Facebook is not very different from the original vision proposed by founder Mark Zuckerberg— "Giving people the power to share, and make the world more open and connected."[10]

A company's vision must be focused. It must also be flexible enough to adapt to changes in the business environment. The ethical standards set by top management are also important to a

vision the ability to perceive marketplace needs and what an organization must do to satisfy them.

firm's long-term relationships with its customers, suppliers, and the general public. Sometimes, ethical standards are made to comply with industry or federal regulations, such as safety or quality standards. Other times, new standards are set after unethical actions have been taken by managers, such as the financial accounting wrongdoings that led to the Sarbanes-Oxley Act. Many firms are now taking a closer look at large compensation packages received by their CEOs and other top executives. Because of public demands, compensation committees are reassessing their guidelines for salaries, bonuses, and other benefits.[11]

SOLVING AN **ETHICAL** CONTROVERSY

Google Stands Alone: When Ethics and Business Don't Mix

When Google first entered the Chinese market, the firm was criticized. Google had agreed to the censorship guidelines set out by the Chinese government, which controls the distribution of information to the Chinese public. Google made this agreement in the hope that the Chinese government would later relax its stand and allow Chinese citizens to have the same open access to Internet information as others have. But that didn't happen. In fact, the censorship seemed to grow tighter. And it also seemed that someone was using Google to identify Chinese citizens who actively disagreed with the government. So, Google decided to shut down operations in China and rerouted Chinese users to a safe site in Hong Kong. Google received praise from the Internet community for its move to Hong Kong, but received only mild support from the business world.

Should the ethical standards set by a business have more weight than undemocratic laws and regulations in the countries where it operates?

PRO

1. Many multinational firms now have global ethics policies. These policies apply to each country where these firms do business, regardless of national law. Global ethics policies help managers to make consistent decisions, even if they have to lose some profits.

2. Firms and their employees must always put ethical standards ahead of practices that restrict human rights. "If any corporate executive finds that he or she is actually thinking about putting profit ahead of humanity," argues Mickey Edwards, vice-president of the international not-for-profit Aspen Institute, "it is time for that person to reflect seriously on how and when the moral compass, and one's own claim to humanity, got lost."

CON

1. Ethical standards are not always the same from one country to the next. Google's move may have a negative impact on Chinese consumers. They at least had access to some information when Google was there. "Leaving may look and feel great to those of us in the West, but exiting a market may not always have the desired impact," writes one expert.

2. Companies that are willing to work with such governments can actually use their influence with consumers to make change happen. For example, companies can create demand for their goods and services. They can also become active in the community through service projects, such as building schools.

Summary

Google's exit from China was a clear decision to some people; to others, it was not clear at all. "China is a very important market," noted one analyst. "What's the incentive for a government or another company to join with Google? There is none and that's why you haven't seen it happen." Others point out that China has a market of more than 1 billion consumers, so it is hard to know how open that market will be in the next five or 10 years. And things are getting tougher, not easier for companies wanting to operate in China. "There is a barrage of new rules and regulations for foreign companies operating in China," notes a businessperson with experience in China. "And everybody is trying to figure out what it means."

Sources: Alexei Oreskovic and Paul Eckert, "Google Finds Few Allies in China Battle," *Reuters*, March 25, 2010, http://www.reuters.com; Steve Pearlstein and Raju Narisetti, "Doing Right at What Cost?" *Washington Post*, March 25, 2010, http://views.washingtonpost.com; Aron Cramer and Dunstan Allison Hope, "Google and China: When Should Business Leave on Human Rights Grounds?" *Huffington Post*, March 22, 2010, http://www.huffingtonpost.com.

The ethical tone set by a top management team can lead to financial and nonfinancial rewards. Setting a high ethical standard does not just keep employees from doing wrong but it also encourages, motivates, and inspires them to achieve goals they never thought possible. Such satisfaction creates a more productive, stable workforce—one that can create a long-term competitive advantage for the organization. In practice, ethical decisions are not always clear, and managers must make difficult decisions. Sometimes, a firm operates in a country where standards differ from our standards in Canada. Other times, a manager might have to make an ethical decision that reduces profits or leads to job losses. You might think that a large firm—because of its size—will have a harder time adopting ethical practices than a small firm. But consider toymaker giant Mattel, which has earned recognition again and again for its ethical standards. Named one of the "World's Most Ethical Companies" by the Ethisphere Institute, Mattel consistently demonstrates high standards. "Our commitment to 'play fair' is at the core of our organization's culture and is the cornerstone of our ethical compliance program," notes chairman and CEO Robert A. Eckert.

Alex Brigham, executive director of the Ethisphere Institute, sees the connection between ethics and good business. "Mattel's promotion of a sound ethical environment shines within its industry and shows a clear understanding that operating under the highest standards for business behaviour goes beyond goodwill and is intimately linked to performance and profitability," he says.[12]

A firm's vision is a focus for its actions. Vision helps to direct the company toward opportunities and sets it apart from its competitors. The current vision for Facebook is not very different from the original vision proposed by founder Mark Zuckerberg—"Giving people the power to share, and make the world more open and connected."

Bloomberg via Getty Images

Taking an ethical stand can actually cost a firm in lost revenues and other support. When Google announced a reversal of its original stance on censorship in China—by shutting down operations there and rerouting traffic to an uncensored site in Hong Kong—not only did the company lose business, it found itself standing alone on the issue. Google's decision and the consequences are discussed in the "Solving an Ethical Controversy" feature.

 ASSESSMENT CHECK

7.2.1 What is meant by a vision for the firm?

7.2.2 Why is it important for a top executive to set high ethical standards?

IMPORTANCE OF PLANNING

LO 7.3 Summarize the major benefits of planning, and distinguish among strategic planning, tactical planning, and operational planning.

Good planning can turn a vision into reality. When Reid Hoffman first got the idea for the professional social network LinkedIn, he was "very interested in this whole notion of each of us as individual professionals who are on the Internet and how that changes the way we do business, our careers, our brand identity. I realized that the world was transforming every individual into a small business." As Hoffman worked on the idea, he thought about how a professional social network could be used. He asked himself and others questions to help develop his plan. "How do you positively influence your brand on the Net? How do you assemble a team fast? Who has the expertise to guide you?" The answers to these questions and more became the plan for LinkedIn.[13]

Types of Planning

Planning can be categorized by scope, or how widely the plan affects other factors. Planning can also be categorized by breadth, or how far into the future the plan extends. For example, some plans are very broad and long range. Other plans are short range and very narrow, affecting only some parts of the organization, not the whole firm. Planning can be divided into four categories: strategic, tactical, operational, and contingency planning. Each step includes more specific information than the step before. Each planning step must also fit into an overall plan, from the mission statement (described in the next section) to objectives to specific plans. This overall plan must also include narrow, functional plans aimed at individual employees and work areas that relate to individual tasks. These plans must fit within the firm's overall plan and help it to reach objectives and achieve its mission.

Strategic Planning

The most far-reaching level of planning is *strategic planning*—the process of deciding on the primary objectives of an organization and then taking action and setting aside resources to achieve those objectives. Generally, strategic planning is done by the top executives in a company. The office supplies retailer Staples has a strategy of using company resources to raise environmental awareness—and develop or improve products. Staples sponsors the annual Staples Global EcoEasy Challenge, where college and university students compete by developing new products or redesigning existing ones in a way that represents a new approach to sustainability.[14]

Tactical Planning

Tactical planning involves carrying out the activities set out in the strategic plans. Tactical plans guide the current and short-term activities required to carry out the overall strategies. The Staples Global EcoEasy Challenge is a tactic that shows strategic planning around environmentally responsible products. Another tactic for the same strategy is Staples' development of its EcoEasy and Sustainable Earth product lines. "Staples' commitment to designing more environmentally responsible products as compared to conventional products is evident by our own EcoEasy and Sustainable Earth brands," notes Staples' vice-president of environmental affairs Mark Buckley.[15]

Operational Planning

Operational planning sets the detailed standards that help to carry out tactical plans. This activity involves choosing specific work targets and assigning employees and teams to carry out plans. Strategic planning focuses on the organization as a whole, but operational planning develops and carries out tactics in specific functional areas. For example, operational planning of the Staples EcoEasy Challenge might include selecting judges; setting deadlines; reviewing contestant applications; and deciding on the competition categories, such as creating a product using eco-friendly materials.

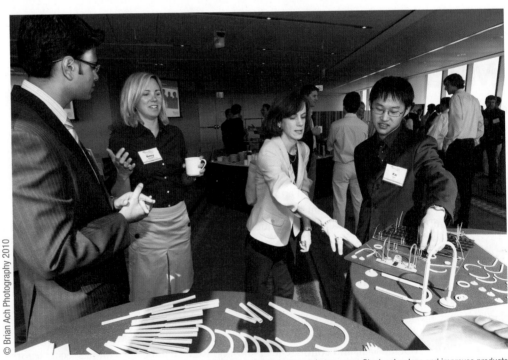

© Brian Ach Photography 2010

Staples's strategic planning includes using company resources to raise environmental awareness. Staples develops and improves products through its annual Staples Global EcoEasy Challenge competition for college and university students.

Contingency Planning

Planning cannot foresee every possibility. Even the best plans may face major accidents, natural disasters, and rapid economic downturns. To handle these disruptions, many firms use *contingency planning*. This type of planning helps firms to resume operations as quickly and as smoothly as possible after a crisis. It also makes it easier for them to openly tell the public what happened. Contingency planning activity involves two components: continuing the business and communicating to the public. Many firms have management strategies that make it easier to recover from the loss of data, breaches of security, product failures, and natural disasters such as floods or fire. When a major disaster occurs or business is disrupted, a company can turn to its contingency plan. This plan usually outlines a chain of command for crisis management and assigns specific emergency functions to some or all managers and employees. But a crisis usually occurs on a smaller scale. For example, a product delivery might get lost, a key person might be sick and unable to attend an important meeting, or the electricity might go out for a day. These events also need contingency planning. For example, when British Airways (BA) cabin crews walked off their jobs, the airline had to cancel or delay hundreds of flights. Many travellers were stranded or rerouted. Others tried to find flights on different airlines. By the second day of the strike, many BA flights were back on schedule. BA said that its contingency planning was successful. Because it sensed a possible strike, BA had retrained some on-ground staffers to work as cabin crew. It also leased planes and crew from some of its competitors. "Our contingency plans are continuing to work well . . . around the world," stated an airline spokesperson.[16]

Planning at Different Organizational Levels

Managers spend time planning every day. The total time spent and the type of planning depends on the level of the manager. As shown in Table 7.1, top managers, including a firm's board of directors and CEO, spend a great deal of time on long-range planning. Middle-level managers and supervisors focus on short-term, tactical, and operational planning. Employees at all levels can help themselves and their company by making plans to meet their own specific goals.

✓ **ASSESSMENT CHECK**

7.3.1 Outline the planning process.

7.3.2 Describe the purpose of tactical planning.

7.3.3 Compare the types of plans made by top managers and middle managers. How does their focus differ?

Table 7.1 Planning at Different Management Levels

PRIMARY TYPE OF PLANNING	MANAGERIAL LEVEL	EXAMPLES
Strategic	Top management	Organizational objectives, fundamental strategies, long-term plans
Tactical	Middle management	Quarterly and semi-annual plans, departmental policies and procedures
Operational	Supervisory management	Daily and weekly plans, rules, and procedures for each department
Contingency	Primarily top management, but all levels contribute	Ongoing plans for actions and communications in an emergency

THE STRATEGIC PLANNING PROCESS

LO 7.4 Describe the strategic planning process.

Strategic planning can make the difference between success and failure. Strategic planning forms the basis of many management decisions. Successful strategic planners often follow the six steps shown in Figure 7.2: defining a mission, assessing the organization's competitive position, setting organizational objectives, creating strategies for competitive differentiation, implementing the strategy, and assessing the results and refining the plan.

FIGURE 7.2
Steps in the Strategic Planning Process

Defining the Organization's Mission

mission statement a written description of an organization's overall business purpose and aims.

The first step in strategic planning is to translate the firm's vision into a **mission statement**. A mission statement is a written description of an organization's overall business purpose and aims. It is a statement of a firm's reason for being. It can highlight the range of its operations, the market it will serve, and how it will try to set itself apart from competitors. A mission statement guides the actions of employees.

Mission statements can be short or long:

- Starbucks: "To inspire and nurture the human spirit—one person, one cup and one neighborhood at a time."

- Disney: "We create happiness by providing the finest in entertainment for people of all ages, everywhere."

- Nike: "To bring inspiration and innovation to every athlete in the world."

- Sony: "To experience the joy of advancing and applying technology for the benefit of the public."

A good mission statement states the firm's purpose for being in business and its overall goal. The most effective mission statements are those that people remember. The "Going Green" feature describes the mission of Johnson & Johnson, a global manufacturer of medicinal drugs and healthcare products.

GOING GREEN

JOHNSON & JOHNSON: CARING FOR THE WORLD

Johnson & Johnson has written a company statement of values. It promises that "We must maintain in good order the property we are privileged to use, protecting the environment and natural resources." It is a simple statement, but a difficult promise to fulfill. Johnson & Johnson makes a wide range of consumer products such as Band-Aids, Listerine, and Johnson's Baby Lotion. It also produces medical devices and prescription drugs. Making these products can result in a giant carbon footprint: the manufacturing process produces emissions, chemicals are used in products and processes, and the company uses a huge amount of energy. But Johnson & Johnson is committed to reaching its environmental goals and has put the management in place to reach those goals.

The firm sets new long-term goals every five years, under its "Healthy Planet" program. Some of these goals have included

setting up and using the direct purchase of low-impact hydro and wind power, on-site solar power, and landfill gas. Other goals include purchasing renewable energy certificates from wind power and biomass facilities. Johnson & Johnson believes these practices will benefit the environment and the company because the firm will use reliable, affordable sources of energy. Johnson & Johnson also operates the largest fleet of hybrid vehicles owned by any corporation in the world.

Part of the Healthy Planet program also involves being truthful about green advertising—avoiding so-called *greenwashing*. Company management believes in transparency, being clear and truthful. That's why the company informs employees, suppliers, consumers, and shareholders about what's green and what's not. It also means being specific about sustainability measures. "Provide your consumers with real numbers that inform and empower them," says the website. Johnson & Johnson doesn't want to overstate its efforts to be green, but the firm is beginning to go public about its efforts to share the news with consumers. For example, the company is the second-largest producer of solar panels in the United States. It was also recently ranked number three on *Newsweek*'s Green Ranking List.

None of these goals could have been reached without support from Johnson & Johnson's leadership. Chairman and CEO William Weldon is committed to his company's sustainability initiatives as they relate to people and the planet. He writes, "More than ever, we know that caring for the health and well-being of people is not only an outstanding business but a mission that truly touches lives."

Questions for Critical Thinking

1. What role does the CEO's leadership play in meeting Johnson & Johnson's green goals?

2. How does the company's mission relate to sustainability?

Sources: Company website, http://www.jnj.com accessed April 12, 2010; "To Our Shareholders," *Annual Report*, http://www.investor.jnj.com, accessed April 12, 2010; "Partner Profile," *Green Power Partnership*, March 22, 2010, http://www.epa.gov.

Assessing Your Competitive Position

After a mission statement has been created, the next step in the planning process is to decide on the firm's current—or hoped-for—position in the marketplace. The company's founder or top managers assess the factors that can help it grow or cause it to fail. The **SWOT analysis** is a tool that is often used in this part of strategic planning. SWOT is a short form for *strengths, weaknesses, opportunities*, and *threats*. By assessing all four factors one by one, a firm can then develop the best strategies for gaining a competitive advantage. The framework for a SWOT analysis is shown in Figure 7.3.

SWOT analysis SWOT is a short form for *strengths, weaknesses, opportunities,* and *threats*. By assessing all four factors one by one, a firm can then develop the best strategies for gaining a competitive advantage.

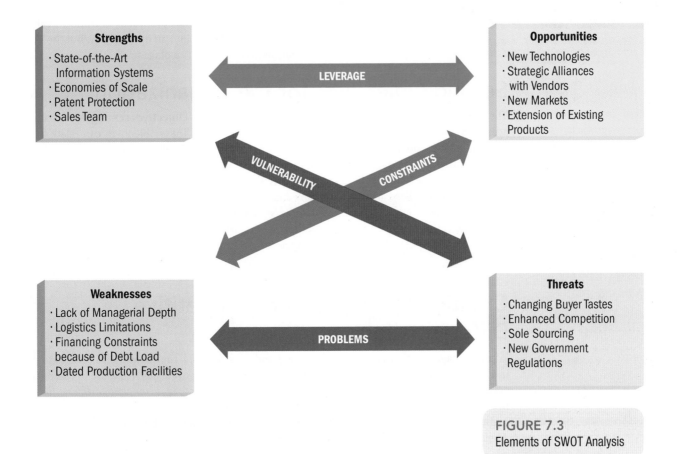

Strengths
- State-of-the-Art Information Systems
- Economies of Scale
- Patent Protection
- Sales Team

LEVERAGE

Opportunities
- New Technologies
- Strategic Alliances with Vendors
- New Markets
- Extension of Existing Products

VULNERABILITY

CONSTRAINTS

Weaknesses
- Lack of Managerial Depth
- Logistics Limitations
- Financing Constraints because of Debt Load
- Dated Production Facilities

PROBLEMS

Threats
- Changing Buyer Tastes
- Enhanced Competition
- Sole Sourcing
- New Government Regulations

FIGURE 7.3
Elements of SWOT Analysis

To assess a firm's strengths and weaknesses, its managers may look at each functional area, such as finance, marketing, information technology, and human resources. Or they might look at the strengths and weaknesses of each office, plant, or store. Entrepreneurs may use a SWOT analysis to focus on the individual skills and experience they bring to a new business.

For Starbucks, a key strength is consumers' positive view of the company's brand. After all, it gets them to stand in line to pay premium prices for coffee. That positive view comes from Starbucks being one of the best 100 companies to work for according to *Fortune*. It also comes from its socially responsible corporate policies. The company's strategic plans include various ways to build on strong brand loyalty by attaching it to new products and expanding into new markets. The expansion efforts have included creating a Music WiFi Community on its website; offering bottled Frappuccino drinks in grocery stores; and opening thousands of Starbucks outlets in Europe, Asia, and the Middle East. Weaknesses include opening too many stores in some markets

and not paying attention to store design. Starbucks eventually had to deal with these weaknesses by closing some stores and redesigning others.[17]

Starbucks continues its SWOT analysis by trying to define the major opportunities and threats the firm may face. Threats might include an economic recession—when consumers are not willing to buy premium products—or a change in government regulations. Starbucks handled the threat of an economic downturn by offering less expensive instant coffee in such stores as Costco and Target. Opportunities included taking advantage of the growth of social media. The Starbucks website now has links to Facebook and Twitter.[18]

A SWOT analysis can change. After all, strengths and weaknesses, like opportunities and threats, may shift over time. A strength may eventually become a weakness, and a threat may turn into an opportunity. But the SWOT analysis gives managers a place to start.

Kevork Djansezian/©AP/Wide World Photos

Starbucks extends its strong brand loyalty to new products and markets. This activity is one example of the company's strategic turnaround plan.

Setting Objectives for the Organization

objectives the targets that managers use to plan for the organization's hoped-for performance. These objectives can relate to such areas as new-product development, sales, customer service, growth, environmental and social responsibility, and employee satisfaction.

The next step in planning is to develop objectives for the firm. **Objectives** set targets so that managers can plan for the organization's hoped-for performance. These objectives can relate to such areas as new-product development, sales, customer service, growth, environmental and social responsibility, and employee satisfaction. The mission statement identifies a company's overall purpose and aims, but objectives are more specific.

For example, Ford Motor Company had an objective to update the styling of its Taurus model. The new Taurus features a T-handle shifter and a built-in navigation system.[19] Quiznos had the objective of reducing the eco-footprint of its packaging. Quiznos now serves its drinks in 100-percent compostable, wax-coated paper cups, and its salad bowls are made from renewable sugarcane.[20]

Creating Strategies for Competitive Differentiation

When managers develop a mission statement and set objectives, they help their business to move in a specific direction. But the firm also needs to decide on the strategies it will use to reach its target ahead of the competition. The basic goal of developing a strategy is *competitive differentiation*—the unique mix of a company's abilities and resources that set it apart from its competitors. A firm might differentiate itself, or set itself apart, by being the first to introduce a product. For example, Apple introduced the iPad to a global market, WestJet decided to focus on providing exceptional customer service, and Costco chose to offer bargains. Becel is the leading margarine brand in Canada. The company has a strong commitment to heart health innovation and education. The firm sets itself apart from other brands by highlighting its association with reducing cholesterol through proper diet and exercise.[21]

Implementing the Strategy

After the first four phases of the strategic planning process are complete, managers are ready to put those plans into action. The middle managers or supervisors are often the people who actually implement a strategy. But studies show that many top company officials don't want to give these managers the power to make decisions that could be helpful for the company. Companies that *are* willing to empower employees usually profit from that decision.[22]

Many firms have a strategy of cutting costs and maintaining a high level of customer service. A strategy that makes sense is to cross-train call-centre representatives. When customers phone in, they don't need to be transferred to someone else if the person who answers the call has been trained to answer the most frequently asked questions. This idea may seem like an obvious strategy that won't have much effect. But research shows that cross-training can reduce the cost of running a call centre, increase customer satisfaction, and improve employee morale.[23]

Monitoring and Adapting Strategic Plans

The final step in the strategic planning process is to monitor and adapt plans when the actual performance fails to meet goals. Monitoring involves gathering feedback about performance. Managers might compare actual sales against forecast sales; compile information from surveys; listen to complaints from the customer hot line; interview employees who are involved; and review reports prepared by production, finance, marketing, or other company units. If an Internet advertisement doesn't result in enough customers or sales, managers might look at whether to continue the advertisement, change it, or discontinue it. If a retailer sees that customers buy more jeans when they are displayed near the front door, the display area will probably stay near the door—and may even be made bigger. Managers can continue to use of such tools as SWOT analysis and forecasting to help adapt their objectives and functional plans as changes occur.

✓ **ASSESSMENT CHECK**

7.4.1 What is the purpose of a mission statement?

7.4.2 Which of a firm's characteristics are compared in a SWOT analysis?

7.4.3 How do managers use objectives?

MANAGERS AS DECISION MAKERS

LO 7.5 Contrast the two major types of business decisions, and list the steps in the decision-making process.

Managers make decisions every day. Some decisions may involve shutting down a manufacturing plant. Other decisions may deal with adding grilled cheese sandwiches to a lunch menu. **Decision-making** is the process of seeing a problem or opportunity, assessing possible solutions, selecting and carrying out the best-suited plan, and assessing the results. Managers make two basic kinds of decisions: programmed decisions and nonprogrammed decisions.

Programmed and Nonprogrammed Decisions

A *programmed decision* involves simple, common, and frequently occurring problems that already have solutions. For example, programmed decisions include reordering office supplies, renewing a lease, and referring to an already decided-on discount for bulk orders. Programmed decisions are made in advance. The firm sets rules, policies, and procedures for managers and employees to follow on a routine basis. Programmed decisions save managers time and save companies money because new decisions don't have to be made each time the situation arises.

decision-making the process of seeing a problem or opportunity, assessing possible solutions, selecting and carrying out the best-suited plan, and assessing the results.

TOBIAS SCHWARZ/Reuters /Landov

Apple made a nonprogrammed decision when it released the iPad. The decision involved a complex and unique opportunity and had important results for the company.

A *nonprogrammed decision* involves a complex and unique problem or opportunity and has important results for the organization. Nonprogrammed decisions include entering a new market, deleting a product from the line, or developing a new product. Apple's decision to develop and launch the iPad was a nonprogrammed decision that involved research and development, finances, technology, production, and marketing. Decisions were made about everything, from what kinds of apps and accessories the iPad would offer, to how much the new device would cost consumers.[24]

How Managers Make Decisions

In a simple view, decision-making is choosing from two or more options, and the chosen option becomes the decision. In a larger view, decision-making is a step-by-step process that helps managers to make effective choices. This process begins when someone sees a problem or an opportunity, develops possible ways of taking action, evaluates the options, selects and carries out one option, and assesses the outcome. It's important to remember that managers are *human* decision makers. Managers may follow the decision-making process shown in Figure 7.4 step-by-step, but the outcome of their decisions depends on many factors: the quality of the information they used and their experience, creativity, and wisdom.

FIGURE 7.4
Steps in the Decision-Making Process

Making good decisions is never easy. A decision might hurt or help the sales of a product; it might insult or disappoint a customer or co-worker; it might affect the manager's own career or reputation. Managers' decisions can have legal and ethical effects. In Canada, *Corporate Knights Magazine* publishes an annual list of "The Best 50 Corporate Citizens." In the United States, *CRO*

Magazine publishes an annual list of "The 100 Best Corporate Citizens." The companies on these lists make decisions that are ethical, environmentally responsible, fair toward employees, and accountable to local communities. These companies also provide responsible goods and services to customers and a healthy return to investors. These organizations prove that good corporate citizenship is good behaviour. The top 10 Canadian corporate citizens named one recent year were: Mountain Equipment Co-op, Cooperators Group, Vancouver City Savings Credit Union, Hydro One, Loblaw Companies Limited, Sherritt International, Mouvement des caisses Desjardins (The Desjardins Group), SNC-Lavalin Group Inc., IGM Financial, and IAMGOLD Corporation. The top 10 U.S. corporate citizens named were Hewlett-Packard, Intel, General Mills, IBM, Kimberly-Clark, Abbott Laboratories, Bristol-Myers Squibb, The Coca-Cola Company, Gap Inc., and Hess Corporation.[25]

> ✓ **ASSESSMENT CHECK**
>
> **7.5.1** Distinguish between programmed and nonprogrammed decisions.
>
> **7.5.2** What are the steps in the decision-making process?

MANAGERS AS LEADERS

> **LO 7.6** Define *leadership*, and compare different leadership styles.

A manager must show **leadership**, by directing or inspiring others to reach goals. All great leaders do not share the same qualities, but three personal qualities are often mentioned: empathy (the ability to imagine being in someone else's position), self-awareness, and objectivity. Empathy and objectivity may seem like opposites, but they do balance each other. Many leaders share other qualities, such as courage, passion, commitment, innovation, and flexibility.

Leadership involves the use of influence or power. This influence may come from one or more sources. One source of power is the leader's position in the company. A national sales manager has the authority to direct the activities of the sales force. Another source of power is a leader's expertise and experience. A first-line supervisor with expert machinist skills will likely be respected by employees in the machining department. Some leaders derive power from their personalities. Employees may admire a leader because they see a person who is exceptionally kind and fair, humorous, energetic, or enthusiastic. Admiration, inspiration, and motivation are especially important during difficult economic times or when a leader needs to make tough decisions for the

leadership the ability to direct or inspire people to reach goals.

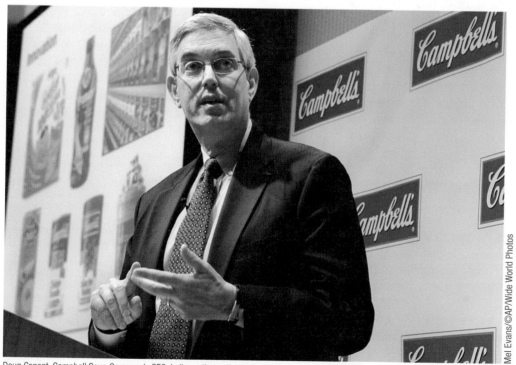

Doug Conant, Campbell Soup Company's CEO, believes that action is the best way to show leadership.

Mel Evans/©AP/Wide World Photos

company. Jeffrey Immelt, chairman and CEO of General Electric (GE) was in this position. His story is described in the "Hit & Miss" feature.

When Doug Conant took over as CEO at Campbell Soup Company in 2001, the company was decidedly a little boring. Instead of being filled with new ideas, the firm wasn't thinking about doing anything new. Conant looked around the company. It produces one of the best-known brands in the world. Conant was frustrated. "The microwave was invented in 1947, but it took us until 2002 to put together a microwaveable soup pack," he told the company's researchers, marketers, and managers. Conant got to work on updating the world's largest soup company. He cut all products that were not number one or number two in their categories. He poured resources into developing products that offered value, nutrition, and convenience. And he engineered a new focus on two of the world's largest soup-eating nations: China and Russia. Conant believes that action is the best demonstration of leadership. "You can't talk your way out of something you behaved your way into," he says.[26]

HIT & MISS

Jeff Immelt Leads GE in a New Direction

GE was once one of the world's most well-known and respected firms. But then it fell on hard times. The company manufactures many products, from toasters to washing machines to jet engines. But GE was forced to make cuts to save the company. The person in charge of GE is its CEO, Jeffrey Immelt.

Over the years, GE became a conglomerate, a company that bought up other companies— and GE didn't just buy other companies in the same business. GE strayed from its roots as a manufacturer of electrical appliances. Its GE Capital unit once accounted for more than half of the company's overall profits. Now it has a huge number of bad loans. GE's ownerships in NBC Universal and the NBC network were sold to cable operator Comcast. But shareholders and others are asking, "Why was GE involved in these businesses in the first place?"

Jeffrey Immelt decided to change the direction of the company. "GE must be an industrial company first," he notes. "We need a new strategy for this economy. We should clear away any arrogance, false assumptions, or a sense that things will be OK just because we are [in] America."

Financially, GE can't just walk away from its GE Capital loans. But Immelt has promised to reduce the size of the loans. He also wants to renew the firm's focus on its industrial background, including by investing in clean energy projects. He takes his leadership role and the leadership role of GE very seriously. "We need to invest more in innovation. We need to target this innovation toward fulfilling big needs like clean energy," he says. "Nothing of consequence is accomplished without leadership."

Immelt knows that today's leaders must have a democratic style that encourages input from employees. "Twenty-first century leaders listen. They use external inputs as a catalyst. They put their ego in check. They ask more questions than they answer. They welcome dissent and debate, and are constantly seeking more intelligence." Immelt has been spending his weekends listening to the 185 officers of GE—one at a time. The weekend sessions create personal relationships with his team.

He also points out the importance of delegating, or assigning, tasks to others so the firm can innovate more easily and regain a competitive standing. "GE is a big organization. The problem with size is that it can be too slow. At GE, we must push decision-making down in the organization and we must delegate more."

Immelt has shown his commitment to GE, his employees, and the firm's shareholders by declining his bonus two years in a row. This doesn't mean he isn't paid well—he still earns more than $5.5 million per year. Immelt is determined to regain the respect for his firm that it once enjoyed. As a leader, he understands this cannot be accomplished without inspired employees. "Leaders must motivate with vision," he observes. His vision includes a much brighter light for GE.

Questions for Critical Thinking

1. How would you describe Immelt's leadership style? Is it suitable for a big organization like GE? Why or why not?

2. Do you think Immelt is an effective motivator? Would you want to work for him? Why or why not?

Sources: Diane Brady, "Can GE Still Manage?" *Bloomberg BusinessWeek*, April 25, 2010, 26–32; GE website, http://www.ge.com, accessed April 9, 2010; "Renewing American Leadership: Immelt at West Point," *GE Reports*, http://www.gereports.com, accessed April 9, 2010; Stephen Manning, "GE's CEO Declines Bonus for 2nd Year," *BusinessWeek*, March 5, 2010, http://www.businessweek.com.

Leadership Styles

A person's leadership style depends on how that person uses power to lead others. Leadership styles range from autocratic leadership at one extreme to free-rein leadership at the other extreme. *Autocratic leadership* is centred on the boss. Autocratic leaders make decisions on their own without consulting employees. They make decisions, communicate the decisions to employees, and expect the decisions to be carried out right away.

Democratic leadership includes employees in the decision-making process. This leadership style centres on employees' contributions. Democratic leaders assign projects, ask employees for suggestions, and encourage participation. An important outcome of democratic leadership in business is the concept of **empowerment**, where employees share authority, responsibility, and decision-making with their managers.

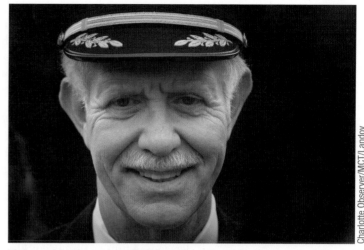

US Airways flight 1549 was forced to land in the Hudson River in New York. The quick thinking and decision-making leadership of Chesley Sullenberger saved the lives of everyone on that flight.

At the opposite extreme from autocratic leadership is *free-rein leadership*. Free-rein leaders believe in minimal supervision. They allow employees to make most of their own decisions. Free-rein leaders communicate with employees frequently. For its first decade in business, Google was proud of its free-rein leadership style. Engineers were encouraged to pursue any and all ideas, teams formed or disbanded on their own, and employees spent as much or as little time as they wanted to on any given project. But then the firm entered its second decade. Not every innovation was worth pursuing—and some valuable ideas were getting lost. CEO Eric Schmidt noted, "We were concerned that some of the biggest ideas were getting squashed." So the firm set up a process for reviewing new project ideas to focus on those ideas most likely to succeed.[27]

empowerment giving employees shared authority, responsibility, and decision-making with their managers.

Which Leadership Style Is Best?

No single leadership style is right for every firm in every situation. Leadership styles sometimes need to be changed for a company to grow. That was the situation for Google. In a crisis, an autocratic leadership style might save the company—and sometimes the lives of customers and employees. That's what happened when US Airways flight 1549 was forced to land in the Hudson River in New York. Quick, autocratic decisions made by pilot Chesley Sullenberger meant that everyone on the flight survived. But US Airways management on the ground used a democratic style of leadership: managers at many levels were empowered to take actions to help the passengers and their families. For example, one executive arrived on the scene with a bag of emergency cash for passengers and credit cards for employees so they could purchase medicines, food, or anything else they needed.[28] Some companies know which leadership style works best for their employees, customers, and business conditions. Those companies are most likely to choose the best leaders for their needs.

✓ **ASSESSMENT CHECK**

7.6.1 How is *leadership* defined?

7.6.2 Identify the styles of leadership as they range from the most to the least amount of employee participation.

CORPORATE CULTURE

LO 7.7 Discuss the meaning and importance of corporate culture.

An organization's **corporate culture** is its collection of principles, beliefs, and values. The corporate culture is influenced by the leadership style of its managers, the way the firm communicates, and the overall work environment. A corporate culture is typically shaped by the leaders who founded and developed the company and by the leaders who were appointed since the founders left. For example, look at Google. It has grown by leaps and bounds since

corporate culture an organization's collection of principles, beliefs, and values.

its launch. The firm tries to continue the culture of innovation, creativity, and flexibility that its co-founders, Larry Page and Sergey Brin, promoted from the beginning. Google now has offices around the world, staffed by thousands of workers who speak many different languages. "We are aggressively inclusive in our hiring, and we favour ability over experience," states the website. "The result is a team that reflects the global audience Google serves. When not at work, Googlers pursue interests from cross-country cycling to wine tasting, from flying to Frisbee."[29]

Managers sometimes use symbols, rituals, ceremonies, and stories to strengthen a corporate culture. The corporate culture at the Walt Disney Company is almost as famous as the Disney characters themselves. In fact, every Disney employee is known as a cast member. All new employees attend training seminars to learn the language, customs, traditions, stories, product lines—everything about the Disney culture and its original founder, Walt Disney.[30]

Corporate cultures can be very strong and lasting. But sometimes they need to change to meet new demands in the business world. A firm that is filled with tradition and bureaucracy might need to shift to a leaner, more flexible culture to respond to shifts in technology or customer demands. A firm that grows quickly—like Google—usually needs to make some adjustments in its culture to make room for more customers and more employees.

In an organization with a strong culture, everyone knows and supports the same principles, beliefs, and values. That's the culture at WestJet Airlines, described in the "Hit & Miss" feature. To reach its goals, a business must also provide structure, which results from the management function of organizing.

✓ ASSESSMENT CHECK

7.7.1 What is the relationship between leadership style and corporate culture?

7.7.2 What is a strong corporate culture?

LO 7.8 Identify the five major forms of departmentalization and the four main types of organization structures.

organization a structured group of people working together to achieve common goals.

ORGANIZATIONAL STRUCTURES

An **organization** is a structured group of people working together to achieve common goals. An organization features three key elements: human interaction, goal-directed activities, and structure. The organizing process is mostly led by managers. It should result in an overall structure that makes it easier for individuals and departments to work together to achieve company goals.

The steps involved in the organizing process are shown in Figure 7.5. Managers first decide on the specific activities needed to carry out plans and achieve goals. Next, they group these work activities into a structure that makes sense. Then, they assign work to specific employees and give them the resources they need. Managers coordinate the work of different groups and employees within the firm. Finally, they evaluate the results of the organizing process to ensure effective and efficient progress toward planned goals. Evaluation sometimes results in changes to the way work is organized.

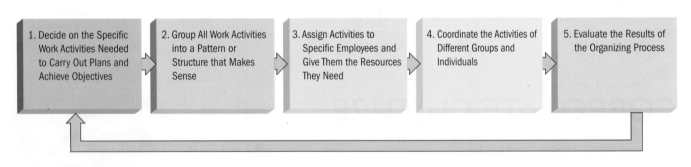

1. Decide on the Specific Work Activities Needed to Carry Out Plans and Achieve Objectives

2. Group All Work Activities into a Pattern or Structure that Makes Sense

3. Assign Activities to Specific Employees and Give Them the Resources They Need

4. Coordinate the Activities of Different Groups and Individuals

5. Evaluate the Results of the Organizing Process

FIGURE 7.5 Steps in the Organizing Process

HIT & MISS

WestJet Airlines: Most Admired Corporate Culture in Canada

WestJet Airlines was named a J.D. Power 2011 Customer Service Champion. The company was also inducted into the Corporate Culture Hall of Fame after being named one of Canada's Most Admired Corporate Cultures every year from 2005 to 2010. The airline is well known for its reasonable fares, cheerful service, convenient schedules, and genuine interest in its passengers. WestJet is both successful and profitable. It is the business model that other service-oriented businesses study to learn how WestJet sets itself apart through its superior customer service.

WestJet's strategic plan is built on four pillars for long-term success:

- People and Culture – Investing in and fostering the growth, development and commitment of our people.

- Guest Experience – Consistently and continuously providing an amazing guest experience.

- Revenue and Growth – Achieving an average annual compound growth rate in available seat miles of between four and seven per cent.

- Costs – Achieving a targeted, sustainable profit margin that will be number one among North American airlines.

Together, these pillars describe the corporate focus and culture that directs the firm. WestJet is also known to have a corporate culture filled with humour and energy that spills over to its customers. When you fly WestJet, the hosts tell jokes over the public address system before giving the formal instructions about flight safety. The jokes help to get passengers' attention and create a more relaxed atmosphere for the flight. Employees are empowered and convey the culture of the company to customers. The idea is that if the company's 8,000 employees are happy, they will want to make sure their customers are happy, too. This simple strategy has been very effective. There's another reason employees feel differently about the company they work for. About 85 percent of eligible employees own shares of the company through an employee share purchase plan.

Questions for Critical Thinking

1. How would you describe the principles, beliefs, and values at WestJet?

2. How important is employee ownership to creating and maintaining the corporate culture?

Sources: Company website, http://www.westjet.com/guest/en/about/index.shtml, accessed January 23, 2012; Fact Sheet, http://www.westjet.com/pdf/investorMedia/investorFactSheet.pdf, accessed January 23, 2012; Canada News Wire, "WestJet Named to Corporate Culture Hall of Fame," February 1, 2010, http://www.newswire.ca/en/story/692931/westjet-named-to-corporate-culture-hall-of-fame, accessed January 23, 2012; "WestJet Culture Seen as Tops in Country," *Calgary Herald*, October 11, 2006, http://www.canada.com/calgaryherald/news/calgarybusiness/story.html?id=1cec87b5-bbab-4e1e-a63a-e64f91b15fa6&k=24339, accessed January 12, 2012.

Many factors can affect the results of organizing. The list includes a firm's goals and competitive strategy, the type of product it offers, the way it uses technology to accomplish work, and its size. Small firms typically create very simple structures. For example, the owner of a dry-cleaning business is often the top manager, who hires several employees to process orders, clean the clothing, and make deliveries. The owner purchases supplies such as detergents and hangers, hires and trains employees, coordinates employees' work, prepares advertisements for the local newspaper, and keeps the accounting records.

As a company grows, its structure becomes more complex. Increased size often means specialization and growing numbers of employees. A larger firm may need to hire many salespeople and a sales manager to direct and coordinate their work, or it may need to organize an accounting department.

An effective structure is clear and easy to understand: employees know what they are expected to do, and they know whom they report to. They also know how their jobs help to achieve the company's mission and overall strategic plan. An *organization chart* can help people to understand the structure of a firm. Figure 7.6 shows a sample organization chart.

FIGURE 7.6 Sample Organization Chart

Not-for-profit organizations also organize themselves using formal structures. These structures help them to function efficiently and to carry out their goals. The organizational structure of non-profits, such as the Salvation Army and the Alberta Society for Prevention of Cruelty to Animals, sometimes includes a mix of paid staff and volunteers.

Departmentalization

departmentalization the process of dividing work activities into units within the organization.

Departmentalization is the process of dividing work activities into units within the organization. In this arrangement, employees specialize in certain jobs—such as marketing, finance, or design. Depending on the size of the firm, usually an executive heads the department, followed by middle-level managers and supervisors. The five major forms of departmentalization divide work by product, geographical area, customer, function, and process.

- *Product departmentalization.* This approach organizes work units based on the goods and services a company offers. Activision Blizzard Inc. recently restructured its organization by product. The videogame publisher is now divided into four divisions: "Call of Duty," a military game; internally owned games, such as "Guitar Hero" and "Tony Hawk"; licensed properties; and Blizzard Entertainment, maker of the online game "World of Warcraft."[31]

- *Geographical departmentalization.* This form organizes units by geographical regions within a country or, for a multinational firm, by region throughout the world. Enterprise Rent-A-Car is organized by geography, staffing 7,000 rental locations in the United States, Canada, Germany, Ireland, and England.[32]

- *Customer departmentalization.* Customer departmentalization might be used by a firm that offers a variety of goods and services for different types of customers. For example,

© R. Alcorn, photographed for John Wiley & Sons

These familiar office products represent only one of 3M Corporation's many product lines. Because 3M serves a broad range of customers, it is organized on the basis of customer departmentalization.

3M's wide range of products is divided among six business units: consumer and office; display and graphics; electro and communications; healthcare; industrial and transportation; and safety, security, and protection services.[33]

- *Functional departmentalization.* Some firms organize work units according to business functions, such as finance, marketing, human resources, and production. An advertising agency may create departments for creative personnel (e.g., copywriters), media buyers, and account executives.

- *Process departmentalization.* Some goods and services require multiple work processes to complete their production. A manufacturer may set up separate departments for cutting material, heat-treating it, forming it into its final shape, and painting it.

As Figure 7.7 shows, a single company may use several forms of departmentalization. When deciding on a form of departmentalization, managers take into account the type of product they produce, the size of their company, their customer base, and the locations of their customers.

FIGURE 7.7
Different Forms of Departmentalization within One Company

Delegating Work Assignments

Managers assign work to employees, a process called **delegation**. For example, employees might be assigned to answer customer calls, scoop ice cream, process returns, make deliveries, open or close a store, cook or serve food, contribute to new-product design, calculate a return on investment, or any of thousands of other tasks. Just as important as the tasks themselves, employees are usually given some authority to make decisions.

Companies like Zappos, the online shoe retailer, give their workers the power to make decisions to better serve their customers. The result is generally happier employees and more satisfied customers.[34] As employees receive more power to make decisions, they also must be accountable for their actions and decisions—that is, they receive credit when things go well and must accept responsibility when things don't go well. Managers also must decide on the best way to delegate responsibilities when employees belong to different age groups, as discussed in the "Business Etiquette" feature.

delegation the managerial process of assigning work to employees.

Span of Management

The *span of management,* or span of control, is the number of employees a manager supervises. These employees are often referred to as *direct reports.* First-line managers often have the widest spans of management because they monitor the work of many employees. The span of management varies, depending on many factors, including the type of work performed and employees' training. In recent years, a growing trend has brought wider spans of control. Many companies have reduced their layers of management to flatten their organizational structures. This process usually increases employees' decision-making responsibility.

Centralization and Decentralization

How widely should managers assign decision-making authority throughout an organization? A company that emphasizes *centralization* keeps decision-making at the top of the management hierarchy. A company that emphasizes *decentralization* shifts decision-making to lower levels. A trend toward decentralization has pushed decision-making down to operating employees in many companies. Firms decentralize because they believe the change will improve their service to customers. For example, a hotel's front desk clerk is better able to help a guest who needs a crib or a wake-up call than the hotel's general manager.

BUSINESS ETIQUETTE

Managing a Multigenerational Workforce

Today's firms employ workers who span a wide range of ages. Management experts warn against stereotyping, or treating people on the basis of an overly simple idea of their characteristics or qualities. The experts do suggest making an effort to understand each group. They suggest taking steps to open up communications so that everyone in the workforce works well together. Baby boomers, those people born between 1946 and 1964, tend to be competitive. Most of them believe that younger employees should work their way up the company ladder. Gen-Xers, born between 1965 and 1977, are more skeptical, independent thinkers. Gen-Yers—also called the Millennials—were born in 1978 or later. They prefer teamwork, feedback, and technology.

Managers can use the following tips to effectively assign work to employees in these groups:

- Offer—and encourage—mentoring, an informal relationship between younger and older employees to guide and advise younger employees. Communication and support that crosses age groups can increase understanding among employees.

- Understand different learning styles and work styles, and make workplace changes to help employees who learn and work differently.

- Involve employees in the workplace through training, education, and career development opportunities.

- Discard strict routines for those who work best without them.

- Use different forms of communication. Older employees may prefer chatting on the phone or in person. Millennials might prefer e-mails, text messages, or social networking.
- Give everyone an equal voice. Everyone wants to be heard and understood. Offer opportunities for all employees to voice their opinions.

Sources: Sally Kane, "The Multigenerational Workforce," *About.com*, http://legalcareers.about.com, accessed March 29, 2010; "How to Manage Different Generations," *Wall Street Journal*, http://guides.wsj.com, accessed March 29, 2010; Tammy Erickson, "Finally, Gen X Takes Over," *BusinessWeek*, January 13, 2009, http://www.businessweek.com.

Types of Organization Structures

The four basic types of organization structures are line, line-and-staff, committee, and matrix. Some companies use one type of structure, but most use a mix of two or more types.

Line Organizations

The oldest and simplest organization structure is a *line organization*. It sets up a direct flow of authority from the chief executive to the employees. The line organization defines a simple, clear *chain of command*—a hierarchy of managers and workers. Everyone knows who is in charge, and decisions can be made quickly. This structure is very effective in a crisis situation. But a line organization also has its downsides. Each manager has complete responsibility for a range of activities. But in a medium-sized or large organization, the manager can't be an expert in all of the tasks. In a small organization, such as a local hair salon or a dentist's office, a line organization is probably the most efficient way to run the business.

Line-and-Staff Organizations

A *line-and-staff organization* combines the direct flow of authority of a line organization with staff departments that support the line departments. Line departments help to make decisions that affect the firm's core operations. Staff departments lend specialized technical support. Figure 7.8 shows a line-and-staff organization. Accounting, engineering, and human resources are staff departments. They support the line authority that extends from the plant manager to the production manager and supervisors.

A line manager and a staff manager have different authority relationships. A line manager forms part of the primary line of authority that flows throughout the organization. Line managers work directly with the production, financing, or marketing departments—the areas that are needed to produce and sell goods and services. A staff manager provides information, advice, or technical assistance to help the line managers. Staff managers do not have authority to give orders outside their own departments or to assign actions to the line managers.

FIGURE 7.8 Line-and-Staff Organization

The line-and-staff organization is common in mid-size and large organizations. It is an effective structure because it combines the line organization's rapid decision-making and direct communication with the expert knowledge of the staff departments.

Committee Organizations

A *committee organization* is a structure that places authority and responsibility in a group of individuals, not a manager. This model often appears as part of a regular line-and-staff structure.

Committees also work in areas such as new-product development. A new-product committee may include managers from accounting, engineering, finance, manufacturing, marketing, and technical research. Having representatives from all areas involved in creating and marketing products is a good idea. It usually improves both the planning process and employee morale because decisions reflect very different viewpoints.

Committees tend to act slowly and make conservative, or safe, decisions. They may make decisions by compromising, or by coming to an agreement with conflicting interests, instead of choosing the best alternative. The definition of a camel as "a racehorse designed by committee" provides a fitting description of the imperfections of committee decisions.

Matrix Organizations

Some organizations use a matrix or product management design to make their structures more suitable to their business. The *matrix structure* links employees from different parts of the organization who work together on specific projects. Figure 7.9 shows a matrix structure. A project manager assembles a group of employees from different functional areas. The employees keep their ties to the line-and-staff structure, as shown by the vertical white lines. As the horizontal gold lines show, employees are also members of project teams. When the project is completed, employees return to their "regular" jobs.

FIGURE 7.9 Matrix Organizations

In the matrix structure, each employee reports to two managers: one line manager and one project manager. Employees who are working on a special project receive instructions from the project manager (horizontal authority), but they continue as employees in their permanent functional departments (vertical authority). The term *matrix* refers to the intersecting grid of horizontal and vertical lines of authority.

The matrix structure is popular at high-technology and multinational corporations, and in hospitals and consulting firms. Dow Chemical and Procter & Gamble have both used matrix structures. The major upsides of the matrix structure come from its flexibility to adapt quickly to rapid changes in the environment. It also focuses resources on major problems or products. The matrix structure also provides an outlet for employees' creativity and initiative. But it challenges project managers to take the skills of specialists from many departments and form a coordinated team. Team members' permanent functional managers must adjust their employees' regular workloads.

The matrix structure is most effective when company leaders give project managers the authority to use whatever resources are available to achieve the project's objectives. Good project managers know how to make the project goals clear and how to keep team members focused. A firm that truly adopts the matrix structure will also encourage a project culture by making sure staffing is adequate, the workload is reasonable, and other company resources are available to project managers.[35]

WHAT'S AHEAD

In the next chapter, we focus on the importance of people in shaping the growth and profitability of the organization. We examine how firms recruit, select, train, evaluate, and compensate employees as they try to attract, retain, and motivate a high-quality workforce. The concept of motivation is examined, and we will discuss how managers apply theories of motivation in the modern workplace. The next chapter also looks at the important topic of labour–management relations.

✔ **ASSESSMENT CHECK**

7.8.1 What is the purpose of an organization chart?

7.8.2 What are the five major forms of departmentalization?

7.8.3 What does *span of management* mean?

RETURN TO INSIDE BUSINESS

Research In Motion: A Question of Management?

Research In Motion Ltd. first introduced the BlackBerry in 1998. It was a hit with mobile business people who liked the value-added feature of a pager they could use to instantly receive, read, and reply to e-mail from their office computers. Laptops were larger, more expensive, and not as easy to connect for communicating with others. The BlackBerry is small, costs under $500, and allows business people to receive their e-mail while away from their office. Their connection fees were reasonably inexpensive, which attracted the business market that believed in the importance of timely communications. When BlackBerry added more features, such as voice, it started competing with cellphones. It seemed that RIM had created the perfect mobile communications device.

As we all know now, Apple's iPhone and iPad offered consumers even more functions. Some people questioned RIM's leadership and management decision-making.

QUESTIONS FOR CRITICAL THINKING

1. Is top management responsible for the decline of RIM share value?

2. Can a restructuring of management return RIM to a leadership position?

SUMMARY OF LEARNING OBJECTIVES

LO 7.1 Define *management* and the three types of skills necessary for managerial success.

Management is the process of achieving organizational goals through people and other resources. The management hierarchy usually has three levels: top managers who provide overall direction for company activities, middle managers who carry out the strategies of top managers and direct the activities of supervisors, and supervisors who deal directly with workers. The three basic managerial skills are technical, human or interpersonal, and conceptual.

✓ ASSESSMENT CHECK ANSWERS

7.1.1 What is management? Management is the process of achieving organizational goals through people and other resources. The manager's job is to combine human and technical resources in the best way possible to achieve the company's goals.

7.1.2 Describe the differences in the jobs of top managers, middle managers, and supervisory managers. Top managers develop long-range plans, set a direction for their organization, and inspire all employees to achieve the company's vision. Middle managers focus their attention on specific operations, products, or customers. They develop plans and procedures to carry out the firm's strategic plans. Supervisory managers deal directly with nonmanagerial employees who produce and sell the firm's goods and services. These managers are responsible for carrying out the plans developed by middle managers and for motivating workers to accomplish immediate goals.

7.1.3 What is the relationship between the manager's planning and controlling functions? Controlling is assessing

an organization's performance to decide whether it is achieving its goals. The basic purpose of controlling is to assess the success of the planning function. Controlling also provides feedback for future rounds of planning.

LO 7.2 Explain the role of vision and ethical standards in business success.

Vision is the founder's ability to perceive marketplace needs and what an organization must do to satisfy them. Vision helps to clarify a firm's purpose and the actions it can take to make the most of opportunities. High ethical standards can help build success for a firm through job satisfaction and customer loyalty.

✓ ASSESSMENT CHECK ANSWERS

7.2.1 What is meant by a vision for the firm? A vision is a focus for a firm's actions. Vision helps to direct the company toward opportunities and sets it apart from its competitors.

7.2.2 Why is it important for a top executive to set high ethical standards? High ethical standards often result in a stable workforce, job satisfaction, and customer loyalty.

LO 7.3 Summarize the major benefits of planning, and distinguish among strategic planning, tactical planning, and operational planning.

The planning process identifies organizational goals and develops the actions needed to reach those goals. Planning helps a company to turn its vision into action. It also helps it to take advantage of opportunities and to avoid costly mistakes. Strategic planning is a far-reaching process. It takes a broad view of the world to decide on the organization's long-range focus and activities. Tactical planning focuses on the current and short-range activities required to carry out the organization's strategies. Operational planning sets the standards and work targets for functional areas such as production, human resources, and marketing.

 ASSESSMENT CHECK ANSWERS

7.3.1 Outline the planning process. Some plans are very broad and long range. These plans focus on the main organizational goals. Other plans are more detailed and show how particular goals will be met. Each planning step—from the mission statement to objectives to specific plans—must fit into an overall plan.

7.3.2 Describe the purpose of tactical planning. The purpose of tactical planning is to decide which short-term activities should be carried out to meet the firm's overall strategy.

7.3.3 Compare the types of plans made by top managers and middle managers. How does their focus differ? Top managers focus on long-range, strategic plans. In contrast, middle-level managers and supervisors focus on short-term, tactical planning.

LO 7.4 Describe the strategic planning process.

The first step in strategic planning is to translate the firm's vision into a mission statement that describes the firm's overall purpose and aims. Next, planners assess the firm's current competitive position using tools such as SWOT analysis. Managers then set specific objectives. The next step is to develop strategies for reaching objectives that will differentiate the firm, or set it apart, from its competitors. Managers then develop an action plan. This plan outlines the specific ways for carrying out the strategy. Finally, the results achieved by the plan are assessed, and the plan is adjusted as needed.

 ASSESSMENT CHECK ANSWERS

7.4.1 What is the purpose of a mission statement? A mission statement is a public description of a firm's purpose, the reason it exists, the customers it will serve, and the way it is different from competitors. A mission statement guides the actions of company managers and employees.

7.4.2 Which of a firm's characteristics are compared in a SWOT analysis? A SWOT analysis assesses a firm's strengths, weaknesses, opportunities, and threats, compared with its competitors. A SWOT analysis helps to decide on a firm's competitive position in the marketplace.

7.4.3 How do managers use objectives? Objectives result from the firm's mission statement. They are used to set performance levels in areas such as profitability, customer service, and employee satisfaction.

LO 7.5 Contrast the two major types of business decisions, and list the steps in the decision-making process.

A programmed decision applies a company rule or policy to solve a frequently occurring problem. A nonprogrammed decision responds to a complex and unique problem that has important results for the organization. The five-step approach to decision-making includes seeing a problem or opportunity, developing possible ways of taking action, evaluating the options, selecting and carrying out one option, and assessing the outcome.

 ASSESSMENT CHECK ANSWERS

7.5.1 Distinguish between programmed and nonprogrammed decisions. Programmed decisions involve simple problems that occur frequently, such as reordering office supplies. The firm usually sets policies and procedures for dealing with these problems to make the process easier. Nonprogrammed decisions require more individual evaluation. For example, buying real estate or equipment is a nonprogrammed decision that needs some research.

7.5.2 What are the steps in the decision-making process? The decision-making steps are seeing a problem or opportunity, developing possible ways of taking action, evaluating the options, selecting and carrying out one option, and assessing the outcome.

LO 7.6 Define *leadership*, and compare different leadership styles.

Leadership is the ability to direct or inspire others to reach goals. The basic leadership styles are autocratic, democratic, and free-rein leadership. The best leadership style depends on three elements: the leader, the followers, and the situation.

 ASSESSMENT CHECK ANSWERS

7.6.1 How is *leadership* defined? Leadership means the ability to direct or inspire people to reach organizational goals. Effective leaders share several personal qualities, such as empathy, self-awareness, and objectivity in dealing with others. Leaders also use the power of their jobs, expertise, and experience to influence others.

7.6.2 Identify the styles of leadership as they range from the most to the least amount of employee participation. At one extreme, autocratic leaders make decisions on their own without consulting employees. At the opposite extreme, free-rein leaders leave most decisions to their employees. In the middle are democratic leaders who ask employees for suggestions and encourage participation.

LO 7.7 Discuss the meaning and importance of corporate culture.

Corporate culture refers to an organization's principles, beliefs, and values. It is typically shaped by a firm's founder and is communicated to all employees through formal programs, such as training, rituals, and ceremonies, and through informal discussions among employees. Corporate culture can influence a firm's success by giving it a competitive advantage.

 ASSESSMENT CHECK ANSWERS

7.7.1 What is the relationship between leadership style and corporate culture? The best leadership style to adopt often depends on the organization's corporate culture, its system of principles, beliefs, and values. Corporate culture is influenced by managers' philosophies, the firm's communications networks, its workplace environments, and its practices.

7.7.2 What is a strong corporate culture? A corporate culture is an organization's collection of principles, beliefs, and values. In an organization with a strong culture, everyone knows and supports the same principles, beliefs, and values.

LO 7.8 Identify the five major forms of departmentalization and the four main types of organization structures.

The division of work activities into units within the organization is called *departmentalization*. The units may be based on products, geographical locations, customers, functions, or processes. Most firms implement one or more of four organization structures: line, line-and-staff, committee, and matrix structures.

✔ **ASSESSMENT CHECK ANSWERS**

7.8.1 What is the purpose of an organization chart? An organization chart is a visual diagram of a firm's structure that shows job positions, job functions, and the reporting hierarchy.

7.8.2 What are the five major forms of departmentalization? Product departmentalization organizes units by the goods and services a company offers. Geographical departmentalization organizes units by geographical regions. Customer departmentalization organizes units by different types of customers. Functional departmentalization organizes units by business functions such as finance, marketing, human resources, and production. Process departmentalization organizes units by the steps or work processes needed to complete production or provide a service.

7.8.3 What does *span of management* mean? The span of management, or span of control, is the number of employees a manager supervises.

BUSINESS TERMS YOU NEED TO KNOW

REVIEW QUESTIONS

1. What are the three levels of management hierarchy? Which management skills are the most important at each level? Why?

2. Identify the four basic managerial functions. Suppose you were hired to be the manager of a local restaurant. Which managerial functions would the biggest part of your job? Why?

3. Describe the link between a company's vision and its ethical standards. Why is it important for top management to communicate a clear vision and ethical standards for a company?

4. Identify the four types of planning. Suppose you planned a barbecue with your friends. When you woke up on the morning of the party, it was pouring rain. What type of planning would help you to deal with the rain? What are your options for the barbecue?

5. What is the link between a firm's vision and its mission statement? Think about your own dream of a career as an entrepreneur. What is your vision? What might be your mission statement?

6. Define *objectives*. Outline objectives you might have for your own college or university education and your career. How can an outline help you carry out your own career strategy?

7. Identify each of the following as a programmed or nonprogrammed decision:

a. reordering printer cartridges

b. selecting a cellphone provider

c. buying your favourite toothpaste or shampoo

d. selecting a college or university to attend

e. filling your car with gasoline

8. From what sources does a leader gain power? Which leadership style works best for a manager whose firm is making cost-cutting decisions? Why?

9. Why is a strong corporate culture important to a company's success? How is the corporate culture linked to leadership style?

10. Which type of organization structure provides the most flexibility to respond to changes in the marketplace and to be innovative? What are the downsides of this structure?

PROJECTS AND TEAMWORK APPLICATIONS

1. Imagine that you've been hired as a supervisor at a bakery shop called Claire's Cakes. The founder, Claire, wants to increase production, expand deliveries, and eventually open several more shops. Create a job description for yourself. Include the managerial functions and the skills you'll need to be successful.

2. On your own or with a classmate, write a mission statement for Claire's Cakes. Think about the type of company it is, the products it offers customers (cakes for special occasions), and the type of growth it is planning.

3. Contingency planning requires a combination of looking ahead and being adaptable. Josh James is the founder of Omniture, the Web analytics firm he recently sold to Adobe. James recalls the importance of being adaptable when his company was having difficulties. "There were times when I lay down on the floor at night, close to crying. Then my wife would come over and kick me and say, 'Get up and figure it out.'"[36] Research the news headlines for situations that required contingency planning. Report to the class what the challenge was and how the managers handled it. Discuss whether the planning was effective or successful.

4. Identify a person you think is a good leader. It can be someone you know personally or a public figure. Describe the personal qualities that are most important in making this person an effective leader. Would this person's leadership style work in situations other than his or her current position? Why or why not?

5. Research a firm whose goods or services you purchase or admire. Learn what you can about the organization's culture. Would you be an effective manager in this culture? Why or why not? Share your findings with the class.

WEB ASSIGNMENTS

1. Strategic planning. Visit the website listed below. It summarizes Johnson & Johnson's strategic planning philosophy. Read up on several recent acquisitions by Johnson & Johnson. Prepare a brief report to discuss how the acquisitions resulted from the company's strategic planning process.

http://www.investor.jnj.com/strategic.cfm

2. Mission statements. Go to the websites of two organizations: one for-profit firm and one not-for-profit organization. Print out the mission statements from both organizations. Take the material with you to class to participate in a discussion on mission statements.

3. Management structure. Visit the website listed below. Click on "corporate governance" and answer the following questions:

a. How would you characterize Target's organizational structure?

b. What is the composition of Target's board of directors?

http://investors.target.com/phoenix.zhtml?c=65828&p=irol-IRHome

Note: Internet Web addresses change frequently. If you don't find the exact sites listed, you may need to access the organization's home page and search from there or use a search engine such as Bing or Google.

Access your WileyPLUS course for:

- The complete digital textbook.

- Question assistance, including links to relevant sections in the online digital textbook.

- Immediate feedback and proof of progress, 24/7

- Integrated, multi-media resources – including MP3 downloads, visual exhibits, animations, and much more – that provide multiple study paths and encourage more active learning.

QUIZ YOURSELF

© Can Stock Photo Inc./wacker

8 | HUMAN RESOURCE MANAGEMENT: FROM RECRUITMENT TO LABOUR RELATIONS

LEARNING OBJECTIVES

LO 8.1 Explain the role and responsibilities of human resource management.

LO 8.2 Describe how recruitment and selection contribute to placing the right person in a job.

LO 8.3 Discuss how orientation, training programs, and performance appraisals help companies develop their employees.

LO 8.4 Describe how firms compensate employees through pay systems and benefit programs.

LO 8.5 Discuss employee separation and the impact of downsizing and outsourcing.

LO 8.6 Explain the different methods and theories of motivation.

LO 8.7 Discuss the role of labour unions, the collective bargaining process, and methods for settling labour–management disputes.

INSIDE BUSINESS

Canadian Apparel Manufacturing: Seeking Solutions in a Global Marketplace

© Can Stock Photo Inc./kadmy

Until the 1950s, one of the largest players in the Canadian economy was the Canadian apparel (clothing) manufacturing industry. This industry provided jobs to thousands in both large and small businesses. But today, the managers of mostly small firms in a shrinking industry try to deal with increasingly difficult global competitive forces.

In 2011, Canadian manufacturers produced more than $7 billion worth of clothing. Some of it, 24 percent, was exported to the United States. Smaller Canadian producers can take advantage of being located close to American customers, smaller production runs, and quick delivery times. Still, the industry faces increasing difficulties due to rising costs for labour, fabrics, marketing, and the rising exchange rate on the American dollar. In 2003, the lower-valued Canadian dollar acted as a subsidy for exporters, by keeping the price of Canadian goods low. Then, the value of the Canadian dollar was at a low of US$0.65. Now, the Canadian and American dollars are close to being at par: a dollar in one country is very close to being worth a dollar in the other country. This situation presents a challenge to Canadian manufacturers. Canadian businesses also face heavier competition from lower-costing imports from China and India.

Each year, about $4 billion worth of clothing is imported into Canada—clothing that once was almost all made in Canada. Today, only 21 percent of all clothing sold in Canada was made in Canada. Canadian clothing manufacturers have moved away from competing against cheaper imported clothing. Some have found success by focusing on higher-quality and higher-priced clothing.

Today, 71 percent of Canadian-made clothing is sold to Canadians, and 24 percent is sold to Americans. Less than 20 years ago, about 70 percent of the textile and clothing products consumed in Canada were made in Canada.

A major factor in the decline of Canadian manufacturing is the dropping of trade barriers. The result was more open trade that shifted jobs in production. As a result of the Uruguay Round

of negotiations, World Trade Organization member-countries agreed to remove all quotas between 1995 and 2005. The end of quotas meant Canadian manufacturers lost their protection from imports. According to the Canadian Apparel Federation, the clothing manufacturing industry lost more than 40,000 jobs from 2001 to 2006. Some economists believe that these jobs will never return. Canada will have to replace these jobs if Canadians are to find well-paid employment in the future.

In response, Canadian manufacturers have increased their investment in more efficient machinery and equipment, automated more of the production process, focused on fewer lines of products, and increased their marketing efforts into new markets. Over the past decade, Canadian companies have outsourced more large-scale production runs to China and India where labour costs are much lower.

Canadian retailers sell more than $34 billion worth of apparel merchandise. The revenues for wholesalers and manufacturers are about $10 billion and $7 billion, respectively. Clearly, the clothing industry is a big business that offers huge rewards to those that can compete. Large-scale retailers, such as Walmart, and chain stores, such as The Gap, have, over the years, pushed thousands of smaller independent retailers out of business. Some large retailers have even set up their own wholesaling and manufacturing divisions. The Canadian industry is moving farther away from manufacturing and more toward being a distribution business. The challenge to the surviving Canadian manufacturers is to find a way to compete both in Canada and internationally.

According to Statistics Canada, the industry is made up of some 2,200 manufacturers, mostly small businesses, located primarily in Quebec (51 percent), Ontario (28 percent), British Columbia (12 percent), Alberta (4 percent), and Manitoba (2 percent). Quebec accounts for 58 percent of all industry activity, with more than 1,000 clothing-related businesses located in Montreal, the historical capital of the industry.

More than 32,000 people work in the apparel manufacturing industry. This industry has traditionally provided semi-skilled jobs, such as sewing, for local people and for new immigrants. About 58 percent of businesses employ fewer than 100 people, and 38 percent employ fewer than five people. Only 4 percent of businesses have between 100 and 499 employees, which means they also likely operate on a large manufacturing scale. Smaller manufacturers sometimes outsource certain steps in the production process to other local firms that might specialize in a particular task, or they might invest in labour-saving machinery. But smaller

production runs and higher average costs due to outsourcing help explain the very small profit margins—of less than 1 percent. These low profits have led to many business closures.

Research by the apparel industry notes that despite the many challenges, new companies continue to enter this industry. This regeneration, or new growth, has been encouraged by relatively few barriers to entry to the industry, particularly capital investment requirements. Many new companies try to set up based on an idea from an entrepreneur who has identified an unmet need, or niche. New niches continue to be found, and many are successful. Today, approximately 7,000 students are registered in post-secondary apparel programs in Canada. That means new talent will likely continue to find its way into the industry.[1]

CHAPTER 8 OVERVIEW

The very basis of management is the importance of employees to the success of any organization. In this chapter, we explore the important issues of human resource management and motivation. We begin by discussing how organizations attract, develop, and retain employees. Then we describe the concepts, or ideas, behind motivation and how human resource managers apply these concepts to increase employee satisfaction and organizational effectiveness.

We discuss the reasons why labour unions exist. We also focus on legislation that affects labour–management relations. We then discuss the process of collective bargaining and the tools that unions and management use in seeking their objectives.

HUMAN RESOURCES: THE PEOPLE BEHIND THE PEOPLE

LO 8.1 Explain the role and responsibilities of human resource management.

human resource management the function of attracting, developing, and retaining employees who can perform the activities needed to meet organizational objectives.

A company is only as good as its workers. At some companies, people come to work each day eager to see each other, to do their very best on the job, to serve their customers, and to help their firm compete. Those companies are very likely to be a success. The best companies value their employees just as much as they value their customers. Without workers, companies would not have any goods or services to offer customers. Firms understand the value of good workers. That's why they do their best to hire top-quality employees and support them. Achieving a high level of job satisfaction and dedication among employees is the goal of **human resource management**, which attracts, develops, and retains the employees who can perform the activities needed to meet organizational objectives. However, when the firm is a small competitor in the Canadian apparel manufacturing industry and has limited financial resources, attracting and keeping top managerial talent can be just one more challenge to face.

Not every firm is large enough to have a separate human resources department. But whoever performs this function generally does the following: plans for staffing needs, recruits and hires workers, provides for training and evaluates performance, decides on compensation and benefits, and oversees employee separation. In accomplishing these five tasks, shown in Figure 8.1, human resource managers achieve the following objectives:

1. Providing qualified, well-trained employees for the organization

2. Maximizing employee effectiveness in the organization

3. Satisfying individual employee needs through monetary compensation, benefits, opportunities to advance, and job satisfaction

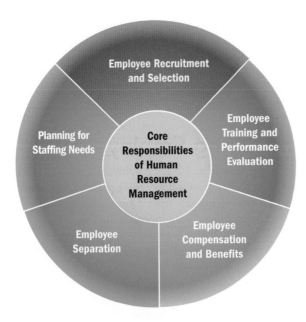

FIGURE 8.1 Human Resource Management Responsibilities

Human resource plans must be based on an organization's overall competitive strategies. Human resource managers work with other managers to predict how many employees a firm or department will need. These managers also decide what skills those workers should bring to the job—and what skills they might learn on the job. Human resource managers are often asked for advice when a firm is thinking about reducing costs by laying off workers or increasing costs by hiring new workers. Human resource managers are also involved in both long-term and short-term planning.

✔ **ASSESSMENT CHECK**

8.1.1 What are the five main tasks of a human resource manager?

8.1.2 What are the three overall objectives of a human resource manager?

RECRUITMENT AND SELECTION

LO 8.2 Describe how recruitment and selection contribute to placing the right person in a job.

Human resource managers recruit and help select the right workers for a company. They need to ensure that job candidates bring the needed skills to the job or have the desire and ability to learn these skills. To help in this task, most firms implement the recruitment and selection process shown in Figure 8.2.

Finding Qualified Candidates

When the economy dips and jobs are lost, many people compete for a limited number of jobs. A company that develops a great reputation for benefits or their working conditions might receive hundreds of job applications. But even with so many job seekers competing for a small number of job openings, companies often have trouble finding the right person. According to a recent survey, more than half the responding firms reported that although they had many applicants, the "quality of candidates" was lacking. "We get tons of résumés from people," laments one director of human resources. "We are just not getting highly qualified candidates."[2]

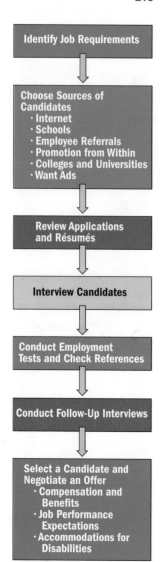

FIGURE 8.2 Steps in the Recruitment and Selection Process

The traditional methods of recruiting workers include college and university job fairs, personal referrals, and want ads. Most companies now rely on their websites for recruiting new workers. A firm's website might include a career section that provides general employment information and a listing of open positions. Job seekers are often able to submit a résumé and apply for an open position online. Appendix G, Careers in Contemporary Business, points out that some firms also post job openings on job websites such as Monster.com.

Internet recruiting is a quick, efficient, and inexpensive way to reach a large number of job seekers. Most companies currently use the Internet, including social networking sites, to fill job openings. Using the Internet is also the best way for firms to reach new college and university graduates and workers in their 20s and 30s.

Recruiting techniques continue to change as technology advances. JobsinPods.com is an online library of podcast interviews with hiring managers and employees at a variety of companies, including Intel and IBM. New podcasts, also called jobcasts, are posted in a blog format, and older podcasts are archived. Some of the people interviewed describe employers' hiring needs, while others talk about what it's like to work at a particular company. Job seekers can also download the podcasts to an iPod and listen to them whenever they want to.[3]

Selecting and Hiring Employees

The human resource manager selects and hires employees, often by working with department managers or supervisors. Every firm must follow provincial and federal employment laws. These laws state that employers cannot discriminate against job applicants, or treat them unfairly, because of their race, religion, colour, sex, national origin, and so forth.

These laws are designed to make the competition for jobs fairer for all job seekers. These laws have also led to many legal cases over the years. For example, UPS Freight recently agreed to pay a $46,000 settlement to a former employee because of religious discrimination. The employee, who is a Rastafarian, was told to shave his beard and cut his hair, which would follow company grooming policy. Because long hair and a beard are part of Rastafarian worship, the employee requested that the company accommodate, or help him to meet, his religious needs. But instead, UPS fired him, which was a violation, or a breach, of his civil rights to be able to practise his religion.[4] Failure to follow the terms of equal employment opportunity laws can result in costly legal fees, expensive fines, bad publicity, and poor employee morale.

Because of the high cost of such lawsuits and settlements, human resource managers must understand the laws that apply to employment so they can prevent unintended actions that might break these laws. Even the process of interviewing a job candidate must be carried out according to law. For example, an interviewer may not ask job applicants about their marital status, children, race or nationality, religion, age, criminal records, mental illness, medical history, or alcohol and substance abuse. For more information about employment law, visit the websites of the Society for Human Resource Management (http://www.shrm.org) and Services Canada (http://www.servicecanada.gc.ca/).

Dealing with hiring restrictions can be a challenge. Some firms try to screen out high-risk employees by requiring drug testing for job applicants. Drug testing is common in industries that deal with public safety—such as air travel and truck driving. But drug testing can lead to strong debates because of privacy issues. Also, positive test results may not be accurate. Another issue is whether employees can be required to speak a particular language in the workplace. Employers may legally establish requirements for specific jobs—true occupational qualifications. For example, a designer of women's clothing can hire only female models to show off new designs.

Recruiting and selecting employees is expensive. There are costs for advertising, interviewing, employment testing, and even medical exams. After an applicant is hired, there are costs for training and for equipment, such as a computer. But a bad hiring decision is even more expensive because the firm has to go through the whole process again to find the right person. One estimate suggests that the total cost of a hiring mistake amounts to 24 times the applicant's annual pay.[5] So it's especially important for human resource managers to make the best choices when it comes to recruitment and selection.

Internet recruiting is a quick, efficient, and inexpensive way to reach a large number of job seekers. Most companies currently fill job openings by using the Internet, including social networking sites. When aerospace giant Boeing needed more employees, it didn't hand out pamphlets at job fairs. Instead, it posted job ads on Facebook.

Daniel Acker/Bloomberg/Getty Images, Inc.

✓ **ASSESSMENT CHECK**

8.2.1 Describe several recruiting techniques used by human resource managers.

8.2.2 Is it unfair to firms that some questions cannot be asked during job interviews?

To avoid these mistakes—and to get the right person for the job the first time—many employers require applicants to complete employment tests. These tests may be used to prove the applicant has certain skills, such as mechanical, technical, language, and computer skills. One example is the Wonderlic Basic Skills Test, which measures basic math and verbal skills. The Wonderlic, a cognitive ability test, measures a person's abilities in understanding words, numbers, and logic. Cognitive ability tests accurately predict job performance on many types of jobs.

ORIENTATION, TRAINING, AND EVALUATION

LO 8.3 Discuss how orientation, training programs, and performance appraisals help companies develop their employees.

After employees are hired, they need to know what is expected of them and how well they are performing. Companies provide this information through orientation, training, and evaluation. A new hire may complete an orientation program prepared by the human resource personnel and the department where the employee will work. During orientation, employees learn about company policies regarding their rights and benefits. They might receive an employee manual that includes the company's code of ethics and code of conduct. And they'll usually receive some form of training.

Training Programs

Training is a good investment for both employers and employees. Training provides workers with an opportunity to build their skills and knowledge. These new skills can also prepare them for new job opportunities within the company. Training also helps employers to keep long-term, loyal, high-performing workers.

On-the-Job Training

One popular teaching method is *on-the-job training*. This type of training prepares employees for job duties by having them perform tasks under the guidance of experienced employees. A variation of on-the-job training is apprenticeship training. An employee who is an apprentice learns a job by working as an assistant to a trained worker. Apprenticeships usually focus on blue-collar trades—such as plumbing and heating services. But many new entrants to white-collar professions also complete apprenticeships. McDonald's now has apprenticeship-training programs in its U.K. restaurants as part of an economic stimulus plan launched by the British government. McDonald's offered 6,000 apprenticeships in the first year of its program, increasing the number to 10,000 the following year. "We're letting people know that we're as serious about education as we are about burgers and fries," notes the company's website.[6]

Classroom and Computer-Based Training

Many firms offer some form of classroom instruction, such as lectures, conferences, workshops, or seminars. Ernst & Young, a large tax-service firm, offers a training program called Ernst & Young and You (EYU). This program focuses on classroom learning, experiential learning, and coaching.[7]

Many firms are replacing classroom training with computer-based training programs. These programs can significantly reduce the cost of training. Computer-based training offers consistent presentations. It can also include videos that simulate the work environment, often by using actors in similar situations. Employees can learn at their own pace without having to sign up for a class. Employees can use online training programs for interactive learning. They might work with a mentor or instructor who is located elsewhere; or they might take part in a simulation where they have to make decisions related to their work. In general, human resources managers agree on the value of training. In a study on training, Accenture discovered that for every hour its competitors spent on training, Accenture spent two hours. Accenture invests heavily in its employees because it believes these workers will be able to help their company gain a competitive edge in the marketplace.[8]

performance appraisal
evaluation of and feedback on an employee's job performance.

Management Development

A *management development program* provides training designed to improve the skills and broaden the knowledge of current or future managers and executives. Training may be aimed at increasing specific technical knowledge or more general knowledge, in areas such as leadership and interpersonal skills. For example, the Conference Board of Canada provides management training in leadership, team development, and strategic implementation. Canadian businesspeople can take the courses online or at selected classroom settings.[9]

Performance Appraisals

The best way for a company—and its employees—to improve is to provide feedback about job performance. Most firms use an annual **performance appraisal** to evaluate an employee's job performance and provide feedback. A performance appraisal can include assessments of everything from attendance to goals met. A manager will use this evaluation to make decisions about compensation, promotion, additional training needs, transfers, or even termination. Performance appraisals are common, but not everyone agrees how useful they are. Some management experts argue that a performance review is based on a single manager's subjective, or personal, opinion, which can be positive or negative. The same experts say that most employees are afraid to speak honestly to their managers during a performance review.[10] If a performance review is to be effective, it should meet the following criteria, or guidelines:

- Take place several times a year
- Be linked to organizational goals
- Be based on objective measures
- Take place in the form of a two-way conversation[11]

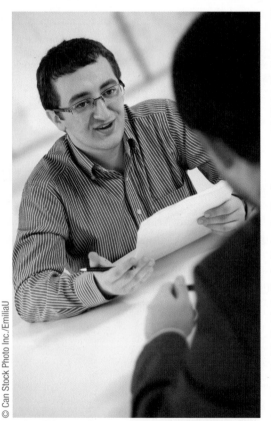

Employees value face-to-face feedback on their job performance. Evaluations that are fair and consistent can improve an organization's productivity and profitability.

Some firms use peer reviews, which have employees assess the job performance of their co-workers. Other firms ask employees to review the job performance of their supervisors and managers. One such performance appraisal is the *360-degree performance review*. This type of appraisal gathers feedback from a review panel of 8 to 12 people, including co-workers, supervisors, team members, people who report to the employee, and sometimes even customers. The idea is to get as much feedback from as many viewpoints as possible. This kind of review involves a lot of work, but employees benefit: they are more involved with the process and they understand more about their own strengths, weaknesses, and roles in the company. Managers also benefit because they get much more in-depth feedback from all parts of the organization. Firms such as Halogen Software, which has headquarters in Kanata, Ontario, offer computer programs to help firms gather and deal with this type of performance review data.[12] A potential weakness of 360-degree performance reviews is their anonymous nature—workers with personal likes and dislikes might try to influence the outcome.

COMPENSATION

LO 8.4 Describe how firms compensate employees through pay systems and benefit programs.

Compensation—the amount employees are paid in money and benefits—is one of the most highly charged issues faced by human resource managers. The amount employees are paid, including any benefits they receive, has a huge effect on where people live, what they eat, and how they spend their leisure time. It also has an effect on job satisfaction. Balancing compensation for employees at all job levels can be a challenge for human resource managers.

compensation the amount employees are paid in money and benefits.

Everyone likes to read about the companies—or the jobs—that pay their employees the most in cash and benefits. *Fortune* magazine publishes an annual list of "100 Best Companies to Work For." This list includes information on compensation. Top executives at large companies earn millions of dollars, which can be a touchy issue among employees and shareholders. The "Hit & Miss" feature discusses this topic.

HIT & MISS

The Good, Bad, and Ugly of Executive Pay

Executives at large institutions—particularly those on Bay Street and Wall Street—often receive huge compensation packages and annual multimillion-dollar bonuses. That may be fine when their firms are raking in profits. But the problem is that they continue to receive large paycheques despite steep financial losses. Making matters worse is that some of the financial institutions they work for accepted government assistance from the economic stimulus package.

The American Congress reacted to taxpayer outrage by enacting new rules that state any top executives at the firms receiving assistance must accept limits on their cash bonuses. Large severance packages are now banned, and shareholders must approve the executives' pay. Despite these new regulations, some firms continue to overpay their executives. For example, one CEO took home a pay increase even though the company did so poorly it had to lay off employees. But others have risen to the occasion on their own. Aflac CEO Daniel Amos declined his bonus of nearly $3 million, and top executives at Ford Motor Company cut their own pay by 30 percent.

At the federal level, Kenneth Feinberg—also known as the pay czar—has proposed new ground rules for executive compensation for companies everywhere. According to Feinberg, executives should be limited to $500,000 annually in cash compensation—anything additional should come in the form of stock or other benefits. Executives should pay for their own entertainment perks—like golf club memberships.

Overall, some true reforms may be on the horizon. Some executives might not like the new practices, but it's better if they agree to them voluntarily. Companies and their boards will have to "adopt a set of core principles like accountability, alignment, fairness, and transparency," predicts compensation expert Donald Delves.

Questions for Critical Thinking

1. Some critics of the proposed changes in executive compensation argue that reducing performance rewards will encourage talented managers to go elsewhere. Is this reasoning a valid objection to pay limits? Why or why not?

2. Do you think shareholders and boards should have input on the size of compensation packages for CEOs? Why or why not?

Sources: Devin Leonard, "Bargain Rates for a CEO?" *New York Times*, April 2, 2010, http://nytimes.com; "Stricter Pay Limits for Bailed Out Execs," *CBS News*, March 23, 2010, http://www.cbsnews.com; "Executive Pay Trends for 2010," *BusinessWeek*, accessed January 8, 2010, http://www.businessweek.com.

wage pay based on an hourly rate or the amount of work accomplished.

salary pay calculated on a periodic basis, such as weekly or monthly.

The terms *wage* and *salary* are often used as if they mean the same thing, but actually the two terms are different. A **wage** is pay that is based on an hourly pay rate or the amount of work accomplished. Typical wage earners are factory workers, construction workers, auto mechanics, retail salespeople, and restaurant wait staff. A **salary** is calculated periodically, often weekly or monthly. Salaried employees receive a set amount of pay that does not rise or fall with the number of hours worked. Wage earners can receive overtime pay, but salaried workers do not. Office personnel, executives, and professional employees usually receive salaries.

An effective compensation system should attract well-qualified workers, keep them satisfied in their jobs, and inspire them to succeed. It's also important to note that certain laws, including minimum wage laws, must be taken into account.

Most firms base their compensation policies on the following factors: (1) what competing companies are paying, (2) government regulation, (3) the cost of living, (4) company profits, and (5) an employee's productivity. Many firms try to find a balance between rewarding workers and maintaining profits. They do this by linking more of employees' pay to superior performance. Firms try to motivate employees to excel by offering some incentive compensation in addition to salaries or wages. These programs include the following:

- Profit sharing, awards that are bonuses based on company profits
- Gain sharing, whereby companies share the financial value of productivity gains, cost savings, or quality improvements with their workers
- Lump-sum bonuses and stock options, such as one-time cash payments and the right to purchase stock in the company based on performance
- Pay for knowledge, which distributes wage or salary increases as employees learn new job tasks

Figure 8.3 summarizes the four types of incentive compensation programs.

FIGURE 8.3 Four Forms of Incentive Compensation

Profit Sharing	Gain Sharing
Bonus based on company profits	Bonus based on productivity gains, cost savings, or quality improvements
Lump-Sum Bonus	**Pay for Knowledge**
One-time cash payment or option to buy shares of company stock based on performance	Salary increase based on learning new job tasks

employee benefits additional compensation—such as vacation time, retirement savings plans, profit-sharing, health insurance, gym memberships, child and elder care, and tuition reimbursement—paid entirely or in part by the company.

Employee Benefits

In addition to paying wages and salaries, firms also provide benefits to employees and their families as part of their compensation. **Employee benefits** are additional compensation that is paid entirely or in part by the company. Employee benefits can include vacation time, retirement savings plans, profit-sharing, health insurance, gym memberships, child and elder care, and tuition reimbursement. Benefits represent a large portion of an employee's total compensation. Wages and salaries account for around 70 percent of the typical employee's earnings. The other 30 percent takes the form of employee benefits. Pensions and other retirement plans make up a large portion of employee benefits.[13]

Some benefits are required by law. Firms may be required to make pension contributions and payments to unemployment insurance and workers' compensation programs, which protect workers in case of job-related injuries or illnesses. Firms voluntarily provide some other employee benefits, such as child care and health insurance, to help them attract and retain employees. As the "Solving an Ethical Controversy" feature discusses, some advocates are pressing lawmakers to require businesses to provide paid sick leave.

In general, large companies often pay for supplementary healthcare benefits, leaving employees paying little of the cost. However, with costs increasing each year, employers now offer incentives for workers to live healthier lives. Gym memberships, nutrition programs, wellness visits to the doctor, and smoking-cessation classes are all examples of these incentives. SAS has its own medical centre *and* a free on-site gym. The firm also provides many other employee benefits, including on-site daycare, unlimited sick days, and a summer camp for kids. In addition, SAS still pays 90 percent of its employees' monthly insurance premiums.[14]

On-site fitness facilities are a company benefit that improves both the company's health and that of its employees.

SOLVING AN **ETHICAL** CONTROVERSY

Should Paid Sick Leave Be Required by Law?

Canada and the United States do not have laws that require paid sick days. Many argue that developed nations should make paid sick days a basic labour standard. Although most full-time employees in North America enjoy the benefits of paid sick days, it is not a universal right—that is, it isn't a right enjoyed by everyone.

Should businesses be required to provide paid sick leave for their employees?

PRO

1. A healthy workforce is important to the competitiveness of any firm. When an employee can't take time off for medical treatment, it puts the company at risk. "Not only is this situation bad for sick workers and their families, but it puts other workers and the public at risk of contracting infectious illnesses," points out one public official.

2. No worker should be penalized for being ill. By making paid sick leave a law, workers cannot be fired because of illness.

CON

1. Requiring firms to pay for sick leave adds to the cost of doing business. To pay for this cost, employers may have to cut other benefits, stop all extra hiring, or lay people off because they can't afford the added expense.

2. Workers may misuse their sick leave. When a worker calls in sick, an employer may have to pay a temporary worker in addition to paying the permanent employee who is off sick.

Summary

Those in favour of paid sick leave argue that it is a matter of basic workers' rights. Paid sick leave would benefit mostly low-income employees who are already struggling to pay for food and shelter. Opponents say that the costs are too great for most businesses. They say that paid sick time would result in lost productivity, a reduction in wages to offset the cost, and maybe even a total reduction in the number of jobs.

Sources: "Editorial: Reject Mandate for Paid Sick Leave," *New Haven Register*, April 1, 2010, http://www.nhregister.com; A. J. Higgins, "Paid Sick Leave Bill Significantly Weakened," *Maine Public Broadcasting Network*, March 29, 2010, http://www.mpbn.net; Laura Fishman, "Paid Sick Leave Strikes Debate," *Houston Employment Law Blog*, February 12, 2010, http://houstonemploymentlawsblog.com; Christine Stuart, "Lamont Not Sold on Paid Sick Days for Small Businesses," *CTNewsjunkie.com*, February 9, 2010, http://www.ctnewsjunkie. com; James Sherk, "Mandatory Paid Sick Leave: The Heritage Foundation 2010 Labor Boot Camp," *Heritage Foundation*, January 14, 2010, http://www.heritage.org.

Flexible Benefits

In today's workplaces, employees now represent a wide range of personalities and lifestyles. In response to this increasing diversity, firms are developing creative ways to tailor their benefit plans to employees' needs. One approach sets up *flexible benefit plans,* also called cafeteria plans. These plans offer a choice of benefits, including different types of medical insurance, dental and vision plans, and life and disability insurance. One working spouse can choose medical coverage for the entire family, while the other spouse can use benefit dollars to buy other types of coverage. Typically, each employee receives a set allowance (called flex dollars or credits) to pay for benefits that suit his or her needs. Contributions to cafeteria accounts can be made by both the employee and employer. Cafeteria plans also offer tax benefits to both employees and employers.

Another way to increase the flexibility of employee benefits involves time off from work. Instead of having a set numbers of holidays, vacation days, and sick days, some employers give each employee a bank of *paid time off (PTO).* Employees can use days from their PTO accounts without having to explain why they need the time. The greatest advantage of PTO is the freedom it gives workers to make their own choices. The greatest disadvantage is that it is an expensive benefit for employers.[15]

A two-career couple heads for the daycare centre and work. Many employees use flextime to mesh their work schedules with opening and closing times at schools and daycare programs.

Comstock Images/Thinkstock/Getty Images

Flexible Work

Some firms offer the option of *flexible work plans.* These plans allow employees to adjust their working hours or their places of work according to their needs. Flexible work plan options include flextime, compressed workweeks, job sharing, and home-based work (telecommuting). These benefit programs reduce employee turnover and absenteeism and boost productivity and job satisfaction. Flexible work has become critical in attracting and keeping talented human resources.

Flextime allows employees to set their own work hours within certain limits. For example, instead of scheduling everyone to work between 8:00 A.M. and 5:00 P.M., a manager might decide that all employees must be at work between the core hours of 10:00 A.M. and 3:00 P.M. Outside the core hours, employees can choose to start and end early, or start and end late. Flextime works well in jobs that are independent. But it does not work so well when the employees work in teams or provide direct customer service. Flextime is popular in Europe, where 56 percent of all companies offer some kind of flextime arrangement.[16]

Flexible scheduling is easier to arrange with a small number of employees. But, with the help of Web-based software programs, the logistics problems of flexible scheduling can be made easier for larger organizations. Managers can post schedules online; then employees can log in and request certain shifts or schedule changes.[17]

Some companies offer a *compressed workweek.* This plan allows employees to work longer hours on fewer days. Employees might work four 10-hour days and then have three days off each week. These work arrangements not only reduce the number of hours employees spend commuting each week but can stretch out the company's overall workday, providing more availability to customers in other time zones. People who work in hospitals, airlines, and police and fire departments often work several long days, then have several days off.

A *job sharing program* allows two or more employees to divide up the tasks of one job. This plan appeals to more and more people who prefer to work part-time rather than full-time—such as older workers, students, working parents, and people of all ages who want more time for personal interests or leisure. Job sharing requires a lot of cooperation and communication between the partners, but a company can benefit from the talents of both people.

Home-based work programs allow employees to perform their jobs from home instead of at the workplace. These *telecommuters* are connected to their employers through the Internet, voice and video conferencing, and mobile devices. Working from home generally appeals to employees who want freedom. It also appeals to persons with disabilities, older workers, and parents. Companies benefit from telework arrangements because they can expand their pool of talent and increase productivity without increasing costs.[18] Telecommuters need to be self-disciplined and reliable employees. They also need managers who are comfortable with setting goals and managing from afar. Forrester Research predicts that telecommuting will grow from its current 34 million North American workers to 63 million by the year 2016.[19]

More than 70 percent of Generation Y professionals—those just entering the workforce—are concerned with balancing career with personal life. Most simply reject the idea of sitting in an office cubicle for 8 to 10 hours a day. They want the flexibility to do their jobs anywhere, any time.[20] Their demands place pressure on companies to offer such options as job sharing, compressed workweeks, and telecommuting.

✓ **ASSESSMENT CHECK**

8.4.1 Explain the difference between *wage* and *salary*.

8.4.2 What are flexible benefit plans? How do they work?

EMPLOYEE SEPARATION

Employee separation is a broad term for the loss of an employee for any reason, voluntary or involuntary. Voluntary separation includes workers who resign to take a job at another firm or to start a business. Involuntary separation includes downsizing and outsourcing.

LO 8.5 Discuss employee separation and the impact of downsizing and outsourcing.

Voluntary and Involuntary Turnover

Turnover occurs when an employee leaves his or her job. Voluntary turnover occurs when the employee decides to resign for his or her own reasons—perhaps to take another job, start a new business, or retire. Some human resource managers will ask the employee for an exit interview to learn why he or she is leaving; this conversation can provide valuable information to a firm. An employee might decide to resign because of lack of career opportunities. The human resource manager who learns of this reason might offer ongoing training.[21] Another employee might resign because of low pay. In that case, the human resource manager might offer a raise. The "Business Etiquette" feature offers some advice on how to ask for a raise. Sometimes, employees choose to resign and accept jobs at other firms because they fear upcoming layoffs. In this case, the human resource manager might be able to put to rest any fears about job security.

Involuntary turnover occurs when employees are terminated because of poor job performance or unethical behaviour in their business practices or in the workplace. Involuntary turnover also occurs when firms are forced to eliminate jobs as a cost-cutting measure, as in the case of downsizing or outsourcing. No matter how necessary a termination may be, it is never easy for either the human resource manager or the employee. The employee may react with anger or tears; co-workers may take sides. Human resource managers should remain calm and professional. They must be educated in employment laws so the termination is handled properly. Some employees who are fired say they have been wrongfully dismissed and file their complaint formally, in a lawsuit.

employee separation a broad term for the loss of an employee for any reason, voluntary or involuntary.

Downsizing

As the economy tightens, companies often face the hard choice of terminating employees to cut costs or streamline the organization. **Downsizing** is the process of reducing the number of employees within a firm by eliminating jobs. Downsizing can be done by offering early retirement or voluntary severance programs. But these options don't always accomplish the goal of downsizing. Read about AOL's recent downsizing effort in the "Hit & Miss" feature.

downsizing the process of reducing the number of employees within a firm by eliminating jobs.

After downsizing, some firms report improvements in profits, market share, employee productivity, quality, and customer service. But research is beginning to show that downsizing doesn't always lead to those improvements. "Much of the conventional wisdom about downsizing—like the fact that it automatically drives a company's stock price higher, or increases profitability—turns out to be wrong," notes Jeffrey Pfeffer of Stanford University.[22] Downsizing can have the following negative effects:

- Anxiety, health problems, and lost productivity among the remaining workers
- Expensive severance packages paid to laid-off workers
- A domino effect on the local economy—unemployed workers have less money to spend, which creates less demand for consumer goods and services, which increases the likelihood of more layoffs and other failing businesses.[23]

BUSINESS ETIQUETTE

How to Ask for a Raise

Have you ever thought about asking for a raise? Just thinking about it might make your hands sweat. You fear rejection—being turned down—or worse, retaliation, such as anger or criticism. But if you know that you are doing a superior job—such as taking the initiative when it's not required—or if it's been more than a year since your last pay increase, then maybe it's time to build a case for a raise. You should be able to at least open the conversation with your boss. Here are a few tips for being successful:

- *Be prepared.* Find out whether your company has a policy for raises. For example, some companies have a pay range or sliding pay scale for each position. If your company has a pay scale, learn where your pay fits on the scale.

- *Gather important data about yourself.* Keep track of your work accomplishments, including extra projects or tasks you've done well. Keep a log of positive feedback from co-workers, other supervisors, and customers. If the praise is already in writing, that's even better.

- *Think through exactly what you want.* Do you want a percentage increase, or a dollar amount? Or maybe you want more vacation time or time off for career education? Make sure your request is reasonable. When you meet with your supervisor, be as specific as possible about what you want.

- *Don't be pushy or hasty in your conversation.* At the same time, state your argument with confidence. Your goal is to get your supervisor to open up to thinking about the possibility of meeting your request.

- If your supervisor turns down your request, *ask for specifics about what you need to do to qualify for the raise*—and when. If possible, ask for a follow-up meeting within a certain period of time, such as two months.

- When you return to your desk or office, *send your supervisor an e-mail thanking him or her for meeting with you.* You can also politely state the results of the conversation. If your request has been granted, make sure your performance lives up to your raise in pay. If your supervisor has put off making a decision, don't give up. Get back to work, document everything, and earn that raise.

Sources: Samantha Maziarz Christmann, "Asking for More: Don't Be Afraid to Ask for a Raise," *Buffalo News*, March 15, 2010, http://www.buffalonews.com; "How to Negotiate for a Raise—Even in a Bad Economy," *EmploymentDigest.net*, March 4, 2010, http://www.employment digest.net; Mary Sevinsky, "Is a Raise in Your Future for 2010?," *CareerRealism.com*, January 15, 2010, http://www.careerrealism.com.

If downsizing is the only option for company survival, then managers can take steps to make sure it is done the best way possible. If a firm is committed to its workforce as part of its mission, it will do everything it can to support both the workers who must leave and the workers who will stay. For example, Xilinx Inc., a North American semiconductor manufacturer, was recently forced to either shrink its operations or close. The company took several steps to avoid layoffs. First, the company temporarily shut down plants and offered voluntary retirement plans and sabbatical leaves. Human resource managers discussed the situation with employees before making pay cuts. By taking these steps—with all employees giving up something—the company survived its downturn without any involuntary terminations.[24]

outsourcing using outside vendors to produce goods or fulfill services and functions that were previously handled in-house or in-country.

Outsourcing

Another way that firms shrink themselves into leaner organizations is by **outsourcing**. Outsourcing involves using outside vendors to produce goods or fulfill services and functions that were previously handled in-house or in-country. Jobs are transferred from inside a firm to outside the firm. Jobs that are most often outsourced include office maintenance, deliveries, food service, and security. However, other job functions can be also outsourced, including manufacturing, design, information technology (IT), and accounting. In general, companies will try to outsource functions that are not part of their core business so they can save on expenses and remain flexible. In some cases, such as with small Canadian apparel manufacturers, outsourcing some parts of the production process to lower-cost specialists is necessary to survive in a highly competitive business environment. As long as the final product delivered to customers is what was planned, it does not matter who actually did the work.

✓ ASSESSMENT CHECK

8.5.1 What is the difference between voluntary and involuntary turnover?

8.5.2 What is downsizing? How is it different from outsourcing?

HIT & MISS

AOL Employees Don't Exit Voluntarily

People don't usually want to leave their jobs, especially when the economy is tighter than usual and unemployment numbers are already high. But that's what AOL asked its workers to do in a recent effort to downsize the company and control costs. AOL asked for 2,500 volunteer separations and received only 1,100. That left a gap of 1,400 workers. The goal was to reduce the firm's workforce by more than 30 percent, from 6,900 to about 4,400.

AOL had been struggling for several years after the merger with Time Warner. It finally spun off as an independent company—but a damaged one. AOL management decided that the only way to turn the company around was to trim as many costs as possible, from every corner of the organization. The turnaround plan, called Project Everest, was led by new CEO Tim Armstrong, a former sales executive for Google. After downsizing the workforce, Armstrong planned to refocus AOL's business in a few select areas, including content, online advertising, and communications. "Project Everest is the completion of phase one of AOL's turnaround," noted a company spokesperson.

If you think all of this sounds a bit cold-hearted and short-sighted, you are not alone. One of the greatest difficulties to a company after layoffs is dealing with the low morale of the remaining workers. Layoffs are distressing to those who are let go and just as traumatic to those who remain. Productivity often slides, as does the image of the company. "There's substantial research into the physical and health effects of downsizing on employees—research that reinforces the notion that layoffs are literally killing people," warns Jeffrey Pfeffer of Stanford University. In the case of AOL, the firm actually hired new salespeople to ensure there would be no breaks in advertising. AOL managers also held meetings with advertisers to tell them of the actions being taken. They also sent notes to some clients containing private contact information for top executives. Despite taking these steps, some advertising clients decided to take their business elsewhere. In an effort to rebuild its business, AOL may have lost one of its most valuable assets—its best people.

Questions for Critical Thinking

1. Was it a good decision for AOL to ask for volunteers to resign before making layoffs? Why or why not?

2. Could AOL managers have better prepared their clients for the downsizing?

Sources: Dustin Ensinger, "Why Layoffs Are Not Beneficial to Companies," *Economy in Crisis*, February 8, 2010, http://www.economyincrisis.org; Nicholas Carlson, "AOL Is Hiring Sales People to Make Sure Layoffs Don't Interrupt Coverage," *Business Insider*, January 13, 2010, http://www.businessinsider.com; "AOL Layoffs Begin: 1,400 Jobs to Be Slashed," *Mashable.com*, January 11, 2010, http://www.mashable.com; Miguel Helft, "AOL Begins 1,200 Layoffs," *New York Times*, January 11, 2010, http://bits.blogs.nytimes.com; Juan Carlos Perez, "AOL Voluntary Layoff Program Falls Short," *ComputerWorld*, January 5, 2010, http://www.computerworld.com.

MOTIVATING EMPLOYEES

LO 8.6 Explain the different methods and theories of motivation.

One of a manager's main goals is to motivate employees to be loyal to their company and to perform their best on the job. Motivation starts with good employee morale. Morale is the employees' mental view toward their employer and jobs, often including a common sense of purpose.

High employee morale occurs when workers feel they are valued, their opinions are heard, and they are empowered to contribute what they do best. High morale generally results from good management, including an understanding of human needs and an effort to satisfy those needs in ways that move the company forward. In contrast, low employee morale usually signals a poor relationship between managers and employees. It often results in absenteeism, voluntary turnover, and a lack of motivation.

Generally speaking, managers use rewards and punishments to motivate employees. Extrinsic rewards are rewards that are external to, or outside of, the work itself, such as pay, fringe benefits, and praise. Intrinsic rewards are feelings related to performing the job, such as feeling proud about meeting a deadline or achieving a sales goal. Punishment involves a negative outcome in response to such undesirable behaviour as being late, skipping staff meetings, or treating a customer poorly.

There are several theories of motivation. All theories relate to the basic process of motivation itself: recognizing a need, moving toward meeting that need, and satisfying that need. For example, if you are hungry, you might be motivated to make yourself a sandwich. Once you have eaten the sandwich, the need is satisfied, and you are no longer hungry. Figure 8.4 illustrates the process of motivation.

Need → produces → **Motivation** → which leads to → **Goal-Directed Behaviour** → resulting in → **Need Satisfaction**

FIGURE 8.4 The Process of Motivation

Maslow's Hierarchy of Needs Theory

Maslow's hierarchy of needs
a theory of motivation proposed by Abraham Maslow. According to the theory, people have five levels of needs that they try to satisfy: physiological, safety, social, esteem, and self-actualization.

Managers can motivate employees by applying the studies of psychologist Abraham H. Maslow. **Maslow's hierarchy of needs** is a widely accepted list of human needs. This list is based on these important assumptions:

- People's needs depend on what they already possess.

- A satisfied need is not a motivator; only needs that remain unsatisfied can influence behaviour.

- People's needs are arranged in a hierarchy of importance; once people satisfy one need, at least partially, another need emerges and demands satisfaction.

Maslow proposed that all people have basic needs such as hunger and protection. People must satisfy these basic needs before they can consider higher-order needs, such as social relationships and self-worth. Maslow identified five types of needs:

1. *Physiological needs.* These basic human needs include food, shelter, and clothing. On the job, employers satisfy these needs by paying salaries and wages and providing a heated or cooled workspace.

2. *Safety needs.* These needs refer to desires for physical and economic protection. Companies satisfy these needs by providing benefits such as health insurance and meeting safety standards in the workplace.

3. *Social (belongingness) needs.* People want to be accepted by family, friends, and co-workers. Managers might satisfy these needs by encouraging teamwork and group lunches.

4. *Esteem needs.* People like to feel valued and recognized by others. Managers can meet these needs by offering special awards or privileges.

5. *Self-actualization needs.* These needs drive people to seek fulfillment of their dreams and capabilities. Employers can satisfy these needs by offering challenging or creative projects and opportunities for education and advancement.[25]

According to Maslow, people must satisfy their lower-order needs (physiological and safety needs) before they are motivated to satisfy higher-order needs (social, esteem, and self-actualization needs).

Everyone, including employees, has a need to belong. Occasional office parties allow workers to relax and socialize, lifting their morale and motivating them to do a good job.

Herzberg's Two-Factor Model of Motivation

More than 50 years ago, Frederick Herzberg—a social psychologist and consultant—came up with a theory of motivation and work that is still popular today. Herzberg surveyed workers to find out when they felt good or bad about their jobs. He learned that certain factors were important to job satisfaction though they might not contribute directly to motivation. These *hygiene factors* (or maintenance factors) refer to aspects of work that do not directly relate to a task but *do* relate to the job environment. These factors include pay, job security, working conditions, status, interpersonal relations, technical supervision, and company policies.

Motivator factors, in contrast, can produce high levels of motivation when they are present. These factors relate directly to specific aspects of a job, including job responsibilities, achievement and recognition, and opportunities for growth. Hygiene factors are extrinsic, or come from outside, while motivators are intrinsic, or come from within. Managers should remember that hygiene factors, though not motivational, can result in satisfaction. Managers who want to motivate employees should emphasize recognition, achievement, and growth. Companies that make

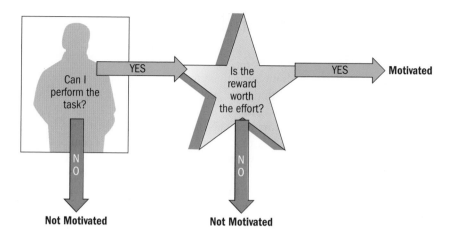

FIGURE 8.5 Vroom's Expectancy Theory

the various lists of "best places to work" always have managers who understand what it takes to motivate employees, whether the firm is large or small. Canada's Top Employers is an organization that promotes recognition of best practices. It has a special designation for "Young People." The factors used to decide on rankings include benefits such as tuition assistance and the availability of co-op or work–study programs; mentorship and training programs, including benefits such as bonuses paid when employees complete certain courses or professional designations; and career management program that look for initiatives—such as companywide skills inventories—that can help younger workers to advance faster in the organization.[26]

Expectancy Theory and Equity Theory

Victor Vroom's work led to his **expectancy theory** of motivation. This theory describes the process people use to evaluate the likelihood that their efforts will lead to the results they want and the degree to which they want those results. Expectancy theory suggests that people use three factors to determine how much effort to put forth. First is a person's subjective, or personal, prediction that a certain effort will lead to the desired result. This is the "can do" component of an employee's approach to work. Second is the value of the outcome (reward) to the person. Third is the person's assessment of how likely a successful performance will lead to a desirable reward. Vroom's expectancy theory is summarized in Figure 8.5. In short, an employee is motivated if he or she thinks he or she can complete a task. Next, the employee assesses the reward for accomplishing the task and is motivated if the reward is worth the effort.

Equity theory is concerned with an individual's view of fair and equitable treatment. In their work, employees first consider their effort and then their rewards. Next, employees compare their results against the results of their co-workers. As shown in Figure 8.6, if employees feel they are under-rewarded for their effort in comparison with others doing similar work, equity theory suggests they will decrease their effort to restore the balance. Conversely, if employees feel they are over-rewarded, they will feel guilty and put more effort into their job to restore equity and reduce guilt.

expectancy theory the process people use to evaluate the likelihood that their efforts will lead to the results they want and the degree to which they want those results.

equity theory an individual's perception of fair and equitable treatment.

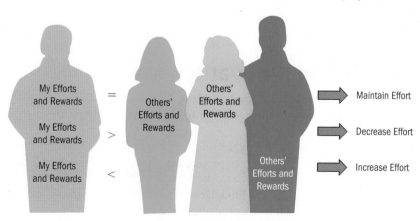

FIGURE 8.6 Equity Theory

Goal-Setting Theory and Management by Objectives

When people have needs, those needs motivate them to direct their behaviour toward something that will satisfy their needs. That something is a goal. A goal is a target, objective, or result that someone tries to accomplish. **Goal-setting theory** says that people will be motivated to the extent to which they accept specific, challenging goals and receive feedback that shows their progress toward goal achievement. As shown in Figure 8.7, the basic components of goal-setting theory are goal specificity, goal difficulty, goal acceptance, and performance feedback.

Goal specificity refers to goals that are clear and concrete. A goal such as "we want to reduce our carbon footprint" is vague and hard to relate to a clear target. But, a goal such as "we want to reduce our carbon footprint by 2 percent" gives employees a clear target. Goal difficulty shows how hard the goal is to reach. A more difficult goal, such as "we want to reduce our carbon footprint by 5 percent in three years" can be more motivating than the easier goal.

Goal acceptance relates to people's understanding of the goal and their agreement with the goal. People are likely to reject a goal that is too challenging—such as reducing the firm's carbon footprint by 20 percent in two years. Finally, performance feedback is information about performance and how well the goal has been met. Goal setting typically won't work unless performance feedback is provided.

Goals help focus workers' attention on the important parts of their jobs. Goals also energize and motivate people. They create a positive tension between the current state of affairs and the desired state. This tension is satisfied by meeting the goal or rejecting it.

Fifty years ago, Peter Drucker introduced a goal-setting technique called **management by objectives (MBO)** in his book, *The Practice of Management*. MBO is a structured approach that helps managers to focus on reachable goals and to achieve the best results based on the organization's resources. MBO helps motivate individuals by aligning their objectives with the goals of the organization. The outcome is an increase in overall organizational performance. MBO clearly outlines people's tasks, goals, and contributions to the company. MBO is a process that is worked out between managers and employees. MBO principles include the following:

- A series of related organizational goals and objectives
- Specific objectives for each person
- Participative decision-making
- A set time period to accomplish goals
- Performance evaluation and feedback

goal-setting theory the idea that people will be motivated to the extent to which they accept specific, challenging goals and receive feedback that shows their progress toward goal achievement.

FIGURE 8.7
Components of Goal-Setting Theory

management by objectives (MBO) a structured approach that helps managers to focus on reachable goals and to achieve the best results based on the organization's resources.

Job Design and Motivation

Today's human resource managers are always looking for ways to motivate employees through their jobs. Jobs can be designed to be more motivating in three ways: through job enlargement, job enrichment, and job rotation.

Job enlargement is a job design that expands an employee's responsibilities by increasing the number and variety of tasks. Redesigning the production process is one way to enlarge a job. For example, on a traditional assembly line, each worker completes the same task over and over again. A firm can redesign the assembly line to a modular work area where employees complete a variety of tasks. These tasks may then result in the production of an entire product.

Job enrichment expands an employee's job duties to empower an employee to make decisions and learn new skills leading toward career growth. A firm might give its managers and sales consultants the power to make decisions about their work, such as how to organize sales presentations and when they prefer to work.

Job rotation involves a system of moving employees from one job to another. Job rotation increases an employee's range of activities. Workers learn more jobs and therefore learn more tasks. The goal is to increase employees' interest in their jobs and to have them learn more about the company. For example, nurses in a hospital might rotate from oncology to the ICU.

Managers' Attitudes and Motivation

A manager's attitude toward his or her employees greatly influences their motivation. Maslow's theory, described earlier, helps managers to understand that employees have a range of needs beyond their paycheques. Psychologist Douglas McGregor, a student of Maslow, studied employee motivation from the viewpoint of managers. McGregor studied managers' interactions with employees. He saw that managers made one of two assumptions about workers' behaviour. McGregor named these two assumptions Theory X and Theory Y. He also showed how these assumptions affect management styles.

- *Theory X* assumes that employees dislike work and try to avoid it whenever possible. Managers must work at getting employees to do their jobs. Theory X managers believe that the average worker prefers to receive instructions, avoid responsibility, and take little initiative. These managers also believe that the average worker views money and job security as the only valid motivators—Maslow's lower order of needs.

- *Theory Y* assumes that the typical person actually likes work and will seek and accept more and more responsibility. Theory Y managers assume that most people can think of creative ways to solve work-related problems. These managers believe in giving employees the opportunity to participate in decision-making. The traditional management philosophy relies on external control and constant supervision, but Theory Y views self-control and self-direction as the main motivators—Maslow's higher order of needs.

Management professor William Ouchi proposed another viewpoint on management, labelled *Theory Z*. Theory Z tries to blend the best of American and Japanese management practices. This approach views worker involvement as the key to increased productivity for the company and improved quality of work-life for employees. Many Canadian firms have adopted the participation aspect of the Japanese management style. These firms ask workers for suggestions to improve their jobs, and then give them the authority to implement changes.

LABOUR–MANAGEMENT RELATIONS

The North American workplace is far different from what it was a century ago. Then, it was common to have child labour, unsafe working conditions, and a 72-hour workweek. The changed workplace is a result of labour unions, labour legislation, and the collective bargaining process. Today's human resource managers must be educated in labour–management relations, the settling of disputes, and the competitive tactics of unions and management.

Development of Labour Unions

A **labour union** is a group of workers who organize themselves to work toward common goals in the areas of wages, hours, and working conditions.

Labour unions are found at the local, national, and international levels. A *local union* represents union members in a specific area, such as a single community. A *national union* is a labour

---

✔ **ASSESSMENT CHECK**

8.6.1 What are the four steps in the process of motivation?

8.6.2 Explain how goal-setting works.

8.6.3 Describe the three ways that managers design jobs for increased motivation.

LO 8.7 Discuss the role of labour unions, the collective bargaining process, and methods for settling labour–management disputes.

labour union a group of workers who organize themselves to work toward common goals in the areas of wages, hours, and working conditions.

organization consisting of numerous local chapters. An *international union* is a national union with membership outside of Canada, usually in the United States. The International Brotherhood of Teamsters is an international union.

Canadian-based labour groups grew and eventually organized into the country's largest national organization of unions, the Canadian Labour Congress (CLC). The CLC represents about 3 million of the 4.6 million unionized Canadians, about 70 percent of the unionized workforce. In Canada, about 30 percent of the entire workforce is unionized.[27] Two other large national organizations are the Canadian Federation of Labour (CFL) and the Confederation of National Trade Unions (CNTU). Some unions belong to more than one of these central union organizations, and some belong to both Canadian and American groups. For example, the United Steel Workers belong to the CLC in Canada and the American Federation of Labour and Congress of Industrial Organizations (AFL-CIO) in the United States.

Labour Relations Board

A labour relations board is a type of judicial organization. It is responsible for overseeing workers' groups that apply to become a union and activities that occur during a labour dispute. Each province has its own labour relations board. People who work in interprovincial communications or transportation are under the legal authority of the national labour board, the Canada Industrial Relations Board. Although some rules vary, they all function in a similar manner.

The Collective Bargaining Process

collective bargaining the process of negotiation between management and union representatives.

Labour unions work to increase job security for their members and to improve wages, hours, and working conditions. These goals are achieved primarily through **collective bargaining**, the process of negotiation between management and union representatives.

Union contracts usually cover a two- or three-year period. They are often the result of weeks or months of discussion, disagreement, compromise, and eventual agreement. After an agreement is reached, the union members must vote to accept or reject the contract. When the contract is rejected, the union members have two choices. They can send union representatives back to the bargaining process with management representatives, or the union members may decide to strike to obtain their demands.

Settling Labour–Management Disputes

We hear about strikes in the news, but most labour–management negotiations result in a signed contract. If a disagreement occurs, it is usually settled through a grievance procedure, mediation, or arbitration. These options are quicker and less expensive than a strike.

The union contract is a guide to relations between the firm's management and its employees. The agreement states the rights of each party. No contract, regardless of how detailed it is, will remove the possibility of disagreement. Disagreements can be the beginning of a *grievance*, a complaint—by a single employee or by the entire union—that management is violating, or is breaking, some portion of the agreed-on contract. Almost all union contracts state that these complaints must be submitted through a formal grievance procedure, such as the process shown in Figure 8.8. A grievance might be a disagreement about pay, working hours, or the workplace itself. The grievance procedure usually begins with an employee's supervisor and then moves up the company's hierarchy. If the highest level of management can't settle the grievance, it is submitted to an outside party for mediation or arbitration.

FIGURE 8.8 Steps in the Grievance Procedure

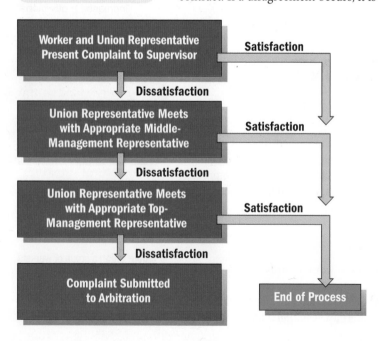

Mediation is the process of settling labour–management disagreements through an impartial, or objective, third party. Although the mediator does not make the final decision, he or she can hear the whole story and make objective recommendations. If the dispute still cannot be settled, then the two parties can turn to *arbitration*. An outside arbitrator is chosen who must be acceptable to both the union and management. The arbitrator will then make a legally binding decision. This decision is final. Both parties are legally required to agree to it. Most union negotiations go to arbitration if union and management representatives cannot reach a contract agreement.

Competitive Tactics of Unions and Management

Both unions and management use tactics to make their views known and to win support.

Union Tactics

The union's main tactics are strikes, picketing, and boycotts. The *strike,* or walkout, is one of the labour union's most effective tools. It involves a temporary work stoppage by workers until a dispute has been settled or a contract signed. A strike generally seeks to disrupt business by calling attention to workers' needs and union demands. Strikes can last for days or weeks and can be costly to both sides. The 2004–05 strike by the National Hockey League Players Association against the National Hockey League lasted 310 days, starting September 16, 2004. This strike resulted in the cancellation of the season without the awarding of the Stanley Cup.[28] Although a strike is powerful, it can also damage a wider portion of the local economy. If fans aren't watching games at local sports bars, those businesses will lose profits on nights that normally bring in large crowds.

Picketing involves workers marching in a public protest against their employer. This activity is another effective form of union pressure. Picketing is protected under law as long as it does not involve violence or intimidation. Picketing may accompany a strike, or it may be a protest against what are believed to be unfair labour practices. On a holiday weekend during a strike, hundreds of British Airways workers picketed a soccer field near Heathrow airport during a tense standoff. Although planes continued to take off and land over the field, passengers could see the angry workers below.[29]

A *boycott* is an organized attempt to keep the public from purchasing the goods or services of a firm. Some unions have been very successful in organizing boycotts. Some unions fine members who do not obey a boycott.

Management Tactics

Management has tactics for competing with organized labour when negotiations break down. In the past, management has used the lockout. It is a management "strike" to put pressure on union members by closing the firm. But companies usually use one of two tactics: they hire strikebreakers in highly visible fields, such as professional sports, or they transfer supervisors and other nonunion employees to continue operations during strikes. In the British Airways strike described earlier, management leased aircraft from other airlines and used volunteer pilots and managers to take the place of the striking cabin crews.[30]

Picket lines went up at British Airways when members of the cabin crews went on strike. Strikes are a last-ditch tactic that can be costly for the union, hurt an entire industry, and even damage the economy.

STEVE PARSONS/PA Photos/Landov

The Future of Labour Unions

Through most of the 20th century, union membership and influence grew. Industrial workers had a voice in decisions about their wages, benefits, and working conditions. But Canada, the United States, Western Europe, and Japan have shifted from manufacturing economies to information and service economies. As a result, union membership and influence have declined. The largest union

GOING GREEN

LABOUR UNIONS AND GREEN CONSTRUCTION

The construction industry has many opportunities to change the look of the world—or at least, make it greener.

One labour union, the Operative Plasterers and Cement Masons International Association (OPCMIA) has already seen this opportunity. The OPCMIA is training its members in the use of new green technologies and processes that will improve the energy efficiency of buildings and reduce their carbon footprint. As the construction industry begins to use these new technologies, particularly to achieve LEED (Leadership in Energy and Environmental Design) status, workers need to know how to use them properly and safely.

The OPCMIA training program is called Green Five. It is being added to existing training to reach about 5,400 participants in 70 programs offered in local chapters, community colleges, vocational/technical schools, and OPCMIA Joint Apprenticeship and Training Centers. The Green Five program trains plasterers and cement masons in the green use and application of the following materials: polished concrete, pervious concrete, exterior insulation finish systems, and American Clay. American Clay is a coloured mineral coating that is toxin-free, free of VOCs (volatile organic compounds), and mould-resistant. Training in American Clay includes the preparation and mixing of the material, hand application, primers, additives and sealers, and maintaining and repairing walls.

The Green Five program includes Green Awareness Training. This training deals with energy-efficient building construction in general, the process of energy assessment and retrofitting of existing buildings, and provides an overview of green products and manufacturing processes. Leadership training and "train-the-trainer" courses are also offered. "Program participants include construction workers, building engineers, and energy auditors as part of our outreach toward making green construction knowledge accessible to the whole of the industry," says Gerry Ryan, director of training, health, and safety for OPCMIA.

Questions for Critical Thinking

1. How does "green" training give OPCMIA an important industry role for the future?

2. What other industries might benefit from unions taking a leadership role in green training? How can taking these steps toward green training result in benefits for workers, unions, and management?

Sources: David Bradley, "TR10: Green Concrete," *Technology Review*, May/June 2010, http://www.technologyreview.com; "About OPCMIA," OPCMIA website, http://www.opcmia.org, accessed April 29, 2010; Gerry Ryan, "The Green Five Program," *Green Labor Journal*, April 29, 2010, http://greenlaborjournal.com.

---

in Canada is the Canadian Union of Public Employees (CUPE). It has more than 600,000 government employee members. After the federal government passed the Public Service Staff Relations Act of 1967, all federal, provincial, and municipal employees were able to organize into unions. Soon after, public sector unions began to grow. Today, public sector unions include more than 70 percent of all employees. They make up three of the largest unions in Canada: the Canadian Union of Public Employees (CUPE), the National Union of Public and General Employees (NUPGE), and the Public Service Alliance (PSA).[31]

How can labour unions change so they continue to play a valuable role? They can be more flexible and adapt to a global economy and a diverse workforce. They can respond to the growing need for environmentally responsible business and manufacturing processes. That's what the Operative Plasterers and Cement Masons International Association (OPCMIA) is doing, as described in the "Going Green" feature. Unions can set up working relationships with human resource managers and other management officials. They can also recognize the potential for prosperity for everyone—management and union workers included.

✓ **ASSESSMENT CHECK**

8.7.1 What is a labour union? What is collective bargaining?

8.7.2 What are the three main tactics used by unions to win support for their demands?

WHAT'S AHEAD

One way to recruit and keep a highly motivated workforce is to treat employees well by improving their work environment. Managers can also help employees to reach their full potential in three ways: by empowering them to make decisions, leading them to work effectively as teams, and encouraging clear, positive communication. The next chapter discusses these three ways of improving performance. Companies that apply these three methods benefit from their employees' knowledge, and employees can have a more meaningful role in the company.

RETURN TO INSIDE BUSINESS

Canadian Apparel Manufacturing: Seeking Solutions in a Global Marketplace

Small business entrepreneurs have always been present in the Canadian garment industry. Entrepreneurs generally learn the business first by working for someone else and then set out on their own. In general, barriers to entry, such as the required financial investment, have remained relatively low, compared with most other manufacturing industries. As anyone in the fashion business will tell you, "You're only as good as your last season." With every new fashion season, the process starts all over again as manufacturers look for the next styles, fabrics, and colours that will bring sales, profits, and sustainability.

QUESTIONS FOR CRITICAL THINKING

1. How can Canadian apparel manufacturers better compete against imports within Canada?

2. How can Canadian apparel manufacturers better compete in international markets?

3. What motivates young people to enter the fashion production business?

SUMMARY OF LEARNING OBJECTIVES

LO 8.1 Explain the role and responsibilities of human resource management.

Human resource managers are responsible for attracting, developing, and retaining the employees who can perform the activities needed to meet organizational objectives. They plan for staffing needs, recruit and hire workers, provide for training and evaluate performance, decide on compensation and benefits, and oversee employee separation.

 ASSESSMENT CHECK ANSWERS

8.1.1 **What are the five main tasks of a human resource manager?** The five main tasks are planning for staffing needs, recruiting and hiring workers, providing for training and evaluating performance, deciding on compensation and benefits, and overseeing employee separation.

8.1.2 **What are the three overall objectives of a human resource manager?** The three overall objectives are providing qualified, well-trained employees for the organization; maximizing employee effectiveness; and satisfying individual employee needs through monetary compensation.

LO 8.2 Describe how recruitment and selection contribute to placing the right person in a job.

Human resource managers use internal and external methods to recruit qualified employees. They may use college and university job fairs, personal referrals, want ads, and other resources. Internet recruiting is now the fastest, most efficient, and least expensive way to reach a large number of job seekers. Firms must abide by employment laws to avoid lawsuits. Before hiring

candidates, human resource managers may require employment tests that evaluate certain skills or aptitudes. When all of this is complete, there is a better chance that the right person will be hired for the job.

 ASSESSMENT CHECK ANSWERS

8.2.1 **Describe several recruiting techniques used by human resource managers.** Techniques include college and university job fairs, personal referrals, want ads, company websites, online job sites, and podcast interviews (known as jobcasts) that feature hiring managers and employees talking about work at their companies.

8.2.2 **Is it unfair to firms that some questions cannot be asked during job interviews?** The firm should only be interested in whether job applicants have the skills or experience to perform a certain job. Any interview questions should be concerned only with the job applicant's abilities. The firm should be free to ask these questions.

LO 8.3 Discuss how orientation, training programs, and performance appraisals help companies develop their employees.

New employees often complete an orientation program where they learn about company policies and practices. Training programs provide opportunities for employees to build their skills and knowledge. These new skills can also prepare them for new job opportunities within the company. Training also helps employers to keep long-term, loyal, high-performing employees. Performance appraisals give employees feedback about their strengths and weaknesses and how they can improve.

ASSESSMENT CHECK ANSWERS

8.3.1 What are the benefits of computer-based training? Computer-based training offers consistent presentations and interactive learning. Employees can also learn at their own pace. Computer-based training is also less expensive than other types of training.

8.3.2 What is a management development program? A management development program provides training designed to improve the skills and broaden the knowledge of current and potential executives.

8.3.3 What are the four criteria, or standards, of an effective performance appraisal? A performance appraisal should take place several times a year, be linked to organizational goals, be based on objective measures, and be a two-way conversation.

LO 8.4 Describe how firms compensate employees through pay systems and benefit programs.

Firms compensate employees with wages, salaries, incentive pay systems, and benefits. Benefit programs vary among firms, but most companies offer healthcare programs, insurance, retirement plans, paid time off, and sick leave. More and more companies offer flexible benefit plans and flexible work plans, such as flextime, compressed workweeks, job sharing, and home-based work.

 ASSESSMENT CHECK ANSWERS

8.4.1 Explain the difference between *wage* and *salary*. Wages are based on an hourly pay rate or the amount of work accomplished. Salaries are paid periodically, such as weekly or monthly. Salaries do not rise or fall with the number of hours worked.

8.4.2 What are flexible benefit plans? How do they work? Flexible benefit plans offer a choice of benefits, including different types of medical insurance, dental and vision benefits, and life and disability insurance. Typically, each employee receives a set allowance (also known as flex dollars) to pay for these benefits that suit his or her needs.

LO 8.5 Discuss employee separation and the impact of downsizing and outsourcing.

Employee separation occurs when a worker leaves his or her job, either voluntarily or involuntarily. Sometimes an employee is terminated because of poor job performance or unethical behaviour. Downsizing is the process of reducing the number of employees within a firm by eliminating jobs. Some negative effects of downsizing include anxiety and lost productivity among the remaining workers, expensive severance packages, and a domino effect in the local economy. Outsourcing involves transferring jobs from inside a firm to outside the firm. While some expenses may be cut, a firm may experience a strong negative reaction in job performance and public image.

 ASSESSMENT CHECK ANSWERS

8.5.1 What is the difference between voluntary and involuntary turnover? Voluntary turnover occurs when employees leave firms for their own reasons, such as to start their own businesses, take jobs with other firms, move to another community, or retire. Involuntary turnover occurs because of employees' poor job performance or unethical behaviour in their business practices or in the workplace. It can also occur when a company is forced to eliminate jobs.

8.5.2 What is downsizing? How is it different from outsourcing? Downsizing is the process of reducing the number of employees within a firm by eliminating jobs. Downsizing is done to cut overhead costs and streamline the organizational structure. Outsourcing occurs when companies contract with other firms to perform noncore jobs or business functions, such as housekeeping, maintenance, or relocation services. Outsourcing allows companies to focus on what they do best. It can also result in a downsized workforce.

LO 8.6 Explain the different methods and theories of motivation.

Employee motivation starts with high employee morale. According to Maslow's hierarchy of needs, people satisfy lower-order needs (such as food and safety) before moving to higher-order needs (such as esteem and fulfillment). Herzberg's two-factor model of motivation is based on the fulfillment of hygiene factors and motivation factors. Expectancy theory suggests that people use these factors to decide whether to make the effort needed to complete a task. Equity theory refers to a person's view of fair and equitable treatment. Goal-setting theory says that people will be motivated to the extent to which they accept specific, challenging goals. Job design is also used by managers for motivation.

 ASSESSMENT CHECK ANSWERS

8.6.1 What are the four steps in the process of motivation? The four steps are need, motivation, goal-directed behaviour, and need satisfaction.

8.6.2 Explain how goal-setting works. People will be motivated to the extent to which they accept specific, challenging goals and receive feedback that shows their progress toward goal achievement.

8.6.3 Describe the three ways that managers design jobs for increased motivation. Jobs can be designed to be more motivating in three ways: through job enlargement, job enrichment, and job rotation. Job enlargement is a job design that expands an employee's responsibilities by increasing the number and variety of tasks. Job enrichment changes the job duties to increase employees' authority in planning their work, deciding how it should be done, and learning new skills that help them grow. Job rotation involves a system of moving employees from one job to another.

LO 8.7 Discuss the role of labour unions, the collective bargaining process, and methods for settling labour–management disputes.

Labour unions have led to improvements in wages, working conditions, and labour laws. Unions achieve these improvements through the collective bargaining process, which results in an agreement. Most labour–management disagreements are settled through the grievance process. Sometimes, third-party mediation or arbitration is needed to settle disagreements.

✓ ASSESSMENT CHECK ANSWERS

8.7.1 **What is a labour union? What is collective bargaining?** A labour union is a group of workers who organize themselves to work toward common goals in the areas of wages, hours, and working conditions. Collective bargaining is the process of negotiation between management and union representatives.

8.7.2 **What are the three main tactics used by unions to win support for their demands?** Unions' main tactics are strikes (walk-outs), picketing, and boycotts.

BUSINESS TERMS YOU NEED TO KNOW

human resource management 214

performance appraisal 218

compensation 219

wage 220

salary 220

employee benefits 220

employee separation 223

downsizing 223

outsourcing 224

Maslow's hierarchy of needs 226

expectancy theory 227

equity theory 227

goal-setting theory 228

management by objectives (MBO) 228

labour union 229

collective bargaining 230

REVIEW QUESTIONS

1. Why has Internet recruiting become an important tool for human resource managers?

2. Recruitment and selection are expensive. What steps can human resource managers take to make sure they hire the right person for each job?

3. Give an example of a type of job that would be suitable for on-the-job training. Describe specifically how on-the-job training would work for this job. Include a list of tasks a new hire might learn on the job.

4. What five factors are compensation policies usually based on? Name three employee benefits that are required by law. Name three employee benefits that firms often provide voluntarily.

5. Describe four types of flexible work plans. Identify an industry that would be well suited to each type of plan, and explain why.

6. Why do companies downsize? What are some of the downsides to downsizing? Why do companies outsource? What are some of the downsides to outsourcing?

7. Select three different theories of motivation. Explain how each theory can be used by managers to motivate employees.

8. Suppose a manager of a popular sandwich shop maintains a Theory X view about employees. At the beginning of each workweek, what might this manager tell his or her employees? Now suppose the manager has a Theory Y view, then a Theory Z view. Describe what a manager with each of these views might say to employees.

9. In what major ways have labour laws changed the workplace over the past century? How would today's workplace be different if we did not have these laws?

10. What are mediation and arbitration? Describe a situation that might lead to arbitration.

PROJECTS AND TEAMWORK APPLICATIONS

1. On your own or with a classmate, research firms that provide management training programs. Prepare a presentation about one of these firms. Describe how the firm uses management training programs and some specific details of the program.

2. Choose one of the following companies, or a company that you might like to work for. Research the company's benefits by using the firm's website and a job search website such as Monster.com. Outline the firm's benefits. Decide whether you still want to work for the company, and why. Suggested firms:

   a. Timberland

   b. SAS

   c. NextEra Energy Resources

   d. Kraft Foods

   e. FedEx

3. With a classmate, choose an on-campus job and outline how you would share that job. Create a schedule and division of tasks.

4. Choose what you think would be your dream job five years from now. Using Maslow's hierarchy of needs, create a chart that shows how this job fulfills each level of need.

5. Research one of the major labour laws mentioned in the text. Learn what circumstances led to the proposal and passing of the law. How will this law affect the work world you will enter when you graduate?

WEB ASSIGNMENTS

1. **Human resources (HR) as a profession.** Go to the website listed below and review the material. Answer the following questions:

   a. How many people are employed in HR?

   b. What are the educational requirements to become an HR manager?

   c. How rapidly is the occupation expected to grow over the next decade?
   http://www.hrsdc.gc.ca/eng/home.shtml

2. **Performance reviews.** Visit the websites listed below. Each website lists some tips for employee performance reviews. Print out the material and bring it to class for a class discussion on performance reviews.
   http://www.squidoo.com/employeeperformancereview
   http://articles.techrepublic.com.com/5100-10878_ 11-1049853.html
   http://smallbusiness.dnb.com/human-resources/workforce-management/1385-1.html

3. **Teamsters.** The Teamsters is one of the North America's largest and oldest labour unions. Go to the union's website (http://www.teamsters-canada.org) and review the material. When was the union founded? The union originally represented workers in what industry? How many members do the Teamsters currently have?

Note: Internet Web addresses change frequently. If you don't find the exact sites listed, you may need to access the organization's home page and search from there or use a search engine such as Bing or Google.

www.wileyplus.com

Access your WileyPLUS course for:

- The complete digital textbook.

- Question assistance, including links to relevant sections in the online digital textbook.

- Immediate feedback and proof of progress, 24/7

- Integrated, multi-media resources – including MP3 downloads, visual exhibits, animations, and much more – that provide multiple study paths and encourage more active learning.

QUIZ YOURSELF

© Can Stock Photo Inc./wacker

9 | TOP PERFORMANCE THROUGH EMPOWERMENT, TEAMWORK, AND COMMUNICATION

LEARNING OBJECTIVES

LO 9.1 Describe why and how organizations empower employees.

LO 9.2 Distinguish among the five types of teams in the workplace.

LO 9.3 Identify the characteristics of an effective team, and summarize the stages of team development.

LO 9.4 Relate team cohesiveness and norms to effective team performance.

LO 9.5 Describe the factors that can cause conflict in teams and ways to manage conflict.

LO 9.6 Explain the importance and process of effective communication.

LO 9.7 Compare the different types of communication.

LO 9.8 Explain external communication and methods of managing a public crisis.

INSIDE BUSINESS

Tony Lamport

Pam Cooley and CarShareHFX

"This is what we do as humans. We move people and we move things. How we do this exposes our intelligence and our values."

Social entrepreneur Pam Cooley co-founded CarShareHFX in Halifax in 2008. Cooley has strong organizational and communications skills. She is also devoted to socially responsible causes. These skills and interests helped her to set up a new way of using automobiles. CarShare Atlantic Limited was the first multi-vehicle CarShare service in Atlantic Canada. The Halifax Chamber of Commerce named the firm the Gold New Business of the Year for 2010. Cooley has succeeded in getting the socially responsible message out—CarShare provides a cost-effective alternative to vehicle ownership. Members pay an annual fee and have 24-hour self-service access to the entire fleet of cars. Cars are booked using a phone-in or online reservation system. Society will benefit from having greater mobility and lower traffic congestion and exhaust emissions. By partnering with CarShareHFX, organizations can reduce parking limitations, decrease the number of parking spots they need to build, and save thousands of dollars. Dalhousie University chose to be a partner to help reduce congestion and to make more space available for people, not vehicles.

For the system to work, participants need to have a high level of cooperation with each other. That means clear communications about everything, from what to do if the gas tank runs low to how to deal with finding dents or scratches on the car.

Much of this customer information is explained in simple step-by-step videos and text on the firm's website, http://carsharehfx.ca/. The promotional information is aimed at drivers who can benefit from the co-operative model of car-sharing rather than car ownership. And it's very persuasive. The highlighted benefits include the freedom from many responsibilities associated with car ownership, such as costs for insurance, maintenance, and parking. Customer members pay only for the time they use a vehicle. All costs are included in the hourly and per kilometre rates.

CarShareHFX vehicles can use privileged parking locations around town, and members can conveniently reserve a car online.

This company appeals to a generation of young drivers who are concerned with socially responsible behaviours. But government and corporate organizations, such as Clean Nova Scotia, also want to encourage and participate in the system. Clean Nova Scotia (http://clean.ns.ca/) is a not-for-profit organization founded in 1988. It is guided by a board of directors with representation from business, academia, government, and the community. Over the last 20 years, Clean Nova Scotia has become an effective, high-profile organization that works with individuals, government, business, and communities to improve the environment. Clean Nova Scotia spokesperson Derek Gillis is a supporter of CarShareHFX. He sees its role as a way for reducing the size of corporate fleets of vehicles. Gillis argues that the co-operative model could be expanded to include trucks and other vehicles that may not be driven very often. These vehicles could be shared between businesses and governments.

Another targeted customer base for CarShareHFX is property managers and their tenants. The program might also appeal to real estate developers looking both to improve the quality of life for their tenants and to reduce their environmental footprint on new apartment or condominium projects. These developers could partner with CarShareHFX to provide on-site vehicles for tenants to share. This service would provide added value by decreasing demand for parking spaces. The idea fits well with developers who want to improve their green initiatives, including LEED (Leadership in Energy and Environmental Design) certification, the gold seal in environmentally superior construction. Some partners currently offering CarShareHFX benefits to their residents are The Westwood, Southwest Properties, Killam Properties, and King's Wharf developments.

Pam Cooley's ongoing efforts to help build more economically sound socially responsible opportunities will definitely benefit from her visible success with CarShareHFX.[1]

CHAPTER 9 OVERVIEW

Well-managed large organizations know that teamwork and communication are essential for empowering employees to perform their best. This chapter focuses on how organizations involve employees by sharing information and empowering them to make critical decisions, by having them work in teams, and by encouraging communication. We begin by discussing how managers can empower their employees' decision-making authority and responsibility. Then we explain why and how more and more firms are relying on teams of workers, not individuals, to make decisions and carry out assignments. Finally, we discuss how effective communication helps workers to share information that improves the quality of decision-making.

LO 9.1 Describe why and how organizations empower employees.

empowerment giving employees shared authority, responsibility, and decision-making with their managers.

EMPOWERING EMPLOYEES

An important component of effective management is the **empowerment** of employees. Organizations promote this goal by giving employees shared authority, responsibility, and decision-making with their managers. Empowerment uses the brainpower of all workers to find better ways of doing their jobs, serving customers, and achieving organizational goals. Empowerment frees managers from hands-on control of workers. It motivates workers by adding challenges to their jobs. Empowerment also gives workers a feeling of ownership. Managers empower employees by sharing company information and decision-making authority and by rewarding them for their own performance—and the company's. The topic of employee empowerment is discussed in the "Solving an Ethical Controversy" feature.

Sharing Information and Decision-Making Authority

One of the most effective ways to empower employees is to keep them informed about the company's financial performance. Research suggests that companies should provide regular reports to their employees on key financial information, such as profit-and-loss statements. Firms show their willingness to practise open-book management by using the company's internal website, or intranet, to post financial statements, training schedules, policy documents, and other information. Employees can visit the website and look up the company's cash flow, its design standards, and its basic measures of financial performance. In this way, employees can understand more about the organization's strategic thinking and how their own work fits into the overall plan. Employees who are trained in how to read financial statements can understand how their work contributes to company profits. These employees are better able to direct their work efforts to make use of company resources. Using information technology to empower employees carries some risks. One risk is that private company information may reach competitors. Management must weigh this risk and other risks against the benefits of sharing information with employees.[2]

The second way that companies empower employees is by giving them broad authority to make decisions that carry out a firm's vision and its competitive strategy. Even among non-management staff, empowerment extends to decisions and activities usually handled by managers. Employees might be responsible for such tasks as purchasing supplies, making hiring decisions, scheduling production or work hours, overseeing the safety program, and granting pay increases.

Linking Rewards to Company Performance

The ultimate step in convincing employees of their role in the success of their firm is worker ownership. Companies offer worker ownership in two ways: employee stock ownership plans and stock options. Table 9.1 compares these two methods of employee ownership.

Employee Stock Ownership Plans

About 7 percent of Canadians participate in *employee stock ownership plans (ESOPs).*[3] These plans are growing in popularity in Canada. ESOPs benefit employees by giving them stock ownership in their companies. These stocks can lead to profits when the value of the firm increases. Under ESOPs, the employer buys shares of the company stock on behalf of the employee as a retirement

SOLVING AN **ETHICAL** CONTROVERSY

Employee Empowerment: Yes or No?

Many firms today recognize the benefits of empowering employees—entrusting them with decision-making authority that may improve sales outcomes, relationships with customers, and the firm's ultimate success. But not all managers are convinced that giving control to their employees is the best way to run a company. They worry about allowing employees to make decisions that could be an expensive lesson if those choices turn out to be wrong.

Should firms empower employees to make decisions that could improve company relationships and overall performance?

PRO

1. Employees who are empowered to make decisions within their job descriptions and their years of expertise can help build both relationships and sales. For example, an employee who has direct contact with customers can market products and solve customer problems more effectively if he or she has the authority to do so. A salesperson who can authorize a return or a discount on the spot can improve a firm's relationship with a customer and ensure repeat business.

2. Empowered employees are motivated to increase their own performance and that of the firm. Workers who are entrusted with making decisions about their own jobs feel a sense of ownership in their company's overall performance. Employees can move their companies into a position of success when they are motivated to display the commitment, initiative, and creativity that decision-making requires.

CON

1. When things at a firm go wrong—such as a major product recall or the discovery of poor working conditions at an outsourced facility—customers, investors, and the public immediately turn their attention to the company's leadership. If the company's top management appears unaware of the decision-making that led to these mistakes, then customers, investors, and the public quickly lose faith in the firm. Employee decision-making can result in this type of communication breakdown within an organization.

2. When employees are empowered but don't receive proper training, customers or suppliers might receive insufficient or inaccurate information. That poor information can lead to failed solutions, damaged relationships, and lost sales.

Summary

Most firms now practise some degree of empowerment among their employees. Some managers, though, are unwilling to pass this kind of decision-making authority to employees. But even those managers who support empowerment agree that employees must be trained in decision-making skills and educated about the goods and services marketed by their firm. The company must create a single and consistent message so all customers are treated fairly by different employees. When empowerment is set up properly, it can be an important force in moving an organization forward.

Sources: George N. Root, "Challenges of Employee Empowerment," *Small Business-Chron.com,* http://smallbusiness.chron.com, accessed August 16, 2010; Cameron Kauffman, "Employee Involvement: A New Blueprint for Success," *Journal of Accountancy,* May 2010, http://www.journalofaccountancy.com; Bob Reynolds, "Thoughts from the Shower—Pros and Cons to Empowering Your Employees," *Snoitulos Ten,* April 30, 2010, http://www.snoitulosten.com; Stacy Blackman, "How to Empower Employees with the Illusion of Control," *Blogs Bnet.com,* April 16, 2010, http://blogs.bnet.com.

Table 9.1 Employee Stock Ownership Plans and Stock Options

EMPLOYEE STOCK OWNERSHIP PLANS	STOCK OPTIONS
Company-sponsored trust fund holds shares of stock for employees	Company gives employees the option to buy shares of its stock
Usually covers all full-time employees	Can be granted to one, a few, or all employees
Employer pays for the shares of stock	Employees pay a set price to exercise the option
Employees receive stock shares (or value of stock) when they retire or leave the company	Employees receive shares of stock when (and if) they exercise the option, usually during a set period

Sources: "Employee Stock Options and Ownership (ESOP)," *Reference for Business,* http://www.referenceforbusiness.com, accessed April 19, 2010; "Employee Stock Options Fact Sheet," The National Center for Employee Ownership, http://www.nceo.org, accessed April 19, 2010.

benefit. The accounts continue to grow in value tax-free. When employees leave the company, they can cash in their stock shares. Employees are motivated to work harder and smarter because, as part owners, they share in their firm's financial success. About 60 percent of surveyed companies that offer ESOPs report an increase in employee productivity. The most definitive study in Canada was done by the Toronto Stock Exchange. It compared ESOP versus non-ESOP public companies. ESOP companies scored better than non-ESOP companies on several factors: their five-year profit growth was 123 percent higher, net profit margin was 95 percent higher, productivity measured by revenue per employee was 24 percent higher, return on average total equity was 92.3 percent higher, and return on capital was 65.5 percent higher.[4]

When ESOPs are used for retirement funds, they must follow government regulations designed to protect pension benefits. Because ESOPs can be expensive to set up, they are more common in larger firms than in smaller firms. ESOPs have one danger: if the majority of an employee's retirement funds are in company stock and the value falls dramatically, the employee may lose financially.[5]

Stock Options

Another popular way for companies to share ownership with their employees is by offering *stock options,* or the rights to buy a specified amount of company stock at a given price within a given time period. In an ESOP, the company holds stock for the benefit of employees. In stock options, employees can own the stock themselves if they choose to exercise, or use, their options by purchasing stock. For example, an employee receives an option on 100 shares at $10 per share. The stock price increases to $20 per share. The employee can choose to exercise, or use, the option to buy those 100 shares at $10 each. The employee can then sell the stocks at the market price of $20 per share, and keep the difference. If the stock price never increases above the option price, the employee doesn't need to exercise the option.[6]

Options were once limited to senior executives and members of the board of directors, but some companies now offer stock options to all employees. An estimated 9 million employees in thousands of North American companies hold stock options.[7] Of all the stock options issued by these corporations, about one-third go to the top five executives at each firm. Much of the remainder goes to other executives and managers, who make up only about 2 percent of the workforce. Solid evidence suggests that stock options motivate regular employees to perform better. Some people argue that for stock options to be most effective as motivators, they need to be offered to a much broader range of employees.

Stock options have turned hundreds of employees into millionaires at such firms as Research In Motion, The Home Depot, Microsoft, and Google. But their success stories don't mean that everyone can make money through stock options. Remember that stock prices drop during economic downturns. And, similar to ESOPs, employees face risks when they rely on a single company's stock to provide for their retirement. In addition to stock options and ESOPs, many firms offer their executives other perks, or special privileges.

✓ **ASSESSMENT CHECK**

9.1.1 What is empowerment?

9.1.2 What kinds of information can companies provide to employees to help them share decision-making responsibility?

9.1.3 How do employee stock ownership plans and stock options reward employees and encourage empowerment?

LO 9.2 Distinguish among the five types of teams in the workplace.

team a group of people with certain skills who share a common purpose, approach, and performance goals.

work teams relatively permanent groups of employees with complementary skills who perform the day-to-day work of organizations.

TEAMS

A **team** is a group of people with certain skills who share a common purpose, approach, and performance goals. All team members hold themselves responsible and accountable for reaching their objectives. Teams are widely used in business and in many not-for-profit organizations, such as hospitals and government agencies. Teams are one of the most frequently discussed topics in employee training programs because teams require that people learn how to work well together. Many firms emphasize the importance of teams during their hiring processes. For example, job applicants are often asked about their previous experiences as team members. Companies want to hire people who can work well with others. Combining all of their talents and ideas will achieve more than they could achieve working alone. Figure 9.1 outlines five basic types of teams: work teams, problem-solving teams, self-managed teams, cross-functional teams, and virtual teams.

About two-thirds of firms use **work teams**. These teams are relatively permanent groups of employees. In this approach, people with complementary skills perform the day-to-day work of the organization. A work team might include all the workers involved in assembling and packaging a product—anything from cupcakes to cars.

In contrast to work teams, a **problem-solving team** is a temporary combination of workers who gather to solve a specific problem. After this problem is solved, the team is no longer needed and is disbanded. Problem-solving teams differ from work teams in important ways. Work teams are permanent groups designed to handle any business problem that arises, but problem-solving teams have specific missions. Toyota faced serious quality problems—unintended acceleration, faulty brakes, and questions about their tires. The company was forced to recall thousands of vehicles. Toyota formed rapid-response Swift Market Analysis Response Teams (SMART) to deal with the technical problems. These teams were made up of field technology specialists, engineers from manufacturing and design, and product engineers from North America. Specialists from Japan were on call, available when they were needed. Together, the SMART members worked with dealers across North America to contact customers and arrange for on-site analyses of each problem vehicle to figure out what went wrong and why. Teams were encouraged to "listen and react" to customers' descriptions of their experiences as part of their investigation.[8] Typically when a problem is solved, the team is no longer needed and disbands. In other cases, the team may develop a more permanent role within the firm.

A **self-managed team** is a work team that has the authority to decide how its members will complete their daily tasks. A self-managed team works most effectively when it combines employees with a range of skills and functions. Members are cross-trained to perform each other's jobs as needed. Distributing decision-making authority in this way can mean that members can concentrate on satisfying customers. Whole Foods Market has a structure that is based on self-managed work teams. Company managers decided that Whole Foods could be most innovative if employees made decisions themselves. Every employee is part of a team, and each store has about 10 teams handling separate functions, such as groceries, bakery, and customer service. Each team handles responsibilities such as setting goals, hiring and training employees, scheduling team members, and purchasing goods to stock. Teams meet at least monthly to review goals and performance, solve problems, and explore new ideas. Whole Foods awards bonuses based on the teams' performance relative to their goals.[9]

A **cross-functional team** is a team made up of members from different functions, such as production, marketing, and finance. Cross-functional teams usually work on specific problems or projects, but they can also serve as permanent work teams. The value of cross-functional teams is their different perspectives and the range of skills that they bring to a work effort. At Harley-Davidson, cross-functional teams work to find new ways to enhance the unique sound of its motorcycles while reducing unwanted noise. "We're aggressively moving from a tribal way of working to a cross-functional approach," notes Alex Bozmoski, manager of the cross-functional teams.[10]

Virtual teams are groups of geographically or organizationally separated co-workers who use telecommunications and information technologies to accomplish an organizational task. Because they use e-mail, video conferencing, and group communication software, members of virtual teams rarely meet face-to-face. The main advantage of virtual teams is their flexibility. Employees can work with each other regardless of physical location, time zone, or their organizational relationship. Because of their very nature, virtual teams that are scattered across the globe can be difficult to manage. Firms that are committed to virtual teams believe that the benefits outweigh the drawbacks.

FIGURE 9.1 Five Types of Teams

Five Types of Teams

Self-Managed Teams: Teams that are empowered to decide how they complete their daily tasks.

Cross-Functional Teams: Teams that are made up of members from different functions, or parts, of a firm.

Virtual Teams: Groups of geographically or organizationally separated co-workers who use technology to communicate and work together.

Work Teams: Work teams do just what their name suggests—the daily work. When empowered, they are self-managed teams.

Problem-Solving Teams: These teams comprise knowledge workers who meet to solve specific problems then disband.

problem-solving team a temporary combination of workers who gather to solve a specific problem and then disband.

self-managed team a work team that has the authority to decide how its members complete their daily tasks.

cross-functional team a team made up of members from different functions, such as production, marketing, and finance.

virtual teams groups of geographically or organizationally separated co-workers who use telecommunications and information technologies to accomplish an organizational task.

 ASSESSMENT CHECK

9.2.1 What is a team?

9.2.2 What are the five types of teams, and how are they different?

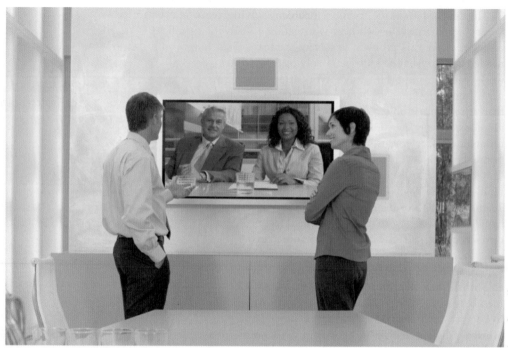

Image Source/Getty Images

Members of a virtual team rarely meet in person, but they stay in touch through new technologies, such as video conferencing. In today's global marketplace, the flexibility of virtual teams is a distinct advantage.

TEAM CHARACTERISTICS

Effective teams share several characteristics. They must be an appropriate size to accomplish their work. In addition to size, teams also can be sorted according to the similarities and differences among team members, called *level* and *diversity*. We discuss these three characteristics next.

Team Size

Teams can range in size from as small as two people to as large as 150 people. Most teams, though, have fewer than 12 members. Although no ideal size limit applies to every team, research on team effectiveness shows that teams achieve their best results with six or seven members. A group of this size is big enough to benefit from a variety of diverse skills, yet small enough that members can communicate easily and feel part of a small and supportive group.

Groups smaller or larger than six or seven can be effective, but they create added challenges for team leaders. Participants in small teams of two to four members often show a desire to get along with each other. They tend to like informal relationships marked by discussions of personal topics, and they make only limited demands on team leaders. A large team with more than 12 members poses a different challenge for team leaders. With this size of group, decision-making may work slowly. Participants may also feel less committed to the team goals. Larger teams also tend to lead to disagreements, absenteeism, and membership turnover. Subgroups may form, leading to possible disagreements about various functions. As a general rule, a team of more than 20 people should be divided into sub-teams, each with its own members and goals.

Team Level and Team Diversity

Team level is the team's average level of ability, experience, personality, or any other factor. Businesses consider team level when they need teams with a particular set of skills to do their jobs well. For example, an environmental engineering firm might put together a team with a high level of experience to write a proposal for a large contract.

team level the team's average level of ability, experience, personality, or any other factor.

Team level represents the average level or capability on a team. **Team diversity** represents the team's differences in ability, experience, personality, or any other factor. Strong teams have talented members—as shown by their team level. They also have members who are different in terms of their ability, experience, or personality. Team diversity is an important consideration for teams that must complete a wide range of different tasks or complex tasks. For example, the British Broadcasting Corporation (BBC) routinely creates teams for events such as the FIFA World Cup or the Olympic Games. These teams involve production and broadcast groups larger than 100 people, many of whom are part-time employees. The team members typically come from more than 15 different countries. Their skills can range from those of an electrician to those of a statistician, and from scheduling to producing. Because an event at the sports venues takes place only once, the BBC teams have one chance to get it right.[11] Ernst & Young, a global firm that provides financial services, relies on team diversity, as described in the "Hit & Miss" feature.

Strong teams not only have talented members but also members who are different in their ability, experience, or personality. Team diversity is an important consideration for teams that need to complete a wide range of different tasks or complex tasks. For example, the British Broadcasting Corporation (BBC) routinely creates teams for events such as the FIFA World Cup or the Olympic Games.

team diversity the team's differences in ability, experience, personality, or any other factor.

HIT & MISS

Team Diversity at Ernst & Young

Ernst & Young has seen it all—economic booms and busts, including the recent recession and fallout from the financial industry. But the company that provides tax, transaction, and advisory services is surviving. It is doing well partly because of its new outlook about the business environment and how it will operate. One focus is how its 144,000 employees can contribute their talents more fully to the company's future.

Specifically, Ernst & Young is changing the way it uses teams. A recent company survey was titled, "The New Global Mindset: Driving Innovation through Diverse Perspective." The survey's results found that companies operating in 25 or more countries base only 5 percent of their senior leadership in those countries. These companies are failing to make the most of the diverse cultures and ideas that could move them forward. "The economic crisis has mandated that companies rethink the way they do business," observes James S. Turley, chairman and CEO of Ernst & Young. "Company leaders need to consider how a lack of diverse perspectives—at the top of their organization and at the individual team level—might affect plans for global growth, new products, or mergers and acquisitions."

Ernst & Young has come up with a strategy for its new team diversity. Managers who are planning or leading teams should consider the following:

- *The mindset.* Managers must think about what needs to happen so that a true cultural change can occur within the organization.

- *The talent.* Managers should search every corner of the organization for true talent—it might be in the cafeteria, at an assistant's desk, or in the human resources office.

  - *Anticipation.* Creative managers need to use the diverse talents of team members to identify new products and services that could be the next "big thing."

  - *Consensus.* Total agreement among team members isn't always necessary. In fact, disagreement can boost a team's energy and force people to come up with new and better ideas and solutions.

"We all know that innovation is critical to economic recovery," says Beth Brooke, global vice chair of Ernst & Young. "In today's environment, the business leaders who have a truly global mindset and can integrate diverse perspectives will be the ones best positioned to drive innovation and long-term success."

Questions for Critical Thinking

1. Why is team diversity so critical for a global firm like Ernst & Young?

2. Think about the nature of Ernst & Young's business. What level would you expect Ernst & Young's teams to operate at? Why?

Sources: Ernst & Young, "LLP Diversity Award," *BAP Forums,* http://www.bap.org, accessed April 19, 2010; "Diversity Drives Innovation," January 27, 2010, Ernst & Young Web site, http://www.ey.com; James S. Turley, "The New Global Mindset," *Bloomberg BusinessWeek,* January 26, 2010, http://www.businessweek.com; "Ernst & Young LLP Starts 2010 with a Three-Day Event for Minority Students and a Faculty Roundtable Focused on Campus Diversity," *PR Newswire,* January 6, 2010, http://www.printthis.clickability.com.

Stages of Team Development

Teams typically progress through five stages of development: forming, storming, norming, performing, and adjourning. Not every team passes through each of these stages, but teams that use each step are usually better performers. These stages are shown in Figure 9.2.

Stage 1: Forming

Forming is the orientation period when team members get to know each other and learn what behaviours are acceptable to the group. Team members begin with curiosity about what they are expected to do and whether they will fit in with the group. An effective team leader provides time for members to get to know each other.

Stage 2: Storming

The personalities of team members begin to emerge at the storming stage. Individual personalities come out, as members clarify their roles and expectations. Conflicts may arise, as people disagree about the team's mission and compete for position and control of the group. Subgroups may form because of common interests or concerns. At this stage, the team leader must encourage everyone to participate. Members need to work through their uncertainties and conflicts. Teams must move beyond this stage to achieve productivity.

Stage 3: Norming

During the norming stage, members resolve their differences, accept each other, and reach broad agreement about the roles of the team leader and other participants. This stage is usually brief. The team leader can use this stage to emphasize the team's unity and the importance of its objectives.

Stage 4: Performing

While performing, members focus on solving problems and accomplishing tasks. They interact frequently and handle conflicts constructively. The team leader encourages all members to contribute. He or she should try to ensure everyone is involved.

Stage 5: Adjourning

The team adjourns after members have completed their assigned task or solved the problem. During this phase, the focus is on wrapping up and summarizing the team's experiences and accomplishments. The team leader may recognize the team's accomplishments with a celebration, perhaps handing out plaques or awards.

FIGURE 9.2 Stages of Team Development

Diagram labels:
- **FORMING** — Orientation, meeting the other team members, and learning what is expected. Leader provides time for members to get to know each other.
- **STORMING** — Conflict, disagreement. Leader encourages participation, differences surface.
- **NORMING** — Establishment of order and cohesion. Leader helps clarify team roles, norms, and values.
- **PERFORMING** — Cooperation, problem solving. Leader encourages participation and task accomplishment.
- **ADJOURNING** — Task completion. Leader brings closure and may celebrate the team's accomplishments.

✔ **ASSESSMENT CHECK**

9.3.1 Explain team level and team diversity.

9.3.2 Explain how teams progress through the stages of team development.

LO 9.4 Relate team cohesiveness and norms to effective team performance.

team cohesiveness the extent to which team members feel attracted to the team and motivated to remain part of it.

TEAM COHESIVENESS AND NORMS

Teams tend to maximize productivity when they form highly cohesive, or unified, units. **Team cohesiveness** refers to the extent to which members feel attracted to the team and motivated to remain part of it. This cohesiveness, or feeling of unity, typically increases when members interact frequently, share common attitudes and goals, and enjoy being together. Cohesive groups have a better chance of retaining their members than groups that do not achieve cohesiveness. As a result, cohesive groups typically experience lower turnover. Team cohesiveness promotes cooperative behaviour, generosity, and a willingness of team members to help each other. When team cohesiveness is high, team members are more motivated to contribute to the team because they want the approval of other team members.

Not surprisingly, studies have clearly shown that cohesive teams quickly achieve high levels of performance and consistently perform better than groups that are not cohesive.

Team-building retreats are sometimes used to encourage team cohesiveness and improve team members' satisfaction and retention. Team retreats allow members to participate in team-building exercises and games away from the office. These retreats provide time and space for people to get to know each other outside of the workplace. These retreats can lead to team members creating bonds with each other. When these bonds return with team members to the workplace, they can lead to benefits for a long period of time.[12] Team training can also build cohesion by cross-training team members in others' roles or by training team members to develop the skills needed to support the team task.[13]

A **team norm** is a standard of conduct shared by team members that guides their behaviour. Norms are not formal written guidelines; they are informal standards that identify key values and clarify team members' expectations. Team norms include standards of conduct during meetings and a shared vision for the team. Norms can be positive or negative. In highly productive teams, positive norms contribute to constructive work and the accomplishment of team goals. Negative norms can contribute to reduced work effort, reduced quality, and poor job attendance.

team norm a standard of conduct shared by team members that guides their behaviour.

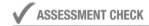 **ASSESSMENT CHECK**

9.4.1 How does cohesiveness affect teams?

9.4.2 Explain how team norms positively and negatively affect teams.

TEAM CONFLICT

LO 9.5 Describe the factors that can cause conflict in teams and ways to manage conflict.

Conflict occurs when one person's, or one group's, needs do not match those of another, and one side may try to block the other side's intentions or goals. Conflict and disagreement are to be expected in most teams. But that shouldn't be a surprise. People who work together are naturally going to disagree about what to do and how to do it. What causes conflict in teams? Almost anything can lead to conflict, but the main cause of team conflict is disagreement over goals and priorities. Other common causes of team conflict include disagreements over task-related issues, personalities that can't get along, being overtired and overstressed, and team diversity.

Earlier in this chapter, we discussed how teams can experience diversity among their members. Diversity brings stimulation, challenge, and energy, but it can also lead to conflict. The job of the manager is to create an environment where differences are appreciated, and a team of diverse individuals can work productively together. Diversity awareness training programs can reduce conflict by bringing these differences out in the open and identifying the unique talents of diverse individuals.

Most people think conflict should be avoided, but management experts know that conflict can actually improve team performance. The key to dealing with conflict is making sure that the team experiences the right kind of conflict. **Cognitive conflict** focuses on problem-related differences of opinion. Resolving these differences strongly improves team performance. In cognitive conflict, team members disagree because their different experiences and expertise lead them to different views of the problem and its solutions. People in a cognitive conflict have a willingness to examine, compare, and resolve their differences to produce the best possible solution. By contrast, **affective conflict** refers to the emotional reactions that can occur when disagreements become personal instead of remaining professional. These differences can strongly decrease team performance. Affective conflict often results in hostility, anger, resentment, distrust, cynicism, and apathy. It can make people uncomfortable, cause them to withdraw, decrease their commitment to a team, lower the satisfaction of team members, and decrease team cohesiveness. Unlike cognitive conflict, affective conflict weakens team performance by preventing teams from taking part in activities that are needed to achieve team effectiveness.

Managers can learn to manage team conflict. They can even make conflict work for them. The team leader's most important contribution to conflict resolution may be encouraging good

conflict the outcome when one person's, or one group's, needs do not match those of another, and one side may try to block the other side's intentions or goals.

cognitive conflict a disagreement that focuses on problem- and issue-related differences of opinion.
affective conflict a disagreement that focuses on individuals or personal issues.

communication and making it possible. Then, teammates will respect each other and are free to disagree with each other. Ongoing, effective communication means that team members view each other accurately, understand what is expected of them, and obtain the information they need. Organizations can extend this strategy by looking at situations or conditions in the workplace that might be causing conflict. Solving a single conflict isn't helpful if the team or the company has deeper problems. Employees can learn to become better team members through team-building exercises, listening exercises, and role-playing.[14]

LO 9.6 Explain the importance and process of effective communication.

THE IMPORTANCE OF EFFECTIVE COMMUNICATION

China, India, and Mexico are home to businesses that provide goods and services to companies and consumers in North America. But the more players are involved in the production process, the harder it is to coordinate communication. Japanese Toyota found itself in the middle of miscommunications when it tried to document a consistent timeline for the discovery and reporting of unintended acceleration in some of its vehicles. Everyone was talking about the cause—loose floor mats, stuck gas pedals, and electronics. But then it came out that European dealers had received information and repair kits from Toyota months earlier.[15]

communication a meaningful exchange of information through messages.

Communication can be defined as a meaningful exchange of information through messages. Few businesses can succeed without effective communication. As shown by the Toyota example, miscommunication can result in damage to the company. Toyota was ordered to pay a record-breaking $16.4 million in fines for its failure to communicate the safety problems quickly enough.[16]

Managers spend about 80 percent of their time—6 hours and 24 minutes of every eight-hour day—in direct communication with others, whether on the telephone, in meetings, via e-mail, or in individual conversations. Company recruiters rate effective communication—listening, conversing, and giving feedback—as the most important skill they look for when hiring new employees. In this last half of the chapter, you'll learn about the communication process, the basic forms of communication, and ways to improve communication within organizations.

The Process of Communication

Every communication follows a step-by-step process that includes interactions among six elements: sender, message, channel, audience, feedback, and context. This process is shown in Figure 9.3.

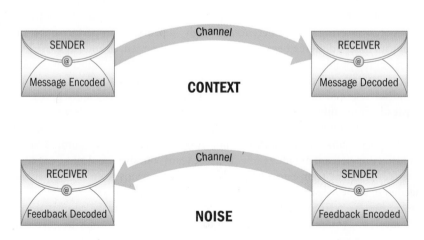

FIGURE 9.3 The Communication Process

In the first step, the *sender* composes the message and sends it through a communication carrier, or channel. Encoding a message means that the sender translates its meaning into understandable terms and puts it in a form so the message can be sent through a chosen channel. The sender can communicate a particular message through many different channels, including face-to-face conversations, phone calls, and e-mail or texting. A promotional message to the firm's customers may be communicated through such forms as radio and television ads, billboards, magazines and newspapers, sales presentations, and social media such as Facebook and Twitter. The audience consists of the people who receive the message. In decoding, the receiver of the message interprets its meaning. Feedback from the audience—in response to the sender's communication—helps the sender to know whether the audience has correctly interpreted the intended meaning of the message.

Every communication takes place in a situational or cultural context. The *context* can exert a powerful influence on how well the process works. For an example of a situational context, consider that a conversation between two people in a quiet office may be a very different experience from the same conversation held at a noisy party. For an example of a cultural context, consider that a Canadian who orders chips in an English tavern will likely receive French fries.

Anthropologists classify cultures as low context or high context. Communication in *low-context cultures* tends to rely on written and verbal messages. Examples of low-context cultures include Switzerland, Austria, Germany, Canada, and the United States. In contrast, communication in *high-context cultures* depends not only on the message itself but also on the conditions that surround it, including nonverbal cues, past and present experiences, and personal relationships between the parties. High-context cultures include Japan, Latin America, and India. Westerners must carefully match their own low-context style to the expectations of colleagues and clients from high-context countries. North Americans tend to favour direct interactions and want to "get down to business" soon after shaking hands or sitting down to a business dinner. Businesspeople in Mexico and Asian countries prefer to become acquainted before discussing details. When conducting business in these cultures, wise visitors allow time for relaxed meals when business-related topics are avoided.

Senders must pay attention to audience feedback. They should even ask for feedback if none is offered. Feedback clarifies whether the communication's intended message was properly received. Feedback can show whether the receiver heard the message and was able to decode it accurately. Even when the receiver tries to understand, the communication may fail if the message contained slang or words that are unclear.

Noise during the communication process is any interference with the transmission of messages and feedback. Noise can result from simple physical factors, such as the poor reception of a cellphone or static that drowns out a radio commercial. Noise can also be caused by more complex differences in people's attitudes and viewpoints. Even when people are sent the same communications, they can have very different understandings of the message because of communication noise.

Noise can be present at any point in the communication process. Managers must learn how to cut through noise when communicating with employees. Managers at i-level, a digital communications agency, found a creative way to cut through noise when communicating its plans to move from a paper-based process to an online system. First, the managers distributed "i" character mugs to office staff. Then they sent messages to employees' mobile phones. Those with iPhones received animated messages. New hires and prospective employees without company phones received a USB stick with the messages. "The communications felt really innovative and it was good using digital media because at the end of the day, that's what we're about as a company," says James Miller, the company's human resource director. "People have found it really good fun and I'm really, really pleased with the concept we have come up with."[17]

Noise during the communication process can result from simple physical factors, such as the poor reception of a cellphone or static that drowns out a radio commercial. Even when people are sent the same communications, they may have very different understandings of the message because of communication noise.

© Can Stock Photo Inc./Vlue

✓ **ASSESSMENT CHECK**

9.6.1 What is the difference between communication in low-context and high-context cultures?

9.6.2 In the context of the communication process, what is noise?

LO 9.7 Compare the different types of communication.

BASIC FORMS OF COMMUNICATION

Managers and co-workers communicate in many different ways. They make phone calls, send e-mail, hold a staff meeting, or chat in the hallway. They also communicate with facial expressions, gestures, and other body language. Small variations can change how a message is received. As Table 9.2 shows, communication takes different forms: oral and written, formal and informal, and nonverbal.

Table 9.2 Forms of Communication

FORM	DESCRIPTION	EXAMPLES
Oral communication	Communication transmitted through speech	Personal conversations, speeches, meetings, voice mail, telephone conversations, video conferences
Written communication	Communication transmitted through writing	Letters, memos, formal reports, news releases, e-mail, faxes, online discussion groups, Internet messaging
Formal communication	Communication transmitted through the chain of command within an organization to other members or to people outside the organization	Internal—memos, reports, meetings, written proposals, oral presentations, meeting minutes
		External—letters, written proposals, oral presentations, speeches, news releases, press conferences
Informal communication	Communication transmitted outside formal channels without regard for the organization's hierarchy of authority	Rumours spread informally among employees via the grapevine
Nonverbal communication	Communication transmitted through actions and behaviours rather than through words	Gestures, facial expressions, posture, body language, dress, makeup

Oral Communication

Managers spend a lot of time using oral communication, both in person and on the phone. Some people prefer to communicate this way, believing that using oral communication means that messages are received more accurately. Face-to-face oral communication allows people to combine words with other cues, such as facial expressions and tone of voice. Oral communication over the telephone lacks visual cues, but people receiving the message can hear the tone of voice. People can also provide immediate feedback by asking questions or restating the message. Because oral communication is immediate, it has drawbacks. If one person is upset or nervous during a conversation, noise enters the communication process. A hurried manager might brush off an employee who has an important message to deliver. A frustrated employee might say some harsh words to an unsupportive supervisor instead of thinking before speaking.

listening receiving a message and interpreting its intended meaning by grasping the facts and feelings the message conveys.

An important part of oral communication is **listening**—receiving a message and interpreting its intended meaning by accurately grasping the facts and feelings the message conveys. Listening may be the most important communication skill, but most of us don't use it enough—or as well as we should.

Listening may seem easy because the listener appears to make no effort. But the average person talks at a rate of 150 words per minute, while the brain can handle up to 400 words per minute. This gap can lead to boredom, inattention, and misinterpretation. In fact, immediately after listening to a message, the average person can recall only half of it. After several days, a listener can recall only 25 percent or less.

Certain types of listening behaviours are common in both business and personal interactions:

- *Cynical or defensive listening.* This type of listening occurs when the receiver of a message feels that the sender is trying to gain some advantage from the communication.

- *Offensive listening.* In this type of listening, the receiver tries to catch the speaker in a mistake or contradiction.

- *Polite listening.* In this mechanical type of listening, the receiver listens to be polite. The listener does not expect to contribute to the communication. Polite listeners usually don't pay attention. They spend their time thinking about what they want to say when the speaker finishes.

- *Active listening.* This form of listening requires involvement with the information and empathy with the speaker's situation. In both business and personal life, active listening is the basis for effective communication.

An especially important goal for business leaders is to learn to be an active listener. Effective communication is essential to their role. Listening is hard work, but it pays off with increased learning, better interpersonal relationships, and greater influence.[18] Both managers and employees can develop skills to make them better listeners, as described in the "Business Etiquette" feature.

Written Communication

Channels for written communication include reports, letters, memos, online discussion boards, social media, e-mails, and text messages. Many of these channels permit only delayed feedback and create a record of the message. The sender of a written communication needs to prepare the message carefully. The sender should also review the message to avoid misunderstandings, especially before pressing the "send" button.

Effective written communication reflects its audience, the channel carrying the message, and a suitable degree of formality. When writing a formal business document, such as a complex marketing research report, a manager must plan in advance and carefully construct the document. The process of writing a formal document involves planning, research, organization, composition and design, and revision. Written communication via e-mail may call for a less formal writing style, including short sentences, phrases, and lists.

E-mail is a very effective communication channel, especially for delivering straightforward messages and information. E-mail's effectiveness also leads to its biggest problem: too much e-mail! Many workers find their valuable time is used up dealing with e-mail. To relieve this task and leave more time for the most important tasks, some companies are looking at ways to reduce the time employees spend sending and reading e-mail and other online data. To meet this need, some firms provide specialized software and services. OpenText Corporation, a company headquartered in Waterloo, Ontario, provides content management solutions to clients, including solutions related to e-mail.[19]

Two other e-mail issues are security and retention. Because e-mail messages are often informal, senders sometimes forget that they are creating a written record. Even if the recipient deletes an e-mail message, other copies exist on company e-mail servers. E-mails on company servers can be used as evidence in a legal case or to build a case for disciplinary action.

Formal Communication

A *formal communication channel* carries messages that flow within the chain of command structure defined by an organization. The most familiar channel is downward communication. This channel carries messages from someone who holds a senior position in the organization to subordinates,

Listening may seem easy because the listener appears to make no effort. But the average person talks at a rate of 150 words per minute, while the brain can handle up to 400 words per minute. This gap can lead to boredom, inattention, and misinterpretation.

© Can Stock Photo Inc./micropix

or the people below. Managers may communicate downward by sending employees e-mail messages, leading discussions at department meetings, giving employees policy manuals, posting notices on bulletin boards, and reporting news in company newsletters. The most important factor in formal communication is to be open and honest. "Spinning" bad news to make it look better almost always doesn't work. In a work environment that has open communication, employees feel free to express opinions, offer suggestions, and even voice their complaints. Research has shown that open communication has the following seven characteristics:

1. *Employees are valued.* Employees are happier and more motivated when they feel they are valued and their opinions are heard.

2. *A high level of trust exists.* Telling the truth maintains a high level of trust. Trust forms the foundation for open communication, which can lead to employee motivation and retention.

3. *Conflict is invited and resolved positively.* Conflict encourages innovation and creativity.

4. *Creative dissent is welcomed.* When employees can express their creative ideas, they feel they are contributing to the company and improving performance.

5. *Employee input is requested.* The key to any company's success is input from employees. Seeking employees' feedback gives them a sense of involvement and improves working relations.

6. *Employees are well informed.* Employees feel valued when they are kept informed about what is happening within the organization.

7. *Feedback is ongoing.* Both positive and negative feedback must be ongoing. Feedback should be provided in a way that builds relationships rather than assigns blame.[20]

Many firms also define formal channels for upward communications. These channels encourage communication from employees to supervisors and upward to top management levels. Some examples of upward communication channels are employee surveys, suggestion boxes, and systems for employees to propose ideas for new products or voice complaints. Upward communication is also needed for managers to evaluate the effectiveness of downward communication. Figure 9.4 shows the different forms of formal and informal organizational communication.

BUSINESS ETIQUETTE

Tune Up Your Listening Skills

Smart managers know that good listening is important to business success. Tuning in to employees, customers, and competitors can provide valuable insight and information. Listening means paying attention to verbal and nonverbal cues. It means turning off your cellphone during a face-to-face conversation or meeting. It involves strategies for understanding the message that is conveyed. Here are a few tips for improving your listening skills:

- *Be attentive.* If it is culturally appropriate, maintain eye contact with the speaker, but don't stare. Nod your head to show that you are listening. Block out distractions such as background noise and unrelated thoughts.

- *Keep an open mind.* Hear the other person all the way through, even if you are certain you will disagree. You will show respect for the speaker, and your own reply will be better informed.

- *Don't interrupt.* Even if you are absolutely certain of what the person is going to say—or if you are sure you have a solution or answer—wait until the speaker is finished. Then, you can ask a question or make your point.

- *Ask questions.* Ask at least one question or paraphrase portions of the speaker's discussion to ensure that you understand the other person's point.

- *Be empathetic.* Laugh or be consoling when it is suitable. You don't have to agree with the speaker, but even in the heat of disagreement, you can show empathy.

Sources: Norma Chew, "Are You a Good Listener?" *Associated Content,* http://www.associatedcontent.com, accessed April 19, 2010; Dianne Schilling, "Listening Skills: 10 Steps to Effective Learning," *WomensMedia.com,* March 20, 2010, http://www.womensmedia.com; "Are You an Active Listener?" *New Horizons,* February 16, 2010, http://www.newhorizons123.com.

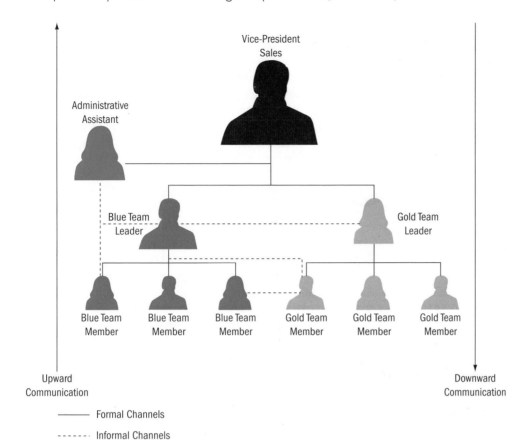

Upward Communication

Downward Communication

——— Formal Channels

------ Informal Channels

FIGURE 9.4 Formal and Informal Channels of Communication

Informal Communication

Informal communication channels carry messages outside the formally authorized channels of an organization's hierarchy. A familiar example of an informal channel is the **grapevine**, an internal channel that passes information from unofficial sources. All organizations, large or small, have grapevines. Grapevines spread information with speed and economy—and they are surprisingly reliable. But company communications must be managed effectively so that the grapevine is not the main source of information. When properly encouraged, the grapevine can help managers in three ways: to get a feel for the morale of companies, to understand the anxieties of the workforce, and to evaluate the effectiveness of formal communications. Managers can improve the quality of information passing through the company grapevine by sharing what they know, even if it is early or partial information. By feeding information to selected people, smart leaders can harness the power of the grapevine.

grapevine an internal information channel that passes information from unofficial sources.

The main drawback of this communication channel is gossip, which usually travels along the grapevine. People who gossip often spread misinformation and weaken morale. A manager should deal directly with the gossiper, taking action that suits the severity of the situation. The manager can then use the grapevine and other communication channels to spread accurate information about the company.[21]

Organizations are becoming more decentralized and more spread out globally. That means that more than ever, informal communication provides an important source of information, through e-mail, texting, and social media. Henry Mintzberg, a McGill University professor, believes that informal communications are essential to good managerial decision-making. The "Hit & Miss" feature discusses Mintzberg's studies.

Nonverbal Communication

So far, this section has discussed different forms of verbal communication, or communication that uses words to convey meaning. Equally important is *nonverbal communication,* which transmits messages through actions and behaviours. Nonverbal actions that become communication cues include gestures, posture, eye contact, tone and volume of voice, and even clothing choices.

(HIT)& MISS

Henry Mintzberg: Observing What Managers Do

McGill University management professor Henry Mintzberg enjoys a well-deserved international reputation for his scholarly work on how managers behave in the workplace. Mintzberg is noted for his study published in 1980. In that study, he reported what managers did while they worked. Mintzberg gathered data by following several senior managers while they were busy at their jobs. Mintzberg found that managers showed several common working methods and played clearly identifiable managerial roles to achieve their objectives at work.

To show the methods managers tended to follow, Mintzberg drew a picture of the fast-paced, driven manager with little or no time to spare. Coffee breaks and lunch were opportunities for meetings and informal communication with people. Work was never one continuous task; instead, it was choppy, constantly interrupted by other tasks, such as phone calls and short conversations with people who entered the office without an appointment. Mintzberg also recognized the existence of a critical network of people. These were the people that managers talked with regularly. Managers also counted on these people to help achieve their work goals.

Mintzberg observed and classified three primary behaviour roles of managers. Interpersonal roles included leadership and managerial actions that connected people in the organizations; informational roles involved the collection and distribution of information; and decisional roles included negotiation, designing change within the organization, and other activities related to decision-making.

These role descriptions helped to provide insights into the work managers did and the skills they would need to be successful. The Mintzberg study also helped to show how work actually got done in a modern corporation, which dismissed many myths about corporate culture.

Today, Mintzberg has triggered more discussion and debate. He argues that formal evidence-based performance output data (e.g., unit sales) are usually too dated for managers to use to make good decisions. Mintzberg believes that managers should put their faith in the flow of informal information, opinions, and even hearsay. Of course, many disagree with this view and strongly support using formal communication reports to guide managerial decision-making.

Mintzberg's study was thought to be groundbreaking. Researchers had always made assumptions about how managers communicated and behaved in a work environment. Those assumptions had seemed logical, but were wrong, according to Mintzberg. Technology plays a big role in how we communicate today. Team members who are not in the same physical location may communicate through the use of computerized video conferencing, smartphones, social media sites, and blogs. Some team members may never actually meet face-to-face. What will today's researchers find when they look at how managers and employees actually work in today's electronic environment?

Mintzberg's recent commentary suggests that managers should pay more attention to informal communications, not wait for formal evidence-based performance output data (e.g., unit sales). His viewpoint speaks to the changes that are taking place in management communications and decision-making.

Questions for Critical Thinking

1. How much value should higher management place on postings to the corporate blog, where any of a firm's managers can comment on their current thoughts, opinions, and activities?

2. How can a firm improve communications within a team of managers located across Canada who have never met face-to-face?

Sources: Henry Mintzberg, *Managing* (San Francisco: Berrett-Koehler, 2009); Henry Mintzberg, *The Nature of Managerial Work*, (New York: Harper & Row, 1973; reprinted by Prentice-Hall, 1983); Ingo Keilitz, "Henry Mintzberg Misses the Mark on Performance Measurement Data," *Made2Measure Blog*, November 15, 2009, http://made2measure. blogspot.com/2009/11/henry-mintzberg-misses-mark-on.html, accessed online January 30, 2012; Proven Models website, http://www.provenmodels.com/88/ten-managerial-roles/mintzberg,-henry, accessed January 30, 2012; Karl Moore, "Porter or Mintzberg: Whose View of Strategy Is the Most Relevant Today?" *Forbes.com*, March 28, 2011, http://www.forbes.com/sites/karlmoore/2011/03/28/porter-or-mintzberg-whose-view-of-strategy-is-the-most-relevant-today/, accessed January 30, 2012; Henry Mintzberg, "The Manager's Job: Folklore and Fact," *Harvard Business Review*, July–August 1975, pp. 49–61; K.M. Bartol and D.C. Martin, *Management* (New York: McGraw-Hill Inc. 1991), pp. 10–14.

Nonverbal cues can have more impact on communications than many people realize. In fact, some people estimate that 70 percent of interpersonal communication is conveyed through nonverbal cues. Top salespeople are particularly good at reading and using these cues. For example, they practise "mirroring" a customer's gestures and body language to show agreement.[22]

Powerful messages are even conveyed through the amount of personal space, or the physical distance, between people who are communicating. Figure 9.5 shows the four zones of personal space and social interaction: intimate, personal, social, and public. In North America, most business conversations occur within the social zone, roughly between 1.25 and 3.75 metres apart. If one person tries to approach closer than that, the other will likely feel uncomfortable or even threatened.

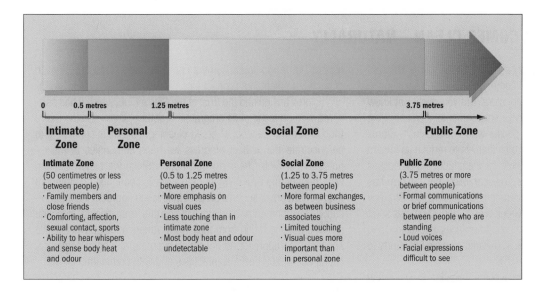

FIGURE 9.5
Influence of Personal Space in Nonverbal Communication

Understanding nonverbal cues can be especially challenging for people from different cultural backgrounds. Cultural ideas of personal space differ widely throughout most of the world. For example, most Latin Americans have business conversations while standing very close to the person they are talking to. Many North Americans find the space uncomfortably close. North Americans often step back to keep their personal space a little wider, but Latin Americans see that gesture as a sign of cold and unfriendly relations. To protect their personal space, some North Americans use desks or tables to separate themselves from their Latin American colleagues. Of course, these people risk their colleagues moving around the furniture to reduce the uncomfortable distance.

People send nonverbal messages even when they try not to. Nonverbal cues can show a person's true feelings and thoughts, which may differ from what they are saying. Generally, when verbal and nonverbal cues conflict, receivers of the communication tend to believe the nonverbal content. In job interviews, managers watch for nonverbal behaviour. When looking to hire people with good attitudes and a team orientation, many firms have several job applicants meet in group sessions. When one applicant gives a good answer, and another applicant frowns or looks discouraged, that nonverbal behaviour suggests that a person may not be a strong team player.

✔ **ASSESSMENT CHECK**

9.7.1 Define the four common listening behaviours.

9.7.2 What are the differences between formal and informal communication?

LO 9.8 Explain external communication and methods of managing a public crisis.

EXTERNAL COMMUNICATION AND CRISIS MANAGEMENT

External communication is an exchange of information using messages sent between an organization and its major audiences: customers, suppliers, other firms, the general public, and government officials. Businesses use external communication to keep their operations going, to maintain their positions in the marketplace, and to build customer relationships by supplying information such as changes to products and prices. Every communication with customers—including sales presentations and advertisements—should create goodwill and contribute to customer satisfaction. Firms such as Clorox use their websites to publish good news about their company, as described in the "Going Green" feature. An important function of external communication is informing the public about new initiatives for environmentally friendly processes, community projects, and the firm's other socially responsible activities.

external communication a meaningful exchange of information through messages sent between an organization and its major audiences.

GOING GREEN

CLOROX COMES CLEAN—NATURALLY

You've probably seen the Green Works brand of household and commercial cleaning solutions at your local grocery store. But you might not know that these natural, environmentally responsible cleaners are made by the same people who make bleach. Clorox is committed to following through on initiatives to reduce its impact on the environment by changing both its manufacturing processes and the ingredients in its products. To accomplish this, the firm has established a department of Environmental Sustainability Strategy and an Eco Office. Clorox's line of Green Works products meets strict environmental standards for ingredients, fragrances, packaging, and manufacturing processes. Clorox is also working on similar efforts to improve its traditional products.

One of the first pieces of external communication about its new focus on product ingredients was a list of ingredients, so consumers would know more about the products they were buying. The list has grown in detail. Clorox now provides more detailed information about its safety processes, the guidelines it uses to screen ingredients, and information on fragrances (a major ingredient in cleaning solutions). Clorox asks all fragrance suppliers to agree to increasingly strict fragrance standards. Clorox is the first major consumer packaged goods company to provide such detail to let consumers know exactly what its products contain and how they are made.

To spread the word farther, Clorox recently launched its own Corporate Social Responsibility (CSR) website. It provides information about Clorox's processes and products. The site is easy to use, includes a complete listing of product ingredients, and provides a glossary of terms so consumers can fully understand the function of each ingredient in a product (see http://www.trygreenworks.ca/).

Clorox has gained the trust of the Sierra Club, which it has partnered with on some of its programs. Together, Clorox and the Sierra Club praise the benefits of green cleaning. "Clorox is continuing to demonstrate the kind of progress we need companies to make," notes Sierra Club Chairman Carl Pope. "Since we began working with them on the Green Works brand, we've seen their commitment to important areas such as product innovation, ingredient communication, environmental stewardship and the transition to eliminate chlorine transportation from their North American supply chain. We applaud their approach to becoming even more open in communicating about their business practices and CSR commitments."

Questions for Critical Thinking

1. Clorox uses its CSR website to publish information and news about its green processes and products. How can the company use a social network, such as Facebook, to increase its online external communication?

2. Is there a downside to using the Internet for this type of communication? Why or why not?

Sources: Clorox website, http://www.cloroxcsr.com, accessed April 29, 2010; "2010 Best Companies for America's Children," *Working Mother*, http://www.workingmother.com, accessed April 29, 1010; "Clorox's New CSR Web Site Features Upgraded 'Ingredients Inside' Product Information," *CSRwire*, February 1, 2010, http://www.csrwire.com.

However, companies can experience a public relations crisis that threatens their reputation or goodwill. Nestlé is one of the world's largest food producers. It faced a crisis when Greenpeace reported that the firm was importing palm oil from suppliers who were damaging the rainforests in Indonesia, home to endangered orangutans and other species at risk. Outraged consumers raced to Nestlé's Facebook page to add their angry comments. Nestlé's response to the problem turned angry, including scolding the Facebook visitors for their aggression. This response angered consumers further, until Nestlé's Facebook moderator apologized "for being rude."[23]

How a company such as Nestlé handles a crisis can affect whether its reputation will be restored. Deciding on a plan of action and dealing with facts and rumours immediately can make the difference between regaining trust and allowing the disaster to grow. The following communication steps can help calm a public relations crisis:

1. When a crisis occurs, a firm should respond quickly. Executives should prepare a written statement—and stick to it. The statement should mention the time, place, and the initial description of what occurred (not the cause), and the number and status of the people involved.

2. As soon as possible, top company management should appear in public with news media present, if possible. The public will hold top management responsible, so it's best that top managers respond to reporters' questions.

3. When answering questions at an initial press conference or in an interview, the management representative must stick to the facts. If the press conference is held immediately, many details about the event, the cause, and the people involved may not yet be known; the spokesperson should not speculate, or create theories, about these details. As information becomes available, the firm can provide accurate updates.

4. If a question is currently unanswerable, the executive can offer to find out the answer. This answer should be quickly found and relayed as soon as possible. It's not a good idea to answer a question by saying, "No comment." It is much better to say, "I don't know."

5. The firm should recognize that problems exist, explain solutions, and welcome feedback. If a question or factual statement puts the organization in a negative light, the manager should accept that there is a problem, and then explain how the firm is correcting it.

6. The press conference or interview will be most effective if the executive speaks briefly and clearly and provides visual images. If available, a video with positive images—such as thriving rainforests—can be useful.[24]

Businesses use external communication to keep their operations going, to maintain their positions in the marketplace, and to build customer relationships. Every communication with customers—including sales presentations and advertisements—should create goodwill and contribute to customer satisfaction.

The crisis faced by Nestlé—the claim that it was purchasing palm oil from a supplier that was contributing to the destruction of rainforests—was made worse by the criticism posted on social media sites. Nestlé announced it would immediately stop purchasing oil from this supplier and added that this supplier represented only 1.25 percent of its total palm oil use. Still, debate over the company's environmental practices continued online. Nestlé spokesperson Nina Backes notes that it in these instances it is difficult "to show that we are listening, which we obviously are, while not getting into a shouting match." Daniel Kessler, press officer at Greenpeace, admits that social media present a new challenge for companies trying to manage their external communication. "This is the place where major corporations are very vulnerable," he remarks.[25]

✓ ASSESSMENT CHECK

9.8.1 What is external communication?

9.8.2 What is the first thing a company should do when a public crisis occurs?

WHAT'S AHEAD

Today's consumers expect the products they buy to be of the highest value for the price. Firms ensure this value by developing efficient systems for producing goods and services and by maintaining high quality. The next chapter examines the ways in which businesses produce world-class goods and services, efficiently organize their production facilities, purchase what they need to produce their goods and services, and manage large inventories to maximize efficiency and reduce costs.

RETURN TO INSIDE BUSINESS

Pam Cooley and CarShareHFX

When Pam Cooley was developing the CarShareHFX concept in the Halifax area, she needed to communicate a message that would attract a particular targeted customer or intermediary. An obvious message to users, both individuals and businesses, is the advantage of saving money and simplifying car ownership. The message directed to real estate developers and property management firms was a little different. For these customers, CarShareHFX partnerships provide a value-added competitive advantage by reducing the number of parking spots needed for residents. For example, a retired couple living in the city core might only occasionally need to use a second vehicle. Instead of paying for a second car that isn't used much, the couple can use a CarShare car that they can access from their building's garage.

QUESTIONS FOR CRITICAL THINKING

1. Identify other potential users that might benefit from the car-sharing model.

2. What message would you use to gain their participation?

SUMMARY OF LEARNING OBJECTIVES

LO 9.1 Describe why and how organizations empower employees.

Organizations empower employees by giving them shared authority and responsibility to make decisions about their work with their managers. Empowerment tries to use the brainpower of all workers to find better ways of doing their jobs, serving customers, and achieving organizational goals. Empowerment often includes linking rewards to company performance through employee stock ownership plans (ESOPs) and stock options.

ASSESSMENT CHECK ANSWERS

9.1.1 What is empowerment? Empowerment is giving employees shared authority and responsibility to make decisions about their work with their managers.

9.1.2 What kinds of information can companies provide to employees to help them share decision-making responsibility? One of the best ways to get employees to share decision-making responsibility is for executives to share information about company performance, particularly financial performance.

9.1.3 How do employee stock ownership plans and stock options reward employees and encourage empowerment? Employee stock ownership plans (ESOPs) benefit employees by giving them ownership stakes in their companies. Employees are motivated to work harder and smarter because they share in their firm's financial success. In an ESOP, the company holds stock for the benefit of employees (when employees leave the company, they cash in their stock). Stock options give employees a chance to own the stock themselves if they exercise, or use, their options by purchasing the stock.

LO 9.2 Distinguish among the five types of teams in the workplace.

The five basic types of teams are work teams, problem-solving teams, self-managed teams, cross-functional teams, and virtual teams. Work teams are permanent groups of co-workers who perform the day-to-day tasks needed to operate the organization. Problem-solving teams are temporary groups of employees who gather to solve specific problems and then disband. Self-managed teams have the authority to make decisions about how their members complete their daily tasks. Cross-functional teams are made up of members from different units, such as production, marketing, and finance. Virtual teams are groups of geographically or organizationally separated co-workers who use telecommunications and information technologies to accomplish an organizational task.

ASSESSMENT CHECK ANSWERS

9.2.1 What is a team? A team is a group of employees who share a common purpose, approach, and set of performance goals.

9.2.2 What are the five types of teams, and how are they different? Work teams are permanent, while problem-solving teams are temporary. Unlike work teams, self-managed teams have the authority to change how they get their work done. Cross-functional teams are composed of people from different work functions, while virtual teams are composed of people from different locations who use technology to communicate and work together.

LO 9.3 Identify the characteristics of an effective team, and summarize the stages of team development.

Three important characteristics of a team are its size, team level, and team diversity. The ideal team size is about six or seven members.

Team level is the team's average level of ability, experience, personality, or any other factor. Team diversity represents the team's differences in ability, experience, personality, or any other factor. Team diversity is an important consideration for teams that must complete a wide range of different tasks or complex tasks. Teams pass through five stages of development: (1) forming is the orientation period when members get to know each other and learn what behaviours are acceptable to the group; (2) storming is the stage when individual personalities come out, as members clarify their roles and expectations; (3) norming is the stage when differences are resolved, members accept each other, and they agree about the roles of the team leader and other participants; (4) performing is characterized by problem solving and a focus on task accomplishment; (5) adjourning is the final stage, with a focus on wrapping up and summarizing the team's experiences and accomplishments.

 ASSESSMENT CHECK ANSWERS

9.3.1 **Explain team level and team diversity.** Team level represents the team's average level or capability. Team diversity represents the team's differences in ability, experience, personality, or any other factor.

9.3.2 **Explain how teams progress through the stages of team development.** Teams pass through five stages of development: forming, storming, norming, performing, and adjourning.

LO 9.4 Relate team cohesiveness and norms to effective team performance.

Team cohesiveness is the extent to which team members feel attracted to the team and motivated to remain on it. Team norms are the standards of conduct shared by team members that guide their behaviour. Highly cohesive teams whose members share certain standards of conduct tend to be more productive and effective.

 ASSESSMENT CHECK ANSWERS

9.4.1 **How does cohesiveness affect teams?** Members of cohesive teams interact frequently, share common attitudes and goals, have high morale, and are likely to help each other. Cohesive teams also perform better.

9.4.2 **Explain how team norms positively and negatively affect teams.** Norms are informal standards that identify key values and clarify team members' expectations. Norms can be positive or negative. Positive norms contribute to constructive work and the accomplishment of team goals. Negative norms can, for example, contribute to reduced work effort, reduced quality, and poor job attendance.

LO 9.5 Describe the factors that can cause conflict in teams and ways to manage conflict.

Conflict and disagreement are to be expected in most teams. Conflict can come from many sources: disagreements about goals and priorities, task-related issues, personalities that can't get along, scarce

resources, and being overtired and overstressed. The key to dealing with team conflict is not avoiding it, but making sure that the team experiences the right kind of conflict. Cognitive conflict focuses on problem-related differences of opinion. Resolving these differences strongly improves team performance. By contrast, affective conflict refers to the emotional reactions that can occur when disagreements become personal instead of remaining professional. These differences can strongly decrease team performance. A team leader can manage team conflict by encouraging good communication so team members view each other accurately, understand what is expected of them, and obtain the information they need.

 ASSESSMENT CHECK ANSWERS

9.5.1 **What is cognitive conflict, and how does it affect teams?** In cognitive conflict, team members disagree because their different experiences and expertise lead them to different views of the problem and its solutions. People in a cognitive conflict have a willingness to examine, compare, and resolve their differences to produce the best possible solution.

9.5.2 **Explain affective conflict and its impact on teams.** Affective conflict often results in hostility, anger, resentment, distrust, cynicism, and apathy. It can make people uncomfortable, cause them to withdraw, decrease their commitment to a team, lower the satisfaction of team members, and decrease team cohesiveness.

LO 9.6 Explain the importance and process of effective communication.

Managers spend about 80 percent of their time in direct communication with others. Company recruiters consistently rate effective communication—listening, conversing, and giving feedback—as the most important skill they look for when hiring new employees. The communication process follows a step-by-step process that involves interactions among six elements: sender, message, channel, audience, feedback, and context. The sender composes the message and sends it through the channel. The audience receives the message and interprets its meaning. The receiver gives feedback to the sender. The communication takes place in a situational or cultural context.

 ASSESSMENT CHECK ANSWERS

9.6.1 **What is the difference between communication in low-context and high-context cultures?** Communication in low-context cultures tends to rely on written and verbal messages. By contrast, communication in high-context cultures depends not only on the message itself but also on the conditions that surround it, including nonverbal cues, past and present experiences, and personal relationships between the parties.

9.6.2 **In the context of the communication process, what is noise?** Noise is any interference with the transmission of messages and feedback. Noise can result from physical factors such as poor reception of a cellphone or differences in people's attitudes and perceptions.

LO 9.7 Compare the different types of communication.

People exchange messages in many ways. Their communication takes many forms: oral and written, formal and informal, verbal and nonverbal. Effective written communication reflects its audience, its channel, and a suitable degree of formality. Formal communication channels carry messages within the chain of command. Informal communication channels, such as the grapevine, carry messages outside the formal chain of command. Nonverbal communication plays a larger role than most people think. Sometimes, verbal and nonverbal cues conflict. When that happens, the receiver of a message tends to believe the meaning conveyed by nonverbal cues.

✓ ASSESSMENT CHECK ANSWERS

9.7.1 Define the four common listening behaviours. Cynical listening occurs when the receiver of a message feels that the sender is trying to gain some advantage from the communication. Offensive listening occurs when the receiver tries to catch the speaker in a mistake or contradiction. Polite listening occurs when the receiver is thinking about what he or she wants to say when the speaker finishes. Active listening requires involvement with the information and empathy with the speaker's situation.

9.7.2 What are the differences between formal and informal communication? Formal communication occurs within the formal chain of command defined by an organization. Informal communication occurs outside the organization's hierarchy.

LO 9.8 Explain external communication and methods of managing a public crisis.

External communication is an exchange of information using messages sent between an organization and its major audiences: customers, suppliers, other firms, the general public, and government officials. Every communication with customers should create goodwill and contribute to customer satisfaction. However, companies can experience a public crisis that threatens their reputations or goodwill. To manage a public crisis, businesses should respond quickly and honestly, and a member of top management should be available to answer questions.

✓ ASSESSMENT CHECK ANSWERS

9.8.1 What is external communication? External communication is an exchange of information using messages sent between an organization and its major audiences.

9.8.2 What is the first thing a company should do when a public crisis occurs? The firm should respond quickly by preparing a written statement. This statement should include the time, place, description of the event, and the number and status of people involved.

BUSINESS TERMS YOU NEED TO KNOW

empowerment 240	cross-functional team 243	team norm 247	listening 250
team 242	virtual teams 243	conflict 247	grapevine 253
work teams 242	team level 244	cognitive conflict 247	external communication 255
problem-solving team 243	team diversity 245	affective conflict 247	
self-managed team 243	team cohesiveness 246	communication 248	

REVIEW QUESTIONS

1. How do companies benefit from empowering their employees? How do employees benefit from empowerment?

2. Suppose that a shoe manufacturer wants to use teams to decide how to improve its environmental standards for products and processes. What type (or types) of teams would be best for this initiative? Why?

3. How do team level and team diversity affect team performance?

4. What are the characteristics of an effective team? Why are these features so significant?

5. At what stages of development might a team not be able to move forward? How should a team leader or manager deal with this situation?

6. Describe the norms associated with your business class. How do these norms influence the way you behave?

7. What steps can managers take to manage team conflict?

8. In what ways is context a powerful influence on the effectiveness of communication? Describe a situation where situational or cultural context affected one of your communication processes.

9. What are the upsides and downsides of oral and written communication?

10. What is the role of external communication? Why is external communication important to companies?

PROJECTS AND TEAMWORK APPLICATIONS

1. Empowerment is having the power and authority to make decisions. For this project, the teacher steps back and allows the class to plan and carry out a day of classes. The students might appoint a leader, divide into teams (to plan a lecture, decide on an assignment, plan a field trip, and other activities). It's completely up to the students how they organize and carry out the day's classes. In the next class, discuss the experience—including any upsides and downsides of empowerment.

2. Divide the class into teams of relatively equal size. Each team can select one of the following two problems to solve or use another problem: arranging for a speaker or expanding the vegetarian menu in the cafeteria. The students do not need to complete the entire problem-solving process. Each team should go through the forming stage of team development and establish norms. Each team should outline a plan for accomplishing the group's task. Is each team cohesive? Why or why not?

3. Try this listening exercise with a partner. First, spend a few minutes writing a paragraph or two about the most important thing that happened to you this week. Second, read your paragraph out loud to your partner. Next, have your partner read his or her paragraph. Finally, take turns stating the most important points in the other person's story. See how well you listened to each other.

4. On your own or with a classmate, visit your school's library, a mall, or anywhere that people gather. Take 10 or 15 minutes to observe the nonverbal cues that people give each other: Does the librarian smile at students? What is the body language of students in groups? Notice any changes in nonverbal communication when someone joins a group or leaves it. After you leave the area, jot down as many of your observations as you can.

5. Choose a company you are familiar, or whose products you use. Research the company's products and its socially responsible and sustainability initiatives (e.g., see whether the firm has set a goal to reduce its energy consumption). Create an advertisement that focuses on one of these initiatives as an example of the company's positive external communication.

WEB ASSIGNMENTS

1. **Team-building exercises.** The website Teampedia is "a collaborative encyclopedia of free team building activities, free icebreakers, teamwork resources, and tools for teams that anyone can edit!" Find some team-building activities to help break down stereotypes.

   http://www.teampedia.net/wiki/index.php?title=Main_Page

2. **Writing better business letters.** Using a search engine, such as Google or Bing, search for websites that offer tips and suggestions to improve letter-writing skills. (One such website is shown below.) Select two of these sites and review the material. Prepare a brief summary.

   http://www.askoxford.com/betterwriting/letterwriting/?view=uk

3. **Employee stock ownership plans.** Visit the website of the ESOP Association (http://www.esopassociation.org). Go to "About ESOPs," then "What Is an ESOP?" then click on "Use of ESOPs." Print out the material and bring it to class to participate in a class discussion on employee stock ownership plans.

Access your WileyPLUS course for:

- The complete digital textbook.
- Question assistance, including links to relevant sections in the online digital textbook.
- Immediate feedback and proof of progress, 24/7
- Integrated, multi-media resources – including MP3 downloads, visual exhibits, animations, and much more – that provide multiple study paths and encourage more active learning.

QUIZ YOURSELF

Note: Internet Web addresses change frequently. If you don't find the exact sites listed, you may need to access the organization's home page and search from there or use a search engine such as Bing or Google.

10 | PRODUCTION AND OPERATIONS MANAGEMENT

LEARNING OBJECTIVES

LO 10.1 Explain the strategic importance of the production function.

LO 10.2 Identify and describe the four main categories of production processes.

LO 10.3 Explain the role of technology in the production process.

LO 10.4 Identify the factors involved in a plant location decision.

LO 10.5 Explain the major tasks of production and operations managers, and outline the three activities involved in carrying out the production plan.

LO 10.6 Identify the steps in the production control process.

LO 10.7 Discuss the importance of quality control.

INSIDE BUSINESS

© MiRafoto.com/Alamy

The World Cup Gets a Kick Out of Jabulani

A soccer ball seems like a simple thing to make—some panels stitched together into a globe and inflated with air. But ask anyone involved in World Cup soccer (called "football" in most of the world), or in production at Adidas, and you'll hear a different story. Manufacturing a soccer ball is a complex process, especially when you're making the official ball for the FIFA World Cup soccer championships. Adidas has won the contract to produce the official championship soccer ball many times since 1970. Adidas is known for its consistent performance, but the firm never stops trying to improve. Instead, its design and production teams work hard to come up with a better product every time.

When the 2010 soccer ball model was unveiled, soccer fans had reason to celebrate. The new soccer ball was called the Jabulani, which means "to celebrate" in isiZulu, the language of South Africa's Zulu people. The soccer ball's name was chosen to pay respect to the 2010 World Cup host nation—the Republic of South Africa. The ball was produced in 11 colours to represent the 11 players on every team, the 11 official languages of South Africa, the 11 South African tribes that make up the nation, and the 11th Adidas World Cup ball. Each ball contained four triangle-shaped figures on a white background, in the style of traditional African designs.

But the new soccer ball offered more than bright colours. The ball featured new technology, including eight 3-D globe-shaped panels that were moulded in the interior of the ball to give the ball perfect roundness. Reducing the number of outer panels and seams gave the ball a 70 percent larger striking surface. The goose-bump surface, a feature that first appeared on the previous model, was improved to give players more control over the ball in all kinds of weather. The players loved the new ball. "Fantastic, the ball

does exactly what I wanted it to," praised one player. Another player agreed: "A very strong ball, true to hit."

Before the Jabulani reached the toes of World Cup soccer players, it was thoroughly tested at Adidas's labs in England and Germany. Robots kicked at early models, and man-made wind gusts attempted to blow them around. When the final product was ready, it was as perfect as Adidas's designers, engineers, production staff, and testers could make it. Of course, the Jabulani had to meet all the required specifications for a World Cup match ball, including weight, circumference, diameter, air pressure, and even water absorption.

Adidas also had to meet the production demand for the World Cup (both for official teams and for consumers). The company contracted the Pakistani manufacturing plant, Forward Group, to produce the entire supply of hand-stitched replica, or imitation, Jabulani models to be sold to the mass market. Forward Group expected to ship 6 million replica balls in one year, although it faced chronic power outages and other production problems. The economy of Sialkot, the town where the balls were produced, depends on soccer ball manufacturing. The official Jabulani match balls were produced by a factory in China, which could produce the thermally bonded balls used in World Cup play. The balls were then shipped from both countries. They soon arrived on the shelves of sporting goods stores around the world and on the bright green fields of the World Cup in South Africa.[1]

CHAPTER 10 OVERVIEW

Businesses satisfy their commitment to society by producing and marketing the goods and services that people want. They create what economists call *utility*—the want-satisfying power of a good or service. Businesses can create or improve four basic kinds of utility: time, place, ownership, and form. A firm's marketing department creates time, place, and ownership utility by offering products to customers at a time and place that are convenient for purchase.

Production creates form utility by converting raw materials and other inputs into finished products, such as Adidas's Jabulani soccer ball. **Production** uses resources, including workers and machinery, to convert materials into finished goods and services. This process can either make major changes to raw materials or combine two or more already finished parts into new products. The task of **production and operations management** is to oversee the firm's production process by managing the people and machinery that convert materials and resources into finished goods and services. This process is shown in Figure 10.1.

People sometimes use the terms *production* and *manufacturing* to mean the same thing, but the two are actually different. Production is used in both manufacturing and nonmanufacturing industries. For example, fishing and mining companies are involved in production, as are firms that deliver packages or offer hotel rooms. Figure 10.2 lists five examples of production systems for goods and services.

The production process can result in a tangible good such as a car or an intangible service such as cable television. The production process always converts inputs into outputs. A cabinetmaker combines wood, tools, and skill to create finished kitchen cabinets. A transit system combines buses, trains, and employees to create its output: passenger transportation. Both production processes create a useful good or service.

This chapter describes the process of producing goods and services. It looks at the importance of production and operations management. It also discusses the new technologies that are changing the production function. The chapter then discusses the tasks of the production and operations manager, the importance of quality, and the methods businesses use to ensure high quality.

production the use of resources, such as workers and machinery, to convert materials into finished goods and services.

production and operations management the process of overseeing the production process by managing the people and machinery that convert materials and resources into finished goods and services.

FIGURE 10.1 The Production Process: Converting Inputs into Outputs

INPUTS
· Resources
· Raw Materials

CONVERSION PROCESS
·Add Value

OUTPUTS
· Goods
· Services

LO 10.1 Explain the strategic importance of the production function.

THE STRATEGIC IMPORTANCE OF PRODUCTION

Production is a vital business activity, as are marketing and finance. Without products to sell, companies cannot generate money to pay their employees, lenders, and shareholders. And without the profits from products, firms quickly fail. The production process is just as important in not-for-profit organizations, such as The Hospital for Sick Children (SickKids) and Goodwill Industries. These organizations offer goods or services that are tied to their existence. When production and operations management are effective, they can lower a firm's costs of production, increase the quality of its goods and services, allow it to be dependable when meeting customer demands, and enable it to renew itself by providing new products. Let's look at the differences among three kinds of production: mass, flexible, and customer-driven production.

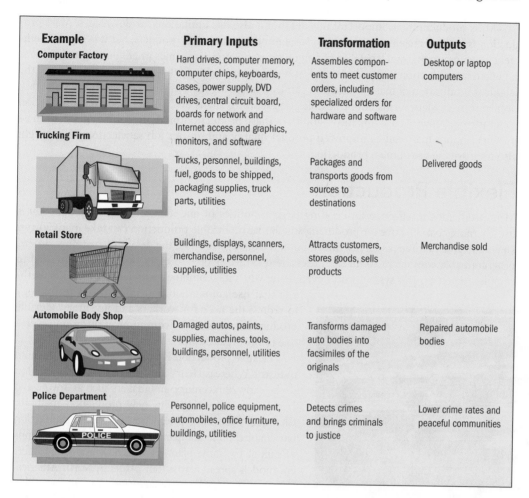

Example	Primary Inputs	Transformation	Outputs
Computer Factory	Hard drives, computer memory, computer chips, keyboards, cases, power supply, DVD drives, central circuit board, boards for network and Internet access and graphics, monitors, and software	Assembles components to meet customer orders, including specialized orders for hardware and software	Desktop or laptop computers
Trucking Firm	Trucks, personnel, buildings, fuel, goods to be shipped, packaging supplies, truck parts, utilities	Packages and transports goods from sources to destinations	Delivered goods
Retail Store	Buildings, displays, scanners, merchandise, personnel, supplies, utilities	Attracts customers, stores goods, sells products	Merchandise sold
Automobile Body Shop	Damaged autos, paints, supplies, machines, tools, buildings, personnel, utilities	Transforms damaged auto bodies into facsimiles of the originals	Repaired automobile bodies
Police Department	Personnel, police equipment, automobiles, office furniture, buildings, utilities	Detects crimes and brings criminals to justice	Lower crime rates and peaceful communities

FIGURE 10.2 Typical Production Systems

Mass Production

Canada began as a colonial supplier of raw materials to Europe and has become an industrial giant. Much of this change has resulted from **mass production**, a system for manufacturing products in large quantities by using effective combinations of employees with specialized skills, mechanization, and standardization. Because of mass production, outputs (goods and services) are available in large quantities at lower prices than individually made items. Mass production has brought us cars, computers, televisions, books, and even homes.

Mass production begins with the specialization of labour, by dividing work into its simplest forms so that each worker can focus on one task. By separating jobs into small tasks, managers create the right conditions for high productivity through mechanization. In mechanization, machines do much of the work previously done by people. Standardization, the third element of mass production, involves producing identical, interchangeable goods and parts. Standardized parts make it easier to replace substandard or worn-out parts. For example, if your car's windshield wiper blades wear out, you can easily buy replacements at a local auto parts store, such as Canadian Tire.

These principles of specialization, mechanization, and standardization led to development of the *assembly line*. This manufacturing method moves the product along a conveyor belt past many workstations, where workers perform specialized tasks, such as welding, painting, installing individual parts, and tightening bolts. Henry Ford's application of the assembly line greatly changed auto assembly. Before the assembly line, Ford's workers took 12 hours to assemble a Model T car. With an assembly line, the same car could be made in just 1.5 hours. Not surprisingly, many other industries soon adopted the assembly-line process.

mass production a system for manufacturing products in large quantities by using effective combinations of employees with specialized skills, mechanization, and standardization.

Mass production has important upsides, but it also has limitations, or downsides. Mass production is highly efficient for producing large numbers of similar products, but it is highly inefficient when producing small batches of different items. Some companies might be tempted to focus on efficient production methods instead of focusing on making what customers want. Also, the labour specialization of mass production can lead to boring jobs, as workers repeat the same task over and over. Many firms adopt flexible production systems and customer-driven production systems to improve their competitive abilities. These production methods won't replace all mass production, but may lead to improved product quality and greater job satisfaction. They might also improve the use of mass production.

Flexible Production

Mass production is effective for creating large quantities of one item, but *flexible production* is usually more cost-effective for producing smaller runs. Flexible production can take many forms. Generally, it uses three resources: information technology to share the details of customer orders, programmable equipment to fill the orders, and skilled people to carry out the tasks needed to complete an order. This system works even better when it is combined with lean production methods that use automation and information technology to reduce the need for workers and inventory. Flexible production needs a lot of communication among everyone in the organization.

Flexible production is now widely used in the auto industry. Whereas Henry Ford changed auto production in the early 20th century, automakers such as Toyota and Honda are innovating with new production methods. Changing from mass production to flexible production has enabled these companies to produce different kinds of cars at the same plant. Honda now builds 15 different models spread across four plants in North America. "Using our flexible manufacturing capacity, we plan to continue to maintain our local production levels at approximately 80 percent of our annual sales," states a company spokesperson.[2] Honda's news is good news for North American workers and consumers.

Paul Vernon/©AP/Wide World Photos

This Honda auto plant uses flexible production techniques to produce several different models. The auto industry developed mass production methods, but now finds more efficiency in flexible production.

Customer-Driven Production

A *customer-driven production* system assesses customer demands to make a connection between the products that are manufactured and the products people want to buy. Many firms use this approach with great success. One method is to set up computer links between factories and retailers' scanners. Data about sales are then used to create short-term forecasts and design production schedules to meet those forecasts. Another approach to customer-driven production systems is to wait until a customer orders a product and then produce it—whether it's a taco or a computer. Shibui Designs creates custom-made dresses in high-end fabrics for female executives and other women over 40. Each item of clothing is made to fit a single customer's measurements. Founder Elizabeth Nill, who is over 60, started the business because she couldn't find clothing that fit well. "I don't have the body of a model, and the bulges are real. Truly made classic clothing that is custom made-to-measure helps camouflage these inevitable imperfections and makes me feel more elegant." Nill's customers agree.[3]

ASSESSMENT CHECK

10.1.1 What is mass production?

10.1.2 What is the difference between flexible production and customer-driven production?

LO 10.2
Identify and describe the four main categories of production processes.

PRODUCTION PROCESSES

It probably won't surprise you that an Apple iPad and a litre of gasoline use different production processes and take different amounts of time to make. Production processes use either an analytic or a synthetic system; time requirements use either a continuous or an intermittent process.

An analytic production system reduces a raw material to its component, or individual, parts to extract one or more marketable products. Petroleum refining breaks down crude oil into several marketable products, including gasoline, heating oil, and aviation fuel. When corn is processed, it results in marketable food products, including animal feed and corn-based sweetener.

A synthetic production system is the reverse of an analytic system. It combines two or more raw materials or parts, or transforms raw materials, to produce finished products. Canon's assembly line produces a camera by assembling various parts such as a shutter or a lens cap. Other synthetic production systems make drugs, chemicals, computer chips, and canned soup.

A continuous production process creates finished products over a long period of time. The steel industry is a good example. Its blast furnaces never completely shut down except for repairs. Other firms that use continuous production are petroleum refineries, chemical plants, and nuclear power facilities. A shutdown can damage sensitive equipment and lead to a costly outcome.

An intermittent production process creates products in short production runs. Machines may be shut down frequently or may be changed so they produce different products. Most services result from intermittent production systems. For example, accountants, plumbers, and dentists do not try to standardize their services because each customer offers a different situation that needs an individual approach. But some companies, such as Mr. Lube (auto service), H&R Block (tax preparation service), and GreenLawn (lawn-care service), offer standardized services. This offering is part of a strategy to operate more efficiently and to compete by offering lower prices. McDonald's is well-known for its nearly continuous production of food. This company has moved toward a more intermittent production model. The fast-food chain invested millions of dollars in new cooking equipment to set up kitchens for preparing sandwiches quickly to order. McDonald's prefers this method instead of producing large batches ahead of time and then keeping them warm under heat lamps.

✔ **ASSESSMENT CHECK**

10.2.1 What are the two main production systems?

10.2.2 What are the two time-related production processes?

TECHNOLOGY AND THE PRODUCTION PROCESS

LO 10.3 Explain the role of technology in the production process.

Production changes rapidly as computer technologies continue to develop. Many manufacturing plants are now known as "lights out" facilities. These facilities are completely automated. That means no workers are needed to build or make the products. This type of manufacturing plant means a big change in the types of jobs available in manufacturing. It also means that companies can design, produce, and adapt products more quickly to meet customers' changing needs.

Green Manufacturing Processes

More and more manufacturing firms are investing resources into developing processes that result in less waste, lower energy use, and little or no pollution. Companies as big as Walmart and as small as your local café are learning to operate in a more sustainable manner. Some companies may use biofuel to power a fleet of delivery trucks or may stop using unnecessary packaging. Firms are proud of the steps they take to be more sustainable. Seventh Generation makes household goods and cleaning products. This company has used sustainable manufacturing processes since it started. The firm's approach is to look at its operations as a whole, by considering the entire impact of its processes and products on the environment. Seventh Generation consistently assesses its processes and makes changes. For example, it might cut emissions from its distribution system or redesign its packages. "It's the best insurance any company can have for long-term success," notes co-founder and top executive Jeffrey Hollender.[4] The "Going Green" feature describes energy firms that are working on new methods for drilling for natural gas. The new methods are much less damaging to the environment than traditional methods.

GOING GREEN

DRILLING FOR NATURAL GAS—CLEAN ALTERNATIVES

Drilling for natural gas doesn't usually lead to images of an undisturbed landscape. In fact, studies by the government and by private environmental groups show that the main method for extracting natural gas from the earth—hydraulic fracturing—can result in contaminated water supplies. Hydraulic fracturing involves injecting millions of litres of water, sand, and chemicals deep into the ground to crack open the beds of shale that contain natural gas. Then, the gas can rise to the surface. Environmental scientists and the people who live near the drilling sites are concerned about two things: the amount of water being used and the possible contamination of their water supplies by the chemicals used in the process. These concerns have been voiced in many communities across Canada. In Quebec, the provincial government decided to go ahead with its planned natural gas development. The Quebec government handling of the decision and how it dealt with public opinion led to much criticism.

But many energy companies *are* paying attention to these concerns—including those that drill for oil and natural gas. Environmental Technologies Ltd. makes a non-toxic alternative to the toxic chemicals. This firm says that its product kills bacteria just as effectively as the toxic chemicals. Ecosphere Technologies Inc. claims antibacterial chemicals aren't needed because its product can completely kill the bacteria at the surface before water is injected into the gas wells. Ecosphere also reduces water use and water waste by helping energy producers to reuse the water used in hydraulic fracturing. That means companies no longer need to pay to ship millions of litres of waste water to treatment plants or disposal sites.

None of these firms suggests that the drilling should stop. Instead, the firms are researching and developing greener technologies. New companies—and divisions or subsidiaries of the larger energy firms—are forming rapidly to take advantage of this business opportunity.

Questions for Critical Thinking

1. What type of production system is used by natural gas drilling companies? Explain your answer.

2. Do you predict that the firms that are investing in greener processes will ultimately be successful? Why or why not?

Sources: Marianne White, "Quebec Moved Too Fast on Shale Gas: Watchdog," *Montreal Gazette,* March 31, 2011, http://www.montrealgazette.com/news/decision-canada/Quebec+moved+fast+shale+watchdog/4532660/story.html#ixzz1JW9Ku1zL, accessed April 14, 2011; "Hydraulic Fracturing," EPA website, http://www.epa.gov, accessed April 29, 2010; "Sustainable Technology," Baker Hughes website, http://www.bakerhughes.com, accessed April 29, 2010; Ben Casselman, "Firms See Green in Natural-Gas Production," *Wall Street Journal,* March 30, 2010, http://www.wsj.com; "EPA Launches Hydraulic Fracturing Study," *Environmental Leader,* March 19, 2010, http://www.environmentalleader.com.

LEED (Leadership in Energy and Environmental Design) a voluntary certification program administered by the Canada Green Building Council, aimed at promoting the most sustainable construction processes available.

Firms that are involved in building construction—or are thinking of building new offices or manufacturing plants—are turning their attention to **LEED (Leadership in Energy and Environmental Design)** certification. LEED is a voluntary certification program offered by the Canada Green Building Council (CaGBC). It is aimed at promoting the most sustainable construction processes available. The LEED certification process is tough. It involves meeting standards in energy savings, water efficiency, carbon dioxide (CO_2) emissions reduction, improved indoor environmental quality (including air and natural light), and other categories.[5]

Robots

More and more manufacturers have freed workers from boring and sometimes dangerous jobs by replacing them with robots. A *robot* is a machine that can be programmed to perform tasks that require the repeated use of materials and tools. Robots can repeat the same tasks many times without changing their movements. Many factories use robots to stack their products on pallets and shrink-wrap them for shipping. Consolidated Technologies Inc. is located in Vaudreuil, Quebec, near Montreal. It produces robotic corrugated paper-box assemblers and product-packaging machines. One machine can assemble more than 120 cartons per minute. Another machine fills the cartons at a rate of 20 cases of products per minute. Both machines work much faster than humans.[6]

In the past, robots were most common in automotive and electronics manufacturing. Today, more and more industries are adding robots to their production lines. Because of improvements in technology, robots are now less expensive and more useful than they once were. Firms operate many different types of robots. The simplest is a pick-and-place robot. It moves in only two or three directions, picking up one item from one spot and placing it in another spot. So-called field robots assist people in nonmanufacturing, often dangerous, environments, such as nuclear power plants, the International Space Station, and even on battlefields. Police use remote-controlled robots to pick up and deal with suspected bombs. The same technology can also be used in factories. By using vision systems, infrared sensors, and bumpers on mobile platforms, robots can move parts or finished goods from one place to another. They can either follow or avoid people, whichever is needed to do the job. For example, machine vision systems are used for complex applications, such as quality assurance in the manufacturing of medical devices. Innovations in machine vision parts, such as cameras, lighting systems, and processors have greatly improved what these systems can do.

Computer-Aided Design and Manufacturing

Computer-aided design (CAD) is a process used by engineers to design parts and entire products on the computer. Engineers who use CAD can work faster and with fewer mistakes than those who use traditional drafting systems. An engineer can use an electronic pen to sketch three-dimensional (3-D) designs on an electronic drafting board or directly on the computer screen. The engineer can then use software tools to make major and minor design changes. The computer can also analyze the results for certain characteristics or problems. Engineers can put a new car design through a simulated road test to project its real-world performance. For example, if they find a problem with weight distribution, the necessary changes can be made virtually—without actually test-driving the car. With advanced CAD software, creating a prototype, or a trial model, is as much "virtual" as it is "hands-on." Actual prototypes or parts aren't built until the engineers are satisfied that the virtual designs are as perfect as they can be. Dentistry has also benefited from CAD, which can design and create, at the dentist's office, such products as caps and crowns that perfectly fit a patient's mouth or jaw.[7]

Remote-controlled robots are well suited for work in dangerous environments. This field robot was developed for use by bomb squads. It can photograph suspicious-looking devices, move them to a safer location, and then blow them up.

© Can Stock Photo Inc./bendicks

The process of **computer-aided manufacturing (CAM)** picks up where the CAD system leaves off. A manufacturer can use CAM to analyze the steps that a machine must take to produce a needed product or part. Electronic signals send instructions to the processing equipment to perform the needed production steps in the correct order. Both CAD and CAM technologies are now used together at most modern production facilities. These so-called CAD/CAM systems are linked electronically so they can automatically transfer computerized designs to the production facilities. These systems save both time and effort. They also allow firms to produce parts that need more precise manufacturing.

Flexible Manufacturing Systems

A **flexible manufacturing system (FMS)** is a production facility that workers can quickly change to manufacture different products. The typical system uses computer-controlled machining centres to produce metal parts, robots to handle the parts, and remote-controlled carts to deliver the materials. All steps of the process are linked by electronic controls that direct activities at each stage of manufacturing. The system can even replace broken or worn-out drill bits and other tools.

Flexible manufacturing systems have been improved by powerful new software that allows machine tools to be reprogrammed while they are running. This capability means that the same machine can make hundreds of different parts, and the operator doesn't need to shut the machine down to load each new program. The software also connects to the Internet to receive updates and to control machine tools at other sites. The software resides on a company's computer network. That means that engineers can use the software to locate production problems any time, from anywhere they can access the network. Nissan Motor Co. recently expanded its

computer-aided design (CAD) a process used by engineers to design parts and entire products on the computer. Engineers who use CAD can work faster and with fewer mistakes than those who use traditional drafting systems.

computer-aided manufacturing (CAM) a computer tool that a manufacturer uses to analyze CAD output and the steps that a machine must take to produce a needed product or part.

flexible manufacturing system (FMS) a production facility that workers can quickly change to manufacture different products.

computer-integrated manufacturing (CIM) an integrated production system that uses computers to help workers design products, control machines, handle materials, and control the production function.

✓ ASSESSMENT CHECK

10.3.1 List some of the reasons businesses invest in robots.

10.3.2 What is a flexible manufacturing system (FMS)?

10.3.3 What are the major benefits of computer-integrated manufacturing (CIM)?

flexible manufacturing system to join its plants in emerging markets, including China, Thailand, and India. In general, Nissan's expanded FMS cuts its new-vehicle lead time and investment in half. But the new system is not without its flaws that will take time to work out.[8]

Computer-Integrated Manufacturing

Companies use robots, CAD/CAM, FMS, computers, and other technologies together to apply **computer-integrated manufacturing (CIM)**. This integrated production system uses computers to help workers design products, control machines, handle materials, and control the production function. This type of manufacturing does not always lead to more automation and fewer people than other options. But it does involve a new type of automation that is organized around the computer. The key to CIM is a centralized computer system running software that integrates and controls separate processes and functions. The advantages of CIM include increased productivity, decreased design costs, increased equipment utilization, and improved quality.

CIM is widely used in the printing industry to coordinate thousands of printing jobs, some very small. CIM saves money by combining many small jobs into one larger job and by automating the printing process from design to delivery. Global printing company Manroland uses CIM to provide printing solutions for its business customers. One of its products, PRINTVALUE, offers a complete line of solutions for every aspect of a pressroom.[9]

LO 10.4 Identify the factors involved in a plant location decision.

THE LOCATION DECISION

The decision of where to locate a production facility depends on transportation, human, and physical factors, as shown in Table 10.1. Transportation factors include the closeness to markets and raw materials and the availability of transportation options for both inputs and outputs. Automobile assembly plants are usually located near major rail lines. Inputs—such as engines, plastics, and metal parts—arrive by rail, and the finished vehicles are shipped out by rail. Shopping malls are often located next to major streets and freeways in suburban areas because most shoppers arrive by car.

Table 10.1 Factors in the Location Decision

LOCATION FACTOR	EXAMPLES OF AFFECTED BUSINESSES
Transportation	
Closeness to markets	Baking companies and manufacturers of other perishable products, dry cleaners, hotels, other services
Closeness to raw materials	Paper mills
Availability of transportation options	Brick manufacturers, retail stores
Physical Factors	
Water supply	Computer chip fabrication plants
Energy	Aluminum, chemical, and fertilizer manufacturers
Hazardous wastes	All businesses
Human Factors	
Labour supply	Auto manufacturers, software developers
Local zoning regulations	Manufacturing and distribution companies
Community living conditions	All businesses
Taxes	All businesses

Physical variables include such issues as weather, water supplies, available energy, and options for disposing of hazardous waste. Theme parks, such as Walt Disney World, are often located in warm climates so they can attract visitors year-round. A manufacturing business that wants to locate near a community must prepare an *environmental impact study*. This study analyzes how a proposed plant will affect the quality of life in the surrounding area. Regulatory agencies usually need these studies to report on the impact on transportation facilities; energy requirements; water and sewage treatment needs; the effects on natural plant life and wildlife; and any possible water, air, and noise pollution.

Deciding where to locate a production facility can often depend on the weather. Some theme parks, such as Walt Disney World, are located in warm climates so they can attract visitors year-round.

Human factors in the location decision include an area's labour supply, local regulations, taxes, and living conditions. Management considers local labour costs and the availability of workers with the needed qualifications. Software makers and other computer-related firms concentrate in areas that have the technical talent they need, including California's Silicon Valley, Boston, Toronto, Montreal, and Austin, Texas. By contrast, some labour-intensive industries have located their plants in rural areas, where there is readily available labour and few other high-wage jobs. Some firms that have headquarters in Canada, the United States, and other industrialized countries have moved their production off-shore in search of low wages. But no matter what type of industry a firm is in, when deciding on a location, a production and operations manager must consider the following factors:

- Closeness to suppliers, warehouses, and service operations

- Costs of insurance and taxes

- Availability of employee needs such as housing, schools, mass transportation, day care, shopping, and recreational facilities

- Size, skills, and costs of the local labour force

- Enough space for current and future needs of the firm

- Distance to the market for goods

- Receptiveness of the community

- Economical transportation for incoming materials and supplies and for outgoing finished goods

- Climate and environment that matches the industry's needs and employees' lifestyle
- Amount and cost of energy services
- Government incentives

A recent trend in location strategy is bringing production facilities closer to the final markets where the goods will be sold. One reason is the reduced time and cost for shipping. Another reason is a closer cultural relationship between the parent company and the supplier (in cases where production remains overseas). This trend has led some business developers to label Central America "the new Asia."[10] German automaker Volkswagen decided to build a $1-billion manufacturing plant in North America to make its new midsize sedan. Volkswagen expects to roll 150,000 vehicles out of the plant each year. The plant site includes the possibility of a major expansion that would further increase production capacity. CEO Stefan Jacoby notes that the plant is part of Volkswagen's overall strategy for capturing more of the North American auto market.[11]

Governments sometimes offer incentives to businesses that are willing to locate in their region. These incentives may take the form of tax breaks, agreements to improve infrastructure, and similar activities. Sometimes, location is all about bringing the right people together in the centre of the action. The "Hit & Miss" feature describes how Toyota's engineering team designs and produces new Formula One racing cars each year in its facility in Germany.

✓ **ASSESSMENT CHECK**

10.4.1 How does an environmental impact study affect the location decision?

10.4.2 What human factors contribute to the location decision?

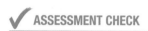

HIT & MISS

Toyota Uses Its Own Formula to Build F1 Cars

In a factory in Cologne, Germany, a scale-model Formula One (F1) race car buzzes around a track. Engineers in white coats assemble a monocoque, the load-supporting shell that makes cars stronger and less expensive. A machine tests an engine to its limits. Toyota is using its well-known team approach to manufacture open-wheel racers from start to finish.

Most carmakers build their F1 racers in several factories; only Ferrari and Toyota build them in one place. In Cologne, Toyota's 650-member team of engineers, designers, drivers, and mechanics use the latest technology and materials—from aerodynamics, lighter materials, and fuel efficiency—to produce a better, faster car. Each F1 car is unique. With careful attention to detail and accuracy, engineers follow a vehicle through every stage of the production process. Half-scale models are made from carbon fibre, aluminum, and other components produced by laser-guided machines. These models are tested in wind tunnels, where the floors move at the same speed as the wind to create conditions found on any of the world's tracks. Machines can create any race condition, such as the humidity and temperature on a tropical circuit at the Malaysian Grand Prix. They can even duplicate a specific race.

The models aren't the only fast-moving items on the factory floor. The production team also races to get new cars ready for each season. Except for the monocoque, car parts change with lightning speed. Seventy percent of parts are changed throughout a season, and 95 percent of parts are new each year. Sometimes, the F1 racing regulations are revised. New regulations can lead to big design changes, such as doing away with traction-control systems that control power to the rear wheels to avoid wheel spin. In response, the

Toyota team built a more aerodynamic car to correct any instability. To meet other regulations, Toyota altered the F1 car's design to reduce the dangerously high G-forces drivers experience during a race, especially during cornering.

Speed and reaction time are crucial during production. Most F1 carmakers depend on one strong leader to make decisions, but not Toyota. It uses the team-management system it perfected in its other auto factories. Says Tadashi Yamashina, manager of the Cologne facility, "We encourage teamwork and always have our minds set on *kaizen*," the Japanese term for continuous improvement. He redesigned the teams, putting one manager in charge of the chassis and one in charge of the engine. He also opened the lines of communication so that all team members can share their expertise. As in all Toyota plants, everyone is encouraged to recommend solutions. And everyone is empowered to stop assembly if a problem is found. Some industry observers say the Toyota manufacturing style is too slow for F1 racing. Yamashina believes the principles that helped Toyota grow to a global power will work in building a F1 car. He admits that results have not come as quickly as he would like but he has no plans to change. After all, it took Toyota years to benefit fully from its production system.

Questions for Critical Thinking

1. What are the upsides and downsides to producing a Formula One race car in one location?

2. Why is F1 production a challenge for the Toyota management system?

Sources: "Traction in Action: Life without Traction Control," Toyota F1 Team site, http://www.toyota-f1.com, accessed March 31, 2008; John Murphy, "Will Toyota's Way Win on the Track?" *Wall Street Journal*, March 14, 2008, p. B1; Heath Reidy, "Ready for the Off," *Professional Engineering*, December 12, 2007, pp. 27–28.

THE JOB OF PRODUCTION MANAGERS

LO 10.5 Explain the major tasks of production and operations managers, and outline the three activities involved in carrying out the production plan.

Production and operations managers supervise the work of people and machinery to convert inputs (materials and resources) into finished goods and services. As Figure 10.3 shows, these managers perform four major tasks.

1. Planning the overall production process.

2. Selecting the best layout for the firm's facilities.

3. Carrying out the production plan.

4. Controlling the manufacturing process to maintain the highest possible quality.

Part of the control process involves continuous assessment of the results. If problems occur, managers return to the first step and make adjustments.

PRODUCTION MANAGEMENT TASKS

Planning the Production Process → Selecting the Most Appropriate Layout → Carrying Out the Production Plan → Controlling the Production Process

FIGURE 10.3 Tasks of Production Managers

Planning the Production Process

Production planning begins by choosing the goods or services to offer to customers. This decision is the essence, or core, of every company's reason for operating. Other decisions follow product planning, such as machinery purchases, pricing decisions, and selection of retail outlets. In product planning, it's not enough to plan products that satisfy customers. Products must satisfy customers *and* be produced as efficiently and inexpensively as possible. Market research is used to gather consumer reactions to proposed products. It is also used to estimate potential sales and profitability. Production departments focus on planning the production process in two ways: (1) by converting original product ideas into final specifications and (2) by designing the most efficient facilities to produce those products.

Production managers need to understand how a project fits into the company's structure because it can affect the success of the project. In a traditional manufacturing organization, each production manager has a specific area of authority and responsibility, such as purchasing or inventory control. One downside to this structure is that it may actually mean that the purchasing manager will compete against the inventory control manager. More organizations have moved toward team-oriented structures. Some organizations assign team members to specific projects, with all team members reporting to the production manager. Each team is responsible for the quality of its products and has the authority to make changes to improve performance and quality. The two approaches have two major differences: all workers on teams are responsible for their output, and teamwork avoids the competitiveness between managers often found in traditional structures.

Selecting the Facility Layout

The next production management task is selecting the best layout for the facility. An efficient facility layout can reduce material handling, decrease costs, and improve product flow through the facility. This decision requires managers to consider all phases of production and the inputs needed at each step. Figure 10.4 shows three common layout designs: process, product, and

(A) Process Layout

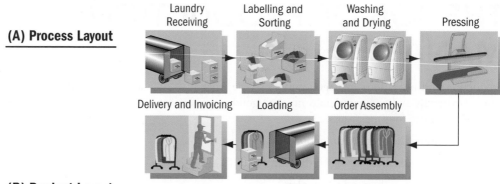

Laundry Receiving   Labelling and Sorting   Washing and Drying   Pressing

Delivery and Invoicing   Loading   Order Assembly

(B) Product Layout

(C) Fixed-Position Layout

Material Storage 1   Material Storage 2   Material Storage 3

Subcontractor A

Subcontractor B

Subcontractor C

Machine Group 1   Machine Group 2   Machine Group 3

Employee Group 1

Employee Group 2

Employee Group 3

(D) Customer-Oriented Layout

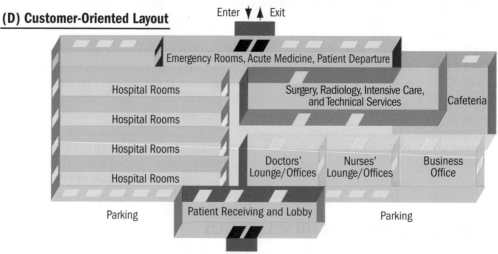

Enter ▼ ▲ Exit

Emergency Rooms, Acute Medicine, Patient Departure

Hospital Rooms

Hospital Rooms

Surgery, Radiology, Intensive Care, and Technical Services

Cafeteria

Hospital Rooms

Hospital Rooms

Doctors' Lounge/Offices

Nurses' Lounge/Offices

Business Office

Parking

Patient Receiving and Lobby

Parking

Exit ▼ ▲ Enter

FIGURE 10.4 Basic Facility Layouts

fixed-position layouts. It also shows a customer-oriented layout typical of service providers' production systems.

A *process layout* groups machinery and equipment according to their functions. The work in process moves around the plant to reach different workstations. A process layout often makes it easier to produce a variety of nonstandard items in relatively small batches.

Its purpose is to process goods and services that have a variety of functions. For example, a typical machine shop has separate departments where machines are grouped by functions such as grinding, drilling, pressing, and lathing. *Process layouts* can suit a variety of production functions and use general-purpose equipment that can be less costly than specialized equipment to purchase and maintain.

A *product layout*, also called an assembly line, sets up production equipment along a product-flow line. The work in process moves along this line past workstations. This type of layout efficiently produces large numbers of similar items, but it may be inflexible, with room for only a few product variations. Although product layouts date back at least to the Model T assembly line, companies are improving this approach with modern touches. Many auto manufacturers continue to use a product layout, but robots perform many of the activities that humans once did. Automation solves one of the major drawbacks of this system—unlike humans, robots don't get bored doing a dull, repetitive job. European automaker Holland Car Plc uses an assembly-line approach called complete knockdown (CKD). In this assembly line, all the auto parts are imported in pieces to be welded, painted, and assembled at its facility in Ethiopia.[12]

A *fixed-position layout* places the product in one spot. The workers, materials, and equipment go to the product's location. This approach suits very large, bulky, heavy, or fragile products. For example, a bridge cannot be built on an assembly line. Fixed-position layouts are in used in several industries, including construction, shipbuilding, aircraft and aerospace, and oil drilling. In all of these industries, the nature of the product generally dictates a fixed-position layout.

Service organizations must also decide on suitable layouts for their production processes. A service firm should arrange its facilities to enhance the interactions between customers and its services—also called a *customer-oriented layout*. If you think of patients as inputs, a hospital uses a form of the process layout. Banks, libraries, dental offices, and hair salons also use process layouts. Sometimes the details surrounding a service require a fixed-position layout. For example, doctors, nurses, and medical devices are brought to patients in a hospital emergency room.

Carrying Out the Production Plan

After production managers plan the production process and select the best layout, the next task is to carry out the production plan. This activity involves (1) deciding whether to make, buy, or lease products or parts; (2) selecting the best suppliers for materials; and (3) controlling inventory to keep enough supplies in stock, but not too much.

Make, Buy, or Lease Decision

Every producer faces a **make, buy, or lease decision**—whether to manufacture a product or part in-house, buy it from an outside supplier, or lease it. This decision is critical in many contemporary business situations.

Several factors affect the make, buy, or lease decision, including the costs of leasing or purchasing parts from outside suppliers compared with the costs of producing the parts in-house. The decision sometimes depends on whether outside suppliers can meet a firm's standards for quality and quantity. The decision may also be affected by the need for confidentiality and whether the firm needs the supplies for a short or long period of time. A firm might not have the technology to produce certain parts or materials, or the technology might be too costly. Goodyear Tire & Rubber Co. has teamed up with Genencor, an industrial biotechnology firm. Together, they are developing a cleaner alternative to the synthetic rubber used as the raw material in many tires. The "Hit & Miss" feature describes how this alliance is contributing to the tires of the future.

When a firm decides to buy goods from outside suppliers, production managers should still keep a relationship going with other supply sources. Having an alternative supplier means that the firm can get the materials it needs even during strikes or when quality-assurance problems

make, buy, or lease decision choosing whether to manufacture a product or part in-house, buy it from an outside supplier, or lease it.

HIT & MISS

Goodyear Tire & Genencor: A Sweet Alliance

For many years, tire manufacturers like Goodyear have added synthetic rubber to the natural rubber used to make truck and automobile tires. Synthetic rubber is made using a chemical called isoprene. It is a volatile, toxic hydrocarbon that is a by-product from refining crude oil. Isoprene is bad for the environment, and producing it requires a supply of crude oil for refining. Until recently, there wasn't any real alternative—Goodyear still needed to purchase its raw materials to manufacture its tires, including the isoprene-based synthetic rubber. But researchers at Genencor, an industrial biotechnology firm based in Rochester, New York, have come up with the answer. This firm has figured out how to produce synthetic rubber from sugar instead of using refined oil waste. Goodyear believes so much in this solution it has decided to work with Genencor to develop the new product.

"An intensive search has been underway for years for alternative sources of isoprene, in particular those from renewable resources such as biomass," explains John McAuliffe, a scientist with Genencor. His company has developed a method that involves fermenting sugar cane, corn, corn cobs, and switch grass to create a new product called Biolsoprene™. This new product will become the basis for synthetic rubber in the next few years. Goodyear makes 200 million tires every year. It has been one of the world's largest users of isoprene—so the conversion to Genencor's Biolsoprene™ will have wide effects.

"We want to make biochemicals from renewable materials," notes McAuliffe, "partially as a hedge against rising crude oil prices and much more so because this approach moves us to a more sustainable future." Genencor has made its first delivery of Biolsoprene™ to Goodyear for use in its manufacturing process. As a result, greener tires will hit the road soon. Both firms see their working together as a win–win for everyone, including consumers. "We believe it's important to look at alternative renewable raw materials in our production processes," says Jesse Roeck of Goodyear. "We chose to work with Genencor based on our strategy of open innovation because they are one of the leaders in industrial biotechnology."

Questions for Critical Thinking

1. Describe the benefits of creating a research relationship with a supplier for future raw materials or supplies.

2. Planning is needed before investing in a future with a supplier. How can this decision affect other aspects of the production process?

Sources: "Revolutionary Technology Promises Green Tires for a More Sustainable Future," *Clean Technology,* March 31, 2010, http://www.azocleantech.com; "Genencor and Goodyear Partnering on Process to Develop Biolsoprene from Sugars," *Green Car Congress,* March 25, 2010, http://www.greencarcongress.com; "On the Road to Sweet Tires Made with a More Sustainable Process," *Physorg.com,* March 24, 2010, http://www.physorg.com; "Biolsoprene™ Product Begins Flowing from Genencor to Goodyear," *Auto Channel,* March 9, 2010, http://www.theautochannel.com.

or other situations affect the inputs. Outsourcing has its downsides, too. Companies say the main reason they use outsourcing is to reduce costs and focus on their core business activities. But outsourcing can also lead to layoffs and a decrease in the quality of the firm's outputs.[13]

Selection of Suppliers

After a company decides what inputs to buy, it must choose the best suppliers for its needs. To make this choice, production managers compare several factors: quality, prices, dependability of delivery, and services offered by competing companies. Different suppliers may offer the same quality and the same prices. The final decision often depends on the firm's past experience with each supplier, speed of delivery, warranties on purchases, and other services.

When a firm is planning for a major purchase, negotiations with suppliers may take several weeks or months. The buying decision may need several managers to look at all the options before the final selection is made. For example, the selection of a supplier for an industrial drill press may require a joint decision by the production, engineering, purchasing, and quality-control departments. These departments often must sort out their different views before they agree on a purchasing decision.

The Internet provides powerful tools for finding and comparing suppliers. Buyers can log on to business exchanges to compare specifications, prices, and availability. Ariba offers online software and other tools that organizations can use to source $120-billion worth of goods and services from suppliers around the world.[14]

Firms often purchase raw materials and parts on long-term contracts. If a manufacturer needs a continuous supply of materials, a one-year or two-year contract with a supplier can ensure availability. Today, many firms build long-term relationships with suppliers and reduce the number of companies they deal with. At the same time, many organizations ask their suppliers to expand their roles in the production process.

BUSINESS ETIQUETTE

Making the Most of Business Meetings

Some people love business meetings because they are a nice change from boring tasks. Others find meetings to be tiresome disruptions from more important work they need to do. But business meetings are sometimes necessary. You might enjoy meetings more if you look at how they can help you to build your career. Think of all meetings—including staff meetings, sales meetings, appointments with customers, and conferences with colleagues—as part of your overall networking strategy. Use these tips to make the most of your next business meeting:

- *Be on time.* Being on time shows that you value your own time and that of others. It also shows that you take the meeting seriously.

- *Turn off your cellphone and any other electronic devices.* Unless you are a doctor on call for emergencies, keep your cellphone turned off. Beeps and ringtones can distract others. They also show that your attention is elsewhere.

- *Pay attention.* Listen actively to what others are saying. Take notes when it is suitable.

- *Participate.* Ask questions and make brief points when appropriate. Stay on the subject. Avoid controlling a discussion.

- *Conduct yourself professionally.* Be polite to others at the meeting. Thank the others for their time at the end of the meeting.

- *Exchange business cards.* At the end of the meeting, exchange business cards or contact information with others that you may want to contact later.

Sources: Karyn Hill, "Business Meeting Etiquette—5 Essential Tips," *Business Coach Site,* http://www.bellaonline.com, accessed April 26, 2010; Donna Reynolds, "Practice Business Meeting Etiquette," *How To Do Things,* http://www.howtodothings.com, accessed April 26, 2010; Shaun Mangan, "7 Tips for More Effective Business Meetings," *Ezine Articles,* http://ezinearticles.com, accessed April 26, 2010.

Production managers use networking to learn about suppliers and to get to know them personally. Managers also meet suppliers, competitors, and colleagues at trade shows, conferences, and seminars, and other meetings. The "Business Etiquette" feature provides tips for making the most of these meetings.

Inventory Control

Production and operations managers are responsible for **inventory control**. They need to balance the costs of storing inventory with the need to have stock on hand to meet demand. Several costs are involved in storing inventory: warehousing costs, taxes, insurance, and maintenance. Firms waste money if they store more inventory than they need. But having too little inventory may lead to a shortage of raw materials, parts, or goods that can be sold. The outcome can be delays and unhappy customers.

Firms lose business when they keep missing promised delivery dates or turn away orders. When farmer Jay Armstrong ordered a combine attachment—just as his family had done for 50 years—the dealer told Armstrong he wouldn't receive the equipment until August, when the farm's growing season would nearly be over. Armstrong was forced to make his purchase from a competitor, who promised delivery in May.[15]

Efficient inventory control can save money. Many firms use *perpetual inventory* systems to continuously assess the amount of their stock and where it is stored. These inventory control systems usually rely on computers, and many automatically generate orders when stock is low. Many grocery stores link their scanning devices to perpetual inventory systems that reorder goods without the need for a human. When the system records a shopper's purchase, it reduces the inventory count stored in the computer. When inventory drops to a certain level, the system automatically reorders the merchandise. Canada's largest supermarket chain, Loblaws, uses a software system designed by SAP. The network of more than 1,000 corporate and franchised Loblaws stores use the SAP system to manage stock. The system is responsible for ordering and receiving inventory. It also counts and selects inventory in the stockrooms. The software can update and confirm the perpetual inventory balances.[16]

inventory control a function that balances the costs of storing inventory with the need to have stock on hand to meet demand.

JIT systems are being used in a wide range of industries, including the medical supplies field.

Some companies hand over their inventory control functions to suppliers. This concept is known as *vendor-managed inventory*. At Dell Computer assembly plants, almost all the parts suppliers also handle Dell's inventory control functions.

Just-in-Time Systems

A **just-in-time (JIT) system** is based on a broad management philosophy that reaches beyond the narrow activity of inventory control. A JIT system affects all production and operations management. A JIT system tries to use only items that add value to operations activities. It does this by providing the right part at the right place at just the right time—just before it is needed in production.

JIT systems are used in a wide range of industries, including the medical supplies field. Hospitals can use a JIT system to manage the distribution of supplies, equipment, and clinical materials. Hospitals partner with their key distributors to keep an inventory of certain emergency supplies on hand. Other supplies are distributed on a JIT basis, which saves time and money.[17]

Production that uses a JIT system shifts most of the responsibility for carrying inventory to suppliers. The suppliers use forecasts to decide how much inventory to carry. They keep stock on hand to respond to manufacturers' needs. When suppliers do not keep enough high-quality parts on hand, the purchasers may hand them penalties. When manufacturers underestimate demand for a product, the JIT system may have trouble adapting. Strong demand can overtax JIT systems. Suppliers and their customers may struggle to keep up with orders without having an inventory of goods to meet the extra demand.

Materials Requirement Planning

Effective inventory control requires efficiency. It also needs careful planning to ensure the firm has all the inputs it needs to make its products. How do production and operations managers work through all of this information? They use **materials requirement planning (MRP)**, a computer-based production planning system that ensures a firm has all the parts and materials it needs to produce its output at the right time and place and in the right amounts.

Production managers use MRP programs to create schedules that list the specific parts and materials needed to produce an item. These schedules show the exact quantities needed. They also show the dates to order those quantities from suppliers so that they will be delivered at the correct time in the production cycle. A small company might get by without an MRP system. If a firm makes a simple product with only a few parts, a production manager can phone in an order for an overnight delivery of crucial parts. But for a complex product, such as a high-definition TV or aircraft, longer lead times are needed.

The Allan Candy Company is a large Canadian candy manufacturer. It uses MRP software from Microsoft to streamline and integrate all of its processes. The software figures out which materials are needed and automatically generates the purchase orders. CEO Steven Dakowsky believes this system gives his firm a competitive edge in the candy market. "I believe in the power of technology and that it is a differentiating factor, especially for companies our size," he says. "So, for me, it is critically important that we are ahead of the game."[18]

just-in-time (JIT) system a broad management philosophy that reaches beyond the narrow activity of inventory control to affect the entire system of production and operations management.

materials requirement planning (MRP) a computer-based production planning system that ensures a firm has all the parts and materials it needs to produce its output at the right time and place and in the right amounts.

✔ ASSESSMENT CHECK

10.5.1 List the four major tasks of production and operations managers.

10.5.2 What is the difference between a traditional manufacturing structure and a team-based structure?

10.5.3 What factors affect the make, buy, or lease decision?

CONTROLLING THE PRODUCTION PROCESS

LO 10.6 Identify the steps in the production control process.

The final task of production and operations managers is controlling the production process to maintain the highest possible quality. **Production control** creates well-defined procedures for coordinating people, materials, and machinery to provide the greatest production efficiency. Suppose that a watch factory must produce 80,000 watches during October. Production control managers divide this total into a daily production assignment of 4,000 watches for each of the month's 20 working days. Next, they decide on the number of workers, raw materials, parts, and machines the plant needs to meet the production schedule. This work is much like the work of a manager in a service business such as a restaurant. A restaurant manager must estimate how many dinners will be served each day. The manager then decides what food to buy and how many people are needed to prepare and serve the food.

Figure 10.5 shows production control as a five-step process: planning, routing, scheduling, dispatching, and follow-up. These steps are part of the firm's overall emphasis on total quality management.

production control creating well-defined procedures for coordinating people, materials, and machinery to provide the greatest production efficiency.

FIGURE 10.5 Steps in Production Control

Production Planning

The first step of production control is *production planning*. In this step, managers decide on the amount of resources (including raw materials and other items) needed to produce a certain output. The production planning process leads to a list of all needed parts and materials. Purchasing staff can compare this list with the firm's perpetual inventory data to identify which items need to be purchased. Employees or automated systems set up the delivery schedules so the needed parts and materials will arrive when they are needed during the production process. Production planning also ensures the availability of needed machines and personnel. At the Wilson Sporting Goods Company factory in Ohio, there's a special excitement leading up to the Super Bowl each year. Workers there have made every football that has ever been used in a Super Bowl game. Each January, construction on the balls begins. The footballs are about 70 percent complete before the final playoff games are decided. When workers know which two team names will be printed on the balls, production speeds up. The plant makes about 120 official game balls and about 6,000 versions for sale to fans. "The market determines how many balls we will make," notes Gregory Miller, the plant controller.[19]

Material inputs contribute to service-production systems, but production planning for services tends to focus on human resources more than materials.

Routing

The second step of production control is *routing*. In this step, the manager decides on the sequence of work throughout the facility, who will perform each part of the work, and where the work will be done. Routing choices depend on two factors: the nature of the good or service and the facility layout. As discussed earlier in the chapter, the common layout designs are product, process, fixed-position, and customer-oriented layouts. Some routing decisions make sense, such as dipping an automobile body into a rust-proofing bath before painting it. Other decisions may need for more study. For example, what is the best sequence when mixing ingredients to make a salad dressing?

Even small service businesses, such as hair salons, use scheduling systems.

Scheduling

The next stage of production control is the *scheduling* phase. In this stage, managers develop timetables that show how long each operation in the production process takes and when workers should perform it. Efficient scheduling means that production will meet the delivery schedules and make efficient use of resources.

Scheduling is important whether the product is complex or simple to produce and whether it is a good or a service. A pencil is simpler to produce than a computer, but each production process has scheduling needs. A stylist may take 25 minutes to complete each haircut using just one or two tools, but every day a hospital schedules procedures and treatments, from X-rays to surgery to follow-up appointments. Sleepmaster is a medium-sized firm that recently moved some of its production from its Australian headquarters to China. But the company's MRP system had very little capacity for scheduling, and the workers in China did not know how to use the technology. Sleepmaster's operations manager set up a new scheduling program called Resource Manager. The new program is easier to use and organize, costs little to operate, and has support available via Skype.[20]

Production managers use several analytical methods for scheduling. One of the oldest methods is the *Gantt chart*. This method tracks projected and actual work progress over time. Many people use Gantt charts, like the one shown in Figure 10.6. One glance at the chart quickly shows the progress of any project. Gantt charts are most effective for scheduling simple projects.

A complex project might require a *PERT (program evaluation and review technique)* chart. This chart tries to reduce the number of delays by coordinating all parts of the production process. PERT was first developed for the military and has been adapted for use in industry. The simplified PERT diagram in Figure 10.7 shows the schedule for purchasing and installing a new robot. The heavy gold line indicates the *critical path*—the sequence of operations that requires the longest time for completion. In this case, the project cannot be completed in less than 17 weeks.

A PERT network may be made up of thousands of events and may take place over months of time. Complex computer programs help production managers to develop a PERT network and to find the critical path among all the events and activities. This type of complex production planning is needed when constructing a huge office building.

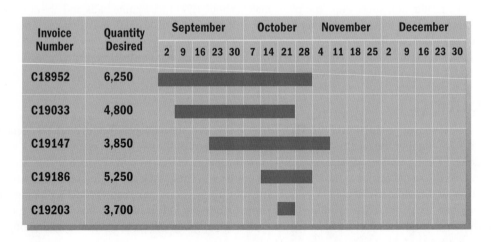

Invoice Number	Quantity Desired	September					October				November				December				
		2	9	16	23	30	7	14	21	28	4	11	18	25	2	9	16	23	30
C18952	6,250																		
C19033	4,800																		
C19147	3,850																		
C19186	5,250																		
C19203	3,700																		

FIGURE 10.6
Sample Gantt Chart

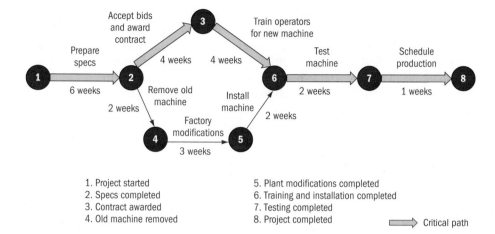

1. Project started
2. Specs completed
3. Contract awarded
4. Old machine removed
5. Plant modifications completed
6. Training and installation completed
7. Testing completed
8. Project completed

➡ Critical path

FIGURE 10.7
PERT Diagram for the Purchase and Installation of a New Robot

Dispatching

In the *dispatching* phase of production control, management instructs each department on the work it needs to do and how long it has to do the work. The dispatcher authorizes performance, provides instructions, and lists job priorities. Dispatching may be the responsibility of a manager or a self-managed work team.

Follow-Up

Sometimes even the best plans fail. That's why production managers need to be aware of any problems. In the *follow-up* phase of production control, managers and employees, or team members, spot problems in the production process and come up with solutions. Problems can take many forms: machinery malfunctions, delayed shipments, and absent employees can all affect production. The production control system must identify and report these delays to managers or work teams so they can adjust schedules and correct the underlying problems.

IMPORTANCE OF QUALITY

LO 10.7 Discuss the importance of quality control.

Next we look at quality in terms of the production of goods and services. In this sense, **quality** is defined as the state of being free of deficiencies or imperfections. Quality matters because it is costly to fix, replace, or redesign imperfect products. If Seagate makes a defective computer hard drive, it must either fix the drive or replace it to keep a customer happy. If Air Canada books too many passengers for a flight, it must offer vouchers worth several hundred dollars to encourage passengers to give up their seats and take a later flight.

For most companies, the costs of poor quality can add up to 20 percent or more of sales revenue. The costs of poor quality include downtime, repair costs, rework, and employee turnover. Low-quality goods and services can also result in lost sales and a poor company image. Facebook experienced a quality crisis when users were confused and upset about its new privacy settings. "Many of you thought our controls were too complex," wrote CEO Mark Zuckerberg in a letter to users. "Our intention was to give you lots of granular controls, but that may not have been what many of you wanted. We just missed the mark."[21]

Companies can use benchmarking to ensure that they always produce high-quality products. When a company uses **benchmarking**, it looks at how well other companies perform business functions or tasks and uses their performance as a standard for measuring its own performance. In other words, benchmarking is the process of comparing one firm's standards and practices to other firms' standards and best practices. Automobile companies routinely purchase each other's cars and then take them completely apart to examine and compare the design, components, and

quality the state of being free of deficiencies or imperfections.

benchmarking the process of looking at how well other companies perform business functions or tasks and using their performance as a standard for measuring another company's performance.

ASSESSMENT CHECK

10.6.1 What five steps are involved in controlling the production process?

10.6.2 What is the difference between a PERT chart and a Gantt chart?

materials used to make even the smallest part. These companies then make improvements to match or exceed the quality found in their competitors' cars. Companies may use many different benchmarks, depending on their objectives. For example, organizations that want to make more money may compare their operating profits or expenses to those of other firms. Retailers concerned with productivity may want to benchmark their sales per square metre.

When a firm is benchmarking, it needs to decide what it wants to accomplish, what it wants to measure, and which company can provide the most useful benchmarking information. A firm might choose a direct competitor for benchmarking, or it might choose a company in an entirely different industry that has processes the firm wants to study and copy.[22]

Quality Control

quality control measuring output against quality standards.

Quality control involves measuring output against quality standards. Firms use quality control to spot defective or imperfect products and to avoid delivering poor-quality goods to customers. Quality standards should be set high enough to meet customer expectations. A 90 or 95 percent success rate might seem to be good, but would you want your phone service or Internet network to work only 90 percent of the time? You would likely feel frustrated, and you would probably switch your phone service or your Internet service provider.

Manufacturing firms can check on quality levels by using visual inspections, electronic sensors, robots, and X-rays. Service organizations can gather quality-control information from surveys. Negative feedback from customers or a high rejection rate on a product or part may mean that production is not meeting quality standards. Firms that outsource their operations face a greater challenge in checking on quality levels. They also have a tougher time assuring customers of the quality of their goods or services, especially when they are highly visible companies, such as airlines. The "Solving an Ethical Controversy" feature discusses the quality of multivitamins manufactured in China for North American companies.

A typical factory can spend up to half its operating budget identifying and fixing mistakes. That means that a company should not rely just on inspections to meet its quality goals. Instead, production managers should identify all processes involved in producing goods and services and then work to increase the efficiency of these processes. They need to find and correct the causes of problems in the processes. A company needs to focus its efforts on better designs of products and processes and to set clear quality targets. These efforts can lead to higher-quality, error-free production.

The Six Sigma concept to achieving quality goals is used by more and more large organizations, including Rogers Communications, the Ontario Lottery and Gaming Corporation, General Electric, Heinz, 3M, and Sears. When a company uses *Six Sigma*, it tries to make error-free products 99.9997 percent of the time. That means it is allowed to make only 3.4 errors for every 1 million opportunities. The goal of Six Sigma programs is for companies to eliminate nearly all defects in output, processes, and transactions.[23]

ISO Standards

International Organization for Standardization (ISO) an international organization whose mission is to develop and promote international standards for business, government, and society. The aim is to improve and encourage global trade and cooperation.

For many organizations, an important measure of quality is being able to meet the standards of the **International Organization for Standardization**, known as **ISO** for short. ISO doesn't stand for anything; that is, it is not an acronym but is a shorter name from the Greek word *isos*, meaning "equal." ISO started in 1947 and is a network of national standards bodies from 163 countries. Its mission is to develop and promote international standards for business, government, and society. The aim is to improve and encourage global trade and cooperation. ISO has developed voluntary standards for all sorts of tasks, from the format of banking and telephone cards to freight containers to paper sizes to metric screw threads. The Standards Council of Canada (SCC) is the Canadian member body, and the American National Standards Institute is the U.S. member. Canadian firms typically deal with both bodies.

The ISO 9000 standards help organizations to ensure that their products and services (1) are of high quality and (2) provide a basis for continual improvement. The ISO 14000 standards for environmental management help organizations to ensure that their operations (1) cause as

---

SOLVING AN **ETHICAL** CONTROVERSY

Multivitamins Produced in China: Are Stricter Quality Controls Needed?

The news is filled with Chinese manufacturing and its quality control issues. We have heard about contaminated, or tainted, pet food and baby food and the harmful paint used on children's toys. Now it's multivitamins, which may contain dangerous levels of lead and toxic bacteria—and are showing up in North American stores. Some people have called for stricter quality standards. Some vitamin firms have decided to source their ingredients elsewhere. One firm offers Opurity, a new premium multivitamin. Its ingredients come from other countries, and the bottle is labelled "China Free."

Should Chinese manufacturers need to meet stricter quality controls for goods made for North American markets?

PRO

1. According to the Chinese Ministry of Commerce, 85 percent of Chinese citizens rank their quality concerns as high for food and drugs made in their own country. Tighter controls would benefit North American and European consumers—and Chinese consumers.

2. Vitamins that are labelled "Made in Germany" or "Made in Canada" might still contain ingredients from China. Because Chinese-made vitamin products have been shown to contain high levels of toxic substances, tighter quality controls are needed.

CON

1. Many vitamins contain ingredients from more than one source, so it is impossible to say that China is the only source of contamination.

2. Chinese production offers companies good value. Chinese labour and other services are far less costly than in other countries. These savings can be passed on to the consumer in the form of lower prices.

Summary

A former senior official at the U.S. Food & Drug Administration (FDA) says that the FDA doesn't have enough inspectors to catch all the quality violations. That means that the incidence of contamination may be much higher than we think. At the very least, consumers should know the origin of ingredients in multivitamins. They can then decide which vitamins to buy. Those who don't want to buy ingredients sourced from China can choose products like Opurity.

Sources: "New Multivitamins Target Concern Over China's Quality Problems," *EIN,* April 27, 2010, http://www.einpresswire.com; "China Outsourcing: A Benefit to Companies Worldwide," *New Articles,* April 27, 2010, http://newarticles.co.tv; Kimberly Palmer, "Explaining China's Quality Control Problems," *U.S. News & World Report,* April 23, 2009, http://www.usnews.com.

---

little harm as possible to the environment and (2) continually improve their environmental performance.

ISO 9001:2008 and ISO 14001:2004 respectively give the requirements for a quality management system and an environmental management system. Both can be used for certification. An organization gains certification when its management system (the way it manages its processes) is independently audited by a certification body (also known in North America as a registration body, or registrar) and is confirmed as meeting the requirements of the standard. The organization is then issued with an ISO 9001:2008 or an ISO 14001:2004 certificate.

Certification is not a requirement of either standard. An organization can follow ISO standards to gain benefits for the organization and its customers—without certification. But many organizations want to be certified because many managers, consumers, and shareholders see an independent audit as adding confidence to a firm's abilities. Business partners, customers, suppliers, and shareholders may prefer to deal with certified organizations. Certifications need to be renewed every few years, which means audits are also needed every few years.

Many consumers prefer to buy from companies that are ISO-certified.

The Canadian Press/Stephen C. Host

The ISO itself develops standards but does not carry out the auditing and certification. These tasks are done independently of ISO by hundreds of certification organizations around the world. The certificates they issue carry their own logo, not that of the ISO because the ISO does not approve or control the activities of the certification organizations.

Many organizations report significant benefits from using ISO's management system standards, such as increased efficiency, better teamwork, improved customer satisfaction, and reduced consumption of resources.[24]

WHAT'S AHEAD

Maintaining high quality is an important part of satisfying customers. The business function of marketing also has the objectives of product quality and customer satisfaction. The next part consists of three chapters that explore the many activities involved in customer-driven marketing. These activities include product development, distribution, promotion, and pricing.

RETURN TO INSIDE BUSINESS

The World Cup Gets a Kick Out of Jabulani

The introduction of Jabulani was not the first time that a soccer ball design has been reworked. In 2006, a new design led to a new surface on the ball. But players complained about the irregular ball movement. They said the new design was wobbly, unstable in flight, and made the goalie's job of blocking the ball even more difficult. In response, Adidas reduced the number of panels to eight and gave the surface aerodynamic ridges to help it move through the air. But laboratory testing by the National Aeronautics and Space Administration (NASA) showed that players would not find any greater control using the newest ball design.

"It's quite obvious. You're seeing a knuckle-ball effect," said Rabi Mehta, an aerospace engineer involved in the testing. Mehta explained that when a relatively smooth ball with seams flies through the air without much spin, the air close to the surface is affected by the seams, producing an unbalanced flow. This imbalance creates side forces that can suddenly push the ball in one direction and cause sharp swerves and swoops.

Mehta believes that the Jabulani ball will tend to knuckle at 70 to 80 kilometres per hour, which is the speed of the ball during a free-kick around the goal area.[25]

QUESTIONS FOR CRITICAL THINKING

1. From a design point of view, what sort of ball should Adidas try to engineer?

2. How important is the look of the soccer ball?

SUMMARY OF LEARNING OBJECTIVES

LO 10.1 Explain the strategic importance of the production function.

Production and operations management is a vital business function. A company needs a quality good or service to create profits; otherwise, it soon fails. The production process is also important in not-for-profit organizations. These organizations offer goods or services that are tied to why they exist. Production and operations management plays an important strategic role. It can lower the costs of production, increase output quality, and allow the firm to respond flexibly and dependably to customers' demands.

✓ ASSESSMENT CHECK ANSWERS

10.1.1 What is mass production? Mass production is a system for manufacturing products in large quantities by using effective combinations of mechanization, standardization, and employees with specialized skills.

10.1.2 What is the difference between flexible production and customer-driven production? Flexible production generally involves using three resources: information technology to receive and share orders, programmable equipment to fill the orders, and skilled people to carry out tasks needed to complete an order. Customer-driven production assesses customer demands to make a connection between the products that are manufactured and the products people want to buy.

LO 10.2 Identify and describe the four main categories of production processes.

The four main categories of production processes are the analytic production system, the synthetic production system, the continuous production process, and the intermittent production process. The analytic production system reduces a raw material to its component, or individual, parts to extract one or more marketable products. The synthetic production system combines two or more raw materials or parts to produce finished products. The continuous production process creates finished products over a long period of time. The intermittent production process creates products in short production runs.

✓ ASSESSMENT CHECK ANSWERS

10.2.1 What are the two main production systems? The two main production systems are analytic production and synthetic production. An analytic production system reduces a raw material to its component, or individual, parts to extract one or more marketable products. A synthetic production system combines two or more raw materials or parts, or transforms raw materials, to produce finished products.

10.2.2 What are the two time-related production processes? The two time-related production processes are the continuous production process and the intermittent production process. The continuous production process creates finished products over a long period of time. The intermittent production process creates products in short production runs.

LO 10.3 Explain the role of technology in the production process.

Computer-driven automation allows companies to design, create, and adapt products quickly. Companies can also produce products in ways that meet customers' changing needs. Important design and production technologies include robots, computer-aided design (CAD), computer-aided manufacturing (CAM), and computer-integrated manufacturing (CIM). Many manufacturing firms invest resources into developing processes that result in less waste, lower energy use, and little or no pollution.

 ASSESSMENT CHECK ANSWERS

10.3.1 List some of the reasons businesses invest in robots. Businesses use robots to free workers from sometimes dangerous jobs and to move heavy items from one place to another in a factory.

10.3.2 What is a flexible manufacturing system (FMS)? An FMS is a production facility that workers can quickly change to manufacture different products.

10.3.3 What are the major benefits of computer-integrated manufacturing (CIM)? The main benefits are increased productivity, decreased design costs, increased equipment utilization, and improved quality.

LO 10.4 Identify the factors involved in a plant location decision.

The factors for choosing the best site for a production facility fall into three categories: transportation, human, and physical factors. Transportation factors include the availability of transportation options and the closeness to markets and raw materials. Physical variables involve such issues as water supply, available energy, and options for disposing of hazardous wastes. Human factors include the area's labour supply, local regulations, taxes, and living conditions.

 ASSESSMENT CHECK ANSWERS

10.4.1 How does an environmental impact study affect the location decision? An environmental impact study analyzes how a proposed plant will affect the quality of life in the surrounding area. The study reports on how transportation, energy use, water and sewer treatment needs, and other factors will affect plants, wildlife, water, air, and other features of the natural environment.

10.4.2 What human factors contribute to the location decision? Human factors in the location decision include an area's labour supply, labour costs, local regulations, taxes, and living conditions.

LO 10.5 Explain the major tasks of production and operations managers, and outline the three activities involved in carrying out the production plan.

Production and operations managers use people and machinery to convert inputs (materials and resources) into finished goods and services. Four major tasks are involved. First, the managers must plan the overall production process. Next, they must select the best layout for their facilities. Then they carry out their production plans. Finally, they control the production process and assess the results to maintain the highest possible quality.

Carrying out the production plan involves deciding whether to make, buy, or lease products or parts; selecting the best suppliers for materials; and controlling inventory to keep enough supplies in stock, but not too much.

 ASSESSMENT CHECK ANSWERS

10.5.1 List the four major tasks of production and operations managers. The four tasks are planning overall production, selecting a layout for the firm's facilities, carrying out the production plan, and controlling manufacturing to achieve high quality.

10.5.2 What is the difference between a traditional manufacturing structure and a team-based structure? In the traditional structure, each manager is responsible for a specific area. In a team-based structure, all workers are responsible for their output.

10.5.3 What factors affect the make, buy, or lease decision? Several factors affect this decision, including the need for confidentiality, whether outside suppliers can meet a firm's standards, and the costs of leasing or purchasing parts from outside suppliers compared with the costs of producing them in-house.

LO 10.6 Identify the steps in the production control process.

The production control process has five steps: planning, routing, scheduling, dispatching, and follow-up. Quality control is an important consideration throughout this process. Coordination of each of these phases should result in high production efficiency and low production costs.

 ASSESSMENT CHECK ANSWERS

10.6.1 What five steps are involved in controlling the production process? The five steps are planning, routing, scheduling, dispatching, and follow-up.

10.6.2 What is the difference between a PERT chart and a Gantt chart? PERT charts try to reduce the number of delays by coordinating all parts of the production process. PERT charts are used for more complex projects. Gantt charts track projected and actual work progress over time. Gantt charts are used for scheduling simple projects.

LO 10.7 Discuss the importance of quality control.

Quality control involves measuring goods and services against quality standards. Firms use quality control to spot defective or imperfect products and to avoid delivering poor-quality goods to customers. Devices for monitoring quality levels of the firm's output include visual inspection, electronic sensors, robots, and X-rays. Companies can increase the quality of their goods and services by using Six Sigma techniques and by becoming ISO 9000 and 14000 certified.

✓ **ASSESSMENT CHECK ANSWERS**

10.7.1 What are some ways that a company can track the quality of its output? Companies can track quality by using benchmarking, quality control, Six Sigma, and ISO standards.

10.7.2 List some of the benefits of ISO 9000 certification. These standards show how a company can ensure that its products meet customers' requirements. Studies show that business partners, customers, suppliers, and shareholders prefer to deal with companies that are ISO 9000 certified.

BUSINESS TERMS YOU NEED TO KNOW

production 264

production and operations management 264

mass production 265

LEED (Leadership in Energy and Environmental Design) 268

computer-aided design (CAD) 269

computer-aided manufacturing (CAM) 269

flexible manufacturing system (FMS) 269

computer-integrated manufacturing (CIM) 270

make, buy, or lease decision 275

inventory control 277

just-in-time (JIT) system 278

materials requirement planning (MRP) 278

production control 279

quality 281

benchmarking 281

quality control 282

International Organization for Standardization (ISO) 282

REVIEW QUESTIONS

1. What is utility? How does production create utility?

2. Why is production such an important business activity? How does production create value for the company and its customers?

3. Why are firms moving toward flexible production and customer-driven production instead of mass production? Describe a product that is better suited to flexible production or customer-driven production than mass production. Explain your choice.

4. Identify whether an analytic production system or a synthetic production system applies to each of the following products:

   a. logging

   b. medical care

   c. cotton farming

   d. fishing

   e. construction

5. The home construction industry and the dental industry benefit from the use of CAD. Both industries can also benefit from using CAM—to manufacture home construction parts and to create dental implants and crowns. Choose another industry that would benefit from the use of both CAD and CAM systems. Explain how the industry can use both systems.

6. The Vancouver Aquarium is the largest aquarium in Canada and one of the five largest in North America. What specific factors might have contributed to the selection and success at this location?

7. What is the best facility layout for each of the following?

   a. a movie rental shop

   b. a nail salon

   c. a car wash

   d. a sandwich shop

8. What factors might be involved in selecting suppliers for a steakhouse restaurant?

9. What is inventory control? Why is the management of inventory crucial to a company's success?

10. What is benchmarking? How can it help a firm improve the quality of its goods and services?

PROJECTS AND TEAMWORK APPLICATIONS

1. Imagine that you recently became the owner of a popular ice cream shop. You want to attract more customers and expand the business. What type of production process—continuous or intermittent—is better for your business? Create a plan that shows the details of how you will use this process and why it will help you to meet your goals as a business owner.

2. On your own or with a classmate, imagine that you've been hired to help a business group design a shopping mall. Using the location factors discussed in the chapter, recommend where the mall should be located—and why. Present your plan to the class.

3. On your own or with a classmate, select one of the following businesses and sketch out or describe the layout that that would be best for attracting and serving customers:

   a. a Mexican restaurant

   b. a home furnishings store

   c. a pet store

   d. a motorcycle dealership

   e. a dentist office

4. Suppose you and your best friend decide to start a house-painting service. Draft a production plan for your business, including the following decisions: (a) make, buy, or lease; (b) suppliers; and (c) inventory control.

5. Choose two firms to compare (one firm should provide a good benchmarking opportunity for its production processes). The benchmarking firm doesn't need to be in the same industry as the other firm. Present your decisions to the class and explain why you made both choices.

WEB ASSIGNMENTS

1. **Just-in-time inventory management systems.** Go to the websites listed below to learn more about just-in-time inventory management systems. Make some notes on what you learned and bring them to class to participate in a class discussion.

   http://www.wisegeek.com/what-is-a-just-in-time-inventory.htm

   http://smallbusiness.dnb.com/manage/finances/12375503-1.html

   http://www.smcdata.com/software-choices/just-in-time-inventory-control-systems-1.html

2. **Plant location decision.** Using an Internet news service, such as Google news (http://news.google.com) or Yahoo! news (http://news.yahoo.com), search for news about a recent decision on a plant location. An example is Toyota's recent decision to expand its production facilities in Woodstock and Cambridge, Ontario. Research the decisions. Prepare a brief report that shows the factors that the firm considered in making its decision to expand in Canada.

   http://www.theglobeandmail.com/report-on-business/toyota-eyes-expansion-of-ontario-plants/article2341364/

3. **ISO certification.** Visit the website of the International Organization for Standardization (http://www.iso.org). Click on "Standards development" and then "Processes and procedures." What products are ISO standards currently being developed for?

Access your WileyPLUS course for:

- The complete digital textbook.

- Question assistance, including links to relevant sections in the online digital textbook.

- Immediate feedback and proof of progress, 24/7

- Integrated, multi-media resources – including MP3 downloads, visual exhibits, animations, and much more – that provide multiple study paths and encourage more active learning.

QUIZ YOURSELF

Note: Internet Web addresses change frequently. If you don't find the exact sites listed, you may need to access the organization's home page and search from there or use a search engine such as Bing or Google.

3 LAUNCHING YOUR . . .

MANAGEMENT CAREER

Part 3, "Management: Empowering People to Achieve Business Goals," covers Chapters 7 through 10. These three chapters discuss management, leadership, and the internal organization; human resource management, motivation, and labour–management relations; improving performance through empowerment, teamwork, and communication; and production and operations management. In those chapters, you read about top executives and company founders who directed their companies' strategy and led others in their day-to-day tasks to keep them on track. You also read about middle managers who make plans to turn the strategies into realities, and supervisors who work directly with employees to create strong teams that satisfy customers. A variety of jobs are available to people who choose management careers. And the demand for managers will continue to grow.

So what kinds of jobs can you choose from if you decide on a management career? As you learned in Chapter 7, three types of management jobs exist: supervisory managers, middle managers, and top managers. Supervisory management, or first-line management, includes positions such as supervisor, office manager, department manager, section chief, and team leader. Managers at this level work directly with the employees who produce and sell a firm's goods and services.

Middle management includes positions such as general managers, plant managers, division managers, and regional or branch managers. These managers are responsible for setting objectives that work with top management's goals. They also plan and carry out strategies for meeting those objectives.

Top managers include such positions as chief executive officer (CEO), chief operating officer (COO), chief financial officer (CFO), chief information officer (CIO), and executive vice-president. Top managers spend most of their time developing long-range plans, setting a direction for their organization, and inspiring a company's executives and employees to achieve their vision for the company's future. Top managers travel frequently between local, national, and global offices so they can meet and work with customers, suppliers, company managers, and employees.

Most managers start their careers in sales, production, or finance. If you are interested in a management career, you will likely start in a similar entry-level job. When you perform that job and other jobs well, you may be considered for a supervisory position. Then, if you are interested in supervising others and you have the technical, human, and conceptual skills to succeed, you'll begin your management career path. But what kinds of supervisory management jobs are available? Let's review the exciting possibilities.

Administrative services managers manage basic services that all organizations need—such as clerical work, payroll, travel, printing and copying, data records, telecommunications, security, parking, and supplies.

Construction managers plan, schedule, and coordinate the building of homes, commercial buildings such as offices and stores, and industrial facilities such as manufacturing plants and distribution centres. While administrative service managers work in offices, construction managers usually work on building sites with architects, engineers, construction workers, and suppliers.

Food service managers run restaurants and services that prepare and offer meals to customers. They coordinate workers and suppliers in kitchens, dining areas, and banquet operations; are responsible for those who order and purchase food inventories; maintain kitchen equipment; and recruit, hire, and train new workers. Food service managers can work for restaurant chains such as Olive Garden, for small locally owned restaurants, or for corporate food service departments in organizations.

Human resource managers help organizations to follow federal and provincial labour laws; effectively recruit, hire, train, and retain talented workers; administer corporate pay and benefits plans; develop and administer organizational human resource policies; and, when necessary, participate in contract negotiations or handle disputes. Human resource management jobs vary widely, depending on how specialized the requirements are.

Lodging managers work in hotels and motels but also help run camps, ranches, and recreational resorts. They may supervise employees that work in guest services, the front desk, the kitchen, the restaurant, banquets, house cleaning, and building maintenance. Because they are expected to help satisfy customers around the clock, they often work long hours and may be on call when not at work.

Medical and health services managers work in hospitals, nursing homes, doctors' offices, and corporate and university settings. They run departments that offer clinical services; ensure that provincial and federal laws are followed; and handle decisions related to the management of patient care, nursing, surgery, therapy, medical records, and financial payments.

Purchasing managers lead and control organizational supply chains that ensure companies purchase materials at reasonable prices and have the materials they need to produce the goods and services they sell. They also oversee deliveries when and where they are needed. Purchasing managers work with wholesale and retail buyers, to buy goods that are then resold to others; purchasing agents, who buy supplies and raw materials for their organizations; and contract specialists, who negotiate and supervise purchasing contracts with key suppliers and vendors.

Production managers direct and coordinate operations that manufacture goods. They work with employees who produce parts and assemble products and help decide which new machines should be purchased and when existing machines need maintenance. They are also responsible for meeting production goals that specify the quality, cost, schedule, and quantity of units to be produced.

The website "Living in Canada" provides a survey of salaries paid for a wide variety of managerial and other positions. You can find out more about managerial salaries by visiting http://www.livingin-canada.com/wages-for-management-jobs-canada.html. The average manager's salary appears to be about $60,000 per year.[1]

CAREER ASSESSMENT EXERCISES IN MANAGEMENT

1. The Canadian Institute of Management (CIM) is a not-for-profit professional organization that provides a range of management development and educational services to individuals, companies, and government agencies. Access the CIM's website at http://www.cim.ca/. Write a one-page summary of CIM's services.

2. Go online to a business news service, such as Yahoo! News or Google News, or look at the business section of your local newspaper. Find a story relating to a first-line supervisor, a middle manager, or a top executive. Write a summary of that person's duties. What decisions does the manager make? How do those decisions affect the manager's organization?

3. From the descriptions above, pick a management position that interests you. Research the career field. What skills do you have that would make you a good candidate for a management position in that field? What work and other experience do you need to help you get started? List your strengths and weaknesses. Draw up a plan to improve your strengths.

© Richard Levine/Alamy

PART 4

MARKETING MANAGEMENT

11 | CUSTOMER-DRIVEN MARKETING

LEARNING OBJECTIVES

LO 11.1 Summarize the ways in which marketing creates utility.

LO 11.2 Discuss the marketing concept.

LO 11.3 Describe not-for-profit marketing, and identify the five major categories of nontraditional marketing.

LO 11.4 Outline the basic steps in developing a marketing strategy.

LO 11.5 Describe the marketing research function.

LO 11.6 Identify and explain each of the methods available for segmenting consumer and business markets.

LO 11.7 Outline the determinants of consumer behaviour.

LO 11.8 Discuss the benefits of and tools for relationship marketing.

INSIDE BUSINESS

Handmade Items: Etsy.com Has Them All

Lisa Lutz, of Kelowna, British Columbia, promotes her handmade beaded jewellery and accessories from her own website, BeadCrazed.com. But she sells to customers online through her personal Etsy.com shop. Unique, handmade items have always been popular alternatives to mass-market products. Not very long ago, many craftspeople physically carried their creations to craft fairs or sold their work through friends and associates. Some still do, but now they also have access to potentially unlimited global markets through websites such as ArtFire, 1000 Markets, and Etsy.

Unlike eBay, where independent artisans compete directly with mass producers and importers, Etsy caters to customers who are looking for one-of-a-kind jewellery, a handmade quilt, or a pair of hand-carved bookends. Artisans use these sites to set up online "shops"; many have shops at more than one website to increase their exposure. These sites also carry knitted goods, clothing for adults and children, vintage items, photographs and other visual artworks, paper goods, spices and other food items, services such as custom DVDs of your special event, and craft supplies for making your own project. Shoppers can see photographs of individual items and ratings of different sellers. They also can choose from various payment options.

Etsy is now the largest online artisan and vintage market. Etsy got a boost from the craft boom. But when the collapse of the job market drove many hobbyists to try to make a living from their crafts, Etsy's membership soared. Etsy now has 3.75 million registered users. In a recent year, it had gross sales of $180.6 million. Looking for a piece of jewellery, maybe a new ring? A jewellery search on Etsy turned up 86,237 rings on 4,107 pages. Their prices range from pennies to almost a hundred thousand dollars for an

© Can Stock Photo Inc./thesupe87

opulent diamond engagement ring. The Etsy community spans the globe with buyers and sellers coming from more than 150 countries, including Canada.

Opening an online shop is cheaper and easier than opening a bricks-and-mortar store. Most websites allow sellers to set up shop for free, then charge a small fee to post an item and take a percentage of each sale. For example, Etsy charges 20 cents to post one item for four months, then takes 3.5 percent when that item is sold. That isn't very much, but if sellers want their items to stay high in search results, they need to renew the listings often. Some sellers renew their listings daily, so the fees can add up. Etsy also offers sellers a support system through blogs and links to social-networking sites such as Facebook and Twitter. It is working to improve its search functions and is planning to set up a customer service phone line.

Many people dream of quitting their day jobs to make a living from selling their handmade products online, but selling online is not easy and is getting harder. Competition has become extreme as more artisans are joining these websites. Working from home or a studio often means spending long hours knitting or sewing or making jewellery, especially during the holiday rush—then more long hours standing in line at the post office, waiting to ship the items sold. And of course, sellers have to spend time promoting their products in every possible medium, from blogs to magazines to, yes, that network of friends and associates.[1]

CHAPTER 11 OVERVIEW

Business success in the 21st century is directly tied to a company's ability to identify and serve its target markets. In fact, all organizations—profit-oriented and not-for-profit, manufacturing and retailing—*must* serve customer needs to succeed. And that's what Etsy does by offering a wide range of unique, handmade items. Marketing is the link between the organization and the people who buy and use its goods and services. Organizations use marketing to figure out buyer needs. They also use marketing to show that they can meet those needs by supplying a quality product at a reasonable price. Marketing is the path to developing loyal, long-term customers.

Consumers purchase goods for their own use and enjoyment. Business purchasers look for products for their firms to use in their business operations. Both types of buyers may seem to be made up of a large number of similar people. But marketers see the separate wants and needs for each group. Buyers can be manufacturers, Web surfers, and shoppers in the grocery aisles. Companies gather huge amounts of data on every detail of consumer lifestyles and buying behaviours. Marketers use the data to understand the needs and wants of both final customers and business buyers. When buyers can satisfy customers, they are on their way toward building relationships with them. But it's not always easy. To start a relationship with the buying public, Whole Foods CEO John Mackey invites e-mails from consumers who may—or may not—be customers. Mackey spent several weeks in an e-mail debate with an animal welfare activist about Whole Foods selling duck meat from a particular source. Mackey then asked the activist to help rewrite his firm's policies on farm animal treatment. This relationship developed through direct communication between the CEO and a consumer. Mackey's open e-mail invitation helps Whole Foods to build a relationship with customers who have certain food-source concerns.

This chapter begins with an examination of the marketing concept and how businesspeople develop a marketing strategy. We then turn to marketing research techniques and an explanation of how businesses apply data to market segmentation to better understand customer behaviour. The chapter closes with a detailed look at the important role customer relationships play in today's highly competitive business world.

WHAT IS MARKETING?

LO 11.1 Summarize the ways in which marketing creates utility.

marketing an organizational function and set of processes for creating, communicating, and delivering value to customers and for managing customer relationships in ways that benefit the organization and its stakeholders.

To succeed, every organization must serve customer needs—from profit-seeking firms such as McDonald's and Bell Canada to such not-for-profits as the Make-a-Wish Foundation of Canada and the Canadian Cancer Society. According to the American Marketing Association, **marketing** is "an organizational function and a set of processes for creating, communicating, and delivering value to customers and for managing customer relationships in ways that benefit the organization and its stakeholders."[2] Marketing techniques don't just sell goods and services, they also help people support ideas or viewpoints and educate others. The Canadian Diabetes Association mails out questionnaires that ask, "Are you at risk for diabetes?" The documents help educate the general public about this widespread disease by listing its risk factors and common symptoms and by describing the work of the association.

The best marketers not only give consumers what they want but anticipate and expect consumers' needs even before consumers see those needs themselves. Ideally, marketers can get ahead of the competition by helping consumers create a link between their new need and the fulfillment of that need by the marketers' products. ScotiaBank and Bank of Montreal promote pre-approved mortgages at low interest rates so customers know what they can borrow before they shop for a house. NetJets offers fractional (or shared) jet ownership to executives who want the luxury and flexibility of private ownership without the cost of owning their own plane. Samsung offers its next generation of high-definition TV with its trademarked Internet@TV. Owners connect their televisions to their home Internet connection, then add widgets to track the weather, check eBay, view Flickr albums, and check for Twitter updates—all in real time. Consumers can also sign up for Video-on-Demand service through Rogers, Bell, and other service providers. "Get the best of the Web right on your TV!" their promotion says.

The best marketers give consumers what they want and anticipate their needs. NetJets offers fractional (shared) jet ownership to executives who want the luxury and flexibility of private ownership without the cost of owning their own plane.

Lexington Herald-Leader, Frank Anderson/AP/Wide World Photos

As these examples show, marketing is more than just selling. Marketing is a process that begins with discovering unmet customer needs and continues with several tasks: researching the potential market; producing a good or service that can satisfy the targeted customers; and promoting, pricing, and distributing that good or service. Throughout the entire marketing process, a successful organization focuses on building customer relationships.

When two or more parties benefit from trading something of value (such as goods, services, or cash), they have entered into an **exchange process**. When you purchase a cup of coffee, the other party in the exchange may be a convenience store clerk, a vending machine, or a Dunkin' Donuts server. The exchange seems simple—you hand over some money, and you receive your cup of coffee. But the exchange process is more complex. The exchange happens because you felt the need for a cup of coffee. It also happens because you saw the convenience store or the vending machine. You might not choose Dunkin' Donuts unless you had heard of the brand. Because of marketing, your desire for a flavoured blend, a decaf, or a plain black coffee is identified—and the coffee manufacturer's business is successful.

exchange process an activity in which two or more parties trade something of value (such as goods, services, or cash) that satisfies each other's needs.

How Marketing Creates Utility

Marketing affects many parts of an organization. It also affects an organization's dealings with its customers. **Utility** is the ability of a good or service to satisfy the wants and needs of customers. A company's production function creates *form utility* by converting raw materials, component parts, and other inputs into finished goods and services. But the marketing function creates three types of utility: time utility, place utility, and ownership utility. *Time utility* is created by making a good or service available when customers want to purchase it. *Place utility* is created by making

utility the power of a good or service to satisfy a want or need.

HIT & MISS

The Pepsi Refresh Project: Viral Marketing

PepsiCo recently launched the Pepsi Refresh Project, a year-long program. Consumers were invited to submit short videos of ideas that would benefit their communities. Pepsi accepted 1,000 videos each month and posted them online so that visitors to the website could vote on them. At the end of each month, Pepsi awarded grants of varying amounts to the winning projects. Over the year, the company gave away a total of $20 million. Instead of advertising the project during the Super Bowl, Pepsi announced that it would *not* be doing so and instead posted a video on the Internet. The video quickly went viral (spreading through the process of Internet sharing). Visits to the Refresh website increased an astonishing 800 percent after the Super Bowl in February—and stayed high.

Facebook and Twitter have made big changes to Internet marketing. Facebook has about 900 million members worldwide. Twitter claims to log 50 million tweets per day. According to Pepsi's CEO, Indra Nooyi, the company is investing one-third of its marketing budget in social media.

Marketing the project on the Internet had its upsides and downsides. Traffic to the website seemed to drop during the first three weeks of each month. It would then spike during the last week in the final round of voting, so announcing winners every month was a good idea. Also, people hoping to win grants set up their own local social media campaigns using Facebook and Twitter. Their efforts generated more publicity for the project. However, as time went on, these contestants and some celebrity contestants became the sources of most of the publicity.

SEO (search-engine optimization) firms watched the campaign closely to follow its successes and to spot features that could be improved for future campaigns.

Questions for Critical Thinking

1. Choose an advertiser with a presence on Facebook and Twitter. Which social medium seems more successful at getting the advertiser's message across?

2. If you have a Facebook page, how would you use it to market either your own business or a cause that inspires you?

Sources: Pepsi Refresh Project website, http://www.refresheverything.com, accessed March 11, 2010; Michael Learmonth, "Pepsi's World Cup Campaign Infiltrates Viral Chart," *Advertising Age,* March 11, 2010, http://adage.com; "Pepsi Refresh Project: Social Media Marketing Splash or Flawed Strategy?" *Online PR News,* March 4, 2010, http://www.onlineprnews.com; Scott Moir, "Facebook vs. Twitter: A Social Media Internet Marketing Strategy and Benefit Comparison," *World Daily News,* February 23, 2010, http://www.jazzou.com "Pepsi Refresh Project—Huge Potential Viral Marketing Success," *Online PR News,* February 13, 2010, http://www.onlineprnews.com; "Pepsi Refresh Project—Huge Potential Viral Marketing Success," *Online PR News,* February 13, 2010, http://www.onlineprnews.com; "Pepsi Refresh Project—Social Media Marketing Strategy or Hype?" *Online PR News,* February 10, 2010, http://www.onlineprnews.com.

---

a product available in a location convenient for customers. *Ownership utility* refers to an organized transfer of goods and services from the seller to the buyer. Some firms can create all three forms of utility. Target was the first North American retailer to offer bar-coded, scannable mobile coupons direct to cellphones. Guests can sign on to the program either on their personal computers or on their cellphones. Each month, they receive either an e-mail or a text message with a link to a mobile website page where they find offers for various products. They can use the mobile coupons at any Target store because Target is the first retailer to have point-of-sale scanning technology for the coupons in all of its stores. Steve Eastman, the president of Target.com, says, "At Target, we know that mobile phones are an integral part of our guests' lives, and mobile coupons are just another way we're providing convenient, on-the-go shopping solutions."[3] PepsiCo has also created several forms of utility for its customers through social networking media, as described in the "Hit & Miss" feature.

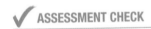 **ASSESSMENT CHECK**

11.1.1 What is utility?

11.1.2 Identify how marketing creates utility.

LO 11.2 Discuss the marketing concept.

EVOLUTION OF THE MARKETING CONCEPT

Marketing has always been a part of business, from the earliest village traders to large 21st-century organizations that produce and sell complex goods and services. Over time, marketing activities have evolved through the four eras shown in Figure 11.1: the production, sales, and marketing

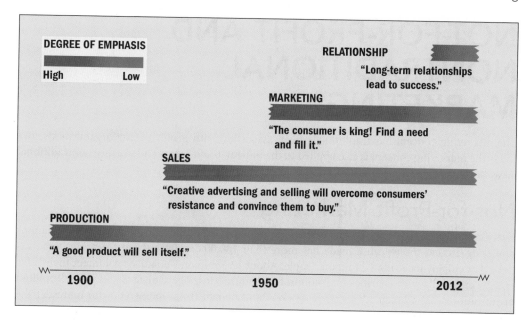

FIGURE 11.1 Four Eras in the History of Marketing

eras, and now the relationship era. These eras run similar to some of the time periods discussed in Chapter 1.

For centuries, organizations of the *production era* stressed their efficiency in producing quality products. Their philosophy could be summed up by the remark, "A good product will sell itself." This focus on production continued into the 20th century, then it gradually gave way to the *sales era*. In the sales era, businesses assumed that consumers would buy as a result of energetic sales efforts. Organizations didn't fully recognize the importance of their customers until the *marketing era* of the 1950s. Then, organizations began to adopt a consumer orientation. This focus has grown stronger in recent years, leading to the *relationship era* in the 1990s, which continues today. In the relationship era, companies focus on customer satisfaction and building long-term business relationships.

Emergence of the Marketing Concept

The term **marketing concept** refers to a companywide customer focus with the goal of achieving long-term success. The basic idea of the marketing concept is that marketplace success begins with the customer. A firm should analyze each customer's needs and then work backward to offer products that fulfill those needs. The emergence of the marketing concept can be explained best by the shift from a *seller's market*, to a market with a shortage of goods and services, to a *buyer's market*, a market with too many goods and services. During the 1950s, North America became a strong buyer's market. As a result, companies were forced to satisfy customers rather than just producing and selling goods and services.

Today, much competition among firms centres on the effort to satisfy customers. Apple's iPhone followed on the heels of its wildly successful iPod. The iPhone combines the features of a cellphone, a widescreen iPod with touch controls, and an Internet link. Like the iPhone models before it, the 3G iPhone operates completely by touch screen, has a 9-centimetre display, contains a full Safari Web browser, and takes pictures with a 3-megapixel camera. The more recent iPod Touch borrowed some of the iPhone's innovative features. Apple then introduced the iPad, a touch-screen tablet computer and reader with WiFi or WiFi plus 3G. The iPad was as big a success as the iPod and the iPhone. Apple is well known for anticipating and responding quickly to consumers' needs. "Apple clearly wants potential buyers to think of the iPad as a casual entertainment device," says one industry watcher.[4]

marketing concept
a companywide consumer focus on promoting long-term success.

 ASSESSMENT CHECK

11.2.1 What is the marketing concept?

11.2.2 How is the marketing concept tied to the relationship era of marketing?

NOT-FOR-PROFIT AND NONTRADITIONAL MARKETING

The marketing concept has traditionally been associated with profit-seeking organizations. But today the marketing concept is also applied to the not-for-profit sector and to other nontraditional areas, such as religious organizations and political campaigns.

Not-for-Profit Marketing

Every continent receives benefits from the approximately 20 million not-for-profit organizations operating around the world. Canada has more than 160,000 registered not-for-profit organizations that employ more than 2 million people. About 12.5 million Canadians volunteer their time, energy, and skills with charities and nonprofit organizations. The United States has 1.9 million organizations that employ 12.9 million workers and benefit from volunteers who represent the equivalent of 9 million full-time employees.[5] When the value of those volunteers is taken into account, Canada leads the world in contributions to its gross domestic product by not-for-profit organizations; the United States is a close second.[6] The largest not-for-profit organization in the world is the Red Cross/Red Crescent. Other not-for-profits range from Habitat for Humanity to the Alberta Society for the Prevention of Cruelty to Animals. These organizations benefit by applying many of the strategies and business concepts used by profit-seeking firms. They apply marketing tools to reach audiences, attract and secure funding, and accomplish their overall missions. Marketing strategies are important for not-for-profit organizations because, just like for-profit businesses, they also compete for dollars. Not-for-profit organizations compete for dollars from individuals, foundations, and corporations.

Not-for-profit organizations operate in both public and private sectors. Public groups include government units and agencies that receive tax funding. For example, a municipal swimming pool receives funding from the local municipal government and might be operated by volunteers. The private not-for-profit sector comprises many different types of organizations, including the Canadian Olympic Committee and the Canadian Medical Association. Although some private not-for-profits generate surplus revenue, their primary goals are not about earning profits. If they earn funds beyond their expenses, they invest the excess in their organizational missions.

Celebrities are particularly visible in their campaigns for not-for-profit organizations—both their own organizations and those of others. The actress Reese Witherspoon is the Avon Global Ambassador and Honorary Chairperson of the Avon Foundation for Women. Witherspoon helped present a $500,000 grant to the Fund for Global Women's Leadership. The grant was intended to help the worldwide movement to end violence toward women.[8]

Nontraditional Marketing

Not-for-profit organizations often use one or more of five major categories of nontraditional marketing: person marketing, place marketing, event marketing, cause marketing, and organization marketing. Figure 11.2 shows

Courtesy of United Way Toronto

In some cases, not-for-profit organizations form a partnership with a for-profit company to promote the firm's message or to distribute its goods and services. This partnership usually benefits both organizations. Calgary-based energy transportation and distribution company Enbridge is the title sponsor of the CN Tower Climb for the United Way Toronto.[7]

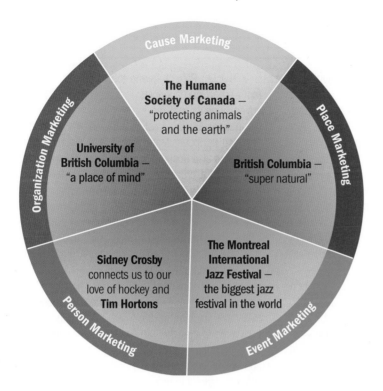

FIGURE 11.2 Categories of Nontraditional Marketing

examples of these types of marketing. As described in the "Going Green" feature, an organization uses each of these types of marketing to connect with the audience that is most likely to offer time, money, or other resources. In some cases, the effort may reach the market the organization intends to serve.

Person Marketing

Person marketing refers to efforts designed to attract the attention, interest, and preference of a target market toward a person. Campaign managers for a political candidate conduct marketing research to identify groups of voters and financial supporters. They then design advertising campaigns, fundraising events, and political rallies to reach that target group. In another example of person marketing, Canon Canada's television advertising campaign spokeswoman Avril Lavigne showed her creative use of Canon's PowerShot camera to a young potential market that knew her more for her musical talents. The message was clear—PowerShot makes creative photography simple and easy, even for people who know very little about the mechanics of a camera.

Many successful job seekers use the tools of person marketing. They research the wants and needs of prospective employers, and then they identify ways they can meet those wants and needs. They look for employers through a variety of channels and send messages that focus on how they can benefit the employer.

Place Marketing

As the term suggests, **place marketing** attempts to attract people to a particular area, such as a city, region, or country. This marketing may focus on a place that may appeal to consumers as a tourist destination or to businesses as a desirable business location. A strategy for place marketing often includes advertising.

Place marketing may be combined with event marketing, such as the Olympics. For example, Vancouver used three mythical cartoon critters, named Quatchi, Miga, and Sumi, to promote the Olympic and Paralympic Winter Games. Merchandise featuring the mascots was available for sale to the public for more than two years before the actual games took place.[9]

person marketing efforts that are designed to attract the attention, interest, and preference of a target market toward a person.

place marketing an attempt to attract people to a particular area, such as a city, region, or country.

GOING GREEN

THE TAP PROJECT

Recently, *Esquire* magazine challenged David Droga, the founder of the Droga5 advertising firm, to prove that his creative thinking deserved the magazine's "Best and Brightest" award. After Droga watched a documentary about Hurricane Katrina's effects on New Orleans, he started thinking about the many people who don't have access to clean, safe drinking water. In North America, we take our drinking water for granted. But when Droga was served a free glass of tap water at a New York City restaurant, he got the idea for his next advertising campaign. Droga remembers thinking, "We have to make people aware of the luxury we have and help others who don't have it." He presented his idea to UNICEF, and the Tap Project was born.

Approximately 900 million people around the world—about half of them children—don't have safe, accessible drinking water. UNICEF and the Tap Project hope to reduce that number by half by 2015. Every day, 4,100 children under age 5 die of water-borne diseases.

During the United Nation's World Water Week, top restaurants in New York City asked their patrons to donate one dollar or more for a glass of tap water. Since then, the Tap Project has raised almost $1.5 million in the United States. All donations go to UNICEF's water, sanitation, and hygiene programs. One dollar allows UNICEF to provide safe drinking water to one child for 40 days. Funds raised in 2010 went primarily to Haiti, the Central African Republic, Guatemala, Togo, and Vietnam. Caryl Stein, the president and CEO of the U.S. Fund for UNICEF, noted, "In Haiti alone, less than 60 percent of people had access to safe water even before the earthquake."

Leading advertising agencies in the United States have also participated in the Tap Project. Casanova Pendrill Publicidad, a marketing firm that is aimed at the Hispanic market, won the top prize in *Advertising Age*'s Non-Traditional/Guerrilla Marketing category. In its "Agua Sucia" ("dirty water") campaign, the firm bottled dirty water as if it were mineral water and sold the bottles for $1 from vending machines on New York City streets. "Customers" could choose from such "flavours" as cholera, typhoid, hepatitis, and dysentery. The agency's slogan was, "You'd never drink dirty water, the rest of the world shouldn't have to, either."

The Tap Project spread to other North American cities and to more advertising agencies. In a recent year, 21 agencies produced advertisements that ran in 19 cities, in addition to their efforts on the Internet. For the most recent World Water Week, the Tap Project changed its focus. More than 1,000 restaurants participated, but volunteers also hosted 250 other fundraising events. The campaign established a presence on Facebook and Twitter and on an online radio station. But only five cities—Chicago, Los Angeles, New York, Seattle, and Washington, DC—and eight advertising agencies were involved. Ryu Mizuno, the director of marketing at the U.S. Fund for UNICEF, said the Tap Project was "maturing as a brand" and that the fund preferred "doing a few things in a great way instead of being all over the map."

Some observers claim that such changes are typical of nontraditional marketing campaigns, especially those where ad agencies have volunteered their services. Another difference from the first years is that the Tap Project's very success has led to other water charities—and all of them are competing for donations and volunteers. The earthquake in Haiti also had an impact. But UNICEF planned to grow the campaign again in 2011. Mizuno said, "Agencies that participated in the past and didn't participate this year are staying in touch with us."

Questions for Critical Thinking

1. What types of nontraditional marketing does the Tap Project use?

2. As this feature mentions, fewer cities and advertisers are participating in World Water Week. What steps would improve participation in future years?

Sources: Tap Project website, http://www.tapproject.org, accessed April 14, 2010; Tap Project online radio station, http://www.tapprojectradio.org, accessed April 14, 2010; Droga5 website, http://www.droga5.com, accessed April 14, 2010; Karyn McCormack, "UNICEF: Tapping the Power of Water," *BusinessWeek*, http://www.businessweek.com, accessed April 14, 2010; Alessandra Bulow, "UNICEF Tap Project," *Food & Wine*, March 22, 2010, http://www.foodandwine.com; Helena Bottemiller, "Restaurants Join in Clean Water Project," *Food Safety News*, March 20, 2010, http://www.foodsafetynews.com; United States Fund for UNICEF, "2010 UNICEF Tap Project Launches to Help Provide Safe Water to Children Worldwide," March 11, 2010, http://www.unicefusa.org.

event marketing marketing or sponsoring of short-term events such as athletic competitions and cultural and charitable performances.

Event Marketing

Event marketing refers to marketing or sponsoring short-term events such as athletic competitions and cultural and charitable performances. The Canadian Diabetes Association sponsors "Walk, Run, Cycle for Diabetes" events throughout the year. This event offers Canadian communities an opportunity to get active while also raising awareness and funds for the Canadian Diabetes Association. These volunteer-led events target local communities, promote a healthy and active lifestyle, and are dedicated to exposing the reality of diabetes and the importance of the cause.[10]

Event marketing often leads to partnerships between not-for-profit and for-profit organizations. Many businesses sponsor events such as 10K runs to raise funds for health-related charities. These occasions require a marketing effort to plan the event and attract participants and sponsors. Events may be intended to raise money or awareness, or both.

Cause Marketing

Cause marketing is marketing that promotes awareness of a cause or social issue or raises money for a cause or social issue, such as drug abuse prevention or childhood hunger. Cause marketing tries to educate the public and may or may not try to raise funds. An advertisement often contains a phone number or website address where people can get more information about the organization or issue. People can either donate money or take other actions of support. The Royal Bank of Canada sponsors the University of Western Ontario's Alternative Spring Break program. This program provides funds that help young adults and student volunteers participate in community activities in Canada and in other locations in need. Projects range from rebuilding housing damaged by natural disaster to teaching health care and English to children.[11]

For-profit companies look for ways to contribute to their communities by joining forces with charities and causes to provide financial resources, marketing resources, and human resources. Timberland is well known for participating in the City Year program, where young adults contract to perform a year of volunteer service in their communities. For-profit firms can also combine their goods and services with a cause. Seventh Generation makes household cleaning and paper products and is committed to educating consumers about how "green" products can make their homes healthier and safer.[12]

Organization Marketing

The final category of nontraditional marketing, **organization marketing**, focuses on an organization. It influences consumers to accept the goals of an organization, receive the services of an organization, or contribute in some way to an organization. Examples of organizations that use marketing include the college or university you are attending, the Canadian Cancer Society, and Oprah Winfrey's Angel Network. These organizations use their own websites, advertise in magazines, and send mail directly to consumers in their efforts to market their organizations. The Angel Network was established by Oprah Winfrey more than a decade ago to "encourage people around the world to make a difference in the lives of others." The organization runs its own charitable projects and supports the projects of other not-for-profits such as Habitat for Humanity.[13]

cause marketing marketing that promotes a cause or social issue, such as preventing child abuse, anti-littering efforts, and stop-smoking campaigns.

organization marketing a marketing strategy that influences consumers to accept the goals of an organization, receive the services of an organization, or contribute in some way to an organization.

✓ **ASSESSMENT CHECK**

11.3.1 Why do not-for-profit organizations use marketing?

11.3.2 What are the five types of nontraditional marketing used by not-for-profit organizations?

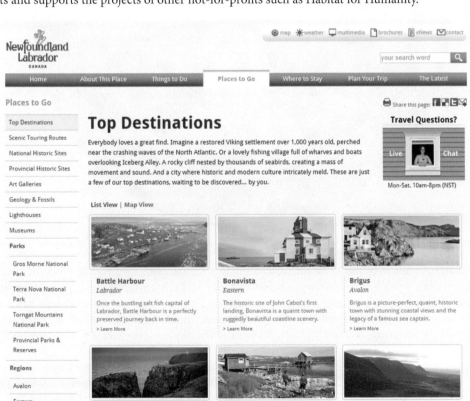

This web page sightseeing guide is an example of *place marketing*. It is published by the government of Newfoundland and Labrador to encourage tourism.

Courtesy of Newfoundland and Labrador Tourism

DEVELOPING A MARKETING STRATEGY

In any successful organization, for-profit or not-for-profit, decision-makers follow a two-step process to develop a *marketing strategy*. First, decision-makers study and analyze all possible target markets and choose the most suitable market. Second, they create a marketing mix to satisfy the chosen market. Figure 11.3 shows the relationships among the target market, the marketing mix variables, and the marketing environment. This section describes the development of a marketing strategy that is designed to attract and build relationships with customers. Sometimes, in an effort to attract customers, marketers use questionable methods, as described in the "Solving an Ethical Controversy" feature.

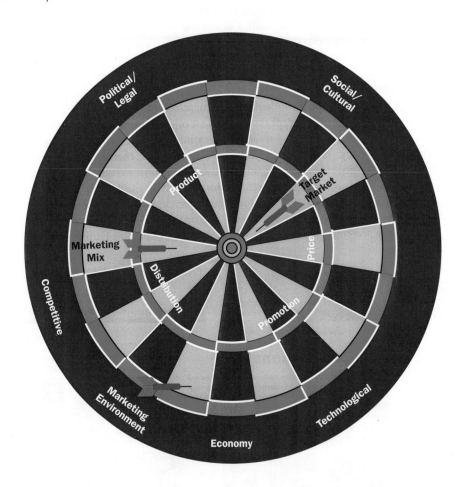

FIGURE 11.3 Target Market and Marketing Mix within the Marketing Environment

Earlier chapters of this book introduced many environmental factors that affect the success or failure of a firm's business strategy, including today's rapidly changing and highly competitive world of business, a wide range of social and cultural factors, economic challenges, political and legal factors, and technological innovations. Although these external forces often operate outside managers' control, marketers must still consider the impact of environmental factors on their decisions.

A marketing plan is a key part of a firm's overall business plan. The marketing plan outlines a firm's marketing strategy. It also includes information about the target market, sales and revenue goals, the marketing budget, and the timing for implementing the elements of the marketing mix.

— SOLVING AN **ETHICAL** CONTROVERSY —

When Free Credit Reports Aren't Free

When times are tough and credit is tight, consumers are more likely to want to look up their credit scores and see what they can do about them. In Canada, the way that credit reporting companies handle a person's personal information is governed by the federal Personal Information Protection and Electronic Document Act (PIPEDA) and Credit Reporting Act and by such provincial acts as the Personal Information Protection Act (PIPA). In the United States, the Fair Credit Reporting Act (FCRA) governs the industry, which deals with the three major consumer reporting companies in North America—Equifax, Experian, and TransUnion. Credit reporting companies often advertise offers for a free credit report on the Internet. That's what TransUnion does at https://www.freecreditreportsincanada.ca/. But many offers have hidden costs or will lead customers to other services that have costs.

Should firms be allowed to use the word "free" when advertising for credit reports if the service contains hidden costs?

PRO

1. If the credit score itself is free, but related services are not, then the advertising is truthful. Ty Taylor, the president of Experian's Consumer Direct Division, says, "You get a free credit report and free score for test-driving our services."

2. Some promotional offers include free credit scores, with a tie-in to additional services for a fee. Other industries make similar offers for a free month of phone, cable, or Internet service.

CON

1. The word "free" is a powerful invitation in advertising. Some companies provide "free" reports, then bill consumers for services they have to cancel.

2. Consumer advocates say that firms work on people's fears. Edgar Dworsky, the founder of ConsumerWorld.org and formerly on Experian's consumer advisory panel, says, "Does the average person really need to see their credit reports more than once every four months? Do you need to look at it daily? That's paranoia."

Summary

Most consumers know that the use of the word "free" in any advertising is generally attached to some kind of cost at some point in time. However, should consumers have to figure out exactly when they might be charged a cost for their dealings with consumer reporting companies—or with any company?

Sources: Ron Lieber, "Free Credit on Credit? No Longer," *New York Times,* April 7, 2010, http://www.nytimes.com; "FREE Annual Credit Reports," Federal Trade Commission, http://www.ftc.gov/freereports, accessed April 2, 2010; Joe Taylor, "New Laws Crack Down on Free Credit Report Marketing," *CardRatings,* March 30, 2010, http://www.cardratings.com; Michelle Singletary, "Free Credit Reports Get Easier to Find," *Washington Post,* March 4, 2010, http://www.boston.com.

Selecting a Target Market

The two elements of a marketing strategy are best described by the expression "find a need and fill it." A firm's marketers study the individuals and business decision-makers in its potential market to find a need. A market consists of people who have purchasing power, a willingness to buy, and the authority to make purchase decisions.

Markets can be classified by type of product. **Consumer products**—often known as business-to-consumer (**B2C**) products—are goods and services that are purchased by end users. Some examples are a Global Positioning System (GPS), tomato sauce, and a haircut. **Business products**—or business-to-business (**B2B**) products—are goods and services purchased to be used, either directly or indirectly, in making other goods that will be resold. Some products can fit either classification depending on who buys them and why. For example, a computer and a credit card can be used by both a business and a consumer.

consumer (B2C) product
a good or service that is purchased by end users.

business (B2B) product
a good or service purchased to be used, either directly or indirectly, in the production of other goods for resale.

target market a group of people that an organization markets its goods, services, or ideas toward, using a strategy designed to satisfy this group's specific needs and preferences.

marketing mix a blending of the four elements of marketing strategy—product, distribution, promotion, and pricing—to satisfy chosen customer segments.

A **target market** is the group of possible customers that an organization directs its marketing efforts toward. Customer needs and wants differ, and no single organization can satisfy everyone. For example, *Popular Science* is a magazine geared toward readers who are interested in science and technology, whereas *Bon Appétit* is aimed at readers who are interested in fine food and cooking.

Decisions about marketing involve strategies for four areas of marketing activity: product, distribution, promotion, and pricing. A firm's **marketing mix** blends the four strategies to fit the needs and preferences of a specific target market. Marketing success depends not on the four individual strategies but on their unique combination.

Product strategy involves more than just designing a good or service by adding needed qualities. It also includes decisions about package design, brand names, trademarks, warranties, product image, new-product development, and customer service. Think about your favourite pair of jeans. Do you like them because they fit the best, or do other qualities—such as styling and overall image—play a role in your brand preference? *Distribution strategy,* the second marketing mix variable, ensures that customers receive their purchases in the proper quantities at the right times and locations. *Promotional strategy,* another marketing mix element, effectively blends advertising, personal selling, sales promotion, and public relations to achieve its goals of informing, persuading, and influencing purchase decisions.

Pricing strategy, the final mix element, is also one of the most difficult areas of marketing decision-making. Firms need to set profitable and justifiable prices for their product offerings. Such actions must sometimes comply with government regulation and may receive considerable public criticism. They also represent a powerful competitive strategy. Pricing strategies frequently lead to responses by the other firms in the industry, which may match price changes to avoid losing customers. Think about your jeans again. Would you continue to purchase them if they were priced much higher or much lower?

Developing a Marketing Mix for International Markets

Marketing a good or service in foreign markets means deciding whether to offer the same marketing mix in every market (*standardization*) or to develop a unique mix to fit each market (*adaptation*). Standardizing the marketing mix can have upsides such as reliable marketing performance and low costs. This approach works best with B2B goods, such as steel, chemicals, and aircraft. These products need little sensitivity to a nation's culture.

Adaptation allows marketers to vary their marketing mix to suit local competitive conditions, consumer preferences, and government regulations. Consumer products tend to be more culture-dependent than business products. For that reason, they often need adaptation. SUBWAY, which already has 144 stores in China, plans to open 500 new stores there.

© Karen Cowled/Alamy

In contrast, adaptation lets marketers vary their marketing mix to suit local competitive conditions, consumer preferences, and government regulations. Consumer tastes are often shaped by local cultures. Consumer products tend to be more culture-dependent than business products. For that reason, they often need adaptation. SUBWAY, which already has 144 stores in China, plans to open 500 new stores in the next five years. SUBWAY hopes to match the Chinese presence of McDonald's in 10 years. As SUBWAY opens stores in different regions, it plans to adapt its menu to local tastes with such offerings as Beijing roast duck sandwiches and "hot spicy Szechuan sauce." Why do these firms go out of their way to adapt to Chinese preferences? China is a market with 1.3 billion potential consumers.[14]

Marketers also try to build adaptability into the designs of standardized goods and services for international and domestic markets. *Mass customization* allows a firm to mass-produce goods and services while also adding unique features to individual or small groups of orders. For example, online firm Blank Label (www.blanklabel.com) specializes in custom-made men's dress shirts. Customers can choose their own fabric, style, individual features, and size. Spreadshirt (www.spreadshirt.com) specializes in customized casual wear, accessories, and even personalized underwear.[15]

✓ **ASSESSMENT CHECK**

11.4.1 Distinguish between consumer products and business products.

11.4.2 What are the steps in developing a marketing strategy?

MARKETING RESEARCH

LO 11.5 Describe the marketing research function.

Marketing research involves more than just collecting data. Researchers must decide how to collect data, then they interpret the results, convert the data into decision-oriented information, and communicate those results to managers for use in decision-making. **Marketing research** is the process of collecting and evaluating information to help marketers make effective decisions. It links business decision-makers to the marketplace by providing data about potential target markets that help them design effective marketing mixes.

marketing research the process of collecting and evaluating information to support marketing decision-making.

Obtaining Marketing Research Data

Marketing researchers need both internal and external data. Firms generate *internal data* within their organizations. Financial records provide useful information, such as changes in unpaid bills; inventory levels; sales generated by different categories of customers or product lines; profitability of particular divisions; or comparisons of sales by territories, salespeople, customers, or product lines.

Researchers gather *external data* from outside sources, including previously published data. Trade associations publish reports on activities in specific industries. Advertising agencies collect information on the audiences reached by various media. National marketing research firms offer information through subscription services. Some professional research firms specialize in specific markets, such as youth or ethnic groups. This information helps companies to make decisions about developing or modifying products.

The largest consumer-goods manufacturer in the world is Procter & Gamble. This firm has excelled in marketing research for a long time; it created its own marketing research department in 1923 and began conducting its research online in 2001. To help the company recover from the global recession, Bob McDonald, the company's chief executive officer, has set the goal of reaching 1 billion new customers by 2015. This expansion involves reaching customers in developing regions. As part of this strategy, he posed as a market researcher and travelled undercover to 30 countries.[16]

Secondary data, or previously published data, are low cost and easy to obtain. Government publications are excellent data sources, and most are available online. The most frequently used government statistics are census data, which contain the population's age, gender, education level, household size and composition, occupation, employment status, and income. Even private research firms such as TRU (formerly Teenage Research Unlimited), which studies the purchasing habits of teens, provide some free information on their websites. This information helps firms evaluate consumers' buying behaviour, look ahead to possible changes in the marketplace, and identify new markets.

Even though secondary data are a quick and inexpensive resource, this information sometimes is not specific or current enough for marketing researchers' needs. Researchers may decide that they need to collect *primary data*—data collected firsthand through such methods as observation and surveys.

Observational studies view the actions of consumers either directly or by using mechanical devices. More retailers are watching their customers by way of video cameras. This kind of observation can solve problems such as by widening a too-narrow aisle to allow shoppers easier access. But such close observation has also raised privacy concerns.[17] Procter & Gamble spends about $200 million on consumer observation each year and says it is the firm's most important type of marketing research. CEO McDonald says, "If we can continue to innovate and continue to mind consumer needs and delight consumers, that ability outweighs any macroeconomic force."[18]

Observing customers cannot provide all the information a marketing researcher needs. For example, a researcher might observe a customer buying a red sweater, but have no idea why the purchase was made—or for whom. When researchers need information about consumers' attitudes, opinions, and motives, they need to ask the consumers themselves. They may conduct surveys by telephone, in person, online, or in focus groups.

A *focus group* gathers 8 to 12 people in a room or over the Internet to discuss a specific topic. A focus group can lead to new ideas, address consumers' needs, and even point out flaws in existing products. Pottery Barn Kids, a division of Pottery Barn, developed its *Learning Toys Collection* through observation, reading, and focus groups. Focus groups that included both parents and children were gathered and observed as they played with and talked about the new toys. Marketing researchers have also begun to take advantage of mobile marketing and social media outlets such as Facebook, Twitter, and blogs.[19]

Applying Marketing Research Data

business intelligence a field of research that uses activities and technologies for gathering, storing, and analyzing data to make better competitive decisions.

Market researchers now collect information that is more accurate than in the past. That means the resulting marketing strategies are also more effective. One field of research, known as **business intelligence**, uses various activities and technologies to gather, store, and analyze data to make better competitive decisions. Dell established its IdeaStorm website to gather information, criticism, compliments, and ideas for developing new computer products and improving its existing products. New users must register at the site and follow guidelines to post their ideas and reactions. Submitted ideas receive scores for their popularity, which helps Dell to sort through the material and decide which ideas to pursue. Recently, Dell added "Storm Sessions," where the company posts a topic and asks visitors to contribute their ideas. To make the discussions specific and relevant to the topic, each session is open only for a limited time. "Our commitment is to listen to your input and ideas to improve our products and services, and the way we do business," reads a welcoming note to the site. "We will do our best to keep you posted on how Dell brings customer ideas to life."[20]

Data Mining

data mining the use of computer searches of customer data to detect patterns and relationships.

data warehouse a customer database that allows managers to combine data from several different organizational functions.

After a company has built a database, marketers must be able to analyze the data and use the information it provides. **Data mining** is part of the broader field of business intelligence. It refers to the task of using computer-based technology to evaluate data in a database and identify useful trends. These trends or patterns may suggest models of real-world business activities. Accurate data mining can help researchers forecast recessions and pinpoint sales prospects.

Data mining uses a **data warehouse**, a sophisticated customer database that allows managers to combine data from several different organizational functions. Rapleaf Inc. collects publicly available personal information from social networking sites such as Facebook, Twitter, and other forums. Rapleaf then sells this information to airlines and credit card companies that view those individuals as potential customers. Such information can include everything from your blogging or posting habits to your credit rating. Among the issues arising from data mining are ownership of Web user data, the targeting capabilities of the Web, government supervision—and, of course, privacy.

Some observers feel that privacy norms are changing. They see confidentiality giving way to increasing openness.[21] Turiya Media's product, Leafnode, mines and analyzes the behaviour of online game players. It works by tracking the number of hours players spend on which games, and then creating behavioural profiles. Game publishers pay a monthly fee for the resulting data, which enable them to "proactively identify and retain their best customers, and target them with personalized recommendations."[22]

✓ ASSESSMENT CHECK

11.5.1 What is the difference between primary data and secondary data?

11.5.2 What is data mining?

MARKET SEGMENTATION

LO 11.6 Identify and explain each of the methods available for segmenting consumer and business markets.

Market segmentation is the process of dividing a market into several relatively similar groups. Both for-profit and not-for-profit organizations use segmentation to help them reach desirable target markets. Market segmentation is often based on the results of research, which tries to identify trends among certain groups of people. For instance, one survey of online teens revealed that the number of online teenagers and young adults who blog dropped from 28 percent in one recent year to 14 or 15 percent just a few years later. Social networking seems to have taken over communications functions among these two groups: its use has grown to 73 percent of all teenagers and 72 percent of all young adults. Only 8 percent of teenagers polled use Twitter.[23] This kind of information helps marketers to decide what types of products to develop and to whom these products should be marketed.

market segmentation the process of dividing a total market into several relatively similar groups.

Market segmentation attempts to isolate the traits that set a certain group of customers apart from the overall market. However, segmentation doesn't automatically produce marketing success. Table 11.1 lists several criteria that marketers should consider. The effectiveness of a segmentation strategy depends on how well the market meets these criteria. Marketers need to first link a market segment to a target, and then they can create a suitable marketing strategy.

Table 11.1 Criteria for Market Segmentation

CRITERION	EXAMPLE
A segment must be a measurable group.	Data can be collected on the dollar amount and number of purchases made by college and university students.
A segment must be accessible for communication.	More and more seniors are now online, so many more seniors can now be reached through Internet channels.
A segment must be large enough to offer profit potential.	In a small community, a store carrying only large-size shoes might not be profitable. For similar reasons, a specialty retail chain may prefer to locate in a large market.

Many retailers know that the holiday season can make or break their entire business year. That's why retailers need to predict accurately—and months ahead of time—customers' spending patterns and trends. Knowing about these trends is especially important during or after difficult economic times. The toy retailing giant Toys "R" Us identified a hot toy trend among children during one recent holiday season, so the firm decided to stock the toy. Zhu Zhu Pets, plush mechanical hamsters, were a huge hit with kids. Their parents camped out in parking lots, waiting to buy them. Gerald Storch, the company's CEO, said, "History has shown that the future rewards companies which are aggressive during economic downturns."[24]

How Market Segmentation Works

The first segmentation distinction involves whether a firm offers goods and services to customers for their own use or to purchasers who will use them directly or indirectly in providing other products for resale (the so-called B2B market). Depending on whether their firms offer consumer or

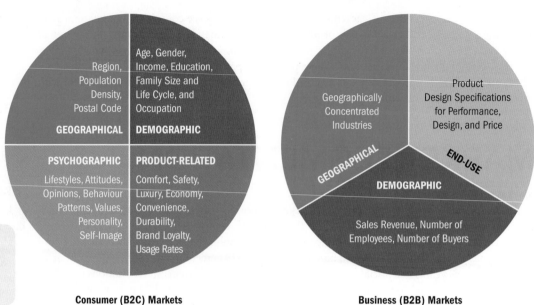

FIGURE 11.4
Methods of
Segmenting Consumer
and Business Markets

Consumer (B2C) Markets

Business (B2B) Markets

business products, marketers segment their target markets differently. Four common bases for segmenting consumer markets are geographical segmentation, demographic segmentation, psychographic segmentation, and product-related segmentation. By contrast, business markets can segment on three criteria: customer-based segmentation, end-use segmentation, and geographical segmentation. Figure 11.4 illustrates the segmentation methods for these two types of markets.

Segmenting Consumer Markets

Market segmentation has been practised since people first began selling products. Tailors made some clothing items for men and others for women. Tea was imported from India for tea drinkers in England and other European countries. In addition to demographic and geographical segmentation, today's marketers also define customer groups based on product-related differences and criteria that are psychographic—relating to lifestyle and values.

Geographical Segmentation

geographical segmentation
dividing an overall market into similar groups on the basis of their locations.

The oldest segmentation method is **geographical segmentation**—dividing a market into similar groups on the basis of their locations. Geographical location does not guarantee that consumers in a certain region will all buy the same kinds of products, but it does provide some information about needs. For examples, people who live in the suburbs buy more lawn-care products than those who live in city centres. But many people in the suburbs choose instead to purchase the services of a lawn maintenance firm. Consumers who live where winter is more severe are more likely than those who live in warmer areas to buy ice scrapers, snow shovels, and snow blowers. They are also more likely to contract with firms to remove the snow from driveways. Marketers also look at the size of the population of an area and who lives there—are the residents old or young? Do they reflect an ethnic background? What is the level of their income?

Job growth and migration patterns are also important to consider. Some businesses combine areas or even entire countries that share similar population and product-use patterns, instead of treating each as an independent segment.

Demographic Segmentation

demographic segmentation
dividing markets on the basis of various demographic or socioeconomic characteristics, such as gender, age, income, occupation, household size, stage in family life cycle, education, or ethnic group.

The most common method of market segmentation is **demographic segmentation**. This type of segmentation separates markets on the basis of various demographic or socioeconomic characteristics. Common demographic measures include gender, income, age, occupation, household size, stage in the family life cycle, education, and racial or ethnic group. Statistics Canada and the U.S. Census Bureau are the best sources of demographic information for their markets. Figure 11.5 lists some of the measures used in demographic segmentation.

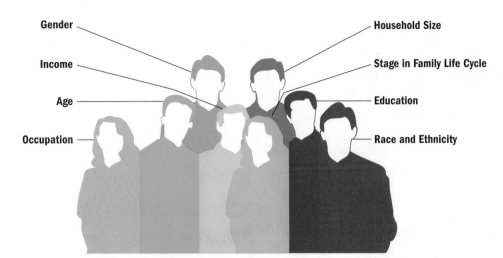

FIGURE 11.5 Common Demographic Measures

North American police departments are a highly specialized occupational demographic group. The Ford Crown Victoria is popular for its durability as a vehicle. It has long held 75 percent of the patrol-car market share. Ford plans to phase out the "Crown Vic" and replace it with the Police Interceptor. The vehicle is modelled on the Taurus sedan but has been adapted for the extreme circumstances of police work. The Interceptor's fuel efficiency is 25 percent better than the Crown Vic's. Its 365-horsepower engine outguns the Crown Vic's by 115 horsepower. Ford's police advisory board helped develop the Interceptor, but it may face competition from General Motors, Chrysler, and Carbon Motors (based in Indiana). These companies either produce or are planning to produce police vehicles of their own.[25]

Gender used to be a simple way to define markets for certain products—jewellery and skin care products for women; tools and motorcycles for men. But that has changed—dramatically. Men now buy jewellery and skin care products, and women buy tools and motorcycles. But marketers have found that there are still differences in the *ways* that women and men shop. These differences may go as far back as humanity's earliest days, when males generally hunted for food and females generally gathered it. One study showed that many male shoppers behave similarly to early hunters, who, once they found a prey animal, tracked it, killed it, and brought it back home as fast as possible. Many female shoppers behave more like early gatherers, who spent time carefully inspecting a variety of plants, choosing only those that were ripe.[26]

Another shift involves purchasing power. North American women now control an estimated 85 percent of the $7 trillion spent each year on personal consumption items.[27] One study predicts that women will soon control 60 percent of all wealth, in part because they live longer than men.[28]

Age may be the most unstable factor in demographic segmentation in Canada and the United States because of our rapidly aging population. Of the 340-plus million people who live in North America, more than one-third will be age 55 or older by the year 2020.[29] Because of these statistics, marketers for travel and leisure products, and marketers for retirement and business investments, are working hard to attract the attention of this age group, the aging baby boomers—those born between 1946 and 1964. Active-adult housing communities are one result of these efforts. Some developers have built communities with a resort-style atmosphere in desirable locations such as Whistler, B.C. ski country or the outskirts of a large city such as Toronto or Montreal. But, because of the recession, many such communities have actually seen their populations decrease. According to Mark Mather, associate vice-president of the Population Reference Bureau, "Baby boomers helped fuel housing and population growth in retirement areas earlier in the decade, and now they are playing an important role in the decline."[30]

Teens are another rapidly growing market. The entire scope of Gen-Yers—those born between 1976 and 1997—takes in about one-third of the total North American population. These consumers, often called the Millennials, are tech-savvy shoppers. They influence not only their own purchases but also those of their families and friends. They are educated consumers who comparison shop and

The image of children on the cover of a kids' catalogue, such as the one shown on the top of this pile, shows demographic segmentation by stage of the family life cycle.

usually avoid impulse purchases, partly because of the recession and partly because they are spending their own money. According to a Nielsen survey, compared with older generations, such as the "greatest generation" (those who lived through World War II) and the baby boomers, Gen-Yers shop less often but when they do shop, they buy more, preferring megastores and big box-retailers.[31]

Statistics can be helpful, but they don't tell the whole story. To serve customers well, marketers must also learn where people live, how old they are, what languages they speak, how much income they have, and their cultural tastes and preferences. Sometimes, marketers must do intensive research to reach a particular age group or gender group, or both, as described in the "Hit & Miss" feature.

Psychographic Segmentation

Lifestyle is the sum of a person's needs, preferences, motives, attitudes, social habits, and cultural background. In recent years, marketing researchers have tried to put together lifestyle portraits of consumers. This effort has led to another strategy for segmenting target markets, **psychographic segmentation**, which divides consumer markets into groups with similar psychological characteristics, values, and lifestyles.

psychographic segmentation dividing consumer markets into groups with similar attitudes, values, and lifestyles.

Psychographic studies are used to evaluate motivations for purchases of hundreds of goods and services, ranging from soft drinks to healthcare services. Firms use the resulting data to tailor their marketing strategies to carefully chosen market segments. A frequently used way of developing psychographic profiles uses *AIO statements*—people's verbal descriptions of their various attitudes, interests, and opinions. Researchers survey a sample of consumers, asking them whether they agree or disagree with each statement. The answers are then organized and analyzed for use in identifying various lifestyle categories.

Another way to get consumers to provide current information about their lifestyles is for organizations to create *blogs* in the hope that consumers may respond. Companies including Research In Motion, The Globe and Mail, and Microsoft have hired bloggers to run online Web journals as a way to connect with consumers and receive information from them. Other firms

HIT & MISS

Disney XD TV: Marketing to Boys

Disney marketing aimed at young girls has been highly successful. Just think of the "Princesses" products, the Jonas Brothers, and *High School Musical*. But the Disney Channel audience is 40 percent male. (*Pirates of the Caribbean* and *Toy Story* have both had successful sequels.)

In North America, about 10 percent of the population are males aged 5 to 19 years old. Worldwide, boys (or their parents) spend $50 billion every year on clothes, toys, and video games.

Recently, Disney bought Marvel Entertainment. It is hoping that Marvel's superheroes will draw viewers to Disney's XD TV channel. The channel is aimed at boys but doesn't exclude girls from its offerings of animation, action-adventure, comedy, movies, sports-themed shows, and music videos. The Disney XD website provides access to games, videos, and TV episodes.

How did Disney research a demographic that is known for not talking about their feelings? It hired a team of social scientists, who learned the following:

- Boys identify with main characters who are trying to grow, and they want to see more characters like themselves in TV shows.

- Boys personalize the undersides of their skateboards and carry them so the tag shows.

- Boys like to share small accomplishments.

- Boys shuttle quickly from one activity to another, moving from TV to video games to sports, and so on.

- Boys want more variety and reality in TV shows, not just all action or all cartoons.

Disney used these results to add a trophy room to the games page at the XD website and by advising its actors to carry their skateboards so the tagging showed, for realism. Viewership at XD increased more than 25 percent—but most of the new audience was girls. Boys aged 6 to 14 increased only 10 percent. The economic downturn also hurt advertising, but didn't discourage Rich Ross, the president of Disney Channels Worldwide. "We've seen cultural resonance, and it doesn't come overnight," he said.

Questions for Critical Thinking

1. What type(s) of segmentation strategy is Disney applying? Will it be effective? Why or why not?

2. What steps can Disney take to increase viewership of Disney XD among boys?

Sources: Company website, http://disney.go.com, accessed April 11, 2010; Tom Lowry and Ronald Grover, "Disney's Marvel Deal and the Pursuit of Boys," *BusinessWeek*, March 9, 2010, http://www.businessweek.com; Seth Lubove and Andy Fixmer, "Disney Beefs Up Marketing to Boys," *Ledger*, March 4, 2010, http://www.theledger.com.

encourage employees at all levels to use blogs to communicate with consumers. General Motors has several blogs at its GMblogs.com site, each set up for a specific brand or consumer interest. The FastLane blog discusses GM cars and trucks and invites consumers to offer their thoughts and ideas. Chevrolet Voltage is aimed at fans of the Volt and other electric vehicles. The Lab is where GM's advanced design team talks about its work and invites feedback from community members.[32]

Although demographic classifications such as age, gender, and income are relatively easy to identify and measure, researchers also need to define psychographic categories. Marketing research firms often conduct wide studies of consumers and then share their psychographic data with clients. Businesses sometimes look to studies done by sociologists and psychologists to help them understand their customers. For example, while children may belong to one age group and their parents to another, both live certain lifestyles together. Recent marketing research shows that today's parents are willing and able to spend more on goods and services for their children than parents were willing and able to spend a generation or two ago. Spending on toys and video games for children topped $41 billion for a recent year in North America.[33] These are just a few trends identified by the researchers, but they provide valuable information to firms that may be considering developing games, designing the interiors of family vehicles, or offering new wireless plans.

Product-Related Segmentation

Sellers who use **product-related segmentation** divide a consumer market into groups that are based on buyers' relationships to the good or service. The three most popular approaches to product-related segmentation are based on benefits sought, usage rates, and brand loyalty levels.

product-related segmentation dividing consumer markets into groups that are based on benefits sought by buyers, usage rates, and loyalty levels.

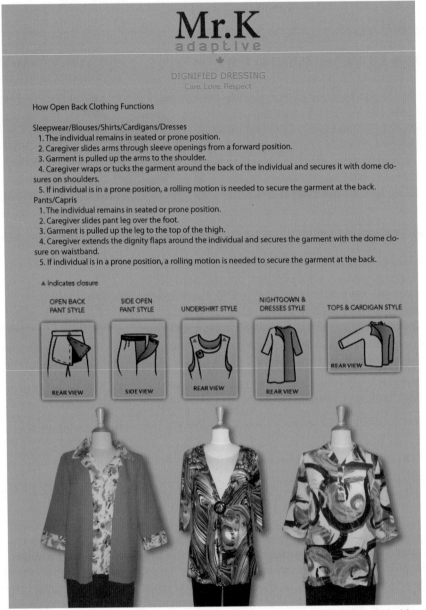

Mr.K
adaptive

DIGNIFIED DRESSING
Care. Love. Respect

How Open Back Clothing Functions

Sleepwear/Blouses/Shirts/Cardigans/Dresses
  1. The individual remains in seated or prone position.
  2. Caregiver slides arms through sleeve openings from a forward position.
  3. Garment is pulled up the arms to the shoulder.
  4. Caregiver wraps or tucks the garment around the back of the individual and secures it with dome closures on shoulders.
  5. If individual is in a prone position, a rolling motion is needed to secure the garment at the back.
Pants/Capris
  1. The individual remains in seated or prone position.
  2. Caregiver slides pant leg over the foot.
  3. Garment is pulled up the leg to the top of the thigh.
  4. Caregiver extends the dignity flaps around the individual and secures the garment with the dome closure on waistband.
  5. If individual is in a prone position, a rolling motion is needed to secure the garment at the back.

▲ indicates closure

OPEN BACK PANT STYLE — REAR VIEW
SIDE OPEN PANT STYLE — SIDE VIEW
UNDERSHIRT STYLE — REAR VIEW
NIGHTGOWN & DRESSES STYLE — REAR VIEW
TOPS & CARDIGAN STYLE — REAR VIEW

Canadian manufacturers can compete in a crowded fashion industry by developing and producing products that cater to niche markets. Kovac Industries of Montreal produces the Mr. K brand of "adaptive fashions" for senior women. Mr. K clothing is specially designed to be suitably fashionable and functional to allow easier placement and removal.

Segmenting by *benefits sought* focuses on the qualities that people look for in a good or service and the benefits they expect to receive. As more firms shift toward consumer demand for products that are eco-friendly, marketers find ways to emphasize the benefits of these products. Home-goods retailer Crate & Barrel has begun to offer tables and chairs made of mango wood. The wood is harvested only after the trees can no longer produce fruit. Consumers can also select a sofa whose cushions are made of recycled fibres that are filled with a natural, soy-based foam. According to the company's website, "While our collection has featured renewable woods and sustainable materials for a number of years, we are now introducing important initiatives that will help make our homes more thoughtful environments."[34]

Consumer markets can also be segmented according to the amounts of a product that people buy and use. Segmentation by *product usage rate* usually defines such categories as heavy users, medium users, and light users. The 80/20 principle states that roughly 80 percent of a product's revenues come from only 20 percent of its buyers. Companies can now pinpoint which of their customers are the heaviest users and even the most profitable customers. Companies then direct most of their marketing efforts to those customers.

The third technique for product-related segmentation divides customers by *brand loyalty*—the degree to which consumers recognize, prefer, and insist on a particular brand. Marketers define groups of consumers with similar degrees of brand loyalty. They then try to tie loyal customers to a good or service by giving away premiums, anything from a logo-imprinted T-shirt to a pair of tickets to a concert or sports event.

Segmenting Business Markets

In many ways, the segmentation process for business markets is like the segmentation process for consumer markets. But some specific methods are different. Business markets can be divided in three ways: through geographical segmentation; demographic, or customer-based, segmentation; and end-use segmentation.

Geographical segmentation methods for business markets are like the geographic segmentation methods used for consumer markets. Many B2B marketers target geographically concentrated industries, such as aircraft manufacturing, automobiles, and oil field equipment. The marketing mix may need to be changed to adapt to the customer needs, languages, and other variables of a different location. These changes will likely be needed when the company is marketing itself internationally.

Demographic, or customer-based, segmentation begins with a good or service being designed to suit a specific organizational market. Sodexho Marriott Services is the largest provider of food services in North America. Its customers include healthcare institutions, business and government offices, schools, colleges, and universities. Within these broad business segments, Sodexho identifies more specific segments, which might include government offices on the west coast or universities that have culturally diverse populations—and their different food preferences or dining styles. Sodexho uses survey data that cover students' lifestyles, attitudes, preferences for consumer products in general, services, and media categories. In addition, Sodexho uses targeted surveys that identify preferences for restaurant brands or certain foods, meal habits, and the amount of spending on meals. Marketers evaluate the data, which sometime reveal surprising trends. At one university, students said that they liked foods with an international flavour. So Sodexho adapted its offerings.[35]

To make it easier to focus on a specific type of business customer, the federal government has developed a system for subdividing the business marketplace into detailed segments. The six-digit *North American Industry Classification System (NAICS)* provides a common classification system used by the United States, Canada, and Mexico, the member-nations of the North American Free Trade Agreement (NAFTA). This system divides industries into broad categories such as agriculture, forestry, and fishing; manufacturing; transportation; and retail and wholesale trade. Each major category is further subdivided into smaller segments, such as gas stations with convenience food and warehouse clubs. The smaller segments provide more detailed information and make it easier to compare data among the member-nations.

Another way to group firms by their demographics is to segment them by size, such as by their sales revenues or numbers of employees. Some firms collect data from visitors to its website and use the data to segment customers by size. Modern information processing also means that companies can segment business markets based on how much they buy, not just how big they are.

End-use segmentation focuses on the precise way a B2B purchaser will use a product. This method is similar to the benefits-sought segmentation used for consumer markets. End-use segmentation helps small and mid-size companies to target specific end-user markets instead of competing directly with large firms for wider customer groups. A company might also design a marketing mix based on certain criteria for making a purchase.

end-use segmentation a marketing strategy that focuses on the precise way a B2B purchaser will use a product.

 ASSESSMENT CHECK

11.6.1 What is the most common form of segmentation for consumer markets?

11.6.2 What are the three approaches to product-related segmentation?

11.6.3 What is end-use segmentation in the B2B market?

LO 11.7 Outline the determinants of consumer behaviour.

CONSUMER BEHAVIOUR

A fundamental marketing task is to find out why people buy one product and not another. The answer requires an understanding of **consumer behaviour**: the activities of end consumers that are directly involved in obtaining, consuming, and disposing of products, and the decision processes before and after these activities.

consumer behaviour end consumers' activities that are directly involved in obtaining, consuming, and disposing of products, and the decision processes before and after these activities.

Determinants of Consumer Behaviour

Businesses study people's purchasing behaviour to identify their attitudes toward products and to learn how they use products. This information also helps marketers reach their targeted customers. Both personal and interpersonal factors affect the way buyers behave. Personal influences on consumer behaviour include individual needs and motives, perceptions, attitudes, learned experiences, and self-concept. For example, people are constantly looking for ways to save time, so firms do everything they can to provide goods and services that are designed for convenience. But when it comes to products such as dinner foods, consumers don't just want convenience—they also want the flavour of a home-cooked meal and quality time with their families. So companies such as Stouffer's offer frozen lasagna and manicotti in family sizes, and grocery stores have entire sections of freshly prepared take-out meals, including roast turkey and filet mignon.

McDonald's is betting that consumers who drink premium coffee beverages will also like to buy them at bargain prices. In many locations, McDonald's has placed McCafé coffee bars near the cash register. These coffee bars offer cappuccinos, lattes, and mochas. Almost 70 percent of McDonald's stores now serve these beverages, putting the company in direct competition with Starbucks.[36]

The interpersonal determinants of consumer behaviour include cultural, social, and family influences. In the area of convenience foods, cultural, social, and family influences come into play as much as an individual's need to save time. Marketers understand that many consumers value the time they spend with their families and want to provide them with good nutrition. Marketers often emphasize these values when advertising convenience food products.

Sometimes external events influence consumer behaviour. One study suggests that because of the recession, consumers may have permanently changed their buying and spending behaviour. The survey found that 72 percent of consumers said that they had significantly or somewhat changed their shopping habits; only 7 percent said they had made no change. Manufacturers and retailers—and especially small businesses—will need to create new marketing strategies in response to these challenges.[37]

Determinants of Business Buying Behaviour

When business buyers need to make a purchase, they have to deal with their own preferences, which may not be their firm's preference. They must also deal with a variety of influences from their organizations because many people can be involved in the decision to purchase B2B products. For example, a design engineer may help set the specifications that potential suppliers must meet. A procurement manager may invite selected companies to bid on a purchase. A production supervisor may evaluate the operational qualities of the proposals that the firm receives, and the vice-president of manufacturing may head a committee making the final decision.

Steps in the Consumer Behaviour Process

Consumer decision-making follows the sequential process shown in Figure 11.6. Interpersonal and personal influences affect every step. The process begins when the consumer recognizes a problem or opportunity. For example, if someone needs a new pair of shoes, that need becomes a problem to solve. If you receive a promotion at work and a 20 percent salary increase, that change may lead to a purchase opportunity.

To solve the problem or take advantage of the opportunity, the consumer looks for information about his or her intended purchase and evaluates options, such as the available brands. The goal is to find the best response to the problem or opportunity.

In the end, the consumer usually reaches a decision and completes the transaction. Later, the customer evaluates the experience by making a post-purchase evaluation. Feelings about the experience serve as feedback that will affect future purchase decisions. The various steps in the sequence are affected by both interpersonal and personal factors.

✓ **ASSESSMENT CHECK**

11.7.1 Define *consumer behaviour*.

11.7.2 What are some determinants of consumer behaviour?

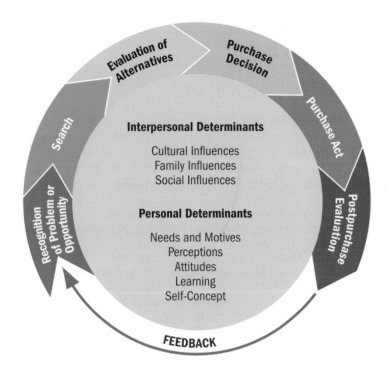

Interpersonal Determinants

Cultural Influences
Family Influences
Social Influences

Personal Determinants

Needs and Motives
Perceptions
Attitudes
Learning
Self-Concept

Evaluation of Alternatives

Purchase Decision

Purchase Act

Search

Postpurchase Evaluation

Recognition of Problem or Opportunity

FEEDBACK

FIGURE 11.6 Steps in the Consumer Behaviour Process

RELATIONSHIP MARKETING

LO 11.8 Discuss the benefits of and tools for relationship marketing.

The past decade has brought rapid change to most industries. Customers have become better informed and more demanding purchasers by closely comparing competing goods and services. They expect, even demand, new benefits from the companies that supply them. These expectations are make it harder for firms to gain a competitive advantage on the basis of product features alone.

In today's hypercompetitive era, businesses need to find new ways of relating to customers to maintain long-term success. Businesses are developing strategies and tactics that create closer relationships with their customers, suppliers, and even employees. As a result, many firms are turning their attention to relationship marketing. **Relationship marketing** goes beyond an effort toward making the sale. This type of marketing develops and maintains long-term, cost-effective exchange relationships with partners. These partners include individual customers, suppliers, and employees. As its ultimate goal, relationship marketing seeks to achieve customer satisfaction.

When businesses manage their relationships instead of just completing sales transactions, they can often develop creative partnerships. But customers will enter into relationships with firms only when they are assured that the relationship will be of benefit to them. As the intensity of commitment increases, so does the likelihood of a business continuing a long-term relationship with its customers. Businesses build relationships by partnering with customers, suppliers, and other businesses. Timberland, maker of footwear and clothing, creates many partnerships that foster long-term relationships. Timberland partners with not-for-profit organizations such as CARE, City Year, and Clean Air–Cool Planet to complete service projects for communities and the environment. Through its Serv-a-Palooza, hundreds of Timberland employees sign up for volunteer tasks in their communities. Those opportunities even extend to customers who have expressed an interest in participating in programs in their own regions. If you want to volunteer for a food drive or to help restore a marsh, just log on to the Timberland website to see what's available. All of these activities help build relationships with customers, communities, and other organizations.[38]

relationship marketing
developing and maintaining long-term, cost-effective exchange relationships with partners.

BUSINESS ETIQUETTE

Calming the Angry Customer

In any business, an angry customer is a challenge. An upset customer represents not only an immediate problem but also a potential loss of future business. The customer may be upset over poor service or a broken product, frustrated by lack of attention from the company, or just plain demanding. You, the businessperson, should look at this customer not as a disruption but as an opportunity to see your company from the outside. With a little bit of common sense, good personal skills, and knowledge of your company and its products, you can turn the customer's dissatisfaction into satisfaction.

- *Remain calm and professional.* The customer isn't angry with you personally. Let the customer speak first, and listen carefully as he or she states the problem. Make written notes. Acknowledge the customer's anger, then assure him or her that you will correct the situation.

- *Repeat the customer's stated problem.* Using your own words assures the customer that you have been listening. For example, you might say, "The shoes you received were the right colour but the wrong size." Make sure you understand the problem before offering a solution.

- *Focus on the solution.* Having procedures in place beforehand can help you resolve a problem quickly. If you can't solve the problem yourself, immediately refer it to someone who can. Fast action will let the customer know that you are on his or her side.

- *Thank the customer for his or her patience.* By bringing the problem to your attention, the customer is actually giving you an opportunity to improve service to all your clients.

- *Follow up.* If appropriate, send an e-mail or make a phone call to make sure the correct pair of shoes arrived. Your professionalism will strengthen the customer's relationship with your firm—and positive word of mouth may even bring you new customers.

Sources: Lynne McClure, "Handling Angry Customers," Impact Publications, http://impactpublications.com, accessed April 4, 2010; Katy Tynan, "Conflict Management Part 2—Calming an Irate Customer," *Ezinearticles.com*, http://ezinearticles.com, accessed April 4, 2010; "How to Calm an Angry Customer," *BusinessKnowledgeSource.com* http://www.businessknowledgesource.com, accessed April 4, 2010.

Benefits of Relationship Marketing

Relationship marketing helps all parties involved. Businesses that create solid relationships with suppliers and customers protect themselves against competitors. These businesses are also often rewarded with lower costs and higher profits than they would generate on their own. Long-term agreements with a few high-quality suppliers can reduce a firm's production costs. Unlike one-time sales, these ongoing relationships encourage suppliers to offer customers preferred treatment. For example, suppliers might quickly correct any quality problems and be willing to adjust shipments to accommodate changes in orders.

Encouraging good relationships with customers can be a vital strategy for a firm. By identifying current purchasers and maintaining positive relationships with them, organizations can efficiently target their best customers. Studying current customers' buying habits and preferences can help marketers to identify potential new customers and establish ongoing contact with them. Attracting a new customer can cost five times as much as keeping an existing customer. Long-term customers do not just reduce marketing costs; they usually buy more, require less service, refer other customers, and provide valuable feedback. Together, these elements contribute to a higher **lifetime value of a customer**—the revenues and intangible benefits (such as referrals and customer feedback) from the customer over the life of the relationship, minus the amount the company must spend to acquire and serve that customer. Keeping that customer may occasionally require some extra effort, especially when the customer has become upset or dissatisfied with a good or service. But good marketers can overcome this particular challenge, as described in the "Business Etiquette" feature.

Businesses also benefit from having strong relationships with other companies. Purchasers who repeatedly buy from one business may find that they save time and gain service quality as

lifetime value of a customer the revenues and intangible benefits (such as referrals and customer feedback) from a customer over the life of the relationship, minus the amount the company must spend to acquire and serve that customer.

the business learns more about their specific needs. Some relationship-oriented companies also customize items based on customer preferences. Because many businesses reward loyal customers with discounts or bonuses, some buyers may even find that they save money by developing long-term relationships. Alliances, or working with other firms, to serve the same customers also can be rewarding. The partners combine their capabilities and resources to accomplish goals that they could not reach on their own. Alliances with other firms may also help businesses to develop the skills and experience they need to improve service to current customers or to successfully enter new markets.

Tools for Nurturing Customer Relationships

Relationship marketing has important benefits for both customers and businesses. Most relationship-oriented businesses quickly learn that some customers generate more profitable business than others. The 80/20 principle mentioned earlier in the chapter suggests that 20 percent of a firm's customers account for 80 percent of its sales and profits. A customer in that category has a higher lifetime value than a customer who buys only once or twice or a customer who makes small purchases.

Businesses shouldn't ignore any customer, but they do need to distribute their marketing dollars wisely. A firm may choose to customize goods or services for high-value customers while working to increase repeat sales of standardized products to less valuable customers. Differentiating between these two groups also helps marketers to focus on each group in an effort to increase their commitment.

frequency marketing a marketing initiative that rewards frequent purchases with cash, rebates, merchandise, or other premiums.

affinity program a marketing effort sponsored by an organization that targets people who share common interests and activities.

Frequency Marketing and Affinity Marketing Programs

Firms try to build and protect customer relationships by using popular techniques, including frequent-buyer or frequent-user programs. These so-called **frequency marketing** programs reward purchasers with cash, rebates, merchandise, or other premiums. Frequency programs have grown more sophisticated over the years. They offer more personalization and customization than in the past. Airlines, hotel groups, restaurants, and many retailers, including grocery stores, use frequency programs. Customers who join the Marriott Rewards program have the option to spend their earned points at nearly 3,000 hotels, resorts, spas, and golf locations in 67 countries and territories worldwide.[39]

Affinity programs are another tool for building emotional links with customers. An affinity program is an organization's marketing effort that targets people who share common interests and activities. Affinity programs are common in the credit card industry. For example, a person can sign up for a credit card that is printed with the logo of a favourite charity, a sports or entertainment celebrity, or a photograph of his or her college or university. MBNA Canada Bank is the largest independent credit card issuer in the world and offers an affinity MasterCard credit card for the University of Toronto.

Affinity programs are a tool for building emotional links with customers. These programs are common in the credit card industry. For example, MBNA Canada Bank offers an affinity MasterCard credit card for the University of Toronto.

Many businesses also use comarketing and cobranding. In a **comarketing** deal, two businesses jointly market each other's products. When two or more businesses link their names to a single product, **cobranding** occurs. Sometimes, two unlikely businesses team up. When that happens, the marketing sparks can fly—and two very different groups of consumers may come together to buy the same product. For example, Nike and Apple have marketed the Nike + iPod Sport kit. To use this kit, a runner inserts a special sensor into a built-in pocket in a Nike + shoe. The sensor matches the runner's activity with workout data and music that plays through the iPod. Consumers can also purchase specially designed Nike workout clothing that has pockets designed to hold an iPod nano itself.[40]

comarketing a cooperative arrangement where two businesses jointly market each other's products.

cobranding a cooperative arrangement where two or more businesses team up to closely link their names on a single product.

One-on-One Marketing

The ability to customize products and rapidly deliver goods and services is increasingly dependent on technology, such as computer-aided design and computer-aided manufacturing (CAD/CAM). The Internet offers a way for businesses to connect with customers in a direct and personal manner. Companies can take orders for customized products, gather data about buyers, and predict what items a customer might want in the future. Computer databases provide strong support for effective relationship marketing. Marketers can maintain databases on customer tastes, price-range preferences, and lifestyles. They can also quickly obtain names and other information about possible customers. Amazon.com greets each online customer with a list of suggested books he or she might like to purchase. Many online retailers send their customers e-mails about upcoming sales, new products, and special events.

Small and large companies often use *customer relationship management (CRM)* software technology to help them gather, sort, and interpret data about customers. Software firms develop this software to help businesses build and manage their relationships with customers. For example, QueueBuster is a software product that offers callers the choice of receiving an automated return call instead of waiting on hold for the next available representative. After putting the software in place, travel agency STA reported that its customer satisfaction ratings had improved to 98 percent. This simple solution to customers' frustration helped STA to build customer loyalty. It also helped save STA from lost business.[41]

✔ **ASSESSMENT CHECK**

11.8.1 What is the lifetime value of a customer?

11.8.2 Discuss the increasing importance of one-on-one marketing efforts.

WHAT'S AHEAD

The next two chapters examine each of the four elements of the marketing mix that marketers use to satisfy their selected target markets. Chapter 12 focuses on products and their distribution through various channels to different outlets. Chapter 13 covers promotion and the various methods marketers use to communicate with their target customers, and strategies for setting prices for different products.

RETURN TO INSIDE BUSINESS

Handmade Items: Etsy.com Has Them All

Lisa Lutz creates her own jewellery and uses Etsy.com to help build her brand recognition and distribution. She also uses Facebook and other social media platforms such as blogs to link online readers back to her business, Bead Crazed, and its website at http://www.beadcrazed.com/. She writes online, "I love to learn and have taken classes in wirework, ArtClay silver and metalsmithing. While looking for the 'perfect' bead, I discovered lampworking. My hobby quickly turned into a bead crazed obsession, and I have been making lampwork beads for about 4 years now." Although she is a full-time medical technician in microbiology and mother of four, she says that she is happily busy producing and selling her creations online as well creating customized pieces for customers.

QUESTIONS FOR CRITICAL THINKING

1. How can Bead Crazed and Lisa Lutz generate more attention online?

2. Does Lutz have an advantage producing and selling jewellery online instead of some other art form?

3. What sort of customer is drawn to the artisans selling on Etsy.com?

SUMMARY OF LEARNING OBJECTIVES

LO 11.1 Summarize the ways in which marketing creates utility.

Utility is the ability of a good or service to satisfy the wants and needs of customers. The production function creates form utility by converting inputs to finished goods and services. Marketing creates three types of utility—time utility, place utility, and ownership utility—by making the product available when consumers what to buy it, where consumers want to buy it, and by arranging for an organized transfer of ownership.

✓ ASSESSMENT CHECK ANSWERS

11.1.1 What is utility? Utility is the ability of a good or service to satisfy the wants and needs of customers.

11.1.2 Identify how marketing creates utility. Marketing creates time utility by making a good or service available when customers want to purchase it, place utility by making the product available in a convenient location, and ownership utility by transferring the product from the buyer to the seller.

LO 11.2 Discuss the marketing concept.

The marketing concept refers to a companywide customer focus with the goal of achieving long-term success. This concept is much needed in today's marketplace, which is mainly a buyer's market, where buyers can choose from many goods and services. Marketing now centres on satisfying customers and building long-term relationships with them.

✓ ASSESSMENT CHECK ANSWERS

11.2.1 What is the marketing concept? The marketing concept is a companywide customer focus with the goal of

achieving long-term success. According to the marketing concept, success begins with the customer.

11.2.2 How is the marketing concept tied to the relationship era of marketing? Most marketing now centres on satisfying customers and building long-term relationships with them. In a previous marketing era, the focus was on simply producing and selling goods and services.

LO 11.3 Describe not-for-profit marketing, and identify the five major categories of nontraditional marketing.

Not-for-profit organizations use marketing just as for-profit firms do. Not-for-profit organizations operate in both the public and private sectors. They use marketing to attract volunteers and donations, to make people aware of their existence, and to achieve certain goals for society. Not-for-profit organizations may use several types of nontraditional marketing—person, place, event, cause, or organization marketing. They may use only one type of marketing or a combination of two or more types.

✓ ASSESSMENT CHECK ANSWERS

11.3.1 Why do not-for-profit organizations use marketing? Not-for-profit organizations use marketing to attract volunteers and donors, communicate their message, and achieve their societal goals.

11.3.2 What are the five types of nontraditional marketing used by not-for-profit organizations? The five types of nontraditional marketing are person, place, event, cause, and organization marketing.

LO 11.4 Outline the basic steps in developing a marketing strategy.

All organizations develop marketing strategies to reach their customers. This process involves two steps: first, analyzing the overall market and selecting a target market; and, second, developing a marketing mix that blends elements related to product, distribution, promotion, and pricing decisions.

 ASSESSMENT CHECK ANSWERS

11.4.1 Distinguish between consumer products and business products. Business products are goods and services purchased to be used, either directly or indirectly, in the production of other goods for resale. Consumer products are goods and services purchased by the end users.

11.4.2 What are the steps in developing a marketing strategy? The steps in developing a marketing strategy are analyzing the overall market, selecting a target market, and developing a marketing mix.

LO 11.5 Describe the marketing research function.

Marketing research is the information-gathering function that links marketers to the marketplace. It provides valuable information about potential target markets. Firms may generate internal data or gather external data. They may use secondary data or conduct research to obtain primary data. Data mining involves computer searches through customer data to detect patterns or relationships. It is a helpful tool in forecasting various trends such as sales revenues and consumer behaviour.

 ASSESSMENT CHECK ANSWERS

11.5.1 What is the difference between primary data and secondary data? Secondary data are previously published facts that are inexpensive to retrieve and easy to obtain. Primary data are collected firsthand through observation or surveys.

11.5.2 What is data mining? Data mining involves using computer searches of customer data to evaluate the data and identify useful trends that may suggest models of real-world business activities.

LO 11.6 Identify and explain each of the methods available for segmenting consumer and business markets.

Consumer markets can be divided according to four criteria: geographical factors; demographic characteristics, such as age and family size; psychographic variables, which involve behavioural and lifestyle profiles; and product-related variables, such as the benefits consumers look for when buying a product or the degree of brand loyalty they feel toward it. Business markets are segmented

according to three criteria: geographical characteristics, customer-based specifications for products, and end-user applications.

 ASSESSMENT CHECK ANSWERS

11.6.1 What is the most common form of segmentation for consumer markets? The most commonly used consumer market segmentation method is demographics.

11.6.2 What are the three approaches to product-related segmentation? The three approaches to product-related segmentation are by benefits sought, product usage rate, and brand loyalty.

11.6.3 What is end-use segmentation in the B2B market? End-use segmentation focuses on the precise way a B2B purchaser will use a product.

LO 11.7 Outline the determinants of consumer behaviour.

Consumer behaviour refers to end consumers' activities that have direct effects on obtaining, consuming, and disposing of products, and the decision processes before and after these actions. Personal influences on consumer behaviour include an individual's needs and motives, perceptions, attitudes, learned experiences, and self-concept. The interpersonal determinants include cultural influences, social influences, and family influences. Many people within a firm may take part in business purchase decisions, so business buyers must consider a variety of organizational influences in addition to their own preferences.

 ASSESSMENT CHECK ANSWERS

11.7.1 Define *consumer behaviour.* Consumer behaviour refers to end consumers' activities that are directly involved in obtaining, consuming, and disposing of products, and the decision processes before and after these actions.

11.7.2 What are some determinants of consumer behaviour? Determinants of consumer behaviour include both personal influences and interpersonal influences. Personal influences include an individual's needs and motives; perceptions, attitudes, and experiences; and self-concept. Interpersonal influences include cultural, social, and family influences.

LO 11.8 Discuss the benefits of and tools for relationship marketing.

Relationship marketing is an organization's attempt to develop long-term, cost-effective links with individual customers for mutual benefit. Encouraging good relationships with customers can be part of a firm's vital strategy. By identifying current purchasers and encouraging a positive relationship with them, an organization can efficiently target its best customers, fulfill their needs, and create loyalty. Information technologies, frequency and affinity programs, and one-on-one efforts all help build relationships with customers.

✓ **ASSESSMENT CHECK ANSWERS**

11.8.1 **What is the lifetime value of a customer?** The lifetime value of a customer is the total of the revenues and intangible benefits from the customer over the life of the customer's relationship with a firm, minus the amount the company must spend to acquire and serve the customer.

11.8.2 **Discuss the increasing importance of one-on-one marketing efforts.** One-on-one marketing is increasing in importance as consumers demand more customization in goods and services. One-on-one marketing is also increasingly dependent on technology such as computer-aided design and computer-aided manufacturing (CAD/CAM). The Internet also offers a way for businesses to connect with customers in a direct and personal manner.

BUSINESS TERMS YOU NEED TO KNOW

marketing 294	organization marketing 301	data warehouse 306	relationship marketing 315
exchange process 295	consumer (B2C) product 303	market segmentation 307	lifetime value of a customer 316
utility 295	business (B2B) product 303	geographical segmentation 308	frequency marketing 317
marketing concept 297	target market 304	demographic segmentation 308	affinity program 317
person marketing 299	marketing mix 304	psychographic segmentation 310	comarketing 317
place marketing 299	marketing research 305	product-related segmentation 311	cobranding 317
event marketing 300	business intelligence 306	end-use segmentation 313	
cause marketing 301	data mining 306	consumer behaviour 313	

REVIEW QUESTIONS

1. Define the four different types of utility and explain how marketing contributes to the creation of utility. Then choose one of the following companies and describe how it creates each type of utility with its goods or services:

   a. Burger King

   b. Polo Ralph Lauren

   c. Chapters bookstore

   d. Supercuts hair salons

   e. Adobe Systems

2. Describe the shift from a seller's market to a buyer's market. Why was this move important to marketers?

3. Describe how an organization might combine person marketing and event marketing. Give an example.

4. Describe how an organization might combine cause marketing and organization marketing. Give an example.

5. Identify each of the following as a consumer product or a business product, or classify it as both:

   a. a cup of coffee

   b. iPad

   c. gasoline

   d. a boat trailer

   e. hand sanitizer

   f. hair gel

6. Identify and describe the four strategies that blend to create a marketing mix.

7. What is a target market? Why is target market selection usually the first step in the development of a marketing strategy?

8. Identify the two strategies that a firm can use to develop a marketing mix for international markets. What are the upsides and downsides of each?

9. Describe the types of data that might be gathered by someone who is thinking of starting an accounting service. How might this businessperson use the data in making the start-up decision?

10. Explain each of the methods used to segment consumer and business markets. Which methods are most effective for each of the following and why? (Note that more than one method might be suitable.)

  a. a grocery store featuring organic foods

  b. hair-care products

  c. a tour bus company

  d. a line of baby food

  e. dental insurance

  f. a dry cleaner

11. What are the three major determinants of consumer behaviour? Give an example of how each one might influence a person's purchasing decision.

12. What are the benefits of relationship marketing? Describe how frequency and affinity programs work toward building relationships.

PROJECTS AND TEAMWORK APPLICATIONS

1. On your own or with a classmate, choose one of the following products and create an advertisement that illustrates how your firm creates time, place, and form utility in its delivery of the product to the customer.

  a. an auto repair service

  b. hiking tours

  c. a craft supply store

  d. a pet-sitting service

2. Choose one of the following not-for-profit organizations or find one on your own. Research the organization online to learn more about it. Outline your proposal for a fundraising event. You can base your event on the chapter discussion of nontraditional marketing, such as cause marketing or organization marketing.

  a. Alberta Society for the Prevention of Cruelty to Animals

  b. Prostate Cancer Foundation

  c. Canadian Red Cross

  d. Salvation Army

3. As a marketer, you may be able to classify your firm's goods and services as both business and consumer products. Your company's sales will likely increase because you will build relationships with a new category of customers. On your own or with a classmate, choose one of the following products, and outline a marketing strategy for attracting the classification of customer that is *opposite* from the one listed in parentheses.

  a. a hybrid car (consumer)

  b. a LCD TV (consumer)

  c. a limousine service (business)

  d. office furniture (business)

4. Think of two situations where you were a customer: one situation when you were satisfied with the merchandise you received and one situation when you were not satisfied. List the reasons you were satisfied in the first case and list the reasons you were not satisfied in the second case. Did the failure occur because the seller did not understand your needs?

5. Comarketing and cobranding are techniques that organizations often use to market their own and each other's products, such as Nike running shoes and the Apple iPod. On your own or with a classmate, choose two firms with goods and/or services you think would work well together for comarketing separate products or cobranding a single product. Create an advertisement for your comarketing or cobranding effort.

WEB ASSIGNMENTS

1. **Demographic trends.** The Canadian Census and the *Statistical Abstract of the United States* are excellent sources of demographic and economic data. Visit the websites listed below. On the StatsCan site, click on "By topic" from the list on the left and then view the population data. On the U.S. website, scroll down the list on the left and select "Population." What do the Canadian and American populations currently look like in terms of age and race? What will the population look like in the decades to come?

   http://www12.statcan.ca/census-recensement/index-eng.cfm

   http://www.census.gov/compendia/statab/

2. **Market segmentation.** Go to the website of Canon Canada and review the company's range of product offerings. Prepare a brief report on how Canon segments its markets.

   http://www.canon.ca/

3. **Customer loyalty programs.** Airlines and hotel chains offer customer loyalty programs. Pick an airline and hotel chain and print out information on the firm's customer loyalty program. (Two examples are listed here.) Bring the material to class to participate in a discussion on this topic.

   http://www.westjet.com/guest/en/business-travel/frequent-guest-program/

   http://www.marriott.com/rewards/rewards-program.mi

WILEY **PLUS**
www.wileyplus.com

Access your WileyPLUS course for:

- The complete digital textbook.

- Question assistance, including links to relevant sections in the online digital textbook.

- Immediate feedback and proof of progress, 24/7

- Integrated, multi-media resources – including MP3 downloads, visual exhibits, animations, and much more – that provide multiple study paths and encourage more active learning.

QUIZ YOURSELF

Note: Internet Web addresses change frequently. If you don't find the exact sites listed, you may need to access the organization's home page and search from there or use a search engine such as Bing or Google.

© Can Stock Photo Inc./Danno44

12 | PRODUCT AND DISTRIBUTION STRATEGIES

LEARNING OBJECTIVES

LO 12.1 Explain marketing's definition of a product; differentiate among convenience products, shopping products, and specialty products; and distinguish between a product mix and a product line.

LO 12.2 Briefly describe the four stages of the product life cycle and their marketing implications.

LO 12.3 Explain how firms identify their products.

LO 12.4 Outline and briefly describe the major components of an effective distribution strategy.

LO 12.5 Distinguish between the different types of wholesaling intermediaries.

LO 12.6 Describe the various types of retailers, and identify retail strategies.

LO 12.7 Identify the various categories of distribution channels, and discuss the factors that influence channel selection.

INSIDE BUSINESS

Montreal's Fitness City Complex: Bringing Fitness Businesses Together Under One Roof

© Can Stock Photo Inc./Kzenon

It is a well-established business model—bring competing businesses together at one location for the convenience of the customer. If customers don't find what they are looking for at one business, they can easily check out the others. That's why we often find car dealerships grouped together in a "car shopping district." Customers can easily visit a few car dealers and compare their products before making a purchase decision. Car dealerships outside of the main car-shopping district need to offer something very special if they expect shoppers to travel to their business.

This clustering, or grouping, strategy is familiar to us. We see it in large cities in their restaurant districts, fashion districts, and theatre districts. The same idea might be successful for other businesses, too. Think about the possibilities for businesses that do not compete directly, but complement each other by offering related services. These businesses tend to be scattered. Because of their locations, they are not very visible to potential customers. But, by clustering together in one location, customers of one business are more likely to become customers of a complementary business.

An example of this kind of strategic thinking is Fitness City, located near the Trans-Canada Highway in Montreal's suburban area known as the West Island. Fitness City instantly became the largest fitness facility in Quebec when it recently opened its doors. The facility brings together a variety of fitness businesses under one 73,000-square-foot roof to serve customers who are both fitness-conscious and health-conscious.

Fitness City's largest fitness provider is Monster Gym, which takes up 45,000 square feet. Monster Gym has been owned and managed by Carmine Petrillo for more than 20 years. His original gym would have been considered large enough at 8,000 square feet. But the move to the new building provides space to offer even more facilities to Monster Gym's 6,000 members. Monster Gym acts as the "anchor" for the complex because of its 24/7 operating hours, its size, and its large and diverse clientele.

As members walk through the building's main entrance, they pass Cielos Studios, the 9,000-square-foot space dedicated to yoga, Pilates, pole dancing, Zumba, tai chi, erotic dance, meditation, and other equipment-free classes. Like Monster Gym, Cielos was an established West Island business that brought along its diverse customers when it relocated to Fitness City.

The same scenario was true for Grant Brothers Boxing and MMA Gyms, operated by former Canadian Middleweight Champion Otis Grant and his brother Howard, a 1988 Olympian and former Canadian Lightweight Champion. (Another brother, Ryan, operates a Grant Brothers Boxing Gym in Toronto). These gyms offer boxing, which tends to attract young men. They also offer kick-boxing, which appeals to women because of the aerobic workout and defensive training. According Howard Grant, men and women are often more likely to try boxing and other classes when they see someone of their own age in the ring working out. This is especially true for young adults who look at boxing and other contact sports as part of an overall effort to build and discipline both their bodies and their minds.

The Fitness City complex also offers the services of the Nuance Spa and massage facility; batting cages, golf simulations, and training at Bergy Baseball & Golf; and professional physiotherapists, dieticians, trainers, and coaches to help fitness-minded individuals reach their goals. Le Bistro Fit is the new restaurant located in the centre of the complex. It provides healthy meals and beverages for clients to enjoy after their workouts. Each of these individually owned businesses hopes to gain new customers—and revenue—from the mix of clientele that use the complex. In time, each business will see how much it benefits from the success of its neighbours.[1]

CHAPTER 12 OVERVIEW

In this chapter we examine the many ways that organizations design and carry out marketing strategies that address customers' needs and wants. Two of the most powerful tools are strategies that relate to products (which include both goods and services) and strategies that relate to the distribution of those products.

As the Fitness City complex shows, successful companies are deeply aware of their customers' needs. Fitness City continues to build business by adding new service providers, such as food supplements stores and more martial arts specialists. The creation of new products is the lifeblood, or life force, of an organization. Companies must constantly develop new products to ensure their survival and long-term growth.

This chapter focuses on the first two elements of the marketing mix: product and distribution. We begin our discussion of product strategy by describing the classifications of goods and services, customer service, product lines and the product mix, and the product life cycle. Companies often shape their marketing strategies differently depending on the stage of the product life cycle: when they are introducing a new product, when the product has established itself in the marketplace, and when the product is declining in popularity. We also discuss product identification through brand name and distinctive packaging. We then look at how companies foster, or encourage, loyalty to their brands to keep customers coming back for more.

Distribution is the second mix variable discussed. It focuses on moving goods and services from producer to wholesaler to retailer to buyers. Managing the distribution process includes making decisions such as what kind of wholesaler to use and where to offer products for sale. Retailers can range from specialty stores to factory outlets and everything in between. To succeed, retailers must choose suitable customer service, pricing, and location strategies. The chapter ends with a look at logistics, the process of coordinating the flow of information, goods, and services among suppliers and on to final consumers.

LO 12.1 Explain marketing's definition of a product; differentiate among convenience products, shopping products, and specialty products; and distinguish between a product mix and a product line.

product a bundle of physical, service, and symbolic characteristics designed to satisfy consumer wants.

PRODUCT STRATEGY

What is a product? Most people answer this question by listing a product's physical features. But marketers take a broader view. To marketers, a **product** is a bundle of physical, service, and symbolic characteristics designed to satisfy consumer wants. The chief executive officer of a major tool manufacturer once startled his shareholders when he said, "Last year our customers bought over 1 million quarter-inch drill bits, and none of them wanted to buy the product. They all wanted quarter-inch holes." Product strategy involves much more than just producing a good or service; it focuses on the benefits of a good or service. The marketing conception of a product includes decisions about package design, brand name, trademarks, warranties, product image, new-product development, and customer service. For example, think about your favourite soft drink. Do you like it for its taste alone? Or are you attracted by other qualities, such as clever ads, attractive packaging, overall image, and ease of purchase from vending machines and other convenient locations? These other qualities may influence your choice more than you think.

Classifying Goods and Services

Marketers have found it useful to classify goods and services as either B2C or B2B, depending on whether the purchasers of the particular item are consumers or businesses. These classifications can be subdivided further. Each classification type needs a different competitive strategy.

Classifying Consumer Goods and Services

Consumer goods and services—that is, goods and services used by end consumers who purchase products for their own use and enjoyment and not for resale—are usually classified on the basis of how consumers buy them. *Convenience products* are items that consumers purchase frequently, immediately, and with little effort. For example, such convenience products as newspapers, snacks, candy, coffee, and bread are usually for sale in gas-station stores, vending machines, and local newsstands.

Shopping products are those products that are usually purchased only after the buyer has compared competing products in competing stores. A person who wants to buy a new sofa or dining room table may visit many stores, examine dozens of pieces of furniture, and spend days making the final decision. *Specialty products* are the third category of consumer products. These are products that a purchaser is willing to make a special effort to obtain. The purchaser is already familiar with the item and considers it to have no reasonable substitute. For example, the nearest MINI Cooper dealer may be 75 kilometres away, but if you have decided you want one, you will make the trip.

Note that a shopping product for one person may be a convenience item for someone else. Each item's product classification is based on the buying patterns of most of the people who purchase it.

The interrelationship of the marketing mix factors is shown in Figure 12.1. Marketing decision-makers need to know the best classification for a specific product. Knowing the most suitable classification helps marketers to understand how the other mix variables will adapt to create a profitable, customer-driven marketing strategy.

Classifying Business Goods

Business products are goods and services such as paycheque services and huge multifunction copying machines used in operating an organization. They also include machinery, tools, raw materials, components, and buildings used to produce other items for resale. While consumer products are classified by how consumers buy them, business products are classified by their basic characteristics and by how they are used. Products that are long-lived and relatively expensive are called *capital items*. Less costly products that are consumed within a year are referred to as *expense items*.

© travelibUK/Alamy

Buying a *specialty product* takes extra effort. The MINI Cooper is sold in a limited number of places.

> **FIGURE 12.1**
> Marketing Impacts of Consumer Product Classification

Marketing Strategy Factor	Convenience Product	Shopping Product	Specialty Product
· Purchase Frequency	· Frequent	· Relatively infrequent	· Infrequent
· Store Image	· Unimportant	· Very important	· Important
· Price	· Low	· Relatively high	· High
· Promotion	· By manufacturer	· By manufacturer and retailers	· By manufacturer and retailers
· Distribution Channel	· Many wholesalers and retailers	· Relatively few wholesalers and retailers	· Very few wholesalers and retailers
· Number of Retail Outlets	· Many	· Few	· Very small number; often one per market area

B2B products have five basic categories: installations, accessory equipment, component parts and materials, raw materials, and supplies. *Installations* are major capital items, such as new factories, heavy equipment and machinery, and custom-made equipment. Installations are expensive and often involve buyer and seller negotiations that may last for more than a year before a purchase is made. Purchase approval often involves the agreement of many different people—production specialists, purchasing department representatives, and members of top management.

Although *accessory equipment* also includes capital items, these items are usually less expensive and shorter lived than installations, and involve fewer decision-makers. Examples include hand tools and fax machines. *Component parts and materials* are finished business goods that become part of a final product, such as disk drives that are sold to computer manufacturers or batteries purchased by automakers. *Raw materials* are farm and natural products used to produce other final products. Examples include milk, wood, leather, and soybeans. *Supplies* are expense items used in a firm's daily operation that do not become part of the final product. Supplies are often referred to as MRO (maintenance, repair, and operating supplies). They include paper clips, light bulbs, and copy paper.

Classifying Services

Services can be classified as either B2C or B2B. Examples of services for consumers include childcare and eldercare centres and auto detail shops. Examples of services for businesses include the Pinkerton security patrol at a local factory and Kelly Services' temporary office workers. Sometimes, a service works in both consumer and business markets. For example, when ServiceMaster cleans the upholstery in a home, it is a B2C service, but when it spruces up the painting system and robots in a manufacturing plant, it is a B2B service.

Services can also be convenience products, shopping products, or specialty products. Which type of product it is will depend on the buying patterns of customers. Services can be distinguished from goods in several ways. First, services are intangible, or immaterial; in contrast, goods are tangible, or material. In addition, services are perishable, or short-lived, because firms cannot store them in inventory. They are also difficult to standardize because they must meet individual customers' needs. Finally, from a buyer's perspective, the service provider *is* the service; the two are inseparable in the buyer's mind.

© Teri Stratford

A *product line* is a group of related products designed to have the same appearance, like these PepsiCo products.

Marketing Strategy Implications

The consumer product classification system is a useful tool in marketing strategy. As shown in Figure 12.1, a new refrigerator is classified as a shopping good. That classification gives its marketers a better idea of how it needs to be promoted, priced, and distributed.

Each group of business products needs a different marketing strategy. Most installations and many component parts are marketed directly from manufacturer to business buyer. That means the promotional emphasis is on personal selling, not on advertising. In contrast, marketers of supplies and accessory equipment rely more on advertising because their products are often sold through an intermediary, such as a wholesaler. Producers of installations and component parts may involve their customers in new-product development, especially when the business product is custom made. Finally, firms selling supplies and accessory equipment place greater emphasis on competitive pricing strategies than do other B2B marketers, who tend to focus more on product quality and customer service.

Product Lines and Product Mix

Few firms do business with only a single product. If their first market entry is successful, they tend to increase their chances for profit and growth by adding new offerings. The iPhone and iPad have touchscreen technology and App Stores. These innovations may be a sign of things to come. Most "mainstream knowledge workers" will probably continue to use conventional computers for some time. But one IT research company predicts that by 2015, more than half of personal computers bought for users aged 15 and under will have touchscreens. The firm also predicts that touchscreen devices will have a huge potential in education. An entire generation may grow up with touchscreen technology.[2]

A company's **product line** is a group of related products that share physical similarities or are targeted toward a similar market. A **product mix** is the assortment of product lines and individual goods and services that a firm offers to consumers and business users. The Coca-Cola Company and PepsiCo both have product lines that include old standards—Coke Classic and Diet Coke, Pepsi and Diet Pepsi. But recently, PepsiCo announced it would start distributing Tampico Plus. Unlike other products from Tampico Beverages, Tampico Plus drinks contain vitamins A, C, and E. They also have half as much sugar as regular Tampico drinks. Thus, they meet the guidelines for beverages that can be sold in high schools that limit the amount of sugar in drinks available to students.[3]

Marketers must continually assess their product mix for a few reasons: to ensure company growth, to satisfy changing consumer needs and wants, and to adjust to competitors' offerings. To remain competitive, marketers look for gaps in their product lines and fill them with new offerings or modified versions of existing products. A helpful tool that is frequently used in making product decisions is the product life cycle.

product line a group of related products that share physical similarities or are targeted toward a similar market.

product mix the assortment of product lines and individual goods and services that a firm offers to consumers and business users.

✓ **ASSESSMENT CHECK**

12.1.1 How do consumer products differ from business products?

12.1.2 Differentiate among convenience products, shopping products, and specialty products.

PRODUCT LIFE CYCLE

After a product is on the market, it usually goes through four stages known as the **product life cycle**: introduction, growth, maturity, and decline. As Figure 12.2 shows, industry sales and profits vary depending on the product's life-cycle stage.

Product life cycles are not set in stone; that is, not all products follow this pattern precisely, and some products may spend different amounts of time in each stage. But the idea of a product life cycle helps the marketing planner to look ahead to new developments throughout the various stages of a product's life. Profits take on a predictable pattern through the stages, and the promotional focus shifts from communicating product information in the early stages to heavy brand promotion in the later stages.

LO 12.2 Briefly describe the four stages of the product life cycle and their marketing implications.

product life cycle the four basic stages in the development of a successful product—introduction, growth, maturity, and decline.

FIGURE 12.2 Stages in the Product Life Cycle

Stages of the Product Life Cycle

In the *introduction stage,* the firm takes on several activities: promoting demand for its new offering; informing the market about the product; offering free samples to interest consumers in making their first purchase; and explaining the product's features, uses, and benefits. Sometimes companies partner to promote new products. That's what General Mills and Warner Bros. Pictures and Legendary Pictures did to launch Yoplait Greek Yogurt. General Mills invited women to "discover their inner goddess" in connection with the film companies' *Clash of the Titans.* Izabella Miko, who played the goddess Athena in the film, was the spokesperson for the new yogurt.[4] The developers of Crocs sandals spent the introduction stage selling their product at boat shows. The Crocs proved popular and quickly moved to the next stage.

New-product development costs are high. Some marketers design fancy promotional campaigns to introduce consumers to the new product. Developing the product and promoting it are important to support later success. But these high expenses sometimes lead to losses in the introductory stage. Some firms try to lower these costs through ultra-low-cost product development. This approach involves meeting customer needs with the lowest-cost innovations possible, designing from scratch with a stripped-down budget and the simplest engineering possible.[5] But all these costs are needed if the firm is to profit later.

During the *growth stage,* sales climb quickly as new customers join the early users who now are repurchasing the item. Word-of-mouth referrals and continued advertising and other special promotions encourage consumers to make their first purchases. At this stage, the company begins to earn profits on the new product. This success encourages competitors to enter the field with similar offerings, leading to price competition. Amazon had early success with the Kindle digital reader. Amazon then faced competition from the Chapters and Indigo Kobo, the Barnes & Noble Nook, and the Sony Reader. Amazon rushed to get its Kindle iPad app to the App Store in time for the launch of Apple's iPad. Allowing Kindle products to be read on the iPad will benefit both Amazon and Apple.[6]

In the *maturity stage,* industry sales first increase, but then reach a saturation level when further expansion is difficult. Competition also gets much stronger, increasing the availability of the product. Firms focus on capturing competitors' customers, often dropping prices to increase the attractiveness of their product. Cellphones are in the maturity stage: competitors compete not only on price but also on features such as calendars, e-mail and attachments, messaging capability, full-colour screens, keyboards, and fax and word-processing functions. Flat-screen TVs are also in the maturity stage, so companies are trying to entice consumers to buy new models by offering even bigger screens. As worldwide production of high-definition TVs increases, some observers believe that makers of LED backlight displays will lower their prices to stay competitive with less expensive display options.[7]

Late in the maturity stage, sales volume fades, and some of the weaker competitors leave the market. During this stage, firms promote mature products aggressively to protect their market share and to set their products apart from those of competitors. Alberto Culver is changing the old tub of Noxzema. The tub itself will remain, but with a new look. Through a new online and print campaign, the product is promoted as a fresh, tingling face-cleansing experience for women.[8]

Sales continue to fall in the *decline stage,* the fourth phase of the product life cycle. Profits decrease and may become losses, as the reduced overall market for the product leads to further price-cutting. Competitors gradually leave the market, making some profits possible for the remaining firms in the shrinking market. The decline stage usually is caused by a product innovation or a shift in consumer preferences. Technology change can hasten the decline stage for a product. Most homes have at least one DVD player. High-definition DVDs, once promoted as the best in DVD technology, have been displaced by Blu-ray. Other major competitors for entertainment are online sites where consumers can download movies or television shows. These sites are popular because the link between the computer and the television is becoming faster and more reliable.[9]

Marketing Strategy Implications of the Product Life Cycle

The product life cycle is a useful concept. Marketers can use it to design a flexible marketing strategy that can adapt to the changing marketplace. A firm's competitive activities may involve developing new products, lowering prices, increasing distribution coverage, creating new promotional campaigns, or

HIT & MISS

Canadian Tire: Changing with the Times

From coast to coast across Canada, the long-respected Canadian Tire Corporation is a retailing institution. About 85 percent of Canadians live within a 15-minute drive of a store. More than 10,000 Canadians have their cars serviced there every day. Canadian Tire is visited by 40 percent of the adult population at least once a week. It is the most visited non-grocery retailer in the country. Not surprising, Canadian Tire is the top national retailer in gardening, home appliances, home-improvement products, power tools—and, of course, auto parts and accessories. Today, Canadian Tire has 487 associated dealer-owned and corporate-owned stores across Canada employing more than 68,000 people.

But it wasn't always this way. It may be hard to imagine, but in 1922, Ontario had about 200,000 automobiles. The same year, brothers John W. and Alfred J. Billes bought the Hamilton Tire & Garage Ltd. in Toronto. Just when Canadians were starting to think about the automobile as a serious form of personal transportation, the Billes brothers were offering parts, a repair service, storage in the winter, and fuel to keep local motorists on the move. As the popularity of automobile ownership increased, companies like Canadian Tire competed for the attention of customers who would need services for their automobile and farm vehicles. The Canadian Tire Corporation has grown tremendously. Over the years, it has become a retail centre for auto, sports, leisure, and home products.

The Canadian Tire catalogue was first introduced in 1928 to reach customers in rural and remote areas of the country. The catalogue is still popular today: 9 million copies are printed each year. One thing may be more appreciated by Canadians than the convenience of their local Canadian Tire store or catalogue—finding a stack of Canadian Tire money in their glove compartment. Canadian Tire money was first introduced in 1961 to reward cash-paying customers and to encourage return visits. It has proven to be a huge success as a customer-loyalty plan.

Today, Canadian Tire Stores in major city centres and regional shopping malls don't look anything like the small retailer that seemed to show up in every small Canadian town, where it sold sports gear and provincial hunting and fishing licences. The pace of store renovations has been speeded up to attract more shoppers after early results showed customers' quick acceptance of the new look and product selections. Canadian Tire has introduced financial services, including bank savings accounts, guaranteed investment certificates, credit cards, and mortgages. In 2002, the company acquired Mark's Work Wearhouse casual clothing. In 2011, it bought The Forzani Group of sports shops. Both acquisitions have helped position the firm for future revenue growth. As customers continue to respond to new, larger store formats, Canadian Tire earnings and profits reach ever higher levels. In 2011, gross revenues rose to $10.8 billion. From humble beginnings, the Billes's small family enterprise has grown to become the huge Canadian franchise corporation we know today.

Questions for Critical Thinking

1. What are the greatest challenges facing Canadian Tire today?

2. Which future retailing acquisition would fit well within the Canadian Tire organization?

Sources: Canadian Tire website, http://corp.canadiantire.ca/EN/Pages/default.aspx, accessed February 8, 2012.

any combination of these approaches. In general, the marketer's goal is to extend the product life cycle as long as the item is profitable. Some products are highly profitable during the later stages of their life cycle because all the initial development costs have already been recovered.

A commonly used strategy for extending the life cycle is to increase customers' frequency of use. Walmart and Shoppers Drug Mart (Pharmaprix in Quebec) offer grocery sections in their stores. Both firms added groceries to increase the frequency of shopper visits. Another strategy is to add new users. Marketers for Old Spice grooming products decided that Old Spice didn't need to be an old-fashioned product. They came up with a campaign to freshen up the product line's image and attract younger men. The new campaign was called "The Man Your Man Could Smell Like." It cleverly poked fun at the idea that merely using Old Spice would make younger men irresistible to women—while promising, with a wink, that it would.[10]

Arm & Hammer used a third approach: it found new uses for its products. The original use of the firm's baking soda was for baking. But Arm & Hammer now promotes its newer uses as a toothpaste, refrigerator freshener, and flame extinguisher. A fourth product life cycle extension strategy is changing package sizes, labels, and product designs. Changing the product design can often mean finding a way to give it an online application. For example, Mattel's doll sales had declined almost 20 percent. The toymaker increased sales by teaming its Barbie doll with the White House Project and the Take Our Daughters and Sons to Work Foundation. Consumers were invited to celebrate Barbie's 125th career by voting online to choose from among architect, computer engineer, environmentalist, news anchor, and surgeon. The winners, announced at the New York Toy Fair, were Computer Engineer Barbie (by popular vote) and News Anchor Barbie (by girls' vote). Both were part of Barbie's "I Can Be" series.[11]

Stages in New-Product Development

New-product development is expensive, time-consuming, and risky. Only about one-third of all new products become success stories. Products can fail for many reasons. Some have not been properly developed and tested, some are poorly packaged, and others don't have enough promotional support or distribution or do not satisfy a consumer need or want. Even successful products reach the end of the decline stage and must be replaced with new-product offerings.

Most of today's newly developed items are aimed at satisfying specific consumer demands. New-product development is more efficient and cost-effective because marketers use a systematic, or organized, approach to develop new products. As Figure 12.3 shows, the new-product development process has six stages. Each stage requires a "go/no-go" decision by management before moving on to the next stages. The development of new products needs large investments in both time and money. The sooner that decision-makers can identify a weak product and drop it from further steps, the less time and money will be wasted.

The starting point in the new-product development process is generating ideas for new offerings. Ideas come from many sources, including customer suggestions, suppliers, employees, research scientists, marketing research, inventors outside the firm, and competitive products.

The most successful ideas are directly related to satisfying customer needs. Procter & Gamble recently expanded its Febreze home collection by adding the Flameless Luminary In-Home Scent Delivery System. Instead of lighting a potentially dangerous candle, consumers can use a battery-operated, flameless light that distributes fragrance from a decorative, scented shade. The light automatically turns off after four hours. The design was a finalist in the Consumer Packaged Goods—Household Segment category of the Edison Best New Product Awards.[12]

In the second stage, screening removes ideas that do not work with overall company goals or that cannot be developed given the company's resources. Some firms hold open discussions of new-product ideas with specialists who work in different functional areas in the organization.

During the concept development and business analysis phase, further screening occurs. The analysis involves assessing the new product's potential sales, profits, growth rate, and competitive strengths. It also tries to determine whether the new product fits with the company's product, distribution, and promotional resources. At this stage, some companies use *concept testing*—marketing research designed to attract consumers' first reactions to new-product ideas. For example, potential consumers might be asked about proposed brand names and other methods of product identification. *Focus groups* are formal sessions where consumers meet with marketers to discuss what they like or dislike about current products. Sometimes the consumers can test or sample a new offering to provide immediate feedback.

Next, an actual product is developed, subjected to a series of tests, and revised. At this stage, developers may create functioning prototypes, or test models, or detailed descriptions of the product. These designs are the joint responsibility of the firm's development staff and its marketers. The marketers provide feedback on consumer reactions to the proposed product design, colour, and other physical features.

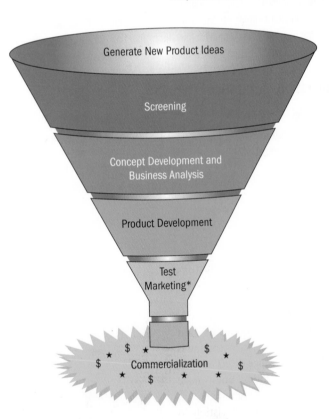

* Some firms skip this step and move directly from product development to commercialization.

FIGURE 12.3 Process for Developing New Goods and Services

Test marketing introduces a new product and a complete marketing campaign to a selected city or TV coverage area. When marketers look for a test location, they prefer a location or television coverage area with a manageable size, where residents match their target market's demographic profile. During the test marketing stage, the item is sold in a limited area while the company examines both consumer responses to the new offering and the marketing effort used to support the product. Test market results can help managers to decide on the product's likely performance in a full-scale introduction. Some firms skip test marketing because of concerns that the test could reveal their product strategies to the competition. Also, many expenses are involved in doing limited production runs of complex products such as a new auto or refrigerator. Sometimes, these costs are so high that the test marketing stage is skipped, and the development process moves directly to the next stage.

In the final stage, commercialization, the product is made available in the marketplace. This stage is also known as a product launch. Much planning goes into this stage. The firm's strategies for distribution, promotion, and pricing must all work together to support the new product. The videogame-maker Electronic Arts (EA) announced a new distribution strategy for future games. EA will release premium downloadable content (PDLC) for a game before releasing the complete, packaged version. The PDLC will be priced at $15 and will include three to four hours of playing time. The company will invite comments from reviewers and players. It will then make changes to the final version before releasing it for sale.[13]

New-product development is a vital process for 21st-century firms: firms need a steady stream of new products to offer their customers, the risks of product failure can be very expensive, and tens of millions of dollars are needed to complete a successful new-product launch. But, as Table 12.1 shows, success is not guaranteed until the new product achieves customer acceptance. Microsoft introduced a new operating system, Windows Vista, but it never caught on. The next version of Windows, Windows 7, has done much better. Another company, DigiScent, launched a new computer device. It was intended to bring the sense of smell to online shopping or browsing. But DigiScent didn't think through its plan carefully. Consumers rejected the idea of having to deal with unwanted aromas. Consumers also gave a thumbs-down on the product's name—iSmell.[14]

test marketing the introduction of a new product and a complete marketing campaign to a selected city or TV coverage area.

Table 12.1 The Worst-Made Cars on the Road

RANK	AUTO	TYPICAL OWNER COMMENT
1	Yugo	"I once test drove a Yugo, during which the radio fell out, the gear shift knob came off in my hand, and I saw daylight through the strip around the windshield."
2	Chevy Vega	"As near as I could tell, the car was built from compressed rust."
3	Ford Pinto	"The barbecue that seats four."
4	AMC Gremlin	"It was entirely possible to read a Russian novel during the pause between stepping on the gas and feeling any semblance of forward motion."
5	Chevy Chevette	"The ad didn't show the car going anywhere fast . . . because it couldn't."

Source: Reported in "Car Talk," http://www.cartalk.com, accessed April 30, 2010; Claire Martin, "The Worst Cars Ever," *MSN Autos,* April 22, 2010, http://editorial.autos.msn.com.

✔ **ASSESSMENT CHECK**

12.2.1 What are the stages of the product life cycle?

12.2.2 What are the marketing implications of each stage?

LO 12.3 Explain how firms identify their products.

PRODUCT IDENTIFICATION

A major part of developing a successful new product is choosing how to identify the product and distinguish it from other products. Both tangible goods and intangible services are identified by brands, brand names, and trademarks. A **brand** is a name, term, sign, symbol, design, or some combination that identifies the products of one firm and shows how they differ from competitors'

brand a name, term, sign, symbol, design, or some combination that identifies the products of one firm and shows how they differ from competitors' offerings.

brand name the part of the brand that is made up of words or letters that form a name. It is used to identify a firm's products and show how they differ from the products of competitors.

trademark a brand that has been given legal protection.

products. Tropicana, Pepsi, and Gatorade are all made by PepsiCo. A unique combination of name, symbol, and package design sets each brand apart from other similar products.

A **brand name** is that part of the brand that is made up of words or letters that form a name. It is used to identify a firm's products and show how they differ from the products of competitors. The brand name is the part of the brand that can be spoken. Many brand names are well known around the world, such as Coca-Cola, McDonald's, American Express, Google, and Nike. McDonald's brand mark, the "golden arches," is also familiar around the world.

A **trademark** is a brand that has been given legal protection. The protection is granted only to the brand's owner. Trademark protection includes the brand name, design logos, slogans, packaging elements, and product features such as colour and shape. A well-designed trademark, such as the Nike "swoosh," can make a difference in how positively consumers perceive a brand.

Selecting an Effective Brand Name

Good brand names are easy to say, easy to recognize, and easy to remember: Crest, Visa, and Dell are good examples. Global firms face a real problem when selecting brand names. An excellent brand name in one country may be a poor choice in another country. Most languages have a short *a*, so *Coca-Cola* is easy to say almost anywhere. But an advertising campaign for E-Z washing machines failed in the United Kingdom. The British pronounce *z* as "zed." They are not as familiar with American "pronunciation" as Canadians are.

Brand names should also send the right image to the buyer. One effective way to create a name is to link the product with its positioning strategy. For example, the name Dial links to the idea of 24-hour protection. Dove soap and beauty products link to the idea of mildness. Taster's Choice instant coffee links to its promotional claim "Tastes and smells like ground roast coffee."

Brand names also must be legally protectable. Trademark law does not allow brand names that contain words in general use, such as *television* or *automobile*. Generic words—words that describe a type of product—cannot be used exclusively by any organization. But sometimes a brand name becomes so popular that it passes into common language and turns into a generic word. Then, the company can no longer use it as a brand name. A long time ago, aspirin, linoleum, and zipper were exclusive brand names. But these words have become generic terms and no longer have legal protection.

Brand Categories

A brand that is offered and promoted by a manufacturer is known as a *manufacturer's* (or *national*) *brand*. Examples are Tide, Cheerios, Windex, Fossil, and Nike. But not all brand names belong to manufacturers; some are the property of retailers or distributors. A *private* (or *store*) *brand* identifies a product that is not linked to the manufacturer; instead, it carries a wholesaler's or retailer's label. Two examples are Sears's Craftsman tools and Loblaw's President's Choice foods.

Another branding decision that marketers must make is whether to use a family branding strategy or an individual branding strategy. A *family brand* is a single brand name used for several related products. Kraft, KitchenAid, Johnson & Johnson, Hewlett-Packard, and Arm & Hammer use a family name for their entire line of products. When a firm using family branding introduces a new product, both customers and retailers recognize the familiar brand name. The promotion of individual products within a product line benefits all the products because the family brand is well known.

Other firms use an *individual branding* strategy by giving a different brand name to each product within a product line. For example, Procter & Gamble has individual brand names for its different laundry detergents—Tide, Cheer, and Gain. Each brand targets a unique market segment.

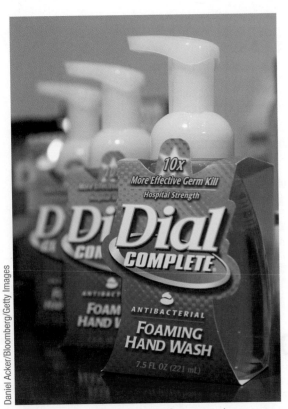

To be effective, *brand names* must be easy for consumers to say, recognize, and remember.

Daniel Acker/Bloomberg/Getty Images

Consumers who want a cold-water detergent can choose Cheer over Tide or Gain, instead of purchasing a competitor's brand. Individual branding also builds competition within a firm and enables the company to increase its overall sales.

Brand Loyalty and Brand Equity

Brands achieve different levels of consumer familiarity and acceptance. For example, a homeowner may insist on Andersen windows when renovating, but may not prefer any brand when buying a loaf of bread. Consumer loyalty can increase a brand's value, so marketers try to strengthen brand loyalty. When a brand image suffers, marketers try to recreate a positive image.

Brand Loyalty

Marketers measure brand loyalty in three stages: brand recognition, brand preference, and brand insistence. *Brand recognition* is brand acceptance that is strong enough that the consumer is aware of the brand, but not strong enough to lead a customer to prefer it over other brands. A consumer might have heard of L'Oréal hair care products, without necessarily preferring those products to Redken products. Marketers can often increase brand recognition through advertising, free samples, and discount coupons.

Brand preference occurs when a consumer chooses one firm's brand over a competitor's. At this stage, the consumer usually uses his or her previous experience when selecting the product. Furniture and other home furnishings fall into this category. Suppose a shopper purchased an IKEA dining room table and chairs and was satisfied with them. This shopper is likely to return to IKEA to purchase a bedroom set. While there, this shopper might also pick up a set of mixing bowls for the kitchen or a lamp for the family room—because this shopper knows and likes the IKEA brand.

During Design Week in New York City, IKEA installed this clever display, which is meant to look like a bus stop. IKEA, the retailer of affordable, well-designed contemporary furniture enjoys *brand insistence*—the ultimate expression of brand loyalty. For devoted IKEA fans, no other brand will do.

Brand insistence is the ultimate degree of brand loyalty. Consumers who have brand insistence will look for a product at another outlet, special-order it from a dealer, order by mail, or search the Internet. Shoppers who insist on IKEA products for their homes may drive an hour or two—making a day excursion of the venture—to visit an IKEA store. The combination of value for the money and the concept of IKEA as a shopping destination have given the brand a unique appeal for shoppers.[15]

Brand-building strategies were once limited to consumer goods, but they are becoming more important for B2B brands. Intel, Xerox, IBM, and service providers such as Krystal Klean and Cisco are among the suppliers who have built brand names among business customers.

Brand Equity

Brand loyalty is at the heart of **brand equity**, the added value that a respected and successful name gives to a product. This value results from a combination of factors: awareness, loyalty, perceived quality, and feelings or images the customer associates with the brand. High brand equity offers financial advantages to a firm because the product represents a large market share. High brand equity can also reduce price sensitivity, which can lead to higher profits. Figure 12.4 shows the world's 10 most valuable brands and their estimated worth.

Brand awareness is high when the product is the first one that comes to mind when you hear a product category. If someone says "coffee," do you think of Starbucks, Dunkin' Donuts, or Tim Hortons? Brand association is the link between a brand and other favourable images.

brand equity the added value that a respected and successful name gives to a product.

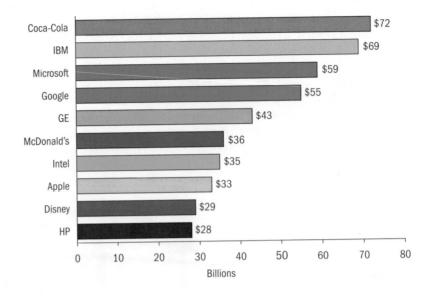

Source: Data from "2011 Rankings of the Top 100 Brands," *Interbrand website* http://www.interbrand.com/en/best-global-brands/best-global-brands-2008/best-global-brands-2011.aspx, accessed May 9, 2012.

FIGURE 12.4 The World's Ten Most Valuable Brands and Their Worth (in billions of dollars)

Coca-Cola — $72
IBM — $69
Microsoft — $59
Google — $55
GE — $43
McDonald's — $36
Intel — $35
Apple — $33
Disney — $29
HP — $28

Billions

Large companies usually assign the task of managing a brand's marketing strategies to a *brand manager*, also called a *product manager*. This marketing professional plans and puts in place the other promotional, pricing, distribution, and product arrangements that lead to strong brand equity. A *category manager*, a newer type of professional, oversees an entire group of products. Unlike traditional brand managers or product managers, category managers have profit responsibility for their product group. These managers are assisted by associates, usually called *analysts*. Part of the shift to category management was started by large retailers. They realized they could benefit from the marketing power of large grocery and household goods producers such as Kraft and Procter & Gamble. As a result, producers began to focus their attention on in-store merchandising instead of mass-market advertising. A few years ago, Kraft reorganized its sales force so that each representative was responsible for a retailer's needs instead of just promoting a single brand.

category advisor the individual that the business customer assigns as the major supplier to deal with all the other suppliers for a project. The category advisor also presents the entire package to the business buyer.

A **category advisor** functions in the B2B context. This individual is the major supplier that a business customer assigns to deal with all the other suppliers for a project. The category advisor also presents the entire package to the business buyer.

Consumer demand has led to more environmentally friendly packages. Box manufacturers and chemical companies are working to create more compact packaging that is made from renewable sources and is recyclable. Frito-Lay introduced compostable packaging for its SunChips multigrain snacks.

Packages and Labels

Packaging and labels are needed for product identification. They also play an important role in a firm's overall product strategy. Packaging affects an item's durability, image, and convenience. It is also one of the biggest costs in many consumer products. Consumer demand has led to smaller, more environmentally friendly packages. Box manufacturers and chemical companies are working to create more compact packaging that is made from renewable sources and is recyclable. As explained in the "Going Green" feature, Frito-Lay introduced compostable packaging for its SunChips multi-grain snacks. One-third of North America's waste consists of containers and packaging, much of it from fast-food chains. Quiznos recently launched its "Eat Toasty, Be Green" campaign to introduce its new, environmentally friendly packaging. The restaurant chain now uses 100 percent compostable, wax-coated paper cups; salad containers made of renewable sugar cane; napkins made from 100 percent recycled materials; and plastic lids made from 30 percent recycled polyethylene terephthalate (PET) bottles. Even the employees' uniforms were changed—the hats and aprons are now made from 100 percent recycled soda bottles.[16]

SUNCHIPS INTRODUCES GREENER PACKAGING

Everybody loves to snack on chips. But nobody can love what happens to the empty bag. It eventually ends up in a landfill—and may never decompose. Frito-Lay's brand SunChips aimed to change all that. On Earth Day 2009, it introduced what it called "the world's first compostable chip bag."

In a recent survey, 75 percent of those questioned thought that recyclable packaging was "somewhat important," and 51 percent felt that compostable packaging was "somewhat important." A recyclable item can be used repeatedly, whereas a compostable item breaks down in the presence of water and oxygen.

The company had to meet the challenge of developing packaging that was ecologically sound while also preserving the contents. After four years of research and testing, the company had a bag made of more than 90 percent plant-based, and therefore renewable, materials. The outer layer is made of corn-based polylactic acid (PLA). Although the bag is 100 percent compostable, researchers are working on an environmentally friendly inner layer that will keep the contents crisp and edible. Frito-Lay makes it clear that the bag decomposes most quickly—in about 14 weeks—in a hot, active composting bin. If the bag is simply left on the ground, it will still break down, but less quickly.

The new bag sounds a little different from its old packaging. But Frito-Lay assured its customers that SunChips still taste the same. It even promoted the difference as the "new sound of green" and included a clip of the sound on its website, along with a link to Facebook.

The Biodegradable Products Institute certified the new packaging, but getting North Americans to recognize the need for composting is another matter. A Frito-Lay executive acknowledged the challenge—and the opportunity to educate consumers. What was not expected was an 11 percent drop in sales and public ridicule over the "noise" made when consumers handled the new packaging material. Marketers learned a hard lesson: although the socially responsible green packaging was popular with most consumers and most of society, many customers avoided the product because of this effort. As a result, the company returned to the original packaging for all but the original flavour chips. Frito-Lay continues to search new materials that are not quite so noisy.

Questions for Critical Thinking

1. What role did the new, compostable packaging play in the overall marketing strategy for SunChips?

2. How do you think SunChips can most effectively educate North Americans about the importance of composting?

Sources: Bruce Horovitz, "Frito-Lay Sends Noisy, 'Green' SunChips Bag to the Dump," *USAToday.com*, October 5, 2010, http://www.usatoday.com/money/industries/food/2010-10-05-sunchips05_ST_N.html, accessed May 9,2012; Company website, http://www.sunchips.com, accessed May 4, 2010; Kate Galbraith, "A Compostable Chips Bag Hits the Shelves," *New York Times,* March 16, 2010, http://greeninc.blogs.nytimes.com; Kathryn Siranosian, "New SunChips Bag: 90% Plant-Based, 100% Compostable," *Triple Pundit,* February 22, 2010, http://www.triplepundit.com.

Choosing the right package is especially important in international marketing. Marketers need to be aware of language variations and cultural preferences. Consumers in African nations often prefer bold colours, but use of the country's flag colours can lead to problems. Some countries don't like to see other uses of their flag. Also, Africans often associate red with death or witchcraft. Package size can vary depending on a country's purchasing patterns and market conditions. In countries where many people have only small refrigerators, consumers may want to buy their beverages one at a time instead of in six-packs. Package weight is another important issue because shipping costs are often based on weight.

Labelling is another important part of the packaging process. In Canada, companies must meet labelling laws by providing enough information so that consumers can compare competitive products. In the case of food packaging, labelling must include nutritional information. Marketers who ship products to other countries must meet the labelling requirements in those nations. They need to know the answers to the following questions:

- Does the information on the labels need to be in more than one language?

- Do ingredients need to be listed?

- Do the labels give enough information about the product to meet government standards?

Another important part of packaging and labelling is the *universal product code (UPC)*. This bar code is read by the optical scanners that link the UPC to a product and print the name of the item and the price on a receipt. For many stores, these identifiers are useful for packaging and labelling, for simplifying and speeding retail transactions, and for evaluating customer purchases and controlling inventory. Radio-frequency identification (RFID) technology uses embedded chips that can broadcast their product information to receivers. RFID may replace the UPC, which we'll discuss later in this chapter.

 ASSESSMENT CHECK

12.3.1 Differentiate among a brand, a brand name, and a trademark.

12.3.2 Define *brand equity*.

DISTRIBUTION STRATEGY

The second element of the marketing mix is the **distribution strategy**. This strategy is a plan that deals with the marketing activities and institutions that get the right good or service to the firm's customers. Distribution decisions involve selecting the suitable types of transportation, warehousing, inventory control, order processing, and marketing channels. Marketing channels are usually made up of intermediaries such as retailers and wholesalers that move a product from producer to final purchaser.

Two major parts of an organization's distribution strategy are distribution channels and physical distribution. **Distribution channels** are the paths that products—and their legal ownership—follow from producer to consumer or business user. All organizations use these channels to distribute their goods and services. **Physical distribution** is the actual movement of products from producer to consumers or business users. Physical distribution covers a broad range of activities, including customer service, transportation, inventory control, materials handling, order processing, and warehousing. As explained in the "Hit & Miss" feature, Gourmet Chips and Sauces, a Montreal food distributor, is building a distribution network of retailers across Canada for its imported and domestic lines of all natural extremely hot products.

Distribution Channels

Marketers' first decision in distribution channel selection is to choose which type of channel will best meet both their firm's marketing objectives and the needs of their customers. As shown in Figure 12.5, marketers can choose to use either a *direct distribution channel* or a *marketing intermediary*. A distribution channel carries goods directly from producer to the consumer or business user. A *marketing intermediary* (also called a *middleman*) is a business firm that moves goods from their producers to consumers or business users. It usually involves several different marketing intermediaries. Marketing intermediaries help the distribution channel operate smoothly through

FIGURE 12.5
Alternative Distribution Channels

HIT & MISS

Gourmet Chips & Sauces Targets a Niche Market

The "heat levels" of these products differ. Some are mild, like Aubrey D.'s Condiments, Sweet Death, Jalapeño Death Sauces, and Chipotle Death Rain Potato Chips. Others are insanely hot, like Ultra Death Sauce and XXX Hot Habañero Salsa. And when Gourmet Chips & Sauces talks about the "heat level," they're talking about the "extreme end" of the market. With every bite, warning labels and fire alarm bells go off.

The gourmet market for high-quality "extremely hot" and spicy chips and sauces is small when compared with the variety and sales volumes offered by the industry's leaders, such as PepsiCo. PepsiCo leads the market by selling products with highly visible and recognizable brands such as Frito-Lay, Tostitos, and Doritos.

To compete with companies like PepsiCo, smaller firms can choose to focus on a niche in the marketplace. They can try to set themselves apart to attract customers who want something that is different from all the mass-market products.

Montreal-based Gourmet Chips & Sauces produces its own line of Aubrey D.'s Gourmet Condiments. It also imports a select line of Blair's sauces and chips from the United States and distributes this product for sale across Canada. This line of hot and spicy potato chips and sauces are all handcrafted to ensure top quality. They are made from natural ingredients, contain no preservatives or trans fats, and are gluten-free. The chips are kettle-cooked in canola or sunflower oil. Along with the sauces, they are a healthier alternative to the mass-market snacks typically found.

The limited distribution is a problem. Customers need to make more of an effort to buy these products, compared with the PepsiCo products that seem to be for sale everywhere. But the limited distribution has led to a growing niche market of premium customers and retailers who recognize the superior quality and unique product value. As a result, many customers who have tried the products are prepared to spend time looking for them. They are also prepared to pay a small premium in price. Retailers want to offer their customers something unique. The premium price is also a welcome contribution to their businesses.

Questions for Critical Thinking

1. How can Gourmet Chips & Sauces build its distribution network of grocery and convenience stores across Canada?

2. What other products could the firm add to its line?

Sources: Company website http://www.gourmetchip.com/ accessed May 23, 2011; interviews with company owner, Aubrey Zelman, November 15, 2011.

---

several activities: buying, selling, storing, and transporting products; sorting and grading bulky items; and providing information to other channel members. The two main categories of marketing intermediaries are wholesalers and retailers.

No one channel suits every product. The best channel depends on the circumstances of the market and on customer needs. The most suitable channel choice may also change over time as new opportunities arise and marketers try to maintain their competitiveness.

Direct Distribution

The shortest and simplest way to connect producers and customers is by direct contact between the two parties. This method is most commonly used in the B2B market. Other examples of direct distribution occur when consumers buy fresh fruits and vegetables at roadside stands or farmers markets. Direct distribution can also be found in services, such as banking, 10-minute oil changes, and ear piercing.

Direct distribution is often found in the marketing of relatively expensive, complex products that may require demonstrations. Direct contacts between producers and business buyers are used to market most major B2B products, such as installations, accessory equipment, component parts, business services, and even raw materials. The Internet has also made direct distribution an attractive option for many retail companies and service providers. FedEx customers have long used online tools to track conventional shipments. FedEx's new International Priority Direct Distribution service allows users to ship more than one package from a single country of origin to different recipients in a single destination country. The packages are cleared through customs as a single shipment. In addition, multiple shipments to multiple recipients in multiple European Union countries can be cleared through customs as a single shipment through Charles de Gaulle Airport near Paris.[17]

Marcy Goldman of Montreal distributes her exquisite baking recipes through her books. They are sold at traditional retailers, such as Chapters Indigo, and at her online magazine www.betterbaking.com.

16 Contacts

8 Contacts

FIGURE 12.6
Reducing Transactions through Marketing Intermediaries

✓ **ASSESSMENT CHECK**

12.4.1 Define *distribution channels*.

12.4.2 What is a marketing intermediary?

LO 12.5 Distinguish between the different types of wholesaling intermediaries.

wholesaler a distribution channel member that sells primarily to retailers, other wholesalers, or business users.

Distribution Channels Using Marketing Intermediaries

Direct channels allow producers to have simple and straightforward connections with their customers. But the list of channel alternatives in Figure 12.5 suggests that direct distribution is not always the best choice. Some products sell in small quantities for relatively low prices to thousands of widely scattered consumers. Makers of such products cannot cost-effectively contact each of their customers. Instead, they distribute products through specialized intermediaries called *wholesalers* and *retailers*.

You might think that adding intermediaries to the distribution process would increase the final cost of products. But adding intermediaries often lowers consumer prices. Intermediaries such as wholesalers and retailers often add significant value to a product as it moves through the distribution channel. They add value by creating utility, providing additional services, and reducing costs.

Marketing utility is created when intermediaries help ensure that products are available for sale when and where customers want to purchase them. For example, if you want something warm to eat on a cold winter night, you don't call Campbell's Soup and ask them to ship a can of chicken noodle soup. Instead, you go to the nearest grocery store, where you find utility in the form of product availability—a can of Campbell's chicken noodle soup on the grocery store shelf. Intermediaries perform important services such as transporting merchandise to convenient locations. Finally, a marketing intermediary represents numerous producers, which can cut the costs of buying and selling. As Figure 12.6 shows, four manufacturers each selling directly to four consumers requires 16 separate transactions. Adding a marketing intermediary, such as a retailer, cuts the number of necessary transactions to eight.

WHOLESALING

A **wholesaler** is a distribution channel member that sells primarily to retailers, other wholesalers, or business users. For example, Sysco is a wholesaler that buys food products from producers and then resells them to restaurants, hotels, and other institutions in the United States and Canada.

Wholesaling is a crucial part of the distribution channel for many products, especially consumer goods and business supplies. Wholesaling intermediaries can be classified on the basis of ownership: some are owned by manufacturers, some are owned by retailers, and others are independently owned. Statistics Canada reports that Canada has approximately 111,500 wholesale enterprises. The United States has about 430,000 wholesalers, and 85 percent of them have fewer than 20 employees. In many product categories, Canadian wholesalers compete with American wholesalers for customers anywhere in North America.[18]

Manufacturer-Owned Wholesaling Intermediaries

A manufacturer's marketing manager may decide to distribute goods directly through company-owned facilities to control distribution or customer service. Firms operate two main types of manufacturer-owned wholesaling intermediaries: sales branches and sales offices.

Sales branches stock the products they distribute and fill orders from their inventories. They also provide offices for sales representatives. Sales branches are common in the chemical, petroleum products, motor vehicle, and machine and equipment industries.

A *sales office* is exactly what its name implies: an office for a producer's salespeople. Manufacturers set up sales offices in various regions to support local selling efforts and improve customer service. Some kitchen and bath fixture manufacturers maintain showrooms to display their products. Builders and decorators can visit these showrooms to see how the finished items will look. Unlike sales branches, sales offices do not store any inventory. When a customer orders from a showroom or other sales office, the merchandise is delivered from a separate warehouse.

Independent Wholesaling Intermediaries

An independent wholesaling intermediary is a business that represents several different manufacturers and sells to retailers, manufacturers, and other business accounts. Independent wholesalers can be either merchant wholesalers or agents and brokers, depending on whether they take title to (legal ownership of) the products they handle.

Merchant wholesalers, like apparel wholesaler WholesaleSarong.com, are independently owned wholesaling intermediaries. They take title to, or legal ownership of, the goods they handle. Within this category, a *full-function merchant wholesaler* provides an assortment of services for retailers or industrial buyers, such as warehousing, shipping, and even financing. A subtype of full-function merchant is a *rack jobber*. This type of firm stocks, displays, and services specific retail products, such as paperback books or greeting cards in a drugstore or supermarket. The retailer usually receives a commission that is based on actual sales. This commission is considered to be payment for providing merchandise space to a rack jobber.

A *limited-function merchant wholesaler* also takes legal title to the products it handles, but it provides fewer services to the retailers it sells to. Some limited-function merchant wholesalers only warehouse products and do not offer delivery services. Others may warehouse products and deliver them but provide no financing. One type of limited-function merchant wholesaler is a *drop shipper*. Drop shippers operate in the coal and lumber industries and in other industries that deal in bulky products, where no single producer can provide a complete assortment. Drop shippers provide access to many related goods by contacting numerous producers and negotiating the best possible prices. To control costs, producers usually ship such products directly to the drop shipper's customers.

Another category of independent wholesaling intermediaries consists of *agents* and *brokers*. They may or may not take physical possession of the goods they handle, but they never take title, or ownership. They work mainly to bring buyers and sellers together. Stockbrokers, such as Scotiabank's ScotiaMcLeod investment dealers, and real estate agents, such as RE/MAX realtors, perform functions similar to those of agents and brokers, but at the retail level. They do not take title to the sellers' property; instead, they create time and ownership utility for both buyer and seller by helping to carry out buying and selling transactions.

Manufacturers' reps act as independent sales forces by representing the manufacturers of related but noncompeting products. These agent intermediaries are sometimes referred to as *manufacturers' agents*. They receive commissions that are based on a percentage of the sales they make.

Retailer-Owned Co-operatives and Buying Offices

Retailers sometimes work together to form their own wholesaling organizations. Such organizations can take the form of either a buying group or a co-operative. The retailers set up the new operation to reduce costs or to provide some service that is not readily available in the marketplace. For example, to achieve cost savings through quantity purchases, independent retailers may form a buying group that negotiates bulk sales with manufacturers. Federated Co-operatives

✓ **ASSESSMENT CHECK**

12.5.1 Define *wholesaling*.

12.5.2 Differentiate between a merchant whole-saler and an agent or broker in terms of title to the goods.

LO 12.6 Describe the various types of retailers, and identify retail strategies.

retailers distribution channel members that sell goods and services to individuals for their own use, not for resale.

Limited (FCL) is a Western Canada–based co-operative that is owned by approximately 250 retail co-operatives. These retail co-ops are the "members" of FCL. FCL provides central whole-saling, manufacturing, and administrative services to its member-owners. Together, FCL and its member-owners are known as the Co-operative Retailing System (CRS).[19] In a co-operative, an independent group of retailers may decide to work together to share functions such as shipping or warehousing.

RETAILING

Retailers, in contrast to wholesalers, are distribution channel members that sell goods and services to individuals for their own use, not for resale. Consumers usually buy their food, cloth-ing, shampoo, furniture, and appliances from some type of retailer. Your grocery store may have bought some of its dairy products from a co-operative wholesaler, such as Quebec-based Agropur, and then resold them to you.

Retailers are the final link—the so-called "last three feet"—of the distribution channel. Retailers are often the only channel members that deal directly with consumers. That means retailers need to remain alert to changing consumer needs. For example, soaring gas prices affect consumers' budgets: they may make fewer trips to the mall and may cut back on nonessential purchases. As a result, retail-ers may need to offer special sales or events to encourage customers to visit their shops. Retailers also need to keep pace with developments in the fast-changing business environment, such as disruptions in the delivery of supplies because of widespread wildfires or storms.

Nonstore Retailers

Retailers are divided into two categories: store retailers and nonstore retailers. As Figure 12.7 shows, nonstore retailing includes four forms: direct-response retailing, Internet retailing, auto-matic merchandising, and direct selling. *Direct-response retailing* reaches consumers through catalogues; telemarketing; and even magazine, newspaper, and tele-vision ads. Shoppers order goods by mail, telephone, computer, and fax machine. Their purchases are delivered to their home, or shoppers pick up their purchases at a local store.

Internet retailing is the second form of nonstore retailing. Tens of thousands of retailers have set up shop online. Internet sales are growing at a rate of about 5 percent a year (as total retail sales decline). Today, North American online sales account for about 3.8 percent of total retail sales.[20] Hundreds of Internet enter-prises shut down during the first few years of the 21st century. The firms that survived have stronger business models than those that failed. Two examples of successful pure dot-com businesses are Amazon and eBay. Retailing has seen a major shift: many traditional bricks-and-mortar retailers have set up online shopping through their own websites to compete with pure dot-com start-ups. Best Buy and Walmart report strong online sales. Shopping sites are among the most popular Internet destinations. Clothing and DVD purchases are especially popular, and their online sales have increased.

The last two forms of nonstore retailing are automatic merchan-dising and direct selling. *Automatic merchandising* provides convenience through the use of vending machines. Automated teller machines (ATMs) may soon join vending machines as a form of automatic merchandising. For example, at some ATMs, consumers can purchase stamps, concert tickets, and road maps. Future ATMs may be able to connect to cellphones to allow custom-ers to download and pay for games and music. Banks are always looking for

FIGURE 12.7 Types of Nonstore Retailing

new ways to compete for customers. *Direct selling* includes direct-to-consumer sales by Pampered Chef kitchen representatives and salespeople for Silpada sterling silver jewellery through party-plan selling methods. Both are forms of direct selling.

Companies that once used telemarketing to attract new customers have been faced with consumer resistance to intrusive phone calls. Among the growing barriers are caller ID, call-blocking devices such as the TeleZapper, and the National Do Not Call List (DNCL). The DNCL makes it illegal for most companies to call people who have registered their phone number. As a result, many companies, including telecommunications and regional utilities, now send direct-mail pieces to promote such services as phones, cable television, and natural gas.

Store Retailers

In-store sales still result in more sales than nonstore retailing such as direct-response retailing and Internet selling. Store retailers range in size from tiny newsstands to multi-storey department stores and large warehouse-style retailers such as Costco. Table 12.2 lists the different types of store retailers with examples of each type. Clearly, retailing can take many approaches. Retail outlets must choose among these approaches to sell a variety of services and product lines offered at a range of prices.

Courtesy of Robert Sommers

This Proactiv Solution kiosk dispenses skin care products, just as an ATM dispenses cash. *Automatic merchandising* is a form of nonstore retailing.

Table 12.2 **Types of Retail Stores**

STORE TYPE	DESCRIPTION	EXAMPLE
Specialty store	Offers a complete selection in a narrow line of merchandise	Choices Markets, Bass Pro Shops, Golf Town, Williams-Sonoma
Convenience store	Offers staple convenience goods, easily accessible locations, extended store hours, and rapid checkouts	7-Eleven, Boni Soir, Mac's
Discount store	Offers wide selection of merchandise at low prices; off-price discounters offer designer or brand-name merchandise	Target, Walmart, Army & Navy
Warehouse club	Large, warehouse-style store selling food and general merchandise at discount prices to membership card-holders	Costco, DirectBuy
Factory outlet	Manufacturer-owned store selling seconds, production overruns, or discontinued lines	Adidas, Tommy Hilfiger, Pottery Barn, Ralph Lauren
Supermarket	Large, self-service retailer offering a wide selection of food and nonfood merchandise	Safeway, Whole Foods Market, Loblaws
Supercentre	Giant store offering food and general merchandise at discount prices	Walmart Supercentre, Super Target, Real Canadian Superstore
Department store	Offers a wide variety of merchandise selections (furniture, cosmetics, housewares, clothing) and many customer services	The Bay

The Wheel of Retailing

Retailers face constant change as new stores replace older stores. In a process called the *wheel of retailing*, new retailers enter the market by reducing services so they can offer lower prices. For example, supermarkets and discount stores gained their market position by offering low prices and limited service. Some of these new retailers slowly add services as they grow. In a few years, they become "older stores" and are the targets of new retailers.

As Figure 12.8 shows, most major developments in retailing appear to fit the wheel pattern. The low-price, limited-service strategy describes supermarkets, catalogue retailers, discount stores, Internet retailers, and "big-box" stores, such as PetSmart and Office Depot. Corner grocery stores have led to supermarkets and then to warehouse clubs such as Costco. Department stores have lost market share to discount clothing retailers such as Target and Winners. Independent bookstores have lost business to giant chains such as Chapters Indigo and online-only sellers such as Amazon.ca and Buy.ca.

But the wheel of retailing does not fit every pattern of retail evolution. For example, automatic merchandising has always been a relatively high-priced retail method. The wheel of retailing has benefits for retailers. It gives retail managers a general idea of what to expect during the evolution of retailing. It also shows that business success involves the "survival of the fittest." Retailers that fail to change will fail to survive.

FIGURE 12.8 The Wheel of Retailing

Mid-1900s
Supermarkets;
Discount
Stores

Early 1900s
Self-Service
Grocers;
Sears
Catalogue

Early 2000s
Internet Retailers;
Big-Box Stores;
Lifestyle Shopping
Centres

Late 1800s
Department
Stores;
Five & Dime
Variety Stores

How Retailers Compete

Retailers compete with each other in many ways. Nonstore retailers focus on making the shopping experience as convenient as possible. Shoppers at store retailers such as Holt Renfrew enjoy a luxurious atmosphere and personal service.

Like manufacturers, retailers must develop marketing strategies that are based on goals and strategic plans. Successful retailers use images that alert consumers to the stores' identities and the shopping experiences they provide. To create that image, all parts of a retailer's strategy must work together and complement each other. Retailers must first identify their target markets, and then choose the strategies for merchandising, customer service, pricing, and location that will attract customers in their target market segments.

Identifying a Target Market

The first step in developing a competitive retailing strategy is to select a target market. This choice requires careful evaluation of the market segment's size, profit potential, and its current level of competition. For example, bargain stores, such as Dollar Store, target consumers who are extremely price-conscious; while convenience stores, such as 7-Eleven, target consumers who want an easy way to purchase items they buy frequently. Seventh Generation makes "green" products for household cleaning and personal care. It began as a mail-order company, then started selling at natural-food stores. It then grew into a major business whose products were featured at supermarkets nationwide and at Target and Amazon.ca. Seventh Generation is committed to increasing consumer awareness of environmentally safe cleaning and household products. It recently began its "Protecting Planet Home" campaign. The company plans to build on its 45 percent profits by launching its first national marketing campaign online, in print, and in TV commercials. The

© Teri Stratford

Seventh Generation identified its *target market* as those people who are committed to using environmentally safe products for household cleaning.

company's goal is to get 45 percent of North American households to try at least one Seventh Generation product.[21]

Selecting a Product Strategy

Next, the retailer must develop a product strategy to decide on the best mix of merchandise to carry to satisfy its target market. Retail strategists must decide on the general product categories, product lines, and the variety to offer. Sometimes this decision involves expanding or reducing the product mix. Polaroid's parent company signed a five-year licensing agreement with Starlight, a leading consumer electronics manufacturer and distributer. Under the agreement, Starlight will develop a range of Polaroid-brand consumer electronics equipment, including Blu-ray players, stand-alone and portable DVD players, e-readers, iPod docking stations, and home theatre systems.[22]

Shaping a Customer Service Strategy

A retailer's customer service strategy focuses on attracting and retaining target customers to maximize sales and profits. Some stores offer a wide variety of services, such as gift wrapping, alterations, returns, interior design services, and delivery. Other stores offer only basic customer service, and they feature their low prices instead. Some grocery shoppers find convenience online, by using a service that selects grocery items, packs the products, and delivers the purchases to the door. Other grocery shoppers choose to visit a bricks-and-mortar store and make their own selections.

Selecting a Pricing Strategy

Retailers base their pricing decisions on their costs of purchasing products from other channel members and offering services to customers. Pricing can play a major role in consumers' view of a retailer. Consumers don't always choose the lower-priced products. For example, Loblaws offers three choices: high-quality products under its President's Choice private brand, lower-priced no-name brands, and higher-priced national brands. Loblaws provides these options, and customers can choose the products they prefer. Pricing strategy is covered in more detail in Chapter 13.

Choosing a Location

A good retail location can often make the difference between success and failure. The location decision depends on the retailer's size, financial resources, product offerings, competition, and, of course, its target market. The decision is also influenced by traffic patterns, the visibility of the store's signage, parking, and the location of complementary stores. Consider the competition between PetSmart and Mondou. Mondou tends to have smaller stores than PetSmart and in greater numbers. Their stores are mostly located in strip malls. In contrast, PetSmart's strategy is to build bigger "power centres" right beside other large discount chains. Some PetSmart stores offer added pet services—adoption, grooming, daycare, and boarding. Mondou stores are thought of more as "convenience stores" for pet supplies—especially food. Both companies have implemented "green" initiatives.[23]

A *planned shopping centre* is a group of retail stores that have been planned, coordinated, and marketed as a unit to shoppers in a geographical trade area. By providing single convenient locations and free parking, shopping centres have replaced downtown shopping in many cities. But time-pressed consumers are always looking for more efficient ways to shop, including using catalogues, Internet retailers, and one-stop shopping at large free-standing stores such as Walmart Supercentres. To lure more customers, shopping centres are now marketing themselves as entertainment destinations, by offering movie theatres, art displays, carousel rides, and musical entertainment. The West Edmonton Mall includes a water park and indoor arena. The giant Mall of America in Bloomington, Minnesota, features a seven-acre amusement park and an aquarium.

Shopping malls attract teens, who often meet there to socialize with friends. Businesses want to welcome their teen customers, but sometimes the group of teens hanging around the mall causes difficulties for other customers and some retailers, as described in the "Solving an Ethical Controversy" feature.

In recent years, some large regional malls have seen a growing shift in shopping centre traffic to smaller strip centres and name-brand outlet centres. Many consumers have also shifted their

SOLVING AN **ETHICAL** CONTROVERSY

Teens at the Mall: Good or Bad for Business?

Some shopping malls have banned unsupervised teenagers on weekend evenings. Others are considering a total ban on teens who are not accompanied by adults. Teenagers go to malls to hang out with their friends but they also spend money there. Mall retailers used to complain about groups of unsupervised teenagers. But now they hope to attract these young spenders to increase sales. Teenagers are more cautious shoppers than they were before the recession, but they are once again snacking at the food court and shopping at Roots, American Eagle, and Abercrombie & Fitch.

Should malls that have banned unsupervised teenagers think about removing those bans to help increase business?

PRO

1. According to Thompson Reuters, spending by teenagers has increased. Malls should encourage teens to shop.

2. Most teenagers are well behaved. They should not be banned as a group because of the bad behaviour of a few.

CON

1. Some merchants are still cautious. One said, "Parents drop their kids off, and they don't know what their kids do while they are away."

2. The attractiveness of teenagers freely spending money needs to be balanced against the risk of crowd behaviour. At one mall, more than a dozen teenagers were arrested after a fight broke out.

Summary

Just as adults spent much less during the recent recession, so did their children. The "bank of Mom and Dad—on pretty much all levels—basically shut down," said one retail analyst. Teenagers have now returned to their impulsive shopping habits. Mall owners and civic leaders will need to find a balance between maintaining order and encouraging these consumers of tomorrow.

Sources: Andrea Chang, "Free-Spending Teens Return to Malls," *Los Angeles Times,* March 28, 2010, http://articles.latimes.com; Erica Shaffer, "City Leaders Recommend Total Ban of Unsupervised Teens at Mall," WTOL, February 18, 2010, http://www.wtol.com; Fran Daniel, "Mall May Limit Teens: Policy Expected to Require Parental Supervision on Friday, Saturday Evenings," *Winston-Salem Journal,* February 9, 2010, http://www2.journalnow.com.

---

shopping to so-called *lifestyle centres*. These open-air complexes house retailers that often focus on specific shopper segments and specific product interests.

Building a Promotional Strategy

A retailer designs advertisements and develops other promotions for two reasons: to create demand and to provide information, such as the store's location, its offerings, prices, and hours. When a recent year proved to be difficult, Starbucks turned to social media for a new promotional strategy. The chain launched MyStarbucksIdea.com. Customers could log onto this forum to ask questions, offer suggestions, and even voice their dislikes. The site's 180,000 registered users have offered 80,000 ideas; Starbucks has carried out 50 of the suggestions. The Starbucks Facebook page has some 5.7 million fans; the chain also has 775,000 Twitter followers. Charles Bruzzo, the chain's vice-president for brand, content, and online, says the company is seeing the beginning of an "intersection between digital and physical."[24]

Nonstore retailers provide their phone numbers and website addresses as part of their promotional strategy. More recently, online retailers have scaled back their big advertising campaigns and worked to build traffic through word of mouth and clever promotions. Promotional strategy is also discussed in depth in Chapter 13.

Creating a Store Atmosphere

A successful retailer designs its merchandising, pricing, and promotion strategies to work with *store atmospherics*, the physical characteristics of a store and its services. The idea is to positively influence consumers' views of the shopping experience. Atmospherics begin with the store's exterior. Eye-catching architectural elements and signage are used to attract customer attention and interest. Interior atmospheric elements include the store layout, merchandise presentation, lighting, colour, sound, and cleanliness. For example, a high-end store like Holt Renfrew may feature high ceilings that highlight tasteful and well-designed displays of high-quality goods. In contrast, Costco stocks an ever-changing offering of moderately priced products in its warehouse-like settings decorated with industrial-style display hardware.

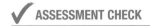

ASSESSMENT CHECK

12.6.1 Define *retailer*.

12.6.2 What are the elements of a retailer's marketing strategy?

DISTRIBUTION CHANNEL DECISIONS AND LOGISTICS

LO 12.7 Identify the various categories of distribution channels, and discuss the factors that influence channel selection.

Every firm faces two major decisions when choosing how to distribute its goods or services: selecting a specific distribution channel and deciding on the level of distribution intensity. When deciding which distribution channel is most efficient, business managers need to consider four factors: the market, the product, the producer, and the competition. These factors are often interrelated and may change over time. In today's global business environment, strong relationships with customers and suppliers are important for survival. One way to help strengthen such relationships online is to practise proper social media manners, as explained in the "Business Etiquette" feature.

BUSINESS ETIQUETTE

Minding Your Social Media Manners

More and more entrepreneurs are using social networking media to promote their small or medium-size businesses. Facebook, Twitter, LinkedIn, and many blogs and forums offer endless marketing opportunities. A recent survey found that 70 percent of small businesses planned to increase their use of social media. Seventy-nine percent did not plan to run TV commercials, and 70 percent didn't use radio ads.

Just as in the real business world, good manners, common courtesy, and common sense will take you far in the virtual business world. Here are a few tips on good manners for social media:

1. *Even though you join social networks to promote your business, don't make it too obvious.* Instead of promoting yourself or your business nonstop, post carefully worded messages to show that you have something of value to offer to interested people. Otherwise, you risk being considered a spammer.

2. *Be aware that you are in social networks for the long haul.* Group members or forum members are real people with real interests and ideas. Get to know the members of your forums. Learn about their interests and how the community, as a whole, works. Virtual networks of "friends" have unwritten rules, just as real networks do.

3. *It's not the numbers that count.* Getting your brand known or achieving other marketing goals doesn't depend on how many Twitter followers you have; it depends on how you connect with them.

4. *Be careful of what you say.* Avoid vulgar language, off-colour jokes, or any hint of racial or gender bias. Don't bring up religion, politics, or other sensitive subjects. Leave any strong opinions out of your marketing profile.

5. *Remember that your customers will be discussing you on their own networks.* Your reputation may travel farther than you know!

Sources: Mickie Kennedy, "Do You Have Good Social Media Manners?" *eReleases,* March 23, 2010, http://www.ereleases.com; Michelle Bowles, "5 Social Media Tips for ecommerce Marketing," *Online Marketing Blog,* March 12, 2010, http://www.toprankblog.com; Kim States, "Five Social Media Tips to Connect Small Businesses," *AzBiz.com,* January 2, 2010, http://www.azbiz.com; Sean Rasmussen.

Selecting Distribution Channels

Market factors may be the most important consideration when choosing a distribution channel. When a firm needs to reach a target market of a small number of buyers or buyers within a small geographical area, the best option may be a direct channel. In contrast, if the firm must reach customers who live in a wide geographical area or who make frequent small purchases, then the channel may need to use marketing intermediaries to make goods available when and where customers want them.

In general, most standardized products or items with low unit values use relatively long distribution channels. On the other hand, products that are complex, expensive, custom made, or perishable move through shorter distribution channels involving few—or no—intermediaries. The increasing use of e-commerce is resulting in changes in traditional distribution practices. The European Commission recently issued an interesting set of rules, effective until 2022. These rules allow makers of goods with less than a 30 percent market share—usually high-end manufacturers—to block Internet-only retailers from carrying their products. The commission declared that "suppliers should normally be free to decide on the number and type of distributors they want to have in their distribution systems… More generally, suppliers may only want to sell to distributors that have one or more physical points of present [actual "bricks-and-mortar" stores] where the suppliers' goods can be touched, smelled, tried, etc." The European Alliance—which represents luxury goods manufacturers such as LVMH Louis Vuitton Moët Hennessey, Gucci, and Burberry—lobbied for and welcomed the new rules as a way to protect the quality image of their products. Online-only retailers, such as Amazon, eBay, and their European equivalents, called for a reversal of the "bricks-and-mortar" requirement and warned that some manufacturers would use the new rules to "restrict the availability" of their products online and thus keep prices high.[25]

But the Greek entrepreneur Stelios Haji-Ioannou finds the Internet to be the perfect channel for easyGroup, the private investment group for his "easy" brand. The company represents a variety of businesses with the "easy" tag—easyJet.com, easyCar.com, easyJobs.com, easyPizza.com, and even an easyBus route between Gatwick Airport and London. Each business offers a no-frills, low-cost approach to services that consumers can order online. EasyJet is one of Europe's biggest Internet retailers, selling 95 percent of its seats online.[26]

Some producers offer a broad product line and have the financial and marketing resources to distribute and promote their products. These producers are more likely than others to choose a shorter channel. Instead of depending on marketing intermediaries, financially strong manufacturers with broad product lines typically use their own sales representatives, warehouses, and credit departments to serve both retailers and consumers.

In many cases, start-up manufacturers turn to direct channels for two reasons: because they can't get intermediaries to carry their products or because they want to extend their sales reach. Some companies use direct channels to carry intangible goods. For example, in New York City, Art Meets Commerce uses the Internet and social networking to promote small Broadway and off-Broadway shows that have tight marketing budgets. The company posts short videos of its clients' shows on YouTube. It also uses Facebook and Twitter to increase traditional word-of-mouth publicity. When celebrities see the shows and post favourable tweets, their followers may also feel encouraged to see the shows.[27]

Competitive performance is the fourth key consideration when choosing a distribution channel. A producer loses customers when an intermediary fails to deliver the promotion or product. Channels used by established competitors and new market entries also can influence decisions. Sometimes a joint venture between competitors can work well. For example, Best Buy and Apple have teamed up to sell their products under the same roof. Under the agreement, Apple controls its own retail space within Best Buy stores. Although Apple has a well-established retail business, it can't match the size of electronics giant Best Buy. Best Buy benefits by generating more traffic from customers who want to see and buy Apple's innovative products in convenient locations. The strategy has worked well—specifically, sales of Macs have increased. Best Buy was the only non-Apple retailer in North America to carry the iPad. All of Best Buy's 673 stores with Apple shops sold out their stock of iPads in four days.[28]

Selecting Distribution Intensity

A second key distribution decision involves *distribution intensity*—the number of intermediaries or outlets a manufacturer uses to distribute its goods. Your community may have only one BMW dealership, but you can likely find Coca-Cola everywhere—in grocery stores, convenience stores, gas stations, vending machines, and restaurants. BMW has chosen a different level of distribution intensity from that used by Coca-Cola. In general, market coverage has three different intensity levels:

Exclusive distribution limits market coverage in a specific geographical region. This approach suits relatively expensive specialty products such as Rolex watches. Retailers are carefully selected to enhance the product's image to the market.

Daniel Acker/Bloomberg/Getty Images

1. *Intensive distribution* involves placing a firm's products in nearly every available outlet. Intensive distribution usually suits low-priced convenience goods such as milk, newspapers, and soft drinks. This kind of market coverage requires co-operation from many intermediaries, including wholesalers and retailers.

2. *Selective distribution* involves a manufacturer selecting only a limited number of retailers to distribute its product lines. Selective distribution can reduce total marketing costs and establish strong working relationships within the channel.

3. *Exclusive distribution* is at the opposite extreme from intensive distribution. This distribution strategy limits market coverage in a specific geographical region. This approach suits relatively expensive specialty products such as Rolex watches. Retailers are carefully selected to enhance the product's image to the market and to ensure that well-trained personnel will contribute to customer satisfaction. Producers may give up some market coverage by granting an exclusive territory to a single intermediary. But the decision usually pays off by developing and maintaining an image of quality and prestige.

When companies are clearing out excess inventory, even high-priced retailers may look to discounters to help them move the merchandise from their warehouses. For example, to satisfy consumers' taste for luxury goods, designer outlet malls offer shoppers a chance to buy originally high-priced items at lower prices. And online vendors like Montreal-based Beyond the Rack provide distributors and manufacturers the opportunity to clear excess merchandise inventories quickly. After all, their fashion-driven shoppers are searching online for the next great deal.[29]

Logistics and Physical Distribution

A firm's choice of distribution channels creates the final link in the **supply chain**, the complete sequence of suppliers that help to create a good or service and deliver it to business users and end consumers. The supply chain begins when the raw materials used in production are delivered to the producer. The supply chain continues with the actual production activities that create finished goods. Finally, the finished goods move through the producer's distribution channels to end customers.

The process of coordinating the flow of goods, services, and information among members of the supply chain is called **logistics**. The term originally referred to strategic movements of military troops and supplies. Today, it describes all of the business activities involved in the supply chain with the ultimate goal of getting finished goods to customers.

Physical Distribution

Physical distribution is a major focus of logistics management. It was identified earlier in the chapter as one of the two basic dimensions of distribution strategy. Physical distribution refers to the activities aimed at efficiently moving finished goods from the production line to the consumer

supply chain the complete sequence of suppliers that help to create a good or service and deliver it to business users and final consumers.

logistics the process of coordinating the flow of goods, services, and information among members of the supply chain.

or business buyer. As Figure 12.9 shows, physical distribution is a broad concept that includes transportation and many other elements that help link buyers and sellers. An effectively managed physical distribution system can increase customer satisfaction by ensuring reliable movements of products through the supply chain. For example, Walmart studies how quickly goods can be shelved after they arrive at the store. Walmart executives know that strategies that may seem to be efficient in the warehouse, such as completely filling pallets with goods, can actually be time-consuming or costly in the store aisles.

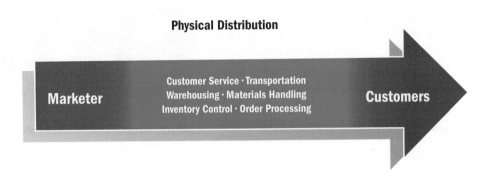

FIGURE 12.9
Elements of a Physical Distribution System

Radio-frequency identification (RFID) technology relies on a computer chip. This chip is implanted on a product or its packaging and emits a low-frequency radio signal to identify the item. The radio signal doesn't need a direct line of sight to register on the store's computers the way a bar code does. That means a hand-held RFID reader can scan crates and cartons before they are unloaded. Because the chip can store information about the product's progress through the distribution channel, RFID can help retailers to better manage inventories, maintain stock levels, reduce loss, track stolen goods, and cut costs. The technology is similar to what is already used to identify lost pets and to help some vehicles move more quickly past toll booths. Walmart, Target, and the German retailer Metro Group already require their suppliers to use RFID technology. Automakers use RFID technology to improve their production processes by tracking parts and other supplies. A new version of the RFID chip can be printed on paper or plastic. The use of RFID technology has led to privacy and counterfeiting concerns. Recently, one company developed a process that uses unique silicon "fingerprints" to generate unclonable RFID chips.[30]

Warehousing is the physical distribution activity that involves the storage of products. *Materials handling* is moving items within factories, warehouses, transportation terminals, and stores. Inventory control involves managing inventory costs, such as storage facilities, insurance, taxes, and handling. The physical distribution activity of *order processing* includes preparing orders for shipment and receiving orders when shipments arrive.

The wide use of electronic data interchange (EDI) and the constant pressure on suppliers to improve their response time have led to **vendor-managed inventory**. It is the process in which the producer and the retailer agree that the producer (or the wholesaler) will decide how much of a product a buyer needs and automatically ship new supplies when needed.

The form of transportation used to ship products depends on the kind of product, the distance involved, and the cost. The logistics manager can choose from several companies and types of transportation. Table 12.3 shows the five major transport modes: trucks (with about 75 percent of total expenditures), railroads (approximately 12 percent), water carriers (6 percent), air freight (4 percent), and pipelines (3 percent). The faster methods usually cost more than the slower methods. When choosing the most suitable method of transportation, the important factors include speed, reliable delivery, shipment frequency, location availability, handling flexibility, and cost.

About 15.5 million trucks operate in the United States, and about 700,000 operate in Canada. They carry most finished goods all or part of the way to the consumer. Nearly 2 million of the U.S. trucks are tractor trailers.[31] Another major form of transportation is the railroads, which compete with many truck routes despite their recent loss of market share. The 565 freight railroads in the

vendor-managed inventory the process in which the producer and the retailer agree that the producer (or the wholesaler) will decide how much of a product a buyer needs and automatically ship new supplies when needed.

Table 12.3 Comparison of Transportation Modes

MODE	SPEED	DEPENDABILITY IN MEETING SCHEDULES	FREQUENCY OF SHIPMENTS	AVAILABILITY IN DIFFERENT LOCATIONS	FLEXIBILITY IN HANDLING	COST
Truck	Fast	High	High	Very extensive	Average	High
Rail	Average	Average	Low	Low	High	Average
Water	Very slow	Average	Very low	Limited	Very high	Very low
Air	Very fast	High	Average	Average	Low	Very high
Pipeline	Slow	High	High	Very limited	Very Low	Low

United States, Canada, and Mexico operate across more than 325,000 kilometres of track and earn almost $75 billion in revenues. Seventy percent of all autos manufactured in North America travel to their destinations by train. A freight train needs only 3.8 litres of diesel fuel to transport 1 tonne of cargo almost 685 miles.[32]

Customer Service

Customer service is a major part of both product and distribution strategies. *Customer service standards* measure the quality of service a firm provides for its customers. Managers often set quantitative guidelines—for example, that all orders be processed within 24 hours after they are received or that salespeople approach shoppers within two minutes after they enter the store. Sometimes customers set their own service standards and then choose suppliers that meet or exceed those standards.

The customer service portions of product strategy include warranty and repair service programs. *Warranties* are firms' promises to repair a defective product, refund money paid, or replace a product if it proves unsatisfactory. Repair services are also important. Consumers want to know that help is available if something goes wrong. For example, shoppers for home computers often choose retailers that feature low prices *and* offer repair services and tech support centres. Products with poor after-sales service quickly disappear from the market as a result of word-of-mouth criticism.

Consumers' complaints of the impersonal service they received at websites led dot-coms to take several steps to "humanize" their customer interactions and deal with complaints. Many websites include help button icons that link the visitor to a company representative.

✔ **ASSESSMENT CHECK**

12.7.1 What is distribution intensity?

12.7.2 Define *supply chain*.

12.7.3 What do customer service standards measure?

WHAT'S AHEAD

This chapter covered two of the elements of the marketing mix: product and distribution. It introduced the key marketing tasks of developing, marketing, and packaging want-satisfying goods and services. It also focused on three major parts of an organization's distribution strategy: the design of efficient distribution channels; wholesalers and retailers who make up many distribution channels; and logistics and physical distribution. We now turn to the remaining two elements of the marketing mix—promotion and pricing—in Chapter 13.

RETURN TO INSIDE BUSINESS

Montreal's Fitness City Complex—Bringing Fitness Businesses Together Under One Roof

The concept of clustering fitness businesses under one roof has proven to be successful. Soon after Fitness City opened, a new tenant launched a service offering indoor golf instruction. It uses computer-generated screens that allow for year-round indoor golf instruction. This business is a welcomed addition to Montreal, where golfers anxiously await the end of winter and the start of a new golf season.

The owners of Fitness City continue to seek new tenants that can benefit from the fitness-oriented customers who regularly spend time—and money—at the complex. One idea is to expand health and wellness services by providing space where professionals such as dieticians and physiotherapists can meet with their clients.

QUESTIONS FOR CRITICAL THINKING

1. Which other health-related and wellness-related professionals should be considered as tenants?

2. How can these professional services be marketed within the complex?

SUMMARY OF LEARNING OBJECTIVES

LO 12.1 Explain marketing's definition of a product; differentiate among convenience products, shopping products, and specialty products; and distinguish between a product mix and a product line.

A product is a bundle of physical, service, and symbolic characteristics designed to satisfy consumer wants. The marketing conception of a product includes the brand, product image, warranty, service attributes, packaging, labelling, and the physical or functional characteristics of the good or service.

Goods and services can be classified as consumer (B2C) or business (B2B) products. Consumer products are those goods and services purchased by end consumers for their own use. They can be convenience products, shopping products, or specialty products, depending on how consumers buy them. Business products are those products purchased for use either directly or indirectly in the production of other goods and services for resale. They can be classified as installations, accessory equipment, component parts and materials, raw materials, and supplies. This classification is based on how the items are used and product characteristics. Services can be classified as either consumer or business services.

A product mix is the assortment of goods and services a firm offers to individual consumers and B2B users. A product line is a series of related products.

✓ ASSESSMENT CHECK ANSWERS

12.1.1 How do consumer products differ from business products? Business products, such as drill presses, are sold to firms or organizations. Consumer products, such as personal-care items, are sold to end users.

12.1.2 Differentiate among convenience products, shopping products, and specialty products. Convenience products are items the consumer seeks to purchase frequently, immediately, and with little effort. Shopping products are typically purchased after the buyer has compared competing products in competing stores. Specialty products are those products that a purchaser is willing to make a special effort to obtain.

LO 12.2 Briefly describe the four stages of the product life cycle and their marketing implications.

Every successful new product passes through four stages in its product life cycle: introduction, growth, maturity, and decline. In the introduction stage, the firm attempts to create demand for the new product. In the product's growth stage, sales climb, and the company earns its first profits. In the maturity stage, sales reach a saturation level. In the decline stage, both sales and profits decrease. Marketers sometimes use strategies such as the following to extend the product life cycle: increasing the frequency of use; adding new users; finding new uses for the product; and changing package size, labelling, or product quality.

The new-product development process for most products has six stages: idea generation, screening, concept development and business analysis, product development, test marketing, and commercialization. At each stage, marketers must decide whether to continue to the next stage, make changes to the new product, or discontinue the development process. Some new products may skip the test marketing stage for various reasons: because they want to quickly introduce a new product with excellent potential, because of a desire not to reveal new-product strategies to competitors, or because of the high costs involved in limited production runs.

✓ ASSESSMENT CHECK ANSWERS

12.2.1 What are the stages of the product life cycle? The product life cycle has four stages: introduction, growth, maturity, and decline. In the introduction stage, the firm tries to attract demand for the new product. In the product's growth stage, sales climb, and the company earns its first profits. In the maturity stage, sales reach a saturation level. In the decline stage, both sales and profits decline.

12.2.2 What are the marketing implications of each stage? Marketers sometimes use strategies to extend the product life cycle, including increasing frequency of use, adding new users, finding new uses for the product, and changing package size, labelling, or product quality.

LO 12.3 Explain how firms identify their products.

Products are identified by brands, brand names, and trademarks. All three are important elements of product images. Effective brand names are easy to say, easy to recognize, and easy to remember. They also project the right images to buyers. Brand names cannot contain generic words. Under certain circumstances, companies can lose the exclusive rights to their brand names if common use transforms the brand names into generic terms for product categories. Some brand names belong to retailers or distributors, not to manufacturers. Brand loyalty is measured in three degrees: brand recognition, brand preference, and brand insistence. Some marketers use family brands to identify several related items in a product line. Other marketers use individual branding strategies by giving a different brand name to each product within a product line.

 ASSESSMENT CHECK ANSWERS

12.3.1 Differentiate among a brand, a brand name, and a trademark. A brand is a name, term, sign, symbol, design, or some combination used to identify the products of one firm and show how they differ from competitive offerings. A brand name is that part of the brand consisting of words or letters. It is used to identify a firm's products and show how they differ from the products of competitors. A trademark is a brand that has been given legal protection.

12.3.2 Define *brand equity*. Brand equity is the added value that a respected and successful brand name gives to a product.

LO 12.4 Outline and briefly describe the major components of an effective distribution strategy.

A firm must decide whether to move products through direct or indirect distribution. After making this decision, the company needs to identify which types of marketing intermediaries, if any, will distribute its goods and services. The Internet has made direct distribution an attractive option for many retail companies.

 ASSESSMENT CHECK ANSWERS

12.4.1 Define *distribution channels*. Distribution channels are the paths that products, and their legal ownership, follow from producer to consumer or business user.

12.4.2 What is a marketing intermediary? A marketing intermediary (also called a middleman) is a business firm that moves goods from their producers to the consumers or business users.

LO 12.5 Distinguish between different types of wholesaling intermediaries.

Wholesaling is a crucial part of the distribution channel for many products, especially consumer goods and business supplies. Wholesaling intermediaries can be classified on the basis of ownership: some are owned by manufacturers, some are owned by retailers, and others are independently owned. Firms operate two main types of manufacturer-owned wholesaling intermediaries: sales branches and sales offices.

An independent wholesaling intermediary is a business that represents several different manufacturers and sells to retailers, manufacturers, and other business accounts. Independent wholesalers can be either merchant wholesalers or agents and brokers, depending on whether they take title to (legal ownership of) the products they handle.

Retailers sometimes work together to form their own wholesaling organizations. Such organizations can take the form of either a buying group or a co-operative.

 ASSESSMENT CHECK ANSWERS

12.5.1 Define *wholesaling*. Wholesaling is a crucial part of the distribution channel for many products, especially consumer goods and business supplies.

12.5.2 Differentiate between a merchant wholesaler and an agent or broker in terms of title to the goods. Merchant wholesalers are independently owned wholesaling intermediaries that take title to the goods they handle. Agents and brokers may or may not take physical possession of the goods they handle, but they never take title, or ownership. They work mainly to bring buyers and sellers together.

LO 12.6 Describe the various types of retailers, and identify retail strategies.

Retailers, in contrast to wholesalers, are distribution channel members that sell goods and services to individuals for their own use, not for resale. Nonstore retailing includes four forms: direct-response retailing, Internet retailing, automatic merchandising, and direct selling. Store retailers range in size from tiny newsstands to multi-storey department stores and warehouse-style retailers such as Costco.

The first step in developing a competitive retailing strategy is to select a target market. Next, the retailer must develop a product strategy to determine the best mix of merchandise to carry to satisfy that market. A retailer's customer service strategy focuses on attracting and retaining target customers to maximize sales and profits. Retailers base their pricing decisions on their costs of purchasing products from other channel members and offering services to customers. A good retail location can often make the difference between success and failure. A retailer designs advertisements and develops other promotions to stimulate demand and to provide information such as the store's location, merchandise offerings, prices, and hours. A successful retailer closely matches its merchandising, pricing, and promotion strategies with store atmospherics, the physical characteristics of a store and its amenities. A good match can help to influence consumers' perceptions of the shopping experience.

 ASSESSMENT CHECK ANSWERS

12.6.1 Define *retailer*. A retailer is a distribution channel member that sells goods and services to individuals for their own use, not for resale.

12.6.2 What are the elements of a retailer's marketing strategy? Retailers must first identify their target markets, and then choose the strategies for merchandising, customer service, pricing, and location that will attract customers in their target market segments.

LO 12.7 Identify the various categories of distribution channels, and discuss the factors that influence channel selection.

Marketers can choose either a direct distribution channel or an indirect distribution channel. A direct distribution channel moves goods directly from the producer to the consumer. An indirect distribution channel uses marketing intermediaries to make goods available when and where customers want them. Ideally, the choice of a distribution channel should support a firm's overall marketing strategy. Before selecting distribution channels, firms must consider their target markets, the types of goods being distributed, their own internal systems and concerns, and competitive factors.

A second key distribution decision involves distribution intensity. The business must decide on the market coverage needed to achieve its marketing strategies: intensive distribution, selective distribution, or exclusive distribution.

 ASSESSMENT CHECK ANSWERS

12.7.1 What is distribution intensity? Distribution intensity is the number of intermediaries or outlets a manufacturer uses to distribute its goods.

12.7.2 Define *supply chain*. A supply chain is the sequence of suppliers that help in creating a good or service and delivering it to business users and end consumers.

12.7.3 What do customer service standards measure? Customer service standards measure the quality of service a firm provides for its customers.

BUSINESS TERMS YOU NEED TO KNOW

product 326

product line 329

product mix 329

product life cycle 329

test marketing 333

brand 333

brand name 334

trademark 334

brand equity 335

category advisor 336

distribution strategy 338

distribution channels 338

physical distribution 338

wholesaler 340

retailers 342

supply chain 349

logistics 349

vendor-managed inventory 350

REVIEW QUESTIONS

1. Classify each of the following products as either a business-to-consumer (B2C) product or a business-to-business (B2B) product. Then choose one product and describe how it can be classified as both a B2C product and a B2B product.

   a. *Runner's World* or *Esquire* magazine

   b. a six-pack of apple juice

   c. a limousine service

   d. tech support for a communications system

   e. a golf course

   f. a Thai restaurant

2. What is the relationship between a product line and a product mix? Give an example of each.

3. Identify and briefly describe the six stages of new-product development.

4. What is the difference between a manufacturer's brand and a private brand? What is the difference between a family brand and an individual brand?

5. What are the three stages of brand loyalty? Why is it so important to marketers to reach the last stage of brand loyalty?

6. What are the upsides of direct distribution? When is a producer most likely to use direct distribution?

7. What is the wheel of retailing? How has the Internet affected the wheel of retailing?

8. Identify and briefly describe the four different types of nonstore retailers. Give an example of at least one type of good or service that would be suited to each type of nonstore retailer.

9. What are the three intensity levels of distribution? Give an example of two products for each level.

10. Define *logistics*. How does it relate to physical distribution?

PROJECTS AND TEAMWORK APPLICATIONS

1. On your own or with a classmate, choose one of the following goods or services. Decide whether you want to market it as a consumer product or a business product. Create a brand name and marketing strategy for your product.

   a. a lawn mower repair service

   b. a hardware store

   c. a soft drink

   d. an English-language class

   e. an accounting firm

2. Choose one of the following products that is either in the maturity stage or the decline stage of its life cycle (or select one of your own). Develop a marketing strategy for extending the product's life cycle.

  a. popcorn

  b. a fast-food restaurant chain

  c. a newspaper

  d. music CDs

  e. paper stationery or notecards

3. Where do you do most of your shopping—in stores or online? Choose your favourite retailer and analyze why you like it. Outline your reasons for shopping there. Suggest two or three areas for improvement.

4. Choose one of the following products. Select a distribution intensity for the product. Describe specifically where and how the product would be sold. Describe the reasons for your strategy.

  a. a line of furniture manufactured from recycled or reclaimed materials

  b. custom-designed jewellery

  c. a house-painting service

  d. handicraft supplies

  e. a radio talk show

WEB ASSIGNMENTS

1. Product classification. Review the chapter's discussion on product classification. Visit the website of Johnson & Johnson (http://www.jnj.com) and click on "Our Products." Classify Johnson & Johnson's wide range of products.

2. Shopping centres. The West Edmonton Mall in Edmonton is North America's largest shopping centre. Go to the mall's website (http://www.wem.ca) to learn more about it. Make a list of five interesting facts you learned about the West Edmonton Mall.

3. Railroad statistics. Visit the website of the Railway Association of Canada (http://www.railcan.ca/). Review the material and answer the following questions:

  a. How big is the railway industry in Canada?

  b. How many people do railroads employ?

  c. How much freight did railroads carry during the most recent year for which data are available?

Access your WileyPLUS course for:

- The complete digital textbook.

- Question assistance, including links to relevant sections in the online digital textbook.

- Immediate feedback and proof of progress, 24/7

- Integrated, multi-media resources – including MP3 downloads, visual exhibits, animations, and much more – that provide multiple study paths and encourage more active learning.

QUIZ YOURSELF

Note: Internet Web addresses change frequently. If you don't find the exact sites listed, you may need to access the organization's home page and search from there or use a search engine such as Bing or Google.

© Can Stock Photo Inc./anizza

13 | PROMOTION AND PRICING STRATEGIES

LEARNING OBJECTIVES

LO 13.1 Discuss how integrated marketing communications relates to a firm's overall promotional strategy, explain the concept of a promotional mix, and outline the objectives of promotion.

LO 13.2 Summarize the different types of advertising and advertising media.

LO 13.3 Outline the roles of sales promotion, personal selling, and public relations in promotional strategy.

LO 13.4 Describe pushing and pulling promotional strategies.

LO 13.5 Outline the different types of pricing objectives.

LO 13.6 Discuss how firms set prices in the marketplace, and describe the four alternative pricing strategies.

LO 13.7 Discuss consumer perceptions of price.

INSIDE BUSINESS

WorkSafeBC: Promoting Safety to Young Workers

WorkSafeBC is an insurance agency serving more than 200,000 employers and 2.3 million workers in British Columbia (BC). It is a workers' compensation board that help workers who have injuries related to the workplace. WorkSafeBC is a quasi-government agency, which means it operates under the guidance of the British Columbia provincial government but is separate from the government. In a recent year, premiums collected from employers totalled about $1 billion and payouts for claims were more than $1.3 billion. About 137,000 claims were made, resulting in 2.8 million lost workdays. The top three causes of injuries that led to lost workdays were strains (excluding back strains) at 1,118,000 days, back strains at 567,000 days, and fractures at 456,000 days. Although the average age of an injured worker is 41 years, 12 percent of young men under age 25 (about 6,300) reported injuries. The agency performance can be improved by reducing the number and the seriousness of worker injuries. One way to achieve this goal is to change people's attitudes toward workplace safety—especially the attitudes of younger men, who are more likely than any other population group to experience an injury.

Back in 2001, Vancouver-based Wasserman & Partners Advertising Inc. first won the contract to create a new promotional program for BC's Workers' Compensation Board (WCB). The agency began with a basic recommendation—make WorkSafeBC the public face of the organization. A total rebrand was needed. The WCB brand referred to claims, insurance, and administration, but it didn't have the heart or the belief that anyone or anything could change workplace behaviour. It also did not capture the passion within the organization that was focused on safety and accident prevention in the workplace.

WorkSafeBC's goal was to change social attitudes toward safety in the workplace. By doing this, it was hoped that workers would learn that work injuries can be avoided. Since putting the rebrand strategy in place, the organization's corporate reputation has increased. WorkSafeBC has a proud internal culture and focus. Statistics show that its promotional campaigns are changing attitudes toward workplace safety—and reducing injuries.

© Can Stock Photo Inc./Lurin

Before developing promotional ideas, research was done to better understand the target audience. This generation of consumers believes that it's cool to care about something; the agency wanted to find an opportunity to use that desire to make a change for the good. This audience also feels in control of their culture, instead of being consumers of culture. They don't want to be spoken at, they want to engage. They are connected 24/7. Technology and community are both important.

Unlike most other safety campaigns that target youth, the firm rejected the traditional "shock and awe" approach of scaring young people into working safely. According to Alvin Wasserman, president and creative strategist:

> "Shock and awe" catches attention, but in our current culture of violence as entertainment, it's too easy to say "That's not me" and it doesn't provide tangible information on what to do. Research shows that it is ineffective in changing behaviour. A successful social marketing campaign presents the magnitude of the problem but also gives the audience something tangible to do in order to address the problem. To develop our approach we asked ourselves and our target audience what would be the first step to making the work environment safer. The answer—ask for help if you don't know what to do.

The strategy developed was to tap into the target audience's desire to make a difference. This strategy led to the launch of the Raise Your Hand campaign, as a blueprint, or a plan, for a young worker movement that focuses on workplace safety and rights: the right to know about hazards at your job and how to protect yourself; the right to participate in making sure your job and workplace are safe and healthy; and the right to refuse unsafe work. The idea was to help create a social environment where all young workers in BC would ask for help to be safer on the job and would feel free to "raise their hand" when the workplace did not appear to be safe.

Raise Your Hand engages with young workers by showing up at all of the popular summertime youth cultural events throughout the province. From music events to major sporting events, the Raise Your Hand team is there. In the fall, Raise Your Hand participates in campus crawls at universities and colleges throughout BC to reach more young people.

But connecting online has always been a major strategy of the campaign. The interactivity of rich media online ads has led to record website results. WorkSafeBC's online presence includes distribution strategies that use social media sites such as Facebook, YouTube, and Twitter.[1]

CHAPTER 13 OVERVIEW

This chapter focuses on the different types of promotional activities and how prices are decided on for goods and services. **Promotion** is the function of informing, persuading, and influencing a purchase decision. This activity is as important to not-for-profit organizations as it is to for-profit companies.

Some promotional strategies try to develop *primary demand*, or consumer desire, for a general product category. The objective of such a campaign is to stimulate sales for an entire industry so that individual firms benefit from the total market growth. A popular example is the dairy industry's "Got Milk?" campaign. Print and television messages about the nutritional benefits of milk feature various celebrities. Another very successful promotional campaign aimed at increasing per-capita consumption is the long-running "Get Cracking" campaign by the Egg Farmers of Ontario. This promotion emphasizes the many easy meal preparations that use eggs.

In contrast, most promotional strategies try to stimulate *selective demand*—desire for a specific brand. Just about every adult needs banking and financial services. TD Canada Trust wants consumers to pick its firm from among the many competitors in the marketplace. Banks tend to promote their friendly customer services, expertise, and convenient locations to set themselves apart from competitors. For most customers, the bank brand is understood in terms of the people they actually come in contact with at their local branch. Marketers choose from among many promotional options to communicate with potential customers. Marketing messages can be communicated through a television or radio commercial, a newspaper or magazine ad, a website, a direct-mail flyer, or a sales call. Each marketing message reflects the product, place, person, cause, or organization promoted in the content. Marketers use **integrated marketing communications (IMC)** to coordinate all promotional activities—media advertising, direct mail, personal selling, sales promotion, and public relations—to produce a unified, customer-focused promotional strategy. This coordination is designed to avoid confusing the consumer and to focus positive attention on the promotional message.

This chapter begins by explaining the role of IMC, and then discusses the objectives of promotion and the importance of promotional planning. Next, it examines the elements of the promotional mix: advertising, sales promotion, personal selling, and public relations. Finally, the chapter addresses pricing strategies for goods and services.

promotion the function of informing, persuading, and influencing a purchase decision.

integrated marketing communications (IMC) the coordination of all promotional activities—media advertising, direct mail, personal selling, sales promotion, and public relations—to produce a unified, customer-focused promotional strategy.

LO 13.1 Discuss how integrated marketing communications relates to a firm's overall promotional strategy, explain the concept of a promotional mix, and outline the objectives of promotion.

INTEGRATED MARKETING COMMUNICATIONS

An integrated marketing communications (IMC) strategy focuses on customer needs to create a unified promotional message in the firm's ads, in-store displays, product samples, and presentations by company sales representatives. To gain a competitive advantage, marketers that use IMC need a broad view of promotion. Media options continue to increase, and marketers cannot rely on traditional broadcast, print media, and direct mail. Marketing plans must include all forms of customer contact. Packaging, store displays, sales promotions, sales presentations, and online and interactive media also communicate information about a brand or organization. Marketers that use IMC create a unified personality and message for the good, brand, or service they promote. Coordinated activities also increase the effectiveness of reaching and serving target markets.

Marketing managers set the goals and objectives for the firm's promotional strategy, while keeping in mind the firm's overall organizational objectives and marketing goals. Using these objectives, marketers weave the various elements of the strategy—personal selling, advertising, sales promotion, publicity, and public relations—into an integrated communications plan. This document becomes a central focus of the firm's total marketing strategy to reach its selected target market. Feedback, including marketing research and sales reports, completes the strategy by identifying any activities that differ from the plan and suggesting improvements.

The job-search engine Monster.com combined several marketing promotions to create its stepped-up IMC campaign "Get a Monster Advantage." The campaign's first TV commercial featured a down-on-his-luck boogeyman who goes to Monster.com to find the perfect new job. A second commercial, featuring another character, aired during a recent Super Bowl game. Other spots were aired on national cable networks and were extended to social media. Humorous interactive links on sites such as Facebook and advertising on other sites further reached out to the online audience. Print ads appeared in *The Wall Street Journal*, in more than 100 regional daily newspapers, in monthly business publications, and in human resource publications, such as *HR Executive*, *Wired*, and *Fast Company*.[2]

The Promotional Mix

Every organization creates a marketing mix by combining product, distribution, promotion, and pricing strategies. In a similar way, each organization also needs to blend the many types of promotion into a unified and organized plan. The **promotional mix** is the combination of personal selling and nonpersonal selling that marketers use to meet the needs of a firm's target customers and to effectively and efficiently communicate its message to them. **Personal selling** is the most basic form of promotion: a direct person-to-person promotional presentation to a potential buyer. The buyer–seller communication can occur in several ways: during a face-to-face meeting, by telephone, videoconference, or an interactive computer link.

Nonpersonal selling consists of advertising, sales promotion, direct marketing, and public relations. Advertising is the best-known form of nonpersonal selling, but sales promotion accounts for about half of the money spent on nonpersonal selling. Spending is increasing for sponsorships, which involve marketing messages that are delivered in association with another activity, such as a golf tournament or a benefit concert. Marketers need to be careful about the types of promotion they choose because they risk alienating, or isolating, the very people they are trying to reach.

Each element in the promotional mix offers its own advantages and disadvantages, as Table 13.1 shows. When a firm selects the most effective combination of promotional mix elements, it may reach its promotional objectives. The spending levels within the promotional mix vary by industry. Manufacturers of many business-to-business (B2B) products typically spend more on personal selling than on advertising because those products—such as a new telecommunications system—may require a significant investment. Consumer-goods marketers may focus more on advertising and sponsorships. Later sections of this chapter discuss how the parts of the mix contribute to effective promotion.

Objectives of Promotional Strategy

Promotional strategy objectives vary among organizations. Some organizations use promotion to expand their markets, while other organizations use promotion to defend their current positions. As Figure 13.1 shows, common objectives include providing information, differentiating a product, increasing sales, stabilizing sales, and highlighting a product's value.

promotional mix the combination of personal and nonpersonal selling that marketers use to meet the needs of a firm's target customers and to effectively and efficiently communicate its message to them.

personal selling the most basic form of promotion: a direct person-to-person promotional presentation to a potential buyer.

nonpersonal selling forms of selling such as advertising, sales promotion, direct marketing, and public relations.

Table 13.1 Comparing the Elements of the Promotional Mix

ELEMENT	ADVANTAGES	DISADVANTAGES
Advertising	Reaches large consumer audience at low cost per contact	Difficult to measure effectiveness
	Allows strong control of the message	Limited value for closing sales
	Message can be modified to suit different audiences	
Personal selling	Message can be tailored for each customer	High cost per contact
	Produces immediate buyer response	High expense and difficulty of attracting and retaining effective salespeople
	Effectiveness is easily measured	
Sales promotion	Attracts attention and creates awareness	Difficult to differentiate from similar programs of competitors
	Effectiveness is easily measured	Nonpersonal appeal
	Produces increases in short-term sales	
Public relations	Improves trust in a product or firm	Difficult to measure effectiveness
	Creates a positive attitude about the product or company	Often devoted to nonmarketing activities
Sponsorships	Viewed positively by consumers	Difficult to control message
	Enhances brand awareness	

positioning a concept whereby marketers try to establish their products in the minds of customers by communicating to buyers the meaningful differences about the attributes, price, quality, or use of a good or service.

FIGURE 13.1 Five Major Promotional Objectives

Marketers often pursue more than one promotional objective at the same time. For example, to promote its Microsoft Office software, Microsoft needs to convince two groups that the product is a worthwhile investment: business owners, who buy the software, and the business owners' employees, who use the software.

Providing Information

A major portion of advertising is information-oriented. Credit card ads provide information about benefits and rates. Ads for hair-care products include information about benefits such as shine and volume. Ads for breakfast cereals often mention nutritional information. Television ads for prescription drugs, a nearly $2 billion industry in North America, are sometimes criticized for relying on emotional appeals rather than providing information about the causes, risk factors, and the prevention of disease.[3] But print advertisements for drugs often contain an entire page of warnings, side effects, and usage guidelines.

Differentiating a Product

Promotion can also be used to differentiate a firm's offerings from the competition. By using a concept called **positioning**, marketers try to establish their products in the minds of customers. The idea is to communicate to buyers some meaningful differences about the attributes, price, quality, or use of a good or service.

When you set out to purchase a car, you can choose from hundreds of brands. How do you decide which car to buy? Carmakers do their best to differentiate their vehicles by style, performance, safety features, and price. They must make their vehicles stand out to individual consumers. General Motors intends its new Chevrolet Cruze compact car to replace the discontinued Cobalt model. Traditionally, compact cars have been less expensive than midsize cars but are also known for being pretty ordinary, or average. The Cruze costs more than the Cobalt, but GM is promoting its higher quality and—especially—its high-quality safety engineering and safety features. A version of the Cruze has been on sale in other countries for a few years. The Cruze received the highest crash-safety score ever in the European New Car Assessment Program.[4]

Increasing Sales

Increasing sales volume is the most common objective of a promotional strategy. Naturalizer became the third-largest seller of women's dress shoes by appealing to baby boomers. But as these women have grown older, they have bought fewer pairs of shoes each year. Naturalizer wants to keep these customers but also wants to attract the younger generation. The firm developed a new line of trendy shoes. The promotional strategy included ads in magazines read by younger women—such as *Elle* and *Marie Claire*— featuring young women in beach attire and Naturalizer shoes. The response to this strategy was a large increase in Naturalizer's sales in department stores.

Stabilizing Sales

Sales stabilization is another goal of promotional strategy. During slow sales periods, some firms use employee sales contests. These contests are meant to motivate salespeople by offering prizes such as vacations, TVs, smartphones, and cash to those who meet certain sales goals. During the off-season, companies may try to stimulate sales from customers by distributing sales promotion materials, such as calendars, pens, and notepads. Jiffy Lube puts that little sticker on your windshield to remind you when to have your car's next oil change. The regular visits help to provide stabilize sales. A stable sales pattern brings several advantages. It evens out the production cycle and reduces some management and production costs. It also simplifies financial, purchasing, and marketing planning. An effective promotional strategy can contribute to these goals.

Highlighting the Product's Value

Some promotional strategies improve a product's value by explaining the hidden benefits of ownership. For example, carmakers offer long-term warranty programs, and life insurance companies promote certain policies as investments. The creation of brand awareness and brand loyalty improves a product's image and increases its desirability. Advertising that includes luxurious images supports the reputation of premium brands such as Jaguar, Tiffany, and Rolex.

product placement a form of promotion where marketers pay placement fees to have their products featured in various media, from newspapers and magazines to television and movies.

Promotional Planning

Today's marketers promote their products in many ways. The lines between the different elements of the promotional mix are blurring. Consider the practice of **product placement**. A growing number of marketers pay placement fees to have their products showcased in various media, ranging from newspapers and magazines to television and movies. For example, Coca-Cola gets prominent placement on *American Idol*. *The Tonight Show with Jay Leno* and *Extreme Makeover: Home Edition* are two popular shows with high product-placement appeal.[5] Product and brand

Coca-Cola gets prominent placement on *American Idol*. Product and brand placements have skyrocketed with the increasing number of reality TV shows and with improving technology that allows viewers to fast forward through conventional, stand-alone commercials.

placements have seen huge increases as a result of two developments: the growing number of reality TV shows and new technology that allows viewers to fast-forward through conventional, stand-alone commercials. NBC's reality show *The Biggest Loser* had the highest number of product placements—more than 6,200—in one recent season. *American Idol* was second, with more than 4,600. The industry report *Product Placement Spending in Media* estimates that product placement spending—also known as brand entertainment spending—totalled more than $3.5 billion in one year.[6]

guerrilla marketing innovative, low-cost marketing efforts designed to get consumers' attention in unusual ways.

Another type of promotional planning is considered by firms with small budgets. **Guerrilla marketing** refers to innovative, low-cost marketing efforts designed to get consumers' attention in unusual ways. Guerrilla marketing is an increasingly popular tactic for marketers, especially those with limited promotional budgets. The Coca-Cola Company recently maximized a humorous guerrilla marketing effort by combining it with social media marketing. How many times have you tried to get a snack or a drink from a vending machine, only to have the machine keep your change, or worse, not give you your paid-for item? A vending machine at a university was apparently broken. It gave the student customer a Coke—and then another, and another, and another. The pleased student handed out the unexpected bonus drinks, getting huge smiles from other students. The whole incident was filmed, guerrilla style, and posted on YouTube. It quickly went viral as viewers tweeted and blogged about it and sent the link to their friends.[7]

Marketers for larger companies have caught on. They are using guerrilla approaches, but with mixed success. The computer-game maker Electronic Arts (EA) faced an unusual challenge when marketing its videogame "Dante's Inferno," which is based on the first part of Dante Alighieri's medieval epic poem *The Divine Comedy*. Before starting its campaign, EA conducted a survey and found that fewer than 20 percent of those questioned knew anything about the "Inferno" besides the name. Not only did EA need to generate excitement about the game, it also needed to educate prospective buyers about the poem. Dante assigned sinners to one of nine regions, or circles, of hell according to their sins. The circles descended from lust, gluttony, greed, and so on, down to treachery, the worst sin, in the lowest circle. The company's campaign, Nine Months of Hell, took Dante's imagined structure as its theme and adapted it to EA's gaming needs. The campaign got off to a rocky start in the form of staged, phony protests against the game by phony religious groups. Although the protests were quickly unmasked as a practical joke, they set up negative expectations about the rest of the campaign. Things went from bad to worse when the promotion referred to the next circle of hell, lust. The blatantly sexist "Sin to Win" contest was launched at Comic-Con, the biggest comic-book and gaming convention in North America. Female gamers—a large portion of the videogame market—were outraged. They had already felt alienated and ignored by the gaming industry; now they also felt demeaned. The marketers said they were sorry, learned from their mistakes, and tried for a more intellectual—though still edgy—approach. Phil Marineau, the senior product manager for the game, said, " 'Sin to Win' was a great eye-opener for us, and we're glad it happened early on, so we could learn from it." In the end, the campaign was both praised and criticized within the marketing industry.[8]

From this overview of the promotional mix, we now turn to discussions of each of its elements. The following sections detail the major promotional mix elements of advertising, sales promotion, personal selling, and public relations.

✓ **ASSESSMENT CHECK**

13.1.1 What is the objective of an integrated marketing communications program?

13.1.2 Why do firms pursue multiple promotional objectives at the same time?

13.1.3 What are product placement and guerrilla marketing?

LO 13.2 Summarize the different types of advertising and advertising media.

ADVERTISING

advertising paid nonpersonal communication usually targeted at large numbers of potential buyers.

Consumers receive 4,000 to 5,000 marketing messages each day, many of them in the form of advertising.[9] Advertising is the most visible form of nonpersonal promotion—and the most effective for many firms. **Advertising** refers to paid nonpersonal communication usually targeted at large numbers of potential buyers. Although we often think of advertising as a typically North American function, it is a multibillion-dollar global activity. More than $10 billion is spent on advertising every year in Canada. According to Statistics Canada, about 5,000 advertising agencies are among nearly 12,000 firms involved in advertising and related services. Advertising agencies account for about 43 percent of advertising revenues generated, with the most being revenues sourced in Ontario (57 percent), Quebec (22 percent), and British Columbia (9 percent).[10]

Advertising expenditures vary among industries, companies, and media. Automotive, retail, and telecommunications firms spend the most on advertising in North America—carmakers spend $20 billion on advertising every year. General Motors spends the most, typically more than $3 billion annually.[11] Because advertising expenditures are so great, and because consumers receive so many advertising messages, firms need to be more and more creative and efficient at attracting consumers' attention.

Types of Advertising

The two basic types of advertisements are product ads and institutional ads. **Product advertising** consists of messages designed to sell a particular good or service. Advertisements for BlackBerry PlayBooks, Apple iPods, and Capital One credit cards are examples of product advertising. **Institutional advertising** involves messages that promote concepts, ideas, or philosophies. It can also promote goodwill toward industries, companies, organizations, or government entities. Each year, the Juvenile Diabetes Research Foundation promotes its "Walk for the Cure," a fundraising event. Your college or university may advertise in local papers or on news shows to promote its activities.

Cause advertising is a form of institutional advertising that is growing in importance. This type of advertising promotes a specific viewpoint on a public issue. It uses advertising to influence public opinion and the political process about such issues as literacy, hunger and poverty, and alternative energy sources. Both not-for-profit organizations and businesses use cause advertising, which is sometimes called *advocacy advertising*. As part of Avon's corporate responsibility, the Avon Foundation promotes its Speak Out Against Domestic Violence program. The ads feature a celebrity endorsement from Reese Witherspoon.[12]

Advertising and the Product Life Cycle

Advertising is designed to inform, persuade, or remind. Both types of advertising—product advertising and institutional advertising—belong to one of these three categories depending on the advertising objectives. For example, a firm uses *informative advertising* to build initial demand for a product in the introductory, or beginning, phase of the product life cycle. Highly publicized new-product entries attract the interest of potential buyers. The buyers then look for information about the advantages of the new products over existing products, the new products' warranties, their prices, and locations that offer the new products. Ads for new cellphones try to attract new customers by boasting about their new features, colours, designs, and pricing options.

Persuasive advertising tries to improve the competitive status of a product, institution, or concept. This type of advertising is usually used in the growth and maturity stages of the product life cycle. *Comparative advertising* is one of the most popular types of persuasive product advertising. This type of advertising compares products directly with their competitors—either by naming the competing product or by suggesting it. For example, Tylenol advertisements mention the possible stomach problems that the generic drug aspirin could cause, and then states that its pain reliever does not irritate the stomach. But advertisers need to be careful when they name competing

New Lipton® Tea & Honey

sweetened with honey   made from real tea leaves   real fruit flavors

Only 5 calories per serving. Find with Iced Tea Mixes.

DRINK POSITIVE

PR NEWSWIRE/AP Images

Product advertising consists of messages designed to sell a particular good or service.

product advertising messages designed to sell a particular good or service.

institutional advertising messages that promote concepts, ideas, or philosophies. It can also promote goodwill toward industries, companies, organizations, or government entities.

cause advertising a form of institutional advertising that promotes a specific viewpoint on a public issue as a way to influence public opinion and the political process.

HIT & MISS

The E*Trade Baby Talks Value

Babies and young children often utter funny, surprising, and insightful comments on the world around them. Online stock trading, investing, and banking firm E*Trade has bet its advertising budget on cuteness. The company created a series of television commercials featuring a talking baby who knows more about investing than the average adult. He's adorable, funny—and smart.

He text-messages friends and even hires a clown with his investment profits, commenting that he underestimated the clown's creepiness. At the end of the most talked-about of the ads, he spits up on his computer keyboard—reminding viewers that, after all, he is just a baby. E*Trade launched new installments of the Talking Baby series during Super Bowl broadcasts over a period of three years. The third commercial was so popular that it was rated higher than ads for Doritos, Coca-Cola, Bud Light, and even ads for Pepsi starring Justin Timberlake.

Making stock trading funny or even memorable is not easy, especially during difficult economic times. But E*Trade succeeded. Viewers remember the cute wisecracking baby. Despite the huge task of trying to understand online stock trading, viewers come away with the impression that E*Trade is so easy that even a smart child can do it. E*Trade took a big risk by advertising during such a visible program as the Super Bowl, and during such challenging economic times. But it was a calculated risk that has always been part of E*Trade's

promotional strategy. "History repeatedly has shown that those who continue to make smart marketing investments when economic times are uncertain are best positioned for success when the economy rebounds," explains Nicholas Utton, chief marketing officer for E*Trade. "That's why, in this uncertain economic climate, reinforcing the strength of our brand and value proposition is critical."

The talking toddler fits E*Trade's image as a firm that thumbs its nose at large, traditional brokerages. E*Trade encourages investors to take control of their own portfolios instead of leaving all the decisions in the hands of professionals.

Questions for Critical Thinking

1. Are these ads targeted at non-investors or people who are currently investing?

2. What risks are associated with this campaign in the future?

Sources: Company website, http://www.etrade.com, accessed March 16, 2009; "E*Trade Super Bowl Commercial—the Cute Baby Hook," *Ad Savvy*, http://www.adsavvy. org, accessed March 4, 2009; Charles Leroux, "E*Trade Baby Ad Puts Shankopotamus in Play," *Chicago Tribune*, February 5, 2009, http://www.chicagotribune.com; "NBC Reportedly Struggling to Sell Out Super Bowl Pregame Ads," *Sports Business Daily*, January 26, 2009, http://www.sportsbusinessdaily.com; "E*Trade Announces Super Bowl XLIII Advertisement," *Yahoo! Finance*, January 23, 2009, http://biz.yahoo.com; Rafael Grillo, "The Online Brokerage Wars: E*Trade Offers Compelling Risk/Reward," *Seeking Alpha*, May 27, 2008, http://seekingalpha.com; "Talking and Trading Baby Blows Away Star-Studded Super Bowl Competition," *Reuters*, February 4, 2008, http://www.reuters.com.

---

brands; they risk leaving themselves open to controversy or even legal action. Notice that Tylenol does not mention a specific aspirin brand in its promotions.

Reminder-oriented advertising is often used for products in the late maturity or decline stages of the product life cycle. This advertising is used to maintain awareness of the importance and usefulness of a product, concept, or institution. For example, Triscuits have been around for a long time, but Nabisco tries to increase sales by using up-to-date advertising that appeals to health and fitness–conscious consumers. The advertising mentions its new no-trans-fat formula.

Advertising Media

Marketers must choose how to distribute their advertising budgets among various media. All media offer advantages and disadvantages. Cost is an important consideration when selecting media, but marketers must also choose the media best suited for communicating their message. As Figure 13.2 shows, the three leading media outlets for advertising are television, newspapers, and magazines. But Internet advertising is growing fast. Consumers now receive ads when they download news and other information to their hand-held wireless devices.

Advertising executives agree that firms need to rethink their traditional ad campaigns to make use of new media. They also need to update their uses of traditional media. Google is looking for ways to combine the targeting capabilities of Internet advertising with the richness of the television medium. Google and Intel are working with the television manufacturer Sony to develop TVs and set-top boxes that allow viewers to navigate the Web, including accessing social-networking sites such as Twitter. The software is based on Google's Android operating system used in its smartphones. Logitech is developing a remote control for the system, including a miniature keyboard.[13] The project has advanced to the point where Google is testing a TV Web-search service. Google is not alone in its efforts to bring television and the Web closer together. It faces stiff competition from Microsoft and Apple, among others.[14]

Television

Television continues to be one of North America's leading national advertising media. Television advertising can be classified as network ads, national ads, local ads, or cable ads. Despite a decline in audience share and growing competition from cable, network television remains the easiest way for advertisers to reach large numbers of viewers—10 million to 20 million North Americans with a single commercial. Automakers, fast-food restaurants, and food manufacturers are heavy users of network TV advertising.

About 90 percent of Canadian households and 58 percent of U.S. households with TVs subscribe to cable television. They are attracted to the more than 800 channels available through cable or satellite services. But the cable and satellite networks are facing new competition. One survey indicates that 60 percent of North American homes have one or more videogame consoles. People are using the consoles to download apps and video-on-demand offerings. And a small but growing number of viewers are discontinuing their cable service and opting instead for online services such as Netflix, Hulu, Apple's iTunes, and the networks' own websites. Recently, 1.3 million people watched at least part of the Masters golf tournament online, double the number who watched online the previous year. People still prefer free, advertising-supported downloads, although online network advertising made up only 2.5 percent of the $62 billion in annual North American advertising revenues. But the number of homes with digital video recorders (DVRs) and high-definition (HD) televisions is increasing steadily. Recent research suggests that even people who can use their DVRs to skip TV ads don't always do so. According to the Nielsen Company, many DVR users still watch shows at their scheduled times and watch the ads; even those who record shows for later viewing watch almost half the ads they could skip. As more people watch playbacks of their favourite shows, the networks' ratings—and commercial watching—increase too.[15]

Although—or maybe because—television reaches the greatest number of consumers at once, it is the most expensive advertising medium. NBC's *Sunday Night Football* has long been the most expensive regularly broadcast program of the fall season. A 30-second ad costs almost $340,000. Super Bowl ads have been known to command prices of nearly $3 million for 30 seconds. More recently, those spots sold for between $2.5 million and $2.8 million.[16] Marketers want to be certain that their commercials reach the greatest number of viewers. Because of the high cost, advertisers may demand guarantees of audience size and receive compensation if a show fails to deliver the promised number of viewers.

Newspapers

Daily and weekly newspapers continue to be the most popular type of local advertising. Marketers can easily tailor newspaper advertising for local tastes and preferences. Advertisers can also coordinate newspaper advertisements with other promotional efforts, such as discount coupons from supermarkets and one-day sales at department stores. A disadvantage comes from the relatively short life span; people usually discard their newspapers soon after reading. Retailers and automobile dealers rank are the biggest newspaper advertisers. Most newspapers now have websites. Some offer separate material and features, which complement their print editions.

Radio

Despite the large number of other media, the average North American household owns five radios—including radios in cars. This high rate of market penetration makes radio an important advertising medium. Advertisers like having a captive audience of listeners as they commute to and from work. As a result, morning and evening drive-time shows have the highest ad rates. In major markets, many stations serve different demographic groups by offering targeted programming. Internet radio programming offers more opportunities for yet more focused targeting.

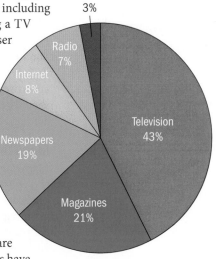

FIGURE 13.2
Dividing Up the Advertising Media Pie

Note: Percentages do not total to 100% due to rounding. Direct mail was not measured in these data.

Source: Data from "100 Leading National Advertisers Index," *Advertising Age,* http://adage.com/datacenter, accessed January 8, 2010.

Satellite stations offer great potential for advertisers. Sirius and XM both offer commercial-free music, but include advertising on their news and talk shows. A recent study predicts that Internet radio will have 185 million listeners by 2020, although 250 million will still listen to AM/FM (sometimes referred to as terrestrial) radio. Internet advertising revenues reached $260 million in a recent year, with an additional $28 million from podcasting.[17] Google recently updated its AdWords application to include ads that can be broadcast by traditional radio stations. An advertiser fills out a questionnaire indicating the target audience and where and how often the ad should be run. The advertiser pays a fee each time the ad is aired. The advertiser can also have the ad tracked to learn the best possible time to reach the desired audience.[18]

Magazines

Magazines include consumer publications and business trade journals. *Time, Reader's Digest,* and *Sports Illustrated* are consumer magazines. *Advertising Age* and *Oil & Gas Journal* are trade publications.

Magazines sometimes customize their publications and target advertising messages to different regions of the country. One method places local advertising in regional editions of the magazines. Other magazines attach wraparounds—half-size covers on top of full-size covers. These wraparounds highlight articles that relate to particular geographic areas; different wraparounds appear in different parts of the country.

Magazines are a natural choice for targeted advertising. Media buyers study demographics of subscribers and select magazines that attract the desired readers. For example, American Express advertises in *Fortune* and *Forbes* to reach businesspeople. PacSun clothes and Clearasil skin medications are advertised in *Teen Vogue*.

Direct Mail

The average North American household receives about 550 pieces of direct mail each year, including 100 catalogues. The huge growth in the variety of direct-mail offerings and the convenience they offer today's busy, time-pressed shoppers has made direct-mail advertising a multibillion-dollar business. Even consumers who like to shop online often page through a catalogue before placing an online order. Although direct-mail advertising is expensive per person, a small business may be able to afford a limited direct-mail campaign but not a television or radio ad. For businesses with a small advertising budget, a carefully targeted direct-mail effort can be highly effective. E-mail is a low-cost form of direct marketing. Marketers can target the most interested Internet users by offering website visitors an option to register to receive e-mail. Companies like Amazon.ca, The Home Depot, and Abercrombie & Fitch routinely send e-mails to regular customers.

Address lists are at the heart of direct-mail advertising. Direct-mail marketers use data-mining techniques to segment markets. They then create profiles that show the types of consumers who are likely to buy their products or donate to their organizations. Catalogue retailers sometimes experiment by sending direct-mail pieces randomly to people who subscribe to particular magazines. Then, they analyze the orders received from the mailings and develop profiles of purchasers. Finally, they rent lists of subscriber names that match the profiles they have developed.

Studies have shown that most consumers are annoyed by the amount of so-called "junk mail" they receive every day, including catalogues, advertising postcards, and flyers. Among Internet users, a major pet peeve is *spam,* or junk e-mail. Many local governments have outlawed sending e-mail promotions without legitimate return addresses, although it is difficult to track down and charge offenders.

The Canadian Marketing Association (CMA; www.the-cma.org) helps marketers by offering its members guidelines on ethical business practices. The American-based Direct Marketing Association (DMA; www.the-dma.org) also provides consumer information at its website. The DMA and Canada Post offer services for consumers to opt out of receiving unsolicited direct mail.

Outdoor Advertising

In one year, outdoor advertising accounted for more than $6 billion in North American advertising spending.[19] Most spending on outdoor advertising is for billboards, but spending is growing fast for other types of outdoor advertising, such as signs in transit stations, stores, airports, and sports stadiums. Advertisers are exploring new forms of outdoor media that involve technology: computerized paintings, video billboards, "trivision" that displays three revolving images on a single billboard, and moving billboards mounted on trucks. Other innovations include ads displayed on the Goodyear blimp, by using an electronic system that offers animation and video.

But outdoor advertising has several disadvantages. The medium requires brief messages, and billboards are often attacked by preservation and conservation groups.

Advertisers are exploring new forms of outdoor media that involve technology: computerized paintings, video billboards, "trivision" that displays three revolving images on a single billboard, and moving billboards mounted on trucks.

© Justin Kase z12z/Alamy

Internet Advertising

Sales from online advertising and marketing are now greater than the sales from print media. In a recent year, North American companies spent more than $120 billion on advertising in online and digital media and more than $112 billion on advertising in newspapers and magazines.[20] Search engine marketing, display ads, and even classified ads are increasing.

Online and interactive media have already changed the nature of advertising. Internet advertising started with simple banner ads but has become much more complex and sophisticated. Miniature television screen images, called *widgets* or *gadgets*, can carry marketing messages only a few inches high on a website, blog, or desktop display. These small images contain embedded links to their home sites. Online advertising can also take other forms. Ford Motor Company's Fiesta subcompact car was available in Europe but not in North America. To educate the North American public about the Fiesta, which was soon to be available, the company launched its Fiesta Movement. Ford gave 100 consumers a European Fiesta for six months and had them use the cars to complete various errands each month. (Ford paid for the gas.) Some people used the cars for charitable work, such as delivering Meals on Wheels. Others used the cars for real adventures or for eloping. As part of the project, the consumers documented their missions and posted the results on YouTube, Flickr, Facebook, and Twitter. In the next phase of the Fiesta Movement, consumers will compete for cash prizes and the chance to win a Fiesta of their own. Google, which owns YouTube, predicts that the website will soon be making money for the first time. Advertising on YouTube was nearly sold out. Eric Schmidt, Google's CEO, predicted that more advertisers would use YouTube in their ad campaigns. He said that YouTube "has gone from being a nice to have to an essential part of the media mix of any display campaign."[21]

Another example of Internet advertising is *viral advertising*. This type of advertising creates a message that is novel or entertaining enough for consumers to forward it to others, spreading it like a virus. Spreading the word online often relies on social networking on sites like MySpace and Facebook. The great advantage to advertisers is that it costs nothing. While viral marketing can be risky, the best campaigns are edgy and often funny. Among the most effective viral video ads of late were "Will It Blend?" which showed what happens when an iPhone met a blender; T-Mobile Dance, a film of a dancing flash mob in London's Liverpool Street Railway Station; and "United Breaks Guitars," about a member of the band Sons of Maxwell, his guitar, and United Airlines.[22]

Some viral campaigns rely on personal word-of-mouth promotions. But when ordinary consumers are recruited as "brand ambassadors" or "buzz agents" for pay, questions are sometimes raised about ethics. One company, BzzAgent, gives its members products instead of money. But these ambassadors are not required to tell others that they're being paid or receiving free gifts to discuss products. Some people view this approach as problematic.[23]

Sponsorship

sponsorship providing funds for a sporting or cultural event in exchange for a direct association with the event.

Marketers can use one of the hottest trends in promotion to integrate several elements of the promotional mix. **Sponsorship** involves providing funds for a sporting or cultural event in exchange for a direct association with the event. Sports sponsorships attract two-thirds of all sponsorship dollars in North America. Entertainment, festivals, causes, and the arts divide up the remaining third of sponsorship dollars. Firms may also sponsor charitable or other not-for-profit awards or events such as the CIBC-sponsored Canadian Breast Cancer Foundation's Run for the Cure.

Sponsors benefit in two major ways: they gain exposure to the event's audience and they gain association with the image of the activity. If a celebrity is involved, sponsors usually earn the right to use the celebrity's name and the name of the event in advertisements. They can set up signs at the event, offer sales promotions, and similar activities. Sponsorships play an important role in relationship marketing, by bringing together the event, its participants, and the sponsoring firms.

Other Media Options

infomercials a form of broadcast direct marketing; 30-minute programs resemble regular TV programs, but sell goods or services.

As consumers filter out familiar advertising messages, marketers look for new ways to catch their attention. Many firms use the major media, but some firms promote through other means, such as infomercials and specialized media. **Infomercials** are a form of broadcast direct marketing, also called *direct-response television (DRTV)*. These 30-minute programs resemble regular television programs but sell goods or services, such as exercise equipment, skin-care products, or kitchenware. The long format allows an advertiser to thoroughly present product benefits, increase awareness, and make an impact on consumers. Advertisers also receive immediate responses in the form of sales or inquiries because most infomercials feature toll-free phone numbers. Infomercial stars may become celebrities, attracting more customers wherever they go. The most effective infomercials tend to be for auto-care products, beauty and personal-care items, investing and business opportunities, collectibles, fitness and self-improvement products, and housewares and electronics.[24]

Advertisers use just about any medium they can find. A more recent development is the use of automated teller machines (ATMs) for advertising. Some ATMs can play 15-second commercials on their screens, and many can print advertising messages on receipts. An ATM screen has a captive audience because the user must watch the screen to complete a transaction. Directory advertising includes the familiar Yellow Pages listings in telephone books. Advertising is also available in thousands of other types of directories; most such advertising is for business-related promotions. Besides local and regional directories, publishers also produce special printed and online versions of the Yellow Pages specifically for ethnic groups.

ASSESSMENT CHECK

13.2.1 What are the two basic types of advertising? Into what three categories do they fall?

13.2.2 What is the leading advertising medium in North America?

13.2.3 In what two major ways do firms benefit from sponsorship?

LO 13.3 Outline the roles of sales promotion, personal selling, and public relations in promotional strategy.

sales promotion forms of promotion such as coupons, product samples, and rebates that support advertising and personal selling.

SALES PROMOTION

Sales promotion was traditionally viewed as a supplement, or add-on, to a firm's sales or advertising efforts. But sales promotion has emerged as an important part of the promotional mix. Promotion now accounts for more than half as many marketing dollars as are spent on advertising, and promotion spending is rising faster than ad spending. **Sales promotion** consists of forms of promotion such as coupons, product samples, and rebates that support advertising and personal selling.

Both retailers and manufacturers use sales promotions to offer consumers extra incentives to buy. Sales promotions can lead to the short-term advantage of increased sales. But sales promotions can also help marketers build brand equity and improve their customer relationships. Examples of sales promotion include samples, coupons, contests, displays, trade shows, and dealer incentives.

Consumer-Oriented Promotions

The goal of a consumer-oriented sales promotion is to get new and existing customers to try products, and ultimately, to buy products. Marketers want to increase sales of complementary products, increase impulse purchases, and encourage repeat business by rewarding product purchasers. Figure 13.3 shows how marketers allocate their consumer-oriented spending among the categories of promotions.

Promotions can also be used to popularize an idea, such as the growing awareness of plastic shopping bags and the pollution they contribute to the environment. The "Going Green" feature discusses the growing trend of banning plastic shopping bags.

Premiums, Coupons, Rebates, and Samples

Nearly six of every 10 sales promotion dollars are spent on *premiums*—items given away for free or at a reduced price when another product is purchased. For example, cosmetics companies, such as Clinique, offer sample kits with purchases of their products. Fast-food restaurants are also big users of premiums. McDonald's and Burger King include a toy with the purchase of every children's meal. The toys are often tie-ins with new movies or popular cartoon shows. Marketers generally choose premiums that are likely to get consumers thinking about and caring about the brand and the product. People who purchase health foods at a grocery store may find an offer for a free personal training session at a local health club printed on the back of their sales receipt.

Customers redeem *coupons* for small price discounts when they purchase the promoted products. Such offers may persuade a customer to try a new or different product. Some large supermarket chains double the face value of manufacturers' coupons. Coupons have the downside of focusing customers on price instead of brand loyalty. Some consumers complain that clipping or printing out coupons is too time-consuming, but others enjoy the savings, especially when money is tight and prices seem high.

North American consumers' use of coupons increased 27 percent in a recent year. Consumers used 3.3 billion coupons with a face value of $3.5 billion. Internet coupon use increased an amazing

FIGURE 13.3
Spending on Consumer-Oriented Promotions

Source: Data from Kathleen M. Joyce, "Higher Gear," *Promo Magazine,* http://promomagazine.com, accessed April 26, 2010.

GOING GREEN — HOW **MUCH WOULD YOU PAY FOR A PLASTIC SHOPPING BAG?**

Many stores in Toronto, Montreal, Vancouver, and other Canadian cities now collect a tax or charge about five cents for giving customers a plastic shopping bag at the checkout counter. This cost is meant to discourage the use of plastic bags and instead encourage the use of longer-lasting reusable and recyclable bags.

In North America, it is estimated that almost 4 billion tons of plastics waste—in the form of bags, sacks, and wrapping—were generated in one year. The plastic is made from oil and can take 1,000 years to break down. Only about 1 percent of this waste is ever recycled.

A growing number of people want to reduce these statistics. For example, more city governments have banned the use of plastic bags, required certain retailers to accept plastic bags for recycling, or imposed a tax on plastic.

But such laws have not always been met with approval. In eco-friendly Seattle, voters overturned a law charging 20 cents per plastic bag, perhaps because they were already recycling and reusing the bags. Big retailers like Walmart and Loblaws sell reusable bags

for about a dollar. These bags carry the store's logo and name and promote the use of reusable bags. Some retailers have reacted to customer complaints and have stopped charging for plastic bags.

Questions for Critical Thinking

1. Can stores that provide eco-friendly shopping bags or other ways to reduce the polluting effects of plastic gain promotional benefits from their efforts? How can cities that ban or tax plastic bags promote their actions?

2. What other ways can you think of to promote the idea of recycling plastic bags or reducing their use?

Sources: "NYCWasteLe$$," Plastic Bag Recycling, http://www.nyc.gov, accessed May 11, 2010; Dave Gram, "Vt. Plastic Bag Tax Proposal Seen Coming Too Late," *Rutland Herald,* April 16, 2010, http:// http://www.rutlandherald.com; Melissa Eddy, "Plastic Bag Ban: Would You Pay 5 Cents for a Bag?" *Huffington Post,* February 22, 2010, http:// www.huffingtonpost.com; Steve Painter, "3 Wal-Marts Testing Purge of Plastic Bags," *Arkansas Democrat-Gazette,* January 24, 2010, http://ww6.lexisnexis.com; Stephen Messenger, "Washington D.C.'s Plastic Bag Tax Takes Effect This Week," *TreeHugger.com,* January 3, 2010, http://www.treehugger.com.

360 percent. Marketers issued 367 billion coupons with a face value averaging $1.44, but shortened the expiration periods by some 10 percent. Consumers can now access coupons on their Web-enabled cellphones while shopping. Some analysts predict that the growing use of paperless mobile coupons could soon make clippable or even printed-out coupons a thing of the past.[25]

Rebates offer cash back to consumers who mail in required proofs of purchase. Rebates help packaged-goods manufacturers increase purchase rates, promote multiple purchases, and reward product users. Other types of companies also offer rebates, especially for electronics, computers and their accessories, and automobiles. Processing rebates gives marketers a way to collect data about their customers, but many shoppers find it awkward to collect the required receipts, forms, and universal product codes (UPCs) and then wait several weeks for the refund.

A *sample* is a gift of a product distributed by mail, door to door, in a demonstration, or inside packages of another product. On any given day, you might receive a sample moisturizer, a bar of soap, or a packet of laundry detergent. Out of every four consumers who receive samples, three will try them.

Games, Contests, and Sweepstakes

Contests, sweepstakes, and games offer cash, merchandise, or travel as prizes to participating winners. Firms often sponsor these activities to introduce new goods and services and to attract new customers. Games and contests require entrants to solve problems or write essays, and they must sometimes provide a proof of purchase. Sweepstakes choose winners by chance and require no product purchase. Consumers typically prefer sweepstakes because they are easy; games and contests require more effort. Companies like sweepstakes, too, because they are inexpensive to run and the number of winners is decided at the beginning. With games and contests, the company doesn't know how many people will correctly complete a puzzle or gather the right number of symbols from scratch-off cards. Sweepstakes, games, and contests can reinforce a company's image and advertising message. But consumer attention may focus on the promotion instead of on the product.

In recent years, court rulings and legal restrictions have limited the use of games and contests. Companies must proceed carefully when advertising their contests and games and the prizes they award. Marketers must show the chances of winning and avoid false promises, such as suggesting that a consumer has already won.

Specialty Advertising

Have you received any free pens, T-shirts, or refrigerator magnets imprinted with a business name? These offers are examples of **specialty advertising** or *advertising specialties*. This type of sales promotion involves the gift of useful merchandise carrying the name, logo, or slogan of a profit-seeking business or a not-for-profit organization. Because those products are useful and sometimes personalized with recipients' names, people tend to keep and use them, giving advertisers repeated exposure. Advertising specialties were originally designed to identify and create goodwill for advertisers. Now they generate sales leads and develop traffic for stores and trade show exhibitors. Like premiums, these promotions should reinforce the brand's image and its relationship with the recipient.

Trade-Oriented Promotions

Sales promotion techniques can also contribute to campaigns directed to retailers and wholesalers. **Trade promotion** is sales promotion geared to marketing intermediaries, not to consumers. Marketers use trade promotion to encourage retailers to stock new products, continue carrying existing products, and promote both new and existing products effectively to consumers. Successful trade promotions offer financial incentives. They require careful timing, attention to costs, and should be easy for intermediaries to apply. These promotions should bring quick results and improve retail sales. Major trade promotions include point-of-purchase advertising and trade shows.

Point-of-purchase (POP) advertising consists of displays or demonstrations that promote products when and where consumers buy them, such as in retail stores. When the Swiffer floor cleaner was being introduced, Procter & Gamble used in-store demonstrations to show consumers how it worked. Marketing research has shown that consumers are more likely to purchase certain products when such displays are used. Sunscreen, painting supplies, and snacks are typically displayed this way. A high-tech version of POP advertising is digital advertising consoles mounted on grocery carts. Impulse

specialty advertising promotional items that prominently display a firm's name, logo, or business slogan.

trade promotion sales promotion geared to marketing intermediaries, not to final consumers.

point-of-purchase (POP) advertising displays or demonstrations that promote products when and where consumers buy them, such as in retail stores.

purchases make up 53 percent of total buying. POP has already begun to evolve into what is being called "mobile advertising." Although privacy is still an issue, more and more websites and other services are now able to locate Internet users, and location-based mobile spending is expected to increase from a current $34 million to $4 billion in 2015. About 25 percent of the millions of Facebook members open the site using mobile electronic devices. Location-based advertising will not be directed primarily to desktop computers but to smartphones, iPads, Kindles, game consoles, and automobiles.[26]

Manufacturers and other sellers often exhibit their products at *trade shows* to promote goods or services to members of their distribution channels. These shows are often organized by industry trade associations. Each year, thousands of trade shows attract millions of exhibitors and hundreds of millions of attendees. Such shows are especially important in fast-changing industries for such products as computers, toys, furniture, and fashions. The annual Consumer Electronics Show is held in Las Vegas. It is North America's largest such show, attracting more than 100,000 visitors. Trade shows are also strong in the fields of medicine, health care, recreational vehicles, camping, and even woodworking machinery. These shows are especially effective for introducing new products and generating sales leads.

Personal Selling

Personal selling refers to a person-to-person promotional presentation to a potential buyer. Many companies consider personal selling to be the key to marketing effectiveness. Unless a seller matches a firm's goods or services to the needs of a certain client or customer, none of the firm's other activities produces any benefits. Today, sales and sales-related jobs employ about 16 million North American workers.[27] Businesses often spend five to 10 times as much on personal selling as on advertising. Personal selling includes the significant costs of hiring, training, benefits, and salaries. Because of these costs, businesses are very concerned with the effectiveness of their sales personnel. One of their continuing concerns is with the way representatives communicate with others. The "Business Etiquette" feature discusses how to negotiate during difficult economic times.

BUSINESS ETIQUETTE

How to Negotiate in a Difficult Economy

Many businesses rely on personal selling. Even when the economy is weak, you can still find ways to negotiate effectively. Here are five tips for successful negotiation in good and difficult economic times:

1. *Be a good listener.* Listening carefully is always a good idea. Like good detectives, good negotiators ask questions—and then listen to what is said by the other negotiator or the prospect (the possible buyer or seller). You'll establish trust—and learn whether your proposal will meet your prospect's needs.

2. *Be prepared.* Before you negotiate, do as much research as you can on your prospect, the prospect's business, the effect of the economy on the prospect's industry, and so on. Preparation is the only part of negotiation that is completely within your control.

3. *Be patient.* North Americans always seem to be in a hurry. In Asia, South America, and the Middle East, people know that if you rush, you may make mistakes. Taking your time may also give you a psychological advantage over the other negotiator.

4. *Decide what is important to you.* What do you absolutely need? What would you be willing to give up?

5. *Keep your options open.* If you feel you can't make a satisfactory agreement and you have offered all you can offer, leave yourself the option of walking away.

Sources: Ed Brodow, "Ten Tips for Negotiating in 2010," Ed Brodow Seminars, http:// www.brodow.com, accessed May 11, 2010; Ken Dooley, "6 Tips for Negotiating in a Tough Economy," *BusinessBrief*, March 9, 2010, http://www.businessbrief.com; Ken Dooley, "The Keys to Successful Negotiation," *BusinessBrief*, February 16, 2010, http://www.businessbrief.com.

How do marketers decide whether to make personal selling the main focus of their firm's marketing mix? In general, firms are likely to focus on personal selling instead of advertising or sales promotion under four conditions:

1. Customers are relatively few in number and are geographically concentrated.

2. The product is technically complex, involves trade-ins, or requires special handling.

3. The product carries a relatively high price.

4. The product moves through direct-distribution channels.

A good example is selling Piper Cub airplanes. Airplane buyers tend to be wealthy people who value their freedom and privacy—and the luxury of owning their own plane. "It is a way of life I am selling," says veteran sales rep Bruce Keller, "not just aluminum. I want the customer to share that with me. If you look at my airplane and you sit in it, you are going flying."[28]

The sales functions of most companies are going through rapid change. Compared with in the past, today's salespeople are more concerned with creating long-term buyer–seller relationships and acting as consultants to their customers. After the recession, salespeople faced a new challenge—consumers who haggle over prices, even on retail items. One survey found that 88 percent of those questioned had haggled over at least one price in the past six months. The Great Depression of the 1930s was the last time North Americans engaged in serious amounts of haggling. Today's consumers have advantages that would surprise their grandparents. Anyone with a Web-enabled cellphone can Google competing prices of merchandise while standing outside a retail store. Many have learned to bargain via websites such as eBay or have used Priceline to negotiate deals on travel. The survey found that hagglers had better than a 75 percent success rate in making deals on clothing, appliances, and jewellery.[29]

Personal selling can occur in several settings; each setting can involve either business-to-business (B2B) or business-to-consumer (B2C) selling. *Field selling* refers to sales representatives who make sales calls on prospective customers at their businesses. Companies that sell major industrial equipment typically rely on field selling. *Over-the-counter selling* describes sales activities in retailing and some wholesale locations, where customers visit the seller's facility to purchase items. *Telemarketing* sales representatives make their presentations over the phone. A later section reviews telemarketing in more detail.

Sales Tasks

All sales activities involve helping customers in some way. A salesperson's work can vary from one company or situation to another, but all sales work usually includes a mix of three basic tasks: order processing, creative selling, and missionary selling.

order processing a form of selling used mostly at the wholesale and retail levels; involves identifying customer needs, pointing out products that meet those needs, and completing orders.

Order Processing Order processing is used in both field selling and telemarketing, but this form of selling is most often related to retail and wholesale firms. In order processing, the salesperson identifies customer needs, points out merchandise to meet those needs, and processes the order. Route sales personnel process orders for such consumer goods as bread, milk, soft drinks, and snack foods. They check each store's stock, report inventory needs to the store manager, and complete the sale. Most of these jobs include at least minor order-processing functions.

creative selling a persuasive type of promotional presentation.

Creative Selling Sales representatives for most business products and some consumer items perform **creative selling**, a persuasive type of promotional presentation. Creative selling promotes a good or service whose benefits are not readily seen or whose purchase decision requires a close look at other options. Creative selling is used to sell intangible products such as insurance, but can also be used to sell tangible goods.

Many retail salespeople just process orders, but many consumers want more customer service. That's where creative selling comes in. For example, training sales staff at women's clothing stores might include holding seasonal wardrobe-building workshops. After attending such a workshop, the sales staff can better help customers select and purchase coordinating clothing, accessories, and shoes. Customers might not have purchased these items if they hadn't received such advice.

missionary selling an indirect form of selling where the representative promotes goodwill for a company or provides technical or operational assistance to the customer.

Missionary Selling Sales work also includes an indirect form of selling, where the representative promotes goodwill for a company or gives the customer technical or operational help. This practice is called **missionary selling**. Many businesses that sell technical equipment, such as Oracle and

Fujitsu, provide systems specialists who act as consultants to customers. These salespeople work to solve problems and sometimes help their clients with questions not directly related to their employers' products. Other industries also use missionary selling techniques. Pharmaceutical company representatives—called *detailers*—visit physicians to describe the firm's latest offerings. Some firms are also finding success with less direct methods, including Web-based sales calls after office hours. The large pharmaceutical maker Pfizer recently cut back its sales force and is turning toward electronic marketing. The company has found electronic detailing especially helpful. It allows doctors to access the latest information on drugs when and where they choose. The information can also be strictly controlled, and the company runs much less risk of its salespeople being accused of marketing drugs for off-label uses—that is, for treating conditions other than those they were originally intended to help.[30] The actual sales, in any case, are handled through pharmacies, which fill the prescriptions.

Telemarketing Telemarketing refers to personal selling by telephone. It provides a firm's marketers with a high return on their expenses, an immediate response, and an opportunity for a personalized two-way conversation. Many firms use telemarketing because expense or other factors keep salespeople from meeting many potential customers in person. Telemarketers can use databases to target prospects based on population data. Telemarketing takes two forms: outbound and inbound. A sales representative who calls you is practising *outbound telemarketing*. On the other hand, *inbound telemarketing* occurs when you call a toll-free phone number to get product information or place an order.

Outbound telemarketers must follow various legal requirements and industry guidelines that guide their behaviour. In general, telemarketers must disclose what they are selling and the organization they represent before making their presentations. Calls are limited to between 9 A.M. and 9:30 P.M. on weekdays and between 10 A.M. and 6 P.M. on weekends. Sellers must also inform the customer about the details of exchange policies. Recent legislation requires telemarketers to respect lists of people who do not want to receive calls. Consumers who want to be on the list must call a special number or visit a website to register. Telemarketers must stop calling registered numbers within 31 days or face stiff fines.[31] Charities, surveys, and political campaign calls are exempt from these restrictions. Also, businesses that already have a relationship with consumers can make telemarketing calls. These businesses include the bank where customers have accounts or the dealership where they bought their car.

telemarketing personal selling by telephone, which provides marketers with a high return on their expenses, an immediate response, and an opportunity for a personalized two-way conversation.

The Sales Process

The sales process typically follows the seven-step sequence shown in Figure 13.4: prospecting and qualifying, the approach, the presentation, the demonstration, handling objections, closing, and the follow-up. Remember the importance of flexibility; a good salesperson will vary the sales process to suit a customer's responses and needs. The process of selling to a potential customer who is unfamiliar with a company's products differs from the process of serving a long-time customer.

Prospecting, Qualifying, and Approaching At the prospecting stage, salespeople identify potential customers. Salespeople may look for leads for prospective sales from such sources as existing customers, friends and family, and business associates. The qualifying process identifies potential customers who have the financial ability and authority to buy.

Companies use different ways to identify and qualify prospects. Some companies rely on business development teams to do this work. They use the responses from direct mail to provide leads to sales reps. Other companies believe in personal visits from sales representatives;

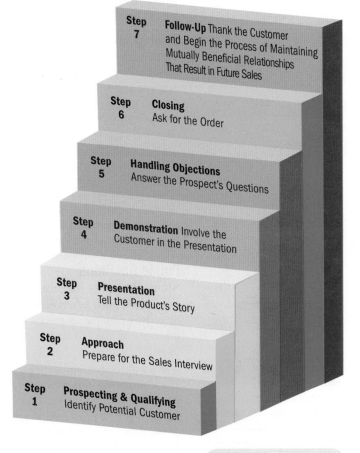

Step 7 Follow-Up Thank the Customer and Begin the Process of Maintaining Mutually Beneficial Relationships That Result in Future Sales

Step 6 Closing Ask for the Order

Step 5 Handling Objections Answer the Prospect's Questions

Step 4 Demonstration Involve the Customer in the Presentation

Step 3 Presentation Tell the Product's Story

Step 2 Approach Prepare for the Sales Interview

Step 1 Prospecting & Qualifying Identify Potential Customer

FIGURE 13.4 Seven Steps in the Sales Process

others use e-mail, which is inexpensive and usually has a good response rate. Many B2B firms use electronic social media such as electronic newsletters, Web events, virtual trade shows, podcasts, videos, online demonstrations, and blogs.[32]

Before making the first contact with a customer, successful salespeople make careful preparations, by analyzing available data about a prospective customer's product lines and other related information. These salespeople know that a good first impression can influence a customer's attitude toward the selling company and its products.

Presentation and Demonstration At the presentation stage, salespeople communicate promotional messages. They may describe the major features of their products, highlight the advantages, and give examples of satisfied consumers. A demonstration is a critical step in the sales process. It helps to reinforce the message that the salesperson has been communicating. For example, department-store shoppers can get a free makeover at the cosmetics counter. And anyone looking to buy a car will take it for a test drive before deciding whether to purchase it.

Some products are too large to transport to prospective buyers or require a special installation to demonstrate. Sales representatives can demonstrate these products for customers by using laptop computers, multimedia presentations, Web conferences, podcasts, and graphic programs like SmartDraw.[33] Services, which are intangible can't be demonstrated in the same way. Salespeople may find it helpful to show a presentation that includes testimonials from satisfied customers or graphs illustrating results.

Handling Objections Some salespeople fear potential customers' objections because they view their questions as criticism. But a good salesperson can use objections as an opportunity to answer questions and explain how the product will benefit the customer. As a general rule, the key is to sell the benefits, not the features: How will this product help the customer?

Closing The critical point in the sales process is the closing. This is the time when the salesperson asks the prospect to buy. If the presentation has matched the product benefits to customer needs, the closing should be a natural conclusion. If there are some bumps in the process, the salesperson can try some different techniques, such as offering alternative products, offering a special incentive for purchase, or restating the product benefits. The ideal outcome of this interaction is closing the sale—and beginning a relationship where the customer builds loyalty to the brand or product. But even if the sale is not closed, the salesperson should still think of the interaction as the beginning of a potential relationship. The prospect might become a customer in the future.

Follow-Up A salesperson's actions after the sale may lead to the customer making another purchase. Follow-up is an important part of building a long-lasting relationship. After closing, the salesperson should process the order efficiently. By calling soon after a purchase, the salesperson reassures customers that they made the right decision to buy. The salesperson also creates an opportunity to correct any problems.

Public Relations

A final element of the promotional mix is public relations (PR). Public relations includes publicity and supports advertising, personal selling, and sales promotion, usually by pursuing broader objectives. Companies use PR to try to improve their image with the public by distributing specific messages or ideas to target audiences. Cause-related promotional activities are often backed up by public relations and publicity campaigns. In addition, PR helps a firm to increase awareness of goods and services and then builds a positive image of those goods and services.

public relations an organization's communications and relationships with its various public audiences.

Public relations refers to an organization's communications and relationships with its various public audiences, such as customers, vendors, news media, employees, shareholders, the government, and the general public. Many of these communication efforts have marketing purposes. Public relations is an efficient, indirect communications channel for promoting products. It can publicize products and help create and maintain a positive image of the company.

The public relations department links a firm with the media. It provides the media with news releases and video and audio clips. It also holds news conferences to announce new products, the formation of strategic alliances, management changes, financial results, and other developments. Publications issued by the department include newsletters, brochures, and reports.

Publicity

The type of public relations that is tied most closely to promoting a company's products is **publicity**—the nonpersonal stimulation of demand for a good, service, place, idea, event, person, or organization by unpaid placement of information in print or broadcast media. Press releases and news coverage generate publicity. Ironically, criticism can sometimes also generate publicity. Spirit Airlines recently got a lot of negative publicity when it started charging fees for carry-on luggage—but the airline's bookings increased 50 percent. The increased bookings resulted from the airline having installed "pre-reclined" seats on its new planes. The new seats meant the airline could add more seating and lower its airfares. Even though "pre-reclined" is a poor name—the seats don't recline but stay permanently upright—some observers say that consumers looking for the cheapest airfares will continue to book on Spirit.[34]

Publicity also benefits not-for-profit organizations when they receive coverage of events such as the 17th Annual Head and Neck Cancer Fundraising Gala for McGill University's Department of Otolaryngology. The event was highly publicized because of the attendance and support of actor and producer Michael Douglas. Douglas has a vacation home in the resort area of Mont Tremblant. When he called his doctor in New York complaining about severe pain, his doctor referred him to his friend and colleague, Dr. Saul Frenkiel, at the Jewish General Hospital in Montreal. Frenkiel diagnosed Douglas as having a tumour. But other health professionals had examined Douglas for the same symptoms and had missed the tumour. After successful treatment in the United States, a grateful Douglas asked how he could show his gratitude. Someone suggested he could help with fundraising. That's how Douglas became the honouree at the event, which raised $2 million. It is an extraordinary amount for what is generally considered to be a little known area of cancer research and treatment. Besides the funds for research, the publicity has helped raise awareness in the general public about this cancer's risks and treatments.[35] When a for-profit firm teams up with a not-for-profit firm in a fundraising effort, the relationship usually generates good publicity for both organizations.

publicity the nonpersonal stimulation of demand for a good, service, place, idea, event, person, or organization by unpaid placement of information in print or broadcast media.

✔ ASSESSMENT CHECK

13.3.1 Why do retailers and manufacturers use sales promotions?

13.3.2 When does a firm use personal selling instead of non-personal selling?

13.3.3 How does public relations serve a marketing purpose?

PUSHING AND PULLING STRATEGIES

LO 13.4 Describe pushing and pulling promotional strategies.

Marketers can choose between two general promotional strategies: a pushing strategy or a pulling strategy. A **pushing strategy** uses personal selling to market an item to wholesalers and retailers in a company's distribution channels. Companies promote the product to members of the marketing channel, not to end users. Sales personnel explain to marketing intermediaries why they should carry particular merchandise. They usually support their promotion by offering special discounts and promotional materials. Some marketers also offer **cooperative advertising** allowances, by sharing with channel partners the cost of local advertising of their firm's product or product line. All these strategies are designed to motivate wholesalers and retailers to push the good or service to their own customers.

A **pulling strategy** tries to promote a product by generating consumer demand for it, mainly through advertising and sales promotion appeals. Potential buyers will then request that their suppliers—retailers or local distributors—carry the product, which pulls it through the distribution channel. Dove used this strategy when it launched its new Men + Care line of men's personal-care products during a recent Super Bowl. The 30-second commercial, with its tagline "Be comfortable in your own skin," generated a large online response. Many consumers searched such terms as "Super Bowl," "ad," and "men" to find retailers that stocked the products.[36]

Most marketing situations require combinations of pushing and pulling strategies, although the main emphasis can vary. Consumer products usually depend more heavily on pulling strategies; and B2B products usually favour pushing strategies.

pushing strategy personal selling to market an item to wholesalers and retailers in a company's distribution channels.

cooperative advertising allowances that marketers provide to share with channel partners the cost of local advertising of their firm's product or product line.

pulling strategy promotion of a product by generating consumer demand for it, mainly through advertising and sales promotion appeals.

✔ ASSESSMENT CHECK

13.4.1 Give an example of a pushing strategy.

13.4.2 Give an example of a pulling strategy.

PRICING OBJECTIVES IN THE MARKETING MIX

price the exchange value of a good or service.

Products offer utility, or want-satisfying power. As consumers, we decide how much value we associate with each product. For example, after a major storm, we may value electricity, food, and water above everything else. If we commute a long distance or are planning a vacation, fuel may be of greater concern. All consumers have limited amounts of money and a variety of possible uses for it. The **price**—the exchange value of a good or service—becomes a major factor in consumer buying decisions.

Businesspeople try to meet certain objectives through their pricing decisions. Pricing objectives vary from firm to firm, and many companies have multiple pricing objectives. Some firms try to improve profits by setting high prices; others set low prices to attract new business. As Figure 13.5 shows, the four basic categories of pricing objectives are (1) profitability, (2) volume, (3) meeting competition, and (4) prestige.

At the cosmetics counter, salespeople offer a free makeup demonstration. They are reinforcing the message that their cosmetic products can improve your look.

© Can Stock Photo Inc./szefei

Profitability Objectives

profitability objectives common goals that are included in the strategic plans of most firms.

volume objectives pricing decisions that are based on market share, the percentage of a market controlled by a certain company or product.

Profitability objectives are the most common goals listed in most firms' strategic plans. Marketers know that profits are the revenue the company brings in, minus its expenses. Usually a big difference exists between revenue and profit. Most automakers try to produce at least one luxury vehicle. They can charge $50,000 or more for it instead of relying entirely on the sale of cars priced at $15,000 to $25,000.

Some firms maximize profits by reducing costs instead of increasing prices. Companies can maintain prices and increase profitability by operating more efficiently or by changing the product to make it less costly to produce. One strategy is to maintain a steady price while reducing the size or amount of the product in the package. Manufacturers of candy, coffee, and cereal often use this strategy.

Volume Objectives

A second approach to pricing strategy—**volume objectives**—bases pricing decisions on market share, the percentage of a market controlled by a certain company or product. One firm may want to have a 25 percent market share in a certain product category; another firm may want to maintain or expand its market share for specific products. As a market becomes oversupplied—like the PC market—firms need to find ways to get consumers to upgrade or try new products. Setting a lower price can meet that objective, as long as the firm still makes a profit. Many PC makers—and retailers—have begun to offer their products at lower prices, especially at the start of the school year. Microsoft's Windows 7 operating system sold well and gave Microsoft and electronics retailer BestBuy big profits. But manufacturers of PCs such as Hewlett-Packard and Dell did not share in the success. They had hoped that consumers would be willing to pay more for their new PCs, which were loaded with Windows 7 and many other new features. Instead, consumers resisted paying more, and retailers offered deep discounts during a recent holiday season.[37]

Pricing Objectives

Profitability
"We want profits to increase by 10 percent a year through 2015."

Volume
"By 2015, we plan to achieve a 28 percent share of the personal watercraft market."

Meeting Competition
"We will meet their prices and achieve profit and volume growth by offering better customer service."

Prestige
"The new perfume has an exquisite package, a beautiful label, and one of the highest retail prices."

FIGURE 13.5 Pricing Objectives

Pricing to Meet Competition

A third set of pricing objectives tries to meet competitors' prices so that price becomes a nonissue. In many lines of business, firms set their own prices to match the prices set by established industry leaders. But companies cannot legally work together to agree on prices.

Price is a highly visible element of a firm's marketing mix. Some businesses may be tempted to use a product's price to gain an advantage over competitors. Sometimes the race to match competitors' prices results in a *price war*, which has happened in the airline and fast-food industries. Because some competitors can match a price cut, many marketers try to avoid price wars by using other strategies, such as adding value, improving quality, educating consumers, and building relationships.

Although price is a major element of the marketing mix, it is not the only one. Electronic readers such as the Kindle and the iPad are in a fierce pricing competition for digital books, as the "Solving an Ethical Controversy" feature explains.

Prestige Objectives

The final category of objectives takes in the effect of prices on prestige. **Prestige pricing** sets a relatively high price to develop and maintain an image of quality and exclusiveness. Marketers set such objectives because they recognize the role of price in communicating an overall image for the firm and its products. People expect to pay more for a Lexus, a Louis Vuitton purse, or a Caribbean vacation on St. Kitts or Nevis. Despite a recession, the British retailer Selfridges has seen a 60 percent increase in sales of "must-have" handbags by the luxury brand Mulberry. Mulberry even has waiting lists for some of its styles.[38]

prestige pricing setting a relatively high price to develop and maintain an image of quality and exclusiveness.

── SOLVING AN **ETHICAL** CONTROVERSY ──

Free E-Books: Good or Bad for Business?

When Amazon's Kindle electronic reader first became available, Amazon charged consumers $9.99 for each e-book they purchased. Publishers insisted that that price was too low to keep their business profitable. But Amazon actually gave some e-books away for free, including those of living authors who earn an income from their writing.

Amazon explained that the free e-books were a way to get consumers to read some unfamiliar writers. The hope was that customers would then buy other works by those writers. But some publishers delay publication of electronic editions for several months after the hardcover books have been issued, in the same way they delay publishing paperback editions.

Should e-books be given away for free?

PRO

1. Some publishers view free e-books as promotions to generate buzz about new or unknown authors.

2. Some publishers that give away e-books on a regular basis have noticed an increase in sales, which, as one executive says, is "all found money."

CON

1. "It is illogical to give books away for free," said David Young of Hachette Book Group, which publishes Stephenie Meyer's *Twilight* series.

2. The relatively low price of e-books may discourage consumers from buying actual books with suggested retail prices of $25 or more.

Summary

When Apple unveiled its iPad, it announced that it had negotiated with five of the six biggest publishers to charge $12.99 to $14.99 for each e-book edition of adult fiction and nonfiction. But insiders say that Apple required the publishers to agree to discounts on bestselling books, so that the publicized price range was the ceiling, and some prices could be lower.

Sources: Stan Schroeder, "The E-Book Price War Isn't Over Yet," *Mashable,* February 18, 2010, http://mashable.com; Motoko Rich, "Apple's Prices for E-Books May Be Lower Than Expected," *New York Times,* February 18, 2010, http://www.nytimes.com; Motoko Rich, "With Kindle, the Best Sellers Don't Need to Sell," *New York Times,* January 23, 2010, http://www.nytimes.com; "The Kindle Pricing Strategy & the Kindle Pricing History," *askDeb.com,* January 20, 2010, http://www.askdeb.com.

Scarcity can also create prestige. Products that are limited in distribution or products that are so popular that they become scarce generate their own prestige. Businesses can then charge more for them. Apple iPhones and iPads always seem to be in short supply when new models are introduced. Eager buyers can be seen camping outside retail locations the day before, in hopes of being among the first to own the latest technological gadgets.

LO 13.6 Discuss how firms set prices in the marketplace, and describe the four alternative pricing strategies.

PRICING STRATEGIES

People from different areas of a company contribute their expertise to set the most strategic price for a product. Accountants, financial managers, and marketers provide relevant sales data, cost data, and customer feedback. Designers, engineers, and systems analysts also contribute important information.

Prices are determined in two basic ways: by applying the concepts of supply and demand discussed in Chapter 3 and by completing cost-oriented analyses. Economic theory assumes that a market price will be set at the point where the amount of a product desired at a given price equals the amount that suppliers will offer for sale at that price. In other words, the market price occurs at the point where the amount demanded and the amount supplied are equal. Online auctions, such as those on eBay, are a popular application of the demand-and-supply approach.

Bloomberg via Getty Images

Some journeys cannot be put into words.

Prestige pricing sets a relatively high price to develop and maintain an image of quality and exclusiveness. People expect to pay more for a Louis Vuitton bag, just like the rock star in this ad.

Price Determination in Practice

Economic theory might lead to the best pricing decisions, but most businesses do not have all the information they need to make those decisions. Most businesses use **cost-based pricing** formulas. These formulas calculate total costs per unit and then add markups to cover overhead costs and generate profits.

Cost-based pricing totals all costs associated with offering a product in the market, including research and development, production, transportation, and marketing expenses. An added amount, the markup, then covers any unexpected or overlooked expenses and provides a profit. The total is the selling price. The actual markup used varies depending on such factors as brand image and type of store. The typical markup for clothing is determined by doubling the wholesale price (the cost to the merchant) to arrive at the retail price for the item.

cost-based pricing calculating total costs per unit and then adding markups to cover overhead costs and generate profits.

Breakeven Analysis

breakeven analysis the pricing-related technique used to calculate the minimum sales volume a product must generate at a certain price level to cover all costs.

Businesses often do a **breakeven analysis** to calculate the minimum sales volume a product must generate at a certain price level to cover all costs. This method involves looking at various costs and total revenues. *Total cost* is the sum of total variable costs and total fixed costs. *Variable costs* change with the level of production, as labour and raw materials do. *Fixed costs* such as insurance premiums and utility rates charged by water, natural gas, and electric power suppliers remain stable regardless of the production level. *Total revenue* is calculated by multiplying price by the number of units sold.

Finding the Breakeven Point

The *breakeven point* is the level of sales that will generate enough revenue to cover all of the company's fixed and variable costs. It is the point where total revenue just equals total costs. Sales beyond the breakeven point will generate profits; sales volume below the breakeven point will result in losses. The following formulas give the breakeven point in units and dollars:

$$\text{Breakeven Point (in units)} = \frac{\text{Total fixed costs}}{\text{Contribution to fixed costs per unit}}$$

$$\text{Breakeven Point (in dollars)} = \frac{\text{Total fixed costs}}{1 - \text{Variable cost per unit/Price}}$$

As an example, a product sells for $20. It has a variable cost of $14 per unit and produces a $6 per-unit contribution to fixed costs. If the firm has total fixed costs of $42,000, then it must sell 7,000 units to break even on the product. The calculation of the breakeven point in units and dollars is as follows:

$$\text{Breakeven Point (in units)} = \frac{\$42,000}{\$20 - \$14} = \frac{\$42,000}{\$6} = 7,000 \text{ units}$$

$$\text{Breakeven Point (in dollars)} = \frac{\$42,000}{1 - \$14/\$20} = \frac{\$42,000}{1 - 0.7} = \frac{\$42,000}{0.3} = \$140,000$$

Marketers use breakeven analysis to calculate the profits or losses that would result from several different proposed prices. Because different prices produce different breakeven points, marketers can compare their calculations of required sales to break even with the sales estimates from marketing research studies. This comparison can identify the best price—the price that would attract enough customers to exceed the breakeven point and earn profits for the firm.

Most firms want to know whether enough customers will buy the number of units the firm needs to sell at a particular price to break even. They develop estimates of consumer demand through surveys of likely customers, interviews with retailers that would sell the product, and reviewing prices charged by competitors. The breakeven points for several possible prices are then calculated and compared with sales estimates for each price. This practice is referred to as *modified breakeven analysis.*

FIGURE 13.6
Breakeven Analysis

Alternative Pricing Strategies

The strategy a company uses to set its prices should grow out of the firm's overall marketing strategy. In general, firms can choose from four alternative pricing strategies: skimming, penetration, discount or everyday low pricing, and competitive pricing.

Skimming Pricing

A **skimming pricing** strategy sets an intentionally high price relative to the prices of competing products. The term comes from the expression "skimming the cream." This pricing strategy often works when introducing a distinctive good or service that has little or no competition, but it can also be used at other stages of the product life cycle. A skimming strategy can help marketers set a price that separates a firm's high-end product from those of competitors. It can also help a firm recover its product development costs before competitors enter the field. This strategy is often used with prescription drugs.

Penetration Pricing

A **penetration pricing** strategy sets a low price as a major marketing tactic. Businesses may price new products much lower than competing products when they enter new industries that have dozens of competing brands. Once the new product achieves some market success, through purchases encouraged by its low price, marketers may increase the price to the level of competing products. But stiff competition can prevent the price increase.

Everyday Low Pricing and Discount Pricing

Everyday low pricing (EDLP) is a strategy of maintaining continuous low prices instead of using short-term price-cutting tactics such as cents-off coupons, rebates, and special sales. This strategy has been used successfully by retailers such as Walmart and GNC to consistently offer low prices to consumers; manufacturers also use EDLP to set stable prices for retailers.

Stores such as Walmart use an everyday low pricing strategy of maintaining continuous low prices instead of using short-term price-cutting tactics such as cents-off coupons, rebates, and special sales.

Businesses that use *discount pricing* hope to attract customers by dropping prices for a set period of time. Automakers usually offer consumers special discounts on most or all of their vehicles during the holiday shopping season. After the holidays, prices usual rise again. Experts warn that discounting must be done carefully, or profits can disappear. Businesses should offer discounts only for a specified period of time and with a clear understanding of what they are trying to accomplish by using the strategy. They should advertise the discount, so customers know it is a special deal. When the time period is over, the discount should be over, too.

HIT & MISS

Will Lower Prices Help Nokia Regain Its Edge?

For years, the Finnish electronics company Nokia owned a huge share of the world's cellphone market, easily outselling early competitors such as Motorola and Sony Ericsson. Recently, Nokia found itself facing competition from Research In Motion's BlackBerry devices and from Apple's iPhone, which has begun to lower its prices.

Nokia seems to be trying various strategies, but some observers think the company has lost its strategic focus. Nokia's chief executive, Olli-Pekka Kallasvuo, announced that the company would focus on software. He also mentioned a deal with Microsoft to create business-oriented mobile applications. Another executive declared that Nokia would become the "world's biggest entertainment media network." Nokia recently launched its "Comes with Music" downloading service, which was the first of its kind in the Middle East. But the service has done poorly elsewhere due to stiff competition from Apple's iTunes. Yet another executive announced the debut of the Booklet 3G, a laptop computer that would make the "personal computer more social, more helpful, and more personal."

At a meeting in New Delhi, India, Tuula Rytilä-Uotila, Nokia's vice-president of products, announced that the company planned to lower the prices of Nokia's smartphones. "We want to take smartphones to a wider audience by bringing down the prices of such phones. The strategy is to be present in all price ranges." The company hopes to increase demand for its low-end mobile phones and may put some indirect pressure on Apple and Research In Motion, whose handsets are more sophisticated.

Questions for Critical Thinking

1. Do you think Nokia will regain lost ground with its new pricing strategy? Why or why not?

2. Will Nokia's low-end cellphones work as good loss leaders (a product sold at a low price to stimulate other sales)? Why or why not?

Sources: Company website, www.nokia.com, accessed May 11, 2010; Arik Hesseldahl, "Nokia's Kallasvuo: We Must 'Move Even Faster,'" *BusinessWeek*, April 22, 2010, http://www.businessweek.com; Mark Ritson, "Nokia Brand Needs Firm Direction," *Branding Strategy Insider*, April 5, 2010, http://www.brandingstrategyinsider.com; Abbas Jaffar Ali, "Nokia Announces the X6 and 'Comes with Music' Service for the Middle East," *T-Break Tech*, February 11, 2010, http://tech.tbreak.com; John Paczkowski, "Nokia Agitating for a Handset Price War?" *All Things Digital*, February 1, 2010, http://digitaldaily.allthingsd.com.

When Nokia saw its market share decrease, it tried various ways to lure consumers back. One strategy was lowering prices on some of its cellphones. This strategy is discussed in the "Hit & Miss" feature.

Competitive Pricing

Many organizations rely heavily on price as a competitive tactic, but even more organizations use **competitive pricing** strategies. These firms try to reduce the emphasis on price competition by matching other firms' prices and by focusing their own marketing efforts on the product, distribution, and promotional elements of the marketing mix. In industries with relatively similar products, competitors must match each other's price reductions to maintain market share and remain competitive. By pricing their products to match the prices of competing offerings, marketers largely remove the price variable from their marketing strategies.

competitive pricing a strategy that tries to reduce the emphasis on price competition by matching other firms' prices and by focusing their own marketing efforts on the product, distribution, and promotional elements of the marketing mix.

✔ **ASSESSMENT CHECK**

13.6.1 What is a cost-based pricing formula?

13.6.2 Why do companies implement competitive pricing strategies?

CONSUMER PERCEPTIONS OF PRICES

LO 13.7 Discuss consumer perceptions of price.

How do you perceive, or view, prices for certain products? Marketers need to consider how customers perceive prices. If large numbers of potential buyers consider a price to be too high or too low, businesses must correct the situation. When setting prices, marketers consider price–quality relationships and the use of odd pricing.

Price–Quality Relationships

Research shows that a consumer's perception of product quality is closely related to an item's price. Most marketers believe that this perceived price–quality relationship remains steady over a relatively wide range of prices, although extremely high or low prices have less credibility. The price–quality relationship can critically affect a firm's pricing strategy.

Many consumers associate prestige, quality, and high price as being related. That is, they believe that paying a high price for an item such as an Infiniti car or a Chanel bag will convey prestige and ensure quality. Others believe that eating at an expensive restaurant means the food will be better than food served at a modestly priced restaurant. The opposite is also true. Many consumers may view an extremely low price as an indication that corners have been cut and quality will be poor. Interestingly, a recent study noted that California wines made from organically grown grapes are less expensive than those made from nonorganic grapes. But this price difference actually seemed to be a disadvantage for the organic wines: labelling a wine as "made from organically grown grapes" drove the price down, but the same wine without the certification notice sold for more. Many factors may contribute to this situation. In the 1970s and 1980s, when organic wines were first produced, the reds gained a bad reputation: many of them quickly turned to vinegar because they were made without preservatives. Some consumers still remember this. Also, "green" consumers are aware of the benefits of organically grown fruits and vegetables, but the benefits of organically grown wines are not so well known. Growers need to communicate to consumers that, in this case at least, price and quality don't necessarily go together.[39]

odd pricing a pricing method that uses uneven amounts to make prices appear to be less than they really are.

Odd Pricing

Have you ever wondered why retailers set prices like $1.99 instead of $2 or $9.95 instead of $10? **Odd pricing** is a pricing method that uses uneven amounts to make prices appear to be less than they really are. Before the age of cash registers and sales taxes, retailers reportedly followed this practice to force clerks to make correct change as part of their cash control efforts. But odd pricing is commonly used today because many retailers believe that consumers prefer uneven amounts or amounts that sound less than they really are. Some retailers also use this method to identify items that have been marked down. The odd price lets people know the item is on sale.

✔ **ASSESSMENT CHECK**

13.7.1 How does the price–quality relationship affect a firm's pricing strategy?

13.7.2 Why is odd pricing used?

WHAT'S AHEAD

The chapters in Part 4 have explained the main principles of marketing management. These chapters also described how each principle fits a firm's overall business strategy. Part 5 will help you to understand how companies manage the technology and information that businesses can use to create value for their customers and improve their competitiveness in the marketplace.

RETURN TO INSIDE BUSINESS

WorkSafeBC: Promoting Safety to Young Workers

For the first two years, Raise Your Hand was expressed simply by using photos of raised hands. Each hand was connected to a story contributed by a young worker. As more and more young workers participated, the website changed daily. The campaign grew to further express the feel of a grassroots movement. It then built on the stories, to give something back to young workers in the form of an empowering message about how to exercise their workplace rights.

Postings to YouTube and other social media sites have exceeded expectations, as measured by the number and quality of stories, event and online interactions, and click-through rates.

QUESTIONS FOR CRITICAL THINKING

1. How would you continue the success of this online program?

2. Describe the concept for a new online promotional campaign.

SUMMARY OF LEARNING OBJECTIVES

LO 13.1 Discuss how integrated marketing communications relates to a firm's overall promotional strategy, explain the concept of a promotional mix, and outline the objectives of promotion.

When a firm practises integrated marketing communications, it coordinates promotional activities to produce a unified, customer-focused message. IMC identifies consumer needs and shows how a company's products meet those needs. Marketers select the promotional media that work best to target and reach customers. The programs rely on teamwork and careful promotional planning to coordinate IMC strategies.

A company's promotional mix combines personal selling and nonpersonal selling. Nonpersonal selling includes advertising, sales promotion, and public relations. By selecting the most suitable combination of promotional mix elements, marketers try to achieve the firm's five major promotional objectives: providing information, differentiating a product, increasing demand, stabilizing sales, and highlighting the product's value.

✓ ASSESSMENT CHECK ANSWERS

13.1.1 What is the objective of an integrated marketing communications program? An IMC strategy focuses on customer needs to create a unified promotional message about a firm's goods or services.

13.1.2 Why do firms pursue multiple promotional objectives at the same time? Firms pursue multiple promotional objectives because they may need to convey different messages to different audiences.

13.1.3 What are product placement and guerrilla marketing? Product placement involves paying a fee to have a product featured in certain media. Guerrilla marketing refers to innovative, low-cost marketing efforts designed to get consumers' attention in unusual ways.

LO 13.2 Summarize the different types of advertising and advertising media.

Advertising is the most visible form of nonpersonal promotion. Advertising is designed to inform, persuade, or remind. Product advertising promotes a good or service, while institutional advertising promotes a concept, idea, organization, or philosophy. Television, newspapers, and magazines are the largest advertising media categories. Other advertising media include direct mail, radio, and outdoor advertising. Interactive advertising directly involves the consumer, who controls the flow of information.

✓ ASSESSMENT CHECK ANSWERS

13.2.1 What are the two basic types of advertising? Into what three categories do they fall? The two basic types are product and institutional. They fall into the categories of informative, persuasive, and reminder-oriented advertising.

13.2.2 What is the leading advertising medium in North America? According to the most recent statistics listed in Figure 13.2, television is the leading advertising medium in North America.

13.2.3 In what two major ways do firms benefit from sponsorship? Firms benefit from sponsorship in two ways: they gain exposure to the event's audience, and they gain from their association with the activity's positive image.

LO 13.3 Outline the roles of sales promotion, personal selling, and public relations in promotional strategy.

Sales promotion accounts for more expenses than advertising. Consumer-oriented sales promotions include coupons, games, rebates, samples, premiums, contests, sweepstakes, and promotional products. This type of sales promotion offers consumers an extra incentive to buy a product. Point-of-purchase advertising displays and trade shows are sales promotions directed to the trade markets. Personal selling involves face-to-face interactions between the seller and buyers. The primary sales tasks are order processing, creative selling, and missionary selling. Public relations is nonpaid promotion that seeks to enhance a company's public image.

✔ ASSESSMENT CHECK ANSWERS

13.3.1 Why do retailers and manufacturers use sales promotions? Retailers and manufacturers use sales promotions to offer consumers extra incentives to buy their products.

13.3.2 When does a firm use personal selling instead of nonpersonal selling? Personal selling is generally used when there are few customers who are geographically concentrated, the product is technically complex or requires special handling, the price is high, or the product moves through direct-distribution channels.

13.3.3 How does public relations serve a marketing purpose? Public relations is an efficient, indirect communications channel for promoting products. It can publicize products and help create and maintain a positive image of the company.

LO 13.4 Describe pushing and pulling promotional strategies.

A pushing strategy relies on personal selling to market a product to wholesalers and retailers in a company's distribution channels. A pulling strategy promotes the product by generating consumer demand for it, through advertising and sales promotion.

✔ ASSESSMENT CHECK ANSWERS

13.4.1 Give an example of a pushing strategy. A pushing strategy is used by drug manufacturers, who used to market only to physicians and hospitals. Today, drug manufacturers also use a pulling strategy by marketing directly to patients through advertising, which encourages patients to ask their doctors about the medications.

13.4.2 Give an example of a pulling strategy. Pulling strategies are used by retailers and by manufacturers of consumer goods such as cosmetics, automobiles, and clothing.

LO 13.5 Outline the different types of pricing objectives.

Pricing objectives can be classified as profitability, volume, meeting competition, and prestige. Profitability objectives are the most common goals. Volume objectives base pricing decisions on market share. Meeting competitors' prices makes price a nonissue in competition. Prestige pricing sets a high price to develop and maintain an image of quality or exclusiveness.

✔ ASSESSMENT CHECK ANSWERS

13.5.1 Define *price*. Price is the exchange value of a good or service.

13.5.2 What is a second approach to pricing strategy? A second approach to pricing strategy is volume objectives. This pricing strategy bases pricing decisions on market share.

LO 13.6 Discuss how firms set prices in the marketplace, and describe the four alternative pricing strategies.

Economic theory determines prices by using the law of demand and supply. But most firms use cost-based pricing, which adds a markup after totalling all costs. Firms usually do a breakeven analysis to calculate the minimum sales volume a product must generate at a certain price to cover all costs. The four alternative pricing strategies are skimming, penetration, everyday low pricing and discounting, and competitive pricing. A skimming strategy sets a high price initially to recover costs and then lowers the price. A penetration strategy sets a lower price and then raises it later. Everyday low pricing and discounting offer a lower price for a period of time. Competitive pricing matches other firms' prices and highlights a product's nonprice benefits.

✔ ASSESSMENT CHECK ANSWERS

13.6.1 What is a cost-based pricing formula? A cost-based pricing formula calculates the total costs per unit and then adds markups to cover overhead costs and generate profits.

13.6.2 Why do companies implement competitive pricing strategies? Companies use competitive pricing strategies to reduce the emphasis on price competition by matching other firms' prices and by focusing their own marketing efforts on the product, distribution, and promotional elements of the marketing mix.

LO 13.7 Discuss consumer perceptions of price.

When setting prices, marketers must consider how consumers perceive the price–quality relationship of their products. Consumers may be willing to pay a higher price if they perceive a product to be of superior quality. Marketers often use odd pricing to convey a message to consumers.

✔ ASSESSMENT CHECK ANSWERS

13.7.1 How does the price–quality relationship affect a firm's pricing strategy? Consumers believe that the price of an item reflects its quality, except in extreme cases. A firm must try to set its prices accordingly.

13.7.2 Why is odd pricing used? Retailers believe that consumers prefer prices that have uneven amounts or amounts that sound like less than they really are. Odd pricing may also be used to indicate a sale item.

BUSINESS TERMS YOU NEED TO KNOW

promotion 358

integrated marketing communications (IMC) 358

promotional mix 359

personal selling 359

nonpersonal selling 359

positioning 360

product placement 361

guerrilla marketing 362

advertising 362

product advertising 363

institutional advertising 363

cause advertising 363

sponsorship 368

infomercials 368

sales promotion 368

specialty advertising 370

trade promotion 370

point-of-purchase (POP) advertising 370

order processing 372

creative selling 372

missionary selling 372

telemarketing 373

public relations 374

publicity 375

pushing strategy 375

cooperative advertising 375

pulling strategy 375

price 376

profitability objectives 376

volume objectives 376

prestige pricing 377

cost-based pricing 378

breakeven analysis 378

skimming pricing 380

penetration pricing 380

everyday low pricing (EDLP) 380

competitive pricing 381

odd pricing 382

REVIEW QUESTIONS

1. What is the purpose of integrated marketing communications?

2. What are the five major objectives of a promotional strategy?

3. Identify and define each of the three categories of advertising based on their purpose. Which of the three categories of advertising would marketers likely use for the following products?

   a. deodorant

   b. an electronic reader

   c. organic produce

   d. healthcare insurance

4. What are the benefits of online and interactive advertising? What might be some drawbacks?

5. For each of the following, describe potential benefits and drawbacks of a sponsorship relationship:

   a. LG and the Snowboard FIS World Cup

   b. ING Bank and Hamilton's Around the Bay 30K Road Race

   c. Wrangler and the Wrangler Football Golf Classic (a golf tournament that raises money for high-school football programs)

6. If you were a marketer for Rolex, what kind of sales promotion might you use for high-end watches?

7. In what situations are firms likely to emphasize personal selling?

8. Describe the seven-step sales process.

9. Define the four basic categories of pricing objectives.

10. What are the four alternative pricing strategies used by marketers? Give an example of the circumstances under which each might be selected.

PROJECTS AND TEAMWORK APPLICATIONS

1. Choose a product that you purchased recently. Identify the various media that were used to promote the product and analyze the promotional mix. Do you agree with the company's marketing strategy, or would you suggest changes to the promotional mix? Why? Create your own print ad for the product you chose, using any business strategies or knowledge you have learned in this course so far.

2. Evaluate the price of the product you selected in the exercise above. What pricing strategy is the manufacturer using? Do you think the price is fair? Why or why not? Choose a different strategy; develop a new price for the product based on the new strategy. Ask your classmates whether they would purchase the product at the new price. Why or why not?

3. Some schools receive financial benefits by allowing companies to promote their goods and services to students. Others have decided against this practice, and some schools ban this type of promotion. Find some examples of corporate sponsors in public elementary and

high schools and on college and university campuses. With your class, discuss the pros and cons of promotion in public schools and on college and university campuses. In your view, is there a difference between a public school and a college or university campus? Why or why not?

4. On your own or with a classmate, research a recent issue that has caused a business, a not-for-profit organization, or a government agency to suffer from bad publicity. Evaluate the situation. Outlining the steps the organization might take to build better public relations.

5. You are the marketing manager at a company that is introducing a new line of video games. How would you set the prices for the new products?

WEB ASSIGNMENTS

1. Top advertisers. *Advertising Age* compiles data annually on the top national advertisers. Visit the website listed below to access the most recent year. Answer the following questions:

    a. Who were the top 10 advertisers that year?

    b. How much did they spend on advertising?

    c. What was the most advertised brand that year?

    http://adage.com/datacenter/article?article_id5106348

2. Online coupon fraud. Go to the websites listed to learn about online coupon fraud. Prepare a brief report. Make sure to answer the following questions: How big a problem is online coupon fraud? What changes have marketers made to try to reduce online coupon fraud?

    http://www.newser.com/story/35962/hackers-spread-coupon-scam.html

    http://online.wsj.com/article/SB124641121217977575.html

    http://multichannelmerchant.com/retail/news/0308-curtailing-online-coupon-fraud/

3. Yield management. Assume you want to fly from St. John's, Newfoundland and Labrador, to Victoria, British Columbia. Visit some travel sites. Search for fares. Change such factors as advance purchase, day of departure, time of departure, and so on. What did this exercise teach you about yield management?

    http://www.expedia.ca

    http://www.kayak.com

    http://www.travelocity.ca

WILEY **PLUS**
www.wileyplus.com

Access your WileyPLUS course for:

- The complete digital textbook.
- Question assistance, including links to relevant sections in the online digital textbook.
- Immediate feedback and proof of progress, 24/7
- Integrated, multi-media resources – including MP3 downloads, visual exhibits, animations, and much more – that provide multiple study paths and encourage more active learning.

QUIZ YOURSELF

4 LAUNCHING YOUR . . .

MARKETING CAREER

In Part 4, "Marketing Management," you learned about the goals and functions of marketing. The three chapters in this part emphasized the central role of customer satisfaction in defining value and developing a marketing strategy in traditional and nontraditional marketing settings. You learned about the role of marketing research and the need for relationship marketing in today's competitive environment. You discovered how new products are developed and how they change through the four stages of the product life cycle, from introduction through growth and maturity to decline. You also learned about the role of different channels in creating effective distribution strategies. Finally, you saw the impact of integrated marketing communications on the firm's promotional strategy, the role of advertising, and how pricing affects consumer behaviour. You may have read about some marketing tasks and functions that sounded especially interesting. Here are a few ideas about careers in marketing.

The first thing to remember is that marketing is more than personal selling and advertising. For example, are you curious about why people behave the way they do? Are you good at spotting trends? Marketing research analysts look for answers to a wide range of questions about business competition, customer preferences, market trends, and past and future sales. They often design and conduct their own consumer surveys, using the telephone, mail, the Internet, or personal interviews and focus groups. They collect the data and analyze it. Their recommendations become input for managerial decisions, such as whether to introduce new products, redesign current products, enter new markets, or discontinue products or markets where profitability is low. Marketing researchers may be included in a new-product development team, where they work directly with scientists, production and manufacturing personnel, and finance employees. Marketing researchers are often asked to help clients put their recommendations in place. With today's highly competitive economy, jobs in this area are expected to grow.

Another career path in marketing is sales. Do you work well with others? Are you good at reading other people's feelings? Are you a self-starter? If so, being a sales representative might be for you. Selling jobs exist in every industry. Many of these jobs use a combination of salary and performance-based commissions, so they can pay very well. Sales jobs are also often a first step on the ladder to upper-management positions. Sales representatives work for wholesalers and manufacturing companies (and even for publishers such as the one that produces this book). They sell automobiles, computer systems and technology, pharmaceuticals, advertising, insurance, real estate, commodities and financial services, and all kinds of consumer goods and services.

If you're interested in mass communications, you should know that print and online magazines, newspapers, and broadcast companies generate most of their revenue from advertising. Sales representatives who sell space and time slots in the media contribute to the success of these firms. If you like to travel, consider that many sales jobs involve travel.

Advertising, marketing management, and public relations are other categories of marketing. In large companies, marketing managers, product managers, promotion managers, and public relations managers often work long hours under pressure; they may travel frequently or transfer between jobs at headquarters and positions in regional offices. Their responsibilities include directing promotional programs, supervising advertising campaigns and budgets, and conducting communications such as press releases with the firm's public audiences. Thousands of new positions are expected to open up in the next several years; the field is expected to grow 14 percent over the next decade. Growth of the Internet and new media has increased demand for advertising and public relations specialists.

Advertising and public relations firms employ thousands of people. Most advertising firms develop specialties; many of the largest advertising firms work internationally. Online advertising is one area where new jobs will be opening in the future, especially as more and more client firms expand their online sales operations.

CAREER ASSESSMENT EXERCISES IN MARKETING

1. Select a field that interests you. Use the Internet to research the types of sales positions available in that field. Locate a few entry-level job openings and see what career steps that position can lead to. (You might want to start with a popular job-posting site such as Monster.ca.) Note the job requirements, the starting salary, and the form of compensation—straight salary or salary plus commission? Write a one-page summary of your findings.

2. Use the Internet to identify and research two or three of the leading advertising agencies in Canada, such as Cossette Communications or Wasserman & Partners. What are some of their recent ad campaigns? Who are their best-known clients? Where do the agencies have offices? What job openings do they currently list, and what qualifications do they ask for? Write a brief report comparing the agencies you selected, decide which agency you would prefer to work for, and give your reasons.

3. Test your research skills. Choose an ordinary product, such as toothpaste or soft drinks. Design a survey to find out why people chose the brand they most recently purchased. For instance, suppose you wanted to find out how people choose their shampoo. List as many decision criteria as you can think of, such as availability, scent, price, packaging, benefits from use (conditioning, dandruff-reducing, and so on), brand name, and ad campaign. Ask eight to 10 friends to rank these decision factors, and note some simple demographics about your research subjects such as their age, gender, and occupation. Chart your results. What did you learn about how your people made their purchase decision? Did any of your findings surprise you? How could have improved the survey?

PART 5
MANAGING TECHNOLOGY AND INFORMATION

Chapter 14 Using Technology to Manage Information

14 USING TECHNOLOGY TO MANAGE INFORMATION

LEARNING OBJECTIVES

LO 14.1 Distinguish between data and information, and explain the role of information systems in business.

LO 14.2 List the components and different types of information systems.

LO 14.3 Outline how computer hardware and software are used to manage information.

LO 14.4 Describe networking and telecommunications technology and the types of computer networks.

LO 14.5 Discuss the security and ethical issues involving computer information systems.

LO 14.6 Explain the steps that companies go through in anticipating, planning for, and recovering from information systems disasters.

LO 14.7 Review the current trends in information systems.

INSIDE BUSINESS

Stock-Trak: Learning about the Stock Market through Simulation

What's the best way to learn about the stock market—a complicated business environment that involves rapidly changing information and special terms that only those involved seem to understand? More importantly, how can someone develop good trading skills, gain a sense of how stocks behave in real time, and experience what they would do in a situation—without actually risking any money?

According to Tom Reti and Mark Brookshire, executives at Stock-Trak, there is no better way to learn about investment trading than real-life experience. To get that experience without risking any money, Stock-Trak provides a Web-based stock market simulation and training products package. Stock-Trak has sold its products to the academic and financial services markets and to the general public.

Wall Street Survivor (www.wallstreetsurvivor.com) is part of Stock-Trak's consumer division. It targets online investing, trading, and game enthusiasts with an investment-oriented simulation and contest website. Anyone interested in learning and developing their trading skills can sign up and experience online trading without the risk of losing real money. Real-time data are provided so that learners can see the immediate results of their decisions. Learners can also use a variety of learning materials and supplements, such as discussion forums with other learners and tutorials, to improve their trading skills. Contest prizes make the experience more exciting and competitive while avoiding the risk of losing money. Stock-Trak's co-branding with newspapers and other media has proven very successful, as shown by the website http://www.marketwatch.com/game/. If you've ever seen a stock market investment contest,

chances are good that Stock-Trak provided the simulation and learning environment.

In the academic market, more than 60,000 students at colleges and universities in 30 countries have used the simulation to learn about trading stocks, options, futures, bonds, and mutual funds. Dedicated websites such http://nipissing.stocktrak.com/home.aspx at Ontario's Nipissing University are typical of websites Stock-Trak has set up for other universities, such as Montreal's McGill University, the University of Toronto, New York University, Yale University, and Columbia University.

The third market for Stock-Trak is the growing financial services industry that uses simulation training for employees before putting them work trading with real clients' money. Stock-Trak has been providing training to employees of Scottrade Inc. since 2008. Under the terms of their agreement, Stock-Trak manages a Web-based employee education and training simulator used by employees of Scottrade's 375 branch offices. Each quarter, new hires are given simulated cash to manage. They are tested for their knowledge of the stock and option markets and their ability to successfully use the various tools and techniques learned through Scottrade's training program.

Stock-Trak Group has three office locations in Montreal, Quebec; Mississauga, Ontario; and Atlanta, Georgia.[1]

CHAPTER 14 OVERVIEW

This chapter explores how businesses manage information as a resource and how they use technology to help in this task. Today, nearly all business functions—from human resources to production to supply chain management—rely on information systems. The chapter begins by looking at the differences between information and data and then defines an information system. The components of information systems are presented, and two major types of information systems are described. The chapter also discusses databases, which are important to all organizations and are the heart of all information systems. Then the chapter looks at the computer hardware and software that drive information systems. Today, specialized networks make information access and information transmission work smoothly; so the chapter examines different types of telecommunications and computer networks to see how businesses are using them for competitive advantage. The chapter then turns to a discussion of the ethical and security issues affecting information systems, followed by a description of how organizations plan for, and recover from, information system disasters. A review of the current trends in information systems concludes the chapter.

LO 14.1 Distinguish between data and information, and explain the role of information systems in business.

DATA, INFORMATION, AND INFORMATION SYSTEMS

Every day, businesspeople ask themselves questions such as the following:

- How well is our product selling in Calgary compared with in Halifax? Have sales among consumers aged 25 to 45 increased or decreased in the past year?

- How will rising energy prices affect production and distribution costs?

- If employees can access the benefits system through our network, will our benefit costs increase or decrease?

- How can we communicate more efficiently and effectively with our workforce that is spread out across the country?

An effective information system can help answer these and many other questions. **Data** consist of raw facts and figures that may or may not be relevant, or meaningful, to a business decision. **Information** is knowledge gained from processing those facts and figures. For example, businesspeople need to gather demographics, or population data, about a target market or the specifications of a certain product. But the data are useless unless they are transformed into relevant information that can be used to make a competitive decision. For example, data might be the sizes of various demographic groups. Information drawn from those data could be how many of those individuals are potential customers for a firm's products. Technology has advanced so quickly that all businesses—large or small, in large cities or in remote areas, now have access to data and information that can make them competitive in a global arena.

An **information system** is an organized method for collecting, storing, and communicating past, present, and projected information on internal operations and external intelligence. Most information systems today use computer and telecommunications technology. A large organization typically assigns responsibility for managing its information systems and related operations to an executive called the **chief information officer (CIO)**. The CIO often reports directly to the firm's chief executive officer (CEO). An effective CIO can understand and control technology so that the company can use one seamless operation to communicate both internally and externally. But small companies rely just as much on information systems as do large ones, even if they do not assign a full-time manager to this area.

The role of the CIO is both expanding and changing as the technology to manage information continues to develop. Over the past 10 years, the role of a CIO has changed from being a technical role to being a business partner who often applies strong influence over a company's strategy. CIOs will need to adapt their roles even further in the future. More and more, CIOs and former CIOs are being appointed to companies' boards of directors.[2]

data raw facts and figures that may or may not be meaningful to a business decision.

information knowledge gained from processing data.

information system an organized method for collecting, storing, and communicating past, present, and projected information on internal operations and external intelligence.

chief information officer (CIO) the executive responsible for managing a firm's information systems and related computer technologies.

Information systems can be designed to assist many business functions and departments—from marketing and manufacturing to finance and accounting. They can manage a huge flood of information by organizing data in a logical and accessible manner. A company can use the system to monitor all areas of its operations and business strategy, identifying problems and opportunities. Information systems gather data from inside and outside the organization; they then process the data to produce information that is meaningful to all aspects of the organization. The processing steps can include storing data for later use, classifying and analyzing it, and retrieving it easily when needed.

Many companies—and nations—combine high-tech and low-tech solutions to manage the flow of information. E-mail, wireless communications, and videoconferencing are increasingly common. But they haven't totally replaced paper memos, phone conversations, and face-to-face meetings. Information can make the difference between staying in business and going bankrupt. The right information can help a firm keep up-to-date with changing consumer demands, competitors' activities, and recent government regulations. A firm can then apply this information to fine-tune existing products, develop new products, and maintain effective marketing.

✓ **ASSESSMENT CHECK**

14.1.1 Distinguish between data and information.

14.1.2 What is an information system?

COMPONENTS AND TYPES OF INFORMATION SYSTEMS

LO 14.2 List the components and different types of information systems.

The definition of *information system* in the previous section does not specifically mention the use of computers or technology. Information systems have been around since the beginning of civilization. Of course, by today's standards, the early information systems were very low-tech. Think about your college or university library. At one time, the library probably had a card catalogue to help students find information. The card catalogue was an information system because it stored data about books and periodicals in an organized manner on index cards. Library users could flip through the cards and locate library materials by author, title, or subject. But the process could be difficult and time-consuming.

When today's businesspeople think about information systems, they most likely think about **computer-based information systems**. These systems rely on computer and related technologies to store information electronically in an organized, accessible manner. Instead of a card catalogue, your college or university library probably uses a computerized information system. Users can search through library holdings quickly and easily.

Computer-based information systems consist of four components and technologies:

- Computer hardware
- Computer software
- Telecommunications and computer networks
- Data resource management

Computer hardware refers to machines that range from supercomputers to smartphones. It also includes the input, output, and storage devices needed to support computing machines. Software includes operating systems, such as Microsoft's Windows 7 or Linux, and applications programs, such as Adobe Acrobat or Oracle's PeopleSoft Enterprise applications. Telecommunications and computer networks refer to the hardware and software needed to provide wired or wireless voice and data communications. Also included are support for external networks, such as the Internet, and private internal networks. Data resource management involves developing and maintaining an organization's databases so that decision-makers can access the information they need when they need it.

In the case of your college or university library, the computer-based information system is usually made up of computer hardware, such as monitors and keyboards, which are linked to the library's network and a database containing information on the library's holdings. Specialized software allows users to access the database. The library's network is likely also connected to a larger private network and the Internet. These connections give users remote access to the library's database and access to other computerized databases, such as LexisNexis.

computer-based information systems information systems that use computer and related technologies to store information electronically in an organized, accessible manner.

Databases

database a centralized integrated collection of data resources.

The heart of any information system is its **database**, a centralized integrated collection of data resources. A company designs its databases to meet specific information processing and retrieval needs of its workforce. Businesses obtain databases in many ways. They can hire a staff person to build them on site, hire an outside source to build them, or buy packaged database programs from specialized vendors, such as Oracle. A database acts as an electronic filing cabinet. It is capable of storing large amounts of data and retrieving a specific piece of data within seconds. A database should be continually updated; otherwise, a firm may find itself with data that are outdated and possibly useless. One problem with databases is that they often contribute to information overload—too much data for people to absorb or data that are irrelevant, or not meaningful, to decision-making. Computer processing speed and storage capacity are increasing rapidly, and data have become more abundant—that is, there is more data and it is more easily available. As a result, businesspeople need to be careful that their databases contain only the facts they need. If they aren't careful, much time can be wasted wading through unnecessary data. Another challenge with databases is keeping them safe, as the "Hit & Miss" feature describes.

Decision-makers can also look up data online. Online systems give access to large amounts of government data, such as economic data from Statistics Canada. One of the largest online databases is that of the Canadian Census. The Canadian Census of Population is conducted every five years. It collects data on households across Canada and tries to count everyone in the country. Selected participants fill out forms, answering questions about marital status, place of birth, ethnic background, citizenship, workplaces, commuting time, income, occupation, type of housing, number of telephones and vehicles, and even the number of grandparents who are caregivers. Although certain restrictions limit how people can access and use specific census data, the general public may access the data through Statistics Canada's website.

© Can Stock Photo Inc./PicsFive

A library's *computer-based information system* is generally made up of computer hardware linked to the library's network and a database of information on the library's holdings. Specialized software allows users to access the database.

HIT & MISS

Business Intelligence Software Helps with Information Overload

According to recent research, about 60 percent of Canadian companies use business intelligence software to help managers deal with all the data they need to process and understand. Sales of analytical software are growing at a 10 percent rate and approaching $11 billion annually.

More than half of executives reported feeling weighed down by the volume of data processing and analysis that they need to do as part of their decision-making responsibilities. But these tasks can be made easier by using software that processes large volumes of data and can produce guidance for management.

For example, most businesses have little if any understanding of their mobile, wireless, and data communications usage. They received invoices from a large telecommunications companies, such as Bell Canada, Rogers, or Telus, and simply pay their bills. They have no way of knowing if they are paying for unneeded services or if they are overpaying for the services they use. A business intelligence software solution can now help large corporations to save time and money. Etelesolv is a start-up consulting firm in Lachine, Quebec. Its TeleManager system provides managers with details of costs and usage to help them control costs, such as an employee who runs up excessive charges. According to Etelesolv's president, Christopher Thierry, the software identified $800,000 of potential savings for one client.

The young company's clients include RBC Financial Group, Canada Post, RONA, GazMet, and SunLife. But even smaller firms need help with analyzing and reconciling their telecommunications invoices.

Questions for Critical Thinking

1. What other areas of managerial decision-making involve large volumes of data and would likely benefit from a software solution?

2. How might software firms price their software solutions to different companies?

Sources: Etelesolv corporate website, http://www.etelesolv.com/, accessed May 19, 2011; Peter Hadekel, "Solving Telecom Mysteries," *Montreal Gazette*, April 7, 2011, pp. B1–B2; Matt Hartley, "Information Overload Burden to Execs: Poll," *National Post*, May 16, 2011, p. A2.

Another source of free information is company websites. Anyone who is interested can visit firms' home pages to look for information about customers, suppliers, and competitors. Trade associations and academic institutions also maintain websites with related information.

Types of Information Systems

Many different types of information systems exist. In general, information systems fall into one of two broad categories: operational support systems or management support systems.

Operational Support Systems

Operational support systems are designed to produce a variety of information on an organization's activities for both internal and external users. Examples of operational support systems include transaction processing systems and process control systems. **Transaction processing systems** record and process data from business transactions. For example, major retailers use point-of-sale systems, which link electronic cash registers to the retailer's computer centres. Sales data are transmitted from cash registers to the computer centre either immediately or at regular intervals. **Process control systems** monitor and control physical processes. For example, a steel mill may have electronic sensors linked to a computer system to monitor the entire production process. The system makes necessary changes and alerts operators to potential problems.

Commercial airplane manufacturer Airbus relies on an advanced information system. It uses RFID (radio-frequency identification) technology to track parts and tools used in the production and maintenance of its products, including its new A350 XWB planes. The high-memory RFID tags are placed on parts. The information system then follows the parts from warehouses to production facilities to the specific production lines where they are attached to aircraft. The system also tracks how and where tools are used. Airbus expects the information system to improve overall supply chain management, reduce required inventory levels, and increase productivity.[3]

operational support systems information systems designed to produce a variety of information on an organization's activities for both internal and external users.

transaction processing systems operational support systems that record and process data from business transactions.

process control systems operational support systems that monitor and control physical processes.

The complex process of airline maintenance is critical to passenger safety. Many airlines use an *operational support system* to track parts, schedule inspections, and manage inventory levels.

© Can Stock Photo Inc./poco_bw

Management Support Systems

Management support systems are information systems that are designed to provide support for effective decision-making. Several different types of management support systems are available. A **management information system (MIS)** is designed to produce reports to managers and other professionals.

A **decision support system (DSS)** gives direct support to businesspeople during the decision-making process. For example, a marketing manager might use a decision support system

management support systems information systems that are designed to provide support for effective decision-making.

management information system (MIS) an information system that is designed to produce reports to managers and other professionals.

decision support system (DSS) an information system that gives direct support to businesspeople during the decision-making process.

executive support system (ESS) an information system that lets senior executives access the firm's primary databases, often by touching the computer screen, pointing and clicking a mouse, or using voice recognition.

expert system a computer program that imitates human thinking through complicated sets of "if-then" rules.

✓ ASSESSMENT CHECK

14.2.1 List the four components of a computer-based information system.

14.2.2 What is a database?

14.2.3 What are the two general types of information systems? Give examples of each.

to analyze how a product's price change will affect sales and profits. MEI Computer Technology Group provides North American consumer products producers with a comprehensive sales and trade promotions tracking software called TradeInsight. This software provides real results that are linked to specific promotional efforts, such as an advertising campaign, a special coupon, or another marketing tactic. Clients such as Kellogg's, Heinz, and L'Oreal can track the impact of their promotional spending on sales. They can then use this information when planning their future promotional strategies.[4]

An **executive support system (ESS)** lets senior executives access the firm's primary databases, often by touching the computer screen, pointing and clicking a mouse, or using voice recognition. In the typical ESS, users can choose from many kinds of data, such as the firm's financial statements and sales figures or stock market trends for the company and for the industry as a whole. Managers can start by looking at summaries, and then access more detailed information when needed.

Finally, an **expert system** is a computer program that imitates human thinking through complicated sets of "if-then" rules. The system applies human knowledge in a specific subject area to solve a problem. Expert systems are used for a variety of business purposes: to set credit limits for credit card applicants, to monitor machinery in a plant to detect potential problems or breakdowns, to arrange mortgage loans, and to design plant layouts. They are typically developed by capturing the knowledge of recognized experts in a field whether within a business itself or outside it.

LO 14.3 Outline how computer hardware and software are used to manage information.

COMPUTER HARDWARE AND SOFTWARE

It may be hard to believe, but only a few decades ago computers were thought of as exotic curiosities, used only for very specialized applications and understood by only a few people. The first commercial computer, UNIVAC I, was sold to the U.S. Census Bureau in the early 1950s. It cost $1 million, took up most of a room, and could perform about 2,000 calculations per second.[5] The invention of transistors and then integrated circuits (microchips) quickly led to smaller and more powerful devices. By the 1980s, computers could perform several million calculations per second. Now, computers perform billions of calculations per second, and some fit in the palm of your hand.

The first personal computers were introduced in the late 1970s and early 1980s. Then, the idea of a computer on every desk, or in every home, seemed unbelievable and not very likely. Today, computers have become a must-have for both businesses and households. Not only have computers become much more powerful and faster over the past 25 years, but they are also less expensive. IBM's first personal computer (PC), introduced in 1981, cost well over $5,000. Today, a PC can sell for less than $800.

Types of Computer Hardware

hardware all tangible, or physical, elements of a computer system.

Hardware consists of all tangible, or physical, elements of a computer system—the input devices, the components that store and process data and perform calculations, and the output devices that present the results to users. Input devices allow users to enter data and commands for processing, storage, and output. The most common input devices are the keyboard and mouse. Storage and processing components include the hard drive and various other storage components, such as DVD drives and flash memory devices. Flash memory devices are becoming increasingly popular because they are small and can hold large amounts of data. Some, called thumb drives, can even fit on a keychain. To gain access to the data they hold, users plug the drives into a USB (universal serial bus) port, standard on today's computers. Output devices, such as monitors and printers, are the hardware elements that transmit or display documents and other results of a computer system's work.

Different types of computers have varying memory capacities and processing speeds. These differences define four broad classifications: mainframe computers, midrange systems, personal computers, and hand-held devices. A mainframe computer is the largest computer system. It has the greatest storage capacity and the fastest processing speeds. Especially powerful mainframes called *supercomputers* can handle extremely rapid, complex calculations that involve thousands of variables, such as weather modelling and forecasting. Today's supercomputers can perform a trillion or more calculations per second.

Midrange systems consist of high-end network servers and other types of computers that can handle large-scale processing needs. They are less powerful than mainframe computers but more powerful than most personal computers. A **server** is the heart of a midrange computer network. It supports applications and allows networked users to share output devices, software, and databases. Many Internet-related functions at organizations are handled by midrange systems. Midrange systems are also commonly used in process control systems, computer-aided manufacturing (CAM), and computer-aided design (CAD).

server the heart of a midrange computer network.

Personal computers are everywhere today—in homes, businesses, schools, not-for-profit organizations, and government agencies. Recent estimates of PC ownership report that more than two-thirds of North American households have at least one personal computer. PCs have earned their increasing popularity because of their ever-expanding capability to handle many of the functions that large mainframes performed only a few decades ago. Most desktop computers are linked to networks, such as the Internet.

Desktop computers were once the standard PC seen in offices and homes. Millions of desktop computers remain on the job, but notebook, or laptop, computers now account for more than half of all new PCs sold. The increasing popularity of notebooks can be explained by their lower prices, improved displays, faster processing speeds, larger storage capacities, and more durable designs. They are more powerful and lighter or thinner than ever before. Notebook computers cost more than desktop computers. For many users, the size, weight, and portability of notebooks are worth the extra cost.

One of the newer types of computer devices is the *tablet*. Apple's iPad and RIM's PlayBook are smaller, lighter, and more portable than laptop computers. They don't have the advanced computing capability of larger, more expensive computers; but tablets can display television and movie videos, magazines, books and other audiovisual content at the time and place convenient to the user. This technology is changing the viewing habits of users. Tablets are quickly becoming an alternative to a laptop. They can perform such basic tasks as e-mail, word processing, and spreadsheet calculations. They can also access the Internet through a wireless connection.

Hand-held devices—made by companies such as Apple, RIM, Nokia, Palm, and Samsung—are even smaller. Two kinds of hand-held devices are available to most business and consumer users. The original type is the personal digital assistant (PDA). PDAs keep schedules and contact information and have limited software applications such as word processing and spreadsheets. Most PDAs today allow users to access the Internet through wireless networks.

The other type of hand-held device is the *smartphone*. A smartphone is a device that combines a cellphone with a PDA. Examples include Apple's iPhone, Google's Android, RIM's BlackBerry, and Samsung's BlackJack. Smartphones can make and receive calls and text messages. They also allow users to surf the Internet, receive and send e-mail, check their schedules, and even open and edit documents. On short

Using smartphones and tablets can boost productivity, but some people overuse or misuse them. Check out the "Business Etiquette" box for some helpful tips for courteous communication while using your hand-held device in a business environment.

© Can Stock Photo Inc./wacker

BUSINESS ETIQUETTE

Courteous Communications via Wireless Devices

Cellphone use in North America is very common. With so many of us communicating instantly—and almost constantly—it is more important than ever to be courteous, or well-mannered, whether speaking or e-mailing on a hand-held device.

1. *Be aware of your surroundings—and your neighbours.* If you're in a meeting or another place where a phone conversation would be unsuitable, turn your ring-tone off. If the call or e-mail simply can't wait, excuse yourself and leave the room to take the call.

2. *Lower your voice when taking a call in a public area.* If you are in area that is quieter than your speaking voice, it's better to have your conversation somewhere else. Find another area more suitable for having a conversation.

3. *When sending e-mail or texting, don't overabbreviate.* A business message can be short without being cute or, worse, hard to understand. It is just as easy to key in "See you at 3" as "cu@3."

4. *Before you send a text message or e-mail, read it over carefully.* Typos and grammatical errors don't look professional, especially in a business message.

5. *Be careful about your Facebook profile photo.* Now that smartphones let users link all their contact information, your photo may appear on the other person's phone when you call. And people beyond those on your "friends" list will see it. Be sure your photo is suitable for both friends and business callers.

Sources: Christopher Elliott, "E-Mail Etiquette for Wireless Devices: 7 Tips," Microsoft Small Business Center, http://www.microsoft.com, accessed May 24, 2010; Taya Flores, "Cell Phone Etiquette Is Important," *JC Online.com,* April 19, 2010, http://www.jconline.com; Mike Elgan, "Here Comes the New Cell Phone Etiquette," *IT World,* January 22, 2010, http://www.itworld.com.

---

trips, many businesspeople find that they rely on their smartphone. Because of smartphones' added capabilities, it's not surprising that smartphone sales are growing much faster than sales of traditional PDAs. Most of the recent overall growth in the sale of cellphones can be traced to sales of smartphones.[6]

In addition to PDAs and smartphones, some specialized hand-held devices are used in a variety of businesses for specific applications. For example, in some restaurants, servers use small wireless devices to swipe a credit card and print out a receipt right at the customer's table. Drivers for UPS and FedEx use special hand-held devices to track package deliveries and accept delivery signatures. The driver scans each package as it is delivered, and the information is transmitted to the delivery firm's network. Within a few seconds, the sender can use an Internet connection to obtain delivery information and view a copy of the receiver's signature.

Computer Software

software all the programs, routines, and computer languages that control a computer and tell it how to operate.

Software includes all of the programs, routines, and computer languages that control a computer and tell it how to operate. The *operating system* is the software that controls the basic workings of a computer system. More than 90 percent of personal computers use a version of Microsoft's popular Windows operating system. Personal computers made by Apple use the Mac operating system. Most hand-held devices use either the Palm or Symbian operating system or a special version of Windows called Windows Mobile. But the Droid, iPhone, and BlackBerry models have their own operating systems. Other operating systems include Unix, which runs on many midrange computer systems, and Linux, which runs on both PCs and midrange systems.

Table 14.1 Common Types of Applications Software

TYPE	DESCRIPTION	EXAMPLES
Word processing	Programs that input, store, retrieve, edit, and print various types of documents.	Microsoft Word, Pages (Apple)
Spreadsheets	Programs that prepare and analyze financial statements, sales forecasts, budgets, and similar numerical and statistical data.	Microsoft Excel, Numbers (Apple)
Presentation software	Programs that create presentations. Users can create bulleted lists, charts, graphs, pictures, audio, and even short video clips.	Microsoft PowerPoint, Keynote (Apple)
Desktop publishing	Software that combines high-quality type, graphics, and layout tools to create output that can look as attractive as documents produced by professional publishers and printers.	Adobe Acrobat, Microsoft Publisher
Financial software	Programs that compile accounting and financial data to create financial statements, reports, and budgets; they perform basic financial management tasks such as balancing a chequebook.	Quicken, QuickBooks
Database programs	Software that searches and retrieves data from a database; it can sort data based on various criteria.	Microsoft Access, Approach
Personal information managers	Specialized database programs that allow people to track communications with personal and business contacts; some combine e-mail capability.	Microsoft Outlook, Lotus Organizer
Enterprise resource planning	Integrated cross-functional software that controls many business activities, including distribution, finance, and human resources.	SAP Enterprise Resource Planning

Application software is a software program that performs the specific tasks that the user wants to carry out—such as writing a letter or looking up data. Examples of application software include Adobe Acrobat, Microsoft PowerPoint, and Quicken. Table 14.1 lists the major categories of application software. Most application programs are stored on individual computers. But the future of applications software is constantly changing. Some believe much of it will become Web-based, with the programs themselves stored in the "cloud," on Internet-connected servers. Others disagree, arguing that most computer users will not want to rely on an Internet connection to perform such tasks as preparing a spreadsheet using Microsoft Excel. The "Going Green" feature explains how some observers believe that cloud computing might help reduce greenhouse gases.

 ASSESSMENT CHECK

14.3.1 List two input and two output devices.

14.3.2 Why are notebook computers so popular?

14.3.3 What is software? List the two categories of software.

CAN **CLOUD COMPUTING ALSO BE "GREEN" COMPUTING?**

The increase in cloud computing has some observers hoping it will also decrease the emission of greenhouse gases. But others are growing concerned that cloud computing will cause emissions to increase because it will lead to larger and larger data storage centres that use more energy.

The environmental organization Greenpeace recently issued the "Cool IT Challenge" to the IT sector. Greenpeace urges firms to reduce emissions by using renewable electricity to power their data

centres. Greenpeace also wants firms to pressure utility companies to improve their access to renewable energy. In a recent report, Greenpeace said that IT energy solutions can even encourage the growth of local, decentralized energy centres as opposed to large grids. These smaller, local networks could result in better energy choices for consumers, improved energy efficiency, and greater use of renewable energy.

Greenpeace has published a chart that rates major data centres' use of power sources. Google's data centre in Oregon was the leading user of renewable energy: almost 51 percent of its energy comes from renewable sources, not from coal and nuclear power.

The Green Grid is a group of IT companies interested in improving energy efficiency. It recently launched a downloadable tool that helps IT professionals lower their overall energy use by using outside air and water to cool their data centres at little or no cost.

Even Greenpeace has come under fire for relying on coal and nuclear energy at some of its data centres, due to long-term agreements with local utilities. Gary Cook, one of the Cool IT Campaign's policy advisors, said, "We're definitely trying to run the greenest operation we can . . . We're in the process of reworking some of our IT infrastructure, and we'll clean that up."

Questions for Critical Thinking

1. Why do devices that rely on cloud computing, such as smartphones or the iPad, contribute to increased greenhouse gas emissions?

2. Will the data centres' voluntary actions be enough to lower greenhouse gas emissions? Why or why not?

Sources: Greenpeace website, http://www.greenpeace.org, accessed May 22, 2010; The Green Grid website, http://www.thegreengrid.org, accessed May 22, 2010; GreenerComputing Staff, "Green Grid Offers Tools for Free Data Center Cooling," *GreenBiz,* April 12, 2010, http://www.greenbiz.com; Rich Miller, "Greenpeace: Cloud Contributes to Climate Change," Data Center Knowledge, March 30, 2010, http://www. datacenterknowledge.com; Matthew Wheeland, "Cloud Computing Is Efficient, But It's Not Green— Yet," *GreenBiz,* March 30, 2010, http://www.greenbiz.com; Rich Miller, "Greenpeace's Hosting: Not 'Truly Green,'" *Data Center Knowledge*, March 3, 2010.

LO 14.4 Describe networking and telecommunications technology and the types of computer networks.

COMPUTER NETWORKS

As mentioned earlier, nearly all computers today are linked to networks. In fact, if your PC has Internet access, you're linked to a network. Local area networks and wide area networks allow businesses to communicate, transmit and print documents, and share data. These networks require businesses to install special equipment and connections between office sites. But Internet technology has also been applied to internal company communications and business tasks, by using a ready-made network. Among these new Internet-based applications are intranets, virtual private networks (VPNs), and voice over Internet protocol (VoIP). Each has contributed to the effectiveness and speed of business processes, so we discuss them next.

local area networks (LANs) computer networks that connect machines within limited areas, such as a building or several nearby buildings.

wide area networks (WANs) computer networks that tie larger geographical regions together by using telephone lines and microwave and satellite transmission.

Local Area Networks and Wide Area Networks

Most organizations connect their offices and buildings by creating **local area networks (LANs)**, computer networks that connect machines within limited areas, such as a building or several nearby buildings. LANs are useful because they link computers and allow them to share printers, documents, and information. LANs also provide access to the Internet. Figure 14.1 shows what a small business computer network might look like.

Wide area networks (WANs) tie larger geographical regions together by using telephone lines, microwave transmission, and satellite transmission. One familiar WAN is long-distance telephone service. Companies such as Bell Canada and Telus provide WAN services to businesses and consumers. Firms also use WANs to conduct their own operations. Typically, companies link their own network systems to outside communications equipment and services for transmission across long distances.

Notebook Computer

Router/Firewall

Notebook Computer

Server

Printer

Desktop Computer   **Desktop Computer**

FIGURE 14.1 A Local Area Network

Wireless Local Networks

A wireless network allows computers, printers, and other devices to be connected without the need for cables that physically link the devices. The current standard for wireless networks is called WiFi, short for *wireless fidelity*. **WiFi** is a wireless network that connects various devices and allows them to communicate with one another through radio waves. Any PC that has a WiFi receptor can connect with the Internet at so-called hot spots—locations with a wireless router and a high-speed Internet modem. There are hundreds of thousands of hot spots around the world. They are found in a variety of places, including college and university campuses, airports, libraries, and coffee shops. Some locations provide free access, while others charge a fee.

WiFi connections are often called *hot spots*—locations with a wireless router and a high-speed Internet modem. There are hundreds of thousands of hot spots around the world. They are found in a variety of places, including college and university campuses, airports, libraries, and coffee shops.

Many believe that WiFi will soon be followed by *Wi-Max*. Unlike WiFi's relatively limited geographic coverage area—generally around 90 metres—a single Wi-Max access point can provide coverage over many kilometres. In addition, cellphone service providers, such as Bell Canada and Rogers, offer broadband network cards for notebook PCs. These devices allow users to access the provider's mobile broadband network from nearly any location where cellphone reception is available.

WiFi a wireless network that connects various devices and allows them to communicate with one another through radio waves.

Intranets

One way to share information in an organization is to set up a company network similar to the Internet. This type of network is called an **intranet**. Intranets are similar to the Internet, but they limit access to authorized users, often an employee group. Intranet users access the system by entering a password. An intranet blocks outsiders who don't have valid passwords by using software and hardware known as a **firewall**. Firewalls limit data transfers to certain locations. They also track system use so that managers can identify threats to the system's security, including attempts to log on with invalid passwords. Highly advanced software will immediately alert system administrators to suspicious activities but will allow authorized personnel to use smart cards to connect from remote terminals.

Intranets solve the problem of linking different types of computers. Like the Internet, intranets can link computers that run different kinds of operating systems. Intranets are relatively easy and inexpensive to set up because most businesses already have some of the required hardware and software. For example, a small business can purchase a DSL router and a few cables to create an intranet using phone jacks and internal phone lines. All the business's computers will be linked to each other and to the Internet.

Intranets also support teamwork among employees who travel or work from home. Any intranet member with the right identification, a PC, and an Internet connection can link to the intranet and gain access to group calendars, e-mail, documents, and other files. Intranets can also be used for videoconferencing and other forms of virtual meetings. Jetstar, an airline serving the Asian Pacific region, has more than 3,000 employees. But three-quarters of them—pilots, cabin crews, and airport staff—will never set foot in the home office. Pilots can visit the company's intranet to access the latest safety information, and home office employees can go online to update the staff directory and transfer paper forms. Corporate and staff communications are transmitted to all employees via Jetstar's intranet. These communications help to build a sense of community among people who may rarely meet in person.[7]

intranet a computer network that is similar to the Internet but limits access to authorized users.

firewall a type of security system for computers that limits data transfers to certain locations; it also tracks system use so that managers can identify threats to the system's security, including attempts to log on with invalid passwords.

Virtual Private Networks

To gain increased security for Internet communications, companies often turn to **virtual private networks (VPNs)**, secure connections between two points on the Internet. These VPNs use firewalls and programs that encrypt, or encode, data to make them more secure during transit. The data are then decrypted, or decoded at the receiving end. In very general terms, a VPN can include a range of networking technologies, from secure Internet connections to private networks from service providers like IBM. A VPN is cheaper for a company to use than leasing several of its own lines. It might take months to install a leased line in some parts of the world, but a new user can be added to a VPN in a day. Because a VPN uses the Internet, it can be wired, wireless, or a combination of the two.

VoIP

VoIP stands for *Voice over Internet Protocol*. It is an alternative to traditional telecommunication services provided by companies such as Bell Canada and Telus. The VoIP telephone is not connected to a traditional phone jack but is connected to a personal computer that has a broadband connection. Special software transmits phone conversations over the Internet, instead of through telephone lines. A VoIP user can access the phone as usual. People can use VoIP to place and receive calls to and from others who have traditional telephone connections (either landline or wireless).

A growing number of consumers and businesses are using VoIP, mainly because of its cost savings and extra features. As technology continues to advance, demand for VoIP has increased. Videotron provides VoIP service to Quebec customers, in addition to providing Internet and cable television services. Google recently announced it is developing its own VoIP service. The various VoIP providers are working together with the goal of creating a single VoIP standard to permit seamless roaming worldwide. This new standard might develop soon, especially since Microsoft acquired the global leader in VoIP technology—Skype.[8]

VoIP has many advantages. But there are also several potential downsides to replacing traditional telephony with Internet telephony. For one thing, an Internet phone service is only as reliable as the broadband connection. If your broadband connection goes out, so will your phone service. Also, without the suitable protection, VoIP can expose a phone system to the threats that can affect the rest of the Internet, such as worms and viruses.

✓ **ASSESSMENT CHECK**

14.4.1 What is a LAN?

14.4.2 What are the differences between an intranet and a VPN?

14.4.3 Briefly explain how VoIP works.

LO 14.5 Discuss the security and ethical issues involving computer information systems.

SECURITY AND ETHICAL ISSUES AFFECTING INFORMATION SYSTEMS

Many security and ethical issues affect information systems. Information systems are becoming more important as business assets; they are also becoming harder and more expensive to replace. Damage to information systems or theft of data can have disastrous results. When computers are connected to a network, a problem at any individual computer can affect the entire network. Two of the major security threats are e-crime and so-called malware.

E-Crime

Computers provide efficient ways for employees to share information. But they may also allow access to information by people who may have criminal intentions. Or they may allow access to private information by pranksters—who have no purpose other than to see whether they can break into a system. Common e-crimes involve stealing or altering data in several ways:

- Employees or outsiders may change or create data to produce inaccurate or misleading information.

- Employees or outsiders may alter computer programs to create false information or illegal transactions or to insert viruses.

- Unauthorized people can access computer systems for their own benefit or knowledge or just to see if they can figure out how to get in.

Individuals, businesses, and government agencies are all vulnerable to computer crime. Computer hackers are unauthorized users. They sometimes work alone and sometimes work in groups. Hackers sometimes break into computer systems just to show that they can do it; other times, they have more disturbing reasons. A recent survey reported that although computer crimes have decreased slightly, many computer crimes may go undetected. Why? Because firms focus on discouraging hackers and blocking pornography but leave themselves open to cybercriminals who are developing increasingly advanced tools. Even Apple computers, which are normally protected from cybercrime, are becoming vulnerable: more and more Mac users now store data in the "cloud"—that is, on the Internet itself, not on their hard drives. Although there is no single uniform system for reporting cybercrime, the Internet Engineering Task Force (IETF) is working toward a common format that will have reliable time stamps, will be available in different languages, and will allow users to attach samples of malicious code. These automated tools will be able to analyze massive amounts of data much faster than human analysts.[9]

Information system administrators use two basic protections against computer crime: they try to prevent access to their systems by unauthorized users and they try to prevent the viewing of data by unauthorized system users. The simplest method of preventing access requires an authorized user to enter a password. The company may also install firewalls, described earlier. To prevent system users from reading sensitive information, the company may use encryption software, which encodes, or scrambles, messages. To read encrypted messages, users must use an electronic key to convert the messages to regular text. But, as fast as software developers invent new and more advanced protective measures, hackers seem to break through their defences. As a result, computer security is an ongoing battle.

Another form of computer theft is as old as crime itself: theft of equipment. Because computers may contain important information for a business, employees need to be especially careful not to leave laptops unattended or within easy reach of others.

As computer hardware becomes smaller, it also becomes more at risk to theft. For example, hand-held devices can easily disappear with a pickpocket or purse snatcher. Many notebook computers and hand-held devices contain special security software or passwords that make it difficult for a thief, or any unauthorized person, to access the computer's data. If you have a notebook computer that contains sensitive personal information, you should consider adding security software.

Computer Viruses, Worms, Trojan Horses, and Spyware

Viruses, worms, Trojan horses, and spyware are collectively referred to as **malware**, malicious software programs designed to infect computer systems. These programs can destroy data, steal sensitive information, and even make it impossible to operate a computer. Recently, malware has been discovered in advertisements on major sites such as Yahoo and Google. Malware attacks cost consumers and businesses billions of dollars every year. Law enforcement has made some progress against cybercrime. But some observers predict that cybercriminals may soon target social-networking sites such as Facebook and Twitter.[10]

malware any malicious software program designed to infect computer systems.

viruses malicious software programs that attach themselves to other programs (called *hosts*) and change them or destroy data.

Computer **viruses** are malicious software programs that attach themselves to other programs (called *hosts*) and change them or destroy data. According to the computer security company Symantec, almost 3 million computer viruses are currently active worldwide.[11] Viruses can be programmed to become active immediately or to remain inactive for a period of time, and then later activate themselves and cause problems. A virus can reproduce by copying itself onto other programs stored in the same drive. It spreads as users install infected software on their systems or exchange files with others, usually by e-mail, by accessing electronic bulletin boards, by trading disks, or by downloading programs or data from unknown sources on the Internet.

worm a small piece of software that uses a security hole in a network to replicate itself.

A **worm** is a small piece of software that uses a security hole in a network to replicate, or copy, itself. A copy of the worm scans the network for another machine that has a specific security hole. It copies itself to the new machine using the security hole and then also starts the same process of copying itself from that machine. Unlike viruses, worms don't need host programs to damage computer systems.

botnet a network of PCs that have been infected with one or more data-stealing viruses.

A **botnet** is a network of PCs that have been infected with one or more data-stealing viruses. Computer criminals tie the infected computers into a network, often without the owners being aware of it, and sell the botnet on the black market. The cybercriminals or others then use the botnet to commit identity theft, send spam, buy blocks of concert tickets for scalping, and attack the Internet itself. About 4,000 to 6,000 botnets are active today. Spanish authorities recently brought down the Mariposa botnet, the world's largest botnet to date—a network of 12.7 million infected computers. Some of the computers were inside *Fortune* 1,000 companies and major banks. Although the authorities made some arrests, the creator of the Mariposa botnet has not been caught.[12]

Trojan horse a program that claims to do one thing but in reality does something else, usually something malicious.

A **Trojan horse** is a program that claims to do one thing but in reality does something else, usually something malicious. For example, a Trojan horse might claim to be a game. But when a user clicks on the Trojan horse to launch it, the program might erase the hard drive or steal personal data stored on the computer.

spyware software that gathers user information through the user's Internet connection without his or her knowledge, usually for advertising purposes.

Spyware is software that gathers user information through the user's Internet connection without his or her knowledge, usually for advertising purposes. Spyware applications are typically bundled with other programs downloaded from the Internet. Once installed, the spyware monitors user activity on the Internet and transmits that information in the background to someone else.

Attacks by malware are not limited to computers and computer networks; hand-held devices, including cellphones, have also been affected. Smartphone users have reported a sharp increase in viruses, worms, and other forms of malware.[13]

Recently, a group of computer scientists cracked the security system that is used in 80 percent of the world's cellphones. The scientists said it was relatively easy and that they did it to encourage development of more advanced security.[14]

As viruses, worms, botnets, and Trojan horses become more complex, the technology to fight them must also become more complex. The simplest way to protect against computer viruses is to install one of the many available antivirus software programs, such as Norton AntiVirus and McAfee VirusScan. These programs also protect against worms and some Trojan horses. Antivirus software programs continuously monitor systems for viruses and automatically get rid of any they spot. Users should regularly update their antivirus software by downloading the latest virus definitions. Computer users should also install and regularly update antispyware programs because many Trojan horses are forms of spyware.

But management must begin to emphasize security at a deeper level: during software design, in corporate servers, at Web gateways, and through Internet service providers. Because more than 90 percent of the world's PCs run on Microsoft operating systems, a single virus, worm, or Trojan horse can quickly spread among PCs. Individual computer users should carefully choose the files they load onto their systems, scan their systems regularly, keep their antivirus software up-to-date, and install only software from known sources. They should also be very careful when opening e-mail attachments from unknown sources because many viruses, worms, and Trojan horses are spread that way.

Information Systems and Ethics

The scope and power of today's information systems raise many ethical issues and concerns. These ethical issues affect both employees and organizations. For example, organizations often have specific ethical standards and policies regarding the use of information systems by employees and vendors. These standards include obligations to protect system security and the privacy and confidentiality of data. Policies may also cover employees' personal use of computers and related technologies, both hardware and software.

Ethical issues also involve an organization's use of information systems. Organizations have an obligation to protect the privacy and confidentiality of data on employees and customers. Employment records contain sensitive personal information, such as bank account numbers. If this information is not protected, it could lead to identity theft. Another ethical issue is the use of computer technology to monitor employees while they are working. The "Solving an Ethical Controversy" feature debates the issue of employee monitoring.

ASSESSMENT CHECK

14.5.1 Explain computer hacking.

14.5.2 What is malware?

14.5.3 How does a computer virus work?

SOLVING AN **ETHICAL** CONTROVERSY

Should Employers Monitor Employees' Internet Use?

According to an American Management Association/ePolicy Institute survey, two-thirds of employers monitor employees' use of the Internet. Technology now allows employers to check which websites their employees visit on company time, the pattern of keystrokes on individual computers, and the amount of time spent online. Employers can even use GPS-enabled phones to track employees.

For most employees, on-the-job access to the Internet and e-mail is a necessity. In some workplaces, employees need to do a certain amount of Internet surfing for research purposes. A company's Facebook page can be either a powerful marketing tool or a liability if employees use their own social media sites to complain about the company.

Should employers monitor their employees' time online?

PRO

1. Surveys estimate that employees spend between one and two hours every day online for personal use. Some employees perform innocent tasks such as banking, but others visit inappropriate websites. Either way, those online hours mean lost productivity for the company.

2. Inappropriate use of office computers can leave a company vulnerable to hacking, viruses, and other security threats.

CON

1. Some employers are concerned that if they monitor employees, they could risk losing a workplace atmosphere of trust, commitment, and motivation.

2. Employees have a reasonable concern about privacy, especially if they have not been informed beforehand that their online activities are being monitored.

Summary

Although the law clearly gives employers the right to monitor computer activity, many debate the acceptable range of monitoring a worker's use of a company-provided device. Most analysts suggest that companies should establish clear policies on computer, Internet, and e-mail use. They should train employees, have them sign a document stating that they understand the policies, and then trust their employees to do the right thing.

Sources: "How Do Employers Monitor Internet Usage at Work," *wiseGEEK*, http://www.wisegeek.com, accessed May 23, 2010; Susan M. Heathfield, "Electronic Surveillance of Employees," *About.com* Human Resources, http://humanresources.about.com, accessed May 23, 2010; Karen Codere, "Managing Social Media in the Workplace," *The Business Ledger*, April 28, 2010, http://www.thebusinessledger.com; Laura Petrecca, "More Employers Use Tech to Track Workers," *USA Today*, March 17, 2010, http://www.usatoday.com.

DISASTER RECOVERY AND BACKUP

LO 14.6 Explain the steps that companies go through in anticipating, planning for, and recovering from information systems disasters.

FalconStor is an IT firm that specializes in servicing engineering companies. FalconStor sets up a system of backups stored on remote servers, which are then transferred to tape and stored off-site.

Even the most advanced computer information systems can be disrupted by natural disasters, power failures, equipment malfunctions, software glitches, human error, and terrorist attacks. These disruptions can cost businesses and other organizations billions of dollars. Even more serious outcomes can occur. For example, one recent study found that more than 93 percent of firms that lost their data centres for 10 days or more went bankrupt within six months.[15]

Disaster recovery planning is a critical function of all organizations. It refers to planning how to prevent computer system failures and planning how to continue operations if computer systems do fail. Disaster prevention programs can avoid some costly problems. The most basic precaution is routinely backing up software and data—at the organizational level and the individual level. But the organization's data centre cannot be the only place where critical data is stored because a single location is vulnerable to threats from both natural and human-caused disasters. As a result, off-site data backup is a necessity, whether in a separate physical location or online on the Internet itself. Companies that do online backups store the encrypted data in secure facilities that also have their own backups. The initial backup may take a day or more, but later backups will take far less time because they usually involve backing up only new or revised files.

According to security experts, an organization has five important tasks when considering off-site data storage. First is planning. The organization needs to decide what data need to be protected. Priority should be given to data that would lead to extreme legal or business consequences if they were lost. Second, a backup schedule must be set up and closely followed. Third, when data are transmitted off-site, they must be protected by the highest level of security possible. Fourth, care should be taken in selecting the right security vendor. Dozens of vendors offer different services in different areas of expertise. Finally, the backup system should be continually tested and evaluated.

✓ ASSESSMENT CHECK

14.6.1 What types of disasters are information systems vulnerable to?

14.6.2 List an organization's tasks when it is considering off-site data storage.

LO 14.7 Review the current trends in information systems.

INFORMATION SYSTEM TRENDS

Computer information systems are continually and rapidly changing. Firms that want to keep their information systems up-to-date must keep up-to-date with changes in technology. Some of the most significant trends in information systems include the growing demands of the so-called distributed workforce, the increased use of application service providers, on-demand computing, and cloud and grid computing.

The Distributed Workforce

As discussed in earlier chapters, many companies are relying more and more on a *distributed workforce*—employees who no longer work in traditional offices but work in *virtual offices*, including at home. Information technology makes a distributed workforce possible. Computers, networks, and other components of information systems make it possible for many workers to do their jobs almost anywhere. For example, none of JetBlue's reservations agents work in offices; they all work at home, connected to the airline's information system. JetBlue is not alone in its use of home-based workers. Boeing, Starbucks, Agilent Technologies, Sun Microsystems, and many other companies maintain virtual offices with thousands of workers. According to recent research, about 10 percent of North American full-time wage and salary workers work at home on any given day. Of the self-employed workforce, more than one-third work at home on any given day.[16] Statistics show that most at-home workers use computers and related technologies. Virtual offices can range from a mailing address, mail forwarding, and a phone answering service to a full office, usually leased by the month. The increasing demands of the distributed workforce will likely lead to more innovative and increasingly powerful information systems.

Application Service Providers

Many firms find that it makes sense to outsource at least some of their information technology functions. Because of the increasing cost and complexity of obtaining and maintaining information systems, many firms hire an **application service provider (ASP)**, an outside supplier that provides both the computers and the application support for managing an information system. An ASP can simplify complex software for its customers so that it is easier for them to manage and use. When an ASP relationship is successful, the buyer can then devote more time and resources to its core businesses instead of trying to manage its information systems. Firms that use an ASP can also make their technology dollar stretch farther. Smaller companies who use an ASP can now access the kind of information power that was previously available only to larger organizations. Even large companies turn to ASPs to manage some or all of their information systems. Recently, Microsoft outsourced much of its internal information technology (IT) services to Infosys Technology to save money and to streamline, simplify, and support its services.[17]

Companies that decide to use ASPs should check the backgrounds and references of these firms before hiring one to manage critical systems. Customers should also ensure that the service provider has strong security measures to block computer hackers or other unauthorized access to the data, that its data centres are running reliably, and that adequate data and applications backups are maintained.

application service provider (ASP) an outside supplier that provides both the computers and the application support for managing an information system.

On-Demand, Cloud, and Grid Computing

Another recent trend is **on-demand computing**, also called *utility computing*. Instead of purchasing and maintaining expensive software, firms rent the software time from application providers. They pay only for their usage of the software, similar to purchasing electricity from a utility. On-demand computing is especially useful for firms that have annual peaks in demand or have seasonal increases in their use of an application. By renting the service they need only when they need it, customers can avoid buying software that is not needed frequently. By using on-demand computing, companies remain current with the most efficient software and avoid having to purchase huge upgrades.

Cloud computing uses powerful servers to store applications software and databases. Users access the software and databases via the Web. They can use any Internet-connected device, such as a PC or a smartphone. The software as a service (SaaS) movement is an example of cloud computing. The "Hit & Miss" feature describes how Cisco Systems provides security for cloud-based applications.

on-demand computing the use of software time from application providers; firms pay only for their usage of the software, not for purchasing or maintaining the software.

cloud computing the use of powerful servers that store applications software and databases that users access by using any Internet-connected device, such as a PC or a smartphone.

HIT & MISS

Cisco Systems Tackles Cloud Security

More and more businesses are managing increasing amounts of e-mail and storing increasing amounts of data. Many save money and physical space by turning to cloud computing and storage, including software as a service (SaaS). Instead of installing software on site, a business can use SaaS to access software over the Internet either by subscription or by using a "pay as you go" plan. These businesses also need to protect their databanks from computer crime. In a traditional local area network, security applications are relatively easy to set up at the network's borders. But this challenge is made more difficult by the borderless environment of cloud computing and because of increasing threats to online security.

Cisco Systems has responded by developing security applications for cloud-based computing. One application directs a business's Web traffic to security towers located in 100 countries around the world. These locations use layers of antivirus and antimalware utilities to scan websites and quickly block access to any websites that have been infected.

Another application offers both cloud-based and on-site e-mail security. The cloud-based application deletes spam and viruses. The on-site application provides data-loss prevention, e-mail encryption, and other services. Another e-mail encryption service provides cloud-based encryption for locally stored messages.

Other applications support security for off-site workers who use desktops computers, laptops, tablets, and smartphones. One feature addresses the problem that occurs when an employee leaves a business. With one click of the mouse, an administrator can disable the departing employee's access to every SaaS application he or she ever used. And the administrator can use another click to set up access for a new employee.

As the vice-president and general manager of Cisco's security technology unit states, "Securing the cloud is highly challenging. But it is one of the top challenges that the industry must rise to meet."

Questions for Critical Thinking

1. What are some pros and cons of storing data "in the cloud"?

2. Why is it important to block a former employee's access to company data, e-mail, or applications?

Sources: Company website, *News@Cisco* press release, http://www.cisco.com, accessed June 4, 2010; James Urquhart, "Cloud Computing and the Economy," *CNET News*, April 13, 2010, http://news.cnet.com; Margaret Steen, "Cloud Services and SaaS: A Smarter Way to Do Business," *Cisco News*, March 29, 2010, http://newsroom.cisco.com; Stuart Young, Andy Taylor, and James Macaulay, "Small Businesses Ride the Cloud: SMB Cloud Watch—U.S. Survey Results," Cisco Internet Business Solutions Group, February 2010, http://www.cisco.com; Mike Kirkwood, "Rulers of the Cloud: Will Cloud Computing Be the Second Coming of Cisco?" *ReadWriteWeb*, February 19, 2010, http://www.readwriteweb.com.

---

grid computing a network of smaller computers that run special software.

✓ ASSESSMENT CHECK

14.7.1 What is an application service provider?

14.7.2 Explain on-demand computing.

Small and medium-size companies occasionally find themselves with jobs that require more computing power than their current systems offer. A cost-effective solution for these firms may be **grid computing**, a network of smaller computers running special software. The software breaks down a large, complex job into smaller tasks and then distributes the tasks to the networked computers. The software then reassembles the results of the individual tasks into the finished job. By combining multiple small computers, grid computing creates a virtual mainframe or even a supercomputer.

WHAT'S AHEAD

Part 5 was devoted to managing technology and information. Part 6 is about managing financial resources in contemporary business and the next chapter, "Understanding Accounting and Financial Statements," focuses on accounting, financial information, and financing reporting. Accounting is the process of measuring, interpreting, and communicating financial information to enable people inside and outside the firm to make informed decisions. The chapter describes the functions of accounting and role of accountants; the steps in the accounting cycle; the types, functions, and components of financial statements; and the role of budgets in an organization.

RETURN TO INSIDE BUSINESS

Stock-Trak: Learning about the Stock Market through Simulation

A major competitive advantage for Stock-Trak is its use of real-time financial information to provide learners with a Web-based stock market simulation. Price changes and analytical reports are sent online to users with little delay, only slightly behind the times that the same data and information are provided to real traders. Stock-Trak traders pay large subscription fees to receive this information so they can learn to make more intelligent trading decisions. The simulation provides a real-time learning experience that is as close to reality as the learner can expect to get. Stock-Trak is looking for ways to grow its business, such as by partnering with organizations that can deliver a large group of users.

QUESTIONS FOR CRITICAL THINKING

1. Which other organizations or groups should Stock-Trak consider partnering with? Why?

2. What other educational products or services could Stock-Trak develop?

SUMMARY OF LEARNING OBJECTIVES

LO 14.1 Distinguish between data and information, and explain the role of information systems in business.

Businesspeople need to understand the difference between data and information. Data are raw facts and figures that may or may not be relevant, or meaningful, to a business decision. Information is knowledge gained from processing those facts and figures. An information system is an organized method for collecting, storing, and communicating past, present, and projected information on internal operations and external intelligence. Most information systems today use computer and telecommunications technology.

 ASSESSMENT CHECK ANSWERS

14.1.1 Distinguish between data and information. Data consist of raw facts and figures that may or may not be relevant to a decision. Information is the knowledge gained from processing data.

14.1.2 What is an information system? An information system is an organized method for collecting, storing, and communicating past, present, and projected information on internal operations and external intelligence.

LO 14.2 List the components and different types of information systems.

When people think about information systems, they generally think of computer-based systems, information systems that use computers and related technologies. Computer-based information systems rely on four components: computer hardware, software, telecommunications and computer networks, and data resource management. The heart of an information system is its database, a centralized integrated collection of data resources. Information systems fall into one of two broad categories: operational support systems or management support systems.

Operational support systems are designed to produce a variety of information for users. Examples include transaction processing systems and process control systems. Management support systems are designed to support effective decision-making. They include management information systems, decision support systems, executive support systems, and expert systems.

 ASSESSMENT CHECK ANSWERS

14.2.1 List the four components of a computer-based information system. The four components of a computer-based information system are computer hardware, software, telecommunications and computer networks, and data resource management.

14.2.2 What is a database? A database is a centralized, integrated collection of data resources.

14.2.3 What are the two general types of information systems? Give examples of each. The two categories of information systems are operational support systems (such as transactions processing systems and process control systems) and management support systems (such as management information systems, decision support systems, executive support systems, and expert systems).

LO 14.3 Outline how computer hardware and software are used to manage information.

Hardware consists of all tangible, or physical, elements of a computer system, including input and output devices. Major categories of computers include mainframes, supercomputers, midrange systems, personal computers (PCs), and hand-held devices. Computer software provides the instructions that tell the hardware what to do. The operating system is the software that controls the basic workings of the computer. Other programs, called application software, perform specific tasks that users want to complete.

✓ ASSESSMENT CHECK ANSWERS

14.3.1 List two input devices and two output devices. Input devices include the keyboard and mouse. Output devices include the monitor and printer.

14.3.2 Why are notebook computers so popular? Notebook computers represent more than half of all new personal computers sold. Their increased popularity is due to better displays, lower prices, more rugged designs, increasing computing power, and slimmer designs.

14.3.3 What is software? List the two categories of software. Computer software provides the instructions that tell the hardware what to do. The two categories of software are the operating system and application software. The operating system is the software that controls the basic workings of the computer. Application software performs the specific tasks that users want to complete.

LO 14.4 Describe networking and telecommunications technology and the types of computer networks.

Local area networks connect computers within a limited area. Wide area networks tie larger geographical regions together by using telephone lines, microwave transmission, or satellite transmission. A wireless network allows computers to communicate through radio waves. Intranets allow employees to share information on a company network. Access to an intranet is restricted to authorized users and is protected by a firewall. Virtual private networks (VPNs) provide a secure Internet connection between two or more points. VoIP—voice over Internet protocol—uses a personal computer running special software and a broadband Internet connection to make and receive telephone calls over the Internet, instead of using traditional telephone networks.

✓ ASSESSMENT CHECK ANSWERS

14.4.1 What is a LAN? A LAN is a local area network, a computer network that connects machines within a limited area, such as a building or several nearby buildings.

14.4.2 What are the differences between an intranet and a VPN? An intranet is a computer network similar to the Internet. Unlike the Internet, access to an intranet is limited to employees or other authorized users. A virtual private network (VPN) is a secure connection between two points on the Internet.

14.4.3 Briefly explain how VoIP works. The VoIP phone is connected to a personal computer that has a broadband connection. Special software transmits phone conversations over the Internet. A VoIP user can place and receive calls to and from others who have traditional telephone connections (either landline or wireless).

LO 14.5 Discuss the security and ethical issues involving computer information systems.

Many security and ethical issues affect information systems. Two of the main security threats are e-crime and malware. E-crimes range from hacking—unauthorized access to an information system—to the theft of hardware. Malware is any malicious software program designed to infect computer systems. Examples include viruses, worms, botnets, Trojan horses, and spyware. Ethical issues affecting information systems include the proper use of the systems by authorized users. Organizations also have an obligation to employees, vendors, and customers to protect the security and confidentiality of the data stored in information systems.

✓ ASSESSMENT CHECK ANSWERS

14.5.1 Explain computer hacking. Computer hacking refers to unauthorized people gaining illegal access to a computer system. Sometimes the hackers' purpose is just to see whether they can get into the system. Other times, hackers have more disturbing reasons, such as stealing or altering data.

14.5.2 What is malware? Malware is any malicious software program designed to infect computer systems.

14.5.3 How does a computer virus work? A virus is a program that attaches itself to another program (called a host). The virus then changes the host, destroys data, or even makes it impossible to operate the computer system.

LO 14.6 Explain the steps that companies go through in anticipating, planning for, and recovering from information systems disasters.

Information system disasters may be caused by humans or may result from natural causes. Such disasters can cost businesses billions of dollars. The impact of a disaster can be decreased by routinely backing up software and data, both at an organizational level and at an individual level. Organizations should back up critical data at an off-site location. Some organizations may also want to invest in extra hardware and software sites, which can be accessed during emergencies.

✓ ASSESSMENT CHECK ANSWERS

14.6.1 What types of disasters are information systems vulnerable to? Even the most powerful and advanced computer information systems can be disrupted by natural disasters, power failures, equipment malfunctions, software glitches, human error, and even terrorist attacks.

14.6.2 List an organization's tasks when it is considering off-site data storage. The five tasks are planning and deciding which data to back up, establishing and following a backup schedule, protecting data when they are transmitted off-site, choosing the right vendor, and continually testing and refining the backup system.

LO 14.7 Review the current trends in information systems.

Computer information systems are continually and rapidly evolving. Some of the most significant trends are the increasing demands of the distributed workforce, the increased use of application service providers, on-demand computing, and grid computing. Many people now work in virtual offices, including at home. Information technology makes this work arrangement possible. Application service providers allow organizations to outsource many of their IT functions. Instead of buying and maintaining expensive software, users of on-demand computing rent software time from outside vendors and pay only for their usage. Grid computing consists of a network of smaller computers running special software creating a virtual mainframe or even supercomputer.

 ASSESSMENT CHECK ANSWERS

14.7.1 What is an application service provider? An application service provider (ASP) is an outside vendor that provides both the computers and the application support for managing an information system. By using an ASP, the organization can effectively outsource some, or all, of its IT function.

14.7.2 Explain on-demand computing. Instead of purchasing and maintaining expensive software, some organizations use on-demand computing. In this arrangement, software is rented from a vendor and the organization only pays for its actual usage.

BUSINESS TERMS YOU NEED TO KNOW

data 392

information 392

information system 392

chief information officer (CIO) 392

computer-based information systems 393

database 394

operational support systems 395

transaction processing systems 395

process control systems 395

management support systems 395

management information system (MIS) 395

decision support system (DSS) 395

executive support system (ESS) 396

expert system 396

hardware 396

server 397

software 398

local area networks (LANs) 400

wide area networks (WANs) 400

WiFi 401

intranet 401

firewall 401

virtual private networks (VPNs) 402

VoIP 402

malware 403

viruses 404

worm 404

botnet 404

Trojan horse 404

spyware 404

application service provider (ASP) 407

on-demand computing 407

cloud computing 407

grid computing 408

REVIEW QUESTIONS

1. Distinguish between data and information. Why is this difference important to businesspeople who manage information?

2. What are the four components of an information system?

3. Describe the two different types of information systems, and give an example of how each type might help a specific business.

4. Explain decision support systems, executive support systems, and expert systems.

5. What are the major categories of computers? What is a smartphone?

6. What is an intranet? Give specific examples of the benefits for firms that have their own intranets.

7. What steps can organizations and individuals take to prevent computer crime?

8. How does a computer virus work? What can individuals and organizational computer users do to reduce the likelihood of acquiring a computer virus?

9. Why is disaster recovery important for businesses? Relate your answer to a natural disaster such as a hurricane or fire.

10. Describe four information system trends.

PROJECTS AND TEAMWORK APPLICATIONS

1. Suppose you've been hired to design an information system for a midsize retailer. Describe what that information system might look like, including the necessary components. Would the system be an operational support system, a management support system, or both?

2. Select a local company and contact the person in charge of its information system for a brief interview. Ask that individual to outline his or her company's information system. Ask the person what he or she likes most about the job. Did this interview make you more or less interested in a career in information systems?

3. Working with a partner, research the current status of Wi-Max. Prepare a short report on its growth, its current uses, and its future for business computing.

4. Your supervisor has asked for your advice. She isn't sure the company's information system needs any major safeguards because the company has very little Web presence beyond a simple home page. But employees use e-mail to contact suppliers and customers. List the threats that the company's information system is vulnerable to. What types of protection would you suggest?

5. Has your computer ever been hacked or attacked by a virus? What steps did you take to recover lost files and data? How would you prevent something similar from happening again?

WEB ASSIGNMENTS

1. Operational support systems. Go to the website http://www.tradeinsight.com/what-is-tradeinsight and watch the videos at http://www.youtube.com/watch?v5N5QcU6TgrTQ&list5UUiaWYUxHK1ssmwEsvBDEMBg&index52&feature5plcp and http://www.tradeinsight.com/about-us. Prepare a brief report on what you learned about the advantages of operational support system software.

2. Computer security. Visit the website listed below. Review the material and answer the following questions:

a. What are two current malware threats? How serious are they?

b. What is a potentially unwanted program (PUP)? What are two recent PUPs?

   http://www.mcafee.com

3. Cloud computing. IBM is one of the largest providers of cloud computing. Visit the IBM website (http://www.ibm.com) and click on "Solutions" and then select "Cloud computing." Print out the material and bring it to class to participate in a class discussion on the subject.

www.wileyplus.com

Access your WileyPLUS course for:

- The complete digital textbook.

- Question assistance, including links to relevant sections in the online digital textbook.

- Immediate feedback and proof of progress, 24/7

- Integrated, multi-media resources – including MP3 downloads, visual exhibits, animations, and much more – that provide multiple study paths and encourage more active learning.

QUIZ YOURSELF

Note: Internet Web addresses change frequently. If you don't find the exact sites listed, you may need to access the organization's home page and search from there or use a search engine such as Bing or Google.

5 LAUNCHING YOUR . . .

INFORMATION TECHNOLOGY CAREER

Part 5, "Managing Technology and Information," consists of Chapter 14. This chapter discussed using computers and related technology to manage information. We discussed well-known technology companies such as Google and Oracle and many smaller organizations that use computer technology to manage information. These examples show that all organizations need to manage technology and information. The complexity and scope of technology and information are likely to increase in the years ahead. As a result, the demand for information systems professionals is expected to grow.

According to research, employment in occupations such as computer software engineering, software support specialists, and network systems administrators is expected to grow faster than the average for all occupations in the next decade. Of the top five occupations where employment is expected to grow the fastest over the next few years, two occupations are related to information systems.[1]

What types of jobs are available in information systems? What are the working conditions like? What are the career paths? Experience in information systems can lead to a wide variety of jobs. In some cases, you'll work in the information systems department of a business such as Enbridge. In other cases, you may work for a specialized information systems firm, such as IBM. A specialized firm provides information services to governments, not-for-profit organizations, and businesses.

Information systems is a popular business major, and many entry-level positions are available each year. Many information systems graduates spend their entire careers in this field, while some move into other areas. People who began their careers in information systems are well represented in senior management positions. Let's look briefly at some of the specific jobs you might find after earning a degree in information systems.

Technical support specialists are troubleshooters who monitor the performance of computer systems; provide technical support and solve problems for computer users; install, modify, clean, and repair computer hardware and software; and write training manuals and train computer users.

Network administrators design, install, and support an organization's computer networks, including its local area network, wide area network, Internet, and intranet systems. They provide administrative support for software and hardware users and ensure that the design of an organization's computer networks and all of the components fit together efficiently and effectively.

Computer security specialists plan, coordinate, and implement an organization's information security. They educate users about how to protect computer systems, install antivirus and similar software, and monitor the networks for security breaches. In recent years, the role and importance of computer security specialists have increased in response to the growing number of attacks on networks and data.

CAREER ASSESSMENT EXERCISES IN INFORMATION SYSTEMS

1. Assume you're interested in a career as a systems administrator. Go to the following website: http://www.itworldcanada.com. Prepare a brief report outlining the responsibilities of a systems administrator, the employers that hire for these positions, and the educational background needed.

2. Examine the website for Trade Insight Inc.: http://www.tradeinsight.com/. Read a few of the case studies. Write a brief report about how the firm's software helps clients to better understand their sales and marketing data.

© Can Stock Photo Inc./monkeybusiness

PART 6
MANAGING FINANCIAL RESOURCES

15 | UNDERSTANDING ACCOUNTING AND FINANCIAL STATEMENTS

LEARNING OBJECTIVES

LO 15.1 Explain the functions of accounting, and identify the three basic activities involving accounting.

LO 15.2 Describe the roles played by public, management, government, and not-for-profit accountants.

LO 15.3 Identify the foundations of the accounting system, including GAAP, IFRS, and the role of the Accounting Standards Board (AcSB).

LO 15.4 Outline the steps in the accounting cycle, and define *double-entry book-keeping* and the *accounting equation*.

LO 15.5 Explain the functions and major components of the four principal financial statements: the balance sheet, the income statement, the statement of changes in equity, and the statement of cash flows.

LO 15.6 Discuss how financial ratios are used to analyze a company's financial strengths and weaknesses.

LO 15.7 Describe the role of budgets in a business.

LO 15.8 Outline the accounting issues facing global business.

INSIDE BUSINESS

Cooking the Books

Charla Jones/Globe and Mail/The Canadian Press

Imagine it is a few weeks after year end. The financial statements have been prepared by a team of experienced accountants. They've also been audited by another team of experienced auditors. This *must* mean that the statements are correct. After all, how complicated can accounting be? The numbers are either right or wrong. These are common misconceptions—or misunderstandings—about the nature of accounting information. Accountants have quite a bit of flexibility when preparing financial statements. But they always need to stay within the limits of generally accepted accounting principles.

Accountants make choices about *when* to recognize, or record, revenue and expenses on the financial statements. For example, suppose the publisher of this textbook sells 100 copies of the textbook to your school bookstore with the option to return any books not purchased by students. When will the publisher's accountant recognize, or record, the revenue? Is it recognized when the books are delivered, or when the books are sold to students? Accountants also estimate how much bad debt or depreciation expense to charge against income in a given year. For example, when a company buys a delivery van, over how many years is the van depreciated? The more years the van is depreciated over, the lower the expense each year. Many people who prepare financial statements choose policies and make estimates at the high or low end of the acceptable ranges. Sometimes, the decision comes down to an individual's personal motivations. Some individuals may want to increase their bonus, which may be tied to the company's net income; or, they may want to lower their income taxes, which may also be based on net income.

Some financial statement preparers go far beyond the prescribed ranges. They commit fraud by changing the statements and providing false information for their personal gain.

One well-known Canadian fraud case involved Livent co-founders Garth Drabinsky and Myron Gottlieb. Both were found guilty of forgery and defrauding their investors of more than $400 million. The two ran Livent, a theatre production company that produced some of Canada's best-known theatrical productions, including Canada's longest running musical at the time, *The Phantom of the Opera*. Part of the Livent scheme involved moving expenses from one period to another, or allocating expenses to certain shows that they did not relate to. Drabinsky was sentenced to seven years, and Gottlieb was sentenced to six years. They were released on $350,000 bail, while waiting to file an appeal.

In the United States, the energy company Enron filed for bankruptcy in 2001. The Enron case was known as one of the world's biggest audit failures. Enron hid billions of dollars in debt by not recording it on the financial statements. Shortly after the Enron case, another fraud case was revealed. It was discovered that corporate executives at the telecommunications company WorldCom were also "cooking the books." They had been recording many expenses as assets and had inflated revenues by using creative accounting. These well-known accounting scandals resulted in the world's largest bankruptcies at the time.

These major fraud cases led to the creation of increased regulatory legislation, such as the Sarbanes-Oxley Act in the United States and Bill 198 in Canada. Canadian, American, and global companies are now required to spend billions of dollars to remain in compliance with these new legislations.[1]

CHAPTER 15 OVERVIEW

Accounting professionals prepare the financial information that organizations present in their annual reports. Whether you begin your career by working for a company or by starting your own firm, you need to understand what accountants do. You also need to understand why their work is so important in contemporary business.

Accounting is the process of measuring, interpreting, and communicating financial information to enable people inside and outside the firm to make informed decisions. In many ways, accounting is the language of business. Accountants gather, record, report, and interpret financial information in a way that describes the status and operation of an organization and aids in decision-making.

Millions of men and women around the world are employed as accountants. In Canada, more than 180,000 people work as accountants or auditors.[2] Accounting is one of the most in-demand disciplines on university campuses. Part of the attraction is the availability of jobs and the high starting salaries for talented graduates. In Canada, salaries for Chartered Accountants (CAs) average more than $186,000 per year. First-year CAs average just under $75,000 per year.[3]

This chapter begins by describing who uses accounting information. We then discuss business activities that involve accounting statements: financing, investing, and operations. Next, we explain the accounting process, define double-entry bookkeeping, and present the accounting equation. We then discuss how information about financial transactions is developed into financial statements. Next we look at the methods of interpreting these statements and the role of budgeting when planning and controlling a business. The chapter concludes with a discussion of the impact of financial information in global business.

accounting the process of measuring, interpreting, and communicating financial information to support internal and external business decision-making.

LO 15.1 Explain the functions of accounting, and identify the three basic activities involving accounting.

USERS OF ACCOUNTING INFORMATION

Both people inside an organization and people outside an organization use accounting information to help them make business decisions. Figure 15.1 lists the users of accounting information and how they apply that information.

FIGURE 15.1 Users and Applications of Accounting Information

The major users of accounting information are managers at a business, government agency, or not-for-profit organization. Accounting information helps them to plan and control daily and long-range operations. Business owners and boards of directors at not-for-profit groups also use accounting data to track managers' progress in operating the organizations. Union officials use accounting data in contract negotiations, and employees refer to it as they monitor their firms' productivity and profitability performance.

Some companies want employees to understand how their work affects the company's bottom line. These companies share sensitive financial information with their employees and teach them how to understand and use financial statements. People who support *open-book management* believe that allowing employees to view financial information helps them to better understand how their work contributes to the company's success, which, in turn, benefits the employees.

Outside a firm, potential investors evaluate accounting information to help them decide whether to buy a firm's stock. As we'll discuss later in the chapter, any company whose stock is traded publicly must report its financial results on a regular basis. That means that anyone can look up RONA's sales last year or how much money Research In Motion made during the last quarter. Bankers and other lenders use accounting information to evaluate a potential borrower's financial soundness. The Canada Revenue Agency (CRA) and provincial tax officials use it to calculate a company's tax liability. Citizens' groups and government agencies use accounting information to assess the efficiency of such operations as Alberta Health Services, BC Hydro, and the Art Gallery of Ontario.

Accountants play important roles in business and in many other aspects of society. Their work influences each of the business environments discussed earlier in this book. Accountants clearly provide important information to help managers deal with the competitive and economic environments.

Some other accounting contributions are less obvious, or less noticed, such as helping others to understand, predict, and react to the technological, regulatory, and social and cultural environments. For example, every year, thousands of volunteers help Canadians to complete their income tax returns. One of the largest organized programs is the Community Volunteer Income Tax Program (CVITP), organized by the CRA. Through this program, more than 16,000 volunteers help more than half a million Canadians to complete their provincial and federal tax returns.

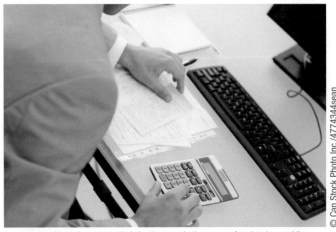

Accountants play an important role in business and other areas of society by providing services to businesses, individuals, government agencies, and not-for-profit organizations.

Business Activities Involving Accounting

The natural progression of a business begins with financing. All the steps after financing, including investing, lead to operating the business. All organizations, for-profit and not-for-profit, perform these three basic activities, and accounting plays a key role in each:

1. Financing activities provide necessary funds to start a business and expand it after it begins operating.

2. Investing activities provide valuable assets that are needed to run a business.

3. Operating activities focus on selling goods and services, but they also view expenses as important elements of sound financial management.

Brian Hill, CEO of Vancouver-based Aritzia, performed all three activities during the start-up and growth of his high-fashion chain. Aritzia targets women between the ages of 15 and 30. Hill's success in Canada led to a major U.S. expansion. Hill could have tried to finance the expansion himself, as he had done before. But he wanted to avoid the financial risk that he had taken on before, when Aritzia was growing. Hill decided to seek financing from Berkshire Partners, who took a majority stake in the company. Aritzia recently moved toward a more vertically integrated model. He chose this model to benefit from "a bigger piece of the pie" by cutting out a third-party retailer. He also made this choice for strategic reasons: Hill believes that part of Aritzia's success is that the company understands customers' needs. He feels that if he and his company are involved at the point of sale, they will have a better feel for the needs of the customers. This strategy has proved very successful thus far.[4]

✓ **ASSESSMENT CHECK**

15.1.1 Define *accounting*.

15.1.2 Who uses accounting information?

15.1.3 What three business activities involve accounting?

LO 15.2 Describe the roles played by public, management, government, and not-for-profit accountants.

ACCOUNTING PROFESSIONALS

Accounting professionals work in many areas in and for business firms, government agencies, and not-for-profit organizations. They can be classified as public accountants, management accountants, government accountants, and not-for-profit accountants.

Public Accountants

public accountant an accountant who provides accounting services to other organizations.

A **public accountant** provides accounting services to individuals or business firms for a fee. Most public accounting firms provide three basic services to clients: (1) auditing, or examining, financial records; (2) tax preparation, planning, and related services; and (3) management consulting. Because public accountants are not employees of a client firm, they can provide unbiased advice about a firm's financial condition.

Canada has hundreds of public accounting firms, but just a few firms attract the largest share of the industry. The four largest public accounting firms—Deloitte, Ernst & Young, KPMG, and PricewaterhouseCoopers—collect almost $4 billion annually from Canadian clients. In contrast, the Toronto-based Grant Thornton, the nation's fifth-largest accounting firm, has annual revenues of approximately $409 million.[5]

Some years ago, public accounting firms were criticized for providing management consulting services to the same firms they audited. Critics argued that when a public accounting firm does both—auditing and management consulting—a conflict of interest is created. This conflict of interest may weaken confidence in the quality of the financial statements that accounting firms audit. The bankruptcies of some high-profile firms increased pressure on public accounting firms to end the practice. Legislation also set strict limits on the types of consulting services auditors can provide. For example, an accounting firm that audits a company's books cannot provide any other services to that company, including tax services. As a result, three of the four largest public accounting firms either sold large portions of their consulting practices or created separate consulting companies. PricewaterhouseCoopers, for example, sold much of its consulting business to IBM. The accounting firms now focus on providing auditing and tax services.

As the "Hit & Miss" feature outlines, more and more public accountants are also being certified as *forensic accountants*. Some smaller public accounting firms have chosen to specialize in forensic accounting. These professionals, and the firms that employ them, focus on uncovering potential fraud in many different organizations.

Chartered Accountants (CAs) are Canada's most recognized group of professional accountants. They demonstrate their accounting knowledge by meeting provincial requirements for education and experience and by successfully completing thorough testing in accounting theory and practice, auditing, law, finance, strategy, and taxation. Other recognized accountants meet specified educational and experience requirements and pass certification exams to earn the title *Certified Management Accountant (CMA)*, *Certified General Accountant (CGA)*, *Certified Fraud Examiner (CFE)*, or *Certified Internal Auditor (CIA)*.

At the time of printing, the three major accounting bodies in Canada (CA, CMA, and CGA) were discussing the possibility of merging into one designation, the Chartered Professional Accountant (CPA).

Management Accountants

An accountant who is employed by a business other than a public accounting firm is called a *management accountant*. A management accountant collects and records financial transactions and prepares financial statements used by the firm's managers in decision-making. Management accountants provide timely, relevant, accurate, and concise information that executives can use to operate their firms more effectively and more profitably than without this input. A management

HIT & MISS

Forensic Accountants: Fraud Busters

When you think of an accountant, do you picture someone poring over stacks of ledgers or computer printouts, calculator in hand? Much of accounting *does* involve ledgers and printouts, but forensic accounting is a little different. Forensic accountants don't take a company's accounting numbers at face value—they are crime fighters who look at what's happening behind those numbers. Forensic accountants work in a growing field. They investigate such white-collar crimes as business fraud, improper financial reporting, and illegal investment schemes.

Forensic accounting is accounting that is done in preparation for legal review. Forensic accountants take the skeptical view. They investigate below the surface of an organization's accounting system to find out what actually happened. They may also testify as expert witnesses if a case goes to trial. In Canada, forensic accountants typically need a professional accounting designation such as a CA (Chartered Accountant) and further training in investigative techniques. Forensic accountants may have a certified fraud examiner (CFE) designation or a diploma in forensic accounting (DIFA).

Nortel Networks was once a large Canadian telecommunications company. It went through multiple financial statement restatements before completely collapsing. As a result, former CEO Frank Dunn, former CFO Douglas Beatty, and former corporate controller Michael Gollogly were charged with fraud, falsification of accounts and documents, and involvement in issuing a false prospectus. Such scandals can have far-reaching and disastrous effects on a firm. Nortel's stock once traded at as high as $124.50 per share and represented more than one-third of the TSE 300 index, the Toronto Stock Exchange's index of 300 influential stocks. After news broke on the accounting charges, Nortel stock became penny stock, trading at less than $1.00 per share.

Al Rosen is one of Canada's best known and possibly its most outspoken forensic accountants. He said, "You can churn out all sorts of rubbish in quarterly and annual reports…and guess what the newspapers do with their databases? They take this crap, they do all this analysis, and they're playing with bogus numbers."

Questions for Critical Thinking

1. Describe how a shift in the economy has created a new career path for accounting students.

2. How can forensic accounting change the world of business?

Sources: "The Wild Ride of Canada's Most-Watched Stock," CBC News website, February 27, 2008, http://www.cbc.ca/news/background/nortel/stock.html, accessed May 18, 2011; CICA website, "The CICA Alliance for Excellence in Investigative and Forensic Accounting," http://www.cica.ca/focus-on-practice-areas/forensic-accounting/the-alliance-for-excellence-in-investigative-and-forensic-accounting/index.aspx, accessed May 18, 2011; "RCMP Lay Fraud Charges against Former Nortel Execs," CTV News website, June 19, 2008, http://www.ctv.ca/CTVNews/TopStories/20080619/rcmp_nortel_080619/, accessed May 18, 2011; David Berman, "Lie Detector," *MoneySense*, December/January 2002, http://www.canadianjusticereviewboard.ca/CJRB_director_Al_Rosen.htm, accessed May 18, 2011.

---

accountant prepares financial statements and plays a major role in interpreting them. A management accountant should be able to provide answers to many important questions:

- Where is the company going?

- What opportunities are in the company's future?

- Will certain situations expose the company to excessive risk?

- Does the firm's information system provide detailed and timely information to all levels of management?

Management accountants often specialize in different aspects of accounting. For example, a cost accountant decides on the costs of goods and services and helps to set their prices. An internal auditor examines the firm's financial practices to ensure that its records include accurate data and that its operations comply with federal, provincial, and local laws and regulations. A tax accountant works to minimize a firm's tax bill and handles its federal and provincial tax returns. Some management accountants achieve a *certified management accountant (CMA)* designation through experience and by passing a thorough examination.

Management accountants are usually involved in the development and enforcement of organizational policies on such items as employee travel. As part of their job, many employees travel and accumulate frequent flyer miles and hotel reward points. Some organizations have strict policies over the personal use of these travel points, but many do not.

In recent years, the federal regulations for accounting and public reporting have changed. The need to adapt to the new regulations has increased the demand for management accountants. As a result, salaries for these professionals are rising.

Government and Not-for-Profit Accountants

Federal, provincial, and local governments also need accounting services. Government accountants and those who work for not-for-profit organizations perform professional services similar to the services provided by management accountants. Accountants in government and not-for-profit sectors are concerned primarily with how efficiently the organizations work to meet their objectives. Many government agencies employ accountants, including the CRA, the Canadian Security Intelligence Service (CSIS), the Province of Manitoba, and the City of St. John's in Newfoundland and Labrador. The federal government employs hundreds of accountants.

Accountants also work for not-for-profit organizations, such as churches, labour unions, charities, schools, hospitals, and universities. The not-for-profit sector is one of the fastest growing segments of accounting practice. More not-for-profits are publishing their financial information because donors want more accountability from these organizations. Donors are interested in how the groups spend the money they raise.

✓ **ASSESSMENT CHECK**

15.2.1 List three services offered by public accounting firms.

15.2.2 What tasks do management accountants perform?

LO 15.3 Identify the foundations of the accounting system, including GAAP, IFRS, and the role of the Accounting Standards Board (AcSB).

generally accepted accounting principles (GAAP) principles that outline the conventions, rules, and procedures for deciding on the acceptable accounting practices at a particular time.

THE FOUNDATION OF THE ACCOUNTING SYSTEM

Accountants need to provide reliable, consistent, and unbiased information to decision-makers. To help them in this task, accountants follow guidelines, or standards, known as **generally accepted accounting principles (GAAP)**. These principles outline the conventions, rules, and procedures for deciding on the acceptable accounting and financial reporting practices at a particular time. GAAP includes International Financial Reporting Standards (IFRS), Accounting Standards for Private Enterprises (ASPE), accounting standards for not-for-profit, accounting standards for pension plans, and accounting standards for governments.

All GAAP standards are based on several basic qualitative characteristics: consistency, relevance, representational faithfulness, reliability, timeliness, understandability, verifiability, and comparability. Consistency means that all data should be collected and presented in the same manner across all periods. Any change in how specific data are collected or presented must be noted and explained. Relevance states that all information being reported should be appropriate and assist users in evaluating financial information. Representational faithfulness means that financial information should reflect the substance of the economic activity during the reporting period. Reliability implies that the accounting data in financial statements are dependable and can be verified by an independent party, such as an outside auditor. Timeliness states that financial information should be made available within a time period that allows the financial information to be useful in decision-making. Understandability requires that financial information be clearly presented to the users. Verifiability means that other independent and knowledgeable individuals would agree that the financial information is fairly presented. Finally, comparability ensures that one firm's financial statements can be compared with those of similar businesses. In Canada, the **Accounting Standards Board (AcSB)** is primarily responsible for evaluating and setting GAAP related to pension plans and to private and not-for-profit businesses. The Public Sector Accounting Board (PSAB) is responsible for accounting standards for governments.

Canadian public companies are required to use International Financial Reporting Standards (IFRS). These standards allow for financial statements to be more easily compared from country to country. This level of comparability is required because of the increase in worldwide trade. The idea of a uniform set of global accounting rules is gaining interest, mainly as a result of the expansion of the European Union and the signing of cross-national trade agreements, such as the North American Free Trade Agreement (NAFTA). Also, more investors are buying shares in foreign multinational corporations, and they need a practical way to evaluate firms in other countries. To assist global investors, more and more firms are reporting their financial information by using international accounting standards. This practice helps investors to make informed decisions.

International Financial Reporting Standards (IFRS) are the standards and interpretations adopted by the **International Accounting Standards Board (IASB)**. The use of IFRS is widespread

Accounting Standards Board (AcSB) the organization that interprets and modifies GAAP in Canada for private and not-for-profit businesses.

International Financial Reporting Standards (IFRS) the standards and interpretations adopted by the IASB.

International Accounting Standards Board (IASB) the organization that promotes worldwide consistency in financial reporting practices.

and growing. More than 120 countries require, permit the use of, or have a policy of working with IFRS, including India, Australia, Canada, Hong Kong, and member-countries of the European Union.

How does IFRS differ from ASPE? IFRS and ASPE share many similarities, but also have some important differences. For example, under ASPE, firms report plant, property, and equipment on the balance sheet at the historical cost minus depreciation; under IFRS, firms have the option to report plant, property, and equipment on the balance sheet at current market value. The IFRS option gives a clearer picture of the real value of a firm's assets. Many accounting experts believe that, overall, IFRS is less complicated than traditional GAAP and more transparent.[6]

In the United States, the **Financial Accounting Standards Board (FASB)** sets GAAP. The FASB is currently working with the IASB on a project to work toward IFRS. The U.S. is one of the few developed countries not currently using IFRS.

In response to accounting fraud and questions about the independence of auditors, the U.S. government enacted the Sarbanes-Oxley Act, commonly known as SOX. SOX then created the Public Company Accounting Oversight Board. This five-member board has the power to set audit standards and to investigate and approve the accounting firms that certify the books of publicly traded firms. All Canadian companies that have publicly traded stock or debt on a U.S. stock exchange must comply with SOX. In Canada, Bill 198 requires similar provisions as SOX for Canadian companies.

SOX and Bill 198 also added to the reporting requirements for publicly traded companies. For example, senior executives, including the CEO and chief financial officer (CFO), must personally certify that the financial information reported by the company is correct. As noted earlier, these additional requirements have increased the demand for accounting professionals, especially managerial accountants. One result of this increased demand has been higher salaries.

Financial Accounting Standards Board (FASB) the organization that interprets and modifies GAAP in the United States.

BUSINESS ETIQUETTE

Tips for Complying with the Corruption of Foreign Public Officials Act

The Corruption of Foreign Public Officials (CFPO) Act is meant to prevent the bribery of foreign officials for the purpose of gaining or keeping business in another country. More companies now do business overseas. They are naturally concerned about being at risk to violations of this law. Enforcement of this act is at an all-time high and is expected to remain high. Penalties are severe, including fines and prison time for anyone convicted. The following are some ways that global firms can improve their compliance and reduce their risk:

1. Assess your firm's risk under the CFPO Act, country by country. Does your firm do business with any government-owned foreign firms or with any foreign government officials? What are the risks of corruption and bribery?

2. Set up a policy for your firm's employees—in Canada and abroad—to comply with the CFPO Act. The policy should cover gifts and payments to foreign officials, charitable donations, accurate and complete records, and other areas at risk.

3. Train your employees in the policies of the CFPO Act. Include these policies in your company's overall compliance process. Have your Human Resources department make these policies part of new-employee orientation.

4. Have a compliance team in place to monitor compliance to the act and to be on the watch for potential risks. The team should include company lawyers, accountants, and auditors. The team should be empowered to make both in-house and external investigations.

5. Plan any international investigations carefully. Many foreign countries do not apply the attorney–client privilege to company lawyers and employees.

Sources: Department of Justice, "The Corruption of Foreign Public Officials Act: A Guide," May 1999, http://www.justice.gc.ca/eng/dept-min/pub/cfpoa-lcape/index.html, accessed May 27, 2011; "Foreign Corrupt Practices Act," Ernst & Young, http://www.ey.com, accessed June 1, 2010; U.S. Department of Justice, "Foreign Corrupt Practices Act: An Overview," http://www.justice.gov, accessed June 1, 2010; Gary Sturisky, "2010 Compliance Challenges: Three More Areas That Matter," *Corporate Compliance Insights*, March 4, 2010, http://www.corporatecomplianceinsights.com; Brian Loughman, Aaron Marcu, and Kerry Schalders, "Top Ten Tips for FCPA Compliance," Association of Corporate Counsel, March 1, 2010, http://www.acc.com; Nina Gross, "Foreign Corrupt Practices Act: Leading Practices to Consider," Deloitte, January 29, 2010, http://www.deloitte.com.

ASSESSMENT CHECK

15.3.1 Define *GAAP*.

15.3.2 What is the role played by the AcSB?

LO 15.4 Outline the steps in the accounting cycle, and define *double-entry bookkeeping* and the *accounting equation*.

accounting cycle the set of activities involved in converting information and individual transactions into financial statements.

It is expensive for firms to meet GAAP standards and the requirements of SOX and Bill 198. For example, audits can cost millions of dollars each year. These expenses can be especially difficult for small businesses. Some people have suggested making changes to GAAP and SOX for smaller firms. They argue that some accounting rules were designed for larger companies. As a result, Canada has multiple sets of standards, such as the Accounting Standards for Private Enterprises (ASPE), which are set by the AcSB.

The **Corruption of Foreign Public Officials Act** is a federal law that prohibits Canadian citizens and companies from bribing foreign officials to win or continue business. The law was later extended to make foreign officials subject to penalties if they cause similar corrupt practices to occur within Canada or its territories. The "Business Etiquette" feature provides some tips on Corruption of Foreign Public Officials Act compliance.

THE ACCOUNTING CYCLE

Accounting deals with a firm's financial transactions with its employees, customers, suppliers, owners, and with bankers and various government agencies. For example, payroll cheques result in a cash outflow to employees. A payment to a supplier results in the delivery of needed materials for the production process. Customers use cash, cheque, and credit to purchase goods, which generate business funds to cover the costs of operations and to earn a profit. Prompt payment of bills keeps the firm's credit rating high and helps its future ability to earn a profit. Accountants gather data on individual buying and selling transactions and convert these data to financial statements through a process called the **accounting cycle**.

Figure 15.2 shows the activities involved in the accounting cycle: recording, classifying, and summarizing transactions. Any transaction that has a financial impact on the business, such as wages or payments to suppliers, should be recorded. These transactions are recorded in journals, which list the transactions in the order they occurred. Journal listings are then posted to ledgers. A ledger shows increases or decreases in specific accounts such as cash or wages. Ledgers are used to prepare the financial statements, which summarize the financial transactions. Management and other interested parties use the resulting financial statements for many different purposes.

FIGURE 15.2 The Accounting Cycle

The Accounting Equation

Three fundamental terms appear in the accounting equation: assets, liabilities, and owners' equity. An **asset** is anything with future benefit owned or controlled by a business. Assets include land, buildings, supplies, cash, accounts receivable (amounts owed to the business as payment for credit sales), and marketable securities.

asset anything with future benefit owned or controlled by a firm.

Tangible assets, such as equipment, buildings, and inventories are the most common assets. But a firm's most important assets may be its intangible assets, such as patents and trademarks. These assets are especially important for such companies as computer software firms, biotechnology companies, and pharmaceutical companies. For example, Johnson & Johnson—which has both biotechnology and pharmaceutical operations—reported more than $31 billion in intangible assets (including goodwill) in one recent year, out of a total of almost $95 billion in assets.[7]

Tangible assets, such as buildings, equipment, and inventories may look impressive. But they are sometimes less important to a company than its intangible assets, such as patents and trademarks.

© Can Stock Photo Inc./imagecom

Two groups have claims against the assets of a firm: creditors and owners. A **liability** of a business is anything owed to creditors—that is, the claims of a firm's creditors. When a firm borrows money to purchase inventory, land, or machinery, the claims of creditors are shown as accounts payable, notes payable, or long-term debt. Wages and salaries owed to employees also are liabilities (known as *wages payable* or *accrued wages*).

Owners' equity is the owners' initial investment in the business plus any profits that were not paid to owners. A strong owners' equity position is often used as evidence of a firm's financial strength and stability.

liability a claim against a firm's assets by creditors.

owners' equity the funds that owners invest in the business plus any profits not paid to owners in the form of cash dividends.

The **accounting equation** (also called the *accounting identity*) states that assets must equal liabilities plus owners' equity. This equation reflects the financial position of a firm at any point in time:

$$\text{Assets} = \text{Liabilities} + \text{Owners' equity}$$

Because financing comes from either creditors or owners, the right side of the accounting equation also represents the business's financial structure.

The accounting equation also illustrates **double-entry bookkeeping**—the process used to record accounting transactions. Because assets must always equal liabilities plus equity, each transaction must have two or more effects on the accounts. For example, if a company increases an asset, one of the following must also happen: another asset must decrease, a liability must increase, or owners' equity must increase. That is, if a company uses cash to purchase inventory, one asset (inventory) is increased while another asset (cash) is decreased by the same amount. Following the same idea, a decrease in an asset must be balanced by either an increase in another asset, a decrease in a liability, or a decrease in owners' equity. If a company uses cash to repay a bank loan, both an asset (cash) and a liability (bank loans) decrease by the same amount.

accounting equation the relationship that should reflect a firm's financial position at any time: assets should always equal the sum of liabilities and owners' equity.

double-entry bookkeeping the process used to record accounting transactions; each individual transaction is always balanced by another transaction.

Two simple numerical examples will help to explain the accounting equation and double-entry bookkeeping.

First, assume the owner of a photo studio uses her own funds to buy a new camera system for $5,000. The accounting transaction would look as follows:

Increase plant, property, and equipment (an asset) by $5,000

Increase owners' equity by $5,000

So, the left side of the accounting equation increases by $5,000 and is balanced by a $5,000 increase on the right side.

Second, assume a firm has a $100,000 loan from a bank and decides to pay it off using some of its cash. The transaction would be recorded as follows:

Decrease bank loan (a liability) by $100,000

Decrease cash (an asset) by $100,000

In this second example, the left side and right side of the accounting equation both decrease by $100,000.

The relationship described by the accounting equation is the basis for developing the firm's financial statements. Three financial statements form the foundation: the balance sheet, the income statement, and the statement of changes in equity. The information in these statements is calculated using the double-entry bookkeeping system and reflects the basic accounting equation. A fourth statement, the statement of cash flows, focuses on the sources and uses of cash in a firm's operating, investing, and financing activities.

The Impact of Computers and the Internet on the Accounting Process

For hundreds of years, bookkeepers have manually recorded, or posted, accounting transactions as entries in journals. They then transferred the information, or posted it, to individual accounts listed in ledgers. Computers have simplified the process, making it both faster and easier. For example, point-of-sale terminals in retail stores perform several functions each time they record sales. These terminals recall product prices from a computer system's memory and keep inventory counts of individual items. They also do the data entry functions that were once entered manually.

Accounting software programs are used widely in both large and small businesses. They allow a do-it-once approach: a single sales entry is automatically converted into a journal entry, which is stored until needed. Decision-makers can then instantly access up-to-date financial statements and financial ratios. Improvements in accounting software continue to make the process faster and easier. CPS is a Canadian company that sells and services machines. Recently CPS decided to use Sage Accpac ERP and Sage CRM to integrate its databases and track its sales processes. This new system means that managers no longer need to wait for reports because they can access the data at anytime. Those who use information on outside sales can now access and share information with management, accounting, and those who use inside sales figures. All the operational data is integrated with CPS's accounting data to reduce the number of duplicate entries.[8]

The accounting needs of entrepreneurs and small businesses differ from the needs of larger firms. Some accounting software programs, such as QuickBooks and Simply Accounting, have been designed specifically for entrepreneurs and small businesses. Software programs designed for larger firms, such as products from Oracle and SAP, often need more sophisticated computer systems.

For firms that conduct business worldwide, software producers have introduced new accounting programs that handle all of a company's accounting information for every country where it operates. The software handles other languages and currencies. It can also deal with the financial, legal, and tax requirements of each nation where the firm does business.

The Internet also influences the accounting process. Several software producers offer Web-based accounting products designed for small and medium-sized businesses. These products allow users to access their complete accounting systems from anywhere using a standard Web browser. The "Going Green" feature explains how Deloitte is integrating sustainability into its infrastructure and its business services.

✔ **ASSESSMENT CHECK**

15.4.1 List the steps in the accounting cycle.

15.4.2 What is the accounting equation?

15.4.3 Briefly explain double-entry bookkeeping.

GOING GREEN

DELOITTE EDUCATES ITSELF—AND OTHERS—ON SUSTAINABILITY

Deloitte is one of the Big Four accounting and auditing firms. Recently, the company made two decisions: to make its own internal operations greener and to offer its clients training in green practices. It seems logical that a firm specializing in financial reporting would enter the area of nonfinancial reporting as the business world begins to value green practices. Firms once thought of "going green" as good public relations but not so good financially. But many firms now see the importance of sustainability in an increasingly energy-limited world.

Kathryn Pavlovsky is a co-leader of Deloitte's Enterprise Sustainability Group. She says, "Nonfinancial reporting is evolving from voluntary communications to mandatory compliance, and the environmental regulatory and financial reporting worlds are converging." The move to add sustainable activities to a company's nonfinancial reporting has been encouraged by many factors: the recent recession, activism from shareholders, and changing consumer attitudes and behaviours. Also, technological advances have made green practices more realistic and affordable.

Deloitte's corporate responsibility policy declares that the company will "advocate the sustainable use of natural resources and the environment." The company began its internal greening campaign by surveying its employees. Called "How Green Is Your Footprint?" the survey measured "greenness" on an individual basis. It then suggested how each employee could improve his or her performance. A second survey, "How Green Is Your *Other* Footprint?" helps employees to measure their sustainability practices at home.

Deloitte also established a Green Leadership Council (GLC) to maintain contact between the various company regions and management. The GLC educates employees about important green issues and promotes a unified message to all the company's offices. Deloitte employees now conduct virtual meetings and conferences whenever possible. When employees need to travel, the company travel arrangements include car rentals and hotel options considered to be green. Deloitte has also adopted Leadership in Energy and Environmental Design (LEED) standards when building new offices and retrofitting existing offices. The company focuses on purchasing supplies that have a minimal impact on the environment, and it has worked with its suppliers to reach greater levels of sustainability.

Deloitte's Centre for Sustainability Performance (CSP) advises businesses on how to reduce their environmental impact and remain profitable. Among the areas covered are planning and strategy, revenue generation, tax incentives, and competitive branding. The CSP also explores sustainability opportunities for employees, offices, IT infrastructure, and communities. The centre's activities include on-site training for client firms, research and development in sustainability measurement and reporting, publication of reports on these topics for corporate sustainability managers, and consulting and sales support.

One of the centre's recent workshops for clients was "Sustainability Measurement and Reporting: Tools, Methods, and Metrics." The course was designed to help clients become familiar with the current methods for measuring and reporting their own sustainability. It also provided a preview of new developments in these areas. According to Mark W. McElroy, the CSP's director, the course covered "tools, methods and metrics across all dimensions of corporate social responsibility and sustainability performance, including carbon, water, solid waste, social impacts, triple bottom line and non-financial measurement and reporting in general, both from an enterprise and product life cycle perspective."

To further develop its internal greening efforts, Deloitte recently introduced its Green Sync tool. It is intended to promote employee and stakeholder involvement. Johanne Gelinas is a partner with Deloitte Canada's Corporate Responsibility and Sustainability practice. She says, "Executives will always be challenged about where to spend time and resources. By adopting a strategic approach to corporate responsibility, they can start to identify environmental, social and governance initiatives that can also improve shareholder value."

Questions for Critical Thinking

1. Why would Deloitte find it relatively easy to expand from financial reporting to nonfinancial reporting?

2. How would you answer the question, "How big is *your* carbon footprint?" What can you do to make your home and/or your workplace greener?

Sources: Deloitte website, http://www.deloitte.com, accessed June 1, 2010; Deborah Fleischer, "Deloitte: Best Practices for Going Green," *Triple Pundit*, February 1, 2010, http:// www.triplepundit.com; Deborah Fleischer, "Deloitte: Green Training on Sustainability Measurement and Reporting," *Green Impact*, January 4, 2010, http://greenimpact.com; "Deloitte Launches Center for Sustainability Performance," press release, August 10, 2009, http://www.csrwire.com; Deloitte, "Sustainability & Climate Change," http://www.deloitte.com/us/sustainability, accessed May 17, 2012.

FINANCIAL STATEMENTS

LO 15.5 Explain the functions and major components of the four principal financial statements: the balance sheet, the income statement, the statement of changes in equity, and the statement of cash flows.

Financial statements provide managers with the information they need to evaluate the firm's profitability, its overall financial health, and its liquidity position—the ability to meet its current obligations and needs by converting assets into cash. Managers can base their decisions on information in the balance sheet, the income statement, the statement of changes in equity, and the statement of cash flows. Managers interpret the data in these statements so they can communicate the appropriate information to internal decision-makers and to interested parties outside the organization.

Of the four financial statements, the only permanent statement is the balance sheet: its amounts are carried over from year to year. The income statement, statement of changes in equity, and statement of cash flows are temporary statements because they are closed out at the end of each year and therefore are not cumulative in nature.

SOLVING AN **ETHICAL** CONTROVERSY

Should Whistle-Blowers Be Rewarded?

The U.S. Sarbanes-Oxley Act of 2002 (SOX) and Canada's Bill 198 were intended to reduce fraud. Both require CEOs and CFOs to sign off on the accuracy of their companies' financial statements. But most reported fraud is revealed by anonymous whistle-blowers or by journalists, auditors, or others.

The Public Servants Disclosure Protection Act protects Canadians who report misconduct in the government. But unlike in the United States, this legislation does not financially reward whistle-blowers. In the United States, the False Claims Act allows citizens to file lawsuits alleging fraud against the federal government. The biggest settlements have involved hospital chains and drug manufacturers; the largest fine was $1 billion. Some whistle-blowers have collected almost $47 million in rewards. The U.S. Foreign Corrupt Practices Act (FCPA) may also result in huge rewards. But whistle-blowers are not always successful; some have been fired, forced to quit, or demoted.

Should whistle-blowers be rewarded for reporting financial fraud in Canada?

PRO

1. A recent survey found that "a strong monetary incentive to blow the whistle does motivate people with information to come forward."

2. People who commit fraud can face strict penalties, such as those outlined under SOX, Bill 198, the FCPA, and the Corruption of Foreign Public Officials Act. One survey reported that 83 percent of fraud examiners believe that internal corporate controls on fraud will actually decline.

CON

1. Some observers feel that some "whistle-blower-friendly" provisions of the FCPA in the United States may discourage accused firms from simply settling with the federal government and paying a fine to avoid costly legal procedures.

2. Not all whistle-blowers are innocent. A former UBS banker exposed tax evasion at the firm but was sentenced to prison because he did not reveal that he had participated in the fraud himself.

Summary

In the United States, legislation before Congress would require the Securities and Exchange Commission (SEC) to award whistle-blowers up to 30 percent of fines the government collects on the basis of "original information." Some observers worry that these changes could result in a "race to disclose" between companies that self-report and current or former employees. Canada has not seen any similar movements to financially reward whistle-blowers.

Sources: Parliament of Canada, "Bill C-25, The Public Servants Disclosure Protection Act," http://www.parl.gc.ca/About/Parliament/LegislativeSummaries/bills_ls.asp?ls=c25&Parl= 37&Ses=3, accessed June 3, 2011; "Sarbanes-Oxley Can Help Curb Company Fraud," McGladrey, http://rsmmcgladrey.com, accessed June 1, 2010; Michael Connor, "Finance Reform Bill Could Increase Big Payouts to Whistleblowers," *Business Ethics*, May 2, 2010, http://business-ethics.com; "Whistle blowers Making Money Thanks to Law," *NewsChannel 8*, May 1, 2010, http://cfc.news.8.net; Deloitte Webcast Poll, "Poll: More Financial Statement Fraud Expected to Be Uncovered in 2010, 2011," *Corporate Compliance Insights*, April 28, 2010, http://www.corporate complianceinsights.com; James Hyatt, "Who Detects Corporate Fraud? (Tip: It's Not Usually the SEC . . .)," *Business Ethics*, February 16, 2010, http://business-ethics.com; Michael Rubinkam, "UBS Tax Evasion Whistle-Blower Reports to Federal Prison," *USA Today*, January 8, 2010, http://www.usatoday.com.

Public companies report their financial statements at the end of each three-month period and at the end of each fiscal year. Annual statements must be examined and verified by the firm's outside auditors. These financial statements are public information available to anyone. The "Solving an Ethical Controversy" feature discusses the problem of financial fraud.

A fiscal year does not need to be the same as the calendar year. Many companies set different fiscal years. For example, the Starbucks fiscal year runs from October 1 to September 30 of the following year. Nike's fiscal year consists of the 12 months between June 1 and May 31. By contrast, GE's fiscal year is the same as the calendar year, running from January 1 to December 31.

balance sheet a statement of a firm's financial position—what it owns and claims against its assets—at a particular point in time.

The Balance Sheet

A **balance sheet** (or *statement of financial position* under IFRS) shows a firm's financial position on a particular date. It is similar to a photograph of the firm's assets, liabilities, and owners' equity at a specific moment in time. Balance sheets must be pre-pared at regular intervals because a firm's managers and other internal parties often need this information every day, every week, or at least every month. External users, such as shareholders and industry analysts, may use this information less often, maybe every quarter (every three months) or once a year.

The balance sheet follows the accounting equation. On the left side of the balance sheet are the firm's assets—what it owns. These assets are shown in a downward order of liquidity. In other words, the assets with the highest ability to convert to cash are shown first. That's why cash is always listed first on the asset side of the balance sheet. The assets represent how management has used its avail-able funds.

On the right side of the equation are the claims against the firm's assets. Liabilities and owners' equity show the sources of the firm's assets. They are listed in the order they are due. Liabilities include the claims of creditors—the financial institutions or bondholders that have loaned the firm money; suppliers that have provided goods and services on credit; and others to be paid in the future, such as federal, provincial, and municipal tax authorities. Owners' equity represents the owners' claims against the firm's assets; in the case of a corporation, owners' equity represents the claims of shareholders. Owners' equity also includes any excess of all assets over liabilities.

The balance sheet is the only permanent statement of the four financial statements. It shows the firm's financial position on a particular date and its amounts are carried over from year to year.

Figure 15.3 shows the balance sheet for Diane's Java, a small coffee wholesaler. The account-ing equation is illustrated by the three classifications of assets, liabilities, and owners' equity on the company's balance sheet. Remember, total assets must always equal the sum of liabilities and owners' equity. In other words, the balance sheet must always balance.

The Income Statement

The **income statement** is a financial record of a company's revenues, expenses, and profits over a specific time period. In contrast, a balance sheet shows a firm's financial record at one specific point in time. You can think of the income statement as a video, while the balance sheet is more like a photograph. The income statement summarizes a firm's financial performance over a specific time period, usually a quarter (three months) or a year.

The income statement also helps decision-makers to focus on overall revenues and the costs needed to generate these revenues. Managers of a not-for-profit organization use the income state-ment to check whether the revenues from contributions and other sources will cover the organiza-tion's operating costs. Finally, the income statement provides many basic data used to calculate the financial ratios that managers use in planning and controlling activities. Figure 15.4 shows the income statement for Diane's Java.

An income statement is also called *a profit-and-loss statement, a P&L statement*, or under IFRS, *a statement of comprehensive income*. It begins with total sales or revenues generated during a year, quarter, or month. The following lines then deduct all of the costs related to producing the revenues. Typical costs include operating expenses, interest, and taxes. After all costs have been subtracted, the remaining net income may be distributed to the firm's owners (the shareholders, proprietors, or partners) or reinvested in the company as retained earnings. The final figure on the income statement—net income after taxes—is the so-called *bottom line*.

Keeping costs under control is an important part of running a business. But, too often, companies focus more on increasing revenue than on controlling costs. It doesn't matter how much money a company collects in revenues—it won't stay in business for long unless it earns a profit.

income statement a financial record of a company's revenues, expenses, and profits over a specific period of time.

1 Current Assets:
Cash and other liquid assets that can or will be converted to cash within one year.

2 Plant, property, and equipment (net):
Physical assets expected to last for more than one year; shown net of accumulated depreciation.

3 Value of assets such as patents and trademarks.

4 Current Liabilities:
Claims of creditors that are to be repaid within one year; accruals are expenses, such as wages, that have been incurred but not yet paid.

5 Long-term debt:
Debts that come due one year or longer after the date on the balance sheet.

6 Owners' (or Shareholders') equity:
Claims of the owners against the assets of the firm; the difference between total assets and total liabilities.

FIGURE 15.3
Diane's Java Balance Sheet (Fiscal Year, Ending December 31)

Diane's Java

Balance Sheet - December 31

($ thousands)	2014	2013
Assets		
Current Assets		
1 Cash	$ 800	$ 600
Short-term investments	1,250	940
Accounts receivable	990	775
Inventory	2,200	1,850
Total current assets	5,240	4,165
2 Plant, property, and equipment (net)	3,300	2,890
3 Goodwill and other intangible assets	250	250
Total Assets	8,790	7,305
Liabilities and Shareholders' Equity		
Current Liabilities		
4 Accruals	$ 350	$ 450
Accounts payable	980	900
Notes payable	700	500
Total current liabilities	2,030	1,850
5 Long-term debt	1,100	1,000
Total liabilities	3,130	2,850
6 Shareholders' equity	5,660	4,455
Total Liabilities and Equity	8,790	7,305

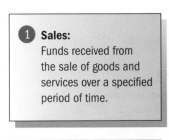

① Sales:
Funds received from the sale of goods and services over a specified period of time.

② Cost of goods sold:
Cost of merchandise or services that generate the firm's sales.

③ Operating expenses:
Salaries and other operational expenses not directly related to the acquisition or production, of the firm's output.

④ Depreciation:
Noncash expenses that reflect the systematic reduction in the value of the firm's plant, property and equipment.

⑤ Net income:
Sales minus total expenses; profit after taxes.

Diane's Java
Income Statement for the year ending December 31

($ thousands)	2014	2013
① Sales	$17,300	$14,200
② Cost of goods sold	10,370	8,804
Gross profit	6,930	5,396
③ Operating expenses	3,550	2,950
Operating profit	3,380	2,446
④ Depreciation	350	300
Interest expense (net)	98	75
Earnings before taxes	2,932	2,071
Income taxes	1,005	650
⑤ Net income	1,927	1,421

FIGURE 15.4
Diane's Java Income Statement (Fiscal Year Ending December 31)

Statement of Changes in Equity

The **statement of changes in equity** is a record of the change in equity from the end of one fiscal period to the end of the next fiscal period. It uses information from both the balance sheet and income statement. A simplified example is shown in Figure 15.5 for Diane's Java.

Note that the statement of changes in equity begins with the shareholders' equity that is shown on the balance sheet at the end of the prior year. Net income is added, and cash dividends paid to owners are subtracted. If owners contributed any additional capital, for example, through the sale of new shares, this amount is added to equity. If owners withdrew capital, for example, through the repurchase of existing shares, equity is reduced by that amount. All of the additions and subtractions, taken together, equal the change in owners' equity from the end of the previous fiscal year to the end of the current fiscal year. The new amount of owners' equity is then reported on the balance sheet for the current year.

statement of changes in equity a record of the change in equity from the end of one fiscal period to the end of the next fiscal period.

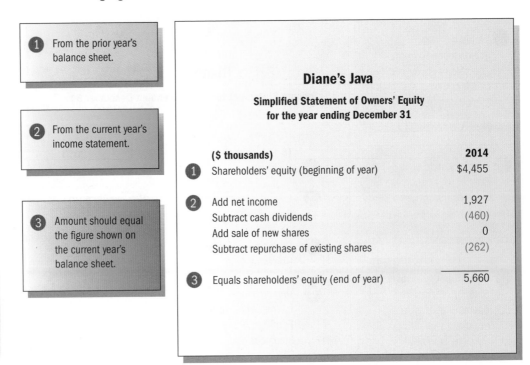

1. From the prior year's balance sheet.

2. From the current year's income statement.

3. Amount should equal the figure shown on the current year's balance sheet.

FIGURE 15.5
Diane's Java Simplified Statement of Changes in Equity (Fiscal Year Ending December 31)

Diane's Java

**Simplified Statement of Owners' Equity
for the year ending December 31**

($ thousands)	2014
1 Shareholders' equity (beginning of year)	$4,455
2 Add net income	1,927
Subtract cash dividends	(460)
Add sale of new shares	0
Subtract repurchase of existing shares	(262)
3 Equals shareholders' equity (end of year)	5,660

The Statement of Cash Flows

statement of cash flows a record of the sources and uses of cash during a period of time.

So far, we have looked at the statement of changes in equity, the income statement, and the balance sheet. Most firms prepare a fourth accounting statement—the **statement of cash flows**. All public companies must prepare and publish a statement of cash flows. Commercial lenders, such as banks, often ask a borrower for a statement of cash flows. The statement of cash flows provides investors and creditors with information about a firm's cash receipts and cash payments for its operations, investments, and financing during an accounting period. Figure 15.6 shows the statement of cash flows for Diane's Java.

accrual accounting an accounting method that records revenues and expenses when they occur, not when cash actually changes hands.

Companies prepare a statement of cash flows because of the wide use of accrual accounting. **Accrual accounting** records revenues and costs when they occur, not when actual cash changes hands. As a result, the amounts may differ between what is reported as sales, expenses, and profits and the amount of cash that actually flows into and out of the business during a period of time. For example, companies depreciate fixed assets—such as machinery and buildings—over a specified period of time. In other words, companies reduce the value of the asset as the asset ages. Depreciation is reported as an expense on the firm's income statement (see item 4 in Figure 15.4), but does not involve the movement of any cash. Depreciation is a noncash expense. That means that the amount a firm reports as net income (profits after tax) for a period actually understates the amount of cash the firm took in, less expenses. As a result, depreciation is added back to net income when calculating cash flow (see item 1 in Figure 15.6).

The lifeblood of every organization is its *cash flow*. Many former owners of failed firms blame poor cash flow for their company's downfall. Many people value the statement of cash flow. They believe that preparing it and having it examined by various people can help to prevent financial distress for otherwise profitable firms. Too many firms are forced into bankruptcy because they lack the cash needed to continue their day-to-day operations.

Even when bankruptcy is not an issue, the statement of cash flows can provide investors and others with vital information. For example, assume that a firm's income statement reports rising earnings. But, at the same time, the statement of cash flows shows that the firm's inventory is rising faster than its sales. This situation is often a signal that demand for the firm's products is dropping, which may, in turn, be a sign of financial trouble.

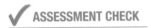 ASSESSMENT CHECK

15.5.1 List the four financial statements.

15.5.2 How is the balance sheet organized?

15.5.3 Define *accrual accounting*.

① Operating Activities:
The nuts and bolts of day-to-day activities of a company carrying out its regular business; Increases in accounts receivable and inventory are like uses of cash, while increases in accruals and accounts payables are like sources of cash; in financially healthy firms, net cash flow from operating activities should be positive.

② Investing Activities:
Transactions to accumulate or use cash in ways that affect operating activities in the future; often a use of cash.

③ Financing Activities:
Ways to transfer cash to or from creditors and to or from owners; can be either positive or negative.

④ Net Cash Flow:
The sum of cash flow from operating, investing, and financing activities, a reconcilement of cash from the beginning to the end of the accounting period (one year in this example).

Diane's Java

Statement of Cash Flows for the year ending December 31

($ thousands)	2014
Cash Flow from Operating Activities	
① Net income	$1,927
Depreciation	350
Change in accounts receivable	(215)
Change in inventory	(350)
Change in accruals	(100)
Change in accounts payable	80
Total cash flow from operating activities	1,692
② Cash Flow from Investing Activities	
Capital expenditures	(760)
Change in short-term investments	(310)
Total cash flow from investing activities	(1,070)
③ Cash Flow from Financing Activities	
Cash dividends	(460)
Sale/repurchase of shares	(262)
Change in notes payable	200
Change in long-term debt	100
Total cash flow from financing activities	(422)
④ Net Cash Flow	200
Cash (beginning of year)	600
Cash (end of year)	800

FIGURE 15.6 Diane's Java Statement of Cash Flows (Fiscal Year Ending December 31)

FINANCIAL RATIO ANALYSIS

Accounting professionals have important responsibilities beyond preparing financial statements. They also help managers interpret the statements by comparing data on the firm's current activities to data for previous periods and to data on other companies in the same industry. *Ratio analysis* is one of the most commonly used tools. It measures a firm's liquidity, profitability, reliance on debt financing, and how effectively management uses the firm's resources. This analysis also allows comparisons with other firms and with the firm's own past performance.

Ratios help managers by interpreting actual performance and making comparisons to what should have happened. Managers compare their firm's ratios with ratios of similar companies to understand their firm's performance compared with competitors' results. These industry standards are important measures and help to focus on problem areas—and areas of excellence. Ratios for the current accounting period can be compared with similar calculations for previous periods to spot developing trends. Ratios can be classified according to their specific purposes. The four major categories of financial ratios are summarized in Table 15.1. The ratios for Diane's Java for the 2013 and 2014 fiscal years are shown in Table 15.2.

Table 15.1 Major Categories of Financial Ratios

CATEGORY	RATIO	DESCRIPTION
Liquidity ratios	Current ratio	Current assets divided by current liabilities
	Quick (acid-test) ratio	Current assets (minus inventory) divided by current liabilities
Efficiency ratios	Inventory turnover	Cost of goods sold divided by average inventory
	Receivables turnover	Credit sales divided by average accounts receivable
	Total asset turnover	Revenue or sales divided by average total assets
Leverage ratios	Debt ratio	Total liabilities divided by total assets
	Long-term debt to equity	Long-term debt divided by owners' equity
Profitability ratios	Gross profit margin	Gross profit divided by revenue or sales
	Net profit margin	Net profit divided by revenue or sales
	Return on equity	Net profit divided by average owners' equity

Table 15.2 Financial Ratios for Diane's Java

FINANCIAL RATIO	2014 FISCAL YEAR	2013 FISCAL YEAR
Current ratio	2.58	2.25
Quick ratio	1.50	1.25
Inventory turnover	5.12	5.03
Receivables turnover	19.60	19.32
Total asset turnover	2.15	2.15
Debt ratio	35.6%	39.0%
Long-term debt to equity	19.4%	22.4%
Gross profit margin	40.0%	38.0%
Net profit margin	11.1%	10.0%
Return on equity	38.1%	36.6%

Liquidity Ratios

Liquidity ratios measure a firm's ability to meet its short-term obligations, such as loans, when they are due. An increase in liquidity reduces the likelihood that a firm will need to raise funds to repay loans. On the other hand, firms with low liquidity may have to choose between defaulting (failing to pay) and borrowing from high-cost lending sources to meet their short-term financial obligations.

Two commonly used liquidity ratios are the current ratio and the acid-test ratio, also called the quick ratio. The current ratio compares current assets to current liabilities. It provides executives with information about the firm's ability to pay its current debts as they mature, or as payments are due. The current ratio of Diane's Java is computed as follows (unless indicated, all amounts from the balance sheet or income statement are in thousands of dollars):

$$\text{Current ratio} = \frac{\text{Current assets}}{\text{Current liabilities}} = \frac{5,240}{2,030} = 2.58$$

In other words, Diane's Java has $2.58 of current assets for every $1.00 of current liabilities. In general, a current ratio of 2:1 is considered to provide satisfactory liquidity. This rule of thumb, or guideline, must be considered along with other factors, such as the nature of the business, the season, and the quality of the company's management team. Diane's Java's management and others are likely to evaluate this ratio of 2.58:1 by comparing it with ratios for previous operating periods and with industry averages.

The acid-test (or quick) ratio measures the ability of a firm to meet its debt payments on short notice. This ratio compares quick assets—the most liquid current assets—against current liabilities. Quick assets generally consist of cash and equivalents, short-term investments, and accounts receivable. In general, quick assets equal total current assets minus inventory.

Diane's Java's current balance sheet lists total current assets of $5.24 million and inventory of $2.2 million. Therefore, its quick ratio is calculated as follows:

$$\text{Acid-test ratio} = \frac{\text{Current assets} - \text{Inventory}}{\text{Current liabilities}} = \frac{(5,240 - 2,200)}{2,030} = 1.50$$

Because the traditional rule of thumb, or guideline, for an adequate acid-test ratio is around 1:1, Diane's Java appears to have a strong level of liquidity. However, the same cautions apply here as for the current ratio. The ratio should be compared with industry averages and data from previous operating periods to decide whether it is adequate for the firm.

Activity Ratios

Activity ratios measure how effectively management uses the firm's resources. One of the most frequently used activity ratios is the inventory turnover ratio. This ratio indicates the number of times merchandise moves through a business:

$$\text{Inventory turnover} = \frac{\text{Cost of goods sold}}{\text{Average inventory}} = \frac{10,370}{[(2,200 + 1,850)]/2} = 5.12$$

Average inventory for Diane's Java is calculated by adding the inventory as of December 31, 2014 ($2.2 million) to the inventory as of December 31, 2013 ($1.85 million) and dividing it by 2. Comparing the 5.12 inventory turnover ratio with industry standards provides a measure of the firm's efficiency. Note that inventory turnover can vary widely depending on the products a company sells and the industry it operates in.

When a company sells a large portion of its products on credit, it can learn useful information by measuring its receivables turnover. Receivables turnover can be calculated as follows:

$$\text{Receivables turnover} = \frac{\text{Credit sales}}{\text{Average accounts receivable}}$$

Because Diane's Java is a wholesaler, let's assume that all of its sales are credit sales. Average receivables equals the simple average of 2014's receivables and 2013's receivables. The receivables turnover for Diane's Java is calculated as follows:

$$\text{Receivables turnover} = \frac{17{,}300}{[(990+775)/2]} = 19.60$$

The average age of receivables is calculated by dividing 365 by the receivables turnover. The average age of Diane's Java receivables is 18.62 days. Assume Diane's Java expects its retail customers to pay outstanding bills within 30 days of the date of purchase. Given that the average age of its receivables is less than 30 days, Diane's Java appears to be doing a good job collecting its credit sales.

Another measure of efficiency is total asset turnover. It measures the amount of sales generated by each dollar invested in assets. The calculations for Diane's Java's total asset turnover are as follows:

$$\text{Total asset turnover} = \frac{\text{Sales}}{\text{Average total assets}}$$
$$= \frac{17{,}300}{[(8{,}790+7{,}305)/2]} = 2.15$$

Average total assets for Diane's Java equals total assets as of December 31, 2014 ($8.79 million) plus total assets as of December 31, 2013 ($7.305 million) divided by 2.

Diane's Java generates about $2.15 in sales for each dollar invested in assets. Although a higher ratio generally shows that a firm is operating more efficiently, care must be taken when comparing firms that operate in different industries. Some industries require a higher investment in assets than other industries.

Profitability Ratios

Some ratios measure the organization's overall financial performance by evaluating its ability to generate revenues that are greater than its operating costs and other expenses. These measures are called *profitability ratios*. To compute these ratios, accountants compare the firm's earnings with total sales or investments. Over a period of time, profitability ratios may show the effectiveness of management in operating the business. Three important profitability ratios are gross profit margin, net profit margin, and return on equity:

$$\text{Gross profit margin} = \frac{\text{Gross profit}}{\text{Sales}} = \frac{6{,}930}{17{,}300} = 40.0\%$$

$$\text{Net profit margin} = \frac{\text{Net income}}{\text{Sales}} = \frac{1{,}927}{17{,}300} = 11.1\%$$

$$\text{Return on equity} = \frac{\text{Net income}}{\text{Average equity}} = \frac{1{,}927}{[(5{,}660 + 4{,}455)/2]} = 38.1\%$$

All these ratios show positive evaluations of the current operations. For example, the net profit margin indicates that the firm realizes a profit of slightly more than 11 cents on each dollar of merchandise it sells. Although this ratio varies widely among business firms, Diane's Java compares well with wholesalers in general, which have an average net profit margin of around 5 percent. But, for a better interpretation of the results, this ratio, like the other profitability ratios, should be evaluated in relation to profit forecasts, past performance, or more specific industry averages. Similarly, although the firm's return on equity of almost 38 percent appears outstanding, any analysis should also consider the degree of risk in the industry.

Leverage Ratios

Leverage ratios measure how much a firm relies on debt financing. These ratios provide interesting information to potential investors and lenders. If management has taken on too much debt to finance the firm's operations, it may face difficulty in meeting future interest payments and repaying outstanding loans. As we discuss in Chapter 17, borrowing money does have advantages. But relying too much on debt financing may lead to bankruptcy. More generally, both investors and lenders may prefer to deal with firms whose owners have invested enough of their own money to avoid having to borrow funds. The debt ratio and the long-term debt to equity ratio help interested parties evaluate a firm's leverage:

$$\text{Debt ratio} = \frac{\text{Total liabilities}}{\text{Total assets}} = \frac{3,130}{8,790} = 35.6\%$$

$$\text{Long-term debt to equity} = \frac{\text{Long-term debt}}{\text{Owners' equity}} = \frac{1,100}{5,660} = 19.4\%$$

This Aflac advertisement is aimed at investors not insurance buyers. It notes the firm's 10-year total return to shareholders of 18.3 percent. *Return on equity* is one measure of a company's profitability.

When the debt ratio (the ratio of total liabilities to total assets) is greater than 50 percent, it shows that a firm is relying more on borrowed money than on owners' equity. Because Diane's Java's debt ratio is 35.6 percent, the firm's owners have invested considerably more than the total liabilities shown on the balance sheet. Also, the firm's long-term debt to equity ratio is only 19.4 percent, which shows that Diane's Java has only about 19.4 cents in long-term debt for every dollar in equity. The long-term debt to equity ratio also shows that Diane's Java hasn't relied very much on borrowed money.

The four categories of financial ratios relate balance sheet and income statement data to one another, help management focus on a firm's strengths and weaknesses, and show the areas in need of further investigation. Large, multiproduct firms that operate in very different markets use their information systems to update their financial ratios every day or even every hour. Each company's management must decide on a suitable review schedule to avoid the costly and time-consuming mistake of excessive monitoring.

Managers, investors, and lenders should pay close attention to how accountants apply accounting rules when preparing financial statements. GAAP gives accountants some flexibility in reporting certain revenues and expenses. Public companies are required to disclose, in footnotes to the financial statements, how the various accounting rules were applied.

✓ **ASSESSMENT CHECK**

15.6.1 List the four categories of financial ratios.

15.6.2 Define the following ratios: *current ratio*, *inventory turnover*, *net profit margin*, and *debt ratio*.

BUDGETING

LO 15.7 Describe the role of budgets in a business.

The financial statements discussed in this chapter focus on past business activities. But these same financial statements also provide the basis for planning in the future. A **budget** is a planning and controlling tool. It is the organization's plan for how it will raise and spend money during a specific period of time. Specifically, it shows the firm's expected sales revenues, operating expenses, cash receipts, and cash expenses. It quantifies the firm's plans for a specified future period. The budget can be thought of as a short-term financial plan. It becomes the standard that actual performance is compared against.

budget an organization's plans for how it will raise and spend money during a specific period of time.

Budget preparation is often a time-consuming task. It may involve many people from various departments within the organization. The complexity of the budgeting process varies with the size and complexity of the organization. Large corporations such as Research In Motion, RBC, and Rogers maintain complex and sophisticated budgeting systems. Their budgets serve as planning and controlling tools and help managers to integrate their numerous divisions. Budgeting in both large and small firms is similar to household budgeting in its purpose: to match income and expenses in a way that accomplishes goals and schedules cash inflows and outflows.

The accounting department is an organization's financial centre. It provides much of the data for budget development. The overall master budget, or operating budget, is composed of many individual budgets for each of the firm's separate units. These individual budgets typically include the production budget, cash budget, capital expenditures budget, advertising budget, and sales budget.

Technology has improved the efficiency of the budgeting process. The accounting software products discussed earlier—such as QuickBooks—all include budgeting features. The software modules designed for specific businesses are often available from third parties. Many banks now offer their customers personal financial management tools (PFMs) developed by software companies. One such tool is Quicken, Canada's most used money management program from Intuit.[9]

One of the most important budgets prepared by firms is the *cash budget*. The cash budget tracks the firm's cash inflows and outflows. It is usually prepared each month. Figure 15.7 illustrates a sample cash budget for Birchwood Paper, a small paper products company. The company has set a $150,000 target cash balance. The cash budget shows the months when the firm will need temporary loans—May, June, and July. It also shows the size of loan the company will need (close to $3 million). The document also shows that Birchwood will generate a cash surplus in August, when it can begin repaying the short-term loan. Finally, the cash budget produces a tangible standard against which to compare actual cash inflows and outflows.

✓ **ASSESSMENT CHECK**

15.7.1 What is a budget?

15.7.2 How is a cash budget organized?

Birchwood Paper Company
Four-Month Cash Budget

($ thousands)	May	June	July	August
Gross sales	$1,200.0	$3,200.0	$5,500.0	$4,500.0
Cash sales	300.0	800.0	1,375.0	1,125.0
One month prior	600.0	600.0	1,600.0	2,750.0
Two months prior	300.0	300.0	300.0	800.0
Total cash inflows	1,200.0	1,700.0	3,275.0	4,675.0
Purchases				
Cash purchases	1,040.0	1,787.5	1,462.5	390.0
One month prior	390.0	1,040.0	1,787.5	1,462.5
Wages and salaries	250.0	250.0	250.0	250.0
Office rent	75.0	75.0	75.0	75.0
Marketing and other expenses	150.0	150.0	150.0	150.0
Taxes		300.0		
Total cash outflows	1,905.0	3,602.5	3,725.0	2,327.5
Net cash flow				
(Inflows – Outflows)	(705.0)	(1,902.5)	(450.0)	2,347.5
Beginnning cash balance	250.0	150.0	150.0	150.0
Net cash flow	(705.0)	(1,902.5)	(450.0)	2,347.5
Ending cash balance	(455.0)	(1,752.5)	(300.0)	2,497.5
Target cash balance	150.0	150.0	150.0	150.0
Surplus (deficit)	(605.0)	(1,902.5)	(450.0)	2,347.5
Cumulative surplus (deficit)	(605.0)	(2,507.5)	(2,957.5)	610.0

FIGURE 15.7 Four-Month Cash Budget for Birchwood Paper Company

HIT & MISS

Accounting: Hong Kong Meets China

Hong Kong was a British colony for almost 200 years. In 1997, Britain transferred Hong Kong to the People's Republic of China. China's rise to global power has led to difficulties in combining its financial environment with that of Hong Kong. Even after the transfer, Hong Kong and mainland China kept two separate accounting systems with different standards and different qualifying examinations. Hong Kong accounting is based on international standards and is conducted in English; Chinese accounting is not.

At the beginning of 2010, Hong Kong accepted Chinese accounting standards. This step shows China's growing attractiveness to international investors. It also advances China's ambition to be part of the international financial system. Until recently, the Chinese accounting system was known for its "book-cooking" scandals. As Hong Kong's transition to Chinese standards continues, Hong Kong accountants risk losing much of their business to Chinese firms.

Tim Lui is a tax partner at the Hong Kong branch of the worldwide accounting firm PricewaterhouseCoopers. He believes that in the short run, at least, Hong Kong accountants have a competitive edge because of their training and international perspective. Foreign investors will be glad to see that Chinese companies will be audited by large, international accounting firms. But he warns against underestimating the Chinese market: "The mainland's development is robust and fast and the market is immense."

Another concern is that small and medium-sized Hong Kong accounting firms simply aren't big enough to succeed in China, especially in Shanghai, China's business and accounting centre. Robert Sawhney of SRC Associations Ltd., a Hong Kong accounting firm, urges smaller firms to market themselves more aggressively and to update their training strategies. He says, "There is substantial scope for Asian accounting firms to provide services to other organizations and in niche areas."

Questions for Critical Thinking

1. How might the mix of Chinese and internationally accepted accounting methods affect Chinese firms' operations and ethical standards?

2. What can Hong Kong accounting firms do to increase their business in mainland China?

Sources: Robert C. Sawhney, "The Competitiveness of Hong Kong & Asian Accounting Firms," white paper, March 2010, http://www.srchk.com; "The Demand for Accountants Is Always There," *China Daily*, January 8, 2010, http://www.chinadaily.com; Alison Leung, "China Auditors Set to Take on Hong Kong Stock Market," *Reuters*, December 30, 2009, http://www.reuters.com.

INTERNATIONAL ACCOUNTING

LO 15.8 Outline the accounting issues facing global business.

Today, accounting procedures and practices must be adapted to work in an international business environment. The BlackBerry maker, Research In Motion, generates more than half of its annual revenues from sales outside Canada. Nestlé, the giant chocolate and food products firm, operates throughout the world. It derives 98 percent of its revenues from outside Switzerland, its home country. Global firms must reliably translate the financial statements of the firm's international affiliated firms, branches, and subsidiaries and convert data about foreign currency transactions to dollars. Also, foreign currencies and exchange rates influence the accounting and financial reporting processes of firms operating internationally.[10]

As market economies have developed in such countries as Poland and China, the demand for accountants has increased. The "Hit & Miss" feature describes recent developments in the accounting profession in China and Hong Kong.

Exchange Rates

As defined in Chapter 4, an exchange rate is the value of one country's currency in terms of the currencies of other countries. Currencies can be treated as if they are goods to be bought and sold. Like the price of any product, currency prices change according to supply and demand. But unlike many products, currency prices change daily—or more often. Exchange rate fluctuations, or ups and downs, complicate accounting entries and accounting practices.

In Pakistan, a truck driver delivers Nestlé food products. Because the Swiss corporation operates around the world, its profits and its financial statements are affected by foreign exchange rates.

Ilyas Dean/NewsCom

Accountants who deal with international transactions must take care when recording their firms' foreign sales and purchases. Today's sophisticated accounting software helps firms handle all of their international transactions within a single program. An international firm's consolidated financial statements must show any gains or losses due to changes in exchange rates during specific periods of time. Financial statements that cover operations in two or more countries need to treat fluctuations consistently to allow for comparison.

In Canada, GAAP requires firms to adjust their earnings to reflect changes in exchange rates. A weakening dollar generally increases the earnings of a Canadian firm that has international operations: the same units of a foreign currency will translate into more Canadian dollars. A strengthening dollar will have the opposite effect on earnings—the same number of units of a foreign currency will translate into fewer dollars. In one recent year, for example, currency fluctuations caused an $11 million drop in earnings from the same quarter of the previous year for PPG, the world's second largest paint manufacturer.[11]

ASSESSMENT CHECK

15.8.1 How are financial statements adjusted for exchange rates?

WHAT'S AHEAD

This chapter describes the role of accounting in an organization. Accounting is the process of measuring, interpreting, and communicating financial information to interested parties both inside and outside the firm. The next two chapters discuss the finance function of an organization. Finance deals with planning, obtaining, and managing the organization's funds to accomplish its objectives in the most efficient and effective manner possible. Chapter 16 outlines the financial system, the system used to transfer funds from savers to borrowers. Organizations rely on the financial system to raise funds for expansion or operations. The chapter includes a description of financial institutions, such as banks; financial markets, such as the Toronto Stock Exchange; financial instruments, such as stocks and bonds; and the role of the Bank of Canada. Chapter 17 discusses the role of finance and the financial manager in an organization.

RETURN TO INSIDE BUSINESS

Cooking the Books

Many feel that accounting information is "black and white"—that is, it is either right or wrong, with no in-between shades of grey. But as described in the stories of accounting fraud, many accountants and high-level executives risk stiff prison sentences when "cooking the books."

QUESTIONS FOR CRITICAL THINKING

1. How is it possible that what seems to be straightforward financial information can be altered by corporate executives who claim it conforms to GAAP?

2. Why do corporate executives risk prison sentences by preparing questionable financial statements?

SUMMARY OF LEARNING OBJECTIVES

LO 15.1 Explain the functions of accounting, and identify the three basic activities involving accounting.

Accountants measure, interpret, and communicate financial information to people inside and outside the firm to support informed decision-making. Accountants gather, record, and interpret financial information for management. They also provide financial information on the status and operations of the firm for evaluation by outside individuals, such as government representatives, shareholders, potential investors, and lenders. Accounting plays key roles in financing activities, which help to start and expand an organization; investing activities, which provide the assets a company needs to continue operating; and operating activities, which focus on selling goods and services and paying expenses incurred in regular operations.

 ASSESSMENT CHECK ANSWERS

15.1.1 Define *accounting*. Accounting is the process of measuring, interpreting, and communicating financial information that describes the status and operation of an organization and aids in decision-making.

15.1.2 Who uses accounting information? Managers in all types of organizations use accounting information to help them plan, assess performance, and control daily and long-term operations. Outside users of accounting information include government officials, investors, creditors, and donors.

15.1.3 What three business activities involve accounting? The three activities involving accounting are financing, investing, and operating activities.

LO 15.2 Describe the roles played by public, management, government, and not-for-profit accountants.

Public accountants provide accounting services to other firms or individuals for a fee. They perform the following activities: auditing, tax return preparation, management consulting, and accounting system design. Management accountants are employed by a firm, where they collect and record financial transactions, prepare financial statements, and interpret financial data for managers. Government and not-for-profit accountants perform many of the same functions as management accountants. But, instead of dealing with profits and losses, they look at how effectively the organization or agency is operating.

 ASSESSMENT CHECK ANSWERS

15.2.1 List the three services offered by public accounting firms. The three services offered by public accounting firms are auditing, management consulting, and tax services.

15.2.2 What tasks do management accountants perform? Management accountants work for an organization. They are responsible for collecting and recording financial transactions, and for preparing and interpreting financial statements.

LO 15.3 Identify the foundations of the accounting system, including GAAP, IFRS, and the role of the Accounting Standards Board (AcSB).

The foundation of the accounting system in Canada is GAAP (generally accepted accounting principles), a set of guidelines or standards that accountants follow. Companies that trade on a public stock exchange are required to use IFRS (International Financial Reporting Standards). Some basic qualitative characteristics of the financial statements are consistency, relevance, representational faithfulness, reliability, timeliness, understandability, verifiability, and comparability. The Accounting Standards Board (AcSB) is an independent body made up of accounting professionals. The AcSB is primarily responsible for evaluating, setting, and modifying GAAP.

✔ **ASSESSMENT CHECK ANSWERS**

15.3.1 Define *GAAP*. GAAP stands for generally accepted accounting principles. It is a set of standards or guidelines that accountants follow when recording and reporting financial transactions.

15.3.2 What is the role played by the AcSB? The Accounting Standards Board (AcSB) is an independent body made up of accounting professionals. It is primarily responsible for evaluating, setting, and modifying Canadian GAAP related primarily to private and not-for-profit organizations. Note that publicly accountable organizations are required to follow IFRS.

LO 15.4 Outline the steps in the accounting cycle, and define *double-entry bookkeeping* and the *accounting equation*.

The accounting process involves recording, classifying, and summarizing data about financial transactions. This information is used to produce financial statements for the firm's managers and other interested individuals. Transactions are recorded chronologically, in the order they occur, in journals, then posted in ledgers, and then summarized in accounting statements. Today, most of this activity takes place electronically. The basic accounting equation states that assets (what a firm owns) must always equal liabilities (what a firm owes creditors) plus owners' equity (the owners' investments in the firm). This equation also illustrates double-entry bookkeeping, the process used to record accounting transactions. In double-entry bookkeeping, each individual transaction must be balanced by another transaction.

 ASSESSMENT CHECK ANSWERS

15.4.1 List the steps in the accounting cycle. The accounting cycle involves the following steps: recording transactions, classifying the transactions, summarizing the transactions, and using the summaries to produce financial statements.

15.4.2 What is the accounting equation? The accounting equation states that assets (what a firm owns) must always equal liabilities (what a firm owes) plus owners' equity (the owners' investments in the firm). An increase or decrease in an asset must be balanced by an increase or decrease in liabilities, owners' equity, or both.

15.4.3 Briefly explain double-entry bookkeeping. Double-entry bookkeeping requires every transaction to be balanced by another transaction.

LO 15.5 Explain the functions and major components of the four principal financial statements: the balance sheet, the income statement, the statement of changes in equity, and the statement of cash flows.

The balance sheet shows a firm's financial position on a particular date. The three major classifications of balance sheet data are the elements of the accounting equation: assets, liabilities, and owners'

equity. The income statement shows the results of a firm's operations over a specific time period. It focuses on the firm's activities—its revenues and expenditures—and the resulting profit or loss during the period. The major entries in the income statement are revenues, cost of goods sold, expenses, and profit or loss. The statement of changes in equity shows the change in owners' equity from the end of the previous year to the end of the current year. Finally, the statement of cash flows shows a firm's cash receipts and cash payments during an accounting period. It outlines the sources and uses of cash in the basic business activities of operating, investing, and financing.

 ASSESSMENT CHECK ANSWERS

15.5.1 List the four financial statements. The four financial statements are the balance sheet, the income statement, the statement of changes in equity, and the cash flow statement.

15.5.2 How is the balance sheet organized? Assets (what a firm owns) are shown on one side of the balance sheet and are listed in a downward order of their convertibility into cash. On the other side of the balance sheet are claims to assets, liabilities (what a firm owes), and owners' equity (the owners' investments in the firm). Claims are listed in the order in which they are due. For example, liabilities are listed before owners' equity. Assets always equal liabilities plus owners' equity.

15.5.3 Define *accrual accounting*. Accrual accounting records revenues and expenses when they occur, not when cash actually changes hands. Most companies use accrual accounting to prepare their financial statements.

LO 15.6 Discuss how financial ratios are used to analyze a company's financial strengths and weaknesses.

Liquidity ratios measure a firm's ability to meet its short-term obligations. Examples are the current ratio and the quick ratio, also called the acid-test ratio. Activity ratios, such as the inventory turnover ratio, the accounts receivable turnover ratio, and the total asset turnover ratio, measure how effectively a firm uses its resources. Profitability ratios assess the overall financial performance of the business. Examples are the gross profit margin, the net profit margin, and the return on owners' equity. Leverage ratios, such as the total liabilities to total assets ratio and the long-term debt to equity ratio, measure the extent to which the firm relies on debt to finance its operations. Financial ratios help managers and outside evaluators compare a firm's current financial information with that of previous years and with results for other firms in the same industry.

 ASSESSMENT CHECK ANSWERS

15.6.1 List the four categories of financial ratios. The four categories of ratios are liquidity, activity, profitability, and leverage.

15.6.2 Define the following ratios: *current ratio, inventory turnover, net profit margin,* and *debt ratio.* The current ratio equals current assets divided by current liabilities; inventory turnover equals cost of goods sold divided by average inventory; net profit margin equals net income divided by sales; and the debt ratio equals total liabilities divided by total assets.

LO 15.7 Describe the role of budgets in a business.

Budgets are financial guidelines for future periods. They show a firm's expected sales revenues, operating expenses, cash receipts, and cash expenses. They reflect management's expected outcomes for the future and are based on plans that have been made. Budgets are important tools for planning and controlling. They provide standards against which actual performance can be measured. One important type of budget is the cash budget, which estimates cash inflows and outflows over a period of time.

✓ **ASSESSMENT CHECK ANSWERS**

15.7.1 What is a budget? A budget is a planning and control tool that reflects the firm's expected sales revenues, operating expenses, cash receipts, cash expenses.

15.7.2 How is a cash budget organized? Cash budgets are usually prepared monthly. Cash receipts are listed first.

They include cash sales and the collection of past credit sales. Cash outlays, or cash expenses, are listed next. These include cash purchases, payment of past credit purchases, and operating expenses. The difference between cash receipts and cash outlays is net cash flow.

LO 15.8 Outline the accounting issues facing global business.

One accounting issue that affects global business is exchange rates. An exchange rate is the value of one country's currency in terms of the currencies of other countries. Daily changes in exchange rates affect the accounting entries for the sales and purchases of firms dealing in international markets. These fluctuations, or ups and downs, create either losses or gains for companies.

✓ **ASSESSMENT CHECK ANSWERS**

15.8.1 How are financial statements adjusted for exchange rates? An exchange rate is the value of one country's currency in terms of the currencies of other countries. Fluctuations, the ups and downs, of exchange rates create either gains or losses for global companies. Data about international financial transactions must be translated into the currency of the country where the parent company resides.

BUSINESS TERMS YOU NEED TO KNOW

accounting 418

public accountant 420

generally accepted accounting principles (GAAP) 422

Accounting Standards Board (AcSB) 422

International Financial Reporting Standards (IFRS) 422

International Accounting Standards Board (IASB) 422

Financial Accounting Standards Board (FASB) 423

Corruption of Foreign Public Officials Act 424

accounting cycle 424

asset 424

liability 425

owners' equity 425

accounting equation 425

double-entry bookkeeping 425

balance sheet 428

income statement 429

statement of changes in equity 431

statement of cash flows 432

accrual accounting 432

budget 437

REVIEW QUESTIONS

1. Define *accounting.* Who are the major users of accounting information?

2. What are the three major business activities where accountants play a major role? Give an example of each.

3. What does the term *GAAP* mean? Briefly explain the role of the Accounting Standards Board.

4. What is double-entry bookkeeping? Give a brief example.

5. List the four major financial statements. Which financial statements are permanent and which are temporary?

6. What is the difference between a current asset and a long-term asset? Why is cash typically listed first on a balance sheet?

7. List and explain the major items found on an income statement.

8. What is accrual accounting? Give an example of how accrual accounting affects a firm's financial statement.

9. List the four categories of financial ratios and give an example of each. What is the purpose of ratio analysis?

10. What is a cash budget? Briefly outline what a simple cash budget might look like.

PROJECTS AND TEAMWORK APPLICATIONS

1. Contact a local public accounting firm and set up an interview with one of the accountants. Ask the accountant about his or her educational background, why he or she was attracted to the accounting profession, and what he or she does during a typical day. Prepare a brief report on your interview. Do you want to learn more about the accounting profession? Are you more interested or less interested in a career in accounting? Why?

2. Suppose you work for a Canadian firm that has extensive operations in various countries. You are preparing your firm's financial statements, and you need to restate data from the various currencies to Canadian dollars. Which financial statements and which parts of these statements will be affected?

3. Identify two public companies operating in different industries. Collect at least three years' worth of financial statements for the firms. Calculate the financial ratios listed in Table 15.1. Prepare an oral report that summarizes your findings.

4. You've been appointed treasurer of a local not-for-profit organization. You want to improve the quality of financial reporting to existing and potential donors. What kinds of financial statements do you ask the organization's accountant prepare? Why do you think better-quality financial statements might help reassure donors?

5. Use the format of the table Figure 15.7 and adapt it to prepare your personal cash budget for next month. Keep in mind the following suggestions as you prepare your budget:

  a. *Cash inflows.* Your sources of cash include your payroll earnings, if any; gifts; scholarships; tax refunds; dividends and interest; and income from self-employment.

  b. *Cash outflows.* When estimating next month's cash outflows, include any of the following that may apply to your situation:

    i. Household expenses (rent or mortgage, utilities, maintenance, home furnishings, telephone/cellphone, cable TV, household supplies, groceries)

    ii. Education (tuition, fees, textbooks, supplies)

    iii. Work (transportation, clothing)

    iv. Clothing (purchases, cleaning, laundry)

    v. Automobile (auto payments, fuel, repairs) or other transportation (bus, train)

    vi. Insurance premiums

      • Renters (or homeowners)

      • Auto

      • Health

      • Life

    vii. Taxes (income, real estate)

    viii. Savings and investments

    ix. Entertainment/recreation (health club, vacation/travel, dining, movies)

    x. Debt (credit cards, installment loans)

    xi. Miscellaneous (charitable contributions, childcare, gifts, medical expenses)

  c. *Beginning cash balance.* This amount can be based on a minimum cash balance you keep in your chequing account. It should include only the cash available for your use; investments in retirement plans should not be included.

WEB ASSIGNMENTS

1. **International Accounting Standards Board (IASB).** The IASB is responsible for setting and modifying international accounting rules. Go to the IASB's website (http://www.iasb.org); click on "About us" and select "About the organisation." Print out the material and bring it to class to participate in a class discussion on the IASB.

2. **Certified Management Accountant (CMA).** As noted in the chapter, managerial accountants often seek the CMA designation. Visit the website of CMA Ontario (http://www.cma-ontario.org/). Click on "Become a CMA," and then "Steps to becoming a CMA." What are the educational and experiential requirements to obtain a CMA? How many exams does a CMA candidate need to pass? What do these exams cover?

3. **Financial reporting requirements.** The chapter discussed the financial reporting requirements of Canadian companies, including public companies whose shares are traded on a stock exchange. Visit the website listed below and type in the name of a public company, and then click on "financials" to view the firm's current financial statements. Prepare a brief report comparing those statements to the ones shown in the chapter.

    http://www.google.com/finance

Access your WileyPLUS course for:

- The complete digital textbook.

- Question assistance, including links to relevant sections in the online digital textbook.

- Immediate feedback and proof of progress, 24/7

- Integrated, multi-media resources – including MP3 downloads, visual exhibits, animations, and much more – that provide multiple study paths and encourage more active learning.

QUIZ YOURSELF

Note: Internet Web addresses change frequently. If you don't find the exact sites listed, you may need to access the organization's home page and search from there or use a search engine such as Bing or Google.

16 | THE FINANCIAL SYSTEM

LEARNING OBJECTIVES

LO 16.1 Outline the structure and importance of the financial system.

LO 16.2 List the various types of securities.

LO 16.3 Define *financial market,* and distinguish between primary and secondary financial markets.

LO 16.4 Describe the characteristics of the major stock exchanges.

LO 16.5 Discuss the organization and functioning of financial institutions.

LO 16.6 Explain the functions of the Bank of Canada and the tools it uses to control the supply of money and credit.

LO 16.7 Understand the impact of regulations and laws affecting the financial system.

LO 16.8 Describe the global financial system.

INSIDE BUSINESS

© Kristoffer Tripplaar/Alamy

Canada Weathers the Credit Crisis

In 2008, much of the world's financial systems melted. But Canada's financial systems were largely unaffected. Europe, Greece and Italy felt a significant impact of the global credit crisis. In the United States, interest rates were low and borrowing was high. The greater access to financing increased both the demand for housing and housing prices. U.S. banks became very aggressive. They tempted clients, including many high-risk clients, by offering very low down payments and low interest rates for the first few years of their mortgage. These mortgages were then packaged and sold to investors who felt assured that the collateral, or security, behind the mortgages (the homes) would reduce any risk of default on the mortgage. The main problem began after clients completed the first few years of low-interest mortgage payments. Their mortgage rates then increased, causing their monthly payments to also increase. Many clients were forced to default on their payments or sell their homes. The increase of homes on the market led to a reverse effect on prices—the "bubble" burst. The result was a high proportion of "toxic" mortgages, which had a higher value than the homes themselves. For example, homes valued at less than $250,000 had mortgages of more than $500,000. This situation was a disaster for creditors. Some lost half or more of their investment.

Why weren't Canadians affected in the same way? And, why were Canadian banks rated the strongest in the world by the World Economic Forum? For starters, Canada's financial system is much more regulated than the U.S. banking system. And, by nature, Canadians tend to be less financially aggressive than Americans. Canadian banks have many more checks and balances related to confirming income, job status, and sales contracts. Canadian *consumers* also carry less debt on average than Americans (20 percent versus 26 percent, respectively). That explains why Canadians had fewer subprime mortgages: one in 20 in Canada versus one in six in the United States.

In Canada, housing values just before the 2008 financial crisis were about 200 percent of what they were in 1989, compared with 260 percent in the United States. During the crisis, the value of U.S. homes dropped to approximately 220 percent of their 1989 values, while little change was felt in Canada. The same type of housing bubble is highly unlikely in Canada because Canadians are generally financially conservative, both on the buyer's side and the lender's side. As a result, Canadian homes are rarely valued at less than their mortgage, which was a problem for Americans after the housing bubble burst. The Canada Mortgage and Housing Corporation (CMHC) is owned by the Canadian government. It insures mortgages for higher-risk clients who have low down payments.

Finally, Canadians receive no tax incentive for having a mortgage whereas mortgage interest is a tax deduction in the United States, providing another reason for Americans to have a mortgage. In Canada, "a mortgage is seen as something you want to get rid of as fast as possible," says Peter Dungan, an economist at the Rotman School of Management at the University of Toronto. It is clear that no single factor preserved the financial system in Canada during the financial meltdown. Instead, a combination of financial conservatism and government policy helped Canadians to weather the crisis.[1]

CHAPTER 16 OVERVIEW

Businesses, governments, and individuals often need to raise capital, or money. For example, suppose a businessperson forecasts a sharp increase in sales for the coming year. This expected sales increase requires additional inventory. If the business lacks the cash to purchase the needed inventory, it may turn to a bank for a short-term loan. On the other hand, some individuals and businesses have incomes that are greater than their current expenses. They may want to earn interest on the extra funds. For example, suppose your income this month is $3,000, but your expenses are only $2,500. You can deposit the extra $500 in a bank account and receive interest.

The two transactions described above are small parts of what is known as the **financial system**, the mechanism by which money flows from savers to users. Almost all businesses, governments, and individuals participate in the financial system. A well-functioning financial system is vital to a nation's economic health. The financial system is the topic of this chapter.

We begin by describing the financial system and its components in more detail. We then outline the major types of financial instruments, such as bonds and stocks (also known as shares). Next we discuss financial markets, where financial instruments are bought and sold. We then describe the world's major stock markets.

Next, banks and other financial institutions are described in depth. We detail the structure and responsibilities of the Bank of Canada and the tools it uses to control the supply of money and credit. The chapter concludes with an overview of the major laws and regulations affecting the financial system and a discussion of today's global financial system.

financial system the mechanism by which money flows from savers to users.

LO 16.1 Outline the structure and importance of the financial system.

UNDERSTANDING THE FINANCIAL SYSTEM

Households, businesses, government, financial institutions, and financial markets together form what is known as the financial system. A simple diagram of the financial system is shown in Figure 16.1.

On the left are savers—those who have excess funds. For different reasons, savers choose not to spend all their current income, so they have a surplus of funds. Users are the opposite of savers; their spending needs are greater than their current income, so they have a shortfall. They need to obtain additional funds to make up the difference. Savings are provided by some households, businesses, and the government, but some other households, businesses, and the government are borrowers. Households may need money to buy automobiles or homes. Businesses may need money to purchase inventory or build new production facilities. Governments may need money to build highways and courthouses.

In Canada, households are generally net savers. That means that, as a whole, households save more money than they use. Businesses and governments are net users. That means that they generally use more funds than they save. You may be surprised that households provide most of the net savings in

FIGURE 16.1 Overview of the Financial System and Its Components

the Canadian financial system. After all, Canadians do not have a reputation for being thrifty. The savings rate of Canadian households is low compared with the savings rates in other countries, but Canadian households still save billions of dollars each year.

How much an individual saves depends on many factors. One of the most important factors is the person's age. As people age, they often move from being net borrowers to being net savers. When you graduate from university or college and begin a career, you likely have very little savings. In fact, you may be in debt. In the early years of your career, you may spend more than you make as you buy major assets, such as a home. In these early career years, your *net worth*—the difference between what you own and what you owe—is very low and may even be negative. But as your career progresses and your income rises, you will begin to build financial savings to fund retirement and other needs. Your net worth will also increase. It will continue to increase until you retire and begin drawing on your retirement savings.

Funds can be transferred between savers and users in two ways: directly and indirectly. A direct transfer means that the user raises the needed funds directly from savers. Direct transfers *do* occur, but most funds flow through either financial markets or financial institutions. For example, assume a local school district needs to build a new high school. The district does not have enough cash to pay for the school construction costs, so it sells bonds to investors (savers) in the financial market. The district uses the funds from the sale to pay for the new school. In return, the bond investors receive interest each year for the use of their money.

The other way that funds can be transferred indirectly is through financial institutions—for example, through a commercial bank such as TD Canada Trust or Scotiabank. The bank pools, or combines, customer deposits and uses the funds to make loans to businesses and households. These borrowers pay the bank interest, and the bank, in turn, pays its depositors interest for the use of their money.

The accompanying "Going Green" feature describes how TD Bank has started to transform all its branches so that they will be "carbon neutral."

✓ ASSESSMENT CHECK

16.1.1 What is the financial system?

16.1.2 In the financial system, who are the borrowers and who are the savers?

16.1.3 List the two most common ways that funds are transferred between borrowers and savers.

GOING GREEN   TD BANK: "AS GREEN AS OUR LOGO"

TD Bank's square, green logo is a familiar sight from Vancouver to Florida. TD Bank announced that it was the first North American bank to go carbon neutral in the United States. The bank achieved carbon neutrality by reducing waste, using alternative sources of energy, and building environmentally friendly buildings from sustainable materials. With 1,000 branches, or "stores," TD has used its resources to pursue an aggressive "green" policy.

To demonstrate its goal of carbon neutrality, TD bank unveiled a new prototype store. The 3,800-square-foot building is designed to reduce energy use by 50 percent, compared with earlier models. Each new store will make up to 20 percent of its own electricity through solar panels on the roof. To keep interior temperatures comfortable, the windows will have specially coated glass that reflects or absorbs heat energy. Sensors will control lighting over the course of the day. The drive-through facility will feature a translucent solar canopy. Outside, the landscaping will include drought-resistant plants and water-efficient plumbing.

Among other measures, TD Bank has bought a block of wind energy large enough to run its 2,300 automated teller machines (ATMs). It plans to encourage its customers to save energy by signing up for online banking and paperless statements. TD Bank has also located many of its branches near public transportation.

TD Bank's first fully green office opened in Queens Village, New York. This branch has applied for LEED (Leadership in Energy and Environmental Design) Platinum Certification, the highest level. The bank eventually plans to have all of its offices meet LEED standards.

In Canada, TD Financial Group has established the TD Friends of the Environment Foundation. It has provided over $53 million to support more than 19,000 grassroots environmental initiatives throughout Canada.

Fred Graziano, TD Bank's head of retail banking, says, "We're taking the environment seriously and we strongly believe this is the right thing to do for our business, customers, employees and the community. We want TD Bank to be as green as our logo."

Questions for Critical Thinking

1. Why does "going green" make good business sense for TD Bank?

2. Think about your own banking practices. What steps can you take to be greener?

Sources: Company website, http://www.tdbank.com, accessed February 22, 2012; James Comtois, "TD Bank's First Green Branch Sprouts in Queens," *Crain's New York Business.com,* February 22, 2012, http://www.crainsnewyork.com; Patrick Lo, "TD Bank Goes Carbon Neutral," *Green Street Journal,* March 16, 2010, http://www.gsjournal.com; "TD Bank Goes Carbon Neutral, Unveils 'Green Store' Prototype," *Environmental Leader,* February 22, 2012, http://www.environmentalleader.com; "TD Bank, America's Most Convenient Bank, Announces It's Now Carbon Neutral and Unveils New 'Green Store' Prototype Design," press release, February 18, 2010, http://multivu.prnewswire.com; TD Friends of the Environment Foundation, "TD Friends of the Environment Foundation: Helping Canadians Make a Difference," http://www.fef.td.com/about.jsp, accessed July 4, 2011.

**LO
16.2**   List the various types of securities.

securities financial instruments that represent the obligations of the issuers to provide the purchasers with the expected stated returns on the funds invested or loaned.

TYPES OF SECURITIES

When businesses and governments borrow funds from savers, they provide different types of guarantees for repayment. **Securities**, also called financial instruments, represent the obligations of the issuers—businesses and governments—to provide the purchasers with the expected or stated returns on the funds invested or loaned. Securities can be grouped into three categories: money market instruments, bonds, and shares (also known as stock). Money market instruments and bonds are debt securities. Shares are units of ownership in public corporations, such as Sun Life Financial, HBC, and BCE.

Money Market Instruments

Money market instruments are short-term debt securities issued by governments, financial institutions, and corporations. All money market instruments mature within one year from the date of issue. The issuer pays interest to the investors for the use of their funds. Money market instruments are generally low-risk securities and are purchased by investors when they have surplus cash. Examples of money market instruments include Canadian Treasury bills, commercial paper, and bank certificates of deposit.

Treasury bills are short-term securities issued by the Canadian Treasury and backed by the full faith and credit of the Canadian government. Treasury bills are sold with a maturity date of 30, 90, 180, or 360 days and must be a minimum of $1,000. They are virtually risk-free and are easy to resell. Commercial paper refers to securities sold by corporations, such as Telus. These securities mature in 1 to 270 days from the date of issue. Although commercial paper is slightly riskier than Treasury bills, it is generally considered to be a very low-risk security.

A certificate of deposit (CD) is a time deposit at a financial institution, such as a commercial bank, a savings bank, or a credit union. The sizes and maturity dates of CDs vary and can often be tailored to meet the needs of purchasers. CDs of $100,000 or less per depositor are insured by the Canada Deposit Insurance Corporation (CDIC). CDs in larger denominations are not federally insured but can be sold more easily before they mature.

Bonds

Bondholders are creditors of a corporation or government body. A firm may sell bonds to obtain long-term debt capital. Federal, provincial, and municipal governments also acquire funds through bonds. Bonds are issued in various denominations, or face values, usually between $1,000 and $25,000. Each issue indicates the rate of interest and the maturity date. The rate of interest to be paid to the bondholder is stated as a percentage of the bond's face value. The maturity date is the date when the bondholder will be paid the bond's full face value. Bondholders are creditors. That means their claim on the firm's assets must be satisfied before any claims of shareholders if the firm enters into bankruptcy, reorganization, or liquidation.

Types of Bonds

A prospective bond investor can choose among a several types of bonds. The major types of bonds are summarized in Table 16.1. *Government bonds,* such as Canada Savings Bonds, are bonds sold by the Canadian government. Government bonds are backed by the full faith and credit of the Canadian government, which means they are the least risky of all bonds. The Treasury sells bonds that mature in 2, 5, 10, and 30 years from the date of issue.

Municipal bonds are bonds issued by municipal governments. Two types of municipal bonds are available: corporate bonds and mortgage-backed *corporate bonds.* Corporate bonds include a diverse group of bonds. They often vary depending on the collateral—the property pledged by the borrower—that backs the bond. For example, a *secured bond* is backed by a specific pledge of company assets. These assets are the collateral, just like a home is collateral for a house mortgage. However, many businesses also issue unsecured bonds, called *debentures*. These bonds are backed only by the financial reputation of the issuing corporation.

Table 16.1 Types of Bonds

ISSUER	TYPES OF SECURITIES	RISK	SPECIAL FEATURES
Government of Canada (government bonds)	Canada Savings Bonds: Mature in 10 years, but can be cashed at any time.	Government bonds carry virtually no risk.	Affordable: can be purchased for as little as $100
Provincial and local governments (municipal bonds)	General obligation: Issued by provincial or local governmental units with taxing authority; backed by the full faith and credit of the province or municipality where the bonds are issued.	Risk varies, depending on the financial health of the issuer. Risk is generally very low.	
Corporations	Secured bonds: Bonds that are backed by specific assets.	Risk varies depending on the financial health of the issuer.	A few corporate bonds are convertible into common shares of the issuing company.
	Unsecured bonds (debentures): Bonds that are backed by the financial health and reputation of the issuer.	Most corporate bond issues are rated in terms of credit risk (AAA or Aaa is the highest rating).	
Financial institutions	Mortgage-backed securities	Generally very low risk.	They pay monthly income consisting of both interest and principal.

The second type of bonds are mortgage-backed corporate bonds, also called *mortgage-backed securities (MBSs)*. These bonds are backed by a pool, or group, of mortgage loans purchased from lenders, such as chartered banks. As borrowers make their mortgage payments, these payments are "passed through" to the holders of the securities. MBSs are very safe because all mortgages in the pool, or group, are insured by CMHC. In the United States, during the period of approximately 2004 to 2008, similar securities were issued. But these securities consisted of so-called *subprime mortgages*, loans made to borrowers with poor credit ratings. Many of these securities turned out to be risky and, in part, triggered what became known as the *credit crisis*, which began in 2008. The extent of the crisis forced the U.S. government to undertake a massive bailout of the financial system. The Office of Financial Stability—part of the U.S. Treasury department—was created to purchase poor-quality, mortgage-backed securities from financial institutions.

Quality Ratings for Bonds

Two factors affect the price of a bond: its risk and its interest rate. Bonds vary in terms of their risk. Bond investors use a tool called a *bond rating* to assess the risk of a bond. Several investment firms rate corporate and municipal bonds. In Canada, the Dominion Bond Rating Service (DBRS) provides bond ratings. The best-known bond rating organizations are Standard & Poor's (S&P), Moody's, and Fitch. Table 16.2 lists the S&P bond ratings. Moody's and Fitch use similar rating systems. Bonds with the lowest level of risk are rated AAA. As ratings descend, risk increases. Bonds with ratings of BBB and above are classified as *investment-grade bonds*. Bonds with ratings of BB and below are classified as *speculative bonds*, or *junk bonds*. Junk bonds attract investors because they offer high interest rates in exchange for greater risk. Today, junk bonds pay about 50 percent more in interest than investment-grade corporate bonds. The recent credit crisis generated a great deal of criticism toward the ratings companies. This criticism centred on the conflict of interest from ratings companies also advising companies on how to structure their bond offerings.

Table 16.2 Standard & Poor's Bond Ratings

Highest	**AAA**	Extremely strong capacity to meet financial commitments; the highest rating
	AA	Very strong capacity to meet financial commitments
	A	Strong capacity to meet financial commitments, but may be at risk during poor economic conditions and changes in circumstances
	BBB	Adequate capacity to meet financial commitments, but more subject to risk during poor economic conditions
	BB	Less vulnerable in the near-term but faces major ongoing uncertainties during poor business, financial and economic conditions
	B	More vulnerable to risks from poor business, financial and economic conditions but currently has the capacity to meet financial commitments
	CCC	Currently vulnerable and dependent on favourable business, financial, and economic conditions to meet financial commitments
	CC	Currently highly vulnerable
	C	Currently highly vulnerable obligations and other defined circumstances
Lowest	**D**	Payment default on financial commitments

Note: Standard & Poor's occasionally assigns a plus or minus following the letter rating. For instance, AA+ means that the bond is higher quality than most AA bonds but hasn't quite met AAA standards. Ratings below C indicate that the bond is currently not paying interest. Source: Standard & Poor's Rating Services, "Credit Ratings Definitions and FAQs." http://www.standardandpoors.com/ratings/definitions-and-faqs/en/us#def_1, accessed February 22, 2012.

The second factor affecting the price of a bond is its interest rate. All other things being equal, the higher the interest rate, the higher the price of a bond. But often everything else is *not* equal: the bonds may not be equally risky, or one bond may have a longer maturity date. Investors must evaluate the individual characteristics of each bond.

Another important influence on bond prices is the *market interest rate*. Bonds pay fixed rates of interest. That means that as market interest rates rise, bond prices fall. The opposite is also true: as market interest rates fall, bond prices rise. For example, the price of a 10-year bond that pays 5 percent per year would fall by about 8 percent if market interest rates rose from 5 percent to 6 percent.

Most corporate and municipal bonds are callable, as are some government bonds. A *call provision* allows the issuer to redeem, or cash, the bond before its maturity at a specified price. Not surprisingly, issuers tend to call bonds when market interest rates are declining. For example, suppose the City of Toronto had $50 million in bonds outstanding with a 5 percent annual interest rate. It would pay $2.5 million annually in interest. Now, suppose interest rates fall to 3 percent. The city may decide to call the 5 percent bonds, by repaying the principal from the proceeds, or funds, from the newly issued 3 percent bonds. Calling the 5 percent bonds and issuing 3 percent bonds will save the city $1 million a year in interest payments. The savings in annual interest expense should be greater than the cost of retiring the old bonds and issuing new bonds.

Shares

common shares the basic form of corporate ownership.

The basic form of corporate ownership is **common shares**. Purchasers of common shares are the true owners of a corporation. Holders of common shares vote on major company decisions, such as purchasing another company or electing a board of directors. In return for the money they invest, holders of common shares expect to receive some sort of return.

This return can be cash dividend payments, expected increases in the value of the shares, or both. Dividends vary widely from firm to firm. As a general rule, faster-growing companies pay less in dividends because they need more funds to finance their growth. As a result, investors expect shares that pay little or no cash dividends to show a greater increase in value compared with shares paying larger cash dividends.

Sometimes unexpected events can have a major effect on dividends. On April 20, 2010, the oil-drilling rig *Deepwater Horizon*, leased by the British oil firm BP, exploded and caught fire, killing 11 oil workers and injuring others. BP launched an advertising campaign in print and on television. The ads featured BP's CEO, Tony Hayward, who promised to "make this right." In early June, more than 40 members of Congress called on BP to suspend its dividends, stop the ad campaign, and use the ad money to instead clean up the oil spill. BP's share prices began to fall. Standard & Poor's downgraded BP's debt rating from AA-minus to A. It was a hint that the rating might be further downgraded. BP's chairman, Carl-Henric Svanberg, announced that BP would cancel dividend payments to shareholders for the first quarter of the fiscal year and suspend dividend payments to shareholders for the second and third quarters.

Before the disaster, BP had been Britain's largest company. But, in the following months, BP's value fell by half. Scientists estimated the well was leaking more than 11.3 million litres each day, making it the largest oil-related disaster in U.S. history.[2]

Investors who hold common shares benefit from a company's success. But they also risk losing their investments if the company fails. If a firm dissolves, claims of the creditors must be satisfied before shareholders receive anything. Because creditors have the first (or senior) claim to assets, holders of common shares are said to have a residual claim on company assets.

The market value of a share is the price that shares are currently selling for. For example, Research In Motion's share price varied between $13 and $69 per share in the 12-month period ending February 21, 2012.[3] What leads to a share's market value? The answer is complicated. Many factors can cause share prices to move up or down. In the long run share prices tend to follow a company's profits.

Preferred Shares

In addition to common shares, a few companies also issue preferred shares. Holders of preferred shares receive preference in the payment of dividends. TransCanada and Bombardier are examples of firms that have issued preferred shares. Also, if a company is dissolved, holders of preferred shares have claims on the firm's assets that are ahead of the claims of holders of common shares. On the other hand, holders of preferred shares rarely have voting rights. Also, they are paid fixed dividends, regardless of how profitable the firm becomes. Preferred shares are legally classified as equity, but many investors consider preferred shares to be more like a bond than common shares.

Convertible Securities

Companies may issue bonds or preferred shares that include a conversion feature. Such bonds or shares are called *convertible securities*. This feature gives the bondholder or holder of preferred shares the right to exchange the bond or preferred shares for a fixed number of common shares. Convertible bonds pay lower interest rates than bonds without conversion features, which helps to reduce the issuing firm's interest expenses. Investors are willing to accept lower interest rates because they value the possibility of additional gains if the price of the firm's shares increase. For example, at a price of $61 per share, Peabody Energy's convertible bond would have a common share value of at least $1,043 ($61 × 17.1). If the price of Peabody's common shares increases by $10 per share, the value of the convertible bond will increase by at least $171.

FINANCIAL MARKETS

Securities are issued and traded in **financial markets**. There are many different types of financial markets. One of the most important differences is between primary and secondary markets. In the **primary markets**, firms and governments issue securities and sell them initially to the general public. A company may sell a bond or issue shares to the investing public when it needs capital to purchase inventory, expand a plant, make major investments, acquire another firm, or pursue other business goals. For example, Russian Nanotechnologies Corporation planned to sell $1.7 billion in bonds to pay for expansion and new projects.[4]

In a share offering, investors are offered the opportunity to purchase ownership shares in a firm and to participate in a firm's future growth, in exchange for providing the firm's current capital.

✓ **ASSESSMENT CHECK**

16.2.1 What are the major types of securities?

16.2.2 What areas of the government issue bonds?

16.2.3 Why do investors purchase common shares?

LO 16.3 Define *financial market*, and distinguish between primary and secondary financial markets.

financial markets markets where securities are issued and traded.

primary markets financial markets where firms and governments issue securities and sell them initially to the general public.

THE CANADIAN PRESS/Frank Gunn

At the Toronto Stock Exchange, current share prices are displayed.

When a company offers shares for sale to the general public for the first time, it is called an *initial public offering (IPO)*. Many of these offerings were from Asian companies.[5] The "Hit & Miss" feature describes an American company's IPO.

Both for-profit corporations and government agencies also rely on primary markets to raise funds by issuing bonds. For example, the federal government sells Treasury bonds to finance some of the federal expenses such as interest payments on outstanding federal debt. Provincial and local governments sell bonds to finance capital projects, such as the construction of sewer systems, streets, and fire stations.

Announcements of new bond and share offerings appear daily in business publications such as *The Globe and Mail* and *The Financial Post*. These announcements are often in the form of a simple black-and-white ad called a *tombstone*.

Securities are sold to the investing public in two ways: in open auctions and through investment bankers. Almost all securities sold through open auctions are Government of Canada securities. Sales of most corporate and municipal securities are made through financial institutions such as TD Securities.

HIT & MISS

A Major Spinoff for Citigroup

Not long ago, the U.S. banking company Citigroup was involved in not just banking but also other interests, including insurance. Following the recent financial crisis, Citigroup's CEO, Vikram Pandit, began to dispose of some of these holdings. He wanted to slim the company down to its original core banking business, by focusing on large institutions and wealthy individuals. The trend in Canada has been the opposite: major Canadian banks are now entering the insurance sector and adding to their core banking business.

Primerica Inc. was one of the Citigroup holdings to go. Based in Duluth, Georgia, Primerica sells life insurance, mutual funds, and other financial products door-to-door. Its middle-class customers earn from $30,000 to $100,000 a year. Primerica never fit well with the rest of Citigroup—and Primerica's 100,000 fiercely independent salespeople liked it that way. As the financial crisis worsened, some of Primerica employees suggested cutting ties with Citigroup.

Citigroup tried to sell Primerica but could not find a buyer willing to pay the asking price. So Citigroup announced that it would spin off Primerica. Primerica would issue an initial public offering (IPO) and sell shares in the company for the first time. Primerica planned to sell 18 million shares at $12 to $14 a share. Under the terms of the IPO, Citigroup would take all the profits and keep Primerica's existing accounts. Primerica would be a smaller company but it would keep any new policies. John Addison and Rick Williams, the co-CEOs of Primerica, said, "We're going to be a smaller, faster-growing company going forward."

The IPO went better than expected. Primerica sold more than 21 million shares at almost $20 each. Addison and Williams feel that the company's focus has contributed to its success. "No one else has our business model," said Williams. "No one else focuses on the middle-income, middle market like we do." Analysts took the IPO's success as a sign that both the life insurance industry and the market were recovering from the recession.

Questions for Critical Thinking

1. Visit the websites of Citibank and Primerica. Why do you think these two companies did not work well together?

2. Although Citigroup failed to find a buyer for Primerica, the IPO was very successful. Why do you think it was so successful?

3. Can you see a similar sale in one of Canada's larger financial institutions, such as RBC Financial Group or TD Bank Financial Group? If so, which line of business can you see being spun off?

Sources: Primerica website, http://www.primerica.com, accessed June 21, 2010; Citigroup website, http://www.citigroup.com, accessed June 21, 2010; Kerri Shannon, "Citigroup Spin-Off Primerica Boasts Strong Stock Debut in Hot IPO Market," *Money Morning*, April 4, 2010, http://moneymorning.com; "Primerica IPO a Success as Shares Jump," *CNBC*, April 1, 2010, http://www.cnbc.com; Maria Aspan and Clare Baldwin, "Citi Spinoff Primerica Soars on Hopes for Economy," *Reuters*, April 1, 2010, http://www.reuters.com; David Enrich, "An IPO of Primerica Will End a Citi Era," *Wall Street Journal*, November 6, 2009, http://www.online.wsj.com.

These institutions purchase the issue from the firm or government and then resell the issue to investors. This process is known as *underwriting*.

Financial institutions underwrite shares and bond issues at a discount. That means they pay the issuing firm or government less than the price that financial institutions charge investors. This discount is compensation for the financial institution's services, including the risk financial institutions take on when they underwrite a new security issue. The discount is often negotiable, but usually averages around 5 percent for all types of securities. The size of the underwriting discount is generally higher for share issues than for bond issues. For example, underwriting discounts for IPOs are generally between 7 and 10 percent.

Corporations and governments are willing to pay for the services provided by financial institutions because they are financial market experts. The underwriter typically locates buyers for the issue and advises the issuer on several details: the general characteristics of the issue, its pricing, and the timing of the offering. Several financial institutions commonly perform the underwriting process. The issuer selects a lead, or primary, financial institution, which forms a syndicate consisting of other financial institutions. Each member of the syndicate purchases a portion of the security issue, and then resells it to investors.

Media reports of share and bond trading are most likely to refer to trading in the **secondary market**, a collection of financial markets where previously issued securities are traded among investors. The corporations or governments that originally issued the securities being traded are not directly involved in the secondary market. The issuers do not make payments when securities are sold, and they do not receive any proceeds when securities are purchased. For example, the Toronto Stock Exchange (TSX) is a secondary market. The secondary market handles four to five times the dollar value of securities as are handled in the primary market. Each day, millions of shares worth billions of dollars are traded on the TSX.[6] The characteristics of the world's major stock exchanges are discussed in the next section.

secondary market a collection of financial markets where previously issued securities are traded among investors.

✔ **ASSESSMENT CHECK**

16.3.1 What is a financial market?

16.3.2 Distinguish between a primary and a secondary financial market.

16.3.3 Briefly explain the role of financial institutions in the sale of securities.

UNDERSTANDING STOCK MARKETS

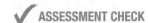

LO **16.4** Describe the characteristics of the major stock exchanges.

Stock markets, or exchanges, are probably the best-known of the world's financial markets. In these markets, shares of stock are bought and sold by investors.

stock markets (exchanges) markets where shares of stock are bought and sold by investors.

The Toronto Stock Exchange

The Toronto Stock Exchange, or TSX, is Canada's largest stock exchange. For a company's shares to be traded on the TSX, the firm must apply for a listing and meet certain listing requirements. The firm must continue to meet requirements each year to remain listed on the TSX. Corporate bonds are also traded on the TSX, but bond trading is less than 1 percent of the total value of securities traded on the TSX during a typical year.

Foreign Stock Markets

The New York Stock Exchange (NYSE) is sometimes referred to as the "Big Board." The NYSE is the most famous stock market and one of the oldest stock markets in the world. Shares traded on this exchange represent most of the largest, best-known companies in the United States and have a total market value of more than $13 trillion. The NYSE is the world's largest stock market.

The Nasdaq Stock Market is the world's second largest stock market. It is very different from the NYSE. Nasdaq stands for National Association of Securities Dealers Automated Quotation System. It is actually a computerized communications network that links member investment firms. It is the world's largest intranet. All trading on Nasdaq takes place through its intranet, not on a trading floor.

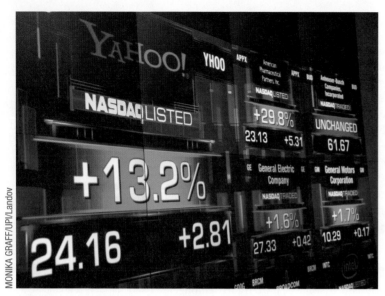

All trading on Nasdaq takes place through its intranet, not on a trading floor.

Stock markets can be found throughout the world. Almost all developed countries and many developing countries have stock exchanges. For example, stock exchanges are located in Mumbai, Helsinki, Hong Kong, Mexico City, and Paris. One of the largest stock exchanges outside the United States is the London Stock Exchange. The London Stock Exchange was founded in the early 17th century. It lists over 3,000 stock and bond issues from more than 70 countries around the world. Trading on the London Stock Exchange takes place using a Nasdaq-type computerized communications network.

The London Stock Exchange is the most international of all stock markets. It handles about two-thirds of all cross-border trading in the world, such as the trading of shares of Canadian companies outside of Canada. Institutional investors in Canada may trade TSX-listed shares or Nasdaq-listed shares in London.

Stock markets around the world are closely interconnected. As a result, changes in one country's economy can affect other countries, as explained in the "Hit & Miss" feature.

(HIT) & MISS

How News Lifts—or Sinks—Shares around the World

The growth of computerized trading has closely connected all the developed nations and many developing nations. A snapshot of the world markets shows how events in one country can affect stock markets everywhere.

Canada was not hit very hard by the global recession of 2008 to 2012. But this recession was the worst in U.S. history since the Great Depression. The Canadian recession was not as damaging as the recessions in the early 1980s or the early 1990s. Still, Finance Minister Jim Flaherty decided to set up an economic action plan.

In the spring of 2010, Americans grew hopeful that their country was starting to climb out of the recession. The U.S. Federal Reserve announced that although American households were not spending as much as before the recession, the U.S. economy was slowly improving. Some companies were making a profit because of rising consumer demand. Earlier in the recovery, some companies had made money by cutting their costs. The share prices increased in some U.S. companies, such as Apple. The computer company Hewlett-Packard announced that it was buying the smartphone maker Palm.

America seemed to be emerging from the credit crisis. But the credit crisis hit Greece, which has had major challenges paying off its debts. As a member of the European Union, Greece had adopted the euro as its currency. Other euro countries, such as Spain and Portugal, also faced financial troubles. Standard & Poor's reduced the bond rating of all three countries.

As Greece tried to recover amid violence and political turmoil, it adopted drastic measures: government spending was reduced on social programs even though the public protested. Prime Minister George Papandreou said that the public sector was "overly grown, overly expensive." He told Greeks that he hoped the austerity program would "give us a cushion" that would "give us quite a bit of money."

Questions for Critical Thinking

1. Why would a financial crisis on the other side of the world affect the Canadian economy? Why was the Canadian economy less affected by the global financial crisis than the United States?

2. As you read this textbook, what has happened in Greece, Spain, and Portugal? Have they recovered from their economic crises?

3. When Standard & Poor's downgraded the U.S. debt, what was the effect on the Canadian economy in 2011?

Sources: Mark Rohner, "Greece Ahead of Targets, Will Not Default, Papandreou Says," *Bloomberg Businessweek*, February 22, 2012, http://www.businessweek.com; European Union website, http://europa.eu, accessed February 22, 2012; Will Swarts, "Stocks Surge as Earnings Stay Robust," *SmartMoney*, April 29, 2010, http://www.smartmoney.com; Christine Hauser, "Stocks Higher as Earnings Lift Sentiment," *New York Times*, April 28, 2010, http://www.nytimes.com; Reuters, "Earnings Lift World Stocks, Greece Stays in Focus," *Economic Times*, April 21, 2010, http://economictimes.indiatimes.com; Spyros Economides, "Viewpoint: The Politics of Greece's Economic Crisis," *BBC News*, June 17, 2011, http://www.bbc.co.uk/news/world-europe-13805391, accessed July 6, 2011; Department of Finance Canada, "Budget 2009: Canada's Action Plan," January 27, 2009, http://www.fin.gc.ca/n08/09-011-eng.asp, accessed July 6, 2011; Tavia Grant, "Was Canada's Recession 'Average'?" *Globe and Mail*, May 6, 2010, http://www.theglobeandmail.com/report-on-business/economy/was-canadas-recession-average/article1535179/, accessed July 6, 2011.

ECNs and the Future of Stock Markets

For years a so-called *fourth market* has existed. The fourth market is the direct trading of exchange-listed stocks off the floor of the exchange. Until recently, trading in the fourth market was limited to institutional investors who were buying or selling large blocks of shares.

The fourth market has begun to open up to smaller, individual investors through markets called *electronic communications networks* (ECNs). In ECNs, buyers and sellers meet in a virtual stock market and trade directly with one another. ECNs have become a significant force in the stock market in recent years. The TSX now uses the services of SAVVIS to facilitate its ECN.[7]

Investor Participation in the Stock Markets

Most investors aren't members of the TSX or any other stock market; they need to use the services of a brokerage firm to buy or sell shares. Two examples of brokerage firms are Edward Jones and TD Waterhouse. Investors establish an account with the brokerage firm and then enter orders to trade shares. The brokerage firm handles the trade for the investor and charges the investor a fee for the service. Some investors phone in their orders or visit the brokerage firm in person. But today, most investors use their personal computers (PCs) to trade stocks online. The requirements for setting up an account vary from broker to broker. Selecting the right brokerage firm is one of the most important decisions investors make.

The most common type of order is a *market order*. This order instructs the broker to obtain the best possible price—the highest price when selling and the lowest price when buying. If the stock market is open, market orders are filled within seconds. Another popular type of order is called a *limit order*. It sets a price ceiling when buying or a price floor when selling. If the order cannot be filled when it is placed, the order is left with the exchange's market maker, a firm who is always ready to buy or sell a specific share at a publicly quoted price. It may be filed later if the price limits are met.

> ✓ **ASSESSMENT CHECK**
>
> **16.4.1** What are the world's two largest stock markets?
>
> **16.4.2** What makes the London Stock Exchange unique?
>
> **16.4.3** Explain the difference between a market order and a limit order.

FINANCIAL INSTITUTIONS

> **LO 16.5** Discuss the organization and functioning of financial institutions.

One of the most important parts of the financial system is its **financial institutions**. They are an intermediary between savers and borrowers. They collect funds from savers and then lend the funds to individuals, businesses, and governments. Financial institutions improve the transfer of funds from savers to users by increasing the efficiency and effectiveness of the process. Financial institutions make it easier for savers to earn more and for users of funds to pay less. It is difficult to imagine how any modern economy can function without well-developed financial institutions. Think about how difficult it would be for a business to obtain financing or for an individual to purchase a new home without using a financial institution. Borrowers would need to identify and negotiate terms with each saver individually.

Traditionally, financial institutions have been classified into depository institutions and non-depository institutions. Depository institutions accept deposits that customers can withdraw on demand. Examples of depository institutions include commercial banks, such as CIBC, RBC, TD Canada Trust, and Scotiabank. Nondepository institutions include life insurance companies, such as Manulife Financial; pension funds, such as the Ontario Teachers' Pension Plan; and mutual funds. Together, Canadian financial institutions have trillions of dollars in assets. Figure 16.2 illustrates the number and types of major financial institutions in Canada.

> **financial institutions**
> intermediaries between savers and borrowers that collect funds from savers and then lend the funds to individuals, businesses, and governments.

Commercial Banks

Commercial banks are the largest and probably the most important financial institutions in Canada and in most other countries. In Canada, the 23 domestic banks and other foreign-based financial institutions manage assets of more than $3.7 trillion. Commercial banks offer the most services of any financial institution. These services include a wide range of chequing and savings

FIGURE 16.2
Financial Institutions
in Canada

Note: P&C insurance companies refers to profit and casualty insurance companies.

Sources: Department of Finance Canada, "The Canadian Financial Services Sector," http://www.fin.gc.ca/toc/2002/fact-cfss_-eng.asp, accessed July 6, 2011.

Servus Credit Union said May 2, 2011, it will partner with 20 credit unions across Alberta to launch province-wide inter-credit union banking services.[10]

deposit accounts, consumer loans, credit cards, home mortgage loans, business loans, and trust services. Commercial banks also sell other financial products, including securities and insurance.[8]

Within the past few years, the number of domestic banks increased significantly from 14 to 23. Despite the strength of the "big banks," many consumers opt to do their banking with smaller financial institutions that offer more personal service, such as Edmonton-based Servus Credit Union.[9]

How Banks Operate

Banks raise funds by offering customers a variety of chequing and savings deposits. The banks then pool, or combine, these deposits and lend most of them out in the form of consumer and business loans. At the end of a recent year, banks held several billion dollars in deposits and outstanding loans.[11] Banks lend a great deal of money to households and businesses for a variety of purposes. Banks currently hold more than $1 trillion in residential mortgages and more than $500 billion in commercial loans.[12] Commercial banks are an especially important source of funds for small businesses. When banks evaluate loan applications, they look at the borrower's ability and willingness to repay the loan. Occasionally, banks reject loan applications.

Banks make money mostly because the interest rate they charge borrowers is higher than the rate of interest they pay depositors. Banks also make money from other sources, such as fees they charge customers for using chequing accounts and ATMs.

After the recent credit crisis, many small business owners have suffered because banks have begun pulling their lines of credit; the "Business Etiquette" feature offers some suggestions if this happens to you.

Electronic Banking

Each year, more and more funds move through electronic funds transfer systems (EFTSs). EFTSs are computerized systems for conducting financial transactions over electronic links. Millions of businesses and consumers now pay bills and receive payments electronically. For example, most employers directly deposit employees' paycheques into their bank accounts, instead of issuing paper cheques. Today, nearly all social assistance payments and other federal payments are sent as electronic data, not as paper documents.

One of the original forms of electronic banking, the automated teller machine (ATM) continues to grow in popularity. ATMs allow customers to make bank transactions at any time by inserting an electronic card into the machine and entering a personal identification number (PIN). Networked systems enable ATM users to access their bank accounts in distant provinces and throughout the world. Most banks now offer debit cards. Customers can use a debit card to pay for purchases directly from their chequing or savings account. A debit card looks like a credit card but acts like a cheque. Many large retailers—including Canadian Tire, Shoppers Drug Mart, and Tim Hortons—have installed special terminals that allow customers to use their debit cards to make purchases. Customers are required to enter their personal identification numbers and can receive cash back. Consumers enjoy the convenience of this feature; at the same time, it eliminates the problem of bad cheques for retailers. The number of annual ATM and debit card transactions in Canada is expected to be more than 4 billion within the next couple of years.[13]

Online Banking

Today, many consumers do some or all of their banking on the Internet. According to a recent survey, Canadians were the highest users of Internet banking (see Figure 16.3).[14] Canadians can choose from two types of online banks: Internet-only banks, such as PC Financial, and traditional bricks-and-mortar banks that also have websites, such as RBC and CIBC. The main reason people use online banking is for convenience. Customers can transfer money, check their account balances, and pay bills at any time.

Deposit Insurance

Most commercial bank deposits are insured by the **Canada Deposit Insurance Corporation (CDIC)**, a federal agency. If a CDIC-insured bank fails, its depositors are paid in full by the CDIC, up to $100,000. The CDIC was formed in 1967 to build public confidence in the banking system. Before deposit insurance, banks often experienced so-called *runs*, where people rushed to withdraw their money, often because of a rumour about the bank's unstable financial condition. As banks experienced more and more withdrawals in a short period, they would reach a point where they were unable to meet all the demands for cash and closed their doors. The remaining depositors who could not get to the bank on time often lost most of their money. Deposit insurance shifts the risk of bank failures from individual depositors to the CDIC. Banks can still fail today, but no insured depositor has ever lost any money within the insurable limit.

Canada Deposit Insurance Corporation (CDIC) the federal agency that insures deposits at commercial and savings banks.

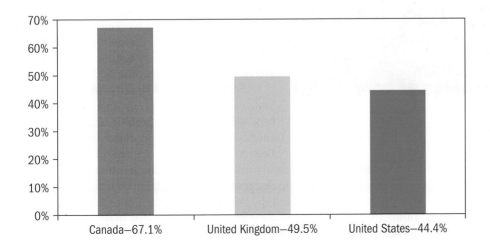

FIGURE 16.3 Online Banking Usages

Source: "Canada Leads World in Online Banking Use," *Marketing VOX*, http://www.marketingvox.com/canada-leads-world-in-online-banking-usage-039784/, accessed July 7, 2011.

BUSINESS ETIQUETTE

What to Do When Your Credit Gets Pulled

For years, banks have issued business credit cards to small business owners. The cards come with a line of credit of usually several thousand dollars or more. The line of credit gives these businesses a safety net in case of a late payment from a client or some other emergency. After the credit crisis hit, banks began to either call those loans in or limit the credit lines to the amount currently outstanding. As a result, millions of small business owners lost that safety net. The Canadian Federation of Independent Businesses (CFIB) reported that 20 percent of small and medium-sized business owners had their applications for credit rejected. In some cases, their credit lines had been decreased or their requests to extend their loans had been denied. Here are some steps to consider if this situation happens to you.

1. Be careful not to use all credit you have left; doing so could have a negative impact on your credit score.

2. Make your current monthly payment as quickly as possible, either online or by phone.

3. Obtain debt counselling to learn how to better manage your debt. Use a trusted organization, such as Credit Canada (www.creditcanada.com).

4. If possible, pay down your existing credit card debt. But, if you know you'll need money in the short term, weigh that need against your credit score before you write the cheque.

5. Keep careful track of your credit score. Equifax Canada and TransUnion Canada provide free credit reports.

Sources: Federal Trade Commission, "Credit and Your Consumer Rights," http://www.ftc.gov, accessed June 21, 2010; Sam Thacker, "Steps to Take When Your Credit Line Is Pulled," *All-Business*, http://www.allbusiness.com, accessed June 21, 2010; Jeffrey Weber, "What to Do When Your Credit Limit Is Decreased," *SmartBalanceTransfers.com,* March 4, 2010, http://www. smartbalancetransfers.com; Julie Bennett, "What to Do When the Bank Pulls Your Line of Credit," *Entrepreneur,* February 2010, http://www.entrepreneur.com; Industry Canada, *Supporting Small Business Innovation: Review of the Business Development Bank of Canada,* http://www.ic.gc.ca/eic/site/ic1.nsf/vwapj/E-BDC.pdf/$file/E-BDC.pdf, accessed July 28, 2011; Equifax website, https://www.econsumer.equifax.ca/index_en.html?transaction_id5100aca537487668e726bba5aaf22a4, accessed July 28, 2011; TransUnion website, http://www.transunion.ca/, accessed July 28, 2011.

© Francis Vachon/Alamy

Credit unions are growing in popularity. The Credit Union Central of Canada is a good place to start when looking for a credit union in your area.

Credit Unions

Commercial banks are the largest depository financial institution in the Canada, but credit unions also serve a significant segment of the financial community. Today credit unions offer many of the same services as commercial banks.

Credit unions are co-operative financial institutions that are owned by their depositors, all of whom are members. More than 5 million Canadians belong to one of the nation's approximately 379 credit unions. Combined, credit unions have more than $131 billion in assets.[15] The number of credit unions in Canada has decreased in recent years because of their efforts to merge to gain economies of scale.[16]

Credit unions are designed to serve consumers, not businesses. Credit unions raise funds by offering members several different chequing and saving accounts. Credit unions then lend these funds to members. Because credit unions are not-for-profit institutions, consumers often prefer them over commercial banks and other financial institutions: credit unions often pay higher rates of interest on deposit, charge lower rates of interest on loans, and charge fewer fees. Deposits at credit unions are insured at the provincial level. The Prince Edward Island Credit Union Deposit Insurance Corporation insures deposits at credit unions in the province of Prince Edward Island. It works essentially the same way that the CDIC does.

Nondepository Financial Institutions

Nondepository financial institutions accept funds from businesses and households, and then invest most of these funds. Generally, these institutions do not offer chequing accounts (demand deposits). Three examples of nondepository financial institutions are insurance companies, pension funds, and finance companies.

Insurance Companies

Households and businesses buy insurance to transfer risk from themselves to the insurance company. The insurance company accepts the risk in return for a series of payments, called *premiums*. Underwriting is the process insurance companies use to determine whom to insure and how much to charge. During a typical year, insurance companies collect more in premiums than they pay in claims. After they pay their operating expenses, they invest the difference. Insurance companies are a major source of short- and long-term financing for businesses. Life insurance companies have total assets of more than $400 billion. They invest their funds in everything from bonds and stocks to real estate.[17] Examples of life insurers include Canada Life and Manulife Financial.

Pension Funds

Pension funds provide retirement benefits to workers and their families. They are set up by employers and are funded by regular contributions from employers and employees. Because pension funds have predictable long-term cash inflows and very predictable cash outflows, they invest heavily in assets, such as common stocks and real estate. The Canada Pension Plan (CPP) fund has assets of more than $148.2 billion. The recovery of global markets led to total investment income of $31.7 billion after the financial crisis era. The fund's current asset mix consists of 48.3 percent in Canadian assets and 51.7 percent in foreign investment assets with only 30 percent of total assets in less risky bonds. Since the financial crisis, the asset mix has shifted to include more foreign investment and fewer Canadian assets.[18]

Finance Companies

Consumer and commercial finance companies offer short-term loans to borrowers. Two examples are Ford Credit and John Deere Capital Corporation. A commercial finance company supplies short-term funds to businesses that use their tangible assets as collateral for the loan. These tangible assets can include inventory, accounts receivable, machinery, or property. A consumer finance company plays a similar role for consumers. Finance companies raise funds by selling securities or by borrowing funds from commercial banks. Many finance companies, such as GMAC, are actually subsidiaries of a manufacturer. GMAC finances dealer inventories of new cars and trucks. It also provides loans to consumers and other buyers of General Motors products.

Mutual Funds

One of the most significant types of financial institutions today is the mutual fund. *Mutual funds* are financial intermediaries that raise money from investors by selling shares. They then use the money to invest in securities that meet the mutual fund's objectives. For example, a share-based mutual fund invests mainly in common shares. Mutual funds have become extremely popular over the last few decades. Canada's more than 830 mutual funds have approximately $378 billion in assets; up from $125 billion in the early 1990s. One reason for this growth is the increased popularity of registered retirement savings plans (RRSPs) and similar types of retirement plans. An estimated 39 percent of all RRSP assets are invested in mutual fund shares. This amount is down from 88 percent in 2008, before the financial crisis led to the major decrease in share prices globally.[19]

Mutual fund investors are indirect owners of a portfolio of securities. As the value of the securities owned by the mutual fund changes, the value of the mutual fund's shares will also change. Investment income, such as bond interest and stock dividends, is passed through to mutual fund shareholders.

Just less than half of mutual fund assets are invested in company shares. Money market mutual funds are also popular. These funds invest in money market instruments such as commercial paper. Money market funds have total assets of just over $2.6 trillion.[20]

 ASSESSMENT CHECK

16.5.1 What are the two main types of financial institutions?

16.5.2 What are the primary differences between commercial banks and credit unions?

16.5.3 What is a mutual fund?

LO 16.6 Explain the functions of the Bank of Canada and the tools it uses to control the supply of money and credit.

THE ROLE OF THE BANK OF CANADA

Created in 1935, the **Bank of Canada (the Bank)** is the central bank of Canada and an important part of the nation's financial system. The Bank, once privately owned, became a government-owned Crown corporation in 1938. The Bank of Canada has four basic responsibilities: regulating monetary policy, designing and issuing bank notes, regulating the financial system, and managing funds for the federal government and other clients.

Bank of Canada (the Bank) the central bank of Canada.

Monetary Policy

The Bank's most important function is regulating monetary policy, which means controlling the supply of money and credit. The Bank's job is to make sure that the money supply grows at a suitable rate, allowing the economy to expand and inflation to remain in check. If the money supply grows too slowly, economic growth will slow, unemployment will increase, and the risk of a recession will increase. If the money supply grows too rapidly, inflationary pressures will build. The Bank uses its policy tools to push interest rates up or down. If the Bank pushes interest rates up, the growth rate in the money supply will slow, economic growth will slow, and inflationary pressures will ease. If the Bank pushes interest rates down, the growth rate in the money supply will increase, economic growth will pick up, and unemployment will fall.

The two common measures of the money supply are called M1 and M2. M1 consists of currency in circulation and the balances in bank chequing accounts. M2 equals M1 plus balances in some savings accounts and money market mutual funds. Figure 16.4 shows the approximate composition of the M2 money supply. The Bank has two major policy tools for controlling the growth in the supply of money and credit: the discount rate and open market operations.

The discount rate is the interest rate at which chartered banks make short-term loans to member banks. The discount rate is often referred to as the bank rate. A bank might need a short-term loan if transactions leave it short of reserves. If the Bank wants to slow the growth rate in the money supply, it increases the bank rate. This increase makes it more expensive for banks to borrow funds. Banks, in turn, raise the interest rates they charge on loans to consumers and businesses. The end result is a slowdown in economic activity. Lowering the bank rate has the opposite effect.

The second policy tool, and the one used more often, is *open market operations*, the technique of controlling the money supply growth rate by buying or selling Canadian government securities. If the Bank buys government securities, the money it pays enters circulation, where it increases the money supply and lowers interest rates. When the Bank sells government securities, money is taken out of circulation and interest rates rise. When the Bank uses open market operations it uses as its benchmark, or guideline, the so-called *overnight rate*—the rate at which banks lend money to each other overnight. Table 16.3 shows how the tools used by the Bank can either stimulate or slow the economy.

The Bank has the authority to use selective credit controls when the economy is growing too rapidly or too slowly. These credit controls include the power to set margin requirements—the percentage of the purchase price of a security that an investor must pay in cash when making credit purchases of shares or bonds.

The Bank can also inject capital into the financial system in response to a financial crisis. For example, during the credit crisis in the United States, which began in 2008, the U.S. Federal Reserve (the American equivalent to the Bank of Canada) pumped hundreds of billions of dollars into the financial system. The Federal Reserve even came to the rescue of AIG, a major U.S. insurance company, by purchasing some of the firm's shares. In Canada, the Bank kept interest rates at historical lows during the global financial crisis.

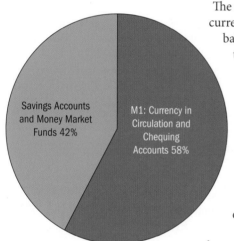

FIGURE 16.4 Total M2 Money Supply

Savings Accounts and Money Market Funds 42%

M1: Currency in Circulation and Chequing Accounts 58%

Source: Statistics Canada, "Exchange Rates, Interest Rates, Money Supply and Stock Prices, 2007–2011," http://www.statcan.gc.ca/tables-tableaux/sum-som/l01/cst01/econ07-eng.htm, accessed May 24, 2012.

Table 16.3 Tools Used by the Bank of Canada to Regulate the Growth in the Money Supply

TOOL	BRIEF DESCRIPTION	IMPACT ON THE GROWTH RATE OF THE MONEY SUPPLY	IMPACT ON INTEREST RATES AND THE ECONOMY	FREQUENCY OF USE
1. Bank rate	The interest rate that the Bank of Canada charges banks for loans.	An increase in the bank rate slows the growth rate in the money supply.	An increase in the bank rate pushes interest rates up and slows economic growth.	Used only with open market operations.
2. Open market operations	The buying and selling of government securities to increase or decrease bank reserves.	Selling government securities reduces bank reserves and slows the growth rate in the money supply.	Selling government securities pushes interest rates up and slows economic growth.	Used frequently.

Transactions in the foreign exchange markets also affect the Canadian money supply and interest rates. The Bank can lower the exchange value of the dollar by selling dollars and buying foreign currencies. It can also raise the dollar's exchange value by doing the opposite—buying dollars and selling foreign currencies. When the Bank buys foreign currencies, the effect is the same as buying securities: the purchase of foreign currencies or securities increases the reserves in Canada's banking system. In contrast, selling foreign currencies is like selling securities: selling foreign currencies or securities reduces bank reserves.

Historically, the Bank also influenced the money supply by controlling the *reserve requirement*. The reserve requirement was the percentage of cash that banks were required to maintain for immediate withdrawal by customers. The lower the reserve requirement, the more the money supply could increase. For example, if you deposited $10,000 at your local bank and the reserve requirement was 3 percent, the bank would then likely lend out $9,700 to someone else (perhaps to purchase a car). The purchaser (the borrower) would then give the $9,700 to the seller of the car who would deposit it in the bank. At this point, the money supply related to the initial deposit is $19,700 (the initial $10,000 plus the $9,700 also in the bank). This process would continue, increasing the money supply further. The original deposit of $10,000 would have a potential impact on the money supply of $333,333 ($10,000/3%). In 1992, the Bank of Canada removed the reserve requirement. Banks now decide themselves the proportion of deposits to keep on hand.

✔ **ASSESSMENT CHECK**

16.6.1 What is the Bank of Canada?

16.6.2 List the two main tools the Bank uses to control the supply of money and credit.

REGULATION OF THE FINANCIAL SYSTEM

LO 16.7 Understand the impact of regulations and laws affecting the financial system.

It is probably not surprising that many parts of the financial system must comply with government regulation and are supervised by government agencies. After all, the financial system is very important to how our economy works. Self-regulation is commonplace in the financial industry.

Bank Regulation

Banks are among the nation's most heavily regulated businesses. The main purpose of bank regulation is to ensure public confidence in the safety and security of the banking system. Banks are critical to the overall functioning of the economy. For example, a collapse of the banking system can have disastrous results. Under the Bank Act, the federal government is responsible for regulating the banking sector. Several regulatory bodies are involved in regulating Canadian banks, including the Department of Finance, the Bank of Canada, the Office of the Superintendent of Financial Institutions (OSFI), and the CDIC. Some regulation is also at the provincial level because of the many lines of business that a commercial bank or credit union may be involved in.[21]

Government Regulation of the Financial Markets

At the provincial level, regulation of Canadian financial markets is primarily administered by organizations such as the Manitoba Securities Commission or the Ontario Securities Commission. These provincial organizations are in turn coordinated by the Canadian Securities Administrators (CSA) to reduce duplication of efforts and provide consistency. But, in the end, responsibility is in the hands of the various provincial bodies.

insider trading use of material nonpublic information about a company to make investment profits.

One area that provincial regulators pay particular attention to is insider trading. **Insider trading** is defined as the use of material nonpublic information about a company to make investment profits. Examples of material nonpublic information include a pending merger or a major oil discovery. Releasing information on these activities before they occur could affect the firm's share price. The definition of insider trading goes beyond corporate insiders—people such as the company's officers and directors. It includes lawyers, accountants, investment bankers, and even reporters—anyone who uses nonpublic information to profit in the stock market at the expense of ordinary investors. Although some actions or communications are clearly insider trading, other activities are more difficult to pin down. As a result, all employees of public companies must keep in mind what is and is not permitted.

Industry Self-Regulation

The securities markets are also heavily self-regulated by professional associations and the major financial markets. The securities industry understands that rules and regulations are designed to ensure fair and orderly markets. The rules and regulations also promote investor confidence and benefit all participants. Two examples of self-regulation are the rules of conduct established by professional organizations and the market surveillance techniques used by the major securities markets.

Market Surveillance

All securities markets use a variety of methods to spot possible violations of trading rules or securities laws. In Canada, the Toronto Stock Exchange (TSX) wants to promote integrity and fairness in all trading across equity marketplaces. The TSX outsources market surveillance to an independent third party—the Investment Industry Regulatory Organization of Canada (IIROC). IIROC's surveillance functions include real-time monitoring of trading activity: a team of experts watch all equity trades as they occur to ensure compliance with the securities trading rules. IIROC is equipped with an experienced team and a dedicated surveillance facility with advanced technology. It monitors company news, stock charts, and chat room activity to detect volume and price anomalies. IIROC also monitors timely disclosure of material information by publicly traded businesses to ensure they comply with Universal Market Integrity Rules (UMIR). State-of-the-art technology and monitoring systems allow IIROC to track trading behaviour in real time and collect evidence needed to pursue cases relating to violations, such as insider trading and manipulative activity.[22] Self-regulation by the financial industry has been an important part of securities market regulation. But some argue that the industry can never truly regulate itself effectively in today's market environment. The "Solving an Ethical Controversy" feature debates the pros and cons of industry self-regulation.

 ASSESSMENT CHECK

16.7.1 Who regulates banks?

16.7.2 Define *insider trading*.

— SOLVING AN **ETHICAL** CONTROVERSY —

Can the Securities Market Regulate Itself?

"Those of us who have looked to the self-interest of lending institutions to protect shareholders' equity, myself included, are in a state of shocked disbelief."

That's what was said by Alan Greenspan, former chairman of the Federal Reserve Board in the United States, in his testimony before Congress, after the credit crisis. He had long supported the idea that the market could always be trusted to regulate itself and should be left free to do so. But with his words, he rejected that policy. The crisis brought an end to a Wall Street bubble that had done well, partly due to unlimited, unregulated speculation. Stricter government regulation of the financial industry seems very likely.

Can the securities market be trusted to regulate itself?

PRO

1. Regulation of the securities market will give the government too much power over private industry.

2. The mere idea of regulation has made some institutions change their behaviour voluntarily. For example, some banks have announced that they will eliminate overdraft fees for consumer accounts.

3. Self-regulation can lead to greater investor confidence.

CON

1. Some analysts feel that existing government regulation is too lax. They believe that the government, which is supposed to regulate the financial industry, was too lenient with some large financial institutions.

2. The TSX has one body that both approves company listings and enforces the rules. Most other exchanges, such as the NYSE and London Stock Exchange, have two separate bodies, one for each purpose.

3. Self-regulation leads to a loss of independence.

Summary

Public disapproval of the securities market is likely to continue as long as people continue to feel the effects of the financial crisis in their everyday lives, especially in the United States. The government has considered new, stricter regulations on financial institutions. Some argue that those regulations are unnecessary and could even be harmful.

Sources: Bill Singer, "Analyzing a Troubling Wall Street Double Standard," *Corporate Compliance Insights,* May 4, 2010, http://www.corporatecomplianceinsights.com; Felix Salmon, "How the SEC Cracks Down on Unethical Behavior," *Reuters,* April 20, 2010, http://blogs.reuters.com; Peter Hamby, "DNC Ad: Wall Street Lobbyists Trying to Block Reform," *CNN,* April 20, 2010, http://politicalticker.blogs.cnn.com; Roger Lowenstein, "*The End of Wall Street* by Roger Lowenstein: Book Excerpt," *Bloomberg Businessweek,* April 8, 2010, http://www.business week.com; Andrew Ross Sorkin, "Extreme Makeover, Wall Street Edition," *New York Times,* April 1, 2010, http://dealbook.blogs.nytimes.com; Charles H. Green, "Fixing What Ails Wall Street: Ethics, or Incentives?" *Trusted Advisor Associates,* September 21, 2009, http://trustedadvisor.com; Tim Kiladze, "TSX Regulation a Conflict of Interest: Report," *Globe and Mail,* July 29, 2010, http://www.theglobeandmail.com/globe-investor/tsx-regulation-a-conflict-of-interest-report/article1653215/, accessed July 28, 2011.

THE FINANCIAL SYSTEM: A GLOBAL PERSPECTIVE

LO 16.8 Describe the global financial system.

Not surprisingly, the global financial system is becoming more and more integrated each year. As we've noted, financial markets exist throughout the world. Shares of Canadian firms trade in other countries, and shares of international companies trade in Canada. Financial institutions have also become a global industry. Major Canadian banks—such as CIBC, RBC

In Frankfurt, Germany, a sculpture of the euro—the symbol for the European Union's currency—stands outside the headquarters of Europe's central bank. The 12 gold stars represent all the peoples of Europe.

and Scotiabank—have extensive international operations. They have offices, lend money, and accept deposits from customers throughout the world.

Of the 50 largest banks in the world (measured by total assets), only three are Canadian—RBC, TD Bank, and the Bank of Nova Scotia. The largest of the three, RBC, ranks 34th. Besides the three Canadian banks on the list, the other 47 are based in Belgium, China, France, Germany, Italy, Japan, the Netherlands, Switzerland, the United Kingdom, and other parts of the world. The world's largest bank, BNP Paribas SA is based in Paris. It has almost $2.7 trillion in assets. These international banks also operate worldwide, including in the United States.[23]

The effects of financial globalization are evident in Canada. Canada's growing cultural diversity has led to an increase in other banking models. Many other financial models exist around the world, including the interest-free Islamic system of banking. Special banks are needed to address the financial needs of devout Muslims who cannot be involved in interest-based transactions, including home mortgages. Islamic finance companies such as Guidance Financial, Hakeem Wealth Management, and Ijara Canada provide financial products to the previously underserved niche market of Islamic finance. Globally, financial institutions, including HBSC, Citigroup, and Lloyds TSB, have seen their assets grow at an annual rate of more than 20 percent in this emerging market. Currently their assets total more than $1 trillion worldwide.[24]

HSBC Amanah was set up to serve the unique financial needs of the Muslim community.

Almost all nations have some sort of a central bank, similar to the Bank of Canada. Examples include the U.S. Federal Reserve (the Fed), the Bank of England, the Bank of Japan, and the European Central Bank. These central banks have a similar role to that of the Bank of Canada—controlling the money supply and regulating banks. Policymakers at the Bank of Canada often respond to changes in the U.S. financial system by making similar changes to the Canadian system. For example, if the Fed pushes U.S. interest rates lower, central banks in Canada, Japan, and Europe may also push their interest rates lower. These changes can influence events in countries around the world. When Canadian and European interest rates are low, they decrease the cost of borrowing for Canadian and European firms but increase the amount of money available for loans to borrowers in other countries, such as Chile and India.

✔ **ASSESSMENT CHECK**

16.8.1 Where do Canadian banks rank compared with international banks?

16.8.2 Do other countries have organizations that play roles similar to those played by the Bank of Canada?

WHAT'S AHEAD

This chapter explored the financial system, a key part of the Canadian economy and a process that affects many aspects of contemporary business. The financial system is the process by which funds are transferred between savers and borrowers. It includes securities, financial markets, and financial institutions. The chapter also described the role of the Bank of Canada and discussed the global financial system. In the next chapter, we discuss the finance functions of a business, including the role of financial managers, financial planning, asset management, and sources of short- and long-term funds.

RETURN TO INSIDE BUSINESS

Canada Weathers the Credit Crisis

The financial crisis has had a significant impact on global financial markets. Countries significantly affected include the United States, Greece, Italy, Australia, Brazil, Russia, and many more.

QUESTIONS FOR CRITICAL THINKING

1. How can financial institutions and countries prevent another major financial crisis?

2. Why was Africa not as affected by the financial crisis as most of the rest of the world?

SUMMARY OF LEARNING OBJECTIVES

LO 16.1 Outline the structure and importance of the financial system.

The financial system is the process by which funds are transferred between those who have excess funds (savers) and those who need additional funds (users). Savers and users are individuals, businesses, and governments. Savers expect to earn a rate of return in exchange for the use of their funds. Financial markets, financial institutions, and financial instruments (securities) make up the financial system. Although direct transfers are possible, most funds flow from savers to users through the financial markets or financial institutions, such as commercial banks. A well-functioning financial system is vital to the overall health of a nation's economy.

 ASSESSMENT CHECK ANSWERS

16.1.1 What is the financial system? The financial system is the mechanism by which funds are transferred between those who have excess funds (savers) and those who need additional funds (users).

16.1.2 In the financial system, who are the borrowers and who are the savers? Savers and borrowers are individuals, businesses, and governments. Generally, individuals are net savers, meaning they spend less than they make. Businesses and governments tend to be net borrowers.

16.1.3 List the two most common ways that funds are transferred between borrowers and savers. The two most common ways funds are transferred are through the financial markets and through financial institutions.

LO 16.2 List the various types of securities.

Securities, also called *financial instruments,* represent the obligations of the issuers—businesses and governments—to provide purchasers with the expected or stated returns on the funds invested or loaned. Securities can be classified into three categories: money market instruments, bonds, and shares. Money

market instruments and bonds are debt instruments. Money market instruments are short-term debt securities and tend to be low-risk securities. Bonds are longer-term debt securities and pay a fixed amount of interest each year. Bonds are sold by the Canadian government (Canada Savings Bonds), provincial and local governments (municipal bonds), and corporations. Mortgage-backed securities are bonds backed by a pool, or group, of mortgage loans. Most municipal and corporate bonds have risk ratings. Common shares represent ownership in corporations. Investors who hold common shares have voting rights and a residual claim on the firm's assets.

 ASSESSMENT CHECK ANSWERS

16.2.1 What are the major types of securities? The major types of securities are money market instruments, bonds, and shares.

16.2.2 What areas of the government issue bonds? Bonds are issued by the federal, provincial, and local governments.

16.2.3 Why do investors purchase common shares? Investors purchase common shares for two reasons. One reason is to receive dividends, which are cash payments made to shareholders by the firm. The other reason is the potential price increase of the shares.

LO 16.3 Define *financial market,* and distinguish between primary and secondary financial markets.

A financial market is a market where securities are bought and sold. The primary market for securities serves businesses and governments that want to sell new security issues to raise funds. Securities are sold in the primary market either through an open auction or through a process called *underwriting.* The secondary market handles transactions of previously issued securities between investors. One example of a secondary market is the Toronto Stock Exchange. The business or government that issued the security is not directly involved in secondary market transactions. The secondary market handles about four to five times the dollar value of securities as are handled in the primary market.

✓ **ASSESSMENT CHECK ANSWERS**

16.3.1 What is a financial market? A financial market is a market where securities are bought and sold.

16.3.2 Distinguish between a primary and a secondary financial market. The primary market for securities serves businesses and governments that want to sell new security issues to raise funds. The secondary market handles transactions of previously issued securities between investors.

16.3.3 Briefly explain the role of financial institutions in the sale of securities. Financial institutions purchase new securities issues from corporations or provincial and local governments and then resell the securities to investors. The institutions charge a fee for their services.

LO 16.4 Describe the characteristics of the major stock exchanges.

The best-known financial markets are the stock exchanges. Stock exchanges can be found throughout the world. Canada's largest stock exchange is the Toronto Stock Exchange, or TSX. The world's two largest stock exchanges are the New York Stock Exchange and Nasdaq. Both are located in the United States. The NYSE is bigger when measured in terms of the total value of shares traded. Larger and better-known companies dominate the NYSE. The Nasdaq stock market is an electronic market where buy and sell orders are entered into a computerized communication system. Most of the world's major stock markets today use similar electronic trading systems. Electronic trading may be the future for stock markets.

✓ **ASSESSMENT CHECK ANSWERS**

16.4.1 What are the world's two largest stock markets? The world's two largest stock markets are the New York Stock Exchange and the Nasdaq Stock Market.

16.4.2 What makes the London Stock Exchange unique? The London Stock Exchange is the most international of the world's stock markets. A large percentage of the shares traded there are not from British firms.

16.4.3 Explain the difference between a market order and a limit order. A market order instructs the investor's broker to obtain the best possible price when buying or selling securities. A limit order sets a maximum price (if the investor wants to buy) or a minimum price (if the investor wants to sell).

LO 16.5 Discuss the organization and functioning of financial institutions.

Financial institutions act as intermediaries between savers and users of funds. Depository institutions accept deposits from customers that can be exchanged for cash on demand. Examples of depository institutions are commercial banks, savings banks, and credit unions. Commercial banks are the largest and most important of the depository institutions. They offer the widest range of services. Savings banks are a major source of home mortgage loans. Credit unions are not-for-profit institutions that offer financial services to consumers. The Canada Deposit Insurance Corporation is a government agency that insures deposits at these financial institutions. Nondepository institutions include pension funds and insurance companies. Nondepository institutions invest a large portion of their funds in stocks, bonds, and real estate. Mutual funds are another important financial institution. These companies sell shares to investors and, in turn, invest the proceeds in securities. Many individuals today invest a large portion of their retirement savings in mutual fund shares.

✓ **ASSESSMENT CHECK ANSWERS**

16.5.1 What are the two main types of financial institutions? The two major types of financial institutions are depository institutions (those that accept chequing and similar accounts) and nondepository institutions.

16.5.2 What are the primary differences between commercial banks and credit unions? Today, commercial banks and credit unions offer many of the same services. Commercial banks lend money to businesses and to individuals. Credit unions banks lend money mostly to individuals, usually in the form of home mortgage loans.

16.5.3 What is a mutual fund? A mutual fund is an intermediary that raises money by selling shares to investors. It then pools, or combines, investor funds and purchases securities that meet the mutual fund's objectives.

LO 16.6 Explain the functions of the Bank of Canada and the tools it uses to control the supply of money and credit.

The Bank of Canada (the Bank) is the central bank of Canada. The Bank regulates monetary policy, designs and issues bank notes, regulates the financial system and manages funds for the federal government and other clients. It controls the supply of credit and money in the economy to promote growth and control inflation. The Bank's main tools include the overnight interest rate and open market operations. Selective credit controls and purchases and sales of foreign currencies also help the Bank to manage the economy.

✓ **ASSESSMENT CHECK ANSWERS**

16.6.1 What is the Bank of Canada? The Bank of Canada is Canada's central bank. It is responsible for regulating the financial system providing banking-related services for the federal government, acting as the banker's bank, designing and issuing bank notes, and setting monetary policy.

16.6.2 List the two main tools the Bank uses to control the supply of money and credit. The two main tools are the overnight interest rate and open market operations.

LO 16.7 Understand the impact of regulations and laws affecting the financial system.

Commercial banks, savings banks, and credit unions in Canada are heavily regulated by federal banking authorities. Banking regulators require institutions to follow sound banking practices. They have the power to close noncompliant banks. In Canada, financial markets are regulated primarily at the provincial level. Markets are also heavily self-regulated by the financial markets and professional organizations. Provincial regulatory bodies set the requirements for both primary and secondary market activity. They ban a number of practices, including insider trading. They also require public companies to disclose financial information regularly. Professional organizations and the securities markets also have rules and procedures that all members must follow.

 ASSESSMENT CHECK ANSWERS

16.7.1 Who regulates banks? All banks are regulated by the federal government.

16.7.2 Define *insider trading*. Insider trading is defined as the use of material nonpublic information to make an investment profit.

LO 16.8 Describe the global financial system.

Financial markets exist throughout the world and are increasingly interconnected. Investors in other countries purchase Canadian securities, and Canadian investors purchase foreign securities. Large Canadian banks and other financial institutions have a global presence. They accept deposits, make loans, and have branches throughout the world. Foreign banks also operate worldwide. The average European or Japanese bank is much larger than the average Canadian bank. Almost all nations have a central bank that performs the same roles as the Bank of Canada. Central bankers often act together, raising and lowering interest rates to control economic conditions.

 ASSESSMENT CHECK ANSWERS

16.8.1 Where do Canadian banks rank compared with international banks? Banks in Asia and Europe are generally much larger than Canadian banks. Only three of the world's 50 largest banks are based in Canada.

16.8.2 Do other countries have organizations that play roles similar to those played by the Bank of Canada? Yes, almost all nations have central banks that perform many of the same functions as the Bank of Canada.

BUSINESS TERMS YOU NEED TO KNOW

financial system 448

securities 450

common shares 452

financial markets 453

primary markets 453

secondary market 455

stock markets (exchanges) 455

financial institutions 457

Canada Deposit Insurance Corporation (CDIC) 459

Bank of Canada (the Bank) 462

insider trading 464

REVIEW QUESTIONS

1. What is the financial system? Why is it rare for funds to be directly transferred from savers to users?

2. What is a security? Give several examples.

3. List the major types of bonds. What is a mortgage-backed security?

4. What are the differences between common shares and preferred shares?

5. Explain the difference between a primary financial market and a secondary financial market.

6. Why are commercial banks and credit unions classified as depository financial institutions? How do commercial banks differ from credit unions?

7. Why are life insurance companies, pension funds, and mutual funds considered financial institutions?

8. Briefly explain the role of the Bank of Canada. List the tools it uses to control the supply of money and credit.

9. What methods are used to regulate banks? Why are Canadian chartered banks also regulated by the CDIC?

10. Explain how the Bank of Canada works with other central banks to affect exchange rates.

PROJECTS AND TEAMWORK APPLICATIONS

1. Collect current interest rates on the following types of bonds: Canada Savings Bonds, AAA-rated municipal bonds, AAA-rated corporate bonds, and BBB-rated corporate bonds. Arrange the interest rates from lowest to highest. Explain the reasons for the ranking.

2. You've probably heard of Canada Savings Bonds. You may even have received some bonds as a gift. What you may not know is that there are *two* different types of Canada Savings Bonds. Do some research and compare the two types of bonds. What are their features? What are their pros and cons? Which of the two bonds do you prefer?

3. Working with a partner, assume you are considering buying shares of RONA or The Home Depot. Describe how you would analyze the two companies' shares to decide which you would buy.

4. Working in a small team, identify a large bank. Visit that bank's website and look up its most recent financial statements. Compare the bank's financial statements to those of a nonfinancial company, such as a manufacturer or retailer. Report on your findings.

5. Assume you're investing money for retirement. What investment criteria are the most important to you? Go to the MSN Money website (http://money.msn.com). Under the "Investing" tab, select "mutual funds." Then on the left side of the screen, under "Fund Finder," choose either "Find top performers by category" or "Find using Power Search." Identify at least three mutual funds that most closely meet your criteria. Choose one of the funds and research it. Answer the following questions:

   a. What was the fund's average annual return for the past five years?

   b. How well did the fund perform relative to its peer group and relative to an index such as the Standard & Poor's 500?

   c. What are the fund's 10 largest holdings?

WEB ASSIGNMENTS

1. **Online stock trading.** To learn more about online trading, visit the website of a brokerage firm that offers online trading, such as BMO InvestorLine (www.bmoinvestorline.com) or Scotia iTRADE (www.scotiaitrade.com). Most electronic brokerage firms also offer a trading demonstration. Use the demonstration to see how to obtain price information, company news, place buy or sell orders, and check account balances. Make some notes about your experience and bring them to class to participate in a class discussion.

2. **Banking statistics.** Visit the website listed below. Access the most recent year you can find and answer the following questions:

   a. How many commercial banks were operating at the end of the year? How many credit unions were operating?

   b. What were the total assets of commercial banks and credit unions at the end of the year?

   c. How many commercial banks had assets greater than $2 billion at the end of the year? How many commercial banks had assets of less than $300 million at the end of the year?

   http://www.bankofcanada.ca/publications-research/periodicals/bfs/

3. **The Bank of Canada.** Go to the website of the Bank of Canada (www.bankofcanada.ca). Locate information on the Bank of Canada's board of directors. Prepare a short report on the 14-member board. Who are the current members? What are their backgrounds? When were they appointed? When do their terms expire?

Access your WileyPLUS course for:

- The complete digital textbook.
- Question assistance, including links to relevant sections in the online digital textbook.
- Immediate feedback and proof of progress, 24/7
- Integrated, multi-media resources – including MP3 downloads, visual exhibits, animations, and much more – that provide multiple study paths and encourage more active learning.

QUIZ YOURSELF

Note: Internet Web addresses change frequently. If you don't find the exact sites listed, you may need to access the organization's home page and search from there or use a search engine such as Bing or Google.

17 | FINANCIAL MANAGEMENT

LEARNING OBJECTIVES

LO 17.1 Define *finance,* and explain the role of financial managers.

LO 17.2 Describe the parts of a financial plan and the financial planning process.

LO 17.3 Outline how organizations manage their assets.

LO 17.4 Compare the two major sources of funds for a business, and explain the concept of leverage.

LO 17.5 Identify sources of short-term financing for business operations.

LO 17.6 Discuss long-term financing options.

LO 17.7 Describe mergers, acquisitions, buyouts, and divestitures.

INSIDE BUSINESS

The Wooing of Ratiopharm

AP Photo/Franka Bruns

Nearly all Canadians know that it is cheaper to buy a generic drug—an over-the-counter drug such as ibuprofen—than the brand-name version, such as Aleve or Advil. Pharmaceutical companies know this, too. Canadian patents on brand-name drugs expire after 20 years. After a patent runs out, a drug company loses its exclusive right to manufacture the brand-name version of the product it has spent time, research, and money to develop. As patents have expired, generic-drug companies have opened all over the world, from Germany to India. The result has been a huge growth in the pharmaceutical industry. Apotex Inc. is Canada's largest generic-drug manufacturer. Every year, it produces more than 300 generic pharmaceuticals for more than 85 million individual prescriptions. Developing a successful new drug can be profitable, but it is a risky and expensive process, and success is never guaranteed. Many big pharmaceutical companies have expanded by buying manufacturers of generic drugs. The decision to buy another firm can be difficult. Financial managers need to carefully forecast the expected increase in profits and then weigh that benefit against the costs of acquisition. But these forecasts are not certain, and success is never guaranteed. In one recent case, several companies wanted to buy a generics maker. They were like gentlemen suitors presenting themselves to an attractive potential bride. In a modern, electronic twist, their courtship was concluded in less than three months.

Ratiopharm, based in Ulm, Germany, is one of the world's five largest producers of generic drugs. It specializes in drugs that treat cardiovascular and respiratory disorders, diseases of the central nervous system, and other illnesses. It also deals with medicines that prevent infections. When the family that owned Ratiopharm announced the company was up for sale, several big pharmaceutical firms were interested. That list was then narrowed down to three: Pfizer Inc., based in New York City; Teva Pharmaceutical Industries of Israel; and Actavis of Iceland.

Ratiopharm was especially attractive because Germans buy more generic drugs than other Europeans, and Ratiopharm was the second biggest seller of generics in Germany. Like young men wooing a potential bride, the companies sent their executives to Ulm to explain why Ratiopharm should accept their offer. Some analysts thought that Ratiopharm's decision would depend on which company promised to keep the greatest number of jobs at Ratiopharm.

Pfizer or its subsidiaries manufacture over-the-counter brands from Advil and ChapStick to Centrum vitamins and Robitussin; prescription drugs for women's health, cardiovascular disease, and cancer; and veterinary medicines. One analyst suggested that buying Ratiopharm would help Pfizer to move its brand-name products into the worldwide generic market when their patents expire. It would also allow Pfizer to expand into developing markets. Pfizer's bid for Ratiopharm was €3 billion (about US$4.08 billion). After Pfizer's presentation, Ratiopharm's management wrote a letter to the company's employees, saying, "The bidder emphasized the high efficiency of Ratiopharm's domestic and foreign production sites and told the meeting it was ready to make investments in Ulm."

Teva was already the world's largest producer of generic pharmaceuticals. Acquiring Ratiopharm would make Teva the leading generics maker in Europe and the second biggest in Germany. According to one analyst, Teva aimed to preserve both Ratiopharm's workforce and its locations in Germany. Teva offered €3.63 billion ($4.97 billion).

The Icelandic company Actavis had about 10,000 employees in 40 countries, making it about the same size as Ratiopharm. It also had about the same sales figures as Ratiopharm. Despite being heavily in debt, Actavis made an offer of about €3.32 billion, or $4.10 billion.

Analysts had predicted that Ratiopharm would not make a decision quickly, but Teva soon made an announcement. It would acquire Ratiopharm for €3.63 billion ($4.97 billion). Shlomo Yani, Teva's president and CEO, announced that Ratiopharm would strengthen Teva's presence "in key European markets, most notably in Germany, as well as rapidly growing generic markets such as Spain, Italy and France."[1]

CHAPTER 17 OVERVIEW

Previous chapters discuss two basic functions that a business must perform. First, the company must produce a good or service or contract with suppliers to produce a good or service. Second, the firm must market its good or service to prospective customers. This chapter introduces a third, equally important, function: a company's managers must ensure that the company has enough money to perform its other tasks successfully, in both the present and the future, and that these funds are invested properly. The company must have enough funds to buy materials, equipment, and other assets; pay bills; and compensate employees. This third business function is **finance**—planning, obtaining, and managing the company's funds to accomplish its objectives as effectively and efficiently as possible.

An organization's financial objectives include meeting expenses, investing in assets, and maximizing its overall worth, which is often measured by the value of the firm's common shares. Financial managers are responsible for meeting expenses, investing in assets, and increasing profits to shareholders. Solid financial management is critical to the success of a business. You can look at the news any day and find examples of firms that may have offered good products to the marketplace, but failed because funds were improperly managed.

This chapter focuses on the finance function of organizations. It begins by describing the role of financial managers, their place in the organizational hierarchy, and the increasing importance of finance. Next, we outline the financial planning process and the parts of a financial plan. Then the discussion focuses on how organizations manage assets as efficiently and effectively as possible. We compare the two major sources of funds—debt and equity. Next, we introduce the concept of leverage. The major sources of short-term and long-term funding are described in the following sections. A description of mergers, acquisitions, buyouts, and divestitures concludes the chapter.

finance the business function of planning, obtaining, and managing the company's funds to accomplish its objectives as effectively and efficiently as possible.

LO 17.1 Define *finance*, and explain the role of financial managers.

THE ROLE OF THE FINANCIAL MANAGER

Organizations face intense pressures today. As a result, organizations need to measure and reduce the costs of their business operations. They also need to maximize their revenues and profits. **Financial managers** are the executives who develop and carry out their firm's financial plan and decide on the most appropriate sources and uses of funds. They are among the most vital people on the corporate payroll.

Figure 17.1 shows the finance function of a typical company. At the top is the chief executive officer (CEO). The chief financial officer (CFO) usually reports directly to the company's chief executive officer (CEO) or chief operating officer (COO). In some companies, the CFO is also a

financial managers the executives who develop and carry out their firm's financial plan and decide on the most appropriate sources and uses of funds.

FIGURE 17.1 The Finance Organization at a Typical Firm

member of the board of directors. In the case of the software maker Oracle, both the current CFO and the former CFO serve on that company's board; the former CFO chairs the board. Moreover, CFOs often serve as independent directors on other firms' boards, such as Telus, Tim Hortons, and Microsoft. As noted in Chapter 15, the CFO and the firm's CEO must both certify the accuracy of the firm's financial statements.

Three senior managers often report directly to the CFO. The titles can vary, but these three executives are commonly called the *vice-president of financial management* (or *planning*), the *treasurer*, and the *controller*. The vice-president for financial management or planning is responsible for preparing financial forecasts and analyzing major investment decisions related to new products, new production facilities, and acquisitions. The treasurer is responsible for all of the company's financing activities, including cash management, tax planning and preparation, and shareholder relations. The treasurer also works on the sale of new security issues to investors. The controller is the chief accounting manager. The controller's functions include keeping the company's books, preparing financial statements, and conducting internal audits. The "Hit & Miss" feature explains the increasing importance of financially sound IT management.

The growing importance of financial professionals is reflected in the number of CEOs who have been promoted from financial positions. For example, Indra Nooyi, CEO of PepsiCo, and Jim Marsh, CEO of the British telecommunications company Cable and Wireless, both served as their firm's CFO prior to assuming the top job. The importance of finance professionals is also reflected in CFOs' salaries. A survey by the executive compensation

Jin Lee/Bloomberg/Getty Images, Inc.

The growing importance of financial professionals is reflected in the growing number of CEOs who have been promoted from financial positions. Indra Nooyi, CEO of PepsiCo, served as CFO prior to assuming the top job.

HIT & MISS

Apptio Calculates the Cost of Information Technology

Software as a service (SaaS) is growing. Many companies are making the change to cloud computing to save money and increase efficiency. But is cloud computing always more economical and efficient? Until recently, there was no reliable way to find out.

Apptio provides hosted Internet technology solutions, including its Technology Business Management package. Recently, Apptio introduced its new Cost Transparency Template. This template generates the formulas a company can use to calculate how much more—or less—it would cost to invest in cloud computing compared with other options, including traditional in-house hardware and storage. Among Apptio's clients are BNP Paribas, Starbucks, Hallmark, and Expedia. Jeff Day, Apptio's director of marketing, says, "We see that cloud computing is going to change the way IT leaders think about how they manage IT."

St. Luke's Health System has 1,200 doctors among its 9,000 employees in 11 hospitals. The chief information officer, Debe Gash, wanted to get rid of all nonessential IT-related costs. A spending-analytics tool from Apptio helped Gash and her team to save millions of dollars. The tool works by highlighting unnecessary or duplicate spending. For example, St. Luke's had too many desktop

software licences, two full-time employees who dealt only with spam management, and large expenses related to electronic storage. Those expenses were reduced or eliminated, and funds are now redirected to pay for needed programs, such as electronic health records. "We were surprised at the efficiencies we were able to derive from getting those insights," Gash said.

In the future, IT managers will need to understand how the cloud works and whether it will be more cost-effective than other in-house or external systems. Day says, "The greatest inhibitor of the cloud is a lack of understanding. IT leaders need better systems and tools to perform accurate analysis."

Questions for Critical Thinking

1. Why have companies recently become so concerned with cost management?

2. Why might it be difficult for very large companies to keep accurate account of spending on such items as computer hardware and software licences?

Sources: Company website, http://www.apptio.com, accessed June 24, 2010; Denise Dubie, "IT Cost Management and the Cloud," *Network World*, April 13, 2010, http://www.networkworld.com; Bob Evans, "Global CIO: St. Luke's CIO Saves Millions with Apptio's Help," *InformationWeek*, April 6, 2010, http://www.informationweek.com; Brian Carlson, "Top 5 Financial Management Predictions for 2010," *CIO*, February 2, 2010, http://www.cio.com.

consulting firm Equilar found the median annual salary for CFOs of *Fortune* 500 companies to be around $3.76 million.[2] The CFO of the investment firm Berkshire Hathaway is actually paid more than the company's famous chairperson, Warren Buffett.[3]

In their jobs, financial professionals continually balance risks with expected financial returns. Risk is the uncertainty of gain or loss; return is the gain or loss that results from an investment over a specified period of time. Financial managers try to maximize the wealth of their firm's shareholders by striking the right balance between risk and return. This balance is called the **risk-return trade-off**. For example, a firm that relies heavily on borrowed funds may increase the return (in the form of cash) to shareholders. But the more money a firm borrows, the greater the risks to shareholders. An increase in a firm's cash on hand reduces the risk of being unable to meet unexpected cash needs. But cash alone does not earn much, if any, return. Firms that fail to invest their surplus funds in an income-earning asset—such as in securities—reduce their potential return or profitability. This chapter provides many examples of the risk-return trade-off.

Every financial manager must balance risks and returns. For example, in the late 1990s, Airbus had to make a major decision: whether to begin development and production of the giant A380 jetliner, the world's largest jetliner. The development costs for the aircraft were first estimated at more than $10 billion. But before committing to such a huge investment, financial managers weighed the potential profits of the A380 against the risks of investing in the aircraft's development. Airbus's future was on the line. It decided to go ahead with the development of the A380. The company spent more than $15 billion on research and development. The A380 entered commercial service a few years ago. Airbus currently has orders for approximately 200 jetliners at a list price of more than $359 million each.[4] At this time, it is still unclear whether the A380 investment was a smart and profitable decision.

Financial managers must also adapt to changes in the financial system. The recent credit crisis has made it more difficult for some companies to borrow money from traditional lenders such as banks. As a result, many firms have scaled back their expansion plans or are looking for funding from other sources, such as commercial financing companies. Financial managers must also adapt to internal changes.

risk-return trade-off the process of maximizing the wealth of the firm's shareholders by striking the right balance between risk and return.

✔ ASSESSMENT CHECK

17.1.1 What is the structure of the finance function at the typical firm?

17.1.2 Explain the risk-return trade-off.

LO 17.2 Describe the parts of a financial plan and the financial planning process.

FINANCIAL PLANNING

Financial managers develop their organization's **financial plan**, a document that specifies the funds needed by a firm for a given period of time, the timing of cash inflows and outflows, and the most appropriate sources and uses of funds. *Operating plans* are short-term financial plans that focus on no more than a year or two in the future. *Strategic plans* are financial plans that have a much longer time horizon, up to five or 10 years.

A financial plan is based on forecasts of several items: production costs, purchasing needs, plant and equipment expenses, and sales activities for the period covered. Financial managers use forecasts to decide on the specific amounts needed and the timing of expenses and receipts. They build a financial plan based on the answers to three questions:

1. What funds will the firm require during the planning period?
2. When will the firm need additional funds?
3. Where will the firm obtain the necessary funds?

Some funds flow into the firm when it sells its goods or services, but funding needs vary. The financial plan must reflect both the amounts and timing of inflows and outflows of funds. Even a profitable firm may face financial difficulties when it needs funds but sales are slow, when the volume of its credit sales increases, or when customers are slow in making payments.

In general, preparing a financial plan consists of three steps. The first step is a forecast of sales or revenue over some future time period. This projection is the key variable in any financial plan: without an accurate sales forecast, the firm will have difficulty accurately estimating other variables, such as production costs and purchasing needs. The best way to forecast sales depends on the type

financial plan a document that specifies the funds needed by a firm for a period of time, the timing of cash inflows and outflows, and the most appropriate sources and uses of funds.

of business. For example, a retailer's CFO might begin by looking at the current sales per store. The CFO would look at the near future, including expected sales growth and any planned store openings or closings. This information can help to provide a forecast of sales for the next period. If the company sells merchandise through other channels, such as online, the forecast is adjusted to include those additional channels.

Next, the CFO uses the sales forecast to decide on the expected level of profits for future periods. This longer-term projection involves estimating expenses such as purchases, employee compensation, and taxes. Many expenses are the result of sales. For example, the more a firm sells, generally the more it purchases. The CFO should also decide what portion of these profits will likely be paid to shareholders in the form of cash dividends.

After coming up with the sales and profit forecast, the CFO then needs to estimate how many additional assets the firm will need to support the projected sales. For example, an increase in sales might mean the company needs additional inventory, faster collection of accounts receivable, or even a new plant and equipment. Depending on the type of industry, some businesses need more assets than other businesses to support the same amount of sales. The technical term for this greater requirement is *asset intensity*. For example, the chemical manufacturer DuPont has approximately $0.68 in assets for every dollar in sales. In other words, for every $100 increase in sales, the firm needs about $68 of additional assets. The warehouse retailer Costco is less asset-intensive. It needs only about $0.34 in assets for every dollar in sales. In other words, Costco would need an additional $34 of assets for every $100 of additional sales. This difference is not surprising; manufacturing is a more asset-intensive business than retailing.

A simplified financial plan illustrates these steps. Assume a growing company is forecasting that sales next year will increase by $40 million to $140 million. After estimating the company's expenses, the CFO believes that after-tax profits next year will be $12 million, and the firm will pay nothing in dividends. The projected increase in next year's sales will require the firm to invest another $20 million in assets. Because increases in assets represent a use of funds, the company will need an additional $20 million in funds. The company's after-tax earnings will contribute $12 million, and the remaining $8 million must come from outside sources. The financial plan tells the CFO how much money will be needed and when it will be needed. Using this knowledge, and knowing that the firm has decided to borrow the needed funds, the CFO can then begin negotiations with banks and other lenders.

The cash inflows and outflows of a business are similar to the cash inflows and outflows of a household. The members of a household depend on weekly or monthly paycheques for funds, but their expenses may vary greatly from one pay period to the next. The financial plan should indicate the amount and timing of funds flowing into and out of the organization. One of the largest business expenses is employee compensation.

A good financial plan also includes financial control. Financial control is a process of comparing actual revenues, costs, and expenses with the forecasted amounts. This comparison may show differences between projected and actual figures. It is important to discover any differences early so quick action can be taken.

Bill Morrison is the CFO of Genco Marketplace, a business that liquidates, or sells off, other companies' excess inventory. Genco buys inventory that is not selling well, then it resells the inventory to wholesalers. In turn, the wholesalers sell the inventory to discount retailers. Genco is always careful about the cost of freight, including fuel. Genco pays the

Costco's *asset intensity* is lower than that of a typical manufacturing business.

Justin Sullivan/Getty Images, Inc.

✓ ASSESSMENT CHECK

17.2.1 What three questions does a financial plan address?

17.2.2 Explain the steps involved in preparing a financial plan.

transportation costs of taking the goods from their current location to where they will be liquidated. Some excess inventory is seasonal. For example, when a retailer has winter coats left over in June, Genco will buy those coats, hold them in inventory, and sell them to a wholesaler in the fall, when demand for winter coats increases. But the longer a product remains unsold, the harder it is to liquidate, even at a deep discount. In all cases, Morrison or members of his team need to prepare a financial plan that takes into account both the benefits and risks of buying the merchandise.[5]

LO 17.3 Outline how organizations manage their assets.

MANAGING ASSETS

As noted in Chapter 15, assets consist of what a firm owns. But assets also represent uses of funds. To grow and prosper, companies need to obtain additional assets. Sound financial management requires assets to be acquired and managed as effectively and efficiently as possible. The "Business Etiquette" feature offers tips for managing assets.

Short-Term Assets

Short-term assets are also called current assets. These assets consist of cash and assets that can be, or are expected to be, converted into cash within a year. The major current assets are cash, marketable securities, accounts receivable, and inventory.

BUSINESS ETIQUETTE

Tips for Managing Assets

These are challenging times for all businesses, whether one-person start-ups or large corporations. One of the most difficult problems is controlling costs. Here are some tips for managing assets—physical, financial, and human—while focusing on both short-term demands and long-term planning:

1. *Define your goals and objectives.* Be realistic when working out the resources you will need to meet both your immediate needs and your long-term plans. If you need to borrow money, be aware that credit is currently very tight, or difficult to access.

2. *Examine your expenses.* You may find some areas where you can reduce or eliminate unnecessary expenditures, such as travel or discretionary spending. Which makes more financial sense for your company—cloud computing or traditional hardware and storage?

3. *Communicate with all your associates.* Be sure that your employees, suppliers, and clients know what is happening with your business. When people hear nothing, especially during difficult times, they often assume the worst has happened.

4. *Cultivate your human assets.* Identify your valued employees and let them know that they are important to the business. In difficult times, companies often try to hire talented personnel from their competitors. Again, communication is important. If your best employees hear nothing from you, they may also assume the worst has happened—and they may be more willing to leave for what may seem to be better opportunities elsewhere.

5. *Have at least one backup plan.* Your goals and objectives may not work out the way you expected them to. You may plan for a certain amount of receivables, but they may suddenly decrease. If possible, keep sufficient financial reserves available to see the company through the unexpected. That way, you may be able to turn disaster to your advantage.

Sources: "Managing Assets in Volatile Times: Nine Ways CFOs Can Adapt to Changing Financial Markets," Deloitte, http://www.deloitte.com, accessed June 24, 2010; Fred Jennings and R. W. Beck, "Leveraging Enterprise Value with Asset Management," *Utility Products,* January 14, 2010, http://www.elp.com; Daniel Solin, "Seven Shocking Tips to Boost Your Returns by 400% (or More)," *DailyFinance,* January 1, 2010, http://www.dailyfinance.com.

Cash and Marketable Securities

The major purpose of cash is to pay for day-to-day expenses. It is similar to individuals who keep a balance in their chequing accounts to pay bills or buy food and clothing. Most organizations try to keep a minimum cash balance so they have funds available for unexpected expenses. As noted earlier, cash earns little, if any, return; most firms invest their excess cash in *marketable securities*. These are low-risk securities that either have short maturities or can be easily sold in secondary markets. Money market instruments—described in Chapter 16—are popular choices for firms that have excess cash. The cash budget, which we discussed and illustrated in Chapter 15, is one tool for managing cash and marketable securities. The cash budget shows expected cash inflows and outflows for a period of time. The cash budget shows which months the firm will have surplus cash and will be able to invest in marketable securities and which months when it will need additional cash.

Critics of some companies' budgeting practices argue that some firms hoard cash. Recently, Cisco Systems had more than $35 billion in cash and marketable securities. But firms may have good reasons for holding large amounts of cash and marketable securities. For example, they may be planning to soon use these funds to make a large investment, pay dividends to shareholders, or repurchase outstanding bonds.

Accounts Receivable

Accounts receivable are uncollected credit sales. They can represent a significant asset. The financial manager's job is to collect the funds owed to the firm as quickly as possible, while still offering sufficient credit to customers to attract and generate increased sales. In general, a more liberal credit policy means higher sales but also increased collection expenses, higher levels of bad debt, and a higher investment in accounts receivable.

Management of accounts receivable is composed of two functions: deciding on an overall credit policy and deciding which customers will be offered credit. Formulating a credit policy involves deciding whether the firm will offer credit and, if so, what terms of credit to offer. For example, will a discount be offered to customers who pay in cash? The overall credit policy is often the result of competitive pressures or general industry practices. If all your competitors offer their customers credit, your firm will likely also need to offer credit. The second aspect of a credit policy is deciding which customers will be offered credit. Managers must consider the importance of the customer and the customer's financial health and repayment history.

One simple tool for assessing how well receivables are being managed is to calculate the accounts receivable turnover over two or more time periods in a row. We showed how this ratio is calculated in Chapter 15. If the receivables turnover shows signs of slowing, it means that, on average, credit customers are paying later. This trend may need further investigation.

Inventory Management

For many firms, such as retailers, inventory represents the largest single asset. For example, at the home furnishings retailer Bed Bath & Beyond, inventory makes up about 49 percent of total assets. Even for nonretailers, inventory is an important asset. At the heavy-equipment manufacturer Caterpillar, inventory is almost 12 percent of total assets. On the other hand, some types of firms, such as electric utilities and transportation companies, have no inventory. Most firms carry inventory. Their proper management of inventory is vital to the business's success.

Managing inventory can be complicated. The cost of inventory includes more than just the cost of acquiring goods. It also includes the costs of ordering, storing, insuring, and financing

At Bed Bath & Beyond, inventory is the most valuable asset. Managing inventory can be a costly and highly complicated task, especially for retailers.

© Patti McConville/Alamy

inventory. In addition, businesses take on the costs of stock-outs and the costs of lost sales due to insufficient inventory. Financial managers try to minimize the cost of inventory. But production, marketing, and logistics also play important roles in determining proper inventory levels. The production considerations of inventory management were discussed in Chapter 10. In Chapter 12, we outlined the marketing and logistics issues surrounding inventory.

Trends in the inventory turnover ratio—described in Chapter 15—can be early warning signs of difficulties ahead. For example, when inventory turnover has been slowing for several quarters in a row, inventory is rising faster than sales. This situation may suggest that customer demand is slowing. The firm may needs to take action, such as reducing production or increasing promotional efforts.

Capital Investment Analysis

In addition to current assets, firms also invest in long-lived assets. Unlike current assets, long-lived assets are expected to produce economic benefits for more than one year. These investments often involve large amounts of money. For example, as noted earlier in the chapter, Airbus invested more than $15 billion in development of the A380. In another example, Target Corp. recently announced its expansion into Canada, buying out the store leases of 220 Zellers stores for $1.83 billion. Target will need to invest in billions of dollars of long-lived assets to support its plans to open 100 to 150 stores over the next few years.[6]

Capital investment analysis is the process financial managers use when deciding whether to invest in long-lived assets. Firms make two basic types of capital investment decisions: expansion and replacement. The A380 and Target investments are examples of expansion decisions. Replacement decisions involve upgrading assets by substituting new assets for older assets. A retailer, such as Walmart, might decide to replace an old store with a new Supercentre, as it did in Concord, Ontario. Walmart Canada also plans to open 40 new Supercentre stores in Canada in the next few years, spending some $500 million on remodelling, expansion, moving, and adding additional locations.[7]

Financial managers must estimate all the costs and benefits of a proposed investment. This task can be very difficult, especially for very long-lived investments. Companies should only pursue those investments that offer an acceptable return—measured by the difference between benefits and costs. Target's financial managers believed that the benefits of expanding into Canada outweighed the high cost. The expansion will allow Target to begin an international strategic expansion project. When deciding whether to expand into Canada, Target's financial managers would have considered the expected profit and the strategic benefits from the expansion. Target's CEO, Gregg Steinhafel, said, "This is earlier than we expected and it is a bigger initial investment." This expansion is a large investment for Target. Steinhafel said they will have to "suspend any serious activity" in other international markets for the time being due to the sheer magnitude of the expansion.[8]

Managing International Assets

Today, firms often have assets worldwide. Waterloo-based Research In Motion generates more than half of its annual sales outside of Canada.[9] Most sales for Unilever and Nestlé occur outside their home countries (the Netherlands and Switzerland, respectively). Managing international assets creates several challenges for financial managers. One of the most important challenges is dealing with exchange rates.

As we discussed in several other chapters, an exchange rate is the rate at which one currency can be exchanged for another currency. Exchange rates can vary widely from year to year, which creates a problem for any company that has international assets. For example, assume a Canadian firm has a major subsidiary in the United Kingdom. Assume that the U.K. subsidiary earns an annual profit of £750 million. Over the past five years, the exchange rate between the U.S. dollar and the British pound has varied between 2.302 (dollars per pound) and 1.523.[10] This means the dollar value of the U.K. profits ranged from $1.73 billion to $1.14 billion.

Many global firms are involved in activities that reduce the risks associated with exchange rate ups and downs. Some of these activities are complicated. But if done correctly, these activities can reduce or even eliminate the risks associated with changes in the value of foreign currencies. Reducing the risks of exchange rate fluctuations will improve the financial performance of the firm, which can have a positive impact on its share price.

✓ **ASSESSMENT CHECK**

17.3.1 Why do firms often choose to invest excess cash in marketable securities?

17.3.2 What are the two aspects of accounts receivable management?

17.3.3 Explain the difference between an expansion decision and a replacement decision.

SOURCES OF FUNDS AND CAPITAL STRUCTURE

LO 17.4 Compare the two major sources of funds for a business, and explain the concept of leverage.

The use of debt for financing can increase both the potential for return and the potential for loss. Recall the accounting equation introduced in Chapter 15:

Assets = Liabilities + Owners' equity

When this equation is viewed from a financial management perspective, it shows that there are only two types of funding: debt and equity. *Debt capital* consists of funds obtained through borrowing. *Equity capital* consists of funds provided by the firm's owners when they reinvest their earnings, make additional contributions, liquidate assets, issue shares to the general public, or raise capital from outside investors. The mix of a firm's debt and equity capital is known as its **capital structure**.

Companies often take very different approaches to choosing a capital structure. As the company uses more debt, the risk to the company increases: the firm needs to make the interest payments on the money borrowed, regardless of the amount of cash flow coming into the company. Choosing more debt increases the fixed costs a company must pay, which makes a company more sensitive to any change in sales revenues. Debt is frequently the least costly method of raising additional financing dollars, which is why it is so frequently used.

Different industries choose varying amounts of debt and equity to use when financing. Information provided by DataMonitor shows the automotive industry has debt ratios (the ratio of liabilities to assets) of more 60 percent for both Toyota and Honda and more than 90 percent for Ford. These companies are primarily using debt to finance their asset expenses. Companies such as McDonald's and Starbucks use only 49 percent debt and 27 percent debt, respectively. The mixture of debt and equity a company uses is a major management decision.

capital structure the mix of a firm's debt and equity capital.

leverage increasing the rate of return on funds invested by borrowing funds.

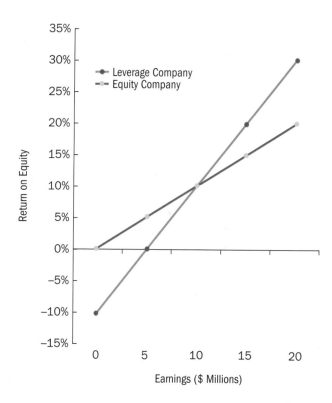

Leverage and Capital Structure Decisions

Raising needed cash by borrowing allows a firm to benefit from the principle of **leverage**, increasing the rate of return on funds invested by borrowing funds. The key to managing leverage is to ensure that a company's earnings remain larger than its interest payments, which increases the leverage on the rate of return on shareholders' investment. Of course, if the company earns less than its interest payments, shareholders lose money on their original investments.

Figure 17.2 shows the relationship between earnings and shareholder returns for two identical imaginary firms that choose to raise funds in different ways. Leverage Company obtains 50 percent of its funds from lenders who purchase company bonds. Leverage Company pays 10 percent interest on its bonds. Equity Company raises all of its funds through sales of company stock.

Notice that if earnings double, from $10 million to $20 million, the returns to the shareholders of Equity Company also double—from 10 percent to 20 percent. But returns to shareholders of Leverage Company more than double—from 10 percent to 30 percent. But leverage can also work in the opposite direction. If earnings fall from $10 million to $5 million (a decline of 50 percent), returns to shareholders of Equity Company also fall by 50 percent—from 10 percent to 5 percent. By contrast, returns to shareholders of Leverage Company fall from 10 percent to zero. Thus, leverage increases potential returns to shareholders but also increases risk.

FIGURE 17.2 How Leverage Works

Note: The example assumes that both companies have $100 million in capital. Leverage Company consists of $50 million in equity and $50 million in bonds (with an interest rate of 10 percent). Equity Company consists of $100 million in equity and no bonds. This example also assumes no corporate taxes.

Another problem with borrowing money is that relying too much on borrowed funds may reduce management's flexibility in future financing decisions. If a company raises equity capital this year and needs to raise funds next year, it will probably be able to raise either debt or equity capital. But if it raises debt capital this year, it may be forced to raise equity capital next year.

Equity capital also has downsides. Because shareholders are owners of the company, they usually elect the board of directors and vote on major company issues. But when new equity is sold, the control of the existing shareholders is weakened, and the outcome of these votes could potentially change. One sensitive subject today between companies and shareholders is whether shareholders should be able to vote on executive pay packages. The "Solving an Ethical Controversy" feature discusses this issue.

Another downside of equity capital is that it is more expensive than debt capital. First, creditors have a senior claim to the assets of a firm before the shareholders' claims. Because of this advantage, creditors will accept a lower rate of return than shareholders will accept. Second, the firm can deduct interest payments on debt, reducing its taxable income and its tax bill. In contrast,

---

SOLVING AN **ETHICAL** CONTROVERSY

Executive Pay: Should Shareholders Decide the Salaries of CEOs?

While the world was suffering through the 2008 financial crisis and its aftermath, the news media were reporting on the huge salaries of CEOs and other top executives at large corporations.

At a recent Royal Dutch Shell annual meeting, shareholders voted down the proposed executive compensation package. In response, the company announced it would freeze executive pay and base its bonuses on performance. The new CEO received a salary 20 percent lower than that of the previous CEO. The company said that the changes would "demonstrate appropriate restraint in the current economic environment. "Say-on-pay" voting by shareholders has become increasingly common—and controversial.

Should company shareholders help decide how much top executives are paid?

PRO

1. Publicly held corporations are owned by their shareholders, who should have the opportunity to vote on compensation for top executives. Robert E. Denham and Rajiv L. Gupta, co-chairs of The Conference Board Task Force on Executive Compensation, said, "Shareholders . . . and the public deserve to see executive compensation programs that serve shareholders' interests and are explained to shareholders . . ."

2. Some analysts believe that lopsided pay structures played a role in the financial crisis in the United States. Federal Reserve Chairman Ben Bernanke said, "Compensation practices at some banking organizations have led to misaligned incentives and excessive risk-taking."

CON

1. Shareholders may not necessarily know what appropriate pay is. Many do not have the time or resources to do their own analysis and to judge whether a pay program is suitable, or whether it promotes a risk-taking, get-rich-quick mentality in executives.

2. Shareholders recently turned down the chance to vote on executive pay at companies such as Johnson & Johnson and Dow Chemical. Many shareholders prefer to discuss pay structures with management and board members before voting.

Summary

The Ontario Securities Commission (OSC) is considering making it a requirement for companies to give shareholders a say on executive compensation. This approach would begin to position Canada in line with many European countries and in the direction of the United States, where "say-on-pay" regulations are either currently in place or are in the planning stage.

Sources: Alix Stuart, "Reform Bill Mandates Say on Pay," *CFO.com,* June 29, 2010, http://www.cfo.com; Jim Kuhnhenn and Alan Fram, "Congress Agrees on Financial Oversight," *Philadelphia Inquirer,* June 26, 2010, http://www.philly.com; Ann Yerger, "Red Flags for Say-on-Pay Voting," Harvard Law School Forum on Corporate Governance and Financial Regulation, May 18, 2010, http://blogs.law.harvard.edu; A. G. Laffey, "Executive Pay: Time for CEOs to Take a Stand," *Harvard Business Review,* May 2010, http://hbr.org; Bryant Ruiz Switzky, "CEO Compensation Down in 2009," *Washington Business Journal,* May 7, 2010, http://washingtonbizjournals.com; "Shell Shareholder 'Rebellion' Leads to New Limits on Executive Pay, Bonuses," *Huffington Post,* February 26, 2010, http://www.huffingtonpost.com; Helen Coster, "The State of the CEO in 2010," *Forbes.com,* January 21, 2010, http://www.forbes.com; David R. Butcher, "Cracking Down on Excessive Executive Pay," IMT Industry Market Trends, October 29, 2009, http://news.thomasnet.com; Danielle Arbuckle, "Should Shareholders Have a Say on Executive Pay?" *Wallet Pop website,* http://www.walletpop.ca/blog/2011/01/19/should-shareholders-have-a-say-on-executive-pay/, accessed August, 2, 2011.

dividends paid to shareholders are not tax-deductible. A key part of the financial manager's job is to weigh the upsides and downsides of debt capital and equity capital, and then create the most suitable capital structure for the firm.

Mixing Short-Term and Long-Term Funds

Financial managers face another decision: deciding on the suitable mix of short-term and long-term funds. Short-term funds consist of current liabilities, and long-term funds consist of long-term debt and equity. Short-term funds are generally less expensive than long-term funds, but they expose the firm to more risk. This risk occurs because short-term funds need to be renewed, or rolled over, frequently. Short-term interest rates can be unstable. For example, during a recent 12-month period, rates on commercial paper, a popular short-term financing option, ranged from a high of 6 percent to a low of less than 2 percent.[11]

Because short-term rates move up and down frequently, the interest expense on short-term funds can vary greatly from year to year. For example, if a firm borrows $50 million for 10 years at 5 percent interest, its annual interest expense is fixed at $2.5 million for the entire 10 years. On the other hand, if the firm borrows $50 million for one year at a rate of 4 percent, its annual interest expense of $2 million is fixed for only that year. If interest rates increase the following year to 6 percent, then $1 million will be added to the interest expense bill. Another potential risk of relying on short-term funds is availability. Even financially healthy firms can occasionally find it difficult to borrow money.

Because of the added risk of short-term funding, most firms choose to finance all of their long-term assets, and even a portion of their short-term assets, by using long-term funds. Johnson & Johnson is typical of this choice. Figure 17.3 shows a recent balance sheet that divides out the short-term and long-term assets, and the short-term and long-term funds.

Dividend Policy

In addition to decisions regarding capital structure and the mix of short-term and long-term funds, financial managers also make decisions regarding a firm's dividend policy. *Dividends* are periodic cash payments to shareholders. The most common type of dividend is paid quarterly and is often called a *regular dividend*. Occasionally, firms make one-time special dividend payment or extra dividend payments, as Microsoft did some years ago. Earnings that are paid in dividends are not reinvested in the firm and don't contribute additional equity capital.

Firms are under no legal obligation to pay dividends to shareholders. Although some companies pay generous dividends, others pay nothing. Until 2010, Starbucks never paid a dividend to its shareholders. In contrast, 3M has paid dividends for 30-plus consecutive years; during that time, the amount of the dividends has more than quadrupled. Companies that pay dividends try to increase the amount of dividends paid or, at the very least, hold the amount of the dividends steady from year to year. But, in rare cases, firms must cut or eliminate dividends. As mentioned in Chapter 16, as a result of the oil spill in the Gulf of Mexico BP announced it was cancelling dividend payments for the first quarter and suspending those payments to shareholders for the second and third quarters of their fiscal year.[12]

Many factors are considered when deciding on a company's dividend policy. One factor is the

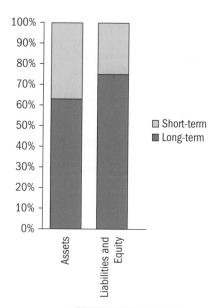

FIGURE 17.3
Johnson & Johnson's Mix of Short-Term and Long-Term Funds

Source: Johnson & Johnson balance sheet, Yahoo! Finance, http://finance.yahoo.com, accessed June 24, 2010.

As a result of the oil spill in the Gulf of Mexico, BP announced it was cancelling dividend payments for the first quarter and suspending them for the second and third quarters of their fiscal year.

Simon Dawson/Bloomberg via Getty Images

ASSESSMENT CHECK

17.4.1 Explain the concept of leverage.

17.4.2 Why do firms generally rely more on long-term funds than short-term funds?

17.4.3 What is an important factor in deciding on a firm's dividend policy?

firm's investment opportunities. Suppose a firm has numerous investment opportunities and wants to finance some or all of them through equity funding. It will likely pay little, if any, of its earnings in dividends. Shareholders may actually want the company to retain earnings, because if they are reinvested, the firm's future profits, and the value of its shares, will increase faster. By contrast, a firm with more limited investment opportunities generally pays more of its earnings in dividends.

In addition to dividends, some firms buy back a portion of their outstanding shares. The Home Depot, for example, has repurchased more than $1 billion of shares over the past few years. Generally, shares are purchased on the secondary markets. The main purpose of share buy-backs is to raise the market value of the remaining shares, which benefits the shareholders.

LO 17.5 Identify sources of short-term financing for business operations.

SHORT-TERM FUNDING OPTIONS

An organization may discover that its cash needs are greater than its available funds. Retailers generate surplus cash for most of the year, but they need to build up inventory during the late summer and fall to get ready for the holiday shopping season. They often need funds to pay for this merchandise until the holiday sales generate revenue. They can then use the incoming funds to repay the amount they borrowed. In this kind of situation, financial managers often look to short-term sources of funds. Short-term sources of funds are repaid within one year. The three major sources of short-term funds are trade credit, short-term loans, and commercial paper. Large firms often rely on a combination of all three sources of short-term financing.

Trade Credit

Trade credit is extended by suppliers when a firm receives goods or services and agrees to pay for them at a later date. Trade credit is common in many industries such as retailing and manufacturing. Suppliers ship billions of dollars of merchandise to retailers each day and are paid at a later date. Without trade credit, the retailing sector would probably look much different—with fewer selections. To record trade credit, the supplier enters the transactions as an account receivable, and the retailer enters it as an account payable. Canadian Tire Corporation currently has more than $1.3 billion of accounts payable on its books.[13] The main upside of trade credit is its easy availability. The main downside to trade credit is that the amount a company can borrow is limited to the amount it purchases.

What is the cost of trade credit? If suppliers do not offer a cash discount, trade credit is effectively free. For example, assume a supplier offers trade credit under the terms net 30. These terms mean that the buyer has 30 days to pay. In other words, companies are borrowing $100 and repaying $100 in 30 days. The effective rate of interest is zero. But some suppliers offer a discount if they are paid in cash. If a discount is offered, trade credit can get expensive. Assume that a 2 percent discount is offered to cash buyers. If buyers do not take the discount, they have 30 days to pay. If the buyer does not pay cash, the terms are the same as borrowing $98 today and repaying $100 in 30 days. The annual interest rate on such a loan is more than 24 percent.

Short-Term Loans

Loans from commercial banks are a significant source of short-term financing for businesses. Businesses often use these loans to finance inventory and accounts receivable. For example, a small manufacturer of ski equipment has its highest sales in late fall and early winter. To meet this demand, it begins building inventory during the summer. The manufacturer also needs to finance accounts receivable (credit sales to customers) during the fall and winter. It takes out a bank loan during the summer. As the inventory is sold, and as accounts receivable are collected, the firm repays the loan.

Borrowers can choose from two types of short-term bank loans: lines of credit and revolving credit agreements. A line of credit specifies the maximum amount the firm can borrow over a period of time, usually a year. The bank is under no obligation to actually lend the money. It will lend the money but only if funds are available. Most lines of credit require the borrower to repay the original amount, plus interest, within one year. In contrast, a revolving credit agreement is basically a guaranteed line of credit—the bank guarantees that the funds will be available when needed. Banks typically charge a fee, on top of interest, for revolving credit agreements.

The cash budget is an important tool when deciding on the size of a line of credit. The cash budget shows the months when additional financing will be needed or when borrowed funds can be repaid. For example, assume the ski manufacturer's cash budget indicates that it will need $2.5 million from June through November. The financial manager might set up a line of credit with the bank for $2.8 million. The extra $300,000 is added to cover any unexpected cash outflows.

Commercial finance companies also make short-term loans to businesses. Most bank loans are unsecured, which means that no specific assets are pledged as collateral, or security. Loans from commercial finance companies are often secured by using accounts receivable or inventory as collateral.

Factoring is another form of short-term financing that uses accounts receivable. The business sells its accounts receivable at a discount to either a bank or a finance company—which is called a *factor*. The cost of the transaction depends on the size of the discount. Factoring allows the firm to convert its receivables into cash quickly without worrying about collections.

The cost of short-term loans depends on the interest rate and on the fees charged by the lender. Some lenders also require the borrower to keep *compensating balances*—5 to 20 percent of the outstanding loan amount—in a chequing account. Compensating balances increase the effective cost of a loan because the borrower does not have full use of the amount borrowed.

For example, suppose a firm borrows $100,000 for one year at 5 percent interest. The borrower will pay $5,000 in interest (5 percent $\times$ $100,000). If the lender requires that 10 percent of the loan amount be kept as compensating balance, the firm has use of only $90,000. But because the firm will still pay $5,000 in interest, the effective rate on the loan is actually 5.56 percent ($5,000/$90,000).

Commercial Paper

Commercial paper is a short-term IOU sold by a company; it was briefly described in Chapter 16. Commercial paper is usually sold in multiples of $100,000 to $1 million and has a maturity date that ranges from 1 to 270 days. Most commercial paper is unsecured. It is an attractive source of financing because large amounts of money can be raised at interest rates that are usually 1 to 2 percent less than the interest rates charged by banks. At the end of a recent year, almost $1.15 trillion in commercial paper was outstanding.[14] Although commercial paper is an attractive short-term financing option, only a small percentage of businesses can issue it. Access to the commercial paper market has traditionally been limited to large, financially strong corporations.

✔ **ASSESSMENT CHECK**

17.5.1 What are the three sources of short-term funding?

17.5.2 Explain trade credit.

17.5.3 Why is commercial paper an attractive short-term financing option?

SOURCES OF LONG-TERM FINANCING

LO 17.6 Discuss long-term financing options.

Funds from short-term sources can help a firm meet its current needs for cash or inventory. But a larger project or plan, such as buying another company or investing in real estate or equipment, usually requires funds for a much longer period of time. Unlike short-term financing, long-term financing is repaid over many years.

Organizations acquire long-term financing from three sources. The first source is long-term loans from financial institutions such as commercial banks, life insurance companies, and pension funds. A second source is bonds—certificates of indebtedness—sold to investors. A third source is equity financing acquired by selling shares in the firm or reinvesting company profits.

Public Sale of Shares and Bonds

Public sales of securities, such as shares and bonds, are a major source of funds for corporations. These sales provide cash inflows for the issuing firm and either a share in its ownership (for a share purchaser) or a specified rate of interest and repayment at a stated time (for a bond purchaser). Because many shares and bonds are traded in the secondary markets, shareholders and bondholders can easily sell these securities. Recently, when a European debt crisis seemed likely, it caused a massive slowdown in bond sales. As fears of a crisis eased later in the year, bond sales reached their highest level in a year. As of late 2010, companies had sold about $78.7 billion of Canadian corporate bonds.[15] Public sales of securities can vary quite a bit from year to year depending on conditions in the financial markets. For example, bond sales tend to be higher when interest rates are low.

In Chapter 16, we discussed how most companies sell securities publicly—through investment bankers, by using a process called *underwriting*. Investment bankers purchase the securities from the issuer and then resell them to investors. The issuer pays a fee to the investment banker, called an *underwriting discount*.

Private Placements

Some new share or bond issues are not sold publicly but are offered instead to a small group of major investors such as pension funds and insurance companies. These sales are referred to as *private placements*. Most private placements involve corporate debt issues. More than $120 billion in corporate bonds were sold privately in a recent year in the United States.[16]

It is often cheaper for a company to sell a security privately than publicly. Private placements are subject to fewer government regulations because registration with Canadian Securities Administration is not required. Institutional investors such as insurance companies and pension funds buy private placements because they typically carry slightly higher interest rates than publicly issued bonds. In addition, the terms of the issue can be designed to meet the specific needs of both the issuer and the institutional investors. Of course, the institutional investor gives up liquidity, or ease of cashability, because privately placed securities do not trade in secondary markets.

Venture Capitalists

Venture capitalists are an important source of long-term financing, especially to new companies. **Venture capitalists** are business firms or groups of individuals that invest in new and growing firms in exchange for an ownership share. They typically raise money from wealthy individuals and institutional investors and invest these funds in promising firms. Venture capitalists also provide management consulting advice and funds. In exchange for their investment, venture capitalists become part owners of the business. If the business succeeds, venture capitalists can earn large profits. The "Going Green" feature describes how new investment vehicles are being created to reflect some investors' interests in corporate sustainability.

One of Canada's largest venture capital firms is Covington Funds. Covington was established in 1994. It has invested in several sectors, including technology and health care. One of the many companies that Covington has invested in is Golf Town. Covington currently manages more than $300 million in assets.[17]

venture capitalists business firms or groups of individuals that invest in new and growing firms in exchange for an ownership share.

Private Equity Funds

Private equity funds are similar to venture capitalists. They are investment companies that raise funds from wealthy individuals and institutional investors. They then invest those funds in both public and privately held companies. Unlike venture capital funds, which tend to focus on small,

GOING GREEN

A **KNIGHT IN SHINING CAPITALISM**

The words *clean* and *capitalism* are not often used together in the same sentence. Many think of capitalism in a negative sense. But can large corporate companies operate under the concept of "clean capitalism"?

Corporate Knights (CK) is a Toronto-based company that understands that many investors have changing objectives. CK publishes an annual "clean capitalism" report. It uses objective measures to assess the environmental, social, and governance (ESG) practices of some of Canada's largest companies. Executives, regulators, investors, and other stakeholders consult this $1,495 report to assess the sustainability practices of these companies. CK also publishes a list of the top 100 companies in the "Global 100 Most Sustainable Corporations in the World." Canadian companies that made the list for 2012 include Suncor Energy Inc. (#47), Enbridge Inc. (#71), Encana Corp. (#76), and the Royal Bank of Canada (#95). Novo Nordisk A/S of Denmark, a healthcare company, was ranked number one.

CK is currently developing a global collection of clean capitalism passive investments to help investors who want to invest in companies that practise clean capitalism.

CK is responding to investors who want to evaluate companies both on their financial performance and on their "extra-financial" performance, including activities that support the environment, labour, and human rights. The measurement of ESG practices by a single organization allows investors to compare various companies. Many believe that these extra-financial measures can significantly influence a company's long-term performance and affect its true overall value.

Questions for Critical Thinking

1. Why does "going green" make good business sense for large corporations?

2. How do ESG practices affect a company's market value and long-term financial potential?

Sources: Corporate Knights, "Clean Capitalism," http://www.corporateknights.com/cleancapitalism, accessed March 6, 2012; "2012 Global 100 Most Sustainable Companies: The Full List," http://www.global100.org/, accessed March 6, 2012; Corporate Knights, "Toronto-based Clean Capitalism Media Company Closes Investment Round to Launch Capital Markets Division," press release, November 16, 2011, http://huffstrategy.com/MediaManager/release/Corporate-Knights/31-12-69/Toronto-based-clean-capitalism-media-company-closes-investment-ro/2386.html, accessed March 6, 2012; Novo Nordisk company website, http://www.novonordisk.com/, accessed March 6, 2012.

start-up companies, private equity funds invest in all types of businesses, including mature companies. For example, Onex Corporation, a private equity fund, recently bought three of Boeing's parts manufacturing plants for $1.5 billion.[18] Often, private equity funds invest in transactions that take public companies private, also known as leveraged buyouts (LBOs). In these transactions, discussed in more detail in the next section, a public company reverts to private status. The "Hit & Miss" feature profiles another large private equity fund, Harvest Partners.

A variation of the private equity fund is the so-called *sovereign wealth fund*. Sovereign wealth funds are owned by governments. They invest in a variety of financial and real assets, such as real estate. Sovereign wealth funds generally make investments that are based on the best risk-return trade-off. But their investment decisions are also influenced by political, social, and strategic considerations.

The television series "Dragons' Den" popularizes entrepreneurs and their search for long-term financing.

PHOTOGRAPH BY RICHARD KENDAL, CAMERA PRESS LONDON

Chinese sovereign wealth funds have recently made several purchases in Canada. The China Investment Corporation made several large investments in major Canadian resource companies and the Alberta oil sands. PetroChina Company paid $5.44 billion for a 50 percent stake in Encana Corporation's natural-gas assets in Western Canada. China Petrochemical Corporation paid $4.65 billion recently to buy a part of Syncrude Canada Ltd., a company that produces bitumen from Alberta oil-sands projects.[19] The assets of the 10 largest sovereign wealth funds are shown in Figure 17.4. Together, these 10 funds have more than $3.9 trillion in assets.

HIT & MISS

Harvest Partners Grows Its Investments

Is it possible to have too much money to spend in too little time? Harvest Partners and other private equity firms have just a few years to invest about $500 billion.

Harvest Partners is a private equity firm that specializes in leveraged buyouts and growth financing. It focuses on companies in North America and Western Europe. The firm manages funds emphasizing private equity and debt investments. Harvest Partners makes equity investments of $30 million to $100 million in companies with revenues of between $100 million and $750 million. It prefers to be a control investor, by becoming a partner in the companies it finances. Those companies tend to be middle-market firms that need investment to adapt to changing times and markets.

Private equity firms usually have three to six years to reinvest the funds they have raised from client investors. If they cannot or do not reinvest during that time, they must return the money. During the boom years, Harvest Partners raised $815 million from client investors. So far it has reinvested about $293 million. The firm now faces a 2012 deadline to reinvest the remaining $522 million.

Not all private equity investments are successful. Harvest Partners had owned the equity of the Natural Products Group (NPG), a manufacturer of organic shampoos and soaps. When NPG went bankrupt, Harvest Partners lost its entire investment.

Recently Harvest Partners joined MTP Energy Management to invest $80 million in Regency Energy Partners, a middle-market natural gas company. Michael DeFlorio is a senior managing director of Harvest Partners. He said that Regency "embodies our investment strategy focused on exceptionally managed . . . midstream service providers participating in the most promising resource plays in the industry."

Questions for Critical Thinking

1. Describe some of the risks faced by a firm such as Harvest Partners.

2. Why do you think Harvest Partners and other equity firms are required to invest their clients' funds within a limited time?

Sources: Company website, http://www.harvpart.com, accessed June 24, 2010; "Harvest Partners," profile from *Bloomberg Businessweek,* http://investing.businessweek.com, accessed June 24, 2010; Julie Cresswell, "On Wall Street, So Much Cash, So Little Time," *New York Times,* June 23, 2010, http://www.nytimes.com; Emily Thornton, "LBO Firms Can't Spend $503 Billion as Deadlines Loom (Update 1)," *Bloomberg.com,* March 10, 2010, http://www.bloomberg.com; Brian Baxter, "The Bankruptcy Files: Curtain Drops on Movie Gallery, Air America Loses Frequency," *AM Law Daily,* February 4, 2010, http://amlawdaily.typepad.com; "Harvest Partners, MTP Energy Invest in Regency Energy Partners," *iStockAnalyst,* September 7, 2009, http://www.istockanalyst.com.

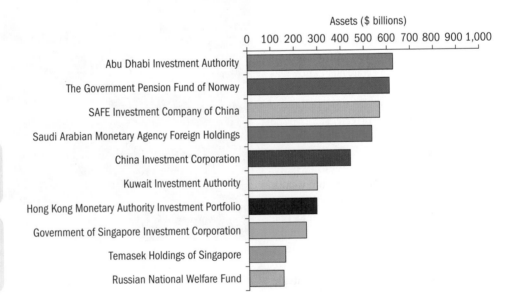

FIGURE 17.4 The World's 10 Largest Sovereign Wealth Funds

Source: Sovereign Wealth Fund Institute, "Sovereign Wealth Fund Rankings," http://www.swfinstitute.org, accessed May 18, 2012.

Hedge Funds

Hedge funds are private investment companies that are available only to qualified large investors. In recent years, hedge funds have become a significant presence in Canadian financial markets, though they have the same relative representation in the United Kingdom and the United States. Before the recent recession, some analysts estimated that Canadian hedge funds and hedge fund–related products totalled more than $20 billion. More recently, hedge fund providers have begun selling these funds, in the form of mutual funds, to smaller investors for as little as $1,000.[20] Hedge funds also make large investments in noninvestment-grade bonds, also known as junk bonds. Globally, hedge funds are estimated to have total assets of more than $1.82 trillion.[21] Traditionally, hedge funds, unlike venture capitalists and private equity funds, did not make direct investments in companies; instead, they usually preferred to purchase existing shares and bond issues.

✔ **ASSESSMENT CHECK**

17.6.1 What is the most common type of security sold privately?

17.6.2 Explain venture capital.

17.6.3 What is a sovereign wealth fund?

MERGERS, ACQUISITIONS, BUYOUTS, AND DIVESTITURES

LO 17.7 Describe mergers, acquisitions, buyouts, and divestitures.

Chapter 5 briefly described mergers and acquisitions. A merger is a transaction where two or more firms combine into one company. In an acquisition, one firm buys the assets of another firm and assumes that firm's obligations. Chapter 5 listed the classifications of mergers and acquisitions—vertical, horizontal, and conglomerate. It also noted that many of these transactions involve large sums of money. A recent example is Hewlett-Packard's acquisition of the smartphone maker Palm. In this section, we focus on the financial implications of mergers and acquisitions, buyouts, and divestitures.

A merger includes a buyer and a seller. The seller is often referred to as the *target*. Financial managers evaluate a proposed merger or acquisition in much the same way they evaluate any large investment—by comparing the costs and benefits. To acquire another company, the buying firm typically needs to offer a premium for the target's shares—in other words, a price higher than the current market price. For example, Hewlett-Packard offered $5.70 for each share of Palm, a premium of almost 20 percent over the existing price.[22]

When the buyer makes what is known as a **tender offer** for the target's shares, it specifies a price and the form of payment. The buyer can offer cash, securities, or a combination of the two. The Hewlett-Packard offer to Palm shareholders was all cash. The tender offer can be friendly, meaning it is backed by the target's board of directors, or unfriendly. Shareholders of both the buyer and target must vote to approve a merger.

tender offer a proposal made by a firm to the target firm's shareholders specifying a price and the form of payment.

Setting a premium requires the financial manager to estimate the benefits of a proposed merger. These benefits can include the cost savings from economies of scale, reduced workforces, or the buyer getting a bargain price for the target's assets. Sometimes, a buyer finds that the most cost-effective method of entering a new market is simply to buy an existing company that serves the market. Johnson & Johnson has a long history of making such acquisitions. When it decided to enter the contact lens market several years ago, Johnson & Johnson bought Vistakon, the firm that invented disposable contact lenses under the brand name Acuvue. *Synergy* is the term used to describe the benefits produced by a merger or acquisition. It refers to the idea that the combined firm is worth more than the buyer firm and the target firm are worth individually.

Leveraged buyouts, or **LBOs**, were briefly introduced in the preceding section. In an LBO, public shareholders are bought out, and the firm reverts to private status. The term *leverage* refers to the financing of many of these transactions with high degrees of debt—often more than 75 percent. Financial companies provide financing for many LBOs. LBO activity decreased sharply during the recent economic downturn. As the economy began to recover, LBO activity increased. According to Standard & Poor's, LBO financing recently grew to $13.6 billion, about 15 times the amount from the same time a year before.[23]

leveraged buyouts (LBOs) transactions where public shareholders are bought out and the firm reverts to private status.

Why do so many LBOs occur? One reason is that private companies enjoy benefits that public companies do not. Private companies are not required to publish financial results, are subject to less regulatory supervision, and are not pressured to produce short-term profits. Some argue that LBOs, because of the high degree of debt, require management to use more discipline to control costs. Although LBOs do have advantages, history has shown that many companies that go private appear as public companies several years later.

divestiture the sale of assets by a firm.

In a sense, a **divestiture** is the reverse of a merger. That is, in a divestiture, a company sells its assets, such as subsidiaries, product lines, or production facilities. Two types of divestitures exist: selloffs and spinoffs. In a *selloff*, assets are sold by one firm to another. For example, when Shell Canada Energy decided to focus its resources on "other options," it sold its stake in the Mackenzie Valley Pipeline Project in the Northwest Territories and other assets in the region. When asked for a statement, the chairperson of the Aboriginal Pipeline Group said, "We're sure that there's . . . a lot of companies out there that would love to step up to the plate and take over." Similarly, Calgary-based Suncor Energy sold its natural gas assets, located in Trinidad and Tobago, for $396 million. Centrica Plc took ownership of all the assets, allowing Suncor to focus on other aspects of its core business.[24]

The other type of divestiture is a *spinoff*. In this transaction, the assets sold form a new firm. For example, Motorola announced that it was splitting into two publicly traded firms. The parent company will handle its core business of mobile converged devices, digital home-entertainment devices, and video voice and data solutions. The spinoff firm will handle heavy-duty two-way radios, mobile computers, public security systems, wireless network infrastructure, and other business-oriented goods and services. Both organizations will continue to use the Motorola brand name, with the parent company now named Motorola Mobile Devices and Home. Motorola shareholders will receive shares of the new company, Motorola Enterprise Mobility and Networks. Bell Canada also recently spun off its regional small-business operations and rural portions of its residential wire line business to Aliant.

Firms divest assets for several reasons. Sometimes divestitures result from previous acquisitions that didn't work out as well as expected. In early 2001, America Online and Time Warner merged to create AOL Time Warner, Inc. Nine years later, Time Warner announced it was spinning off AOL. The merger is now considered one of the worst mistakes in corporate history. It had failed to generate the expected synergies between the two companies. Shortly after the merger, AOL had 27 million subscribers; more recently, that number had shrunk to about 6.3 million.

In other cases, a firm makes a strategic decision to focus on its core businesses. It then decides to divest any assets that fall outside this core. That was the explanation that Motorola gave when criticized that the company had become too large and after its mobile-device business was taken over first by Nokia, then Samsung, and then Apple. A similar explanation was given by Bell Alliant CEO Karen Sheriff. She explained that the company had sold xwave to Bell to "focus on our core priorities such as fibre-to-the home, improve our balance sheet and ensure long-term value to our investors."

ASSESSMENT CHECK

17.7.1 Define *synergy*.

17.7.2 What is an LBO?

17.7.3 What are the two types of divestitures?

WHAT'S AHEAD

Contemporary Business concludes with seven appendices. Appendix A contains additional case studies, while video case studies are provided in Appendix B. Appendix C outlines the main legal issues concerning business. It reviews the types of laws, the regulatory environment of business, and the core of business law, including discussions of contract law and property law. Appendix D examines risk management and insurance. It describes the concept of risk, alternative ways of dealing with risk, and the various kinds of insurance available to business and individuals. Appendix E discusses some of the important areas of personal financial planning, such as budgeting, credit, and retirement planning. Appendix F describes how to write an effective business plan, and Appendix G discusses career searches and options to help you prepare for your future in business.

RETURN TO INSIDE BUSINESS

The Wooing of Ratiopharm

Financial managers make key decisions related to a company's most liquid asset—cash.

QUESTIONS FOR CRITICAL THINKING

1. When making a key investment decision what projections does management need to prepare?

2. What key external factors can affect the reliability of a manager's financial forecasts?

SUMMARY OF LEARNING OBJECTIVES

LO 17.1 Define *finance*, and explain the role of financial managers.

Finance deals with planning, obtaining, and managing a company's funds to accomplish its objectives efficiently and effectively. The major responsibilities of financial managers are developing and carrying out financial plans and deciding on the most appropriate sources and uses of funds. The chief financial officer (CFO) heads a firm's finance organization. Three senior executives reporting to the CFO are the vice-president for financial management, the treasurer, and the controller. When making decisions, financial professionals continually balance risks with expected financial returns.

✓ ASSESSMENT CHECK ANSWERS

17.1.1 What is the structure of the finance function at the typical firm? The head of the finance function of a firm has the title of chief financial officer (CFO) and generally reports directly to the firm's chief executive officer. Reporting to the CFO are the treasurer, the controller, and the vice-president for financial management.

17.1.2 Explain the risk-return trade-off. Financial managers try to maximize the wealth of their firm's shareholders by striking the right balance between risk and return. Often, the decisions that involve the highest potential returns expose the firm to the greatest risks.

LO 17.2 Describe the parts of a financial plan and the financial planning process.

A financial plan is a document that specifies the funds needed by a firm for a given period of time, the timing of cash inflows and outflows, and the most appropriate sources and uses of funds. The financial plan addresses three questions: What funds will be required during the planning period? When will funds be needed? Where will funds be obtained? Three steps are involved in the financial planning process: forecasting sales over a future period of time, estimating the expected level of profits over the planning period, and deciding on the additional assets needed to support the additional sales.

✓ ASSESSMENT CHECK ANSWERS

17.2.1 What three questions does a financial plan address? The financial plan addresses three questions: What funds will be required during the planning period? When will funds be needed? Where will funds be obtained?

17.2.2 Explain the steps involved in preparing a financial plan. The first step is to forecast sales over a future period of time. Second, the financial manager must estimate the expected level of profits over the planning period. The final step is to decide on the additional assets needed to support the additional sales.

LO 17.3 Outline how organizations manage their assets.

Assets consist of what a firm owns. They also represent the uses of its funds. Sound financial management requires assets to be acquired and managed as effectively and efficiently as possible. The major current assets are cash, marketable securities, accounts receivable, and inventory. The goal of cash management is to have enough funds to meet day-to-day transactions and pay for any unexpected expenses. Excess cash should be invested in marketable securities, which are low-risk securities with short maturity dates. Accounts receivable are uncollected credit sales. Managing accounts receivable involves collecting funds owed the firm as quickly as possible, while also offering enough credit to customers to attract and generate increased sales. The main goal of inventory management is to minimize the overall cost of inventory. Production, marketing, and logistics also play roles in determining proper inventory levels. Capital investment analysis is the process financial managers use when deciding whether to invest in long-lived assets. This process involves comparing the benefits and costs of a proposed investment. Managing international assets poses additional challenges for the financial manager, including the problem of fluctuating exchange rates.

✓ ASSESSMENT CHECK ANSWERS

17.3.1 Why do firms often choose to invest excess cash in marketable securities? Cash in hand earns no rate of return. Excess cash should be invested in marketable securities.

Marketable securities are low-risk securities that have short maturity dates and can be easily sold in the secondary markets. As a result, they are easily converted into cash, when needed.

17.3.2 What are the two aspects of accounts receivable management? The two aspects of accounts receivable management are deciding on an overall credit policy (whether to offer credit and, if so, what terms of credit to offer) and deciding which customers will be offered credit.

17.3.3 Explain the difference between an expansion decision and a replacement decision. An expansion decision involves decisions about offering new products or building or acquiring new production facilities. A replacement decision considers whether to replace an existing asset with a new asset.

LO 17.4 Compare the two major sources of funds for a business, and explain the concept of leverage.

Businesses have two sources of funds: debt capital and equity capital. Debt capital refers to funds obtained through borrowing, and equity capital consists of funds provided by the firm's owners. The mix of debt and equity capital is known as the firm's capital structure, and the financial manager's job is to find the proper mix. Leverage is a technique of increasing the rate of return on funds invested by borrowing. But leverage also increases risk. Also, relying too much on borrowed funds may reduce management's flexibility in future financing decisions. Equity capital also has its downsides. When additional equity capital is sold, the control of existing shareholders is weakened. In addition, equity capital is more expensive than debt capital. Financial managers also face decisions concerning the suitable mix of short-term and long-term funds. Short-term funds are generally less expensive than long-term funds but expose firms to more risk. Financial managers are also involved in deciding the firm's dividend policy.

✓ ASSESSMENT CHECK ANSWERS

17.4.1 Explain the concept of leverage. Leverage is a technique of increasing the rate of return by borrowing funds. But leverage also increases risk.

17.4.2 Why do firms generally rely more on long-term funds than short-term funds? Although short-term funds are generally less expensive than long-term funds, short-term funds expose the firm to additional risks. The cost of short-term funds can vary greatly from year to year. In addition, short-term funds can sometimes be difficult to obtain.

17.4.3 What is an important factor in deciding on a firm's dividend policy? The main factor in deciding on a firm's dividend policy is its investment opportunities. Firms with more profitable investment opportunities often pay less in dividends than firms that have fewer such opportunities.

LO 17.5 Identify sources of short-term financing for business operations.

The three major short-term funding options are trade credit, short-term loans from banks and other financial institutions, and commercial paper. Trade credit is extended by suppliers when a firm receives goods or services and agrees to pay for them at a later date. Trade credit is relatively easy to obtain and costs nothing unless a supplier offers a cash discount. Loans from commercial banks are a significant source of short-term financing and are often used to finance accounts receivable and inventory. Loans can be either unsecured or secured. In unsecured loans, no assets are pledged as collateral, or security. In secured loans, accounts receivable or inventory are pledged as collateral. Commercial paper is a short-term IOU sold by a company. Large amounts of money can be raised through the sale of commercial paper, usually at interest rates lower than those charged by banks. Access to the commercial paper market is limited to large, financially strong corporations.

✓ ASSESSMENT CHECK ANSWERS

17.5.1 What are the three sources of short-term funding? The three sources of short-term funding are trade credit, short-term loans from banks and other financial institutions, and commercial paper.

17.5.2 Explain trade credit. Trade credit is extended by suppliers when a buyer agrees to pay for goods and services at a later date. Trade credit is relatively easy to obtain and costs nothing unless a cash discount is offered.

17.5.3 Why is commercial paper an attractive short-term financing option? Commercial paper is an attractive financing option because large amounts of money can be raised at interest rates that are usually lower than the interest rates charged by banks.

LO 17.6 Discuss long-term financing options.

Long-term financing is repaid over many years. Organizations acquire long-term financing from three sources: long-term loans from financial institutions, bonds sold to investors, and equity financing. Public sales of securities, such as shares and bonds, are a major source of funds for corporations. These securities can generally be traded in secondary markets. Public sales can vary quite a bit from year to year depending on the conditions in the financial markets. Private placements are securities—new share or bond issues—sold to a small number of institutional investors. Most private placements involve debt securities. Venture capitalists are an important source of long-term financing for new companies. If the business succeeds, venture capitalists can earn large profits. Private equity funds are investment companies that raise funds from wealthy individuals and institutional investors. They then invest the funds in both public and private companies. Unlike venture capitalists, private equity funds invest in all types of businesses. Sovereign wealth funds are investment companies owned by governments.

ASSESSMENT CHECK ANSWERS

17.6.1 What is the most common type of security sold privately? Corporate debt securities are the most common type of security sold privately.

17.6.2 Explain venture capital. Venture capitalists are important sources of funding, especially for new companies. Venture capitalists invest in new companies by taking an ownership position. If the business succeeds, venture capitalists can earn large profits.

17.6.3 What is a sovereign wealth fund? A sovereign wealth fund is a government-owned investment company. These companies invest in a variety of financial and real assets, such as real estate. Although most investments are based on the best risk-return trade-off, investment decisions are also influenced by political, social, and strategic considerations.

LO 17.7 Describe mergers, acquisitions, buyouts, and divestitures.

A merger is a transaction where two or more firms combine into one company. An acquisition is a transaction where one company buys another. A merger includes a buyer and a seller (called the *target*). The buyer offers cash, securities, or a combination of the two in return for the target's shares. Mergers and acquisitions should be evaluated the same way any large investment is evaluated—by comparing the costs with the benefits. Synergy is the term used to describe the benefits a merger or acquisition is expected to produce. A leveraged buyout (LBO) is a transaction where shares are purchased from public shareholders, and the company reverts to private status. LBOs are usually financed with large amounts of borrowed funds. Private equity companies are often major financers of LBOs. Divestitures are the opposite of mergers—companies sell their assets such as subsidiaries, product lines, or production facilities. A selloff is a divestiture where assets are sold to another firm. In a spinoff, a new firm is created from the assets divested. Shareholders of the divesting firm become shareholders of the new firm.

ASSESSMENT CHECK ANSWERS

17.7.1 Define *synergy*. Synergy is the term used to describe the benefits produced by a merger or acquisition. It refers to the idea that the combined firm is worth more than the buyer firm and the target firm are worth individually.

17.7.2 What is an LBO? In an LBO—a leveraged buyout—public shareholders are bought out, and the firm reverts to private status. LBOs are usually financed with large amounts of borrowed money.

17.7.3 What are the two types of divestitures? The two types of divestitures are selloffs and spinoffs. In a selloff, assets are sold by one firm to another firm. In a spinoff, a new firm is created from the assets divested. Shareholders of the divesting firm become shareholders of the new firm.

BUSINESS TERMS YOU NEED TO KNOW

finance 474

financial managers 474

risk-return trade-off 476

financial plan 476

capital structure 481

leverage 481

venture capitalists 486

tender offer 489

leveraged buyouts (LBOs) 489

divestiture 490

REVIEW QUESTIONS

1. Explain the risk-return trade-off and give two examples.

2. Describe the financial planning process. How does asset intensity affect a financial plan?

3. What are the main considerations when deciding on an overall credit policy? How do the actions of competitors affect a firm's credit policy?

4. Why do exchange rates pose a challenge for financial managers at companies that operate internationally?

5. Discuss the idea of leverage. Use a numerical example to illustrate the effect of leverage.

6. What are the advantages and disadvantages of debt financing and equity financing?

7. Compare and contrast the three sources of short-term financing.

8. Define *venture capitalist*, *private equity fund*, *sovereign wealth fund*, and *hedge fund*. Which of the four invests the most money in start-up companies?

9. Briefly describe the mechanics of a merger or acquisition.

10. Why do firms divest assets?

PROJECTS AND TEAMWORK APPLICATIONS

1. Assume you would like to start a business. Create a rough financial plan that addresses the three financial planning questions listed in the text.

2. Working with a partner, assume that a firm needs $10 million in additional long-term capital. It currently has no debt and $40 million in equity. The firm's options are issuing a 10-year bond (with an interest rate of 7 percent) or selling $10 million in new equity. You expect next year's earnings will be $5 million before interest and taxes. (The firm's tax rate is 35 percent.) Prepare a memo outlining the advantages and disadvantages of debt financing and equity financing. Using the numbers provided, prepare a numerical illustration of leverage similar to Figure 17.2.

3. Your new small business has grown, but it now needs a large amount of capital. A venture capital firm has agreed to provide the money you need. In return, the venture capital firm will own 75 percent of the business, and you will be replaced as CEO by someone chosen by the venture capitalist. You will be considered the founder of the company and the chairperson of the board. Are you willing to take the money in return for losing control over your business? Why or why not?

4. Working in a small team, select three publicly traded companies. Visit each firm's website. Find the part of the website that includes information for investors. Review each firm's dividend policy. Does the company pay dividends? If so, when did it begin paying dividends? Have dividends increased each year, or have they had ups and downs from year to year? Is the company currently repurchasing shares? Has it done repurchased shares in the past? Prepare a report to summarize your findings.

5. As noted in the chapter, one of the most unfortunate mergers in corporate history involved Time Warner and America Online. Research this merger. Why did analysts expect it to be successful? Why did it fail? What has happened to AOL since then? What are some examples of failed Canadian mergers?

WEB ASSIGNMENTS

1. **Jobs in financial management.** Visit the website listed below to explore careers in finance. How many people currently work as financial managers? What is the projected increase in employment over the next 10 to 20 years? What is the average level of compensation?

   http://www.servicecanada.gc.ca/eng/qc/job_futures/statistics/0111.shtml

2. **Capital structure.** Go to the website listed below to access recent financial statements for Canadian Tire. Access the most recent annual report and locate the balance sheet. What is the firm's current capital structure (the relationship between debt and equity)? Has it changed over the past five years? Why would Canadian Tire choose this capital structure?

   http://corp.canadiantire.ca/EN/Investors/FinancialReports/Pages/AnnualReports.aspx

3. **Mergers and acquisitions.** Using a news source, such as the CBC (http://www.cbc.ca) or The Globe and Mail (http://www.theglobeandmail.com), search for an announcement of a recent merger or acquisition. An example would be Centric Health Corporation's acquisition of LifeMark Health. (A link is shown below.) Print out the articles and bring them to class.

   http://www.lifemark.ca/DynamicContent/Default.aspx?ID=30

Access your WileyPLUS course for:

- The complete digital textbook.
- Question assistance, including links to relevant sections in the online digital textbook.
- Immediate feedback and proof of progress, 24/7
- Integrated, multi-media resources — including MP3 downloads, visual exhibits, animations, and much more — that provide multiple study paths and encourage more active learning.

QUIZ YOURSELF

Note: Internet Web addresses change frequently. If you don't find the exact sites listed, you may need to access the organization's home page and search from there or use a search engine such as Bing or Google.

6 LAUNCHING YOUR . . .

ACCOUNTING OR FINANCE CAREER

Part 6, "Managing Financial Resources," describes the finance function in organizations. Finance deals with planning, obtaining, and managing an organization's funds to accomplish its objectives in the most effective way possible. In Chapter 15, you read about accounting firms and variety of large and small public and private organizations that generate and use accounting data. In Chapter 16, we discussed the financial system, including the various types of securities, financial markets and institutions, the Bank of Canada, financial regulators, and global financial markets. In Chapter 17, we examined the role that financial managers play in an organization; financial planning; short-term and long-term financing options; and mergers, acquisitions, buyouts, and divestitures. In both chapters, we described the finance functions of a variety of businesses, governments, and not-for-profit organizations. As Part 6 illustrates, finance is a diverse profession and includes many different occupations. According to Human Resources and Skills Development Canada, over the next decade, most finance-related occupations are expected to experience a little better than average employment growth. Employment in several finance occupations is expected to grow much faster than average. Employment in the financial investment industry should be strong because of two reasons: the globalization of securities markets and the large number of baby boomers in their peak earning years who have funds to invest.[1]

In most business schools, accounting and finance are popular majors among undergraduates. Many accounting graduates start their careers working for a public accounting firm. At first, their job duties may include auditing or tax services, usually working with more senior accountants. As their careers progress, accounting graduates may take on more supervisory responsibilities. Some may move from public accounting firms to take accounting positions at other organizations. Many accounting graduates spend their entire careers in these fields, while others move into other areas. Let's look briefly at some of the specific jobs you might find after earning a degree in accounting.

Public accountants perform a broad range of accounting, auditing, tax, and consulting services for their clients, which include businesses, governments, not-for-profit organizations, and individuals. Auditing is one of the most important services offered by public accountants, and many accounting graduates begin their careers in this field. Auditors examine a client's financial statements and accounting policies to make sure they conform to all applicable standards and regulations. Public accountants either own their own businesses or work for public accounting firms. Many public accountants are Chartered Accountants (CAs). To become a CA, you must meet educational and experience requirements and pass three sets of examinations. Certified Management Accountants (CMAs) and Certified General Accountants (CGAs) are also required to meet educational, experience, and examination requirements.

Many accountants work for an organization other than a public accounting firm. They record and analyze financial information and financial statements for their organizations. Management accountants are also involved in budgeting, tax preparation, cost management, and asset management. Internal auditors verify the accuracy of their organization's internal controls and check for irregularities, waste, and fraud.

Combining finance with accounting is a common choice for a double major. Individuals who have degrees in finance also enjoy relatively high starting salaries. A recent survey found that the average starting salary for a person with an undergraduate degree in finance was nearly $58,000 per year and could be as high as $73,500 per year.[2]

All organizations need to obtain and manage funds. They employ finance professionals to handle these tasks. Financial institutions and other financial services firms employ a large percentage of all finance graduates. These businesses provide important finance-related services to businesses, governments, and not-for-profit organizations. Some graduates with finance degrees take jobs with financial services firms such as Royal Bank Financial Group and Scotia Capital. Others begin their careers working in the finance departments of businesses in other industries, such as Canadian Tire, Bell Canada, governments, or not-for-profit organizations. You may begin your career by evaluating commercial loan applications for a bank, analyzing capital investments for a business, or helping a not-for-profit organization decide how to invest its endowed funds. Finance professionals often work as members of a team that advises top management. Some individuals spend their entire careers working in finance-related occupations; others use their finance experience to move into other areas of the firm. Today, the chief financial officer—the most senior finance executive—holds one of the most important jobs in any organization. Today, an increasing number of CEOs began their careers in finance.

Finance is a diverse, exciting profession. Here are a few of the specific occupations you might find after earning a degree in finance.

Financial managers prepare financial reports, direct investment activities, raise funds, and carry out cash management strategies. Computer technology has reduced the time needed to produce financial reports. Many financial managers spend less time preparing reports and more time analyzing financial data. All organizations employ financial managers. About 30 percent of all financial managers work for financial services firms such as commercial banks and insurance companies.[3] Specific responsibilities vary depending on the job title. For example, credit managers supervise the firm's issuing of credit, establish credit standards, and monitor the collection of accounts receivable. Cash managers control the flow of cash receipts and disbursements to meet the needs of the organization.

Most *loan officers* work for commercial banks and other financial institutions. They find potential clients and help them apply for loans. Loan officers usually specialize in commercial, consumer, or mortgage loans. Loan officers often act in a sales role, by contacting individuals and organizations about their need for funds and trying to persuade them to borrow the funds from the loan officer's institution. As a result, loan officers often need marketing skills in addition to their finance skills.

Security analysts generally work for financial services firms such as Sunlife Financial or Manulife Financial. Security analysts review economic data, financial statements, and other information to predict the outcome for securities such as common shares and bonds. They recommend investment strategies to individual investors and institutional investors. Many senior security analysts hold a chartered financial analyst (CFA) designation. Obtaining a CFA requires a specific educational background, several years of related experience, and a passing grade on a thorough, three-stage examination.

Portfolio managers manage money for an individual client or an institutional client. Many portfolio managers work for pension funds or mutual funds; they make investment decisions to benefit the funds' beneficiaries. Portfolio managers generally have extensive experience as financial managers or security analysts, and many are CFAs.

Personal financial planners help individuals to make decisions related to insurance, investments, and retirement planning. Personal financial planners meet with their clients, assess their needs and goals, and make recommendations. Approximately 30 percent of personal financial planners are self-employed. Many hold certified financial planner (CFP) designations. Obtaining a CFP requires a specific educational background, related experience, and passing a thorough examination.

CAREER ASSESSMENT EXERCISES IN ACCOUNTING AND FINANCE

1. The Canadian Institute of Chartered Accountants is a professional organization for the public accounting profession. Visit the organization's website (http://www.cica.ca). Review the information on CICA standards and examinations. Write a brief summary on what you learned about how to become a CA.

2. Suppose you are interested in a career as a security analyst. You've heard that the CFA is an important designation and can help enhance your career. Visit the CFA's website (http://www.cfainstitute.org) to learn more about the designation. What are the requirements to obtain a CFA designation? What are the professional benefits of having a CFA designation?

3. Arrange for an interview with a commercial loan officer at a local bank. Ask the loan officer about his or her educational background, what a typical day is like, and what the loan officer likes and does not like about the job.

4. TD Waterhouse offers financial planning services to individuals and organizations. Visit the firm's careers website (http://www.td.com/careers/job-profiles/td-waterhouse-td-mutual-funds/waterhouse.jsp). Review the material and write a brief summary of what you learned about being a personal financial planner. Are you interested in a career as a financial planner? Why or why not?

APPENDIX A
ADDITIONAL CASES

Part 1 Business in a Global Environment

SAS Is Still a Great Place to Work

SAS is a global leader in analytics and statistical software solutions. The company employs thousands of employees around the world, including many working in major cities across Canada. SAS employees enjoy the benefits that come with working for a company that values loyal employees and treats them particularly well. So much so, that in 2011 and 2012, SAS headed the list of *Fortune* magazine's Top 100 Companies to work for. To get an idea of why employees rate the company so highly, let's look at the company's 300-acre (120-hectare) main campus located in Raleigh, North Carolina. Here you will find a gym, weight room, meditation garden, sauna, and Olympic-size swimming pool. It seems unlikely any of the complex's 4,200 employees would fall ill with such health-building options to choose from, but just in case, there's a healthcare centre with a staff of 56, including four doctors, 10 nurses, physical therapists, and a psychologist. All care is free. "We charge you for one thing," says the health service director, "if you miss your appointment and don't give us notice. That's $10."

Free or subsidized programs include Pilates, Zumba, yoga, weight management, smoking cessation, Wii bowling, massage, and aerobics. Two subsidized daycare centres care for 600 children, and there's a summer camp. The company offers job sharing, telecommuting, and domestic partner benefits for same-sex couples. Employees can get their clothes dry cleaned, car detailed, and income tax return prepared while they work. They can eat in any of three subsidized cafeterias during the day (one has a piano player who takes requests) and grab take-out for the family at day's end. They can prepare their own snacks in one of the many kitchens. But with free snacks every day, including Krispy Kremes (on Fridays) and M&Ms (a long-standing Wednesday tradition), why would they?

Jim Goodnight, the company's only chief executive officer (CEO) in its 34 years, believes treating employees well is simply good business. Rather than thinking it's unusual for SAS to be so generous, he wonders why other companies don't follow suit. And he should wonder, especially when SAS's revenues that have risen every year of the firm's existence and recently topped $2.3 billion despite the global recession. SAS has been one of *Fortune*'s best companies to work for in each of the last 13 years and recently earned the number-one spot on the list. "Some may think that because SAS is family-friendly and has great benefits we don't work hard," says a communications employee. "But people do work hard here, because they're motivated to take care of a company that takes care of them." That sentiment expresses the culture of trust that Goodnight has worked to create. "What we don't do is treat our employees like they're all, you know, criminals," says his vice-president of human resources.

Employee turnover among the 11,000 SAS employees worldwide is 2 percent, well below the industry average, and the company receives about 100 résumés for every open position. (About half its employees work in the United States.) The typical employee works 35 hours per week, and many make their own schedules; no one counts sick days. Average tenure is 10 years.

About 17,000 customers worldwide use SAS data mining software, including IBM, Microsoft, Oracle, national retailers, banks, insurance and pharmaceutical firms, universities, the U.S. Census Bureau, and even professional baseball teams. Goodnight spends much of his time on the road meeting and talking with these clients, though he sometimes admits he would rather be programming. But he knows where the real value of the company lies, and that's the reason he's willing to spend so much on making SAS a great place to work. "My chief assets drive out the gate every day," he says. "My job is to make sure they come back."

Questions for Critical Thinking

1. Explain how flexible and family-friendly policies have played a role in SAS's success.

2. What kind of relationship does SAS seem to have with its employees? With its customers?

Sources: "100 Best Companies to Work For," *CNNMoney.com*, http://money.cnn.com/magazines/fortune/bestcompanies/2011/, accessed February 24, 2011; "100 Best Companies to Work For: #1 SAS," *CNNMoney.com*, http://money.cnn.com, accessed February 4, 2010; David A. Kaplan, "SAS: A New No. 1 Best Employer," *CNNMoney.com*, January 22, 2010, http://money.cnn.com; Stefan Stern, "A Good Day for Dr. Goodnight and SAS," *Financial Times*, January 22, 2010, http://blogs.ft.com; Rick Smith, "'We're Hiring' Sign Remains Out at SAS for 2010," *Local Tech Wire*, January 21, 2010, http://localtechwire.com.

Cause-Related Marketing—Give a Day, Get a Disney Day

Cause-related marketing began in 1976, when the March of Dimes, which fights birth defects, wanted to raise funds in the West. A typical cause-related marketing campaign teams one or more not-for-profit organizations with for-profit organizations. The for-profit organization announces publicly that it will donate some or all of the proceeds from a product or products to the not-for-profit organization. Cause-related marketing has grown from almost nothing to roughly $1.57 billion. Social networking groups such as Facebook and Twitter have become official or unofficial resources for information and for spreading the word about causes such as education, fighting disease, clean water, and environmental issues.

After the recent recession, consumers started spending less and turning instead to inexpensive, family-oriented activities. In this economic climate, a new type of cause-related partnership was created.

Disney Parks announced its new "Give a Day, Get a Disney Day" program for 2010. In partnership with the HandsOn Network, a U.S. volunteer network, Disney offered free one-day, one-park admission to the first million people who performed one day of certified volunteer work for a participating charity or other program. Habitat for Humanity and Ronald McDonald House were just two of the programs, but volunteers could also clean up a local park; work at a homeless shelter, museum, or other institution; or walk or run for a cause such as diabetes or heart disease. Many of the activities were family oriented and were intended to help parents teach their children about volunteering. Families of up to eight could volunteer together, and children as young as six could participate. Jay Rasulo, the chairman of Walt Disney Parks and Resorts, said, "we want to recognize … the contributions people make to their communities every day. We want to inspire 1 million volunteers—people who will invest time and energy to make their own communities and neighbourhoods a better place."

Visitors can check the Disney website to find opportunities, arranged by location, for volunteering through the HandsOn network. So many people visited the sign-up page that it crashed several times. Although Disney had no official social network pages, multiple unofficial ones were created. In addition, HandsOn publicized the program through its Facebook, Twitter, and

YouTube accounts. Volunteer Canada has teamed up with HandsOn Network to expand the initiative and include up to 50,000 Canadians.

The program was closing in on its goal of 1 million volunteers.

Disney has also launched many lower-profile sustainability programs. For example, Disney's Animal Kingdom resort composts its horticulture clippings, and food leftovers are used locally as fertilizer. Even the cooking oil is recycled and used to create biofuel that is used by local businesses. The Walt Disney Company Healthy Cleaning Policy focuses on minimizing the environmental impact of their cleaning products both from a toxicity perspective and a quantity-used perspective. Educational programs have also been set up to educate guests on the importance of environmental sustainability.

It may be too soon to tell whether volunteer cause-related marketing and corporate environmental sustainability programs will become more common. But the success of these programs has set a standard that future projects can aspire to.

Questions for Critical Thinking

1. How does Disney fulfill its responsibility to the general public through its various initiatives?

2. Which organization benefits more from the "Give a Day, Get a Disney Day" program—Disney or HandsOn? Explain your answer.

Sources: Walt Disney Company and Affiliated Companies, "Give a Day of Volunteer Service in 2010, Get a Day of Disney Theme Park Fun— Free," September 29, 2009, http://corporate.disney.go.com, accessed February 2010; HandsOn Network, "Give a Day. Get a Disney Day," n.d., http://handsonnetwork.org; Carrie Urban Kapraun, "Disney and the HandsOn Network: Give a Day, Get a Disney Day," *IEG,* January 22, 2010, http://www.sponsorship.com; Nancy Osborne, "Give a Day, Get a Disney Day," *KFSN,* January 22, 2010; http://abclocal.go.com/kfsn; Rachael Chong, "Cause-Related Marketing: Just Plain Ol' Marketing?" *Huffington Post,* January 4, 2010; http://www.huffingtonpost.com; Product Red website, http://www.joinred.com; Joe Waters, "Why Social Media and Cause Marketing Belong Together," *Selfish Giving,* February 16, 2010, http://selfishgiving.com; Volunteer Canada website, http://www.govolunteer.ca/gadgaddfaq_volunteers.html, accessed February 22, 2011; "Disney Sustainability," Benefits-of-Recycling.com, http://www.benefits-of-recycling.com/disneysustainability.html, January 31, 2012.

Greener Shipping—At Sea and in Port

For many years, environmentalists have advocated slower driving and slower flying as ways to save fuel and reduce emissions of greenhouse gases. This equation applies equally at sea as it does on land and in the air. When the price of oil reached $145 a barrel, the container shipping company Maersk Line decided to take action.

Based in Copenhagen, Maersk is the largest shipping line in the world, with more than 500 vessels. Instead of the standard speed of 24 or 25 knots (just under 45 km per hour), the *Ebba Maersk* sails at 12 knots (just under 23 km per hour), a speed known in the industry as "super slow steaming." Super slow steaming reduces fuel consumption from 317 metric tons per day to 90 to 136 metric tons per day and saves $5,000 an hour. Maersk has shifted hundreds of its ships to super slow steaming. Other shipping lines resisted slowing their vessels down at first, but now many of them have adopted "slow steaming" speed (20 knots, or 37 km per hour) or super slow steaming.

The recent recession created a further incentive for container shipping lines to reduce costs and save energy. Among other measures, Maersk's ships have lowered their interior lighting and substituted rolls of paper towels for paper napkins in their dining salons. "The previous focus has been on 'What will it cost?' and 'Get it to me as fast as possible,'" said Søren Stig Nielsen, the director of environmental sustainability at Maersk. "But now there is a third dimension. What's the CO_2 footprint?"

Then there are the containers themselves. Whether empty or full, they occupy the same amount of space. Made of steel, they are still heavy even when empty. The Dutch company Cargoshell has devised a container, called a Cargoshell. When empty, the Cargoshell collapses in less than half a minute to one-quarter the size of a full one. Cargoshells can also be stacked more compactly than steel containers. Steel containers usually have outward-opening doors that take up an entire side panel. The Cargoshell's door simply rolls up or down. Cargoshells are made of fibre-reinforced composite materials, so they weigh 25 percent less than steel containers. They need no paint because they do not corrode. The composites are good insulators, important for temperature control. Manufacturing Cargoshells generates less carbon dioxide than manufacturing steel containers. All these factors add up to reduced costs, energy savings, and lower carbon emissions.

The ports where cargo ships arrive and depart are crowded with cranes, trucks, trains, tugboats, and ferries—all of which emit diesel exhaust into the atmosphere. Diesel exhaust has been declared as a possible carcinogen by the World Health Organization, CAREX Canada, and other organizations. The government of Canada has made a significant commitment to provide funding to install greener technology at Canadian ports. It recently decided to install BC Hydro–powered cables at the Prince Rupert Port Authority's Fairview terminal. The cables will connect directly to ships, reducing their need to rely solely on diesel fuel. The $2.5-million investment is expected to reduce greenhouse gas emissions by up to 4,000 tonnes. Taken separately, all these measures are worthy efforts to fight global warming. Taken together, they could add up to a "green" integration of almost all aspects of the shipping industry.

Questions for Critical Thinking

1. How do Maersk and Cargoshell carry out their responsibilities to society?

2. Many of the goods you buy and use are imported from overseas and sold more cheaply than if they were made in Canada. But do they have hidden, nonmonetary costs? Use the information in this case as a guide.

Sources: Steven Greenhouse, "Clearing the Air at American Ports," *New York Times,* February 26, 2010, http://www. newyorktimes.com; Maersk website, http://www.maersk.com, accessed February 18, 2010; "Maersk Cuts Fuel Use, Emissions 30% by Slowing Down," *Environmental Leader,* February 18, 2020, http://www.environmentalleader.com; Elisabeth Rosenthal, "Slow and Steady Across the Sea Aids Profit and the Environment," *New York Times,* February 17, 2010, http://www.newyorktimes.com; John W. Miller, "Maersk: Container Ship Cuts Costs to Stay Afloat," Polaris Institute, February 2010, http://www.polarisinstitute.org; Cargoshell website, http://www.cargoshell.com, accessed February 12, 2010; Clean Ports USA, U.S. Environmental Protection Agency, http://epa.gov, accessed February 12, 2010; Jace Shoemaker-Galloway, "Cargoshell Collapsible Shipping Containers: A Greener and Flatter Way to Transport Goods," *Triple Pundit,* February 5, 2010, http://www.triplepundit.com, Carex Canada website, http://www.carexcanada. ca/en/diesel_engine_exhaust.pdf, accessed February 22, 2011, Transport Canada, "Government of Canada Funds Green Port Project in Prince Rupert," press release, September 14, 2010, http://www.tc.gc.ca/eng/mediaroom/releases-2010-h103e-6078.htm, accessed February 22, 2011.

Smartphones: Recession-Proof and Growing

The rise of the smartphone has been one of the most innovative developments in electronics. Among the many models available are the Apple iPhone, the Research In Motion (RIM) BlackBerry, and the Motorola Droid. Many other models are in the works.

Despite the 2008–10 recession, smartphones have remained very popular. Competition among the smartphones will likely remain strong and become even stronger. One factor influencing this trend is the availability of applications.

The iPhone is ahead of any other smartphone in terms of applications, or "apps." It leads in number of app developers, number of apps, and number of downloaded apps. The iPhone applications number in the hundreds of thousands; the Apple iStore boasts more than 500,000 apps, and many more are expected. Most are free; others (about 18 percent) cost just a few dollars. Apps range in content from weather to games to music to news. A typical user downloads 20 apps, and games are the most popular. Apple recently celebrated its one-billionth iPhone download.

The following are some predictions for the smartphone industry:

- Some analysts forecast that sales of smartphones will increase four-fold by 2013, and fees for smartphone apps in the United States alone will increase ten-fold to $4.2 billion. As smartphones become more powerful and capable of more functions, they could replace laptops in the future.

- Smartphones will account for an increasing share of the mobile-phone market. In a recent year, 1.2 billion mobile phones were shipped worldwide; of these, 190 million, or 15.8 percent, were smartphones. That percentage is expected to rise.

- As we have seen, application stores have experienced much growth. The iPhone already has plenty of games available, so analysts suggest app developers should work on other types of software, such as apps for business purposes. In contrast, RIM's BlackBerry has plenty of business applications, so its developers should work on producing more game apps.

- Location-based services, which already include the Global Positioning System (GPS), will increase. Droid users can download step-by-step spoken directions via Google. Soon, smartphones will be able to trace a package or find your friends so you can meet for a movie. Advertisers may be able to add pop-up ads to the maps you download.

Manufacturers are expected to launch other devices in addition to smartphones. Amazon's e-reader Kindle is facing competition from the Barnes & Noble Nook. Apple's iPad tablet is functions as a media viewer as well as an e-reader. As this decade unfolds, devices and applications will be limited only by the developers' imaginations.

Questions for Critical Thinking

1. How has the rapid development of technology affected competition in the mobile-phone industry?

2. How does this technology affect supply and demand in the mobile-phone industry?

Sources: Apple website, http://www.apple.com, accessed February 4, 2010; Amazon website, http://www.amazon.com, accessed February 4, 2010; Barnes & Noble website, http://barnesandnoble.com, accessed February 4, 2010; Marguerite Reardon, "Microsoft Readies Smartphone Assault on Apple," *cnet news,* February 9, 2010, http://news.cnet.com; "Smart Phones Leading the Handset Industry Out of Recession," *Mobile Entertainment,* February 1, 2010, http://www.mobile-ent.biz; Matt Hamblen, "7 Smartphone Predictions for 2010," *Computerworld Mobile & Wireless,* December 4, 2009, http://www.computerworld.com; Matt Hamblen, "Big Money Seen for iPhone, Smartphone App Developers," *InfoWorld,* September 22, 2009, http://www.infoworld.com; Sarah Perez, "The State of the Smartphone: iPhone Is Way, Way Ahead," *ReadWriteWeb,* April 20, 2009, http://www.readwriteweb.com.

Google and Facebook Face Off in India's Social Networking Wars

India is the world's largest democracy. With a population of 1.2 billion people, it is also the second most populous country (after China). India is considered a major growth Internet market because it has a tradition of free speech, a growing middle class that is still discovering the Internet (only a small portion of the Indian population is online so far), and huge market opportunities for providers of Web search and advertising.

Orkut, owned by Google, has long been India's most popular social networking site, growing 35 percent a year and averaging 15 million to 16 million unique visitors a month. Facebook, its closest rival, was launched around the same time, in 2004. Despite steady growth, Facebook has since been running a fairly distant second to Orkut, recently reaching 7.5 million to 8.2 million visitors a month. But Facebook has been competing fiercely in the social networking wars. In one recent month, Facebook gained 700,000 visitors; in the same month, Orkut's numbers dropped by 800,000, the largest dip in a year. Many observers of India's Internet scene believe these two statistics signal a major advance for Facebook, and it may soon overtake Google's Orkut as India's premier online social network.

Facebook grew its audience about 230 percent in one recent year. What is the reason for its success? One factor is a special software tool the site is promoting to let new users easily import their friends from Orkut and other sites. The tool speeds the process of establishing a Facebook presence and was created especially for Orkut users. Facebook is also available in many of the widely used Indian languages, including Hindi, Punjabi, Bengali, Telugu, Tamil, and Malayalam. Facebook also hired away a top Google advertising executive and has been buying ads on Google's India portal. Finally, Facebook recently added a "lite" version of its social media site, designed for users in developing countries that have limited access to high-speed Internet connections.

Meanwhile, Google faces some potential problems in India that are common to many multinational and Internet companies. Fearing a backlash in the midst of emotional public mourning for an Indian official killed in a helicopter crash, Google recently took two actions: it removed offensive comments posted about the official on Orkut and removed the entire user group to which the comments had been posted. Says one leading civil liberties lawyer in India, "Communal tensions become largely an excuse for denial of civil liberties and denial of freedom of speech. It's a very thin line that's being tread."

"In those gray areas it is really hard," agrees Google's deputy general counsel. Company policy is to review posted material that Orkut users have flagged. The company will remove any content that violates Orkut's global bans on child pornography and hate speech, or the laws of the country in which it is operating.

Questions for Critical Thinking

1. Do you think Facebook can become India's leading social networking site? Why or why not? What else can Facebook do to ensure success?

2. How well do you think Google is handling the problem of censoring content on its international sites such as Orkut? How do you think its solutions of these problems will affect its plans to keep ahead of Facebook?

Sources: Robin Wauters, "In India Facebook Uses Google AdWords to Leapfrog Orkut," *Tech Crunch,* http://techcrunch.com, January 22, 2010; Amol Sharma and Jessica E. Vascellaro, "Google and India Test the Limits of Liberty," *Wall Street Journal,* www.online.wsj.com, January 2, 2010; Leena Rao, "Facebook's Plan to Trounce Orkut in India May Be Working," *Tech Crunch,* http://techcrunch.com, November 30, 2009; "Orkut Vs. Facebook: What the Indians Are Looking For," *Social Media News,* http://socialmedia.globalthoughtz.com, November 19, 2009.

Part 2 Starting and Growing Your Business

Small Meets Big: Patagonia and Walmart Join Forces for the Environment

When Yvon Chouinard started rock climbing as a teenager, he never dreamed his love of rock climbing would lead to the ownership of two companies and a lifelong desire to help preserve the planet. But 55 years later, the climber-businessman has joined forces with Walmart—an unlikely partner—to spread the word that sustainability is cool.

Chouinard founded Chouinard Equipment to make safer, more environmentally friendly equipment for rock climbers and mountaineers. He didn't like the way previous generations of climbers had destroyed mountain environments. Patagonia, founded in 1972, offered the "soft" side of the outdoors—specialized clothing, boots, packs, luggage, and other gear. From the very beginning, Chouinard and his design team worked hard to develop products whose materials and manufacturing processes were eco-friendly. "The reason I am in business is I want to protect what I love," Chouinard explains. "I used to spend 250 days a year sleeping on the ground. I've climbed on every continent. I'm old enough to have seen the destruction."

In the mid-1990s Chouinard discovered that the cotton Patagonia was using for many of its garments came from industrial farms that used toxic chemicals. His response was swift and definite. He gave his company just 18 months to switch to organic cotton. Chouinard has also been successful at persuading other businesses to go green.

For the past few years, Chouinard's team has been working with Walmart to develop a sustainability index for its products, by sharing valuable information that Patagonia has gained over the years. Walmart is 1,300 times as large as Patagonia, but Patagonia has knowledge and experience that Walmart can use to reinvent itself as an environmentally responsible firm. Chouinard doesn't mind sharing with a company that has such a huge impact on both the marketplace and the planet. And Walmart officials are eager to learn. The company plans to post scorecards in its stores, rating products on their eco-friendliness and social impact. Walmart is also developing a system to give preference to suppliers who comply with these steps. At one conference of Walmart buyers and executives, Chouinard pointed out that Walmart's use of little light-emitting diode (LED) lights in its stores—which seem to use minimal energy—actually requires 19 plants in California to power them. On hearing this statement, a Walmart buyer stood in the audience and shouted, "We're going to get rid of those!"

Questions for Critical Thinking

1. The alliance between Patagonia and Walmart is an excellent example of a small business and a large business working together to achieve an objective. Do you think the same results would be possible if Walmart acquired Patagonia? Why or why not?

2. Walmart is learning from Patagonia. But what can Patagonia learn from Walmart?

Sources: Patagonia website, http://www.patagonia.com, accessed July 7, 2010; "Patagonia," in "Inc. Top Workplaces 2010," *Inc.*, http://www.inc.com, accessed July 7, 2010; Monte Burke, "Wal-Mart, Patagonia, Team to Green Business," *Forbes,* May 6, 2010, http://www.forbes.com; Kent Garber, "Yvon Chouinard: Patagonia Founder Fights for the Environment," *US News & World Report,* October 22, 2009, http://politics.usnews.com.

Small Businesses Are Big into Social Networking

One of the biggest challenges for entrepreneurs is getting their new business known to potential investors, suppliers, the media, and customers. Maybe that's why entrepreneurs have been so quick to turn to social media as a tool for communicating to as many people as possible.

Many believe that when social media is used skillfully, it can help level the playing field between small businesses and their giant competitors. David avRutick, co-owner of Folbot, a small kayak retailer, claims that Twitter has increased his sales. "You can't buy that kind of exposure," avRutick says. Folbot competes against such outdoor-gear retailers as L.L. Bean and Cabela's—the smaller company needed widespread interactive communication to challenge the larger competitors. Stephen Bailey, who tracks social-media marketing for the footwear retailer John Fluevog Boots & Shoes, notes, "The people coming from social media have been buying." How else could Bailey's company lure customers away from Zappos.com?

But critics point out that using Facebook, Twitter, LinkedIn, and the more recent Yelp have a wide range of value to small businesses. "The hype right now exceeds the reality," observes Larry Chiagouris, a professor of marketing at Pace University's Lubin School of Business. The use of social media by firms with fewer than 100 employees doubled in one recent year; but only 22 percent of those who responded to a separate survey reported a direct increase in profits as a result of social media use, and half said they only broke even on the investment. Others warn that social media networking eats up valuable time, especially for an entrepreneur whose day is usually filled with tasks ranging from design to distribution, and manufacturing to marketing. "If you spend two hours a day on Twitter and Facebook, that's 25 percent of your day!" points out Chaitanya Sagar, founder of a small business outsourcing company called p2w2.

Most experts, including experienced entrepreneurs, support the use of social media, but with moderation. Chris Lindland, owner of Cordarounds.com, an online clothing retailer, advises patience. "My business has been visited millions of times, but I haven't made millions of sales," he comments. But he believes that his patience will pay off. "People have told me they finally got around to buying from my business after reading about it on social media two years ago." Sagar agrees, "If you expect immediate sales from social media, you will be disappointed." Sagar suggests that entrepreneurs focus instead on marketing their brands instead of expecting direct sales. "If you have this perspective, you will be able to use social media for the right reasons and save a lot of time."

Questions for Critical Thinking

1. How do you think social networking will change the business environment for entrepreneurs?

2. How can entrepreneurs use social networking media to secure financing for their businesses?

Sources: Kasey Wehrum, "Is Social Media Worth Your Time?," *Inc.com,* March 16, 2010, http://www.inc.com; Sarah E. Needleman, "Entrepreneurs Question Value of Social Media," *Wall Street Journal,* March 16, 2010, http://online.wsj. com; Ross Kimarovsky, "10 Small Business Social Media Marketing Tips," *Mashable.com,* http://mashable.com, accessed March 16, 2010; Paul Frederic, "Smart Social Networking for Your Small Business," *Forbes.com,* June 5, 2009, http://www. forbes.com; Claire Cain Miller, "Yelp Will Let Businesses Respond to Web Reviews," *New York Times,* April 10, 2009, http://www.nytimes.com.

Part 3 Management: Empowering People to Achieve Business Goals

The Coca-Cola Company: Training for the Future Right Now

Coca-Cola is one of the most recognizable brands in the world—it has also stood the test of time, having survived more than 125 years. But the firm has come a long way from its first fizzy drink; it is now a global empire with products sold in more than 200 countries. The Coca-Cola Company maintains that the key to its success and longevity isn't its secret recipe for the famous cola in the red can; it's the people behind the fizz. The company has become especially expert in two areas of human resource management: wellness benefits and training. As a result, the company employs healthy, skilled, and knowledgeable workers.

Several years ago, The Coca-Cola Company revamped its health and wellness programs to make them a central part of the firm's overall strategy. "We now have a strategy in which our health care benefits and our wellness programs are mixed together," explains Mary Williams, senior counsel of global compensation and benefits. Prior to the new initiative, "we had no communication with the employee that having a healthy worker within our workforce was important to the company."

The company now offers real incentives for employees to participate in its wellness programs. For example, one recent year the company gave $120 to any worker who completed a wellness assessment. The following year, the company increased the amount, offering up to $180 to any employee who agreed to participate in health coaching. Also included are fitness challenges, where workers earn redeemable points by getting enough sleep at night or by eating fruits and vegetables. Perhaps the most important part of the wellness effort is reaching employees with the right information and encouraging them to participate—wellness benefits are promoted through e-mail blasts and ads running on in-house television monitors. The new company mantra is "Live Positively," observes Williams.

Just as important as keeping employees healthy is the company's effort to train and educate them, preparing them for future changes and leadership roles. A few years ago, the company founded Coca-Cola University (CCU) as part of an overall strategy to develop the global workforce to reach its greatest potential. "No longer can we think of career development as a step up in job grade or organization level, or of training as the sole source of skill development," explains Katharine Nisbet, head of the management university. "Today, career development is about gathering critical experiences, necessary skills, and leadership capabilities that will be vital to the company's and individual's success today and in the future."

Coca-Cola University operates on a 70-20-10 model of employee development: 70 percent of learning takes place on the job, 20 percent takes place through coaching and mentoring, and 10 percent is acquired through formal, structured training. Within this model, the company's human resource managers strive to match the right training to each worker's needs. One employee might receive classroom teaching, online lessons, and on-the-job support, but another employee might receive a different combination of training methods.

An important aspect of CCU's management training strategy is that it works for everyone. "Our leadership training applies to every Coca-Cola associate," says Nisbet. "It is helping them build core competencies such as innovation, collaboration, and teamwork." Some of the seminars to which all staff are invited to participate include "Driving Innovative Business Improvements," "Collaborating to Win," and "Developing and Inspiring Others." At their performance appraisal meetings, employees are encouraged to sign up for these and other offerings through CCU. Using this strategy means that The Coca-Cola Company always has a group of employees from which to draw management talent. CCU-trained employees are already knowledgeable about the company's strategies and objectives, now and for the future.

Questions for Critical Thinking

1. In addition to cash payments, what other incentives could encourage The Coca-Cola Company employees to participate in its wellness programs?

2. The Coca-Cola Company has developed a comprehensive, worldwide training program. Its management training strategy increases the number of employees who are ready to move into leadership roles. What other positive effects do you predict this strategy may have on the company's future success?

Sources: "Associate Training," The Coca-Cola Company, http://www.thecoca-colacompany.com, accessed April 15, 2010; "Behind the Fizz," HRM, April 12, 2010, http://www.hrmasia.com; Lydell C. Bridgeford, "Coca-Cola Retools Wellness Strategy," *SMB Human Resources,* March 15, 2010, http://smbhr.benefitnews.com.

SeaWorld Faces a Public Relations Crisis

Over the years, thousands of visitors to Orlando's SeaWorld have been entertained by the skills of SeaWorld's resident whales and their trainers. Most people understand the risk the whales' trainers face because of the huge size and strength of the whales. But no one expected tragedy when a long-time trainer was pulled into the water by one of her favourite partners, Tilikum, the orca, or killer whale. Within moments, the trainer died.

SeaWorld faced a huge public crisis. Proper communication was crucial. The company faced many questions. Were visitors in danger? Should SeaWorld be shut down? And what would happen to Tilikum ("Tilly")—should he be safely kept apart from the other whales, or should his life be ended? Were other, equally dangerous animals also performing at SeaWorld? SeaWorld managers and employees needed to deal with these troubling questions. They also needed to deal with their loss of a much-loved co-worker. SeaWorld immediately stopped all whale shows at its Orlando location and at its sister parks in San Antonio and San Diego. SeaWorld took this time to review the details of the tragedy. Orlando SeaWorld's president, Dan Brown, held a press conference shortly after the event. Crisis experts said that he made a mistake when he didn't correct the statement by the local sheriff's spokesman that the trainer had accidentally fallen into the water alongside the whale. Brown only said, "She drowned in an incident with one of our killer whales." Later, when it came out that Tilly had pulled the trainer into the water, Brown lost credibility, his ability to be trusted. After the truth came out, SeaWorld's head trainer was available to answer further questions from the press and to explain more about how SeaWorld trained the orcas.

SeaWorld received many accusations and attacks—from frightened families and animal rights advocates. Rumours began about Tilly's background and what would happen to him. Everyone knew there would be no easy solution. "If [SeaWorld] were to make even the slightest hint or suggestion that [Tilly] should be put down, I can only imagine the backlash that would come from animal rights groups from around the world on that one," observed Steve Huxter, the former head trainer at Sealand of the Pacific, where Tilly lived before moving to SeaWorld.

Meanwhile, another kind of wave was getting ready to cross SeaWorld—in the form of Facebook and Twitter. SeaWorld was one of the early big companies to see the value of direct interaction with its customers by establishing both a Facebook site and Twitter account. Both accounts were now filled with comments from worried fans—and from critics. In the end, SeaWorld had to shut down its Facebook wall temporarily because of reports of inappropriate photos relating to the tragedy. And no tweets were posted from @Shamu, the popular Twitter blog "ghostwritten" by Shamu the whale.

But the Facebook site was soon started up again, and SeaWorld spokesman Fred Jacobs asked people to log on to it again. He said that SeaWorld would only stop postings that contained swearing or harassment and those that could be seen as being insensitive, or thoughtless, to the trainer's family and friends. "If you were to get on Facebook right now and ask a question about the morality of keeping whales in captivity, we'll get back to you," Jacobs promised. "Now is not the time to circle the wagons. There's a value proposition between a company and the people who follow it on social media." Some people weren't sure that it was a good idea for SeaWorld to open itself up to so much direct interaction with the public. But SeaWorld executives were firm: this was their cue to listen.

Questions for Critical Thinking

1. How could SeaWorld's Dan Brown have better handled the press conference after the accident?

2. How can SeaWorld use social media to heal and strengthen its relationship with the public?

Sources: "New Details About Whale Attack Responsible for SeaWorld Trainer's Death," *Radar,* March 1, 2010, http://www.radaronline.com; Laura Wides-Munoz, "SeaWorld Faces Major Public Relations Challenge," *The Examiner,* February 26, 2010, http://www.washingtonexaminer.com; Larry Rice, "Trainer: Orca Whale's Instinct Was to Play," *MyNorthwest.com,* February 26, 2010, http://www.mynorthwest.com; Beth Kassab, "Shamu Attack Exposes Social Media Risks," *OrlandoSentinel.com,* February 25, 2010, http://www.orlandosentinel.com.

Windy City Fieldhouse: It's All about Teams

Team building has become its own industry. More managers now understand the importance of encouraging strong, effective teams. And that has led to new companies that specialize in creative way to build teams. Chicago's Windy City Fieldhouse is one such firm. Even the name sounds like fun and games—and that's this firm wants to hear.

Windy City Fieldhouse (WCF) develops and offers programs that are designed to bring people together in a way that they don't even realize they are taking part in team-building and communication exercises. The WCF staff hosts outdoor corporate picnics, fun runs/walks, carnivals and block parties, and even Grand Prix racing events. If a client wants a more traditional training program, WCF will do that too—but most companies go for the fun. "Striving to provide programs that enhance meaningful relationships and add tremendous value, WCF continues to develop a variety of corporate event packages in order to respond to its clients' needs," states the website.

WCF is perhaps best known for its "Scavenger Hunts in Chicago" (SHIC) division. SHIC creates, organizes, and leads the corporate event. The employee teams must work together to solve clues and find their way to a location chosen by the client company. The location may be a cocktail party or a dinner at a Chicago Cubs game—it's up to the client. Each team is assigned a Scavenger Hunt facilitator. Once they reach their goal, the final destination, team members must complete certain tasks, such as taking funny photographs or finding special objects. With a facilitator acting as team leader, the team members learn how to set goals, establish guidelines, and make the most of their differences.

Participants enjoy the activities. "The feedback from my team was overwhelmingly positive," says one client. Another reports, "It has been a long time since this team has had a team gathering and when they did, we never had this much participation. Everyone really enjoyed the event." Windy City Fieldhouse is certainly on to something—for three years in a row, the firm has been named "Best Teambuilding Company" in Chicago.

Questions for Critical Thinking

1. Imagine that you had an opportunity to participate in one of SHIC's scavenger hunts. How do you think you would benefit from the experience as a team member?

2. Why is it important for SHIC to provide a facilitator for each team-building experience?

Sources: "Who Is Scavenger Hunts in Chicago?" and "Client Testimonials," Company website, http://www. scavengerhuntsinchicago.com, accessed April 20, 2010; "Scavenger Hunts in Chicago," *Here's Chicago,* http:// www.hereschicago.com, accessed April 20, 2010; Toddi Gutner, "Applicants' Personalities Put to the Test," *Previsor,* http://www.previsor.com, accessed April 20, 2010.

GM: Putting Workers in the Driver's Seat

At GM, the autoworkers do many tasks as part of their jobs. They operate machinery, run computer programs, and manage schedules and logistics. But until recently, there's one thing most GM workers hadn't been asked to do: drive the cars.

Workers were recently given the chance to volunteer for a new program—to "check out" a vehicle from the plant lot, take it home for a night or a weekend, and drive it as if it were their own car or SUV. In return, the test drivers were asked for detailed comments about the vehicles, giving them a powerful voice in the design and construction of the cars they spend hours and weeks building. "We had so much interest in [the program] we had to use a lottery to determine who would get to be a volunteer," reports Enrique Flores Jr., president of the United Auto Workers Local 276, the union representing 2,400 workers at the GM plant.

The test-drive idea isn't new—executives and managers have done it for years—but bringing the program to the workers represents a new attitude toward empowering employees. "We want to engage employees to do underground marketing," explains Wendy Stachowicz, coordinator of the GM Vehicle Advocate Program. "You look at where the company has been and where it has to go. Everyone has to help."

Employees were selected by a lottery and by their driving records. If they decided to purchase the vehicle they test drove or another vehicle in the program, they qualified for discounts that reduced the cost to almost the wholesale price. But participants didn't receive commissions or other rewards for test driving the cars—that wasn't the idea. "This is a tool to empower people, to get them really engaged with our products," explains Stachowicz. Next, GM is considering expanding the program to include GM retirees and suppliers.

Questions for Critical Thinking

1. In what ways does the GM test-drive program empower workers?

2. How can GM benefit from this type of empowerment of its assembly plant workers?

Sources: "GM Employees Getting Up-Close Look at New Line-up," *FinChannel.com,* April 20, 2010, http://www.finchannel. com; "GM Launches Plant-City Tour to Showcase Line-up, Empower Employees to Promote New Vehicles," GM website, http://www.gm.com, accessed April 20, 2010; Terry Box, "Arlington GM Workers to Take Home New Cars to Try Out," *Dallas Morning News,* February 27, 2010, http://www.dallasnews.com.

Macedonia: The New Hub of Apparel Manufacturing?

If you're not sure where to find the Republic of Macedonia, you're probably not alone. The small country with a population of about 2 million is located in the heart of Eastern Europe. It shares borders with Bulgaria, Serbia, Kosovo, Albania, and Greece. Macedonia is quickly becoming a major centre for apparel manufacturing. Although the manufacture of textiles and clothing is already one of the country's largest industries, Macedonian manufacturers are pushing for more because their factories are working at only half their capacity.

Currently, Macedonian factories are equipped to fulfill cut-make and cut-make-trim orders, but the goal is to offer full-package production, including producing fabric design and production. "We need customers to move their design and product development here, so we become their partners in production, offering a fast, flexible approach and something cheaper than the client is used to," says Vladimir Icokaev, a manager at textile and clothing exporter Global Plus.

Macedonian factories already supply major European brands and retailers with jackets, coats, skirts, pants, and shirts. The 500 textile and clothing firms in Macedonia are small by international standards—most employ from 30 to 500 workers. What they can't provide in volume they offer in flexibility. Competitors from countries as nearby as Bulgaria and as far away as China and India are focusing on mass production, offering high volume at the lowest cost. But Macedonian manufacturers prefer to focus on short production runs and high quality. "If buyers want capacity they can get it anywhere in the world," says Ilijev Nikolco, general manager for manufacturer INT, which provides a range of services from design through finished garments. "The future for Macedonia is exclusively in higher quality, more complicated styles and lower lead times."

Unlike the competitive situation in other countries, many of the small Macedonian manufacturers work together to serve the same customers. "The appeal for buyers and retailers is that they can deal with one factory that has a network to put garments out to individual suppliers—a one-stop shop," notes Gabriela Pavloska, export manager at Okitex, a women's wear company that is headquartered in Germany. Okitex actually works with 20 factories in Macedonia to produce a complete collection of women's items—such as coats, blazers, and blouses. "Our idea is to combine factories to provide a source because a client doesn't just want one type of garment," explains Pavloska.

Location is another factor that works in Macedonia's favour, particularly with its European customers. Delivery to the United Kingdom takes about three days; to Germany, about two days. Macedonia is also located near the high-end fabric producers in Turkey and Italy. The average lead time from receiving the fabric to delivery of a finished product is around three weeks. The small, flexible Macedonian factories can easily produce minimum orders of just 100 pieces per style and colour—and deliver them to a customer anywhere in Western Europe in less than a month.

Macedonia still needs to overcome some difficulties. For example, workers do not always have the necessary technical skills, and Macedonia is not yet a member of the European Union. But some Macedonian factories are sending their workers to Germany and other countries for training, and Macedonia recently held an international business event sponsored by the Macedonian Competitiveness Project and USAID (the U.S. Agency for International Development). During the event, 29 manufacturers showcased their capabilities to buyers that included such popular European brands as Topshop, Monsoon, Whistles, and BMB Clothing. Buyers were surprised— and impressed—by the facilities, the quality, the flexibility, and the easy location of Macedonian manufacturers. "It really is a brilliant way to meet a new manufacturing partner," said Leonie Barrie, an industry expert. So the next time you buy an item of clothing, check the label—it might read, "made in Macedonia."

Questions for Critical Thinking

1. In the long run, will Macedonia be successful in its strategy of focusing on flexibility, quality, and proximity rather than trying to compete with the high-volume, low-price strategy of its rivals? Why or why not?

2. How might Macedonian apparel manufacturers attract North American buyers?

Sources: "Macedonian Apparel on Buyers' Radar," *Carana Corporation,* http://www.carana.com, accessed April 26, 2010; "Macedonia: Stip on Radar of UK Apparel Retailers," *Fibre2Fashion,* April 20, 2010, http://www.fibre2fashion.com; Leonie Barrie, "Analysis: Macedonian Makers Eye Fast Fashion Partnerships," *Just-Style,* March 23, 2010, http://www. just-style.com.

Part 4 Marketing Management

Advertising on Facebook: Unlimited Potential?

At 900 million members, Facebook is a huge global social network—with the potential for large revenue. Users are familiar with the advertisements in the right-hand margin of certain pages. Some big names, such as Walmart and PepsiCo, post ads, but so do many smaller companies. What users may not know is that advertisers can use members' personal information—their age, location, interests, level of education, and Facebook connections—to carefully target their ads. For example, women who change their relationship status to "engaged" will see ads from local caterers, planners, wedding-gown stores, photographers, and so on. In contrast, Google uses keywords and search histories to target ads.

Facebook recently overtook Google as the most visited site in the United States. Eager to reach Facebook's much larger membership, many advertisers are switching from Google to Facebook. Some predict that Facebook will earn $2 billion from global advertising. One study found that 78 percent of Facebook users return to Facebook to see more news stories; but only 67 percent of Google News users do the same. Facebook traffic is up 185 percent; Google is up only 9 percent.

Facebook's "self-service" ads usually appear on a user's profile page and consist of a small photo and some text. An advertiser sets a daily budget—there is no minimum—and uses Facebook's ad-creation tool. When the advertiser has spent the day's entire budget, Facebook stops running the ad. If money is left over, the advertiser can roll it over to the next day's budget. Advertisers pay either "by impression," each time a user views the ad, or "per click," every time a user actually clicks on the link in the ad to open the company's website.

Facebook members can become "fans" of an advertiser's Facebook page or can reply to an invitation on Facebook to attend a company-sponsored event. But as in other media, consumers have a deep mistrust of Web advertising as a trustworthy source of information. With so many ads on Facebook, the click-through rates (CTRs) have fallen from close to 3 percent to about 0.3 percent. Of course, the point of the ads is to get people to look at them, but most users ignore the ads. When promoting a contest, one advertiser found that humour—and pictures of cute puppies and kittens—increased his CTR even more than the offers of prizes.

Some Facebook users find the ads off-putting—or worse—because advertisers can target them precisely. But Dan Rose, the vice-president for business development at Facebook, has predicted that the quality of the ads will improve as more companies use the system.

Facebook requires the text and photo in an ad to work with what is being advertised. But Facebook does not review ads before they are posted. The only review system is user feedback. If a user reports an ad as misleading, offensive, uninteresting, irrelevant, repetitive, or "other," then Facebook deletes the ad from that user's page. The more people who ask for an ad to be removed, the less likely Facebook will allow it be posted on other people's pages.

Some observers predict that Facebook will change Web advertising and even the advertising industry itself. Facebook's "Connect" technology allows members to take their social networks with them as they browse the Internet. And just as in the real world, in the virtual world, people are much more likely to value the opinions of their friends than the opinions of people—or advertisers—they don't know.

Questions for Critical Thinking

1. Why do advertisers continue to post ads on Facebook, even though the click-through response rate is so low?

2. How does Web advertising affect consumer behaviour? Does it help build customer relationships or not?

Sources: Claire Cain Miller, "Twitter Unveils Plan to Draw Money from Ads," *New York Times*, April 12, 2010, http://www.nytimes.com; Courtney Rubin, "Should You Advertise on Facebook?" *Inc.com*, March 23, 2010, http://www.inc.com;

Carmen Nobel, "Facebook Ad Model Is Friend to Small Business," *The Street,* March 22, 2010, http://www.thestreet.com; Steve Rubal, "Facebook Will Rule the Web During the Next Decade," *Advertising Age,* March 15, 2010, http://www.adage. com; Jonathan L. Yarmis, "How Facebook Will Upend Advertising," *BusinessWeek,* March 9, 2010, http://www.business week.com; Brad Stone, "Ads Posted on Facebook Strike Some as Off-Key," *New York Times,* March 3, 2010, http://www. nytimes.com; Kunur Patel, "Will E-Commerce Help Facebook's Ad Sales?" *Advertising Age,* March 1, 2010, http://www. adage.com; Taylor Pratt, "Fun Ways to Improve Facebook Ad CTRs," *Search Engine Journal,* n.d. [March 2010], http:// www.searchenginejournal.com.

Marketing Gone Wrong: Johnson & Johnson and Risperdal

Several years ago, the U.S. Food and Drug Administration (FDA) approved Johnson & Johnson's drug Risperdal for the treatment of psychotic disorders, such as schizophrenia, in adults. But the National Institute of Mental Health found that schizophrenia affects only about 1.1 percent of U.S. adults. According to a lawsuit filed by the state of Louisiana, Johnson & Johnson therefore decided to seek a wider market for the drug by indirectly promoting it for other purposes.

Under U.S. law, if the FDA has approved a drug for treating at least one disorder, then doctors are permitted to prescribe it "off label,"—that is, for any other disorder they think the drug will help—even if the FDA has not approved the drug for treating that other disorder. (The condition the drug is intended to treat must be stated on the labelling.) Drug manufacturers are forbidden to promote a drug for any use other than the FDA-approved use.

Recently, the U.S. Department of Justice charged Johnson & Johnson with paying hundreds of millions of dollars in kickbacks to Omnicare Inc. to buy and promote Risperdal, among other drugs, for off-label uses. According to the charge, Omnicare, the largest pharmacy for U.S. nursing-home patients, promoted prescribing Risperdal for elderly patients who had Alzheimer's disease—even though the FDA never approved Risperdal for treating Alzheimer's. Johnson & Johnson stated, "We believe airing the facts will confirm that our conduct, including rebating programs like those the government now challenges, was lawful and appropriate. We look forward to the opportunity to present our evidence in court."

As far back as 1994—just one year after the FDA approved Risperdal for psychotic disorders—the FDA ordered Johnson & Johnson to stop its claims that Risperdal was more effective than competing drugs. In 1999, the FDA warned the company that its marketing literature overstated Risperdal's benefits for elderly patients with Alzheimer's disease and understated the risks. Nonetheless, a Johnson & Johnson business plan showed the company aimed to increase Risperdal's sales to these vulnerable patients well into the 21st century (as baby boomers aged). Sales of Risperdal peaked at $4.5 billion in 2007, before the patent expired, and other companies could legally manufacture cheaper, generic versions of the drug.

In 2005, the FDA issued a public health advisory, warning that Risperdal and similar drugs actually increased the chances of death among elderly Alzheimer's patients, usually as a result of heart failure or pneumonia. The FDA has also required Risperdal labelling to note this increased risk in a "black box" warning, the FDA's strictest type of warning.

Ten states have filed lawsuits against Johnson & Johnson for promoting Risperdal off-label. Louisiana sued to force the company to pay millions of dollars in fines and to regain public money spent on Risperdal. Johnson & Johnson's lawyers argued that Louisiana did not cite any evidence of misrepresentation or off-label promotion. The company also claimed there was no connection between its marketing and the decision by Louisiana doctors to prescribe Risperdal. The judge rejected this argument, and the trial date was set. A spokesman for Johnson & Johnson said that the case "should be decided on the body of evidence, including testimony, not on the basis of excerpts from documents." The company has not put any money aside toward a settlement.

Omnicare paid $98 million to settle charges of running kickback plans with nursing homes and other drug manufacturers. Neither Omnicare nor Johnson & Johnson acknowledged having done anything wrong.

Questions for Critical Thinking

1. Is it an appropriate marketing strategy to recommend nonapproved uses of a drug? Why or why not?

2. Which market segmentation strategy was Johnson & Johnson using when it decided to promote Risperdal for Alzheimer's patients? What did the company fail to take into account when developing this strategy?

Sources: Margaret Cronin Fisk, Jef Feeley, and David Voreacos, "Did J&J Plan to Break Rules?" *BusinessWeek,* March 11, 2010, http://www.businessweek.com; Margaret Cronin Fisk, Jef Feeley, and David Voreacos, "J&J Pushed Risperdal for Elderly after U.S. Warning, Files Show," *Bloomberg.com,* March 10, 2010, http://www.bloomberg.com; Natasha Singer, "Johnson & Johnson Accused of Drug Kickbacks," *New York Times,* January 16, 2010, http://www.nytimes.com; Michael Winter, "Johnson and Johnson Accused of Drug Kickbacks," *USA Today,* January 15, 2010, http://content.usatoday.com; Jim Edwards, "J&J Nursing Home Kickback Scheme Tripled Sales, DOJ Alleges," *BNET,* January 15, 2010, http://industry. bnet.com.

Luxury Brands Market to Millennials

Chanel. Armani. BMW. Cartier. These long-established, high-end brands are very interested in Generation Y, also known as the Millennials—those born during the 1980s and who are now in their mid-twenties to early thirties. The newest challenge these once-exclusive brands face is marketing to this age group.

According to a recent American marketing survey, which also applies to Canada, Millennials are the "largest consumer group in U.S. history," even bigger than the baby-boom generation, the previous record holders. The 70 million to 85 million Millennials make up 25 percent of the American population. They are the most ethnically diverse population group ever and the age group that is the least limited by gender stereotypes. They spend more than $200 billion a year on purchases. As they enter the workforce and set up their own households, their spending power will overtake the soon-to-retire baby boomers.

Even more important is how Millennials receive information and communicate. Unlike any previous generation, they have grown up with digital technology. The take for granted such things as cellphones, video games, and other high-speed electronic devices and media. They are used to having instantly available information and communication. A recent survey by the Pew Research Center notes that 75 percent of Generation Y use social networking, in contrast to 50 percent of Generation X (those in their mid-thirties to late forties) and 30 percent of baby boomers (those in their late forties to late sixties).

Millennials are very aware of the value of what they buy. The marketing survey found that 65 percent of female Millennials and 61 percent of male Millennials describe themselves as brand conscious. But the marketing tools of heritage and exclusivity, which have traditionally been used to promote prestige brands, mean little to Millennials. Instead, they value quality, authenticity, and image. They shun anything that resembles self-promotion in either brands or people, including prominently displayed corporate logos.

Burberry, a maker of high-end clothing and accessories, established in 1836, recently began an ambitious multimedia effort to reach Millennials. One of the company's first moves was to hire Emma Watson, an actress famous for playing the role of Hermione Granger in the Harry Potter movies. Watson, a Millennial born in 1990, was the new face of Burberry's spring–summer campaign. In addition to promoting its business through traditional print advertising and its website, Burberry has also used live streaming and 3-D filming of its fashion shows. Burberry also hired the photo blogger Scott Schuman, known as the Sartorialist, to launch a special website, Art of the Trench, to promote its classic trench coat. Burberry's Facebook page calls Art of the Trench "a living celebration of the trench coat and the people who wear it." The website, essentially a social networking blog, invites owners to submit photos of themselves wearing their trench coats—and to submit videos to its YouTube channel. Links allow visitors to "view details," "like," "share," and "leave comments" on the photos. They can also sort the photos by popularity, gender, styling, trench colour, and weather. The site features music by the Maccabees, White Lies, and other groups, with links to their websites. Burberry's chief executive officer, Angela Ahrendts, said, "Attracting the Millennial customer to luxury started two years ago—I said that we can either get crushed or ride the greatest wave of our life."

Scott Galloway of New York University's School of Business says, "Gen Y goodwill is arguably the closest thing to a crystal ball for predicting a brand's long-term prospects. Just as Boomers drove the luxury sector for the last 20 years, brands that resonate with Gen Y, whose purchasing power will surpass that of Boomers by 2017, will be the new icons of prestige."

Questions for Critical Thinking

1. Millennials are brand conscious but generally dislike conspicuous, flashy brand logos. How might these likes and dislikes affect a company's brand equity?

2. Burberry is basing its product strategy on how Millennials use the Internet and social media, not on the preferences of their parents. Will this difference in strategy continue as the Millennials mature? If so, how might Burberry change its product strategy?

Sources: Company website, http://us.burberry.com, accessed August 3, 2010; Art of the Trench, http://artofthetrench.com, accessed August 3, 2010; Sharalyn Hartwell, "Millennials Love Brands, Not Branding," Examiner.com, May 6, 2010, http://www.examiner.com; Scott Galloway, "Gen Y Prestige Brand Ranking," May 3, 2010, http://l2thinktank.com/Gen_Y_Report.pdf; Pew Research Center, "The Millennials: Confident. Connected. Open to Change," February 24, 2010, http://pewresearch.org/pubs/1501/millennials-new-survey-generational-personality-upbeat-open-new-ideas-technology-bound; Jessica Bumpus, "Millennial Burberry," Vogue.com, March 3, 2010, http://www.vogue.co.uk; Suzy Menkes, "Marketing to the Millennials," *New York Times,* March 2, 2010, http://www.nytimes.com.

Brand Names versus Store Brands

Shoppers who buy brand-name products usually say they prefer them because of their quality. Shoppers who buy store-brand products usually say they prefer them because of their price. What about shopper who want both good quality and a good price?

Some retailers such as Loblaws and Target have found they have had too many of the same products under different brand names. Their shoppers were buying less and looking for bigger bargains. Items that weren't selling well were replaced by more popular brands or by in-house generics. This trend was especially true for such basic items as household and personal products and food staples. As one observer said, "People don't want to have to choose between among 15 or 20 different brands of toilet paper or paper towels or even basic food stuff." The retailers were sure that shoppers would be eager to snap up these bargains.

Target guessed that consumers would buy their in-house brands, and it looks like they were correct. The high-quality store lines that Target stocks have yielded a 2 percent increase in same-store sales for one recent month. The in-store brands of up & up, Archer Farms, and Market Pantry account for more than 20 percent of all food products sold at Target. A retailing analyst wrote in a recent report, "the company has unique top-line drivers that aren't dependent on macro recovery."

In general, this overall strategy has worked. The market share of store brands has grown between 2 and 6 percent. And 77 percent of consumers who bought less expensive store-brand items were satisfied with their choice.

Questions for Critical Thinking

1. Why do chain stores carry brand-name products alongside their own in-house brands?

2. What are some of the ways that stores such as Target are able to keep their prices low?

Sources: "Target's Comeback Plan on Track," *Store Brands Decisions,* August 10, 2010, http://www.storebrandsdecisions.com; Parija Kavilanz, "Dumped! Brand Names Fight to Stay in Stores," CNN Money.com, February 16, 2010, http://money.cnn.com; Kevin Cokeley, "Retailers Replacing Big Names with House Brands," NBC Dallas–Fort Worth, February 19, 2010, http://www.nbcdfw.com; Sara Zucker, "Wal-Mart Reintroduces Brands after Customer Complaints," Brandchannel.com, March 12, 2010, http://www.brandchannel.com.

Marketing to the Teenage Crowd

Today's teenagers were born just before the turn of the 21st century. They represent billions of dollars in buying power. The big question for marketers is how to reach this teenage crowd.

Unlike their parents, today's teens have grown up in this electronic age and take it for granted. Like teenagers of earlier generations, today's teens like to communicate with each other. Unlike teenagers of previous generations, today's teens can keep in touch with each other almost constantly. One study estimates that teenagers spend more than seven hours a day using media of various kinds, mostly electronic. How do they find this amount of time? By sacrificing sleep and by multi-tasking. Some older teens can perform seven activities at once. Parents often find their teens listening to music, watching a TV program, doing homework, playing a videogame, and text messaging.

What media do teenagers neglect or ignore? They rarely read newspapers. Jeffrey Cole, the director of the Center for the Digital Future at the University of Southern California, predicts that printed newspapers will eventually disappear as social media steadily increase. Teens want news, he explains, but only about the narrowly focused community of their peers.

Teenagers don't communicate with their friends through e-mail. One survey shows that although 73 percent of teens visit social-networking sites, only about 8 percent use Twitter. They like smartphones, especially those with apps for constant status updates, but they don't make many phone calls. Instead, they text-message, sometimes sending up to 10 messages every hour.

Marketers will need to learn how to reach teenagers. For example, teens like to be invited to be involved; they don't like being told to be involved. So marketers need to ask for their input and to listen with genuine respect. They need to adopt some of their suggestions and to continue to ask for their feedback. Morgan Stewart of ExactTarget surveyed teens to find out which brand they thought did the best job of communicating with them. To his surprise, Amazon got more write-in votes than any other brand, including Facebook. He says of Amazon, "Teens can read reviews, they can submit their own, and they can get recommendations based on what they like." Stewart believes that "managing your Amazon presence is more important than building out a Facebook strategy."

Of course, even Amazon is only one part of an integrated marketing plan. Teenagers are highly suspicious of anything that seems even remotely like advertising. When shopping, they depend heavily on the opinions of their friends. They also enjoy fun sites such as Sporcle.com, FunnyOrDie.com, and FailBlog.org. YouTube is another important tool for viral marketing—and it's free.

Jeffrey Cole thinks that as today's teens move into adulthood, the desire to know everything about their friends will fade. What will last will be something that every generation wants: they will still want to have "total control over their media" as a way of having "real control over their lives."

Questions for Critical Thinking

1. Do you think marketers can reach teens with specially tailored promotional campaigns for such goods and services as video games, smartphone apps, and concert tickets? Why or why not?

2. How can marketers best target teens so they appeal to them but without making them feel talked down to? Suggest a marketing or promotional theme for one product that you think would appeal to a teen.

Sources: Steve Bauer, "Reaching the Elusive Teenager," *Word of Mouth,* April 13, 2010, http://wom.fleishmanhilliard.com; Carol Phillips, "Where Teens Hang Out Digitally," *Millennial Marketing,* March 12, 2010, http://millennialmarketing. com; Tim Loc, "Teens Love Social Media, Detest Newspapers," *iMedia Connection,* March 3, 2010, http://www. imediaconnection.com; Steve McClellan, "Teens into Social Media, Not Newspapers," *Mediaweek,* March 2, 2010, http://www.mediaweek.com; Tamar Lewin, "If Your Kids Are Awake, They're Probably Online," *New York Times,* January 20, 2010, http://www.nytimes.com; "Teen Marketing: A Look Ahead," Pangea Media, January 1, 2010, http://www.pangeamedia.com.

Part 5 Managing Technology and Information

Kaspersky Lab Busts Computer Bugs

Computer viruses can affect large and small businesses. They can also affect people who own home computers or smartphones. Once a virus has invaded a network or a device—such as a computer, tablet, PDA, or cellphone—it copies itself and begins causing slowdowns or, worse, destroying data or stealing a user's identity.

Many software programs are available to catch and/or stop viruses and worms. The programs produced by Kaspersky Lab are among the most popular and the most effective. The company was founded by Russian-born Eugene Kaspersky, an engineer. He became interested in computer viruses when his own computer was attacked by the notorious Cascade virus in 1989.

He developed a disinfection utility for the virus, then went on to set up a catalogue of viruses and disinfection utilities. This database now includes 4 million entries. In 1997, he and several colleagues founded Kaspersky Lab.

The company has headquarters in Moscow and branches worldwide. The company has won many awards for its antivirus software packages. Only four years after setting up a location in the Americas, Kaspersky Lab won an award for best e-mail security system. Today, Kaspersky Lab is the world's largest privately held antimalware company. It offers products for both corporate networks and home personal computer (PC) users in almost every country in the world. More than 300 million users rely on Kaspersky products for their security, and 150,000 new users sign up every week.

One of Kaspersky Lab's success stories involves the Austrian National Tourist Office, the country's official tourist organization. It has 250 employees in 30 offices in Austria and in cities around the world, including New York, Sydney, Beijing, and Singapore. The tourist office's international website has pages in many languages and features Austria's many attractions for visitors. The office's travel services are Web-based, and its employees rely constantly on the Internet for online research and e-mail from their colleagues in different branches. Because of the growing worldwide risk of viruses and other malware, the tourist office decided it needed a better security system.

The tourist office consulted the Austrian information technology (IT) subsidiary Austrian Info Systems GmbH, which decided that the best solution would be to adopt the entire range of products in the Kaspersky Anti-Virus Business Optimal package. From the tourist bureau's home office in Vienna, the Kaspersky Administration Kit runs centralized monitoring and supervises all the office's servers and all of its antivirus protection. Other Kaspersky antivirus utilities protect all of the 250 workstations worldwide, the 25 file servers, and the 550 mailboxes that make up the exchange infrastructure. A free administration kit helps Austrian Info Systems make regular searches of the tourist office's network for viruses.

For the home computer user, Kaspersky Lab offers programs that help prevent various forms of identity theft; provide protection against viruses, Trojan horses, and spyware; and scan websites for malware. Because more Mac users now store data in the "cloud," on Internet servers, their computers can also become infected with viruses and other malware. For these users, Kaspersky Lab offers a Mac version of its antivirus software. And because smartphone users increasingly use their hand-held devices as PCs, the company now offers a mobile security program.

The company recently celebrated its 12th anniversary. Its website declares that its "most valuable asset is the wealth of experience and knowledge it has gained in ... combating viruses and other IT threats, enabling us to pre-empt trends in malware development. This helps us to remain one step ahead of the competition and provide our users with the most reliable protection from new types of attack."

Questions for Critical Thinking

1. Why is it so important for Kaspersky Lab—as a business—to stay ahead of new computer threats?

2. How do you protect your own computer or hand-held device from viruses and other malware? What steps would you take to improve your protection?

Sources: Company website, http://usa.kaspersky.com, accessed May 24, 2010; Austrian National Tourist Office website, http://www.austria.info, accessed May 24, 2010; Maxine Cheung, "Kaspersky CMO Outlines New Partner Initiatives and Resources," *IT Business Canada*, February 18, 2010, http://www.itbusiness.ca.

Part 6 Managing Financial Resources

Intacct Provides Accounting Software as a Service

More businesses are turning to cloud computing. These businesses make use of SaaS, or software as a service, instead of buying, installing, and maintaining software packages. A company that uses SaaS subscribes to a website that leases software. The software remains on that provider's servers. Any approved company employee can access the software from anywhere—an in-office computer; an off-site notebook; or even a BlackBerry, iPhone, or other hand-held device that has Internet capability. All data are saved and stored on the website's servers. Smaller companies find that using SaaS offers many benefits. They don't need to buy expensive software packages, administer the software and on-site servers, or hire information technology (IT) personnel.

Intacct was one of the first online SaaS providers of accounting software. More than 30,000 people across 3,000 companies use its products. Intacct provides two basic packages: Intacct Accounting Edition and Intacct. Intacct Accounting Edition allows accounting firms and their clients to work on the same financial data at the same time. It is used mostly by accounting firms whose clients have from five to 100 employees. The second package, which is simply called Intacct, is used by businesses that have grown too large to use QuickBooks or similar applications from Microsoft or Sage. These businesses generally have 25 to 1,000 employees. These businesses have the software and control access to the software; the accounting firm logs in as a user.

Daniel Druker, a senior vice president at Intacct, says, "Our research with the AICPA [American Institute of Certified Public Accountants] shows a 50 percent productivity improvement for accounting firms that switch to SaaS—plus roughly doubling in proactive consultation hours. And firms can serve around 10 percent more clients with the same staff, by reducing time for travel and error fixing."

One of Intacct's clients is ASP Global Services (ASPGS), a warehouse management solutions provider. Intacct's software has made it possible for ASPGS to modernize and streamline its financial processes. The General Ledger program has improved ASPGS's ability to plan, budget, report, and analyze its business. The software also means ASPGS can enter data faster and more efficiently without having to export those data into a program such as Microsoft Excel. Intacct allows ASPGS to see a real-time income statement at any given moment. As a result, ASPGS has more accurate financial reporting and saves a great deal of time and resources.

Mike Mullane, the CEO of ASPGS, says, "Intacct is a huge time saver for us. With Intacct, there are a lot of processes you can set up once and then let them run automatically going forward. This allows us to be more effective in managing the company and enables us to spend more time looking forward instead of constantly looking at what has already happened."

Intacct recently unveiled the latest edition of its financial management and accounting package. The program, called Winter 2010, enables GAAP (Generally Accepted Accounting Principles) and analysis without the need for additional software. It also includes modules for such options as accounting, purchasing, business intelligence, multicurrency support, and sales-tax management, among many others. Druker says about the new edition, "Our mindset is: If you're a small business, why run a system like this yourself? You don't have to install or configure a thing. We turn it on for you, and you use it as you would use Google or Amazon."

Questions for Critical Thinking

1. What are the potential disadvantages of using software to automate administrative processes such as accounting and financial reporting?

2. Why is it important for users of financial accounting and other software packages to restrict access to certain kinds of information in the system?

Sources: Intacct website, http://us.intacct.com, accessed June 1, 2010; ASPGS website, http://unicode.com, accessed June 1, 2010; "Using Cloud Financial Applications from Intacct Cuts Monthly Close Process by More Than Two Weeks and Delivers $100,000 in Annual Salary Savings," *MarketWire,* March 29, 2010, http://www.marketwire.com; Daniel Dern, "Are You Being Served?" *Insight Magazine,* February–March 2010, http://www.icpas.org; "Intacct Launches Upgraded Online Accounting Program," *SmallBusinessComputing.com,* February 3, 2010, http://www.smallbusinesscomputing.com; "Intacct Winter 2010 Named One of the Top 10 Small Business Financial Applications by SmallBusinessComputing.com," press release, February 2, 2010, http://us.intacct.com.

Emerging-Market Stocks: The New Leaders?

Electronic trading means that the click of a mouse can set in motion a financial transaction on the other side of the world. But this interconnected market has its dark side because almost all the nations of the world were affected by the financial crisis. Many of the developed nations struggled to recover, but some developing nations were more fortunate than others. Many developing nations did not play a role in what turned out to be the housing market bubble and so they were relatively unaffected when it burst. As a result, the economies of nations in Asia and Latin America, oil-rich Russia, and the former Soviet-bloc countries of Eastern Europe could move ahead of their more highly developed counterparts.

Emerging markets—that is, financial markets in developing nations—are not new. They have been around since the 19th century. Traditionally, developing nations provided raw materials, such as petroleum and other resources, to the industrialized West but imported relatively few goods in return. Until a few years ago, these nations' markets were best known for the extremes of their boom-and-bust cycles. As recently as 1997, many East Asian countries fell like dominoes under a series of bankruptcies, recessions, and other financial woes. In 1998, Russia defaulted on its debt, causing its market to tumble more than 80 percent. Since then, many developing countries have managed to balance their budgets and have improved in other ways that made their economies grow. This growth has brought wealth. Low interest rates on loans have made it possible for local companies to do very well. These countries also have less national, corporate, and household debt than most developed nations. People can afford to spend money on imported goods—and are ready and willing to invest in their own countries.

The Morgan Stanley Capital International (MSCI) Emerging Markets Index measures the performance of financial markets in 25 developing countries. These countries include Egypt, the Czech Republic, Peru, Thailand, and the so-called BRIC countries—Brazil, Russia, India, and China. In a recent year, the MSCI Emerging Markets Index grew 70 percent.

Antoine Van Agtmael, the chairman and chief investment officer of Emerging Markets Management, created the term *emerging markets*. He believes that after the crash of 2008 and the revival of 2009, "We have just had the best gains in the history of emerging markets; we need a bit of a breather. It's not going to be the panic of 2008 and it's not going to be the fabulous year we had last year."

Some investors warn that emerging markets also have a dark side. For example, look at the small Middle Eastern country of Dubai, which is perhaps best known to Americans for its palm tree–shaped artificial islands. Dubai spent generously on these and other fanciful construction projects and then fell heavily into debt. When it failed to attract buyers or even renters for these sites, Dubai's bubble economy burst and the country fell into a recession. Some investors also worry that housing bubbles like the one in the United States may be growing in China and Hong Kong.

But other investors, such as David Cohen of Action Economics in Singapore, are more hopeful. Cohen said, "The economic picture is brightening despite all the caution flagged by the central banks and finance ministry officials around the world. The data still continues [*sic*] to show a global recovery led by Asia."

So far, emerging markets account for less than 3 percent of assets managed by American investment firms. But if these markets continue to do well, that number could double over the next five years.

Questions for Critical Thinking

1. Suppose one or more developing nations falls into a recession. What effect might this situation have on world markets?

2. Why do you think Canadians have invested so little in emerging markets? If you wanted to convince a friend to join you in investing in an emerging market, what arguments would you use?

Sources: Ed Johnson and Ron Harui, "Emerging-Market Stocks Gain, Erasing 2010 Loss; Yen Weakens," *Bloomberg Businessweek,* June 23, 2010, http://www.businessweek.com; "MSCI Emerging Markets Index," *Investopedia,* http://www.investopedia.com, accessed June 21, 2010; Jeremy Gaunt, "Global Investors Cut Stocks, Emerging Markets: Poll," *Reuters,*

March 31, 2010, http://www.reuters.com; "Emerging Market Stocks May Need a 'Breather,'" *Economic Times,* March 17, 2010, http://economictimes.indiatimes.com; Tina Russo, "Big Upside for Small Stocks in Emerging Markets," *Forbes.com,* February 8, 2010, http://www.forbes.com; Heather Timmons, "Emerging Markets Soar Past Their Doubters," *New York Times,* December 30, 2009, http://www.nytimes.com; "Dubai Property Prices Could Drop 20% More," *Property Frontiers,* July 2, 2009, http://news.propertyfrontiers.com.

Credit Unions Find a Silver Lining in the Financial Crisis

Like the rest of the North America, Meigs County, Tennessee, a mostly rural county, had suffered during the recent financial crisis and the recession that followed. As the three largest employers in the county heard many times, it was a bad year to try to start a credit union. But the Middle Tennessee Federal Credit Union, now worth $3 million, recently celebrated its first birthday.

The founders of the credit union, originally named the Mid East Tennessee Community Credit Union, had begun seeking a charter before the economic trouble. Their employees were relying on high-interest payday loans to meet their financial needs, and the founders wanted to help them to access small, short-term loans on more reasonable terms. The credit union opened for business in the midst of the recession. Jim Pitt, the chairman of the credit union's board and the chief executive officer (CEO) of Polyform Plastics, says, "Mostly I am proudest of our loans for the first year."

A bank is a for-profit institution that must report to its board members and shareholders, but a credit union is a not-for-profit cooperative owned by its members. Credit unions place priorities on the basic finances of everyday life: savings and chequing accounts, credit cards, and small loans for homes or cars. Compared with banks, credit unions generally pay more interest on savings accounts and charge less interest on loans. Credit unions direct any excess funds back to its members. Just as the Canada Deposit Insurance Corporation (CDIC) insures bank deposits, the provincial credit union centrals, such as Credit Union Central of New Brunswick, insures deposits of up to $250,000.

Credit unions are chartered to serve particular groups. Originally, most credit unions were affiliated with employers. About 10 years ago, credit unions began to ease their membership requirements. With the big banks pulling or tightening consumer credit, some consumers have had difficulty getting even the most routine loans, for example, for a used car. Small-business owners have also been affected. Credit unions have filled the gap, especially in the United States. In Canada, one in three Canadians is a member of a credit union or caisse populaire. The recent mergers of some credit unions has led to more combined resources to better serve their clients, as was the case in the recent merger of Desjardins and Meridian.

Credit unions don't perform all the services of traditional banks. Some credit unions do not even issue automated teller machine (ATM) cards. The Credit Union Central of Canada (CUCC) has online tools to help you find a credit union near you.

"It is gratifying that Canadians continue to feel valued and well served by their local credit unions," said David Phillips, president and CEO of Credit Union Central of Canada (Canadian Central).

Questions for Critical Thinking

1. Why is an organization such as the Credit Union CUCC important to the credit union industry?

2. Do you think that Canadian credit unions were affected by the credit crisis the same way as their American counterparts were affected?

3. Use the CUCC or your provincial credit union locator tool to find a credit union near you. If you are eligible to join, compare the credit union's interest rates and service charges with those of your current financial institution. What are the advantages of joining the credit union? What are the advantages to staying with your financial institution?

Sources: "Credit Union vs. Bank," Star Community Credit Union, http://www.starcreditunion.com, accessed June 21, 2010; Middle Tennessee Federal Credit Union website, http://www.midtenfcu.com, accessed June 21, 2010; National Credit Union Administration Web site, http://www.ncua.gov, accessed June 21, 2010; Credit Union National Association website, http://www.cuna.org, accessed June 21, 2010; David Morrison, "Year-Old Tenn. Credit Union Finds Success Despite Great Recession," *Credit Union Times*, April 28, 2010, http://www.cutimes.com; Bob Trebilcock, "Bye, Banks: Time to Join a Credit Union," *MoneyWatch/CBS News*, January 12, 2010, http://www.cbsnews.com; James Briggs, "Credit Unions Thrive as Big Banks Cut Back on Lending," *Oakland Press*, January 4, 2010, http://www.theoaklandpress.com; CBC website, "Desjardins and Meridian Credit Unions to Merge," March 1, 2011, http://www.cbc.ca/news/business/story/2011/03/01/desjardins-meridian.html, accessed July 28, 2011; Credit Union Central of Canada website, http://www.cucentral.ca/, accessed July 28, 2011; PEI Credit Unions website, http://www.peicreditunions.com/news.php?id=29, accessed July 28, 2011.

SunOpta Divests to Grow

SunOpta Inc. focuses on integrated business models in the natural and organic foods and natural health products markets. SunOpta Inc. is based in Brampton, Ontario, and has three business units, including the well-known SunOpta Food Group. This division specializes in sourcing, processing, and packaging natural and organic food products. On June 14, 2010, SunOpta Inc. announced that it had completed the divestiture of the company's Canadian food distribution assets to United Natural Foods Inc. (UNFI) and UNFI Canada Inc. The food distribution assets included in the divestiture were part of the SunOpta Distribution Group (SDG), but SunOpta did not give up all of its operations. SunOpta ensured that it retained the natural health products distribution and manufacturing assets—which represent the balance of the assets in SDG.

SunOpta was pleased that this divestiture resulted in no jobs lost. All employees involved in the Canadian food distribution operations were offered employment with UNFI (the leading distributor of natural, organic, and specialty foods in the United States).

But the question remains—why the divestiture? This divestiture was done purely for growth. SDG explains that for fiscal 2009, SDG brought in revenues of US$237.3 million. In the same period, its Canadian food distributions operations alone generated revenues of US$169.6 million and raised positive operating earnings. But the natural health products operation was a different story. Despite its revenues of US$67.7 million, this sector had negative operating earnings due to the cost of relaunching some of its natural health product brands. SunOpta could not continue without divesting.

Steve Bromley, the president and chief executive officer (CEO) of SunOpta, was not discouraged. Instead, he was optimistic about the growth opportunities the divestiture could bring. "Completing this divestiture is an important step in our strategy to focus on our core food manufacturing platform, strengthening our balance sheet and positioning the Company for the future," he commented. Again, Bromley showed his employee-focused mindset, "Once again we want to express our sincere appreciation to our dedicated employees for their years of hard work and dedication and wish them continued success under UNFI's leadership."

It appeared that everyone involved in the deal was pleased with the outcome, which is unusual in these types of divestitures. Steve Spinner, the president and CEO of UNFI, was even more than pleased about the divestiture. He commented, "We are very happy to have closed this acquisition as it represents the latest step in our strategy to grow our business in the Canadian market and we look forward to working closely with our new UNFI Canada associates." United Natural Foods Inc. carries and distributes more than 60,000 products to more than 17,000 customer locations across North America.

SunOpta continued with its divestures well after the sale to UNFI. In May 2011, SunOpta sold some of its equipment for processing frozen fruit to Cal Pacific Specialty Foods for $1.8 million. "This divestiture is another step in simplifying our frozen fruit business model to focus on value-added private label frozen fruit products for the retail and food service channels and improve long-term profitability," said Bromley. Similar to earlier divestitures, SunOpta plans to reinvest the funds from the divestiture in growth projects.

Questions for Critical Thinking

1. What are some of the reasons that companies divest their assets?

2. How can SunOpta's divestitures assist the company in meeting its growth prospects?

Sources: Newsfile website, "SunOpta Completes Divestiture of Canadian Food Distribution Assets," press release, June 14, 2010, http://www.newsfilecorp.com/release.aspx?id=540, accessed August 5, 2011; Winnipeg Free Press website, http://www.winnipegfreepress.com/business/breakingnews/122860644.html, accessed August 5, 2011; SunOpta website, http://www.sunopta.com/, accessed August 5, 2011, UNFI website, http://www.unfi.com/AboutUs.aspx, accessed August 5, 2011.

Top Hedge Fund Managers Earn Record Paycheques

During the recent recession, the banking and investment industry experienced steep drops in income. But, as the economy began to revive, the 25 top-earning hedge fund managers earned $25.3 billion. Those earnings topped even the old record, set in the boom days before the crisis.

One of those hedge fund managers was David Tepper of Appaloosa Management. While other investors feared that the banking sector would collapse again, Tepper bet that the U.S. federal government would step in to prevent the biggest banks from failing. In late 2008 and early 2009, Tepper invested heavily in funds that others would have looked at as bad investments, including preferred shares and bonds of the big banks. But Tepper, formerly of Goldman Sachs, won big, earning $4 billion. "We bet on the country's revival," he said. "Those who keep their heads while others are panicking do well." The U.S. Treasury Department agreed with Tepper, because it also bought preferred stock in troubled banks to help them recover. The Treasury has since sold many of those stocks at a good profit.

Hedge funds are elite, private investment companies that are open only to highly qualified, large investors. Unlike mutual funds, hedge funds are not regulated by the Securities and Exchange Commission in the United States but they are subject to regulation in Canada by organizations such as the Ontario Securities Commission. During the heady days before the financial crisis, hedge funds earned huge profits. Their managers did well, too, because they usually take a significant percentage of a hedge fund's annual earnings. When the crisis struck, even these funds experienced losses in the double digits, and their managers' incomes dropped by as much as 50 percent. But when the market rallied, hedge funds also did well. Of the 25 top hedge fund managers, the lowest earner made $350 million.

As the world economies recovered, the news media reported the immense salaries of chief executive officers (CEOs) and other top corporate executives at banks and large brokerage houses. The stories stirred the critics, especially because ordinary people were losing their jobs, homes, and health insurance. But some analysts believe that hedge fund managers such as David Tepper earned their huge salaries because they dared to take big risks in the hope of big rewards.

Of course, not all hedge funds did well when the stock market revived. The gap between the highest-earning hedge funds and the losing hedge funds grew wider. Nadia Papagiannis, a hedge fund analyst at Morningstar Inc., said, "The hedge funds that survived 2008 were able to capture the gains on the way up in 2009. This year is not going to be as lucrative as last year. There's not enough of room [*sic*] for another rally as big as we saw in '09."

Questions for Critical Thinking

1. Compare hedge funds with mutual funds.

2. Do you agree that the top hedge fund managers deserve their high salaries? Why or why not?

Sources: Jim Pavia, "Hedge Fund Manager Made $4B Last Year. And He Deserved It," *InvestmentNews*, April 8, 2010, http://www.investmentnews.com; Ben Rooney, "Hedge Fund Manager Paycheck: $4 Billion," *CNNMoney.com*, April 1, 2010, http://money.cnn.com; Jim Kim, "Hedge Fund Managers Earn Record Pay in 2009," *FierceFinance*, April 1, 2010, http://www.fiercefinance.com; Edward Helmore, "Hedge Fund Pay Soars—But 2010 Could be Tougher," *First Post*, April 1, 2010, http://www.thefirstpost.co.uk; Nelson D. Schwartz and Louise Story, "Pay of Hedge Fund Managers Roared Back Last Year," *New York Times*, March 31, 2010, http://www.nytimes.com.

WILEY
PLUS
www.wileyplus.com

Access your WileyPLUS course for:

- The complete digital textbook.

- Question assistance, including links to relevant sections in the online digital textbook.

- Immediate feedback and proof of progress, 24/7

- Integrated, multi-media resources – including MP3 downloads, visual exhibits, animations, and much more – that provide multiple study paths and encourage more active learning.

APPENDIX B
VIDEO CASES

Part 1 Business in a Global Environment

Secret Acres: Selling Comics Is Serious Business

Just about everyone remembers a favourite comic book hero from childhood—whether it was Spiderman, Tin Tin, or even Garfield. Leon Avelino and Barry Matthews readily admit that they are kids in grown-up bodies with real day jobs (Avelino works for *Sports Illustrated* and Matthews is an accountant for an e-commerce firm). They just happen to love comic books and their latest form—graphic novels. Their love for comics in all forms—and their desire to start their own business—led them to found Secret Acres, a comic book and graphic novel publisher based in New York City. Secret Acres has published several works from up-and-coming authors (they have eight books on their list so far). The company also sells books from independent distributors. Often asked whether they think Secret Acres will succeed or fail in the next few years, Avelino quips, "People think we're too small to fail." He laughs but then adds, "That pisses me off. I think we can totally fail."

But Avelino and Matthews do not intend to fail. They admit that Secret Acres faces many economic challenges if it's going to continue and eventually succeed, Matthews says, "Every decision we make, we know what the outcome is going to be because it's all small and it's very close to us." Right now, Secret Acres can use its small size to build relationships with its customers. "We are able, because we're small, to produce a very specific kind of comic book, a specific kind of graphic novel, that appeals to a specific audience," explains Matthews. "I love that. We have a lot of control over what we do and we're not doing anything specifically to turn a buck." That said, the accountant in Matthews knows that, to stay in business, Secret Acres must sell enough books to push unit costs down, keeping production expenses and prices as low as possible.

Matthews also refers to Secret Acres' relationships with bookstores, which are personal because he and Avelino do all the work themselves. "When you have a small group of stores you are selling from, you have to collect from them on a one-to-one basis," says Matthews. Sometimes the relationship becomes awkward when Matthews or Avelino needs to remind a bookstore owner of an unpaid balance.

Another challenge facing the duo is the uncertain future of the print publishing market. The introduction of e-readers such as Amazon's Kindle and Barnes & Noble's Nook created a new delivery system for printed work. The e-reader hasn't led to the buying frenzy that its manufacturers had hoped (some competing models have already disappeared), online delivery of printed matter is alive and well—and it's likely that some form of e-reader will eventually catch on. "Publishers are nervous because no one knows how popular e-readers will be in the long run," says Matthews.

Another popular product over the last decade is the graphic novel, the fiction genre that combines comic book techniques with the longer, more complex structure of a novel. Graphic novels are especially popular among teens and college and university students. They have also received serious attention from the literary world. College and university courses are now taught around the graphic novel. And, each year, the American Library Association publishes a list of recommended graphic novels for teens. A firm like Secret Acres may be able to capitalize and succeed on a literary trend that continues to gain in popularity.

Matthews and Avelino haven't quit their day jobs yet. They know it will take some time before they can call themselves full-time publishers. But they love the comic book business and they are willing to wait for the good times they believe are ahead. "We have faith in the fact that if these books find the right audience, they'll do fine," says Avelino. "I'm OK with being patient. We need to keep going long enough to build a back list that is self-supporting." And Secret Acres already has a following among comic fans—their secret is out.

Questions for Critical Thinking

1. What steps can Matthews and Avelino take to create demand for their books? How does a small business like Secret Acres balance supply with demand?

2. How can Secret Acres make the most of an economy that is recovering slowly? What are the firm's pros and cons compared with a large publishing company?

3. How would you describe the Secret Acres' competition?

4. Do you think Secret Acres should pursue online distribution through e-readers and other delivery systems? Why or why not?

Sources: Secret Acres website, http://www.secretacres.com, accessed August 19, 2010; "Great Graphic Novels for Teens," Young Adult Library Services Association, http://www.ala.org/yalsa, accessed August 19, 2010; Harry McCracken, "E-Readers May Be Dead, But They're Not Going Away Yet," *PC World*, August 17, 2010, http://www.pcworld.com.

Smart Design: Life Is in the Details

When you peel a potato or use a pizza cutter, you probably don't think about the tool you are using unless it doesn't work right—if it sticks or snags, gouges the potato, or tears the pizza crust. The team at Smart Design doesn't mind not being noticed. They operate quietly behind the scenes, developing a wide range of designs for products made and sold by companies around the world. They come up with designs that make everything from toothbrushes to automobiles function better in human hands. Smart Design engineers developed the popular OXO Good Grips line of kitchen utensils and the SmartGauge instrument cluster for the Ford Fusion Hybrid.

"Smart Design is about designing products for people in their everyday life," explains Richard Whitehall, vice-president of industrial design for Smart Design. "There are little things you might see in a product that you'd think, 'I wish I'd thought of that—it's a great idea.'" Sometimes it's the simplest or smallest detail in the engineering of a product that leads consumers to continue using the product or to purchase it again. Smart Design tries to make universal products that work well for a wide range of people in different situations. And this is where the global challenge comes in—differences in cultural preferences, product use, language, and other factors can make universal product development difficult. But Smart Design has offices in both the United States and abroad. It has testing locations in Europe and Asia, and its employees represent more than 20 different countries.

Ted Booth, director of interactive design says, "Interactive design is anything with a 'chip' in it. I can't imagine approaching interactive design without a global perspective." Booth explains how Smart Design develops the design for a mobile phone. "The way people use it varies from country to country," he notes. "So what might look like a new feature in one country is really old hat in another." Booth says that it is very common for consumers in Finland and South Korea to pay for most goods and services from their mobile phones, but this is not yet a common practice for North American consumers. Some of this practice is driven by industry standards, but much of it has to do with cultural expectations. "It's important to have a global perspective [in design] so you know the trends in other countries. You need to design and shape the experience to hit the market and bring something new to the market, but also adapt to individual markets," concludes Booth.

Booth describes his company's work on the "Q" control for HP—a single navigation controller that can be used across all HP products, ranging from TV remotes to printers to cameras. Smart Design tested the Q control in the United States, Germany, Spain, and South Korea. Researchers discovered a few local changes were needed. And there was one universal preference among all consumers—everyone needed a "back" button. Booth explains that everyone needs know that there is an escape, undo—or back button—for every function so that users feel comfortable working through an interactive task.

Smart Design has an impressive list of worldwide clients, including Ford, Bell Canada, ESPN, World Kitchen, Microsoft, Samsung, and Kellogg's, among many others. The firm has won many honours, including nationally recognized design awards. But Smart Design remains focused on the details. For example, the firm recently developed the Reach Wondergrip children's toothbrush for Johnson & Johnson. Traditional children's toothbrushes were basically just scaled-down versions of the adult models. Kids couldn't hold them easily and so were less likely to brush their teeth. The new Wondergrip children's model changed the industry standard for children's toothbrushes—and children's brushing habits. Smart Design also developed a women's sports watch for Nike—based on the needs and preferences of women runners. And there's that line of kitchen tools that make food preparation and cooking just a little bit easier and more fun.

Richard Whitehall began his career working for a firm that manufactured mountaineering gear. He describes the importance of design in every product used by consumers. "We were trying to think of a situation people were in and trying to design a product in a way that people from different countries—whether they were stuck in the Alps or on a boat—could use in all these different situations." Whether you are climbing a mountain in Switzerland or cutting your pizza in Boston, you need your tools to work perfectly—and that is the goal of Smart Design.

Questions for Critical Thinking

1. Ted Booth and Richard Whitehall mention some of the cultural barriers that Smart Design faces in developing products for worldwide use. Give examples of other barriers the firm might face in international trade.

2. Describe what you believe would be the best level of involvement for Smart Design to have when doing business in Europe. Remember to consider the role of the European Union.

3. Smart Design already has a presence in South Korea. How might the firm best approach developing products for the market in India? In China?

4. Do you believe it is possible to develop truly universal products? Why or why not?

Sources: Smart Design website, http://www.smartdesignworldwide.com, accessed August 19, 2010; "National Design Awards," Cooper-Hewitt, National Design Museum, http://www.nationaldesignawards.org, accessed August 19, 2010; Alissa Walker, "Biomimicry Challenge: For IBM, Smart Design Draws Water Inspiration from Ecosystems," Fast Company.com, May 17, 2010, http://www.fastcompany.com.

Part 2 Starting and Growing Your Business

Comet Skateboards: It's a Smooth Ride

Jason Salfi loves skateboarding. And that is how many small businesses begin. The founder has a passion for something—whether it's cooking or surfing or creating video games—and decides to turn it into a business. For Salfi, it's skateboarding. The company, now in business for more than a decade, is Comet Skateboards. When Salfi graduated from Cornell University, he did what many recent graduates do—he headed west. He lived on a boat off the coast of California. He partnered with a friend and together they tinkered around with making skateboards, which they sold to other skateboard fans in their circle of friends. But Salfi wanted something more. He wanted to find a better way to make skateboards and a way to support his newly started family. "Back then, skateboards were made with seven layers of maple and sprayed with a lacquer-based coating," he recalls. "Skateboards were accounting for 35 to 40 percent of the natural maple being harvested each year." Salfi loved skateboarding, but he didn't like the way boards were made. He believed that a skateboard could be built with more environmentally sustainable processes and materials. "I wanted to start a company that would make an impression on people and build an awareness around the use of natural resources," Salfi says.

Not long after he launched Comet Skateboards, Salfi moved his company and his family back east to Ithaca, New York. There, he partnered with e2e Materials, a small start-up out of Cornell. The firm specializes in regionally sourced bio-composite materials; they manufacture their own soy-based resin and bio-composites that Salfi describes as "incredibly strong and biodegradable." The formula was exactly what Salfi was looking for. He set up shop and hired several employees, including Bob Rossi, now head of Web development for Comet and president of the Green Resource Hub, an organization that focuses on helping businesses to practise sustainability.

Rossi is impressed with Salfi's total commitment to finding the best way to make his products, even if it meant moving across the country. "To move your business into the opportunity, to create a greener product, that is pretty impressive to me . . . There's a lot of green-washing out there," says Rossi. He knows the difference. Comet goes much farther than simply purchasing e2e's materials; the firm has adopted a closed-loop manufacturing process, which means that it reduces or eliminates waste by examining the life cycle of all the materials used in its manufacturing process.

It might seem like Salfi and Rossi aren't cut from the same cloth as the previous generation of skateboarders—they're busy doing good things for the environment and for their community instead of rolling along the fringes of society like the original bad-boy image of skateboarding. But Salfi remains true to his skateboarding background (though Rossi admits to being new to the sport). Comet's boards have names like The Voodoo Doll and Shred City. They are built for specialists who prefer downhill, or freeriding. Riders are invited to contribute ideas for the shapes, graphics, and names of new boards. Comet has found a way to increase profit potential by using green materials. Its efforts have led to praise from both business bloggers and committed skateboarding bloggers. Salfi seems to have found a way to blend doing good with doing good business—in a sport that was once far from the mainstream.

Salfi hopes that Comet Skateboards will serve as an example of a small business that can make a big difference—while making products that provide fun. "We look at everything we do through the lens of how we can create a model that people can replicate in the future," he says. Salfi observes proudly that although Comet has only been in Ithaca for a few years, the company has a 100-percent retention rate of employees. He wants Comet to be a company that is known for its positive working environment, a place where people can develop long-term careers.

"We know that in the grand scheme of things, we're a small company, but through the many means of getting the message out—the Internet, video, music, and photography—we can actually have a broad footprint and make the idea of sustainability and social justice appealing to a broader market," predicts Salfi. While the bottom line—turning a profit—is vital to Comet's survival and growth, Salfi believes that this new way of doing business is more important in the long run. "We like to think we're creating a blueprint for the kind of company that will be around for 100 or 200 years," he muses. Then the skateboarder emerges. With a grin Salfi adds, "At the end of the day we're making skateboards, and we don't want to bum anybody out."

Questions for Critical Thinking

1. In which category, or categories, does Jason Salfi fit as an entrepreneur? Why? Give examples.

2. Salfi notes that the use of information technology—part of the environment for entrepreneurs—can help Comet Skateboards reach a broader audience. Can you identify

any population and economic trends that might provide opportunities for Comet Skateboard's growth as a business?

3. Which traditional characteristics of entrepreneurs best describe Jason Salfi? Why?

4. As Comet Skateboards reaches the next level of growth, where might the firm have the best chance of obtaining further financing? Why?

Sources: Comet Skateboards website, http://www.cometskateboards.com, accessed August 20, 2010; "GOOD Products," Halogen TV, http://www.halogentv.com, accessed August 20, 2010; Nadia Hosni, "Triple Bottom Line: Comet Skateboards," *Tonic*, April 27, 2010, http://www.tonic.com.

Part 3 Management: Empowering People to Achieve Business Goals

Dan Formosa: At the Forefront of Smart Design

Like many new businesses, Smart Design was founded by a group of college classmates who wanted to change something. Dan Formosa and several of his college friends had a background in design and ergonomics. The group believed that design should be about people, not things—and Smart Design was born. In the beginning, it was a hard sell—not the designs themselves, but the idea that the needs of individual people should be involved in the development of design. Formosa was interested in "how design can affect our quality of life, improve performance, and affect behaviour." The original Smart Design team "pulled together techniques in biomechanics and cognitive psychology," recalls Formosa. "This was a type of an approach that no other design group was undertaking in the U.S. at the time, so it was an early test of our beliefs about what and where design should be." Smart Design was successful throughout the 1980s, but Formosa admits that it was an uphill battle to convince clients that design was, indeed, for everyone.

Then came OXO. Around 1990, Smart Design acquired a new client, the manufacturing firm OXO. Formosa's team had a chance to re-invent the design of common household products, ranging from can openers to scissors. The result was the OXO Good Grips line of kitchen utensils. Because of the unexciting nature of these products—consumers weren't used to shopping for a potato peeler that actually felt comfortable in the hand—once the Good Grips tools caught on, the idea that everyday design is important began to take hold in the marketplace. Smart Design's client base grew significantly, as did the company. Firms such as Ford, ESPN, Samsung, Nike, and Microsoft began to ask for Smart Design's services, and the number of employees increased.

Managing a company of designers can be like trying to herd cats. Everyone has an idea, and everyone is running in a different direction. That means leadership is critical to the firm's success. Paulette Bluhm-Sauriol, director of brand communication, says that while most designers are detail oriented, "Someone has to make sure that the team is keeping the big picture in mind, not just the details." That's part of her job and Formosa's: keeping the overall vision. She also notes that, as a leader, Formosa has the natural gift of connecting and empathizing with people, whether it is employees or potential end-users of Smart Design's products. "Dan has the ability to make going into people's lives and becoming part of their lives comfortable," she observes.

This was particularly true during the development of a new type of pre-filled medical syringe that Smart Design undertook for UCB/OXO Cimzia. The medication Cimzia is a solution that relieves chronic pain in patients with certain conditions. Patients' lives could be improved if they could give themselves the solution in a comfortable way. When the pharmaceutical maker UCB and OXO partnered to develop the new product, they went to Smart Design for help. Formosa asked his team to go straight to the patients themselves to ask them what they needed. Designers met and observed patients in their own environment, giving them a chance to express their wishes. "It can be uncomfortable, but it's amazing how you can get to the big ideas by approaching the project his way," says Paulette Bluhm-Sauriol.

The syringe has met with marketplace success and has won an International Design Excellence Award. Most important, patients are getting what they need, which is exactly what Formosa strives for in each product his firm designs. "If someone buys a product or signs up for a service, they expect it to work. If you actually encounter a product or service that exceeds expectations, that is the sign of a great design," he says. Formosa also argues that the same principles that are applied to the design of a delicate hospital instrument can—and should—be applied to a pizza cutter. "Since our focus is designing for people, then that is the common ground," he asserts.

At Smart Design, the corporate culture supports the belief that the ideas of every employee are important. Regardless of job title, each person is considered a designer, who can contribute value to the process. Formosa doesn't mind the chaos of this kind of organization—it's how he operates. "When we have everybody thinking everything, it's a positive sign," he says. It's a formula that works.

Questions for Critical Thinking

1. Describe Dan Formosa's vision for Smart Design. Why do you think it took so long to gain popularity in the marketplace?

2. Identify Smart Design's strategy for competitive differentiation.

3. How would you describe Dan Formosa's leadership style? Do you think it is the best style for Smart Design? Why or why not?

4. Discuss Smart Design's corporate culture. Do you think it is effective for the kind of business the company engages in? Why or why not?

Sources: Smart Design website, http://www.smartdesignworldwide.com, accessed August 24, 2010; "Smart Design," National Design Awards, http://www.nationaldesignawards.org/2010, accessed August 19, 2010; Ralph Goldsworthy, "Dan Formosa of Smart Design, Designer Q&A," Design Droplets.com, April 28, 2010, http://designdroplets.com.

Seventh Generation Promotes Company Ownership

Common sense suggests that companies who treat their employees well—from fair compensation to dignity in the workplace—will attract and retain the best workers. But then the picture becomes a bit muddy. Traditional models of human resource management are being re-evaluated and sometimes tossed out by firms whose goals and values don't fit with these models. Seventh Generation is one of those companies. "When we win an award for being one of the best places to work in America, that to me is the most important award we can win because it's the hardest thing we do," says co-founder Jeffrey Hollender.

Seventh Generation was founded on the principle of sustainability—that every product it manufactures, whether laundry detergent or paper towels, must be designed and produced in a way that it leaves little or no impact on the environment. Sustainability also applies to how Seventh Generation recruits and develops its human resources over the long term.

Most of the 100-plus employees at Seventh Generation have had at least some experience with another employer. Hollender points out that these employees arrive at Seventh Generation with all of the relationship patterns, values, and attitudes toward work they have learned elsewhere. "Most businesses teach us not to have a voice, not to speak up, not to challenge authority, not to unleash the maximum potential we have as individuals," he says. But Seventh Generation is different. It adds a different set of values into its organizational culture, "the responsibility at Seventh Generation is to unteach people all of those habits and patterns, and unleash the potential that all of those other businesses have stifled," Hollender asserts.

Stephanie Lowe works in human resources at Seventh Generation. When she was hired, the company had only 30 employees—it now has more than 100. The increase in employees has presented a challenge. Not only have people arrived from other firms with a variety of experience and expectations, the logistics of managing 100 employees are different from managing 30. "We can't do things as casually," says Lowe with some regret. "Things just wouldn't get done. It's a hard line to walk, and it's a challenge." In addition, the core value of sustainability is built into every decision the firm makes. "How do you do compensation in a socially responsible company?" asks Lowe. "How do you do that in a company that values different things, where people are asked to value themselves and bring more of themselves to work?"

Seventh Generation's answer to the compensation versus social responsibility and sustainability question is ownership. Every person who works at Seventh Generation has a financial stake in the company. "The most significant way Seventh Generation's philosophy translates into HR [human resources] is ownership," remarks Hollender. He points out that a firm can give employees health insurance, time off, grants for the purchase of hybrid vehicles, on-site fitness centres, and other benefits; but none of these will translate to the benefit of ownership. "The most important thing is to let the people who are creating value by building the business participate in the value they create," Hollender asserts.

Stephanie Lowe echoes this philosophy. "We aren't trying to distinguish between the employees and the corporation," she explains. At Seventh Generation, the people are the company. Employees participate in company ownership. They are viewed as contributors in ways that reach outside their job descriptions. "We are shifting away from traditional performance management to personal development plans," says Lowe. "We do look at what employees need to work on to hit company goals, but also what each person needs to grow personally—and we let them define that." Employees write personal initiatives that help the company to see the talents and potential that may not be obvious during the performance of a particular job. "It's based on the concept that you measure what you value," explains Lowe. "We value volunteer time, making a difference in the world, raising more responsible global citizens." To that end, Seventh Generation encourages employees at every level to speak out with ideas for more sustainable products and processes.

When speaking about the Seventh Generation workforce, Hollender sounds more like a tribal elder than a business manager. But maybe there's a reason for that. Seventh Generation's mission is based on the Great Law of the Iroquois, which counsels each tribe member to consider the impact of all decisions on the next seven generations. "The thing I'm most proud of is the success of our employees at Seventh Generation," boasts Hollender, "their growth, the things they have thought of that I would never have dreamed of, the tough questions that they ask me that I wouldn't ask myself. Unleashing that potential—that is the most magical thing about running a business."

Questions for Critical Thinking

1. Visit the Seventh Generation website at http://www.seventhgeneration.com and view the current job listings there. What qualities does the firm look for in job candidates? How do these qualities differ from the qualities other companies look for?

2. What might be the potential pros and cons of Seventh Generation's view of performance and compensation?

3. Choose one of the motivational theories described in the textbook. Discuss how the theory applies to Seventh Generation's approach to motivating employees.

4. Do you think employees at Seventh Generation will try to unionize? Why or why not? If they did, how do you think the firm would respond?

Sources: Seventh Generation website, http://www.seventhgeneration.com, accessed August 21, 2010; "Sustainability Study," Accenture, http://microsite.accenture.com, accessed August 21, 2010; "Study Says Companies Should Train Managers in Sustainability," 7GenBlog, July 2, 2010, http://www.seventhgeneration.com; Danielle Sacks, "Jeffrey Hollender: Seventh Generation, Triple Bottom Line Entrepreneur," Fast Company.com, February 2, 2010, http://www.fastcompany.com.

Part 4 Marketing Management

Secret Acres: Getting the Word Out

No matter how powerful they are, comic book heroes can't do everything. They still need a little help to get themselves into bookstores—and readers' hands. Leon Avelino and Barry Matthews, co-founders of Secret Acres, know that one of the greatest challenges of publishing is getting books onto the shelves and then into readers' shopping carts. The task is even more difficult for small publishers—in this case, small publishers of comic books and graphic novels. They just don't have the wide distribution network of major publishers. But Avelino and Matthews are fearless.

And their authors think of them as the superheroes of comic book publishing. They know what they are trying to achieve and work hard to make it happen.

"Distribution is a difficult thing right now," admits Matthews. "The publishing industry is changing and comic books themselves have a different distribution methodology and wholesale methodology than traditional books do." For example, conventional bookstores receive a small discount when they purchase books from a publisher, but then have the option to return any unsold books to the publisher. But comic book shops do not operate on a return basis. Comic book shops take a deeper discount but make no returns. Matthews also notes there is only one major distributor of comic books—Diamond Distributors—which has the influence to dictate much of what happens in the business of comic book distribution. Matthews says that Secret Acres' graphic novels could easily be sold to the general book market, but many general book distributors don't want to deal with smaller publishers because they simply don't produce enough books to be profitable.

Matthews explains that he and Avelino are learning alternative ways to distribute their books. "Amazon is great," he says. "They make it very easy for smaller publishers. They treat your books as if they are Amazon books, giving them the sheen of being part of a larger retail channel." Amazon does take a big cut of sales, but Matthews says it's worth it to broaden the distribution of Secret Acres products. Of course, Secret Acres also sells its entire line directly through its website at http://www.secretacres.com, where it also sells books from other independent authors and publishers. This sales method is the most profitable for Secret Acres. It also allows Matthews and Avelino to keep closer tabs on their readers. Because orders are filled on an individual basis, when Matthews recognizes a customer's name and knows that person's preferences, he can add promotional materials, notices of upcoming events or new books, and tie-ins right into the delivery package. This one-on-one interaction helps Secret Acres manage its customer relationships.

Matthews and Avelino also enjoy one other form of distribution—selling at comic book conventions around the country, such as the Stumptown Comics Fest in Portland, Oregon. There, they can interact with readers, other publishers, comic book authors and artists, and even some smaller distributors. Readers, in particular, love to meet the authors and artists. "It feeds the interest in what we're doing," says Matthews. While at an event, Matthews and Avelino try to find time to meet with other small publishers. "A lot of small publishers are in the same position" in terms of distribution, Matthews explains. "So we have been talking with them to see if we can band together to share resources."

For the future, Matthews admits that he and Avelino have no idea how some of the new technologies, including e-readers, will affect their distribution, but they plan to research the possibility of digitizing some of Secret Acres' titles for online distribution.

Despite the company's small size, Secret Acres' authors consider the firm to be mighty. Theo Ellsworth, author of such titles as *Capacity* and *Sleeper Car*, praises Secret Acres for its personal attention and its efforts to market and distribute his books. "It feels good to have the distribution part in someone else's hands," says Ellsworth. He explains that having someone else take care of that aspect of publishing frees him up to concentrate on his art, producing more posters and books—which is, after all, the author's job.

Questions for Critical Thinking

1. Visit Secret Acres' website at http://www.secretacres.com to learn more about the firm's product line. Write a marketing piece describing the product line to a potential distributor.

2. What steps can Secret Acres take to develop brand loyalty and, ultimately, brand equity for its products?

3. How might Secret Acres expand its Internet retailing presence?

4. Secret Acres is a tiny firm with limited distribution. How can the company use customer service to create a competitive advantage, increase distribution, and help it grow?

Sources: Secret Acres website, http://www.secretacres.com, accessed August 25, 2010; Stumptown Comics Fest, http://www.stumptowncomics.com, accessed August 25, 2010; "Great Graphic Novels for Teens," Young Adult Library Services Association, http://www.ala.org/yalsa, accessed August 19, 2010; Harry McCracken, "E-Readers May Be Dead, But They're Not Going Away Yet," *PC World*, August 17, 2010, http://www.pcworld.com.

Pet Airways Handles Pets with Loving Care

Pet owners want the best for their dogs and cats, as shown by the $50-billion pet industry in the United States, including everything from grooming services to squeaky toys. One area that has received little attention is travel. Although owners can find lodging that allows pets, and they can purchase travel carriers and gear, until recently, they had very little choice when it came to transport. If the animal had to travel long distance, it was kept in the cargo hold of a plane. A couple of years ago, all that changed when Dan Wiesel and Alysa Binder wanted to be able to transport their Jack Russell terrier safely and comfortably. So they started a pet transport business called Pet Airways.

"There are 80 million pets traveling around the U.S.," says Alysa Binder. "There's definitely a market for this. We're part of the pet community—we understand." Wiesel and Binder contracted with a firm that flies Beechcraft 1900 aircraft, selecting this plane for its versatility and safety record. They had the planes retrofitted to accommodate pet carriers in the main cabin. They launched their reservation system online and spread the word via social media. When traditional media heard of the new company, Wiesel and Binder appeared on such television shows as *Good Morning America* and *The Today Show*, and in magazines and newspapers. Because of this publicity, Pet Airways has spent nothing on advertising. Its greatest marketing challenge has been educating the public about its service. "Because we're the first to market, we have to tell people what we're all about," explains Binder.

Pet owners who want to book their animals on a Pet Airways flight make a reservation on the airline's website, http://www.petairways.com. One hour before departure, owners check in at the Pet Lounge. Pet passengers are boarded in their carriers, attended to by professional pet attendants who travel with the animals, checking on them every 15 minutes to ensure they are secure and comfortable. Once the plane has landed, owners (or designated recipients) collect their pets in the Pet Lounge.

Pet Airways currently operates flights to nine cities around the United States. Alysa Binder says the firm's goal is to reach 20 cities in the next 18 months. She notes that customers are willing and eager to pay for the service, considering it reasonable compared with the costs of using traditional airlines.

Pet Airways fares start at $149. By comparison, American Airlines charges $100 for a pet to travel beneath a seat and $150 for it to travel as baggage; Delta charges $150 and $275, respectively; and Northwest charges $150 and $225, respectively. Binder says that her customers don't usually consider price anyway because "we aren't the same as general carriers. It's a completely different service. People know that."

Pet Airways customers can register to receive the company's newsletter, which includes insider news on special flight deals and other promotions. They can join the MyPAWS Club, which offers a 40 percent discount on pet supplies at the Pet Airways online store, a 10 percent discount at pet-friendly hotels, 10 percent off at 1-800-PetMeds, 5 percent off on pet health insurance from Pets Best Insurance, and discounts and free samples from other Pet Airways partners.

Wiesel and Binder saw an opportunity in the marketplace and jumped at the chance to offer a safe, reliable solution for pet owners to transport their pets. "On Pet Airways, your pets aren't packages, they're passengers."

Questions for Critical Thinking

1. At this stage of Pet Airway's life cycle, what should the company have as its main promotional objectives? Why?

2. Pet Airways has not yet used any major advertising. Which media would probably be most effective at reaching the firm's intended market? Why?

3. Pet Airways already offers some consumer-oriented promotions. Describe or outline an idea for a new promotion and explain your choice.

4. Outline Pet Airways' pricing objectives. How might these change over the next five years? Ten years? What is the best pricing strategy for Pet Airways? Why?

Sources: Pet Airways website, http://www.petairways.com, accessed August 25, 2010; "Pet Airways Combines with a Public Company Through Share Exchange with American Antiquities," *PR Newswire*, August 16, 2010, http://www.prnewswire.com; "Doctors Call for Airline Pet Ban," *The Independent*, February 21, 2010, http://license.icopyright.net;" "Bone Voyage as Pets Get Airline," *BBC News*, April 17, 2009, http://news.bbc.co.uk.

Part 5 Managing Technology and Information

Zipcar: Technology Fuels Its Business

When you need a car, you want one. When you don't need a car, you don't want to be bothered with the trouble or the expense. That's what makes Zipcar so great. Zipcar is a car-sharing network based in Cambridge, Massachusetts. It operates in urban and metropolitan areas and on university campuses around the United States, Canada, and the United Kingdom. Currently, Zipcar serves more than 200 colleges and universities, and the number is growing steadily. "The service provides a new level of freedom for students, faculty, and staff," says Matthew Malloy, vice-president of international university operations for Zipcar. "Members can use Zipcars to run errands, attend meetings, or get away for the weekend on a pay-as-you-go basis. You no longer need to own to be free."

Once members sign up for the program, they receive a Zipcard that gives them access to any Zipcar parked around campus (or around town). The annual fee for the service is $35, and it includes fuel, insurance, and 180 travel miles (nearly 300 km) per day. A member who wants to use a Zipcar simply goes online to reserve it, then picks up the designated car at the reserved time. "It's easy," says Erin Badger, a senior marketing student at the University of New Hampshire, where the Zipcar program is now in full swing. "You swipe your Zipcard [over a sensor] on the windshield and it unlocks the car. You get in, turn the key, and go." Each Zipcar comes equipped with an individually numbered Zipcard gas card that the driver uses to fill the tank with fuel. So members—including budget-conscious students—don't need cash or their own credit cards when the gas gauge runs low. Members are asked to return each car with at least one-quarter of a tank of gas in it, so no one picks up a car with an empty tank.

Technology plays a huge role in the success of the Zipcar system. "When you think about the member experience, what makes it a seamless and enjoyable experience for the consumer is the technology infrastructure," observes Rob Weisberg, chief marketing officer at Zipcar. When marketing and setting up the system at colleges and universities, Zipcar looks at how students use cars on campus, asking such questions as: Are there places on campus where use is more frequent, or do students want hybrids? "Any time you understand your consumers better, you are able to cater to them more effectively," says Weisberg. He notes that Zipcar puts a lot of effort into understanding the demographic (population-based) and psychographic (life style) trends on and around a campus.

Erin Badger likes that she can use her iPhone app to reserve a Zipcar or extend the reservation if she is driving a car and isn't ready to return it. "The iPhone app relates to the student age group," she says. "They care about us." The Zipcar app was named to *Time* magazine's annual list of "Best Travel Gadgets," "Beyond helping you manage reservations, find nearby pickup locations and browse car models available, the app offers clever capabilities like remote locking and unlocking and honking your car's horn from your phone when you inevitably forget what it looks like in a crowded lot," praises the *Time* review.

Zipcar is always looking toward the future and for ways to better serve its customers. Rob Weisberg predicts that Zipcar technology will someday offer customized seat settings and even pre-set radio station settings that automatically click into place when a member reserves a car. Still, Weisberg highlights the importance of the personal touch. He recalls a student member who posted a note on Twitter joking that he loved everything about Zipcar except that there wasn't a package of Skittles waiting for him when he unlocked the car. So the next time that student reserved a car, a Zipcar employee left a package of Skittles on the dashboard.

"Technology will never replace human interaction," warns Weisberg. "You'd never take the recommendation of a computer over the recommendation of a friend or family member or colleague. So our laser focus on the customer experience and ensuring that it is second to none is really where we need to play. Technology enables that, but it's never going to replace the human touch."

Questions for Critical Thinking

1. Through member surveys and social media postings, Zipcar collects information about members and their lifestyles to design the best system for a community. Write 10 questions that might lead to useful information for Zipcar about students at your own college or university.

2. What kind of data would Zipcar's operational support systems likely collect? What kind of information might they provide?

3. The Zipcar iPhone app already takes care of several tasks. If you were a Zipcar member, what new task would you add to the app?

4. Do you think your campus would be a good candidate for the Zipcar system? Why or why not? If your college or university already has Zipcar, are you a member? Why or why not?

Sources: Zipcar website, http://www.zipcar.com, accessed August 26, 2010; "Zipcar and SCVNGR, East Cambridge Neighbors, Partner on New Rewards Program," Boston.com, August 26, 2010, http://www.boston.com; "Zipcar, Inc.," *Bloomberg Business Week*, http://investing.businessweek.com, accessed August 24, 2010; University of New Hampshire Transportation Services, http://www.unh.edu/transportation, accessed August 24, 2010; Peter Ha, "The Best Travel Gadgets of 2009," *Time*, November 2, 2009, http://www.time.com.

Part 6 Managing Financial Resources

Pet Airways Is a "Feel-Good" Business

It's great to love the business you're in. Just ask Alysa Binder and Dan Wiesel, co-founders of Pet Airways. They love their business, and they also care for their customers, who happen to be furry and four-legged. But Pet Airways, the only service devoted entirely to transporting cats and dogs around the country by air, is also a business. That means that Binder and Wiesel must pay attention to the financial aspects of their company. "We're doing something that's a feel-good, do-good service and it's absolutely rewarding," says Dan Wiesel. But Wiesel knows that, without a thorough accounting of finances, any small business can crash shortly after takeoff.

Binder and Wiesel started Pet Airways based on their personal experiences—they wanted a better, safer travel option for their Jack Russell terrier than having to travel in the cargo hold. The cargo hold's fluctuating temperatures and dark, cramped quarters make a trip on a commercial airline both unsafe and distressing for many animals. Binder and Wiesel both have backgrounds in business. They decided they could do a better job than the passenger airlines and decided to offer pet owners a choice.

As soon as they agreed on their business idea, Wiesel jumped into the financial questions. "I had to ask, 'Is this a viable financial enterprise? What would people pay for a service like this?'" He researched such issues as the cost to retrofit the climate-controlled cabin of a plane to carry animals, the cost to fly a plane from one location to another, and the cost to staff the company. He also researched the demand for a pet airline, and how many pets would need to be booked on each flight for the trip to be profitable. He put all of these variables—and more—onto a spreadsheet so he could see what he and Binder needed to do for Pet Airways to take off.

Wiesel says that financial modelling, financial spreadsheets, and good research on costs and pricing can make or break any small business. "Accounting itself is an absolute full-time, big job," he admits. He wants to "know how much money is coming in, how much is going out, and what's the bottom line." In addition, someone needs to deal with taxes, payroll, benefits, and other financial documentation. Wiesel advises that, in many cases, it's a good idea for small businesses to contract out their accounting to professionals. He prefers this option because outsourcing actually is a deductible expense like any other and allows the small business owner to focus attention on things he or she can do more efficiently.

Running a business is a balancing act, says Wiesel. "You have to be able to reconcile how much cash you have with how you are going to spend it." For example, as Pet Airways looks to expand to more cities, the firm needs to look at the cost of adding more flights and more staff compared with how many more customers those changes might attract. Binder points out that, although it's exciting to dream about growing, they have to think about the costs of everything from additional hiring to developing a more sophisticated website and online reservation system.

All of this leads to the need for a sound financial plan, says Wiesel. "The financial plan is really the core of it because you can play the 'what if' game. You can look at the implications of certain decisions." For example, if Binder and Wiesel want to fly to a certain city, they can research which passenger airlines already serve that city. If it's United Airlines, they know that pet owners will be charged $175 for an animal to fly beneath a passenger's seat, or $250 to fly in the cargo hold. They can look at how many flights a day these airlines fly to the city, and they can probably learn how many pets are booked. And they can look at which terminal Pet Airways would use and the costs of any airport taxes and fees. They can enter all this data into the financial plan and see how it works, before making the final decision.

Binder and Wiesel usually agree on their company's goals and objectives. Wiesel says it all boils down to one question: "What's it going to cost you to achieve your plan?" Recently, Pet Airways announced its merger with the firm American Antiquities in a share-exchange agreement, a major step toward expansion. "We are delighted to complete this transaction … and believe this event represents a significant step in implementing our business plan and continued expansion," stated Wiesel.

Questions for Critical Thinking

1. In Pet Airways' accounting equation, what might be some of the firm's liabilities? What might be some of its assets?

2. Identify the types of costs that Pet Airways might list on its income statement.

3. Why is it important for a small company like Pet Airways to prepare a regular budget?

4. If Pet Airways decides to expand its operations overseas, what kinds of accounting issues would the firm need to consider?

Sources: Pet Airways website, http://www.petairways.com, accessed August 25, 2010; "Pet Airways Combines with a Public Company through Share Exchange with American Antiquities," *PR Newswire*, August 16, 2010, http://www.prnewswire.com; "Doctors Call for Airline Pet Ban," *The Independent*, February 21, 2010, http://license.icopyright.net.

New Harvest Coffee Goes Beyond Fair Trade

"Fair trade has always been part of my legacy in coffee," says Rik Kleinfeldt, president and co-founder of New Harvest Coffee Roasters. "That's where I started with New Harvest." But in less than a decade, New Harvest's business model has grown beyond fair trade to something different.

New Harvest is a small-batch coffee roaster specializing in certified organic coffee that is grown and harvested by farms that use sustainable practices. Kleinfeldt notes that he built his company on two pillars: the highest quality coffee, and sustainable sourcing practices. "But these two weren't really gelling at first," he admits. At the beginning, Kleinfeldt tried to source from fair trade cooperatives, but this approach didn't really fulfill his objective. "Fair trade is based on the commodity system," Kleinfeldt explains, "which creates a floor price at which coffee can't drop below. But it does not really address the issue of quality." The groups that work with fair trade are large co-operatives, sometimes taking in several thousand small farms. All the coffee is blended together as a commodity, so it is impossible for a roaster like New Harvest to deal directly with each farm, to select the specific harvest that it wants to buy.

Kleinfeldt is quick to point out that when fair trade began around a decade ago, it was a lifeline to small farmers because coffee prices were at an all-time low—the growers were selling their crops for less than it cost to produce them. Without fair trade, many of these farms would have gone out of business. Now that the coffee market is a bit more stable, commodity pricing leads its own set of problems. "The commodity pricing usually has nothing to do with the coffee itself," says Kleinfeldt. Prices are set at the New York Stock Exchange, not in the growing fields of Costa Rica or Colombia. He notes that roasters, retailers, and consumers may pay way too much or way too little for a particular year's crop.

Kleinfeldt has become part of what he calls the artisan coffee movement—growers, roasters, and retailers who prefer to deal directly with each other as individual businesses. "We connect directly with our growers and determine price based on quality," he explains. Kleinfeldt and his staff, along with some of his retailers, such as the owner of Blue State Coffee and the owner of Pejamajo Café, travel to coffee farms in Costa Rica and Colombia. There, they taste the coffee before purchasing a crop. Kleinfeldt believes that this approach is the only way to get the best coffee on the market. These visits help develop strong relationships, find solutions to problems, and develop strategies for surviving and thriving as businesses. Through visiting, he says, "we can understand their challenges." At one farm in Colombia, the farmer decided he didn't want to be part of a large fair trade co-operative—instead, he wanted to develop a market for his own coffee. He approached New Harvest with the idea, and New Harvest agreed. This farmer is now one of New Harvest's premier growers.

Sourcing the coffee beans directly from individual farms also helps New Harvest keep close track of organic and sustainability practices. Gerra Harrigan, director of business development for New Harvest Coffee Roasters, notes that tracking organic and sustainability practices is an important part of the firm's business. The owners of local coffee shops—and their customers—like knowing that New Harvest stands behind all of its claims. Harrigan takes the hands-on approach. "When we deal direct-trade coffee, the coffee has to be cared for a little more," she explains. Harrigan grades the coffee on several factors before pricing it for New Harvest.

Kleinfeldt wants consumers to know they are getting a great deal when they ask for New Harvest at their local shop. He points out that the price difference is not as much as people might think. A visit to the supermarket shows that Starbucks and Green Mountain sell for about $9 to $11 per pound ($4 to $5 per kg), whereas most New Harvest coffee sells for about $11 to $13 a pound ($5 to $6 per kg). Because of the richness of New Harvest coffees, most customers actually get more cups of coffee from New Harvest than they do from the other premium brands.

Kleinfeldt hopes that the artisan coffee movement, as he refers to his company's practices, will flourish and grow. He believes that if you're going to drink a cup of coffee, it should be really fresh and of the highest quality—with beans preferably roasted by New Harvest.

Questions for Critical Thinking

1. What are the pros and cons of treating coffee as a commodity in the marketplace? What do you predict will be the future of fair trade?

2. Should the entire coffee market be regulated in any way? Why or why not? If so, how?

3. How would New Harvest change as a business if it made an initial public offering (IPO)?

4. What is your opinion of the so-called artisan coffee movement as a business model? Do you think it will be successful in the long run? Why or why not?

Sources: New Harvest Coffee Roasters website, http://www.newharvestcoffee.com, accessed August 18, 2010; "New Harvest Coffee Roasters," *GreenPeople*, http://www.greenpeople.org, accessed August 29, 2010; Richard Garcia, "Pejamajo Café & New Harvest Coffee Roasters," *Chefs Daily Food Bank*, May 4, 2010, http://www.chefsdailyfoodbank.com.

Comet Skateboards Rides the Triple Bottom Line

Jason Salfi, co-founder and president of Comet Skateboards, is the first to admit he can let the wheels get away from him. Since the launch of Comet Skateboards, he estimates that he has personally "tanked the company four times. I started the company with a friend and we would sacrifice everything for quality," Salfi admits. It's easy to see how this could happen. Salfi loves skateboarding. He's also a fanatic about building the best skateboards on the market with the most sustainable materials available.

During the first years of production, Salfi and his partner paid top dollar for all the materials they used in building the boards. "We weren't really watching how much money we were making," Salfi says sheepishly. They were so wrapped up in the excitement of developing and manufacturing an entirely new class of skateboard, they forgot to watch the bank account balance. Salfi recalls that they did all the usual things that small start-ups do to obtain financing—maxed out their credit cards, got friends and family to co-sign loans, and found angel investors. But Comet Skateboards just seemed to roll through the money without enough return to ensure its survival.

Then the firm hired a manager to specialize in financial details. With a professional in place, Salfi began to understand the real and potential effect of certain buying decisions on the bottom line, and the way cash flow could affect getting products to the marketplace. Now, Comet can forecast better how a product release will affect cash flow, and how that cash flow, in turn, will affect the way the business can reach customers. "Ultimately we're trying to create a sustainable business platform to get our sustainable business vision out there in the marketplace," explains Salfi. But they couldn't do this without managing the company's financial resources.

Comet Skateboards is considered a triple-bottom-line company, carrying the B Corporation logo. This means that Comet strives to create benefit for the company owners (profit), the community (people), and the environment (planet). Currently, there are more than 500 B Corporations in 60 industries. Each company has gone through thorough evaluation and has put written standards in place to address social and environmental responsibility. Everything that Comet does, from its closed-loop manufacturing process to its community involvement, refers to its triple-bottom-line commitment.

Jason Salfi insists that managing the finances for a triple-bottom-line company is pretty much the same as managing the finances for a traditional company. But there are some differences, especially when sourcing raw materials, energy use, and waste disposal. Triple-bottom-line companies are held accountable for the way they treat employees and how they are involved in the community. "The 'magic' is making sure we can afford all that," observes Salfi. "It's just a matter of prioritization. We're not going on $50,000 golf retreats. We're reinvesting the capital we have in the materials we use and the way we interact with people."

Although Salfi didn't pay attention to finances in the company's early days, he now has a good grasp on Comet's role in the larger economic picture. He likes the idea of projecting the impact Comet has on consumers' buying decisions, particularly young people. Teenagers who choose Comet skateboards are choosing products that are made by a triple-bottom-line firm. "If you look at the way a 14-year-old decides to buy things for the rest of his or her life, and you look at the number of decisions that young person is going to make over the span of 50 or 60 years, you could extrapolate that we have impacted 1,000 people in a certain way that could eventually transfer billions of dollars toward socially responsible businesses," explains Salfi. "We're influencing the buying decisions of youth."

Salfi believes that, decades ago, "commerce used to be about improving the quality of life, but somewhere along the line, profits skewed motivations." He likes the idea of the triple-bottom-line rebalancing the priorities of business. "We like to think that as a B Corporation, we are part of a group that wants to bring back the original motivation for business, which was all about creating an improved quality of life for everyone, not just a select few." It might actually be possible for a few well-engineered skateboards to change the world.

Questions for Critical Thinking

1. Hiring a financial manager was a major step for Comet Skateboards. Identify some of the factors the manager would need to consider when creating a plan for risk-return trade-off.

2. What might be some short-term funding options for Comet? Some long-term options? Which would be best for this company, and why?

3. Suppose a larger firm approached Comet with an offer of acquisition. Create a chart outlining the major pros and cons of such an offer.

4. How might Comet's designation as a B Corporation affect the way it answers the three essential questions for building a financial plan?

Sources: Comet Skateboards website, http://cometskateboards.com, accessed August 20, 2010; "GOOD Products," *Halogen TV*, http://www.halogentv.com, accessed August 20, 2010; Nadia Hosni, "Triple Bottom Line: Comet Skateboards," *Tonic*, April 27, 2010, http://www.tonic.com.

Access your WileyPLUS course for:

- The complete digital textbook.

- Question assistance, including links to relevant sections in the online digital textbook.

- Immediate feedback and proof of progress, 24/7

- Integrated, multi-media resources – including MP3 downloads, visual exhibits, animations, and much more – that provide multiple study paths and encourage more active learning.

APPENDIX C
BUSINESS LAW

Apple's iPhone: Don't Touch the Patents!

Smartphone users knew right away they really liked the iPhone. And the iPhone quickly grabbed a big chunk of the cellphone market. The innovative device also led to a long line of imitators. The iPhone has many ground-breaking features. Apple either already has the patents to protect those features or is in the process of filing those patents. A patent gives an inventor exclusive rights to an invention for a period of time.

Several years ago, Apple applied for a patent for the iPhone's multi-function touchscreen. The United States Patent and Trademark Office recently granted Apple patent number 7,479,949. This patent covers the touchscreen and the technology behind the phone's hardware and some of its software, including its operating system and some of its phone and camera functions. But patent protection doesn't mean that Apple is protected from lawsuits. Since the iPhone was launched, Apple has been the target of patent infringement lawsuits by other firms. The lawsuits include claims that Apple copied multi-touch technology, visual-voice technology, and digital-camera and imaging technology. The biggest suit so far has come from Nokia, the world's largest manufacturer of mobile phones. Nokia says that Apple has infringed on 10 of its patents related to wireless handsets. But Apple has countersued Nokia, claiming that Nokia is infringing upon 13 of Apple's patents.

Do these lawsuits sound childish to the average consumer? Maybe. But the technology industry is very complex. Innovations happen so fast that it can be hard to know who came up with an idea first—and at what stage of development an idea should be considered proprietary, or under the ownership of its inventor. Patents take a long time to process, and patent infringement cases can take even longer. Many firms are turning to the U.S. International Trade Commission (ITC) instead of other courts and agencies because the ITC can move these cases along more quickly. But because these cases often involve more than two companies, they can become a tangled web of suits and countersuits.

Apple recently sued the Taiwanese mobile phone manufacturer HTC for infringement of 20 Apple patents relating to the iPhone, mostly patents related to iPhone's graphical user interface. Apple was seeking a permanent injunction that would ban HTC from selling its phones in the United States. "We can sit by and watch competitors steal our patented inventions, or we can do something about it," said Steve Jobs, Apple's co-founder and CEO at the time. "We think competition is healthy, but competitors should create their own original technology, not steal ours."

HTC claimed that it was completely surprised by Apple's lawsuit. "HTC is a mobile-technology innovator and patent holder that has been very focused over the past 13 years on creating many of the most innovative smartphones," said a company spokesperson in response to the suit. "HTC values patent rights and their enforcement, but is also committed to defending its own technology innovations."

Some business law experts find it interesting that Apple did not name software makers Google or Microsoft in its legal action against HTC, which makes such popular phones as the Nexus One. The Nexus One is sold by Google, and several other phones named in the suit use Microsoft's Windows Mobile software.

And in case you thought that things are different in Canada, consider Research In Motion's (RIM's) lawsuit against Ted Livingston and his company, Kik Interactive Inc. Livingston was accused of using proprietary software knowledge gained while he was a student at the University of Waterloo and while he was employed at RIM. Livingston's comment on his blog speaks volumes about the hurt feelings and assumptions made at one's own risk:

> RIM **sued us yesterday. A courier came to drop off a package. I opened up the letter to see a stack of papers with a big gold seal on the first page. Plaintiff: Research In Motion Inc. The company I worked for as a co-op student. The company I loved. The company I thought could benefit from Kik's vision of a mobile community. The company that placed Kik on BlackBerry App World without issue. The company I shared our entire plan with every step of the way, is suing us. I'm not afraid. I'm not surprised. But I am disappointed.**

These cases highlight the importance of every businessperson understanding the basics of business law. It doesn't matter whether you plan to market high-tech devices such as smartphones or sell a simple pair of shoes online—as a businessperson, you will need to know the laws that govern your business activities.[1]

APPENDIX C OVERVIEW

Legal issues affect every part of business. Despite the best efforts of most businesspeople, legal cases are filed against businesses. A disagreement may happen over a contract, an employee may protest being passed over for a promotion, or a town may challenge the environmental impact of a new gas station. Unfortunately, the United States is known as the world's most litigious society because of what seems like an unreasonable fondness for filing lawsuits. Canadian businesses are often participants because of their involvement in the American economy. In the United States, lawsuits are as common as business deals. Consider Walmart, which is involved in as many as 7,000 legal cases at any one time. Even if you are never personally involved in a lawsuit, the cost of these legal actions will still affect you. It is estimated that the average U.S. family pays a hidden "litigation tax" of 5 percent each year because the costs of lawsuits force businesses to increase their prices. Small businesses, such as dentists' offices, doctors' offices, and daycare providers, are often the hardest hit. They may cut back on their services or be forced to close. These problems are as much a Canadian concern as they are American because of the high level of business exchange that takes place across our common border. A Canadian businessperson needs to appreciate both the legal similarities and differences between Canada and the United States.[2]

Legislation that specifically affects business functions is analyzed in each chapter of this book. Chapter 2 presents an overview of the legal environment. Legislation affecting international operations is covered in Chapter 4. Chapter 5 discusses laws related to small businesses. Laws regarding human resource management and labour unions are examined in Chapter 8. Laws affecting other business operations, such as environmental regulations and product safety, are discussed in Chapter 12. Marketing-related legislation is examined in Chapter 13. Finally, legislation relating to banking and the securities markets is discussed in Chapters 16 and 17.

In this appendix, we provide a general overview of legislation at the federal, provincial, and local levels. We point out that, although business executives may not be legal experts, they do need to be knowledgeable in their specific area of responsibility. Some common sense also helps to avoid potential legal problems. This appendix looks at the general nature of business law, the court system, basic legal concepts, and the changing regulatory environment for business. Let's start with some initial definitions and related examples.

LEGAL SYSTEM AND ADMINISTRATIVE AGENCIES

The **judiciary**, or court system, is the branch of government responsible for applying laws to settle disagreements between two or more parties. This court system consists of several types and levels of courts, each with a specific jurisdiction, or area of responsibility. Court systems are organized at the federal, provincial, and local levels. Administrative agencies, such as the Canadian Radio-television and Telecommunications Commission (CRTC), also perform some limited judicial functions, but administrative agencies are more properly viewed as regulatory branches of government.

Canada's court system is divided between the federal and provincial legislatures. Generally, the federal government has exclusive powers over areas that concern the entire country, including criminal law, defence, currency, and telecommunications. The provinces rule mainly on civil matters such as property law. The provinces may empower municipal governments to pass local laws. Both the federal and provincial courts hear civil and criminal cases.

The Supreme Court of Canada will hear only lower-level appeal court cases that they select. These cases are chosen on the basis of their perceived importance to the entire country. Generally speaking, each province has a similar court structure with a *provincial court* level and a *superior court* level. Provincial courts deal with minor criminal and civil cases. The superior courts, which include trial and appeal courts, will generally deal with more serious matters, including murder. There are also several specialized courts, such as *tax court*.

judiciary the branch of government that is responsible for applying laws to settle disagreements; also known as the court system.

TYPES OF LAW

Law consists of the standards set by government and society in the form of either legislation or custom. This broad set of principles, regulations, rules, and customs govern the actions of all members of society, including businesspeople. Our laws come from several sources. **Common law** refers to laws that result from judicial decisions, some of which can be traced to early England. For example, in many countries, provinces, and states, an unmarried couple who have lived together for a certain period of time are said to be legally husband and wife by common law.

Statutory law is written law and includes provincial, state, and federal constitutions; legislative enactments; treaties of the federal government; and ordinances of local governments. Statutes must be drawn precisely and reasonably to be constitutional, and thus enforceable. Still, courts must frequently interpret the intentions and meanings of statutes.

As the global economy grows, knowledge of international law becomes more crucial. **International law** refers to the numerous regulations that govern international trade. Companies must be aware of the domestic laws of their trading partners, trade agreements such as the North American Free Trade Agreement (NAFTA), and the rulings by such groups as the World Trade Organization. International law affects trade in all kinds of industries. Recently, defective or tainted products manufactured in China—but sold in North America—were recalled. Although the goods came from China, the companies that imported and sold these products in Canada and United States were liable, or legally responsible, for the products' defects. Tainted or defective toothpaste, pet food, toys, tires, and shrimp were dealt with by the various government regulatory bodies and agencies that hold manufacturers and distributors responsible for the quality of their foreign-made products. Recent cases involve lawsuits against Chinese manufacturers of construction drywall. Evidence suggests that the drywall contains high levels of corrosive gases that have led to health problems among people who live in homes built with the drywall. In the end, billions of dollars in damages may be awarded to affected homeowners.[3]

In a broad sense, all law is business law because all firms are subject to all laws, the entire body of law, just as individuals are. But, in a narrower sense, **business law** consists of those parts of law that most directly influence and regulate the management of various types of business activity. Specific laws vary widely in their intent from business to business and from industry to industry. The legal interests of airlines, for example, differ from the legal interests of oil companies.

law the standards set by government and society in the form of either legislation or custom.

common law laws that result from judicial decisions, some of which can be traced to early England.

statutory law written law that includes provincial, state, and federal constitutions; legislative enactments; treaties of the federal government; and ordinances of local governments.

international law the numerous regulations that govern international trade.

business law those parts of law that most directly influence and regulate the management of business activity.

A Toronto PetSmart store collects recalled pet food in a bin. Although the tainted food was manufactured in China, the North American companies that outsourced its production were held liable for damages to consumers.

NORM BETTS/Landov

Provincial and local statutes also differ in how widely their laws apply. Some laws affect all businesses that operate in a province. One example is the workers' compensation laws, which cover payments to workers for workplace injuries. Other provincial laws apply to only certain firms or business activities. Provinces have specific licensing requirements for businesses such as law firms, funeral directors, and hair salons. Many local ordinances deal with specific business activities. Local regulations often guide the sizes and types of business signs allowed. Some communities even restrict the sizes of stores, including height and square footage.

REGULATORY ENVIRONMENT FOR BUSINESS

Government regulation of business in North America has changed over time. Depending on public opinion, the economy, and the political climate, governments swing between increased regulation and deregulation. But the goal of both types of legislation is the protection of healthy competition.

The federal Competition Act guards against monopolies, price-fixing, and other limitations on competition. The act protects consumers by ensuring that they have a choice in the marketplace. The same act protects businesses by ensuring that they are free to compete. The objectives of the Competition Act are to encourage competition and to prevent monopolies. The act specifically prohibits any contract or agreement for the purpose of limiting trade. *Price-fixing* is an agreement between two or more businesses to set a price for the goods they sell in the marketplace. A *market allocation* is an agreement to divide the market among potential competitors. A *boycott in restraint of trade* is an agreement between businesses not to sell or buy from a particular entity.

THE CORE OF BUSINESS LAW

Business law includes contract law and the law of agency; sales law and negotiable instruments law; property law and the law of bailment; trademark, patent, and copyright law; tort law; bankruptcy law; and tax law. The following sections set out the key provisions of each of these legal concepts.

Contract Law and Law of Agency

contract a legally enforceable agreement between two or more parties regarding a specified act or thing.

Contract law is the legal foundation on which business dealings are conducted. A **contract** is a legally enforceable agreement between two or more parties regarding a specified act or thing.

Contract Requirements

As Figure C.1 shows, the four elements of an enforceable contract are agreement, consideration, legal and serious purpose, and capacity. The parties must reach agreement about the act or thing specified. For such an agreement, or contract, to be valid and legally enforceable, each party must supply consideration—the value or benefit that each party provides to the others with whom the contract is made. For example, assume that a builder hires an electrician to install electrical wiring in a new house. The wiring job and the resulting payment are the considerations. In addition to consideration, an enforceable contract must involve a legal and serious purpose. Agreements made as a joke or involving the commission of crimes are not enforceable as legal contracts. An agreement between two competitors to fix the prices for their products is not enforceable as a contract because the subject matter is illegal.

The last element of a legally enforceable contract is capacity, the legal ability of a party to enter into agreements. The law does not permit legally enforceable contracts by certain people, such as those judged to be insane. Contracts govern almost all types of business activities. For example, you might sign a contract to lease an apartment or to purchase a car or cellphone service.

Breach of Contract

A violation of a valid contract is called a *breach of contract*. The injured party can go to court to enforce the contract provisions and, in some cases, collect *damages*—financial payments to compensate for a loss and related suffering.

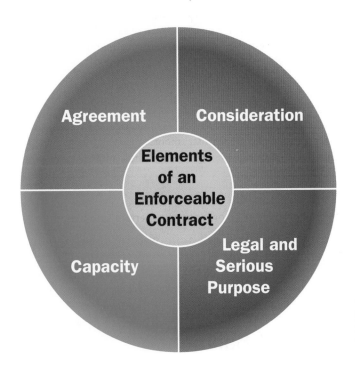

FIGURE C.1
Four Elements of an
Enforceable Contract

Law of Agency

All types of firms conduct business affairs through a variety of agents, such as partners, directors, corporate officers, and sales personnel. An agency relationship exists when one party, called the principal, appoints another party, called the agent, to enter into contracts with third parties on the principal's behalf.

The law of agency is based on common-law principles and case law decisions of provincial and federal courts. Relatively little agency law has been enacted into statute. The law of agency is important because the principal is generally limited by the actions of the agent.

The legal basis for holding the principal liable for acts of the agent is the Latin maxim *respondeat superior* ("let the master answer"). In a case involving agency law, the court must decide the rights and obligations of the various parties. Generally, the principal is held liable if an agency relationship exists and the agent has some type of authority to do the wrongful act. In such cases, the agent is liable to the principal for any damages.

Sales law governs the sales of goods or services for money or on credit. Such agreements are based on the conduct of the parties. The law generally requires written agreements for enforceable sales contracts, but the form of a sales contract is quite flexible: if a written contract is missing certain terms or includes unclear terms, the contract can still be legally enforced. A court will look at past dealings, commercial customs, and other standards of reasonableness to evaluate whether a legal contract exists.

Courts also consider these variables when the buyer or the seller tries to enforce his or her rights as a result of the other party (either the seller or buyer) failing to meet the terms of the

sales law the law governing the sale of goods or services for money or on credit.

contract, meeting the terms only partially, or meeting the terms in a defective or unsatisfactory way. The legal solutions usually involve the award of monetary damages to the injured parties. The law defines the rights of the parties to have the terms of the contract met, to have the contract terminated, and to reclaim the goods or place a lien—a legal claim—against them.

Warranties

Products carry two basic types of warranties: an express warranty and an implied warranty. An express warranty is a specific representation made by the seller regarding the product. An implied warranty is only legally imposed on the seller. Generally, unless implied warranties are disclaimed by the seller in writing, they are automatically in effect. Other provisions govern the rights of the buyer to inspect, accept, and reject products; the rights of both parties during the manufacture, shipment, delivery, and passing of title to products; the legal significance of sales documents; and the placement of the risk of loss if products are destroyed or damaged during manufacture, shipment, or delivery.

Negotiable Instruments

A *negotiable instrument* is commercial paper that is transferable among individuals and businesses. The most common example of a negotiable instrument is a cheque. Drafts, certificates of deposit (CDs), and notes are also sometimes considered negotiable instruments.

The law specifies that a negotiable instrument must be written and must meet the following conditions:

1. It must be signed by the maker or drawer.

2. It must contain an unconditional promise or an order to pay a certain sum of money.

3. It must be payable on demand or at a definite time.

4. It must be payable to order or to the bearer.

Cheques and other forms of commercial paper are transferred when the payee signs the back of the instrument, a process known as endorsement.

Property Law and Law of Bailment

Property law is a key feature of the private enterprise system. *Property* is something for which a person or firm has the unrestricted right of possession or use. Property rights are guaranteed and protected by law.

As Figure C.2 shows, property can be divided into three basic categories: tangible personal property, intangible personal property, and real property. Tangible personal property consists of physical items such as equipment, supplies, and delivery vehicles. Intangible personal property is nonphysical property such as mortgages, shares, and cheques. This type of property is most often represented by a document or other written instrument, but it may also be a computer entry. You are probably familiar with certain types of intangible personal property such as cheques and money orders. Other examples include bonds, notes, letters of credit, and receipts.

A third category of property is real property, or real estate. Most firms have some interaction with real estate law because of the need to buy or lease the space where they operate. Some companies are created to serve these real estate needs. Various aspects of real property law are dealt with by real estate developers, builders, contractors, brokers, appraisers, mortgage companies, escrow companies, title companies, and architects.

The law of bailment deals with the surrender of personal property by one person to another when the property is to be returned at a later date. The person delivering the property is known as the bailor, and the person receiving the property is the bailee. Some bailments benefit bailees, others benefit bailors, and still others provide benefits to both. Most courts now require that all parties practise reasonable care in all bailment situations. The degree of benefit received from the bailment can be a factor in court decisions when deciding whether the parties have met the reasonable-care standards.

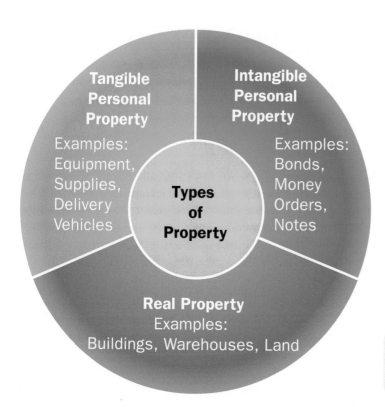

FIGURE C.2
Three Basic Types of Property

Bailment disagreements are most likely to arise in business settings, such as hotels, restaurants, banks, and parking lots. A series of rules are used to govern the settlement of these disagreements. The law focuses on actual delivery of an item. For example, a restaurant owner is not liable if a customer's coat or purse is stolen from the back of his or her chair. This is because the customer has not given the item to the restaurant for safekeeping. But, if the customer delivers the coat or purse to the restaurant checkroom, receives a claim check, and the item is stolen, then the restaurant is liable.

TRADEMARKS, PATENTS, AND COPYRIGHTS

Trademarks, patents, and copyrights provide legal protection by giving a firm the exclusive right to use its key business assets. A **trademark** is a brand that has been given legal protection. It consists of words, symbols, or other designations used by firms to identify their products. Trademarks are a valuable commercial property. Coca-Cola and McDonald's are two of the world's most widely recognized trademarks, so they are very valuable to the companies that own them.

If a product becomes too well known, its fame can create problems. After a trademark becomes a part of everyday language, it loses its protection as a legal trademark. Consider the words *aspirin*, *cola*, *nylon*, *kerosene*, and *linoleum*. All these product names were once the exclusive property of their manufacturers, but they have passed into common language, and now anyone can use them. More recent examples are *Xerox*, *Kleenex*, and *Velcro*. Although these names are legally trademarked, people often use them in everyday language instead of the correct generic terms of *photocopy*, *facial tissue*, and *hook-and-loop*.

trademark a brand that has been given legal protection; words, symbols, or other designations used by firms to identify their products.

Companies understand the value of their trademarks. That's why they fight hard to protect them. Louis Vuitton sued Google for allowing other companies to bid for and use the firm's trademarked brand names as keywords to trigger ads on Google's site. Louis Vuitton lost the lawsuit, but a European court ruled that companies borrowing such keywords must be clearer about who they are and what they are actually selling.[4]

By law, a **patent** guarantees an inventor exclusive rights to an invention for 20 years.

A **copyright** protects written or printed material such as books, designs, cartoon illustrations, photos, computer software, music, and videos. This class of business property is referred to as *intellectual property*. Unsurprisingly, the Internet has opened up a whole new world of copyright infringement, ranging from downloading music files to illegally sharing video footage.

Google faces a challenge both in North America and abroad as it compiles a massive digital library in an effort to create the world's largest online library. Google has given consumers online access to nearly 10 million books from around the world. Google has been challenged by authors and publishers on potential copyright infringement. The U.S. Department of Justice is trying to reach a settlement that benefits all parties. Meanwhile, France and Germany oppose any kind of settlement; these countries are supporting a European book-scanning project that complies with their own laws—which includes requiring permission from copyright holders before the books are scanned. [5]

Despite publicity about Internet copyright infringement, many people break copyright laws unknowingly. Some schools are now trying to educate students about the practice so they can make better and more informed choices about downloading material from the Internet.

> **patent** legal protection that guarantees an inventor exclusive rights to an invention for 20 years.

> **copyright** legal protection of written or printed material such as books, designs, cartoons, photos, computer software, music, and videos.

Law of Torts

A **tort** (French for "wrong") refers to a civil wrong inflicted on another person or on another person's property. The law of torts is closely related to the law of agency because a business entity, or principal, can be held liable for torts committed by its agents in the course of business dealings. Tort law differs from both criminal and contract law. While criminal law is concerned with crimes against the state or society, tort law deals with compensation for injured people who are the victims of noncriminal wrongs.

> **tort** a civil wrong inflicted by one person on another person or on another person's property.

Types of Torts

A tort may be intentional, or it may be caused by negligence, or carelessness. Examples of intentional torts include assault, slander, libel, and fraud. Businesses can become involved in tort cases through the actions of both owners and employees. A security guard who uses excessive force to capture a suspected shoplifter may have committed a tort. Under agency law, the guard's employers, such as a shopping mall or retailer, can be also held liable for any damages or injury caused by the security guard.

The other major group of torts results from negligence. This type of tort is based on carelessness, not on intentional behaviour that causes injury to another person. Under agency law, businesses can also be held liable for the negligence of their employees or agents. A delivery truck driver who injures a pedestrian while transporting goods creates a tort liability for his or her employer if the accident results from negligence, such as failure to keep the vehicle's side-view mirrors clean.

Product Liability

An area of tort law known as *product liability* has been developed by both statutory and case law. These laws hold businesses liable for negligence in the design, manufacture, sale, or use of products. Some jurisdictions have extended the theory of tort law to cover injuries caused by products, regardless of whether the manufacturer is proven negligent. This legal concept is known as strict product liability.

The business response to product liability has been mixed. To avoid lawsuits and fines, some businesses recall defective products voluntarily; others decide to fight recall mandates if they believe the recall is not justified. Auto manufacturers and toy makers typically issue voluntary recalls, as do drug manufacturers.

BANKRUPTCY LAW

Bankruptcy, legal nonpayment of financial obligations, is a common occurrence in contemporary society. Bankruptcy has two purposes. One is to protect creditors by providing a way to obtain compensation through debtors' assets. The second goal is to also protect debtors, allowing them to get a fresh financial start.

bankruptcy the legal non-payment of financial obligations.

The law recognizes two types of bankruptcy: voluntary bankruptcy and involuntary bankruptcy. Under voluntary bankruptcy, a person or firm asks to be judged bankrupt because of the inability to repay creditors. Under involuntary bankruptcy, creditors may request that a party be judged bankrupt. Businesses can go bankrupt for a variety of reasons—mismanagement, plunging sales, or an inability to keep up with changes in the marketplace.

TAX LAW

A branch of law that affects every business, employee, and consumer in the country is tax law. A **tax** is an assessment by a governmental unit. Federal, provincial, and local governments and special taxing authorities all levy, or charge, taxes. Appendix E, "Personal Financial Planning," also covers tax law.

tax an assessment by a governmental unit.

Some taxes are paid by individuals, and some taxes are paid by businesses. Both types of taxes have an impact on contemporary business. Business taxes reduce profits, and personal taxes decrease individuals' disposable incomes that they spend on the products of industry. Governments spend the revenue from taxes to buy goods and services produced by businesses. Governments also act as transfer agents: they move tax revenue to other consumers and transfer funds from the working population to retired or disabled people.

Governments can charge taxes on the basis of several different terms: income, sales, business receipts, property, and assets. The type of tax varies from one taxing authority to the other. Individual income tax is the biggest source of revenue for the federal government. The provinces rely heavily on income taxes and on sales taxes. Cities and towns may collect property taxes, which are then used to provide police and security services. So-called *luxury* taxes are charged on items such as yachts and expensive sports cars; so-called *sin* taxes are charged on items such as cigarettes and alcohol.

BUSINESS TERMS YOU NEED TO KNOW

judiciary 537	international law 537	trademark 541	bankruptcy 543
law 537	business law 537	patent 542	tax 543
common law 537	contract 538	copyright 542	
statutory law 537	sales law 539	tort 542	

PROJECTS AND TEAMWORK APPLICATIONS

1. Consumer protection is an idea that started in the early 1900s and continues today. Choose an industry that you think should—or will—be the next area of concern for consumer protection law. For example, you could choose travel, organic foods, health care, or any area that interests you. Research the consumer protections that may already be in place in this industry. Outline a plan for future protections.

2. To be effective, laws must be practical and enforceable; they must also be updated periodically to reflect changes in societal views and values. Go online and research your home community. Can you find any outdated, unenforceable, or strange laws that affect businesses? Present these laws in class and discuss how they could be revised so that they actually work.

3. The business world is filled with tort cases, and many involve product liability. One of the most famous cases is the customer who sued McDonald's because she spilled a cup of hot McDonald's coffee in her lap, suffering burns and scalding. A jury awarded her $2.7 million damages, an amount that a judge later reduced to less than $500,000. On your own or with a classmate, go online to research other famous product liability cases. Choose a case and learn as much as you can about it, including the effect of the case's outcome on the firm or firms involved. Present your findings in class.

WILEY PLUS
www.wileyplus.com

Access your WileyPLUS course for:

- The complete digital textbook.

- Question assistance, including links to relevant sections in the online digital textbook.

- Immediate feedback and proof of progress, 24/7

- Integrated, multi-media resources – including MP3 downloads, visual exhibits, animations, and much more – that provide multiple study paths and encourage more active learning.

QUIZ YOURSELF

APPENDIX D
INSURANCE AND RISK MANAGEMENT

Residents under Water without Insurance

The risk from flooding is common for people who live near rivers throughout North America. Some communities, like those along the Red River in Manitoba, are at greater risk because of the geography of where they live. What happened in Nashville, Tennessee, is the story of communities where the risk was often considered low and where insurance was often not purchased.

Nashville looked like a set for a disaster movie: muddy water lapped at the stage of the Grand Ole Opry, the nearby Opryland resort was drowned and deserted, cars were sitting in water up to their windows, and tired citizens waded through the streets. But the disaster was real. In one spring weekend, a record 35 centimetres of rain fell on the city and surrounding areas, causing the Cumberland River to crest nearly 8.5 metres above flood level, resulting in major flood damage. More than 11,000 properties sustained a total of $2 billion in direct damage from the floods; Nashville alone had $1 billion in damage. But those numbers don't include the costs of lost businesses, lost jobs, and lost possessions. And they also don't include the estimated cost to clean up and repair the public infrastructure, buildings, and overtime for city workers—which ultimately could run more than $250 million.

As the waters receded, Tennessee residents were grateful to be alive and uninjured. They located relatives and pets. And they began the grim task of mopping up what was left of their homes and possessions. But most soon discovered that rebuilding was going to be a huge task, if not impossible—they didn't have flood insurance. In fact, only 1.5 percent of all homes in the counties surrounding Nashville were covered by flood insurance. Most homeowners who had purchased it did so because their mortgage lenders required it. Many of those who didn't have it had once asked lenders, real estate agents, and builders about flood insurance—but all had been reassured that they didn't need it, despite living close to a major river. "They all said, 'You're not in a flood plain, so you don't need it,'" recalled one homeowner who left her house in a rescue boat with her dog.

The lack of flood insurance meant that the Federal Emergency Management Agency (FEMA) and personal savings—if any—would pay the repair bills for these homeowners. For the homeowners who were covered by flood insurance, their insurance companies would be paying out large claims.

How can something like this happen? If flood insurance is not required by a lender, it's an added expense to homeowners. Insurance rates can vary greatly, and flood insurance doesn't cover everything. For example, personal belongings in a flooded basement aren't generally covered by flood insurance. And any water entering the home must be from the flood itself (not from rainwater or a burst pipe). Flood insurance is a gamble both for the homeowner and the insurer. It's also a gamble for the mortgage holder. Still, FEMA points out that having flood insurance is better than not having it. "Anyone who has flood insurance is way ahead of the game," says Eugene Brezany, public affairs officer for FEMA. "FEMA's assistance is designed to get people back on their feet, not to bring people to their pre-disaster conditions." For example, if a homeowner has a $150,000 flood insurance policy and the house sustains $120,000 in damage, it can be restored. But without the policy, the homeowner is out of pocket $120,000 minus the $5,000 or $10,000 FEMA might contribute.

It comes down to a calculated risk: Will there be a flood? If so, how bad will it be? How much will it cost to repair the damage? Insurance companies use complex formulas to calculate the risks associated with natural disasters. Homeowners must decide whether it's worth paying expensive premiums for coverage if a flood never occurs. After the Nashville flood, both sides—homeowners and insurance companies—would be re-examining their position. Meanwhile, residents who could return to their homes would try to recover what they could. "You have to laugh to keep from crying," said one homeowner. That outlook might well apply to the insurance companies, too.[1]

APPENDIX D OVERVIEW

Risk is a daily fact of life for both individuals and businesses. Sometimes, risk appears in the form of a serious illness or injury. Other times, it takes the form of property loss, such as the damage to Nashville homes and businesses due to flooding. Risk can also occur as the result of the actions of others—such as a driver who is busy texting and runs a stop sign. In still other cases, risk may occur as a result of our own actions—we might go out in a boat during a thunderstorm or fail to listen to warnings about high blood pressure.

Businesspeople must understand the types of risk they face and develop ways to deal with risk. One approach to risk is to shift it to the specialized expertise of insurance companies. This appendix discusses the concept of insurance in a business setting. It begins with a definition of risk. We then describe the various ways that a business can manage risk. Next, we list some of the major insurance concepts, such as the definition of an insurable risk. The appendix concludes with an overview of the major types of insurance.

THE CONCEPT OF RISK

risk uncertainty about loss or injury.

Risk is uncertainty about loss or injury. Think about the risks faced by a typical business. A factory or warehouse faces the risk of fire and smoke, burglary, and storm damage. Others risks faced by businesses include data loss, injuries to workers, and loss of facilities. Risks can be divided into two major categories: speculative risk and pure risk.

Speculative risk gives the firm or individual the chance of a profit or a loss. A firm that expands operations into a new market may experience higher profits or the loss of invested funds. A contractor who builds a house without a specific buyer may sell the house at a profit or lose money if the house sits unsold.

Pure risk, in contrast, involves only the chance of loss. Motorists, for example, always face the risk of accidents. If an accident occurs, the result may be both financial and physical losses. But if an accident doesn't occur, drivers do not profit. Insurance often helps individuals and businesses protect themselves against financial loss resulting from some types of pure risk.

RISK MANAGEMENT

Because risk is an unavoidable part of business, managers must find ways to deal with it. The first step in any **risk management** plan is to recognize what is at risk and why it is at risk. The manager must then decide how to handle the risk. In general, businesses have four alternatives in handling risk: avoid it, minimize it, assume it, or transfer it.

Executives must consider many factors when evaluating risks, both at home and abroad. These factors include a nation's economic stability; social and cultural factors, such as language; available technologies; distribution systems; and government regulations. International businesses are typically exposed to less risk in countries that have stable economic, social and cultural, and political and legal environments.

risk management calculations and actions a firm takes to recognize and deal with real or potential risks to its survival.

Avoiding Risk

Some of the pure risks facing people can be avoided by living a healthful life. Not smoking and not swimming alone are two ways of avoiding personal risk. Businesses can also avoid some of the pure risks they face. For example, a manufacturer can locate a new production facility away from an area that is at risk of hurricanes or tornadoes.

Reducing Risk

Managers can reduce or even eliminate many types of risk by removing hazards or by taking preventive measures. Many companies develop safety programs to educate employees about potential hazards and the proper methods of performing certain dangerous tasks. Any employee who works at a hazardous waste site is required to have training and medical monitoring that meet government standards. The training and monitoring reduce risk and can help increase the bottom line. In addition to the human tragedy of accidents, accidents cost companies time and money.

Many actions can reduce the risk involved in business operations, but they cannot do away with risk entirely. Most major insurers help their clients avoid or minimize risk by offering the services of loss-prevention experts, who conduct thorough reviews of the clients' operations. These health and safety professionals evaluate customers' work environments and recommend procedures and equipment to help firms minimize worker injuries and property losses.

Individuals can also take actions to reduce risk. For example, obeying the rules of the road and doing regular maintenance on a car can reduce the risks associated with driving. Boarding up windows in preparation for a hurricane can reduce the risk of wind damage. But taking these actions can't entirely eliminate risk.

Self-Insuring against Risk

Instead of purchasing insurance against certain types of pure risk, some companies accumulate funds to cover potential losses. These self-insurance funds are special funds created by periodically setting aside cash reserves that the firm can draw on in the event of a financial loss resulting from a pure risk. A firm makes regular payments to the fund, and it charges losses to the fund. Such a fund typically works side-by-side with a risk-reduction program aimed at minimizing losses.

Shifting Risk to an Insurance Company

Although organizations and individuals can take steps to avoid or reduce risk, the most common method of dealing with risk is to shift it to others in the form of **insurance**—a contract in which an insurer, for a fee, agrees to reimburse an insured firm or individual a sum of money if a loss occurs. A *premium* is the insured party's fee to the insurance company for coverage against losses. Insurance substitutes a small, known loss—the insurance premium—for a larger, unknown loss

insurance a contract in which the insurer, for a fee, agrees to reimburse an insured firm or individual a sum of money if a loss occurs.

that may or may not occur. In the case of life insurance, the loss—death—is a certainty; the main uncertainty is the date when it will occur.

It is important for the insurer to understand the customer's business, risk exposure, and insurance needs. Firms that operate in several countries usually do business with insurance companies that maintain global networks of offices.

BASIC INSURANCE CONCEPTS

Figure D.1 shows how an insurance company operates. The insurer (the insurance company) collects premiums from policyholders (consumers or businesses) in exchange for insurance coverage. The insurance company uses some of these funds to pay current claims and operating expenses. The remaining funds are held in the form of reserves, which are invested. Reserves can be used to pay for unexpected losses. The returns from insurance company reserves may allow the insurer to reduce premiums, generate profits, or both. By investing reserves, the insurance industry represents a major source of long-term financing for other businesses.

An insurance company is a professional risk taker. For a fee, it accepts risks of loss or damage to businesses and individuals. Four basic principles underlie insurance: the concept of insurable interest, the concept of insurable risk, the rule of indemnity, and the law of large numbers.

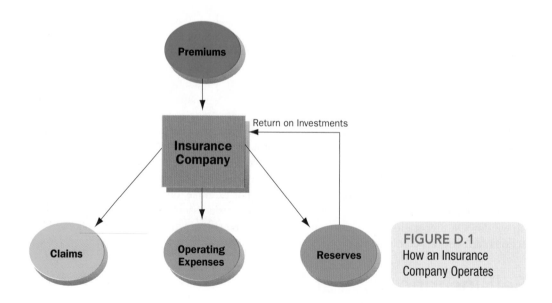

FIGURE D.1
How an Insurance
Company Operates

Insurable Interest

To purchase insurance, an applicant must show an *insurable interest* in the property or life of the insured. In other words, the policyholder must stand to suffer a loss, financial or otherwise, due to fire, storm damage, accident, theft, illness, death, or lawsuit. Homeowners have an insurable interest in their home and its contents. When life insurance coverage is purchased for a family's main income provider, the policyholder's spouse and children have a clear insurable interest.

A firm can purchase property and liability insurance on physical assets—such as an office or warehouse—to cover losses due to fire and theft because the company has an obvious insurable interest. Because top executives are important assets to a company, a business often purchases key-person life insurance, which compensates the business should an important individual die.

Insurable Risk

Insurable risk refers to the requirements that a risk must meet for the insurer to provide protection. Only some pure risks are insurable. No speculative risks are insurable. A pure risk must meet four requirements to be considered an insurable risk:

1. The likelihood of loss should be reasonably predictable. If an insurance company cannot reasonably predict losses, it has no basis for setting affordable premiums.

2. The loss should be financially measurable.

3. The loss should be accidental, or fortuitous, the result of chance.

4. The risk should be spread over a certain geographic area.

The insurance company has the right to set standards for accepting risk. This process of setting these standards, and deciding what to charge, is known as *underwriting*.

Rule of Indemnity

The **rule of indemnity** states that the insured individual or firm cannot collect more than the amount of the loss. The insured cannot collect for a loss more than once. Assume that a florist's delivery van is damaged in an accident. If the damage totals $2,500, then that is the most the business can collect from the insurance company.

Occasionally, a loss may be covered by more than one policy. For example, assume that a $5,000 loss is covered by two different policies. The rule of indemnity means that the insured individual or business can collect a total of $5,000 from both insurance companies. The insurers decide how much each pays based on each policy's details.

rule of indemnity the requirement that the insured cannot collect more than the amount of the loss and cannot collect for the same loss more than once.

The Law of Large Numbers

Insurance is based on the law of averages, or statistical probability. Insurance companies cannot afford to sell insurance policies unless they can reasonably predict losses. As a result, insurance companies have studied the chances of occurrences of deaths, injuries, property damage, lawsuits, and other types of hazards. Table D.1 is an example of the kind of data insurance companies examine. It shows the automobile accident rate, by the age of the driver, for a recent year. From their investigations, insurance companies develop *actuarial tables*. These tables predict the number of fires, automobile accidents, or deaths that will occur in a given year. Premiums charged for insurance coverage are based on these tables. Actuarial tables are based on the law of large numbers. In essence, the **law of large numbers** states that seemingly random events will follow a predictable pattern if enough events are observed.

Let's look at an example to show how insurers use the law of large numbers to calculate premiums. Previously collected statistical data on a city with 50,000 homes indicates that the city will experience an average of 500 fires a year, with damages averaging $30,000 per occurrence. What is the minimum annual premium an insurance company would charge to insure one residence?

To simplify the calculations, assume that the premiums would not produce profits or cover any of the insurance company's operating expenses—they would just produce enough income to pay policyholders for their losses. In total, fires in the city would generate claims of $15 million (500 homes damaged × $30,000). If the cost of these losses was spread over all 50,000 homes, each homeowner would be charged an annual premium of $300 ($15 million ÷ 50,000 homes). In reality, though, the insurer would likely set the premium at a higher figure to cover operating expenses, build reserves, and earn a reasonable profit. For example, during a recent year, the purchase of individual life insurance policies totaled $10 trillion in premiums, but the payout of claims was less.[2]

Some losses are easier for insurance companies to predict than others. Life insurance companies can predict with high accuracy the number of policyholders who will die within a specified period of time. But losses from such hazards as automobile accidents and weather events are much more difficult to predict. For example, the number of damage claims on homeowners' policies due to lightning has increased dramatically. During one recent year, more than 185,000 claims were made, costing insurers nearly $800 million.[3]

law of large numbers the idea that seemingly random events will follow predictable patterns if enough events are observed.

Table D.1 Relationship between the Age of the Driver and the Number of Motor Vehicle Accidents

AGE GROUP	ACCIDENT RATE (PER 100 DRIVERS)
19 years old and under	21
16 years old	28
17 years old	23
18 years old	22
19 years old	18
20 to 24 years old	15
20 years old	21
21 years old	16
22 years old	14
23 years old	13
24 years old	12
25 to 34 years old	10
35 to 44 years old	8
45 to 54 years old	7
55 to 64 years old	7
65 to 74 years old	5
75 years old and over	4

Source: "2010 Statistical Abstract," *The National Data Book,* from *Injury Facts*, National Safety Council, Itasca, IL; http:// www.nsc.org; accessed May 9, 2010.

SOURCES OF INSURANCE COVERAGE

The insurance industry includes both for-profit companies—such as The Co-operators, Empire Life, and Manulife Financial—and public agencies that provide insurance coverage for business firms, not-for-profit organizations, and individuals.

Public Insurance Agencies

A *public insurance agency* is a government unit established to provide specialized insurance protection for individuals and organizations. It provides protection in such areas as job loss (employment insurance) and work-related injuries (workers' compensation). Public insurance agencies also sponsor specialized programs, such as deposit, flood, and crop insurance. The biggest public insurance program in every province is the health insurance that provides health services.

Private Insurance Companies

Most insurance is provided by private firms. These companies provide protection in exchange for the payment of premiums. Some private insurers are owned by shareholders and must be run like any other business. Other insurers are so-called mutual associations. Most but not all mutual insurance companies specialize in life insurance. Technically, mutual insurance companies are owned by their policyholders, who may receive premium rebates in the form of dividends. But there is no evidence that an insurance policy from a mutual company costs any less than a similar policy from a shareholder-owned insurer. In recent years, some mutual insurance companies have reorganized as shareholder-owned companies, including Prudential, one of the world's largest insurers.

TYPES OF INSURANCE

Individuals and businesses spend hundreds of billions of dollars each year on insurance coverage. Figure D.2 shows the annual premiums that insurance companies collected for selected types of insurance in a recent year. Unfortunately, both business firms and consumers make poor decisions when buying insurance. Here are four basic tips to remember when buying insurance:

1. Buy insurance against large losses, not small ones. It is usually much more cost effective to self-insure against small losses.

2. Buy insurance with broad coverage, not narrow coverage. For example, it is usually much less expensive to buy a homeowners policy that protects from multiple events (perils such as fire and theft) than to buy several policies that cover individual events.

3. Shop around. Premiums for similar policies can vary widely from company to company.

4. Buy insurance only from financially strong companies. Insurance companies occasionally go bankrupt. If that happens, the insured have no coverage and little hope of getting their premiums back.

Although insurers offer hundreds of different policies, they all fall into three broad categories: property and liability insurance, health and disability insurance, and life insurance.

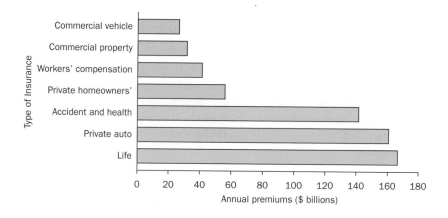

FIGURE D.2
Premiums Collected by Insurance Companies for Selected Types of Insurance

Note: Accident and health includes long-term care and disability insurance.

Source: Insurance Information Institute, *Insurance Fact Book*, http://www.iii.org.

Property and Liability Insurance

Insurance that protects against fire, accident, theft, or other destructive events, or perils, is called **property and liability insurance**. Examples of this insurance category include homeowners' insurance, auto insurance, business or commercial insurance, and liability insurance. Most property and liability policies are subject to deductibles. A deductible is the amount of the loss the insured pays out of pocket.

Homeowners' Insurance

Homeowners' insurance protects homeowners from damage to their residences due to various perils. For example, if a home is destroyed by fire, the homeowners' policy will pay to replace the home and its contents. Nearly all homeowners carry this type of insurance.

Homeowners' insurance premiums have risen sharply in recent years. Homeowners in coastal areas are finding it increasingly difficult to obtain insurance because of the growing number of claims related to erosion, hurricanes, and floods. If homeowners can obtain private coverage, those plans may be very expensive.

property and liability insurance a general category of insurance that protects against losses due to a number of perils, such as fire, accident, and theft.

Although standard policies cover a wide range of perils, most policies do not cover damage from widespread catastrophes such as floods and earthquakes. Homeowners must purchase separate policies to protect against damage caused by these perils.

Auto Insurance

At more than $150 billion in total annual premiums, automobile insurance is North America's largest category of property and liability insurance. Automobile insurance policies cover losses due to automobile accidents or theft, including personal and property claims.

Commercial and Business Insurance

Commercial and business insurance protects firms from financial losses resulting from the suspension of business operations (*business interruption insurance*) or physical damage to property as a result of destructive events. These policies may also protect employers from employee dishonesty or losses resulting from the nonperformance of contracts.

Liability Insurance

Liability insurance protects an individual or business against financial losses to others that the individual or business was responsible for. For example, if a business sells a defective product, the firm's liability insurance will pay for financial losses sustained by customers. A standard amount of liability coverage is usually attached to auto, homeowners', and commercial insurance policies. Additional amounts of liability insurance can be purchased if needed. Adequate liability insurance is critically important today for both businesses and individuals. For example, Walmart requires its suppliers to have at least $2 million in liability coverage for their products; some "high-risk" products require a minimum of $10 million.[4]

Health and Disability Insurance

Each of us faces the risk of getting sick or becoming injured. Even a relatively minor illness can result in substantial health care bills not covered by provincial health care plans. To guard against this risk, many people have some form of supplementary **health insurance**—insurance that provides additional coverage for expenses that result from sickness or accidents. Because of the increasing costs in health care, this type of insurance has become an important consideration for both businesses and individuals.

health insurance insurance that pays for losses due to illness or injury.

Disability Income Insurance

Disability income insurance is one of the most overlooked forms of insurance. And many workers don't have enough coverage. The odds of a person developing a disability are considerably higher than most people think. Take a group of five randomly selected 45-year-olds. There is approximately a 95 percent chance that one of the five will develop some form of a disability during the next 20 years. Disability income insurance is designed to replace lost income when a wage earner cannot work because of an accident or illness.

Private disability insurance is available on either an individual or group basis. Similar to health insurance, a group policy is much cheaper than an individual policy. Many employers provide some disability coverage as an employee benefit. Employees often have the option of obtaining additional coverage by paying more.

Life Insurance

life insurance a type of insurance that protects people against the financial losses that occur with premature death.

Life insurance protects people against the financial losses that occur with premature death. Three of every four North Americans have some form of life insurance. The main reason people buy life insurance is to provide financial security for their families in the event of their death. The life insurance industry has assets of more than $4 trillion, making it one of North America's largest businesses.

Types of Life Insurance

As with health and disability insurance, both individual and group life insurance policies are available. Many employers offer life insurance to employees as part of the firm's benefit program. But, unlike health and disability insurance, an individual life insurance policy is usually cheaper than a group policy for younger people.

The different types of life insurance fall neatly into two categories: term policies and cash value policies. Term policies provide a death benefit if the policyholder dies within a specified period of time. It has no value at the end of that period. Cash value policies—sometimes called whole life and universal life—combine life insurance protection with a savings or investment feature. The cash value represents the amount of the savings or the investment portion of the policy. Although some people prefer cash value policies, many experts believe that term life insurance is a better choice for most consumers. For one thing, a term policy is much cheaper than a cash value policy.

How Much Life Insurance Should You Have?

Life insurance policies can be purchased for almost any amount. The value of the policy is limited only by the amount of premiums people can afford and their ability to meet medical qualifications. But the amount of life insurance a person needs is a very personal decision. The general rule of thumb is that life insurance is needed when family members are financially dependent on an individual's earnings. For example, a young parent with three small children could easily need $500,000 or more in life insurance. A single person with no dependents would reasonably see little or no need for a life insurance policy.

Businesses also buy life insurance. The death of a partner or a key executive is likely to result in a financial loss to an organization. Key person insurance reimburses the organization for the loss of an essential senior executive and to cover the expenses of an executive search to find a replacement. Life insurance policies may also be purchased for each member of a partnership. These policies will repay the deceased partner's survivors for his or her share of the firm and permit the business to continue.

© Can Stock Photo Inc./Kurhan

Many businesses offer life insurance as part of their employee benefits. Although groups usually get a better deal on insurance than individuals, it may be cheaper for young employees to purchase an individual insurance policy.

BUSINESS TERMS YOU NEED TO KNOW

risk 546

risk management 547

insurance 547

rule of indemnity 549

law of large numbers 549

property and liability insurance 551

health insurance 552

life insurance 552

PROJECTS AND TEAMWORK APPLICATIONS

1. Choose one of the following companies or select another one that interests you. Research the company online. Learn what you can about the firm's goods and services, work processes, and facilities. Create a chart to identify risks that you believe the company faces—and show ways the firm can avoid or reduce its risks.

    a. VIA Rail

    b. Toronto Maple Leafs

    c. MEGA Brands Inc.

    d. Laura Secord

2. Assess your own personal insurance needs. What types of coverage do you currently have? How do you see your insurance needs changing in the next five to 10 years?

3. Go online and research one of these man-made disasters: the BP oil spill in the Gulf of Mexico or the Westray Mine disaster in Nova Scotia. Learn what you can about the role of insurance companies. Did they meet or exceed their obligations, or did they fall short? Report your findings in class.

4. Table D.1 shows the relationship between the age of a driver and the number of motor vehicle accidents. The greatest number of accidents occurs between the ages of 16 and 19 and the fewest occur starting at age 65. Research the causes of these accidents. Note the similarities and differences. Create a report that outlines your research. Suggest steps you think the younger group of drivers might take to reduce their risks.

APPENDIX E
PERSONAL FINANCIAL PLANNING

The Credit CARD Trick: Will It Work?

North American college and university students are similar in many ways. What we know about students on one side of the Canada–U.S. border is probably true for students on the other side. In one recent student-loan survey of American college graduates, nearly half said they wished they had learned more in college about managing their finances—specifically, their credit cards. The average college student has 4.6 credit cards and a balance of more than $3,000—and that's on top of any student loans. Only 17 percent of college students pay off their credit card balances in full each month. That means most of them are racking up debt, interest charges, and fees. Critics of the credit card industry point to the credit card issuers that advertise on campus, literally handing out credit cards along with free promotional items, such as backpacks, T-shirts, and water bottles. The water bottles and T-shirts don't build up debt, the credit cards do.

The American government has decided that this situation represents a financial crisis. Students are graduating from college with large debt in addition to their student loans—some have debts of $10,000 or more. The Credit CARD Act (Credit Card Accountability, Responsibility, and Disclosure Act) was signed into law in 2010. This act includes reforms aimed at limiting both the access credit card companies have to students and the amount of credit students are given. Under the new law, credit card issuers cannot offer free incentives such as T-shirts and teddy bears. Also, firms cannot market their cards at a college-sponsored event or within 1,000 feet (300 m) of a college campus. The firms must also have clearer communications with students and with colleges, such as disclosing the terms of their agreements. Students will also have a tougher time actually obtaining credit cards; those under age 21 must have adult co-signers or prove they earn enough income to make payments. Many of these controls, such as the need for co-signing of applications, are already in place under Canadian law.

Some welcome the restrictions in the new law, while others find them too restrictive. "It's my safety line," says one student who happens to have a good summer job and can handle the card. "I use my credit card for everything, from gas to my books to my food and clothes." Another college student thinks that the credit limit should be matched to a student's income and age. "I agree there should be new standards in place. Freshman shouldn't get credit limits of $5,000. However, I don't agree that it should be difficult for them to get credit at all." Others point out the difficulty of finding a co-signer willing to put his or her credit score on the line.

But many adults and students agree that, in general, the steps taken by the Credit CARD Act are positive. "I think it's going to keep a lot of students from getting into trouble," says Irene Leach, associate professor in consumer studies at Virginia Tech University. "I hope it means we'll have more responsible lending and parents don't get surprised that a young person has taken out this debt." And there are options other than the traditional credit card. College students can piggyback on their parents' cards simply by having parents add their name to the card account—that way, parents can monitor their children's credit card spending. Or students can apply for prepaid cards, which are similar to bank debit cards but can have high fees. Visa and other companies file regular reports with credit bureaus, a practice that can help students build a good credit standing without getting into debt.

Students themselves may make the best argument for credit card reform. One student got her first credit card while in college. She built up more than $7,500 in debt and says she has "regretted it ever since."[1]

APPENDIX E OVERVIEW

You are studying business, but much of what you learn in this course also applies to your personal life. For example, you learn about each of the important functions of a business—from accounting to marketing, from finance to management. Learning about each business function will help you choose a career. A career choice is one of the most important personal financial decisions you will make. You will learn why firms prepare budgets and financial statements. But budgets and financial statements are also important tools for individuals and households.

All of us—young or old, rich or poor—can improve how we manage our finances. As a group, North Americans are much better at making money than managing money. This appendix introduces you to personal financial management. **Personal financial management** is the study of economic factors and personal decisions that affect a person's financial well-being. It includes basic money management, credit, tax planning, major consumer purchases, insurance, investing, and retirement planning.

This appendix will draw from many of the topics you will learn while studying business. But it will also introduce you to some new concepts. After you complete this appendix, we hope you will be a better-informed financial consumer and personal money manager. We also hope you will be motivated to learn more about personal finance. The rewards, both financially and otherwise, can be huge.

personal financial management the study of the economic factors and personal decisions that affect a person's financial well-being.

THE MEANING AND IMPORTANCE OF PERSONAL FINANCE

Personal finance is the study of the economic factors and personal decisions that affect a person's financial well-being. Personal finance affects, and is affected by, many things we do and many decisions we make.

On one level, personal finance involves money know-how. Everyone needs to know how to earn money. But we also need to know how to save, spend, invest, and control it so we can achieve goals. The reward of good money management is an improved standard of living. **Standard of living** consists of the necessities, comforts, and luxuries a person wants to achieve or maintain.

On another level, personal finance affects our lifestyles—the way we live our daily lives. Our choice of careers, friends, hobbies, communities, and possessions is shaped by our personal finances—and our personal finances can also be shaped by our lifestyles. If you're a university student living on a tight budget, you may have to make serious financial decisions to achieve your educational goals. Where you live depends on what school you attend and how much you can pay for room and board. Your vacation is set by your academic schedule and your savings account. Your clothing depends on the climate and your budget. All these lifestyle decisions are largely affected by your personal finances.

standard of living the necessities, comforts, and luxuries a person wants to achieve or maintain.

The Importance of Personal Finance Today

Good money management has always been important. But major changes in the economic environment over the past few years have made personal finance even more important today. And this is true whether you're a 20-year-old college student with big tuition bills, a 40-year-old parent with a mortgage to pay, or a 60-year-old thinking about retirement. Let's look at three reasons personal financial planning is so important in today's environment.

Your lifestyle affects your finances. Skiing at expensive resorts won't leave much money in your savings account.

Slow Growth in Personal Income

Personal income in North America has grown very slowly in recent years. The economy is now moving forward, but most analysts predict that, in the coming years, annual increases in wages and salaries will barely keep pace with the rate of inflation.

The slow growth in personal income makes sound money management very important. You cannot count on rising personal income to improve your standard of living. Instead, you need to save and invest more money, stick to a budget, and make major purchases wisely.

Changes in the Labour Market

Job security and how we think about work have changed in recent years. The traditional model of working for the same company for one's entire career is very rare today. The average length of employment in one job is five years.[2]

You and your classmates will likely change jobs and employers several times during your careers. Some of you will work part-time or on a contract basis, with little job security and fewer benefits. Others will take time off to care for small children or elderly parents. And many of you will want to start your own business and work for yourselves.

An estimated one in four workers today will be unemployed sometime during their working lives. Your employer may "downsize" and take your job with it, or "outsource" your job to someone else. Take a look at today's headlines. You'll see that big companies are downsizing, and outsourcing is common.

These changes make sound personal financial management even more important. You need to keep your career skills up-to-date. You also need to build up sufficient financial resources to get you through any unexpected crisis.

More Options

The number of choices today in banking, credit, investments, and retirement planning can be confusing. Today, you can do most of your banking with a brokerage firm and then buy mutual fund shares at a bank. Even the simple chequing account has become more complicated. Most banks offer several different types of chequing accounts, each with its own features and fees. Choosing the wrong account could cost you $100 or more in unnecessary fees each year.

Twenty years ago, few students carried credit cards, and those who did had cards that were tied to their parents' accounts. Banks and other credit card issuers didn't think college and university students represented good risks. Then the situation changed. Now we have a credit card debt crisis among students, as described at the beginning of this appendix. One of the first things you'll do when you start a full-time job is make decisions about employee benefits. Many employers offer lots of choices in such areas as health insurance, disability insurance, group life insurance, and retirement plans. Selecting the right insurance plans can save you thousands of dollars each year. And choosing the right retirement plan can improve your financial security many years from now.

Personal Financial Planning— A Lifelong Activity

Personal financial planning is an important activity whether you're 20, 40, or 60; whether you're single or married with children; or whether your annual income is $20,000 or $200,000. Many experts say that if you can't stick to a budget and control your spending when you're making $25,000 a year, you'll find it difficult to live within your means even if your income doubles or triples.

Good financial planning is a lifelong activity. But that doesn't mean your financial goals and plans will remain the same throughout your life—they won't. The major goal when you're young may be to buy your first home or pay off your student loans. For older people, the major goal is to pay off their home mortgage and save as much as possible for retirement.

A PERSONAL FINANCIAL MANAGEMENT MODEL

personal financial plan a guide to help a person reach his or her desired financial goals.

A **personal financial plan** is a guide to help you reach your targeted goals in the future. It helps you to close the gap between where you are right now and where you'd like to be in the future. Your goals might include buying a home, starting your own business, travelling extensively, sending your children to university, or retiring early. Developing a personal financial plan consists of several steps, as illustrated in Figure E.1.

FIGURE E.1 A Model of Personal Financial Management

The first step is to create a clear picture of where you currently stand financially. Next, develop a series of short-term and long-term goals. These goals will be influenced by your values and by your assessment of your current financial situation. The next step is to decide on a set of financial strategies—in each of the personal planning areas. These strategies will help you to close the gap between where you are now and where you want to be in the future. Next, put your plan into action and closely track its performance. Every few months, evaluate how effective your financial plan has been and make adjustments when necessary.

Financial plans cannot be developed in isolation. Your financial plan should reflect your available resources—especially your salary and your employment benefits, such as health insurance and retirement plans. For example, your goals and financial strategies should be based on a realistic estimate of your future income. If you cannot reach your financial goals through your present career path, you will need to scale back your goals or think about switching careers.

External factors—such as economic conditions and employment prospects—will affect your financial plan and decisions. For example, assume you currently rent an apartment but want to buy a home. Maybe you can afford to buy a home right now, but you think you might be offered a much better job in a new city in the next year. A wise financial move might be to *not* buy a home now but to wait until your employment future is clearer.

General Themes Common to All Financial Plans

All financial plans revolve around three general themes: (1) maximizing income and wealth, (2) using money more effectively, and (3) monitoring expenditures.

Maximizing Income and Wealth

Maximizing your income and wealth means making more money. For example, you can decide to work smarter; look for retraining so you can get a better, higher-paying job; take career risks that may pay off in the long run; and make sound investment decisions. The amount of money you earn is a big part of any financial plan. It is up to you to make the most of your opportunities.

Using Money More Effectively

Money has two basic uses: consumption and savings. Even if you are a regular saver, you'll still spend most of your income, probably more than 90 percent. You must try to spend every dollar wisely and make every major buying decision part of your overall financial plan. Avoid impulsive spending or giving in to a fast-talking salesperson.

It's not just major purchases that you need to watch. When you cut back your spending on small items, you can make a difference. Little purchases add up. For example, packing your own lunch a few times a week instead of always buying your lunch can save you about $15 a week. Invest that savings at 3 percent interest (per year) and you'll have almost $38,000 in 30 years.

Monitoring Expenditures

Budgeting is the key to controlling expenditures. A budget focuses on where the money is going and whether a person's goals are being met. It also suggests when it's time to re-evaluate your priorities. If your budget doesn't match what you want from life both now and in the future, change it.

Information also helps you to keep your expenditures under control. The more you know about real estate, consumer loans, credit-card rates

Small expenses add up. Over time, taking your own lunch to the office instead of eating out can add to your bank account.

© Can Stock Photo Inc./piedmont_photo

and laws, insurance, taxes, and major purchases, the more likely you are to spend the least money to purchase products with the greatest value.

The Pitfalls of Poor Financial Planning

Unfortunately, too many people fail to plan effectively for their financial future. Many people find it difficult to improve their standard of living. And others find themselves with growing debts and a general inability to make ends meet.

We have some laws that try to help consumers who run into difficulty, and credit counselling services can help people organize and pay their debt. But foreclosure and bankruptcy are actions of last resort that you want to avoid.

SETTING PERSONAL GOALS

Whatever your personal financial goals, they should work with your values. Values are a set of basic beliefs about what is important, desirable, and worthwhile in your life. Your values will influence how you spend your money. That's why values should be the foundation of your financial plan. Each person's financial goals will be shaped by the individual's values because every individual thinks of some things as more desirable or important than others. Start by asking yourself some questions about your values, the things that are most important to you, and what you would like to do in your life.

Your goals are also influenced by your current financial situation. Prepare a set of current financial statements for yourself and update them at least once a year. Just like a business, a personal income statement shows your income and expenditures during a year. A balance sheet is a statement of what you own (your assets) and what you owe (your liabilities) at a specific point in time. For an individual or household, the difference between assets and liabilities is called **net worth**. As you build assets over your life, your net worth increases.

net worth the difference between an individual's or a household's assets and liabilities.

After reviewing your current financial statements, prepare a budget. A budget is an excellent tool for tracking your spending and cash flow. It helps you to track past and current spending and plan future spending. Budgets are usually prepared on a monthly basis, but make a weekly budget if that works better. Most budgets divide spending into fixed expenses (those that don't change much from month to month) and variable expenses (those that vary). Your monthly apartment rent or your meal plan at school is probably a fixed expense, but the amount you spend on gas for your car or on entertainment is a variable expense. One key to effective budgeting is to make sure that the budgeted amounts are realistic.

Next, set up a series of financial goals based on your values and your current financial situation. Separate your goals into short-term goals (those you want to achieve within the next six months or year) and long-term goals (those you plan to achieve over the next five or 10 years). A short-term goal might be to pay off your credit card balances by the end of this year, or to save enough money to take a vacation next summer. A long-term goal might be to buy a house by age 30. Your goals are reinforced if they support each other. For example, if you pay off your credit cards, you might have enough money saved to take that vacation or to help toward the down payment for a house. Some goals are monetary—such as paying off the credit card. Others are nonmonetary, such as planning to retire by age 55.

Whether your financial goals are short-term or long-term, monetary or nonmonetary, the best goals are defined specifically and are focused on results. Goals also need to be realistic. You might not be able to pay off all of your credit cards by the end of this year, but you might be able to pay off one credit card. You might not buy the house by age 30, but maybe by age 35. Be sure to set goals that you can actually attain. Keep in mind also that your financial goals will change over your lifetime. It's a good idea to review them every few months and adjust them when necessary, such as when you lose or get a job, relocate to another area of the country, or have children.

YOUR PERSONAL FINANCIAL DECISIONS

You can use financial strategies to help chart your economic future in such areas as career choice, credit management, and tax planning. These strategies should work with your goals. They should be designed to close the gap between where you are and where you want to be.

Career Choice

No factor has a stronger influence on your personal finances than your career choice. Nearly all of your income, especially when you're just starting out, will come from wages and salaries. Through working, we acquire the income we need to build a lifestyle; to buy goods and services, including insurance protection; to save and invest; and to plan for retirement. Your job is also the source of many important fringe benefits that are important to your financial future, such as health insurance and retirement savings plans. Throughout *Contemporary Business*, we've discussed how you can select a career that fits your skills and interests, find a job, and perform in that job.

Basic Money Management

Basic money management includes managing chequing and savings accounts. Properly managing these fairly simple financial assets is an important first step toward proper management of more complicated financial assets such as investment and retirement accounts. You must choose a bank or another financial institution and then select the right chequing account. Financial institutions offer several different types of chequing accounts, each with its own features and fees.

Table E.1 lists several tips for selecting and managing a chequing account. Managing a savings account involves understanding the importance of savings, setting savings goals, and picking the best savings option.

Table E.1 Some Commonsense Tips for Choosing and Managing a Chequing Account

- Shop around. Most financial institutions offer chequing accounts. Fees and services can vary widely.
- Choose the right account for the way you bank. Think about how many cheques you write each month, how often you use ATMs, and your average monthly balance.
- Keep good records and regularly balance your chequing account.
- Use your personal computer to pay bills electronically, balance your chequebook, and do other banking tasks.
- Watch how you use your ATM card. Know which ATMs are owned by your bank and how much you're charged to use another bank's ATM. When using an ATM, check your current balance.
- Notify your bank immediately if your ATM card is lost or stolen.
- Sign up for overdraft protection.
- Understand how your bank calculates your minimum monthly balance.
- Read the fine print in your monthly statement.

Credit Management

Of all areas of personal finance, credit is the area that gets the most people into financial difficulties.

Credit allows a person to purchase goods and services by borrowing the necessary funds from a lender, such as a bank. The borrower agrees to repay the loan over a specified period of time, paying a specified rate of interest. The **finance charge** is the difference between the amount

credit receiving money, goods, or services on the basis of an agreement between the lender and the borrower that the loan is for a specified period of time with a specified rate of interest.

finance charge the difference between the amount borrowed and the amount repaid on a loan.

borrowed and the amount repaid. Credit is available from many sources, but rates vary, so it pays to shop around.

Consumers can choose from two broad types of consumer credit: revolving (or open-end) credit and installment credit. Revolving credit is a credit arrangement where consumers can make a number of different purchases up to a credit limit, specified by the lender. The consumer has the option of repaying some or all of the outstanding balance each month. If the consumer carries a balance from month to month, finance charges (interest) are added to the account. An example of revolving credit is a credit card, such as Visa or MasterCard.

An installment loan is a credit arrangement in which the borrower takes out a loan for a specified amount and agrees to repay the loan in regular installments over a specified period of time. Part of each payment goes toward interest and part goes to repay principal (the amount borrowed). Generally, installment loan payments are made monthly and are for the same amount. Examples of installment loans are most student loans, car loans, and home mortgage loans.

People have good reasons for borrowing money. For example, people borrow money to purchase high-priced goods and services (cars, homes, or a post-secondary education), to deal with financial emergencies, to take advantage of opportunities, and to establish or improve their credit rating. These reasons are suitable uses of credit if you can repay the loans in a timely manner.

A wrong reason for borrowing money is to use credit to live beyond your means. For example, you may want to go to Cancun for a vacation but really cannot afford the cost, so you charge the trip to your credit card. Using credit to live beyond your means can lead to financial problems. Watch for these warning signs of potential credit problems:

- You use credit to meet your basic living expenses.

- You use credit to make impulse purchases.

- You take a cash advance on one credit card to repay another.

- The unpaid balance on your credit cards increases every month.

Consumers who think of credit purchases as a series of small monthly payments are fooling themselves. How long would it take to become debt free if you had $2,200 on your credit card and you paid only the minimum payment each month? The answer is nearly 11 years—and you would have paid more than $2,000 in interest.

If you feel you might have a problem with credit, or may be developing a problem, get help as soon as possible. Your college or university may offer credit counselling services. According to the experts, one of the keys to the wise use of credit is education. By learning about the pros and cons of borrowing money and by learning about responsible spending, you can avoid many problems with credit.

Tax Planning

Everyone pays a variety of taxes to federal, provincial, and local governments. The major taxes paid by individuals are federal and provincial income taxes, local real estate taxes, and sales taxes. Think about your own situation and the taxes you pay. Federal and provincial income taxes are withheld from each paycheque. If you rent an apartment, part of your monthly rent goes to pay the landlord's real estate tax bill. Every time you buy something, you pay sales tax to various governments.

By law, you must pay your taxes. You can use some of the popular computer software to calculate your federal and provincial income taxes, or you can pay a professional to handle them. These two options will likely find the legal deductions you can take. If you do the tax return yourself—even with the help of software—you will learn more about your personal finances.

Major Purchases

Even if you follow a strict budget and manage to save money regularly, you will still spend most of your income each year. Effective buying is an important part of your financial plan. Within personal budget limits, an individual uses his or her rights as a consumer to select or reject from a wide range of goods and services. As you purchase an automobile, a home, or any other major item, you need to carefully evaluate your options, separate needs from wants, and decide how you are going to finance the purchase. Your goal is to make every dollar you spend count.

North Americans spend more than $900 billion annually on transportation. Most of that expense goes to purchasing and maintaining automobiles. New vehicles average more than $20,000 today, and even good used cars can cost more than $15,000. Buying an automobile is a major purchase. On top of that, most car purchases are financed. Buying a car involves weighing many factors, including whether you want a new or used car, what makes and models appeal to you, and how much you can afford to pay. Many consumers today choose not to buy a new car but to lease one. Leasing has advantages, but it also has drawbacks. Overall, leasing is often more expensive than buying.

For most people, housing takes up a large share of their monthly budgets, whether in rent or mortgage payments. Home ownership is a goal of most people. Owning a home has advantages, both financial and nonfinancial. The financial benefits include the potential increase in the home's value and, usually, no taxes on those gains. Nonfinancial benefits include pride of ownership and the freedom to improve or change the home as you want. The major barriers to home ownership are the money required for a down payment and the income required to obtain a mortgage loan.

The other major housing option is renting. Renting offers many advantages, including cost savings (the landlord takes care of maintenance and repairs) and mobility. It is much easier to move when you rent than when you own a home. People who plan on staying in an area for a short period of time are usually better off renting even if they can afford to buy a home. The choice between buying and renting is a major financial decision that needs to be approached rationally, not emotionally.

Insurance

Another important personal planning area is insurance. Insurance is an expensive but necessary purchase. North Americans spend about $150 billion each year on car insurance. Some of the basic principles and the various types of insurance are described in Appendix D. Although the focus of that appendix is business insurance, much of the discussion also applies to your personal insurance needs.

Your goal is to have adequate and appropriate coverage in each of the major insurance types—life, health, disability, and property and liability. Insurance needs can vary from individual to individual. As noted earlier in *Contemporary Business*, some types of insurance are provided to employees as fringe benefits. Employer-provided insurance typically includes supplementary health insurance, disability insurance, and life insurance. In the standard arrangement, employers pay a portion of the premium. A few employers contract with insurance companies to offer employees car and homeowners' insurance at discounts.

Investment Planning

Investing is a process by which money acquired through work, inheritance, or other sources is preserved and increased. Sound investment management

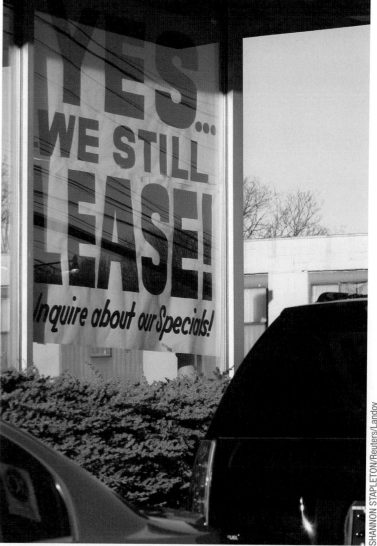

SHANNON STAPLETON/Reuters/Landov

Leasing a car has some advantages, but over the long run it may cost more than buying the same car.

is an important part of the financial plan and can make it easier to reach other personal goals, such as buying a home, financing children's education, starting a business, or retiring comfortably. It is very difficult today to increase your wealth significantly without investing. Because of the changes in the external environment—such as employer-sponsored retirement plans—you will likely need to make investment decisions at some point during your life.

The investment process consists of four steps. The first step is to complete some preliminary tasks, such as setting overall personal goals, contributing to a regular savings program, and managing credit properly. The second step is to establish a set of investment goals—why you want to invest, what you want to accomplish, and your time frame. Your investment goals should be closely related to your overall personal goals. Next, you need to assess risk and return. You invest because you expect to earn some future rate of return. But all investing will expose you to a variety of risks. You need to find the proper balance between risk and return; investments that offer the highest potential returns also expose you to more risk. Your age, income, and your short-term or long-term investment time frames all have an impact on the risk-return trade-off.

The final step is to select the appropriate investments. As discussed in Chapter 16 of *Contemporary Business*, you can choose from three general types of investments: money market instruments, bonds, and common shares. The proper mix of these three investments depends on several factors, including your investment goals and your investment time horizon. For example, a 25-year-old who is investing for retirement should have almost 100 percent of his or her funds invested in common shares because growth in capital is the main investment objective. Even with the recent turmoil in the stock market, common shares generally outperform all other investment alternatives over longer periods of time. On the other hand, if the 25-year-old is investing to have sufficient funds for a down payment on a house within the next couple of years, the investor should have a portion of his or her funds invested in money market instruments or bonds because of the short time horizon. Even after selecting the appropriate investments, the investor must monitor the investments' performance and be prepared to make changes when necessary.

Financial Planning for Tomorrow

The last major personal planning area deals with future financial issues, such as paying for children's college or university education and retirement and estate planning. As you know, post-secondary education is expensive. The costs are rising at a rate greater than the overall rate of inflation. By beginning an education savings program early, parents will have a better chance of offering their children more choices when the time comes. While parents might not have enough savings to cover tuition entirely, they (and their children) can likely borrow less and will add less debt if an education savings program is in place. A variety of educational savings programs exist, including some that offer tax benefits. You can learn more about Canada's educational savings plans at the Human Resources and Skills Development Canada website http://www.hrsdc.gc.ca/eng/learning/education_savings/index.shtml.

Most people want to retire with sufficient funds to ensure their financial security. Canadian government pensions will provide only a fraction of what you will need; you will be responsible for the rest. Depending on the standard of living you hope to have, you will probably need savings of at least $1.5 million by the time you retire. Four important principles apply when it comes to saving for retirement: start early, save as much as you can each month, take advantage of all tax-deferred retirement savings plans you can, and invest your retirement savings appropriately.

Consumers can choose from two major sources of retirement income: employer-sponsored retirement plans and individual retirement plans. Most employers offer their workers a retirement plan; some offer more than one plan. For most people, employer-sponsored retirement plans will likely provide most of their retirement income. Two types of employer-sponsored retirement plans exist. A defined benefit plan guarantees a worker a certain retirement benefit each year. The size depends on many factors, including the worker's income and the length of time he or she worked for the employer. Pension plans are classified as defined benefit plans.

The other type of employer-sponsored retirement plan is the defined contribution plan. In this type of retirement plan, you contribute to your retirement account and so does your employer.

You are given some choice of where your retirement funds can be invested. For example, you may be given a list of mutual funds where you can invest your money. Defined contribution plans are widely used. They are now often replacing defined benefit plans.

Millions of North Americans have some sort of individual retirement plan that is not tied to any employer. These workers may be self-employed or may want to add to their employer-sponsored retirement savings. Examples of individual retirement plans include regular RRSPs (Registered Retirement Savings Plans) and TFSAs (Tax-Free Savings Accounts). Although the TFSA can be thought of as a general savings plan, most people think of it as part of their retirement planning. To set up one of these retirement plans, you must meet certain eligibility requirements.

Another element of financial planning for tomorrow is estate planning. Of all the personal planning areas, estate planning is probably the least meaningful for you today, although your parents and grandparents probably face some estate-planning issues. All adults, regardless of age, need to have two documents: a valid will (naming a guardian if you have any minor children) and a durable power of attorney (a document that gives someone else the power to make financial and medical decisions if you cannot).

This appendix has just scratched the surface of personal financial planning. We hope it has encouraged you to learn more. Consider taking a class in personal financial planning if your college or university offers one. It may be one of the most helpful classes you take while you're in school.

BUSINESS TERMS YOU NEED TO KNOW

personal financial management 556

standard of living 556

personal financial plan 558

net worth 560

credit 561

finance charge 561

PROJECTS AND TEAMWORK APPLICATIONS

1. Prepare a chart outlining your current standard of living, the standard of living you had while growing up, and the standard of living you expect or hope to achieve after you complete your education.

2. Create a chart detailing how you think you could use your money most effectively. What are your pitfalls—late-night pizza, downloading music, trips to the city? In what areas do you already use your money well?

3. Create a weekly budget and a monthly budget. Keep a daily journal of your expenses for the next month to see how well you stick to the budget. Compare your results in class. In what areas did you do well? In what areas do you need improvement? For additional help, you can go to the website http://www.globecampus.ca/money-finder/financial-calculators/student-budget/ to fill out the budget worksheet.

4. Even though you are still in school, you face many important financial issues, from paying college or university expenses to dealing with credit cards. Visit the website http://www.youth.gc.ca/eng/topics/money/manage_finances.shtml. Look at some of the helpful websites for more suggestions on managing your money while in school.

5. Analyze your current credit situation. What are your existing debts? How much are you paying each month? Did you borrow for the right reasons? List some steps you think you should take to improve your management of credit. Go to the website http://www.canlearn.ca/eng/after/index.shtml. Check out the links for more advice on managing your credit.

Access your WileyPLUS course for:

- The complete digital textbook.
- Question assistance, including links to relevant sections in the online digital textbook.
- Immediate feedback and proof of progress, 24/7
- Integrated, multi-media resources – including MP3 downloads, visual exhibits, animations, and much more – that provide multiple study paths and encourage more active learning.

QUIZ YOURSELF

APPENDIX F
DEVELOPING A BUSINESS PLAN

What's Next? A New Business Model for Restaurants

You're probably familiar with buying airline tickets and concert tickets in advance—but what about a restaurant meal? We're not talking about a fast-food chain; we're talking about a fine dining restaurant. Usually, restaurant customers walk in the door and hope to find a vacant table; if they plan ahead, they might call for a reservation. But the idea of purchasing advance tickets for a restaurant is new to most of us.

Grant Achatz is a well-known chef and restaurant owner. He has a new restaurant called Next—based on a new kind of business plan. Instead of taking reservations, the restaurant sells tickets. The plan makes sense. Next will probably be as popular as Achatz's other restaurant, Alina, which is sold out many weeks in advance. "We now pay three or four reservationists all day long to basically tell people they can't come to the restaurant," explains Achatz. When customers purchase tickets in advance, they are assured of a ready table just as they would with a reservation. Achatz and his partner, Nick Kokonas, will be able to save the costs of the full-time reservation staff. They plan to pass along savings like this to their diners. Selling tickets "allows us to give an experience that is actually a great value," notes Achatz.

Diners who want a meal at Next simply visit the restaurant's website. They can look at the menu, which changes four times a year, and then lock into the fixed price for the entire six-course meal. They can also choose to dine at peak or off-peak hours, which will be reflected in the ticket price. For example, a table at 9:30 on a Tuesday night will cost less than a table at 8:00 on Saturday night. Meals range from $45 to $75, with wine and other beverages costing extra. A service charge—instead of a traditional tip—is included in the ticket price. This way, Achatz and Kokonas can distribute the gratuities among the staff as they see fit.

Achatz is known to offer unique dining experiences that many customers are willing to pay for. Next offers patrons a total experience in the cuisine of a specific place and time. It isn't just a theme; it's an experience that re-creates an era, with everything researched by Achatz and his team. The first offering was based on Paris in 1912, with Escoffier-era cuisine prepared, cooked, and served down to the last detail. When the menu changes, every three months, the chef may choose recipes that take diners to postwar Sicily or a fantasy of Chinese cuisine in the year 2020.

In the same way that sports fans buy season tickets, customers of Next can purchase a year's subscription to Next. That way they lock in the price and are guaranteed a reserved table for each of the seasonal menus. Achatz believes that once people get used to the idea of a prepaid meal, they will enjoy the experience. The dinner is paid for, and there's no fumbling for the wallet. "There's no transaction in the restaurant at all," Achatz points out. "So you can literally come in, sit down, start your experience, and when you're done, you just get up and leave."[1]

Many entrepreneurs and small-business owners write business plans to help them organize their businesses, get them up and running, and raise money for expansion. In this appendix, we cover the basics of business planning: what business plans are, why they're important, and who needs them. We also explain the steps involved in writing a good plan and the major elements it should include. Finally, we cover additional resources to get you started with your own business plan—to help you bring your unique ideas to reality with a business of your own.

WHAT IS A BUSINESS PLAN?

You may wonder how the millions of different businesses operating throughout the world today got their start. Many of them got started with a formal business plan. A *business plan* is a written document that defines what a company's objectives are, how these objectives will be achieved, how the business will be financed, and how much money the company expects to bring in. In short, it describes where a company is, where it wants to go, and how it intends to get there.

Why a Business Plan Is So Important

A well-written business plan serves two key functions:

1. It organizes the business and validates (or gives justification for) its central idea.
2. It summarizes the business and its strategy to obtain funding from lenders and investors.

First, a business plan gives a business formal direction, whether it is just starting, going through a phase of growth, or struggling. The business plan forces the principals—the owners—to do some thorough planning, to think through the realities of running and financing a business. In their planning, they consider many details. How will inventory be stored, shipped, and stocked? Where should the business be located? How will the business use the Internet? And most important, how will the business make enough money to make it all worthwhile?

A business plan also gives the owners a well-thought-out blueprint, or plan, to refer to when daily challenges come up. It also acts as a benchmark by which successes and disappointments can be measured. A solid business plan will sell the potential owner on the real possibilities of the idea. In some cases, the by-product of developing the plan is demonstrating to a dreamy person that he or she is trying to start a business that won't work. In other words, the process of writing a plan benefits a would-be businessperson as much as the final plan benefits potential investors.

Finally, a business plan communicates the business's strategy to financiers who may fund the business. A business plan is usually required to obtain a bank loan. Lenders and venture capitalists need to see that the business owner has thought through the critical issues and has presented a promising idea before they will consider investing. After all, they're really interested in whether investing in the business will bring them significant returns.

Who Needs a Business Plan?

Every business owner who expects to be successful needs a business plan. Some people mistakenly believe that they need a business plan only if it will land on the desk of a venture capitalist or the loan committee of a bank. Others think that writing a plan is unnecessary if their bank or lending institution doesn't need it. But these people miss the point of planning. A business plan acts as a map to guide the way through the often tangled roads of running a business. Every small-business owner should develop a business plan because it empowers that person to take control.

HOW DO I WRITE A BUSINESS PLAN?

Developing a business plan should mean something different to everyone. Think of a business plan as a clear statement of a business's identity. A construction company has a different identity from a newly launched magazine, which has yet a different identity from a restaurant hoping to expand its share of the market. Each business has unique objectives and processes, and each faces different obstacles.

At the same time, good business plans contain some similar elements no matter who the business owner is, what he or she sells, or how far the owner is into the venture. A smart business owner shapes the elements of a business plan into a professional and personal representation of the firm's needs and goals. The plan should also be realistic in its assessment of the risks and obstacles specific to the business, and then present solutions for overcoming them.

Because the document is important, it takes time to collect needed information and organize it. Don't be misled into believing that you will simply sit down and begin writing. Before any writing begins, the business owner must become an expert in his or her field. Gathering important information about the company and the market will make the writing easier and faster. The following items are some critical pieces of information that you should have on hand:

- The company's name, legal form of organization, location, financial highlights, and owners or shareholders (if any).

- Organization charts, list of top managers, consultants or directors, and employee agreements.

- Marketing research, customer surveys, and information about the company's major competitors.

- Product information, including goods and services offered; brochures; patents, licences, and trademarks; and research and development plans.

- Marketing plans and materials.

- Financial statements (both current and forecasted).

The business owner also must do a lot of soul searching and brainstorming to answer important questions necessary to build a healthy business. Figure F.1 lists some critical questions to ask yourself.

Once you have answered these questions, you can begin writing the document. It can be between 10 and 50 pages long. The length of the plan depends on the complexity of the company, whether the company is a start-up (established companies have longer histories to detail), and how the plan will be used. Regardless of size, the document should be well organized and easy to use, especially if the business plan is intended for external uses, such as to secure financing. Number all pages, include a table of contents, and make sure the format is attractive and professional. Include two or three charts or graphs, and highlight the sections and important points with headings and bulleted lists. Figure F.2 outlines the major sections of a business plan.

The following paragraphs discuss the most common elements of an effective business plan. When you need additional instruction or information, refer to the "Resources" section at the end of the appendix.

Executive Summary

The primary purpose of an executive summary is to interest readers so that they want to learn more about the business. An *executive summary* is a one- to two-page snapshot of what the overall business plan explains in detail. Consider it a business plan within a business plan. By expressing enthusiasm and energy, the summary should capture the reader's imagination. Describe your strategy for succeeding in a positive, intriguing, and realistic way. Briefly yet thoroughly answer the first questions anyone would have about your business: who, what, why, when, where, and how. Financiers always turn to the executive summary first. If it isn't well presented or is missing the proper information, they will quickly move on to the next business plan in the stack. The executive

**Take a few minutes to read and answer these questions.
Don't worry about answering in too much detail at this point.
The questions are preliminary and
intended to help you think through your venture.**

1. In general terms, how would you explain your idea to a friend?

2. What is the purpose or objective of your venture?

3. What service are you going to provide, or what goods are you going to manufacture?

4. Is there any significant difference between what you are planning and what already exists?

5. How will the quality of your product compare with competitive offerings?

6. What is the overview of the industry or service sector you are going to enter? Write it out.

7. What is the history, current status, and future of the industry?

8. Who is your customer or client base?

9. Where and by whom will your good or service be marketed?

10. How much will you charge for the product you are planning?

11. Where is the financing going to come from to initiate your venture?

12. What training and experience do you have that qualifies you for this venture?

13. Does such training or experience give you a significant edge?

14. If you lack specific experience, how do you plan to gain it?

FIGURE F.1 Self-Evaluation Questions

summary is also important to people funding the business with their own resources. The business plan channels their motivations into a clear, well-written mission statement. It is a good idea to write the executive summary last because it will almost always be revised again, when the business plan takes its final shape.

To write an effective executive summary, focus on the issues that are most important to your business's success, and save the supporting information for the body of the business plan. The executive summary should describe the firm's strategy and goals, the good or service it is selling, and the advantages it has over the competition. It should also give a quick overview of how much money will be required to launch the business, how the money will be used, and how the lenders or investors will recoup their funds.

Introduction

The introduction follows the executive summary. After the executive summary has offered an attractive overview, the introduction should begin to discuss the fine details of the business. It should include any material the upcoming marketing and financing sections do not cover. The introduction should describe the company, the management team, and the product in detail. If one of these topics is particularly noteworthy for your business, you may want to present that topic as its own section. Listen to what you write and respond as the plan takes shape.

The Business Plan

I. Executive Summary
- Who, what, when, where, why, and how?

II. Table of Contents

III. Introduction
- The concept and the company
- The management team
- The product

IV. Marketing Strategy
- Demographics
- Trends
- Market penetration
- Potential sales revenue

V. Financing the Business
- Cash flow analysis
- Pro forma balance sheet
- Income statement

VI. Résumés of Principals

FIGURE F.2 Outline of a Business Plan

Include basic information about the company—its past, present, and future. What are the company's roots, what is its current status, and what actions does it need to take to achieve its goals? If you are starting a company, include a description of the evolution of the concept. Be sure to tie all of the business's goals and plans to the industry it will operate in, and describe the industry itself.

A business doesn't run itself, of course. People are the heart of a business, so write an interesting profile of the business's management team. Who are the key players and how does their experience support the company's goals? Describe their—or your, if you are a sole proprietor (an owner–operator)—education, training, and experience, and highlight and refer to résumés included later in the plan. Be honest—not all businesses are started by experts. If you lack demonstrated experience in a certain area, explain how you plan to gain experience.

Also describe the product, which is the driving force behind the venture. What are you offering, and why is it special? What are the costs of the service or the price tag on the good? Analyze the features of the offering and the effect these features have on the overall cost.

Marketing Strategy

Next comes the marketing strategy section. The *marketing strategy* describes the market's need for the item and the way the business will fulfill it. Marketing strategies are not based on informal projections or observations. They are the result of a careful market analysis. Putting together a marketing strategy allows the business owner to become familiar with every aspect of the particular market. If done properly, it will allow you to define your target market and position your business within that sector to get its share of sales.

The marketing strategy will include discussing the size of the customer base that will want to purchase your good or service and the projected rate of growth for the product or category. Highlight information on the demographics of your customers. *Demographics* are statistical characteristics of the segment of the market, such as income, gender, and age. What types of people will purchase your product? How old are they, and where do they live? What is their lifestyle like? For example, someone starting an interior design business will want to report how many homeowners live within a certain distance from the firm and their median income. Of course, this section of the marketing analysis will be quite different for a company that does all of its business online. You will want to know the types of people who will shop at your website, but your discussion won't be limited to one geographic area. It is also a good idea to describe the trends in your product category. Trends are consumer and business tendencies or patterns that business owners can use to gain market share.

The marketing strategy should also detail your distribution, pricing, and promotional goals. Discuss the average price of your offering and the reasons behind the price you have chosen. How do you intend to let your potential customers know that you have a product to sell? How will you sell it—through a catalogue, in a retail location, online, or maybe a combination of all three? The effectiveness of your distribution, pricing, and promotional goals will determine the extent to which you will be able to gain market share.

Competitors are another important part of your marketing strategy. What companies are already selling products similar to yours? Include a list of your competitors to show that you know exactly who they are and what you are up against. Describe what you think are their major strengths and weaknesses and how successful they have been within your market.

Also include the *market penetration,* which is the percentage of total customers who have purchased a company's product. For example, if there are 10,000 people in your market, and 5,000 have purchased your product, your market penetration is 50 percent. The *potential sales revenue,* also an important figure to include, is the total revenue of a company if it captured 100 percent market penetration. In other words, this figure represents the total dollar value of sales you would bring in if everyone who is a potential customer purchased your product.

Financing the Business

The goal of a business is to make money. Everything in the business plan lays the foundation for the *financing section.* Business owners should not skip this section even if they are not seeking outside money. It is crucial to have an accurate financial analysis to get financing, but it also is a necessary exercise for business owners funding the venture themselves. The financing section shows the cost of the product, operating expenses, expected sales revenue and profit, and the amount of the business owner's personal funds that will be invested to get the business up and running. The financial projections should be encouraging but also accurate and based on realistic assumptions. The owner should be able to defend the numbers projected.

Any assumptions made in the body of the business plan should be tied into the financial section. For example, if you think you will need a staff of five, your cash flow analysis should explain how you are going to pay them. A cash flow analysis, a required section of a financial analysis, shows how much money will flow through your business throughout the year. It helps you plan for staggered purchasing, high-volume months, and slow periods. Your business may be cyclical or seasonal; the cash flow projection lets you know whether you need to arrange a line of credit to cover periodic shortfalls. An income statement is another critical document. The income statement is a statement of income and expenses your company has taken on over a period of time.

Remember that leaving out important details can reduce your credibility, so be thorough. The plan must include your assumptions about the conditions under which your business will operate. It should cover details such as market strength; date of start-up; sales buildup; gross profit margin; equipment, furniture, and fixtures required; and payroll and other key expenses that will affect the financial plan. In addition, a banker will want a pro forma balance sheet, which provides an estimate of what the business owns (its assets), what it owes (its liabilities), and what it is worth (the owner's equity). Refer to Chapters 15, 16, and 17 of *Contemporary Business* for additional details on accounting, financial statements, and financial management.

Résumés of Principals

The final element of the business plan is the inclusion of the résumés of the principals behind the business: the management team. Each résumé should include detailed employment information and accomplishments. Consider expanding on the traditional résumé by including business affiliations, professional memberships, hobbies, and leisure activities, but only if this information applies to your business.

Whichever method you choose to develop a business plan, make sure that *you* develop the plan. It should sound as though it was written by the entrepreneur, not by some outside "expert."

RESOURCES

Whether a person has been in business for decades or is just starting out, many resources are available. A tremendous amount of material can help business owners write effective business plans. The biggest task is narrowing down the resources to the ones that are right for you. The Internet offers many sound business-planning tools and advice, much of which are free. You can look up different examples and opinions, which is important. Remember that no one source will match your situation exactly. Your library and career centre also offer many resources. Following are some helpful resources for business planning.

Books

Dozens of books describe how to write a business plan. Examples include the following:

- Edward Blackwell, *How to Prepare a Business Plan,* 7th ed. (London: Kogan Page Ltd., 2011).
- Steven D. Peterson, Peter E. Jaret, and Barbara Findlay Schenck, *Business Plans Kit for Dummies,* 3rd ed. (Wiley Publishing, 2010).
- Mike McKeever, *How to Write a Business Plan,* 10th ed. (Berkeley, CA: Nolo Press, 2010).
- John W. Mullins, *The New Business Road Test: What Entrepreneurs and Executives Should Do Before Writing a Business Plan,* 3rd ed. (*Prentice Hall Financial Times,* 2010).
- Michael Gerber, *The E-Myth Enterprise: How to Turn a Great Idea into a Thriving Business* (New York: Harper Collins, 2009).

Websites

- *Entrepreneur, Inc.* and *BusinessWeek* magazines offer knowledgeable guides to writing a business plan. *Entrepreneur*'s website also contains sample business plans.

  http://www.entrepreneur.com

  http://www.inc.com

  http://www.businessweek.com

- If you are hoping to obtain funding with your business plan, it is a good idea to become familiar with what investors are looking for. The following are professional associations for the venture capital industry:

  http://www.cvca.ca/ (Canada's Venture Capital & Private Equity Association)

  http://www.nvca.org (National Venture Capital Association)

  http://www.nasbic.org (National Association of Small Business Investment Companies)

  http://www.bdc.ca/EN/solutions/venture_capital/Pages/venture_capital.aspx (Business Development Bank of Canada - BDC Venture Capital)

  http://www.nea.com

  http://www.pwc.com

Software

Business-planning software can help to give an initial shape to your business plan. But a word of caution if you write a business plan using a software template—bankers and potential investors, such as venture capitalists, read so many business plans that the plans that are based on templates may sink to the bottom of the pile. Also, if you aren't looking for funding, using software can undercut a chief purpose of writing a plan—learning about your unique idea. Think twice before you deprive yourself of that experience. Remember, software is a tool. It can help you get started, stay organized, and build a professional-looking business plan, but it can't actually write the plan for you.

Associations and Organizations

Many government and professional organizations provide assistance to would-be business owners. Here is a partial list:

- The Business Development Bank of Canada (BDC) is Canada's business development bank providing Canadian businesses with flexible financing, venture capital and consulting services.

  http://www.bdc.ca/Pages/SplashPage.aspx

- The U.S. Small Business Administration offers planning materials, along with other resources.

  http://www.sba.gov/smallbusinessplanner

- The SBA also has a centre specifically designed for female entrepreneurs.

  http://www.sba.gov/aboutsba/sbaprograms/onlinewbc

PROJECTS AND TEAMWORK APPLICATIONS

1. Visit the website for Next Restaurant at http://www.nextrestaurant.com to learn more about the restaurant's innovative method of selling tickets in advance. Think of another business that doesn't usually sell tickets in advance—yet. Write a brief plan for converting that business to the pre-selling business model. Why do you think this business would be successful? What might be the drawbacks?

2. Do you dream of starting your own business? Take your idea and answer as many of the self-evaluation questions in Figure F.1 as you can. Share your answers with the class. Then file your answers away to read at a future date—either when you have graduated from college or university or when you think you are ready to pursue your own business.

3. Write the executive summary portion of the business plan for your potential business. You may use the answers to the questions in Figure F.1 to help you get started.

www.wileyplus.com

Access your WileyPLUS course for:

- The complete digital textbook.

- Question assistance, including links to relevant sections in the online digital textbook.

- Immediate feedback and proof of progress, 24/7

- Integrated, multi-media resources – including MP3 downloads, visual exhibits, animations, and much more – that provide multiple study paths and encourage more active learning.

APPENDIX G
CAREERS IN CONTEMPORARY BUSINESS

You'll be hitting the job market soon—if you haven't already. Regardless of what industry you want to work in—financial services, marketing, travel, construction, hospitality, manufacturing, wireless communications—you need an education. Attending college or university and taking a business course like this one will help you in your job search. Business skills and knowledge are needed in many different fields. But education comes in many forms. In addition to taking classes, you should try to gain related real-life experience. A summer job, an internship, or even a volunteer opportunity can give you excellent experience that you can build on after you graduate. Cooperative education programs and work–study programs can also give you hands-on experience while you pursue your education. Many students across the country will be doing the same thing, but you can set yourself apart through your work ethic and initiative.

Once you leave school, you will need to earn a living—if you aren't already doing so. Your level of education will probably affect your earnings. There is a wide gap between earnings for high-school graduates and earnings for college or university graduates. And there is still a gap between earnings for men and women.[1]

Keep in mind that a degree may help you get in the door for certain job interviews and may put you on a path for advancement, but a degree doesn't guarantee success—you have to achieve that yourself.

Companies plan their hiring strategies carefully to attract and keep the most productive, creative employees and to avoid the cost of rehiring. So, soon-to-be graduates need to be on their toes. But creativity is common among business students. By the time you finish this class—and your college or university education—you will be well equipped to take on the challenge. You can think of your job hunt as a course in itself; at the end of it, you will have a job. And you will be well on your way toward a rewarding business career.

This course exposes you to all the functional areas of business. You learn how firms are organized and operated. You find out who does what in a company. Gradually, you identify industries and disciplines—such as sales, finance, or product design—that interest you. And you learn about many organizations, large and small—who founded them, what products they offer, how they serve their customers, and what types of decisions they make. In short, you gain knowledge about business that you can apply to your career search and life.

Choosing a career is an important life decision. It sets you on a path that will influence where you live, how much money you earn, what type of people you meet, and what you do every day. Whether your goal is to operate an organic farm or to rise high in the ranks of a major corporation, you'll need to understand the principles of business. Even if you think you're headed down a different path, business skills almost always prove to be helpful. Also, many fields are beginning to recognize the importance of a broader base of knowledge than specialized technical skills—and business knowledge is part of that base.

For example, engineers once relied almost solely on a foundation of technical skill and expertise. But experts in the industry now report a trend toward a more well-rounded education. Engineers still need a strong technical foundation, but they need additional skills. "There's no question that the employee who can do five things is harder to get rid of than the one who can only do one or two," says an engineer who held onto his job during the economic downturn. "The more diverse your toolset, the more stable your job will be."[2] That's why this appendix discusses the best way to approach career decisions and to prepare for an *entry-level job*—your first permanent employment after leaving school. We then look at a range of business careers and discuss employment opportunities in a variety of fields.

It's important to remember that you'll be looking for a job regardless of the state of the overall economy, whether it's slow or booming. You'll read about job cuts and unemployment rates, hiring freezes and wage increases. But if you stay flexible and are ready to work—just about any time and anywhere—you'll succeed.[3]

INTERNSHIPS—A GREAT WAY TO ACQUIRE REAL-WORLD EXPERIENCE

Many business students complete one or more *internships* prior to completing their academic careers. Some arrange internships during the summer, while others work at an internship during a semester away from school. An internship gives you hands-on experience in a real business environment, whether it's in banking, the hotel industry, or retailing. An internship does two helpful things: it teaches you how a business runs and can help you decide whether you want to pursue a career in that industry. You might spend a summer interning in the admissions department of a hospital and then graduate with your job search focused on hospital administration. Or you might decide you'd much rather work for a magazine publisher or a construction company.

When you apply for an internship, don't expect to be paid much, if at all. The true value of an internship lies in its hands-on experience. An internship bridges the theory–practice educational gap. It will help carry you from your academic experience to your professional future. Keep in mind that, as an intern, you will not be running a department. People may not ask for your input or ideas. You may work in the warehouse or copy centre. You might be answering phones or entering data. But it is important to make the most of your internship. Many companies make permanent job offers—or offers to enter paid training programs—to the best interns, so you'll want to stand out.

Internships can serve as critical networking and job-hunting tools. They often lead to future employment opportunities, allowing students to demonstrate their technical skills while providing cost-effective employee training for the company. Even if you aren't hired by the company where you interned, the experience is valuable to your job hunt. One study estimates that almost one-third of all entry-level hires had internships prior to being hired. In a recent year, PricewaterhouseCoopers hired 91 percent of its entry-level employees from those who had interned.[4]

With this information in mind, start thinking the way a professional does. Here are some tips for a successful internship experience. These guidelines are also helpful for your first job.

- **Dress like a professional.** Dress appropriately for your future career. During an interview visit, look around to see what the employees are wearing. If you have any questions, ask your supervisor.

- **Act like a professional.** Arrive on time to work. Be punctual for any meetings or assignments. Ask questions and listen to the answers carefully. Complete your work thoroughly and on time. Maintain good etiquette. Be polite on the phone, in meetings, and in all interactions with other people.

- **Stand out.** Work hard and show initiative, but behave appropriately. Don't try to use authority that you do not have. Show that you are willing to learn.

- **Be evaluated.** Even if your internship does not include a formal evaluation, ask your employer how you are doing so you can learn about your strengths and weaknesses.

- **Keep in touch.** Once you complete your internship, stay in touch periodically with the firm so that people know what you are currently doing.

An excellent source of information to begin your search for an internship can be found at the Canadian government's Youth Canada website, http://www.youth.gc.ca/eng/topics/career_planning/internships.shtml.

In addition to an internship, you can build your résumé with work and life experience through volunteer opportunities, extracurricular activities, and summer or off-campus study programs. *Cooperative education* also provides valuable experience. Cooperative education programs are similar to internships, but the jobs themselves usually pay more. These programs may take place during the summer or during the school year. Students typically take classes one semester and hold jobs the next semester. Most cooperative programs are specific to a major field of study, such as retailing or information technology. At your cooperative job, you'll be treated like a real full-time employee, meaning you'll work long hours and probably have more responsibility than you would as an intern. And depending on how these programs are scheduled, you might add a semester or two to your college education. But in the long run, you will gain knowledge and work experience that will serve you well as you build your career.[5]

SELF-ASSESSMENT FOR CAREER DEVELOPMENT

You are going to spend much of your lifetime working, so why not find a job—or at least an industry—that interests you? To choose the line of work that suits you best, you must first understand yourself. Self-assessment involves looking in the mirror and seeing the real you—with all your strengths and weaknesses. It means answering some tough questions. But being honest with yourself pays off because it will help you find a career that will be challenging, rewarding, and meaningful. As you get to know yourself better, you may discover that helping other people really makes you happy. You may realize that to feel secure, you need to earn enough to put away substantial savings. Or you might learn that you are drawn to risks and the unknown, which might point you toward owning your own business. Each of these discoveries provides you with valuable information in choosing a career.

Many resources are available to help you in selecting a career. They include school libraries, career guidance and placement offices, counselling centres, and online job-search services. They include alumni from your college, friends, family, and neighbours. Don't forget the contacts you make during an internship—they can help you in many ways. Ask questions of anyone you know—a local retailer, banker, or restaurant owner. Most people will be happy to speak with you or arrange a time to do so.

If you are interested in a particular industry or company, you might be able to arrange an informational interview—an appointment with someone who can provide you with more knowledge about an industry or career path. This type of interview is different from an interview after you've applied for a specific job, although it may ultimately lead to a job. The informational interview can help you decide whether you want to pursue a particular type of work. It also gives you some added experience in the interview process—without the pressure. To arrange an interview, talk to anyone you know—friends of your parents, local businesspeople, or coordinators of not-for-profit organizations. Your school may have a database of graduates who are working in various fields and who are willing to talk with students on an informational basis—so be sure to start your search right at your own school.

To help you get started asking and answering the questions that will help you begin looking in the right direction, you can visit a number of websites that offer online career assessment tests. Career Explorer, at http://www.careerexplorer.net is one such site; LiveCareer at http://www.livecareer.com is another. These sites and others, such as Monster's Career Tools and Career Advice areas at http://www.monster.com, help you identify your interests, strengths, and weaknesses—including some that may surprise you.[6] In addition, follow the self-assessment process outlined in the next section to learn more about yourself.

The Self-Assessment Process

For a thorough assessment of your goals and interests, follow these steps:

1. **Outline your career interests.** What field or work activities interest you? What rewards do you want to gain from work?

2. **Outline your career goals.** What do you want to achieve through your career? What type of job can you see yourself doing? Where do you see yourself in a year? In five years? Do you have an ultimate dream job? How long are you willing to work to reach it? Write your goals down so that you can refer to them later.

3. **Make plans to reach your goal.** Do you need more education? Does the career require an apprenticeship or a certain number of years on the job? Outline the requirements you'll need to meet to reach your goal.

4. **List your skills and specific talents.** Write down your strengths—job skills you already have and skills you have developed in life. For example, you might know how to use financial software, and you might be good at negotiating with people. In addition, your school's career development office probably has standardized tests that can help test your aptitude for specific careers. However, take these only as a guideline. If you really want to pursue a certain career, go for it.

5. **List your weaknesses.** This can be tough—but it can also be fun. If you are shy about meeting new people, put shyness on your list. If you are quick to argue, admit it. If you aren't the best business-letter writer or think you're terrible at math, confess to yourself. This list gives you an opportunity to see where you need improvement—and take steps to turn weaknesses into strengths.

6. **Briefly sketch out your educational background.** Write down the schools, colleges, universities, and special training programs you have attended, along with any courses you plan to complete before starting full-time employment. Make an honest assessment of how your background matches up with the current job market. Then make plans to complete any further education you may need.

7. **List the jobs you have held.** Include jobs that paid, internships, and volunteer opportunities. They all gave you valuable experience. As you make your list, think about what you liked and disliked about each. Maybe you liked working with the general public as a supermarket cashier. Perhaps you enjoyed caring for animals at a local shelter.

8. **Consider your hobbies and personal interests.** Many people have turned hobbies and personal pursuits into rewarding careers. Mick Jagger, lead singer of the Rolling Stones,

has a master's degree from the London School of Economics. Without it, he probably wouldn't have been able to manage his rock group's vast business dealings. Jake Burton Carpenter earned a bachelor's degree in economics, but he loved winter sports. So he started a snow-board manufacturing company—and revolutionized the way people get from the top of a snowy mountain to the bottom. Cooking and catering star Paula Deen needed to support her young family. She loved the cooking from her own region—the South—so she opened a small business where she and her boys delivered freshly made bag lunches to local businesses. Today she is a celebrity with her own television show, cookbooks, website, retail products, and more.[7] Turning a hobby into a career doesn't happen overnight, and it's not easy. It requires the same amount of research and hard work as any other business. But for many people, it is a labour of love—and it ultimately succeeds because they refuse to give up.

JOB SEARCH GUIDELINES

Once you have narrowed your choice of career possibilities to two or three that seem right for you, get to work on your job search. Think about the qualities that made these career choices attractive to you. The same qualities also likely caught the attention of others, so you must expect competition. Locate available positions that interest you; then be resourceful! Your success depends on gathering as much information as possible.

Register at Your Career Centre

Register at your school's career centre. Set up an applicant file, including letters of recommendation and supporting personal information. Most placement offices send out periodic lists of new job vacancies by e-mail, so be sure to get your name and e-mail address on the list. Visit the office regularly, and become a familiar face. Find out how the office arranges interviews with company representatives who visit campus. If your school has a career event, make sure you attend.

Preparing Your Job Credentials

Most placement or credential files include the following information:

1. Letters of reference from people who know you well—instructors and employers
2. Transcripts of course work to date
3. Personal data form to report factual information
4. Statement of career goals.

The career centre will provide you with special forms to help you to develop your file. Often, these forms can be completed online. Prepare the forms carefully because employers are always interested in your written communication skills. Keep a copy of the final file for later use in preparing similar information for other employment sources. Check back with the career centre to make sure your file is in order. Update it whenever necessary to reflect additional academic accomplishments and added work experiences.

Letters of reference are very important because they give prospective employers some personal and professional insights about you. They can influence a hiring decision. Make a careful list of people who might be willing to write letters of reference. Your references should not be family members or close friends. Instead, choose a coach, an instructor, a former employer, or someone else whose knowledge could help your job application. A soccer coach could vouch for your hard work and determination. A music teacher might be able to detail how well you accept instruction. A former employer might describe your punctuality and ability to get along with others. If possible, include someone from your school's business faculty on your list of references, or at least one of your current instructors.

Always ask people personally for letters of reference. Be prepared to give them a brief outline of your academic preparation and information about your job interests and career goals. This information will help them prepare their letters quickly and efficiently. It also shows that you are serious about the task and respect their time. Remember that these people are very busy. Allow them at least a couple of weeks to prepare their reference letters; then follow up politely if you haven't heard back. Always call or write to thank them for writing the letters.

Finding Employment through the Internet

The Internet plays an important role in connecting employers and job seekers. Companies of all sizes post their job opportunities on the Web, both on their own sites and on job sites such as Monster.ca, HotJobs.ca, and CareerBuilder.ca. Specialized, or niche, sites such as AccountingJobs.ca and TechJobsCanada.com are also gaining popularity. Some sites are free to applicants, while others charge a subscription fee. Figure G.1 provides a sampling of general and focused career sites.

General and Staffing Sites

Monster.ca

HotJobs.ca

CareerBuilder.ca

KellyServices.ca

Government Sites

http://jobs-emplois.gc.ca/index-eng.htm

http://www.govjobs.ca/

Industry

Health care—http://www.healthcarejob.ca/

Business & finance—http://accountingjobs.ca/; http://www.efinancialcareers-canada.com/

Marketing—http://www.marketing-jobs.ca/

Sales—http://www.salesjobscanada.com/

Technology—http://www.techjobscanada.com/

FIGURE G.1 Internet Job Sites

Career websites typically offer job postings, tips on creating an effective résumé, a place to post your résumé, and advice on interviews and careers. If this sounds easy, keep in mind that these sites may receive hundreds of thousands of hits each day from job hunters, which means you have lots of competition. You can still use one of these sites as part of your job search; just don't make it your only source. Smart job seekers often find that their time is better spent on specialized job boards that offer more focused listings. Naturally, if a particular company interests you, go to the firm's website, where available positions will be posted. If you are interested in applying for a job at the accounting firm Ernst & Young, go to http://www.ey.com. If you are looking for a job with Whole Foods Market, visit http://www.wholefoods.com. And if you fancy yourself working for an outdoor retailer, go to Mountain Equipment Co-op (MEC) at http://www.mec.ca.

Newspapers, the source for traditional classified want ads, also post their ads on the Web. Job seekers can even visit sites that merge ads from many different newspapers into one searchable database, such as CareerBuilder (http://www.careerbuilder.ca). Some sites go a step farther and create separate sections for each career area. For example, entire sections may be devoted to accounting, marketing, and other business professions. Searches can then be narrowed according to geographic location, entry level, company name, job title, job description, and other categories.

As mentioned earlier, you can connect with potential employers by posting your résumé on job sites. Employers search the résumé database for prospects with the right qualifications. One commonly used approach is for an employer to list one or more *keywords* to select candidates for personal interviews—for example, "retail sales experience," "network architecture," or "spa management"—and then browse the résumés that contain all the required keywords. Employers also scan résumés into their human resource database. Then, when a manager requests, for example, 10 candidates, the database can be searched by keywords that apply to the request. Job seekers need to respond to this type of computer screening of applicants by ensuring that right keywords appear on their résumés.

Finding Employment through Other Sources

Earlier, we mentioned the importance of registering at your school's career planning or placement office. If you have completed formal academic coursework at more than one institution, you may be able to set up a placement file at each school. In addition, you may want to contact private and public employment services available in your location or in the area where you would like to live.

Private Employment Agencies

These firms often specialize in certain types of jobs, such as marketing, finance, sales, or engineering. They help both employers and job candidates by offering services that are not available elsewhere. Many private agencies interview, test, and screen job applicants so that potential employers do not have to. Job candidates benefit from the service by being accepted by the agency and because the agency makes the first contact with the potential employer.

A private employment agency usually charges the employer a fee for finding a suitable employee. Other firms charge job seekers a fee for helping find them a job. Make sure that you understand the terms of any agreement you sign with a private employment agency.

Employment Offices

Don't forget to check the government employment offices in your area. Because of the mix of duties, some people view government employment agencies as providing services for semiskilled or unskilled workers. However, these agencies *do* list jobs in many professional categories and are often intimately involved with identifying job finalists for major new facilities moving to your area. In addition, many of the jobs listed at government employment offices may be with government agencies and may include professionals such as accountants, attorneys, healthcare professionals, and scientists.

Learning More about Job Opportunities

Carefully study the various employment opportunities you have identified. Obviously, you will like some more than others, but you can examine a variety of factors when assessing each job possibility:

- Actual job responsibilities
- Industry characteristics
- Nature of the company
- Geographic location
- Salary and opportunities for advancement
- How it supports your long-range career objectives.

Too many job applicants consider only the most striking features of a job, such as its location or the salary offer. But a comprehensive review of job openings should provide a balanced view of the overall employment opportunity, including both long-term and short-term factors.

BUILDING A RÉSUMÉ

Regardless of how you locate job openings, you must learn how to prepare and submit a *résumé*, a written summary of your personal, educational, and professional achievements. The résumé is a personal document covering your educational background, work experience, career preferences and goals, and any related major interests. It also includes such basic contact information as your home and e-mail addresses and your telephone number. It should *not* include information on your age, marital status, race, or ethnic background.

Your résumé is usually your formal introduction to an employer, so it should present you in the best light, highlighting your strengths and your ability to contribute to a firm. But it should *never* contain inflated statements or wrong information. You don't want to begin your career with unethical behaviour, and an employer is bound to discover any conflicts in fact—either immediately or during the months following your employment. Either event will result disrupt your career path.

Organizing Your Résumé

The primary purpose of a résumé is to highlight your qualifications for a job, usually on a single page. An attractive layout makes it easier for the employer to review your qualifications. You can prepare your résumé in several ways. You may use narrative sentences to explain job duties and career goals, or you may present information in outline form. A résumé included as part of your credentials file at the career centre on campus should be quite short. Remember to design it around your specific career objectives.

Figures G.2, G.3, and G.4 illustrate different ways to organize your résumé—by *reverse chronology*, or time; by *function*; and by *results*. Regardless of which format you select, you will want to include the following: a clearly stated objective, your work or professional experience, your education, your personal interests such as sports or music, and your volunteer work. While all three formats are acceptable, one study showed that 78 percent of employers preferred the reverse chronological format—with the most recent experience listed first—because it was the easiest to follow.

Tips for Creating a Strong Résumé

Your résumé should help you stand out from the crowd, just as your college or university admissions application did. A company may receive hundreds or even thousands of résumés, so you want yours to be on the top of the stack. Here are some do's and don'ts:

Do:

- State your immediate objective clearly. If you are applying for a specific job, say so. State why you want the job and why you want to work at this company.

- Use terms related to your field, so that a human resource manager can spot those terms quickly. If you are submitting your résumé online, use words that will create an automatic "match" with a job description or field. If you are applying for an entry-level job in marketing, the phrase "communication skills" is likely to generate a match. You can identify such words and phrases by reading job descriptions online.

- Provide facts about previous jobs, internships, cooperative education programs, or volunteer work, including results or specific achievements. Include any projects or tasks you undertook through your own initiative.

- Emphasize your education if you are a recent graduate. Place it closer to the top of your résumé instead of near the bottom.

- Highlight your strengths and skills, such as research, writing, or organizing.

- Write clearly and concisely.

- Proofread your résumé carefully for grammar, usage, and typographical errors. Refer to a dictionary or style manual.

- Keep your résumé to a single page.

FELICIA SMITH-WHITEHEAD
4265 Popular Lane
Toronto, ON, M4Y 2K2,
416-555-3296
FeliciaSW@gmail.com

OBJECTIVE
Challenging office management position in a results-oriented company where my organizational and people skills can be applied; leading to an operations management position.

WORK EXPERIENCE
ADM Distribution Enterprises, Toronto, ON   2010–Present
Office Manager of leading regional soft-drink bottler. Coordinate all bookkeeping, correspondence, scheduling of 12-truck fleet to serve 300 customers, promotional mailings, and personnel records, including payroll. Install computerized systems.

Merriweather, Hicks & Bradshaw Attorneys, Toronto, ON   2008–2010
Office Supervisor and Executive Assistant for Douglas H. Bradshaw, Managing Partner. Supervised four clerical workers and two paraprofessionals, automated legal research and correspondence functions, and assisted in coordinating outside services and relations with other firms and agencies. Promoted three times from Secretary to Office Supervisor.

Conner & Sons Custom Coverings, Toronto, ON   2004–2008
Secretary in father's upholstery and awning company. Performed all office functions over the years, running the office when the owner was on vacation.

EDUCATION

Humber College, Associate's Degree in Business   2008

North Toronto Collegiate, Honours   2004

COMPUTER SKILLS
Familiar with Microsoft Office and Adobe Acrobat

LANGUAGE SKILLS
Fluent in French (speaking and writing)
Adequate speaking and writing skills in Portuguese

PERSONAL
Member of various community associations; avid reader; enjoy sports such as camping and cycling; enjoy volunteering in community projects.

FIGURE G.2
Chronological Résumé

Don't:

- Offer any misleading or inaccurate information.
- Make vague statements, such as "I work well with others," or "I want a position in business."
- State your objective as, "to run this company" or to "advance as quickly as possible."
- Include a salary request.
- Make demands about vacation time, work hours, or excessive benefits.
- Highlight your weaknesses.
- Submit a résumé with typos or grammatical errors.
- Use slang or other inappropriate phrases or comments.
- Include pictures or graphics, or use fancy fonts.[8]

Eric Greene
Five Oceanside Drive, Apt. 6B
Cavendish, Prince Edward Island
902-444-3838
egreene87@gmail.com

Objective
Joining a growth-oriented company that values highly productive employees. Seeking an opportunity that leads to senior merchandising position.

Professional Experience
Administration
Management responsibilities in a major retailing buying office, coordinated vendor-relation efforts. Supervised assistant buyers.

Category Management
Experience in buying home improvement and sport and recreation categories.

Planning
Chaired a team charged with reviewing the company's annual vendor evaluation program.

Problem Solving
Successfully developed a program to improve margins in the tennis, golf, and fishing lines.

Work Experience
Senior Buyer for Island Department Store   2009–Present

Merchandiser for Maritime Inc.   2007–2009

Education
Bachelor's Degree
McGill University, Montreal
                                                                 2005–2007

Associate's Degree
Dalhousie University, Halifax   2003–2005

FIGURE G.3
Functional Résumé

Take your time with your résumé; it is one of the most important documents you'll create during your career. If you need help, go to your school's career centre. If you are dealing with an employment agency, a counsellor there can help.

Keep in mind that you will probably need to tailor your résumé to each company or job. Again, take the time to do this; it may mean the difference between standing out and being lost in a sea of other applicants.

Preparing Your Cover Letter

In most cases, your résumé will be sent with a *cover letter*. This letter should introduce who you are, explain why you are submitting a résumé (cite the specific job opening if possible), and inform the recipient where you can be reached for an interview. An effective cover letter will make the recipient want to take the next step and read your résumé. Here are a few tips for preparing an outstanding letter:

- Write the letter to a specific person, if possible. A letter addressed to "to whom it may concern" may never reach the right person. Call the company or check its website for the name of the person you should address your letter to. It might be someone in human resources or a person in the department where you'd actually be working. Be sure to obtain the

ANTONIO PETTWAY
101 Beverly Road
Victoria, BC V8N 1S3
778-224-5764
apettway@yahoo.com

OBJECTIVE

To apply my expertise as a construction supervisor to a management role in an organization seeking improvements in overall production, long-term employee relationships, and the ability to attract the best talent in the construction field.

PROFESSIONAL EXPERIENCE

DAL Construction Company, Victoria, BC   2010–Present
   Established automated, on-site recordkeeping system improving communications and morale between field and office personnel, saving 400 work hours per year, and reducing the number of accounting errors by 20 percent. Developed a crew selected as "first choice crew" by most workers wanting transfers. Completed five housing projects ahead of deadline and under budget.

Alberta Housing Authority, Lethbridge, AB   2008–2010
   Created friendly, productive atmosphere among workers enabling first on-time job completion in 4 years and one-half of usual materials waste. Initiated pilot materials delivery program with potential savings of 3.5 percent of yearly maintenance budget.

Essex County Housing Authority, Windsor, ON   2008
   Produced information pamphlets increasing applications for county housing by 22 percent. Introduced labor-management discussion techniques saving jobs and over $29,000 in lost time.

Payton, Durnbell & Associates Architects, London, ON   2007–2008
   Developed and monitored productivity improvements, saving 60 percent on information transfer costs for firm's 12 largest jobs.

EDUCATION

University of Windsor, Bachelor's degree in Business   2003–2007

COMPUTER SKILLS

Familiar with Microsoft Office and Adobe Acrobat

PERSONAL

Highly self-motivated. Willing to relocate. Enjoy tennis and hiking.

FIGURE G.4 Results-Oriented Résumé

person's title if possible (such as general manager or director)—and spell the person's name correctly.

- Introduce yourself and explain the purpose of your letter—to apply for a job.

- Describe briefly an example of your best work or your most ambitious project.

- Keep it short—a page is acceptable, half a page even better.

- Request an interview.

- Thank the person for his or her time and consideration.

- Make sure all your contact information is in the letter—name, address, home phone number, cellphone number, and e-mail address.

- Proofread your letter carefully.[9]

Submitting Your Online Résumé

You may write a sparkling cover letter and an expert résumé. But if your online submission is blocked or tossed aside by an automated processing system, you'll never have a chance to impress the person it was intended for. Here are a few tips for making certain your letter and résumé reach their destination.

- Review the formatting of your résumé to make sure it will appear the same to the recipient as it does to you. Delete any unusual symbols or fonts.
- Use keywords that create a match and allow your résumé through the company's filter. This tip also applies to the subject line of your e-mail, which should be specific and contain keywords such as "application for sales trainee job."
- Include your cover letter in the e-mail.
- Send your résumé in the body of the e-mail—not as an attachment. This is more convenient for the recipient. It also avoids the disaster of having your attachment automatically deleted by an antivirus system.
- Do not send graphics, because they may be blocked or deleted.
- If you are answering an ad, read the instructions for application and follow them exactly.[10]

THE JOB INTERVIEW

Congratulations! You've prepared an effective résumé, and you've been contacted for an interview. An interview is more than a casual conversation. During an interview, at least one manager will learn about you, and you'll learn more about the company and the job. Although you may feel nervous about the interview, you can control some of its outcome by doing your homework: planning and preparing for this important encounter with your potential employer. Before you meet with an interviewer, learn everything you can about the firm. The simplest way to do this is to visit the company's website. You can also check with your school's career centre. If you know anyone who works for the company, ask that person about the firm. Try to learn the answers to the following questions about the organization:

- What does the firm do—manufacture clothing, market snack foods, produce films, sell cars? If you are applying for a job at a large corporation, zero in on the division where you would be working.
- What is the company's mission? Many firms include a statement about their purpose in the business world—to supply affordable energy to communities, to serve fresh food, to make communication easier. Understanding why the company exists will help you grasp where it is headed and why.
- Where, when, and by whom was the company founded? Learn a little about the history of the firm.
- What is its position in the marketplace? Is it a leader or is it trying to gain a competitive advantage? Who are its main competitors?
- Where is the firm based? Does it have operations located around the country and the world, or is it purely local?
- How is the company organized? Are there multiple divisions and products?
- Learning about the firm shows the interviewer that you have initiative and motivation, and an interest in the firm's culture and history. You have taken the time and effort to find out more about the organization, and your enthusiasm shows.

Tips for Successful Interviewing

An interview is your personal introduction to the company. You want to make a good impression. But you also want to learn whether you and the firm are a good fit. Although the interviewer will be asking most of the questions, you will also want to ask some questions. People who conduct interviews say that the most important qualities candidates can exhibit are self-confidence, preparedness, and an ability to communicate clearly.

When you are contacted for an interview, find out the name(s) of the person or people who will be interviewing you. You can also ask whether the initial interview will be with a human resource manager or with the person to whom you would be reporting on the job, or both. Many people who conduct initial job interviews work in their firms' human resource divisions. These interviewers act as gatekeepers and can make recommendations to managers and supervisors about which individuals to interview further, or hire. Managers who head the units where an applicant will be employed may get involved later in the hiring process. Some hiring decisions come from human resource personnel together with the immediate supervisor of the prospective employee. In other cases, immediate supervisors make the decision alone. At your interview, keep in mind the following tips.

Do:

- **Dress appropriately.** Dress as if it is your first day of work at the firm. Conceal any tattoos or body piercings and wear simple jewellery.

- **Arrive a few minutes early.** These few minutes will give you time to relax and take in the surroundings. It also shows that you are punctual and care about other people's time.

- **Introduce yourself with a smile and a handshake.** Be friendly, but not overly familiar.

- **Be yourself—at your best.** Don't suddenly adopt a new personality. Be confident, polite, respectful, and interested in the people who are spending time with you. Be sure to thank each person who interviews you.

- **Listen.** Pay attention to what the interviewer is saying. If something is unclear, ask for clarification. Turn off your cellphone. Your full attention should be on the conversation you are having in the interview.

- **Use appropriate language.** As in your résumé and cover letter, be sure to use correct English. You don't need to be stiff or formal, but avoid slang or phrases that you know are inappropriate for the situation.

- **Be positive in your outlook.** Be enthusiastic about the firm and the job, but don't go overboard.

Don't:

- **Talk too much.** Avoid telling the interviewer a lot about your personal life, or why you left a particular job. Answer questions honestly and thoroughly, but don't dip into meaningless details.

- **Be arrogant or aggressive.** Self-confidence is a good trait, but don't go overboard by behaving in a superior or snobbish manner. Never be aggressive. Do not demand that the interviewer offer you the job or even another interview.

- **Act indifferent or bored.** This may not be the job you ultimately want, but treat the interview and the interviewer with respect and attention. If you make a good impression, the firm is likely to keep your name on file—and that dream job may appear after all.

- **Don't get ahead of yourself.** This is not the time to discuss salary, vacation, or benefits.[11]

Answering and Asking Questions

In a typical format, the interviewer gives you enough time to talk about yourself and your goals. You want to present your thoughts clearly and concisely, in an organized fashion, without rambling on to unrelated topics. The interviewer may wait until you are finished or prompt you to talk about certain subjects by asking questions. Be as specific as possible when answering questions. The questions that interviewers ask often include the following:

- "Why do you want this job?"
- "Why do you want to work in this field?"

- "What are your short-term goals? Long-term objectives?"
- "Where do you see yourself in five years? In 10 years?"
- "What are your strengths? What are your weaknesses?"
- "What motivates you?"
- "Describe a situation in which you made a tough decision or solved a problem."
- "What did you like best about your last job? What did you like least?"
- "Why did you leave your last job?"
- "Why should my firm hire you?"
- "Are you considering other jobs or companies?"

Some of these questions may seem tougher than others, but you can reduce your anxiety by preparing for them. First, think about which questions you fear the most. Then think about possible answers that are both truthful and positive. Rehearse your delivery in front of a mirror or with a friend.[12]

At some point, the interviewer will probably ask you whether you have any questions of your own. It's a good idea to come prepared with some questions, but you may think of other questions during the interview. Try to keep your list short, to three or four of your most important questions. The questions you ask show who you are—just as you revealed yourself when you answered the interviewer's questions. Here is a sample of appropriate questions for the initial interview:

- "Could you clarify a certain aspect of the job responsibilities for me?"
- "Do people who start in entry-level jobs at this company tend to develop their careers here?"
- "In what ways could I perform above and beyond the job requirements?"

At some point during your conversation, the interviewer may give you an idea of the salary range for the job. If not, he or she will do so during a subsequent interview. You may ask about the range, but do not ask exactly how much you will be paid if you get the job. Keep in mind that usually there is little or no negotiation for an entry-level salary. You can ask whether there is a probationary period with a review at the end of the period. Here are a few other questions *not* to ask:

- "When will I be promoted?"
- "How much time off do I get?"
- "When will I get my first raise?"
- "How many people are applying for this job?"
- "What are my chances of getting this job?"

At the end of the interview, be sure to thank the interviewer with a smile and a handshake, even if you both know the job is not for you. Again, another opportunity may come along in the future and you want to leave the door open. When you get home, write a note or e-mail the interviewer, thanking him or her for time spent with you. Thank-you notes really do make a lasting impression on a person, and it gives you another chance to reinforce your interest.

A successful first interview will often lead to a second interview. The purpose of this interview is to learn more about your specific qualifications and fit with the company. You may be introduced to more people—potential co-workers, people in other divisions, or sales staff. You may have another meeting with human resource staff, where you'll learn more about salary, employee benefits, and the firm's code of ethics. Depending on the type of job, you might be asked to take some skills tests. If you are entering a training program for a bank, you might be required to take some math-oriented tests. If you are going to work for a publisher, you might be asked to take an editing test or do some proofreading. If you are applying for a job as a sales representative, you may be given a test that assesses your personality traits. Don't be intimidated by these tests—you are not expected to know everything or be perfect—just do your best.

Making the Employment Decision

After receiving your résumé, conducting one or two interviews, and administering a skills test, a potential employer knows a lot about you. You should also know a lot about the company. If the experience has been positive on both sides, you may be offered a job. If you have interviewed at several companies and are offered more than one job, congratulations! You may receive a phone call, followed by a letter outlining the offer in writing. Whether you receive one offer or several, thank the person making the offer. If you choose to accept immediately, feel free to do so. If you have doubts about the job or need to decide between two, feel free to ask for 24 hours to respond. If you must decline an offer, do so promptly and politely. After all, you may end up working for that firm sometime in the future. If you get a few rejections before you receive an offer, don't give up. Every application and interview adds to your experience.

Congratulations! You've accepted an offer for your first job. You are now a member of the workforce.

As you think about an offer, consider the parts of the job that are most important. You'll want to choose a job that comes closest to your career interests and objectives. But don't rule out the element of surprise—you might wind up with a job you like in an industry you'd never considered before. Don't worry too much about the salary. The point of an entry-level job is to get moving on a forward path. And keep in mind that your first job won't be your last. Once you have accepted an offer, you'll be given a start date and the name of the person to report to. Congratulations, you are now a member of the workforce!

Nontraditional Students

Take a quick glance around your class. You'll likely see classmates of all ages. Some will fall into the traditional college age group of 18 to 22, but many don't. Perhaps you are a Canadian Armed Forces recruit returning from military duty overseas. Maybe you have been working in a full-time career but want to broaden your education. Students who fall outside the 18- to 22-year-old age group are often referred to as *nontraditional students,* but these students have become the norm on many campuses. Other examples of nontraditional students are homemakers returning to school to freshen up their résumés before returning to the workforce and workers who have been laid off due to an economic downturn. As diverse as this group is, they share one thing in common: they are older than traditional students. That means they face different challenges—but also enjoy some advantages over their younger classmates.

One major challenge faced by nontraditional students is scheduling. Often they are juggling the responsibilities of work, school, and family. They may have to study at odd times—during meals, while commuting, or after putting the kids to bed. If they are switching careers, they may also be learning an entirely new set of skills. But nontraditional students have an important advantage: experience. Even experience in an unrelated field is a plus. Older students know how organizations operate. Often, they have developed useful skills in human relations, management, budgeting, and communications. Even a former stay-at-home parent has skills in all of these areas. By observing other people's successes and failures—and by living through a few of their own—they have developed a knowledge of what to do and what not to do. So, in some ways, these students have a head start on their younger counterparts. But they also face the reality that they have fewer years for developing a career.

THE JOB MARKET: WHERE DO YOU FIT IN?

The industry you choose, and the career path you follow within it, are part of a bigger picture. They reflect the needs of society, changing populations, developing technology, and the overall economy. For example, the North American population is expected to increase at a slower rate of growth for the near future than during the previous two decades.

As the North American baby-boom generation ages, the age group between 55 and 64 will increase by about one-third. Thus, we will need more healthcare services and other services for an aging population, such as assisted living facilities and leisure and hospitality. Today's younger workers are receiving more education and training to fill the need for professional and business service workers. These projections affect both the workforce and the types of goods and services needed to satisfy consumers. So jobs in education and healthcare services and in professional and business services will increase substantially.

Careers in service-providing industries continue a long-term rise. Service jobs in health-care and social assistance will increase while manufacturing jobs will continue to shrink. But industries that produce certain types of goods, such as those related to the needs of an aging population and those related to green technologies or products, will probably increase.

The good news is that even in a weaker job market, employers are looking to hire recent college and university graduates. In fact, some continue to offer signing bonuses and other incentives to recruit the best workers. Why? Continuing to hire entry-level employees makes good business sense. Some of the hot jobs can be found in accounting, sales, management training, engineering, and business services. So celebrate your graduation. Keep your résumé current and your outlook positive: a job is out there for you.

A LONG-RANGE VIEW OF YOUR CAREER

Choosing a career is an important life decision. A career is a professional journey—whether you want to run a small restaurant or a branch bank, whether you are fascinated by language or math, whether you prefer to work with animals or people. In the end, you hope to contribute something good to society while enjoying what you do—and make a reasonable living at it.

Throughout your career, it is important to stay flexible and to continue learning. Challenging new skills will be required of managers and other businesspeople during these first decades of the 21st century. Remain open to unexpected changes and opportunities that can help you learn and develop new skills. Keep in mind that your first job will not be your last. But tackle that first job with the same energy and excitement you'd have if someone asked you to run the company itself. Everything you learn on that job will be valuable at some point during your career, and who knows—someday, you may actually run the company.

Finally, if you haven't already started your career search, begin now. Start by talking with various people, lining up an internship, looking for a part-time job on or off campus, or volunteering for an organization. Register with the campus career centre long before you graduate. Then, when you reach your final semester, you'll be well on your way to beginning the career you want.

We are confident that this textbook presents a selection of career options. Whatever you decide, be sure it is right for you—not your friends, your instructors, or your parents. As the old saying goes, "You pass this way just once." Enjoy the journey!

PROJECTS AND TEAMWORK APPLICATIONS

1. Visit one of the job websites such as CareerBuilder.ca or Monster.ca and research an industry you think you might be interested in. Prepare a report on what you learned about the field. Was the site helpful? What types of jobs were available in the field? Based on your report, do you plan to pursue this industry or select another field?

2. Prepare your résumé following the procedures outlined earlier in this section. Exchange your résumé with a classmate so you can critique each other's resume. Then revise and proofread your résumé.

3. Go online to the website for a specific company that you might be interested in working for. Click on the "Careers" or "Job Opportunities" section of the site, and read carefully the job descriptions for any entry-level positions and the procedure for applying for them. Also review any general information about career development at the firm. Write a cover letter as if you were actually applying for one of the jobs.

4. With a classmate, practise interviewing for the job you selected in the previous question. Prepare questions for each other and take turns interviewing and being interviewed. What parts of the interview did you handle well? What can you improve?

5. Think about where you would like to be in your career in five years and write about your plans. Share your plans with the class, then seal them in an envelope. Keep the envelope and open it in five years to see how close you came to your predictions.

www.wileyplus.com

Access your WileyPLUS course for:

- The complete digital textbook.

- Question assistance, including links to relevant sections in the online digital textbook.

- Immediate feedback and proof of progress, 24/7

- Integrated, multi-media resources – including MP3 downloads, visual exhibits, animations, and much more – that provide multiple study paths and encourage more active learning.

GLOSSARY

accounting the process of measuring, interpreting, and communicating financial information to support internal and external business decision-making.

accounting cycle the set of activities involved in converting information and individual transactions into financial statements.

accounting equation the relationship that should reflect a firm's financial position at any time: assets should always equal the sum of liabilities and owners' equity.

Accounting Standards Board (AcSB) the organization that interprets and modifies GAAP in Canada for private and not-for-profit businesses.

accrual accounting an accounting method that records revenues and expenses when they occur, not when cash actually changes hands.

acquisition an agreement in which one firm purchases another.

advertising paid nonpersonal communication usually targeted at large numbers of potential buyers.

affective conflict a disagreement that focuses on individuals or personal issues.

affinity program a marketing effort sponsored by an organization that targets people who share common interests and activities.

angel investors wealthy individuals who invest directly in a new venture in exchange for an equity stake.

application service provider (ASP) an outside supplier that provides both the computers and the application support for managing an information system.

asset anything with future benefit owned or controlled by a firm.

balance of payments the overall money flows into and out of a country.

balance of trade the difference between a nation's exports and imports.

balance sheet a statement of a firm's financial position—what it owns and claims against its assets—at a particular point in time.

balanced budget a situation where total revenues raised by taxes and fees equal the total proposed government spending for the year.

Bank of Canada (the Bank) the central bank of Canada.

bankruptcy the legal nonpayment of financial obligations.

benchmarking the process of looking at how well other companies perform business functions or tasks and using their performance as a standard for measuring another company's performance.

board of directors the governing body of a corporation.

botnet a network of PCs that have been infected with one or more data-stealing viruses.

brand a name, term, sign, symbol, design, or some combination that identifies the products of one firm and shows how they differ from competitors' offerings.

brand equity the added value that a respected and successful name gives to a product.

brand name the part of a brand that is made up of words or letters that form a name. It is used to identify a firm's products and show how they differ from the products of competitors.

branding the process of creating in consumers' minds an identity for a good, service, or company; a major marketing tool in contemporary business.

breakeven analysis the pricing-related technique used to calculate the minimum sales volume a product must generate at a certain price level to cover all costs.

budget an organization's plan for how it will raise and spend money during a specific period of time.

budget deficit a situation where the government spends more than it raises through taxes.

budget surplus the excess funding when government spends less than it raises through taxes and fees.

business all profit-seeking activities and enterprises that provide goods and services necessary to an economic system.

business (B2B) product a good or service purchased to be used, either directly or indirectly, in the production of other goods for resale.

Business Development Bank of Canada (BDC) a governmental agency that assists, counsels, and protects the interests of small businesses in Canada.

business ethics standards of conduct and moral values regarding right and wrong actions in the business environment.

business incubator a local program designed to provide low-cost, shared business facilities to small start-up companies.

business intelligence a field of research that uses activities and technologies for gathering, storing, and analyzing data to make better competitive decisions.

business law those parts of law that most directly influence and regulate the management of business activity.

business plan a formal document that details a company's goals, methods, and standards.

Canada Deposit Insurance Corporation (CDIC) the federal agency that insures deposits at commercial and savings banks.

capital production inputs consisting of technology, tools, information, and physical facilities.

capital structure the mix of a firm's debt and equity capital.

capitalism an economic system that rewards firms for their ability to perceive and serve the needs and demands of consumers; also called the private enterprise system.

category advisor the individual that the business customer assigns as the major supplier to deal with all the other suppliers for a project. The category advisor also presents the entire package to the business buyer.

cause advertising a form of institutional advertising that promotes a specific viewpoint on a public issue as a way to influence public opinion and the political process.

cause marketing marketing that promotes a cause or social issue, such as preventing child abuse, anti-littering efforts, and stop-smoking campaigns.

Central America–Dominican Republic Free Trade Agreement (CAFTA-DR) an agreement among the United States, Costa Rica, the Dominican Republic, El Salvador, Guatemala, Honduras, and Nicaragua to reduce tariffs and trade restrictions.

chief information officer (CIO) the executive responsible for managing a firm's information systems and related computer technologies.

classic entrepreneur a person who sees a business opportunity and sets aside resources to gain access to that market.

cloud computing the use of powerful servers that store applications software and databases that users access by using any Internet-connected device, such as a PC or a smartphone.

cobranding a cooperative arrangement where two or more businesses team up to closely link their names on a single product.

code of conduct a formal statement that defines how an organization expects its employees to resolve ethical issues.

cognitive conflict a disagreement that focuses on problem- and issue-related differences of opinion.

collective bargaining the process of negotiation between management and union representatives.

comarketing a cooperative arrangement where two businesses jointly market each other's products.

common law laws that result from judicial decisions, some of which can be traced to early England.

common shares the basic form of company ownership; shares that give owners voting rights but only residual claims to the firm's assets and income distributions.

communication a meaningful exchange of information through messages.

communism an economic system where all property is shared equally by the people in a community under the direction of a strong central government.

compensation the amount employees are paid in money and benefits.

competition the battle among businesses for consumer acceptance.

competitive differentiation the unique combination of organizational abilities, products, and approaches that sets one company apart from its competitors in the minds of customers.

competitive pricing a strategy that tries to reduce the emphasis on price competition by matching other firms' prices and by focusing their own marketing efforts on the product, distribution, and promotional elements of the marketing mix.

computer-aided design (CAD) a process used by engineers to design parts and entire products on the computer. Engineers who use CAD can work faster and with fewer mistakes than those who use traditional drafting systems.

computer-aided manufacturing (CAM) a computer tool that a manufacturer uses to analyze CAD output and the steps that a machine must take to produce a needed product or part.

computer-based information systems information systems that use computer and related technologies to store information electronically in an organized, accessible manner.

computer-integrated manufacturing (CIM) an integrated production system that uses computers to help workers design products, control machines, handle materials, and control the production function.

conflict the outcome when one person's, or one group's, needs do not match those of another, and one side may try to block the other side's intentions or goals.

conflict of interest a situation in which an employee must choose between a business's welfare and personal gain.

conglomerate merger a merger that combines unrelated firms, usually with the goal of diversification, increasing sales, or spending a cash surplus to avoid a takeover attempt.

consumer (B2C) product a good or service that is purchased by end users.

consumer behaviour end consumers' activities that are directly involved in obtaining, consuming, and disposing of products, and the decision processes before and after these activities.

consumer orientation a business philosophy that focuses first on consumers' unmet wants and needs, and then designs products to meet those needs.

Consumer Price Index (CPI) a measurement of the monthly average change in prices of goods and services.

consumerism public demand that a business consider the wants and needs of its customers when making decisions.

contract a legally enforceable agreement between two or more parties regarding a specified act or thing.

controlling the function of assessing an organization's performance against its goals.

cooperative advertising allowances that marketers provide to share with channel partners the cost of local advertising of their firm's product or product line.

copyright legal protection of written or printed material such as books, designs, cartoons, photos, computer software, music, and videos.

core inflation rate the inflation rate after energy prices and food prices are removed.

corporate culture an organization's collection of principles, beliefs, and values.

corporate philanthropy an organization's contribution to the communities where it earns profits.

corporation a legal organization with assets and liabilities separate from the assets and liabilities of its owners.

Corruption of Foreign Public Officials Act a federal law that prohibits Canadian citizens and companies from bribing foreign officials to win or continue business.

cost-based pricing calculating total costs per unit and then adding markups to cover overhead costs and generate profits.

countertrade a barter agreement whereby trade between two or more nations involves payment made in the form of local products instead of currency.

creative selling a persuasive type of promotional presentation.

creativity the capacity to develop novel solutions to perceived organizational problems.

credit receiving money, goods, or services on the basis of an agreement between the lender and the borrower that the loan is for a specified period of time with a specified rate of interest.

critical thinking the ability to analyze and assess information to pinpoint problems or opportunities.

cross-functional team a team made up of members from different functions, such as production, marketing, and finance.

cyclical unemployment the joblessness of people who are out of work because of a cyclical contraction in the economy.

data raw facts and figures that may or may not be meaningful to a business decision.

data mining the use of computer searches of customer data to detect patterns and relationships.

data warehouse a customer database that allows managers to combine data from several different organizational functions.

database a centralized integrated collection of data resources.

debt financing borrowed funds that entrepreneurs must repay.

decision-making the process of seeing a problem or opportunity, assessing possible solutions, selecting and carrying out the best-suited plan, and assessing the results.

decision support system (DSS) an information system that gives direct support to businesspeople during the decision-making process.

deflation the opposite of inflation, occurs when prices continue to fall.

delegation the managerial process of assigning work to employees.

demand the willingness and ability of buyers to purchase goods and services.

demand curve a graph of the amount of a product that buyers will purchase at different prices.

demographic segmentation dividing markets on the basis of various demographic or socioeconomic characteristics, such as gender, age, income, occupation, household size, stage in family life cycle, education, or ethnic group.

departmentalization the process of dividing work activities into units within the organization.

devaluation a reduction in a currency's value in terms of other currencies or in terms of a fixed standard.

directing guiding and motivating employees to accomplish organizational goals.

discrimination biased treatment toward a job candidate or employee.

distribution channels the paths that products—and their legal ownership—follow from producer to consumers or business users.

distribution strategy a plan that deals with the marketing activities and institutions that get the right good or service to the firm's customers.

diversity the blending of individuals of different genders, ethnic backgrounds, cultures, religions, ages, and physical and mental abilities to enhance a firm's chances of success.

divestiture the sale of assets by a firm.

double-entry bookkeeping the process used to record accounting transactions; each individual transaction is always balanced by another transaction.

downsizing the process of reducing the number of employees within a firm by eliminating jobs.

dumping selling products in other countries at prices below production costs or below typical prices in the home market to capture market share from domestic competitors.

economics the social science that studies the choices people and governments make when dividing up their scarce resources.

embargo a total ban on importing specific products or a total stop to trading with a particular country.

employee benefits additional compensation—such as vacation time, retirement savings plans, profit-sharing, health insurance, gym memberships, child and elder care, and tuition reimbursement—paid entirely or in part by the company.

employee separation a broad term for the loss of an employee for any reason, voluntary or involuntary.

Employment Equity Act (EEA) an act created (1) to increase job opportunities for women and members of minority groups and (2) to help end discrimination based on race, colour, religion, disability, gender, or national origin.

empowerment giving employees shared authority, responsibility, and decision-making with their managers.

end-use segmentation a marketing strategy that focuses on the precise way a B2B purchaser will use a product.

entrepreneur a person who seeks a profitable opportunity and takes the necessary risks to set up and operate a business.

entrepreneurship the willingness to take risks to create and operate a business.

equilibrium price the current market price for an item.

equity financing funds invested in new ventures in exchange for part ownership.

equity theory an individual's perception of fair and equitable treatment.

European Union (EU) a 27-nation European economic alliance.

event marketing marketing or sponsoring of short-term events such as athletic competitions and cultural and charitable performances.

everyday low pricing (EDLP) a strategy of maintaining continuous low prices instead of usingshort-term price cuts such as cents-off coupons, rebates, and special sales.

exchange control a restriction on importing certain products or a restriction against certain companies to reduce trade and the spending of foreign currency.

exchange process an activity in which two or more parties trade something of value (such as goods, services, or cash) that satisfies each other's needs.

exchange rate the value of one country's currency in terms of the currencies of other countries.

executive support system (ESS) an information system that lets senior executives access the firm's primary databases, often by touching the computer screen, pointing and clicking a mouse, or using voice recognition.

expansionary monetary policy a plan to increase the money supply to try to decrease the cost of borrowing. Lower interest rates encourage businesses to make new investments, which leads to employment and economic growth.

expectancy theory the process people use to evaluate the likelihood that their efforts will lead to the results they want and the degree to which they want those results.

expert system a computer program that imitates human thinking through complicated sets of "if-then" rules.

exports domestically produced goods and services sold in other countries.

external communication a meaningful exchange of information through messages sent between an organization and its major audiences.

factors of production four basic inputs for effective operation: natural resources, capital, human resources, and entrepreneurship.

fair trade a market-based approach of paying higher prices to producers for goods exported from developing countries to developed countries in an effort to promote sustainability and to ensure the people in developing countries receive better trading conditions.

finance the business function of planning, obtaining, and managing the company's funds to accomplish its objectives as effectively and efficiently as possible.

finance charge the difference between the amount borrowed and the amount repaid on a loan.

Financial Accounting Standards Board (FASB) the organization that interprets and modifies GAAP in the United States.

financial institutions intermediaries between savers and borrowers that collect funds from savers and then lend the funds to individuals, businesses, and governments.

financial managers the executives who develop and carry out their firm's financial plan and decide on the most appropriate sources and uses of funds.

financial markets markets where securities are issued and traded.

financial plan a document that specifies the funds needed by a firm for a period of time, the timing of cash inflows and outflows, and the most appropriate sources and uses of funds.

financial system the process by which money flows from savers to users.

firewall a type of security system for computers that limits data transfers to certain locations; it also tracks system use so that managers can identify threats to the system's security, including attempts to log on with invalid passwords.

fiscal policy a plan of government spending and taxation decisions designed to control inflation, reduce unemployment, improve the general welfare of citizens, and encourage economic growth.

flexible manufacturing system (FMS) a production facility that workers can quickly change to manufacture different products.

foreign licensing agreement international agreement in which one firm allows another firm to produce or sell its product, or use its trademark, patent, or manufacturing processes, in a specific geographical area, in return for royalties or other compensation.

franchise a contract-based agreement in which a franchisee can produce and/or sell the franchisor's products under that company's brand name if the franchisee agrees to the operating terms and requirements.

franchisee the individual or business firm purchasing a franchise.

franchising a contract-based business arrangement between a manufacturer or other supplier, and a dealer, such as a restaurant operator or retailer.

franchisor the firm whose products are sold to customers by the franchisee.

frequency marketing a marketing initiative that rewards frequent purchases with cash, rebates, merchandise, or other premiums.

frictional unemployment the joblessness of people in the workforce who are temporarily not working but are looking for jobs.

General Agreement on Tariffs and Trade (GATT) an international trade accord that has greatly reduced worldwide tariffs and other trade barriers.

generally accepted accounting principles (GAAP) principles that outline the conventions, rules, and procedures for deciding on the acceptable accounting practices at a particular time.

geographical segmentation dividing an overall market into similar groups on the basis of their locations.

global business strategy the offering of a standardized, worldwide product and the selling of it in basically the same way throughout a firm's domestic and foreign markets.

goal-setting theory the idea that people will be motivated to the extent to which they accept specific, challenging goals and receive feedback that shows their progress toward goal achievement.

grapevine an internal information channel that passes information from unofficial sources.

green marketing a marketing strategy that promotes environmentally safe products and production methods.

grid computing a network of smaller computers that run special software.

gross domestic product (GDP) the sum of all goods and services produced within a country during a specific time period, such as a year.

guerrilla marketing innovative, low-cost marketing efforts designed to get consumers' attention in unusual ways.

hardware all tangible, or physical, elements of a computer system.

health insurance insurance that pays for losses due to illness or injury.

home-based businesses firms operated from the residence of the business owner.

horizontal merger a merger that joins firms in the same industry for the purpose of diversification, increasing customer bases, cutting costs, or expanding product lines.

human resource management the function of attracting, developing, and retaining employees who can perform the activities needed to meet organizational objectives.

human resources production inputs consisting of anyone who works, including both the physical labour and the intellectual inputs contributed by workers.

hyperinflation an economic situation marked by soaring prices.

imports foreign goods and services purchased by domestic customers.

income statement a financial record of a company's revenues, expenses, and profits over a specific period of time.

inflation rising prices caused by a combination of excess consumer demand and higher costs of raw materials, component parts, human resources, and other factors of production.

infomercials a form of broadcast direct marketing; 30-minute programs resemble regular TV programs, but sell goods or services.

information knowledge gained from processing data.

information system an organized method for collecting, storing, and communicating past, present, and projected information on internal operations and external intelligence.

infrastructure the basic systems of a country's communication, transportation, and energy facilities.

insider trading use of material nonpublic information about a company to make investment profits.

institutional advertising messages that promote concepts, ideas, or philosophies. It can also promote goodwill toward industries, companies, organizations, or government entities.

insurance a contract in which the insurer, for a fee, agrees to reimburse an insured firm or individual a sum of money if a loss occurs.

integrated marketing communications (IMC) the coordination of all promotional activities—media advertising, direct mail, personal selling, sales promotion, and public relations—to produce a unified customer-focused message.

integrity behaving according to one's deeply felt ethical principles in business situations.

International Accounting Standards Board (IASB) the organization that promotes worldwide consistency in financial reporting practices.

International Financial Reporting Standards (IFRS) the standards and interpretations adopted by the IASB.

international law the numerous regulations that govern international trade.

International Monetary Fund (IMF) an organization created to promote trade, eliminate barriers, and make short-term loans to member-nations that are unable to meet their budgets.

International Organization for Standardization (ISO) an international organization whose mission is to develop and promote international standards for business, government, and society. The aim is to improve and encourage global trade and cooperation.

intranet a computer network that is similar to the Internet but limits access to authorized users.

intrapreneurship the process of promoting innovation within the structure of an existing organization.

inventory control a function that balances the costs of storing inventory with the need to have stock on hand to meet demand.

joint venture a partnership between companies for a specific activity.

judiciary the branch of government that is responsible for applying laws to settle disagreements; also known as the court system.

just-in-time (JIT) system a broad management philosophy that reaches beyond the narrow activity of inventory control to affect the entire system of production and operations management.

labour union a group of workers who organize themselves to work toward common goals in the areas of wages, hours, and working conditions.

law the standards set by government and society in the form of either legislation or custom.

law of large numbers the idea that seemingly random events will follow predictable patterns if enough events are observed.

leadership the ability to direct or inspire people to reach goals.

LEED (Leadership in Energy and Environmental Design) a voluntary certification program administered by the Canada Green Building Council, aimed at promoting the most sustainable construction processes available.

leverage increasing the rate of return on funds invested by borrowing funds.

leveraged buyouts (LBOs) transactions where public shareholders are bought out and the firm reverts to private status.

liability a claim against a firm's assets by creditors.

life insurance a type of insurance that protects people against the financial losses that occur with premature death.

lifestyle entrepreneur a person who starts a business to reduce work hours and create a more relaxed lifestyle.

lifetime value of a customer the revenues and intangible benefits (such as referrals and customer feedback) from a customer over the life of the relationship, minus the amount the company must spend to acquire and serve that customer.

listening receiving a message and interpreting its intended meaning by grasping the facts and feelings the message conveys.

local area networks (LANs) computer networks that connect machines within limited areas, such as a building or several nearby buildings.

logistics the process of coordinating flow of goods, services, and information among members of the supply chain.

macroeconomics the study of a nation's overall economic issues, such as how an economy maintains and divides up resources and how a government's policies affect its citizens' standards of living.

make, buy, or lease decision choosing whether to manufacture a needed product or part in-house, buy it from an outside supplier, or lease it.

malware any malicious software program designed to infect computer systems.

management the process of achieving organizational goals through people and other resources.

management by objectives (MBO) a structured approach that helps managers to focus on reachable goals and to achieve the best results based on the organization's resources.

management information system (MIS) an information system designed to produce reports for managers and other professionals.

management support systems information systems that are designed to provide support for effective decision-making.

market segmentation the process of dividing a total market into several relatively similar groups.

marketing an organizational function and set of processes for creating, communicating, and delivering value to customers and for managing customer relationships in ways that benefit the organization and its stakeholders.

marketing concept a companywide consumer focus on promoting long-term success.

marketing mix a blending the four elements of marketing strategy—product, distribution, promotion, and pricing—to satisfy chosen customer segments.

marketing research the process of collecting and evaluating information to support marketing decision-making.

Maslow's hierarchy of needs a theory of motivation proposed by Abraham Maslow. According to the theory, people have five levels of needs that they try to satisfy: physiological, safety, social, esteem, and self-actualization.

mass production a system for manufacturing products in large quantities by using effective combinations of employees with specialized skills, mechanization, and standardization.

materials requirement planning (MRP) a computer-based production planning system that ensures a firm has all the parts and materials it needs to produce its output at the right time and place and in the right amounts.

merger an agreement in which two or more firms combine to form one company.

microeconomics the study of small economic units, such as individual consumers, families, and businesses.

mission statement a written description of an organization's overall business purpose and aims.

missionary selling an indirect form of selling where the representative promotes goodwill for a company or provides technical or operational assistance to the customer.

mixed market economy an economic system that draws from both private enterprise economies and planned economies, to different degrees.

monetary policy a government plan to increase or decrease the money supply and to change banking requirements and interest rates to affect bankers' willingness to make loans.

monopolistic competition a market structure where large numbers of buyers and sellers exchange similar products so each participant has some control over price.

monopoly a market situation where a single seller controls trade in a good or service, and buyers can find no close substitutes.

multidomestic business strategy a plan to develop and market products to serve different needs and tastes in separate national markets.

multinational corporation (MNC) a firm with many operations and marketing activities outside its home country.

national debt the money owed by government to individuals, businesses, and government agencies who purchase Treasury bills, Treasury notes, and Treasury bonds.

natural resources all production inputs that are useful in their natural states, including agricultural land, building sites, forests, and mineral deposits.

nearshoring the outsourcing of production or services to locations near a firm's home base.

net worth the difference between an individual's or a household's assets and liabilities.

nonpersonal selling forms of selling such as advertising, sales promotion, direct marketing, and public relations.

North American Free Trade Agreement (NAFTA) an agreement among the United States, Canada, and Mexico to break down tariffs and trade restrictions.

not-for-profit corporations organizations whose goals do not include pursuing a profit.

not-for-profit organizations organizations whose primary aims are public service, not returning a profit to its owners.

objectives the targets that managers use to plan for the organization's hoped-for performance. These objectives can relate to such areas as new-product development, sales, customer service, growth, environmental and social responsibility, and employee satisfaction.

odd pricing a pricing method that uses uneven amounts to make prices appear to be less than they really are.

offshoring the relocation of business processes to lower-cost locations overseas.

oligopoly a market situation where relatively few sellers compete and high start-up costs act as barriers to keep out new competitors.

on-demand computing the use of software time from application providers; firms pay only for their usage of the software, not for purchasing or maintaining the software.

operational support systems information systems designed to produce a variety of information on an organization's activities for both internal and external users.

order processing a form of selling used mostly at the wholesale and retail levels; involves identifying customer needs, pointing out products that meet those needs, and completing orders.

organization a structured group of people working together to achieve common goals.

organization marketing a marketing strategy that influences consumers to accept the goals of and organization, receive the services of an organization, or contribute in some way to an organization.

organizing the process of blending human and material resources through a formal structure of tasks and authority: arranging work, dividing tasks among employees, and coordinating them to ensure plans are carried out and goals are met.

outsourcing using outside vendors to produce goods or fulfill services and functions that were previously handled in-house or in-country.

owners' equity the funds that owners invest in the business plus any profits not paid to owners in the form of cash dividends.

partnership an association of two or more persons who operate a business as co-owners by voluntary legal agreement.

patent legal protection that guarantees an inventor exclusive rights to an invention for 20 years.

penetration pricing a strategy that sets a low price as a major marketing tactic.

performance appraisal evaluation of and feedback on an employee's job performance.

person marketing efforts that are designed to attract the attention, interest, and preference of a target market toward a person.

personal financial management the study of the economic factors and personal decisions that affect a person's financial well-being.

personal financial plan a guide to help a person reach his or her desired financial goals.

personal selling the most basic form of promotion: a direct person-to-person promotional presentation to a potential buyer.

physical distribution the actual movement of products from producer to consumers or business users.

place marketing an attempt to attract people to a particular area, such as a city, state, or country.

planned economy an economic system where business ownership, profits, and resource allocation are shaped by a plan to meet government goals, not goals set by individual firms.

planning the process of looking forward to future events and conditions and deciding on the courses of action for achieving organizational goals.

point-of-purchase (POP) advertising displays or demonstrations that promote products when and where consumers buy them, such as in retail stores.

positioning a concept whereby marketers try to establish their products in the minds of customers by communicating to buyers the meaningful differences about the attributes, price, quality, or use of a good or service.

preferred shares shares that give owners limited voting rights and the right to receive dividends or assets before owners of common shares.

prestige pricing setting a relatively high price to develop and maintain an image of quality and exclusiveness.

price the exchange value of a good or service.

primary markets financial markets where firms and governments issue securities and sell them initially to the general public.

private enterprise system an economic system that rewards firms for their ability to identify and serve the needs and demands of customers.

private property the most basic freedom under the private enterprise system; the right to own, use, buy, sell, and hand down land, buildings, machinery, equipment, patents, individual possessions, and various intangible kinds of property.

privatization the conversion of government-owned and -operated companies to privately held businesses.

problem-solving team a temporary combination of workers who gather to solve a specific problem and then disband.

process control systems operational support systems that monitor and control physical processes.

product a bundle of physical, service, and symbolic attributes designed to satisfy buyers' wants.

product advertising messages designed to sell a particular good or service.

product liability the responsibility of manufacturers for injuries and damages caused by their products.

product life cycle the four basic stages in the development of a successful product—introduction, growth, maturity, and decline.

product line a group of related products that share physical similarities or are targeted toward a similar market.

product mix the assortment of product lines and individual goods and services that a firm offers to consumers and business users.

product placement a form of promotion where marketers pay placement fees to have their products featured in various media, from newspapers and magazines to television and movies.

production the use of resources, such as workers and machinery, to convert materials into finished goods and services.

production and operations management the process of overseeing the production process by managing the people and machinery that convert materials and resources into finished goods and services.

production control creating well-defined procedures for coordinating people, materials, and machinery to provide the greatest production efficiency.

productivity the relationship between the number of units produced and the number of human and other production inputs needed to produce them.

product-related segmentation dividing consumer markets into groups that are based on benefits sought by buyers, usage rates, and loyalty levels.

profitability objectives common goals that are included in the strategic plans of most firms.

profits rewards for businesspeople who take the risks involved to offer goods and services to customers.

promotion the function of informing, persuading, and influencing a purchase decision.

promotional mix the combination of personal and nonpersonal selling that marketers use to meet the needs of a firm's target customers and to effectively and efficiently communicate its message to them.

property and liability insurance a general category of insurance that protects against losses due to a number of perils, such as fire, accident, and theft.

psychographic segmentation dividing consumer markets into groups with similar attitudes, values, and lifestyles.

public accountant an accountant who provides accounting services to other organizations.

public relations an organization's communications and relationships with its various public audiences.

publicity the nonpersonal stimulation of demand for a good, service, place, idea, event, person, or organization by unpaid placement of information in print or broadcast media.

pulling strategy promotion of a product by generating consumer demand for it, mainly through advertising and sales promotion appeals.

pure competition a market structure where large numbers of buyers and sellers exchange similar products, and no single participant has a large influence on price.

pushing strategy personal selling to market an item to wholesalers and retailers in a company's distribution channels.

quality the state of being free of deficiencies or imperfections.

quality control measuring output against quality standards.

quota a limit set on the amounts of particular products that can be imported.

recession a cycle of economic contraction that lasts for six months or longer.

recycling reprocessing of used materials for reuse.

regulated monopoly a firm that is granted exclusive rights in a specific market by a local, provincial, or federal government.

relationship era the business era where firms seek to actively promote customer loyalty by carefully managing every interaction.

relationship management the collection of activities that build and maintain ongoing, mutually beneficial ties with customers and others.

relationship marketing developing and maintaining long-term, cost-effective exchange relationships with partners.

restrictive monetary policy a plan to reduce the money supply to control rising prices, overexpansion, and concerns about overly rapid economic growth.

retailers distribution channel members that sell goods and services to individuals for their own use, not for resale.

risk uncertainty about loss or injury.

risk management calculations and actions a firm takes to recognize and deal with real or potential risks to its survival.

risk-return trade-off the process of maximizing the wealth of the firm's shareholders by striking the right balance between risk and return.

rule of indemnity the requirement that the insured cannot collect more than the amount of the loss and cannot collect for the same loss more than once.

salary pay calculated on a periodic basis, such as weekly or monthly.

sales law the law governing the sale of goods or services for money or on credit.

sales promotion forms of promotion such as coupons, product samples, and rebates that support advertising and personal selling.

Sarbanes-Oxley Act U.S. federal legislation designed to deter and punish corporate and accounting fraud and corruption. It is also designed to protect the interests of workers and shareholders by requiring enhanced financial disclosures, criminal penalties for CEOs and CFOs who defraud investors, and safeguards for whistle-blowers. The act also established a new regulatory body for public accounting firms.

seasonal unemployment the joblessness of workers in a seasonal industry.

secondary market a collection of financial markets where previously issued securities are traded among investors.

securities financial instruments that represent the obligations of the issuers to provide the purchasers with the expected stated returns on the funds invested or loaned.

seed capital the initial funding needed to launch a new venture.

self-managed team a work team that has the authority to decide how its members complete their daily tasks.

serial entrepreneur a person who starts one business, runs it, and then starts and runs more businesses, one after another.

server the heart of a midrange computer network.

sexism discrimination against members of either sex, but usually against women.

sexual harassment unwelcome and inappropriate actions of a sexual nature.

shareholders owners of a corporation as a result of their purchase of shares in the corporation.

skimming pricing a strategy that sets an intentionally high price relative to the prices of competing products.

small business an independent business with fewer than 100 employees and revenues less than $2 million, not dominant in its market.

social audits formal procedures that identify and evaluate all company activities that relate to social issues, such as conservation, employment practices, environmental protection, and philanthropy.

social entrepreneur a person who sees societal problems and uses business principles to develop new solutions.

social responsibility business's consideration of society's well-being and consumer satisfaction, in addition to profits.

socialism an economic system where the government owns and operates the major industries, such as communications.

software all the programs, routines, and computer languages that control a computer and tell it how to operate.

sole proprietorship a business ownership in which the sole proprietor's status as an individual is not legally separate from his or her status as a business owner.

specialty advertising promotional items that prominently display a firm's name, logo, or business slogan.

sponsorship providing funds for a sporting or cultural event in exchange for a direct association with the event.

spyware software that gathers user information through the user's Internet connection without his or her knowledge, usually for advertising purposes.

stakeholders customers, investors, employees, and public affected by or with an interest in a company.

standard of living the necessities, comforts, and luxuries a person wants to achieve or maintain.

statement of cash flows a record of the sources and uses of cash during a period of time.

statement of changes in equity a record of the change in equity from the end of one fiscal period to the end of the next fiscal period.

statutory law written law that includes provincial, state, and federal constitutions; legislative enactments; treaties of the federal government; and ordinances of local governments.

stock markets (exchanges) markets where shares of stock are bought and sold by investors.

strategic alliance a partnership formed to create a competitive advantage for the businesses involved; in international business, the business strategy of one company partnering with another company in the country where it wants to do business.

structural unemployment the joblessness of people who remain unemployed for long periods of time, often with little hope of finding a job.

subcontracting an agreement that involves hiring other companies to produce, distribute, or sell goods or services; in international subcontracting, local companies in a specific country or geographical region are hired to produce, distribute, or sell goods or services.

supply the willingness and ability of sellers to provide goods and services.

supply chain the complete sequence of suppliers that help to create a good or service and deliver it to business users and final consumers.

supply curve a graph that shows the relationship between different prices and the amount of goods that sellers will offer for sale, regardless of demand.

sustainable the capacity to endure in ecology.

SWOT analysis SWOT is a short form for *strengths, weaknesses, opportunities,* and *threats.* By assessing all four factors one by one, a firm can then develop the best strategies for gaining a competitive advantage.

target market a group of people that an organization markets its goods, services, or ideas toward, using a strategy designed to satisfy this group's specific needs and preferences.

tariffs taxes imposed on imported goods.

tax an assessment by a governmental unit.

team a group of people with certain skills who share a common purpose, approach, and performance goals.

team cohesiveness the extent to which team members feel attracted to the team and motivated to remain part of it.

team diversity the team's differences in ability, experience, personality, or any other factor.

team level the team's average level of ability, experience, personality, or any other factor.

team norm a standard of conduct shared by team members that guides their behavior.

technology the business application of knowledge based on scientific discoveries, inventions, and innovations.

telemarketing personal selling by telephone, which provides marketers with a high return on their expenses, an immediate response, and an opportunity for a personalized two-way conversation.

tender offer a proposal made by a firm to the target firm's shareholders specifying a price and the form of payment.

test marketing the introduction of a new product and a complete marketing campaign to a selected city or TV coverage area.

tort a civil wrong inflicted by one person on another person or on another person's property.

trade promotion sales promotion geared to marketing intermediaries, not to final consumers.

trademark a brand that has been given legal protection; words, symbols, or other designations used by firms to identify their products.

transaction management building and promoting products in the hope that enough customers will buy them to cover costs and earn profits.

transaction processing systems operational support systems that record and process data from business transactions.

Trojan horse a program that claims to do one thing but in reality does something else, usually something malicious.

unemployment rate the percentage of the total workforce actively seeking work but currently unemployed.

utility the power of a good or service to satisfy a want or need.

vendor-managed inventory the process in which the producer and the retailer agree that the producer (or the wholesaler) will decide how much of a product a buyer needs and automatically ship new supplies when needed.

venture capital money invested in a business by another business firm or group of individuals in exchange for an ownership share.

venture capitalists business firms or groups of individuals that invest in new and growing firms in exchange for an ownership share.

vertical merger a merger that combines firms operating at different levels in the production and marketing process.

virtual private networks (VPNs) secure connections between two points on the Internet.

virtual teams groups of geographically or organizationally separated co-workers who use a combination of telecommunications and information technologies to accomplish an organizational task.

viruses malicious software programs that secretly attach themselves to other programs (called *hosts*) and change them or destroy data.

vision the ability to perceive marketplace needs and what an organization must do to satisfy them.

VoIP an alternative to traditional telecommunication services provided by companies such as Bell Canada and Telus; uses the Internet instead of telephone lines to transmit messages.

volume objectives pricing decisions that are based on market share, the percentage of a market controlled by a certain company or product.

wage pay based on an hourly rate or the amount of work accomplished.

whistle-blowing disclosure to company officials, government authorities, or the media of illegal, immoral, or unethical practices committed by an organization.

wholesaler a distribution channel member that sells primarily to retailers, other wholesalers, or business users.

wide area networks (WANs) computer networks that tie larger geographical regions together by using telephone lines and microwave and satellite transmission.

WiFi a wireless network that connects various devices and allows them to communicate with one another through radio waves.

work teams relatively permanent groups of employees with complementary skills who perform the day-to-day work of organizations.

World Bank an organization established by industrialized nations to lend money to less developed countries.

World Trade Organization (WTO) a 157-member international institution that monitors GATT agreements and mediates international trade disputes.

worm a small piece of software that uses a security hole in a network to replicate itself.

NOTES

Chapter 1

1. Justin Bieber Music Site, http://www.justinbiebermusic.com/default.aspx, accessed January 2, 2012; Justin Bieber Facebook, http://www.facebook.com/JustinBieber, accessed January 2, 2012; Justin Bieber MySpace, http://www.myspace.com/justinbieber, accessed January 2, 2012; Justin Bieber Twitter Site, http://twitter.com/justinbieber, accessed January 2, 2012; Justin Bieber Zone, http://www.justinbieberzone.com/, accessed January 2, 2012; Marcus Hondro, "Bieber hits 16 million Twitter followers on New Year Day," January 3, 2012, DigitalJourna.com, http://www.digitaljournal.com/article/317183#ixzz1iP4EpfDS, accessed January 3, 2012.

2. Summary of the Findings of the National Survey of Nonprofit and Voluntary Organizations (NSNVO), Statistics Canada website, http://www.statcan.gc.ca/pub/61-533-s/61-533-s2005001-eng.htm#5, accessed January 23, 2011.

3. "Facts, Figures and Funding," Toronto's Hospital for Sick Children (SickKids) website, http://www.sickkids.ca/Research/AbouttheInstitute/Facts-Figures-and-Funding/Fact-Figures-and-Funding.html, accessed January 25, 2011.

4. Ginger Thompson, "As Haiti's Focus Turns to Shelter, Families Press Search for Missing," *New York Times*, January 15, 2010, http://www.nytimes.com; Liz Robbins, "Haiti Relief Effort Faces 'Major Challenge,'" *New York Times*, January 25, 2010, http://www.nytimes.com.

5. Toronto's Hospital for Sick Children (SickKids) book series website, http://www.sickkids.ca/Learning/PatientsandFamilies/SickKids-book-series/index.html, accessed January 25, 2011.

6. LIVESTRONG, The Lance Armstrong website, www.livestrong.org.

7. Andrew Cunningham, "Amazon Kindle (4th Gen) Review," http://www.anandtech.com/show/4988/amazon-fourthgeneration-kindle-review, accessed March 10, 2012.

8. "100 Best Companies to Work For: #1 SAS," CNNMoney.com, http://money.cnn.com, accessed February 4, 2010.

9. Beyond the Rack website, www.beyondtherack.com , accessed January 25, 2011.

10. "Google to Launch Google Docs App Store?" PCMag.com, February 2, 2010, http://www.pcmag.com.

11. "Tech's Top Ten," *Financial Post*, December 29, 2011, p. FP12; Iain Marlow, "Small ISPs Lament CRTC Fee Change, Look to Invest in Own infrastructure," January 13, 2011, *Globe and Mail*, http://www.theglobeandmail.com/news/technology/tech-news/small-isps-lament-crtc-fee-change-look-to-invest-in-own-infrastructure/article1868429/, accessed January 27, 2011.

12. "Small Business Forum 2010," *Canadian Business Journal*, http://www.canadianbusinessjournal.ca/business_in_action/november_10/small_business_forum_2010.html, accessed January 27, 2011; Iain Marlow, "Small ISPs Lament CRTC Fee Change, Look to Invest in Own Infrastructure," January 13, 2011, *Globe and Mail*, http://www.theglobeandmail.com/news/technology/tech-news/small-isps-lament-crtc-fee-change-look-to-invest-in-own-infrastructure/article1868429/, accessed January 27, 2011.

13. *Key Small Business Statistics, July 2010*, Industry Canada, http://www.bdc.ca/EN/Documents/about/KSBS-PSRPE_July-Juillet2010_eng.pdf, accessed January 27, 2011.

14. Jason Magder, "Homegrown Tablet, the Vibe, Takes on iPad," *Montreal Gazette*, January 27, 2011, http://www.montrealgazette.com/technology/Homegrown+tablet+Vibe+takes+iPad/4175127/story.html, accessed February 18, 2011; Exopc website, http://www.exopc.com/en/index.php, accessed February 18, 2011; Ciara website, http://www.ciaravibe.com/index-en.html, accessed February 18, 2011; TMC, "At Dumoulin Électronique First! The CIARA VIBE Tablet, Powered by EXOPC, Now Available to the public," *TMCnet*, January 26, 2011, http://www.tmcnet.com/usubmit/2011/01/26/5269403.htm, accessed February 18, 2011.

15. Patrick May, "So Many Apps, So Little Time," *San Jose Mercury News*, February 7, 2010, www.mercurynews.com.

16. Company website, http://ir.homedepot.com, accessed February 4, 2010.

17. Mack Collier, "Examples of Great Company Blogs," http://www.searchengineguide.com, accessed February 4, 2010.

18. Company Web site, www.overstock.com, accessed February 9, 2010.

19. CNW Canada Newswire, "Endura Energy Begins Construction of Inaugural Rooftop Solar Power System," March 4, 2011, http://cnw.ca/UO3x, accessed January 2, 2012; Endura Energy website, http://www.enduraenergy.ca/, accessed January 2, 2012.

20. John Teresko, "Ford's Light Idea," *Industry Week*, November 1, 2007, http://www.industryweek.com.

21. Endura Energy website, http://www.enduraenergy.ca/, accessed January 2, 2012.

22. "A Change in Climate," *Economist*, January 17, 2008, http://www.economist.com.

23. "The Diversity Inc. Top 50 Companies for Diversity," *Diversity Inc.*, http://www.diversityinc.com, accessed February 4, 2010.

24. "Survey: Workplace Discrimination Still Prevalent," *Inc.com*, March 1, 2007, http://www.inc.com, accessed March 2, 2010.

25. James Cameron Online: The Home of James Cameron Fans website, http://www.jamescamerononline.com/, accessed February 18, 2011.

26. Michael Wilson, "Flight 1549 Pilot Tells of Terror and Intense Focus," *New York Times*, February 8, 2009, http://www.nytimes.com.

27. "America's Most Admired Companies 2008," *Fortune*, http://money.cnn.com, accessed February 9, 2010.

Chapter 2

1. Best of Vegas website, http://www.bestofvegas.com/Shows-Tickets/O/, accessed February 15, 2011; Cirque du Soleil website, http://www.cirquedusoleil.com/en/home.aspx#/en/home/about/details/cirque-du-soleil-at-a-glance.aspx, accessed February 15, 2011; One Drop Foundation website, http://www.onedrop.org/en/DiscoverOneDrop_Canada/WhoWeAre.aspx, accessed February 15, 2011; BSR Website, http://www.bsr.org/, accessed February 15, 2011; Ellen Barry, "What a Dump!," *Metropolis Magazine*, April 1998, http://www.metropolismag.com/html/content_0498/ap98dump.htm, accessed February 15, 2011; "Global Warming Fast Facts," *National Geographic News*, June 14, 2007, http://news.nationalgeographic.com/news/2004/12/1206_041206_global_warming.html, accessed February 15, 2011.

2. Industry Canada, "New Standard on Social Responsibility Launched," http://www.ic.gc.ca/eic/site/csr-rse.nsf/eng/rs00583.html, accessed February 17, 2011.

3. "Lights to Go out on Inefficient Bulbs by 2012," http://www.cbc.ca/canada/story/2007/04/25/lunn-bulbs.html, accessed February 14, 2011; "IKEA Canada to Phase out Incandescent Lighting by January 2011," June 15, 2010, http://www.ikea.com/ca/en/about_ikea/newsitem/2010_incandescent_lighting, accessed February 14, 2011.

4. CNN, "World's Most Admired Companies," http://money.cnn.com/magazines/fortune/mostadmired/2010/full_list/, accessed

December 30, 2011; Johnson & Johnson website, http://www.jnj.com, accessed February 2010.

5. Walmart Canada, "Walmart Corporate Social Responsibility," http://www.walmartcsr.ca/, accessed February 14, 2011.

6. Cliff Kuang, "The GOOD 100: Wal-Mart's Sustainability Push," *Good*, October 7, 2009; Michael Garry, "Wal-Mart Cites Progress on Sustainability Index," *Supermarket News*, November 23, 2009.

7. Ethics Resource Center, "2009 National Business Ethics Survey," November 2009.

8. Daniel Franklin, "Just Good Business," *Economist*, January 17, 2008, http://www.economist.com.

9. Ethics Resource Center, "2009 National Business Ethics Survey," November 2009.

10. John Cox, "Radisson Hotels: Data Breach Affected 'Limited' Number of Sites, Guests," *ComputerWorld*, August 19, 2009, http://www.computerworld.com.

11. Jim Dwyer, "H & M Says It Will Stop Destroying Unworn Clothing," *New York Times*, January 6, 2010; Jim Dwyer, "A Clothing Clearance Where More Than Just the Prices Have Been Slashed," *New York Times*, January 5, 2010, http://www.nytimes.com.

12. "Obama Renews Ban on Ruby, Jade from Myanmar," *National Jeweler*, July 30, 2009, http://www.nationaljewelernetwork.com.

13. Jessica Murphy, "One in 5 Job Seekers Lie on Resume: Poll," *Toronto Sun*, October 27, 2010, http://www.torontosun.com/news/canada/2010/10/27/15855051.html, accessed January 15, 2011; Dale Brazao, "Osgoode Hall Law School Vows to Weed out Fakes," *Toronto Star*, December 30, 2008, http://www.thestar.com/news/gta/article/559484, accessed February 12, 2011.

14. Heather Tooley, "Personal Internet Usage in the Workplace—A Serious Epidemic," *Associated Content*, January 17, 2010, http://www.associatedcontent.com; Jeffrey R. Smith, "No 'LOL' over Misuse of Email and Internet at Work," *Canadian HR Reporter*, September 28, 2009, http://chrremploymentlaw.wordpress.com.

15. "Whistleblower Legislation Bill C-25, Disclosure Protection," *CBC News Online*, April 28, 2004, http://www.cbc.ca/news/background/whistleblower/, accessed February 23, 2011.

16. Ibid.

17. "Alberta Whistleblower Faces $10M Lawsuit from Gaming Company," *CBC News*, October 27, 2006, http://www.cbc.ca/news/canada/edmonton/story/2006/10/27/alberta-gaming.html, accessed February 23, 2011.

18. Air Canada, "Corporate Policy and Guidelines on Business Conduct," http://www.aircanada.com/en/about/media/codeofconduct.pdf, accessed February 17, 2011

19. The Skald Group, "Ethical Awareness and Leadership," http://www.skaldgroup.com/, accessed February 17, 2011.

20. SAI Global website, http://www.saiglobal.com/compliance, accessed March 20, 2012.

21. Umaimah Mendhro and Abhinav Sinha, "Three Keys to Staying Ethical in the Age of Madoff," Forbes.com, February 6, 2009, http://www.forbes.com.

22. PricewaterhouseCoopers Canada Foundation, "Helping to Build and Empower Community Leadership," http://www.pwc.com/ca/en/foundation/index.jhtml#Team, accessed February 17, 2011.

23. Tim Horton Children's Foundation, "One Dream Transforming Many Lives," http://www.timhortons.com/ca/en/difference/childrens_about.html, accessed February 17, 2011.

24. Canada.com website, http://www.canada.com/health/Canada+smoking+leads+drop+hospitalizations/2852120/story.html, accessed February 23, 2011.

25. Childhood Obesity Foundation Website, http://www.childhoodobesityfoundation.ca/, accessed February 17, 2011.

26. SUBWAY website, http://www.subway.com, accessed February 4, 2010; Jared Foundation, http://www.jaredfoundation.org, accessed February 4, 2010; "The Jared Foundation," North American Association of SUBWAY Franchises, http://www.naasf.org, accessed February 10, 2010; Bison Franchise, "SUBWAY's Jared Fogle Retires Famous Fat Pants," February 12, 2009, http://www.bison.com.

27. "Ben Johnson: Canada's Shame," *CBC Digital Archives*, September 26, 1988, http://archives.cbc.ca/sports/drugs_sports/clips/8702/, accessed February 17, 2011; "1988: Johnson Stripped of Olympic Gold," *BBC on This Day*, http://news.bbc.co.uk/onthisday/hi/dates/stories/september/27/newsid_2539000/2539525.stm, accessed February 17, 2011.

28. "Oilsands Giant Suncor Fined for Dumping Pollution into Alberta River," *Toronto Star*, December 22, 2010, http://www.thestar.com/business/article/911071--oilsands-giant-suncor-fined-for-dumping-pollution-into-alberta-river, accessed February 17, 2011.

29. US Environmental Protection Agency, "Where Can I Donate or Recycle My Old Computer and Other Electronic Products?" http://www.epa.gov, accessed February 4, 2010; Best Buy, "We Now Offer Electronics Recycling at All Best Buy Stores Nationwide," http://www.bestbuy.com, accessed February 4, 2010.

30. Recycling Council of Ontario, "Take back the Light," http://www.takebackthelight.ca/, accessed February 17, 2011.

31. Tony Quiroga, "2011 Chevrolet Volt First Drive – Car News," *Car and Driver*, April 2009, http://www.caranddriver.com.

32. Statistics Canada, "Waste Management Industry: Business and Government Sectors," *Daily*, December 22, 2010, http://www.statcan.gc.ca/daily-quotidien/101222/dq101222b-eng.htm, accessed February 17, 2011.

33. Ontario Ministry of Finance, "Ontario Electronic Stewardship Fees," http://www.rev.gov.on.ca/en/notices/rst/74.html, accessed February 17, 2011.

34. Competition Bureau of Canada, *Environmental Claims: A Guide for Industry and Advisors*, June 2008, http://www.competitionbureau.gc.ca/eic/site/cb-bc.nsf/eng/02701.html, accessed February 18, 2011.

35. Martin LaMonica, "Bill Gates Investing in Vinod Khosla Green-Tech Fund," *CNET News*, January 25, 2010, http://news.cnet.com.

36. Tim Hortons, "Tim Hortons Coffee Partnership," http://www.timhortons.com/ca/en/difference/coffee-partnership.html, accessed February 18, 2011.

37. Tim Hortons, "Our Scholarship Program," http://www.timhortons.com/ca/en/join/scholarship.html, accessed February 18, 2011.

38. COSTI Immigrant Services, "Programs and Services," http://www.costi.org/programs/service_details.php?stype_id=53, accessed February 18, 2011.

39. Coca-Cola, "Diversity," http://www.thecoca-colacompany.com, accessed February 12, 2010.

40. "Canadian Breast Cancer Foundation Run for the Cure," http://www.runforthecure.com/site/PageServer?pagename=about_the_run, accessed February 22, 2011.

41. Marlene Rego, "Tickled Pink: Top Breast Cancer Products," *Chatelaine website*, http://www.chatelaine.com/en/article/3972--tickled-pink-top-breast-cancer-products, accessed February 22, 2011.

42. "UPS Pilots Volunteer to Help Haiti Relief Effort," Forbes.com, January 14, 2010, http://www.forbes.com.

43. Consumers' Association of Canada, "About Us," http://www.consumer.ca/1480, accessed February 18, 2011.

44. "15th Listeria Death Linked to Maple Leaf Foods, *CBC News*, September 10, 2008, http://www.cbc.ca/consumer/story/2008/09/10/listeria-ontario.html, accessed February 18, 2011; "How Maple Leaf Foods is Handling the Listeria Outbreak," *CBC News*, http://www.cbc.ca/money/story/2008/08/27/f-crisisresponse.html, accessed February 18, 2011.

45. Sharon Oosthoek, "Rogers Faces $10M Fine over Dropped-Call Ads," *CBC News*, November 19, 20120, http://www.cbc.ca/news/business/story/2010/11/19/consumer-chatr-rogers-competition-bureau.html, accessed February 21, 2011.

46. Canada, Department of Justice Website, *Food and Drugs Act*, http://laws.justice.gc.ca/en/f-27/, accessed February 21, 2011.

47. "Ontario Seeks Appeal of Private-Label Drug Ruling, *CBC News*, February 19, 2011, http://www.cbc.ca/news/health/story/2011/02/19/ontario-drug-ruling-appeal.html, accessed February 21, 2011.

48. "eBay Rules and Policies Overview," eBay, http://pages.ebay.com/help/policies/overview.html, accessed February 14, 2010.

49. Human Resources and Skills Development Canada, "Work—Work-Related Injuries," http://www4.hrsdc.gc.ca/.3ndic.1t.4r@-eng.jsp?iid=20, accessed February 21, 2011.

50. "Canada's Top 100 Employers," http://www.canadastop100.com/, accessed March 20, 2012.

51. Robert Smithson, "Is Unlimited Vacation Time a Recipe for Business Success?" *Kelowna Capital News*, February 16, 2010, http://www.bclocalnews.com.

52. Research In Motion, "Search Full Time Opportunities: Explore the World of RIM," http://www.rim.com/careers/search/index.shtml, accessed January 31, 2012; WestJet, "Great Jobs," http://www.westjet.com/guest/en/jobs.shtml, accessed, January, 31, 2012.

53. Canadian Charter of Rights and Freedoms, http://laws.justice.gc.ca/en/charter/1.html#anchorbo-ga:l_I-gb:s_15, accessed February 22, 2011.

54. "Exotic Dancer Files Age Discrimination Complaint," *CBC News*, http://www.cbc.ca/news/canada/story/2008/11/03/dancer-ohrt-complaint.html, accessed February 22, 2011.

55. Liz Wolgemuth, "20 Ways Older Workers Can Sell Themselves," *U.S. News & World Report*, November 26, 2008, http://www.usnews.com.

56. "Baby Boomers Swell Ranks of Retirement-Aged Canadians, *CBC News*, July 17, 2007, http://www.cbc.ca/news/canada/story/2007/07/17/census-canada.html, accessed February 21, 2011.

57. Margaret Wente, "The Nightmare Gender Gap," *Globe and Mail*, March 2, 2010, http://www.theglobeandmail.com/news/opinions/the-nightmare-gender-gap/article1488609/, accessed February 21, 2011.

58. Gail Zoppo, "Why Are Women Still Earning Less Than Men?" *Diversity Inc.*, April 28, 2009, http://www.diversityinc.com.

59. "Livent Co-founders Drabinsky, Gottlieb Convicted of Fraud and Forgery," *CBC News*, March 25, 2009, http://www.cbc.ca/news/business/story/2009/03/25/livent-decision-fraud.html, accessed February 23, 2011.

Chapter 3

1. Kent Spencer, "Signs of Life in Olympic Village," *The Province*, December 28, 2011, http://www.theprovince.com/technology/Signs+life+Olympic+Village/5917801/story.html; Kent Spencer "Vancouver Drops Prices on Olympic Condo Units," *National Post*, February 11, 2011, p. A6; Canada Mortgage and Housing Corporation, Housing Market Information, Housing Market Outlook – Fourth Quarter 2010, http://www.cmhc-schl.gc.ca/odpub/esub/61500/61500_2010_Q04.pdf?fr=1297379904219, accessed February 15, 2011; Canada Mortgage and Housing Corporation, Housing Market Information, Housing Market Outlook – Fall 2010, http://www.cmhc-schl.gc.ca/odpub/esub/64363/64363_2010_B02.pdf?lang=en, accessed February 15, 2011; Canada Mortgage and Housing Corporation, Housing Market Information, Housing Market Outlook Vancouver and Abbotsford CMAs, Date Released: Fourth Quarter 2007, http://dsp-psd.pwgsc.gc.ca/collection_2007/cmhc-schl/nh12-56/NH12-56-2007-2E.pdf, accessed February 15, 2011; Canada Mortgage and Housing Corporation, Canadian Housing at a Glance 2010, http://www.cmhc-schl.gc.ca/en/corp/about/cahoob/upload/dashboard_en.pdf, accessed February 15, 2011.

2. Nathan Eddy, "Video Game Sales Down 8 Percent in 2009," eWeek.com, http://www.eweek.com, accessed February 4, 2010.

3. Jeff Bercovici, "Soon, You'll Have to Pay for Hulu," *Daily Finance*, June 3, 2009, http://www.dailyfinance.com; Dawn C. Chmielewski and Alex Pham, "At Hulu, 'Free' May Turn to 'Fee,' *Los Angeles Times*, January 21, 2010, http://articles.latimes.com.

4. Jad Mouawad, "Demand for Oil Set to Rise Anew," *New York Times*, February 15, 2010, http://www.nytimes.com.

5. David P. Schulz, "Top 100 Retailers," *Stores*, NRF Stores, http://www.stores.org, accessed February 4, 2010.

6. Pascal Fletcher, "Freeze Mauls Florida Citrus, Significant Damage Seen," *Reuters*, January 11, 2010, http://www.reuters.com.

7. Sustainable Produce Urban Delivery website, www.spud.ca/, accessed March 26, 2012; Eat Local website, http://www.eatlocal.org/, accessed March 26, 2012.

8. Bettina Wassener, "Fed's Move Prompts Drop in Asian Stocks, Oil and Gold, but Dollar Rises," *New York Times*, February 20, 2010, http://www.nytimes.com; Lewa Pardomuan, "Gold Slips 1 Percent after Fed Raises Discount Rate," *Reuters*, February 19, 2010, http://www.reuters.com.

9. "10 Year Gold Price in CAD/oz," http://goldprice.org/charts/history/gold_10_year_o_cad.png, accessed January 10, 2012.

10. William Spain, "Fast-Food Outlook: Intense Competition, Margin Pressures," *MarketWatch*, January 14, 2010, http://www.marketwatch.com.

11. Michael Liedtke, "Yahoo-Microsoft Deal Set, Taking Aim at Google," *Associated Press*, February 18, 2010, http://hosted.ap.org; Hosting News; "Microsoft Exchange Server or Google Apps? A Comparison," September 5, 2009, http://www.thehostingnews.com; Sharon Gaudin, "Google vs. Microsoft: It's Going to Get Worse in 2010," *PC World*, December 23, 2009, http://www.pcworld.com.

12. "CRTC Issues Video-on-Demand Licence Conditions," January 31, 2011, http://www.thewirereport.ca/reports/content/11903-crtc_issues_video_on_demand_licence_conditions, accessed February, 11, 2011.

13. Air Canada website, http://www.aircanada.com, accessed February 4, 2010.

14. Central Intelligence Agency, *World Factbook*, https://www.cia.gov, accessed February 4, 2010.

15. Alexis Leondis, "U.S. Millionaires' Ranks Rose 16% in 2009, Study Says," *BusinessWeek*, March 9, 2010, http://www.businessweek.com.

16. Statistics Canada, Canada Year Book 2010, p. 278, Table 21.7, "Employment, by industry, 1995 to 2009," CANSIM table 282-0008, http://www.statcan.gc.ca/pub/11-402-x/2010000/pdf/labour-travail-eng.pdf, accessed February 3, 2011.

17. World Bank website, http://web.worldbank.org, accessed February 4, 2010; "Disaster Experts Share Lessons for Haiti," http://web.worldbank.org; Jack Ewing, "Emerging Economies Gain a Voice at Davos," *New York Times*, January 26, 2010, http://www.nytimes.com.

18. Central Intelligence Agency, "Country Comparison: Population," *World Factbook*, https://www.cia.gov/library/publications/the-world-factbook/rankorder/2119rank.html, accessed February 3, 2011.

19. U.S. and World Population Clocks, U.S. Census Bureau, http://www.census.gov, accessed February 4, 2010.

20. Justin Pritchard, "U.S. Agency Goes after Cadmium in Children's Jewelry," *ABC News*, January 11, 2010, http://abcnews.go.com.

Chapter 4

1. PotashCorp website, http://www.potashcorp.com, accessed January 23, 2011; Business News Network, "Reaction to Conference Board Report on Potash [10-04-10 4:45 PM], The Close, October 4, 2010, http://watch.bnn.ca/the-close/october-2010/the-close-october-4-2010/#clip356483, accessed

February 18, 2011; Brenda Bouw and Boyd Erman, "PotashCorp Value Tops $170/share: CEO," *Globe and Mail*, October 7, 2010, http://www.bnn.ca/News/2010/10/7/PotashCorp-value-tops-170-share-CEO.aspx, accessed February 11, 2011; Brenda Bouw, "Potash Corp. Doubles Profit, Vows to Avoid Dramatic Price Spike, *Globe and Mail*, January 28, 2011, http://www.theglobeandmail.com/globe-investor/potash-corp-doubles-profit-vows-to-avoid-dramatic-price-spike/article1884428/, accessed February 11, 2011.

2. Statistics Canada website, "Exports of Goods on a Balance-of-Payments Basis, by Product, http://www40.statcan.ca/l01/cst01/gblec04.htm, accessed February 27, 2011,; Central Intelligence Agency, "Canada," *World Factbook*, www.cia.gov, accessed February 27, 2011; Statistics Canada, "International Trade," *Canada Year Book*, pp. 255–266, http://www.statcan.gc.ca/pub/11-402-x/2010000/pdf/international-eng.pdf, accessed February 27, 2011.

3. U.S. Census Bureau, "International Data Base," www.census.gov, accessed March 8, 2010; "You Think! But Do You Know?" *World Bank*, http://youthink.worldbank.org, accessed March 8, 2010.

4. Central Intelligence Agency, *World Factbook*, www.cia.gov, accessed March 8, 2010.

5. Matthew Boyle, "Wal-Mart's Painful Lessons," *BusinessWeek*, www.businessweek.com, October 13, 2009.

6. Sahar Saffron company website, http://safarsaffron.com, accessed March 8, 2010; http://www.spiceadvice.com, accessed March 8, 2010.

7. Steve Hamm, "Big Blue's Global Lab," *BusinessWeek*, www.businessweek.com, August 27, 2009.

8. Statistics Canada, Table 20.a "Canada's Top International Trade Partners, 2009," *Canada Year Book*, p. 256, http://www.statcan.gc.ca/pub/11-402-x/2010000/pdf/international-eng.pdf, accessed March 1, 2011.

9. Central Intelligence Agency, "Canada," *World Factbook*, https://www.cia.gov/library/publications/the-world-factbook/geos/ca.html, accessed March 2, 2011.

10. Illinois Oil and Gas Association, "History of Illinois Basin Posted Crude Oil Prices," http://www.ioga.com/Special/crudeoil_Hist.htm, accessed March 2, 2011.

11. U.S. Census Bureau, "Exhibit 1. U.S. International Trade in Goods and Services, January 2007 to December 2009," www.census.gov, accessed March 8, 2010.

12. Bank for International Settlements, http://www.bis.org., accessed March 8, 2010.

13. Vivian Wai-yin Kwok, "How Kraft Won in China," *Forbes.com*, www.forbes.com, December 8, 2009.

14. Tanya Mohn, "Going Global, Stateside," *New York Times*, www.nytimes.com, March 8, 2010.

15. "India Needs 400 Airports to Cater to People's Needs," *LiveMint*, www.livemint.com, posted March 3, 2010; Samar Halarnkar, "Delhi Airport's T3: Bags Packed, Ready to Go," *LiveMint*, www.livemint.com, posted February 28, 2010.

16. "China Tightens Internet Controls," *BBC News*, http://news.bbc.co.uk, February 23, 2010.

17. Transparency International, "Foreign Bribery and OECD Countries: A Hollow Commitment? Progress Report 2009," www.transparency.org, June 22, 2009.

18. "British Kids Swamped with Sexual Images," *ABC News*, www.abc.net.au, February 27, 2010.

19. Canada Border Services Agency, "Fact Sheet," http://www.cbsa-asfc.gc.ca/media/facts-faits/060-eng.html, accessed March 2, 2011.

20. Louis Uchitelle, "Glassmaking Thrives Offshore, But Is Declining in U.S.," *New York Times*, www.nytimes.com, January 19, 2010.

21. World Trade Organization, "Lamy Calls for March Stocktaking to 'Inject Political Energy and Momentum' in the Negotiations," www.wto.org, February 22 and 23, 2010.

22. "G7 to Forgive Haiti Foreign Debt," *ABC News*, www.abc.net.au, February 7, 2010; press release, "World Bank Statement on Haiti Debt," The World Bank, www.worldbank.org, January 21, 2010.

23. CIA, "United States," *World Factbook*, https://www.cia.gov, accessed March 17, 2010.

24. CIA, "Canada," *World Factbook*, https://www.cia.gov, accessed March 17, 2010.

25. CIA, "Mexico," *World Factbook*, https://www.cia.gov, accessed March 17, 2010.

26. CIA, "European Union," *World Factbook*, https://www.cia.gov, accessed March 17, 2010.

27. "The Story of Tim Hortons," company website, http://www.timhortons.com/ca/en/about/index.html, accessed January 14, 2012.

28. Morinaga Co., company website, www.morinagamilk.co.jp, accessed March 9, 2010.

29. Kate O'Sullivan, "Best Buys in Offshore Manufacturing," CFO.com, www.cfo.com, February 18, 2010.

30. CBC.ca, "Target Buys Zellers Leases for $1.8B," January 13, 2011, http://www.cbc.ca/news/business/story/2011/01/13/target-zellers-takeover.html, accessed March 3, 2011.

31. Company website, www.alcoa.com, accessed March 17, 2010.

Part 1: Launching Your Global Business and Economics Career

1. U.S. Department of Labor, "Tomorrow's Jobs," *Occupational Outlook Handbook*, 2010–2011 edition, U.S. Bureau of Labor Statistics, http://www.bls.gov.

2. U.S. Department of Labor, "Economists," *Occupational Outlook Handbook*, 2010–2011 edition, U.S. Bureau of Labor Statistics, http://www.bls.gov.

3. Adapted from Michael R. Czinkota, Ilkka A. Ronkainen, and Michael H. Moffett, "Criteria for Selecting Managers for Overseas Assignments," in *International Business*, 7th ed. (Mason, OH: SouthWestern, 2005), Table 19.2, p. 634.

4. "MBA Still Packs a Punch," January 28, 2008, *Financial Times*, http://www.ft.com.

5. Sattar Bawany, "Transition Coaching Helps Ensure Success for Global Assignments," *Today's Manager*, January 2008, accessed at Entrepreneur.com, March 17, 2010.

Chapter 5

1. Pi Athlete Management Inc. website, http://www.piathlete.com, accessed January 6, 2012; Interviews with Martin Bindman and Daniel Smajovits of Pi Athlete Management Inc., January 2012; Vimeo, "Pro Baseball Player Marc Bourgeois Visits Home Base in Granby," CTV Montreal, Pi Athlete Management Inc., http://vimeo.com/31769085, accessed January 6, 2012; National Collegiate Athletic Association website, http://ncaa.org/, accessed January 6, 2012; Ron Sirak, "The Golf Digest 50: Golf's Top Earners," *Golf Digest*, February 2012, http://www.golfdigest.com/golf-tours-news/2012-02/top-earners#intro, accessed January 13, 2012; Kurt Badenhausen, "Sports' First Billion-Dollar Man," *Forbes.com*, September 29, 2009, http://www.forbes.com/2009/09/29/tiger-woods-billion-business-sports-tiger.html, accessed January 13, 2012; Businessweek.com, "The Average NFL Player," January 27, 2011, http://www.businessweek.com/magazine/content/11_06/b4214058615722.htm, accessed January 13, 2012; Steve Aschburner, NBA.com, "NBA's 'Average' Salary—$5.15M—A Trendy, Touchy Subject," August 11, 2011, http://www.nba.com/2011/news/features/steve_aschburner/08/19/average-salary/index.html, accessed January 13, 2011; National Hockey League Players' Association, "NHL Player Compensation," http://www.nhlpa.com/Players/compensation, accessed January 13, 2012; CBSSPORTS.com, "MLB Salaries," http://www.cbssports.com/mlb/salaries/avgsalaries, accessed January 13, 2012.

2. "Employer Businesses, by Firm Size and by Province and Territory, 2005 to 2009," *Canada Year Book 2010*, Table 4.2, pp. 42–43, http://www.statcan.gc.ca/pub/11-402-x/2010000/pdf/busperfown-rendentappart-eng.pdf, accessed March 4, 2011.

3. Industry Canada, Small Business Branch, *Key Small Business Statistics*, July 2011, http://www.ic.gc.ca/eic/site/sbrp-rppe.nsf/vwapj/KSBS-PSRPE_July-Juillet2011_eng.pdf/$FILE/KSBS-PSRPE_July-Juillet2011_eng.pdf, accessed March 21, 2012.

4. Paul Delean, "Riding the Health Wave," *Montreal Gazette*, February 28, 2011, p. A16; Nutrisoya website, http://www.nutrisoya,ca/, accessed March 4, 2011.

5. Mary Teresa Bitti, "Running on the Fitness Regimen," *Financial Post*, Canada's 50 Best Special Report, February 22, 2011, p. SR 28; The Running Room website, http://www.runningroom.com/hm, accessed March 4, 2011.

6. Industry Canada, "Small Business Research and Statistics: Key Small Business Statistics—July 2010," http://www.ic.gc.ca/eic/site/sbrp-rppe.nsf/eng/rd02491.html, accessed March 9, 2011.

7. Statistics Canada, "The Financial Picture of Farms in Canada," *2006 Census of Agriculture*, http://www.statcan.gc.ca/ca-ra2006/articles/finpicture-portrait-eng.htm#A1, accessed March 9, 2011.

8. Industry Canada, "Small Business Research and Statistics: Key Small Business Statistics—July 2010: What Is the Contribution of Small Businesses to Canada Gross Domestic Product?" http://www.ic.gc.ca/eic/site/sbrp-rppe.nsf/eng/rd02499.html, accessed March 9, 2011.

9. Industry Canada, "Small Business Research and Statistics: Key Small Business Statistics—July 2010: What Is the Contribution of Small Businesses to Canada's Exports?" http://www.ic.gc.ca/eic/site/sbrp-rppe.nsf/eng/rd02507.html, accessed March 9, 2011.

10. Industry Canada, "Small Business Research and Statistics: Key Small Business Statistics—July 2010: How Many Jobs Do Small Businesses Create?" http://www.ic.gc.ca/eic/site/sbrp-rppe.nsf/eng/rd02497.html, accessed March 9, 2011.

11. Facebook website, http://www.facebook.com/press, accessed April 2, 2010.

12. John Tozzi, Stacy Perman, and Nick Leiber, "America's Best Young Entrepreneurs 2009," *BusinessWeek*, October 12, 2009, http://www.businessweek.com.

13. "Advocacy Small Business Statistics and Research," U.S. Small Business Administration, http://web.sba.gov/faqs, accessed April 2, 2010.

14. Industry Canada, "Small Business Research and Statistics: Key Small Business Statistics—July 2010: How Many Businesses Appear and Disappear Each Year? http://www.ic.gc.ca/eic/site/sbrp-rppe.nsf/eng/rd02494.html, accessed March 9, 2011.

15. Carol Kopp, "The Tragedy of Krispy Kreme," *Yahoo! Finance*, October 13, 2009, http://finance.yahoo.news.

16. Patricia Schaefer, "The Seven Pitfalls of Business Failure and How to Avoid Them," *BusinessKnowHow.com*, http://www.businessknowhow.com/Startup/business-failure.htm, accessed April 2, 2010.

17. Ibid.

18. "Advocacy Small Business Statistics and Research."

19. Leona Liu, "Meet the Celebrity Gardener," *BusinessWeek*, October 13, 2009, http://www.businessweek.com/smallbiz.

20. Statistics Canada, "Survey of Regulatory Compliance Costs, 2008," *The Daily* July 9, 2010, http://www.statcan.gc.ca/daily-quotidien/100709/dq100709c-eng.htm accessed March 10, 2011.

21. "Government of Canada, Canada Business Network website, Small Business Investor Tax Credit, http://www.canadabusiness.ca/eng/summary/6038/, accessed March 21, 2012.

22. "One for One," TOMS Shoes website, http://www.tomsshoes.com/Our-Movement, accessed April 2, 2010.

23. "Top 10 Tips for Writing Your Business Plan," *AllBusiness*, http://www.allbusiness.com/business-planning-structures, accessed April 2, 2010.

24. Business Development Bank of Canada (BDC) website, http://www.bdc.ca/EN/Pages/home.aspx, accessed March 10, 2011,

25. Industry Canada, "Canada Small Business Financing Program," http://www.ic.gc.ca/eic/site/csbfp-pfpec.nsf/eng/home, accessed March 10, 2011 .

26. Robert Joseph, Michael Bordt, and Daood Hamdani, *Characteristics of Business Incubation in Canada, 2005*, Statistics Canada, http://dsp-psd.pwgsc.gc.ca/Collection/Statcan/88F0006X/88F0006XIE2006007.pdf, accessed March 10, 2011,

27. James Langton, "Venture Capital Investment up 10% Last Year: CVCA," *Investment Executive,* February 16, 2011, http://www. investmentexecutive.com/client/en/News/DetailNews.asp?Id=56 941&cat=147&IdSection=147&PageMem=&nbNews=&IdPub=, accessed March 10, 2011; John Tozzi, "Venture Capital's Favorite Startups," *BusinessWeek,* December 19, 2008, http://www. businessweek.com.

28. Industry Canada, "Small Business Research and Statistics: Sustaining the Momentum: An Economic Forum on Women Entrepreneurs—Summary Report," http://www.ic.gc.ca/eic/site/ sbrp-rppe.nsf/eng/rd01309.html, accessed March 9, 2011.

29. Website for Arlene Dickinson, http://arlenedickinson.com/, accessed January 15, 2012; "The Dragons: Arlene Dickinson," website for CBC *Dragons Den,* http://www.cbc.ca/dragonsden/ dragons_arlene.html, accessed January 15, 2012.

30. Franchiseek Canada, "Franchise Statistics: Canadian Franchise Statistics and Information," http://www.franchiseek.com/Canada/ Franchise_Canada_Statistics.htm, accessed March 11, 2011.

31. Franchise Industries LLC, "Statistics," http://www. franchisindustries.com, updated November 24, 2009.

32. Baskin-Robbins, "Franchise Opportunities," http://www. baskinrobbins.com/franchiseopportunities, accessed April 2, 2010; "2009 Franchise 500," *Entrepreneur,* http://www. entrepreneur.com, accessed April 2, 2010.

33. Subway website, http://www.subway.com, accessed April 2, 2010.

34. Edward N. Levitt, "What's So Great About Franchising?" *Franchise Trade,* http://www.franchisetrade.com, accessed April 2, 2010.

35. Ibid.

36. "Why People Are Drawn to Franchising," http://www.articles. directory.com, accessed April 2, 2010.

37. Levitt, "What's So Great About Franchising?"

38. "How Much Does a Franchise Cost?," *AllBusiness.com,* http:// www.allbusiness.com, accessed April 2, 2010.

39. Levitt, "What's So Great About Franchising?"

40. Guard-a-Kid, http://www.entrepreneur.com/business- opportunities, accessed April 2, 2010.

41. Ashley M. Heher, "Food Fight: Burger King Franchisees Sue Chain," *Associated Press,* November 12, 2009, http://finance. yahoo.com.

42. Laura Northrup, "Recent Class Action Lawsuits: Are You Eligible?" *Consumerist,* May 22, 2009, http://consumerist.com.

43. Sun Youth Organization website, http://sunyouthorg.com/, accessed March 13, 2011.

44. The Electricity Forum, "Canadian Electricity Generation, Transmission and Distribution Company Sites," http://www. electricityforum.com/links/cdautil.html, accessed March 13, 2011.

45. VIA Rail website, http://www.viarail.ca/, accessed March 13, 2011.

46. "Cabot's Cooperative Heritage," Cabot Creamery, http://www. cabotcheese.coop, accessed April 2, 2010.

47. Government of Canada, Co-operatives Secretariat, "About Co-ops in Canada," http://www.coop.gc.ca/COOP/display- afficher.do?id=1232131333489&lang=eng, accessed March 13, 2011.

48. Peter Koven and Kim Covert, "Canada Leads in Mining M&As, China Well Back, *Calgary Herald*, March 4, 2011, http://www. calgaryherald.com/business/Canada+leads+mining+China+well +back/4382198/story.html, accessed March 13, 2011.

49. Canadian Breast Cancer Foundation's Run for the Cure website, http://www.runforthecure.com/site/PageServer?pagename=run_ home, accessed March 13, 2011.

50. Barbara Quinn, "Partnering on Sustainability," *Pollution Engineering,* January 2009, p. 17.

Chapter 6

1. Allan Swift, "Stretching with the Times," *Montreal Gazette,* November 20, 2006, pp. B1–B2; Peter Diekmeyer, "On the Flip Side of a Weak Loonie," *National Post,* October 17, 2006, p. SR 1, SR3; Industry Canada, Strategis, "Canadian Apparel," http:// strategis.ic.gc.ca/epic/internet/inapparel-vetements.nsf/en/ ap03282e.html#industry, accessed December 18, 2006; Ville de Montreal, "L'industrie du Vêtement à Montréal," http://ville. montreal.qc.ca/pls/portal/docs/page/MTL_STATISTIQUES_FR/ media/documents/Profil_vetement_v2.pdf, accessed December 18, 2006.

2. The Jim Pattison Group, "About Us," http://www.jimpattison. com/corporate-info/about-us.aspx, accessed January 16, 2012.

3. "Juha Christensen," *CrunchBase,* http://www.crunchbase.com, accessed March 10, 2010.

4. Navkirat Sodhi, "Meet India's Leading Ladies," *Women Entrepreneur,* September 22, 2009, http://www. womenentrpreneur.com.

5. Industry Canada, "The State of Entrepreneurship in Canada, *Small Business Quarterly,* Vol. 11, No. 4, February 2010, http:// www.ic.gc.ca/eic/site/sbrp-rppe.nsf/vwapj/SBQ-BTPE_Feb- Fev2010_eng.pdf/$FILE/SBQ-BTPE-Feb-Fev2010_eng.pdf, accessed March 23, 2011; "Kauffman Index of Entrepreneurial Activity, http://www.kauffman.org, accessed March 10, 2010.

6. Monster Gym website, http://www.monstergym.net, accessed March 25, 2011.

7. Coramark Inc., "Our History," http://www.chezcora.com/our- company/history, accessed January 18, 2012.

8. Office of Advocacy, U.S. Small Business Administration, "The Facts about Small Businesses," http://www.sba.gov, accessed March 10, 2010.

9. Hannah Seligson, "Nine Young Chinese Entrepreneurs to Watch," *Forbes.com,* February 28, 2010, http://www.forbes.com.

10. Eve Gumpel, "Gypsy Tea Steeped in Health and Fun," *Women Entrepreneur*, January 24, 2010, http://www.womentrepreneur. com.

11. Halo by Shoshana website, http://www.halobyshoshana.com/, accessed March 25, 2011.

12. Niels Bosma, Kent Jones, Erkko Autio and Jonathan Levie, "Global Entrepreneurial Monitor: Executive Report," http://www.gemconsortium.org, accessed March 11, 2010.

13. Sodhi, "Meet India's Leading Ladies."

14. Simon Fraser University website, "Beedie School of Business News: Beedie Looks Back at Extraordinary Year at Surrey," http://beedie.sfu.ca/blog/tag/sfu-student-entrepreneur-of-the-year/, accessed January 18, 2012.

15. Students in Free Enterprise, "Leadership and Career Connections," http://www.sife.org, accessed March 11, 2010.

16. Mark Henricks, "Honor Roll," *Entrepreneur,* http://www.entrepreneur.com, accessed March 11, 2010.

17. "Cool College Startups 2010," *Inc.com,* http://www.inc.com, accessed March 10, 2010.

18. Tamara Schweitzer, "Study: Inc. 500 CEOs Aggressively Use Social Media for Business," *Inc.,* November 25, 2009, http://www.inc.com.

19. "Kauffman Index of Entrepreneurial Activity."

20. Newswire, "23-year-old Donates US$1 million to Support University of Waterloo Student Entrepreneurs," accessed March 29, 2011, http://www.newswire.ca/en/releases/archive/March2011/29/c7314.html

21. Play It Again website, http://www.playitagainsports.com/, accessed January 18, 2012.

22. Eve Gumpel, "The Accidental Inventor," *Women Entrepreneur,* August 18, 2009, http://www.womenentrepreneur.com.

23. "A Day in the Life of an Entrepreneur," *Princeton Review,* http://www.princetonreview.com, accessed March 14, 2010.

24. "Oprah Winfrey—About.com Readers' Most Admired Entrepreneur," http://www.entrepreneurs.about.com, accessed March 14, 2010.

25. Dan Moren, "Forget Oprah: Jobs Is Teens' Most Admired Entrepreneur," *About.com,* October 13, 2009, http://pcworld.about.com.

26. Sodhi, "Meet India's Leading Ladies."

27. Company website, http://www.bobbibrowncosmetics.com, accessed March 15, 2010; Bobbi Brown and Athena Schindelheim, "How I Did It," *Inc.,* http://www.inc.com, accessed March 15, 2010.

28. Donna Fenn, "The Kid Behind a $170 Million Website," *Inc.com,* http://www.inc.com, accessed March 15, 2010.

29. Amy S. Choi, "Entrepreneurs Who Thrive on Risky Business," *BusinessWeek,* December 4, 2009, http://www.businessweek.com.

30. Kasey Wehrum, "How I Did It: Ralph Braun of BraunAbility," *Inc.,* December 1, 2009, http://www.inc.com.

31. "Entrepreneurial America: A Comprehensive Look at Today's Fastest-Growing Private Companies," *Inc. The Handbook of the American Entrepreneur,* http://www.inc.com, accessed April 9, 2010.

32. Darren Dahl, "How to Read a Term Sheet," *Inc.,* March 1, 2010, http://www.inc.com.

33. Alexandra Paul, "City First Urban Reserve Open," *Winnipeg Free Press,* January 10, 2012, accessed on January 20, 2012, http://www.winnipegfreepress.com/breakingnews/136997393.html

34. Michael Goldman Inc., http://www.michaelgoldman.com, accessed March 16, 2010.

35. 3M, "A Culture of Innovation," http://www.3M.com, accessed March 16, 2010; Michael Goldman Inc., http://www.michaelgoldman.com.

36. 3M, "A Culture of Innovation."

Part 2: Launching Your Entrepreneurial Career

1. Michael Ames, cited in "Is Entrepreneurship for You?" Small Business Administration, http://www.sba.gov, accessed April 9, 2010.

2. Business Development Bank of Canada, "A Quick Refresher on Patents and Trademarks for Business Services," http://www.bdc.ca/EN/advice_centre/articles/Pages/a_quick_refresher_on_patents_trademarks_for_business_services.aspx, accessed May 1, 2012.

Chapter 7

1. Based on information from the Research In Motion website, http://www.rim.com/, accessed January 23, 2012; " Research In Motion Names Thorsten Heins President and CEO," press release, January 22, 2012, http://www.rim.com/investors/documents/pdf/financial/2012/Research_In_Motion_Names_Thorsten_Heins_President_and_CEO.pdf, accessed January 23, 2012; RIM stock chart, *Globe and Mail,* http://www.theglobeandmail.com/globe-investor/markets/stocks/chart/?q=RIM-T, accessed January 23, 2012; Tim Kiladze and Iain Marlow, "RIM Shakeup Brings Muted Market response," *Globe and Mail,* January 23, 2012, http://www.theglobeandmail.com/globe-investor/rim-shakeup-brings-muted-market-response/article2311427/, accessed January 23, 2012.

2. Loblaw website, http://www.loblaw.ca/, accessed April 5, 2011.

3. John Greenwood, "Canada's Outstanding CEO of the Year", *Financial Post,* January 14, 2011, http://www.financialpost.com/executive/ceo/Canadas+Outstanding+Year+Clark/4110716/story.html, accessed April 5, 2011.

4. "*BusinessWeek* Names Customer Service Champs," *Customers 1st Blogspot,* February 23, 2010, http://www.customers1stblogspot.com.

5. Cold Stone Creamery website, http://www.coldstonecreamery.com, accessed March 28, 2010.

6. "Zappos.com Power by Service," http://about.zappos.com, accessed March 28, 2010.

7. Helen Coster, "The State of the CEO in 2010," *Forbes.com,* January 21, 2010, http://www.forbes.com.

8. John Shmuel and Scott Deveau, "Stronach Resigns as Chairman of Magna," *Financial Post,* March 31, 2011, http://www.canada.com/business/Frank+Stronach+step+down+Magna+chairman/4536966/story.html, accessed online April 5, 2011.

9. Christopher Steiner, "Go Green and Stay in the Black," *Forbes. com,* March 8, 2010, http://www.forbes.com.

10. Facebook website, http://www.facebook.com/facebook, accessed April 5, 2011.

11. Coster, "The State of the CEO in 2010."

12. "Mattel Named One of the World's Most Ethical Companies Again in 2010," *Forbes.com,* March 22, 2010, http://www.forbes.com.

13. Reid Hoffman, as told to Mark Lacter, "How I Did It: Reid Hoffman of LinkedIn," *Inc.com,* May 1, 2009, http://www.inc.com.

14. Staples Announces Finalists of Global Search for the Next Green Office Product," *Boston.com,* March 24, 2010, http://finance.boston.com.

15. Ibid.

16. Sylvia Hui, "British Airways Cabin Crews Strike for 2nd Day," *Associated Press/Forbes.com,* March 21, 2010, http://www.forbes.com.

17. Company website, http://www.starbucks.com, accessed March 31, 2010; "Starbucks News! 2010," *Coffee Club Network,* January 22, 2010, http://www.cofeeclubnetwork.com.

18. "Starbucks News! 2010," *Coffee Club Network.*

19. Aaron Gold, "2010 Ford Taurus Drive," *About.com,* January 2010, http://www.about.com.

20. "Quiznos Helps Customers Eat Green," Quiznos Public Relations, February 25, 2010, http://pr.quiznos.com.

21. Becel website, http://www.loveyourheart.ca/en_ca/about_becel/default.aspx, accessed April 5, 2011.

22. "How Companies Manage the Front Line Today," *McKinsey & Company,* pp. 1–2.

23. Jena McGregor, Alli McConnon, and David Kiley, "Customer Service in a Shrinking Economy," *BusinessWeek,* March 9, 2010, http://www.businessweek.com.

24. Company website, http://www.apple.com, accessed April 1, 2010.

25. "Best 50 Corporate Citizens 2010," *Corporate Knights Magazine,* Issue 32, http://www.corporateknights.ca/report/9th-annual-best-50-corporate-citizens-canada/best-50-corporate-citizens; accessed April 5, 2011; "CR's 100 Best Corporate Citizens 2010," *CR Magazine,* http://www.thecro.org, accessed March 16, 2010.

26. Bruce Horovitz, "CEO Profile: Campbell Exec Nears Extraordinary Goal," *USA Today,* January 26, 2009, http://www.usatoday.com.

27. Scott D. Anthony, "Google's Management Style Grows Up," *BusinessWeek,* March 9, 2010, http://www.businessweek.com.

28. Dean Foust, "US Airways: After the Miracle on the Hudson," *BusinessWeek,* March 9, 2010, http://www.businessweek.com.

29. "Corporate Information," Google website, http://www.google.com/corporate/culture.html, accessed March 30, 2010.

30. "Culture," Walt Disney Company website, http://corporate.disney.go.com/careers/culture.html, accessed March 30, 2010.

31. Ben Fritz, "Company Town," *Los Angeles Times,* March 30, 2010, http://latimesblogs.latimes.com.

32. "Enterprise Facts," Enterprise Rent-A-Car website, http://www.erac.com, accessed March 30, 2010.

33. "Products and Services," 3M website, http://www.3M.com, accessed April 5, 2010.

34. Brandon Gutman, "Zappos' Marketing Chief: 'Customer Service Is the New Marketing!'" *Fast Company,* March 15, 2010, www.fastcompany.com.

35. Mike Gordon, Chris Musso, Eric Rebentisch, and Nisheeth Gupta, "The Path to Successful New Products," *McKinsey Quarterly,* January 7, 2010, http://www.forbes.com.

36. Jason Del Rey, "How I Did It: Omniture's Josh James," *Inc.com,* March 1, 2010, http://www.inc.com.

Chapter 8

1. Charles Duhigg and Keith Bradsher, "Iron Law of Economics," New York Times, published in National Post, January 23, 2012, p. FP3; Allan Swift, "Stretching with the Times," *Montreal Gazette,* November 20, 2006, pp. B1–B2; Industry Canada, "Canadian Apparel Profile," http://www.ic.gc.ca/eic/site/026.nsf/eng/h_00070.html#statistical, accessed January 29, 2012; Industry Canada, "Clothing Manufacturing," http://www.ic.gc.ca/cis-sic/cis-sic.nsf/IDE/cis-sic315empe.html, accessed January 29, 2012 ; Apparel Human Resources Council, *Pressing Ahead: Canada's Transforming Apparel Industry, 2011 Labour Market Information Study,* March 31, 2011, http://www.apparelconnexion.com/apparel/tools/files/b891ecaf-4376-7b1f.pdf, accessed January 29, 2012; The Conference Board of Canada, "Canada's Textiles and Apparel Industry," Spring 2011.

2. Jessica Dickler, "Great Job Openings, No Candidates," *CNNMoney.com,* November 7, 2009, http://cnn.money.com.

3. Jobs in Pods, http://www.jobsinpods.com, accessed April 13, 2010.

4. Peter M. LaSorsa, "UPS Settles EEOC Lawsuit for $46,000," *Illinois Sexual Harassment Attorney Blog,* February 20, 2010, http://www.illinoissexualharassmentblog.com.

5. "Executive Recruiting Advice—Don't Underestimate the Cost of a Mis-Hire," *Fortune 100 Best Companies to Work For,* http://www.fortune100bestcompaniestoworkfor.com, accessed April 13, 2010.

6. "McDonald's Puts Apprenticeships on the Menu," http://www.aboutmcdonalds.com, accessed April 15, 2010.

7. "Welcome to EYU," http://www.ey.com, accessed April 15, 2010.

8. "Systems Integration Consulting Training," https://microsite.accenture.com, accessed April 13, 2010.

9. The Conference Board of Canada, "Education and Learning," http://www.conferenceboard.ca/topics/education/default.aspx, accessed January 30, 2012.

10. Samuel A. Culbert, "Yes, Everyone Really Does Hate Performance Reviews," *Wall Street Journal,* April 19, 2010, http://finance.yahoo.com.

11. "Turn Your Performance Review System into One That Works," *Quality Digest Magazine,* http://www.qualitydigest.com, accessed April 14, 2010.

12. "Gather and Analyze 360 Degree Feedback More Quickly and Easily," Halogen Software, http://www.halogensoftware.com, accessed April 13, 2010.

13. "Employer Costs for Employee Compensation," Bureau of Labor Statistics, March 10, 2010, http://www.bls.gov.

14. Lance Whitney, "SAS, Google Top Fortune's Best-Employer List," *CNET News,* January 25, 2010, http://news.cnet.com.

15. "Advantages and Disadvantages of Paid Time Off," *The Thriving Small Business,* March 19, 2010, http://www.thethrivingsmallbusiness.com.

16. Eugene Eteris, "European Social Market Economy: Flexibility Issues," *The Baltic Course,* March 16, 2010, http://www.baltic-course.com.

17. "Things You Should Know about BidShift," San Angelo Community Medical Center, http://www.sacmc.com, accessed April 14, 2010.

18. "Study: Remote-Work Programs Benefit Employers Too," *Microsoft News Center,* March 11, 2010, http://www.microsoft.com.

19. Anita Cooper, "Telecommuting," *Associated Content,* http://www.associatedcontent.com, accessed April 14, 2010.

20. Lisa Orrell, "5 Tips to Retain Gen Y Talent," *Women Entrepreneur,* April 12, 2010, http://www.womenentrepreneur.com.

21. Marshall Goldsmith, "How to Keep Good Employees in a Bad Economy," February 26, 2010, http://blogs.hbr.org.

22. Dustin Ensinger, "Why Layoffs Are Not Beneficial to Companies," *Economy in Crisis,* February 8, 2010, http://www.economyincrisis.org.

23. Ibid.

24. Christopher D. Zatzik, Mitchell L. Marks, Roderick D. Iverson, "Downsizing Case Studies," *MIT Sloan Management Review,* January 7, 2010, http://www.nationalpost.com.

25. "Maslow's Hierarchy of Needs," *Accel-Team.com,* http://www.accel-team.com, accessed April 14, 2010.

26. Mediacorp Canada Inc., "Canada's Top Employers for Young People," http://www.canadastop100.com/young_people/, accessed January 30, 2012.

27. Canadian Labour Congress website, http://www.canadianlabour.ca/home, accessed January 30, 2012; Human Resources and Skills Development Canada, "Union Membership in Canada 2010," http://www.hrsdc.gc.ca/eng/labour/labour_relations/info_analysis/union_membership/2010/unionmembership2010.shtml#results, accessed January 30, 2012,

28. Jim Baillie, *An Investigation into the Collective Bargaining Relationship Between the NHL and the NHLPA 1994–2005* (Kingston, ON: Queens University Industrial Relations Centre, 2005), http://irc.queensu.ca/gallery/1/dps-nhl-lockout.pdf, accessed January 30, 2012.

29. Jamie Doward, "BA Strike: Airline and Union Swap Barbs on Second Weekend of Walkouts," *Guardian,* March 27, 2010, http://www.guardian.co.uk.

30. Ibid.

31. Human Resources and Skills Development Canada, "Union Membership in Canada 2010."

Chapter 9

1. Interview with Pam Cooley, March 16, 2012; Corporate website, http://www.pamcooley.ca/, accessed March 12, 2012; Corporate website CarShareHFX, www.carsharehfx.ca/, accessed March 12, 2012; "CarShareHFX Welcomes a New Mobility Option at Dalhousie University," *CNW CanadaWire,* March 11, 2011, http://www.newswire.ca/en/story/753625/carsharehfx-welcomes-a-new-mobility-option-at-dalhousie-university, accessed online March 16, 2012.

2. Anderson & Associates website, http://www.andassoc.com, accessed April 19, 2010.

3. Chris Atchison, "Pride of Ownership," *Globe and Mail*, October 7, 2011, http://www.theglobeandmail.com/report-on-business/careers/top-employers/top-employers-2012/pride-of-ownership-works-both-ways/article2193177/, accessed February 1, 2012.

4. The ESOP Association Canada (Employee Share Ownership Plan) website, http://www.esop-canada.com/, accessed April 12, 2011; "Employee Stock Options and Ownership (ESOP)," http://www.referenceforbusiness.com, accessed April 19, 2010.

5. "Employee Ownership as a Retirement Plan," The National Center for Employee Ownership, http://www.nceo.org, accessed April 19, 2010.

6. "Employee Stock Options Fact Sheet," The National Center for Employee Ownership, http://www.nceo.org, accessed April 19, 2010.

7. Ibid.

8. Toyota website, http://www.toyota.com/recall, accessed May 10, 2010.

9. "Our Core Values," Whole Foods Market website, http://www.wholefoodsmarket.com, accessed April 19, 2010.

10. "Harley-Davidson: The Sound of a Legend," http://www.lmsintl.com, accessed April 19, 2010.

11. BBC website, http://www.bbc.co.uk, accessed May 10, 2010; Lynda Gratton, Andreas Voigt, and Tamara Erickson, "Bridging Faultlines in Diverse Teams," *MIT Sloan Management Review,* summer 2007, pp. 22–29.

12. Kate Rogers, "Commitment to Standards, Mission, Clients and Fun," *Nonprofit Times,* April 1, 2010, http://nptimes.com.

13. Robert Grice, "How to Build a Unified Team," *Helium,* http://www.helium.com, accessed April 19, 2010.

14. Nick Grabbe, "Experts: Don't Fear Workplace Conflict," *Gazettenet.com,* March 1, 2010, http://www.gazettenet.com.

15. Ken Thomas and Larry Margasak, "Toyota Waited Months to Tell U.S. about Sticking Accelerator Fixes It Gave to Dealers in Europe," *Associated Press,* April 6, 2010, http://blog.cleveland.com.

16. Ibid.

17. David Woods, "i-level Redesigns Its Employee reward Communication Strategy," *HR Magazine,* March 8, 2010, http://www.humanresourcesmagazine.co.uk.

18. Norma Chew, "Are You a Good Listener?" *Associated Content,* http://www.associatedcontent.com, accessed April 19, 2010.

19. Open Text Corporate website, accessed February 1, 2012, http://www.opentext.com/2/global.htm

20. "Expand Trust in Your Organization," *Peter Stark.com,* http://www.peterstark.com, accessed April 19, 2010.

21. Joni F. Johnston, "How to Deal with Office Gossip," *Ezine Articles,* http://ezinearticles.com, accessed April 19, 2010.

22. John Boe, "How to Read Your Prospect Like a Book!," John Boe International, http://johnboe.com, accessed April 19, 2010.

23. Amar Toor, "Nestlé's Palm Oil PR Crisis Pervades Facebook," *Switched,* March 22, 2010, http://www.switched.com.

24. "Nestlé's Social Media PR Crisis: How Would You Handle It?" Pierce Mattie Public Relations, http://www.piercemattiepublicrelations.com, accessed April 19, 2010.

25. Emily Steel, "Nestlé Takes a Beating on Social-Media Sites," *Wall Street Journal,* March 29, 2010, http://online.wsj.com.

Chapter 10

1. NASA website, "NASA Scores Big with Student Soccer Players in the U.S.A. and Canada," http://www.nasa.gov/topics/nasalife/features/soccer_ball.html, June 18, 2011, accessed February 3, 2012; Tom Wright, "Pakistan Defends Its Soccer Industry," *Wall Street Journal*, April 26, 2010, http://online.wsj.com; "Adidas Unveils World Cup Final Match Ball—Jo'bulani," *Shine2010,* April 20, 2010, http://www.shine2010.co.za; "Official 2010 FIFA World Cup Match Ball," *For Men Only,* March 1, 2010, http://toffsmen.com; Andrew Nusca, "The Science Behind the 2010 World Cup Soccer Ball, Adidas Jabulani," *SmartPlanet,* December 7, 2009, http://www.smartplanet.com; "Adidas Jabulani Official Match Ball of the 2010 FIFA World Cup," *Adidas Press Room,* December 4, 2009, http://www.press.adidas.com.

2. "Honda Builds Record 84% of 2009 U.S. Auto Sales in North America," *Auto Channel,* http://www.theautochannel.com, accessed April 26, 2010.

3. Lydia Dishman, "Retire? Forget about It," *Entrepreneur,* January 11, 2010, http://www.entrepreneur.com.

4. Barbara Quinn, "Carving a Roadway to Sustainability," *Pollution Engineering,* May 2010, p. 17.

5. Canada Green Building Council (CaGBC) website, http://www.cagbc.org, accessed April 14, 2011; "LEED," U.S. Green Building Council website, http://www.usgbc.org, accessed May 27, 2010.

6. Consolidated Technologies website, http://consolidatedtechnologies.ca/, accessed April 14, 2011.

7. Clara Maria Cabrera, "CAD/CAM Dental Technology," *Associated Content,* http://www.associatedcontent.com, accessed April 26, 2010.

8. Roger Schreffler, "Nissan's Flexible Manufacturing Moves to India, Other JVs," *Wards Auto.com,* February 3, 2010, http://www.wardsauto.com.

9. Vince Lapinski, "We Are Print," manroland website, http://www.manroland.us.com.

10. Anupam Govil, "Shifting of the Global Sourcing Axis," *Near Shore Americas,* April 6, 2010, http;//www.nearshoreamericas.com.

11. Mike Pare, "VW Prototypes on Local Horizon," *Chattanooga Times Free Press,* January 11, 2010, http://www.timesfreepress.com.

12. "Holland Car's Assembly Line to Evolve," *Fortune,* April 18, 2010, http://www.addisfortune.com.

13. "Advantages and Disadvantages of Outsourcing," *The Thriving Small Business,* February 8, 2010, http://www.thethrivingsmallbusiness.com.

14. "Supplier Mangement," Ariba website, http://www.ariba.com, accessed April 26, 2010.

15. Shruti Date Singh, "Deere Shortage Prompts Kansas Farmer to Buy Dragotec," *Bloomberg Businessweek,* April 26, 2010, http://www.businessweek.com.

16. SAP website, "Loblaw Selects SAP to Strengthen Its Business Processes in Canada," November 10, 2008, http://www.sap.com/press.epx?pressid=10365, accessed April 14, 2011.

17. "Seattle Children's Hospital Saves $2.5 Million in First Year with Streamlined Inventory Distribution," http://www.hfma.org, accessed April 26, 2010.

18. "Allan Candy Company," *Microsoft Case Studies,* April 19, 2010, http://www.microsoft.com.

19. Judy Miller, "Still Made in America: The Super Bowl Footballs from Ada, Ohio," *Encyclopedia Britannica Blog,* February 1, 2010, http://www.britannica.com.

20. "Success Stories: Sleepmaster, LTD," *User solutions.com,* http://www.usersolutions.com, accessed April 26, 2010.

21. "Contrite Facebook CEO Promises new Privacy Controls," *Yahoo! News,* May 24, 2010, http://news.yahoo.com.

22. Jamie Liddell, "Top Ten Tips for Better Benchmarking," *SSON Network,* http://www.ssonetwork.com, accessed April 26, 2010.

23. Six Sigma Inc. Canada website, http://www.sixsigmacanada.net/, accessed February 3, 2012; Vic Nanda, "Preempting Problems," *Six Sigma Forum Magazine,* February 2010, pp. 9–18.

24. "Maintaining the Benefits and Continual Improvement," International Organization for Standardization, http://www.iso.org, accessed April 26, 2010.

25. NASA website, "NASA Scores Big with Student Soccer Players in the U.S.A. and Canada"; Tom Wright, "Pakistan Defends Its Soccer Industry"; "Adidas Unveils World Cup Final Match Ball—Jo'bulani"; "Official 2010 FIFA World Cup Match Ball"; Andrew Nusca, "The Science Behind the 2010 World Cup Soccer Ball, Adidas Jabulani"; "Adidas Jabulani Official Match Ball of the 2010 FIFA World Cup."

Part 3: Launching Your Management Career

1. Living in Canada, "Canadian Salary Survey," http://www.livingin-canada.com/wages-for-management-jobs-canada.html, accessed May 1, 2012.

Chapter 11

1. Etsy website for Linda Lutz, accessed February 3, 2012, http://www.etsy.com/people/BeadCrazed; Etsy website, http://www.etsy.com, accessed March 25, 2010; Artfire website, http://www.artfire.com, accessed March 25, 2010; 1000 Markets website, http://www.1000markets.com, accessed March 25, 2010; Janell Mooney's website, http://www.etsy.com/shop/dancingmooney, accessed March 25, 2010; Janell Mooney, "What You Should Know about Etsy.com," *Associated Content*, http://associatedcontent.com, accessed March 25, 2010; Cyndia Zwahlen, "Independent Artisans Are Crowding onto the Web," *Los Angeles Times*, March 1, 2010, http://www.latimes.com; Alex Williams, "That Hobby Looks Like a Lot of Work," *New York Times*, December 17, 2009, http://www.nytimes.com.

2. American Marketing Association, "AMA Adopts New Definition of Marketing," *Marketing-Power,* www.danavan.net, accessed March 25, 2010.

3. Company website, http://www.target.com, accessed March 25, 2010; Brad Gilligan, "Target Starts Mobile Coupon Program," *All Tech Considered,* March 11, 2010, http://www.npr.org; Business Wire, "Target Launches First-Ever Scannable Mobile Coupon Program," *MarketWatch,* March 10, 2010, http://www.marketwatch.com; Marguerite Reardon, "Attention Shoppers: Target Offers Mobile Coupons," *CNET News,* March 10, 2010, http://news.cnet.com.

4. Company website, http://www.apple.com, accessed March 25, 2010; "Apple IPAD: Get to Know the Apple iPad," *NY Breaking News,* n.d., http://www.nybreakingnews.com; Arik Hesseldahl, "Apple's Hard iPad Sell," *Business Week,* February 5, 2010, http://www.businessweek.com; Erica Ogg, "Who Will Buy the iPad?" *CNET News,* January 28, 2010, http://news.cnet.com.

5. Michael Hall, David Lasby, Steven Ayer, and William David Gibbons, *Caring Canadians, Involved Canadians: Highlights from the Canada Survey of Giving, Volunteering and Participating,* Catalogue no. 71-542-XWE, Chapter 2, Volunteering (Ottawa: Statistics Canada, 2007), http://www.statcan.gc.ca/pub/71-542-x/2009001/chap/ch2-eng.htm, accessed May 8, 2012; *Summary of the Findings of the National Survey of Nonprofit and Voluntary Organizations* (NSNVO), Statistics Canada website, http://www.statcan.gc.ca/pub/61-533-s/61-533-s2005001-eng.htm#5, accessed January 23, 2011; "Facts and Figures about Charitable Organizations," *Independent Sector,* October 30, 2009, http://www.independentsector.org.

6. Lester M. Salamon, Megan A. Haddock, S. Wojciech Sokolowski, and Helen S. Tice, *Measuring Civil Society and Volunteering: Initial Findings from Implementation of the UN Handbook on Nonprofit Institutions,* Working Paper No. 23 (Baltimore: Johns Hopkins Center for Civil Society Studies, 2007), http://www.jhu.edu.

7. The Enbridge CN Tower Climb for United Way website, http://www.unitedwaytoronto.com/climbforunitedway/main.php.

8. Company website, http://www.avoncompany.com, accessed March 25, 2010; "Avon Foundation for Woman Grants $500,000 to the U.S. Department of State Secretary's Fund for Global Women's Leadership," press release, March 11, 2010, http://multivu.prnewswire.com.

9. "The Adventures of Quatchi, Miga, and Sumi Begin in Earnest," Vancouver 2010, http://www.vancouver2010.com, accessed March 25, 2010.

10. The Canadian Diabetes Association website, http://www.diabetes.ca/, accessed April 28, 2011.

11. The University of Western Ontario's Alternative Spring Break website, http://www.asb.uwo.ca/, accessed April 28, 2011.

12. Company website, http://www.seventhgeneration.com, accessed March 25, 2010.

13. Oprah's Angel Network website, http://oprahsangelnetwork.org, accessed March 25, 2010.

14. Marco Lui, "Subway Plans to Open 500 Stores across China in Next Five Years," *BusinessWeek*, March 11, 2010, http://www.businessweek.com; Farah Master, "Subway Eyes Matching McDonalds in China in 10 Years," *Reuters*, March 8, 2010, http://www.reuters.com.

15. Blank Label website, http://www.blank-label.com, accessed March 25, 2010; Spreadshirt website, http://www.spreadshirt.com, accessed March 25, 2010.

16. Christopher T. Heun, "Procter & Gamble Readies Online Market-Research Push," *InformationWeek,* http://www.informationweek.com, accessed March 29, 2010; Mark Clothier, "P&G's McDonald Pins Growth on Closer Shave than Mumbai Barber," *BusinessWeek,* March 11, 2010, http://www.businessweek.com.

17. Stephanie Rosenbloom, "In Bid to Sway Sales, Cameras Track Shoppers," *New York Times*, March 20, 2010, http://www.nytimes.com.

18. Clothier, "P&G's McDonald Pins Growth on Closer Shave."

19. Pottery Barn Kids website, http://www.potterybarnkids.com, accessed March 25, 2010; "Unica Releases 'The State of Marketing 2010' Results," *CNNMoney.com*, March 10, 2010; http://money.cnn.com.

20. "About Idea Storm," Dell website, http://www.ideastorm.com, accessed March 25, 2010.

21. Declan McCullagh, "Why No One Cares about Privacy Anymore," *CNET News,* March 12, 2010, http://news.cnet.com; Leah Betancourt, "How Companies Are Using Your Social Media Data," *Mashable,* March 2, 2010, http://mashable.com; Jim Cooper, "Yahoo's Carol Bartz Touts Data," *Mediaweek,* March 1, 2010, http://www.mediaweek.com.

22. Company website, http://turiyamedia.com, accessed March 25, 2010; "Turiya Media Targets Game Publishers with Behavioral Data Mining," *GamesBeat,* March 10, 2010, http://games.venturebeat.com.

23. Amanda Lenhart, Kristen Purcell, Aaron Smith, and Kathryn Zickuhr, "Social Media and Young Adults," Pew Internet and American Life Project, February 3, 2010, http://www.pewinternet.org.

24. Andrea Chang, "Buyers at Toy Fair in New York Foresee Another Cutthroat Holiday Season," *Los Angeles Times,* February 15, 2010, http://articles.latimes.com; Stephanie Rosenbloom, "Toys 'R' Us Trims Losses by Making a Hamster Hot," *New York Times*, December 19, 2009, http://www.nytimes.com.

25. Nelson Ireson, "2012 Ford Police Interceptor: Taurus Does Law and Order," *Motor Authority*, March 12, 2010, http://www.motorauthority.com; Brent Snavely, "Ford to Unveil Police Interceptor," *Frreep.com*, March 12, 2010, http://www.freep.com; "Ford Unveils Next-Generation, V-6-Only Taurus Police Car," *USA Today*, March 12, 2010, http://content.usatoday.com.

26. Emily Sohn, "Why (Most) Women Like to Shop," *DiscoveryNews*, December 11, 2009, http://news.discovery.com.

27. Marissa Miley and Ann Mack, "The New Female Consumer: The Rise of the Real Mom," *Advertising Age* White Paper, November 16, 2009, http://adage.com.

28. Constance Waschull, ed., "Women: The Fragile Financial Superpower," *Allianz Knowledge*, updated February 4, 2010, http://knowledge.allianz.com.

29. U.S. Census Bureau, "Resident Population Projections by Sex and Age: 2010 to 2050," *Statistical Abstract of the United States*, http://www.census.gov, accessed March 25, 2010.

30. Paul Briand, "Baby Boomers Shunning Usual Retirement Haunts," *Examiner.com*, March 26, 2010, http://www.examiner.com.

31. "Nielsen: Shopping Habits by Generation," *Convenience Store News*, March 29, 2010, http://www.csnews.com.

32. Company website, http://www.gmblogs.com, accessed March 25, 2010.

33. Ruth Mantell, "Despite Tough Times, Parents Spend Big on Kids," *MarketWatch*, May 4, 2010, www.marketwatch.com.

34. Company website, http://www.crateandbarrel.com, accessed March 25, 2010.

35. "Sodexho Marriott Services," *Claritas*, www.claritas.com, accessed March 29, 2010.

36. Katherine Glover, "More Bad News for Starbucks as McCafé Moves in for the Kill," *BNET*, April 20, 2009, http://industry.bnet.com.

37. Resources for Entrepreneurs staff, "Consumer Habits Could Be Permanently Changed by Recession," *Resources for Entrepreneurs*, March 25, 2010, http://www.gaebler.com.

38. Company website, http://www.timberland.com, accessed March 29, 2010.

39. Company website, http://www.marriott.com, accessed March 29, 2010.

40. Company website, http://www.apple.com/ipod/nike, accessed March 29, 2010.

41. Company website, http://www.netcall.com, accessed March 29, 2010.

Chapter 12

1. Monster Gym website, http://www.monstergym.net/, accessed May 16, 2011; Cielo Studios website, http://www.cielostudios.ca/, accessed May 16, 2011; Grant Brothers Boxing & MMA Gym website, http://grantbrothersmma.com/, accessed May 16, 2011; interviews with Carmine Petrillo and Howard Grant.

2. Stan Schroeder, "Gartner: Most Kids Will Use PCs with Touchscreens by 2015," *Mashable*, April 7, 2010, http://mashable.com.

3. Associated Press, "Pepsi to Distribute New Line of Tampico Drinks," *msn.com*, April 9, 2010, http://news.moneycentral.msn.com.

4. General Mills, "Nourish Your Inner Goddess with the Goodness of New Yoplait Greek Yogurt," press release, March 4, 2010, http://www.generalmills.com; Company websites, http://www.generalmills.com, http://www.warnerbros.com, http://www.legendarypictures.com, accessed April 30, 2010.

5. Joachim Ebert, Shiv Shivaraman, and Paul Carrannanto, "Driving Growth through Ultra-Low-Cost Product Development," *Industry Week*, February 17, 2010, http://www.industryweek.com.

6. Tony Bradley, "Kindle Apps Blur the Line Between Gadgets," *PC World*, January 21, 2010, http://www.pcworld.com; Dan Frommer, "Amazon Rushes Kindle iPad App, Available in Time for iPad Launch," *SF Gate*, April 2, 2010, http://www.sfgate.com.

7. Alfred Poor, "HDTV Almanac—LED Backlight Prices Falling," *HDTV Magazine*, February 22, 2010, http://www.hdtvmagazine.com.

8. Elaine Wong, "Noxzema Tells Consumers to 'Come Clean,' " *Brandweek*, May 17, 2010, www.brandweek.com.

9. Matthew Moskovciak, "Blu-ray Quick Guide," *CNET Reviews*, February 25, 2010, http://reviews.cnet.com.

10. Adam Tschorn, "Old Spice Talks to the Ladies, Man," *Los Angeles Times*, March 6, 2010, http://articles.latimes.com; Drew Grant, "Old Spice's Spicy Ad Campaign," *Mediaite*, February 20, 2010, http://www.mediaite.com; Liz Shannon Miller, "The Viral Genius of Wieden+Kennedy's New Old Spice Campaign," *NewTeeVee*, February 19, 2010, http://newteevee.com.

11. Company website, http://www.mattel.com, accessed April 30, 2010; Amy Graff, "Are Today's Girls Abandoning Their Dolls Too Soon?" *SF Gate*, April 6, 2010, http://www.sfgate.com; Andrea Chang, "Toy Fair 2010: After Strong Holiday Sales, Barbie Flaunts New Jobs and Fashions," *Los Angeles Times*, February 14, 2010, http://latimesblogs.latimes.com; The White House Project, "Barbie Celebrates 125th Career with Global Initiative to Inspire Girls," press release, January 21, 2010, http://thewhitehouseproject.org.

12. Company website, http://www.febreze.com, accessed April 30, 2010; *PR Newswire*, "P&G Leads 2010 Edison Best New Product Award Finalists with Five Nods," press release, February 11, 2010, http://www.prnewswire.com.

13. Company website, http://www.ea.com, accessed April 30, 2010; Ben Gilbert, "Report: EA Planning Premium, Pre-Launch DLC for Retail Games at $10–$15," *Joystiq*, March 22, 2010, http://www.joystiq.com.

14. Tom Merritt, "Top 10 Worst Products," *CNET*, www.cnet.com, accessed April 30, 2010; John Biggs, "Ten Years: The Biggest Product Flops of the Decade," *CrunchGear*, December 31, 2009, http://www.crunchgear.com.

15. CBS4, "Centennial IKEA Construction Begins May 4," April 20, 2010, http://cbs4denver.com; Paula Moore, "IKEA Tackles Tricky Terrain," *Denver Business Journal*, October 16, 2009, http://denverbizjournals.com.

16. Company website, http://www.quiznos.com, accessed April 30, 2010; Quiznos, "Quiznos Rolls Out Green Packaging," press release, February 23, 2010, http://www.chainleader.com.

17. Company website, http://www.fedex.com, accessed April 30, 2010.

18. Statistics Canada, "Annual Wholesale Trade Survey–2009," March 29, 2011, http://www.statcan.gc.ca/cgibin/imdb/p2SV.pl?Function=getSurvey&SDDS=2445&lang=en&db=imdb&adm=8&dis=2, accessed May 8, 2011; U.S. CensusBureau, *County Business Patterns*, http://www.census.gov, accessed May 24, 2010; Bureau of Labor Statistics, "Occupational Outlook Handbook, 2010–11 Edition," http://www.bls.gov, accessed April 30, 2010.

19. Federated Co-operatives Limited website, www.coopconnection.ca, accessed May 8, 2011.

20. U.S. Census Bureau, "Quarterly Retail E-Commerce Sales, 4th Quarter 2009," February 16, 2010, http://www.census.gov.

21. Company website, http://www.seventhgeneration.com, accessed April 30, 2010; Romy Ribitzky, "Talking about an Ad Generation," *Portfolio.com*, February 11, 2010, http://www.portfolio.com; Romy Ribitzky, "7 Facts about Seventh Generation," *Portfolio.com*, February 11, 2010, http://www.portfolio.com; Elaine Wong, "How Seventh Generation Is Going Mainstream," *Brandweek*, January 26, 2010, http://www.brandweek.com.

22. Company website, http://www.polaroid.com, accessed April 30, 2010; "Starlight to Expand Digital Entertainment Product Category under the Polaroid Brand," press release, March 24, 2010, http://www.foxbusiness.com.

23. Mondou Corporate website, http://www.mondou.com/, accessed May 11, 2012.

24. My Starbucks Idea website, http://mystarbucksidea.force.com, accessed April 30, 2010; Emily Bryson York, "Starbucks Gets Its Business Brewing Again with Social Media," *Advertising Age*, February 22, 2010, http://adage.com.

25. James Kanter, "Luxury Goods May Pick and Choose Venues for Sales," *New York Times*, April 20, 2010, http://www.nytimes.com.

26. Company website, "About Us," http://www.easy.com, accessed April 30, 2010.

27. Samuel Axon, "How Small Businesses Are Using Social Media for Real Results," *Mashable*, March 22, 2010, http://mashable.com.

28. Brooke Crothers, "iPad Sold Out at Best Buy Nationwide," *CNET News*, April 7, 2010, http://news.cnet.com; Mary Ellen Lloyd, "Best Buy Shares Benefit from Apple iPad Launch," *Dow Jones Newswires*, April 5, 2010, http://www.foxbusiness.com; Michael Grothaus, "Best Buy to Carry iPad on April 3 at ASC-Stores Only," *TUAW*, March 26, 2010, http://www.tuaw.com.

29. Beyond the Rack Web site, www.beyondtherack.com, accessed May 10, 2011.

30. "Nano-Based RFID Tags Could Replace Bar Codes," *Science Daily*, March 19, 2010, http://www.sciencedaily.com; "Verayo Launches Next Generation of Unclonable RFID Chips," *BusinessWire*, March 2, 2010, http://www.businesswire.com.

31. Gord Baldwin, "Too Many Trucks on the Road?" Statistics Canada, November 12, 2009, http://www.statcan.gc.ca/pub/11-621-m/11-621-m2005028-eng.htm, accessed May 10, 2011;

"Trucking Statistics," *Truck Info*, http://www.truckinfo.net, accessed April 30, 2010.

32. Association of American Railroads, "Class I Railroad Statistics," April 12, 2010, http://www.aar.org; Vince Bond Jr., "Freight Trains Pull Their Weight in Energy Savings," *Great Lakes Echo*, January 12, 2010, http://greatlakesecho.org.

Chapter 13

1. Wasserman & Partners Advertising Inc., interview with Alvin Wasserman, May 13, 2011; Wasserman & Partners Advertising Inc. website, http://www.wasserman-partners.com/, accessed May 18, 2011; WorkSafeBC website, http://www.worksafebc.com/, accessed May 19, 2011; WorkSafeBC, *WorkSafeBC Statistics 2009 Report*, http://www.worksafebc.com/publications/reports/statistics_reports/assets/pdf/stats2009.pdf, accessed May19, 2011.

2. "Monster.com Launches New Integrated Marketing Campaign to Help Job Seekers and Employers 'Get a Monster Advantage,' " press release, January 25, 2010, http://www.pr-inside.com.

3. Rebecca Ruiz, "Ten Misleading Drug Ads," *Forbes.com*, February 2, 2010, http://www.forbes.com.

4. Michelle Krebs, "For Upcoming Chevrolet Cruze, GM Bets Safety Will (Up) Sell," *Edmunds Auto Observer*, April 19, 2010, http://www.autoobserver.com.

5. Nielsen IAG PlaceViews Product-Placement Activity Report, *Advertising Age*, February 22, 2010, http://adage.com; Wayne Friedman, " 'Idol' Gives Coke Millions in Media Value," *MediaPost*, January 14, 2010, http://www.mediapost.com.

6. Christopher Wolf, "Let Me Entertain You," *QSR Magazine*, December 2009, http://www.qsrmagazine.com.

7. Mark Wyatt, "Guerilla [sic] Marketing Meets Social Media," *Articlesbase*, February 8, 2010, http://www.articlesbase.com.

8. David Griner, "To Hell and Back: EA's Guerrilla Marketing Campaign for 'Dante's Inferno,' " *AdFreak.com*, spring 2010, http://adweek.blogs.com.

9. Jim Tierney, "Live from NEMOA: Why Your Brand Should Be Like Elvis," *Multichannel Merchant*, March 11, 2010, http://www.multichannelmerchant.com.

10. Research and Management, *WSI Internet Marketing Trends Report, 2010 Executive Summary*, http://www.wsisme.com/files/Articles/TrendsReport10_Canada.pdf, accessed February 4, 2012; Statistics Canada, "Advertising and related services 2009; accessed February 04, 2012, http://www.statcan.gc.ca/pub/63-257-x/2011001/part-partie1-eng.htm

11. Laurel Wentz and Bradley Johnson, "Top 100 Global Advertisers Heap Their Spending Abroad," *Advertising Age*, November 30, 2009, http://adage.com; "Global Marketers 2009," *Advertising Age*, November 30, 2009, http://adage.com.

12. Avon company website, http://responsibility.avoncompany.com, accessed June 14, 2010.

13. Nick Bilton, "Google and Partners Seek TV Foothold," *New York Times*, March 17, 2010, http://www.nytimes.com.

14. Jessica E. Vascellaro, "Google Tests TV Search Service," *Wall Street Journal*, March 8, 2010, http://online.wsj.com.

15. CRTC website, "How Many Canadians Subscribe to Cable TV or Satellite TV?" August 2006, http://www.crtc.gc.ca/eng/publications/reports/radio/cmri.htm, accessed May 11, 2011; Erick Schonfeld, "Estimate: 800,000 U.S. Households Abandoned Their TVs for the Web," *TechCrunch*, April 13, 2010, http://techcrunch.com; John Latchem, "More U.S. Homes Have Game Consoles than Cable Boxes," *Home Media Magazine*, March 3, 2010, http://www.homemediamagazine.com; Bill Carter, "DVR, Once TV's Mortal Enemy, Helps Ratings," *New York Times*, November 2, 2009, http://www.nytimes.com.

16. "Super Bowl Ad Prices Dip, But Still Pricey," *CBS News*, January 11, 2010, http://www.cbsnews.com; Brian Steinberg, "'Sunday Night Football' Remains Costliest TV Show," *Advertising Age*, October 26, 2009, http://adage.com.

17. "Internet Radio—Traditional Radio's Future?" *Radio News*, April 7, 2010, http://www.radiostreamingnews.com.

18. "Google Audio Ads—The Future of Radio Advertising?" *Broadcast Advertising*, February 14, 2010, http://broadcastadvertising.doodig.com.

19. Outdoor Advertising Association of America, "Facts and Figures," n.d., http://www.oaaa.org.

20. Mike Sachoff, "Online Ad Spending to Outpace Print in 2010," *WebProNews*, March 8, 2010, http://www.webpronews.com.

21. Ford Motor Company website, http://www.fiestamovement2.com, accessed May 14, 2010; Jay Yarow, "YouTube Turning a Profit? Eric Schmidt 'Assumes' It Is," *Business Insider*, January 22, 2010, http://www.businessinsider.com; Grant McCracken, "How Ford Got Social Marketing Right," *Harvard Business Review*, January 7, 2010, http://blogs.hbr.org.

22. Jimm Fox, "The 5 Most Effective Viral Video Ads of 2009," *One Market Media*, January 4, 2010, http://www.onemarketmedia.com.

23. BzzAgent website, http://aboutbzzagent.com, accessed May 2010; Andrew M. Kaikati, "Let's Make a Deal," *Wall Street Journal*, January 25, 2010, http://online.wsj.com.

24. "Effective Infomercials," Infomercial DRTV, http://www.infomercialdrtv.com, accessed May 14, 2010.

25. Edward C. Baig, "Target Puts Mobile Coupons on Customers' Cellphones," *USA Today*, March 11, 2010, http://www.usatoday.com; Phil Wahba, "Coupon Use Up 27 Pct Last Year—Inmar," *Shop Talk*, January 25, 2010, http://blogs.reuters.com.

26. Dan Fletcher, "How Facebook Is Redefining Privacy," *Time*, May 20, 2010, http://www.time.com; "Point of Purchase Marketing Turns to Digital Options," *POP Displays*, April 3, 2010, http://popdisplays.theproductjudge.com; Kunur Patel, "Forget Foursquare: Why Location Marketing Is New Point-of-Purchase," *Advertising Age*, March 22, 2010, http://adage.com.

27. U.S. Department of Labor, Economic News Release, Table 5. Employment by Major Occupational Group, 2008 and Projected 2018, December 11, 2009, http://data.bls.gov, accessed May 14, 2010.

28. Mark Huber, "Life of a Salesman," *Air Space Magazine*, February–March 2007, http://www.airspacemag.com.

29. Matthew Hathaway, "Recession-Weary Consumers Find Haggling Can Cut Costs," *Chicago Tribune*, March 14, 2010, http://articles.chicagotribune.com; Michael S. Rosenwald, "In Tough Economic Times, Shoppers Take Haggling to New Heights," *Washington Post*, January 31, 2010, http://www.washingtonpost.com.

30. Lee Howard, "Pfizer Ups Its Commitment to E-Marketing," *The Day*, January 21, 2010, http://www.allbusiness.com.

31. Canadian Radio-television Telecommunications Commission, "Canadian Radio-television Telecommunications Commission Unsolicited Telecommunication Rules," http://www.crtc.gc.ca/eng/trules-reglest.htm, accessed May 21, 2012.

32. Bruce Wilson, "Generating B2B Sales Leads Using Social Media," *Many Doors Marketing*, February 24, 2010, http://manydoors.net.

33. Nat Robinson, "SlideRocket Presentation Tip—4 Ways For Using MultiMedia Strategically," *SlideRocket*, April 1, 2010, http://www.sliderocket.com.

34. David Parker Brown, "Spirit Airlines Installs 'Pre-Reclined' Seats on New Airbus A320's," *Airline Reporter*, April 21, 2010, http://www.airlinereporter.com.

35. Jennifer Campbell, "Social Notes," *Montreal Gazette*, May 14, 2011, http://www.montrealgazette.com/sports/Social+Notes/4783511/story.html#ixzz1MRJHiWPy, accessed May 15, 2011.

36. Elaine Wong, "Dove Super Bowl Spot Scores Initial Points with Men," *Brandweek*, February 9, 2010, http://www.brandweek.com; Jack Neff and Rupal Parekh, "Dove Takes Its New Men's Line to the Super Bowl," *Advertising Age*, January 5, 2010, http://adage.com.

37. Justin Scheck, "Windows 7 Fails to Boost Profits of PC Makers," *WSJ.com*, January 31, 2010, http://online.wsj.com.

38. Sean Poulter, "The High Price of Fashion: Sales of Luxury It Bags Soar by 60%," *Mail Online*, March 12, 2010, http://www.dailymail.co.uk.

39. "For California Vintners, It's Not Easy Being Green," *Science Daily*, March 5, 2010, http://www.sciencedaily.com.

Chapter 14

1. Stock-Trak, "Academic Solutions," http://www.stocktrak.com/public/products/Stock-Trak.aspx, accessed May 23, 2012; Stock-Trak, "Stock-Trak Group Partners with Scottrade to Provide Stock and Option Simulation Training Tools," press release, October 29, 2008, http://www.stocktrak.com/pdf/Scottrade_102908.pdf, accessed May 23, 2012.

2. Fred Cummins, "The Changing Focus of the CIO in 2010," hp Community Home, February 3, 2010, http://www.communities.hp.com; Galen Gruman, "2010 CIO Priorities Shift to Lightweight Services, Virtualization," *InfoWorld*, January 19, 2010, http://www.infoworld.com; SearchCIO.com staff, "IT Salary Survey: How CIO, IT Salaries Vary by Industry," *SearchCIO.com*, January 7, 2010, http://searchcio.techtarget.com.

3. Rhea Wessel, "Airbus Signs Contract for High-Memory RFID Tags," *RFID Journal*, January 19, 2010, http://www.rfidjournal.com.

4. Corporate website for TradeInsight, http://www.tradeinsight.com/, accessed February 8, 2012.

5. IEEE Computer Society, "History of Computing Timeline," http://www.computer.org; Computer History Museum website, http://www.computerhistory.org, accessed May 24, 2010; Roy Schestowitz, "Computer History Development Timeline: Microsoft Perspective," *Techrights,* February 4, 2010, http://techrights.org.

6. Gary C, "STATS: Android Popularity UP among Future Smart Phone Buyers, Market Share Nearly DOUBLED," *EuroDroid,* March 31, 2010, http://www.eurodroid.com; "Gartner Says Consumers Will Spend $6.2 Billion in Mobile Application Stores in 2010," press release, January 18, 2010, http://www.gartner.com; Lance Whitney, "Smartphones Continue to Surge," *CNET News,* January 5, 2010, http://news.cnet.com.

7. " 'Come Together'—Intranets Are Re-emerging as a Way to Connect Dislocated Employees," *HR Monthly,* April 12, 2010, http://www.intranetdashboard.com.

8. Elliott Drucker, "Tech Insights—The Future of Voice," *Wireless Week,* March 7, 2010, http://www.wirelessweek.com; "Future of VoIP in 2010, a New Beginning?" Cheapest VoIP Calls.net, January 2010, http://cheapestvoipcalls.net.

9. Diane Bartz, "Apple Users Lose Some Immunity to Cybercrime," *Reuters,* April 20, 2010, http://ca.news.yahoo.com; IDG News Service, "E-Crime Reporting Format Draws Closer to a Standard," *Reuters,* March 23, 2010, http://www.reuters.com; Sue Marquette Poremba, "Report: Dangers of Cyber Crime on the Rise," *IT Business Edge,* January 27, 2010, http://www.itbusinessedge.com.

10. Elinor Mills, "Malware Delivered by Yahoo, Fox, Google Ads," *CNET News,* March 22, 2010, http://newsss.cnet.com; Joseph R. Perone, "Expect New, Evolving Computer Viruses in 2010," *Star-Ledger,* December 31, 2009, http://blog.nj.com.

11. Tony Bradley, "McAfee Debacle Shows Why Malware Defense Must Evolve," *TechWorld,* April 28, 2010, http://www.techworld.com.

12. Associated Press, "Mastermind of World's Worst Computer Virus Still at Large," *Fox News,* March 4, 2010, http://www.foxnews.com.

13. "New Security Threat Against 'Smart Phone' Users, Researchers Show," *Science Daily,* February 22, 2010, http://www.sciencedaily.com.

14. Erica Naone, "Experts Break Mobile Phone Security," *Technology Review,* December 29, 2009, http://www.technologyreview.com.

15. "Data Loss Statistics," Boston Computing Network, http://www.bostoncomputing.net, accessed May 24, 2010.

16. "Bureau of Labor Statistics, "Work-at-Home Patterns by Occupation," *Issues in Labor Statistics,* March 2009, http://www.bls.gov.

17. "Infosys Technologies to Manage Microsoft's Internal IT Service," press release, April 13, 2010, http://www.infosys.com.

Part 5: Launching Your Information Technology Career

1. U.S. Department of Labor, "Tomorrow's Jobs," *Occupational Outlook Handbook, 2010–2011,* Bureau of Labor Statistics, accessed June 28, 2010, http://www.bls.gov.

Chapter 15

1. "SEC Charges 4 More Former Nortel Execs with Fraud," CBC website, September 12, 2007, http://www.cbc.ca/news/business/story/2007/09/12/sec-nortel.html, accessed June 2, 2011; "Toronto's Longest-Running Musical Returns," Broadway World website, http://toronto.broadwayworld.com/article/TORONTOS_LONGESTRUNNING_MUSICAL_RETURNS_20061017, accessed, June 2, 2011; "Livent Co-founders Drabinsky, Gottlieb Convicted of Fraud and Forgery," CBC website, March 25, 2009, http://www.cbc.ca/news/business/story/2009/03/25/livent-decision-fraud.html, accessed June 2, 2011; Dave Itzkoff, "Convicted Producers Suggest Lecture Tour Instead of Prison," Arts Beat website, July 8, 2009, http://artsbeat.blogs.nytimes.com/2009/07/08/convicted-producers-suggest-lecture-tour-instead-of-prison/, accessed June 2, 2011; Allison Jones, "Drabinsky, Gottlieb, Found Guilty of Livent Fraud, Take Case to Appeal Court," *Canadian Press*, April 30, 2011, CityNews website, http://www.citytv.com/toronto/citynews/entertainment/news/article/128137--drabinsky-gottlieb-found-guilty-of-livent-fraud-take-case-to-appeal-court, accessed June 2, 2011; Anders Ross, "22 Largest Bankruptcies in World History," Instant Shift website, February 3, 2010, http://www.instantshift.com/2010/02/03/22-largest-bankruptcies-in-world-history/, accessed June 2, 2011; Ronald Fink, "Beyond Enron: The Fate of Andrew Fastow and Company Casts a Harsh Light on Off-Balance-Sheet Financing," *CFO Magazine*, February 1, 2002, http://www.cfo.com/article.cfm/3003186/c_3036065; "How to Hide $3.8 Billion in Expenses," Bloomberg Businessweek website, http://www.businessweek.com/magazine/content/02_27/b3790022.htm, accessed June 2, 2011.

2. Statistics Canada, 2006 Census data, http://www12.statcan.gc.ca/census-recensement/2006/dp-pd/tbt/Rp-eng.cfm?LANG=E&APATH=3&DETAIL=0&DIM=0&FL=A&FREE=0&GC=0&GID=0&GK=0&GRP=1&PID=92105&PRID=0&PTYPE=88971,97154&S=0&SHOWALL=0&SUB=0&Temporal=2006&THEME=74-&VID=0&VNAMEE=&VNAMEF=, accessed May 11, 2011.

3. Canadian Institute of Chartered Accountants, *CA Profession Compensation Survey 2009–Summary Report*, http://cica.ems01.com/CA_Profession_Compensation_Survey_2009-En.pdf, accessed May 11, 2011; Institute of Chartered Accountants of Ontario, "How Many Worlds Do CAs Rule?" http://guidetorulingtheworld.ca/Truth/DollarsSense.aspx, accessed May 11, 2011

4. Imran Ahmed, "CEO Talk: Brian Hill, Chief Executive Officer, Aritzia," Business of Fashion website, August 25, 2009, http://www.businessoffashion.com/2009/08/ceo-talk-brian-hill-chief-executive-officer-aritzia.html#more-5968, accessed June 3, 2011.

5. "Top Accounting Firms 2008," Western Libraries website, http://www.lib.uwo.ca/programs/companyinformationcanada/30topaccounting.html#2008, accessed May 18, 2011.

6. "IFRS FAQs," IFRS.com website, http://www.ifrs.com/ifrs_faqs.html#q3, accessed May 27, 2011.

7. Johnson & Johnson financial statements, *MSN Investor,* http://moneycentral.msn.com, accessed June 1, 2010.

8. "Sage Accpacc ERP: Extending Enterprise Suite—Industry Examples," CA-Plus website, http://www.caplus.com/articles.aspx?aid=150, accessed May 27, 2011.

9. Quicken website, http://quicken.intuit.ca/personal-finance-software/index.jsp, accessed February 20, 2012.

10. *Research in Motion 2011 Annual Report*, http://www.rim.com/investors/documents/pdf/annual/2011rim_ar.pdf, accessed June 1, 2011.

11. Thomas Black, "Weak Dollar Is "Welcome Change' for McDonald's, PPG Profits," *Bloomberg.com*, October 29, 2009, http://www.bloomberg.com.

Chapter 16

1. CTV News website, "U.S.-style Meltdown Won't Happen Here: Harper," http://www.ctv.ca/CTVNews/TopStories/20080924/mortgage_meltdown_080924/, accessed May 25, 2012; Keith B. Richburg, "Worldwide Financial Crisis Largely Bypasses Canada," *Washington Post*, October 16, 2008, http://www.washingtonpost.com/wp-dyn/content/article/2008/10/15/AR2008101503321.html, accessed July 14, 2011; Anthony Haddad, "Ever-Growing Yields from Post-Crisis Winners," October 13, 2009, Street Authority website, http://www.streetauthority.com/a/ever-growing-yields-post-crisis-winners-909, accessed, July 14, 2011; Anup Shah, "Global Financial Crisis," December 11, 2010, Global Issues website, http://www.globalissues.org/article/768/global-financial-crisis, accessed July 14, 2011.

2. Andrew Ross Sorkin, ed., "S&P Cuts BP Ratings, Citing Liabilities and Politics," *New York Times*, June 17, 2010, http:dealbook.blogs.nytimes.com; "BP Suspends Dividend after Deepwater Horizon Spill," MarketWatch, June 16, 2010, http://www.marketwatch.com; Peter Nicholas, "BP Will Create Fund to Pay Claims," *Los Angeles Times*, June 16, 2010, http://articles.latimes.com; AP/1010WINS, "Scientists: BP Oil Spill Leaking Up to 2.52M Gallons a Day," 1010WINS.com, June 15, 2010, http://www.1010wins.com; Ben Baden, "The Case for (and against) BP Cutting Its Dividend," *U.S. News & World Report*, June 14, 2010, http://www.usnews.com; Jeff Plungis and Christopher Condon, "U.S. Lawmakers Say BP Should Suspend Dividends, Ads (Update 2)," *Bloomberg Businessweek*, June 9, 2010, http://www.businessweek.com; "Gulf of Mexico Oil Spill Worst in U.S. History," *MarketWatch*, May 27, 2010, http://www.marketwatch.com; Campbell Robertson, "Search Continues after Oil Rig Blast," *New York Times*, April 21, 2010, http://www.nytimes.com.

3. *Globe and Mail* website, http://www.theglobeandmail.com/globe-investor/markets/stocks/summary/?q=rim-T, accessed February 22, 2012.

4. Catarina Saraiva, William Selway, and Brendan A. McGrail, "California Markets Second-Biggest Taxable Bond Sale of 2010," *Bloomberg.com*, March 25, 2010, http://www.bloomberg.com; Katrina Nicholas, "Russian Nanotechnology Corporation Considers $1.7 Billion Bond Sale," *Nanowerk*, March 11, 2010, http://www.nanowerk.com.

5. "Strong Global IPO Market in Q1 Sets Tone for 2010," news release, Ernst & Young, April 8, 2010, http://www.ey.com; Eric Fox, "The Worst IPOs of 2009," *Investopedia*, December 16, 2009, http://stocks.investopedia.com.

6. "NYSE Euronext Announces First Quarter 2010 Financial Results," news release, May 4, 2010, http://www.nyse.com; "New York Stock Exchange," *Money-Zine*, http://www.money-zine.com, accessed June 21, 2010.

7. Savvis, "Financial Services: Toronto Stock Exchange Connectivity," http://www.savvis.com/en-US/Info_Center/Documents/FIN-US-TorontoStockExchangeConnectivity.pdf, accessed July 6, 2011.

8. Canadian Bankers Association, "Banks Operating in Canada," February 16, 2012 http://www.cba.ca/en/component/content/category/61-banks-operating-in-canada, accessed May 18, 2012.

9. Department of Finance Canada, "Canada's Banks," http://www.fin.gc.ca/toc/2002/bank_-eng.asp, accessed July 6, 2011.

10. Dave Cooper, "Credit Union Connect Launches across Alberta," *Edmonton Journal*, May 2, 2011, http://www.edmontonjournal.com/business/Credit+Unions+Connect+launches+across+Alberta/4710413/story.html?cid=megadrop_story, accessed July 6, 2011.

11. Federal Deposit Insurance Corporation, "Statistics on Depository Institutions Report," http://www2.fdic.gov, accessed June 21, 2010.

12. David Johnston, "Web Exclusive: Is the Canadian Consumer Overextended with Debt?" *Mortgage Brokers News*, http://www.mortgagebrokernews.ca/forum/web-exclusive-is-the-canadian-consumer-overextended-with-debt/75546, accessed July 27, 2011.

13. Interac, "Interac 2011 Statistics," http://www.interac.ca/media/stats.php, accessed July 7, 2011.

14. "Canada Leads World in Online Banking Use," *Marketing VOX*, http://www.canada-leads-world-in-online-banking-usage-039784, accessed July 7, 2011.

15. "America's Largest Credit Unions," *Credit Union Access*, http://creditunionaccess.com, accessed June 21, 2010; Donna Fuscaldo, "Can You Join a Credit Union?" Bankrate.com, April 21, 2010, http://www.bankratecom.

16. Credit Union Central website, http://www.cucentral.com/Q1Results14JUN11, accessed June 14, 2011.

17. Canadian Life and Health Insurance Association Inc., *Response to the Competition Policy Review Panel Consultation Review Panel: Sharpening Canada's Competitive Edge*, January 11, 1008, http://www.ic.gc.ca/eic/site/cprp-gepmc.nsf/vwapj/Canadian_Life_Health.pdf/$FILE/Canadian_Life_Health.pdf, accessed May 18, 2012.

18. CPP Investment Board, "CPP Fund Totals $148.2 Billion at 2011 Fiscal Year-End," press release, May 19, 2011, http://cppib.ca/News_Room/News_Releases/nr_05191101.html, accessed July 28, 2011.

19. The Investment Funds Institute of Canada, "History of Mutual Funds," https://www.ific.ca/Content/Content.aspx?id=4580, accessed, July 7, 2011; Jonathan Chevreau, "One in Four Don't Contribute to RRSPs at All; 28 Percent will Contribute Less ING Finds," Wealthy Boomer blog, January 20, 2010, http://network.nationalpost.com/np/blogs/wealthyboomer/archive/2010/01/20/one-in-four-don-t-contribute-to-rrsps-at-all-28-will-contribute-less-ing-finds.aspx, accessed July 7, 2011.

20. Investment Company Institute, "Trends in Mutual Fund Investing, March 2010."

21. Bank of Canada, "Regulation of the Canadian Financial System," http://www.bankofcanada.ca/wp-content/uploads/2010/11/regulation_canadian_financial.pdf, accessed May 18, 2012.

22. Investment Industry Regulator Organization of Canada's website, http://www.iiroc.ca/English/Pages/home.aspx, accessed July 28, 2011.

23. Banker's Almanac, "Top Banks in the World," http://www.bankersalmanac.com/addcon/infobank/bank-rankings.aspx, accessed July 14, 2011.

24. Emily Mathieu, "No-interest MasterCard Aims at Devout Muslims," *Toronto Star*, April 12, 2010, http://www.thestar.com/business/article/794124--operating-financies-in-good-faith?bn=1, accessed July 12, 2011.

Chapter 17

1. Company website, Ratiopharm GmbH, http://www1.ratiopharm.com, accessed June 24, 2010; Company website, Pfizer Inc., http://www.pfizer.com, accessed June 24, 2010; Company website, Teva Pharmaceutical Industries Ltd., http://www.tevapharm.com, accessed June 24, 2010; Company website, Actavis, http://www.actavis.com, accessed June 24, 2010; Yoram Gabison, "Teva Snubs Israelis: Ratiopharm Purchase Being Financed Abroad," *Haaretz*, May 14, 2010, http://www.haaretz.com; Robert Daniel and Polya Lesova, "Teva to Acquire Ratiopharm in Deal Valued Near $5 Billion," *MarketWatch*, March 18, 2010, http://www.marketwatch.com; Frank Siebelt, Ludwig Burger, and Lewis Krauskopf, "Pfizer to Make Bid for Ratiopharm: Source," *Reuters*, March 16, 2010, http://www.reuters.com; Andrew Ross Sorkin, ed., "Bidding War Pits Pfizer against Teva," *New York Times DealBook*, March 9, 2010, http://dealbook.blogs.nytimes.com; Frank Siebelt, "Pfizer Woos Ratiopharm with Ramp-Up Pledge—Sources," *Reuters*, March 7, 2010, http://www.reuters.com; Aaron Kirchfeld, "Pfizer Chief Said to Make Case for Ratiopharm Deal (Update 2)," *Bloomberg.com*, March 5, 2010, http://www.bloomberg.com; Cyrus Sanati, "Pfizer Said to Set Sights on German Drug Maker," *New York Times DealBook*, March 2, 2010, http://dealbook.blogs.nytimes.com; Ludwig Burger, "Pfizer, Teva Set to Tussle for Ratiopharm: Report," *Reuters*, January 18, 2010, http://www.reuters.com., Apotex Inc., "About Apotex," http://www.apotex.com/global/about/default.asp, accessed August 1, 2011.

2. "2010 CEO Pay Analysis & Strategies for Mid-Caps," *Equilar*, May 2010, http://www.equilar.com.

3. Josh Funk, "Warren Buffet Still Gets $100K Salary at Berkshire Hathaway, But Security Costs Grow to $345K," *Business News*, March 10, 2010, http://blog.taragana.com.

4. Aude Lagorce, "Emirates in Record Airbus A380 Order," *MarketWatch*, June 8, 2010, http://www.marketwatch.com; Andrea Rothman, "Airbus A380 Order Dearth Risks Double-Decker-Dud Fate (Update 1)," *Bloomberg Businessweek*, May 13, 2010, http://www.businessweek.com; David Kaminski-Morrow, "A380 to Remain a Financial Burden for Years: Airbus Chief," *Flightglobal*, January 12, 2010, http://www.flightglobal.com.

5. Sarah Johnson, "CFO: Stop Treating Your Inventories Like Fine Wine," *CFO.com*, September 10, 2009, http://cfo.com.

6. Lauren Coleman-Lochner, "Target Sets Canada for First Expansion Outside U.S.," *Business Week*, January 13, 2011, http://www.businessweek.com/news/2011-01-13/target-sets-canada-for-first-expansion-outside-u-s-.html, accessed August 8, 2011.

7. Stefania Moretti, "Walmart Canada to Open 40 Supercenters," *CNews*, http://cnews.canoe.ca/CNEWS/Canada/2011/01/26/17039171.html, accessed August, 2, 2011.

8. Lochner, "Target Sets Canada for First Expansion Outside U.S."

9. Research In Motion, "Research In Motion Reports First Quarter Fiscal 2012 Results and Revises Full Year Guidance, press release, June 16, 2011, http://www.rim.com/investors/documents/pdf/financial/2012/Q1_FY2012_Financial_Information.pdf, accessed August 2, 2011.

10. X-Rates, "2007—Canadian dollars to GBP," http://www.x-rates.com/d/CAD/GBP/hist2007.html, accessed August 2, 2011.

11. Federal Reserve Board, "Commercial Paper," Federal Reserve Release, May 13, 2010, http://federalreserve.gov.

12. "BP Suspends Dividend after Deepwater Horizon Spill," *MarketWatch*, June 16, 2010, http://www.marketwatch.com; "The Case for (and against) BP Cutting Its Dividend," *U.S. News & World Report*, June 14, 2010, http://www.usnews.com; Jeff Plungis and Christopher Condon, "U.S. Lawmakers Say BP Should Suspend Dividends, Ads (Update 2)," *Bloomberg Businessweek*, June 9, 2010, http://www.businessweek.com; Whitney Kisling, "Dividend Slump Ending as Record Profits Lift Payouts for S&P 500," *China Post*, April 29, 2010, http://www.chinapost.com.tw.

13. Canadian Tire, *2010 Annual Report*, http://corp.canadiantire.ca/EN/Investors/FinancialReports/Annual%20Reports%20Library/CTC_AR_2010.pdf, accessed August 2, 2011.

14. Federal Reserve Board, "Commercial Paper Outstanding," Federal Reserve Release, May 12, 2010, http://federalreserve.gov.

15. Frederick Tomesco, "Corporate Bond Prices May Rise from 3-Year High: Canada Credit, *Bloomberg Businessweek*, http://www.bloomberg.com/apps/news?pid=newsarchive&sid=aZ_zmI6BqxmE, accessed August 2, 2011.

16. Board of Governors of the Federal Reserve System, "Federal Reserve Statistical Release, Z.1, Flow of Funds Accounts of the United States," March 12, 2009, http://www.federalreserve.gov.

17. Covington website, http://www.covingtonfunds.com, accessed August 3, 2011.

18. CBC News, "Onex Buys Boeing Parts Plant for $1.5 Billion," February 22, 2005, http://www.cbc.ca/news/business/story/2005/02/22/onex-050222.html, accessed August 2, 2011.

19. Andy Hoffman and Tara Perkins, "China's Sovereign Wealth Fund Sets up Shop in Toronto," *Globe and Mail*, January 17, 2011, http://www.theglobeandmail.com/report-on-business/chinas-sovereign-wealth-fund-sets-up-shop-in-toronto/article1867917/, accessed August 3, 2011; Jeremy van Loon and Jim Polson, "Albert to Win Chinese Oil-Sands Investment, Minister Says." *Bloomberg*, May 17, 2011, http://www.bloomberg.com/news/2011-05-17/alberta-to-win-chinese-oil-sands-investment-minister-says-1-.html, accessed August 3, 2011.

20. Richard C. Wilson, "Hedge Funds Canada," *Hedge Funds Blogger website*, http://richard-wilson.blogspot.com/2008/06/

hedge-funds-in-canada-canadian-hedge.html, accessed August 3, 2011; Andrew Ross Sorkin, ed., "Hedge Fund Strategies, at Smaller Prices," *New York Times.com*, January 11, 2010, http://dealbook.blogs.nytimes.com.

21. Margie Lindsay, "Global Hedge Fund AUM Hits $1.8 Trillion," *Hedge Funds Review*, March 8, 2010, http://www.hedgefundsreview.com.

22. Jon Swartz, "HP to Acquire Palm for about $1.2B," *USA Today*, April 29, 2010, http://www.usatoday.com; "HP to Acquire Palm for $1.2 Billion," press release, April 28, 2010, http://www.hp.com.

23. Emre Peker, "Cerberus Taps Banks for LBO as Leveraged Loan Rally Spurs M&As," *Bloomberg Businessweek*, May 14, 2010, http://www.businessweek.com; David Russell, "LBOs Loom as Credit Market Recovers," *Nasdaq*, March 19, 2010, http://www.nasdaq.com.

24. Oilweek website, http://www.oilweek.com/news.asp?ID=34515, accessed August 5, 2011; "Canadian Company Sells Natural Gas Assets in T&T," Caribbean 360 website, March 4, 2010, http://www.caribbean360.com/business/canadian_company_sells_natural_gas_assets_in_t_t.rss#axzz1Tzqz6XRf, accessed August 5, 2011.

Part 6: Launching Your Finance Career

1. Human Resources and Skills Development Canada, "Looking Ahead: A 10-Year Outlook for the Canadian Labour Market (2006–2015), http://www.hrsdc.gc.ca/eng/publications_resources/research/categories/labour_market_e/sp_615_10_06/supply.shtml, accessed May 20, 1012.

2. Prince Edward Island Campus Starter, "Top 10 Canadian University Degrees Majors," http://princeedwardisland.campusstarter.com/Top10CanadianUniversityDegreesMajors.cfm, accessed August 5, 2011.

3. U.S. Department of Labor, "Financial Managers," *Occupational Outlook Handbook, 2010–2011*, Bureau of Labor Statistics, http://www.bls.gov, accessed July 8, 2010.

Appendix C

1. Arik Hesseldahl, "Apple's Smartphone Battle Plan," *Bloomberg Businessweek*, April 26, 2010, http://wwwbusinssweek.com; Philip Elmer-DeWitt, "Apple Talks Tough to Handset Makers," *Fortune Technology*, March 9, 2010, http://tech.fortune.com; "Will Apple's Patents Banish HTC Phones?" *MIS Asia*, March 4, 2010, http://wwwmis-asia.com; Marguerite Reardon, "Apple Sues HTC Over iPhone Patents," *CNET News*, March 2, 2010, http://news.cnet.com; Brad Stone, "Apple Sues Nexus one Maker HTC," *New York Times*, March 2, 2010, http://www.nytimes.com; Ted Livingston, "A Sad Day in Waterloo," blog entry posted December 1, 2010, Kik Interactive Blog, www.kik.com/blog/2010/12/a-sad-day-in-waterloo, accessed March 30, 2011.

2. "Frivolous Lawsuits," *NFIB*, http://www.nfib.com, accessed May 7, 2010.

3. Peter J. Brown, "US Lawsuit May Flood China Drywalls," *Asia Times*, April 10, 2010, http://www.atimes.com.

4. Mark Sweney, "Google Wins Louis Vuitton Trademark Case," *Guardian*, March 23, 2010, http://www.guardian.co.uk.

5. B. Smith, "Google Digital Library Faces Major Public Outcry at NYC Hearing," *New York Daily News*, February 18, 2010, http://www.nydailynews.com.

Appendix D

1. Michael Cass, "Nashville Property Damage Now At $1.9 Billion," *Tennessean*, May 16, 2010, http://www.tennessean.com; Tom Weir, "In Nashville, a Way of Life Washed Away," *USA Today*, Mary 9, 2010, http://www.usatoday.com; Melinda Hudgins, "Few Take Advantage of Flood Insurance, *DNJ.com*, May 9, 2010, http://www.dnj.com; "Stories of Tragedy, Survival Surface as Tennessee Flood Waters Recede," *CNN.com*, May 9, 2010, http://www.cnn.com; Emily Holbrook, "Few in Tennessee Covered by Flood Insurance," *Risk Management Monitor*, May 6, 2010, http://www.riskmanagementmonitor.com; Geert de Lombaerde, "Less Than 4,000 Davidson Homes Insured Against Floods," *City Paper*, May 4, 2010, http://nashvillecitypaper.com.

2. *ACLI Lilfe Insurance Fact Book 2009*, http://www.acli.com, accessed May 9, 2010.

3. "Lightning Sparks Concern for Insurance Industry; Homeowners Claims Rise Sharply Over Last Five Years," Insurance Information Institute, March 31, 2010, http://www.iii.org.

4. Walmart, "Insurance Requirements," http://walmartstores.com, accessed May 9, 2010.

Appendix E

1. Patrick Lohmann, "Campus Debtors," *Alibi*, May 6–12, 2010, http://alibi.com; David Ellis, "Credit Card Relief Is Here, But Watch Out for New Traps," *CNN Money.com*, February 22, 2010, http://money.cnn.com; Jennifer Liberto, "Under 21? Getting a Credit Card Just got Tougher," *CNN Money.com*, February 22, 2010, http://money.cnn.com; George Gombossy, "New Credit Card Rules Go into Effect Monday," *Connecticut Watchdog*, February 20, 2010, http://ctwatchdog.com; David K. Randall, "New Credit Card Choices for Students," *Forbes.com*, February 4, 2010, http://www.forbes .com.

2. "Employee Tenure, 2008, and Retiree Health Benefit Trends among the Medicare-Eligible Population," *Employee Benefit Research Institute*, 31, no. 1 January 2010, http://www.ebri.org.

Appendix F

1. Next website, http://nextrestaurant.com, accessed May 9, 2010; Pete Wells, "In Chicago, the Chef Grant Achatz Is Selling Tickets to His New Restaurant," *New York Times*, May 5, 2010, http://www.nytimes.com; "US' Next Hot Restaurant Will Require Prepaid Tickets," *AOL News*, May 5, 2010, http://www.aolnews.com; Chuck Sudo, "Achatz's Next Two Projects: Time Travel, Cocktails," *Chicagoist*, May 4, 2010, http://chicagoist.com; Paul Frumkin, "Grant Achatz to Open New Restaurant and Bar," *Nation's Restaurant News Today*, May 4, 2010, http://www.nrn.com.

Appendix G

1. "Average Earnings of Year-Round, Full-Time Workers by Educational Attainment," *Current Population Reports,* U.S. Census Bureau, http://www.census.gov, accessed May 10, 2010.

2. Henry Devries, "How to Get a Job in Embedded Engineering," *San Diego News Network,* April 27, 2010, http://www.sdnn.com.

3. "College Grad Job Search Strategies," *JobDoc,* March 15, 2010, http://www.boston.com.

4. Lindsey Gerdes, "Best Places to Intern," *Bloomberg Businessweek,* December 10, 2009, http://www.businessweek.com.

5. "The Cooperative Education Model, National Commission for Cooperative Education, http://www.co-op.edu, accessed May 10, 2010.

6. "More Free Assessment Tests," *Career Explorer,* http://www.careerexplorer.net, accessed May 10, 2010; "Assessment Exercises," *Monster Careers,* http://www.monstercareeres.com, accessed May 10, 2010.

7. "Paula's Story," *Paula Deen.com,* http://www.pauladeen.com, accessed May 10, 2010.

8. Kim Isaacs, "Five Resume Tips for College Students," *Monster.com,* accessed May 10, 2010; "Top 10 Professional Resume Writing Tips for 2010," *An Elite Resume,* http://aneliteresume.com, accessed May 10, 2010; "Five Tips for Better Resume Writing," *Resume Writing for Dummies,* http://www.dummies.com, accessed May 10, 2010.

9. Kat Neville, "What Makes a Great Cover Letter, According to Companies?" *Smashing Magazine,* March 25, 2010, http://www.smashingmagazine.com.

10. "Tips for Submitting Your Online Resume," *An Elite Resume,* http://aneliteresume.com, accessed May 10, 2010.

11. Carole Martin, "Ten Tips to Boost Your Interview Skills," *Monster.com,* http://career-advice.monster.com, accessed May 10, 2010.

12. Jerome Young, "How to Answer the Hard Interview Questions," *Forbes.com,* April 9, 2010, http://www.forbes.com.

NAME INDEX

SUBJECT INDEX

Contents

Introduction

1 *The* Ginkgo biloba *or Maidenhair Tree is so called because of the resemblance of its sometimes deeply divided leaves to those of the maidenhair fern. Goethe's poem on the tree comments on the division and asks 'Do you not see from my songs that I too am one yet double?', reflecting the well-known lines from Faust: 'Two souls dwell, alas, within my breast, the one attempting to separate from the other.' The picture shows a unique pair of Ginkgos, male and female, raised in the Botanic Garden and planted against the wall of the Department of Botany in the Downing Site as a symbol of the happy co-operation between professor and Garden in the provision of living plant material. The pair now cover a large area of the building.*

If you take a walk along the Cam from Sheep's Green to the Pike and Eel – from one end of town to the other – you are in gardens and parks nearly all the way, and cross only three roads. The whole centre of the city is surrounded by wide open spaces: Jesus Green, Midsummer Common, Parker's Piece, the Botanic Garden, Coe Fen. To the east the large grounds of Jesus, Sidney Sussex, Emmanuel and Downing Colleges, to the west those of Newnham, Selwyn, Robinson and Wolfson Colleges and the gardens of private houses add to the profusion of lawns, shrubberies, avenues of trees, and herbaceous borders. As a garden city Cambridge has no rival.

To describe all this in full detail would take a large volume and is not what this book sets out to do. The reader will find here a concise guide to the pleasures of almost all the college gardens, of the University Botanic Garden, and of most of the gardens cared for by the City of Cambridge Parks Department. Sometimes there has been more to say about the layout or individual species, sometimes more about the history or the literary associations of a garden, the aim being to characterise the whole rather than provide a comprehensive list. In several colleges, as also in the Botanic Garden, a suggested tour dictates the arrangement; occasionally a summary of seasonal highlights is most appropriate. All really remarkable trees have been included, but shrubs and climbers are so abundant that only selective mention has been possible.

Not all gardens are individually described – most of the newer ones have yet to mature, and some of the older colleges, enclosed by other buildings in the city centre, have scarcely room for more than a few borders and window boxes. St Catharine's provides a display along its short street-front, and enhances the summer season with colourful hanging baskets. It is developing gardens around its hostel, St Chad's, in Grange Road. Fitzwilliam is also still in its early days, but will have a good deal worth seeing by the 1990s. The small garden of Ridley Hall is a pleasant retreat, as is the unexpectedly rustic one at Westcott House, where there is also a massive wisteria, nourished by pigeon manure collected from the belfry of neighbouring All Saints Church.

Private gardens are not included in this survey, but many in the city and surrounding countryside are open annually under the National Gardens Scheme. Two participants in the scheme, the Bell School of Languages and Unwins Seeds Ltd, within two or three miles of the city centre, are specially worth visiting.

The Broughton collection of flower paintings at the Fitzwilliam Museum should not be missed, though only a little of it is shown at any one time.

About the History of Cambridge College Gardens

Walking between a double line of trees up the flank of Castle Hill and climbing the Mound, you would have looked out from the flat top on to parkland stretching as far as Sheep's Green, a mile and a half away – if the plan that Lancelot ('Capability') Brown submitted to the University in 1779 had ever been realised. In the foreground the River Cam would have broadened into a lake with two long islands; the barges going to the mills at Mill Lane were to slip through to one side in a serpentine channel, scarcely noticeable unless they hoisted sail. To the west you would have seen a leg-of-mutton sleeve of lawns and clumps of trees narrowing towards Queens'; beyond, carriages driving along an avenue with semi-circular *ronds-points*, roughly on the line of the present Queen's Road; further west, four broad expanses dividing the area between Madingley Road and Newnham, all edged with more double lines of trees. Pointing your Claude glass more to the east again, you would have seen the centrepiece of the composition, the Gibbs Building at King's, a nobleman's mansion overlooking the new landscape.

It would have been magnificent. Even the barges could have lent local colour to this lord's-eye view. But in a place where tenants could not be evicted, and at least half a dozen colleges were in contention for the squireship of the riverside, it was never in with a chance. It would have done very well for Chatsworth. At Cambridge, Brown, who had already done some work for St John's, had to be content with the reward of £50 for an inscribed silver dish. As they say, not altogether truly, no designer ever works for the same college or for the University twice.

The layout as far as Queen's Road, haphazardly achieved, was not so very different, even 64 years later, from the one proposed by Brown. Queen Victoria and Prince Albert, on their visit in 1843, saw no lake or islands, but just such a span of tree-lined lawns, uninterrupted as yet by the splendid gardens of Clare, as Brown had in mind. The beauty of the Backs today is for the most part the beauty of parks and bridges, rather than of intimate gardens, though within the frame there is great variety, and away from the Backs there is even more.

By and large the colleges have decided to be stately homes. A front court with arbours and seats along the walls, and borders of privet, rosemary, sweetbriar, and shady trees, is unthinkable now. Except at Gonville and Caius, which has an avenue of whitebeams inside its entrance (**25**), front courts are treeless smooth lawns, never meant for sitting on or around. Unlike some modern universities, the colleges have no open forums where students and teachers naturally congregate. A visitor's first impression is to be one of noble simplicity and classical calm.

When the first colleges and halls were founded in the 13th and 14th centuries

2 *Autumn leaves on Trinity College Backs, where students have recently revived the sport of archery. In medieval times most colleges had butts for archery practice.*

7

they would have had either 'flowering meads', meadows of long grass with larkspur and primulas growing in it, or a 'yarde' with camomile lawns, a turf seat, and a few flowers – if they could afford such luxuries at all. It mattered more to use the ground either for profit, by growing saffron for dyes, or for nourishment. The accounts of Peterhouse for 1374–5 show that seeds for parsley, cress, garlic, leeks, saffron and vegetables in general were bought. Vines were often planted at that time, for grapes and shade. Hops were grown in the 16th century, and at King's crab-apple orchards for cider-making were planted soon after the foundation in 1446.

In 1608, James I decreed that 'such as are of ability' should be persuaded and required to buy and distribute mulberry plants, 10,000 in each county, for the breeding of silkworms. Jesus, Christ's and Emmanuel bought 300 each, though one only of these remains, the famous 'Milton's mulberry' at Christ's. More exotic fruits were planted in the 17th century: apricots at Queens', quince trees in the Fellows' Orchard and asparagus at Jesus. Gardens became formal, with sundials and geometrical arrangements of privet hedges. More luxuries came with summerhouses of stone or wood, which sometimes had classical pediments. Dovecots provided for pigeon-pies both for undergraduates and as perks for Fellows. Several colleges kept swans, for the Fellows' table in particular. There are records of swan-uppings, and of 'an action entred agaynst Cole of Horn-ingsay for kyllyng a colledge Swanne'. Other birds kept by colleges include a raven bought by Peterhouse in 1635–6, and a pair of ravens bought by Queens' in 1673–4 and 1737–8; an eagle on a perch in Trinity Great Court in 1683–4 and again in 1744–5; and lapwings at Queens' in 1708–9 and 1736–7.

From very early times, many colleges had a tennis court and a bowling green. The earliest reference to a court for hand-tennis is at Corpus Christi about 1500.

3 The beehives in Christ's Fellows' Garden, providing jars of honey for the Fellows.

Butts for archery are often mentioned in the records, and the swimming pools at Emmanuel and Christ's are two of many 'cold baths' introduced in the 17th and 18th centuries. The numerous pools at St John's at that time were, however, meant for stocking fish.

There is no certainty that in post-medieval times large areas of college grounds were given over to raising crops, whether for use or profit. John Hamond's map of Cambridge of 1592 shows the area behind the present Fitzwilliam Museum as 'Peter Howse backeside of Walkes', and other colleges are shown with trees, sometimes planted in rows and surrounded by walls, without many signs of vegetable beds or any sign of fields used for crops. There were, after all, farms in the neighbourhood, many of them belonging to colleges, which could have supplied them with necessities.

There is no need now to think of college grounds in such practical terms. Nor is there any need for the war-time vegetable gardens that once contributed to hall meals. Yet behind those sacred lawns there are sometimes surprising provisions for personal tastes. Christ's has its row of beehives (3), from which, it is rumoured, Fellows receive an annual jar of honey. Trinity is said to have a spaliered apricot hidden from tourists' eyes. Magdalene has a Victorian pets' cemetery, with miniature tombstones (5). Emmanuel has a herb garden, stocked with marjoram, hyssop, rue and rosemary, tansy and thyme, Scotch lovage tasting like celery and parsley, winter savory (good with trout), and tall elecampane with its spread of sunflower-like heads, not specially good with anything, though still used in cough mixtures, it is said. True, there are

4 The chronological bed in the Botanic Garden shows in chronological order at what period flowers and plants, beginning with woad, were introduced into England. Argemone platyceras, *introduced 1811–30, was formerly supposed to cure cataracts on the eye, the white colour of the flower being associated with the whiteness of the cataract.* Platyceras *refers to its broad prickles.*

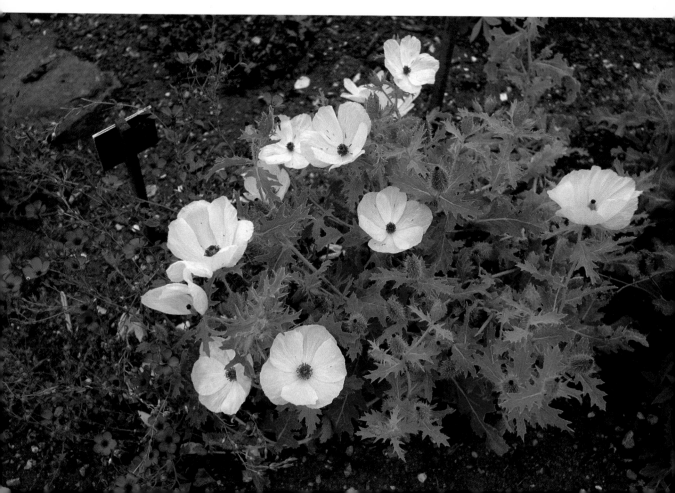

surprisingly few fruit trees, though Peterhouse has a good avenue of apple trees. Only Homerton and Girton go in for orchards, and at Girton you find not only five genuine original Blenheim Oranges, reputed to have come from Woodstock, but a unique collection of 83 cultivars; not that such plenty is always usable. According to one report, a catering manager hesitated to serve home-grown apples at high table because they varied in size, and another declined a gardener's offer of Arthur Turners because, not being spherical, they would not fit peeling machines. Grapes would not give such trouble, yet there are no fruit-bearing vines except, again, at Girton, where pink strawberry grapes are abundant; nor are there any asparagus beds in sight. Where cannabis may have flourished secretly, in its heyday, is another matter.

The front courts do not suggest, either, what special collections are to be found within. In its small densely crowded rock garden Pembroke's collection of conifers mixes bright blue spruce with white broom and the giant rhubarb leaves of *Gunnera manicata* (**6**). St John's gardeners claim world fame for the beds of martagon lilies which fill the Wilderness in June and July with seraglio turbans dangling jewels – though these are perhaps threatened by the loss of the elms that used to protect them. Earlier in the year St John's commemorates Wordsworth well and truly with a display of daffodils rivalling even the one by King's bridge (**7, 43**). Corpus, in the private gardens of Leckhampton, crowns its own spring flowers with an acre or two of lupins in tall grass, following up with the thousands of blooms in the formal rose-garden: 'English Miss', and incongruously 'Whisky Mac', with a touch of gold that would help the best of malts go down.

Christ's commemorates its chief poet more avowedly than St John's, with a garden of flowers and shrubs mentioned in Milton's 'Lycidas'. It is, sadly, not in the best of conditions, having little sunlight. But if the excellent plan is ever realised in another part of the garden it should keep the choice of the Flanders poppy rather than the hyacinth for 'that sanguine flower inscribed with woe'. This memorial to the dead of the First World War is moving and, whatever footnotes say, one prefers not to think Milton meant the hyacinth merely because its leaves seem to have the cry 'AI' printed on them. That is an explanation worthy of 17th-century emblematics, and Milton favoured natural-ness in gardens:

> the crisped brooks . . .
> Ran nectar, visiting each plant, and fed
> Flowers worthy of Paradise which not nice art
> In beds and curious knots, but nature boon
> Poured forth profuse on hill and dale and plain . . .

He surely cannot have taken to the knot-gardens many colleges had in 1688 (as shown in David Loggan's series of engravings of that date), if they existed in his day. Nor, for that matter, can Marvell, at Trinity in the 1630s. His paradise is closer to the Bermudas. Even at Appleton House, where tulips, pinks and roses appear to have been planted in separate beds, each in the shape of five-bastioned forts, Marvell preferred nature that would cling round him, ensnare and fold him in like a lover.

He might have found something like that in Victorian times, as Saint-Saëns did, coming here at the beginning of this century to discover 'a nest of ogival effects embosomed in verdure'. But the shaggy ivy that once created such Romantically russet and seemingly ruined walls has been stripped away in the

5 *The pets' cemetery in Magdalene Fellows' Garden, like the one in Hyde Park, London, contains tombs of cats and dogs. In the last century members of colleges were sometimes allowed to keep pets in their rooms (Byron, prohibited by Trinity's regulations from keeping a dog, brought in a bear 'to sit for a Fellowship').*

interests of the stonework and of the classical 'noble simplicity' idea. On the other hand, the little clumps of wall-rue (*Asplenium ruta-muraria*) are treasured and celebrated for their impudence in growing by the side of the Senate House steps, as they have done without let or hindrance since the plant was recorded there by Babington in 1860.

Apart from allowing walls to be covered with creepers, Cambridge did little to follow 19th-century gardening fashions. St John's had not given Capability Brown much free play in the 1790s, though he may have established the 'natural' Wilderness. In the 1840s Christ's seems to have adopted the 'gardenesque' style of Loudon, with winding paths that still remain. Trinity in the 1870s employed a garden designer who had worked on royal estates. Most other colleges kept the broad lawns and tree-lined avenues as they had developed in the previous century. Only in the present century have garden designers really come into their own. Nevill Willmer at Clare and St John's in the late 1940s adopted some of his ideas from Miss Jekyll; Thomas Sharp at St John's, assisted by Sylvia Crowe, planned on a really large scale to keep the character of the Backs alive. Emmanuel employed John Codrington in the 1960s to design a herb garden and turn the Paddock into a livelier place. Sheila Haywood designed for Churchill; J. St Bodfan Gruffyd began the landscaping of Robinson. Nearly every other college has allowed its garden to grow without any overall plan. Colleges seldom like overall plans, which conflict with their decentralised federalism, and that shows in their gardens. Sometimes, as at Darwin, a former domestic garden

6   *The giant leaves of* Gunnera manicata *by the rockery planted by the late Dean of Pembroke are small in comparison with those plants, sometimes 30 ft across, that grow in the deep valleys of rich alluvial earth and decayed leaved of southern Brazil.* Gunnera *is named after a Scandinavian botanist.* Manicata *means 'sleeved', in reference to the stems.*

suddenly flourishes in perfect unity with its neighbours, and sometimes, as at New Hall, a multiplicity of old gardens joins in a rustic mosaic. The resulting variety from college to college makes for a garden scene in Cambridge with more places of individual character than planned gardens tend to have. The fact that a Fellow has special interests in Bosnia or New Zealand, or that a Prime Minister has decided to present a particular tree, is likely to produce the unexpected round any corner.

Thanks to this distaste for uniformity the gardens sometimes merge into the landscape. The country comes close in to the centre even now. Friesians and tired-looking horses graze outside Jesus in the summer, followed in autumn by flocks of redwings on Midsummer Common, and in bad winters by cormorants that come upstream as far as Jesus Lock. Sheep crop the grass opposite what would have been the centre of Capability Brown's estate, where it is often so wet that fungi abound, unfortunately not really edible: olive-brown caps of *Boletus subtomentosus* and Ink Cap (*Coprinus atramentarius*) alongside the golden brown *Coprinus micaceus*. A heron fishes the ditch along Garret Hostel Lane, while undergraduates on bikes fly past to nine-o'clock lectures. A gardener remembers a shrew in that neighbourhood, which at any rate lived up to its name: 'Stand up and offer to fight you, they will.' Kingfishers flash electric blue, though that is about all, and tree-creepers hop up any remaining elms on the Backs. It is only a short walk from there by way of Sheep's Green to the massed comfrey, butterbur and codlins-and-cream of Paradise. (There is a notice, these days, as you go in, announcing the Owlstone Croft Nature Reserve, but the old name still sticks.) And if you are tempted further, there are strawberries and cream in the orchard at Grantchester, not many minutes' walk in the same direction.

College Gardens

Christ's College

For flowers and shrubs, First Court is the most attractive college court in Cambridge, all the year round (**8**). Beds of begonias and window boxes of very diverse fuchsias, a grand wisteria, a *Hydrangea petiolaris*, a *Garrya elliptica*, winter jasmine, and a brilliant red firethorn provide colour and interest in every season. The hybrid *Prunus × blireana* makes a splendid show in March, there is a fine *Magnolia grandiflora* by the chapel, and the winter sweet *Chimonanthus praecox* grows against the hall.

Second Court is made glorious in autumn by a Virginia creeper that is allowed to cover the whole façade of the 19th-century building from top to bottom before being periodically cut back. On the other side of the court is a *Callicarpa bodinieri* 'Giraldii', with bright purple flowers in November, and two *Robinia pseudoacacia*. Along the medieval wall (to the left behind the Fellows' Building) are three members of the Hydrangea family, seldom planted all together: *Schizophragma hydrangeoides*, *Hydrangea petiolaris* and *Pileostegia viburnoides*.

Third Court is planted with irises flowering in May and June, surrounding the whole central lawn with an unrivalled show (**9**). The largest tree in the court is *Sophora japonica*, the Japanese Pagoda Tree, planted in 1955. Recently it has begun to flower, in August. Against the walls are *Prunus triloba*, introduced from China in 1855, and *Punica granatum* 'Flore Pleno', the double pomegranate.

Christ's are generous in opening the Fellows' Garden (**10**) to the public morning and afternoon throughout the year. The design, with winding paths affording constantly fresh glimpses, is in the style of John Claudius Loudon, the advocate of the 'gardenesque' (meaning 'as a gardener would like', just as the 'picturesque' had been taken earlier to mean 'worthy of painting', or 'as a painter would like'). Loudon's intention was 'to display the individual beauty of trees, shrubs and plants in a state of nature', by means of island beds and promontary beds. He may well have been responsible for the layout at Christ's; he designed the cemetery grounds in Histon Road in 1842. The vista from the middle of the garden towards the spire of Bodley's All Saints Church in Jesus Lane is particularly good.

The garden is most colourful in summer, with reddish-brown *Canna indica* alternating with begonias in the bed on the left, in front of the white beehives. Further on, to the right, is a pool first referred to in 1748 by Thomas Salmon, now the setting for busts of Milton and the Platonist philosopher Ralph Cudworth and for a memorial to the novelist C. P. Snow. The water comes via Emmanuel from Hobson's Conduit, the 17th-century channel dug to bring drinking water to the town. Overshadowed by trees, the pool has a summer-house of brick with a stuccoed portico at one end, and makes a romantic spot. To

8 Christ's First Court is never without flowers. Here it is colourfully dressed in August.

the west is the famous 'Milton's mulberry tree', now in venerable condition. It is extremely unlikely that Milton planted it, or that in 1628, while in residence, he stole some of the recently planted mulberry trees to give to his boyhood tutor at Stowmarket. For a time it was even uncertain whether the mulberry existed in his day. According to the *Cambridge Chronicle* for 14 November 1795, the original tree traditionally associated with Milton was blown down in a hurricane on 6 November that year. But there is a reference to the 'repair' of the mulberry in 1810, and Tennyson saw it, 'old and hollow, somewhat crookèd in the shoulders', as he described it in a poem written while he was at Cambridge (1827–31). Protective lead sheeting inside the trunk was already in position in 1820, and since 1856 the tree has been supported by a mound. There can really be no doubt that it is one of the 300 bought in 1608 to comply with the order of James I (the college accounts record 'Item for 300 mulberrye plants, xviii.s.'), and it may thus claim to be the oldest tree in Cambridge. It produces on average 50 pounds of fruit a year. Recently a sculpture by the distinguished old member of Christ's Anthony Caro has been set up nearby.

Among other trees in the Fellows' Garden are an extremely tall London Plane, a grand chestnut planted with winter aconites to the full circumference of its branches, and (near the rear of the Fellows' Building) the unusual *Sorbus aria* 'Lutescens', with its cups of five leaves at the ends of the stems. A Caucasian Wing-Nut planted in memory of Reginald Harry Noble can be found in the garden in front of the new building behind the Fellows' Garden. The rarer hybrid Rehder Wing-Nut *Pterocarya* × *rehderana* which overhangs Hobson Street by the Master's Lodge entrance was planted in 1963 and is now very handsome, bearing long catkins throughout summer and autumn.

Churchill College

The impression of a vast open space – 42 acres – is not quite true: residential courts are turfed and have climbers, the Master's and Fellows' Garden is being developed as an enclosed feature, and the College Flats are being surrounded with shrubs and climbers. The landscaping and planting plan prepared by Mrs Sheila Haywood of London provides for a perimeter of lime, Oriental Plane and Silver Willow, with an inner framework of oaks and *Mahonia aquifolium.* There are many large or flowering specimen trees, and an oak and a mulberry planted by Sir Winston Churchill in 1959. The garden also contains well-positioned bronzes by Henry Moore and Barbara Hepworth.

Clare College

The cherry by the chapel (**15**) is a delicate pink bouquet in spring; later, blue lavender (Hidcote var.) lines the path to the college gates. Between the college and the river the garden on the south is open to the public at most times, that on the north is private to the Master.

The first view of the Fellows' Garden (**11**) is likely to be from the 17th-century causeway leading to Robert Grumbold's bridge of 1638–40; the limes here are probably of the same date (one side of the former avenue has had to be felled). In spring both sides of the path are crowded with a succession of winter aconites, crocuses, daffodils, anemones, scillas and fritillaries, while through the gaps in the bushes the first signs of life can be seen in the garden itself. It can be entered at either end of the causeway or by the semicircular steps near the middle. First

16

to appear after the early spring flowers are the alpines around the pool, later in the year the yellow and blue herbaceous garden and the scented garden reach their peaks, and later still the stretch of red flowers blooms parallel with the river. Beyond the pool is the white garden and the Dean's Walk, named after William Telfer, a former Fellow. On the side nearer Queen's Road is a dark path hemmed in by yews.

No gardens in Cambridge have been laid out with more thought. The broad lawn which you cross as you come in from the semicircular steps affords a view of the old college buildings and is purposely wide and welcoming; the dark path, entered from the causeway between two close-set chestnut trunks, is a contrast from which you emerge gratefully to a brighter world. The pool garden with its irises, reeds and lilies and its four trees, two of them remaining from the earlier orchard, provides a calm centre (**12**). The vista through the wrought-iron gates (by R. Lister) leads across the pool as though through a nave, towards a curved apse of yew hedges beyond and a perron of York stone leading up the slope further off, all devised to lend distance. Looking across the pool from the opposite direction the garden seems like a theatre: gaps in the yew hedges either side serve as entrances and exits, and a raised stage is dominated by two cypresses. This is one of the most popular scenes in Cambridge for May Week productions of Shakespearean and Elizabethan plays. The cypresses grow too fast to be suitable for more than a few years at a time, but their upright forms are indispensable accompaniments to the two which stand sentry by the gap in the apse: four pillars for the four-sided pool. The yellow and blue garden is peaceful,

10 *The herbaceous border in Christ's Fellows' Garden, in July.*

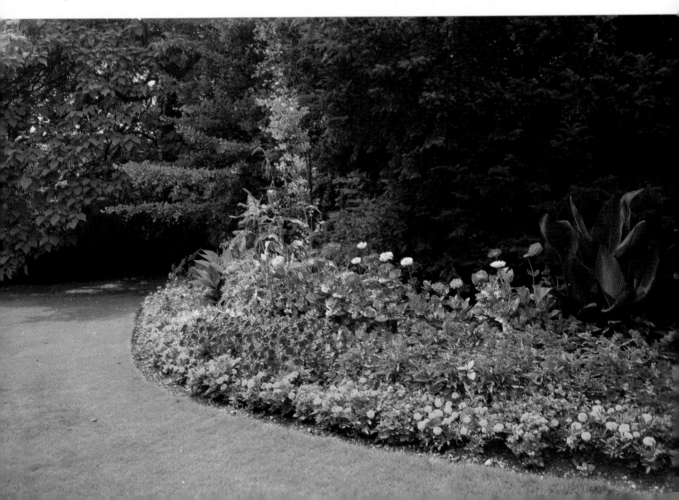

perhaps because the complementary colours, carefully disposed, make a balanced picture to which the eye responds. The original plan of providing a canal or channel where the path now runs would have made for still more tranquillity, but had too many practical disadvantages: in particular, the water-table is often high (many Cambridge residents will remember the dramatic flooding of the whole area as far as the ditch to the west in 1978).

The red border along the Cam, like the yellow and blue garden, is designed to please the eye, though this time with a little deceptiveness. When planted according to plan, though this cannot always be maintained, the reds nearer the bridge are of a more orange shade than those further away, which verge on crimson and purple, so that the vista seen from the causeway seems longer than the measuring-tape would show it to be. The general effect is not spoiled if, for example, an orange splash of gaillardias in some years makes a mild explosion against the Renaissance walls beyond – walls that are visible thanks to the care with which the low Weeping Cherries, *Prunus subhirtella* 'Pendula', have been planted on the river bank.

Standing on the lawn by the orange end of the border, you have to your right a gap through which the ancient bridge, one of the most beautiful in England, can be seen between the venerable Judas Tree on the left and a guelder rose and a medlar on the right. The Judas Tree, bright purplish pink in May (**14**), has white Christmas roses at its foot in December, closing the year's displays. As midsummer approaches, the white of the medlar and guelder rose are answered by the tall *Davidia involucrata*, or Handkerchief Tree, rising above the old kitchen garden wall from Dean Telfer's garden. Once the handkerchiefs have fallen, its beautifully veined leaves are the more visible. Still standing on the lawn in the same place, you see, if you come in autumn, the fine reds of a Buckeye Chestnut, preserved from the old garden and again provided with a gap to make it fully visible. To the right of the chestnut is an old Swamp Cypress, *Taxodium distichum*, pale green in spring and a lively brown in autumn. But the glory at that time of the year is the Copper Beech on the college side of the bridge, masking most of the Master's Garden from public view.

This is a subtle yet frank layout, full of surprises the more you reflect on it, but withholding no secrets, not even the narrow damp passages between the curved yew hedges, where primulas and Himalayan poppies enjoy life, or the narrowing edges of the path beneath the dark yews, which give a false perspective as the gradations of red do. It is mainly the work of Professor Nevill Willmer, a Fellow of Clare with a strong interest in the physiology of colour-perception, advised by two botanists in the college, Professor Sir Harry Godwin and John Gilmour, sometime Director of the Botanic Garden. The work was carried out by the former head gardener William Barlow, who died in 1961, and by the present head gardener, Mr Arbon. The garden is normally open on weekday afternoons (not Saturdays), but sometimes has to be closed to the public because of the damage that could be caused by over-visiting.

Across Queen's Road the garden of Memorial Court contains not only a Tree of Heaven (**13**) and a *Robinia pseudoacacia* of great age, but a Caucasian Wing-Nut by the main gate, a *Sophora japonica* on the lawn, a wellingtonia and two cedars. A sculpture by Barbara Hepworth adorns the front lawn, while Henry Moore's 'Falling Warrior' lies in Thirkill Court, an inner court off Memorial Court. Mounting the steps from the lawn you reach the main court, where there is a giant Black Pine (*Pinus nigra* 'Cebennensis') of Van Gogh-like intensity.

Corpus Christi College

The uncommonly fine display of windowboxes (**16**) does a lot to make up for the absence of gardens in the very small area available for flowers in this college. The court behind the chapel, off Free School Lane, has its own charm; it contains another of Cambridge's veteran mulberries. The churchyard of neighbouring St Bene't's, which has close historical associations with the college, is carefully tended, as is that of St Botolph's, to the south (**17**). The real gardens of Corpus are private, part of the Leckhampton grounds off Grange Road, where there is one of the best rose-gardens in Cambridge, to be seen when the public is allowed access under the National Gardens Scheme. There is also a 'meadow' area, affording a remarkable display of cowslips, including some in startling shades of red (possibly the result of crossing with garden primulas), and, in June, a forest of lupins. A greenish bronze by Henry Moore of a seated man makes a particularly suitable focal point for the cedars and other well-established trees of the old domestic garden.

Darwin College

The whole place is idyllic; its setting on the edge of pastoral Coe Fen is unlike anything else in Cambridge. Newnham Grange, now part of the college, and some of the riverside garden and islands belonged to George Darwin, one of Charles Darwin's sons. The two bridges to the islands where his children played pirates, the Copper Beech and several of the buildings are illustrated in wood-engravings by his daughter Gwen Raverat, in her amusing autobiography *Period Piece* – which is essential reading for anyone who enjoys Cambridge.

Downing College

A fascinating experiment is in progress here, to design trees and gardens so as to alter the impression created by the layout of the buildings. When Wilkins first made a model for the college in 1805 he intended an avenue out of Downing Street towards a 'Propylea', leading to a great rectangle of neo-Grecian chambers, with a chapel and library in the same style across most of the south side. Of this only the east and west sides were built, with some late Victorian modifications. The north side was added in 1929–53, and has drawn some fire from Pevsner, though he is kinder to the central part of it. With this addition a whole aspect of the design was altered. The site of the intended central avenue had already been swallowed up by the laboratories of the Downing Site. The entrance by the Porters' Lodge being to one side, the path from it in front of the north range tended to be seen as a thoroughfare towards Old Addenbrooke's Hospital. What remained apart from Wilkins' beautifully proportioned units was a great open campus with splendid views towards the trees along the southern boundary, and above all towards the often maligned Catholic church, which from within the grounds always presents a striking unity of spire and tower (**18**).

In 1968 Dame Sylvia Crowe was engaged to plan the gardens anew, and devised a scheme which, if ever fully carried out (it is expensive and problematic), would surely be a great enhancement. The proposed rectangular pool in front of the centrally placed chapel would create a strong emphasis on the north–south axis and is just the thing a benefactor might very usefully offer.

11 *Part of the wide sweep of lawn and the red border in Clare Fellows' Garden: a Swamp Cypress dominates the view.*

Then a double row of limes was suggested south of the east–west gravel path, at right angles to chestnuts lining the pool, in order to create an impression of two small courts within the larger court framed by the chapel and its L-shaped wings and re-establish something of Wilkins' design. This plan has already been partly carried out, though not all the plantings have taken successfully. Eventually the gravel path may even be deflected to pass under the limes, breaking the straight line from the Regent Street entrance to the exit in Tennis Court Road.

For the southern end, the plan involved limes and planes planted on diagonals pointing towards the chapel (perhaps too vestigially) and then a special emphasis on the vista to the church spire. Disaster struck from about 1974 onwards when some 150 elms, mostly ringing the perimeter, died of disease, and in the same period a glorious cedar, and beeches and poplars near Lensfield Road, were lost in gales.

The Crowe plan for this end is now in abeyance, and there is debate on the merits of all-green English plantings as against the introduction of other colours: red and variegated maples have already been planted, regrettably, as the view to the spire is otherwise so reminiscent of Constable. The making of a gap in the hedge of the Fellows' Garden to create another view of the spire has been proposed.

But the (private) Fellows' Garden is a great treasure in itself. An old winding path is being restored to something like its former appearance: it leads under a lofty cedar, and there are great quantities of newly planted spring bulbs, a fine Copper Beech, a pinetum devised to mask the chimneys at the rear of the hospital, and a herbaceous border. It can be viewed from the corner of the dining hall. On the opposite side, in the Master's Garden, a huge Holm Oak and even bigger Turkey Oaks with deep-fissured bark can be seen from the old Paddock beyond the isolated gnarled hawthorn, which marks a boundary dating back to a time before the college existed.

Emmanuel College

This is one of the finest gardens in Cambridge, as the flowering crabs, the Bird Cherries and the herbaceous borders along the St Andrew's Street front intimate. Front Court, presided over by Wren's Chapel, has a carefully kept square of lawn walked on only by the Fellows and by the ducks which come in from the pond in the Paddock. To the left of Front Court, through the Hall Screens, lies New Court, with a herb garden planted as recently as 1960, though its box hedges might wrongly suggest an earlier date. The give-away is the triangular form of the beds, devised to allow paths to cross fan-wise from two corners to the doors of the 19th-century staircases and archways. This was the design of John Codrington, who was asked to redesign the court after renovation of the kitchen had destroyed its earlier lawn. Here there are marjoram, rue, tansy, thyme, hyssop, wormwood, pokeweed, burnet roses, angelica with its large spherical heads, borage, scotch lovage, winter savory, elecampane, applemint and parsley. The coloured stones used for backgrounds are worth noting; the shining nuggets of coal, known to undergraduates as Merthyr Tydfil, come as a surprise.

If there is time, it is worth going through the archway at the far end to the tunnel leading to North Court, where three Columnar Hornbeams make a fine group of flame-shapes in foliage. Most of the oval lawn is taken up by a

Paulownia tomentosa (named, according to Humphrey Gilbert-Carter, after Princess Anna Paulowna of the Netherlands), which is covered with what look like pale lilac foxgloves in late May or early June. In Japanese legend this is the tree where the Oriental phoenix nests, as Sei Shōnagon mentions in her 10th-century *Pillow Book*.

Returning to Front Court and walking beneath the cloisters until you are past the entrance to the chapel, you see the arches open out on the left to the Paddock, the former equivalent of the modern garages and car-park. The view is deliberately confined at first by the two Arizona Cypresses on the right, the cherries by the chapel, and the *Pyrus salicifolia* straight ahead, surrounded by the contrasting green of three Irish Yews. Like the herb garden, the layout of these, and of the Black Walnut in front of them (already showing its criss-crossed bark), is due to John Codrington, the former head gardener George Sealy being responsible for the planting. Codrington also introduced the *Koelreuteria paniculata*, or Pride of India, in front of the 17th-century Old Court. This specimen has not yet reached the grandeur of the one in King's Fellows' Garden, but it is more easily seen by the public.

Here in the Paddock (**23**) the real glory of the garden begins. The long pool, with water-lilies and a recent island crowned by a Swamp Cypress and *Cornus stolonifera* 'Flaviramea', is shown on the earliest maps, made not long after the college was founded in 1584 (the serpentine banks were created in the 1960s). It may have been the fish-pond of the Dominican monastery on this site dissolved

12 *After lectures and examinations have finished the cypresses and pool in the formal part of Clare Fellows' Garden make an ideal setting for performances of Shakespeare in May Week. The whole garden is subtly devised, using perspective illusion and skilful colour-gradations for a variety of unusual effects.*

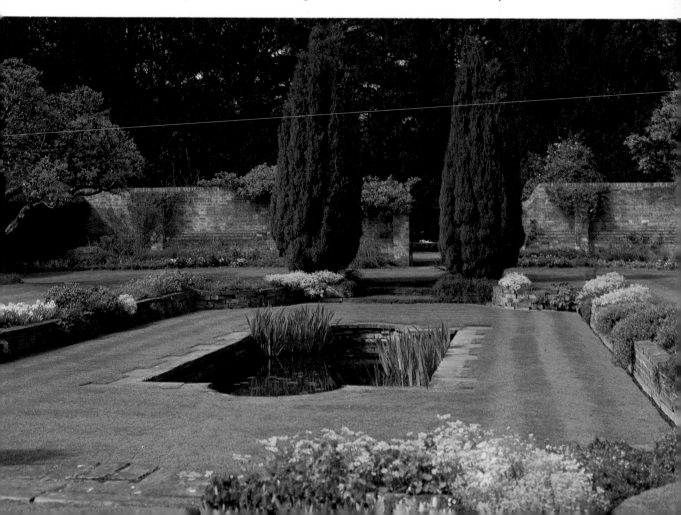

in 1539. Loggan's print of 1688 shows a brewery at the far end, which may have used the water that flows into the pool from Hobson's Conduit (dug in 1610). The pool is now surrounded by bamboos, the giant rhubarb-like *Gunnera manicata,* flags, seakale, and the curious *Podophyllum peltatum,* which can be seen in May putting out thin pink and purple arms bristling with small hairs, from a mat of gnarled roots, like some strange moon-plant.

But the best view of all at Emmanuel is from the steps of the library at the corner of the Paddock, looking out at the quarter-mile semicircle of free-standing trees: two Copper Beeches on the left, the great Oriental Plane – one of the treasures of England (**21, 22**) – and two limes, a *Tilia tomentosa* now some 80 or 90 years old, showing signs of splitting apart under its own weight, and a graceful *Tilia petiolaris,* with a full-grown London Plane alongside it. Seen across the low wall and wooden arch dividing the Paddock from the Fellows' Garden, with the flare of valerians, red-hot pokers, day-lilies and rambler roses, these trees are among the best sights in Cambridge. A focal point is made by Henry Moore's bronze 'Warrior with Shield'. The age of the Oriental Plane is not known; it may have been planted in 1802 or soon after, at the same time as the one at Jesus. Its weeping habit is, however, unusual. It is a tree often seen in Greece and Turkey, giving shelter to assemblies or markets; this particular specimen was celebrated by the Spanish poet Luis Cernuda, who was at the college during the Second World War, in his poem 'El árbol'. Beyond it in the private Fellows' Garden is a swimming pool, possibly 300 years old and claimed to be the oldest in England still in existence.

Heading west from the library enter Chapman's Garden (**19**), to find another pool (connected with the first by a channel under the buildings), a willow alongside and a 'fossil' tree, the *Metasequoia glyptostroboides,* a species once known only in fossil form, but discovered growing in China at the end of the Second World War; the great height of this one has been achieved in less than 40 years. Nearby are two Tulip Trees, *Liriodendron tulipifera,* covered in June with large green and yellow tulip-shaped flowers (**24**). The one at the east end of the pool, whose splayed trunk seems to rise out of a mound, shows why this is sometimes called the 'elephant's-foot tree'. Along the path is a white garden, followed by a red garden, which leads to a covered passageway returning to Front Court.

A pamphlet by Mr Sealy with maps naming all the trees growing in the college in 1984 is available at the Porters' Lodge. The gardens are open to the public, except for the Fellows' Garden, which was opened for the first time under the National Gardens Scheme in 1984.

Girton College

Girton College was started at Hitchin in 1869 and moved to its present site in 1873, most of the buildings being erected between 1876 and 1902. The gardens are unrivalled in size by those of any college in Cambridge, extending over 46 acres; they are enabled to survive in their exposed situation on poor soil only by lorry loads of compost. In 1977–8, one of the worst years for gales, 26 trees were blown down, mostly pines, and scores of other trees were badly damaged. Despite this recent disaster, the not so very long journey to the edge of the city is well worth making.

The former head gardener Mr Stringer recommends a walk circling the main

13 *The Tree of Heaven bears fruit better in Clare Memorial Court than in many other parts of the country. The tree was introduced to England in 1751. In China the larva of a silk-moth feeds on the foliage.*

buildings, beginning at the front drive, to see the aconites and snowdrops in January, and the ceanothus 'Cascade' blossoming on the walls in spring. A Maidenhair Tree, one of the most ancient kinds of living tree in the world, is recognisable by its divided leaf (**1**), which inspired Goethe's poem *Ginkgo biloba*. In this area are a European Larch, not often seen as a specimen tree, an *Acer platanoides* 'Drummondii' recognisable by the white margin on its leaves, and a Copper Beech planted by the Queen Mother in the centenary year. Under the chapel window is a Brown Turkey Fig, cut back in 1962 and now providing up to 100 fruits; near the library are a medlar, and a *Catalpa bignonioides* replacing a mature specimen uprooted by a gale in 1962.

Between the library and the chapel are two beds of hybrid tea roses surrounded by Bourbons, perpetual musk and *rugosa*. They include 'City of New York' (single red), 'Queen of Denmark' (cabbage rose), 'Penelope' and 'The Fairy', and a 'Mermaid' thought to be 50 years old. A yellow and a white Banksian rose grow on the library wall.

Woodlands Court lies north-east of the rosebeds; its irises flower in June and are mostly *Iris germanica*, though there are also *I. foetidissima*, the dwarf flag *I. pumila* (by the entrance) and *I. chamaeiris*. The climbing roses in this court include 'Clos Vougeot', 'Crimson Glory', 'Étoile de Hollande', 'New Dawn', and 'Albertine'.

Leaving Woodlands Court by the same entrance and turning left you come to the strawberry grapes. To your right near the iron kissing-gate are magnolias; turning left round the corner of the New Wing you see on the right a Tree of Heaven and a Cutleaved Beech. At the end of the New Wing is a bluebell glade with periwinkles as ground cover. Turn left again round the far end of the New Wing, and the hockey pitch comes into sight. Here are some *Laburnum vossii* and the unusual *Parrotia persica*, named after the French professor of medicine F. W. Parrot (1792–1841); it has bright-red stamens in March and crimson foliage in autumn.

Turn right past the garages at the end of the hockey pitch and go through the Home Garden, formerly used for vegetables but now grassed over. The collection of delphiniums includes 'Black Knight', the tallest. On your left are the pond and (private) Fellows' Garden; the pond is a pleasing wild place, with willows, yellow flags in June and July, and purple loosestrife a little later. The mound is named after a former Mistress of Girton, Miss K. T. Butler, sometime professor of Italian, and is mostly covered with *Buddleia alternifolia*. It is reached by a bridge from the Fellows' Garden.

Passing along the back (north-east) side of the pond towards the north-west you come to the Yew Walk planted by Miss Welch, who was appointed garden steward in 1883. Further on lies the Honeysuckle Walk, 100 yards long, also created by her (**26**). This is a popular spot for undergraduate picnics after exams, when the hawthorn blossoms above and periwinkle below combine with the honeysuckle to make it one of the most strikingly colourful and fragrant of all Cambridge gardens. At the far end lies the Grange, formerly a private house,

15 *Another of Clare's beautifully positioned trees, the cherry beside the college chapel.*

with Irish Yews and a Golden Yew on the lawns. The Judas Tree was removed as a seedling from a ventilator on one of the roofs in 1965.

Return now through the Old Orchard. Its five original Blenheim Oranges are almost a century old, and there are some 40 other varieties of apple tree, many of them prizewinners. (The New Orchard lies north-east of the Honeysuckle Walk.) Go down the north-west face of the college buildings, then left round the end of the wing, towards the main entrance: on your left is Emily Davies Court, containing many shrubs and a large clump of the blue winter-flowering *Iris unguicularis*, a *Clematis armandii* and ivy with its uncommon parasitical broomrape. On the lawn between the court and the main road the trees include an Atlantic Cedar, a deodar and a Black Mulberry. From here it is a short distance to the starting-place of the walk.

Gonville and Caius College

Space does not allow for many gardens in the main college grounds, though the avenue of whitebeams and the wisteria in the corner give Tree Court a distinctive character (**25**). St Michael's Court, on the other side of Trinity Street, deserves a visit for its blend of dark red and dark green foliage against the background of St Michael's Church. The hostel at Harvey Court, West Road, has taken over some of the gardens of the houses that stood or still stand there; these are of great extent and beauty, and include the only dell in Cambridge. In the depths of the garden is a triangle of three very large cedars with a wellingtonia, and to one side of them a little grove of Judas Trees presided over by a Blue Cedar. An ancient mulberry and an island of conifers near the Court are also worth looking for. A path leads through to Sidgwick Avenue, where the locked Fellows' Garden lies across the road: it contains another mulberry and perhaps the largest Lombardy Poplar in Cambridge.

Homerton College

The grounds, well away from the centre, are vast, and though the best gardens are close to the buildings, a tour should include the boundary hedge of Columnar Hornbeam and hawthorn along the railway line. (Visitors to the grounds should let the Porters' Lodge know of their visit, on arrival.) Near the hedge is a collection of North American trees, useful at this College of Education for teaching children and others. The orchard still supplies fruit to the college, an unusual thing these days. An oak was planted for the Queen's Jubilee Year in 1977. Particularly worth seeing in spring is a Purple-Leaved Maple with yellow and dark-red blossoms like clusters of bees.

Entering from Hills Road, traffic noise is almost left behind, thanks to recent successful plantings along the fence of shrubs between trees that include a Willow-Leaved Pear and a Tree of Heaven. Species roses are supported by wooden pole tripods – an idea borrowed from Sissinghurst. The plantings here, as in many other parts of the college, were designed by the head gardener, Miss Joan Salter.

The white and black buildings to the right of the red brick Victorian building have been enhanced with sensitive plantings that afford colour at most seasons. The brick perron leads to the entrance, alongside which there is a tall *Paulownia tomentosa* – an unusual tree in Cambridge – with a pink-flowered *Prunus tenella* nearby. The most interesting court within is a pleasant paved garden with seats,

dominated by a fine Snakebark Maple and a Swamp Cypress, and surrounded by gorse, broom, potentilla and a rosemary (Miss Jessop's 'upright' variety). In the middle is a statue, 'Stretching Figure', by the Cambridge sculptress Betty Rea (1905–65). On the further side is a Copper Beech preserved so close to the building that you seem to climb into it up the glass-enclosed staircase. Beyond, in the former garden of Trumpington House, is a mulberry so riven with age as to have fallen apart like a Henry Moore three-piece. Can it be as old as Milton's at Christ's? A wellingtonia and a Weeping Wych Elm are close by.

The long wall bordering the car-park, formerly rather desolate, has been transformed by recent plantings, notably a *Prunus triloba* (often difficult to grow), a strikingly red quince (*Chaenomeles superba* 'Knaphill Scarlet'), ceanothus, wisteria and *Akebia quinata*. This should be seen by all owners of bare walls, preferably in spring.

Turning back to the Victorian buildings (if you are not making for the railway line), you come round to the south face, where long grass is no sign of indolence: the various species are left for biology classes to study. An oak grows by the Combination Room, and the rather shady three-sided deep recess to the east is suitably planted with spurges, hellebores, fatsia and bergenia. The new building running north–south, at right angles, has a long row of *Gallica versicolor* 'Rosa mundi', replacing one of lavender.

17 *The churchyard of St Botolph's, adjoining Corpus Christi College in Trumpington Street, is one of the best of many beautiful churchyards in Cambridge. Springtime daffodils, forsythias and cherries are followed in summer by roses and foxgloves.*

On the way out, the Cutleaved Beech dating from the Victorian origins of the college should not be missed: a splendid specimen with delicately formed leafage.

Jesus College

The 'Chimney', the long narrow path leading between high brick walls from Jesus Lane to the entrance of the college, has been called dull. It is, as E. M. Forster replied, of a calculated dullness, concentrating attention on the rich red, gold and black Gothic of the gate-tower. But the famous Oriental Plane on the left can hardly be missed either. It stands in the (private) Fellows' Garden, where it has grown since 1802 from seeds that Edward Daniel Clarke, a Fellow who had been on a tour of Europe with Malthus (also a Fellow), brought back from Thermopylae – a reminder of the Greek victory there which saved European civilisation. As you pass through the entrance arch, the wisteria on the further side of First Court is equally impressive: rising to the second floor, it spans eight window-bays.

The courts form an island surrounded by playing fields and a former orchard which now has a great variety of trees, including a Weeping Ash. In Second Court are vestiges of a Victorian formal garden that existed till 1961. Four couples of trimmed yews shaped like comice pears lean towards each other at the ends of an imaginary cross, as though in a square-dance. The square is in fact the basic form at Jesus. Cloister Court, by the square-towered chapel, is itself a square, with vines on all four sides that are splendid in autumn, and with hanging baskets all through the summer. Chapel Court beyond has a large square of lawn with a holly tree at each corner, and a Cedar of Lebanon planted in 1984. Of the shrubs along the walls the ceanothus flourishes best, being warmed by the Combination Room. Now that the row of pleached limes across the open end of the court has died, there is a grand view of the belt of trees along the perimeter, curving behind the steep thatch of the cricket pavilion. (Behind you, on the wall facing the chapel, is a large sculpture by Eric Gill which should not be overlooked.)

From here there is a choice of routes. The left-hand path will take you through an avenue of limes almost lost in the tree belt (now sadly depleted by elm disease) to the Park Street entrance, where there is another very old Oriental Plane and a *Metasequoia glyptostroboides.* Alternatively, circling the red-brick building to the right, you come to the avenue of chestnuts (**27**) planted in memory of Henry Arthur Morgan, Master till 1912. The tree belt on this side serves as a barrier against traffic noise, and is being thickened with a shrubbery. The Bursary, of red brick, has a *Magnolia grandiflora* against the wall. Turning to the right after passing it, you have a good view of the best steeple in Cambridge, All Saints (by Bodley, 1864), above a triangle of Judas Trees and a colourful shrubbery. From here, Jesus Lane can be regained through the car-park entrance.

The visitor privileged to see the Fellows' Garden will find a mulberry possibly dating from the early 17th century, thanks to which Fellows used to receive an annual pot of mulberry jam; a four-stemmed Holm Oak; and some enigmatically shaped plants supposedly planted by the medieval nuns who formerly occupied this site, *Aristolochia durior.* The name means 'best for childbirth', and the plant has also been known as 'birthwort'.

King's College

King's bridge (**31**), designed by William Wilkins, the architect of the screen fronting King's Parade and the dining hall, was built in 1818, replacing the earlier bridge that stood opposite the chapel. The path leading to it from Queen's

19 *A July scene: the willow (planted in 1923) and pool in Chapman's Garden, Emmanuel. The fish are protected from early-morning herons by taut cables stretched across the bottom of the pool. Emmanuel's pools and gardens are inhabited by many varieties of duck – mandarin, wigeon, mallard, cayuga, tufted, shellduck – some of them presented and given names by the Fellows.*

20 Magnolia ×
soulangeana *in*
Emmanuel Paddock
in April. Magnolia
was named by the
Swedish father of
modern botany,
Linnaeus, after the
16th-century French
botanist Pierre
Magnol; Soulange-
Bodin was also a
French botanist.

Road was made soon after, with a curving line like Capability Brown's curving
avenue at Madingley, carefully planned to reveal the buildings only at the most
dramatic moment. The bridge itself is a curved version of a Greek Ionic
architrave. It gives a fine view across the great expanse of well-kept lawn to the
chapel and the side of Clare College. Along the path from January onwards is the
famous succession of winter aconites, crocuses, chionodoxa and daffodils, worth
coming a long way to see (**30**).

Apart from this and the great beech by the bridge (**29**) there is little of
gardening interest in the main part of the college accessible to the public. The
chestnuts in the bridge avenue are mostly recovering from tree surgery; the elms
along Queen's Road that used to give the Gibbs Building the aspect of a stately
home glimpsed through parkland have died and are replaced by limes and oaks
flanked with protecting hawthorns. The meadow across the river from the chapel
is interesting for its mounds, which look natural enough, but are part of the new
design of the 1820s.

Across the road, however, the Fellows' Garden is a place to visit whenever it is
open to the public, as it is occasionally under the National Gardens Scheme. The
entrance is close to the back gate of the college, and a guide to the trees has been
published, by Dr S. M. Walters. Immediately to the right as you enter is a
Lucombe Oak, a hybrid between the Cork Oak and the Turkey Oak, but nearer
to the Cork Oak, being evergreen. Named after the Exeter nurseryman in whose

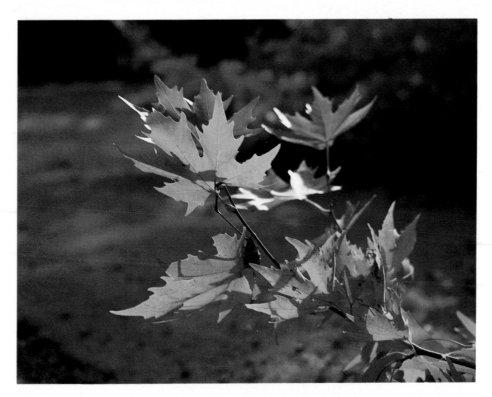

21 *Leaves of the Oriental Plane in the Fellows' Garden at Emmanuel; they are more indented than those of the better-known London Plane. Medieval Persian poets compared them to slender hands.*

nursery it arose about 1762, it is often seen in the West Country. Further to the right is a *Catalpa bignonioides,* one of the oldest trees in the Fellows' Garden. Catalpa derives its name from the language of the Indians of Carolina, and is also known as the Indian Bean. Continuing along beyond the sundial you come to a Black Walnut, and beyond that the site of a Golden Poplar, recently replaced by Columnar Cherries. Next to Clare Memorial Court, close together, are a mulberry transplanted in 1965 – a cutting from one of the mulberries planted in London in the reign of James I – and two Wig Trees flanking a lime, a *Cotinus obovatus* and a *Cotinus coggygria.* Their English name comes from a resemblance of their flowers to fine-haired wigs. A little further on is a very fine Oriental Plane, the kind of plane Virgil speaks of in the *Georgics* (IV. 146), and along the side bordering the college hostel a rare tree, *Gleditsia sinensis,* or Chinese Honey Locust, and another evergreen, a Holm Oak. From here it is easy to see the two wellingtonias, rising high above everything, one in the central island, the other free-standing. They were probably planted about 1860, not long after the first specimens were brought to Britain in 1853. The wellingtonia's soft bark earns it the name 'Punching-Tree', the lighter coloured band near the base possibly being due to the practice of punching it. Near the free-standing wellingtonia is a young Atlantic Cedar.

In the island-bed opposite this last tree is a young *Pyrus salicifolia* or Willow-Leaved Pear, planted in front of an older one, and the glory of the garden: a *Koelreuteria paniculata* or Pride of India (also known as Golden Rain Tree), the finest example in Cambridge, its bright yellow flowers in large panicles appearing in July and August. It is getting on for 80 years old.

In the central island-bed, nearer the entrance, are a *Thuja orientalis* 'Flabelli-formis', planted before 1904, recognisable by its long thin drooping twigs, and, on the further side, a young *Ginkgo biloba* or Maidenhair Tree, and a *Pinus pinaster* or Maritime Pine, a species familiar to visitors to the coast of the South of France and of the Landes. Beyond the wellingtonia are a *Metasequoia glyptostroboides* planted in the early 1960s (slightly later than the ones at Emmanuel and in the Botanic Garden), a Scots Pine, and an enormous Judas Tree.

Magdalene College

The Fellows' Garden is usually open to visitors in the afternoon. Occupying part of the grounds of Buckingham College, a monks' hostel of the 15th century, it is on the site of the ancient pondyards, where a branch of the Cam had been closed off to make fish-ponds; these were filled in in 1586. In the north-west corner of the garden is a pets' cemetery (**5**), with figures of cats and dogs on tombstones bearing their names. The large oak in the middle was planted in 1887 in celebration of Queen Victoria's Jubilee.

The First Court's mellowed red brick walls are pleasantly matched first by the wallflowers and then by the geraniums usually planted there. Hanging baskets add colour to the charming classical yet domestic building that houses the Pepys Library (**33**). The grassy river bank by the road bridge has recently become the largest and most resplendent bed for tulips in Cambridge.

22 *The Oriental Plane in Emmanuel Fellows' Garden in full sail. It is thought to be nearly two hundred years old, and in 1984 it was 92 ft high and 16 ft in girth. The Oriental Plane has been cultivated in England since the 16th century; the well-known aria from Handel's* Xerxes, *'Ombra mai fu', is in praise of the shade it affords.*

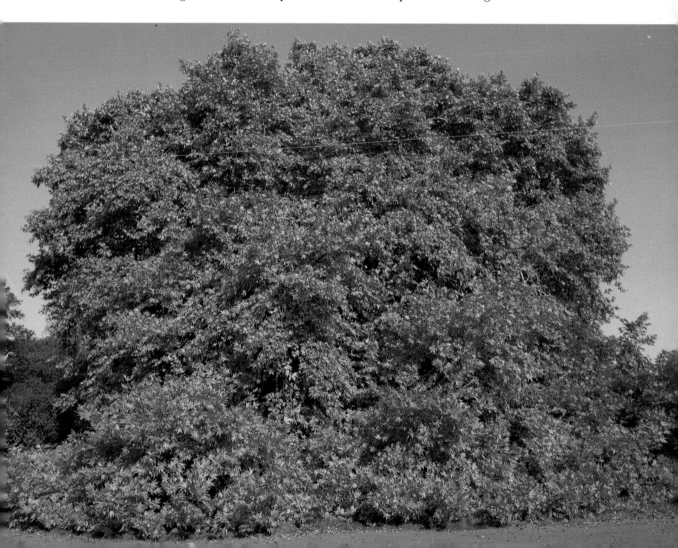

New Hall

The two courts of New Hall are unlike any others in the University, and quite unlike each other. The one on your left as you come from the Porters' Lodge is all cool and white; the architecture of the library, suggesting Indian influence, is answered by the tall fountain jet and its side-canals and carp – not quite Taj Mahal, but you might expect someone in a sari to look down from the high dining hall balcony at the tubs of tulips. (The objection to artificial stagnant water made by William Robinson in *The English Flower Garden* (1883) is still valid, all the same.) The court on your right, partly obscured by the added lecture-room, is greensward from side to side, without paths, but with shade in one half provided by hornbeam and yew, hawthorn and beech, and with a springtime waterfall of crab-apple blossom in the other. To avoid making this half shady too, the pear tree is columnar, and the mulberry a shrub. The well-fenestrated walls are being enhanced by over 100 shrubs – photinia, magnolia, *Robinia hispida*, berberis, *Prunus tenella, Salix hastata* 'Wehrhahnii' and several different weigelas and escallonias, providing something in flower or with coloured leaves throughout the year. The sundial on the west-facing wall, which has a graph for adding or subtracting minutes to convert to Greenwich Mean Time, was given in honour of Dame Rosemary Murray, first President of the College (1954–81). For many years from 1967 onwards, when the builders finally put the new buildings in her care, the President was weekend planter, pruner and weeder of the shrubs you see all round you here.

23 *The herbaceous border in the Paddock, Emmanuel.*

24 *'Tulips' of the Tulip Tree,* Liriodendron tulipifera, *also called Lily Tree and Yellow Poplar, in Chapman's Garden, Emmanuel. A native of North America, it sometimes reaches there a height of almost 200 ft.*

The houses that stood and in some cases still stand along the west side of Huntingdon Road between Buckingham Road and Storey's Way used to be called the 'Darwinnery', since three sons of Charles Darwin lived in them side by side. The buildings of New Hall and Fitzwilliam College now occupy most of this area, while Trinity Hall has developed another part for its hostel Wychfield. New Hall has been particularly lucky in acquiring about ten acres, including not only some of the area of the Darwin gardens, but also some gardens belonging to houses in Storey's Way. The result is unique. Looking at the college from the roadway you have no inkling of the glades and orchards, country lanes and kissing-gate, terraces and hedgerows beyond. There is no route that can be easily described, but any stroller will find, according to the time of year, yards and yards of lily of the valley, a flaming *Parrotia persica*, a blue 'Maidwell Hall' clematis climbing as though casually up a tree, a woodland garden of aconites, crown imperials, hellebores, martagon lilies and cuckoopint, a herbaceous border of peonies and poppies (again the work of Dame Rosemary), a medlar, snake's-head fritillaries, a neo-Georgian house with a neo-Georgian herbaceous border and a rockery flanked with cypresses, a Black Poplar with mistletoe high up and an apple tree almost smothered with it, and a semicircular yew hedge that deserves a garden statue. Into the network of paths and ditches surrounding all these some new low-profiled buildings have been smuggled so that it is now possible to live and study at New Hall as though in the countryside, with squirrels, hedgehogs and small birds of all kinds joining in. It will be a pity if this constantly surprising variety ever becomes unified and ordinary.

On the way out, turn north at the kitchen entrance for a brief look at the garden by the squash court, to see a Columnar Oak, five beeches oddly huddled together (the remains of a beech hedge), a prosperous fig, *Ceanothus* 'Topaz', and, along the foot of the wall, a varied collection of irises presented by the Botanic Garden.

Newnham College

Some sense of the history of this huge garden helps in making out its patterns, so it is a good idea to start at the Old Hall gate in Newnham Walk rather than by the main entrance in Sidgwick Avenue. You then have on your right Sidgwick Hall (**35**), standing well forward, the tall bay windows of Clough Hall further away, the Kennedy Building out of sight in the right-hand corner, and Peile Hall facing you from the far end.

The first garden, of two acres, was begun in 1875 and surrounded Old Hall. Miss A. J. Clough, the first Principal, superintended the layout, and the Irish Yews along the west side of the building remain from her time. Originally, a public bridle-path ran from Old Hall to Grange Road: its course can still be traced by the lime trees on the edge of Clough Hall lawn and the hawthorns nearer to Peile. When Sidgwick was built in 1880 it was divided from Old Hall by the bridle-path, and had its own separate garden, which now takes the form of a fountain and rosebeds (crossing the line of the bridle-path) in memory of Dr Sidgwick, a 'founding father' of the college and husband of the second Principal.

Since Sidgwick was built, the garden has grown by the addition of a piece here, a commemorative tree there, so that the pleasure it gives is due not so much to the layout, which is agreeably casual, but to the variety of plants, trees and shrubs, which make a small Botanic Garden in themselves. So from Old Hall

25 *Whitebeams at Gonville and Caius grow, appropriately, in Tree Court. They lead to the Gate of Virtue, seen on the left, through which students pass each day. In former times, having completed their studies, they left the college by the Gate of Honour, in Senate House Passage, to receive their degrees in Great Saint Mary's Church. 'Whitebeam' means 'white tree' (German Baum), referring to the colour of the underside of the leaves in spring.*

you go down into the sunken garden to see the roses and read the inscription round the pool, come up again, and see on your right a Cutleaved Beech very much admired for its shape; beyond it is an English Oak sent by the Prime Minister W. E. Gladstone from Hawarden in 1887, the year that Clough Hall was built (Gladstone's daughter Helen was a Fellow of Newnham). Continuing in the same direction you come to the mound almost opposite Kennedy, made in 1892 for the college observatory, which is now some way to the south at the end of the sports field. The stone seat and sundial were added in 1910 to commemorate the Principalship of Mrs Sidgwick. These are the main landmarks, though the Hazelnut Walk south of the mound is also a special feature.

No college is so well provided for all seasons. In autumn the pink nerines flower along the north side of Old Hall, as does the bright yellow *Sternbergia lutea* near the door of Clough (**34**). In the same season *Celastrus orbiculatus* on the eastern end of Peile bears scarlet and gold fruits, and many varieties of Michaelmas daisies opposite Kennedy make a bright show against the red brick.

In winter, the yellow flowers of *Chimonanthus praecox* appear on the west face of Sidgwick, and just beyond, between the semicircular bays of Clough's dining hall, is a clump of *Iris unguicularis* like the one in Emily Davies court at Girton. Further along the front of Clough is the white-flowered *Viburnum farreri*, scenting the air from November to February, and still further down, in the corner between Kennedy and Peile, is *Garrya elliptica* with long drooping catkins, a native of California and Oregon. Near the mound is an *Arbutus unedo*, flowering in autumn and winter, sometimes with orange-red fruits at the

26   The Honeysuckle Walk at Girton, scene of picnics during and after the examination weeks. Honeysuckle is the woodbine spoken of by Shakespeare's Puck; its curving flowers are compared (by male chauvinists) to ladies' fingers.

same time – these are like strawberries and can be used for making liqueurs. Further south, towards the Nut Walk, is a *Hamamelis japonica*, Japanese Witch Hazel, with yellow flowers. A few yards to the east is another *Chimonanthus praecox* and a blue-flowered *Hepatica nobilis*, not flowering till February. Also in February appear the bright red stamens of *Parrotia persica*, in the corner south-west of Old Hall.

Spring brings out *Clematis armandii* near the door of Clough – an unusual climber also to be found in Emily Davies court at Girton. Daffodils and cherry-blossoms abound. On the mound masses of yellow flowers appear in April on *Berberis stenophylla*. But by this time of the year there are too many flowerings to mention more than a few (most of the plants are provided with labels). The globe artichokes down the path leading from the door of Clough are worth special notice (*37*), and so are the lemon peonies nearby. Further north along the wall of Clough is a *Rosa × pteragonis* 'Cantabrigiensis', raised in the Botanic Garden, which won the Royal Horticultural Society Award of Merit in 1931. At the corner of Kennedy is a *Wisteria sinensis* planted not long after 1906 and now threatening the brickwork. On the mound, amidst great variety, there is a *Clerodendrum trichotomum*, its star-shaped white flowers surrounded by red calyces in August and September. Pasque flowers grow here at Easter.

Among the trees south of the mound is a *Sorbus latifolia* or Broad-Leaved Whitebeam, rarely planted in gardens, and also flowering in spring; this

27 *The gates and the chestnut avenue leading from Victoria Avenue to Jesus College, a memorial to a former Master of the college.*

28 Spiraea trilobata 'Vanhouttei' *blossoms unstintingly in King's Fellows' Garden. The name* Spiraea *may allude to the spiralling stems of the flowers. The English name for the species is meadow-sweet.*

40

specimen is held to be one of the biggest in Britain. There are seven kinds of honeysuckle in this area, another plant specially favoured here as at Girton, and almost at the edge is a Yellow Tree Peony, *Paeonia lutea* 'Ludlowii', flowering in May and June. The *Parrotia persica*, already mentioned, turns crimson in autumn. The Atlantic Cedar on the perimeter of the sports field (south of the garden) was planted in 1971 at the college's centenary celebrations.

A broadsheet with a map and illustrations and descriptions of many of the trees and plants is available at the Porters' Lodge.

Pembroke College

The formal courts have always been to the west of a wall beyond which the garden proper really begins. Within the courts the great sight in May is the Japanese cherry 'Shimidsu sakura', near the back of Wren's chapel; the blossoms are thick as white fur. Near this, framing the Pitt statue by the library wall, are *Actinidia kolomikta* with particoloured leaves, and *Actinidia polygama*; the same court contains a *Catalpa bignonioides* and a *Photinia frazeri* 'Red Robin', its bright red leaves startling the visitor in early spring. In autumn, the pillars of the gateway through the wall are mounds of wine-red Virginia creeper.

The area beyond this gate, to the east, is shown on Loggan's engraving of 1688 as an orchard formally arranged in parallel lines. By the 1920s there were still some pears, though the dank laurels and yews made it gloomy. The plantings seen today (**39**) are due to several Fellows, but chiefly the former Dean, the Reverend Meredith Dewey, who died in 1983, leaving his rock garden as his memorial. This long pile of Cumberland stone near the buildings is planted with a profusion of evergreens and rockery plants and a huge *Gunnera manicata* nearby, barbaric in its Amazonian luxuriance (**6**). Much replanting has gone on recently. Dewey used to plant and weed here, chatting to passers-by and indulging his delight in the striking and unusual. His personality is still felt in several parts of the whole garden.

The small pool in the rock garden is connected by an alkathene pipe with the lily pond to the south. On the way there it bypasses the mound built round 'Spenser's mulberry', planted probably not by Spenser, who was at Pembroke in the late 1560s, but, like 'Milton's mulberry' at Christ's, as part of James I's ill-conceived plan for promoting a silk industry. 'Long lopped and propped, tied and trussed', as Dewey said, it died in 1977, its mound of earth (said to have come from Great Saint Mary's) being unable to prolong its life any further. But a root-cutting from the old tree was planted on the mound and may yet flourish for another 370 years. The lily pond was ingeniously converted from a static water tank built for firefighting in the Second World War. It is fed from Hobson's Conduit, the channel dug in 1610 to provide drinking water for the town. Walking along the path from the Virginia creeper gate to reach the lily pond, you pass on your right a patch that is colourful with pansies, primulas and fanciful tulips; heathers, unusual cyclamens and hellebores make it a miniature winter garden.

Running east from the lily pond is the Avenue, bordered on one side by gaunt, incredibly tall planes planted in the mid-19th century, not unlike Monet's painting of trees by the Seine in the Fitzwilliam Museum. The area to the right of the Avenue is private, and leads to the Master's Garden; a flaming urn in stone, preserved from Wren's chapel, makes an unusual garden ornament. Near here is a Blue Cedar planted at the suggestion of Professor Basil Willey: it has been the custom at Pembroke to ask Fellows to choose trees for planting, and the Honey Locust var. 'Sunburst', as well as the variegated Incense Cedar and the salmon-pink blossoming *Acer pseudoplatanus* 'Brilliantissimum' on the north side of the Avenue, mark the tenth anniversaries of elections to Fellowships – a more visible commemoration than giving items of silver to be put away in the vaults, though the practice does contribute to a lack of overall planning. Few colleges do make overall garden plans: it is out of keeping with colleges altogether.

In the same area south of the Avenue is the remarkable 'citronge' (*Citrus sinense* × *Poncirus trifoliata*), producing a fruit like oranges and lemons, and *Abelia sepiaria*, green and spiky like some strange seabed plant. Beyond, near the hedge of the Master's Garden, is a *Betula albosinensis* transplanted from Dewey's garden in Millington Road.

Near the eastern end of the avenue is Orchard Building (1956); here, close to a sundial and a *Magnolia grandiflora*, near the north corner, are a Tulip Tree and a *Betulus papyrifera*. Dewey explained this latter planting as being intended to veil the architecture of the building, which not all the Fellows admired. It would also, he felt, be something for Canadians, since the *Betulus* is used for birch-bark canoes – Australians being already provided for in Cambridge with eucalyptus.

31 *King's Backs under an April snowfall.*

This Empire touch continues in the plantings along the terraces of New Court, to the north of Orchard Building, where New Zealand plants and shrubs are in evidence. However, Dewey's suggestion of a wallaby for the crown green bowls court used by Fellows, in front of the Orchard Building, was never taken up. But bearing in mind all these Imperial references, a *Malus* 'Red Sentinel' at the corner of New Court has almost a suggestion of a Guards regiment, while its shining winter berries last.

Returning towards the main entrance, you now walk on a York stone path alongside the buildings known as 'Ridley's Walk', where the martyred bishop of Reformation times used to exercise. In his *Farewell* Ridley addressed the college: 'In thy orchard (the wals, buts and trees, if they could speake, would beare me witnes) I learned without booke [by heart] almost all Paules epistles.' In Greek, he meant.

This Walk leads past the rock garden again, and through the 17th-century stone porch that used to stand as entrance to the old dining hall. The symmetrically placed Golden and Irish Yews either side of it, in the next court, stand where two similar rows, perhaps planted in Ridley's time, appear in Loggan's engraving. Here in the 18th century the Master, Roger Long, erected a planetarium large enough to seat 30 people. Pass through the Screens into the First Court, where a newly planted walnut promises a return to the old Cambridge custom of ornamenting front courts with trees.

A walk across the road and to the left leads to Little St Mary's churchyard, one of the loveliest 'wild' gardens to be seen.

Peterhouse

The oldest college in Cambridge also has the oldest gardens. The croft of a house conveyed to the Brothers of the Sack about 1270 by Walter le Brasur of Shelford and his wife Andreada became, with its companion strips, the *arboretum* or Grove of the college, and this in turn became the Deer Park, where deer were kept until the late 1930s. The Deer Park, still so called, is the part of the gardens to the south of the main college buildings, west of the Fellows' Garden, and has suffered not only the loss of deer but the loss of elms too; the replantings begun in the 1950s have still to make their presence felt. The spaces between, however, have been filled with as grand a show of daffodils as any in Cambridge, and a Pendulous Silver Lime (*Tilia petiolaris*) appropriately planted by the Master in 1977 to mark the Silver Jubilee of Queen Elizabeth II is a token of future growth. A magnificent *Tilia petiolaris* is in the garden beyond the wall; it is at its best in August.

The path through the Deer Park is lined with apple trees that make a fine show in spring, though they are of an age now when they need to be replaced. Limes will gradually take over. Near the buildings two Oriental Planes have very recently been planted. There is also a Judas Tree within the park. To the west, the medieval boundary wall runs parallel to this path; in it can be seen the water-gate of Bishop Alcock (founder of Jesus College, whose three cocks and mitre are

33 Hanging baskets under the arches of the Pepys Building at Magdalene. Samuel Pepys was a member of the college and bequeathed to it his library (including his famous diary), which is housed here in its original twelve bookcases of red oak made for him in 1666.

32 One of the finest cherries in Cambridge, Prunus *'Shirotae', blossoms in King's between the chapel and Clare College (seen in the background).*

on the shield above the arch), a reminder of the time when the Cam had many more branches than it has now. The shallow channel inside the grounds which used to lead to the gate has over many years mysteriously become a round, slightly raised mound. Somewhere near here there was, until at least the early 19th century, a 'College Bath', fed from Hobson's Conduit in Trumpington Street and 'much frequented of the students'. It has left no trace, like the Tennis Court, which was 'now fallen down' in 1727, the dovecot, from which the bursar once drove a thriving trade in 'pigeon pullets', and the kitchen garden.

Beyond the wall of the Deer Park lies the Scholars' Garden, containing many old yews – a feature of all Peterhouse gardens. Some 50 clumps of peonies along its south face make a fine display (**41**). Near the tower block is a bizarre hybrid, *Laburnocytisus adamii*, producing flowers both of broom and of laburnum. It is a 'chimaera', to quote Alan Mitchell, mixing *Laburnum anagyroides* with the dwarf shrub *Cytisus purpureus* 'Scop.', and was popular in Victorian times; not sightly, but still a curiosity.

Turn east beyond the tower block to another part of the Scholars' Garden, containing one of Cambridge's many ancient gnarled mulberries. It has not been claimed for Thomas Gray as Pembroke's and Christ's mulberries have been claimed for their poets Spenser and Milton, though Gray could well have had his old college in mind when he wrote of

> Ye brown o'er-arching Groves,
> That Contemplation loves,
> Where willowy *Camus* lingers with delight!

This mulberry still delivers several stone of fruit each year.

34 Sternbergia lutea *(named after a Count von Sternberg), flowering in October at Newnham. Its flowers withstand bad weather better than crocuses do. Also known as the autumn or winter daffodil, it is thought by some writers to be the Biblical 'lily of the field'; it grows abundantly in Palestine.*

35 *Virginia creepers turning autumnal red on Sidgwick Hall, Newnham.*

Leaving by the tower block you can regain Trumpington Street; the return route to the centre of Cambridge passes the very beautiful 18th-century Master's Lodge opposite the main entrance, graced by several of the best blossoming cherries in the city.

Queens' College

Old Court, perhaps the most picturesque court in Cambridge, has little of special gardening interest, but the famous sundial on the wall (1733) must attract anyone so dependent on the sun as gardeners are. It is also, by the way, a moon-dial; a pamphlet by G. C. Shephard explains its numerous functions. To the west you enter the celebrated Cloister Court, an entirely architectural pleasure. A little passage at the north-east corner leads to Walnut Tree Court, the home of a walnut for centuries; the present beautifully shaped specimen dates from the early 1930s, and stands on the line of a vanished wall belonging to the Carmelite monastery dissolved in 1539. Roses face it, growing by the wall of the President's Garden. The so-called Mathematical Bridge is often attributed to Newton, but was actually designed in the 'Chinese' taste by William Etheridge in 1749 (and later rebuilt).

The ancient Fellows' Garden across the Cam disappeared when Cripps Court was built in the mid-1970s. The only survivor there is the mulberry, now replanted in the middle of the court; the Handkerchief Tree in the corner is a newcomer. But the adjoining Grove, full of daffodils and tulips in spring, leads along the Cam almost as far as King's bridge, making a woodland triangle that invites to exploration. Across the river from the Grove is the new (private) Fellows' Garden, bounded on the north by a clunch wall dating from the Carmelite buildings. The crown bowling green by the Erasmus Building, very like the one at Pembroke, has been in use for centuries. An extremely old mulberry stump may well date from the early-17th-century plantings of which Christ's still has an example.

Robinson College

Dramatic contrasts are the first impression, as you stand high above the Bin Brook after coming in by the entrance near Burrell's Walk. Beneath you a long sturdy wooden bridge, almost a viaduct, curves across the foreground. At the end of a vista ahead, like the backcloth of a stage, is the handsome neo-Tudor gabled house Thorneycreek, better framed now by wings of tree-clusters than its previous owners can ever have foreseen. To the left five strikingly tall Lombardy Poplars rise even higher than the high buildings of the college, at once reducing the impression of their – for Cambridge – unusual size, and yet paradoxically increasing it. Beyond the pool, recently formed in the course of the brook, many fine old trees remain from the gardens of houses now gone: a Copper Beech, a propped mulberry, two cedars – making a mass of foliage advancing to the water's edge. This is a semi-wild area, allowed to remain unmown until May Ball time.

If you take the left-hand path, past the mound under the dining hall windows which is planted now with rock-roses but is intended for more diverse 'maquis-type' planting, you skirt the edge of the semi-wild area, disturbing a duck or two, and suddenly find yourself in completely wild woodland, the brook running between steep slopes lined with close-packed trunks, more rural even than

Addison's Walk at Oxford. The path winds through to a bridge and a broad drive leading to Thorneycreek, where there is a white wisteria and a magnolia by the wall. Turn left, and again there is surprise – a long level of lawn with a flowering crab leading through the old garden of 5 Adams Road, which is now also college territory. A *Parrotia persica* here is worth coming to see in autumn. The path of bluish grey and creamy brown Cotswold stone, and some other features of the gardens, were designed by Henry Woolston, who, as bursar of the college, has been closely involved with the initial development of the college buildings and its gardens. (Building operations were concluded as recently as 1980.)

The back garden of 1 Sylvester Road is (in 1984) still being developed for simple maintenance. So come back past Thorneycreek and perhaps rest on the seat in the small formal garden with yew hedge designed by J. St Bodfan Gruffyd, who initially planned much of the landscaping between here and the college. The view towards the college, with the poplars now on your right, is just as striking as the view from it, the shelving and curving banks contrasting with the tall red curve of the buildings.

After crossing the bridge, with a 'wild' island half-way, you mount up to the college again. There are no gardens within, but the intention is to bring scent and colour into the first-floor courts, which present the problem of brick paving surrounded by high walls. As you leave, you become aware of the architect's square-patterned frames for climbers, which with time will make an original contribution to the façade. Alders, crabs, birches and Columnar Beeches will combine to dress the front with green, and more mature limes and other trees will embellish the Herschel Road frontage.

37 Globe artichokes, Cynara cardenculus, against a woodland background at Newnham.

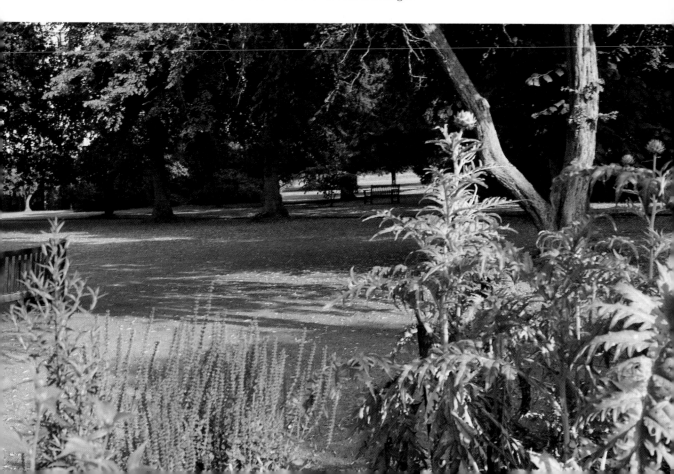

St John's College

Two tall Dawyck Beeches at the corner of Bridge Street and St John's Street, planted about 1940, act sentinel to the broad gates: they and the other pair, further down Bridge Street, are among the most striking trees in Cambridge. The metal flowers on the gates are marguerites, in honour of the foundress Lady Margaret Beaufort, and forget-me-nots (not myosotis but a speedwell like *Veronica chamaedrys*), which allude to the loyal motto of the Beauforts and of the college, 'Souvent me souvient' ('I often remember'), the family's response to a royal plea. The same flowers are carved in stone, with a vine above, over the turreted main entrance further down St John's Street. The strange animals are yales, mythical beasts like antelopes which can swivel their horns.

The first three courts have little by way of gardens, though in First Court the sites of the 12th-century hospital (the college's predecessor) and its 13th-century chapel (demolished to make way for the 19th-century one) are marked by flowers. But Second Court, at first glance four squares of turf surrounded by paths, has a Japanese simplicity and serenity. The squares (or rectangles) are of the intense green that people expect in a college court, while the cobbles are selected with all the care in the world, graded in size from sides to centre, laid in close parallels, harmonising in colour with the brick of the walls (though the dappled colours vary with the great mixture of minerals brought down during the Ice Age and left behind in the Cam valley), laid at right angles where a runnel is needed, and rising in a kind of false mitre joint at the corners of the lawns to make corner-cutting across the grass not merely prohibited but uninviting. To bring the paths into a similar colour-range, the Cambridge architect Peter Bicknell selected from the pink of Teg's Nose quarry near Macclesfield and the grey, beige and pale yellow of the Elland flags from Hipperholme near Halifax.

Third Court is bright all through the year; in the spring it is decked out with polyanthus, somehow a proper Tudor flower, mingling plum-velvet with orange and saffron. Beyond lies the Bridge of Sighs. Visitors are usually diverted to the left and soon have a view of it from the 'Wren' bridge (completed in 1712), for which Wren's drawings are preserved, and whose balustrade is not unlike his conception, though the work was carried out by his mason Robert Grumbold. A letter from Wren is extant suggesting a diversion of the river-bed to create here 'a parterre to the river'. He would have liked to see it flow in a straight line over the college grounds from Trinity Bridge, which would no doubt have enhanced the view of Trinity Library.

All the area to the west of the river was surveyed and replanned by Thomas Sharp, author of the Cambridge Plan, in 1950 and 1951. Crossing the bridge you enter what used to be called St John's Meadow, with the Broad Walk ahead leading to the distant gates on Queen's Road. The parallel path may have been used by horsemen, as the mounting-block nearby suggests. To your right is Rickman's New Court, 'wedding-cake' to some, Romantic palace to others, at all events a theatrical setting for one of the most colourful herbaceous borders in Cambridge, the mounting ranges of flowers being echoed in the ranges of screens and towers behind them (**42**). Until 1825, when building of the court began, this area contained a score of fish-ponds rented out by the college. No trace of such utilities remains.

Further up Broad Walk on the right is a remarkably large yew, Babington's Yew, planted in 1843 by Charles Cardale Babington, taxonomist, polymath and

38 *The Wig Plant (Cotinus coggygria 'Purpureus') gets its name from a resemblance to the fine hair of a wig, but this one growing at Newnham suggests a cloud of spray.*

Fellow of St John's. Its wide-spreading branches and pendulous spray may cause doubt as to whether it really is a yew at all. But it is in fact a Dovaston or Westfelton Yew, *Taxus baccata* var. *dovastoniana*, authenticated by Dr S. M. Walters. Its parent tree, as John Dovaston attests, was 'of most striking and distinguished beauty', its foliage 'like that of the Asparagus, admirably adapted for retaining the dew-drops'. It was also, by Dovaston's account, a tree that 'has food for the philosopher, as well as for the poet; for strange to tell, and what few unseeing believed, although a male . . . it has one entire branch self-productive and exuberantly profuse in female berries . . .'. The yew being dioecious, it is still a curious question whether this one has ever borne fruit or ever does so now.

Near here is a wellingtonia recorded in 1851 as 'planted by Dr Reyner'. Further on still an iron bridge (1822) crosses the Bin Brook, once the 'Binne-brok' or the brook along the 'binnan' field, 'within' the boundary of city and college. Crossing this and continuing towards the gates you have on your left the (private) Fellows' Garden (**43**), renowned for its succession of aconites, daffodils, anemones, bluebells, and particularly martagon lilies. Here in 1860 Babington recorded the wild meadow saxifrage (*Saxifraga granulata*) as 'prob-

39 *Daffodils and hyacinths near the rock garden, part of the Fellows' Garden at Pembroke; in the background is Orchard Building.*

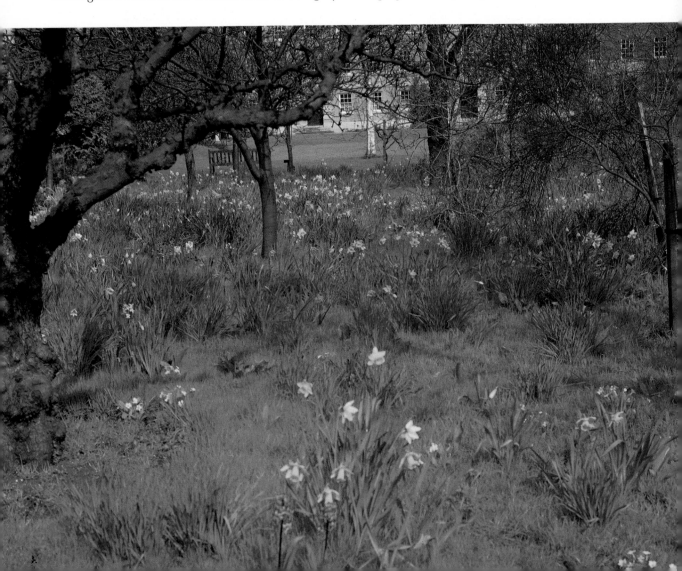

ably brought in with turf formerly'; it can still be seen. Another ancient introduction is tower rock-cress, *Arabis turrita*, which botanists come miles to see in its only 'wild' British locality. In the late 18th century Capability Brown was given by the college money for a piece of plate worth £50 for his 'services in improving the walks', and though there is no clear evidence it is thought he may have given this Wilderness, as it is called, a more natural appearance than it had when its trees were in regular rows. Tradition has it that the paths used to be laid out in the form of the nave, transepts and chancel of a cathedral. All that remains is the nave, now that the north-eastern part has been cleared to make a bowling green, but Loggan's print of 1688 does show it in its present position. Clumps of Fenland alders and viburnums along the brook afford glimpses of the garden from Queen's Road. Many hundreds of trees have been lost in recent years, including elms killed by disease – Thomas Sharp reckoned there were 500 in the early 1950s, of which at least half have gone – and the Wilderness must wait for replanting to take effect. Meanwhile the loss of the trees threatens the woodland flowers too.

The avenue of limes and yews leading to the gates (1822) was proposed by Sharp. From the gate can be seen across the road the continuation of the avenue into the playing fields, also his layout. Balancing the Wilderness, however, is a garden, formerly an orchard (only one quince remains), open to the public; it was laid out in the early 1950s by Sylvia Crowe and has special interest as one of the few formal gardens in Cambridge. 'Since this is the end of the Backs proper,' Sharp wrote, 'the firm definition given by a closed garden will be beneficial to the local landscape as a whole.' The wrought-iron gates and the summerhouse were designed by David Wyn Roberts, a member of the college whose neat architectural designs can be seen in many places in Cambridge. Returning now to the bridge, if you turn right you can see into the Wilderness across the brook, and eventually reach the early Georgian iron gates.

To see more of St John's, turn back towards the prizewinning Cripps Building, across the Bin Brook and through Dame Sylvia's garden: the trees in the old garden of Merton Hall were carefully preserved by the architects Powell and Moya. It may be here that the ash mentioned in Book VI of Wordsworth's *Prelude* stood, for there is a record in 1805 of an ash, marked with a cross (probably as a boundary mark), which seems most likely to have stood just north of the iron bridge near the right bank of the brook. The ash, not a common tree in Cambridge, has always had a mysterious hold on poets since the times of Norse folklore. Wordsworth concludes:

> Oft have I stood
> Foot-bound, uplooking at this lovely Tree
> Beneath a frosty moon. The hemisphere
> Of magic fiction, verse of mine perhaps
> May never tread; but scarcely Spenser's self
> Could have more tranquil visions in his youth,
> More bright appearances could scarcely see
> Of human forms with superhuman Powers,
> Than I beheld, standing on winter nights
> Alone, beneath this fairy work of earth.

A short detour to the left brings you to the very beautiful Merton Hall, a half-timbered building acquired by the college in 1959. A paved garden with a pool

and roses remains from the days when it was a private residence, and there is a greenhouse of remarkably pleasing design. From here pass to the front of the house and so down to the 12th-century 'School of Pythagoras'. Beyond the rear entrance to the Cripps Building the punt-lagoon and its small island, where swans nest, is straight ahead of you. The weir by the sluice is cobbled, to provide the tinkle of running water. Looking towards the river you can just see the corner of a grassy area, once shaded by elms, now covered with crocuses in spring. Being close to the rooms usually allocated to a blind student, this is known as Dog Island, from the fact that the guide-dog is allowed free exercise there. From the river end of the Cripps Building a fairly good view can be had of the Master's absolutely private garden, designed by Nevill Willmer, author-in-chief of Clare Fellows' Garden. The three *Prunus subhirtella* 'Pendula' by the ancient water-gate echo the pair by the river at Clare, and there is a glimpse of the fine terrace by the Master's Lodge, faced with Barnack stone from the medieval hospital and chapel.

To regain the Backs go through New Court by the back entrance. From the porch it is possible to continue along the Backs, crossing into Trinity meadow via the pleasing iron bridge erected in 1874 as a happy mark of co-operation between the rival colleges.

Selwyn College

In late April or early May the whole façade along Grange Road is completely hidden by white cherry blossom. The main court, through the entrance gate, is remarkable for some rare and unusual Mediterranean plants set by Dr Alexis Vlasto, to whom the rejuvenation of all the gardens is largely due. In the north-west corner to your left, *Dracunculus vulgaris*, with a thick white stem flecked with black, and crinkled dark green leaves, deserves its name of Snake Plant. The large spathe is deep chocolate. There is a rare blue-flowered *Lithodora zahnii* from Southern Greece, *Halacsya sendtneri*, of the borage family, from Bosnia, and *Cistus lusitanicus* 'Decumbens' from Portugal. These are all in the beds by the south-facing wall of the court.

Through the railings separating off the garden can be seen *Forsythia europea*, another rarity, collected by Dr Vlasto in Southern Serbia. In summer agapanthus grows either side of the gate, and the myrtle by the chapel entrance is another reminder of Greece. Coming down the perron into the garden you have on your left another clump of *Dracunculus vulgaris*, and nearby the winter-growing *Arum creticum* and *Cistus populifolius*; *Iris xiphioides* was collected in the Pyrenees.

Of the many plants and trees in the bed to the right of the perron the still young Handkerchief Tree (*Davidia involucrata*) deserves special mention. In line with the wall of the chapel, facing the East window, *Cornus kousa* 'Chinensis' was planted in 1978; *Acer saccharinum* from the U.S.A. is also a recent planting.

By now the winding path crossing the garden from north to south is easily seen. A clump of lilac, quince, white and pink cherries, and a magnolia planted in 1977 by the Duke of Edinburgh, makes a colourful centre in spring. But the great distinction of the garden, apart from the Mediterranean collection, is its rosebeds, containing chiefly damask, *gallica* ('Ipsilante', 'Cardinal de Richelieu', 'Belle de Crecy' and some 30 others), and *rugosa* (a very large Chinese *Rosa soulieana* in the centre of a diamond-shaped bed with *Rosa glauca* at three of the corners), besides 15 species of roses in the Fellows' Garden near the summerhouse. Yellow early-flowering roses (*Rosa × pteragonis* 'Cantabrigiensis' being one first raised in the Botanic Garden) are planted together in a rectangular bed close to the main buildings. This is one of the finest rose-gardens in Cambridge, with over 220 species and cultivars.

The variety of other plants and shrubs is almost as great. On the walls leading to the Sidgwick site are *Passiflora caerulea*, *Solanum crispum autumnale* and *Fremontodendron* 'California Glory', with an underplanting of autumn-flowering *Sternbergia lutea*. Of the trees, a fine Holm Oak should be looked for, and a cedar planted in 1890 by Dr Courtney Kenny, near the path. From here can be seen the other exit, a lane bordered with young cherries, *Prunus* 'Taihaku', and *Wisteria sinensis* 'Alba' against a background of equally young *Clematis montana*. Following this to West Road and turning left, you can visit Cripps Court, across Grange Road, where the entrance path is lined with *Gallica versicolor* 'Rosa mundi', the favourite medieval rose, blossoming in July.

Sidney Sussex College

Turning left from the entrance in Sidney Street and crossing the court to the entrance to C staircase, you come out on the far side near the wall-memorial to Duns Scotus and enter the garden which now occupies the area of the Greyfriars'

42 *The herbaceous border in front of St John's New Court.*

41 *Peonies in the Scholars' Garden at Peterhouse. Possibly the first flowers ever grown for ornament, they are mentioned in the Chinese* Book of Songs *of 3300 BC. In recent times Madame Mao tried to prohibit them as images of superfluous wealth; she owed her downfall partly to champions of them.*

churchyard. The trees here, including a Tree of Heaven, are provided with labels, as they are in most of the garden. Turning right, past the far end of the neo-Jacobean building, you enter the garden proper, landscaped originally in the late 18th century. A *Malus tschonowskii* straight ahead makes a pyramid of flaming red in autumn (**45**). To the right is a superb and uncommon Weeping Chestnut (**46**), and below it is a trace of the course of the King's Ditch, the moat which formerly surrounded the town on its eastern side. Its position is indicated by the course of Hobson Street and Park Street, to either side of the college.

A small landmark is made by the sculpture of a mother and child by Karin Jonzen, placed here in memory of the wife of a former Fellow. Beyond this, through a carefully provided gap, a classical arch can be seen in the northern-most corner. This was built in 1762 to the design of James Burrough for the entrance to the college, and was moved in about 1825 to its present position, where it forms a summerhouse fronted by a hedge of Golden Yew. The wall nearby was that of the Franciscan friars. A fruit-bearing fig tree grows by it, as does a *Cytisus battandieri*.

A large part of the garden space is occupied by the Master's private garden, separated from the remainder by a rose pergola. It includes a splendid Weeping Ash. A fine view of the whole can be had from the terrace of Blundell Court, the building to the south completed in 1969.

Trinity College

The space to your right as you come in by Great Gate is immediately interesting. Not only is this Newton's Lawn, formerly his garden, and laid out in his day in a chequerboard of small plots; the apple tree is from the same stock as the one at his home, Woolsthorpe Manor near Grantham, of which so much has been said. Newton's friend William Stukely recorded a conversation in 1726 in which Newton gave an account of the famous occasion: 'After dinner, the weather being warm, we went into the garden and drank tea, only he and myself. Amidst other discourse, he told me, he was just in the same situation as when formerly the notion of gravitation came into his mind. It was occasioned by the fall of an apple, as he sat in a contemplative mood. Why should that apple always descend perpendicularly to the ground, thought he to himself. Why should it not go sideways or upwards, but constantly to the earth's centre? . . .'. This Trinity descendant first bore fruit in 1954. Another like it is in the Botanic Garden.

Great Court, seen from under Great Gate, may not be a garden, but it is the finest open space in Cambridge, to say the least, and still retains the layout of paths it had in Newton's day: 'of immense extent,' Henry James wrote in *English Hours*, 'and the buildings that surround it, with their long, rich fronts of time-deepened gray, are the stateliest in the world'. Between November and March big clumps of *Iris unguicularis* add splashes of bright blue to the area around Great Gate; the east wall is a long line of climbing roses, interrupted by a massive *Magnolia grandiflora*. The rare *Xanthoceras sorbifolium* tucked away in the north-east corner by the chapel should be looked for: its white blossoms with red eye appear in May.

New Court, beyond the diagonally opposite corner, is fresh every winter with jasmine blossom. The chestnut, planted about the turn of the century, was saved

44 *Tulips and anemones announce spring at St John's.*

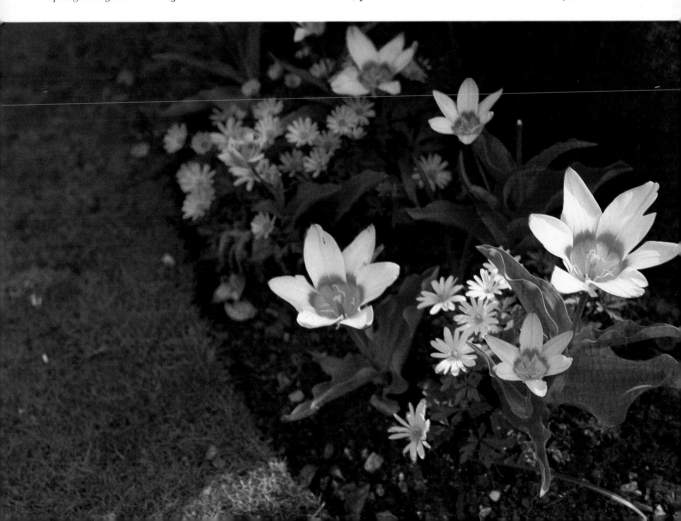

soon after by a Boat Club bodyguard from vandalising infanticides. The court has also many climbers, vegetable and human, some preparing for Alpine environments. Notable are three clematis – *C. patens* 'Hagley Hybrid', *C. viticella* 'Étoile violette' and *C. montana* 'Alba' – and a *Piptanthus laburnifolius*.

From here the gate on the west side leads to the river. The limes, to which Tennyson refers in *In Memoriam*, were planted by the autocratic 18th-century Master, Richard Bentley, on his own authority. The fine bridge by James Essex was erected in 1764–5. The willows on the further bank are known to some as Napoleon's willows; a willow in Downing College is said to have come from a cutting taken from a willow at the first grave of Napoleon on St Helena, and these may have a similar origin.

The path to Queen's Road is raised on a causeway; when the old Magdalene Bridge downstream consisted of three narrow tubes supporting a road, the Backs were often flooded and causeways were the best counter-measures. (Wren's library may have been built on an upper storey precisely to prevent the books getting soaked.) The old limes have been replaced here, but the broad expanses either side are a glowing carpet of crocuses in March (**47**), and a little later narcissi and red tulips make an equally festive show, especially when they come out together with the white cherry blossoms. The cherries themselves are often (wrongly) said to have been planted by A. E. Housman (Fellow 1911–36), probably because of his poem that begins 'Loveliest of trees, the cherry now . . .'. In the far corner of the field to the right, towards St John's, is an oak, sometimes called Trevelyan's Oak after the historian and Master of the college (1940–51), who planted it in 1956 to mark his eightieth birthday.

The garden proper is the Fellows' Garden, straight ahead across Queen's Road. It is private, except that Trinity undergraduates can now use it en route from their hostels in Grange Road, but it is opened to the public on special days under the National Gardens Scheme, and is well worth seeing even in its crippled state. The great avenue of elms planted by the Master, William Whewell, in 1843, was not welcomed at that time – 'a decided mistake', said the senior bursar – but it used to be one of the pleasures of Cambridge to look through the wrought-iron gates at them towering away, inaccessible giants. Now that this tall double palisade has succumbed to Dutch elm disease the garden looks bare, and will do till the new London Planes establish themselves.

The present layout dates from 1873 and is due to W. Brodrick Thomas, who also designed for Sandringham and Buckingham Palace. It is bounded by a perimeter path, hence the name 'The Roundabout', used by the Fellows for the whole garden. If you fork left at the entrance, rather than going straight along the avenue, you see on your left a sundial erected in memory of three Fellows, all members of the Garden Committee, all killed in the First World War. It has a curious history, having been seen in a dream by another Fellow, who remembered its details with such vividness that he felt it was an inspiration meant to be carried out, 'and so the dream was biblically fulfilled', as his widow Maisie Fletcher records in *The Bright Countenance*. Opposite is a mound known as Monte Cobbeo, after the Fellow who is said to have erected the summerhouse on it in order to propose marriage, as Gwen Raverat relates in *Period Piece*. Further left beyond the sundial is a large area of grass, mown only once a year, which is not only beautiful but also of scientific interest. As well as the introduced snake's-head fritillaries and martagon lilies, it has many native species charac-

45 *The Japanese* Malus tschonowskii *at Sidney Sussex turns from green to red in late October or early November.*

teristic of old, unimproved meadows, such as cowslip, quaking grass and salad burnet. To reach it, you may need to take one of the mowed paths often connected with the name of the philosopher Wittgenstein, who used to be thought to have designed them in accordance with mysterious mathematical principles (rather like 'Newton's' Mathematical Bridge at Queens', and no more mysterious in fact). Leading westwards from the Wittgenstein paths is the Lilac Walk, specially beautiful in May, and opening out on to a broad expanse of grass dominated by a Tree of Heaven and a Copper Beech. It has recently been closed off on the north by a long low mound to screen passers-by from sight as they go down the main path of the avenue. The brick octagonal surface joining the paths at the end of the avenue is due to Richard J. Bisgrove of Reading University, who also, in the early 1980s, widened Bin Brook, and afforded an extremely pleasant vista alongside the garden. The landscaping of the whole area here, and much of the planting, is due to him.

But the Fellows' Garden will not for a long time provide again the awe-inspiring surroundings that led to one of the famous occasions of the 19th century. It was here in 1873, shortly before Brodrick Thomas' redesigning, that George Eliot walked beneath the trees on a dark May evening with F. W. H. Myers, who listened to her pronouncing, 'with terrible earnestness', how inconceivable was God, how unbelievable immortality, and how peremptory and absolute duty. As they stood 'amid that columnar circuit of the forest-trees',

46 *An unusual Weeping Chestnut in Sidney Sussex garden, covered with a great wealth of blossom in May.*

Myers recalled, he seemed to be gazing 'like Titus at Jerusalem, on vacant seats and empty halls – on a sanctuary with no Presence to hallow it, and heaven left lonely of a God'. Now that the forest trees have nearly all gone such a *Götterdämmerung* mood is hard to conjure up, but something like it can be imagined.

Trinity Hall

'If I were called upon . . . to mention the prettiest corner of the world', Henry James wrote in 1883, 'I should draw out a thoughtful sigh and point the way to the garden of Trinity Hall.' The original garden was to the right and across the road from the main entrance, where the University offices now are. In 1731 a 'Felos Fruit Garden' occupied the present North Court, while the Fellows' Garden of today (48) was explicitly 'for walking'. A deep herbaceous border runs in front of the whole of its south-facing wall. The very tall Horse Chestnuts over towards Clare, with a gnarled bark looking more like that of Black Poplars, seem to be the ones planted in about 1710, or slightly later. In James' day they were 'of prodigious size'. 'They occupy half the garden,' he wrote, 'and are remarkable for the fact that their giant limbs strike down into the earth, take root again and emulate, as they rise, the majesty of the parent stem. The manner in which this magnificent group of horse-chestnuts sprawls about over the grass, out into the middle of the lawn, is one of the most heart-shaking features of the garden of Trinity Hall.'

The modern visitor's eye will be caught by the late Elizabethan library with Vermeer-style stepped gables in dark red brick, adorned with the Saracen crescent of the founder's arms, those of a Crusader. This building is bordered on two sides by deep beds of spring flowers, followed later in the year by the special

47 A broad sweep of crocuses, one of two beds either side of the avenue on Trinity Backs; in the background, Trinity Library, designed by Sir Christopher Wren.

glory of the place, delphiniums, achilleas, hollyhocks, peonies and sweet williams, celebrating the ancient building (**49**). A *Magnolia grandiflora* in the corner stretches to the eaves.

48 *Trinity Hall Fellows' Garden with chestnut blossoms and a view of the ancient terrace, beyond which flows the Cam.*

The college's achievement is the greater when you consider that it is small in ground area – though with large hostels not far away – and has to spare what room it can for gardens. This is ingeniously done in the new Cherry Tree Court, where a steep-stepped wall has pansies, daisies, aubretia and alyssum in terraced beds, seen from the main area outside as a long vista of colour. Terracing comes naturally to Trinity Hall: both the Fellows' Garden and the students' one next to it have terraces along the river front, and have had since at least the early 18th century. From this vantage point there is a view over Clare Fellows' Garden one way and Garret Hostel Bridge the other, the bridge half masked by a huge willow. An inscription on the terrace wall says it was erected in 1939 to celebrate the sixth centenary of the college's foundation. Here is a comfortable four-seater, where the punt-poles shoot up in front of you and slant away like so many ambling giraffes.

The path leading past the library follows the course of the old Town Ditch, which used to flow into the King's Ditch in what is now Garret Hostel Lane. It leads past Latham, Gatehouse and Thornton Buildings round a grass plot which has a sizeable Copper Beech, a yew, and three cherries. Leaving through the gatehouse, you can enjoy the view of the Cam from the top of the steep bridge, with James' words again in mind: 'grassy banks and mossy balustrades of sun-chequered avenues and groves, of lawns and gardens and terraces, of single-arched bridges spanning the little stream, which is small and shallow and looks as if it had been turned on for ornamental purposes'. There has not been much change here in a hundred years.

Wolfson College

The college occupies the grounds of a former house, and has taken over several houses and their gardens. A ceremonial approach avenue has been planted with Columnar Hornbeams, and the entrance court has a Judas Tree and an old mulberry. The library gardens on the right are exceptionally pleasant: a sundial, copied from one at Trinity, and set up in honour of the first President, James Morrison, forms a bold centre for shrubs and herbaceous borders.

To the rear of East Court are the remnants of a grove of Morello Cherries, while to the left of West Court is a row of cedars, also remaining from a much larger planting. A magnolia has been planted in East Court which, it is hoped, will blossom in about 20 years and reach an unusual height.

49 *The border by the late-16th-century library at Trinity Hall, the best library in Cambridge of its date. The upper floor is kept in its original state, with the books on chains to prevent theft, attached to their Jacobean bookcases.*

The Botanic Garden

Of the five entrances, the one from Bateman Street might have been designed to provide surprises, its narrow path suddenly giving on to a wide choice of routes. If you go in this way no. 1 Brookside is on your right, like a picturesque lodge. On the lawn just inside is an apple tree descended from the one said to have inspired Newton (see Trinity College), on the left of the path a towering Black Walnut with deep bark fissures, and opposite it a giant spray of suckers 70 feet high from a Caucasian Wing-Nut that blew down about the year 1886, each of them big enough for a tree in itself. Here the garden opens out: to the left the path goes to the glasshouses, to the right it leads to the chestnut collection. Our walk, however, goes almost straight on around the end of the stream and down the woodbark path. (Just off a side path to the right is the rarest tree in the Garden, a *Tetracentron sinese*.) Bear left by the end of the lake and cross the stream, which is specially fed with peat for growing ferns and mares' tails. By the path the purple *Lathraea clandestina* can be seen on the ground, a much admired early-flowering parasitic plant. Turn right through the bamboo to the Water Garden, lush with royal fern, great spearwort (a huge buttercup) and great fen ragwort, rediscovered in the Fens in 1972 after being thought extinct in Britain since the 1850s. From the high bank above the Water Garden you get a good panoramic view.

On the horizon is a superb horseshoe of trees surrounding the older part, lining it like a park with great oaks, beeches, birches, pines, and so round to limes and chestnuts, on your right. There are also a few elms remaining, and experiments are underway to see which varieties can survive. Straight ahead to the south are the systematic beds, arranged in curving areas, each containing a single natural order, or a division of one – monocotyledons such as lilies, irises and grasses in an oval, and dicotyledons, a much larger group, around them. Thanks to this layout even the strictly botanic areas are a pleasure to look at, a combination of science and art that typifies the Garden's policy of providing for layman and expert alike. One can contemplate a bed of varieties of mulleins either with a botanist's eye for fine differentiations or with memories of traditional names like hag-leaf or hag-taper, aptly given to their stick-like furry clusters. From here too mistletoe can be seen high on a tree to the south-east.

Across the lake to the south-west, looking from above the Water Garden, are the fine wrought-iron gates, moved here in 1909. They came originally from the first Botanic Garden, founded in 1760 on a plot of land given by the Vice-Master of Trinity, Richard Walker, to discover the virtues of plants 'for the benefit of mankind', and are a reminder of the Garden's essentially unchanging role. For the last 150 years, at all events, an 'enthusiasm for the whole plant "in the field", involving scientific study in the garden and in the laboratory', to quote Dr S. M. Walters, has flourished in a continuous tradition. The Common Lime

50 *The globe artichoke,* Cynara cardenculus, *introduced into England in the mid-17th century, growing in the chronological bed of the Botanic Garden.*

just to the south of the gates was planted when the present Garden was officially opened in 1846. Along this side runs Hobson's Conduit, a stream dug in 1610 to bring drinking water to Cambridge from the Gog Magog hills, and now still useful as a supply to the lake, as well as to several College gardens.

The water lilies growing in the lake (**51**) are of the kind that crowd the water in summer with foliage; the moorhens find this an advantage for stalking about. Turn east and cross the stepping-rocks, one of which has a prehistoric imprint, and you are in the Rock Garden, one of the great attractions. Most of the world's continents are represented in separate divisions, and a special feature is the limestone doline or pit, showing plants found in the 'Karst' area of Carinthia in Austria, and in Yugoslavia. Nearby are clumps of pasque flower, blooming at Easter. Its purple and gold colours explain why it is called 'Danes' Blood' in regions where Danes were thought to have fought against Anglo-Saxons, as at Fleam Dyke, south of the city. East of the Rock Garden is Henslow Walk, named after the Professor of Botany who not only aroused Charles Darwin's interest in the subject, but by his vision and enthusiasm initiated the present Garden. Beyond it, a curious but beautiful bed contains a collection of saxifrages on rocks, shooting out small 'trees' of flowers from every crevice.

The Main Walk leading from the fountain to the Trumpington Gate is planted with deodars, cedars and wellingtonias, an avenue fit to lead up to a stately home. South of this is the Gilbert-Carter Memorial Area, planted in memory of the first scientific Director (as distinct from Curator) of the Garden, appointed in 1921. It is to Humphrey Gilbert-Carter that the printed labels still fixed to some of the trees are due, many of them reflecting his knowledge of

51 *Autumn colours of* Cotinus obovatus, *the American Smoke Tree, seen across the lake in the Botanic Garden. In the centre, white plumes of pampas grass; in the background, some of the collection of willows.*

Greek, Latin, Sanskrit and other languages (their texts were published in a memorial volume in 1975). One of the pleasures of the Garden today is reading such things as his translation of the Persian poem on the flowers of the *Cercis siliquastrum* (by the edge of the systematic beds): 'Ruby ear-rings of Badakh-shán sparkle on the Judas tree.' Gilbert-Carter observes that a beautiful complexion is often likened in Islamic literature to the flowers of this tree; Geoffrey Grigson says the same of foxgloves mentioned in the *Mabinogion,* suggesting that a hectic flush was once admired in Europe too. But there is also a good deal in these labels about practical use: that walnuts were considered good and safe toys for Roman children, that hornbeam is used for piano keys, and *Betula papyrifera* for wigwams.

Beyond lies the New Pinetum, planted in the 1960s along what was then the south-western margin of the Garden. Retrace your steps eastward along South Walk. Two trees stand out in this area: the rare and puzzling *Quercus warburgii,* a garden hybrid of doubtful parentage, and the *Prunus serrula* from China, with bark that looks like dark burnished copper. You soon come out into the open, with 300 yards of 'new' gardens, reaching as far as the Cherry Hinton gate on Hills Road (**53**). These, amounting to one half of the site acquired in 1846, were planted under the direction of John Gilmour in the 1950s and 1960s. Dominating the view is a lofty Tree of Heaven, a species once worshipped in China for reasons not hard to guess. It is one of very few trees surviving from before the 1950s when the ground was used for allotments. On the nearer side of it are the beds illustrating the history of the rose: medieval damasks, ramblers, China roses and hybrid teas instructively arranged. Beyond are the cherries, and beyond them the herbaceous island beds (**55**) full of phlox, asters, salvias, poppies, achillea, astilbe, and in one part a rolling sea of peonies. From here,

52 Chrysanthemums in the Botanic Garden conservatory. These are truly what their name implies, 'golden flowers'. In the Japanese Noh play The Chrysanthemum Child *the chrysanthemum is the source of the elixir of life, giving immortality.*

you can leave by the gate ahead or turn back, following Bateson Walk to the older gardens again. But first there is the scented garden specially created for the blind, planted with *Pelargonium fragrans, Pelargonium odoratissimum, Chrysanthemum balsamita* with its small buttons like tansy, and rosemary, thyme, stock, mint, tobacco and carnations. The shelter here affords a rest half-way.

On the return, leave on the right the picnic area and its poplars, where the hedge of *Cotoneaster lacteus* is covered with dark red berries every Christmas. The chronological beds were planted by the second Director, John Gilmour, in an original arrangement showing the introduction of plants to Britain. Woad naturally comes near the beginning, along with the almond, *Prunus dulcis*. A bed of turf set with columbines, daisies, gillyflowers, periwinkles, primroses, sweet william and violets shows the kind of flowers that would have been seen in the garden of Chaucer's 'Franklin's Tale'. But it is surprising how quickly the beds pass from Anglo-Saxon to Elizabethan times, and how many familiar plants are fairly recent arrivals. Michaelmas daisies came from New England in the 17th century, nasturtiums from Peru and golden rod from Canada not long after. As horizons widened, roses came from China, eschscholtzias from California and kerria from Japan in the 18th century, *Senecio przewalskii* from Mongolia in the mid-19th, and *Cytisus battandieri* from the Atlas mountains in the 20th.

North of the chronological beds is the new Winter Garden, a dazzling sight in the dark days (**54**). Fiery red *Salix alba* 'Chermesina' stands behind yellow *Cornus stolonifera* 'Flaviramea', which in turn crosses branches with purplish *Cornus alba* 'Sibirica'. Glowing yellow Japanese Witch Hazel and the white-

53 *A* Paulownia tomentosa, *home of the Japanese phoenix, catching the winter sun in the 'new' section of the Botanic Garden. A native of China, it was introduced to France from Japan in 1834.*

54 Salix alba *'Chermesina' and* Cornus stolonifera *'Flaviramea' glow with colour in the Winter Garden of the Botanic Garden. Their brightness is achieved by regular cutting back.*

wash of *Rubus biflorus* add to the brilliant confusion. Heathers have stretched across the ground in a few years to cover it almost completely, and variegated ivies complement them. Dwarf conifers and the orange bark of *Sorbus aucuparia* 'Beissneri' make this part of the Garden seem brighter even than the most colourful summer beds.

The next areas are strictly educational, devoted to varieties of juniper, pollination, self-propagation, and the conservation display, including a white-beam whose total wild population in the world amounts to only 15 trees, and further along, the limestone mound, faced by a patch of artificial fen. (Even the National Trust Fen at Wicken is artificial now, water being pumped in to keep it from drying out.)

We are almost back in the old Garden as we pass under the group of planes, leaving on the left a Monkey-Puzzle Tree whose label says that the first seeds brought to Britain were 'abstracted' from the dinner-table of the Viceroy of Chile in 1795. This tree is in the Old Pinetum, which still has fine specimens of Scots Pine and *Pinus nigra*. In summer the giant hogweed jungle here grows to nearly giraffe height in a few weeks. The stems and umbels of hogweed are dried and sliced by the local artist David Keate for making pictures. There is a glimpse of Cory Lodge, till recently the Director's residence. It is named after Reginald Cory, whose large bequest in 1951 was used for the eastern extension, the 'New Garden'. The library and offices are to be housed here.

Continuing along Middle Walk, that is northwards, and leaving the fountain on the left, pass under the larches, rusty gold in autumn, to the old rockery, now the Terrace Garden, which is planted today mainly with conifers. The 'wishing-

55 *A herbaceous island in the 'new' section of the Botanic Garden.*

56 *Springtime pansies, polyanthus and wallflowers outside the hothouses of the Botanic Garden; in the distance, cedars and a wellingtonia by the Main Walk.*

well' is an attraction especially for children; built like the doline and providing a dank wall for ferns, it is more cranny than well. Stretching across the front of the teak glasshouses (built in 1888–92 and rebuilt in 1934) are the only formal beds in the Garden, a richly coloured combination of fuchsias, calceolarias, cinerarias and other plants throughout the warmer seasons (**56**).

After the open air the warmth inside the door of the glasshouses is a preparation for the exotic and the bizarre. Down the corridor at various seasons are the purple and yellow heron's heads of strelitzia with their cockatoo plumes, tree tomatoes, hibiscus, bougainvillaea, and *Aloe arborescens* with a touch of the demonic in its saw-edged leaves. Start from the east: the Succulent House has cactuses like stones, or like hydra-headed worms with a rash of delicate blooms, repulsive and beautiful at once. Geometrical symmetry in one plant is answered by a rank chaos of limbs sprouting from anywhere in another. Even in the Orchid House next door there are similarly uncanny combinations. A spray of *Cymbidium* would suit a bridal gown, but there are orchids that decorate themselves to look like butterflies and hover malevolently with a deep red mouth waiting for prey. *Nepenthes rafflesiana*, source of a tranquilliser but named after the adventurous Raffles of Singapore, has a much larger mouth at the end of a speckled bag several inches long, holding enough water for tadpoles to start their lives in, which some do. The fleshiness and flaunting colours of these traps make them look absurdly menacing, even to humans. Alongside are epiphytes, platyceriums resembling masks of 'wild men' with stems coming out of their mouths, such as you see in church carvings.

The Tropical Fern House is possibly not for the layman. Ferns look much alike and have no striking features. Even the Palm House and the Stove House disappoint slightly. They are not tall enough to house huge jungle trees, and the ground cover, though it includes ten tropical families, is kept in neat order, as it has to be. It is instructive to see the economic plants in the south-west corner: tea, rubber, rice; and the dwarf banana is a sight to watch from week to week as it pushes a purple beak out of its scrolled-up stem, to let it break open and dangle a cluster of baby fruits. On the north-east side are several specimens of *Encephalartos* with bases like pineapples. These are cycads, of which many Mesozoic fossils exist. At a time when reptiles were the dominant form of animal life their swordfish leaves protected them so well that they spread everywhere. Some further sense of the prolific life of the jungle is given by the roots of *Pandanus utilis,* drooping obscenely to the ground.

The Aquarium extending from the Palm House seldom has much of interest to the occasional visitor, though *Nelumbo nucifera* is worth seeing in flower. But the Alpine House, so called, is a model of classical decorum, its saxifrages with neatly radiating leaves in circular pots creating a calm which the dainty flowers do not disturb. In the smaller room beyond, by which you can leave the glasshouses, are more small saxifrages, miniature daffodils from the Pyrenees, irises, cyclamens, yellow Siberian fritillarias and primulas, often arranged along and inside a miniature ravine, or down a very small rocky slope.

Last but one of the glasshouses is a conservatory (**52**, **58**) that would have graced any Victorian home. Cinerarias and poinsettias, coleus, arum lilies, daffodils, chrysanthemums and passion flowers crowd together crimson on purple, prussian blue on billiards green, gold on orange, regardless of designers' rules of harmony. Last of all is the Temperate House, with plants that would be killed by frost outdoors. A 'Mediterranean' climate fosters such trees as the large Australian *Melaleuca sparsiflora*, with small hard evergreen leaves, and quite a few plants come from Atlantic islands – St Helena, Tenerife (the Dragon Tree) and Madeira, the *Geranium maderense* being a showy purple-flowered specimen (not always on display). Oranges and lemons are transferred here in tubs

57 Magnolia liliiflora, *considered by some to be the most beautiful magnolia in the Botanic Garden. Magnolia has about 30 species, many of which can be seen near the Bateman Street entrance of the Garden.*

when their season comes. The very old She-Oak from Australia, *Casuarina stricta,* is hunched and crabbed like a witch.

Leaving the glasshouses by the south-west door, turn to your right to find a small hut filled with carnivorous plants. The ingenious *Drosera rotundiflora* or sundew secretes a sticky substance which holds an insect while the tentacles, or rather glands, fold over it to hold it fast during digestion. Pitcher plants like *Sarracenia* tempt the prey into their 'pitchers' by colour and perfume till it slips down inside; downward-pointing hairs prevent escape and the insect usually drowns in rainwater at the bottom. *Darlingtonia californica,* another pitcher plant, looks like a Medusa-head swarming with green snakes. It has mock windows in the roof of its entrance chamber, against which insects hit themselves in trying to escape: they fall into the pitcher, where they are decomposed by bacterial action. You come away from this section feeling that plants are almost human in their cunning.

To reach the Bateman Street gate again, follow the path westwards. In late winter there will be blossoms of *Chimonanthus praecox,* in early spring daffodils in great variety, then tulips of all kinds, and later peonies. At the corner is a zone of magnolia: from April to June a particularly lovely *Magnolia liliiflora* blossoms here (**57**).

The office of CAMBIENT (the local Naturalists' Trust) at the entrance sells the official guide to the Garden (1979) by Dr S. M. Walters, Director till 1983, as well as guides to the trees and shrubs and the medicinal, economic and carnivorous plants, general books on botany and wildlife, and gifts and cards.

58 *A colourful July display in the Botanic Garden conservatory.*

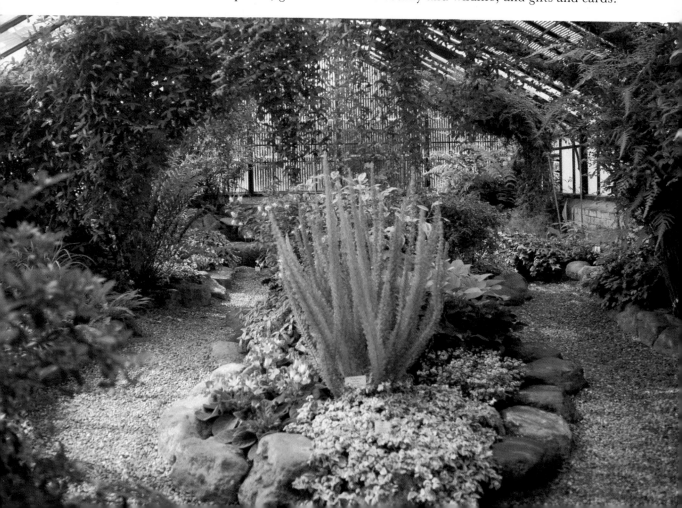

City Gardens

A good start for a perambulation in Pevsner style is Drummer Street bus-station – the shape, if nothing else, still suggests the medieval origin of 'Drummer': *drusemere*, 'muddy pool'. The contrast with Christ's Pieces behind it is then even more marked, the avenue of limes seeming to lead to instant peace. To your right beyond the bowling green French formal beds are patterned every spring with narcissi, forget-me-nots, polyanthus, pansies, wallflowers and above all tulips, about 12,000 bulbs, as in a spa (**59**). Later, look for rudbeckia, geraniums, begonias and cineraria. To the left, near Milton's Walk by Christ's wall, is a well-grown chestnut, and here there used to be a bandstand, which it would be good to have again. The Caucasian Wing-Nut, a large *Salix alba* and in autumn the *Malus tschonoskii* are among the best items. By the tennis courts are some 'self-maintaining' beds planted with wig-plant, Christmas rose, ivy, witch hazel, mahonia, philadelphus, bergenia and other species.

Make for the Four Lamps traffic roundabout, and Victoria Avenue begins: several hundred yards of chestnut candles in May, and conkers galore later on. This is one of the great avenues of Cambridge; there are several more. Milton Road, across the river, is well known for its succession of cherry, almond and hawthorn blossoms, stretching for half a mile. The leaves of whitebeam are worth a trip to De Freville Avenue, off Chesterton Road, while they are still young and peppermint white. Brooklands Avenue, to the south of the city centre, alternates Columnar Hornbeams with Dawyck Beeches, broad next to slim green flames. The planes of Sidgwick Avenue are on the lanky side but still make the street a pleasure.

But keep on with Victoria Avenue for the time being, and at the pelican crossing an over-arching avenue of some 50 plane trees opens up on the left (**60**): why go to the Tuileries? At the end of this arcade of planes you reach the open-air swimming bath, screened with conifers, and Jesus Lock, neat in the best Boulter's Lock tradition. Here there is a choice: the hawthorn avenue to the left crosses Jesus Green back towards St John's, while Carlyle Road ahead leads to a sloping park, Alexandra Gardens, which is bordered with planes and has an avenue of limes that takes you past the bowling green to Alpha Road and so down to Jesus Green again. Having come so far, push on perhaps to the ancient church of St Peter's on Castle Hill; in spring its small churchyard is thick with cow-parsley. Look in at the pretty cottage garden of Kettle's Yard (a University house and exhibition centre). Further up Castle Hill climb the mound, which has interesting wild flowers and a large population of attractive striped snails, and affords a good view over the city in all directions.

Or come straight back to the centre, down St John's Street and Trinity Street, passing the triangular site of All Saints Church – now maintained by the City

59 *The flower beds that greet the traveller who arrives by coach, on Christ's Pieces next to the bus station.*

Parks Service, like most places in this perambulation. Seasonal plantings round the Charing Cross-style memorial make a setting for the summer Craft Markets.

Great Saint Mary's churchyard is now also looked after by the Parks Service. A Weeping Cherry bending over one of the tombs looks exactly like a Romantic vignette; a Weeping Birch faces Bowes and Bowes bookshop, and there is another Weeping Cherry on the Market side. Across the Market lies the controversial Lion Yard. Few find the garden, named after Cambridge's twinned city Heidelberg (go up the spiral staircase in the L-bend). It is formed of symmetrically arranged raised beds in brick frames, vandal-resistant and sealed off from the shops below. Self-maintenance is the watchword here, so far as that means anything: ivy, lavender, bergenia, acanthus, yucca, lamb's ears, sea-holly, euphorbia – a green and grey effect, enlivened a little by *Iris pallida* 'Variegata' round the centrepiece. Tired shoppers could use this retreat more often.

Further afield, Histon Road cemetery has fantastically looming yews and cypresses from the mid-19th century design of J. C. Loudon, setting off marble urns and tall angels. Cherry Hinton Park, with a large collection of wildfowl, has a garden still maturing, but a visit taking in the old quarry just beyond at Limekiln Close in autumn, when traveller's joy is on the rampage, is strongly recommended.

60 *The fan-vaulted tunnel of plane trees leading from Victoria Avenue to the lock on the Cam by Jesus Green.*

In Praise of Cambridge Gardens

St Johns College Garden is very pleasant for the fine walks, both close shady walks and open rows of trees and quickset hedges, there is a pretty bowling green with cut arbours in the hedges; Queens College is old but a stately and lofty building; Clare Hall [Clare College] is very little but most exactly neate; in all parts they have walks with rows of trees and bridges over the river and fine painted gates into the fields.

From *The Journeys of Celia Fiennes* (1697), ed. C. Morris (London, 1947).

I wandered up and down, feeding my greedy eyes, till I found myself again upon the bridge where I had stood that morning, gazing with admiration and astonishment at a scene which I have often expected to see painted or described, and which, nevertheless, in spite of its unique magnificence, seems strangely overlooked by those who cater for the public taste, with pen and pencil: the vista of bridges, one after another spanning the stream; the long line of great monastic palaces, all unlike, and yet all in harmony, sloping down to the stream, with their trim lawns and ivied walls, their towers and buttresses; and opposite them, the range of rich gardens and noble timber trees, dimly seen through which, at the end of the gorgeous river avenue, towered the lofty buildings of St. John's. The whole scene, under the glow of a rich May afternoon, seemed to me a fragment out of 'The Arabian Nights' or Spenser's 'Fairy Queen'.

Charles Kingsley, from *Alton Locke*, 1850.

As I approached I enquired the shortest way to Queens' College, and instead of passing through the town, was directed along that beautiful range of gardens, groves and meadows, which fringe the banks of the Cam, as it rolls lazily along that picturesque line of Colleges which form the western suburbs. My strength seemed to be renewed as I strode with all the freshness of morning through the fine avenues of towering elms which intersect each other in every direction. Daylight was not quite gone; there was light sufficient to enable me to see faintly the beauty and magnificence by which I was surrounded, while yet the impending darkness threw an air of melancholy grandeur round a spot consecrated to my heart by every association that I loved, cherished, and venerated.

Solomon Atkinson, from 'Struggles of a Poor Student through Cambridge', *London Magazine and Review*, 1 April, 1852.

Flotillas of frail canoes of varnished wood glide over the surface of the river . . . You see coming towards you, through the secular trees, the monumental façade of St. John; the river bathes its walls and passes under a 'bridge of sighs' deliciously carved and pierced with barred windows. Then we are out of the town, and the Cam broadens as it sweeps to the right. A lock stops us; beyond this navigation is serious, it is the realm of the 'eight-oars.' In the opposite direction the landskip is greener, with bridge after bridge covered with ivy and wistaria, and little transverse channels losing themselves under the foliage.

Pierre de Coubertin, from *L'Education en Angleterre*, 1888.

CAMBRIDGE GARDENS
MAP SHOWING SITES

MAIN ENTRANCES ARE
SHOWN THUS

N